T0180331

Lecture Notes in Computer Science 14105

Founding Editors

Gerhard Goos
Juris Hartmanis

Editorial Board Members

Elisa Bertino, *Purdue University, West Lafayette, IN, USA*
Wen Gao, *Peking University, Beijing, China*
Bernhard Steffen ⑩, *TU Dortmund University, Dortmund, Germany*
Moti Yung ⑩, *Columbia University, New York, NY, USA*

The series Lecture Notes in Computer Science (LNCS), including its subseries Lecture Notes in Artificial Intelligence (LNAI) and Lecture Notes in Bioinformatics (LNBI), has established itself as a medium for the publication of new developments in computer science and information technology research, teaching, and education.

LNCS enjoys close cooperation with the computer science R & D community, the series counts many renowned academics among its volume editors and paper authors, and collaborates with prestigious societies. Its mission is to serve this international community by providing an invaluable service, mainly focused on the publication of conference and workshop proceedings and postproceedings. LNCS commenced publication in 1973.

Osvaldo Gervasi · Beniamino Murgante ·
Ana Maria A. C. Rocha · Chiara Garau ·
Francesco Scorza · Yeliz Karaca ·
Carmelo M. Torre
Editors

Computational Science and Its Applications – ICCSA 2023 Workshops

Athens, Greece, July 3–6, 2023
Proceedings, Part II

Springer

Editors
Osvaldo Gervasi [ID]
University of Perugia
Perugia, Italy

Ana Maria A. C. Rocha [ID]
University of Minho
Braga, Portugal

Francesco Scorza [ID]
University of Basilicata
Potenza, Italy

Carmelo M. Torre [ID]
Polytechnic University of Bari
Bari, Italy

Beniamino Murgante [ID]
University of Basilicata
Potenza, Italy

Chiara Garau [ID]
University of Cagliari
Cagliari, Italy

Yeliz Karaca [ID]
University of Massachusetts Medical School
Worcester, MA, USA

ISSN 0302-9743   ISSN 1611-3349 (electronic)
Lecture Notes in Computer Science
ISBN 978-3-031-37107-3   ISBN 978-3-031-37108-0 (eBook)
https://doi.org/10.1007/978-3-031-37108-0

© The Editor(s) (if applicable) and The Author(s), under exclusive license
to Springer Nature Switzerland AG 2023
Chapter "Spatial Tools and ppWebGIS Platforms for Sustainable Urban Development and Climate Change Adaptation: Participatory Planning in Urban Areas with Special Conditions" is licensed under the terms of the Creative Commons Attribution 4.0 International License (http://creativecommons.org/licenses/by/4.0/). For further details see license information in the chapter.

This work is subject to copyright. All rights are reserved by the Publisher, whether the whole or part of the material is concerned, specifically the rights of translation, reprinting, reuse of illustrations, recitation, broadcasting, reproduction on microfilms or in any other physical way, and transmission or information storage and retrieval, electronic adaptation, computer software, or by similar or dissimilar methodology now known or hereafter developed.
The use of general descriptive names, registered names, trademarks, service marks, etc. in this publication does not imply, even in the absence of a specific statement, that such names are exempt from the relevant protective laws and regulations and therefore free for general use.
The publisher, the authors, and the editors are safe to assume that the advice and information in this book are believed to be true and accurate at the date of publication. Neither the publisher nor the authors or the editors give a warranty, expressed or implied, with respect to the material contained herein or for any errors or omissions that may have been made. The publisher remains neutral with regard to jurisdictional claims in published maps and institutional affiliations.

This Springer imprint is published by the registered company Springer Nature Switzerland AG
The registered company address is: Gewerbestrasse 11, 6330 Cham, Switzerland

Preface

These 9 volumes (LNCS volumes 14104–14112) consist of the peer-reviewed papers from the 2023 International Conference on Computational Science and Its Applications (ICCSA 2023) which took place during July 3–6, 2023. The peer-reviewed papers of the main conference tracks were published in a separate set consisting of two volumes (LNCS 13956–13957).

The conference was finally held in person after the difficult period of the Covid-19 pandemic in the wonderful city of Athens, in the cosy facilities of the National Technical University. Our experience during the pandemic period allowed us to enable virtual participation also this year for those who were unable to attend the event, due to logistical, political and economic problems, by adopting a technological infrastructure based on open source software (jitsi + riot), and a commercial cloud infrastructure.

ICCSA 2023 was another successful event in the International Conference on Computational Science and Its Applications (ICCSA) series, previously held as a hybrid event (with one third of registered authors attending in person) in Malaga, Spain (2022), Cagliari, Italy (hybrid with few participants in person in 2021 and completely online in 2020), whilst earlier editions took place in Saint Petersburg, Russia (2019), Melbourne, Australia (2018), Trieste, Italy (2017), Beijing, China (2016), Banff, Canada (2015), Guimaraes, Portugal (2014), Ho Chi Minh City, Vietnam (2013), Salvador, Brazil (2012), Santander, Spain (2011), Fukuoka, Japan (2010), Suwon, South Korea (2009), Perugia, Italy (2008), Kuala Lumpur, Malaysia (2007), Glasgow, UK (2006), Singapore (2005), Assisi, Italy (2004), Montreal, Canada (2003), and (as ICCS) Amsterdam, The Netherlands (2002) and San Francisco, USA (2001).

Computational Science is the main pillar of most of the present research, industrial and commercial applications, and plays a unique role in exploiting ICT innovative technologies, and the ICCSA series have been providing a venue to researchers and industry practitioners to discuss new ideas, to share complex problems and their solutions, and to shape new trends in Computational Science. As the conference mirrors society from a scientific point of view, this year's undoubtedly dominant theme was the machine learning and artificial intelligence and their applications in the most diverse economic and industrial fields.

The ICCSA 2023 conference is structured in 6 general tracks covering the fields of computational science and its applications: Computational Methods, Algorithms and Scientific Applications – High Performance Computing and Networks – Geometric Modeling, Graphics and Visualization – Advanced and Emerging Applications – Information Systems and Technologies – Urban and Regional Planning. In addition, the conference consisted of 61 workshops, focusing on very topical issues of importance to science, technology and society: from new mathematical approaches for solving complex computational systems, to information and knowledge in the Internet of Things, new statistical and optimization methods, several Artificial Intelligence approaches, sustainability issues, smart cities and related technologies.

In the workshop proceedings we accepted 350 full papers, 29 short papers and 2 PHD Showcase papers. In the main conference proceedings we accepted 67 full papers, 13 short papers and 6 PHD Showcase papers from 283 submissions to the General Tracks of the conference (acceptance rate 30%). We would like to express our appreciation to the workshops chairs and co-chairs for their hard work and dedication.

The success of the ICCSA conference series in general, and of ICCSA 2023 in particular, vitally depends on the support of many people: authors, presenters, participants, keynote speakers, workshop chairs, session chairs, organizing committee members, student volunteers, Program Committee members, Advisory Committee members, International Liaison chairs, reviewers and others in various roles. We take this opportunity to wholehartedly thank them all.

We also wish to thank our publisher, Springer, for their acceptance to publish the proceedings, for sponsoring part of the best papers awards and for their kind assistance and cooperation during the editing process.

We cordially invite you to visit the ICCSA website https://iccsa.org where you can find all the relevant information about this interesting and exciting event.

July 2023

Osvaldo Gervasi
Beniamino Murgante
Chiara Garau

Welcome Message from Organizers

After the 2021 ICCSA in Cagliari, Italy and the 2022 ICCSA in Malaga, Spain, ICCSA continued its successful scientific endeavours in 2023, hosted again in the Mediterranean neighbourhood. This time, ICCSA 2023 moved a bit more to the east of the Mediterranean Region and was held in the metropolitan city of Athens, the capital of Greece and a vibrant urban environment endowed with a prominent cultural heritage that dates back to the ancient years. As a matter of fact, Athens is one of the oldest cities in the world, and the cradle of democracy. The city has a history of over 3,000 years and, according to the myth, it took its name from Athena, the Goddess of Wisdom and daughter of Zeus.

ICCSA 2023 took place in a secure environment, relieved from the immense stress of the COVID-19 pandemic. This gave us the chance to have a safe and vivid, in-person participation which, combined with the very active engagement of the ICCSA 2023 scientific community, set the ground for highly motivating discussions and interactions as to the latest developments of computer science and its applications in the real world for improving quality of life.

The National Technical University of Athens (NTUA), one of the most prestigious Greek academic institutions, had the honour of hosting ICCSA 2023. The Local Organizing Committee really feels the burden and responsibility of such a demanding task; and puts in all the necessary energy in order to meet participants' expectations and establish a friendly, creative and inspiring, scientific and social/cultural environment that allows for new ideas and perspectives to flourish.

Since all ICCSA participants, either informatics-oriented or application-driven, realize the tremendous steps and evolution of computer science during the last few decades and the huge potential these offer to cope with the enormous challenges of humanity in a globalized, 'wired' and highly competitive world, the expectations from ICCSA 2023 were set high in order for a successful matching between computer science progress and communities' aspirations to be attained, i.e., a progress that serves real, place- and people-based needs and can pave the way towards a visionary, smart, sustainable, resilient and inclusive future for both the current and the next generation.

On behalf of the Local Organizing Committee, I would like to sincerely thank all of you who have contributed to ICCSA 2023 and I cordially welcome you to my 'home', NTUA.

On behalf of the Local Organizing Committee.

Anastasia Stratigea

Organization

ICCSA 2023 was organized by the National Technical University of Athens (Greece), the University of the Aegean (Greece), the University of Perugia (Italy), the University of Basilicata (Italy), Monash University (Australia), Kyushu Sangyo University (Japan), the University of Minho (Portugal). The conference was supported by two NTUA Schools, namely the School of Rural, Surveying and Geoinformatics Engineering and the School of Electrical and Computer Engineering.

Honorary General Chairs

Norio Shiratori	Chuo University, Japan
Kenneth C. J. Tan	Sardina Systems, UK

General Chairs

Osvaldo Gervasi	University of Perugia, Italy
Anastasia Stratigea	National Technical University of Athens, Greece
Bernady O. Apduhan	Kyushu Sangyo University, Japan

Program Committee Chairs

Beniamino Murgante	University of Basilicata, Italy
Dimitris Kavroudakis	University of the Aegean, Greece
Ana Maria A. C. Rocha	University of Minho, Portugal
David Taniar	Monash University, Australia

International Advisory Committee

Jemal Abawajy	Deakin University, Australia
Dharma P. Agarwal	University of Cincinnati, USA
Rajkumar Buyya	Melbourne University, Australia
Claudia Bauzer Medeiros	University of Campinas, Brazil
Manfred M. Fisher	Vienna University of Economics and Business, Austria
Marina L. Gavrilova	University of Calgary, Canada

Sumi Helal   University of Florida, USA and University of
                                    Lancaster, UK
Yee Leung   Chinese University of Hong Kong, China

International Liaison Chairs

Ivan Blečić   University of Cagliari, Italy
Giuseppe Borruso   University of Trieste, Italy
Elise De Donker   Western Michigan University, USA
Maria Irene Falcão   University of Minho, Portugal
Inmaculada Garcia Fernandez   University of Malaga, Spain
Eligius Hendrix   University of Malaga, Spain
Robert C. H. Hsu   Chung Hua University, Taiwan
Tai-Hoon Kim   Beijing Jaotong University, China
Vladimir Korkhov   Saint Petersburg University, Russia
Takashi Naka   Kyushu Sangyo University, Japan
Rafael D. C. Santos   National Institute for Space Research, Brazil
Maribel Yasmina Santos   University of Minho, Portugal
Elena Stankova   Saint Petersburg University, Russia

Workshop and Session Organizing Chairs

Beniamino Murgante   University of Basilicata, Italy
Chiara Garau   University of Cagliari, Italy

Award Chair

Wenny Rahayu   La Trobe University, Australia

Publicity Committee Chairs

Elmer Dadios   De La Salle University, Philippines
Nataliia Kulabukhova   Saint Petersburg University, Russia
Daisuke Takahashi   Tsukuba University, Japan
Shangwang Wang   Beijing University of Posts and
                                    Telecommunications, China

Local Organizing Committee Chairs

Anastasia Stratigea	National Technical University of Athens, Greece
Dimitris Kavroudakis	University of the Aegean, Greece
Charalambos Ioannidis	National Technical University of Athens, Greece
Nectarios Koziris	National Technical University of Athens, Greece
Efthymios Bakogiannis	National Technical University of Athens, Greece
Yiota Theodora	National Technical University of Athens, Greece
Dimitris Fotakis	National Technical University of Athens, Greece
Apostolos Lagarias	National Technical University of Athens, Greece
Akrivi Leka	National Technical University of Athens, Greece
Dionisia Koutsi	National Technical University of Athens, Greece
Alkistis Dalkavouki	National Technical University of Athens, Greece
Maria Panagiotopoulou	National Technical University of Athens, Greece
Angeliki Papazoglou	National Technical University of Athens, Greece
Natalia Tsigarda	National Technical University of Athens, Greece
Konstantinos Athanasopoulos	National Technical University of Athens, Greece
Ioannis Xatziioannou	National Technical University of Athens, Greece
Vasiliki Krommyda	National Technical University of Athens, Greece
Panayiotis Patsilinakos	National Technical University of Athens, Greece
Sofia Kassiou	National Technical University of Athens, Greece

Technology Chair

Damiano Perri	University of Florence, Italy

Program Committee

Vera Afreixo	University of Aveiro, Portugal
Filipe Alvelos	University of Minho, Portugal
Hartmut Asche	University of Potsdam, Germany
Ginevra Balletto	University of Cagliari, Italy
Michela Bertolotto	University College Dublin, Ireland
Sandro Bimonte	CEMAGREF, TSCF, France
Rod Blais	University of Calgary, Canada
Ivan Blečić	University of Sassari, Italy
Giuseppe Borruso	University of Trieste, Italy
Ana Cristina Braga	University of Minho, Portugal
Massimo Cafaro	University of Salento, Italy
Yves Caniou	Lyon University, France

Ermanno Cardelli	University of Perugia, Italy
José A. Cardoso e Cunha	Universidade Nova de Lisboa, Portugal
Rui Cardoso	University of Beira Interior, Portugal
Leocadio G. Casado	University of Almeria, Spain
Carlo Cattani	University of Salerno, Italy
Mete Celik	Erciyes University, Turkey
Maria Cerreta	University of Naples "Federico II", Italy
Hyunseung Choo	Sungkyunkwan University, Korea
Rachel Chieng-Sing Lee	Sunway University, Malaysia
Min Young Chung	Sungkyunkwan University, Korea
Florbela Maria da Cruz Domingues Correia	Polytechnic Institute of Viana do Castelo, Portugal
Gilberto Corso Pereira	Federal University of Bahia, Brazil
Alessandro Costantini	INFN, Italy
Carla Dal Sasso Freitas	Universidade Federal do Rio Grande do Sul, Brazil
Pradesh Debba	The Council for Scientific and Industrial Research (CSIR), South Africa
Hendrik Decker	Instituto Tecnológico de Informática, Spain
Robertas Damaševičius	Kausan University of Technology, Lithuania
Frank Devai	London South Bank University, UK
Rodolphe Devillers	Memorial University of Newfoundland, Canada
Joana Matos Dias	University of Coimbra, Portugal
Paolino Di Felice	University of L'Aquila, Italy
Prabu Dorairaj	NetApp, India/USA
Noelia Faginas Lago	University of Perugia, Italy
M. Irene Falcao	University of Minho, Portugal
Cherry Liu Fang	U.S. DOE Ames Laboratory, USA
Florbela P. Fernandes	Polytechnic Institute of Bragança, Portugal
Jose-Jesus Fernandez	National Centre for Biotechnology, CSIS, Spain
Paula Odete Fernandes	Polytechnic Institute of Bragança, Portugal
Adelaide de Fátima Baptista Valente Freitas	University of Aveiro, Portugal
Manuel Carlos Figueiredo	University of Minho, Portugal
Maria Celia Furtado Rocha	PRODEB–PósCultura/UFBA, Brazil
Chiara Garau	University of Cagliari, Italy
Paulino Jose Garcia Nieto	University of Oviedo, Spain
Raffaele Garrisi	Polizia di Stato, Italy
Jerome Gensel	LSR-IMAG, France
Maria Giaoutzi	National Technical University, Athens, Greece
Arminda Manuela Andrade Pereira Gonçalves	University of Minho, Portugal

Andrzej M. Goscinski	Deakin University, Australia
Sevin Gümgüm	Izmir University of Economics, Turkey
Alex Hagen-Zanker	University of Cambridge, UK
Shanmugasundaram Hariharan	B.S. Abdur Rahman University, India
Eligius M. T. Hendrix	University of Malaga, Spain and Wageningen University, The Netherlands
Hisamoto Hiyoshi	Gunma University, Japan
Mustafa Inceoglu	EGE University, Turkey
Peter Jimack	University of Leeds, UK
Qun Jin	Waseda University, Japan
Yeliz Karaca	University of Massachusetts Medical School, Worcester, USA
Farid Karimipour	Vienna University of Technology, Austria
Baris Kazar	Oracle Corp., USA
Maulana Adhinugraha Kiki	Telkom University, Indonesia
DongSeong Kim	University of Canterbury, New Zealand
Taihoon Kim	Hannam University, Korea
Ivana Kolingerova	University of West Bohemia, Czech Republic
Nataliia Kulabukhova	St. Petersburg University, Russia
Vladimir Korkhov	St. Petersburg University, Russia
Rosa Lasaponara	National Research Council, Italy
Maurizio Lazzari	National Research Council, Italy
Cheng Siong Lee	Monash University, Australia
Sangyoun Lee	Yonsei University, Korea
Jongchan Lee	Kunsan National University, Korea
Chendong Li	University of Connecticut, USA
Gang Li	Deakin University, Australia
Fang Liu	AMES Laboratories, USA
Xin Liu	University of Calgary, Canada
Andrea Lombardi	University of Perugia, Italy
Savino Longo	University of Bari, Italy
Tinghuai Ma	Nanjing University of Information Science & Technology, China
Ernesto Marcheggiani	Katholieke Universiteit Leuven, Belgium
Antonino Marvuglia	Research Centre Henri Tudor, Luxembourg
Nicola Masini	National Research Council, Italy
Ilaria Matteucci	National Research Council, Italy
Nirvana Meratnia	University of Twente, The Netherlands
Fernando Miranda	University of Minho, Portugal
Giuseppe Modica	University of Reggio Calabria, Italy
Josè Luis Montaña	University of Cantabria, Spain
Maria Filipa Mourão	Instituto Politécnico de Viana do Castelo, Portugal

Louiza de Macedo Mourelle	State University of Rio de Janeiro, Brazil
Nadia Nedjah	State University of Rio de Janeiro, Brazil
Laszlo Neumann	University of Girona, Spain
Kok-Leong Ong	Deakin University, Australia
Belen Palop	Universidad de Valladolid, Spain
Marcin Paprzycki	Polish Academy of Sciences, Poland
Eric Pardede	La Trobe University, Australia
Kwangjin Park	Wonkwang University, Korea
Ana Isabel Pereira	Polytechnic Institute of Bragança, Portugal
Massimiliano Petri	University of Pisa, Italy
Telmo Pinto	University of Coimbra, Portugal
Maurizio Pollino	Italian National Agency for New Technologies, Energy and Sustainable Economic Development, Italy
Alenka Poplin	University of Hamburg, Germany
Vidyasagar Potdar	Curtin University of Technology, Australia
David C. Prosperi	Florida Atlantic University, USA
Wenny Rahayu	La Trobe University, Australia
Jerzy Respondek	Silesian University of Technology Poland
Humberto Rocha	INESC-Coimbra, Portugal
Jon Rokne	University of Calgary, Canada
Octavio Roncero	CSIC, Spain
Maytham Safar	Kuwait University, Kuwait
Chiara Saracino	A.O. Ospedale Niguarda Ca' Granda - Milano, Italy
Marco Paulo Seabra dos Reis	University of Coimbra, Portugal
Jie Shen	University of Michigan, USA
Qi Shi	Liverpool John Moores University, UK
Dale Shires	U.S. Army Research Laboratory, USA
Inês Soares	University of Coimbra, Portugal
Elena Stankova	St. Petersburg University, Russia
Takuo Suganuma	Tohoku University, Japan
Eufemia Tarantino	Polytechnic of Bari, Italy
Sergio Tasso	University of Perugia, Italy
Ana Paula Teixeira	University of Trás-os-Montes and Alto Douro, Portugal
M. Filomena Teodoro	Portuguese Naval Academy and University of Lisbon, Portugal
Parimala Thulasiraman	University of Manitoba, Canada
Carmelo Torre	Polytechnic of Bari, Italy
Javier Martinez Torres	Centro Universitario de la Defensa Zaragoza, Spain

Giuseppe A. Trunfio	University of Sassari, Italy
Pablo Vanegas	University of Cuenca, Equador
Marco Vizzari	University of Perugia, Italy
Varun Vohra	Merck Inc., USA
Koichi Wada	University of Tsukuba, Japan
Krzysztof Walkowiak	Wroclaw University of Technology, Poland
Zequn Wang	Intelligent Automation Inc, USA
Robert Weibel	University of Zurich, Switzerland
Frank Westad	Norwegian University of Science and Technology, Norway
Roland Wismüller	Universität Siegen, Germany
Mudasser Wyne	SOET National University, USA
Chung-Huang Yang	National Kaohsiung Normal University, Taiwan
Xin-She Yang	National Physical Laboratory, UK
Salim Zabir	France Telecom Japan Co., Japan
Haifeng Zhao	University of California, Davis, USA
Fabiana Zollo	University of Venice "Cà Foscari", Italy
Albert Y. Zomaya	University of Sydney, Australia

Workshop Organizers

Advanced Data Science Techniques with Applications in Industry and Environmental Sustainability (ATELIERS 2023)

Dario Torregrossa	Goodyear, Luxemburg
Antonino Marvuglia	Luxembourg Institute of Science and Technology, Luxemburg
Valeria Borodin	École des Mines de Saint-Étienne, Luxemburg
Mohamed Laib	Luxembourg Institute of Science and Technology, Luxemburg

Advances in Artificial Intelligence Learning Technologies: Blended Learning, STEM, Computational Thinking and Coding (AAILT 2023)

Alfredo Milani	University of Perugia, Italy
Valentina Franzoni	University of Perugia, Italy
Sergio Tasso	University of Perugia, Italy

Advanced Processes of Mathematics and Computing Models in Complex Computational Systems (ACMC 2023)

Yeliz Karaca   University of Massachusetts Chan Medical
                               School and Massachusetts Institute of
                               Technology, USA
Dumitru Baleanu   Cankaya University, Turkey
Osvaldo Gervasi   University of Perugia, Italy
Yudong Zhang   University of Leicester, UK
Majaz Moonis   University of Massachusetts Medical School,
                               USA

Artificial Intelligence Supported Medical Data Examination (AIM 2023)

David Taniar   Monash University, Australia
Seifedine Kadry   Noroff University College, Norway
Venkatesan Rajinikanth   Saveetha School of Engineering, India

Advanced and Innovative Web Apps (AIWA 2023)

Damiano Perri   University of Perugia, Italy
Osvaldo Gervasi   University of Perugia, Italy

Assessing Urban Sustainability (ASUS 2023)

Elena Todella   Polytechnic of Turin, Italy
Marika Gaballo   Polytechnic of Turin, Italy
Beatrice Mecca   Polytechnic of Turin, Italy

Advances in Web Based Learning (AWBL 2023)

Birol Ciloglugil   Ege University, Turkey
Mustafa Inceoglu   Ege University, Turkey

Blockchain and Distributed Ledgers: Technologies and Applications (BDLTA 2023)

Vladimir Korkhov   Saint Petersburg State University, Russia
Elena Stankova   Saint Petersburg State University, Russia
Nataliia Kulabukhova   Saint Petersburg State University, Russia

Bio and Neuro Inspired Computing and Applications (BIONCA 2023)

Nadia Nedjah   State University of Rio De Janeiro, Brazil
Luiza De Macedo Mourelle   State University of Rio De Janeiro, Brazil

Choices and Actions for Human Scale Cities: Decision Support Systems (CAHSC–DSS 2023)

Giovanna Acampa   University of Florence and University of Enna Kore, Italy
Fabrizio Finucci   Roma Tre University, Italy
Luca S. Dacci   Polytechnic of Turin, Italy

Computational and Applied Mathematics (CAM 2023)

Maria Irene Falcao   University of Minho, Portugal
Fernando Miranda   University of Minho, Portugal

Computational and Applied Statistics (CAS 2023)

Ana Cristina Braga   University of Minho, Portugal

Cyber Intelligence and Applications (CIA 2023)

Gianni Dangelo   University of Salerno, Italy
Francesco Palmieri   University of Salerno, Italy
Massimo Ficco   University of Salerno, Italy

Conversations South-North on Climate Change Adaptation Towards Smarter and More Sustainable Cities (CLAPS 2023)

Chiara Garau	University of Cagliari, Italy
Cristina Trois	University of kwaZulu-Natal, South Africa
Claudia Loggia	University of kwaZulu-Natal, South Africa
John Östh	Faculty of Technology, Art and Design, Norway
Mauro Coni	University of Cagliari, Italy
Alessio Satta	MedSea Foundation, Italy

Computational Mathematics, Statistics and Information Management (CMSIM 2023)

Maria Filomena Teodoro	University of Lisbon and Portuguese Naval Academy, Portugal
Marina A. P. Andrade	University Institute of Lisbon, Portugal

Computational Optimization and Applications (COA 2023)

Ana Maria A. C. Rocha	University of Minho, Portugal
Humberto Rocha	University of Coimbra, Portugal

Computational Astrochemistry (CompAstro 2023)

Marzio Rosi	University of Perugia, Italy
Nadia Balucani	University of Perugia, Italy
Cecilia Ceccarelli	University of Grenoble Alpes and Institute for Planetary Sciences and Astrophysics, France
Stefano Falcinelli	University of Perugia, Italy

Computational Methods for Porous Geomaterials (CompPor 2023)

Vadim Lisitsa	Russian Academy of Science, Russia
Evgeniy Romenski	Russian Academy of Science, Russia

Workshop on Computational Science and HPC (CSHPC 2023)

Elise De Doncker	Western Michigan University, USA
Fukuko Yuasa	High Energy Accelerator Research Organization, Japan
Hideo Matsufuru	High Energy Accelerator Research Organization, Japan

Cities, Technologies and Planning (CTP 2023)

Giuseppe Borruso	University of Trieste, Italy
Beniamino Murgante	University of Basilicata, Italy
Malgorzata Hanzl	Lodz University of Technology, Poland
Anastasia Stratigea	National Technical University of Athens, Greece
Ljiljana Zivkovic	Republic Geodetic Authority, Serbia
Ginevra Balletto	University of Cagliari, Italy

Gender Equity/Equality in Transport and Mobility (DELIA 2023)

Tiziana Campisi	University of Enna Kore, Italy
Ines Charradi	Sousse University, Tunisia
Alexandros Nikitas	University of Huddersfield, UK
Kh Md Nahiduzzaman	University of British Columbia, Canada
Andreas Nikiforiadis	Aristotle University of Thessaloniki, Greece
Socrates Basbas	Aristotle University of Thessaloniki, Greece

International Workshop on Defense Technology and Security (DTS 2023)

Yeonseung Ryu	Myongji University, South Korea

Integrated Methods for the Ecosystem-Services Accounting in Urban Decision Process (Ecourbn 2023)

Maria Rosaria Guarini	Sapienza University of Rome, Italy
Francesco Sica	Sapienza University of Rome, Italy
Francesco Tajani	Sapienza University of Rome, Italy

Carmelo Maria Torre	Polytechnic University of Bari, Italy
Pierluigi Morano	Polytechnic University of Bari, Italy
Rossana Ranieri	Sapienza Università di Roma, Italy

Evaluating Inner Areas Potentials (EIAP 2023)

Diana Rolando	Politechnic of Turin, Italy
Manuela Rebaudengo	Politechnic of Turin, Italy
Alice Barreca	Politechnic of Turin, Italy
Giorgia Malavasi	Politechnic of Turin, Italy
Umberto Mecca	Politechnic of Turin, Italy

Sustainable Mobility Last Mile Logistic (ELLIOT 2023)

Tiziana Campisi	University of Enna Kore, Italy
Socrates Basbas	Aristotle University of Thessaloniki, Greece
Grigorios Fountas	Aristotle University of Thessaloniki, Greece
Paraskevas Nikolaou	University of Cyprus, Cyprus
Drazenko Glavic	University of Belgrade, Serbia
Antonio Russo	University of Enna Kore, Italy

Econometrics and Multidimensional Evaluation of Urban Environment (EMEUE 2023)

Maria Cerreta	University of Naples Federico II, Italy
Carmelo Maria Torre	Politechnic of Bari, Italy
Pierluigi Morano	Polytechnic of Bari, Italy
Debora Anelli	Polytechnic of Bari, Italy
Francesco Tajani	Sapienza University of Rome, Italy
Simona Panaro	University of Sussex, UK

Ecosystem Services in Spatial Planning for Resilient Urban and Rural Areas (ESSP 2023)

Sabrina Lai	University of Cagliari, Italy
Francesco Scorza	University of Basilicata, Italy
Corrado Zoppi	University of Cagliari, Italy

Gerardo Carpentieri   University of Naples Federico II, Italy
Floriana Zucaro   University of Naples Federico II, Italy
Ana Clara Mourão Moura   Federal University of Minas Gerais, Brazil

Ethical AI Applications for a Human-Centered Cyber Society (EthicAI 2023)

Valentina Franzoni   University of Perugia, Italy
Alfredo Milani   University of Perugia, Italy
Jordi Vallverdu   University Autonoma Barcelona, Spain
Roberto Capobianco   Sapienza University of Rome, Italy

13th International Workshop on Future Computing System Technologies and Applications (FiSTA 2023)

Bernady Apduhan   Kyushu Sangyo University, Japan
Rafael Santos   National Institute for Space Research, Brazil

Collaborative Planning and Designing for the Future with Geospatial Applications (GeoCollab 2023)

Alenka Poplin   Iowa State University, USA
Rosanna Rivero   University of Georgia, USA
Michele Campagna   University of Cagliari, Italy
Ana Clara Mourão Moura   Federal University of Minas Gerais, Brazil

Geomatics in Agriculture and Forestry: New Advances and Perspectives (GeoForAgr 2023)

Maurizio Pollino   Italian National Agency for New Technologies,
                             Energy and Sustainable Economic
                             Development, Italy
Giuseppe Modica   University of Reggio Calabria, Italy
Marco Vizzari   University of Perugia, Italy
Salvatore Praticò   University of Reggio Calabria, Italy

Geographical Analysis, Urban Modeling, Spatial Statistics (Geog-An-Mod 2023)

Giuseppe Borruso	University of Trieste, Italy
Beniamino Murgante	University of Basilicata, Italy
Harmut Asche	Hasso-Plattner-Institut für Digital Engineering Ggmbh, Germany

Geomatics for Resource Monitoring and Management (GRMM 2023)

Alessandra Capolupo	Polytechnic of Bari, Italy
Eufemia Tarantino	Polytechnic of Bari, Italy
Enrico Borgogno Mondino	University of Turin, Italy

International Workshop on Information and Knowledge in the Internet of Things (IKIT 2023)

Teresa Guarda	Peninsula State University of Santa Elena, Ecuador
Modestos Stavrakis	University of the Aegean, Greece

International Workshop on Collective, Massive and Evolutionary Systems (IWCES 2023)

Alfredo Milani	University of Perugia, Italy
Rajdeep Niyogi	Indian Institute of Technology, India
Valentina Franzoni	University of Perugia, Italy

Multidimensional Evolutionary Evaluations for Transformative Approaches (MEETA 2023)

Maria Cerreta	University of Naples Federico II, Italy
Giuliano Poli	University of Naples Federico II, Italy
Ludovica Larocca	University of Naples Federico II, Italy
Chiara Mazzarella	University of Naples Federico II, Italy

Stefania Regalbuto   University of Naples Federico II, Italy
Maria Somma   University of Naples Federico II, Italy

Building Multi-dimensional Models for Assessing Complex Environmental Systems (MES 2023)

Marta Dell'Ovo   Politechnic of Milan, Italy
Vanessa Assumma   University of Bologna, Italy
Caterina Caprioli   Politechnic of Turin, Italy
Giulia Datola   Politechnic of Turin, Italy
Federico Dellanna   Politechnic of Turin, Italy
Marco Rossitti   Politechnic of Milan, Italy

Metropolitan City Lab (Metro_City_Lab 2023)

Ginevra Balletto   University of Cagliari, Italy
Luigi Mundula   University for Foreigners of Perugia, Italy
Giuseppe Borruso   University of Trieste, Italy
Jacopo Torriti   University of Reading, UK
Isabella Ligia   Metropolitan City of Cagliari, Italy

Mathematical Methods for Image Processing and Understanding (MMIPU 2023)

Ivan Gerace   University of Perugia, Italy
Gianluca Vinti   University of Perugia, Italy
Arianna Travaglini   University of Florence, Italy

Models and Indicators for Assessing and Measuring the Urban Settlement Development in the View of ZERO Net Land Take by 2050 (MOVEto0 2023)

Lucia Saganeiti   University of L'Aquila, Italy
Lorena Fiorini   University of L'Aquila, Italy
Angela Pilogallo   University of L'Aquila, Italy
Alessandro Marucci   University of L'Aquila, Italy
Francesco Zullo   University of L'Aquila, Italy

Modelling Post-Covid Cities (MPCC 2023)

Giuseppe Borruso   University of Trieste, Italy
Beniamino Murgante   University of Basilicata, Italy
Ginevra Balletto   University of Cagliari, Italy
Lucia Saganeiti   University of L'Aquila, Italy
Marco Dettori   University of Sassari, Italy

3rd Workshop on Privacy in the Cloud/Edge/IoT World (PCEIoT 2023)

Michele Mastroianni   University of Salerno, Italy
Lelio Campanile   University of Campania Luigi Vanvitelli, Italy
Mauro Iacono   University of Campania Luigi Vanvitelli, Italy

Port City Interface: Land Use, Logistic and Rear Port Area Planning (PORTUNO 2023)

Tiziana Campisi   University of Enna Kore, Italy
Socrates Basbas   Aristotle University of Thessaloniki, Greece
Efstathios Bouhouras   Aristotle University of Thessaloniki, Greece
Giovanni Tesoriere   University of Enna Kore, Italy
Elena Cocuzza   University of Catania, Italy
Gianfranco Fancello   University of Cagliari, Italy

Scientific Computing Infrastructure (SCI 2023)

Elena Stankova   St. Petersburg State University, Russia
Vladimir Korkhov   St. Petersburg University, Russia

Supply Chains, IoT, and Smart Technologies (SCIS 2023)

Ha Jin Hwang   Sunway University, South Korea
Hangkon Kim   Daegu Catholic University, South Korea
Jan Seruga   Australian Catholic University, Australia

Spatial Cognition in Urban and Regional Planning Under Risk (SCOPUR23)

Domenico Camarda   Polytechnic of Bari, Italy
Giulia Mastrodonato   Polytechnic of Bari, Italy
Stefania Santoro   Polytechnic of Bari, Italy
Maria Rosaria Stufano Melone Polytechnic of Bari, Italy
Mauro Patano   Polytechnic of Bari, Italy

Socio-Economic and Environmental Models for Land Use Management (SEMLUM 2023)

Debora Anelli   Polytechnic of Bari, Italy
Pierluigi Morano   Polytechnic of Bari, Italy
Benedetto Manganelli   University of Basilicata, Italy
Francesco Tajani   Sapienza University of Rome, Italy
Marco Locurcio   Polytechnic of Bari, Italy
Felicia Di Liddo   Polytechnic of Bari, Italy

Ports of the Future - Smartness and Sustainability (SmartPorts 2023)

Ginevra Balletto   University of Cagliari, Italy
Gianfranco Fancello   University of Cagliari, Italy
Patrizia Serra   University of Cagliari, Italy
Agostino Bruzzone   University of Genoa, Italy
Alberto Camarero   Politechnic of Madrid, Spain
Thierry Vanelslander   University of Antwerp, Belgium

Smart Transport and Logistics - Smart Supply Chains (SmarTransLog 2023)

Giuseppe Borruso   University of Trieste, Italy
Marco Mazzarino   University of Venice, Italy
Marcello Tadini   University of Eastern Piedmont, Italy
Luigi Mundula   University for Foreigners of Perugia, Italy
Mara Ladu   University of Cagliari, Italy
Maria del Mar Munoz Leonisio University of Cadiz, Spain

Smart Tourism (SmartTourism 2023)

Giuseppe Borruso	University of Trieste, Italy
Silvia Battino	University of Sassari, Italy
Ainhoa Amaro Garcia	University of Alcala and University of Las Palmas, Spain
Francesca Krasna	University of Trieste, Italy
Ginevra Balletto	University of Cagliari, Italy
Maria del Mar Munoz Leonisio	University of Cadiz, Spain

Sustainability Performance Assessment: Models, Approaches, and Applications Toward Interdisciplinary and Integrated Solutions (SPA 2023)

Sabrina Lai	University of Cagliari, Italy
Francesco Scorza	University of Basilicata, Italy
Jolanta Dvarioniene	Kaunas University of Technology, Lithuania
Valentin Grecu	Lucian Blaga University of Sibiu, Romania
Georgia Pozoukidou	Aristotle University of Thessaloniki, Greece

Spatial Energy Planning, City and Urban Heritage (Spatial_Energy_City 2023)

Ginevra Balletto	University of Cagliari, Italy
Mara Ladu	University of Cagliari, Italy
Emilio Ghiani	University of Cagliari, Italy
Roberto De Lotto	University of Pavia, Italy
Roberto Gerundo	University of Salerno, Italy

Specifics of Smart Cities Development in Europe (SPEED 2023)

Chiara Garau	University of Cagliari, Italy
Katarína Vitálišová	Matej Bel University, Slovakia
Paolo Nesi	University of Florence, Italy
Anna Vaňová	Matej Bel University, Slovakia
Kamila Borsekova	Matej Bel University, Slovakia
Paola Zamperlin	University of Pisa, Italy

Smart, Safe and Health Cities (SSHC 2023)

Chiara Garau	University of Cagliari, Italy
Gerardo Carpentieri	University of Naples Federico II, Italy
Floriana Zucaro	University of Naples Federico II, Italy
Aynaz Lotfata	Chicago State University, USA
Alfonso Annunziata	University of Basilicata, Italy
Diego Altafini	University of Pisa, Italy

Smart and Sustainable Island Communities (SSIC_2023)

Chiara Garau	University of Cagliari, Italy
Anastasia Stratigea	National Technical University of Athens, Greece
Yiota Theodora	National Technical University of Athens, Greece
Giulia Desogus	University of Cagliari, Italy

Theoretical and Computational Chemistry and Its Applications (TCCMA 2023)

Noelia Faginas-Lago	University of Perugia, Italy
Andrea Lombardi	University of Perugia, Italy

Transport Infrastructures for Smart Cities (TISC 2023)

Francesca Maltinti	University of Cagliari, Italy
Mauro Coni	University of Cagliari, Italy
Francesco Pinna	University of Cagliari, Italy
Chiara Garau	University of Cagliari, Italy
Nicoletta Rassu	University of Cagliari, Italy
James Rombi	University of Cagliari, Italy

Urban Regeneration: Innovative Tools and Evaluation Model (URITEM 2023)

Fabrizio Battisti	University of Florence, Italy
Giovanna Acampa	University of Florence and University of Enna Kore, Italy
Orazio Campo	La Sapienza University of Rome, Italy

Urban Space Accessibility and Mobilities (USAM 2023)

Chiara Garau	University of Cagliari, Italy
Matteo Ignaccolo	University of Catania, Italy
Michela Tiboni	University of Brescia, Italy
Francesco Pinna	University of Cagliari, Italy
Silvia Rossetti	University of Parma, Italy
Vincenza Torrisi	University of Catania, Italy
Ilaria Delponte	University of Genoa, Italy

Virtual Reality and Augmented Reality and Applications (VRA 2023)

Osvaldo Gervasi	University of Perugia, Italy
Damiano Perri	University of Florence, Italy
Marco Simonetti	University of Florence, Italy
Sergio Tasso	University of Perugia, Italy

Workshop on Advanced and Computational Methods for Earth Science Applications (WACM4ES 2023)

Luca Piroddi	University of Malta, Malta
Sebastiano Damico	University of Malta, Malta
Marilena Cozzolino	Università del Molise, Italy
Adam Gauci	University of Malta, Italy
Giuseppina Vacca	University of Cagliari, Italy
Chiara Garau	University of Cagliari, Italy

Sponsoring Organizations

ICCSA 2023 would not have been possible without the tremendous support of many organizations and institutions, for which all organizers and participants of ICCSA 2023 express their sincere gratitude:

Springer Nature Switzerland AG, Switzerland
(https://www.springer.com)

Computers Open Access Journal
(https://www.mdpi.com/journal/computers)

National Technical University of Athens, Greece
(https://www.ntua.gr/)

University of the Aegean, Greece
(https://www.aegean.edu/)

University of Perugia, Italy
(https://www.unipg.it)

University of Basilicata, Italy
(http://www.unibas.it)

 Monash University, Australia
(https://www.monash.edu/)

 Kyushu Sangyo University, Japan
(https://www.kyusan-u.ac.jp/)

 University of Minho, Portugal
(https://www.uminho.pt/)

Universidade do Minho
Escola de Engenharia

Referees

Francesca Abastante	Turin Polytechnic, Italy
Giovanna Acampa	University of Enna Kore, Italy
Adewole Adewumi	Algonquin College, Canada
Vera Afreixo	University of Aveiro, Portugal
Riad Aggoune	Luxembourg Institute of Science and Technology, Luxembourg
Akshat Agrawal	Amity University Haryana, India
Waseem Ahmad	National Institute of Technology Karnataka, India
Oylum Alatlı	Ege University, Turkey
Abraham Alfa	Federal University of Technology Minna, Nigeria
Diego Altafini	University of Pisa, Italy
Filipe Alvelos	University of Minho, Portugal
Marina Alexandra Pedro Andrade	University Institute of Lisbon, Portugal
Debora Anelli	Polytechnic University of Bari, Italy
Mariarosaria Angrisano	Pegaso University, Italy
Alfonso Annunziata	University of Cagliari, Italy
Magarò Antonio	Sapienza University of Rome, Italy
Bernady Apduhan	Kyushu Sangyo University, Japan
Jonathan Apeh	Covenant University, Nigeria
Daniela Ascenzi	University of Trento, Italy
Vanessa Assumma	University of Bologna, Italy
Maria Fernanda Augusto	Bitrum Research Center, Spain
Marco Baioletti	University of Perugia, Italy

Ginevra Balletto	University of Cagliari, Italy
Carlos Balsa	Polytechnic Institute of Bragança, Portugal
Benedetto Barabino	University of Brescia, Italy
Simona Barbaro	University of Palermo, Italy
Sebastiano Barbieri	Turin Polytechnic, Italy
Kousik Barik	University of Alcala, Spain
Alice Barreca	Turin Polytechnic, Italy
Socrates Basbas	Aristotle University of Thessaloniki, Greece
Rosaria Battarra	National Research Council, Italy
Silvia Battino	University of Sassari, Italy
Fabrizio Battisti	University of Florence, Italy
Yaroslav Bazaikin	Jan Evangelista Purkyne University, Czech Republic
Ranjan Kumar Behera	Indian Institute of Information Technology, India
Simone Belli	Complutense University of Madrid, Spain
Oscar Bellini	Polytechnic University of Milan, Italy
Giulio Biondi	University of Perugia, Italy
Adriano Bisello	Eurac Research, Italy
Semen Bochkov	Ulyanovsk State Technical University, Russia
Alexander Bogdanov	St. Petersburg State University, Russia
Letizia Bollini	Free University of Bozen, Italy
Giuseppe Borruso	University of Trieste, Italy
Marilisa Botte	University of Naples Federico II, Italy
Ana Cristina Braga	University of Minho, Portugal
Frederico Branco	University of Trás-os-Montes and Alto Douro, Portugal
Jorge Buele	Indoamérica Technological University, Ecuador
Datzania Lizeth Burgos	Peninsula State University of Santa Elena, Ecuador
Isabel Cacao	University of Aveiro, Portugal
Francesco Calabrò	Mediterranea University of Reggio Calabria, Italy
Rogerio Calazan	Institute of Sea Studies Almirante Paulo Moreira, Brazil
Lelio Campanile	University of Campania Luigi Vanvitelli, Italy
Tiziana Campisi	University of Enna Kore, Italy
Orazio Campo	University of Rome La Sapienza, Italy
Caterina Caprioli	Turin Polytechnic, Italy
Gerardo Carpentieri	University of Naples Federico II, Italy
Martina Carra	University of Brescia, Italy
Barbara Caselli	University of Parma, Italy
Danny Casprini	Politechnic of Milan, Italy

Omar Fernando Castellanos
  Balleteros — Peninsula State University of Santa Elena,
  Ecuador
Arcangelo Castiglione — University of Salerno, Italy
Giulio Cavana — Turin Polytechnic, Italy
Maria Cerreta — University of Naples Federico II, Italy
Sabarathinam Chockalingam — Institute for Energy Technology, Norway
Luis Enrique Chuquimarca
  Jimenez — Peninsula State University of Santa Elena,
  Ecuador
Birol Ciloglugil — Ege University, Turkey
Elena Cocuzza — Univesity of Catania, Italy
Emanuele Colica — University of Malta, Malta
Mauro Coni — University of Cagliari, Italy
Simone Corrado — University of Basilicata, Italy
Elisete Correia — University of Trás-os-Montes and Alto Douro,
  Portugal
Florbela Correia — Polytechnic Institute Viana do Castelo, Portugal
Paulo Cortez — University of Minho, Portugal
Martina Corti — Politechnic of Milan, Italy
Lino Costa — Universidade do Minho, Portugal
Cecília Maria Vasconcelos Costa e
  Castro — University of Minho, Portugal
Alfredo Cuzzocrea — University of Calabria, Italy
Sebastiano D'amico — University of Malta, Malta
Maria Danese — National Research Council, Italy
Gianni Dangelo — University of Salerno, Italy
Ana Daniel — Aveiro University, Portugal
Giulia Datola — Politechnic of Milan, Italy
Regina De Almeida — University of Trás-os-Montes and Alto Douro,
  Portugal
Maria Stella De Biase — University of Campania Luigi Vanvitelli, Italy
Elise De Doncker — Western Michigan University, USA
Luiza De Macedo Mourelle — State University of Rio de Janeiro, Brazil
Itamir De Morais Barroca Filho — Federal University of Rio Grande do Norte, Brazil
Pierfrancesco De Paola — University of Naples Federico II, Italy
Francesco De Pascale — University of Turin, Italy
Manuela De Ruggiero — University of Calabria, Italy
Alexander Degtyarev — St. Petersburg State University, Russia
Federico Dellanna — Turin Polytechnic, Italy
Marta Dellovo — Politechnic of Milan, Italy
Bashir Derradji — Sfax University, Tunisia
Giulia Desogus — University of Cagliari, Italy
Frank Devai — London South Bank University, UK

Piero Di Bonito	University of Campania Luigi Vanvitelli, Italy
Chiara Di Dato	University of L'Aquila, Italy
Michele Di Giovanni	University of Campania Luigi Vanvitelli, Italy
Felicia Di Liddo	Polytechnic University of Bari, Italy
Joana Dias	University of Coimbra, Portugal
Luigi Dolores	University of Salerno, Italy
Marco Donatelli	University of Insubria, Italy
Aziz Dursun	Virginia Tech University, USA
Jaroslav Dvořak	Klaipeda University, Lithuania
Wolfgang Erb	University of Padova, Italy
Maurizio Francesco Errigo	University of Enna Kore, Italy
Noelia Faginas-Lago	University of Perugia, Italy
Maria Irene Falcao	University of Minho, Portugal
Stefano Falcinelli	University of Perugia, Italy
Grazia Fattoruso	Italian National Agency for New Technologies, Energy and Sustainable Economic Development, Italy
Sara Favargiotti	University of Trento, Italy
Marcin Feltynowski	University of Lodz, Poland
António Fernandes	Polytechnic Institute of Bragança, Portugal
Florbela P. Fernandes	Polytechnic Institute of Bragança, Portugal
Paula Odete Fernandes	Polytechnic Institute of Bragança, Portugal
Luis Fernandez-Sanz	University of Alcala, Spain
Maria Eugenia Ferrao	University of Beira Interior and University of Lisbon, Portugal
Luís Ferrás	University of Minho, Portugal
Angela Ferreira	Polytechnic Institute of Bragança, Portugal
Maddalena Ferretti	Politechnic of Marche, Italy
Manuel Carlos Figueiredo	University of Minho, Portugal
Fabrizio Finucci	Roma Tre University, Italy
Ugo Fiore	University Pathenope of Naples, Italy
Lorena Fiorini	University of L'Aquila, Italy
Valentina Franzoni	Perugia University, Italy
Adelaide Freitas	University of Aveiro, Portugal
Kirill Gadylshin	Russian Academy of Sciences, Russia
Andrea Gallo	University of Trieste, Italy
Luciano Galone	University of Malta, Malta
Chiara Garau	University of Cagliari, Italy
Ernesto Garcia Para	Universidad del País Vasco, Spain
Rachele Vanessa Gatto	Università della Basilicata, Italy
Marina Gavrilova	University of Calgary, Canada
Georgios Georgiadis	Aristotle University of Thessaloniki, Greece

Ivan Gerace	University of Perugia, Italy
Osvaldo Gervasi	University of Perugia, Italy
Alfonso Giancotti	Sapienza University of Rome, Italy
Andrea Gioia	Politechnic of Bari, Italy
Giacomo Giorgi	University of Perugia, Italy
Salvatore Giuffrida	Università di Catania, Italy
A. Manuela Gonçalves	University of Minho, Portugal
Angela Gorgoglione	University of the Republic, Uruguay
Yusuke Gotoh	Okayama University, Japan
Mariolina Grasso	University of Enna Kore, Italy
Silvana Grillo	University of Cagliari, Italy
Teresa Guarda	Universidad Estatal Peninsula de Santa Elena, Ecuador
Eduardo Guerra	Free University of Bozen-Bolzano, Italy
Carmen Guida	University of Napoli Federico II, Italy
Kemal Güven Gülen	Namık Kemal University, Turkey
Malgorzata Hanzl	Technical University of Lodz, Poland
Peter Hegedus	University of Szeged, Hungary
Syeda Sumbul Hossain	Daffodil International University, Bangladesh
Mustafa Inceoglu	Ege University, Turkey
Federica Isola	University of Cagliari, Italy
Seifedine Kadry	Noroff University College, Norway
Yeliz Karaca	University of Massachusetts Chan Medical School and Massachusetts Institute of Technology, USA
Harun Karsli	Bolu Abant Izzet Baysal University, Turkey
Tayana Khachkova	Russian Academy of Sciences, Russia
Manju Khari	Jawaharlal Nehru University, India
Vladimir Korkhov	Saint Petersburg State University, Russia
Dionisia Koutsi	National Technical University of Athens, Greece
Tomonori Kouya	Shizuoka Institute of Science and Technology, Japan
Nataliia Kulabukhova	Saint Petersburg State University, Russia
Anisha Kumari	National Institute of Technology, India
Ludovica La Rocca	University of Napoli Federico II, Italy
Mara Ladu	University of Cagliari, Italy
Sabrina Lai	University of Cagliari, Italy
Mohamed Laib	Luxembourg Institute of Science and Technology, Luxembourg
Giuseppe Francesco Cesare Lama	University of Napoli Federico II, Italy
Isabella Maria Lami	Turin Polytechnic, Italy
Chien Sing Lee	Sunway University, Malaysia

Marcelo Leon	Ecotec University, Ecuador
Federica Leone	University of Cagliari, Italy
Barbara Lino	University of Palermo, Italy
Vadim Lisitsa	Russian Academy of Sciences, Russia
Carla Lobo	Portucalense University, Portugal
Marco Locurcio	Polytechnic University of Bari, Italy
Claudia Loggia	University of KwaZulu-Natal, South Africa
Andrea Lombardi	University of Perugia, Italy
Isabel Lopes	Polytechnic Institut of Bragança, Portugal
Immacolata Lorè	Mediterranean University of Reggio Calabria, Italy
Vanda Lourenco	Nova University of Lisbon, Portugal
Giorgia Malavasi	Turin Polytechnic, Italy
Francesca Maltinti	University of Cagliari, Italy
Luca Mancini	University of Perugia, Italy
Marcos Mandado	University of Vigo, Spain
Benedetto Manganelli	University of Basilicata, Italy
Krassimir Markov	Institute of Electric Engineering and Informatics, Bulgaria
Enzo Martinelli	University of Salerno, Italy
Fiammetta Marulli	University of Campania Luigi Vanvitelli, Italy
Antonino Marvuglia	Luxembourg Institute of Science and Technology, Luxembourg
Rytis Maskeliunas	Kaunas University of Technology, Lithuania
Michele Mastroianni	University of Salerno, Italy
Hideo Matsufuru	High Energy Accelerator Research Organization, Japan
D'Apuzzo Mauro	University of Cassino and Southern Lazio, Italy
Luis Mazon	Bitrum Research Group, Spain
Chiara Mazzarella	University Federico II, Naples, Italy
Beatrice Mecca	Turin Polytechnic, Italy
Umberto Mecca	Turin Polytechnic, Italy
Paolo Mengoni	Hong Kong Baptist University, China
Gaetano Messina	Mediterranean University of Reggio Calabria, Italy
Alfredo Milani	University of Perugia, Italy
Alessandra Milesi	University of Cagliari, Italy
Richard Millham	Durban University of Technology, South Africa
Fernando Miranda	Universidade do Minho, Portugal
Biswajeeban Mishra	University of Szeged, Hungary
Giuseppe Modica	University of Reggio Calabria, Italy
Pierluigi Morano	Polytechnic University of Bari, Italy

Filipe Mota Pinto	Polytechnic Institute of Leiria, Portugal
Maria Mourao	Polytechnic Institute of Viana do Castelo, Portugal
Eugenio Muccio	University of Naples Federico II, Italy
Beniamino Murgante	University of Basilicata, Italy
Rocco Murro	Sapienza University of Rome, Italy
Giuseppe Musolino	Mediterranean University of Reggio Calabria, Italy
Nadia Nedjah	State University of Rio de Janeiro, Brazil
Juraj Nemec	Masaryk University, Czech Republic
Andreas Nikiforiadis	Aristotle University of Thessaloniki, Greece
Silvio Nocera	IUAV University of Venice, Italy
Roseline Ogundokun	Kaunas University of Technology, Lithuania
Emma Okewu	University of Alcala, Spain
Serena Olcuire	Sapienza University of Rome, Italy
Irene Oliveira	University Trás-os-Montes and Alto Douro, Portugal
Samson Oruma	Ostfold University College, Norway
Antonio Pala	University of Cagliari, Italy
Maria Panagiotopoulou	National Technical University of Athens, Greece
Simona Panaro	University of Sussex Business School, UK
Jay Pancham	Durban University of Technology, South Africa
Eric Pardede	La Trobe University, Australia
Hyun Kyoo Park	Ministry of National Defense, South Korea
Damiano Perri	University of Florence, Italy
Quoc Trung Pham	Ho Chi Minh City University of Technology, Vietnam
Claudio Piferi	University of Florence, Italy
Angela Pilogallo	University of L'Aquila, Italy
Francesco Pinna	University of Cagliari, Italy
Telmo Pinto	University of Coimbra, Portugal
Luca Piroddi	University of Malta, Malta
Francesco Pittau	Politechnic of Milan, Italy
Giuliano Poli	Università Federico II di Napoli, Italy
Maurizio Pollino	Italian National Agency for New Technologies, Energy and Sustainable Economic Development, Italy
Vijay Prakash	University of Malta, Malta
Salvatore Praticò	Mediterranean University of Reggio Calabria, Italy
Carlotta Quagliolo	Turin Polytechnic, Italy
Garrisi Raffaele	Operations Center for Cyber Security, Italy
Mariapia Raimondo	Università della Campania Luigi Vanvitelli, Italy

Bruna Ramos	Universidade Lusíada Norte, Portugal
Nicoletta Rassu	University of Cagliari, Italy
Roberta Ravanelli	University of Roma La Sapienza, Italy
Pier Francesco Recchi	University of Naples Federico II, Italy
Stefania Regalbuto	University of Naples Federico II, Italy
Rommel Regis	Saint Joseph's University, USA
Marco Reis	University of Coimbra, Portugal
Jerzy Respondek	Silesian University of Technology, Poland
Isabel Ribeiro	Polytechnic Institut of Bragança, Portugal
Albert Rimola	Autonomous University of Barcelona, Spain
Corrado Rindone	Mediterranean University of Reggio Calabria, Italy
Maria Rocco	Roma Tre University, Italy
Ana Maria A. C. Rocha	University of Minho, Portugal
Fabio Rocha	Universidade Federal de Sergipe, Brazil
Humberto Rocha	University of Coimbra, Portugal
Maria Clara Rocha	Politechnic Institut of Coimbra, Portual
Carlos Rodrigues	Polytechnic Institut of Bragança, Portugal
Diana Rolando	Turin Polytechnic, Italy
James Rombi	University of Cagliari, Italy
Evgeniy Romenskiy	Russian Academy of Sciences, Russia
Marzio Rosi	University of Perugia, Italy
Silvia Rossetti	University of Parma, Italy
Marco Rossitti	Politechnic of Milan, Italy
Antonio Russo	University of Enna, Italy
Insoo Ryu	MoaSoftware, South Korea
Yeonseung Ryu	Myongji University, South Korea
Lucia Saganeiti	University of L'Aquila, Italy
Valentina Santarsiero	University of Basilicata, Italy
Luigi Santopietro	University of Basilicata, Italy
Rafael Santos	National Institute for Space Research, Brazil
Valentino Santucci	University for Foreigners of Perugia, Italy
Alessandra Saponieri	University of Salento, Italy
Mattia Scalas	Turin Polytechnic, Italy
Francesco Scorza	University of Basilicata, Italy
Ester Scotto Di Perta	University of Napoli Federico II, Italy
Nicoletta Setola	University of Florence, Italy
Ricardo Severino	University of Minho, Portugal
Angela Silva	Polytechnic Institut of Viana do Castelo, Portugal
Carina Silva	Polytechnic of Lisbon, Portugal
Marco Simonetti	University of Florence, Italy
Sergey Solovyev	Russian Academy of Sciences, Russia

Maria Somma	University of Naples Federico II, Italy
Changgeun Son	Ministry of National Defense, South Korea
Alberico Sonnessa	Polytechnic of Bari, Italy
Inês Sousa	University of Minho, Portugal
Lisete Sousa	University of Lisbon, Portugal
Elena Stankova	Saint-Petersburg State University, Russia
Modestos Stavrakis	University of the Aegean, Greece
Flavio Stochino	University of Cagliari, Italy
Anastasia Stratigea	National Technical University of Athens, Greece
Yue Sun	European XFEL GmbH, Germany
Anthony Suppa	Turin Polytechnic, Italy
David Taniar	Monash University, Australia
Rodrigo Tapia McClung	Centre for Research in Geospatial Information Sciences, Mexico
Tarek Teba	University of Portsmouth, UK
Ana Paula Teixeira	University of Trás-os-Montes and Alto Douro, Portugal
Tengku Adil Tengku Izhar	Technological University MARA, Malaysia
Maria Filomena Teodoro	University of Lisbon and Portuguese Naval Academy, Portugal
Yiota Theodora	National Technical University of Athens, Greece
Elena Todella	Turin Polytechnic, Italy
Graça Tomaz	Polytechnic Institut of Guarda, Portugal
Anna Tonazzini	National Research Council, Italy
Dario Torregrossa	Goodyear, Luxembourg
Francesca Torrieri	University of Naples Federico II, Italy
Vincenza Torrisi	University of Catania, Italy
Nikola Tosic	Polytechnic University of Catalonia, Spain
Vincenzo Totaro	Polytechnic University of Bari, Italy
Arianna Travaglini	University of Florence, Italy
António Trigo	Polytechnic of Coimbra, Portugal
Giuseppe A. Trunfio	University of Sassari, Italy
Toshihiro Uchibayashi	Kyushu University, Japan
Piero Ugliengo	University of Torino, Italy
Jordi Vallverdu	University Autonoma Barcelona, Spain
Gianmarco Vanuzzo	University of Perugia, Italy
Dmitry Vasyunin	T-Systems, Russia
Laura Verde	University of Campania Luigi Vanvitelli, Italy
Giulio Vignoli	University of Cagliari, Italy
Gianluca Vinti	University of Perugia, Italy
Katarína Vitálišová	Matej Bel University, Slovak Republic
Daniel Mark Vitiello	University of Cagliari

Marco Vizzari	University of Perugia, Italy
Manuel Yañez	Autonomous University of Madrid, Spain
Fenghui Yao	Tennessee State University, USA
Fukuko Yuasa	High Energy Accelerator Research Organization, Japan
Milliam Maxime Zekeng Ndadji	University of Dschang, Cameroon
Ljiljana Zivkovic	Republic Geodetic Authority, Serbia
Camila Zyngier	IBMEC-BH, Brazil

Plenary Lectures

A Multiscale Planning Concept for Sustainable Metropolitan Development

Pierre Frankhauser

Théma, Université de Franche-Comté, 32, rue Mégevand, 20030 Besançon, France
pierre.frankhauser@univ-fcomte.fr

Keywords: Sustainable metropolitan development · Multiscale approach · Urban modelling

Urban sprawl has often been pointed out as having an important negative impact on environment and climate. Residential zones have grown up in what were initially rural areas, located far from employment areas and often lacking shopping opportunities, public services and public transportation. Hence urban sprawl increased car-traffic flows, generating pollution and increasing energy consumption. New road axes consume considerable space and weaken biodiversity by reducing and cutting natural areas. A return to "compact cities" or "dense cities" has often been contemplated as the most efficient way to limit urban sprawl. However, the real impact of density on car use is less clear-cut (Daneshpour and Shakibamanesh 2011). Let us emphasize that moreover climate change will increase the risk of heat islands on an intra-urban scale. This prompts a more nuanced reflection on how urban fabrics should be structured.

Moreover, urban planning cannot ignore social demand. Lower land prices in rural areas, often put forward by economists, is not the only reason of urban sprawl. The quality of the residential environment comes into play, too, through features like noise, pollution, landscape quality, density etc. Schwanen et al. (2004) observe for the Netherlands that households preferring a quiet residential environment and individual housing with a garden will not accept densification, which might even lead them to move to lower-density rural areas even farther away from jobs and shopping amenities. Many scholars emphasize the importance of green amenities for residential environments and report the importance of easy access to leisure areas (Guo and Bhat 2002). Vegetation in the residential environment has an important impact on health and well-being (Lafortezza et al. 2009).

We present here the Fractalopolis concept which we developed in the frame of several research projects and which aims reconciling environmental and social issues (Bonin et al., 2020; Frankhauser 2021; Frankhauser et al. 2018). This concept introduces a multiscale approach based on multifractal geometry for conceiving spatial development for metropolitan areas. For taking into account social demand we refer to the fundamental work of Max-Neef et al. (1991) based on Maslow's work about basic human needs. He introduces the concept of satisfiers assigned to meet the basic needs of "Subsistence, Protection, Affection, Understanding, Participation, Idleness, Creation, Identity and Freedom". Satisfiers thus become the link between the needs of everyone and society and may depend on the cultural context. We consider their importance, their location and their accessibility and we rank the needs according to their importance for individuals or households. In order to enjoy a good quality of life and to shorten trips and to reduce automobile use, it seems important for satisfiers of daily needs to be easily accessible. Hence, we consider the purchase rate when reflecting on the implementation of shops which is reminiscent of central place theory.

The second important feature is taking care of environment and biodiversity by avoiding fragmentation of green space (Ekren and Arslan 2022) which must benefit, moreover, of a good accessibility, as pointed out. These areas must, too, ply the role of cooling areas ensuring ventilation of urbanized areas (Kuttler et al. 1998).

For integrating these different objectives, we propose a concept for developing spatial configurations of metropolitan areas designed which is based on multifractal geometry. It allows combining different issues across a large range of scales in a coherent way. These issues include:

- providing easy access to a large array of amenities to meet social demand;
- promoting the use of public transportation and soft modes instead of automobile use;
- preserving biodiversity and improving the local climate.

The concept distinguishes development zones localized in the vicinity of a nested and hierarchized system of public transport axes. The highest ranked center offers all types of amenities, whereas lower ranked centers lack the highest ranked amenities. The lowest ranked centers just offer the amenities for daily needs. A coding system allows distinguishing the centers according to their rank.

Each subset of central places is in some sense autonomous, since they are not linked by transportation axes to subcenters of the same order. This allows to preserve a linked system of green corridors penetrating the development zones across scales avoiding the fragmentation of green areas and ensuring a good accessibility to recreational areas.

The spatial model is completed by a population distribution model which globally follows the same hierarchical logic. However, we weakened the strong fractal order what allows to conceive a more or less polycentric spatial system.

We can adapt the theoretical concept easily to real world situation without changing the underlying multiscale logic. A decision support system has been developed allowing to simulate development scenarios and to evaluate them. The evaluation procedure is based on fuzzy evaluation of distance acceptance for accessing to the different types of amenities according to the ranking of needs. We used for evaluation data issued from a great set of French planning documents like Master plans. We show an example how the software package can be used concretely.

References

Bonin, O., et al.: Projet SOFT sobriété énergétique par les formes urbaines et le transport (Research Report No. 1717C0003; p. 214). ADEME (2020)

Daneshpour, A., Shakibamanesh, A.: Compact city; dose it create an obligatory context for urban sustainability? Int. J. Archit. Eng. Urban Plann. 21(2), 110–118 (2011)

Ekren, E., Arslan, M.: Functions of greenways as an ecologically-based planning strategy. In: Çakır, M., Tuğluer, M., Fırat Örs, P.: Architectural Sciences and Ecology, pp. 134–156. Iksad Publications (2022)

Frankhauser, P.: Fractalopolis—a fractal concept for the sustainable development of metropolitan areas. In: Sajous, P., Bertelle, C. (eds.) Complex Systems, Smart Territories and Mobility, pp. 15–50. Springer, Cham (2021). https://doi.org/10.1007/978-3-030-59302-5_2

Frankhauser, P., Tannier, C., Vuidel, G., Houot, H.: An integrated multifractal modelling to urban and regional planning. Comput. Environ. Urban Syst. **67**(1), 132–146 (2018). https://doi.org/10.1016/j.compenvurbsys.2017.09.011

Guo, J., Bhat, C.: Residential location modeling: accommodating sociodemographic, school quality and accessibility effects. University of Texas, Austin (2002)

Kuttler, W., Dütemeyer, D., Barlag, A.-B.: Influence of regional and local winds on urban ventilation in Cologne, Germany. Meteorologische Zeitschrift, 77–87 (1998) https://doi.org/10.1127/metz/7/1998/77

Lafortezza, R., Carrus, G., Sanesi, G., Davies, C.: Benefits and well-being perceived by people visiting green spaces in periods of heat stress. Urban For. Urban Green. **8**(2), 97–108 (2009)

Max-Neef, M. A., Elizalde, A., Hopenhayn, M.: Human scale development: conception, application and further reflections. The Apex Press (1991)

Schwanen, T., Dijst, M., Dieleman, F. M.: Policies for urban form and their impact on travel: The Netherlands experience. Urban Stud. **41**(3), 579–603 (2004)

Graph Drawing and Network Visualization – An Overview – (Keynote Speech)

Giuseppe Liotta

Dipartimento di Ingegneria, Università degli Studi di Perugia, Italy
giuseppe.liotta@unipg.it

Abstract. Graph Drawing and Network visualization supports the exploration, analysis, and communication of relational data arising in a variety of application domains: from bioinformatics to software engineering, from social media to cyber-security, from data bases to powergrid systems. Aim of this keynote speech is to introduce this thriving research area, highlighting some of its basic approaches and pointing to some promising research directions.

1 Introduction

Graph Drawing and Network Visualization is at the intersection of different disciplines and it combines topics that traditionally belong to theoretical computer science with methods and approaches that characterize more applied disciplines. Namely, it can be related to Graph Algorithms, Geometric Graph Theory and Geometric computing, Combinatorial Optimization, Experimental Analysis, User Studies, System Design and Development, and Human Computer Interaction. This combination of theory and practice is well reflected in the flagship conference of the area, the *International Symposium on Graph Drawing and Network Visualization,* that has two tracks, one focusing on combinatorial and algorithmic aspects and the other on the design of network visualization systems and interfaces. The conference is now at its 31st edition; a full list of the symposia and their proceedings, published by Springer in the LNCS series can be found at the URL: http://www.graphdrawing.org/.

Aim of this short paper is to outline the content of my Keynote Speech at ICCSA 2023, which will be referred to as the "Talk" in the rest of the paper. The talk will introduce the field of Graph Drawing and Network Visualization to a broad audience, with the goal to not only present some key methodological and technological aspects, but also point to some unexplored or partially explored research directions. The rest of this short paper briefly outlines the content of the talk and provides some references that can be a starting point for researchers interested in working on Graph Drawing and Network Visualization.

2 Why Visualize Networks?

Back in 1973 the famous statistician Francis Anscombe, gave a convincing example of why visualization is fundamental component of data analysis. The example is known as the *Anscombe's quartet* [3] and it consists of four sets of 11 points each that are almost identical in terms of the basic statistic properties of their x– and y– coordinates. Namely the mean values and the variance of x and y are exactly the same in the four sets, while the correlation of x and y and the linear regression are the same up to the second decimal. In spite of this statistical similarity, the data look very different when displayed in the Euclidean plane which leads to the conclusion that they correspond to significantly different phenomena. Figure 1 reports the four sets of Anscombe's quartet. After fifty years, with the arrival of AI-based technologies and the need of explaining and interpreting machine-driven suggestions before making strategic decision, the lesson of Anscombe's quartet has not just kept but even increased its relevance.

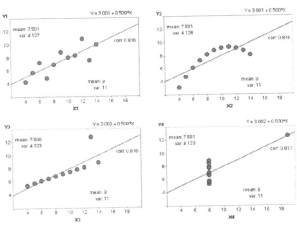

Fig. 1. The four point sets in Anscombe's quartet [3]; the figure also reports statistical values of the x and y variables.

As a matter of fact, nowadays the need of visualization systems goes beyond the verification of the accuracy of some statistical analysis on a set of scattered data. Recent technological advances have generated torrents of data that area relational in nature and typically modeled as networks: the nodes of the networks store the features of the data and the edges of the networks describe the semantic relationships between the data features. Such networked data sets (whose algebraic underlying structure is a called graph in discrete mathematics) arise in a variety of application domains including, for example, Systems Biology, Social Network Analysis, Software Engineering, Networking, Data Bases, Homeland Security, and Business Intelligence. In these (and many other) contexts, systems that support the visual analysis of networks and graphs play a central role in critical decision making processes. These are human-in-the-loop processes where the continuous interaction between humans (decision makers) and data mining or optimization algorithms (AI/ML components) supports the data exploration, the development of verifiable theories about the data, and the extraction of new knowledge that is used to make strategic choices. A seminal book by Keim et al. [33] schematically represents the human-in-the-loop approach to making sense of networked data sets as in Fig. 2. See also [46–49].

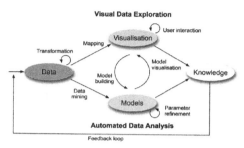

Fig. 2. Sense-making/knowledge generation loop. This conceptual interaction model between human analysts and network visualization system is at the basis of network visual analytics system design [33].

To make a concrete application example of the analysis of a network by interacting with its visualization, consider the problem of contrasting financial crimes such as money laundering or tax evasion. These crimes are based on relevant volumes of financial transactions to conceal the identity, the source, or the destination of illegally gained money. Also, the adopted patterns to pursue the illegal goals continuously change to conceal the crimes. Therefore, contrasting them requires special investigation units which must analyze very large and highly dynamic data sets and discover relationships between different subjects to untangle complex fraudulent plots. The investigative cycle begins with data collection and filtering; it is then followed by modeling the data as a social network (also called *financial activity network* in this context) to which different data mining and data analytic methods are applied, including graph pattern matching, social network analysis, machine learning, and information diffusion. By the network visualization system detectives can interactively explore the data, gain insight and make new hypotheses about possible criminal activities, verify the hypotheses by asking the system to provide more details about specific portions of the network, refine previous outputs, and eventually gain new knowledge. Figure 3 illustrates a small financial activity network where, by means of the interaction between an officer of the Italian Revenue Agency and the MALDIVE system described in [10] a fraudulent pattern has been identified. Precisely, the tax officer has encoded a risky relational scheme among taxpayers into a suspicious graph pattern; in response, the system has made a search in the taxpayer network and it has returned one such pattern. See, e.g., [9, 11, 14, 18, 38] for more papers and references about visual analytic applications to contrasting financial crimes.

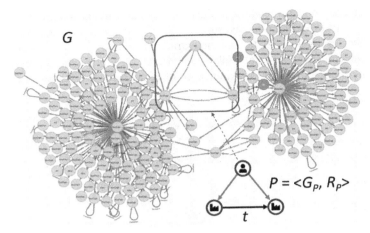

Fig. 3. A financial activity network from [10]. The pattern in the figure represents a SuppliesFromAssociated scheme, consisting of an economic transaction and two shareholding relationships.

3   Facets of Graph Drawing and Network Visualization

The Talk overviews some of the fundamental facets that characterize the research in Graph Drawing and Network Visualization. Namely:

- Graph drawing metaphors: Depending on the application context, different metaphors can be used to represent a relational data set modeled as a graph. The talk will briefly recall the matrix representation, the space filling representation, the contact representation, and the node-link representation which is, by far, the most commonly used (see, e.g., [43]).
- Interaction paradigms: Different interaction paradigms have different impacts on the sense-making process of the user about the visualized network. The Talk will go through the full-view, top-down, bottom-up, incremental, and narrative paradigms. Pros and cons will be highlighted for each approach, also by means of examples and applications. The discussion of the top-down interaction paradigm will also consider the hybrid visualization models (see, e.g., [2, 24, 26, 28, 39]) while the discussion about the incremental paradigm will focus on research about graph storyplans (see, e.g., [4, 6, 7]).
- Graph drawing algorithms: Three main algorithmic approaches will be reviewed, namely the force-directed, the layered), and the planarization-based approach; see, e.g., [5]. We shall also make some remarks about FPT algorithms for graph drawing (see, e.g., [8, 19, 20, 25, 27, 40, 53]) and about how the optimization challenges vary when it is assumed that the input has or does not have a fixed combinatorial embedding (see, e.g., [12, 13, 16, 17, 23]).
- Experimental analysis and user-studies: The Talk will mostly compare two models to define and experimentally validate those optimization goals that define a "readable"

network visualization, i.e. a visualization that in a given application context can easily convey the structure of a relational data set so to guarantee efficiency both in its visual exploration and in the elaboration of new knowledge. Special focus will be given to a set emerging optimization goals related to edge crossings that are currently investigated in the graph drawing and network visualization community unedr the name of "graph drawing beyond planarity" (see, e.g., [1, 15, 29, 35]).

The talk shall also point to some promising research directions, including: (i) Extend the body of papers devoted to user-studies that compare the impact of different graph drawing metaphors on the user perception. (ii) Extend the study of interaction paradigms to extended reality environments (see, e.g., [21, 30, 36, 37]); (iii) Engineer the FPT algorithms for graph drawing and experimentally compare their performances with exact or approximate solutions; and (iv) Develop new algorithmic fameworks in the context of graph drawing beyond planarity.

We conclude this short paper with pointers to publication venues and key references that can be browsed by researchers interested in the fascinating field of Graph Drawing and Network Visualization.

4   Pointers to Publication venues and Key References

A limited list of conferences where Graph Drawing and Network Visualization papers are regularly part of the program includes *IEEE VIS, EuroVis, SoCG, ISAAC, ACM-SIAM SODA, WADS,* and *WG.* Among the many journals where several Graph Drawing and Network Visualization papers have appeared during the last three decades we recall *IEEE Transactions on Visualization and Computer Graphs, SIAM Journal of Computing, Computer Graphics Forum, Journal of Computer and System Sciences, Algorithmica, Journal of Graph Algorithms and Applications, Theoretical Computer Science, Information Sciences, Discrete and Computational Geometry, Computational Geometry: Theory and Applications, ACM Computing Surveys,* and *Computer Science Review.* A limited list of books, surveys, or papers that contain interesting algorithmic challenges on Graph Drawing and Network Visualization include [5, 15, 22, 29, 31–35, 41–45, 50–52].

References

1. Angelini, P., et al.: Simple k-planar graphs are simple (k+1)-quasiplanar. J. Comb. Theory, Ser. B, **142**, 1–35 (2020)
2. Angori, L., Didimo, W., Montecchiani, F., Pagliuca, D., Tappini, A.: Hybrid graph visualizations with chordlink: Algorithms, experiments, and applications. IEEE Trans. Vis. Comput. Graph. **28**(2), 1288–1300 (2022)
3. Anscombe, F.J.: Graphs in statistical analysis. Am. Stat. **27**(1), 17–21 (1973)
4. Di Battista, G., et al.: Small point-sets supporting graph stories. In: Angelini, P., von Hanxleden, R. (eds.) Graph Drawing and Network Visualization. GD 2022, LNCS, vol. 13764, pp. 289–303. Springer, Cham (2022). https://doi.org/10.1007/978-3-031-22203-0_21

5. Battista, G.D., Eades, P., Tamassia, R., Tollis, I.G.: Graph Drawing: Algorithms for the Visualization of Graphs. Prentice-Hall, Hoboken (1999)
6. Binucci, C., et al.: On the complexity of the storyplan problem. In: Angelini, P., von Hanxleden, R. (eds.) Graph Drawing and Network Visualization. GD 2022. LNCS, vol. 13764, pp. 304–318. Springer, Cham (2023). https://doi.org/10.1007/978-3-031-22203-0_22
7. Borrazzo, M., Lozzo, G.D., Battista, G.D., Frati, F., Patrignani, M.: Graph stories in small area. J. Graph Algorithms Appl. **24**(3), 269–292 (2020)
8. Chaplick, S., Giacomo, E.D., Frati, F., Ganian, R., Raftopoulou, C.N., Simonov, K.: Parameterized algorithms for upward planarity. In: Goaoc, X., Kerber, M. (eds.) 38th International Symposium on Computational Geometry, SoCG 2022, June 7–10, 2022, Berlin, Germany, LIPIcs, vol. 224, pp. 26:1–26:16. Schloss Dagstuhl - Leibniz-Zentrum für Informatik (2022)
9. Didimo, W., Giamminonni, L., Liotta, G., Montecchiani, F., Pagliuca, D.: A visual analytics system to support tax evasion discovery. Decis. Support Syst. **110**, 71–83 (2018)
10. Didimo, W., Grilli, L., Liotta, G., Menconi, L., Montecchiani, F., Pagliuca, D.: Combining network visualization and data mining for tax risk assessment. IEEE Access **8**, 16073–16086 (2020)
11. Didimo, W., Grilli, L., Liotta, G., Montecchiani, F., Pagliuca, D.: Visual querying and analysis of temporal fiscal networks. Inf. Sci. **505**, 406–421 (2019)
12. W. Didimo, M. Kaufmann, G. Liotta, and G. Ortali. Didimo, W., Kaufmann, M., Liotta, G., Ortali, G.: Rectilinear planarity testing of plane series-parallel graphs in linear time. In: Auber, D., Valtr, P. (eds.) Graph Drawing and Network Visualization. GD 2020. LNCS, vol. 12590, pp. 436–449. Springer, Cham (2020). https://doi.org/10.1007/978-3-030-68766-3_34
13. Didimo, W., Kaufmann, M., Liotta, G., Ortali, G.: Rectilinear planarity of partial 2-trees. In: Angelini, P., von Hanxleden, R. (eds.) Graph Drawing and Network Visualization. GD 2022. LNCS, vol. 13764, pp. 157–172. Springer, Cham (2023). https://doi.org/10.1007/978-3-031-22203-0_12
14. Didimo, W., Liotta, G., Montecchiani, F.: Network visualization for financial crime detection. J. Vis. Lang. Comput. **25**(4), 433–451 (2014)
15. Didimo, W., Liotta, G., Montecchiani, F.: A survey on graph drawing beyond planarity. ACM Comput. Surv. **52**(1), 4:1–4:37 (2019)
16. Didimo, W., Liotta, G., Ortali, G., Patrignani, M.: Optimal orthogonal drawings of planar 3-graphs in linear time. In: Chawla, S. (ed.) Proceedings of the 2020 ACM-SIAM Symposium on Discrete Algorithms, SODA 2020, Salt Lake City, UT, USA, January 5–8, 2020, pp. 806–825. SIAM (2020)
17. Didimo, W., Liotta, G., Patrignani, M.: HV-planarity: algorithms and complexity. J. Comput. Syst. Sci. **99**, 72–90 (2019)
18. Dilla, W.N., Raschke, R.L.: Data visualization for fraud detection: practice implications and a call for future research. Int. J. Acc. Inf. Syst. **16**, 1–22 (2015)
19. Dujmovic, V., et al.: A fixed-parameter approach to 2-layer planarization. Algorithmica **45**(2), 159–182 (2006)
20. Dujmovic, V., et al.: On the parameterized complexity of layered graph drawing. Algorithmica **52**(2), 267–292 (2008)

21. Dwyer, T., et al.: Immersive analytics: an introduction. In: Marriott, K., et al. (eds.) Immersive Analytics, LNCS, vol. 11190, pp. 1–23. Springer, Cham (2018)
22. Filipov, V., Arleo, A., Miksch, S.: Are we there yet? a roadmap of network visualization from surveys to task taxonomies. Computer Graphics Forum (2023, on print)
23. Garg, A., Tamassia, R.: On the computational complexity of upward and rectilinear planarity testing. SIAM J. Comput. **31**(2), 601–625 (2001)
24. Di Giacomo, E., Didimo, W., Montecchiani, F., Tappini, A.: A user study on hybrid graph visualizations. In: Purchase, H.C., Rutter, I. (eds.) Graph Drawing and Network Visualization. GD 2021. LNCS, vol. 12868, pp. 21–38. Springer, Cham (2021). https://doi.org/10.1007/978-3-030-92931-2_2
25. Giacomo, E.D., Giordano, F., Liotta, G.: Upward topological book embeddings of dags. SIAM J. Discret. Math. **25**(2), 479–489 (2011)
26. Giacomo, E.D., Lenhart, W.J., Liotta, G., Randolph, T.W., Tappini, A.: (k, p)-planarity: a relaxation of hybrid planarity. Theor. Comput. Sci. **896**, 19–30 (2021)
27. Giacomo, E.D., Liotta, G., Montecchiani, F.: Orthogonal planarity testing of bounded treewidth graphs. J. Comput. Syst. Sci. **125**, 129–148 (2022)
28. Giacomo, E.D., Liotta, G., Patrignani, M., Rutter, I., Tappini, A.: Nodetrix planarity testing with small clusters. Algorithmica **81**(9), 3464–3493 (2019)
29. Hong, S., Tokuyama, T. (eds.) Beyond Planar Graphs. Springer, Singapore (2020). https://doi.org/10.1007/978-981-15-6533-5
30. Joos, L., Jaeger-Honz, S., Schreiber, F., Keim, D.A., Klein, K.: Visual comparison of networks in VR. IEEE Trans. Vis. Comput. Graph. **28**(11), 3651–3661 (2022)
31. Jünger, M., Mutzel, P. (eds.) Graph Drawing Software. Springer, Berlin (2004). https://doi.org/10.1007/978-3-642-18638-7
32. Kaufmann, M., Wagner, D. (eds.): Drawing Graphs, Methods and Models (the book grow out of a Dagstuhl Seminar, April 1999), LNCS, vol. 2025. Springer, Berlin (2001). https://doi.org/10.1007/3-540-44969-8
33. Keim, D.A., Kohlhammer, J., Ellis, G.P., Mansmann, F.: Mastering the Information Age - Solving Problems with Visual Analytics. Eurographics Association, Saarbrücken (2010)
34. Keim, D.A., Mansmann, F., Stoffel, A., Ziegler, H.: Visual analytics. In: Liu, L., Özsu, M.T. (eds.) Encyclopedia of Database Systems, 2nd edn. Springer, Berlin (2018)
35. Kobourov, S.G., Liotta, G., Montecchiani, F.: An annotated bibliography on 1-planarity. Comput. Sci. Rev. **25**, 49–67 (2017)
36. Kraus, M., et al.: Immersive analytics with abstract 3D visualizations: a survey. Comput. Graph. Forum **41**(1), 201–229 (2022)
37. Kwon, O., Muelder, C., Lee, K., Ma, K.: A study of layout, rendering, and interaction methods for immersive graph visualization. IEEE Trans. Vis. Comput. Graph. **22**(7), 1802–1815 (2016)
38. Leite, R.A., Gschwandtner, T., Miksch, S., Gstrein, E., Kuntner, J.: NEVA: visual analytics to identify fraudulent networks. Comput. Graph. Forum **39**(6), 344–359 (2020)

39. Liotta, G., Rutter, I., Tappini, A.: Simultaneous FPQ-ordering and hybrid planarity testing. Theor. Comput. Sci. **874**, 59–79 (2021)
40. Liotta, G., Rutter, I., Tappini, A.: Parameterized complexity of graph planarity with restricted cyclic orders. J. Comput. Syst. Sci. **135**, 125–144 (2023)
41. Ma, K.: Pushing visualization research frontiers: essential topics not addressed by machine learning. IEEE Comput. Graphics Appl. **43**(1), 97–102 (2023)
42. McGee, F., et al.: Visual Analysis of Multilayer Networks. Synthesis Lectures on Visualization. Morgan & Claypool Publishers, San Rafael (2021)
43. Munzner, T.: Visualization Analysis and Design. A.K. Peters visualization series. A K Peters (2014)
44. Nishizeki, T., Rahman, M.S.: Planar Graph Drawing, vol. 12. World Scientific, Singapore (2004)
45. Nobre, C., Meyer, M.D., Streit, M., Lex, A.: The state of the art in visualizing multivariate networks. Comput. Graph. Forum **38**(3), 807–832 (2019)
46. Sacha, D.: Knowledge generation in visual analytics: Integrating human and machine intelligence for exploration of big data. In: Apel, S., et al. (eds.) Ausgezeichnete Informatikdissertationen 2018, LNI, vol. D-19, pp. 211–220. GI (2018)
47. Sacha, D., et al.: What you see is what you can change: human-centered machine learning by interactive visualization. Neurocomputing **268**, 164–175 (2017)
48. Sacha, D., Senaratne, H., Kwon, B.C., Ellis, G.P., Keim, D.A.: The role of uncertainty, awareness, and trust in visual analytics. IEEE Trans. Vis. Comput. Graph. **22**(1), 240–249 (2016)
49. Sacha, D., Stoffel, A., Stoffel, F., Kwon, B.C., Ellis, G.P., Keim, D.A.: Knowledge generation model for visual analytics. IEEE Trans. Vis. Comput. Graph. **20**(12), 1604–1613 (2014)
50. Tamassia, R.: Graph drawing. In: Sack, J., Urrutia, J. (eds.) Handbook of Computational Geometry, pp. 937–971. North Holland/Elsevier, Amsterdam (2000)
51. Tamassia, R. (ed.) Handbook on Graph Drawing and Visualization. Chapman and Hall/CRC, Boca Raton (2013)
52. Tamassia, R., Liotta, G.: Graph drawing. In: Goodman, J.E., O'Rourke, J. (eds.) Handbook of Discrete and Computational Geometry, 2nd edn., pp. 1163–1185. Chapman and Hall/CRC, Boca Raton (2004)
53. Zehavi, M.: Parameterized analysis and crossing minimization problems. Comput. Sci. Rev. **45**, 100490 (2022)

Understanding Non-Covalent Interactions in Biological Processes through QM/MM-EDA Dynamic Simulations

Marcos Mandado

Department of Physical Chemistry, University of Vigo, Lagoas-Marcosende s/n, 36310 Vigo, Spain
mandado@uvigo.es

Molecular dynamic simulations in biological environments such as proteins, DNA or lipids involves a large number of atoms, so classical models based on widely parametrized force fields are employed instead of more accurate quantum methods, whose high computational requirements preclude their application. The parametrization of appropriate force fields for classical molecular dynamics relies on the precise knowledge of the non-covalent inter and intramolecular interactions responsible for very important aspects, such as macromolecular arrangements, cell membrane permeation, ion solvation, etc. This implies, among other things, knowledge of the nature of the interaction, which may be governed by electrostatic, repulsion or dispersion forces. In order to know the balance between different forces, quantum calculations are frequently performed on simplified molecular models and the data obtained from these calculations are used to parametrize the force fields employed in classical simulations. These parameters are, among others, atomic charges, permanent electric dipole moments and atomic polarizabilities. However, it sometimes happens that the molecular models used for the quantum calculations are too simple and the results obtained can differ greatly from those of the extended system. As an alternative to classical and quantum methods, hybrid quantum/classical schemes (QM/MM) can be introduced, where the extended system is neither truncated nor simplified, but only the most important region is treated quantum mechanically.

In this presentation, molecular dynamic simulations and calculations with hybrid schemes are first introduced in a simple way for a broad and multidisciplinary audience. Then, a method developed in our group to investigate intermolecular interactions using hybrid quantum/classical schemes (QM/MM-EDA) is presented and some applications to the study of dynamic processes of ion solvation and membrane permeation are discussed [1–3]. Special attention is paid to the implementation details of the method in the EDA-NCI software [4].

References

1. Cárdenas, G., Pérez-Barcia, A., Mandado, M., Nogueira, J.J.: Phys. Chem. Chem. Phys. **23**, 20533 (2021)
2. Pérez-Barcia, A., Cárdenas, G., Nogueira, J.J., Mandado, M.: J. Chem. Inf. Model. **63**, 882 (2023)

3. Alvarado, R., Cárdenas, G., Nogueira, J.J., Ramos-Berdullas, N., Mandado, M.: Membranes **13**, 28 (2023)
4. Mandado, M., Van Alsenoy, C.: EDA-NCI: A program to perform energy decomposition analysis of non-covalent interactions. https://github.com/marcos-mandado/EDA-NCI

Contents – Part II

Cyber Intelligence and Applications (CIA 2023)

**Conversations South-North on Climate Change Adaptation Towards
Smarter and More Sustainable Cities (CLAPS 2023)**

Computational Mathematics, Statistics and Information Management (CMSIM 2023)

Computational Optimization and Applications (COA 2023)

Workshop on Computational Science and HPC (CSHPC 2023)

Cities, Technologies and Planning (CTP 2023)

Computational and Applied Statistics
(CAS 2023)

Oversampling Methods for Handling Imbalance Data in Binary Classification

Theodorus Riston[1], Sandi Nurhibatulloh Suherman[1], Yonnatan Yonnatan[1],
Fajar Indrayatna[1], Anindya Apriliyanti Pravitasari[1], Eka Novita Sari[2],
and Tutut Herawan[3,4(✉)]

[1] Department of Statistics, Universitas Padjadjaran, Jl. Ir. Soekarno KM. 21, Jatinangor,
Sumedang, West Java 45363, Indonesia
{theodorus19001,sandi19002,yonnatan19001}@mail.unpad.ac.id,
{fajar.indrayatna,anindya.apriliyanti}@unpad.ac.id
[2] AMCS Research Center, Jalan Griya Taman Asri, Sleman, Yogyakarta, Indonesia
eka@amcs.co
[3] Sekolah Tinggi Pariwisata Ambarrukmo Yogyakarta, Jl. Ringroad Timur No. 52, Bantul,
Daerah Istimewa Yogyakarta 55198, Indonesia
tutut@um.edu.my
[4] Institute for Big Data Analytics and Artificial Intelligence, UiTM Shah Alam, 40450 Shah
Alam, Selangor Darul Ehsan, Malaysia

Abstract. Data preparation occupies the majority of data science, about 60–80%.
The process of data preparation can produce an accurate output of information to be
used in decision making. That is why, in the context of data science, it is so critical.
However, in reality, data does not always come in a predefined distribution with
parameters, and it can even arrive with an imbalance. Imbalanced data generates a
lot of problems, especially in classification. This study employs several oversampling methods in machine learning, i.e., Random Oversampling (ROS), Adaptive
Synthetic Sampling (ADASYN), Synthetic Minority Over-sampling Technique
(SMOTE), and Borderline-SMOTE (B-SMOTE), to handle imbalanced data in
binary classification with Naïve Bayes and Support Vector Machine (SVM). The
five methods will be run in the same experimental design and discussed in search
of the best and most accurate model for the datasets. The evaluation was assessed
based on the confusion matrices with precision, recall, and F1-score calculated
for comparison. The AUC and ROC curve is also provided to evaluate the performance of each method via figures. The proposed work reveals that SVM with
B-SMOTE has better classification performance, especially in datasets with high
similarity characteristics between the minority and majority classes.

Keywords: Imbalance Data · Oversampling · SMOTE · Naïve Bayes · SVM

1 Introduction

One of the most common problems in data preparation is imbalanced binary classification. A dataset is considered to be imbalanced if one of the target classes has a much
smaller number of instances in comparison to the other classes, hence we name the

© The Author(s), under exclusive license to Springer Nature Switzerland AG 2023
O. Gervasi et al. (Eds.): ICCSA 2023 Workshops, LNCS 14105, pp. 3–23, 2023.
https://doi.org/10.1007/978-3-031-37108-0_1

larger class as the majority class, and the smaller class as the minority class. We need to generate a model that can correctly classify new data that belongs to the minority class, because, in most cases, the minority class is often the intended class to be predicted. Having imbalanced data leads to inaccurate classification results, because imbalanced data leads to a bias towards the majority class during the classification process. One way to handle the imbalanced data is to resample the original dataset, using either under-sampling for the majority class or over-sampling for the minority class until the two classes are almost balanced.

In the under-sampling approach used in [1], several instances of the majority class are randomly removed in order to get a new dataset that is balanced between majority and minority classes. However, this method causes inaccurate results, because it might eliminate important information needed in modeling. The over-sampling approach assigns new instances to the minority class with the aim of balancing the new dataset.

There are several methods used in the over-sampling technique. First, Random Over-Sampling (ROS), which will randomly select the instances of the minority class to be replicated, which results in a balanced class. However, the disadvantage of the ROS method is that it can cause overfitting by randomly replicating instances of the minority class [2]. Chawla *et al.* then proposed the Synthetic Minority Over-Sampling Technique (SMOTE) as another method of handling imbalanced data [3]. There are also many other synthetic over-sampling techniques, such as Borderline-SMOTE [4] and Adaptive Synthetic Sampling (ADASYN) [5]. In this study, the four techniques are employed to handle the imbalance data from binary labels. To discover the most effective approach, several unbalanced open datasets were used in this study. The Support Vector Machine (SVM) and Naive Bayes (NB) Classifier methods are utilized to carry out the classification, since these two well-known methods produce effective results for binary classification. The SVM classifier [6, 7] has gained popularity in various classification tasks due to its improved performance in binary classification scenarios [8]. Given a data set, SVM aims to find a discriminant hyperplane that preserves the optimal edges of boundary instances, called support vectors. Therefore, SVM focuses on increasing the generalizability of the training data. In addition to the SVM, the NB classification is a popular and widely used classification [9]. The Bayesian classifier assigns the most likely class to a given instance, described by its feature vector. Although independence is generally a bad assumption, in practice, NB often competes well with more sophisticated classifiers [10].

There are many over-sampling methods that require research to study and determine which technique is better to use in handling imbalanced data. Therefore, we will test oversampling techniques to overcome several imbalanced datasets, then compare the classification results of each method to determine which method is the best in handling imbalanced data. In evaluating the classification with concentration in the minority class, precision and recall are more effective [11]. In addition, F-value [11] integrating recall and precision is used instead of recall and precision. Its value is large when both recall and precision are large. Moreover, in evaluating the classification, we can use Receiver Operating Characteristic (ROC) Curve, a standard technique that can summarize classifier performance over a range of tradeoffs between True Positive Rate and False Positive Rate [12].

The remainder of the paper is organized as follows. In Sect. 2, more comparable studies are provided and discussed in order to lead to the research question. Section 3 details the methodology, including the tools used to gather tweets and comments, as well as to support the method employed in this research. For Sect. 4, the findings are presented and discussed, and in Sect. 5, we conclude this research and highlight future research.

2 Related Works

Data sampling techniques are used to deal with imbalance issues as they can improve the quality and robustness of the learning algorithm. In its development, there are many techniques to handle imbalanced data, ROS, SMOTE, BSMOTE and ADASYN. However, we need to know which technique works best for binary data so that we can create new high-quality datasets. Jian et al. [13] has investigated by comparing two methods of oversampling, Random Oversampling (ROS) and SMOTE, to handle imbalanced data. The research uses 19 datasets from various sources, including engineering, finance, information, and medical sciences. This research uses the SVM as its classification method. The result of this research was that SMOTE is better than ROS, which was concluded by comparing the recall and area under curve (AUC) values of the two methods. Similarly, Pereira and Saraiva [14] performed a comparative analysis on the handling of imbalanced data. SVM is one of the classification methods used in this analysis, and the imbalance data processing methods included was SMOTE and ROS. In this analysis, the ROS method was found to be not as good as SMOTE because the F-Value and AUC values in ROS were smaller than in SMOTE.

On the other hand, Khemakhem et al. [15], also conducted research related to handling imbalance data using ROS and SMOTE for classification using SVM. The results of the credit risk assessment for the imbalance data set with this method show that the ROS method is better than the SMOTE method with the AUC measurement. Additionally, Hordri et al. [16] conducted research on handling imbalance data on credit card fraud. One of the classification methods used is NB, along with methods of handling imbalanced data such as ROS and SMOTE. The results of the study with a training data ratio of 30:70, concluded that the SMOTE method was better than ROS in Naive Bayes classification when using a precision measurement. However, it is inversely proportional to the use of the F-Value and AUC measurement.

Oreški and Oreški [17] conducted a research on 30 different datasets to compare SVM and Naive Bayes classification methods to handle imbalanced data with SMOTE. The average AUC of various datasets in the research using the SVM classification method before handling imbalance data is 0.6087 and after handling imbalance data increases the AUC to 0.7889. Meanwhile, with NB, there was a decrease in AUC after handling imbalance data, from 0.7928 to 0.7596. The research has shown that in the domain of class imbalance datasets, SMOTE resampling technique has statistically significant positive influence on the performance of SVM classifiers, measured by the AUC measure.

In 2020, Lu *et al.* [18] conducted research related to telecom fraud using ADASYN. The results of this research, handling imbalance data using ADASYN, Recall and F1 values with SVM classification is better than using Naive Bayes classification. Then, Gosain and Sardana [19] conducted follow-up research comparing SMOTE, BSMOTE and ADASYN. On 6 datasets, the SMOTE method outperforms BSMOTE and ADASYN using the Precision and F-Value measurement scales with Naive Bayes classification. Meanwhile, with SVM classification, SMOTE method is better than BSMOTE and ADASYN evaluated using the Precision, F-Value, and AUC.

Table 1. Related Work of Binary Classification with Imbalanced Data

References	Data	Model	Evaluation	
			Type	%
Jian *et al.* [13]	19 datasets from various sources, including engineering, finance, and medical sciences	SVM-ROS	Recall (Average)	54.73
		SVM-SMOTE	Recall (Average)	55.45
		SVM-ROS	AUC	89.69
		SVM-SMOTE	AUC	91.18
Pereira and Saraiva [14]	Electricity consumption data from normal consumers and electricity thieves	SVM-No Balance	AUC	56.14
		SVM-ROS	AUC	59.69
		SVM-SMOTE	AUC	63.42
		SVM-No Balance	F-Value	18.42
		SVM-ROS	F-Value	20.56
		SVM-SMOTE	F-Value	22.81
Khemakhem *et al.* [15]	Tunisian credit risk assessment	SVM-No Balance	AUC	87.9
		SVM-ROS	AUC	97.4
		SVM-SMOTE	AUC	96.1
Hordri *et al.* [16]	Credit card fraud detection	NB-ROS	Precision	93.27
		NB-SMOTE	Precision	93.28
		NB-ROS	F-Value	88.81
		NB-SMOTE	F-Value	88.02
		NB-ROS	AUC	91.07
		NB-SMOTE	AUC	90.38
Oreški and Oreški [17]	30 different datasets from KEEL repository	SVM-No Balance	AUC (Average)	60.87
		SVM-SMOTE	AUC (Average)	78.89
		NB-No Balance	AUC (Average)	79.28

(continued)

Table 1. (*continued*)

References	Data	Model	Evaluation	
			Type	%
Lu *et al.* [18]	Telecom fraud Identification	NB-SMOTE	AUC (Average)	75.96
		SVM-ADASYN	Recall	66.30
		NB-ADASYN	Recall	57.50
		SVM-ADASYN	F-Value	66.70
		NB-ADASYN	F-Value	60.80
Gosain and Sardana [19]	Pima India Diabetes, Breast Cancer Wisconsin, Statlog (Heart) Dataset, Ionosphere, Spam Base Dataset, and German	NB	Precision (Average)	74.33
		NB-SMOTE	Precision (Average)	84.78
		NB-BSMOTE	Precision (Average)	79.07
		NB-ADASYN	Precision (Average)	81.48
		NB	F-Value (Average)	76.10
		NB-SMOTE	F-Value (Average)	80.95
		NB-BSMOTE	F-Value (Average)	77.73
		NB-ADASYN	F-Value (Average)	76.55
		NB	AUC (Average)	90.17
		NB-SMOTE	AUC (Average)	89.17
		NB-BSMOTE	AUC (Average)	89.75
		NB-ADASYN	AUC (Average)	87.98
		SVM	Precision (Average)	85.30
		SVM-SMOTE	Precision (Average)	91.70
		SVM-BSMOTE	Precision (Average)	88.62
		SVM-ADASYN	Precision (Average)	89.82
		SVM	F-Value (Average)	79.18

(*continued*)

Table 1. (*continued*)

References	Data	Model	Evaluation	
			Type	%
		SVM-SMOTE	F-Value (Average)	81.65
		SVM-BSMOTE	F-Value (Average)	79.95
		SVM-ADASYN	F-Value (Average)	78.03
		SVM	AUC (Average)	83.85
		SVM-SMOTE	AUC (Average)	83.92
		SVM-BSMOTE	AUC (Average)	83.48
		SVM-ADASYN	AUC (Average)	81.83
P. Pereira *et al.* [29]	8 datasets from a major automotive assembly company related with a distinct type of steering wheel angle sensor	None	AUC (Average)	57.24
		GC	AUC (Average)	67.31
		SMOTE	AUC (Average)	60.12
		RU	AUC (Average)	60.98
		TL	AUC (Average)	57.32

In 2021, Pereira *et al.* [29] conducted research comparing several balancing techniques with some Machine Learning methods and has found that while Gaussian Copula is the best oversampling technique combined with Random Forest (RF) base learner, SMOTE has shown competitive results on individual basis on several datasets, and is aggregately better results compared to no use of balancing techniques at all, evaluated with AUC. Table 1 summarizes the state-of-the-art techniques presented by many researchers for dealing with imbalance data using SVM and Naive Bayes classification.

3 Material and Proposed Method

3.1 Data

The data used for this research is public data taken from UCI and kaggle sources, taking 8 datasets that have different numbers of samples and characteristics (See Table 2). Also, heterogeneous data means that it contains mixed data types; categorical and numeric features.

3.2 Data Preprocessing

3.2.1 Data Standardization

Normalize all continuous feature values to the same scale in order to avoid having different scales of feature values. All feature values are normalized to the range [0, 1] using the Min-Max Scalar standardization procedure. The equation for the Min-Max

Table 2. Summary Description of Datasets

Source	Number of Samples	Number of Features	Labels
Attrition [27]	1,470	34	{Yes, No}
Flare 1 [25]	323	12	{0, 1}
Flare 2 [25]	1,066	12	{0, 1}
Haberman [25]	306	3	{1, 2}
Mammography [26]	111,183	6	{−1, 1}
Telcochurn [28]	7,043	19	{Yes, No}
Wine-Red [25]	1,590	11	{1, 2}
Wine-White [25]	4,898	11	{1, 2}

Scalar is as follows:

$$u_i' = \frac{u_i - \min(u)}{\max(u) - \min(u)},\qquad (1)$$

where u_i is original data and u_i' is standardized data with $i = 1, \ldots, n$. Moreover $min(u)$ and $max(u)$ are the feature's minimum and maximum values, respectively [20].

3.2.2 Data Split

Data split stage which data is prepared before it is processed. At this stage, the qualities are chosen first. The attributes with 80% missing value and redundant information were not used in the study. The data is translated to a numerical format without losing its real meaning, so the software could read the data.

3.3 Methodology for Binary Classification

3.3.1 Naïve Bayes

Naïve Bayes (NB) classification is a supervised learning approach that employs Bayes' theorem as a framework for categorizing observations into one of a predefined set of classes based on predictor variables' information. NB classifiers estimate the conditional probability that an observation belongs to a certain class based on the values of the predictor variables, assuming that the predictor variables are class-conditionally independent, and hence ignore predictor variable covariance.

The NB classifier is a subset of Bayesian networks. The class variable is at the root of a two-level structure used by NB Classifiers, with all characteristics in the next level. From one class feature to another, directed arcs link them. This structure expresses a strong independence assumption, implying that all characteristics are independent of the class value. Despite the fact that the conditional independence requirement is impractical, the NB classifier works well. According to Bayes theorem, the posterior probability that an observation Y has class index k given the values of predictor variables are described as:

$$\hat{P}\left(Y = k | X_1, \ldots, X_p\right) = \frac{\pi (Y = k) \prod_{j=1}^{P} P(X_j | Y = k)}{\sum_{k=1}^{K} \pi (Y = k) \prod_{i=1}^{P} P(X_j | Y = k)}. \qquad (2)$$

The prior probability in Eq. (2) that the class index is k is $P(Y = k)$. The process calculates a distinct Bayes distribution for each class for each predictor X and observations are allocated to the class with the highest posterior probability given the predictor values. For binary classification the class index k is set to 2.

3.3.2 Support Vector Machine

The Support Vector Machine (SVM) is a supervised learning approach for regression and clarifying issues that uses linear combinations of kernel basis functions to create predictions. SVM employs the structural risk minimization (SRM) concept, which aims to reduce the upper limit of generalization error rather than empirical error. The kernel is used to translate the input data into a high-dimensional space where the data will be segregated linearly in classification issues. The kernel is used to discover the best hyperplane that minimizes the distance between two data sets in the regression issue.

In N-dimensional space, SVM is used to discover the optimum hyperplane. The optimal hyperplane on the Support Vector Machine, which divides the two data sets included in the N-dimensional space, is depicted in Fig. 1. Support Vectors are vectors that are close to the ideal hyperplane (SVs). The correctness of the SVM model is determined by the kernel parameters used, since these parameters have a substantial influence on the kernel method's performance. The number of parameters is determined by the distance between several data sets.

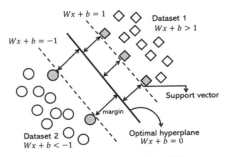

Fig. 1. SVM Hyperplane [7]

Find that $\{x_i, y_i\}_{i=1,\ldots,n}$, input vector $x_i \in \mathfrak{R}^d$ denoted as $y_i \in \mathfrak{R}$. Objective model SVM to find linear function as follows:

$$f(x) = \langle w, \phi_i(x) \rangle + b, \qquad (3)$$

with w and b are weight vector and constants that have been estimated from data, while ϕ_i is a non-linear function. So, regression problem can defined as follows:

$$R(C) = \frac{C}{n} \sum\nolimits_{i=1}^{n} L_\varepsilon(f(x_i), y_i) + \frac{1}{2}\|w\|^2, \tag{4}$$

which $L_\varepsilon(f(x_i), y_i)$ denoted as loss function intensive as in Eq. (5).

$$L_\varepsilon(f(x_i), y_i) = \begin{cases} |f(x) - y| - \varepsilon; \, for |f(x) - y| \geq \varepsilon, \\ 0; \, for \, everything \, else. \end{cases} \tag{5}$$

Variable slack ξ_i and ξ_i^* barrier is done by

Minimize :

$$R(w, \xi_i^*) = \frac{1}{2}\|w\|^2 + C \sum\nolimits_{i=1}^{n} (\xi_i + \xi_i^*),$$

Subject to : \hfill (6)

$$\begin{cases} y_i - \langle w, x_i \rangle - b \leq \varepsilon + \xi_i^*, \\ \langle w, x_i \rangle + b - y_i \leq \varepsilon + \xi_i^*, \\ \xi_i, \xi_i^* \geq 0, \end{cases}$$

where C is a regularized constant greater than 0 to perform balancing between the training error and flatness model which C represents penalty for prediction error that greater than ε. ξ_i *and* ξ_i^* slack extension from actual values to boundary values of ε. Optimization from Eq. (6) can be converted to Lagrange multipliers quadratic problem:

$$f(x) = \sum\nolimits_{i=1}^{n} (\alpha_i - \alpha_i^*) K(x_i, x) + b, \tag{7}$$

where α_i dan α_i^* in Eq. (7) are *Lagrange multipliers*:

$$\sum\nolimits_{i=1}^{n} (\alpha_i - \alpha_i^*) = 0, \tag{8}$$

which satisfies $0 \leq \alpha_i \leq C; 0 \leq \alpha_i^* \leq C; i = 1, \ldots, n$.

The $K()$ in Eq. (7) is a Keren function with value that contain product from 2 vector x_i and x_j inside feature $\phi(x_i)$ and $\phi(x_j)$, such $K(x_i, x_j) = \phi(x_i).\phi(x_j)$.

3.4 Methodology for Handling Imbalanced Data

3.4.1 Random Over-Sampling

The Random Over-Sampling approach works by repeating certain cases and randomly adding some observations in the minority class. The main disadvantage of ROS is that it might cause overfitting due to information replications [21] and increased processing time [22]. The majority and minority classes are represented by the red and purple bars in Fig. 2. The Random Oversampling procedure, as shown in the diagram, selects samples from the minority class and duplicates them to ensure that the classes are evenly represented.

Random Over-sampling depends on a direct application of the distributional hypothesis and is based on the premise that related documents (such as minority-class texts) may be predicted to include semantically comparable terms.

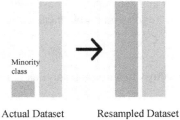

Actual Dataset   Resampled Dataset

Fig. 2. Data Resampling Using Random Over-Sampling [24]

3.4.2 Synthetic Minority Oversampling Technique (SMOTE)

Synthetic Minority Oversampling Techniques is an oversampling approach that works by generating false observations between neighboring minority observations. The benefit of SMOTE over the ROS technique is that it eliminates the problem of machine learning classifiers overfitting [22]. By finding a straight line between existent locations, SMOTE generates random synthetic points. The feature vector and its closest neighbor in a minority class are then identified, and the additional data points are multiplied by a random value between 0 and 1. These synthetic data points are added to the training data collection that will be used to train the models. However, two key limitations of this method are that it is unsuccessful with high-dimensional data, and while generating synthetic data, SMOTE does not hunt for neighboring instances from other classes, which might lead to more noisy data owing to class overlapping. The SMOTE method is shown in Fig. 3, with pink squares representing the minority (positive) class and blue circles indicating the majority class. SMOTE developed synthetic positive samples in the minority class, which are shown as orange triangles between pink squares. The original positive samples and manufactured samples together make up the minority group. This will bring the majority and minority classes closer together.

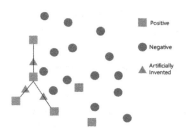

Fig. 3. SMOTE Synthetic Data [3]

To find SMOTE algorithm, choose k and N to represent the number of closest neighbors and synthetic observations, respectively. The algorithm is given as follows;

1. Let x_i, $i = 1, 2, \ldots, n_s$, denote the observations belonging to the minority class and let A denote the set of all x_i, such that $A \ni x_i$. For every x_i;

2. Calculate the Euclidean distance between x_i and all other elements of A to obtain the k-nearest neighbors of x_i;
3. Let S_{ik} denote the set of the k-nearest neighbors of x_i;
4. Randomly sample N synthetic observations denoted x_{ij}, $(j = 1, 2, \ldots, N)$ drom S_{ik} with replacement;
5. Let λ denote a number in the range $[0,1]$. For a given x_{ij}, draw a λ uniformly and then generate a synthetic observations by the formula $x_k = x_i + \lambda(x_i + x_{ij})$;
6. Execute Step 5 for every x_{ij};
7. Stop Algorithm.

3.4.3 Borderline-SMOTE

One of the SMOTE variations is Borderline-SMOTE. Rather than just constructing false observations between neighboring observations in the minority, it focuses on samples closer to the decision border [4]. Borderline-SMOTE like standard SMOTE oversamples observations in the minority class and its immediate neighbors. BorderlineSMOTE has two different parameter variations: borderline-1 and borderline-2. Based on the number of closest neighbors each sample has from the majority class samples samples in the minority class are initially categorized into three sets: danger noise and safe.

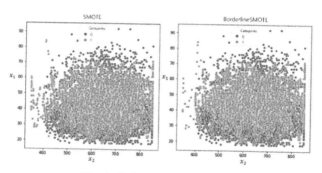

Fig. 4. B-SMOTE Case data [4]

The difference between oversampling data with SMOTE and Borderline-SMOTE is seen in the Fig. 4. Although it may seem to be comparable, there are distinctions in how the synthetic data is generated. B-SMOTE divided the data into 3 classes; "D", "S", and "N", which are danger, safe, and noise, respectively. Then it loops the algorithm below until all the data points are classified;

a Iterates over all instances in minority class $x_i \, \varepsilon \, S_{min}$, using K-NN algorithm on x_i and gets k neighbors of x_i;
b Calculates the number of sample belonging to majority class in the k nearest neighbors of x_i;
c Sample assignation as follows: $\frac{k}{2} \leq |S_i \cap S_{max}| < k$;
d x_i will be assigned to D;
e The sample x_i is to be judged as a noice instance and its divided into N and S set.

3.4.4 Adaptive Synthetic (ADASYN)

Another synthetic data oversampling strategy is the Adaptive Synthetic (ADASYN) sampling approach, which was initially proposed in [23], with the goal of achieving data class balance by adaptively producing data samples in the minority class depending on their distribution with a given balance level. There are two goals in this algorithm. For starters, the algorithm can figure out how many samples are needed for each sample in the minority class. Second, ADASYN pushes machine learning algorithms to recognize or learn the difficult-to-learn examples. The ADASYN method improves classification performance by minimizing the bias induced in the original unbalanced data sets, as seen in Fig. 5. Furthermore, when the equilibrium level is improved by ADASYN, it shows a trend for error reduction.

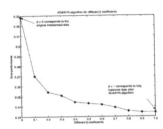

Fig. 5. ADASYN Algorithm for Data Balancing [23]

Choose k and β which denote the number of nearest neighbors and the desired levek if class balance after generating the synthetic data, then;

a. Let n_i denote the number of observation of the majority class and let n_s denote the number of observations of the minority class. Calculate $G = n_l - n_s.\beta$;
b. Let x_i, $i = 1, \ldots, n_s$, denote the observations belonging to the minority class and let A denote the set of all xi, such that A $\ni x_i$. For every x_i;
c. Calculate the Euclidean distance between x_i and all other elements of A to obtain the k-nearest neighbors of x_i;
d. Let S_{ik} denote the set of the k-nearest neighbors of x_i;
e. Define Δ_i as the number of the observations in the k-nearest neighbors region of x_i that belong to the majority class. Calculate the ratio r_i defines as $r_i = \frac{\Delta_i}{k}, i = 1, .., n_s$;
f. Normalize r_i according to $\hat{r} = \frac{r_i}{\sum r_i}$, so that probability equal 1;
g. Calculate $g_i = r_i.G$ which is the number of synthetic observations that need to be generated for each x_i;
h. Randomly sample g_i synthetic observations denoted x_{ij} from S_{ik} with replacement;
i. Let λ denote a number in the range [0,1]. For a given x_{ij}, generate a synthetic obser-vations according to $x_k = x_i + \lambda(x_i - x_{ij})$, where λ is uniformly drawn for each x_k;
j Stop Algorithm.

3.4.5 Receiver Operator Characteristics (ROC) and Precision-Recall (PR) Curve

A classifier identifies instances as positive or negative in a binary decision issue. A confusion matrix, also known as a contingency table, may be used to illustrate the classifier's choice. There are four categories in the confusion matrix: True positives (TP) are positive instances that have been appropriately categorized as such. False positives (FP) are negative cases that have been mistakenly categorized as positive. True negatives (TN) are negatives that have been appropriately identified as such. Finally, false negatives (FN) are positive cases that have been mislabeled as negative. ROC and PR curves are often used to assess a machine learning algorithm's performance on a given dataset. There are a specified number of good and negative instances in each dataset. We demonstrate that the ROC and PR worlds have a strong link.

In ROC space, the aim is to be in the upper-left-hand corner, and the ROC curves on the left of Fig. 6 seem to be quite near to ideal. The aim in PR space is to be in the upper-right-hand corner, and the PR right curves illustrate that there is still a lot of potential for growth.

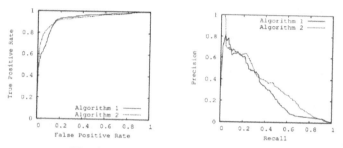

Fig. 6. Comparison of ROC and PR [12]

In this study, the F1-score and accuracy are employed to assess system performance. Precision and recall are required to compute F1-Score. Precision and recall may be determined as shown in Table 3 below.

Table 3. Confusion Matrix for Binary Classed Problems.

		Actual Class	
		1	0
Prediction	1	TP	FP
	0	FN	TN

The following Equation are the formula for Overall Accuracy (OA), precision, recall, F-measure, respectively

$$OA = \frac{TP + TN}{TP + FN + FP + TN}, \tag{9}$$

$$Precision = \frac{TP}{TP + FN}, \tag{10}$$

$$Recall = \frac{TP}{TP + FN},$$ (11)

$$F - Measure = \frac{(1 + \theta^2).Recall.Precision}{\theta^2.Recall + Precision},$$ (12)

where θ is a coefficient to adjust the importance relative of precision and recall.

4   Results and Discussion

4.1   Results

In our experiments, five performance measures are used; precision, recall, F-value, and the area under curve for both ROC and Precision-Recall curves. All of the calculations were made and concluded using R software. The measures were used to evaluate performance of four over-sampling techniques; Random Over Sampling (ROS), Adaptive Synthetic (ADASYN), Synthetic Minority Oversampling Technique (SMOTE), and Borderline-Synthetic Minority Oversampling Technique (B-SMOTE). The value of θ used for F-value is set to 1 and the value of k in all oversampling techniques are set to 5. The classifiers used as classifiers in the experiment are NB and SVM. Eight datasets were used from UCI Machine Learning Database and Kaggle as defined in Table 4 below. Prior to classifying and performing oversampling on the dataset, Principal Component Analysis (PCA) were used to transform the categorical data into numeric-float data in order for it to be oversampled using ADASYN, SMOTE, and B-SMOTE. PCA reduces the number of variables/dimensions of a dataset, while preserving as much information as possible. A percentage split of "80:20" were then used for testing and validation of data. Eighty percent (80%) of the data is for training and twenty percent (20%) is for testing. For the Flare 1 and Flare 2 datasets, we choose the class label "0" as minority and regard the others (>0) as class label "1" being the majority, as we only study two-class problem in this paper.

Table 4. Description of Datasets Used in the Experiments.

Name	Instances	Attributes	Positive	Negative	%Minority
Attrition	1470	35	1233	237	16.12
Flare 1	323	10	265	58	17.96
Flare 2	1066	10	865	201	18.86
Haberman	306	3	225	81	26.47
Mammography	11183	6	10923	260	2.32
Telcochurn	7043	20	5174	1869	26.54
Wine-Red	1599	12	1382	217	13.57
Wine-White	4898	12	3838	1060	21.64

Upon choosing the dataset for this experiment, we adopted an imbalance threshold of 40% while considering them, which states if the number of minority instances is less than 40% of the total instances in the dataset, it is considered as an imbalanced dataset, and therefore chosen for our experiment and evaluation. Table 4 shows the description of the datasets and that all of them fulfills the 40% threshold. Tables 5, 6, and 7 shows the results of actual Precision, Recall, and F-value, on the datasets using both SVM and NB for classification, and by four different methods of oversampling (ROS, ADASYN, SMOTE, and B-SMOTE) to tackle the imbalance on the data. Table 8 and 9 shows the result of the area under curve for the Receiver Operating Characteristic (ROC) Curve and the Precision-Recall (PR) Curve using the same methods of classification and oversampling to tackle the imbalanced datasets. Individually, for B-SMOTE, three stars (***) means that it has the highest value compared to other methods and the actual data without oversampling; two stars (**) means it has the highest value compared to other methods but not the actual data without oversampling; one star (*) means it is nor the lowest or the highest value; and no stars () means it is the lowest value. As for the mean of each method, **bold** denotes a significantly higher or lower value than actual mean, with an α of 5%, tested with two dependent samples t-test in Rstudio.

Figures 7, 8, 9 and 10 shows the curves for the ROC Curve and the PR Curve using SVM and NB before and after applying B-SMOTE to handle imbalanced data.

Table 5. Results in Terms of Precision Measure in the Experiments on Datasets.

Precision (SVM)					Precision (NB)					
Name	Actual	ROS	ADASYN	SMOTE	B-SMOTE	Name	Actual	ROS	ADASYN	SMOTE	B-SMOTE
Attrition	0.8493	1.0000	0.6534	0.6803	0.8000*	Attrition	0.8511	1.0000	0.5906	0.6069	0.6065*
Flare 1	0.9608	1.0000	1.0000	0.9804	1.0000***	Flare 1	0.9167	1.0000	0.7541	0.8214	0.8364*
Flare 2	0.9062	0.9620	0.9620	0.9105	0.9755***	Flare 2	0.8930	0.6866	0.6866	0.7321	0.7171**
Haberman	0.8000	0.6792	0.6944	0.6833	0.7381***	Haberman	0.8036	0.6061	0.5000	0.6557	0.6923**
Mammography	0.9887	0.9059	0.8873	0.9270	0.9949***	Mammography	0.9934	0.8349	0.7915	0.8875	0.9141**
Telcochurn	0.8213	0.7763	0.8468	0.8185	0.8307*	Telcochurn	0.9102	0.8036	0.7648	0.8324	0.7966*
Wine-Red	0.8987	0.9303	0.9077	0.8968	0.9237*	Wine-Red	0.9380	0.7719	0.8403	0.8419	0.8387*
Wine-White	0.8326	0.8681	0.8681	0.8636	0.8601*	Wine-White	0.9175	0.7595	0.7727	0.7877	0.7987*
Mean	0.8822	0.8902	0.8525	0.8376	0.8904	**Mean**	0.9029	0.8078	**0.7126**	**0.7670**	**0.7751**

From Table 5, Borderline-SMOTE (B-SMOTE) has shown to be the most effective method for SVM classifier, because it has the highest point of precision (number of positive class predictions that actually belong to the positive class) in 50% of the datasets, and scored higher points than the actual method without oversampling on 37.5% of the datasets. It can be concluded that B-SMOTE is a good method of oversampling for imbalance data that are classifying true positives using an SVM model. For the NB classifier however, B-SMOTE performs excellent on 40% of the datasets, but still couldn't beat the actual precision when oversampling is not used, but still the best method if oversampling is used.

However, the performance of B-SMOTE while being evaluated using Recall on Table 6 is contradictive. When SVM is used, B-SMOTE shows better results only for two out of eight datasets. And when NB classifier is used, B-SMOTE perform better

Table 6. Results in Terms of Recall Measure in the Experiments on Datasets.

Recall (SVM)						Recall (NB)					
Name	Actual	ROS	ADASYN	SMOTE	B-SMOTE	Name	Actual	ROS	ADASYN	SMOTE	B-SMOTE
Attrition	1.0000	1.0000	0.6777	0.7562	0.6833*	Attrition	0.9677	1.0000	0.7273	0.7273	0.7000
Flare 1	0.9800	0.9787	1.0000	0.9615	1.0000***	Flare 1	0.8800	0.9787	0.8846	0.8846	0.9200***
Flare 2	0.9721	0.8352	0.8362	0.9719	0.8983*	Flare 2	0.9330	0.8187	0.8187	0.9213	0.8305*
Haberman	0.9167	0.7826	0.5814	0.9318	0.6889*	Haberman	0.9375	0.8696	0.7674	0.9091	0.8000*
Mammography	0.9986	0.9240	0.9461	0.9623	0.9726**	Mammography	0.9616	0.8841	0.7471	0.8395	0.7775*
Telcochurn	0.9267	0.7017	0.8032	0.8513	0.8070*	Telcochurn	0.8456	0.7042	0.7160	0.7483	0.7034
Wine-Red	0.9821	0.7937	0.8520	0.8309	0.8364*	Wine-Red	0.8643	0.7098	0.7220	0.7243	0.7564**
Wine-White	0.9710	0.7700	0.7332	0.7902	0.7575*	Wine-White	0.7335	0.6307	0.6295	0.6308	0.6291
Mean	0.9684	**0.8482**	**0.8037**	**0.8820**	**0.8305**	**Mean**	0.8904	0.8245	**0.7516**	0.7982	**0.7646**

at two out of eight datasets, and perform worst at three out of eight datasets. By these results, we conclude that B-SMOTE is not the best to measure Recall (number of positive class predictions made out of all positive examples in the dataset) when using SVM classifier, and is the worst method when NB classifier is used. And by the F-measure from Table 7, B-SMOTE shows that it is not the best method either when using SVM or NB classification.

Table 7. Results in Terms of F-value Measure in the Experiments on Datasets.

F-value (SVM)						F-value (NB)					
Name	Actual	ROS	ADASYN	SMOTE	B-SMOTE	Name	Actual	ROS	ADASYN	SMOTE	B-SMOTE
Attrition	0.9185	1.0000	0.6653	0.7162	0.7371*	Attrition	0.9057	1.0000	0.6519	0.6617	0.6499
Flare 1	0.9703	0.9892	1.0000	0.9709	1.0000**	Flare 1	0.8980	0.9892	0.8142	0.8519	0.8762*
Flare 2	0.9380	0.8941	0.8941	0.9402	0.9353*	Flare 2	0.9126	0.7469	0.7469	0.8159	0.7696*
Haberman	0.8544	0.7273	0.6329	0.7885	0.7126*	Haberman	0.8654	0.7143	0.6055	0.7619	0.7423*
Mammography	0.9936	0.9148	0.9158	0.9443	0.9836*	Mammography	0.9772	0.8588	0.7687	0.8628	0.8403*
Telcochurn	0.8401	0.7371	0.8244	0.8346	0.8187*	Telcochurn	0.8912	0.6266	0.7396	0.7882	0.7471*
Wine-Red	0.9386	0.8566	0.8790	0.8626	0.8779*	Wine-Red	0.8996	0.7395	0.7767	0.7787	0.7954**
Wine-White	0.8965	0.8162	0.7949	0.8252	0.8056*	Wine-White	0.8152	0.6892	0.6938	0.7006	0.7038**
Mean	0.9188	0.8669	0.8258	0.8478	0.8589	**Mean**	0.8956	0.7956	**0.7247**	**0.7777**	**0.7656**

The presence of data balancing does not appear to have any significant effect on the classification results when comparing the average precision and F-value of the SVM classifier. While there are several significant values for recall in the SVM method and precision, recall, and F-value in NB, However, those metric values are less than the actual imbalanced data; hence, this is not a worthwhile outcome.

When measuring using curves like ROC or PR, we need to take a look at the value of area under curve (AUC). The Receiver Operator Characteristic (ROC) plots the True Positive Rate (TPR) against False Positive Rate (FPR) to measure the ability of a classifier to distinguish between classes, and the higher the AUC (the closer it is to one) the better the performance at distinguishing between positive and negative classes. The PR Curve summarizes the trade-off between the TPR and Positive Predictive Value (PPV) using different probability threshold, and the higher the AUC (the closer it is to one) the better.

Table 8. Results Score on Area Under Curve for ROC in the Experiments on Datasets.

Area Under ROC Curve (SVM)					Area Under ROC Curve (NB)				
Name	Actual	ROS	ADASYN	SMOTE	B-SMOTE	Name	Actual	ROS	ADASYN	SMOTE	B-SMOTE
Attrition	0.4252	0.5000	0.4908	0.4721	0.5360***	Attrition	0.4422	0.5000	0.4427	0.4504	0.4619*
Flare 1	0.4923	0.5047	0.5000	0.5051	0.5000*	Flare 1	0.5154	0.5047	0.4579	0.4798	0.4755*
Flare 2	0.4695	0.5347	0.5347	0.4820	0.5206*	Flare 2	0.4812	0.4494	0.4494	0.4311	0.4588*
Haberman	0.4426	0.4611	0.5380	0.3961	0.5174*	Haberman	0.4344	0.3889	0.3750	0.3896	0.4593***
Mammography	0.4951	0.4951	0.4833	0.4902	0.5056***	Mammography	0.5156	0.4855	0.5142	0.5140	0.5375***
Telcochurn	0.4901	0.5232	0.5133	0.4882	0.5077*	Telcochurn	0.4298	0.5531	0.5164	0.5297	0.5314*
Wine-Red	0.4875	0.5374	0.5156	0.5186	0.5242*	Wine-Red	0.4938	0.5205	0.5356	0.5354	0.5251*
Wine-White	0.4357	0.5280	0.5402	0.5228	0.5309*	Wine-White	0.5776	0.5420	0.5479	0.5534	0.5550**
Mean	0.4673	**0.5105**	**0.5145**	0.4844	**0.5178**	**Mean**	0.4863	0.4930	0.4799	0.4854	0.5006

Table 9. Results Score on Area Under Precision-Recall in the Experiments on Datasets.

Area Under Precision-Recall Curve (SVM)					Area Under Precision-Recall Curve (NB)				
Name	Actual	ROS	ADASYN	SMOTE	B-SMOTE	Name	Actual	ROS	ADASYN	SMOTE	B-SMOTE
Attrition	0.4270	0.5000	0.4937	0.4807	0.5248***	Attrition	0.4397	0.5000	0.4607	0.4657	0.4738*
Flare 1	0.4927	0.5031	0.5000	0.5036	0.5000*	Flare 1	0.5146	0.5031	0.4713	0.4857	0.4832*
Flare 2	0.4670	0.5246	0.5246	0.4872	0.5145*	Flare 2	0.4796	0.4642	0.4642	0.4511	0.4710**
Haberman	0.4450	0.4728	0.5256	0.4248	0.5123*	Haberman	0.4378	0.4238	0.4177	0.4204	0.4713***
Mammography	0.4905	0.4966	0.4884	0.4931	0.5039***	Mammography	0.5295	0.4900	0.5099	0.5098	0.5260**
Telcochurn	0.4511	0.5158	0.5094	0.4911	0.5055*	Telcochurn	0.4861	0.5362	0.5116	0.5224	0.5225*
Wine-Red	0.4917	0.5261	0.5108	0.5130	0.5169*	Wine-Red	0.4958	0.5143	0.5248	0.5246	0.5176*
Wine-White	0.4401	0.5193	0.5282	0.5163	0.5218*	Wine-White	0.5731	0.5290	0.5336	0.5382	0.5387**
Mean	0.4631	**0.5073**	**0.5101**	0.4887	**0.5125**	**Mean**	0.4945	0.4951	0.4867	0.4897	0.5005

In Table 8 and Table 9, we can see that, in general, data balancing on SVM has a significant effect. Different from the metric results in Tables 5, 6 and 7, the AUC indicates that balanced data has better values than imbalanced data. NB has the same results, although the difference in value is not statistically significant. When viewed individually, we conclude that B-SMOTE is the best-performing method to produce higher AUC scores when both the NB and SVM classification techniques are used.

Figures 7 and 8 shows the results of ROC and PR curves for Attrition dataset using BSMOTE as a method of oversampling to handle imbalanced data. These curves show an increase in the areas under the curve, while also decreasing the elbow angles of the curves. We can see before BSMOTE, the ROC curves for Attrition dataset were in quite steep and sharp elbow shapes, and after BSMOTE they became duller angles. This meant that BSMOTE has increased Sensitivity, FPR, Precision, and Recall in a more consistent manner also, decreasing the rate of error. While AUC is increased over several instances of observation and methods, further research is needed because an AUC of 0.5 or close to 0.5 is quite common for a balanced dataset.

Lastly, Fig. 10 show the results of ROC and PR curves for Mammography dataset using BSMOTE as method of oversampling to handle imbalanced data. These curves show an increase in both the AUC and also a decrease in the angles of the curve. Same as the results for Attrition dataset, this meant that BSMOTE has successfully increased

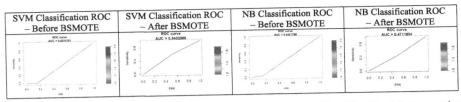

Fig. 7. Results of ROC curve in the experiment of Employee Attrition (Attrition) Dataset using BSMOTE as method of handling imbalanced dataset.

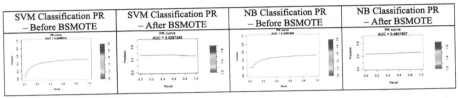

Fig. 8. Results of PR curve in the experiment of Employee Attrition (Attrition) Dataset using BSMOTE as method of handling imbalanced dataset.

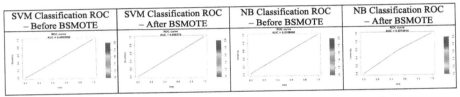

Fig. 9. Results of ROC curve in the experiment of Mammography Dataset using BSMOTE as method of handling imbalanced dataset.

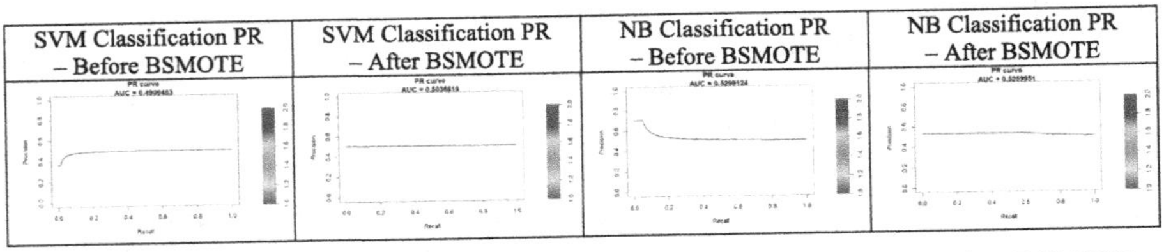

Fig. 10. Results of PR curve in the experiment of Mammography Dataset using BSMOTE as method of handling imbalanced dataset.

these statistics, while maintaining, or even increasing the consistency of these curves, decreasing the rate of error.

4.2 Discussion

The results show that, in general, balancing data does not always result in a good classification, but when you examine the findings from each of the balancing techniques utilized separately, B-smote clearly demonstrates its class. Even though B-SMOTE might not be the best at each and every measure of evaluation, it has shown great performance in the evaluations. It even performed to be the best method in a few datasets. This is due to the nature of the Borderline-SMOTE method.

According to Han *et al.* [4], B-SMOTE is a method that expands the original distribution of the dataset inwards from the borders. B-SMOTE first see the real distribution of the datasets and concludes the minority, then it calculates which of the data points are borderline minority data points, and it calculates and makes new data points by pointing inwards from these borderline minority data points. Therefore, if the distribution is definitive, then B-SMOTE will only add inside these borders and doesn't increase the number of noise or the majority class. This makes B-SMOTE a more precise method of oversampling because it does not affect the majority or the other classes, and it might even increase the precision, if the dataset supports it. However, if we look at the F-value and the recall, B-SMOTE performed the worst on some of the datasets. This is due to the distribution of the datasets. These datasets are not synthetic or randomized/generated datasets. The borders of each class in these datasets are blurry, and sometimes it might even mix with other classes. By nature, they have no set or definitive shapes for B-SMOTE to use in order to determine the borders. This makes B-SMOTE harder to predict and make points that does not intersect with other classes, making the data even more blurry, and reducing the possibility of the model correctly predicting the class and increasing the number of misclassified points and false negatives, reducing the score of recall. In short, it can be said that Borderline-SMOTE is a precise and good method of oversampling to tackle imbalanced dataset, if the dataset has a good shape, or at least a definitive border between the majority class and the minority class, in order to minimize the number of misclassified synthetic data points later in the calculations.'

5   Conclusion and Future Research

Imbalanced Data has been a problem for a long time, and has recently got more attention, especially from data scientists and data miners. There are many techniques one can use to tackle this problem. However, some of the traditional techniques are still unsatisfactory. Borderline-SMOTE presents a new modern technique that might be used to handle the class imbalance problem. The experiments show that the performance of B-SMOTE, evaluated by precision, recall, and F-value are better than ROS, ADASYN, and SMOTE at some datasets, when either SVM or NB classifiers are applied. This is due to the fact that B-SMOTE carefully samples the dataset and expands it inside the borders of the class for it to decrease the misclassification of the data. We can conclude in individual examination, that it does increase the precision, recall, f-value, and area under curves of ROC and PR, for some of the datasets, and it may improve prediction on those datasets. However, the experiments also shows that while it may be more precise when used on correct datasets, it may increase misclassification when use on datasets with blurry borders or intersecting classes. In handling imbalanced data with no set shapes or borders, there needs to be a new method of classification, that may increase the accuracy and area under curve, in a way that the B-SMOTE cannot do, due to the fact that the datasets are mixed.

Future research might also use B-SMOTE and modify the parameters in order to increase the performance by reducing the radius of the borders, the distance between synthetic data, etc. B-SMOTE might not be the best at handling imbalanced data, but it has shown great performance and may be one of the better alternatives to tackle an imbalanced dataset.

Acknowledgement. The authors thanks to the Department of Statistics and Research Center for Artificial Intelligence and Big Data, Universitas Padjadjaran which supports this research. The work of Tutut Herawan and Eka Novita Sari is supported by AMCS Research Center.

References

1. Bach, M., Werner, A., Żywiec, J., Pluskiewicz, W.: The study of under- and over-sampling methods' utility in analysis of highly imbalanced data on osteoporosis. Inf. Sci. **384**, 174–190 (2017)
2. Bekkar, M., Alitouche, D., Akrouf, T., Alitouche, T.A.: Imbalance data learning approaches review. Data Min. Knowl. **3**(4), 15–33 (2013)
3. Chawla, N.V., Bowyer, K.W., Hall, L.O., Kegelmeyer, W.P.: SMOTE: synthetic minority oversampling technique. J. Artif. Intell. Res. **16**, 321–357 (2002)
4. Han, H., Wang, W.-Y., Mao, B.-H.: Borderline-SMOTE: a new over-sampling method in imbalanced data sets learning. In: Huang, D.-S., Zhang, X.-P., Huang, G.-B. (eds.) ICIC 2005. LNCS, vol. 3644, pp. 878–887. Springer, Heidelberg (2005). https://doi.org/10.1007/11538059_91
5. He, H., Bai, Y., Garcia, E.A., Li, S.: ADASYN: adaptive synthetic sampling approach for imbalanced learning. In: 2008 IEEE International Joint Conference on Neural Networks, pp. 1322–1328 (2008)
6. Vapnik, V.N.: The Nature of Statistical Learning Theory. Springer, New York (2000). https://doi.org/10.1007/978-1-4757-3264-1
7. Schlkopf, B., Smola, A.J.: Learning with Kernels: Support Vector Machines, Regularization, Optimization, and Beyond. The MIT Press, Cambridge (2001)
8. Begg, R., Palaniswami, M., Owen, B.: Support vector machines for automated gait classification. IEEE Trans. Biomed. Eng. **52**(5), 828–838 (2005)
9. Kotsiantis, S.B., Pintelas, P.E.: Mixture of expert agents for handling imbalanced data sets. Ann. Math. Comput. Teleinformat. **1**(1), 46–55 (2003)
10. Rish, I.: An empirical study of the Naive Bayes classifier. In: IJCAI 2001 Workshop on Empirical Methods in Artificial Intelligence (IJCAI), pp. 41–46 (2001)
11. Buckland, M., Gey, F.: The relationship between recall and precision. J. Am. Soc. Inf. Sci. **45**(1), 12–19 (1994)
12. Bradley, A.: The use of the area under the ROC curve in the evaluation of machine learning algorithms. Pattern Recogn. **30**(6), 1145–1159 (1997)
13. Jian, C., Gao, J., Ao, Y.: A new sampling method for classifying imbalanced data based on support vector machine ensemble. Neurocomputing **193**, 115–122 (2016)
14. Pereira, J., Saraiva, F.: A comparative analysis of unbalanced data handling techniques for machine learning algorithms to electricity theft detection. In: 2020 IEEE Congress on Evolutionary Computation (CEC), pp. 1–8. IEEE Press (2020)
15. Khemakhem, S., Said, F.B., Boujelbene, Y.: Credit risk assessment for unbalanced datasets based on data mining, artificial neural network and support vector machines. J. Model. Manag. **13**(4), 932–951 (2018)
16. Hordri, N.F., Yuhaniz, S.S., Azmi, N.F.M., Shamsuddin, S.M.: Handling class imbalance in credit card fraud using resampling methods. Int. J. Adv. Comput. Sci. Appl. **9**(11), 390–396 (2018)

17. Oreški, G., Oreški, S.: An experimental comparison of classification algorithm performances for highly imbalanced datasets. In: 25th Central European Conference on Information and Intelligent Systems, Faculty of Organization and Informatics Varazdin, pp. 1–4 (2014)

18. Lu, C., Lin, S., Liu, X., Shi, H.: Telecom fraud identification based on ADASYN and random forest. In: 2020 5th International Conference on Computer and Communication Systems (ICCCS), pp. 447–452. IEEE Press (2020)

19. Gosain, A., Sardana, S.: Handling class imbalance problem using oversampling techniques: a review. In: 2017 International Conference on Advances in Computing, Communications and Informatics (ICACCI), pp. 79–85. IEEE Press (2017)

20. Azeem, M., Usman, M., Fong, A.C.M.: A churn prediction model for prepaid customers in telecom using fuzzy classifiers. Telecommun. Syst. **66**(4), 603–614 (2017). https://doi.org/10.1007/s11235-017-0310-7

21. Batista, G.E., Prati, R.C., Monard, M.C.: A study of the behavior of several methods for balancing machine learning training data. ACM SIGKDD Explor. Newslett. **6**(1), 20–29 (2004)

22. Hartati, E.P., Bijaksana, M.A., et al.: Handling imbalance data in churn prediction using combined SMOTE and RUS with bagging method. J. Phys. Conf. Ser. **971**(1), 012007 (2018)

23. He, H., Bai, Y., Garcia, E.A., Li, S.: ADASYN: adaptive synthetic sampling approach for imbalanced learning. In: 2008 IEEE International Joint Conference on Neural Networks (IEEE World Congress on Computational Intelligence) (IEEE 2008), pp. 1322–1328 (2008)

24. Lahera, G.: Unbalanced datasets what to do about them medium (2018). https://medium.com/strands-tech-corner/unbalanced-datasetswhat-to-do-144e0552d9cd

25. UCI Machine Learning Repository: https://archive.ics.uci.edu/ml/datasets.php. Accessed 2 June 2022

26. Mammography Dataset. OpenML. https://www.openml.org/search?type=data&sort=runs&id=310&status=active. Accessed 2 June 2022

27. IBM HR Analytics Employee Attrition & Performance. Kaggle. https://www.kaggle.com/datasets/pavansubhasht/ibm-hr-analytics-attrition-dataset. Accessed 2 June 2022

28. Telco customer churn: IBM dataset. Kaggle. https://www.kaggle.com/datasets/yeanzc/telco-customer-churn-ibm-dataset. Accessed 22 June 2022

29. Pereira, P.J., Pereira, A., Cortez, P., Pilastri, A.: A comparison of machine learning methods for extremely unbalanced industrial quality data. In: Marreiros, G., Melo, F.S., Lau, N., Lopes Cardoso, H., Reis, L.P. (eds.) EPIA 2021. LNCS (LNAI), vol. 12981, pp. 561–572. Springer, Cham (2021). https://doi.org/10.1007/978-3-030-86230-5_44

Team Member Satisfaction, Teamwork Management, and Task Conflict: A Multilevel Model

Isabel Dórdio Dimas[1]([⊠]) [ID], Marta Alves[2] [ID], Teresa Rebelo[3] [ID],
and Paulo Renato Lourenço[3] [ID]

[1] CeBER, Faculty of Economics, University of Coimbra, Coimbra, Portugal
idimas@fe.uc.pt
[2] University of Beira Interior, NECE-UBI, Covilhã, Portugal
mpalves@ubi.pt
[3] CeBER, Faculty of Psychology and Education Sciences, University of Coimbra, Coimbra, Portugal
{terebelo,prenato}@fpce.uc.pt

Abstract. This study investigates how teamwork management influences the levels of team members' satisfaction both directly and indirectly, through its influence on reducing task conflict. Three hundred and fifty-eight team members from 88 teams were surveyed. A two-wave data collection procedure was implemented with a time lag of about two months. Due to the multilevel nature of data (while teamwork management and task conflict are conceptualized as team-level constructs, team member satisfaction is at the individual level), hypotheses were tested through Multilevel Path Analysis in Stata. Results revealed that teamwork management presented a positive relationship with the levels of satisfaction of team members towards the team. Moreover, task conflict presented a mediating role between teamwork management and satisfaction. The findings emphasize the importance of team members planning the work, organizing resources and providing support to each other to reduce conflict and generate a positive attitude of members towards the team.

Keywords: Team member satisfaction · teamwork management · task conflict

1 Introduction

Organizations have adopted team-based work to give an answer to the challenges of an increasingly complex and volatile environment (Mathieu et al. 2019). Although teams can potentially generate better results than individuals working separately, research shows that not all teams succeed, because they do not develop a functioning that leads to effective collaboration and to the achievement of team goals (DeChurch and Mesmer-Magnus, 2010). In order to achieve collective goals and to contribute to team effectiveness, team members need to be involved in teamwork processes, that is, to develop teamwork (Salas et al. 2008).

© The Author(s), under exclusive license to Springer Nature Switzerland AG 2023

O. Gervasi et al. (Eds.): ICCSA 2023 Workshops, LNCS 14105, pp. 24–34, 2023.
https://doi.org/10.1007/978-3-031-37108-0_2

Although most of the research has considered team performance as the main criterion of effectiveness (Mathieu et al. 2008), there is consensus in the literature regarding the need to consider multiple criteria when studying team effectiveness (Aubé and Rousseau, 2005).

In this context, Hackman (1987) identifies three criteria to be considered when assessing team effectiveness: (a) the degree to which the group's products/services correspond to the standards of quality and quantity of those who receive and/or analyse its output; (b) the degree to which the social processes used to accomplish the work contribute to maintain or enhance the ability of group members to work together in the future; (c) the degree to which the group experience contributes to team members' growth and well-being. In the present study, we focus on members' satisfaction with the group, which is aligned with the last criterion, being one of the most frequent ways to operationalize it. Team member satisfaction is an essential aspect of team effectiveness, and previous research have shown that employees' experiences at work have a significant impact on their work-related attitudes (e.g., personal well-being, turnover) and on their present and future commitment and performance (Nerkar et al. 1996; Spector, 1997).

Recognizing the importance of increasing team member satisfaction among teams, our study is focused on the processes that contribute to it. Specifically, adopting a multi-level design, we explore how individual satisfaction with the team can be influenced by the way the team cooperates, organizes, and plans its activities (i.e., by teamwork management). Moreover, we also intend to explore how teamwork management contribute to reducing conflicts regarding the task, indirectly influencing in a positive way the levels of satisfaction of team members. Our hypothesized model is depicted in Fig. 1.

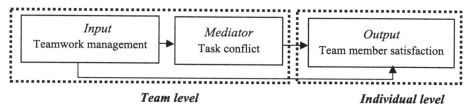

Fig. 1. Hypothesized model under analysis

1.1 Team Member Satisfaction

Job satisfaction has been a central theme in organizational research, and multiple studies can be found supporting its effects on organizations in aspects such as individual work performance (Riketta, 2008), firm performance (van de Voorde et al. 2012), productivity (Hoboubi et al. 2017) or organizational citizenship behaviour and turnover intentions (Tsai and Wu, 2010). Judge and Kammeyer-Mueller (2012) have proposed an integrating definition, which considers job satisfaction as an evaluative state that expresses contentment with the experiences provided by one's job.

In the work group context, satisfaction with the work group, specifically, can be defined as an affective response of members towards the group, its characteristics and functioning (Wiiteman, 1991) and can be conceptualized as a criterion of team effectiveness.

Li et al. (2009) highlight that the level of satisfaction with the team may vary according to the existing personal and interpersonal relationships, the characteristics of the task (e.g., task identity and significance, autonomy and responsibility, and feedback about the results), the result of the work performed (performance), the participation of group members in the work performance, among other factors external or internal to the group. Accordingly, group member satisfaction with the group integrates both aspects related to the task system (e.g., work accomplishment) and aspects related to the affective system of the group (e.g., work climate in the team).

1.2 Teamwork Management and Team Member Satisfaction

The concept of teamwork management was introduced by Rousseau et al. (2006) as part of the construct of teams' internal functioning. Teamwork management refers to the way team members organize themselves to plan their tasks and carry out their work in order to improve team effectiveness (Rousseau et al. 2006).

Teamwork management is associated with the degree team members structure and plan their work to facilitate the implementation of new practices and monitor the work progress (Dimas et al. 2016; Rousseau et al. 2006). According to Rousseau et al. teamwork management involves the following dimensions: work planning/organization, resource management and support for innovation dimensions (Pinto and Lourenço, 2014; Rousseau et al. 2006). Work planning/organization is related to team members' knowledge of their colleague's responsibilities and functions and involve coordinating and planning the work so that tasks are carried out within the deadline (Ilgen et al. 2005; Marks et al. 2001; Rousseau et al. 2006), in order to avoid unnecessary efforts (Cohen et al. 1996). Resource management refers to the way team members manage the available resources (Anderson and West, 1996), allocating the necessary resources to achieve the desired objectives. Finally, support for innovation is defined as the degree team members generate new ideas and practices and promote their practical use (Anderson and West, 1996; Cohen et al. 1996).

These behaviours adopted in the teamwork context are important determinants of team effectiveness (Rousseau et al. 2006). By providing support to each other, allocating resources more efficiently and planning appropriately the work that needs to be done, teamwork management will generate a positive attitude of team members towards their team (i.e., high levels of satisfaction). Accordingly, we hypothesize that:

Hypothesis 1: Teamwork management will have a positive relationship with team member satisfaction.

1.3 The Mediating Role of Task Conflict

Intragroup conflict has been defined as a disagreement that is perceived as tense by at least one of the parties involved in an interaction (De Dreu and Weingart, 2003) and is usually conceptualized as task or relationship oriented (Jehn, 1994). Task conflict emerges when there is tension in the group due to the presence of different opinions regarding the task, while relationship conflict involves situations of interpersonal tension between group members based on differences in personality, beliefs, and attitudes.

Previous studies support the negative influence of both types of intragroup conflict on satisfaction (De Dreu and Weingart, 2003; Dimas and Lourenço, 2015). Indeed, as noted by Tekleab et al. (2009), high levels of conflict may generate stress and harm psychological well-being. Thus, the usual reaction to conflict is dissatisfaction (De Dreu et al. 2004).

Previous studies have found that conflicts in teams are influenced by different factors, namely by the levels of diversity in the group (Jehn et al. 1999), faultlines (Choi and Cho, 2011), trust (Curşeu and Schruijer, 2010), or team climate (Jehn and Mannix, 2001).

Regarding conflicts related to the task, important sources of disagreements include deadlines management and coordination (Gevers and Peeters, 2009). Moye and Langfred (2004) have highlighted the importance of information sharing in reducing task conflicts. Indeed, sharing information among team members help to create a common understanding of the work developed, improving coordination and resources allocation.

Establishing cooperation and a pleasant collaboration is essential to reduce conflicts related to the way tasks are developed and aims are defined and achieved. Accordingly, a better teamwork management will contribute to reducing task conflicts among teams, increasing, in turn, the levels of satisfaction of team members. Accordingly, the following hypothesis is established:

Hypothesis 2: Teamwork management will have an indirect relationship with team member satisfaction through task conflict.

2 Materials and Methods

2.1 Data Collection Procedures

Organizations were identified using both the authors' personal and professional networks and national company databases that are accessible online. In the first contact with the company's representatives, the research purpose was presented, as well as the requirements for the company to participate. In these meetings, companies were also informed that a report on the companies' results could be provided if required. According to the criteria for defining a team (Cohen and Bailey, 1997), teams were considered for inclusion in the study if they (a) consisted of at least three members, (b) were perceived by themselves and others as a team, (c) and worked interdependently to achieve a common goal.

In order to reduce common method variance (Podsakoff et al. 2003), data was collected at two moments about two months apart from each other. A two-month time lag was chosen to reduce common method variance and, simultaneously, to have a period short enough for the antecedents to exert an influence on the outcome considered.

Data collection was carried out through surveys filled in mostly online (in a few cases, surveys were answered in paper format). A team was considered valid only if half of the team members responded to the surveys in both waves. The cut-off of 50% response rate is in line with previous studies that used team-level aggregated data (e.g., Keem et al. 2022).

2.2 Sample

The sample is composed of 358 members of 88 teams from different companies. Most of the companies were small and mid-size enterprises (SMEs) (76%) from the services sector (71%). Team size varied from 3 to 43 members with an average of approximately six members ($SD = 5.37$) and teams have been working together for about eight years ($SD = 10.50$). Teams develop different types of activities, most of them are services teams (46%). Team members have on average 34 years ($SD = 11.63$), 52% are female and have been working in the team for about four years ($SD = 5.84$).

2.3 Measures

Teamwork Management. This variable was evaluated using the scale developed by (Rousseau et al. 2006), which has been adapted to the Portuguese language by Pinto and Lourenço (2014). This scale is composed of six items that are measured using a 5-point Likert-type scale, from 1 (not true) to 5 (completely true). A sample item is "We organize our work activities".

Task Conflict. The scale developed by Dimas and Lourenço (2015) was used to evaluate task conflict. This scale is composed of five items and respondents are asked to rate how often they perceive tension in the team due to the presence of disagreements related to the task. A sample item is "different opinions about the work being done". Items are answered on a 7-point Likert scale, ranging from 1 (never) to 7 (always).

Team Member Satisfaction. Team member satisfaction was evaluated with the scale developed by Dimas and Lourenço (2015). This scale is composed of seven items that measure members' satisfaction with different aspects related to the team. A sample item is "team functioning". Statements are evaluated on a 7-point Likert scale ranging from 1 (totally dissatisfied) to 7 (totally satisfied).

Control Variables. Team size and team tenure were considered as control variables in the present study since previous research revealed that these variables may influence team outcomes (Robert and You, 2018; Standifer et al. 2015). Given that while some teams were surveyed before the COVID-19 pandemic (2020) has started and others already during the pandemic (2021, 2022), a dummy variable (0 = collected before the pandemic; 1 = collected during pandemic) was introduced to account for the possible influence of this pandemic crisis on the explained variables.

3 Results

3.1 Data Aggregation

Since teamwork management and task conflict were operationalized at the team level but obtained at the individual level using referent shift consensus, within-team homogeneity and between-team heterogeneity need to be assured. Accordingly, we calculated the inter-rater reliability index r_{wg} (James et al. 1993) and the intra-class correlation coefficients $ICC(1)$ and $ICC(2)$ (Bliese, 2000).

The r_{wg} index relates the within-group variance of a single item j in a group of K raters (S_{jk}^2) to an expected variance that assumes all ratings were due to random responding (σ_{EU}^2). Since our scales have multi-items, $r_{wg(j)}$ was implemented which is given by the following formula:

$$r_{wg(j)} = \frac{J \times \left(1 - \frac{S_{jk}^2}{\sigma_{EU}^2}\right)}{1 + (j - 1) \times \left(1 - \frac{S_{jk}^2}{\sigma_{EU}^2}\right)}$$

Following Bliese (2000), *ICC(1)* was calculated using Bartko (1976) formula:

$$ICC(1) = \frac{MSB - MSW}{MSB + [(k - 1) \times MSW]}$$

MSB is the between-group mean square, *MSW* is the within-group mean square, and K is the group size. This formula is a way of contrasting the between-group and within-group variance components from the ANOVA model. Since group sizes were different among teams, the group size average was used. While *ICC(1)* may be considered as a measure of the reliability associated with a single assessment of the group mean, *ICC(2)* provides an estimate of the reliability of the group means and is given by the following formula (Bliese, 2000):

$$ICC(2) = \frac{MSB - MSW}{MSB}$$

The results showed adequate average r_{wg} values for teamwork management (M = .89, SD = .21) and task conflict (M = .88, SD = .17), well above the recommended cut-off of point of .70 (James et al. 1993). Results for *ICC(1)* and *ICC(2)*, were .30 and .67, for team work management, and .29 and .66 for task conflict, respectively. Taken together, the r_{wg}, *ICC(1)* and *ICC(2)* values provide sufficient justification for aggregating the data to the team level (Bliese, 2000).

3.2 Measurement Model Assessment

We conducted a confirmatory factor analysis using the maximum likelihood method of estimation to ensure that the variables presented adequate convergent and discriminant validity. The three-factor measurement model revealed some adjustment problems (χ^2 (132) = 592.69, p < .001, CFI = .93, RMSEA = .099). The analysis of the Modification Indices that revealed the model would benefit from estimating the covariances between two errors of the task conflict scale and two errors of the satisfaction scale. After adding those covariances to the model, the adjustment indices presented adequate values (χ^2 (130) = 459.23, p < .001, CFI = .95, RMSEA = .08).

All standardized factorial loadings of the items on respective latent variables were significant (p < .001) and ranged between .68 and .95, indicating convergent validity. The correlation between teamwork management and task conflict was $-.14$ (p < .001) and with satisfaction was .19 (p < .001), while the correlation between task conflict and satisfaction was $-.27$ (p < .001) indicating satisfactory discriminant validity (Kline, 2005).

3.3 Hypotheses Testing

Descriptive statistics and intercorrelations among studied variables are presented in Table 1. Regarding control variables, team tenure was positively and significantly related to team member satisfaction ($R = -.22$, P $< .01$) but not with task conflict ($R = .09$, ns). Teams collected during the pandemic presented higher team member satisfaction ($R = .11$, P $< .05$) and lower levels of task conflict ($R = -.47$, P $< .01$). Team size was not significantly related to the explained variables. Thus, it was dropped from further analyses (Becker et al. 2016). Teamwork management was negatively related to task conflict ($R = -.34$, P $< .01$) and positively related to team member satisfaction ($R = .33$, P $< .01$). Task conflict was negatively related to team member satisfaction ($R = -.34$, P $< .01$).

Table 1. Descriptive statistics and intercorrelation matrix.

Variables	1	2	3	4	5	6	M	SD
1. Team tenure	–						8.72	10.76
2. Team size	−.04	–					8.53	7.72
3. Pandemic situation	.03	.03	–				–	–
4. Teamwork management	−.26**	−.01	.22**	–			3.95	0.50
5. Task conflict	.09	.06	−.47**	−.35**	–		2.90	0.80
6. Team member satisfaction	−.22**	.03	.11*	.33**	−.34**	–	5.60	1.00

Note: N = 358 members/88 teams. * p $< .05$; ** p $< .01$. M = Mean; SD = Standard Deviation; Pandemic situation (0 = before the pandemic; 1 = after the beginning of the pandemic). Team member satisfaction was collected two months after the remaining variables

Data for this study is hierarchical in nature since we are interested in exploring the effect of two variables that are operationalized at the team level, teamwork management and task conflict, on one variable from the individual level, member's satisfaction with the team. Because individuals in the same group share common influences, using ordinary regression analysis would possibly lead to unreliable results since the assumption of independent observations would be violated (Bryk and Raudenbush, 1992). Accordingly, the first step is partitioning the variance (σ^2) in team member satisfaction into its within- and between-group components. If it turns out that there is little or no variation (less than 5%) in team member satisfaction between groups, ordinary regression analysis can be used (Heck et al. 2013).

In this way, the intraclass correlation coefficient (Bliese, 2000) was calculated to examine the ratio of between-group to the total variance (ICC). ICC is computed as follows:

$$ICC = \frac{\sigma_b^2}{\sigma_b^2 + \sigma_w^2},$$

where σ_b^2 is the between-group variance and σ_w^2 is the within-group variance. The ICC value confirmed that 34% of the variance in member's satisfaction is explained by team membership, suggesting the need to use Hierarchical Linear Modelling to test hypotheses.

Thus, we tested our hypothetical model through generalized structural equation modeling (GSEM) with Stata (version 16), including a random intercept in the equation that accounts for group membership. Additionally, teamwork management and task conflict were grand-mean centered (Kreft et al. 1995).

Results of GSEM analysis are presented in Table 2. Teamwork management presented a negative influence on task conflict ($B = -.55$, $p < .001$) and a positive influence on member's satisfaction with the team ($B = .42$; $p < .01$). Thus hypothesis 1 was supported. To test hypothesis 2, we computed the indirect effect of teamwork management on team member satisfaction via task conflict. Results revealed that the indirect effect was significant ($B = .13$, $p < .01$, 95% CI $= .05$; $.22$) providing support for hypothesis 2. The total effect of teamwork management on members' satisfaction was also significant ($B = .56$, $p < .001$, 95% CI $= .31$; $.80$).

Table 2. Generalized structural equation modeling analysis.

Predictor variables	Task conflict	Member's satisfaction
Team tenure	–	−.01*
Pandemic	−.65***	−.15
Teamwork management	−.40***	.42**
Task conflict	–	−.33***
var(M1[Group])	–	.14
var(e.taskconflict)	–	.46
var(e.satisfaction)	–	.69
Log-likelihood	−831.57	−831.57

Note. The random intercept was included in the path analysis. * $p < .05$; ** $p < .01$.; *** $p < .001$

4 Discussion and Conclusions

In the present study we explored how teamwork management influence team member satisfaction, both directly and indirectly through its influence on reducing task conflict. As predicted, a better planning of teamwork generates a positive attitude of team members towards the group. Indeed, when teams organize the work that needs to be done, allocating resources, and providing support to achieve deadlines, the team tend to be more effective and team members more satisfied with the group (Rousseau Et Al. 2006). Additionally, a better organization and planning of the work, translates into a better coordination and improve collaboration (Gevers and Peeters, 2009; Moye and Langfred, 2004), Reducing, in turn, the conflicts that may arise concerning the task. Since conflict, regardless of type, produces tension and discomfort, when task conflicts among the team are less frequent, team members tend to be more satisfied with their team.

Overall, our results highlight the importance of teamwork management for team effectiveness. To the best of our knowledge this is the first study that explores the direct and indirect influence of teamwork management on team member satisfaction. Being member's satisfaction one of the main criteria of team effectiveness (Hackman, 1987), this study contributes to the literature on team effectiveness by exploring the conditions that promote a positive attitude of team members towards the group.

Regarding practical implications, our findings suggest that leaders should coach their teams to develop their ability to plan and organize their work, to contribute to team functioning and to team effectiveness.

The findings of this study should be considered in light of some limitations. although we implemented a two-wave data collection procedure, teamwork management and task conflict were collected at the same time, what can contribute to common-method variance (Conway, 2002). Additionally, although we predicted an influence of teamwork management on task conflict, the reverse could also be possible. Indeed, more task conflicts could reduce the ability of team members work together, coordinate efforts, plan and organize their activities. Accordingly, future studies should implement a three-wave data collection. Finally, in future studies, it would be relevant to adopt a multi-method approach (e.g., direct observation, or interviews), for better data triangulation.

Acknowledgments. This work has been supported by the Fundação para a Ciência e a Tecnologia (FCT) under project grant UIDB/05037/2020.

References

Anderson, N., West, M.A.: The team climate inventory: development of the TCI and its applications in teambuilding for innovativeness. Eur. J. Work Organ. Psy. **5**(1), 53–66 (1996)

Aubé, C., Rousseau, V.: Team goal commitment and team effectiveness: the role of task interdependence and supportive behaviors. Group Dyn. **9**(3), 189–204 (2005)

Bartko, J.J.: On various intraclass correlation reliability coefficients. Psychol. Bull. **83**(5), 762–765 (1976)

Becker, T.E., Atinc, G., Breaugh, J.A., Carlson, K.D., Edwards, J.R., Spector, P.E.: Statistical control in correlational studies: 10 essential recommendations for organizational researchers. J. Organ. Behav. **37**(2), 157–167 (2016)

Bliese, P.D.: Within-group agreement, non-independence, and reliability: implications for data aggregation and analysis. In: Klein, K.J., Kozlowski, S.W.J. (eds.), Multilevel Theory, Research, and Methods in Organizations: Foundations, Extensions, and New Directions, pp. 349–381. Jossey-Bass (2000)

Bryk, A.S., Raudenbush, S.W.: Hierarchical Linear Models: Applications and Data Analysis Methods. Sage Publications, California Inc (1992)

Choi, K., Cho, B.: Competing hypotheses analyses of the associations between group task conflict and group relationship conflict. J. Organ. Behav. **32**(8), 1106–1126 (2011)

Cohen, S.G., Bailey, D.E.: What makes teams work: group effectiveness research from the shop floor to the executive suite. J. Manag. **23**(3), 239–290 (1997)

Cohen, S.G., Ledford, G.E., Spreitzer, G.M.: A predictive model of self-managing work team effectiveness. Hum. Relat. **49**(5), 643–676 (1996)

Conway, J.M.: Method variance and method bias in industrial and organizational psychology. In: Rogelberg, S.G. (ed.), Handbook of Research Methods in Industrial and Organizational Psychology, pp. 344–365. Blackwell Publishing, Malden (2002)

Curşeu, P.L., Schruijer, S.G.L.: Does conflict shatter trust or does trust obliterate conflict? Revisiting the relationships between team diversity, conflict, and trust. Group Dyn. Theory Res. Pract. **14**(1), 66–79 (2010)

de Dreu, C.K.W., van Dierendonck, D., Dijkstra, M.T.M.: Conflict at work and individual well-being. Int. J. Confl. Manag. **15**(1), 6–26 (2004)

de Dreu, C.K.W., Weingart, L.R.: Task versus relationship conflict, team performance, and team member satisfaction: a meta-analysis. J. Appl. Psychol. **88**(4), 741–749 (2003)

DeChurch, L.A., Mesmer-Magnus, J.R.: The cognitive underpinnings of effective teamwork: a meta-analysis. J. Appl. Psychol. **95**(1), 32–53 (2010)

Dimas, I.D., Alves, M.P., Lourenço, P.R., Rebelo, T.: Equipas de trabalho: instrumentos de avaliação. Edições Sílabo, Lisboa (2016)

Dimas, I.D., Lourenço, P.R.: Intragroup conflict and conflict management approaches as determinants of team performance and satisfaction: two field studies. Negot. Confl. Manage. Res. **8**(3), 174–193 (2015)

Gevers, J.M.P., Peeters, M.A.G.: A pleasure working together? The effects of dissimilarity in team member conscientiousness on team temporal processes and individual satisfaction. J. Organ. Behav. **30**(3), 379–400 (2009)

Hackman, J.R.: The design of work teams. In: Lorsch, J. (ed.) Handbook of Organizational Behavior, pp. 315–342. Englewood Cliffs, Prentice-Hall (1987)

Hoboubi, N., Choobineh, A., Kamari Ghanavati, F., Keshavarzi, S., Akbar Hosseini, A.: The impact of job stress and job satisfaction on workforce productivity in an Iranian petrochemical industry. Saf. Health Work **8**(1), 67–71 (2017)

Heck, R.H., Thomas, S.L., Tabata, L.N.: Multilevel and Longitudinal Modeling with IBM SPSS. Routledge, New York (2013)

Ilgen, D.R., Hollenbeck, J.R., Johnson, M., Jundt, D.: Teams in organizations: from input-process-output models to IMOI models. Annu. Rev. Psychol. **56**, 517–543 (2005)

James, L.R., Demaree, R.G., Wolf, G.: RWG: an assessment of within-group interrater agreement. J. Appl. Psychol. **78**(2), 306–309 (1993)

Jehn, K.A.: Enhancing effectiveness: an investigation of advantages and disadvantages of value-based intragroup conflict. Int. J. Confl. Manag. **5**(3), 223–238 (1994)

Jehn, K.A., Mannix, E.A.: The dynamic nature of conflict: a longitudinal study of intragroup conflict and group performance. Acad. Manag. J. **44**(2), 238–251 (2001)

Jehn, K.A., Northcraft, G.B., Neale, M.A.: Why differences make a difference: a field study of diversity, conflict and performance in workgroups. Adm. Sci. Q. **44**(4), 741–763 (1999)

Judge, T.A., Kammeyer-Mueller, J.D.: Job attitudes. Ann. Rev. Psychol. **63**(1), 341–367 (2012)

Keem, S., Koseoglu, G., Jeong, I., Shalley, C.E.: How does ethical leadership relate to team creativity? The role of collective team identification and need for cognitive closure. Group Organ. Manage. (2022)

Kline, R.B.: Principles and Practice of Structural Equation Modelling, 2nd edn. The Guilford Press, New York (2005)

Kreft, I.G.G., de Leeuw, J., Aiken, L.S.: The effect of different forms of centering in hierarchical linear models. Multivar. Behav. Res. **30**(1), 1–21 (1995)

Li, F., Li, Y., Wang, E.: Task characteristics and team performance: the mediating effect of team member satisfaction. Soc. Behav. Personal. Int. J. **37**(10), 1373–1382 (2009)

Marks, M.A., Mathieu, J.E., Zaccaro, S.J.: A temporally based framework and taxonomy of team processes. Acad. Manage. Rev. **26**(3), 356–376 (2001)

Mathieu, J.E., Gallagher, P.T., Domingo, M.A., Klock, E.A.: Embracing complexity: reviewing the past decade of team effectiveness research. Annu. Rev. Organ. Psych. Organ. Behav. **6**, 17–46 (2019)

Mathieu, J., Maynard, M.T., Rapp, T., Gilson, L.: Team effectiveness 1997–2007: a review of recent advancements and a glimpse into the future. J. Manage. **34**(3), 410–476 (2008)

Moye, N.A., Langfred, C.W.: Information sharing and group conflict: Going beyond decision making to understand the effects of information sharing on group performance. Int. J. Conflict Manage. **15**(4), 381–410 (2004)

Nerkar, A.A., McGrath, R.G., MacMillan, I.C.: Three facets of satisfaction and their influence on the performance of innovation teams. J. Bus. Ventur. **11**(3), 167–188 (1996)

Pinto, A.L., Lourenço, P.R.: The work teams internal functioning: bidimensionality, interdependence and performance. Rev. Gestão Tecnol. **14**(1), 5–23 (2014)

Podsakoff, P.M., MacKenzie, S.B., Lee, J.-Y., Podsakoff, N.P.: Common method biases in behavioral research: a critical review of the literature and recommended remedies. J. Appl. Psychol. **88**(5), 879–903 (2003)

Riketta, M.: The causal relation between job attitudes and performance: a meta-analysis of panel studies. J. Appl. Psychol. **93**(2), 472–481 (2008)

Robert, L.P., You, S.: Are you satisfied yet? Shared leadership, individual trust, autonomy, and satisfaction in virtual teams. J. Am. Soc. Inf. Sci. **69**(4), 503–513 (2018)

Rousseau, V., Aubé, C., Savoie, A.: Le fonctionnement interne des équipes de travail: Conception et mesure. Can. J. Behav. Sci./Rev. Can. Sci. Comportement **38**(2), 120–135 (2006)

Salas, E., Goodwin, G.F., Burke, C.S.: Team Effectiveness in Complex Organizations: Cross-Disciplinary Perspectives and Approaches. Taylor & Francis, New York (2008)

Spector, P.E.: Job Satisfaction. Application, Assessment, Causes, and Consequences. Sage Publications, Thousand Oaks (1997)

Standifer, R.L., Raes, A.M.L., Peus, C., Passos, A.M., Santos, C.M., Weisweiler, S.: Time in teams: cognitions, conflict and team satisfaction. J. Manage. Psychol. **30**(6), 692–708 (2015)

Tekleab, A.G., Quigley, N.R., Tesluk, P.E.: A longitudinal study of team conflict, conflict management, cohesion, and team effectiveness. Group Org. Manage. **34**(2), 170–205 (2009)

Tsai, Y., Wu, S.W.: The relationships between organisational citizenship behaviour, job satisfaction and turnover intention. J. Clin. Nurs. **19**(23–24), 3564–3574 (2010)

van de Voorde, K., Paauwe, J., van Veldhoven, M.: Employee well-being and the HRM-organizational performance relationship: a review of quantitative studies. Int. J. Manage. Rev. **14**(4), 391–407 (2012)

Wiiteman, H.: Group member satisfaction. Small Group Res. **22**(1), 24–58 (1991)

Impact of Organizational Factors on Accident Prediction in the Retail Sector

Inês Sena[1,3]([✉]) [iD], João Mendes[1,3] [iD], Florbela P. Fernandes[1,2] [iD],
Maria F. Pacheco[1,2] [iD], Clara B. Vaz[1,2] [iD], José Lima[1,2] [iD],
Ana Cristina Braga[3] [iD], Paulo Novais[3] [iD], and Ana I. Pereira[1,2,3] [iD]

[1] Research Center in Digitalization and Intelligent Robotics (CeDRI),
Instituto Politécnico de Bragança, Campus de Santa Apolónia,
5300-253 Bragança, Portugal
{ines.sena,joao.cmendes,fflor,pacheco,clvaz,jllima,apereira}@ipb.pt
[2] Laboratório Associado para a Sustentabilidade e Tecnologia em Regiões de
Montanha (SusTEC), Instituto Politécnico de Bragança, Campus de Santa Apolónia,
5300-253 Bragança, Portugal
[3] ALGORITMI Research Centre, LASI, University of Minho, Campus de Gualtar,
4710-057 Braga, Portugal
acb@dps.uminho.pt, pjon@di.uminho.pt

Abstract. Although different actions to prevent accidents at work have
been implemented in companies, the number of accidents at work continues to be a problem for companies and society. In this way, companies
have explored alternative solutions that have improved other business
factors, such as predictive analysis, an approach that is relatively new
when applied to occupational safety. Nevertheless, most reviewed studies focus on the accident dataset, i.e., the casualty's characteristics, the
accidents' details, and the resulting consequences. This study aims to
predict the occurrence of accidents in the following month through different classification algorithms of Machine Learning, namely, Decision Tree,
Random Forest, Gradient Boost Model, K-nearest Neighbor, and Naive
Bayes, using only organizational information, such as demographic data,
absenteeism rates, action plans, and preventive safety actions. Several
forecasting models were developed to achieve the best performance and
accuracy of the models, based on algorithms with and without the original datasets, balanced for the minority class and balanced considering
the majority class. It was concluded that only with some organizational
information about the company can it predict the occurrence of accidents
in the month ahead.

Keywords: Predictive analytics · Occupational accidents ·
Preprocessing techniques · Machine Learning algorithms

1 Introduction

Over the years, companies have invested and implemented several preventive
measures to improve security and working conditions, such as safety training,

© The Author(s), under exclusive license to Springer Nature Switzerland AG 2023
O. Gervasi et al. (Eds.): ICCSA 2023 Workshops, LNCS 14105, pp. 35–52, 2023.
https://doi.org/10.1007/978-3-031-37108-0_3

updating tools and machines, safety equipment, strengthening of Safety and Health at Work (OSH) teams, awareness actions, a more significant number of audits, collection of non-conformities, among others [6].

These actions have achieved good results in reducing accidents at the workplace: for example, in 2020, Portugal recorded the lowest number of workplace accidents compared to the previous ten years [1]. Despite the growing efforts of organizations, there was an increase in the number of fatal accidents compared to 2018, accounting for 131 fatalities from work accidents in 2020 [1]. Considering the associated costs, these events continue to be a critical issue for companies, affecting their productivity, competitiveness, and capital. Such occurrences also generate a sense of resentment and anger in society, affecting personal lives and brand image and even causing loss of lives [7,10].

Therefore, to reduce and prevent the occurrence of accidents, companies began to look for new solutions such as Artificial Intelligence (AI) methods and data analysis since they have achieved good results when applied to other business fields: increase in productivity, forecasting sales, identification of buying behavior, among others [16].

It was found in the literature that predictive analytics exists in several domains, from clinical analysis to forecasting stock markets; however, it is relatively new when applied in predicting the outcome of occupational safety incidents [13]. There are already several areas, such as industry [14], construction [15,24], and agribusiness [13], that explore these methods and achieve good results in predicting accidents. However, no studies have been found so far regarding the retail sector, where there is a perception that employees are generally at low risk of accidents at work. However, retail workers are involved in various demanding work activities, thus being exposed to multiple risks and hazards [4].

In Portugal, the wholesale and retail trade activity, vehicle and motorcycle repair is the second economic activity with the highest percentage of workplace-related accidents, 14.62% [1]. Due to this fact and the gap in the bibliographic review, this study aims to identify the occurrence of workplace accidents in a retail company. Specifically, this paper seeks to analyze and process data referring to the company's demographic information, absenteeism rates, preventive safety actions, action plan, and accident history, followed by the application of Machine Learning (ML) algorithms (Decision Tree, Gradient Boost Model, K-Nearest Neighbor, Naive Bayes, and Random Forest) to classify accident or non-accident behavior.

The article is organized into five sections. Section 2 presents a bibliographical review regarding the application of Machine Learning in classifying and predicting work-related accidents. Section 3 introduces the discussion of the methodology, in particular, datasets, pre-processing, theoretical concepts of the used forecasting algorithms, the developed predictive models, and the performance evaluation of the models. Section 4 aims at comparing the forecast results achieved. Finally, Sect. 5 concludes the study by enumerating possible directions for future research.

2   Related Work

This section aims to present state of art related to applying Machine Learning (ML) approaches in predicting occupational accidents.

Although the use of predictive analysis for the minimization, prevention, and prediction of accidents at work is recent, there are already several studies that claim that with Machine Learning algorithms, it is possible to identify and predict with high precision the occurrence of injuries and accidents at work in various business sectors [22].

During the bibliographical review, the construction industry was the business sector that presented a more significant number of studies on applying ML algorithms for predicting workplace accidents, which is justifiable due to the high frequency of accidents at work in this industry [15]. There are several approaches, one of which is through the application of time series data using the coupling of the Discrete Wavelet Transform (DWT) with different methods of Machine Learning, Support Vector Machine (SVM), Multivariate Adaptive Regression Splines (MARS), and Artificial Neural Network (ANNs) to predict the number of daily work accidents for periods of 1 day (short term), 7 days (medium term) and 30 days (long time), with the wavelet-ANN pair achieving the best performance with high accuracy rates in the short and medium term, 0.9275 and 0.7678 respectively, based on the Nash-Sutcliffe efficiency index [24].

There are also many accidents at work in the steel industry. In the paper [14], the authors aim to predict the outcome of accidents at work using two types of Decision Trees, Classification and Regression Trees (CART) and Automatic Chi-square Interaction Detection (CHAID). To do so, they collected 12 variables (age, working days of the worker, number of past accidents of the worker, number of past calamities in the company, daily wage, number of workers in the company, gender, education level, construction type, cause material, severity level, date) for 2127 accidents, and created five predictions for each method. CART achieved better accuracy, 81.78%, and the most predictive variables are age, cause of the accident, and level of education. Therefore, the authors claim that these methods can be used to predict the outcome of workplace accidents in the steel industry [14].

In addition to using ML techniques to predict accidents at work, several studies use these techniques to predict injuries and the severity of accidents at work [7,13,27]. In the agribusiness industry, the authors tested the performance of ML techniques, such as Support Vector Machine (with linear, quadratic, and RBF kernels), Boosted Trees, and Naïve Bayes, in modeling and predicting the severity of occupational accidents using workers' complaints injured. The authors state that through the injured part of the body, the body group, the nature of the injury, the heart of the group, the cause of the injury, the group of reasons, age, and stability of the injured workers, they can classify the severity of the damage with an accuracy rate of 92–98% [13].

Also, in the construction area, the severity of accidents is worrying, as the involved tasks can easily cause victims and property losses; it is, therefore, essential to predict the severity of construction accidents. The authors of this study used 16 critical accident factors, 39 attributes, and eight ML algorithms (Logistic Regression, Decision Tree, Support Vector Machine, Naive Bayes, K-Nearest Neighbor, Random Forest, Multi-Layer Perceptron, and AutoML) and achieved the best F_{score} of 78.3% with Naive Bayes and logistic regression [27].

Apart from ML algorithms, there are other approaches to be explored: for example, the fuzzy logic of Artificial Intelligence that helps to map inputs and outputs efficiently to build the inference engine so that various types of accidents can be predicted [6].

In summary, most of the studies analyzed rely only on data about the characteristics of the victims, events, causes, and injuries for predicting accidents at work. In this context, this work intends to study whether, with only some organizational data, it is possible to identify the number of accidents and non-accidents.

3   Methodology

This research uses information from a Portuguese retail company and ML classification and/or regression algorithms to identify the number of accidents and non-accidents during January 2023.

The developed datasets, pre-processing techniques, ML algorithms, prediction models, and metrics are applied for the best results and performance.

3.1   Dataset Characterization

For this case study, the intention is to use information that all companies generally store without using it to predict accidents to find out if, with this information, it is possible to identify the occurrence of accidents in the month ahead. For this purpose, two sets of data called "internal information" and "safety actions" were prepared, which will be associated individually and simultaneously with the history of accidents and subsequently implemented in different forecasting algorithms.

The set of internal information consists of a combination of demographic data and absenteeism rates for 2022. Demographic data is information about the different characteristics of a population; in this case, it includes information on the number of working hours, average age, percentage the average length of service, percentage of female employees, number of employees, number of full-time and part-time employees, and levels of education per organizational unit among others. Absenteeism at work represents the absence of an employee or more during the working period, whether due to delays, for a few hours, or even missing for several days. This study includes total absenteeism rates for sick leave, covid-19, unjustified absences, parenting, accidents, and other causes. Thus, the set of internal information is composed of 25 input variables.

The set of security actions includes the record of preventive security actions and the action plans established to resolve the identified situations. The descriptions of preventive safety actions are nonconformities observed by those responsible for the unit and Safety and Health at Work (OSH) elements when they visit the field. For each nonconformity, action plans are developed for the intervention of others to repair and improve conditions to prevent workplace incidents. This dataset was created by dividing the information by the status of the action (in progress or concluded) and by its sum per month and the organizational unit, adding up to 50 variables, with information only from August since the company only started collecting these records from that month onwards.

In this way, the data from the internal information set was understood for the same period so that the connection between the groups and the comparison of results was coherent. Therefore, this study will be applied to the internal information dataset, the security actions dataset, and the combined dataset, in which the standard fields, organizational unit, and month will make their integrated.

In addition to these two sets, the accident history was used, including the date of the occurrence and the organizational unit to which the victim belonged, to classify the information from the remaining datasets into non-accident (0) or accident (1), accounting for a total of 22138 data representative of the non-accident class, and 369 referring to accident situations.

3.2   Data Preprocessing

Data preprocessing is a fundamental step when intending to use Machine Learning algorithms for data classification/regression since the quality of the data and the valuable information that can be derived from them directly affect the model's learning capacity.

In this case, when analyzing the datasets in detail, some problems that can influence the learning of the intended model were identified, such as duplicate data, invalid data, and imbalance between the output variables. Therefore, preprocessing techniques were applied to remove duplicates and null values and balance the data before inserting it into the developed model.

Removing duplicate values is critical because such values can distort the analysis and cause incorrect predictions [15]. Likewise, eliminating null values is also essential. Null values can indicate missing information or errors in the dataset. These values can significantly affect the accuracy of predictions since ML algorithms may have difficulty dealing with missing data or may misinterpret it [15].

Furthermore, it is essential to balance the dataset so that each class has the same number of samples and therefore has the same weight in the analysis, avoiding vices [9]. In this case, data on the non-occurrence of accidents are much higher than data on the occurrence of accidents, which may lead to machine learning algorithms favoring this class and leading to high prediction values, but inaccurate predictions and distortions in the analysis. For this reason, it is essential to use the confusion matrices to validate the prediction results.

For this study, we intend to apply two methods that solve the problem of data imbalance, namely the Synthetic Minority Oversampling Technique (SMOTE) and Random Undersampling, and compare the results of classification and/or prediction.

SMOTE's main objective is to increase the number of minority samples by inserting n synthetic minority samples among the k samples closest to a given model with a smaller dimension [27]. Random Undersampling is the contrast, a form of subsampling of the majority class, balancing the data up to the size of the minority class, reducing the sample size and the pressure on storage which will improve the execution time; however, the removal of data can lead to the loss of helpful information [9].

Finally, the categorical variables that specify the unit of work were converted into integer variables since ML algorithms produce better results with data of numerical typology [22].

3.3 Methods

Accident occurrence classification is a typical recent classification problem [13]. This study will evaluate the intended result by comparing five supervised classification algorithms.

Decision Tree (DT) is a supervised learning algorithm that can be used for both classification and regression, which relates decisions and possible consequences [16]. This recursive partitioning technique creates a decision tree with several nodes obtained and divided through division criteria [3]. The tree-building procedure stops when the learning dataset is fitted with predictions. Classification trees are developed for categorical and continuous dependent variables that can assume a finite number of unordered values [20].

Gradient Boost Model (GBM) is an ensemble model that combines several weak predictive models that relate predictors to an outcome. This tree construction method is used to reduce the errors of previous trees, which makes the current model focus on data that previous models failed to predict or classify when fitting an underlying model [3]. It is a reinforcement method in which the dataset is resampled repeatedly, with the results produced as a weighted average of the resampled datasets [16].

K-Nearest Neighbor (KNN) is a non-parametric method used in classification and regression problems, which assumes that similar objects are close to each other [16]. This method examines the k most immediate observations and categorizes a statement. Using the closest point of a group of previously classified matters is used as a basis for categorizing a new topic using the nearest neighbor decision rule [22]. The necessary parameters for the algorithm are the value of k and the distance function; the correct value of k is the value, which after several runs with different values of k, reduces the number of errors found. The distance function is calculated using the Euclidean distance, understood as the physical separation between two-dimensional points [22].

Naive Bayes (NB) is a technique to build classifiers with high bias and low variance that can make a solid model even with a small dataset [8]. It is based on Bayes' theory which uses conditional probabilities to classify a categorical target variable based on the input variables [13]. This algorithm predicts the likelihood of different categories through different attributes [8]. When the response variable has two classes, as in injury severity with non-severe and severe types, NB models typically exhibit excellent accuracy [13].

Random Forest (RF) is a popular Machine Learning technique that uses several independent decision trees created from randomly selected variables [3]. RF models are composed of multiple decision trees, each trained using a portion of the original training data and looking only at a randomly chosen subset of the input variables to find a split. Each tree casts a single vote to define the final categorization further, and the classifier's output is finally chosen by the majority of tree votes [20].

Machine learning algorithms undoubtedly guarantee good results in most of their applications, however, it is necessary to ensure some basic conditions for obtaining results. Within these conditions, it is possible to highlight the dataset, which is the basis of all learning. Getting good results with these methods will be difficult without a sufficiently large and concise dataset. Another condition essential to ensure when applying this type of method is a good combination of hyperparameters; these can guarantee a boost in the results obtained, noting that they must be optimized for each model and each dataset used, with no fixed optimal combination. To carry out this optimization, there are different ways, starting with manual fitting, which consists of trial and error, applying different values, and observing the behavior of the results with them. Evaluating the number of hyperparameters present in most artificial intelligence algorithms is easily concluded that it was necessary to evolve these optimization techniques, with several others emerging, such as grid search [2], random search [5], and later gradient-based algorithms like Bayesian Optimization [26], SMAC [18] as well as metaheuristic algorithms like Genetic Algorithm [21] Particle Swarm Optimization [25].

In this specific case, the random search method was chosen mainly because of its effectiveness combined with a less expensive computational cost when compared to some of the other hyperparameter optimization methods.

Another reason that led us to choose the random search was its ability to cover a broader range of values compared to the grid search since it is a method that does not require prior knowledge of the hyperparameter space, which can be quite complex for some models. It randomly samples hyperparameters from a distribution, which becomes useful when working with more than one algorithm, which is the case when comparing five different algorithms; it is notoriously difficult to know all their hyperparameters.

3.4   Model Development

To develop the model, combining all the previously collected information is necessary. Focusing on identifying the number of accidents and non-accidents in January 2023, it is necessary to train the different models with data from the year 2022. The proposed methodology will be applied to the internal information dataset to ensure the security of the action and both of them together.

Starting with the division of the dataset by months, four months were used for training - 15078 events, approximately 80% of the total data - and the remainder for testing (3799 events) corresponds to approximately 20%. Remembering that to predict the next month is needed to ensure that the model is trained with data from the previous month, using the information of the months from August to November as predictors and the accidents or non-accidents information from September to December as outputs to train the five models. Likewise, for testing the models, the same strategy was used. All the information from December was used as predictors and as output, the predicted data will be the accident or non-accident information from January.

To identify cases of accidents and non-accidents, the value of 0 was associated with each existing information of each dataset when there was no accident, and the value of 1 when there were accidents, accounting for a total of 22138 non-accidents and 369 accident occurrence data (September to January). This connection was made taking into account the previous month, that is, an accident that occurred in September will be connected to August information from the remaining datasets.

Observing the accident and non-accident values, it is notorious that the data is not balanced. Due to this data imbalance, pre-processing techniques were applied to balance the data as mentioned in topic 3.2. The proposed methodology was applied to datasets without balancing, with data balancing through the SMOTE method, and with data balancing from Random Undersampling to compare results. A similar process was used to optimize the algorithms, using or without it to compare results.

To simplify the methodology and all the referred information, a flowchart represented in Fig. 1 was created.

In summary, five classification algorithms will be used for three datasets, internal information, security actions, and a total set, which joins the two previous pieces of information. Each dataset will be applied, with the original data, with the training data balanced for the majority class, and with the data balanced considering the minority class, to the algorithms with and without optimization of the hyperparameters. Noting that the test set did not undergo any type of balancing, maintaining the original results with 62 occurrences of accidents and 3737 occurrences without accidents. This is to conclude better the results of using this information to predict the occurrence of accidents in the following month.

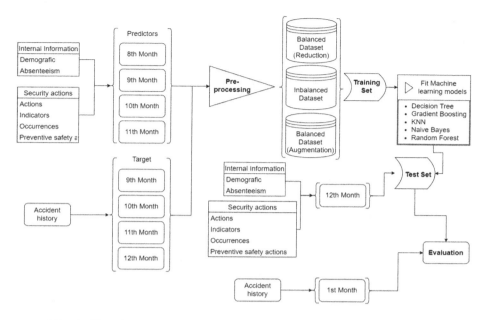

Fig. 1. Flowchart representative of the methodology used in this study.

3.5 Performance Evaluation

To evaluate the performance of the classification model under study, metrics by class were used, such as *Accuracy*, *Precision*, *Recall*, and F_{score}. The metrics are based on the confusion matrix generated for each algorithm [20], which indicates:

- True Positives (TP) - data that were not accidents and were predicted correctly.
- True Negatives (TN) - data points to the model correctly projected as an accident.
- False Positives (FP) - data that the model projected as non-accidents and actually represented the occurrence of accidents.
- False Negatives (FN) - results that were non-accidents and the model identified as an accident.

Accuracy is the most common metric to be used in problems of this magnitude and represents the number of correct predictions as a function of all predictions made, Eq. 1 [20]:

$$Accuracy = \frac{TP + TN}{TP + FP + TN + FN} \tag{1}$$

The *Precision*, defined in Eq. 2, is calculated to evaluate the total correct predictions for a specific class [20]:

$$Precision = \frac{TP}{TP + FP} \tag{2}$$

The *Recall* measures the number of true positives that were classified correctly through Eq. 3 [20]:

$$Recall = \frac{TP}{TP + TN} \tag{3}$$

The F_{score}, defined in Eq. 4, is the harmonic mean of *Precision* and *Recall*, which reaches its best value at one and its worst at zero [20]:

$$F_{score} = \frac{2 * Precision * Recall}{Precision + Recall} \tag{4}$$

The confusion matrix for the specific case study is based on the occurrence of accidents, as shown in Table 1.

Table 1. Confusion matrix example based [20].

	Predict Label	
True label	Not an accident (0)	Accident (1)
Not an accident (0)	TP	FN
Accident (1)	FP	TN

4   Results

In this section, the obtained results are presented and analyzed for each data set, internal information, security actions, and combining the two.

To obtain the best results by the ML algorithms, the hyperparameters of the five algorithms used were optimized with the random search method, as demonstrated in Sect. 3.3, with equal parameters in terms of evaluation, using 5-fold cross-validation, the random state was used, and a number of 100 iterations for each of the algorithms, and for each of the datasets used. The hyperparameters studied for each algorithm and the chosen values are presented in Table 2. Here, Randint represents uniform random integer values, and Logspace means log-spaced floating point values, with 100 samples evenly spaced on a logarithmic scale.

Noting that all the algorithms presented in this work were tested, trained, and implemented on a computer equipped with an Intel(R) Core(TM) i7-10875H processor, with a RAM DDR4 32GB memory and Python version 3.8 as well as the libraries scikit-learn in version 1.2.1 [23], Pandas in version 1.3.4 [19], numpy in version 1.19.2 [11], imblearn in version 0.10.1 [17] and finally matplotlib in version 3.5.0 [12].

In this way, several forecast models were developed for each dataset to compare the results taking into account whether the training set is balanced with the SMOTE technique or with Random Undersampling and if the hyperparameters of the algorithms are optimized or not, originating six approaches for the comparison of results:

Table 2. Hyperparameter values obtained for each Machine Learning algorithm used in this study.

	Methods
Hyperparameter	**Decision Tree**
max_depth	Randint(2,10)
splitter	Either "best" or "random"
min_samples_split	Randint (2,20)
min_samples_leaf	Randint (1,10)
max_features	Either "auto", "sqrt", "log2", or None
max_leaf_nodes	Randint (1, 10)
criterion	Either "gini", "entropy", or "log_loss"
	Random Forest
max_depth	Randint (2,10)
min_samples_split	Randint (2,20)
min_samples_leaf	Randint (1,10)
max_features	Either "auto", "sqrt", "log2" or None
criterion	Either "gini" or "entropy"
n_estimators/neighbors	Randint (1,200)
	K-Nearest Neighboor
n_estimators/neighbors	Randint (1, 200)
leaf_size	Randint (2, 50)
p	Randint (1, 20)
weights	Either "uniform", "distance" or None
algorithm	Either "auto", "ball_tree", "kd_tree" or "brute"
	Naive Bayes
var_smoothing	Logspace (0, -9, num=100)
	Gradient Boost Model
min_samples_split	Randint (2, 20)
min_samples_leaf	Randint (1, 10)
criterion	Either "friedman_mse" or "squared_error"
n_estimators/neighbors	Randint (1, 200)
loss	Either "exponential", "deviance" or "log_loss"
learning_rate	Logspace(0,-7, num = 100)

– Default - In this approach, the original training set is used in the algorithms without optimizing the hyperparameters.
– Optimized - In this case, the original training set is applied in the algorithms to optimize the hyperparameters.

- Reduction Default (RD) - In this strategy, the training set is balanced according to the minority class and implemented in the different algorithms without optimizing the hyperparameters.
- Reduction Optimized (RO) - In this approach, the training set is balanced according to the minority class and implemented in the different algorithms with hyperparameter optimization.
- Augmentation Default (AD) - In this case, the training dataset is balanced with the datasets technique, and in turn, it is applied to the five algorithms without optimizing the hyperparameters.
- Augmentation Optimized (AO) - In this last comparison strategy, the training dataset is balanced with SMOTE technique, and in turn, it is applied to the algorithms taking into account the optimization of the hyperparameters.

4.1   Internal Information Dataset

After obtaining all the results, it is possible to make some observations about using this dataset for accident prediction. Figure 2 shows the confusion matrices that presented the best results.

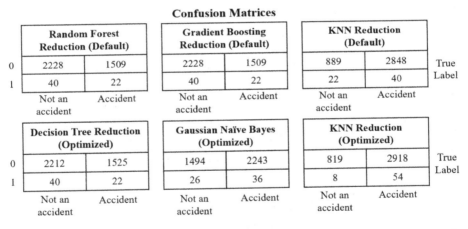

Fig. 2. Confusion matrices of the approaches and method that presented better results for the internal information set.

Analyzing Fig. 2, it appears that the approach that presents the best results in the different methods is the Reduction Default, except the Naive Bayes method, which is the Optimized approach, and KNN where the Reduction Optimized (RO) approach also demonstrates promising results. Observing all matrices, these approaches reached higher true negative and lower actual positive values than the others.

The Random Forest, Gradient Boost Model, and Decision Tree methods, on the other hand, present very similar confusion matrices, so it is necessary to

Table 3. Metric values obtained for the methods and approaches that presented better results in the confusion matrices.

		Metrics			
Method/Strategy	Predict Label	*Precision*	*Recall*	F_{score}	*Accuracy*
RF with RD	Not an accident	0.98	0.70	0.82	0.70
RF with RD	Accident	0.02	0.31	0.03	
DT with RD	Not an accident	0.98	0.59	0.74	0.59
DT with RD	Accident	0.01	0.35	0.03	
GBM with RD	Not an accident	0.98	0.60	0.74	0.59
GBM with RD	Accident	0.01	0.35	0.03	

resort to evaluation metrics so that it is possible to draw a conclusion on which approach and method best predicts the occurrence of accidents with this dataset. The metrics obtained for each mode can be seen in Table 3.

According to the metrics achieved for each strategy and method, it is possible to mention that with the dataset of internal information of a retail company, it is possible to predict with 70% accuracy the occurrence of accidents in the next month through the Random Forest algorithm in the approach Reduction Default.

4.2   Security Actions Dataset

For this dataset, Naive Bayes obtained the best results in predicting the accident event, ranging from 84 to 100% accuracy, however, it was less assertive than the other algorithms in identifying non-accidents, reaching between 2 to 15% accuracy. Considering the final accuracy, the maximum reached was 16% in the Default approach.

The Decision Tree, Random Forest, and Gradient Boost Model methods presented similar results for the Reduction Default and Reduction Optimized approaches. However, when approaching the optimized algorithm, the value of false negatives increases considerably, although there is an increase in true negatives. Of these three methods, the GBM is the one with the least assertiveness, reaching 10% in Reduction Default and 11% in Reduction Optimized, because it has an acceptable value of true negatives (45 accidents predicted out of 62) but a reduced number of true positives (330 in 3737 no accidents). Also, the K-Nearest Neighbor algorithm performs well in Reduction Optimized.

In Fig. 3, one can visualize the confusion matrices of the approaches that obtained the best results for the set of security actions.

Confusion Matrices

	Random Forest Reduction (Default)		Decision Tree Reduction (Default)		KNN Reduction (Default)		
0	3200	537	3251	486	2981	756	True Label
1	47	15	49	13	51	11	
	Not an accident	Accident	Not an accident	Accident	Not an accident	Accident	

Fig. 3. Confusion matrices of the approaches and method that demonstrated better results for the security actions dataset.

Since the results presented in Fig. 3 are very similar, the values of the metrics that can be seen in Table 4 were used.

Table 4. Metric values obtained for the methods and approaches that presented better results in the confusion matrices.

Method/Strategy	Predict Label	Metrics			
		$Precision$	$Recall$	F_{score}	$Accuracy$
RF with RD	Not an accident	0.95	0.86	0.92	0.85
RF with RD	Accident	0.03	0.24	0.05	
DT with RD	Not an accident	0.99	0.87	0.92	0.86
DT with RD	Accident	0.01	0.21	0.05	
KNN with RO	Not an accident	0.98	0.80	0.88	0.79
KNN with RO	Accident	0.01	0.18	0.03	

Analyzing the presented results in detail, the most appropriate model to achieve the intended objective is the Random Forest in the Reduction Default approach.

4.3 Total Dataset

After obtaining results individually, the two data sets were merged through common factors, thus obtaining the total set. The same methodology was applied to see if they achieved better precision in predicting accidents together or separately.

Therefore, from the 30 calculated confusion matrices, Fig. 4 will show those that present better results considering the listed objective.

Analyzing Fig. 4, it appears that the Naive Bayes method is not illustrated because comparatively, the confusion matrices presented, the NB shows values of true negatives and false positives lower than the other methods, which indicates high accuracy values but with lower assertiveness in the occurrence of accidents.

Confusion Matrices

Random Forest Reduction (Default)		Decision Tree Reduction (Default)		KNN Reduction (Default)		Gradient Boosting Reduction (Default)		
0	2530	1207	2319	1418	2000	1737	2549	1188	True
1	31	31	32	30	20	32	32	30	Label
	Not an accident	Accident	Not an accident	Accident	Not an accident	Accident	Not an accident	Accident	

Random Forest Reduction (Optimized)		Decision Tree Reduction (Optimized)		KNN Reduction (Optimized)		Gradient Boosting Reduction (Optimized)		
0	2721	1016	2739	998	2134	1607	2665	1072	True
1	37	25	38	24	25	37	33	29	Label
	Not an accident	Accident	Not an accident	Accident	Not an accident	Accident	Not an accident	Accident	

Fig. 4. Confusion matrices of the approaches and method that demonstrated better results for the total dataset.

It can also be drawn that there is a considerable amount of true negatives and true positives compared to the results observed in the individual datasets. However, it is necessary to use the metrics so that it is possible to draw a more assertive conclusion about the accuracy, approach, and method that makes the dataset reaches the objective. The value of the metrics can be seen in Table 5.

Table 5. Metric values obtained for the methods and approaches that presented better results in the confusion matrices.

Method/Strategy	Predict Label	Metrics			
		$Precision$	$Recall$	F_{score}	$Accuracy$
RF with RD	Not an accident	0.99	0.68	0.80	0.67
RF with RD	Accident	0.03	0.50	0.05	
RF with RO	Not an accident	0.99	0.73	0.84	0.72
RF with RO	Accident	0.02	0.40	0.05	
DT with RD	Not an accident	0.99	0.62	0.76	0.62
DT with RD	Accident	0.02	0.48	0.04	
DT with RO	Not an accident	0.99	0.73	0.84	0.73
DT with RO	Accident	0.02	0.39	0.04	
KNN with RD	Not an accident	0.99	0.54	0.69	0.53
KNN with RD	Accident	0.02	0.52	0.03	
KNN with RO	Not an accident	0.99	0.57	0.72	0.53
KNN with RO	Accident	0.02	0.60	0.04	
GBM with RD	Not an accident	0.99	0.68	0.81	0.68
GBM with RD	Accident	0.02	0.48	0.05	
GBM with RO	Not an accident	0.99	0.71	0.83	0.71
GBM with RO	Accident	0.03	0.47	0.05	

Analyzing Table 5, it can be noted that the methods that obtain a higher accuracy value are the Random Forest, Decision Tree, and the Gradient Boost Model in the Reduction Optimized approach. Observing the results in more detail and taking into account the recall metric, the GBM Reduction Optimized is the one that presents the highest value for the accident class and values for the non-accident class similar to those of the other methods that were mentioned; therefore with the combination of the two datasets it is also possible to predict the occurrence of accidents with an accuracy of 71%.

5   Conclusion and Future Work

The present study aimed to predict the occurrence of accidents in the month ahead of the current one in a retail company, with only organizational data classified as an accident or non-accident event. Taking into account the information provided by the company, two sets of data were developed that were individually applied and combined into five Machine Learning classification algorithms.

Throughout the data analysis, some obstacles were faced, such as the period not being of the same dimension for the different data; therefore, it was necessary to reduce the information to understand the same period. The imbalance of the data was high, with a greater number for the non-accident class, therefore, the results were used and compared with two data balancing approaches. As these mishaps can influence performance and harm the results, hyperparameters optimization was also used for each algorithm to obtain the best possible performance from them.

In this way, six approaches were developed for comparing results and obtaining the best ones considering different techniques to solve the problems encountered. Among the different approaches that were used, the one that achieved the best results in different datasets and methods was the Reduction Default.

It can also be mentioned that the best accuracy achieved was 85% for the safety actions dataset in the RF Reduction Default. However, if we analyze the values of the metrics in detail, the total set reached a higher recall value for the accident class in the GBM method in the Reduction Default approach; however, its accuracy is lower (71%).

In addition, it can also be mentioned that NB is an algorithm that obtains higher values of true negatives; however, it reaches low values of precision due to the values of false positives being higher than those of true positives.

It is possible to conclude that with the information used and without any details of the accidents and characteristics of the victim, it is possible to predict the occurrence of accidents at work in the next month. However, it is necessary to explore this study further to find solutions that increase the value of true negatives and decrease those of false positives.

In this way, and considering the number of workplace accidents and the existing gap in the literature, it is important to deepen the exploration of factors and algorithms that predict the occurrence of accidents at work in any business sector.

As future work, it is intended to explore further the information used, find solutions to the fact that there is a limitation of information regarding the accident event, experiment with other types of organizational information, and add new information to the study.

Acknowledgement. The authors are grateful to the Foundation for Science and Technology (FCT, Portugal) for financial support through national funds FCT/MCTES (PIDDAC) to CeDRI (UIDB/05757/2020 and UIDP/05757/2020), ALGORITMI UIDB/00319/2020 and SusTEC (LA/P/0007/2021). This work has been supported by NORTE-01-0247-FEDER-072598 iSafety: Intelligent system for occupational safety and well-being in the retail sector. Inês Sena was supported by FCT PhD grant UI/BD/153348/2022.

References

1. Pordata. https://www.pordata.pt/portugal. Accessed 03 Apr 2023
2. Abreu, S.: Automated architecture design for deep neural networks. arXiv preprint arXiv:1908.10714 (2019)
3. Ajayi, A., et al.: Optimised big data analytics for health and safety hazards prediction in power infrastructure operations. Saf. Sci. **125**, 104656 (2020)
4. Anderson, V.P., Schulte, P.A., Sestito, J., Linn, H., Nguyen, L.S.: Occupational fatalities, injuries, illnesses, and related economic loss in the wholesale and retail trade sector. Am. J. Ind. Med. **53**(7), 673–685 (2010)
5. Belete, D.M., Huchaiah, M.D.: Grid search in hyperparameter optimization of machine learning models for prediction of HIV/AIDS test results. Int. J. Comput. Appl. **44**(9), 875–886 (2022)
6. Beriha, G., Patnaik, B., Mahapatra, S., Padhee, S.: Assessment of safety performance in Indian industries using fuzzy approach. Expert Syst. Appl. **39**(3), 3311–3323 (2012)
7. Carnero, M.C., Pedregal, D.J.: Modelling and forecasting occupational accidents of different severity levels in Spain. Reliab. Eng. Syst. Saf. **95**(11), 1134–1141 (2010)
8. Chaipanha, W., Kaewwichian, P., et al.: Smote vs. random undersampling for imbalanced data-car ownership demand model. Communications **24**, D105–D115 (2022)
9. Cherian, S.A., Hameed, A.S.: Numerical modelling of concrete filled frp tubes subjected under impact loading (2017)
10. Fernández-Muñiz, B., Montes-Peón, J.M., Vázquez-Ordás, C.J.: Relation between occupational safety management and firm performance. Saf. Sci. **47**(7), 980–991 (2009)
11. Harris, C.R., et al.: Array programming with NumPY. Nature **585**(7825), 357–362 (2020)
12. Hunter, J.D.: Matplotlib: a 2D graphics environment. Comput. Sci. Eng. **9**(03), 90–95 (2007)
13. Kakhki, F.D., Freeman, S.A., Mosher, G.A.: Evaluating machine learning performance in predicting injury severity in agribusiness industries. Saf. Sci. **117**, 257–262 (2019)
14. Koc, K., Ekmekcioğlu, Ö., Gurgun, A.P.: Accident prediction in construction using hybrid wavelet-machine learning. Autom. Constr. **133**, 103987 (2022)

15. Koc, K., Gurgun, A.P.: Scenario-based automated data preprocessing to predict severity of construction accidents. Autom. Constr. **140**, 104351 (2022)
16. Kumar, V., Garg, M.: Predictive analytics: a review of trends and techniques. Int. J. Comput. Appl. **182**(1), 31–37 (2018)
17. Lemaître, G., Nogueira, F., Aridas, C.K.: Imbalanced-learn: a python toolbox to tackle the curse of imbalanced datasets in machine learning. J. Mach. Learn. Res. **18**(1), 559–563 (2017)
18. Li, H., Liang, Q., Chen, M., Dai, Z., Li, H., Zhu, M.: Pruning SMAC search space based on key hyperparameters. Concurr. Comput. Pract. Exp. **34**(9), e5805 (2022)
19. McKinney, W.: Data structures for statistical computing in python. In: van der Walt, S.J., Millman, J. (eds.) Proceedings of the 9th Python in Science Conference, pp. 56–61 (2010). https://doi.org/10.25080/Majora-92bf1922-00a
20. Mendes, J., et al.: Machine learning to identify olive-tree cultivars. In: Pereira, A.I., Kosir, A., Fernandes, F.P., Pacheco, M.F., Teixeira, J.P., Lopes, R.P. (eds.) Optimization, Learning Algorithms and Applications. OL2A 2022. CCIS, vol. 1754, pp. 820–835. Springer, Cham (2023). https://doi.org/10.1007/978-3-031-23236-7_56
21. Nikbakht, S., Anitescu, C., Rabczuk, T.: Optimizing the neural network hyperparameters utilizing genetic algorithm. J. Zhejiang Univ.-Sci. A **22**(6), 407–426 (2021)
22. Oyedele, A., et al.: Deep learning and boosted trees for injuries prediction in power infrastructure projects. Appl. Soft Comput. **110**, 107587 (2021)
23. Pedregosa, F., et al.: Scikit-learn: machine learning in python. J. Mach. Learn. Res. **12**, 2825–2830 (2011)
24. Shirali, G.A., Noroozi, M.V., Malehi, A.S.: Predicting the outcome of occupational accidents by CART and CHAID methods at a steel factory in Iran. J. Public Health Res. **7**(2), jphr-2018 (2018)
25. Singh, P., Chaudhury, S., Panigrahi, B.K.: Hybrid MPSO-CNN: multi-level particle swarm optimized hyperparameters of convolutional neural network. Swarm Evol. Comput. **63**, 100863 (2021)
26. Snoek, J., Larochelle, H., Adams, R.P.: Practical bayesian optimization of machine learning algorithms. Adv. Neural Inf. Process. Syst. **25**, 1–9 (2012)
27. Zhu, R., Hu, X., Hou, J., Li, X.: Application of machine learning techniques for predicting the consequences of construction accidents in China. Process Saf. Environ. Prot. **145**, 293–302 (2021)

SAGA Application for Generalized Estimating Equations Analysis

Luís Moncaixa[1,2]([✉]) [iD] and Ana Cristina Braga[1,2] [iD]

[1] School of Engineering, University of Minho, Braga, Portugal
luismoncaixa@hotmail.com
[2] ALGORITMI Research Centre, LASI, University of Minho, Campus de Gualtar,
4710-57 Braga, Portugal

Abstract. Logistic regression models seek to identify the influence of different variables/factors on a response variable of interest. These are normally used in the field of medicine as it allows verifying which factors influence the presence of certain pathologies. However, most of these models do not consider the correlation between the variables under study. In order to overcome this problem, GEE (Generalized Estimating Equations) models were developed, which consider the existing correlation in the data, resulting in a more rigorous analysis of the influence of different factors. There are different packages in R that allow analysis using GEE models, however, their use requires some prior knowledge of the R programming language. In order to fill this gap and enable any user to perform analysis through GEE models, a Shiny application called SAGA (**S**hiny **A**pplication for **G**EE **A**nalysis) was developed. The developed web application is available for use at the following link http://geemodelapp2022.shinyapps.io/Shiny_App. The main purpose of the SAGA application is to develop and analyse GEE models using a dataset selected by the user, where it will be possible to describe all the variables of interest in the development of the model, as well as validate the same models developed through validation by ROC analysis. In addition to the results of the GEE models, shown in the application, the ROC curves of each developed model are also represented.

Keywords: Logistic Regression · Correlated Data · GEE · Shiny · SAGA

1 Introduction

The use of statistical methods and associated research in human investigation, especially in the field of medicine, has demonstrated in recent decades to be a fundamental element for the development of treatments for diseases as well as for scientific research [3].

This work has been supported by FCT – Fundação para a Ciência e Tecnologia within the R&D Units Project Scope: UIDB/00319/2020.

© The Author(s), under exclusive license to Springer Nature Switzerland AG 2023
O. Gervasi et al. (Eds.): ICCSA 2023 Workshops, LNCS 14105, pp. 53–68, 2023.
https://doi.org/10.1007/978-3-031-37108-0_4

Longitudinal data indicate repeated observations over time for the same sample/individual, with observations more identical within the same individual than across different individuals, thus indicating that these observations will be correlated [5].

This type of data, given the correlation among observations, represents an additional difficulty when applying regression models for analysis, since one of the main assumptions of these models is based on the independence of observations, that is, the correlation is non-existent. Several biomedical analyses of longitudinal data demonstrate that the use of regression models disregarding the correlation of observations results in a less precise estimation of standard errors, influencing all indicators such as confidence intervals or p-values, which allow for a good analysis and can lead to incorrect inferences [8].

The GEE models (Generalized Estimating Equations), developed by *Liang and Zeger* [9], represent a class of models that are often used for data in which the responses are correlated. These models are an extension of GLMs (Generalized Linear Models), as they take into account the correlation present in the data, allowing their application to longitudinal data.

Unlike GLMs, which are based on maximum likelihood theory, the structure of GEE models is related to quasi-likelihood theory, so it does not require specifying the distribution of the data, only requiring the specification of the relationship between the response variable and the covariates, as well as the relationship between the mean and variance of the responses through a correlation structure [2,18]. The inclusion of this correlation structure distinguishes GEE models from any conventional logistic regression model, however, it is not necessary to specify this same structure since GEE models can estimate consistent parameters without any specified correlation structure, as demonstrated by *Liang and Zeger* [9].

Although the inclusion of the correlation structure is not necessary in the development of GEE models, the presence of a structure appropriate to the data being studied allows for better parameter estimates, resulting in more valid statistical inferences. There are several types of correlation structures with the most commonly used being the independence, exchangeable, autoregressive and unstructured. The independent correlation structure indicates that the repeated observations within an individual are independent, meaning they are not correlated. The exchangeable correlation structure assumes that any two or more responses within the same cluster have the same correlation, and the order of the responses is arbitrary. The autoregressive correlation structure commonly applied to studies where time dependence is assumed, meaning that the correlation between responses depends on the time interval between them, with responses with shorter time being more correlated. Finally, the unstructured correlation structure represents different correlations between each observation [21,23].

According to *Horton and Lipsitz* [6], each correlation structure presented earlier should be selected depending on the sample being analyzed. However, there are situations where it is difficult to identify the correlation structure that best fits the sample. To assist in the selection of the correlation structure, *Pan* [12] developed a method called quasi-likelihood under the independence model criterion, QIC. This method is an adaptation of the Akaike information criterion method (AIC), used to estimate the quality of different models, allowing for the selection of the best model, used in GLM models. Since the AIC method is based on the properties of maximum likelihood and these do not apply to GEE models, the QIC method was developed based on the quasi-likelihood method developed by *Wedderburn* [19], thus allowing for its applicability in GEE models.

For different GEE models with different correlation structures, several QIC values are generated, so the best model and, in turn, the best correlation structure will be the model with the lowest QIC value. If different correlation structures present equal QIC values, one should consider the QICu value, which represents a simplified version of QIC [12].

Several authors use GEE models to identify the influences of different factors in biomedical research. *Mitchell et al.* [10] sought to verify if pseudoexfoliation would influence risk factors for the development of glaucoma. Through logistic regression models, they found that the presence of ocular pseudoexfoliation is related to glaucoma in older individuals. However, through GEE models, they found that the risk factors associated with glaucoma are independent of the presence of pseudoexfoliation.

The Shiny package enables the creation of dynamic applications that simplify the use and analysis of GEE models for biomedical studies by allowing users to apply these models without prior programming or code-typing experience in order to derive statistical inferences that allow for the quick and accurate performance of analyses through statistical tests or graphical displays [1].

The objective of this article is to present the new application developed for GEE analysis, SAGA, detailing all the sections and menus existing in it, applied to a case study. Initially, the methodology and approaches to be used in the development of the application will be described, as well as a description of the software and packages that will be used. The case study used in the demonstration of the application will also be introduced. Next, all the menus of the developed application will be demonstrated in detail, ending with a brief conclusion and future prospects.

2   Material and Methods

Statistical programs for GEE models are available in different statistical analysis software products such as *Stata*, *R*, *SPSS*, among others. To verify limitations between different packages, *Nooraee et al.* [11] used a set of packages available in different languages, including *GENMOD*, *SAS*, *GENLIN*, *SPSS*, `repolr`, `multgee`, and `geepack` in R. This author found that the *multgee* and `repolr` packages have more functionalities than the others, but all of them showed limitations in parameter estimation when the number of individuals is very low.

Several packages are available in R for GEE analysis, the `geepack` [22] package was selected for implementation in the Shiny SAGA application, as this package allows for parameter estimation using the GEE methodology, generating statistical inferences and making it possible to use the models developed for validation. Implemented together with the `geepack` package is the `ROCR` package [17], which allows for validation of the developed models, enabling analysis between models, and complementing this analysis with graphical representation of the generated ROC curves.

2.1 Case of Study

To perform the GEE analysis a dataset related to the identification of the presence of ocular pseudoexfoliation in several patients undergoing cataract removal surgery during June 1 to December 31 of 2016 was used, this dataset was provided by the Department of Ophthalmology of the Vila Nova de Gaia/Espinho Hospital Center situated in Vila Nova de Gaia, Portugal.

In addition to personal information about the patients such as age, sex, and date of consultation, over time, information was collected on the eye under analysis, presence of pseudoexfoliation, pupil dilation, presence of intraocular lens and associated diopters, as well as the location where it is inserted.

Pseudoexfoliation syndrome (PEX) is an age-related pathology characterized by fibrillar material deposits, usually identified by a white color, present in the ocular structures of the anterior segment bathed by the aqueous humor [13,15]. This disease is associated with abnormal behaviors and changes in the LOXL1 gene, responsible for synthesizing the fibrous material present in ocular pseudoexfoliation, as reported by *Sangal and Chen* [14], *Govetto et al.* [4] and *Jammal et al.* [7]. Despite this association, there are also external factors associated with ocular pseudoexfoliation, such as age, sex, and geographical area of residence, as reported by *Sangal and Chen* [14] and *Shazly et al.* [16].

2.2 Shiny

The development of web applications for statistical analysis presented itself as a challenge, as it required some deep knowledge of other languages, such as JavaScript, HTML or CSS to develop the application interface and establish a connection with the R language for statistical processing and analysis [20].

Shiny is an R package that enables the development of web applications without requiring prior knowledge of other programming languages, using only the R language. The application developed in Shiny is composed of two components, the interface, which represents the component that corresponds to the structure of the application responsible for receiving all the instructions provided by the user, which will be used to perform the desired tasks in order to visualize the results obtained, and the server, which represents the component responsible for all the processing of the instructions provided by the user in order to perform the desired statistical analysis through functions/algorithms developed in R.

Shiny uses reactive programming, which allows updating in real-time all the results and processes performed, when a change occurs in the instructions provided by the user. After developing the two essential components, described previously, the application is available on the web for any user for free.

Although there are several packages in different programming languages for the application of GEE model analysis, there are not actually web applications that allow the use of these GEE analysis in an intuitive way without programming knowledge. The SAGA application seeks to solve the presented gap, making it possible through it:

– Load the relevant dataset for analysis;
– Select the type of variables, correlation structure, as well as edit the data;
– Validate the developed models and compare them;
– Analyze the obtained results intuitively;
– Export the generated graphical representations;
– Obtain help in the application's functioning.

To describe all the steps to be performed by the user during the use of SAGA for GEE analysis, a flowchart was constructed, as presented in Fig. 1.

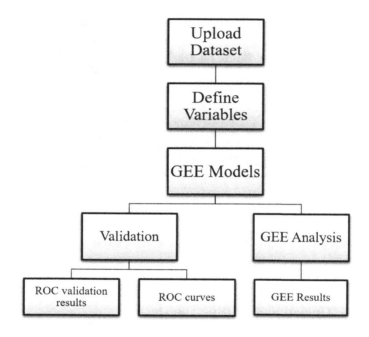

Fig. 1. Flowchart of the structure of the Shiny SAGA application.

Initially, the user must load the dataset to be used, then select all the variables of interest for the construction of the GEE model. Subsequently, the user can view the results of the GEE analysis or validate the created model through receiver operating characteristic validation, where the results from the respective validation as well as the generated ROC curves are obtained.

3 Results

In this section, all the menus and sections existing in the developed SAGA application will be described in detail. The language used will be English in order to facilitate the use among various users.

The application is divided into three sub-menus as described in Fig. 2, which are:

A. Upload and editing of the dataset;
B. Selection of variables for the GEE model;
C. Validation and results of the generated models.

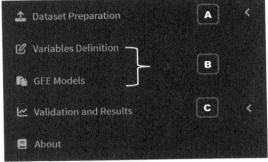

Fig. 2. SAGA menu.

Throughout this section, all menus and submenus of the SAGA application will be described in detail using the dataset corresponding to the case study as an example.

3.1 SAGA: Upload and Editing the Dataset

This menu is based on the user's introduction of the dataset and, if necessary, making changes to it for further development of GEE models, and it is divided into two submenus, upload dataset and dataset changes.

SAGA: Upload Dataset. In this menu, the user will introduce the dataset by clicking the "browse..." button, a new window will appear to select the dataset, limited only to EXCEL files with the `.xlsx` extension and CSV files with .csv extension. Any other data structure will generate an error when imported. The dataset will appear in the background window. In addition to downloading the dataset, there are also some features that can improve or change the visualization of the dataset, as represented in Fig. 3.

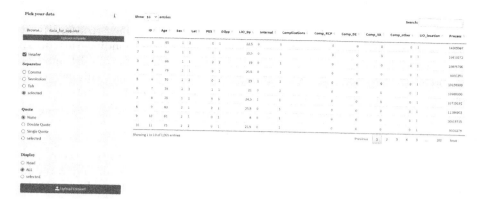

Fig. 3. Importing the dataset as .xlsx file.

SAGA: Data Changes. After the upload of the dataset, there may be some changes that can be made, for example the name of the respective existing columns. In the case of GEE models, column names containing spaces between names should be avoided, as these names often generate errors when the model analysis is performed. The change of the column names can be made in the "Columns Names" section, where all the names of the columns existing in the previously downloaded dataset are displayed, and a text box where the new column name will be entered. To make the change, the desired column will be selected, and its new name will be entered in the text box, and the change will be changed automatically. An example of the use of this section is shown in Fig. 4.

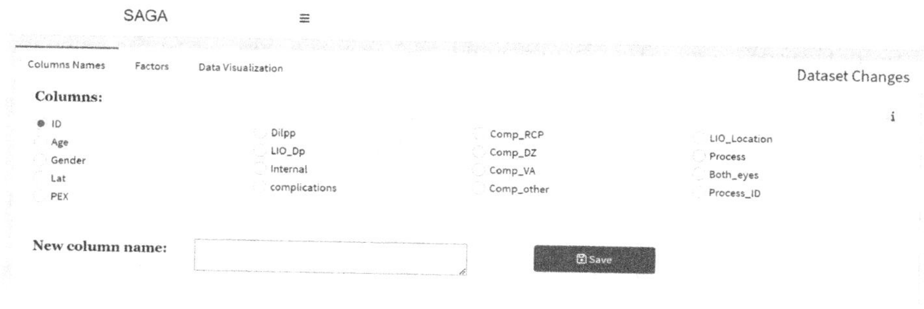

Fig. 4. Column name change from Data Changes menu.

In addition to changing the column names of the dataset, the user can factorize columns whose values are categorical variables. With factorization, these values will be divided into levels, one level for each corresponding variable in the selected column, making it easier to use in the development of GEE models. This process can be done on the sub-menu "Factors". The last sub-menu will show again the uploaded dataset with all the changes made by the user.

3.2   SAGA: Selection of Variables for GEE Models

As described earlier, the variable selection menu corresponds to the second part of the application, and is one of the most fundamental, as all the variables necessary for the development of GEE models will be defined here. The variables that will be selected are:

- Response variable;
- Covariates;
- Identification column, represents the column corresponding to the sample/observation identification;
- Distribution Family, represents the type of distribution of the response variable (e.g. Binomial, Poisson, etc.);
- Correlation Structure.

SAGA: Variables. The selection of variables begins with the selection of the response variable of the GEE model and its corresponding covariates. In the selection of the response variable, all columns corresponding to the dataset uploaded previously are present, and the column corresponding to the variable of interest will be selected. The selection of covariates and their relationship can be defined in two ways:

- **Selection of covariates:** Represented as **A** in Fig. 5. Similar to the response variable, all columns of the dataset will be presented, and the user can select the columns he/she wants. Through this selection process, the covariates will be added to each other. (Example: Age + Gender... + Latency)

- **Introduction of the relationship between covariates:** Represented as **B** in Fig. 5. Another method for selecting covariates is by introducing them and their relationship to each other. The user must input the names of the columns of interest and specify the relationship between the selected covariates.

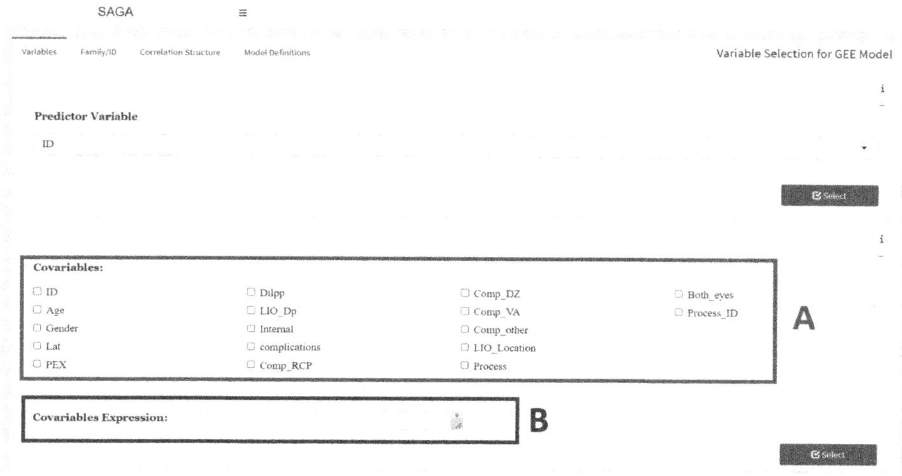

Fig. 5. Selection of the response variable and the process of selecting covariates.

The user can only choose one of the processes for selecting covariates. If both processes are used, the process **A** will be assumed.

SAGA: Family/ID. In this sub-menu, the distribution family of the response variable and the column corresponding to the sample/observation identification are defined. The process for selecting these two variables is the same as described for the response variable, where all the columns of the dataset will be presented, and the user should choose the column of interest.

SAGA: Correlation Structure. The selection of the correlation structure will be the last step in developing the GEE model. The user can select one of the three available correlation structures, described before, which are:

- Independent correlation structure;
- Exchangeable correlation structure;
- Autoregressive correlation structure;

If the user is unsure which correlation structure best fits the model, there is an option to display QIC values by selecting the "Display QIC values" option. This option will present a table with the corresponding QIC and QICu values for each correlation structure, considering the variables previously selected, as represented in Fig. 6. If any variable from the previous sub-menus are missing, this option will deliver an error.

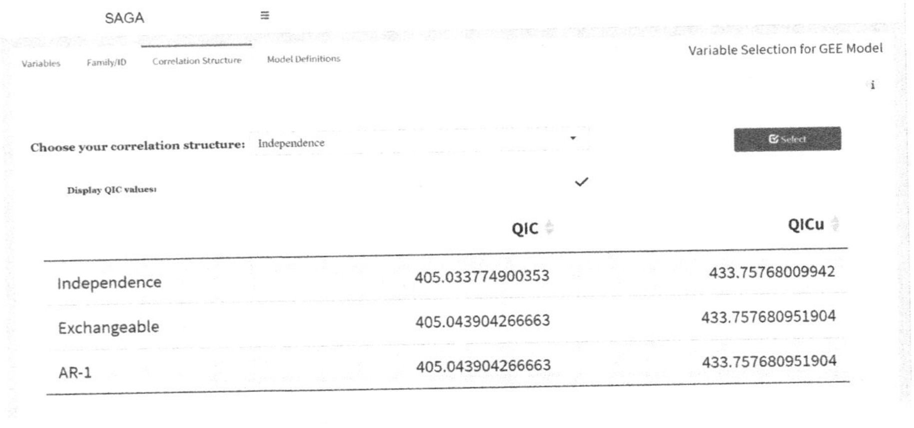

Fig. 6. Selection of the correlation structure with QIC values option.

For the case study, based on the results shown regarding the correlation structure, it is observed that the QIC values are very similar in all structures. However, the independent correlation structure has a slightly lower value. Therefore, the selected structure for developing the GEE models will be the independent correlation structure.

SAGA: Model Definitions. In this final sub-menu, a name will be assigned to the newly developed GEE model and a brief description of the model. This section will not influence the developed model, it is only necessary to label the generated results.

3.3   SAGA: GEE Models

In this menu, the GEE models created are presented, describing the previously selected variables, an example of this menu is shown in Fig. 7. There are 3 functionalities in this menu:

- **Add:** This functionality allows the construction of a new GEE model in addition to the first created model. When the button is executed, the user will return to the variable selection process in the Model Definitions sub-menu, and should select "Variables" as the initial section and continue the procedure described above. The new model will be added to the menu when the "Select" button in the "Model definitions" sub-menu is executed. There is a limit of 3 models created, and the button will become inactive after creating that number of models.

- **Edit:** To execute this button, one of the created models must be selected, and the button will be inactive when two or more models are selected. When this button is executed, the user can change the variables selected in the previous procedure. The model change occurs when the "Save" button in the "Model definitions" sub-menu is executed, so it is suggested to check all sections corresponding to the previously described variables.
- **Run:** The execution of this button occurs when one or more models are selected. Through this button, the variables selected by the user will be considered, and there is no possibility of changing them. The considered variables allow the GEE analysis to be performed, as well as their use in the ROC validation phase, which will be described next.

Fig. 7. Representation of the GEE models menu with three models as an example.

As shown in Fig. 7, for the case study, three different models were developed: one considering only the personal variables of the patients, another considering the ocular variables, and finally a model considering all variables together.

3.4   Validation: ROC Analysis

The validation through ROC analysis of the developed models is an additional and optional functionality, that means, that the user is not required to perform the validation to access the results of the GEE analysis. However, through this validation, the user can obtain additional information about the model or compare them through the metrics obtained during the analysis. Through the ROC validation, the ROC curves will be generated and the value of two metrics, accuracy and area under the curve. These two metrics will help to check the performance of the model. This validation procedure can be done in the "Validation and Results" menu.

Data Split. The first step to proceed with the validation of the models is to define the division of the dataset into training and testing. At this stage, the user can select three different divisions, and in case they are not sure which division to use, there is a default selection that divides the dataset considering its size. After choosing the desired division for validation, the user must press the button "Run ROC" to perform the validation.

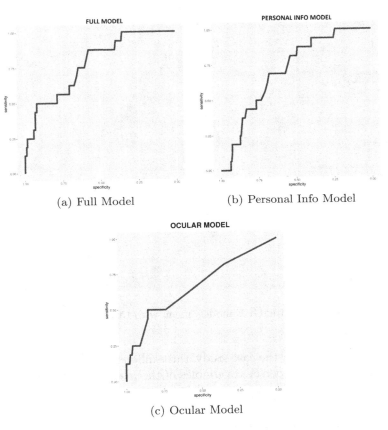

(a) Full Model   (b) Personal Info Model

(c) Ocular Model

Fig. 8. Generated ROC curves for the three different models.

ROC: Graph Visualization. After initializing the ROC analysis in the previous sub-menu, the ROC curves generated for each of the models selected in the previous sections are presented. Below each of the generated curves, there is a "download" button where the user can download the obtained curves to their local computer. The file is in .png format. Figure 8 shows the respective ROC curves considering three different models and their respective download buttons.

ROC: Results. As a complement to the graphical representation of ROC curves generated for different models, this section presents the results obtained in the ROC analysis considering the two metrics referenced in previous sections, Accuracy, it shows how accurate a collection of measurements are in relation to their true value, and AUC. For each previously selected model, the values of the described metrics will be presented, allowing the user to verify, through the obtained results, the model that presents better validation results. Figure 9 show how the results from ROC validation are presented for each developed model.

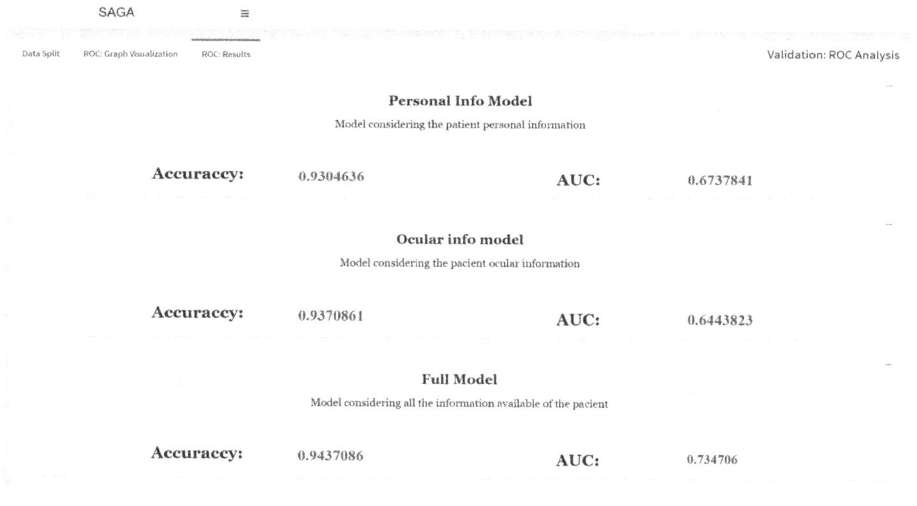

SAGA	≡			
Data Split	ROC: Graph Visualization	ROC: Results		Validation: ROC Analysis

Personal Info Model
Model considering the patient personal information

Accuraccy: 0.9304636   **AUC:** 0.6737841

Ocular info model
Model considering the pacient ocular information

Accuraccy: 0.9370861   **AUC:** 0.6443823

Full Model
Model considering all the information available of the pacient

Accuraccy: 0.9437086   **AUC:** 0.734706

Fig. 9. Example of results from ROC validation for different models.

Based on the ROC validation, it is possible to verify that the model considering all variables presents higher values in both metrics (ACC and AUC) compared to the other models. Therefore, this will be the model considered for the GEE analysis of the case study.

3.5 GEE Results

The results obtained from the models created in the previous menus are presented in this menu. For each developed model, a table describing the results obtained from the GEE analysis will be presented. The obtained table allows the user to analyze the influence of covariates on the response variable, through their estimate values, confidence interval values and the Wald test. These results enable the user to perform a rigorous analysis of the developed model throughout all the steps. The results' table can be downloaded to the user's personal computer in the `.csv` format, allowing for download through the download button for further analysis or visualization. Figure 10 shows a table with the results obtained from one of the models created during the description of all previous menus.

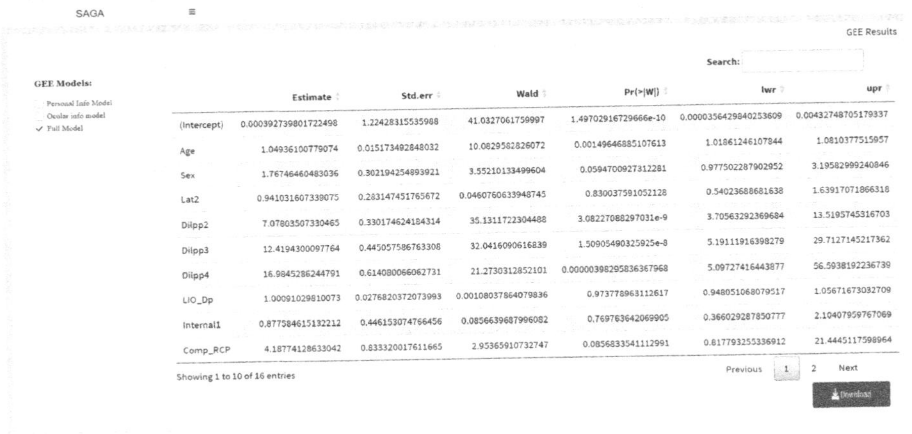

	Estimate	Std.err	Wald	Pr(>|W|)	lwr	upr
(Intercept)	0.000392739801722498	1.22428315535988	41.0327061759997	1.49702916729666e-10	0.0000356429840253609	0.00432748705179337
Age	1.04936100779074	0.015173492848032	10.0829582826072	0.00149646885107613	1.01861246107844	1.0810377515957
Sex	1.76746460483036	0.302194254893921	3.55210133499604	0.0594700927312281	0.977502287902952	3.19582999240846
Lat2	0.941031607339075	0.283147451765672	0.0460760633948745	0.830037591052128	0.54023688681638	1.63917071866318
Dilpp2	7.07803507330465	0.330174624184314	35.1311722304488	3.08227088297031e-9	3.70563292369684	13.5195745316703
Dilpp3	12.4194300097764	0.445057586763308	32.0416090616839	1.50905490325925e-8	5.19111916398279	29.7127145217362
Dilpp4	16.9845286244791	0.614080066062731	21.2730312852101	0.00000398295836367968	5.09727416443877	56.5938192236739
LIO_Dp	1.00091029810073	0.0276820372073993	0.00108037864079836	0.973778963112617	0.948051068079517	1.05671673032709
Internal1	0.877584615132212	0.446153074766456	0.0856639687996082	0.769763642069905	0.366029287850777	2.10407959767069
Comp_RCP	4.18774128633042	0.833320017611665	2.95365910732747	0.0856833541112991	0.817793255336912	21.4445117598964

Fig. 10. Results obtained for one of the models created in the previous menus.

In general, it can be observed through GEE analysis using the SAGA application, that the covariates corresponding to age, pupillary dilation and two complications that appear during cataract removal surgery, have a positive influence on the presence of ocular pseudoexfoliation.

The validation of this influence is based on the obtained p-values lower than 0.05, the estimates values for the influential covariates are positive, and the confidence intervals, which have values greater than 1, demonstrate the covariates' significance.

As already discussed by other authors and demonstrated in the results, age and pupil dilation continue to have an influence on the presence or development of ocular pseudoexfoliation. Also, through the results, it is observed that complications during cataract removal surgery, observed when a zonular dehiscence occurs, may indicate the presence of ocular pseudoexfoliation, as infections resulting from the registered dehiscence may arise, including pseudoexfoliation itself.

In Table 1, all results obtained from the GEE analysis using the SAGA application applied to the case study are described.

Table 1. Results of GEE analysis for the case study

	B	SE(B)	W	$Pr(> |W|)$	CI - 95%
Intercept	0.000399	1.253	39.005	4.23e−10	[3.42e-05–0.005]
Age	1.049	0.015	10.700	0.001	[1.020–1.080]
Gender	1.769	0.301	3.582	0.058	[0.980–3.192]
Lat (LE)	0.941	0.283	0.046	0.830	[0.540–1.638]
LIO DP	1.000	0.028	1.09e-03	0.974	[0.948–1.060]
LIO Location (Sulcus)	2.152	0.786	0.952	0.329	[0.460–10.040]
LIO Location (CA)	9.65e+17	1.346	946.875	0.0	[6.90e+16–1.35e19]
LIO Location (S/LIO)	4.60e−17	1.943	374.704	0.0	[1.012e-18–2.07e-15]
Dilpp (≥7–8)	7.078	0.330	35.142	3.07e−09	[3.706–13.519]
Dilpp (≥6–7)	12.414	0.444	32.211	1.38e−08	[5.20–29.63]
Dilpp (≥5–6)	16.999	0.614	21.272	3.99e−06	[5.10–56.62]
Internal (S)	0.877	0.446	0.086	0.769	[0.37–2.10]
Comp RCP (S)	4.188	0.833	2.954	0.086	[0.82–21.45]
Comp DZ (S)	10.769	0.803	8.767	0.003	[2.23–51.93]
Comp VA (S)	0.365	1.373	0.540	0.463	[0.02–5.38]
Comp other (S)	14.718	0.748	12.916	0.0003	[3.40–63.79]

B: Parameter estimate; SE(B): Standard Error; W: Wald statistic; CI 95%: 95% confidence interval.

4   Conclusions and Future Work

To address the lack of an application exclusively designed for GEE analysis of longitudinal data, SAGA was developed and completed. The application allows for the development of different GEE models considering various scenarios, performs validation through ROC curves for each model, generates the obtained curves and their respective metrics, enabling a more rigorous analysis of the developed models. Finally, it describes the results of the GEE analysis for each model, allowing users to save the obtained results on their personal computer throughout the various processes. This application allows for a more interactive and faster GEE analysis by the user.

This article represents the first release of the SAGA application. The application can suffer bug fixes and improvements on the visual component. SAGA requires the input dataset to be pre-processed, meaning that there are not many tools in the application that allow for data pre-processing before constructing GEE models, such as removing missing data. The introduction of a limitation to access to all the menus before select the variables, can enable a better analysis and reduce the likelihood of errors or undefined parameters.

References

1. Chang, W., et al.: shiny: Web Application Framework for R (2023). https://shiny.rstudio.com/, r package version 1.7.4.9002
2. Christopher, Z.: Generalized estimating equation models for correlated data: a review with applications. Am. J. Polit. Sci. **45**(2), 470–490 (2001)
3. Fitzmaurice, G.M., Laird, N.M., Ware, J.H.: Applied Longitudinal Analysis, vol. 998. John Wiley & Sons (2012)
4. Govetto, A., et al.: Frequency of pseudo exfoliation among patients scheduled for cataract surgery. J. Cataract Refract. Surg. **41**(6), 1224–1231 (2015)
5. Hedeker, D., Gibbons, R.D.: Longitudinal Data Analysis. Wiley-Interscience (2006)
6. Horton, N.J., Lipsitz, S.R.: Review of software to fit generalized estimating equation regression models. Am. Stat. **53**(2), 160–169 (1999)
7. Jammal, H., et al.: Characteristics of patients with pseudoexfoliation syndrome at a tertiary eye care center in jordan: a retrospective chart review. Ophthalmol. Therapy **10**(1), 51–61 (2021)
8. Kleinbaum, D.G., Klein, M.: Logistic regresion for correlated data: Gee. Logist. Regression Self-learn. Text 327–375 (2002)
9. Liang, K.Y., Zeger, S.L.: Longitudinal data analysis using generalized linear models. Biometrika **73**(1), 13–22 (1986)
10. Mitchell, P., Wang, J.J., Hourihan, F.: The relationship between glaucoma and pseudoexfoliation: the blue mountains eye study. Arch. Ophthalmol. **117**(10), 1319–1324 (1999)
11. Nooraee, N., Molenberghs, G., van den Heuvel, E.R.: Gee for longitudinal ordinal data: comparing R-geepack, R-multgee, R-repolr, SAS-GENMOD, SPSS-GENLIN. Comput. Stat. Data Analy. **77**, 70–83 (2014)
12. Pan, W.: Akaike's information criterion in generalized estimating equations. Biometrics **57**(1), 120–125 (2001)
13. Ritch, R., Schlötzer-Schrehardt, U.: Exfoliation syndrome. Surv. Ophthalmol. **45**(4), 265–315 (2001)
14. Sangal, N., Chen, T.C.: Cataract surgery in pseudoexfoliation syndrome. In: Seminars in Ophthalmology, vol. 29, pp. 403–408. Taylor & Francis (2014)
15. Schlötzer-Schrehardt, U., Naumann, G.O.: Ocular and systemic pseudoexfoliation syndrome. Am. J. Ophthalmol. **141**(5), 921–937 (2006)
16. Shazly, T.A., Farrag, A.N., Kamel, A., Al-Hussaini, A.K.: Prevalence of pseudoexfoliation syndrome and pseudoexfoliation glaucoma in upper Egypt. BMC Ophthalmol. **11**(1), 1–6 (2011)
17. Sing, T., Sander, O., Beerenwinkel, N., Lengauer, T.: Package 'ROCR'. Visualizing the performance of scoring classifiers, 1–14 (2015)
18. Wang, Y.G., Fu, L., Paul, S.: Analysis of Longitudinal Data with Examples (2022)
19. Wedderburn, R.W.: Quasi-likelihood functions, generalized linear models, and the gauss-newton method. Biometrika **61**(3), 439–447 (1974)
20. Wickham, H.: Mastering Shiny. O'Reilly Media, Inc. (2021)
21. Wilson, J.R., Lorenz, K.A.: Modeling Binary Correlated Responses using SAS, SPSS and R, vol. 9. Springer (2015)
22. Yan, J., Højsgaard, S., Yan, M.J., False, B.: Package 'geepack' (2012)
23. Ziegler, A., Vens, M.: Generalized estimating equations. Meth. Inf. Med. **49**(05), 421–425 (2010)

Performance Evaluation of Portfolio Stocks Selected with the EU–EV Risk Model

Irene Brito[1]([✉]) [iD] and Gaspar J. Machado[2] [iD]

[1] Center of Mathematics, Department of Mathematics, University of Minho, 4800-045 Guimarães, Portugal
ireneb@math.uminho.pt
[2] Physics Center of Minho and Porto Universities, Department of Mathematics, University of Minho, 4800-045 Guimarães, Portugal
gjm@math.uminho.pt

Abstract. In this paper, the performance of portfolios consisting of stocks selected with the recently proposed expected utility, entropy and variance (EU–EV) risk model is analysed. The portfolios were constructed using data of the PSI 20 index, from January 2019 to December 2020, by reducing the number of stock components to the half with the EU–EV risk model. The efficiency of these portfolios in terms of the mean–variance model was shown to be approximately equal to the efficiency of portfolios obtained from the whole set of stocks. The aim is to evaluate the performance of the constructed portfolios, by comparing their in-sample and out-of-sample results with those of the benchmark. For that purpose, cumulative returns in the in-sample period from January 2019 to December 2020 and in the out-of-sample period from January 2021 to December 2022, considering both an one-year and a two-year time horizon, as well as different performance metrics, such as Sharpe ratio, Sortino ratio, Beta and Alpha, are analysed. The results reveal that the portfolios constructed with the EU–EV risk model outperform the benchmark portfolio in the given periods, where a better performance was obtained in the one-year out-of-sample period. These results suggest that the strategy of constructing portfolios using the best ranked stocks according to the EU–EV risk model can be useful for short-term investment objectives.

Keywords: EU–EV risk model · Stock selection · Portfolio performance evaluation

1 Introduction

Classifying stock risks and the selection of efficient stocks is an important task for the construction of portfolios. The mean–variance model was proposed by Markowitz [11] to assess and construct portfolios by minimizing risk, expressed by variance, and maximizing the expected return. Several other stock selection

© The Author(s), under exclusive license to Springer Nature Switzerland AG 2023
O. Gervasi et al. (Eds.): ICCSA 2023 Workshops, LNCS 14105, pp. 69–83, 2023.
https://doi.org/10.1007/978-3-031-37108-0_5

models were proposed in the literature, where also entropy was used for measuring risk and combined with other measures, for example the mean–variance-entropy model [8], the expected utility and entropy (EU–E) model [16], the fuzzy cross-entropy model [14], or the expected utility, entropy and variance model (EU–EV) model [2]. Also machine learning methodologies were developed for stock selection and portfolio optimization. Huang [7] used support vector regression together with genetic algorithms, and Paiva et al. [12] applied the support vector machine method to compose optimal portfolios. In [5], extreme gradient boosting were used for preselecting stocks with higher potential returns before employing the mean–variance model. Other portfolio construction strategies depend on factor investing criteria (e.g. value, profitability, momentum) [1] or on environmental, social and governance investment criteria, see e.g. [15]. In several of the research works the proposed methodologies lead in certain applications to portfolios that can outperform the benchmark portfolios.

Recently, the expected utility, entropy and variance model (EU–EV model), developed in [3] and in [4], was applied to the selection of stocks for portfolio construction [2]. In the EU–EV risk model, entropy and variance are used as uncertainty risk factors, that are combined with expected utility, as preference factor, using a trade-off parameter. The model was applied in [2] to the PSI 20 index to form subsets with half the number of stocks with lower EU–EV risk. Using the mean–variance model, the efficiencies of the subsets' portfolios were compared with the efficiency of the whole stock set. The results revealed that the risk model selects the relevant stocks for an optimal portfolio construction.

The aim of the present work is now to evaluate the performance of portfolios constructed with the EU–EV risk model by analysing in-sample and also out-of-sample results of different performance indicators and comparing these results with those obtained with the benchmark portfolio, in order to further test the reasonability and adequacy of the EU–EV risk model for stock selection. In this study cumulative returns and perfomance metrics such as Sharpe ratio, Sortino ratio, Beta and Alpha were considered.

This paper is organized as follows. In Sect. 2, the methodology of selecting stocks with the EU–EV risk model is explained and the application to data of the PSI 20 index in order to obtain sets with the best ranked stocks for the portfolio construction is presented. Section 3 deals with the performance evaluation of the portfolios, where cumulative returns, Sharpe and Sortino ratios, Beta and Alpha values of the portfolios are compared with those of the benchmark. Section 4 contains the conclusions of this work.

2 Stock Selection Using the EU–EV Risk Model

2.1 EU–EV Risk Model

The EU–EV model for classifying stock risks is defined as follows. Consider a set of stocks $S = \{S_1, \ldots, S_I\}$ and the action space $A = \{a_1, \ldots, a_I\}$, where $a_i = (x_{i1}, p_{i1}; x_{i2}, p_{i2}; \ldots; x_{iN}, p_{iN}) \in A$ is the action of selecting stock S_i, $i = 1, \ldots, I$, yielding the frequency distribution of stock returns, where x_{in} are the outcomes occurring with probabilities p_{in}, $n = 1, \ldots, N$, that are represented by the discrete random variable X_i. The EU–EV risk for the action a_i is defined by (see [2])

$$R(a_i) = \frac{\lambda}{2}\left[H(X_i) + \frac{\text{Var}[X_i]}{\max\limits_{a_i \in A}\{\text{Var}[X_i]\}} \right] - (1 - \lambda)\frac{\mathbb{E}[u(X_i)]}{\max\limits_{a_i \in A}\{|\mathbb{E}[u(X_i)]|\}}, \qquad (1)$$

where $0 \leq \lambda \leq 1$, $u(\cdot)$ is the utility function and $H(X_i) = -\sum_{n=1}^{N} p_{in} \ln p_{in}$ is the entropy. If $\lambda = 0$, then the risk measure depends only on the expected utility and if $\lambda = 1$ the risk measure uses only the uncertainty factors entropy and variance to assess risk. For $\lambda \in (0, 1)$, the effect of the expected utility on the risk measure is bigger if $\lambda < 0.5$, for $\lambda > 0.5$ the risk measure is more influenced by the uncertainty than by the expected utility and if $\lambda = 0.5$, it is equally influenced by both factors. The stocks are ranked according to the EU–EV risk, where given two stocks S_{i_1} and S_{i_2}, $i_1, i_2 \in \{1, \ldots, I\}$, if $R(a_{i_1}) < R(a_{i_2})$, then the optimal stock is S_{i_1}.

2.2   Data and Portfolio Formation

The PSI 20 index consists, from January 2019 to December 2020, of 18 component stocks of companies denoted by $S = \{S_1, \ldots, S_{18}\}$ (see [2] for more details). These stocks were classified, using the daily returns' frequency distributions, according to the EU–EV risk (1) with utility function

$$u(x) = \begin{cases} \ln(1 + x), & x \geq 0, \\ -\ln(1 - x), & x < 0. \end{cases}$$

The daily returns were calculated from the daily closing prices, collected from Yahoo Finance. The best 9 stocks with lower risk were selected for different ranges of λ to construct portfolios. The following five stock subsets were obtained:

$$\begin{aligned}
Q_1 &= \{S_1, S_3, S_5, S_6, S_8, S_9, S_{11}, S_{16}, S_{18}\}, & \lambda &\in [0, 0.1260), \\
Q_2 &= \{S_1, S_3, S_4, S_5, S_6, S_9, S_{11}, S_{16}, S_{18}\}, & \lambda &\in [0.1260, 0.4685), \\
Q_3 &= \{S_1, S_3, S_5, S_6, S_9, S_{11}, S_{16}, S_{17}, S_{18}\}, & \lambda &\in [0.4685, 0.5311), \\
Q_4 &= \{S_3, S_5, S_6, S_9, S_{11}, S_{13}, S_{16}, S_{17}, S_{18}\}, & \lambda &\in [0.5311, 0.7771), \\
Q_5 &= \{S_3, S_5, S_6, S_9, S_{12}, S_{13}, S_{16}, S_{17}, S_{18}\}, & \lambda &\in [0.7771, 1].
\end{aligned}$$

The mean–variance optimization problem was applied in [2] to the whole set of stocks S and to subsets $Q_1, \ldots, Q_5$. A comparison of the efficient frontiers of S with those of the five subsets revealed that the performance of the sets $Q_1, \ldots, Q_4$ corresponding to $\lambda \in [0, 0.7771)$ was similar to those of S. As for Q_5, with λ close to 1 and therefore privileging stocks with lower uncertainty and almost ignoring expected utility, it performed less well than S, considering the mean–variance performance.

In the following analysis, we will consider also the following sets:

$$Q_6 = \{S_2, S_4, S_7, S_8, S_{10}, S_{12}, S_{13}, S_{14}, S_{15}\},$$
$$Q_7 = \{S_3, S_4, S_{10}, S_{11}, S_{12}, S_{14}, S_{15}, S_{16}, S_{17}\},$$
$$Q_8 = \{S_1, S_2, S_4, S_6, S_8, S_{14}, S_{15}, S_{16}, S_{18}\}.$$

Q_6 consists of the worst ranked stocks by the EU–EV risk (stocks that were mostly left out by the EU–EV selection) and Q_7 and Q_8 contain randomly picked stocks that were presented in [2] and shown to be less efficient than sets $Q_1, \ldots, Q_5$.

The aim is to analyse the performance of portfolios formed with the best ranked stocks, that is, with stocks of Q_i, $i = 1, \ldots, 5$, and compare it with the benchmark S portfolio's performance using the in-sample and also out-of-sample data. We will also investigate if the portfolios constructed with stocks of Q_6, Q_7, Q_8 underperform the benchmark portfolio with respect to the performance indicators, since these were formed with less well classified stocks by the EU–EV risk model and one would therefore expect a poorer performance.

We will denote the five portfolios, favourite in terms of the EU–EV risk, by $Q_1, \ldots, Q_5$, where each portfolio is formed as an equally weighted combination of the stocks of each corresponding set Q_i, $i = 1, \ldots, 5$. The other three portfolios will be denoted by Q_6, Q_7, Q_8 and are built in an analogous way. The stragtegy of using equal weights (in this case $1/9$) is chosen, since it has been reported in the literature that equal-weighted portfolios outperform value-weighted strategies (see e.g. [6,9]). The portfolios contain thus half the number of stocks than the benchmark porfolio PSI 20 index, here represented by S.

3   Performance Evaluation of the Portfolios

In order to analyse the perfomance of the portfolios, different performance indicators and metrics will be determined, using in-sample data from January 2019 to December 2020 and out-of-sample data from January 2021 to December 2022. The performance evaluation will be conducted considering a time horizon of one year and a time horizon of two years and comparing the portfolios' performances with those of the benchmark portfolio PSI 20 index S.

3.1   Cumulative Returns and Performance Metrics

As a first performance indicator, the cumulative returns, obtained from the daily returns, are calculated for the five portfolios $Q_1, \ldots, Q_5$ and for the benchmark index. The cumulative returns are presented in Fig. 1 for the in-sample data. Figure 2 and Fig. 3 contain the cumulative returns corresponding to the out-of-sample data for the one-year and two-year period, respectively. Observing the

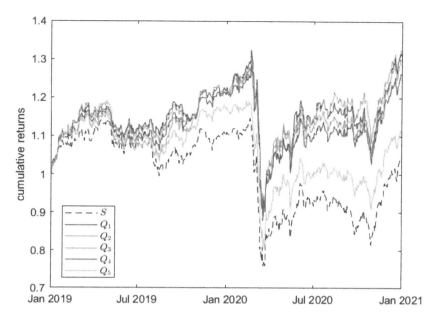

Fig. 1. Cumulative returns of S and $Q_1, \ldots, Q_5$ from January 2019 to December 2020.

evolution of the cumulative returns in Fig. 1, all portfolios, $Q_1, \ldots, Q_5$, outperform the benchmark portfolio S in the given time horizon, where Q_5 underperforms Q_1, Q_2, Q_3, Q_4, and Q_2 seems to outperform the other portfolios in the second half of 2020. These results indicate that the portfolios containing stocks selected with the EU–EV risk model, by weighting more the expected utility than the variance and entropy components, achieve also higher cumulative returns in the considered time interval, whereas Q_5, constructed with stocks weighting more the variance and entropy component than the expected utility component, is the worst performing portfolio among the five. Note that, in the mean–variance efficiency analysis, Q_5 also performed less well than Q_1, Q_2, Q_3 and Q_4.

Considering the one-year out-of-sample period, the portfolios $Q_1, \ldots, Q_5$ continue exhibiting higher cumulative returns than the PSI index S (see Fig. 2), and also in the two-year period, however with an exception in the last quarter of 2022, where Q_1 underperforms S (see Fig. 3). Q_2 is the best performing portfolio in the one-year period and over a larger time interval in the two-year period and Q_1 the worst. But notable is the strong performance of Q_4 and Q_5 in 2022 and, in particular, that of Q_5 in the last quarter of 2022. The portfolios Q_4 and Q_5 contain the best ranked stocks that were selected by the EU–EV risk model weighting more the variance and entropy component than the expected utility, and a higher variance can lead to higher returns, which may explain the higher cumulative returns obtained by these portfolios in further time intervals in the out-of-sample period. However, in general, the portfolios formed with the best

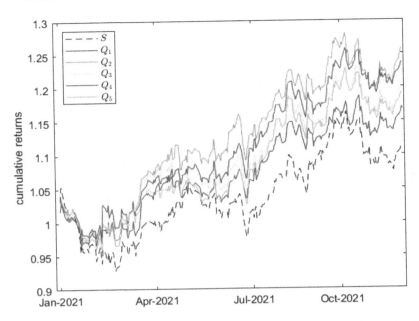

Fig. 2. Cumulative returns of S and $Q_1, \ldots, Q_5$ from January 2021 to December 2021.

ranked stocks according to the EU–EV risk lead also in the out-of-sample periods to higher cumulative returns, when compared to the benchmark returns.

As for portfolio Q_6, constructed with the worst ranked stocks by the EU–EV risk model, and for the portfolios Q_7 and Q_8, that were shown to be less efficient using the mean–variance model, the evolution of the cumulative returns in the in-sample period is illustrated in Fig. 4 and in the out-of-sample periods in Fig. 5 and Fig. 6. In the in-sample period, these portfolios underperform the benchmark portfolio, as it would be expected, with a slight exception during the first quarter of 2019, where Q_7 surpasses S. And, the portfolio that leads in the in-sample period over a wider time range to the lowest cumulative returns is in fact Q_6. Regarding the out-of-sample periods, the cumulative returns of these portfolios exceed the cumulative returns of the benchmark portfolio for several months in 2021 and 2022. Afterwards, in the second half of 2022, the cumulative returns of the portfolios tend to approach and there are periods where S outperforms again the other three portfolios.

For the evaluation of the portfolios' performances we will also consider the following metrics (see e.g. [10, 13]). The Sharpe ratio measures the excess return (the return of the portfolio less the risk-free rate of interest) per unit of total risk of the portfolio (the standard deviation of the porfolio's returns) and is defined by

$$\text{Sharpe} = \frac{r_\text{P} - r_\text{f}}{\sigma_\text{P}},$$

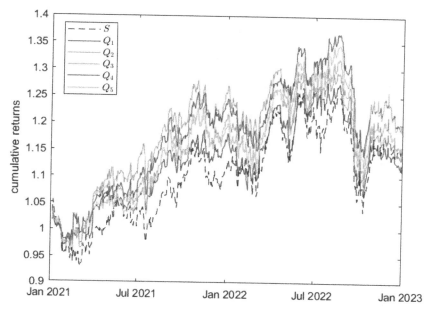

Fig. 3. Cumulative returns of S and $Q_1, \ldots, Q_5$ from January 2021 to December 2022.

where r_P represents the expected return of the portfolio, r_f the risk-free rate, and σ_P is the standard deviation of the portfolio returns. Here we will consider a zero risk-free rate $r_\mathrm{f} = 0$ and the Sharpe ratio quantifies in this case the relation between the expected returns and the standard deviation of the returns of the portfolio. Portfolios with higher Sharpe ratios perfom better according to this measure.

The Sortino ratio is a modification of the Sharpe ratio, where only the downside deviation is taken into account, and it is expressed by

$$\text{Sortino} = \frac{r_\mathrm{P} - r_\mathrm{f}}{\sigma_\mathrm{P}^-},$$

where σ_P^- denotes the standard deviation of the negative portfolio returns. Here we will consider a zero risk-free rate $r_\mathrm{f} = 0$, as in the determination of the Sharpe ratio.

The risk metric Beta quantifies the risk or volatility of a portfolio compared to the market and is given by

$$\text{Beta} = \frac{\text{Cov}(r_\mathrm{P}, r_S)}{\sigma_S^2},$$

where $\text{Cov}(r_\mathrm{P}, r_S)$ is the covariance between the expected return of the portfolio and the expected market return r_S of the benchmark S, and σ_S^2 is the variance of the market returns. Portfolios having Beta> 1 can be interpreted to be more

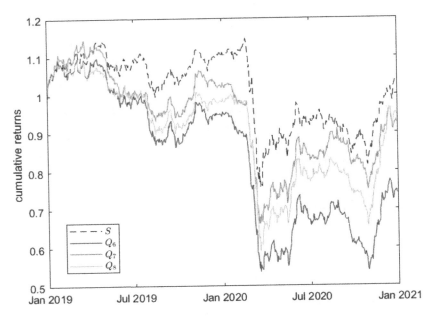

Fig. 4. Cumulative returns of S and Q_6, Q_7, Q_8 from January 2019 to December 2020.

volatile or riskier than the benchmark. In that case the portfolio is also said to be less sensitive to the benchmark volatility. If Beta < 1 the portfolio is less volatile than the benchmark and if Beta= 1, it has the same volatility as the benchmark.

Jensen's Alpha is a performance metric that measures the portfolio return relative to the market return and represents the amount by which the average return of the portfolio deviates from the expected return given by the Capital Asset Pricing Model. The metric is defined by

$$\text{Alpha} = r_P - [r_f + \text{Beta}(r_S - r_f)],$$

with r_P, r_f, r_S and Beta defined above. Here, again, we set $r_f = 0$. A value of Alpha greater than zero indicates that the portfolio has performed better than the market index, a negative value, that the portfolio underperformed the market index and a zero value means that the portfolio's performance is in line with that of the market.

The results of the metrics for the portfolios Q_i, $i = 1, \ldots, 5$, and for the benchmark portfolio S in the in-sample period are listed in Table 1. The Sharpe and Sortino ratios of Q_i, $i = 1, \ldots, 5$, are higher than those of S, as expected, where Q_2 is the best performing portfolio (values of the best performing portfolios are highlighted in bold) and Q_1, Q_2 and Q_3 perform better than Q_4 and Q_5. The portfolio Q_5 attains the lower ratios. The results of the Alpha values, indicating a slight excess return with respect to the market, are in agreement

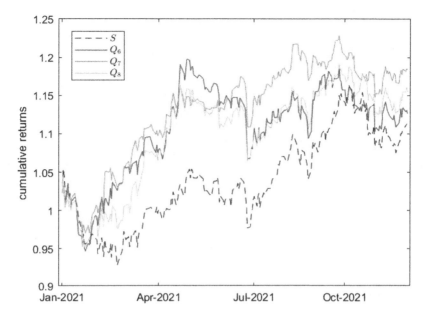

Fig. 5. Cumulative returns of S and Q_6, Q_7, Q_8 from January 2021 to December 2021.

with these conclusions. Since Beta < 1 for all portfolios, one can conclude that the portfolios are less volatile than the benchmark.

Table 1. Performance metrics for $S, Q_1, \ldots, Q_5$ from January 2019 to December 2020.

	S	Q_1	Q_2	Q_3	Q_4	Q_5
Sharpe	0.1938	0.7860	**0.8078**	0.7532	0.6867	0.3737
Sortino	0.2289	0.8748	**0.9306**	0.8626	0.7924	0.4331
Beta	1	0.8215	0.8650	0.8703	0.8562	0.8683
Alpha	0	0.1272	**0.1298**	0.1194	0.1027	0.0359

Considering the out-of-sample period of one year, the Sharpe and Sortino ratios of the five portfolios remain higher than those of the benchmark (see Table 2), where Q_2 has again the best Sharpe ratio, however the best Sortino ratio is now associated with Q_4 and the second best with Q_2. The lowest ratios are now associated with Q_1. The Alpha values replicate the observed behaviour of the Sharpe ratio. According to the Beta values, the portfolios are less volatile than S.

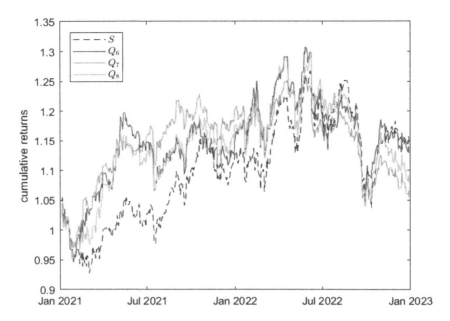

Fig. 6. Cumulative returns of S and Q_6, Q_7, Q_8 from January 2021 to December 2022.

Table 2. Performance metrics for S, $Q_1, \ldots, Q_5$ from January 2021 to December 2021.

	S	Q_1	Q_2	Q_3	Q_4	Q_5
Sharpe	0.7724	1.2771	**1.6830**	1.4251	1.6312	1.3202
Sortino	1.1478	1.8703	2.3443	2.2183	**2.5713**	2.1677
Beta	1	0.7504	0.8443	0.8087	0.7891	0.8290
Alpha	0	0.0792	**0.1528**	0.1098	0.1403	0.0914

The results for the out-of-sample period of two years in Table 3 reveal that now Q_4 and Q_5 provide the best Sharpe and Sortino ratios, where the highest Sharpe ratio is observed for Q_4 and the highest Sortino ratio, for Q_5. The Sharpe and Sortino ratios of S are closer to those of the five portfolios. Indeed, the benchmark performs better than Q_1 and Q_2. The positive Alpha values can be considered approximately equal to zero, which means that the portfolios' performances are in line with the benchmark performance. A closer look reveals that Q_4 attains the highest Alpha, followed by Q_5, whereas Q_1 has the lowest Alpha. The Beta values indicate again that the portfolios are less volatile than S.

Table 3. Performance metrics for $S, Q_1, \ldots, Q_5$ from January 2021 to December 2022.

	S	Q_1	Q_2	Q_3	Q_4	Q_5
Sharpe	0.4863	0.4416	0.4790	0.5292	**0.6712**	0.6534
Sortino	0.7364	0.6322	0.6741	0.7782	1.0359	**1.0459**
Beta	1	0.7594	0.8457	0.8040	0.7571	0.8048
Alpha	0	0.0022	0.0060	0.0144	**0.0344**	0.0310

Examining the results of the performance metrics obtained for the portfolios Q_6, Q_7 and Q_8 in the in-sample period (see Table 4), one can confirm that, in fact, these portfolios underperform the benchmark, not only in terms of lower cumulative returns, as seen before, but also taking into account the Sharpe ratios, the Sortino ratios and the Alpha values. The ratios are all negative, indicating that it is probable to get negative expected returns (losses) with these portfolios. In particular, the ratios of Q_6 are the worst ones, which is consistent with the graphical conclusion of Q_6 yielding the lowest cumulative returns (cf. Fig. 4). Note that Q_6 contains the worst classified stocks by the EU–EV risk model. The negative Alpha values also indicate that the portfolios underperform the benchmark, where Q_6 is the worst classified portfolio according to this indicator. As for the Beta values, one can observe that these portfolios (except Q_7) have higher values than the other portfolios Q_i, $i = 1, \ldots, 5$. The portfolio Q_6 can be considered more volatile than the benchmark, since Beta > 1.

Table 4. Performance metrics for S, Q_6, Q_7, Q_8 from January 2019 to December 2020.

	S	Q_6	Q_7	Q_8
Sharpe	**0.1938**	−0.4683	−0.0840	−0.0123
Sortino	**0.2289**	−0.5909	−0.1025	−0.0144
Beta	1	1.0415	0.8421	0.9336
Alpha	**0**	−0.1471	−0.0498	−0.0393

In contrast, in the one year out-of-sample period, all three portfolios exhibit higher Sharpe and Sortino ratios and a higher Alpha than the benchmark (see Table 5), with the ratios and Alpha of portfolio Q_7 being the highest ones. In fact, this portfolio achieved in this period the highest cumulative returns over a wider time range (cf. Fig. 5). The Beta values are all less than 1.

Table 5. Performance metrics for S, Q_6, Q_7, Q_8 from January 2021 to December 2021.

	S	Q_6	Q_7	Q_8
Sharpe	0.7724	0.8251	**1.3583**	1.0230
Sortino	1.1478	1.2870	**2.0375**	1.5203
Beta	1	0.8107	0.6402	0.8756
Alpha	0	0.0375	**0.1091**	0.0545

In the two-year out-of-sample period, the results in Table 6 indicate that the benchmark outperforms again the portfolios Q_6, Q_7 and Q_8 in terms of the Sharpe and Sortino ratios. Considering the Alpha values, the negative values of Q_7 and Q_8 express the outperformance of the benchmark over these portfolios and the positive value of Q_6 indicates that this portfolio surpasses the benchmark. However the Alpha values are close to zero, suggesting that the differences between the portfolios' and benchmark's returns may be small.

Table 6. Performance metrics for S, Q_6, Q_7, Q_8 from January 2021 to December 2022.

	S	Q_6	Q_7	Q_8
Sharpe	**0.4863**	0.4401	0.2646	0.3131
Sortino	**0.7364**	0.6252	0.3787	0.4445
Beta	1	0.7990	0.5870	0.8766
Alpha	0	**0.0106**	−0.0120	−0.0182

3.2   Summary Analysis

The previous obtained results and analysis can be summarized as follows. The results of the performance evaluation show that the portfolios built with the best classified stocks according to the EU–EV risk model outperform the benchmark in the in-sample period. Among these portfolios, it is Q_5 that provides the worst performance indicators. These results are in accordance to the results obtained in the mean–variance efficiency analysis, where the stocks of Q_1, Q_2, Q_3 and Q_4 led to approximately equal efficient portfolios than S and the stocks of Q_5 led to less effcicient portfolios. On the contrary, the portfolios containing the worst and less well classified stocks underperform the benchmark in the same period, where the worst results were obtained with Q_6, containing the lowest ranked stocks according to the EU–EV risk model.

Considering the out-of-sample period, the results of the performance indicators also confirm that the portfolios Q_i, $i = 1, \ldots, 5$, can beat the benchmark, especially in the one-year time horizon. In the two-year time horizon, two of the five portfolios performed less well than the benchmark considering the Sharpe and Sortino ratios. The Alpha values are very close to zero, however, positive and indicating therefore that the portfolios outperform the benchmark. Surprisingly, the portfolios Q_6, Q_7, Q_8 reach higher cumulative returns, better Sharpe ratios and Sortino ratios (except Q_6, which attains a lower Sortino ratio) and better Alpha values than S in the one-year period. However, in the two-year period these portfolios present again a lower performance than the benchmark, except the cumulative returns, that only in the second half of 2022 decay below the benchmark returns, and the positive Alpha of Q_6, this being however approximately equal to zero.

Based on the obtained results, one can conclude that the selection of stocks with the EU–EV risk model provides portfolios (with half the number of stocks than the benchmark) that are not only efficient in terms of the mean–variance model when compared with the benchmark, but can lead also in a short term horizon to higher cumulative returns and perform better than the benchmark with respect to the measures Sharpe and Sortino ratios and Alpha. The Beta values indicate that the portfolios are less volatile than the benchmark. The positive performance of the portfolios can be explained due to the fact that the EU–EV risk model ranks stocks taking into account the expected utility, the variance and the entropy of the stock returns and these factors play an important role in the evolution, at least in the short term, of the cumulative returns and in the determination of performance factors, such as e.g. the Sharpe ratio, Sortino ratio or Alpha.

4   Conclusions

In this work we have analysed the performance of portfolios, formed with equally weighted stocks that were previously selected with the expected utility, entropy and variance (EU–EV) risk model. The portfolios were constructed using data of the PSI 20 index, from January 2019 to December 2020, and were formed with half the number of stocks than the index portfolio. In order to evaluate the performance, indicators and metrics of the portfolios were compared with those of the benchmark portfolio. Cumulative returns, Sharpe ratios, Sortino ratios, Beta and Alpha values were calculated for the in-sample period and for two out-of-sample periods: a one-year period ranging from January 2021 to December 2021 and a two-year period ranging from January 2021 to December 2022.

In the in-sample period, the portfolios formed with the best ranked stocks outperform the benchmark, as expected, in all the considered performance evaluation indicators, where the Beta values indicate that the portfolios are less volatile than the benchmark. In contrast, examples of other three portfolios, one of them constructed with the worst ranked stocks by the EU–EV risk, underperform the benchmark in the in-sample period. In the one-year out-of-sample period, the results show again that all favourite portfolios outperform the benchmark. In the two-year out-of-sample period, in general, the portfolios again perform better than the benchmark. Only two portfolios have slightly lower Sharpe and Sortino ratios than the benchmark and the cumulative returns of these two portfolios are exceeded by those of the benchmark in a time interval contained in the last quarter of 2022.

The results indicate that for short-term investments the strategy of constructing portfolios using the EU–EV risk model can be profitable. The EU–EV risk measure captures the relevant characteristics of stocks, such as expected utility, variance and entropy of stock returns, that have influence on the evolution of the cumulative returns and on the other considered performance indicators.

In the future, we will perform this analysis considering different in-sample periods and a wider time horizon for the out-of-sample period. We will also investigate the performance of portfolios, constructed with selected stocks using the EU–EV risk model, for markets containing more stocks. The applicability of the model to other investments/funds will also be analysed.

Acknowledgements. IB thanks support from FCT ("Fundação para a Ciência e a Tecnologia") through the Projects UIDB/00013/2020 and UIDP/00013/2020.

GJM acknowledges the financial support from FCT through the Project UIDB/04650/2020.

References

1. Bermejo, R., Figuerola-Ferretti, I., Hevia, T., Santos, A.: Factor investing: a stock selection methodology for the European equity market. Heliyon **7**(10), e08168 (2021). https://doi.org/10.1016/j.heliyon.2021.e08168
2. Brito, I.: A portfolio stock selection model based on expected utility, entropy and variance. Expert Syst. Appl. **213**, Part A, 118896 (2023). https://doi.org/10.1016/j.eswa.2022.118896
3. Brito, I.: A decision model based on expected utility, entropy and variance. Appl. Math. Comput. **379**, Article 125285 (2020). https://doi.org/10.1016/j.amc.2020.125285
4. Brito, I.: The normalized expected utility - entropy and variance model for decisions under risk. Int. J. Approx. Reason. **148**, 174–201 (2022). https://doi.org/10.1016/j.ijar.2022.06.005
5. Chen, W., Zhang, H., Mehlawat, M.K., Jia, L.: mean-variance portfolio optimization using machine learning-based stock price prediction. Appl. Soft Comput. **100**, Article 106943 (2021). https://doi.org/10.1016/j.asoc.2020.106943
6. DeMiguel, V., Garlappi, L., Uppal, R.: Optimal versus naive diversification: how inefficient is the 1/N portfolio strategy? Rev. Financ. Stud. **22**(5), 1915–1953 (2009). https://doi.org/10.1093/rfs/hhm075
7. Huang, C.F.: A hybrid stock selection model using genetic algorithms and support vector regression. Appl. Soft Comput. **12**, 807–818 (2012). https://doi.org/10.1016/j.asoc.2011.10.009
8. Li, B., Zhang, R.: A new mean-variance-entropy model for uncertain portfolio optimization with liquidity and diversification. Chaos Solitons Fractals **146**, 110842 (2021). https://doi.org/10.1016/j.chaos.2021.110842
9. Malladi, R., Fabozzi, F.J.: Equal-weighted strategy: why it outperforms value-weighted strategies? Theory and evidence. J. Asset Manag. **18**, 188–208 (2017). https://doi.org/10.1057/s41260-016-0033-4

10. Marhfor, A.: Portfolio performance measurement: review of literature and avenues of future research. Am. J. Ind. Bus. Manag. **6**, 432–438 (2016). https://doi.org/10.4236/ajibm.2016.64039
11. Markowitz, H.: Mean-Variance Analysis in Portfolio Choice and Capital Markets. Wiley, Hoboken (2000)
12. Paiva, F.P., Cardoso, R.T.M., Hanaoka, G.P., Duarte, W.M.: Decision-making for financial trading: a fusion approach of machine learning and portfolio selection. Expert Syst. Appl. **115**, 635–655 (2019) https://doi.org/10.1016/j.eswa.2018.08.003
13. Samarakoon, L.P., Hasan, T.: Portfolio Performance Evaluation. In: Lee, CF., Lee, A.C. (eds.) Encyclopedia of Finance. Springer, Boston, MA (2006). https://doi.org/10.1007/978-0-387-26336-6_60
14. Qin, Z., Li, X., Ji, X.: Portfolio selection based on fuzzy cross-entropy. J. Comput. Appl. Math. **228**, 188–196 (2009). https://doi.org/10.1016/j.cam.2008.09.010
15. Xidonas, P., Essner, E.: On ESG portfolio construction: a multi-objective optimization approach. Comput. Econ. (2022).https://doi.org/10.1007/s10614-022-10327-6
16. Yang, J., Feng, Y. Qiu, W.: Stock selection for portfolios using expected utility-entropy decision model. Entropy **19**, Article 508 (2017). https://doi.org/10.3390/e19100508

Computational Procedures for Improving Extreme Value Estimation in Time Series Modelling

Dora Prata Gomes[1]($\boxtimes$) (iD), Clara Cordeiro[2,4] (iD), and Manuela Neves[3,4] (iD)

[1] Center for Mathematics and Applications (NOVA Math) and Department of Mathematics, NOVA SST, Caparica, Portugal
`dsrp@fct.unl.pt`
[2] Faculdade de Ciências e Tecnologia, Universidade do Algarve, Faro, Portugal
`ccordei@ualg.pt`
[3] Instituto Superior de Agronomia, Universidade de Lisboa, Lisboa, Portugal
`manela@isa.ulisboa.pt`
[4] CEAUL - Centro de Estatística e Aplicações, Faculdade de Ciências, Universidade de Lisboa, Lisboa, Portugal

Abstract. In the last decades, some work has been developed in parameter estimation of extreme values jointly with time series analysis. Those results show relevant asymptotic properties. However, for finite samples, limiting results provide approximations that can be poor. Some challenges have been developed by combining Extreme Value Theory and time series modelling to obtain more reliable extreme value parameter estimates. In classical time series modelling a key issue is to determine how many parameters must be included in the model. Special care must be given to extreme events in the series that need specific statistical procedures based on the behaviour of extremes. Resampling procedures such as the jackknife and the bootstrap have been used to improve parameters estimation in Extreme Value Theory combined with time series modelling. New approaches, based on bootstrap procedures are shown and are illustrated with a real data set using the ⓡ software.

Keywords: Extreme value theory · Parameter estimation · Resampling procedures · Time series

1 Introduction and a Few Details on EVT

Extreme Value Theory (EVT) aims to study and to predict the occurrence of extreme or even rare events, outside of the range of available data. These events are part of the real world but environmental extreme or rare events may have

This work is funded by national funds through the FCT - Fundação para a Ciência e a Tecnologia, I.P., under the scope of the projects UIDB/00006/2020 (CEAUL), UIDB/00297/2020 and UIDP/00297/2020 (Center for Mathematics and Applications).

ⓒ The Author(s), under exclusive license to Springer Nature Switzerland AG 2023
O. Gervasi et al. (Eds.): ICCSA 2023 Workshops, LNCS 14105, pp. 84–96, 2023.
https://doi.org/10.1007/978-3-031-37108-0_6

a massive impact on everyday life and may have catastrophic consequences for human activities. Most environmental datasets have a time-dependent variation and short-term clustering are typical phenomena for extreme value data, and it is crucial that both are properly accounted for when making inferences.

Let us assume that we have a sample $(X_1, \ldots, X_n)$ of independent and identically distributed (iid) or possibly stationary, weakly dependent random variables (r.v.'s) from an unknown cumulative distribution function (cdf) F. The interest is focused on the distribution of the maxima, $M_n := \max(X_1, \ldots, X_n)$, for which we have

$$P(M_n \leq x) = P(X_1 \leq x) \ldots P(X_n \leq x) = F^n(x). \tag{1}$$

As n goes to ∞, the distribution F^n in (1) has a trivial limit: 0, if $F(x) < 1$ and 1, if $F(x) = 1$. So the idea for M_n was the same of *central limit theorem*: first, subtract a n-dependent constant, then rescale by a n-dependent factor. Assuming that there exist two sequences of real constants, $\{a_n\} \in R^+$ and $\{b_n\} \in R$ such that the maximum, linearly normalized, has a non-degenerate limiting distribution function, G,

$$\lim_{n\to\infty} P((M_n - b_n)/a_n \leq x) = G(x).$$

First results on the G distribution are due to [9,10,13,24]. But were [11] and [14] who gave conditions for the existence of those sequences $\{a_n\} \in R^+$ and $\{b_n\} \in R$ such that, when $n \to \infty$ and $\forall x \in R$,

$$\lim_{n\to\infty} P\left(\frac{M_n - b_n}{a_n} \leq x\right) = \lim_{n\to\infty} F^n(a_n x + b_n) = \mathrm{EV}_\xi(\mathrm{x}), \tag{2}$$

where EV_ξ is a nondegenerate distribution function, denoted as the Extreme Value cdf, and given by

$$\mathrm{EV}_\xi(\mathrm{x}) = \begin{cases} \exp[-(1 + \xi x)^{-1/\xi}], & 1 + \xi x > 0 \text{ if } \xi \neq 0 \\ \exp[-\exp(-x)], & x \in R \qquad \text{ if } \xi = 0. \end{cases} \tag{3}$$

When the above limit holds we say that F is in the domain of attraction (for maxima) of EV_ξ and write $F \in \mathcal{D}_\mathcal{M}(\mathrm{EV}_\xi)$.

The cdf in (3) can also incorporate location (λ) and scale ($\delta > 0$) parameters, and in this case, the EV_ξ cdf is given by,

$$\mathrm{EV}_\xi(x; \lambda, \delta) \equiv \mathrm{EV}_\xi((x - \lambda)/\delta). \tag{4}$$

2   Some Parameters of Interest in EVT

There is a large variety of parameters of extreme events, but the estimation of the *extreme value index* (EVI), the parameter denoted by ξ, in (3), is of primordial importance by itself and because it is the basis for the estimation of all other parameters of extreme events.

Among the most relevant parameters of extreme events, and assuming that we are interested in large values, i.e. in the right tail of the underlying model F, we can mention a few parameters such as the *probability of exceedance*, the *return period* of a high level and the *right endpoint* of the underlying model F. In this paper, we consider the problem of estimating the *high quantile* of probability $1 - p$ (p small), χ_{1-p}, defined by

$$\chi_{1-p} := \inf\{x : F(x) \geq 1 - p\},$$

$$\chi_{1-p} := \lambda - \frac{\delta}{\xi} \left[1 - \{-\log(1-p)\}^{-\xi}\right], \quad \xi \neq 0.$$

Whenever independence is no longer valid, some important dependent sequences have been studied and the limit distributions of their order statistics under some dependence structures are known. Stationary sequences are examples of such sequences and are realistic for many real problems.

Suppose we have n observations from a stationary process $\{Y_n\}_{n \geq 1}$ with marginal distribution function F. For large n and a high level u_n, we have

$$F_n(u_n) = P\left(\max(Y_1, ..., Y_n) \leq u_n\right) \approx F^{n\theta}(u_n),$$

where $\theta \in [0, 1]$ is a constant for the process and is known as the *extremal index*. This concept, even appearing in papers from [23,25,26], was only well characterized by [21]. It is still appropriate to model the distribution of the maximum, $\max(Y_1, ..., Y_n)$, using EV_ξ cdf, in (3), but location and scale parameters are different from those that would have been obtained in the independent setup. In this article, the parameter θ will not be considered.

EVT has been developed under two frameworks. The first one is the parametric framework that considers a class of models associated with the limiting behaviour of the maxima, given in (2). The main assumption behind the parametric approach is that estimators are calculated considering the data following approximately an exact EV probability distribution function defined by a number of parameters.

The other framework, the semi-parametric one, the only assumption made is that the limit in (2) holds, i.e., that the underlying distribution verifies the extreme value condition. In this framework, we do not need to fit a specific parametric model based on scale, shape and location parameters. Estimates are now usually based on the largest k order statistics in the sample, assuming only that the model F underlying the data is in $\mathcal{D}_\mathcal{M}(EV_\xi)$.

The parameter ξ is estimated, on the basis of the k top statistics, with k intermediate, i.e. such that $k = k_n \to \infty$ and $k/n \to 0$, as $n \to \infty$. However, most estimators show a strong dependence on that value k. They usually present a small bias and a high variance for small values of k; bias increases and variance decreases when k increases. To overcome this difficulty, Jackknife and Bootstrap procedures are known as giving more stable estimates around the target value.

2.1   Some Semi-parametric Estimators of ξ

Suppose we have a sample $(X_1, X_2, \ldots, X_n)$ of iid random variables with a heavy regularly varying right tail.

Let $X_{1:n} \leq X_{2:n} \leq \ldots \leq X_{n:n}$ denote the associated non-decreasing order statistics from the sample of size n. The most popular semi-parametric EVI-estimator is the Hill estimator, H, [16]. This estimator can be defined as the average of the log-excesses, $V_{ik} := \ln X_{n-i+1:n} - \ln X_{n-k:n}$, $1 \leq i \leq k < n$, above the high threshold $X_{n-k:n} > 0$,

$$\widehat{\xi}_n^H(k) \equiv H(k) := \frac{1}{k} \sum_{i=1}^{k} V_{ik}, \quad 1 \leq k < n. \tag{5}$$

There are several alternatives to the Hill estimator that are less sensitive to the choice of the level k. We shall consider the simplest class of reduced-bias EVI-estimators, the Corrected Hill (CH) estimator, [2], defined by

$$\hat{\xi}_n^{CH}(k) \equiv \hat{\xi}_{\hat{\beta},\hat{\rho}}^{CH}(k) \equiv \mathrm{CH}(k) := \mathrm{H}(k)\left(1 - \frac{\hat{\beta}(n/k)^{\hat{\rho}}}{1 - \hat{\rho}}\right), \quad 1 \leq k < n, \tag{6}$$

with $(\hat{\beta}, \hat{\rho})$ an adequate estimator of the vector of second-order parameters (β, ρ). For the estimation of this vector of parameters, see [1,12].

2.2   A Semi-parametric Estimator of Extreme Quantiles

Let us consider again the sample $(X_1, X_2, \ldots, X_n)$ of iid random variables with a regularly varying right tail. For these heavy tailed models and for small values of p, we want to extrapolate beyond the sample, estimating not only the EVI, ξ, but also an extreme quantile χ_{1-p}, i.e., a value such that $F(\chi_{1-p}) = 1 - p$, or equivalently,

$$\chi_{1-p} := F^{\leftarrow}(1 - p) = U(1/p), \quad p = p_n \to 0, \quad \text{as } n \to \infty,$$

with the notation $F^{\leftarrow}(y) := \inf\{x : F(x) \geq y\}$ for the generalized inverse function of F and $U(t) := F^{\leftarrow}(1 - 1/t)$, $t \geq 1$, for the reciprocal quantile function. The classical semi-parametric extreme quantile estimator for heavy right-tails was proposed by [32] as

$$Q_{p,\hat{\xi}_n^{\bullet}}(k) = X_{n-k:n}\, r_n^{\hat{\xi}_n^{\bullet}(k)}, \quad 1 \leq k < n, \quad r_n \equiv r_n(k;p) = \frac{k}{np}, \tag{7}$$

where $X_{n-k:n}$ is the $(k+1)$-th upper order statistic and $\hat{\xi}_n^{\bullet}$ can be any consistent estimator of the EVI, ξ.

3   Some Notes on Time Series Analysis

Time series analysis significantly impacts various scientific, economic, and social applications and arises in numerous contexts. A time series is a sequence of observations indexed by time, denoted as $\{X_1, \cdots, X_T\}$, and are typically ordered at evenly spaced intervals with a correlation between the observations.

One of the important aspects of time series analysis is the selection of a model that could have generated them. In order to have a deep analysis of these time series, a statistical model should be considered to capture the stochastic movement of the time series. AutoRegressive Integrated Moving Average (ARIMA) and Exponential Smoothing are commonly used time series models. ARIMA models use past observations of the dependent variable to forecast its values based on a linear regression model. In contrast, Exponential Smoothing methods are more versatile approaches that continually update forecasts, emphasizing the most recent experience. This means recent observations are given more weight than older observations [18]. Exponential Smoothing models consider trend and seasonality patterns in the data, while ARIMA models aim to explain the autocorrelations in the data [18].

4   The Role of Bootstrap Methodology

Computer-intensive methods, which emerged when computers became more powerful, have been developed in the last decades. The most well-known are perhaps the Jackknife [27, 28, 31], and the Bootstrap [7, 19] methodologies. Recently, these two methodologies have been used with success in EVT, revealing themselves as being promising in parameter estimation.

In their classical form, as first proposed by [7], nonparametric bootstrap methods are designed for being used in samples collected under an independent setup. The bootstrap method involves iteratively resampling a dataset with replacement. The nonparametric bootstrap method works without assuming the nature of the distribution underlying the sample. From the original sample, a new sample is resampled with replacement and on the basis of the estimator of interest, an estimate is calculated. This procedure is repeated a large number of times, let us say B times, and the average of the estimates calculated is referred to as "the bootstrap estimate".

In the context of dependent data, the situation is more complicated since the population is not characterized entirely by the one-dimensional marginal distribution F alone, but requires the knowledge of the joint distribution of the whole sequence $X_1, ..., X_T$. Singh [29] presented an example of the inadequacy of the classical bootstrap under dependence. Several attempts have been made to extend the bootstrap method to the dependent case. A breakthrough was achieved when resampling of single observations was replaced by block resampling, an idea that was put forward by [3, 15, 20, 22], and others in various forms and in different inference problems. Several ways of blocking appeared.

Another idea to overcome that issue consists in performing the bootstrap methodology on the residuals after fitting an adequate model, see [4, 5].

In this article the parametric bootstrap approach is proposed. This approach was studied by Efron [8], among other authors. An adequate model is fitted to the data and the model parameters are estimated. When it can be applied, this type of bootstrap method can give better results since it considers the nature of the distribution underlying the data instead of being used the empirical distribution function as is done in the nonparametric bootstrap.

The parametric bootstrap will be applied to the residuals of the time series obtained after an adequate modelling procedure. See the detailed description below.

Step 1: Fit a model to the time series using AIC criterion;
Step 2: Select the best model using accuracy measures;
Step 3: Fit a GEV distribution to the residuals of the best model, $e_1, e_2, \cdots e_T$;
Step 4: For each b $\in B$ a large number
    a) Generate a $e_1^b, e_2^b, \cdots e_T^b$ from the distribution estimated in Step 3;
    b) Combine $e_1^b, e_2^b, \cdots e_T^b$ with the fitted values (from Step 2). A reconstructed sample path of the original time series is obtained;
    c) Repeat Step 4;
Step 5: Obtain the mean of the B values simulated.

This algorithm is an adapted version of a first one developed for forecasting in time series and fully described in [4] and successfully applied in [5]. Here a GEV distribution is fitted to the residuals, and the parametric bootstrap is performed. Computational time depends on the sample size, for moderately sized samples it takes a few minutes. Several accuracy measures were considered in previous applications, such as the *Mean Absolute Error* (MAE), the *Root Mean Squared Error* (RMSE), the *Mean Absolute Percentage Error* (MAPE). They have been also used here.

A very preliminary version of the approach here described joining EVT and time series in order to improve the estimation of extreme quantities of interest was submitted for publication in the Proceedings of the 9th International Conference on Risk Analysis (ICRA9) [6].

The following packages in **ℝ** software are used: `forecast` [17], `ets()`-EXPOS methods and `auto.arima()`-ARIMA models; and the function `fgev()` - Extreme value distributions, from package evd [30].

5   Estimation of Extreme Quantiles for Real-Data Sets

The high quantiles estimation of heavy tailed has many important applications. Studying and modelling river flow discharge rates is required for river management, including water resources planning, pollution prevention, and flood control. This study considers the daily mean flow discharge rate values (m^3/s) of two Portuguese rivers, Tejo and Guadiana. The time horizon for Tejo and Guadiana are January 1974 until June 2022 and from January 2002 until June

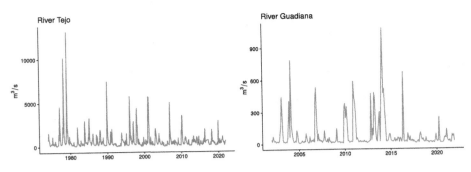

Fig. 1. Monthly maximum flow discharge for river Tejo and river Guadiana.

2022, respectively[1]. As we are interested in studying the maximum values of the series, the maximum of each month is taken (see Fig. 1).

As seen in Fig. 2 and Table 1, the descriptive study of these data revealed a tail heavier than that of the normal.

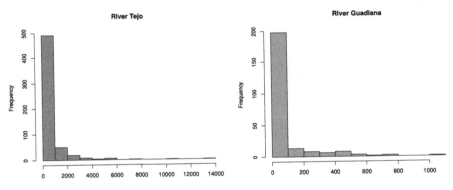

Fig. 2. The histograms for data: Tejo and Guadiana.

For quantiles estimation, it is crucial the estimation of EVI parameter. Fig. 3 shows the sample paths of the EVI estimates obtained when using the aforementioned semiparametric estimators (Sect. 2.1) over the original data.

Considering the time series of monthly maximum values (see Fig. 1) the ARIMA and the Exponential Smoothing models were fitted, and some accuracy measures are obtained and presented in Table 2. According to this table, Exponential Smoothing is the best model because it has the lowest values of the accuracy measures. In fact for the Tejo river, MAE is a little smaller in the `auto.arima` model, but the RMSE and MAPE measures reveal a better performance of the `ets` model, so we continued the work with `ets` The EV distribution is fitted to the residuals of the best model. The graphical representation of these

---

[1] Download at "http://snirh.apambiente.pt".

Table 1. Descriptive statistics measures for both rivers.

River	n	min	max	skewness	kurtosis
Tejo	576	0.99	13102.55	5.7495	47.373
Guadiana	240	3.35	1080.1	3.2483	12.38033

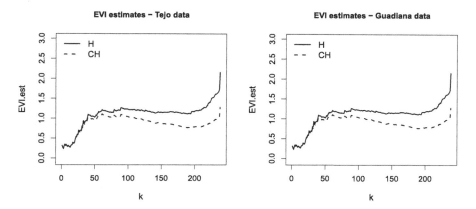

Fig. 3. Sample paths of the EVI-estimates considered.

residuals in Fig. 4 and the positive values for the skewness as well as the high kurtosis, given in Table 3, suggest a right heavy tail.

Table 2. Results of the accuracy measures.

	Tejo			Guadiana		
R function	RMSE	MAE	MAPE	RMSE	MAE	MAPE
ets	869.76	432.96	98.93	115.34	63.68	145.80
auto.arima	922.19	426.81	195.99	123.58	67.28	176.53

Using EV parameters estimates, the parametric bootstrap was performed and the reconstructed time series was obtained. This procedure was repeated $B = 1,000$ times, and mean values for each month were calculated. In Fig. 5 are represented three simulated time series and the mean of all simulated time series, whereas in Fig. 6 are represented the original and the reconstructed time series.

For both rivers can be seen that the reconstructed time series captures the extreme values of the original time series, see Fig. 6.

The quantile estimates are calculated when considering the original time series and the reconstructed time series. For both shape parameter estimators,

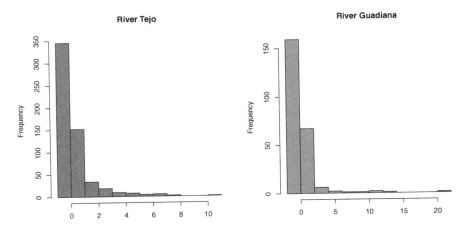

Fig. 4. The histograms for residuals.

Table 3. Descriptive statistics measures for residuals.

River	n	min	max	skewness	kurtosis
Tejo	576	−0.9695	10.4015	3.194409	13.04744
Guadiana	240	−0.9422	21.1081	5.802513	41.72199

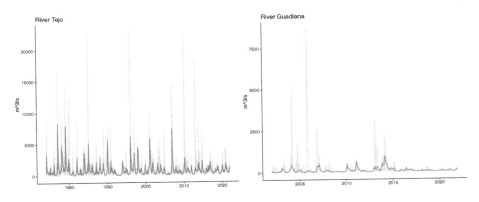

Fig. 5. Simulated time series (gray) and the mean of all.

the sample path of the quantile estimates reveals an underestimation relatively to the sample path obtained over the reconstructed time series, as seen in Fig. 7 and Fig. 8.

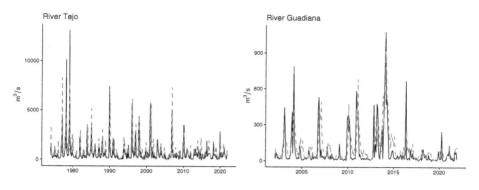

Fig. 6. Time series and the time series reconstructed (dashed).

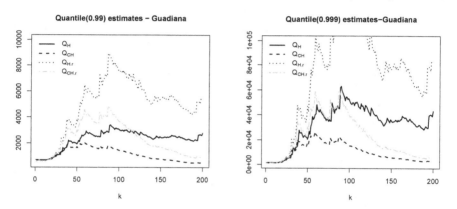

Fig. 7. Sample path of the quantile estimates based on the original time series and on the reconstructed associated for river Guadiana. These are denoted with subscript ".r".

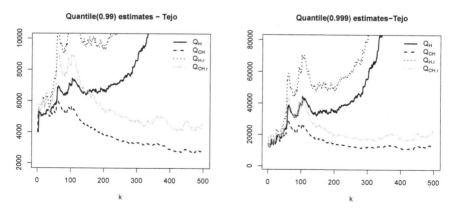

Fig. 8. Sample path of the quantile estimates based on the original time series and on the reconstructed associated for river Tejo. These are denoted with subscript ".r".

6   Concluding Remarks

Several attempts have been made in recent literature to improve the quality of extreme quantile estimators. Estimation of very extreme quantiles is complicated by the lack of observed values. The accuracy of the estimates depends on the estimation of key parameters in EVT, as well as the quantile estimators themselves. Research into both types of estimators is ongoing.

Modeling and forecasting in time series analysis, together with EVT methods, have proven to be valuable procedures for estimating extreme values when capturing time series features. Resampling methods have recently been applied in EVT, but they require special procedures because the resampling of a given sample does not allow obtaining values greater than the observed maximum.

Some procedures to overcome that difficulty were proposed and in this work, we present another one performing the parametric bootstrap on the residuals.

The method is illustrated considering two time series, but other time series were studied, verifying a good performance of the approach presented here.

In future work, an extensive application will be carried out, involving various sets of time series of similar features to those here considered (note that we intend to capture the highest values of a time series, as these may be responsible for catastrophic situations).

Acknowledgments. The authors thank the three referees for their constructive comments and valuable suggestions, which led to substantial improvements to this work. Clara Cordeiro and Manuela Neves are partially financed by national funds through FCT - Fundação para a Ciência e a Tecnologia under the project UIDB/00006/2020 (CEAUL). This work is funded by national funds through the FCT - Fundação para a Ciência e a Tecnologia, I.P., under the scope of the projects UIDB/00297/2020 and UIDP/00297/2020 (Center for Mathematics and Applications).

References

1. Fraga Alves, M.I., Gomes, M.I., de Haan, L.: A new class of semi-parametric estimators of the second order parameter. Portugaliae Math. **60**(2), 193–214 (2003)
2. Caeiro, F., Gomes, M.I., Pestana, D.: Direct reduction of bias of the classical hill estimator. REVSTAT-Stat. J. **3**(2), 113–136 (2005)
3. Carlstein, E.: The use of subseries values for estimating the variance of a general statistic from a stationary sequence. Ann. Stat. **14**(3), 1171–1179 (1986). https://doi.org/10.1214/aos/1176350057
4. Cordeiro, C., Neves, M.M.: Forecasting time series with boot.expos procedure. REVSTAT-Stat. J. **7**(2), 135–149 (2009)
5. Cordeiro, C., Neves, M.M.: Boot.EXPOS in NNGC competition. In: The 2010 International Joint Conference on Neural Networks (IJCNN), pp. 1–7. IEEE (2010). https://doi.org/10.1109/ijcnn.2010.5596361
6. Cordeiro, C., Prata Gomes, D., Neves, M.M.: Time series procedures to improve extreme quantile estimation. In: Statistical Modelling and Risk Analysis: Selected contributions from ICRA9, Springer Proceedings in Mathematics & Statistics, submitted. Springer (2023)

7. Efron, B.: Bootstrap methods: another look at the jackknife. Ann. Stat. **7**(1) (1979). https://doi.org/10.1214/aos/1176344552
8. Efron, B.: Estimation and accuracy after model selection. J. Am. Stat. Assoc. **109**(507), 991–1007 (2014). https://doi.org/10.1080/01621459.2013.823775
9. Fisher, R.A., Tippett, L.H.C.: Limiting forms of the frequency distribution of the largest or smallest member of a sample. Math. Proc. Cambr. Philos. Soc. **24**(2), 180–190 (1928). https://doi.org/10.1017/s0305004100015681
10. Fréchet, M.: Sur la loi de probabilité de l'écart maximum. Ann. Soc. Math. Polon. **6**, 93–116 (1927)
11. Gnedenko, B.: Sur la distribution limite du terme maximum d'une serie aleatoire. Ann. Math. **44**(3), 423–453 (1943). https://doi.org/10.2307/1968974
12. Gomes, M.I., Martins, M.J.: "asymptotically unbiased" estimators of the tail index based on external estimation of the second order parameter. Extremes **5**(1), 5–31 (2002). https://doi.org/10.1023/a:1020925908039
13. Gumbel, E.: Les valeurs extrêmes des distributions statistiques. Ann.de l'institut Henri Poincaré **5**(2), 115–158 (1935)
14. Haan, L.: Regular variation and its application to the weak convergence of sample extremes. Math. Centre Tracts **32** (1970)
15. Hall, P.: Resampling a coverage pattern. Stoch. Process. Appl. **20**(2), 231–246 (1985). https://doi.org/10.1016/0304-4149(85)90212-1
16. Hill, B.M.: A simple general approach to inference about the tail of a distribution. Ann. Stat. **3**(5) (1975). https://doi.org/10.1214/aos/1176343247
17. Hyndman, R., et al.: forecast: Forecasting functions for time series and linear models (2023). https://pkg.robjhyndman.com/forecast/, R package version 8.21
18. Hyndman, R., Athanasopoulos, G.: Forecasting: Principles and Practice, 2nd edn. OTexts, Australia (2018)
19. Krause, J.: Introduction to Bootstrap. Apress (2016). https://doi.org/10.1007/978-1-4842-2382-6-2
20. Kunsch, H.R.: The jackknife and the bootstrap for general stationary observations. Ann. Stat. **17**(3) (1989). https://doi.org/10.1214/aos/1176347265
21. Leadbetter, M.R.: Extremes and local dependence in stationary sequences. Tech. rep. (1982). https://doi.org/10.21236/ada120180
22. Liu, R.Y.: Moving blocks jackknife and bootstrap capture weak dependence. Explor. Limits Bootstrap (1992)
23. Loynes, R.M.: Extreme values in uniformly mixing stationary stochastic processes. Ann. Math. Stat. **36**(3), 993–999 (1965). https://doi.org/10.1214/aoms/1177700071
24. Mises, R.V.: La distribution de la plus grande de n valeurs. Rev. Math. Union Interbalcanique **1**, 141–160 (1936)
25. Newell, G.F.: Asymptotic extremes for m-dependent random variables. Ann. Math. Stat. **35**(3), 1322–1325 (1964). https://doi.org/10.1214/aoms/1177703288
26. O'Brien, G.L.: The maximum term of uniformly mixing stationary processes. Adv. Appl. Prob. **7**(2), 248–248 (1975). https://doi.org/10.1017/s0001867800045729
27. Quenouille, M.H.: Approximate tests of correlation in time-series. J. R. Stat. Soc. Series B (Methodol.) **11**(1), 68–84 (1949). https://doi.org/10.1111/j.2517-6161.1949.tb00023.x
28. Quenouille, M.H.: Notes on bias in estimation. Biometrika **43**(3/4), 353 (1956). https://doi.org/10.2307/2332914
29. Singh, K.: On the asymptotic accuracy of Efron's bootstrap. Ann. Stat. **9**(6), 1187–1195 (1981). https://doi.org/10.1214/aos/1176345636

30. Stephenson, A.G.: EVD: extreme value distributions. R News **2**(2) (2002). https:// CRAN.R-project.org/doc/Rnews/
31. Tukey, J.: Bias and confidence in not quite large samples. Ann. Math. Statist. **29**, 614 (1958)
32. Weissman, I.: Estimation of parameters and large quantiles based on the k largest observations. J. Am. Stat. Assoc. **73**(364), 812–815 (1978). https://doi.org/10. 1080/01621459.1978.10480104

Sleep Disorders in Portugal Based on Questionnaires

Ana Rita Antunes[1,2,3](✉) , Ana Cristina Braga[1] , Marta Gonçalves[4],
and Joaquim Gonçalves[2,3]

[1] ALGORITMI Research Centre, LASI, University of Minho, Campus de Gualtar,
4710-057 Braga, Portugal
id9069@alunos.uminho.pt, acb@dps.uminho.pt
[2] 2Ai – School of Technology, IPCA, 4750-810 Barcelos, Portugal
jgoncalves@ipca.pt
[3] LASI – Associate Laboratory of Intelligent Systems, Guimarães, Portugal
[4] Sleep Medicine Center, Cuf Porto Hospital, Porto, Portugal

Abstract. Sleep disorders are a public safety concern that can influence
the individual's quality of life by reducing cognitive functions, decreasing
alertness, causing mood disturbances and exhaustion, and affecting memory. The evaluation of daytime sleepiness, the risk of developing sleep
apnea, sleep quality, and the respective circadian rhythm are important
aspects to consider. This research aimed to evaluate sleep disorders, in
the Portuguese population, districts, since it is still a gap in the literature. 2087 complete answers were collected, with most of the participants
being female, and their ages ranging from 18 to 78 years old. In terms of
sleep disorders, 21.37% of the participants have a high risk of developing
obstructive sleep apnea, 39.29% have excessive daytime sleepiness, and
61.38% have bad sleep quality. For the circadian rhythm, 57.74% of them
are morning type, 36.85% are evening type, and the remaining 5.41% are
intermediate type. In this research, it was proved that few elements of
the Portuguese population are aware of their sleep quality, and most of
the people with excessive daytime sleepiness have bad sleep quality. In
addition, it was also demonstrated that the work schedule is adjusted to
the circadian rhythm, and the risk of sleep apnea in participants with
excessive daytime sleepiness is about 1.8 times higher than in the ones
with normal daytime sleepiness. This study is innovative since it integrates four questionnaires on sleep disorders, considers a representative
sample from the Portuguese population, and has the largest number of
participants when compared with the studies available.

Keywords: sleep disorders · Pittsburgh · morningness-eveningness ·
Epworth · STOP-Bang · Portugal · questionnaire

This work has been supported by FCT – Fundação para a Ciência e Tecnologia within
the R&D Units Project Scope: UIDB/00319/2020.

© The Author(s), under exclusive license to Springer Nature Switzerland AG 2023
O. Gervasi et al. (Eds.): ICCSA 2023 Workshops, LNCS 14105, pp. 97–113, 2023.
https://doi.org/10.1007/978-3-031-37108-0_7

1   Introduction

Sleep disorders damage one's health, mood, and quality of life, which also affects sleep duration, the incidence of cardiovascular disease, diabetes, and respiratory problems [1,2]. Different epidemiological surveys [3,4] proved that a patient with the following diseases has disturbed sleep: allergic rhinitis, sleep apnea, asthma, or obstructive pulmonary disease. Furthermore, it was also found in [5] a positive association between insomnia and diabetes, obesity, hypertension, congestive heart failure, anxiety, or depression. This means that it is critical to understand how mental and physical health can influence sleep duration and quality [3]. According to [6], sleep is a critical indicator of our health and should be regarded as an essential component of a healthy lifestyle. Furthermore, it has been demonstrated that sleep disorders worsen with age [7]. Poor sleep quality has an impact on individual performance since it affects working memory, processing speed, and cognitive throughput. It is regarded as a major public safety concern since it can increase work accidents, and sometimes people are not aware of their sleep problems [7,8].

Several studies were carried out to determine the prevalence of sleep disorders in the Portuguese population. Some of them intended to understand the impact of sleepiness while driving and the respective consequences [9,10]. There are also studies to analyze the general sleep quality of the Portuguese population [11,12]. In 2014 [9] a study assessed excessive daytime sleepiness and sleep apnea risk among Portuguese truck drivers. Participant recruitment was achieved via e-mail sent to commercial truck companies operating from the north and center of Portugal. From a total of 714 drivers, 20% of them had excessive daytime sleepiness, and 29% had a risk of developing obstructive sleep apnea. A different approach was developed in [10], in which the sample size selection (900 drivers) was chosen using stratified sampling while taking into account the number of driver's licenses in Portugal. The phone numbers of the participants were chosen at random, and they had to be regular drivers, that is, they had to drive vehicles at least once a week. According to the results achieved, 35.30% of the drivers had bad sleep quality, 9.11% had excessive daytime sleepiness, and 10% had a risk of developing sleep apnea. In 2018 [11] the sleep quality of 1119 Portuguese adults was assessed, without identifying how the sample size was achieved. Some participants (28.2%) reported sleep disorders, and 54.8% had poor sleep quality. According to the sleep difficulties index, the majority of the participants have some sleep problems, which are likely to increase with age. Moreover, 62.9% of adults sleep between 6 and 8 h during the week, whereas 44% only need 1 to 15 min to fall asleep. As early as 2020 [12], new information was added about the previous study. Thus, 51.4% of adults reported difficulty falling asleep, 80.5% woke up during the night, and 75.3% awoke spontaneously.

Therefore, there is still a gap, in the literature, on sleep disorders in the Portuguese population, using a representative sample that considers the various districts of Portugal, taking into account the territorial distribution of NUTS II in Portugal. This comprises seven divisions, or regions, five of which are located on the mainland and the remaining two being the autonomous regions of the

Azores and Madeira's territories. For that reason, this research aims to evaluate different sleep disorders, in the adult Portuguese population, using a representative sample. Hence, it is intended to evaluate sleep quality, daytime sleepiness, the risk of obstructive sleep apnea, and circadian rhythm. With this study, it is expected to answer the following questions:

1. The Portuguese population is aware of their sleep quality?
2. Is it true that people with excessive daytime sleepiness have bad sleep quality?
3. The circadian rhythm is adjusted with the work schedule? If not, does it influence their sleep quality and daytime sleepiness?
4. Is it true that people with a risk of developing sleep apnea also have excessive daytime sleepiness?

This article is structured as follows. Section 2 presents a literature review, where the available questionnaires are presented to evaluate daytime sleepiness, developing obstructive sleep apnea, sleep quality, and circadian rhythm. The questionnaire's format, the duration of its availability, the software that was utilized, and the methodology used to determine the representative sample are all described in Sect. 3. The statistical analysis is described in Sect. 4, and the discussion of the results is in Sect. 5. Finally, the main conclusions are reported in Sect. 6.

2   Literature Review

This section will introduce daytime sleepiness, the risk of developing obstructive sleep apnea, sleep quality, and circadian rhythm. Firstly, a brief introduction of each theme will be brought in, and then an identification of different questionnaires available in the literature will be presented.

2.1   Daytime Sleepiness

Daytime sleepiness can affect individual health, which leads to serious consequences, like the risk of motor vehicle accidents and work-related incidents. This means that the individual's cognitive functions are reduced, by affecting their ability to gain or maintain employment. The main causes of daytime sleepiness are sleep deprivation, medication effects, illicit substance use, and obstructive sleep apnea [13].

Thus, the Epworth Sleepiness Scale (ESS) [14] is widely used to measure daytime sleepiness. There are eight questions based on different situations, where the subject has to rate on a scale of 0 to 3 how likely they are to fall asleep, considering their recent routine. So, the final score can be between 0 and 24. If the final score is greater than 10, the subject has excessive daytime sleepiness. The Portuguese version is available at [15].

Sleep-Wake Activity Inventory (SWAI) [16] also evaluates excessive daytime sleepiness, considering six components like excessive daytime sleepiness, distress, social desirability, energy level, ability to relax, and nighttime sleep. This questionnaire is composed of fifty-nine items that are answered on a Likert scale from 1 to 9 which means the behavior is always present, or it never occurs, respectively. The respondents must answer questions regarding their habits only during the last seven days, where lower scores indicate more daytime sleepiness. There is no validation for this questionnaire in Portuguese.

2.2   Developing Obstructive Sleep Apnea

Obstructive sleep apnea is considered a sleep disorder and is defined by episodes of partial or complete upper airway obstruction during sleep [17]. This disorder has several adverse effects, such as excessive daytime sleepiness (the main symptom), decreased alertness, and, in turn, greater difficulty concentrating, and mood disturbances [18].

Therefore, STOP-Bang questionnaire [19] is applied to identify the risk of developing obstructive sleep apnea. This one considers snoring, tiredness, observed apnea, high blood pressure, body mass index, age, neck circumference, and male gender. Thus, there are eight dichotomous questions, and the final score is between 0 and 8. Those with scores equal to or greater than 5 have a high risk of developing moderate to severe obstructive sleep apnea. The Portuguese validation version of the STOP-Bang can be found in [20].

Berlin Questionnaire [21] is another alternative to evaluate the risk of developing sleep apnea. It considers snoring behavior, wake-time sleepiness or fatigue, and the presence of obesity or hypertension. There is also information about the participant's age, weight, height, sex, neck circumference, and ethnicity. This questionnaire is divided into three sections: snoring and apnea (five questions), daytime sleepiness (four questions), and hypertension or obesity (one question). The identification of a high or low risk for developing sleep apnea is based on the responses in each category. If two or more categories have a positive score, then the participant has a high risk, otherwise, the participant is not at risk. The Berlin validation version in Portuguese can be seen in [22].

Quebec Sleep Questionnaire [23] is also used for obstructive sleep apnea, with 32 questions. This questionnaire is divided into five domains, hypersomnolence, diurnal symptoms, nocturnal symptoms, emotions, and social interactions. Each question is scored on a 1 to 7-point Likert scale. The final result is achieved by computing the mean score (1 to 7) within each domain and summing the results. Smaller scores represent a higher impact on the participant's life due to sleep apnea. The Portuguese validation of this questionnaire is available in [24].

2.3   Sleep Quality

Sleep quality is commonly used in the medical field, where it is needed to evaluate different sleep metrics such as total sleep time, sleep onset latency, fragmentation, total wake time, sleep efficiency, and sleep disruptive events [25]. Poor sleep quality can have an impact on an individual's mood, attention, memory, and exhaustion [26].

Mini Sleep Quality (MSQ) [27] evaluates both insomnia and excessive daytime sleepiness, considering 10 questions. It takes into consideration a seven-point Likert scale ranging from never (1) to always (7). In terms of final classification, it's possible to define the participants as having good sleep quality (total sum of scores between 10 and 24), mild sleep difficulties (25 to 27), moderate sleep qualities (28 to 30), and severe sleep difficulties (over 31). There is only a Brazilian Portuguese version of the MSQ questionnaire [28].

Pittsburgh Sleep Quality Index (PSQI) [29] is commonly used, to assess the previous month's sleep quality. This one has 19 questions that are divided into seven components: subjective sleep quality, sleep latency, sleep duration, habitual sleep efficiency, sleep disturbances, use of sleeping medications, and daytime dysfunction. Each component has a score of 0 to 3 and, the final score (0 to 21) is the sum of the scores of each component. The subjects with a final score over 5 have bad sleep quality. The PSQI questionnaire validation in Portuguese can be found in [30].

Sleep Quality Scale (SQS) [31] is another questionnaire to measure sleep quality, also about the previous month. In terms of structure, it is composed of 28 items that are divided into six factors: daytime dysfunction, restoration after sleep, difficulty falling asleep, difficulty getting up, satisfaction with sleep, and difficulty maintaining sleep. A four-point Likert scale was used, with scores ranging from 0 (few) to 3 (almost always), with higher scores indicating poor sleep quality. For this questionnaire, there is no Portuguese validation version.

2.4 Circadian Rhythm

The circadian rhythm, our twenty-four-hour rhythm, is another aspect to analyze when sleepiness is being studied since it is possible to identify when the subject wants to be awake or to asleep. For example, a morning person has a preference to get up early in the morning and go to bed early at night. Evening people, on the other hand, have a preference for going to bed later and, consequently, waking up later than a morning person [32]. When the circadian rhythm is not adjusted to the person's living, it has negative consequences on the resting cycles and physiological and behavioral functions of the individual. Thus, sleep disorders can be caused due to work schedules that are not in accordance with the circadian rhythm [33].

The Morningness-Eveningness questionnaire, developed by Horne and Ostberg [34], consists of 19 questions, and the final score is between 16 and 86. The subjects with classifications between 16 and 30 are a definitely evening type, 31 to 41 moderately evening type, 42 to 58 neither type, 59 to 69 moderately morning type and 70 to 86 definitely morning type. Since the previous questionnaire is very extensive, five questions were extracted to identify the circadian rhythm. This study aimed to reduce the time and effort of the researchers and participants [35]. In 2002 [36], a Portuguese adaptation version was developed and the number of questions was reduced to 16, and the time scales were changed.

Recently, in 2016 [37], an improved scale to measure the circadian rhythm was developed to improve the limitations of the Horne and Ostberg questionnaire. It was intended to improve the four and five Likert scales, eliminate self-assessment questions, add at least two dimensions, one for morningness and the other for eveningness, and reduce the number of questions. Thus, the questionnaire developed has 15 questions using a Likert scale of one to five points. Furthermore, it allows identifying three factors, separately, like distinctness, morning and eveningness affect. Note that the factor distinctness is used to identify if the participant has strong changes in performance and mood, during the day. Each factor has five questions, where higher values represent more changes during the day, morning, and evening preference. This questionnaire is known as Morningness-Eveningness-Stability-Scale improved (MESSi) and the Portuguese version is available in [38].

3   Procedure

Firstly, it was necessary to decide which questionnaires would be used in order to evaluate daytime sleepiness, the risk of developing obstructive sleep apnea, sleep quality, and circadian rhythm. The questionnaires were chosen based on the advice of a sleep physician, and their availability in Portuguese, who recommended using the following: ESS, STOP-Bang, PSQI, and MESSi.

Thereby, the next step was the construction of the final questionnaire to assess sleep disorders. The LimeSurvey platform was used, and it was divided into five parts. The first one is about personal information, such as sex, age, weight, height, geographic distribution, profession, driving questions, work schedule, and weekly hours. The driving questions were the following ones.

3.1: Do you have a driver's license? Yes or no.

3.2: Do you usually drive? Yes or no.

3.3: What type of vehicle do you usually drive? Light passenger car, light goods vehicle, or other.

3.4: What type of course do you usually take? Long or short distance.

3.5: How many years do you have a driver's license? 0 to 5 years, or more than 5 years.

3.6: In the last year, have you ever driven with drowsiness that forced you to stop? Yes or no.

3.7: In the last year, have you ever fallen asleep at the wheel? Yes or no.

3.8: In the last year, have you ever come close to having a traffic accident because you fell asleep at the wheel? Yes or no.

3.9: In the last year, have you had any traffic accidents because you fell asleep at the wheel? Yes or no.

3.10: In the last year, have you had any car accidents for any other reason? Yes or no.

The remaining parts were related to the sleep disorders questionnaires (ESS, STOP-Bang, PSQI, and MESSi), in the Portuguese version.

The third step was the definition of the target audience and the determination of the sample size, in order to be representative of the Portuguese population.

Thereby, it was decided to focus on the adult population, by region, since getting answers about infants, children, and adolescents would be difficult. Portugal's regions are divided into the North, Center, Lisbon Metropolitan Area, Alentejo, Algarve, Autonomous Region of Azores, and Madeira according to the NUTS II classification system. Stratified sampling was applied to determine the representative sample, by region, for the Portuguese adult population. This type of stratification uses probabilities, and the population is divided into different strata, which are exclusive and homogeneous segments, where the next step is the definition of a simple random sample for each stratum, known as a stratum. Moreover, from the proportion of the stratum in the population, the size of the stratum, in the sample, is determined. This approach is known as proportionate stratified sampling [39].

In order to identify the sample size, by region, a confidence interval for the population proportion was considered, which can be expressed like Eq. 1, and the estimation error is given by Eq. 2. It is important to understand all the parameters used, so $\hat{p}_i$ is the estimated proportion, $z_{\left(1-\frac{\alpha}{2}\right)}$ is the chosen z-value, also known as the critical value for the standard Normal distribution, α the level of significance, and n_i the sample size to being identified [40].

$$\hat{p}_i \pm z_{\left(1-\frac{\alpha}{2}\right)} \times \sqrt{\frac{\hat{p}_i \times (1 - \hat{p}_i)}{n_i}} \tag{1}$$

$$\text{Estimation Error} = z_{\left(1-\frac{\alpha}{2}\right)} \times \sqrt{\frac{\hat{p}_i \times (1 - \hat{p}_i)}{n_i}} \tag{2}$$

After defining the level of significance (α), and the estimation error, the sample size, by region, can be computed as in Eq. 3.

$$n_i = \left(\frac{z_{\left(1-\frac{\alpha}{2}\right)} \times \sqrt{\hat{p}_i \times (1 - \hat{p}_i)}}{\text{Estimation Error}}\right)^2 \tag{3}$$

In this research, it was opted to consider both the level of significance and the estimation error as 5%, which means the final expression can be computed as in Eq. 4.

$$n_i = \left(\frac{z_{\left(1-\frac{0.05}{2}\right)} \times \sqrt{\hat{p}_i \times (1 - \hat{p}_i)}}{0.05}\right)^2 = \left(\frac{1.96 \times \sqrt{\hat{p}_i \times (1 - \hat{p}_i)}}{0.05}\right)^2 \tag{4}$$

According to the National Institute of Statistics of Portugal[1], in 2020, it was identified almost 8.6 million adults, in Portugal. After identifying the number of adults by region, the proportion was computed by dividing the number of adults in each region and the total number of Portuguese adults. Thereby, the northern region has the highest number of adults, followed by the Lisbon Metropolitan Area and the Center. The number of adults (N_P), in Portugal, by region, the respective proportion (P), and the minimum value of the representative sample size (N_S) to be achieved are given in Table 1.

Table 1. Adult Population by region and respective proportion.

Region	N_P	P	N_S
North	3012972	35%	350
Center	1898999	22%	264
Lisbon Metropolitan Area	2323345	27%	303
Alentejo	592869	7%	99
Algarve	358763	4%	61
Autonomous Region of Azores	197084	2%	34
Autonomous Region of Madeira	212533	2%	37
Total	8596565	100	1149

Finally, it was time to collect the answers. The sleep disorder questionnaire for the Portuguese adult population was made available on December 3rd, 2021, and it was closed one year later. In terms of dissemination, social networks such as Facebook and LinkedIn, as well as e-mail contact with companies, universities, and town halls in various districts, were considered.

After one year of disclosure, two lines had to be eliminated after analyzing the responses, since the participants answered all the questions with the same number. Then, some of the values in the height, time to bed, and time to be awake features had to be corrected. For example, some participants, instead of inputting 130 cm in height, introduced 1.30. Besides that, the hours to go to bed or wake up also had inconsistencies, instead of 23:00 it was only introduced 23.

For the classification of sleep disorders, the instructions from the STOP-Bang, ESS, and PSQI were considered, however, in the MESSi the questionnaire is only divided into three factors (distinctness, morning affect, and eveningness) and higher values represent more changes during the day, morning and evening preferences, respectively. Therefore, if the morning factor was greater than the evening one, the circadian rhythm was set as the morning type. If the evening factor was greater than the morning factor, it was considered an evening type. Otherwise, it was set as an intermediate circadian rhythm type.

---

[1] Available in https://www.ine.pt/xportal/xmain?xpid=INE&xpgid=ine_indicadores &indOcorrCod=0007307&contexto=bd&selTab=tab2, accessed: 2021-10-26.

4   Statistical Analysis

In this section, the sample description is detailed, where the number of responses achieved by the regions of Portugal and personal information are presented. Then, the sleep disorders analysis was conducted to answer all the research questions with the appropriate methods. McNemar and proportion tests were implemented to evaluate two dependent and independent categorical features, respectively. The independence and strength of the association between two categorical features were assessed using the χ^2 test and odds ratio. The results displayed were computed using the Python software (version 3.8.5), considering the `pandas`, `matplotlib`, `seaborn`, `statsmodels`, and `scipy` libraries.

4.1   Sample Description

In terms of responses, values well above what was initially set as a minimum value were achieved, with 2089 complete answers. The results are presented in Table 2, and it is possible to identify that the North, Lisbon Metropolitan area, and Center have more responses than the other regions, followed by the Azores, Madeira, Alentejo, and Algarve.

Table 2. Sample Stratification by Region.

Region	N
North	468
Center	338
Lisbon Metropolitan Area	455
Alentejo	159
Algarve	97
Autonomous Region of Azores	297
Autonomous Region of Madeira	273
Total	2087

From the achieved results, 73.93% were female, where 34.49% had normal weight, 28.94% were overweight, 20.36% were at risk of being overweight, 13.90% were obese, and the remaining 2.31% were underweight. In terms of age, the median value is equal to 44 years old, which means 50% of the participants are younger than 44 years old. The minimum and maximum values were 18 and 78 years old, respectively. Figure 1a presents the age distribution, where it is visible that most of the participants are young (between 18 and 29 years old) and middle age (40 to 60 years old). Using the age by sex, Fig. 1b, it is perceptive that the ages are similar between males and females, even though there are more females in the study.

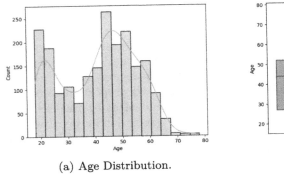

(a) Age Distribution.

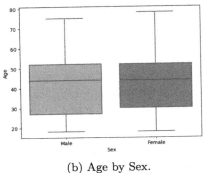

(b) Age by Sex.

Fig. 1. Participants Age.

Table 3 presents the answers achieved about driving. Therefore, most of the participants have a driving license (91.57%), usually drive (92.26%) light passenger cars (95.41%), short course routes (77.82%), and 88.60% have more than 5 years of driving license. Moreover, a few of the participants were forced to stop the car due to drowsiness (12.37%), in the last year, where 2.21% fell asleep at the wheel. Of those who fell asleep, 74.36% were close to having a traffic accident, and 20.69% had actually a traffic accident due to drowsiness. Conversely, of those who have a driver's license and usually drive, only 6.07% have had an accident for any reason other than drowsiness at the wheel.

Table 3. Answers about driving.

Question	Options	Values	Question	Options	Values
3.1	Yes	91.57%	3.6	Yes	12.37%
	No	8.43%		No	87.63%
3.2	Yes	92.26%	3.7	Yes	2.21%
	No	7.74%		No	97.79%
3.3	Light passenger car	95.41%	3.8	Yes	74.36%
	Light goods vehicle	2.95%		No	25.64%
	Other	1.64%			
3.4	Short Course	77.82%	3.9	Yes	20.69%
	Long Course	22.19%		No	79.31%
3.5	0 to 5 years	11.40%	3.10	Yes	6.07%
	More than 5 years	88.60%		No	93.93%

Another piece of information collected was about the work schedule and the respective duration, Fig. 2. It is perceptible that most of the participants work during the day (89.70%), 4.36% shift work, only 1.29% during the night, and 4.65% do not fit into the previous options. In terms of work duration, per week, most of the participants work between 35 and 40 h. These are the durations for the public and private sectors, respectively. Although three students defined the work duration as zero, others' values of less than 35 h, per week, may be of those who work part-time. There are also participants (25%) that work more than 40 h, per week.

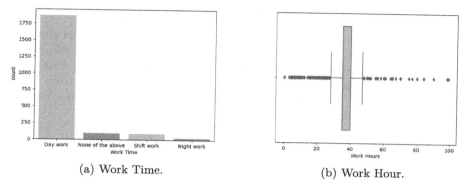

(a) Work Time.   (b) Work Hour.

Fig. 2. Work Information.

In terms of sleep disorders, the results achieved are presented in Table 4. Using the STOP-Bang questionnaire, 21.37% of the participants have a high risk of developing obstructive sleep apnea. Furthermore, 29.29% have excessive daytime sleepiness, and 61.38% have bad sleep quality. With the PSQI questionnaire, it was identified that most of the participants (50%) normally get 6 to 8 h of sleep, per night. Besides that, 50% of them need 10 to 30 min to fall asleep. For the circadian rhythm, 57.74% have morning preferences, 36.85% have evening preferences, and the ones that do not have morning or evening preferences can be considered intermediate or neither type. Regarding the distinctness effect, the first quartile (Q_1) was equal to 14, the second (Q_2) to 17, and the third (Q_3) to 19. In other words, 25% of the participants have a distinctness affect less than 14, 50% of them between 14 and 17, and the remaining 25% have values higher than 19.

Table 4. Sleep Disorders Results.

Questionnaire	Options	Values
STOP-Bang	Low Risk	78.63%
	High Risk	21.37%
ESS	Normal	60.71%
	Excessive	39.29%
PSQI	Bad Quality	61.38%
	Good Quality	38.62%
MESSi	Morning Type	57.74%
	Evening Type	36.85%
	Intermediate	5.41%

4.2   Sleep Disorders Analysis

The Portuguese Population is Aware of Their Sleep Quality? Two aspects must be considered for this research question: subjective sleep quality (SSQ), as reported by each participant in the PSQI questionnaire, and the PSQI final result. All the participants had to identify their sleep quality, divided into four levels: very good, fairly good, fairly bad, and very bad. For this analysis, the options "very good" and "good" were aggregated and defined as good sleep quality. The same approach was applied to the remaining options that were considered to have bad sleep quality. Thereby, the statistical hypotheses to be tested were defined 5, where π_1 is the proportion of subjective sleep quality and π_2 is the proportion of Pittsburg Sleep Quality.

$$H_0 : \pi_1 = \pi_2 \text{ vs } H_1 : \pi_1 \neq \pi_2 \tag{5}$$

The appropriate method to answer the research question is the McNemar Test [41], which is used for two dependent categorical features, with two classes each (2×2). The statistic test (χ^2) was equal to 457, and the p-value was less than 0.001. Considering the level of significance of 5%, the proportion of subjective sleep quality and the Pittsburg Sleep Quality are different. After this conclusion, it is important to understand whether the participants are aware that their quality of sleep is good or bad. Table 5 presents the contingency table between the SSQ and PSQI final results, where it is visible that 532 participants defined their sleep quality as good, however, it is bad. Therefore, some parts of the Portuguese population are not aware of their sleep quality.

Table 5. Contingency Table of Pittsburgh by SSQ for the 1st Research Question.

SSQ	Pittsburgh		
	Bad	Good	Total
Bad	749	26	775
Good	532	780	1312
Total	1281	806	2087

Is it True that People with Excessive Daytime Sleepiness Have Bad Sleep Quality? For this research question, the ESS and the PSQI final results are the features to be analyzed since they identify who has normal or excessive daytime sleepiness, and good or bad sleep quality, respectively. Firstly, it is necessary to select all the participants with excessive daytime sleepiness, and then evaluate the proportions of good and bad sleep quality. In the null hypothesis, the proportions are considered equal, that is, there are no differences in the sleep quality of the participants with excessive daytime sleepiness. Thus, a proportion test for two independent samples was performed, where $z = 17.38$, and the $p - value < 0.001$. Thus, there are differences between the proportions of good and bad sleep quality among those who have excessive daytime sleepiness. In terms of proportional values, 71.46% of the participants with excessive daytime sleepiness have bad sleep quality, and the rest of the participants (28.54%) have a good quality of sleep. Thereby, the research question was proved, so people with excessive daytime sleepiness indeed have bad sleep quality.

The Circadian Rhythm is Adjusted with the Work Schedule? If Not, Does it Influence Their Sleep Quality and Daytime Sleepiness? For this research question, the MESSi final result (morning, evening type, or intermediate) and the work time (day, night, shift work, or none of the above) were considered. It is intended to test if the circadian rhythm and work time features are independent of each other. The appropriate test for this research question is the χ^2 test, where the null hypothesis is about the independence of the features under study. Therefore, the results achieved were $\chi^2(6) = 33.80$, and $p-value < 0.001$. Thus, there is a significant association between work time and circadian rhythm. Using the visualization in Fig. 3, it is clear that individuals who are considered to be morning type (green color) are more prevalent in daytime work, and those who are evening type (blue color) are associated with night work. For the shift work, the proportions are balanced between morning and evening types. Therefore, the work schedule is adjusted to the circadian rhythm.

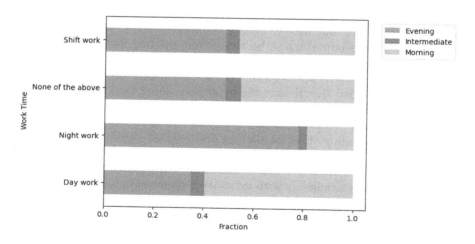

Fig. 3. Circadian Rhythm by Work Time.

Is it True that People with a Risk of Developing Sleep Apnea Also Have Excessive Daytime Sleepiness? To answer the present research question, the comparison between STOP-Bang and ESS final results was the main goal of the analysis. Aside from that, it was decided to evaluate the odds ratio between the two features in order to determine the strength of the association.

The odds ratio achieved was equal to 1.79, indicating that the possibility of detecting a high risk of sleep apnea with excessive daytime sleepiness is about 1.8 times higher when compared with the group that presents normal daytime sleepiness. The 95% confidence interval was equal to]1.44; 2.21[and since the unit does not belong to the interval, there is a significant association between the apnea risk and excessive daytime sleepiness.

5 Discussion

There was an increase in individuals with excessive daytime sleepiness (39.29%) in this study when compared to the results in [9,10], which achieved 20% and 9.11%, respectively. On the other hand, the study developed in 2014 [9] had a high risk of developing obstructive sleep apnea for 29% of the participants, and in 2015 [10] only 10% of the participants had a high risk. However, in our study, it was achieved 21.37%. In terms of sleep quality, there are values of 35.30% [10] and 54.8% [11] of bad sleep quality. In our study, the number of individuals with bad sleep quality was higher (61.38%). It is also possible to compare the values of the sleep duration and the respective time to fall asleep. According to [11] 62.9% of adults sleep between 6 and 8 h, per night, and 44% of adults need 1 to 15 min to fall asleep. In our analysis, it was identified that 50% of adults sleep 6 to 8 h, and it takes 10 to 30 min to fall asleep. Although, 48.78% of adults fell asleep for less than 15 min. Most of the results achieved are higher than the ones presented in other studies, however, it is important to understand that the sample numbers differ and were extracted in different ways. What can impact the results. It is also important to be aware that the responses are subjective since they will depend on how the person understands the question.

According to [8] people are not aware of their sleep deficiency and the effects of sleep deprivation. For that reason, the hypothesis about the Portuguese population was investigated, and it was verified that 41.53% of the adult participants were unaware of their bad sleep quality. Thus, it is essential to identify strategies to address this problem so that people can find reliable solutions to their sleep problems. Furthermore, excessive daytime sleepiness is a consequence of bad sleep quality [42], and when this was evaluated, it was possible to conclude that 71.46% of the adult participants with excessive daytime sleepiness actually have bad sleep quality. Which is in line with the literature. Sleep disorders can also occur when work schedules are not aligned with the circadian rhythm, according to the literature [33]. For the Portuguese adults, in the study, it was proven that the work schedule is adjusted to the circadian rhythm. Another aspect available in the literature is that excessive daytime sleepiness is the main symptom of obstructive sleep apnea [18]. Using the odds ratio, it was possible to conclude that people with excessive daytime sleepiness have a 1.8 times higher risk of developing obstructive sleep apnea than people with normal daytime sleepiness.

6   Conclusions

Sleep disorders are a concerning topic since they can influence an individual's health, mood, and, at the same time, quality of life. For that reason, there are several questionnaires available to evaluate different sleep disorders, such as daytime sleepiness, the risk of developing obstructive sleep apnea, sleep quality, and the type of circadian rhythm. Sleep disorder questionnaires were established with the help of a sleep physician, and the chosen ones were the Epworth Sleepiness Scale, STOP-Bang, Pittsburgh Sleep Quality Index, and Morningness-Eveningness-Stability-Scale improved.

A sleep disorders study was conducted for the adult Portuguese population, whereas stratified sampling was used to achieve representative values for each district of Portugal.

After one year of disclosure, 2087 complete answers were collected, 73.93% of the participants are female, only 34.49% have normal weight, and most of them are young and middle age. Participants range in age from 18 to 78 years old. In terms of sleep disorders, the vast majority of participants have poor sleep quality (61.38%), 21.37% have a high risk of developing sleep apnea, 39.29% have excessive daytime sleepiness, 57.74% are morning type, 36.85% are evening type, and the rest are intermediate.

After defining four research questions about sleep disorders, it was possible to prove that comparing the subjective sleep quality and the sleep quality achieved from the questionnaire, the Portuguese population is not aware of their sleep quality. Another interesting finding was that analyzing the individuals with excessive daytime sleepiness, 71.46% had bad sleep quality. Using a statistical method, it was proven that individuals with excessive daytime sleepiness have bad sleep quality. It was also evaluated the work schedule and the circadian rhythm to verify if it was adjusted. Considering the appropriate method, it was identified that the work schedule was adjusted to the individual's circadian rhythm. Finally, the risk of developing sleep apnea with excessive daytime sleepiness is around 1.8 times higher than the ones with normal daytime sleepiness. The results achieved are in agreement with what is present in the literature about sleep disorders.

Thereby, the novelty of this study is the integration of four questionnaires that evaluate different sleep disorders, apart from personal information, and the high number of responses from the Portuguese population that are representative of the different districts. In the future, the same analysis can be conducted for the usual drivers, and the sample can be increased.

Acknowledgements. We want to thank all the participants for their involvement in this study.

References

1. Foley, D., Ancoli-Israel, S., Britz, P., Walsh, J.: Sleep disturbances and chronic disease in older adults: results of the 2003 national sleep foundation sleep in america survey. J. Psychosom. Res. **56**(5), 497–502 (2004)

2. Gangwisch, J.E., et al.: Short sleep duration as a risk factor for hypertension: analyses of the first national health and nutrition examination survey. Hypertension **47**(5), 833–839 (2006)

3. Quan, S., Zee, P.: A sleep review of systems: evaluating the effects of medical disorders on sleep in the older patient. Geriatrics (2004)

4. Léger, D., et al.: Allergic rhinitis and its consequences on quality of sleep: an unexplored area. Arch. Intern. Med. **166**(16), 1744–1748 (2006)

5. Pearson, N.J., Johnson, L.L., Nahin, R.L.: Insomnia, trouble sleeping, and complementary and alternative medicine: analysis of the 2002 national health interview survey data. Arch. Intern. Med. **166**(16), 1775–1782 (2006)

6. Zee, P.C., Turek, F.W.: Sleep and health: everywhere and in both directions. Arch. Intern. Med. **166**(16), 1686–1688 (2006)

7. Grandner, M.A.: Sleep, health, and society. Sleep Med. Clin. **12**(1), 1–22 (2017)

8. Filip, I., et al.: Public health burden of sleep disorders: underreported problem. J. Public Health **25**, 243–248 (2017)

9. Catarino, R., Spratley, J., Catarino, I., Lunet, N., Pais-Clemente, M.: Sleepiness and sleep-disordered breathing in truck drivers: risk analysis of road accidents. Sleep Breath. **18**, 59–68 (2014)

10. Gonçalves, M., Peralta, A., Monteiro Ferreira, J., Guilleminault, C.: Sleepiness and motor vehicle crashes in a representative sample of Portuguese drivers: the importance of epidemiological representative surveys. Traffic Injury Prevent. **16**(7), 677–683 (2015)

11. Almeida, T., Ramos, C., Cardoso, J.: Sleep quality in the general Portuguese population. Ann. Med. **50**, S144–S145 (2018)

12. Cascalho, M., Sousa, S., Ramos, C., Almeida, T., Cardoso, J.: Hábitos e problemas de sono na população adulta portuguesa. Rev. Psicol. Saúde Doenças **21**, 110–111 (2020)

13. Pagel, J.: Excessive daytime sleepiness. Am. Fam. Phys. **79**(5), 391–396 (2009)

14. Johns, M.W.: A new method for measuring daytime sleepiness: the Epworth sleepiness scale. Sleep **14**(6), 540–545 (1991)

15. Dos Santos, J.M.: Abordagem do doente com patologia do sono. Rev. Portuguesa Med. Geral Familiar **22**(5), 599–610 (2006)

16. Rosenthal, L., Roehrs, T.A., Roth, T.: The sleep-wake activity inventory: a self-report measure of daytime sleepiness. Biol. Psychiat. **34**(11), 810–820 (1993)

17. Bower, C.M., Gungor, A.: Pediatric obstructive sleep apnea syndrome. Otolaryngol. Clin. North Am. **33**(1), 49–75 (2000)

18. Aguiar, M., et al.: Síndroma de apneia obstrutiva do sono como causa de acidentes de viação. Rev. Port. Pneumol. **15**(3), 419–431 (2009)

19. Chung, F., Abdullah, H.R., Liao, P.: Stop-bang questionnaire: a practical approach to screen for obstructive sleep apnea. Chest **149**(3), 631–638 (2016)

20. Reis, R., et al.: Validation of a Portuguese version of the stop-bang questionnaire as a screening tool for obstructive sleep apnea: Analysis in a sleep clinic. Rev. Portuguesa Pneumol. (English Edn.) **21**(2), 61–68 (2015)

21. Netzer, N.C., Stoohs, R.A., Netzer, C.M., Clark, K., Strohl, K.P.: Using the berlin questionnaire to identify patients at risk for the sleep apnea syndrome. Ann. Intern. Med. **131**(7), 485–491 (1999)

22. Vaz, A., Drummond, M., Mota, P.C., Severo, M., Almeida, J., Winck, J.C.: Tradução do questionário de berlim para língua portuguesa e sua aplicação na identificação da saos numa consulta de patologia respiratória do sono. Rev. Port. Pneumol. **17**(2), 59–65 (2011)

23. Lacasse, Y., Bureau, M., Series, F.: A new standardised and self-administered quality of life questionnaire specific to obstructive sleep apnoea. Thorax **59**(6), 494–499 (2004)
24. Sampaio, R., Pereira, M.G., Winck, J.C.: Adaptação portuguesa do questionário de qualidade de vida (saqli) nos doentes com síndrome de apneia obstrutiva do sono. Rev. Port. Pneumol. **18**(4), 166–174 (2012)
25. Krystal, A.D., Edinger, J.D.: Measuring sleep quality. Sleep Med. **9**, S10–S17 (2008)
26. Edinger, J.D., et al.: Derivation of research diagnostic criteria for insomnia: report of an American academy of sleep medicine work group. Sleep **27**(8), 1567–1596 (2004)
27. Zomer, J.: Mini sleep questionnaire (MSQ) for screening large populations for EDS complaints. Sleep **84** (1985)
28. Falavigna, A., et al.: Consistency and reliability of the Brazilian Portuguese version of the mini-sleep questionnaire in undergraduate students. Sleep Breath. **15**, 351–355 (2011)
29. Buysse, D.J., Reynolds, C.F., III., Monk, T.H., Berman, S.R., Kupfer, D.J.: The Pittsburgh sleep quality index: a new instrument for psychiatric practice and research. Psychiatry Res. **28**(2), 193–213 (1989)
30. João, K.A.D.R., Becker, N.B., de Neves Jesus, S., Martins, R.I.S.: Validation of the Portuguese version of the Pittsburgh sleep quality index (PSQI-PT). Psychiatry Res. **247**, 225–229 (2017)
31. Yi, H., Shin, K., Shin, C.: Development of the sleep quality scale. J. Sleep Res. **15**(3), 309–316 (2006)
32. Walker, M.: Why we sleep: unlocking the power of sleep and dreams (2017)
33. Zee, P.C., Attarian, H., Videnovic, A.: Circadian rhythm abnormalities. Continuum: Lifelong Learn. Neurol. **19**(1 Sleep Disorders), 132 (2013)
34. Horne, J.A., Östberg, O.: Individual differences in human circadian rhythms. Biol. Psychol. **5**(3), 179–190 (1977)
35. Chelminski, I., Petros, T.V., Plaud, J.J., Ferraro, F.R.: Psychometric properties of the reduced Horne and Ostberg questionnaire. Personality Individ. Differ. **29**(3), 469–478 (2000)
36. Silva, C.F.D., et al.: The Portuguese version of the Horne and Ostberg morningness-eveningness questionnaire: its role in education and psychology (2002)
37. Randler, C., Díaz-Morales, J.F., Rahafar, A., Vollmer, C.: Morningness-eveningness and amplitude-development and validation of an improved composite scale to measure circadian preference and stability (MESSi). Chronobiol. Int. **33**(7), 832–848 (2016)
38. Rodrigues, P.F., Vagos, P., Pandeirada, J.N., Marinho, P.I., Randler, C., Silva, C.F.: Initial psychometric characterization for the Portuguese version of the morningness-eveningness-stability-scale improved (MESSi). Chronobiol. Int. **35**(11), 1608–1618 (2018)
39. Daniel, J.: Sampling Essentials: Practical Guidelines for Making Sampling Choices. Sage Publications (2011)
40. Montgomery, D.C., Runger, G.C.: Applied Statistics and Probability for Engineers. Wiley, Hoboken (2010)
41. Fisher, M.J., Marshall, A.P., Mitchell, M.: Testing differences in proportions. Aust. Crit. Care **24**(2), 133–138 (2011)
42. Hangouche, A.J.E., et al.: Relationship between poor quality sleep, excessive daytime sleepiness and low academic performance in medical students. Adv. Med. Educ. Pract. 631–638 (2018)

The Multiscale Maximum Change Algorithm for Subsurface Characterization

Abdullah Al Mamun[1], Alsadig Ali[1], Abdullah Al-Mamun[2], Felipe Pereira[1], and Arunasalam Rahunanthan[3(✉)]

[1] Department of Mathematical Sciences, The University of Texas at Dallas, Richardson, TX 75080, USA
[2] Institute of Natural Sciences, United International University, Dhaka, Bangladesh
[3] Department of Mathematics and Computer Science, Central State University, Wilberforce, OH 45384, USA
aRahunanthan@centralstate.edu

Abstract. The characterization of subsurface formations is a formidable task due to the high dimension of the stochastic space involved in the solution of inverse problems. To make the task computationally manageable, one needs to apply a dimensional reduction technique. In this paper we are considering the Karhunen Loève expansion (KLE) as the aforementioned technique. Considering the subsurface properties of interest, such as permeability and porosity, it may be suitable to localize the sampling method so that it can better accommodate the large variation in rock properties. In a Bayesian framework we investigate the solution of an inverse problem involving an elliptic partial differential equation for porous media flows. We propose a new multiscale sampling algorithm in which the prior distribution is expressed in terms of local KL expansions in non-overlapping subdomains of the domain of the inverse problem. We solve the inverse problem using multiple Markov Chain Monte Carlo (MCMC) simulations performed on a multi-GPU cluster. The simulation results indicate that the proposed algorithm significantly improves the convergence of a preconditioned MCMC method.

Keywords: Preconditioned MCMC · MCMC convergence · Inverse Problem · Multiscale Sampling · Domain Decomposition

1 Introduction

It is of great economic importance to find solutions to large scale inverse problems in geophysics [33] and petroleum engineering [1]. To find the solutions to these problems, we first need to numerically solve the partial differential equations that are used to mathematically model the problem. Then, in a Bayesian statistical framework, we simulate the numerical solver repeatedly to solve the inverse problem [2,11,15,23].

Multiscale numerical solvers have been quite successful in producing computationally inexpensive, accurate numerical solutions in porous media applications [10,16,18]. These methods are based on a domain decomposition

© The Author(s), under exclusive license to Springer Nature Switzerland AG 2023
O. Gervasi et al. (Eds.): ICCSA 2023 Workshops, LNCS 14105, pp. 114–129, 2023.
https://doi.org/10.1007/978-3-031-37108-0_8

technique [28]: local solutions computed at subdomains are combined to construct the global solution.

In the context of uncertainty quantification problems in [20] a domain decomposition approach was used for uncertainty analysis of PDEs. In this approach the authors independently performed the analysis on each local component offline and assembled the global uncertainty analysis using the precomputed local information. An efficient method to solve large scale KL decomposition problems was presented in [7]. In this method, the computational domain is divided into nonoverlapping subdomains, and on each subdomain a KL decomposition problem is solved to generate local bases. The local bases are used to discretize the global modes over the entire domain.

We investigate the application Markov Chain Monte Carlo methods to solve large inverse problems in the area of multiphase flows in porous media. The MCMC methods are known to converge slowly to the stationary distribution and we developed methods to speedup the convergence of these methods. In the Multiscale Sampling Method (MSM) [3,4] we combined local KL expansions with a new local averaging technique to improve drastically the convergence rates of the preconditioned MCMC method of [6,9]. The MSM algorithm consists of two steps: a global search in all the subdomains of the domain of the problem and a local search within each subdomain. In the work reported here we present a new development of this two step algorithm. We use the first step of the MSM to select the subdomain that shows the best acceptance of MCMC proposals and the second step of the MSM algorithm is modified to perform the search in the selected subdomain in the first step. Our simulation results show improved convergence of the new algorithm in comparison to the previous MSM.

The paper is organized as follows. In Sect. 2, we start by outlining the governing equations for pollutant transport in a porous medium. A Bayesian framework for subsurface characterization and KLE to reduce the dimension of the stochastic space are presented in Sect. 3. We also present the convergent assessments of the MCMC methods in Sect. 4. The simulation results are presented in Sect. 5. Section 6 is dedicated to provide conclusions of the study.

2   Model Problem

Let us consider a mathematical model that describes the subsurface transport of pollutants in a heterogeneous permeability field. In this model, the system of governing equations consists of an elliptic equation coupled with a hyperbolic equation. The elliptic equation is given by

$$\begin{cases} \boldsymbol{u} & = -k(\boldsymbol{x})\nabla p \quad \text{in } \Omega \\ \nabla \cdot \boldsymbol{u} & = f \qquad\qquad \text{in } \Omega, \end{cases} \tag{1}$$

where $\Omega \subset \mathbb{R}^2$ is a bounded domain with a Lipschitz boundary $\partial\Omega$, $\boldsymbol{u}$ is the Darcy velocity, p represents the fluid pressure, $k(\boldsymbol{x})$ is a positive definite tensor also known as the absolute permeability field of the rock and $f \in L^2(\Omega)$ denotes the sources and the sinks. Note that the typical boundary conditions for porous media flow problems are Dirichlet and Neumann and in this case the pressure and the normal component of the velocity is defined by

$$p = g_p \in H^{\frac{1}{2}}(\partial \Omega_p), \qquad \boldsymbol{u} \cdot \hat{\boldsymbol{n}} = g_u \in H^{-\frac{1}{2}}(\partial \Omega_u),$$

where $\partial \Omega = \overline{\partial \Omega_p} \cup \overline{\partial \Omega_u}$, $\overline{\partial \Omega_p} \cap \overline{\partial \Omega_u} = \varnothing$ and $\hat{\boldsymbol{n}}$ is the outward unit normal vector. The weak formulation of the pressure-velocity equation is used to derive the numerical approximation of the elliptic equation given by Eq. (1). Refer [10] for the weak formulation.

The hyperbolic equation is given by

$$\phi(\boldsymbol{x}) \frac{\partial s(\boldsymbol{x}, t)}{\partial t} + \nabla \cdot [s(\boldsymbol{x}, t) \boldsymbol{u}(\boldsymbol{x})] = 0, \tag{2}$$

where $\phi(\boldsymbol{x})$ represents the rock porosity and $s(\boldsymbol{x}, t)$ is the pollutant concentration in the water.

The aquifer contains spill and monitoring wells. To characterize the permeability field of the domain we use fractional flow data defined by

$$F(t) = 1 - \frac{\int_{\partial \Omega_{\text{out}}} u_n(\boldsymbol{x}) s(\boldsymbol{x}, t) \, dl}{\int_{\partial \Omega_{\text{out}}} u_n(\boldsymbol{x}) \, dl},$$

where $\partial \Omega_{\text{out}}$ is the well outflow boundary and $u_n(\boldsymbol{x})$ is the normal components of the velocity field [26]. In this paper, we consider only the elliptic equation Eq. (1) to demonstrate the significance of the proposed algorithm.

3 Characterization of Subsurface

3.1 The Bayesian Framework

The focus of this study is to characterize the permeability field using the available pressure data on the domain of the problem. We take that the pressure measurements are available on all the black (or white) squares on a chess board. That is, we have the measurements on one half of the discretized domain [34]. The characterization is done in a Bayesian statistical framework, which consists a preconditioned MCMC method. The preconditioned MCMC method will be discussed in Sect. 4.3.

Let us use $\boldsymbol{\eta}$ and R_p, respectively, for the (log of the) permeability field and the pressure measurement data. Using the Bayes' theorem, the posterior probability for the pressure data R_p can be written by

$$P(\boldsymbol{\eta}|R_p) \propto P(R_p|\boldsymbol{\eta}) P(\boldsymbol{\eta}), \tag{3}$$

where $P(\boldsymbol{\eta})$ is a Gaussian prior distribution. The normalizing constant is not required for an MCMC algorithm and is therefore ignored. We use KLE to construct the (log of) permeability field $\boldsymbol{\eta}(\boldsymbol{\theta})$ and the MCMC algorithm is used to generate the chain of $\boldsymbol{\theta}$s. KLE will be discussed in Sect. 3.2. A likelihood function for our problem, which is considered to be Gaussian [9], is given below

$$P(R_p|\boldsymbol{\eta}) \propto \exp\left(-(R_p - R_{\boldsymbol{\eta}})^\top \Sigma(R_p - R_{\boldsymbol{\eta}})\right), \tag{4}$$

where $R_{\boldsymbol{\eta}}$ represents the simulated pressure data. We constructed the covariance matrix Σ to be $\Sigma = \boldsymbol{I}/2\sigma_R^2$, where $\boldsymbol{I}$ is the identity matrix and σ_R^2 is the precision parameter associated with the measured pressure data.

To sample from the posterior distribution (3) the MCMC algorithm is used. The algorithm has an instrumental distribution $I(\boldsymbol{\eta}_p|\boldsymbol{\eta})$, where $\boldsymbol{\eta}$ is the previously accepted sample, and $\boldsymbol{\eta}_p = \boldsymbol{\eta}(\boldsymbol{\theta}_p)$ is proposed at each iteration. For a given permeability field, the forward problem is solved numerically to give $R_{\boldsymbol{\eta}}$. In the MCMC algorithm the acceptance probability is calculated as in [25]. The probability is given by

$$\alpha(\boldsymbol{\eta}, \boldsymbol{\eta}_p) = \min\left(1, \frac{I(\boldsymbol{\eta}|\boldsymbol{\eta}_p)P(\boldsymbol{\eta}_p|R_p)}{I(\boldsymbol{\eta}_p|\boldsymbol{\eta})P(\boldsymbol{\eta}|R_p)}\right). \tag{5}$$

3.2 Dimensional Reduction

In the MCMC algorithm, at each iteration we need a permeability value of each computational cell of the physical domain. This leads to a huge parameter space and the problem becomes impractical as the number of computational cells increases. In order to reduce the parameter space, we consider a Karhunen Loève expansion [12, 21]. Here we briefly discuss the expansion.

For $\boldsymbol{x} \in \Omega$, let $\log[k(\boldsymbol{x})] = Y^k(\boldsymbol{x})$ to be a Gaussian field sample. In addition, we also assume that $Y^k(\boldsymbol{x}) \in L^2(\Omega)$ is a second order stochastic process with unit probability. The assumption $E[(Y^k)^2] = 0$ allows us to express the permeability field $Y^k(\boldsymbol{x})$ for a given orthonormal basis $\{\varphi_i\}$ of $L^2(\Omega)$ as follows:

$$Y^k(\boldsymbol{x}) = \sum_{i=1}^{\infty} Y_i^k \varphi_i(\boldsymbol{x}), \tag{6}$$

with random coefficients $Y_i^k = \int_\Omega Y^k(\boldsymbol{x})$. The eigenfunctions $\varphi_i(\boldsymbol{x})$ for the corresponding eigenvalues λ_i satisfy the integral equation

$$\int_\Omega R(\boldsymbol{x}_1, \boldsymbol{x}_2)\varphi_i(\boldsymbol{x}_2)d\boldsymbol{x}_2 = \lambda_i\varphi_i(\boldsymbol{x}_1), \quad i = 1, 2, \dots \tag{7}$$

where $R(\boldsymbol{x}_1, \boldsymbol{x}_2)$ is a covariance function. Note that the eigenvalues are positive, i.e., $\lambda_i = E[(Y^k)^2] > 0$ and arranged in descending order. Using $\theta_i^k = Y_i^k/\sqrt{\lambda_i}$, Eq. (6) becomes

$$Y^k(\boldsymbol{x}) = \sum_{i=1}^{\infty} \sqrt{\lambda_i}\theta_i^k \varphi_i(\boldsymbol{x}), \tag{8}$$

where the pair (λ_i, φ_i) satisfy Eq. (7). The series written in the Eq. (8) is called KLE. To make sure that the energy E is above 95% [19] we need the first N dominating eigenvalues in KLE, i.e.,

$$E = \frac{\sum_{i=1}^{N} \lambda_i}{\sum_{i=1}^{\infty} \lambda_i} \geq 95\%. \tag{9}$$

We, therefore, calculate the truncated KLE by

$$Y_N^k(\boldsymbol{x}) = \sum_{i=1}^{N} \sqrt{\lambda_i} \theta_i^k \varphi_i(\boldsymbol{x}). \tag{10}$$

3.3 MCMC Convergence Assessment

In the MCMC algorithm we need to address two critical questions: (i) How do we pick an initial seed for an MCMC simulation? and (ii) What are the stopping criteria of an MCMC simulation? In the past the researchers in [27, 29, 31] worked on establishing a theoretical approach for the stopping criteria. However, in practice, we often use empirical diagnostic tools, such as in [5, 22, 24, 30] to analyze the convergence of an MCMC algorithm. In this subsection, we consider two mostly used diagnostics namely the Potential Scale Reduction Factor (PSRF) and the multivariate PSRF (MPSRF). MPSRF is more reliable than PSRF for parallel chains because MPSRF takes all the parameters into account.

We choose l posterior draws from each of the m chains and a parameter vector $\boldsymbol{\theta}$ of dimension N. We consider $\boldsymbol{\theta}_j^c$ as the value of the vector $\boldsymbol{\theta}$ generated at iteration c in the jth chain of the MCMC algorithm. The pooled variance estimate $\widehat{\mathbf{V}}$ is calculated by the weighted average of the between ($\mathbf{B}$) and within chain variance estimates ($\mathbf{W}$) and is given by

$$\widehat{\mathbf{V}} = \frac{l-1}{l}\mathbf{W} + \left(1 + \frac{1}{m}\right)\frac{\mathbf{B}}{l}. \tag{11}$$

The covariance matrices are defined as

$$\mathbf{W} = \frac{1}{m(l-1)} \sum_{j=1}^{m} \sum_{c=1}^{l} \left(\boldsymbol{\theta}_j^c - \bar{\boldsymbol{\theta}}_{j\cdot}\right)\left(\boldsymbol{\theta}_j^c - \bar{\boldsymbol{\theta}}_{j\cdot}\right)^T, \tag{12}$$

and

$$\mathbf{B} = \frac{l}{m-1} \sum_{j=1}^{m} \left(\bar{\boldsymbol{\theta}}_{j\cdot} - \bar{\boldsymbol{\theta}}_{\cdot\cdot}\right)\left(\bar{\boldsymbol{\theta}}_{j\cdot} - \bar{\boldsymbol{\theta}}_{\cdot\cdot}\right)^T, \tag{13}$$

where $\bar{\boldsymbol{\theta}}_{j\cdot}$ represents within chain mean and $\bar{\boldsymbol{\theta}}_{\cdot\cdot}$ denotes the mean between m combined chains. The superscript T indicates the transpose of a matrix. The PSRFs are estimated as

$$\text{PSRF}_i = \sqrt{\frac{\text{diag}(\widehat{\mathbf{V}})_i}{\text{diag}(\mathbf{W})_i}}, \quad \text{where } i = 1, 2, ..., N. \tag{14}$$

If m chains start sampling from the stationary distribution, the estimators $\widehat{\mathbf{V}}$ and $\widehat{\mathbf{W}}$ should be very close to each other and thus the horizontal line drawn at 1 becomes a horizontal asymptote for the maximum of PSRF curves and indicates the convergence of the MCMC simulations. Using the maximum root statistic, as in [5] MPSRF is defined by

$$
\begin{aligned}
\text{MPSRF} &= \sqrt{\max_{\mathbf{a}} \frac{\mathbf{a}^T \widehat{\mathbf{V}} \mathbf{a}}{\mathbf{a}^T \mathbf{W} \mathbf{a}}} \\
&= \sqrt{\max_{\mathbf{a}} \frac{\mathbf{a}^T \left[\frac{l-1}{l} \mathbf{W} + \left(1 + \frac{1}{m}\right) \frac{\mathbf{B}}{l} \right] \mathbf{a}}{\mathbf{a}^T \mathbf{W} \mathbf{a}}} \\
&= \sqrt{\frac{l-1}{l} + \left(\frac{m+1}{m}\right) \max_{\mathbf{a}} \frac{\mathbf{a}^T \frac{\mathbf{B}}{l} \mathbf{a}}{\mathbf{a}^T \mathbf{W} \mathbf{a}}} \\
&= \sqrt{\frac{l-1}{l} + \left(\frac{m+1}{m}\right) \lambda},
\end{aligned}
$$

where $\mathbf{a} \in \mathbb{R}^N$ is an arbitrary vector and λ is the largest eigenvalue of the matrix $\mathbf{W}^{-1}\mathbf{B}/l$. The equality in means of between chains makes the covariance matrix $\mathbf{B}$ zero and eventually MPSRF approaches 1 and thus indicates the convergence of the MCMC simulations.

4   Multiscale Maximum Change Algorithm

4.1   The Multiscale Prior Distribution

The Multiscale Maximum Change strategy consists of two non-overlapping partitions of the domain Ω: the first one is a uniform fine Cartesian mesh Ω^f and the other one is a coarse Cartesian mesh Ω^c. The coarse mesh Ω^c is constructed as a set of elements of Ω^f (see Fig. 1) in which we use the values of the absolute permeability field as piecewise constant. We use KLE for the local dimensional reduction. Let Ω^γ be a partitions into rectangles $\{\Omega_i^\gamma,\ i = 1, \ldots, M_\gamma\}$, such that

$$
\overline{\Omega^\gamma} = \bigcup_{i=1}^{M_\gamma} \overline{\Omega_i^\gamma}; \quad \Omega_i^\gamma \cap \Omega_k^\gamma = \varnothing, \quad i \neq k, \quad \gamma = c, f.
$$

Define $\Gamma = \partial \Omega$ and, for $i = 1, \ldots, M_\gamma$:

$$
\Gamma_{ik}^\gamma = \Gamma_{ki}^\gamma = \partial \Omega_i^\gamma \cap \partial \Omega_k^\gamma, \quad \gamma = c, f.
$$

For the coarse partition $\{\Omega_i^\gamma,\ i = 1, \ldots, M_c\}$ elements, we define the set

$$
\mathcal{S}_i = \{j : \Omega_j^f \subset \Omega_i^c\}.
$$

We apply two length scales in the description of the new multiscale procedure: H and h for the coarse and the underlying fine grid mesh size, respectively. We decompose the vector $\boldsymbol{\theta}$ in Eq. (10) by using random walk sampler (RWS) [17]:

$$
\boldsymbol{\theta}_p = \sqrt{1 - \beta^2}\, \boldsymbol{\theta} + \beta\, \boldsymbol{\varepsilon}, \tag{15}
$$

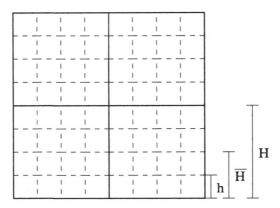

Fig. 1. The coarse Ω^c and fine Ω^f partitions of Ω represented by solid and dashed lines respectively along with three spatial scales.

where $\boldsymbol{\theta}_p$ and $\boldsymbol{\theta}$ are respectively the current and the previously accepted sample, β is used for tuning the sampler and $\boldsymbol{\varepsilon} \in \mathcal{N}(0,1)$.

The samples produced in this approach are Gaussian samples with discontinuities in Γ_{ik}^c. To remove the flux discontinuities at boundaries, downscaling strategies have been developed for multiscale methods [17]. Inspired by the strategies, we complete the construction of a sample from our multiscale prior distribution by using an averaging method. The method is used to condition each sample on the available data at nearest neighbor subdomains [4]. The method is illustrated in Fig. 2.

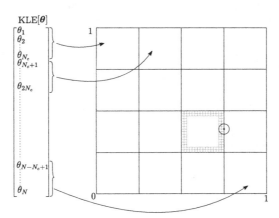

Fig. 2. Correspondence between blocks of theta variables and elements of the coarse partition Ω^c (solid lines) of Ω. Each block of thetas generates a localized Gaussian field in its corresponding subdomain.

A length scale $\overline{H}$ smaller than H is set and, for each i, all the current values of the cells of $\mathcal{S}_i$ are replaced by the local averages (that preserves mean and variance for uncorrelated data). Note that the replacement is done based on the distance of $\overline{H}$ (or less) to Γ_{ik}^c. A sample before and after this averaging procedure is depicted in Fig. 3. The circle for the averaging shown in Fig. 2 is replaced by an ellipse if the correlation lengths are unequal. The averaging is applied on the top right subdomain boundary using $H = 0.25$. The multiscale prior distribution needs two parameters H and $\overline{H}$ from the user.

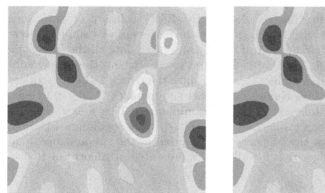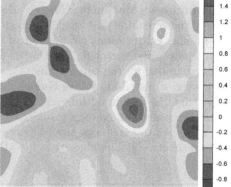

Fig. 3. Permeability field sample before (left) and after (right) local averaging is implemented on the top right subdomain of a domain decomposition with $H = 0.25$.

We define the local stochastic dimension to be $N_c = N/M_c$ and L to be the largest correlation length of the prior distribution. For $L < H$, it is expected that an improved convergence for MCMCs should be observed [4].

4.2   The Multiscale Sampling Method

When the number of subdomains $M_c = 1$, the MSM algorithm reduces to the classic preconditioned MCMC [6,9].

Let us first discuss the preconditioned MCMC algorithm. The preconditioned MCMC algorithm requires a coarse-scale model approximation to the pressure-velocity equation Eq. (1). This approximation is the basis for the filtering step of this method. The discretization for both scales, coarse and fine, is similar to each other. An upscaling procedure [8] is applied to produce effective permeability field. The coarse-grid pressure field R_c is calculated by running the numerical simulator on the coarse-scale grid. The coarse-scale acceptance probability α_c and fine-scale acceptance probability α_f are defined by

$$
\alpha_c(\boldsymbol{\eta}, \boldsymbol{\eta}_p) = \min\left(1, \frac{I(\boldsymbol{\eta}|\boldsymbol{\eta}_p)P_c(\boldsymbol{\eta}_p|R_p)}{I(\boldsymbol{\eta}_p|\boldsymbol{\eta})P_c(\boldsymbol{\eta}|R_p)}\right), \text{ and}
$$

$$
\alpha_f(\boldsymbol{\eta}, \boldsymbol{\eta}_p) = \min\left(1, \frac{P_f(\boldsymbol{\eta}_p|R_p)P_c(\boldsymbol{\eta}|R_p)}{P_f(\boldsymbol{\eta}|R_p)P_c(\boldsymbol{\eta}_p|R_p)}\right),
$$

(16)

respectively, where P_c and P_f refer to the posterior probabilities calculated at coarse-scale and fine-scale, respectively. In MSM, the global permeability field is constructed by taking the local averages. The local permeability field $\boldsymbol{\eta}(\boldsymbol{\theta}^i)$ for each subdomain $\Omega_i^c, i = 1, \ldots M_c$ is constructed by generating local KLE using Eq. (10).

4.3   The Multiscale Maximum Change Method

The Multiscale Maximum Change Method (MMCM) consists of two steps namely the screening and local search steps. In the first step, we complete a certain number of iterations (N number of iterations) and update all the stochastic parameters of the vector $\boldsymbol{\theta}$. Next, we pick a specific subdomain (the winner subdomain) among all the subdomains M_c and localize the search to better explore the posterior distribution. We choose the winner subdomain ($M_i, i \leq c$) in such a way that the likelihood function in Eq. (4) is minimized. That means the subdomain that gives maximum change, i.e., $|E_i - E_{i-1}|$ is the maximum, where E_i and E_{i-1} are the errors of the last accepted proposal in the subdomains i and $i - 1$, respectively. The algorithm for MMCM is presented in Algorithm 1.

Algorithm 1. The Multiscale Maximum Change Method (MMCM)

1: For all the subdomains, $\Omega_i^c, i = 1, \ldots, M_c$, solve Eq. (7) to get a KLE in Eq. (10) by using a given covariance function R.
2: **for** $j = 1$ to M_{mcmc} **do**
3:     **for** $i = 1$ to M_c **do**
4:         **for** $k = 1$ to N_c **do**
5:             Generate Gaussian variables i.i.d., $\mathcal{N}(0,1)$ to construct $\boldsymbol{\theta}_p$ using Eq. (15) in Ω_i^c.
6:             The Gaussian preliminary value sample at the $\mathcal{S}_i$ cells are constructed by a local Gaussian sample using the KLE.
7:             Remove discontinuities by using the averaging method.
8:             Estimate the upscaled permeability on the coarse-scale using $\boldsymbol{\eta}_p$.
9:             Solve the forward problem on the coarse-scale to get R_c.
10:             Calculate the acceptance probability $\alpha_c(\boldsymbol{\eta}, \boldsymbol{\eta}_p)$.
11:             **if** $\boldsymbol{\eta}_p$ is accepted **then**
12:                 Use $\boldsymbol{\eta}_p$ to get R_f.
13:                 Compute the acceptance probability $\alpha_f(\boldsymbol{\eta}, \boldsymbol{\eta}_p)$.
14:                 **if** $\boldsymbol{\eta}_p$ is accepted **then** $\boldsymbol{\eta} = \boldsymbol{\eta}_p$.
15:                 **end if**
16:             **end if**
17:             $j = j + 1$.
18:         **end for**
19:     **end for**
20:     Pick the winner subdomain by using the winning criterion.
21:     Continue with the steps from 5-17 for $2 \times N_c$ times.
22: **end for**

---

5   Numerical Results

In this section we discuss the MCMC simulations using MSM and MMCM. The pressure-velocity equation Eq. (1) is numerically solved on the domain $\Omega = [0, 1] \times [0, 1]$. The numerical simulator is run repeatedly in the MCMC algorithm on a GPU cluster. At each iteration in the MCMC simulation, the numerical simulator needs the distribution of permeability values on the physical domain. For that we first construct a permeability field for each subdomain by applying KLE and then the global permeability field is constructed. In KLE, we define the covariance function as follows:

$$R(\boldsymbol{x}_1, \boldsymbol{x}_2) = \sigma_Y^2 \exp\left(-\frac{|x_1 - x_2|^2}{2L_x^2} - \frac{|y_1 - y_2|^2}{2L_y^2} \right), \tag{17}$$

where L_x and L_y are the correlation lengths. We take $L_x = L_y = 0.2$ and $\sigma_Y^2 = \text{Var}[(Y^k)^2] = 1$. Moreover, we set a zero source term and impose Dirichlet boundary conditions $p = 1$ on the left and $p = 0$ on the right boundaries. No-flow (Neumann-type boundary condition) condition is set on the top and bottom boundaries.

We generate a KLE in each of MSM and MMCM. In both methods, we use $H = 0.5$. The first 20 eigenvalues preserving 97% of the total energy are chosen, and five eigenvalues are chosen for each subdomain. Figure 4 shows the decay of the eigenvalues. We run four MCMCs in parallel for each method.

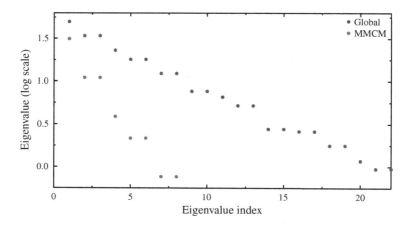

Fig. 4. The decay of the global and local eigenvalues.

On our computational domain of size 16×16 (fine-grid), we generate a reference synthetic permeability field. We then run the GPU numerical simulator [13,14] to generate the pressure field corresponding to this reference permeability field. The pressure values at alternate cells (similar to the black squares of a chessboard) are referred to as pressure measurements. The reference permeability field and the corresponding pressure values are shown in Fig. 5.

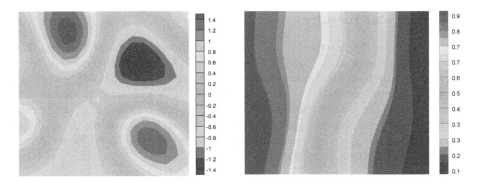

Fig. 5. Reference log permeability field (left) and the corresponding reference pressure field (right).

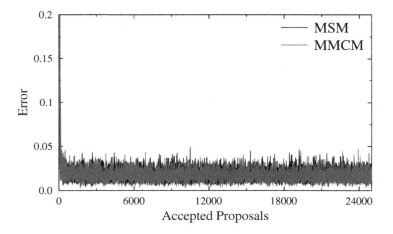

Fig. 6. Error curves of the MSM and MMCM.

We use the maximum of PSRFs and MPSRF to examine the convergence of the MCMC simulations as discussed in Subsect. refmpsrfsps3. If both the MPSRF value and the maximum value of PSRFs approach 1.2, an MCMC simulation can be considered converged to the stationary distribution [32]. Figure 7 shows that both preconditioned MCMC algorithms (MSM and MMCM) converged. The MMCM simulation, however, converges to the stationary distribution faster than the MSM as shown by the bottom plots of Fig. 7. Figure 6 displays the errors for both algorithms. The error at each iteration is calculated by the absolute value of the difference between the reference and simulated pressure data.

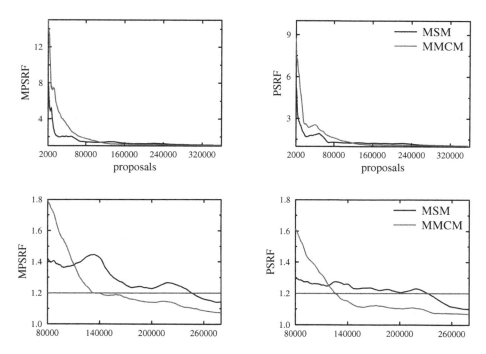

Fig. 7. Top: The maximum of MPSRF and PSRFs for the MSM and MMCM method. Bottom: Tails of the maximum of MPSRF and PSRFs curves.

Figure 8 and Fig. 9 show the accepted permeability fields in two sets of MCMC simulations. The permeability fields generated by MMCM resemble closer to the reference permeability field than those of MSM despite the fact that both methods converged. A similar behavior was observed in other MCMC simulations, as well.

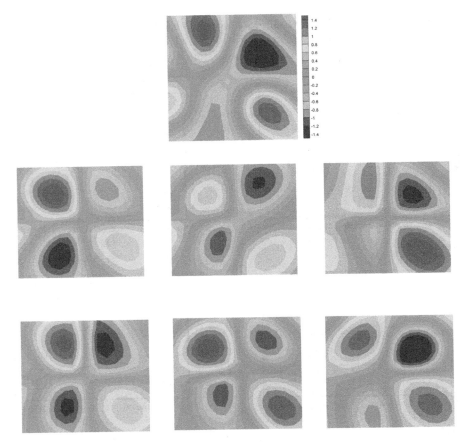

Fig. 8. First row: Reference log permeability filed. Second row: Accepted permeability fields in MSM. Third row: Accepted permeability fields in MMCM. From left to right, log permeability fields at 20000, 40000 and 60000 iterations, respectively, from a set of chains.

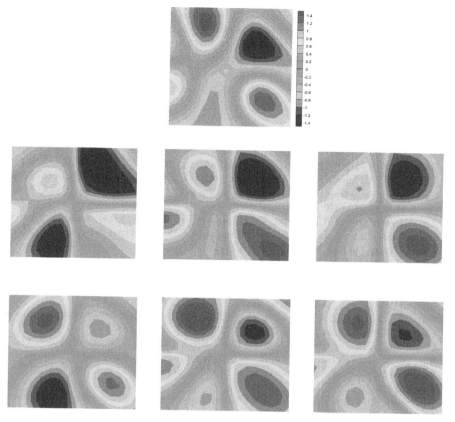

Fig. 9. First row: Reference log permeability filed. Second row: Accepted permeability fields in MSM. Third row: Accepted permeability fields in MMCM. From left to right, log permeability fields at 20000, 40000 and 60000 iterations, respectively, from another set of chains.

6   Conclusions

In this paper we considered the permeability characterization of an aquifer conditioned on measured pressure data. A Bayesian framework was used for the characterization. To improve the convergence rate of the MCMC algorithm in the framework, the new Multiscale Maximum Change Method was introduced. This method is an improvement of the Multiscale Sampling Method. MMCM consists of two steps. In the screening step, we complete a fixed number of iterations on each subdomain and update all the parameters in the stochastic space. In the local search step, we pick the winner subdomain and localize the search to better explore the posterior distribution. The numerical simulations show that both MSM and MMCM converge, but MMCM shows improved convergence.

Acknowledgements. A. Rahunanthan research was supported by NIFA/USDA through Central State University's Evans-Allen Research Program.

All the numerical simulations presented in this paper were performed on the GPU Computing cluster housed in the Department of Mathematics and Computer Science at Central State University.

References

1. Akbarabadi, M., Borges, M., Jan, A., Pereira, F., Piri, M.: A Bayesian framework for the validation of models for subsurface flows: synthetic experiments. Comput. Geosci. **19**(6), 1231–1250 (2015). https://doi.org/10.1007/s10596-015-9538-z
2. Al-Mamun, A., Barber, J., Ginting, V., Pereira, F., Rahunanthan, A.: Contaminant transport forecasting in the subsurface using a Bayesian framework. Appl. Math. Comput. **387**, 124980 (2020)
3. Ali, A., Al-Mamun, A., Pereira, F., Rahunanthan, A.: Multiscale sampling for the inverse modeling of partial differential equations (2023). https://doi.org/10.48550/ARXIV.2302.11149
4. Ali, A.A.H.: Multiscale Sampling for Subsurface Characterization. The University of Texas at Dallas (2021)
5. Brooks, S., Gelman, A.: General methods for monitoring convergence of iterative simulations. J. Comput. Graph. Stat. **7**, 434–455 (1998)
6. Christen, J.A., Fox, C.: Markov chain Monte Carlo using an approximation. J. Comput. Graph. Stat. **14**(4), 795–810 (2005)
7. Contreras, A.A., Mycek, P., Maître, O.P., Rizzi, F., Debusschere, B., Knio, O.M.: Parallel domain decomposition strategies for stochastic elliptic equations. part a: local Karhunen-Loève representations. SIAM J. Sci. Statist. Comput. **40**(4), C520–C546 (2018)
8. Durlofsky, L.: Numerical calculation of equivalent grid block permeability tensors for heterogeneous porous media. Water Resour. Res. **27**(5), 699–708 (1991)
9. Efendiev, Y., Hou, T., Luo, W.: Preconditioning Markov chain Monte Carlo simulations using coarse-scale models. SIAM J. Sci. Comput. **28**, 776–803 (2006)
10. Francisco, A., Ginting, V., Pereira, F., Rigelo, J.: Design and implementation of a multiscale mixed method based on a nonoverlapping domain decomposition procedure. Math. Comput. Simul. **99**, 125–138 (2014)
11. Ginting, V., Pereira, F., Rahunanthan, A.: Multiple Markov chains Monte Carlo approach for flow forecasting in porous media. Procedia Comput. Sci. **9**, 707–716 (2012)
12. Ginting, V., Pereira, F., Rahunanthan, A.: A multi-stage Bayesian prediction framework for subsurface flows. Int. J. Uncertain. Quantif. **3**(6), 499–522 (2013)
13. Ginting, V., Pereira, F., Rahunanthan, A.: A prefetching technique for prediction of porous media flows. Comput. Geosci. **18**(5), 661–675 (2014). https://doi.org/10.1007/s10596-014-9413-3
14. Ginting, V., Pereira, F., Rahunanthan, A.: Rapid quantification of uncertainty in permeability and porosity of oil reservoirs for enabling predictive simulation. Math. Comput. Simul. **99**, 139–152 (2014)
15. Ginting, V., Pereira, F., Rahunanthan, A.: Multi-physics Markov chain Monte Carlo methods for subsurface flows. Math. Comput. Simul. **118**, 224–238 (2015)
16. Guiraldello, R.T., Ausas, R.F., Sousa, F.S., Pereira, F., Buscaglia, G.C.: The multiscale Robin coupled method for flows in porous media. J. Comput. Phys. **355**, 1–21 (2018)

17. Guiraldello, R.T., Ausas, R.F., Sousa, F.S., Pereira, F., Buscaglia, G.C.: Velocity postprocessing schemes for multiscale mixed methods applied to contaminant transport in subsurface flows. Comput. Geosci. **24**(3), 1141–1161 (2020). https://doi.org/10.1007/s10596-019-09930-8
18. Jaramillo, A., et al.: Towards HPC simulations of billion-cell reservoirs by multiscale mixed methods. arXiv preprint arXiv:2103.08513 (2021)
19. Laloy, E., Rogiers, B., Vrugt, J., Mallants, D., Jacques, D.: Efficient posterior exploration of a high-dimensional groundwater model from two-stage Markov chain Monte Marlo simulation and polynomial chaos expansion. Water Resour. **49**(5), 2664–2682 (2013)
20. Liao, Q., Willcox, K.: A domain decomposition approach for uncertainty analysis. SIAM J. Sci. Comput. **37**(1), A103–A133 (2015)
21. Loève, M.: Probability Theory. Springer, Berlin (1997)
22. Cowles, M.K., Carlin, B.P.: Markov chain Monte Carlo convergence diagnostics: a comparative review. J. Am. Stat. Assoc. **91**, 883–904 (1996)
23. Mamun, A., Pereira, F., Rahunanthan, A.: Convergence analysis of MCMC methods for subsurface flow problems. In: Gervasi, O., et al. (eds.) ICCSA 2018. LNCS, vol. 10961, pp. 305–317. Springer, Cham (2018). https://doi.org/10.1007/978-3-319-95165-2_22
24. Mengersen, K.L., Robert, C.P., Guihenneuc-Jouyaux, C.: MCMC convergence diagnostics: a review. In: Bernardo, M., Berger, J.O., Dawid, A.P., Smtith, A.F.M. (eds.) Bayesian Statistics, vol. 6, pp. 415–440. Oxford University Press (1999)
25. Metropolis, N., Ulam, S.: The Monte Carlo method. J. Am. Stat. Assoc. **44**(247), 335–341 (1949)
26. Pereira, F., Rahunanthan, A.: A semi-discrete central scheme for the approximation of two-phase flows in three space dimensions. Math. Comput. Simul. **81**(10), 2296–2306 (2011)
27. Polson, N.G.: Convergence of Markov chain Monte Carlo algorithms. In: Bernardo, J.M., Berger, J.O., Dawid, A.P., Smith, A.F.M. (eds.) Bayesian Statistics, vol. 5, pp. 297–322 (1996)
28. Quarteroni, A.M., Valli, A.: Domain Decomposition Methods for Partial Differential Equations. Oxford University Press, Oxford (1999)
29. Rosenthal, J.S.: Minorization conditions and convergence rates for Markov chain Monte Carlo. J. Am. Stat. Assoc. **90**(430), 558–566 (1995)
30. Roy, V.: Convergence diagnostics for Markov chain Monte Carlo. Annu. Rev. Stat. Appl. **7**, 387–412 (2019)
31. Brooks, S.P., Roberts, G.O.: Convergence assessment techniques for Markov chain Monte Carlo. Stat. Comput. **8**, 319–335 (1998)
32. Smith, B.J.: boa: an R package for MCMC output convergence assessment and posterior inference. J. Stat. Softw. **21**, 1–37 (2007)
33. Stuart, G.K., Minkoff, S.E., Pereira, F.: A two-stage Markov chain Monte Carlo method for seismic inversion and uncertainty quantification. Geophysics **84**(6), R1003–R1020 (2019)
34. Tong, X.T., Morzfeld, M., Marzouk, Y.M.: MALA-within-Gibbs samplers for high-dimensional distributions with sparse conditional structure. SIAM J. Sci. Comput. **42**(3), A1765–A1788 (2020)

Anonymized Data Assessment via Analysis of Variance: An Application to Higher Education Evaluation

Maria Eugénia Ferrão[1,2] , Paula Prata[1,3(✉)] , and Paulo Fazendeiro[1,3]

[1] University of Beira Interior, Covilhã, Portugal
{meferrao,fazendeiro}@ubi.pt, pprata@di.ubi.pt
[2] Centre for Applied Mathematics and Economics (CEMAPRE), Lisbon, Portugal
[3] Instituto de Telecomunicações (IT), Covilhã, Portugal

Abstract. The assessment of the utility of an anonymized data set can be operationalized by the determination of the amount of information loss. To investigate the possible degradation of the relationship between variables after anonymization, hence measuring the loss, we perform an *a posteriori* analysis of variance. Several anonymized scenarios are compared with the original data. Differential privacy is applied as data anonymization process. We assess data utility based on the agreement between the original data structure and the anonymized structures. Data quality and utility are quantified by standard metrics, characteristics of the groups obtained. In addition, we use analysis of variance to show how estimates change. For illustration, we apply this approach to Brazilian Higher Education data with focus on the main effects of interaction terms involving gender differentiation. The findings indicate that blindly using anonymized data for scientific purposes could potentially undermine the validity of the conclusions.

Keywords: Data anonymization · Differential privacy · Data utility · Data quality · ENADE

1 Introduction

The challenge of monitoring sociodemographic gaps in educational outcomes shares some characteristics with other regulatory problems. Regarding the achievement of social justice, the cycle of public policies requires statistical evidence to inform policymakers. How can they promote a just society and what actions can they take to achieve this goal? The Brazilian education evaluation system is mentored to provide such evidence. Specifically, the Exame Nacional de Desempenho dos Estudantes [National Examination of Students Performance] (ENADE) [1] refers to higher education, and allows the computing of several indicators and measures. In addition, ENADE data have been used for scientific research in several scientific fields [2]. For instance, researchers [3] may ask "Are exam-based evaluative methods really adequate to evaluate institutions and courses?", "Does students' performance in standardized tests enable a reliable assessment about the quality of undergraduate courses?" These are just a few valuable research

© The Author(s), under exclusive license to Springer Nature Switzerland AG 2023
O. Gervasi et al. (Eds.): ICCSA 2023 Workshops, LNCS 14105, pp. 130–141, 2023.
https://doi.org/10.1007/978-3-031-37108-0_9

questions on the topic. It is not our main concern to answer any of these questions in this study. Instead, we stand the need of conducting scientific research to support these or other related research questions. We are also certain on the benefits of leveraging evidence-based public policy and, thus, on the potential use of educational data assessment for improvement of education systems. The same is to say that making science for policy in social sciences implies the statistical modeling of administrative data. Thus, with such promising potential benefits in mind, our main concern is the data privacy issues which have emerged with the General Data Protection Regulation (GDPR) initiatives in effect across several regions around the world. In fact, restrictions to microdata access, even when the access intends scientific use, may compromise the contribution of scientific research for social justice.

At least since the 1970s, the subject of data privacy has been discussed in the specialized literature [4, 5]. Despite the great methodological developments, the adoption of data anonymization procedures still does not meet the needs for scientific research purposes in social and behavioral sciences [6]. Following previous work [7, 8], we intend to show obstacles of anonymized data by differential privacy for statistical modelling applied to higher education data.

The article is organized as follows: Sect. 2 presents methodological aspects related to ENADE database, it includes some details of differential privacy as the method applied here for the purpose of data anonymization and its implementation. It also includes a subsection on methods to assess the quality and utility of anonymized data. Section 3 presents the main results and interpretation. Finally, the conclusion is in Sect. 4.

2 Methodology

2.1 Dataset Description

Since 2004, the National Student Performance Exam (ENADE) has been held annually in Brazil to evaluate the performance of graduates from higher education institutions across various dimensions and skills [1, 9]. As a component of Brazilian higher education evaluation system (Sinaes), which includes institutional and program evaluations, the ENADE is instrumental in monitoring the quality indicators of higher education. Participation in the exam is mandatory for all students, and the assessment instruments cover multiple domains based on their field of study. The evaluation cycle for various academic programs is conducted over a three-year period, with different disciplinary areas being assessed each year, including baccalaureate and degree courses in health sciences, agrarian sciences, engineering, architecture, humanities, social sciences, and higher technology courses in various domains.

In 2019, 433930 students were involved (ENADE 2019 - version updated in May 13th, 2021). The exam generates a set of detailed information on the participating students, as well as the courses and Higher Education Institutions evaluated, that is, the microdata composed of 139 variables. This article considers both the students' specific score, such as their grade point average, $gpa1$, and their general score, $gpa2$, as well as their sociodemographic variables, including gender, age, self-declared race/skin color, mother's and father's education levels, working status, family income, and region. We introduced two new variables: (i) the "number of years needed to finish the graduate studies", *years2finish*, computed by the difference between the current year (2019) and the "year of beginning graduation" plus one, and (ii) the number of years of school leave, *years_leave*, computed by the difference between the starting year of graduation, *year_in*, and the last year of secondary school, *year_hs*. Since some values recorded in the data set were not plausible according to the purposes of ENADE and the Brazilian Educational System, it was necessary to pre-process the dataset.

After removing missing and duplicated data, the original data set was reduced to 89.68% of the original size, that is, 389180 rows. Moreover, it was necessary to remove nonsensical data. Notice that in Brazil the academic year agrees with the civil year, the exam occurs at the end of the course (2019 in the present case) and the course takes at least 3 years to be concluded. We selected only the cases where the starting year of graduation, *year_in*, lies in the interval [2002, 2017]. To further remove outliers, the values of the last year of secondary school, *year_hs* were filtered to the interval [1992, 2017]. The cases where the last year of secondary school was bigger than the starting year of graduation were eliminated. Students aged under 16 were also removed from the dataset. This whole process of data cleansing resulted in the elimination of 72343 records from the downloaded data set. Thus, the resulting data set, with 361587 (83.32% of the initial size) records, will be hereafter referred to in this paper as the original (prior to anonymization) data set, DS0.

Table 1, shows for each of the selected variables, the label used in the experiments, its range in the original data set and its classification for the purpose of data anonymization. In the process of data anonymization the attributes are classified as direct identifiers, quasi-identifiers, sensitive, or insensitive, according to their characteristics [10]. Direct identifiers, that is, the ones that are associated with a high risk of re-identification were not present in the ENADE data. A quasi-identifier is an attribute that in combination with quasi-identifiers from other data sets can be useful for re-identification. Six quasi-identifiers were considered in this study: region, age, gender, race/skin color and the two computed variables *years2finish* and *years_leave*. The other attributes were considered as insensitive, that is, they are not associated with any privacy risk.

2.2 Differential Privacy

The concept of differential privacy (DP) was introduced in 2006 [11, 12] as a mathematical definition of privacy designed to statistical data analysis. According to [11], a randomized function R gives ε-Differential Privacy (ε-DP) if for all data sets D1 and D2 differing on at most one record, and for all potential output of R that could be predicted, $S \subseteq \text{Range}(R)$,

$$\Pr[R(D1) \in S] \leq \exp(\varepsilon) * \Pr[R(D2) \in S] \tag{1}$$

Informally speaking, "differential privacy protects the privacy of individuals by requiring that the information of an individual does not significantly affect the output" of any computation that can be performed on the data [13]. The ε parameter, called privacy budget, is a measure of privacy loss. A variant of DP is "approximate differential privacy" introduced in [14] and called (ε, δ)-DP. It is a relaxation of pure DP where the guarantee of Eq. (1) needs to be satisfied only for events whose probability is at least $\approx$ 1–δ [15, 16].

Table 1. Selected variables, respective scales in DS0 and attribute classification.

Variable	Label	Range	Attribute type
University id	uni_id	Between 1 and 23410	Insensitive
Program id	prog_id	Between 3 and 5,001,378	Insensitive
Region	reg	1 = North (N) 2 = Northeast (NE) 3 = Southeast (SE) 4 = South (S) 5 = Central-West (C-W)	Quasi-identifier
Age	age	Between 19 and 86	Quasi-identifier
Gender	gen	M = Male F = Female	Quasi-identifier
Grade point average (specific score)	gpa1	Minimum = 0; Maximum = 93.0	Insensitive
Grade point average (general score)	gpa2	Minimum = 0; Maximum = 98.0	Insensitive
Race / skin color	race	A = White B = Black C = Yellow D = Pardo E = Indigenous F = Not declared	Quasi-identifier
Father's education	edu_f	1 = None 2 = 1st – 5th grade 3 = 6th – 9th grade	Insensitive
Mother's education	edu_m	4 = Secondary school 5 = Graduation 6 = Post-graduation	Insensitive
Family's income	inco	1 = Up to 1.5 minimum wages 2 = 1.5 to 3 minimum wages 3 = 3 to 4.5 minimum wages 4 = 4.5 to 6 minimum wages 5 = 6 to 10 minimum wages 6 = 10 to 30 minimum wages 7 = Above 30 minimum wages	Insensitive
Working status	work	A = Not working B = Work eventually C = Work up to 20 h a week D = Work 21 to 39 h a week E = Work 40 h a week or more	Insensitive

(continued)

Table 1. (*continued*)

Variable	Label	Range	Attribute type
Scholarship for non-local college attendance	schol	A = None B = Housing allowance C = Meal allowance D = Housing and food allowance E = Permanence allowance F = Other type of aid	Insensitive
Academic Scholarship	ac_schol	A = None B = Scientific initiation scholarship C = Extension scholarship D = Monitoring/tutoring sch E = PET scholarship F = Other type of academic sch	Insensitive
Number of years to finish the graduation	years2finish	Between 3 and 18	Quasi-identifier
Years between high school and college	years_leave	Between 0 and 25	Quasi-identifier

Nowadays, several implementations of DP techniques are ready to use. Some change the data by addition of random noise [17–20] and others by random sampling [16, 21]. In this work, we used the SafePub algorithm [16] that implements (ε, δ)-DP using the last approach. This algorithm, available in the open source ARX - Data Anonymization Tool, starts by randomly sampling the dataset. Usually, in a previous step users define generalization hierarchies for the quasi-identifiers for which they intend to decrease precision, for instance by changing the scale or order of magnitude. In the ENADE data, some of the attributes are already generalized as can be seen in Table 1 (see e.g., Father's and Mother' education or Family's income). In this work no hierarchy was defined for the studied attributes. From the parameters ε and δ the algorithm derives a value of k and proceeds performing k-anonymization [22]. This means that all the records appearing less than k times in the current dataset are suppressed. That process is repeated for each possible generalization hierarchy, searching for an optimal solution for a utility model chosen by the user. Finally, the output satisfies k-anonymity and has approximate differential privacy, (ε, δ)-DP, as shown in [16].

2.3 Utility and ANOVA Modelling

The assessment of the utility of an anonymized dataset should be based on data purpose, i.e. utility models typically evaluate data utility by quantifying the amount of information loss. For example, by measuring differences or similarities between the input and the output dataset [23]. Other examples include the sum of squared errors, average distinguishability [24], non-uniform entropy [25] and discernibility [26].

In addition, the analysis of variance (ANOVA) is a useful statistical tool for analyzing differences between groups and can provide valuable insights into the relationships between different variables. In this work the analysis of variance model ($\alpha = 0.05$) is used to statistically compare the results between the original and the anonymized datasets. It is applied to identify student's sociodemographic characteristics (gender, race/skin color, mother's education, family's income, working status, region) which, *ceteris paribus*, may influence (specific) grade point average, *gpa1*, and (general) grade point average, *gpa2*. The statistical model includes the main effects and the following 1st order interactions: gender–working status, gender–race/skin color, gender–family's income, gender–region. Other significant interactions were explored with a Bonferroni correction. The substantive evidence will be presented in Table 5 with the purpose of showing the terms that become not statistically significant depending on the anonymization scenario. Details about the ANOVA model may be found in Scheffé [27].

3   Results

After preprocessing the ENADE 2019 data, the resulting data set, DS0, was anonymized using the ARX tool (version 3.9.1). The privacy model (ε, δ)-DP was applied varying the values of ε and δ for five cases illustrated in Table 2. In the data sets DS1, DS2 and DS3 the value of δ was fixed ($\delta = 0.01$) and the value of ε decreases from 3 to 1. In the data sets DS3, DS4 and DS5 the value of ε was fixed ($\varepsilon = 1$) and the value of δ decreases from 0.01 to 0.0001. For all data sets the process of anonymization was configured with the following parameters: suppression limit, 100%; utility measure, loss; aggregate function, rank; the search strategy was "best-effort, button up" with a limited number of 5 000 steps; all the remaining parameters took the ARX default values.

Table 2. Privacy model, number of records, value of k and estimated risk for each dataset.

Dataset	Privacy model	N° of records	K value	Estimated risk
DS0	-	361587	-	100%
DS1	(3, 0.01)-DP	186245	68	1.5%
DS2	(2, 0.01)-DP	185636	38	2.6%
DS3	**(1, 0.01)-DP**	**144332**	**19**	**5.2%**
DS4	(1, 0.001)-DP	127032	33	3.0%
DS5	(1, 0.0001)-DP	117145	45	2.2%

From Table 2, it is possible to observe that, for the studied data set, the number of records remaining after anonymization decreases when the value of ε decreases keeping the value of δ, as well as the number of records decreases when the value of δ decreases keeping the value of ε. Despite DS1 having the largest number of records, it has the highest value of k. This may seem counter-intuitive because a high value of k could lead to the assumption of a large deletion of records, but as rightfully noted in [28] "privacy is a subjective concept, it varies from person to person, from time to time, even for the same person".

Finally, the last column of Table 2 presents the re-identification risk estimated by ARX for each data set. Usually, three attacker's profiles are considered leading to journalist, prosecutor, and marketer risk. These classifications are related with the way of modelling the adversary's background knowledge about an individual [29]. The models are described in [30] and it is shown that prosecutor risk $\geq$ journalist risk $\geq$ marketer risk. We present the value obtained for the attacker's model that results in the highest risk of re-identification, that is, the estimated prosecutor risk. As can be observed, DS1 has the lowest risk, there just 1.5% of the records are at risk of re-identification. The data set with the lowest value of k, DS3, has the highest risk, that is, 5.2% of the records are at risk of re-identification.

Following the three main steps of data anonymization, apply a privacy model, quantify the risk of re-identification and assess data utility [23], next we present the results of measuring the quality of the studied data sets starting by quality models provided by ARX. Table 3 shows for each data set and for each quasi-identifier the value of the non-uniform entropy [31]. It compares the frequencies of quasi-identifier values in each anonymized dataset with the according frequencies in the original dataset. The ARX tool scales and normalizes the values returned by all the implemented quality models into the range [0, 1] where 0 represents a dataset from which all information has been removed and 1 represents the unmodified input dataset [23]. From Table 3, we can see that DS3 has the best values for the non-uniform entropy and DS5 the worst ones.

Table 3. Quality models: non-uniform entropy for the quasi-identifiers.

Dataset	region	age	gender	race	years2finish	years_leave
DS1	51.5%	48.4%	54.8%	45.4%	48.1%	43.5%
DS2	58.2%	55.0%	61.1%	52.2%	54.9%	50.5%
DS3	**63.9%**	**61.1%**	**67.8%**	**58.3%**	**60.8%**	**57.3%**
DS4	55.8%	52.6%	58.8%	49.6%	52.3%	48.0%
DS5	51.0%	47.9%	54.2%	44.9%	47.6%	42.9%

Table 4 presents for each data set and for each quasi-identifier the values of the sum of squared errors (SSE). The SSE [32] calculates the sum of squares of attribute distances between records in DS0 and their versions in the anonymized data set.

As can be seen from Table 4, the best results are obtained again for DS3. If we notice that DS3 is the data set with the highest re-identification risk, this is an expected result. More useful information means greater risk.

Beyond these standard quality metrics to further enhance the quality assessment we apply the ANOVA model to the studied data sets with *gpa2* as the dependent variable. Considering DS0 as the data reference, the estimates obtained suggest that main effects

Table 4. Quality models: sum of squared errors for the quasi-identifiers.

Dataset	region	age	gender	race	years2finish	years_leave
DS1	49.8%	60.2%	55.2%	59.1%	55.65	61.0%
DS2	56.4%	66.6%	61.5%	65.1%	61.8%	67.1%
DS3	**62.3%**	**72.4%**	**67.1%**	**68.0%**	**67.5%**	**72.1%**
DS4	54.1%	64.7%	59.2%	60.2%	60.0.%	64.8%
DS5	49.3%	60.1%	54.6%	55.9%	55.0%	60.5%

and interactions on *gpa2* are statistically different from zero. The proportion of variance explained by the model (R^2) is 38.3%. The Table 5 pinpoints the terms that do not present interactions statistically different from zero at a level of significance of 5%, i.e., the 'X' marks terms not statistically different from zero at 5%. Depending on the dataset the results change. For example, ANOVA model applied to DS4 and DS1 suggests that gender has no effect on *gpa2*, nor gender interactions with race/skin color or family income. Another example, by applying the model to DS2 the only interaction term that is statistically non-significant is gender-income.

Table 5. Original and anonymized data ANOVA results: gpa2 as dependent variable.

Dataset Variable	DS0	DS1	DS2	DS3	DS4	DS5
Region	X	-	-	-	-	-
Gpa1	X	-	-	-	-	-
Gender	X	X	-	-	X	-
Race/Skin color	X	-	-	-	-	-
Mother's education	X	-	-	-	-	-
Family's income	X	-	-	-	-	-
Working Status	X	-	-	-	-	-
Gender – Working status	X	-	-	-	-	-
Gender – Race/skin color	X	X	-	X	X	X
Gender – Family's income	X	X	X	X	X	X
Gender – Region	X	-	-	-	-	-
Adjusted R^2	38.3%	36.8%	36.8%	37.0%	36.9%	36.7%

As a matter of fact, it is possible to verify that several terms cease to present statistically significant effects according to the remaining data modelling of the anonymized datasets. For instance, DS3 and DS5 seem to indicate that the interactions of gender with race/skin color or with family income potentially have no effect on gpa2 — contrary to what is verified in the original dataset. Please notice that the variance explained is approximately 37% for every model.

To emphasize the difficulty of identifying the loss of the effects of some of the interaction Gender-Income term after anonymization Fig. 1, 2 and 3 depict the results of some visualization tools traditionally used in exploratory data analysis. The estimated marginal means of *gpa2* for the interaction gender with family income is reported in Fig. 1 for DS0 and in Fig. 2 for DS3, whereas the correlation between all the variable pairs is visually conveyed via bivariate association in the heatmap of Fig. 3.

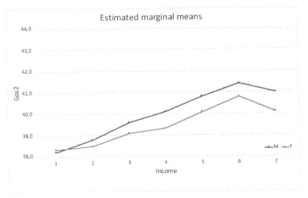

Fig. 1. Gender–Family's income estimated marginal means for DS0

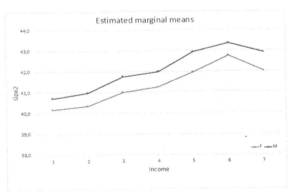

Fig. 2. Gender–Family's income estimated marginal means for DS3

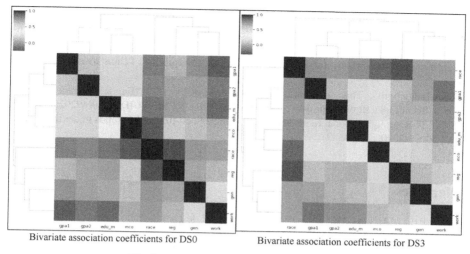

Bivariate association coefficients for DS0

Bivariate association coefficients for DS3

Fig. 3. Correlation matrix for DS0 and DS3

4 Conclusion

In this study, we used the research topic of equity in higher education to demonstrate that even the most suitable anonymization method for big data sets, i.e. differential privacy [20], can become ineffective for anonymizing data whose primary purpose is scientific research in social and behavioral sciences. The quantitative research on equity in higher education is based on the correlational structure between the variables involved. Therefore, we used as an example the Brazilian data from the National Student Performance Exam (ENADE) to investigate the relationship between various sociodemographic variables and the specific performance of students at the end of the course through an ANOVA model.

We particularly focused on the main effects of interaction terms involving gender differentiation. The risk of re-identification for anonymized datasets is around 5% or less. Considering the dataset that is closest to the original, based on two quality and/or utility metrics (entropy and sum of squared errors), the substantive conclusion that can be drawn from modeling anonymized data is that the two interactions "Gender – Race" and "Gender - Family's income" are not statistically significant (at a significance level of 5%). In fact, we found the opposite with the original data! This means that the object of research, that is equity in higher education, may be distorted based on anonymized data. The same is to say that anonymization may lead to a reduction in the amount of information available, and in turn, to a loss of statistical power to detect significant effects or interactions.

While the analysis and modeling of microdata from administrative records are essential for scientific research in various fields [6], the implementation of GDPR has brought additional challenges. In some countries, its implementation makes such research impossible. At the time of publication of this article, neither in Portugal nor in Brazil would it be possible to conduct research on equity in higher education based on recently collected microdata from administrative records outside of the secure rooms located in Lisbon [8] and Brasilia, respectively. Researchers in these countries often work outside of the capital cities. Unfortunately, when the primary or sole method of accessing microdata is through anonymized data, it can negatively impact the quality of their research.

Acknowledgements. This work was partially funded by FCT- Fundação para a Ciência e a Tecnologia through project number CEMAPRE/REM - UIDB/05069/2020 and by FCT/MCTES through national funds and when applicable co-funded EU funds under the project UIDB/50008/2020.

References

1. An, P.E.: MANUAL DO ENADE Exame Nacional de Desempenho dos Estudantes. Dados (2004)
2. Fernandes, A. de O., Gomes, S. dos S.: Exame Nacional de Desempenho de Estudantes (Enade): Tendências da produção científica brasileira (2004–2018). Educ. Policy Anal. Arch. 30 (2022). https://doi.org/10.14507/epaa.30.6547
3. Bertolin, J.C.G., Marcon, T.: O (des)entendimento de qualidade na educação superior brasileira – Das quimeras do provão e do ENADE à realidade do capital cultural dos estudantes. Avaliação. **20**, 105–122 (2015). 10.590/S1414-40772015000100008
4. Dalenius, T.: Towards a methodology for statistical disclosure control. Stat. Tidskr. Stat. Rev. 15, 429–444 (1977)
5. Dalenius, T.: Finding a needle in a haystack. J. Off. Stat. **2**, 329–336 (1986)
6. Hand, D.J.: Statistical challenges of administrative and transaction data. J. R. Stat. Soc. Ser. A Stat. Soc. **181**, 555–605 (2018). https://doi.org/10.1111/rssa.12315
7. Santos, W., Sousa, G., Prata, P., Ferrao, M.E.: Data anonymization: K-anonymity sensitivity analysis. In: 2020 15th Iberian Conference on Information Systems and Technologies (CISTI), pp. 1–6. IEEE, Sevilla (2020)
8. Ferrão, M.E., Prata, P., Fazendeiro, P.: Utility-driven assessment of anonymized data via clustering. Sci. Data. **9**, 1–11 (2022). https://doi.org/10.1038/s41597-022-01561-6
9. INEP - Instituto Nacional de Estudos e Pesquisas Educacionais Anísio Teixeira: ANRESC (Prova Brasil). https://www.gov.br/inep/pt-br/acesso-a-informacao/dados-abertos/microdados
10. Cox, L.H.: Suppression methodology and statistical disclosure control. J. Am. Stat. Assoc. **75**, 377–385 (1980). https://doi.org/10.1080/01621459.1980.10477481
11. Dwork, C.: Differential privacy. In: Bugliesi, M., Preneel, B., Sassone, V., Wegener, I. (eds.) ICALP 2006. LNCS, vol. 4052, pp. 1–12. Springer, Heidelberg (2006). https://doi.org/10.1007/11787006_1
12. Dwork, C.: Differential privacy: a survey of results. In: Agrawal, M., Du, D., Duan, Z., Li, A. (eds.) TAMC 2008. LNCS, vol. 4978, pp. 1–19. Springer, Heidelberg (2008). https://doi.org/10.1007/978-3-540-79228-4_1
13. Beimel, A., Nissim, K., Stemmer, U.: Private learning and sanitization: pure vs. approximate differential privacy. Theory Comput. **12**, 1–61 (2016). https://doi.org/10.4086/toc.2016.v012a001
14. Dwork, C., Kenthapadi, K., McSherry, F., Mironov, I., Naor, M.: Our data, ourselves: privacy via distributed noise generation. In: Vaudenay, S. (ed.) EUROCRYPT 2006. LNCS, vol. 4004, pp. 486–503. Springer, Heidelberg (2006). https://doi.org/10.1007/11761679_29

15. Kasiviswanathan, S.P., Smith, A.: On the "semantics" of differential privacy: a bayesian formulation. J. Priv. Confidentiality. **6** (2014). https://doi.org/10.29012/jpc.v6i1.634

16. Bild, R., Kuhn, K.A., Prasser, F.: SafePub: a truthful data anonymization algorithm with strong privacy guarantees. Proc. Priv. Enhancing Technol. **2018**, 67–87 (2018). https://doi.org/10.1515/popets-2018-0004

17. Avraam, D., Boyd, A., Goldstein, H., Burton, P.: A software package for the application of probabilistic anonymisation to sensitive individual-level data: a proof of principle with an example from the ALSPAC birth cohort study. Longit. Life Course Stud. **9**, 433–446 (2018). https://doi.org/10.14301/llcs.v9i4.478

18. Goldstein, H., Shlomo, N.: A probabilistic procedure for anonymisation, for assessing the risk of re-identification and for the analysis of perturbed data sets. J. Off. Stat. **36**, 89–115 (2020). https://doi.org/10.2478/jos-2020-0005

19. Jagannathan, G., Pillaipakkamnatt, K., Wright, R.N.: A practical differentially private random decision tree classifier. ICDM Work. In: 2009 - IEEE International Conference on Data Mining, pp. 114–121 (2009). https://doi.org/10.1109/ICDMW.2009.93

20. Jain, P., Gyanchandani, M., Khare, N.: Differential privacy: its technological prescriptive using big data. J. Big Data **5**(1), 1–24 (2018). https://doi.org/10.1186/s40537-018-0124-9

21. Li, N., Qardaji, W., Su, D.: On sampling, anonymization, and differential privacy or, k - anonymization meets differential privacy. In: Proceedings of the 7th ACM Symposium on Information, Computer and Communications Security - ASIACCS 2012, p. 32. ACM Press, New York (2012)

22. Sweeney, L.: A model for protecting privacy. Ieee S&P '02. 10, 1–14 (2002)

23. Prasser, F., Eicher, J., Spengler, H., Bild, R., Kuhn, K.A.: Flexible data anonymization using ARX—Current status and challenges ahead. Softw. Pract. Exp. **50**, 1277–1304 (2020). https://doi.org/10.1002/spe.2812

24. LeFevre, K., DeWitt, D.J., Ramakrishnan, R.: Mondrian multidimensional K-anonymity. In: 22nd International Conference on Data Engineering (ICDE 2006), p. 25. IEEE (2006)

25. Gionis, A., Tassa, T.: k-anonymization with minimal loss of information. In: Arge, L., Hoffmann, M., Welzl, E. (eds.) ESA 2007. LNCS, vol. 4698, pp. 439–450. Springer, Heidelberg (2007). https://doi.org/10.1007/978-3-540-75520-3_40

26. Bayardo, R.J., Agrawal, R.: Data privacy through optimal k-anonymization. In: 21st International Conference on Data Engineering (ICDE 2005), pp. 217–228. IEEE (2005)

27. Scheffé, H.: The Analysis of Variance. Wiley, Hoboken (1999)

28. Yu, S.: Big privacy: challenges and opportunities of privacy study in the age of big data. IEEE Access. **4**, 2751–2763 (2016). https://doi.org/10.1109/ACCESS.2016.2577036

29. El Emam, K.: Guide to the De-Identification of Personal Health Information. Auerbach Publications, Boca Raton (2013)

30. Kniola, L.: Plausible adversaries in re-identification risk assessment. In: PhUSE Annual Conference (2017)

31. Prasser, F., Bild, R., Kuhn, K.A.: A generic method for assessing the quality of De-identified health data. Stud. Health Technol. Inform. **228**, 312–316 (2016). https://doi.org/10.3233/978-1-61499-678-1-312

32. Soria-Comas, J., Domingo-Ferrer, J., Sanchez, D., Martinez, S.: t-closeness through microaggregation: Strict privacy with enhanced utility preservation. IEEE Trans. Knowl. Data Eng. **27**, 3098–3110 (2015)

Cyber Intelligence and Applications (CIA 2023)

Mitigating User Exposure to Dark Patterns in Cookie Banners Through Automated Consent

Lorenzo Porcelli$^{(\boxtimes)}$ [iD], Massimo Ficco [iD], and Francesco Palmieri [iD]

Department of Computer Science, University of Salerno, Fisciano, SA, Italy
{lporcelli,mficco,fpalmieri}@unisa.it

Abstract. The General Data Protection Regulation (GDPR) has established a de facto standard for presenting consent banners to users. To comply with the GDPR, websites are required to obtain user consent before processing their personal data, both for the provision of services and the monitoring of user behavior. Despite this, the most commonly adopted paradigm involves informing and requesting user preferences when visiting a website, often without adhering to GDPR standards and including dark patterns, such as dark nudges. In this paper, we propose a Personal Information Management Service that automatically generates consent responses based on user preferences, leveraging a Large Language Model. We demonstrate the feasibility of the proposed approach in a case study involving ChatGPT.

Keywords: Personal Information Management Service (PIMS) · GDPR · Transparency and Consent Framework (TCF) · Cookie banner · Dark pattern · Nudging · Large Language Model (LLM) · Generative Pre-trained Transformer (GPT)

1 Introduction

Modern computing technologies enable the collection, manipulation, and sharing of large amounts of data. This has led to the emergence of a thriving trade in personal information. However, users are often unaware or unable to evaluate the increasingly sophisticated methods designed to collect information about them [34]. With the introduction of the General Data Protection Regulation (GDPR) [19], privacy concerns regarding online services have gained greater prominence. One of the most visible aspects of the GDPR is the emergence of cookie banners for profiling choices (also known as cookie consent notices or consent dialogs). In fact, to comply with GDPR regulations, websites are required to display cookie consent notices that provide users with information about the use of cookies and tracking practices. It should be noted that the rules outlined in the GDPR apply to the handling of personal data of individuals located in the EU, regardless of whether the processing is carried out by an entity outside of the EU. Therefore, compliance with GDPR is mandatory not

© The Author(s), under exclusive license to Springer Nature Switzerland AG 2023
O. Gervasi et al. (Eds.): ICCSA 2023 Workshops, LNCS 14105, pp. 145–159, 2023.
https://doi.org/10.1007/978-3-031-37108-0_10

only for European companies, but also for non-European entities that create software and services intended for use by EU citizens [23].

As service and content providers are required to obtain users' consent before processing their personal data, users can communicate their privacy preferences through digital signals that specify how their data will be processed. The Transparency and Consent Framework (TCF) standardized by the Interactive Advertising Bureau (IAB) is the prevailing approach for collecting user privacy signals, and it is deemed as the only GDPR consent solution designed by the industry for the industry [22]. However, several Consent Management Platforms (CMPs) that adopt this framework often do not fully or only partially comply with the requirements established by the GDPR [28]. In more detail, several studies have highlighted that:

- cookie banners on web pages do not necessarily respect people's choices [30];
- about half of EU websites violate the EU directive on cookies, installing profiling cookies before user consent [37];
- opting out is much more complicated than opting in, and especially changing or revoking previously accepted settings is very difficult [31];
- dark patterns as nudging and implicit consent are ubiquitous [32, 36].

Our proposal aims to introduce a Personal Information Management Service (PIMS) as an intermediary between the user and the CMP within the Transparency and Consent Framework (TCF). The novelty of the proposed approach is the use of a Large Language Model (LLM) for generating and applying rules to enable automatic responses to cookie consent notices. By reducing user interaction with cookie banner on websites, we can effectively mitigate the potential negative effects of dark patterns and provide a seamless browsing experience for users. The latter part of this article is structured as follows. Section 2 provides an introduction to privacy preference signals. Section 3 outlines previous research in the field. In Sect. 4, we conceptually describe the proposed PIMS and place it within the TCF, and then in Sect. 5, report a practical case study. Section 6 delves into a discussion of our proposal and the results we obtained. Finally, we draw our conclusions and future works in Sect. 7.

2   Privacy Preference Signals

Hils et al. [27] identify two waves of privacy preference signals, which are digital representations of how users want their personal data to be processed. The first wave includes the Platform for Privacy Preferences (P3P), Do Not Track (DNT), and the opt-out standards of the Network Advertising Initiative (NAI). The second wave includes signals that have a legal basis, such as the Global Privacy Control (GPC) signal and the Transparency and Consent Framework (TCF). The GPC signal is based on the California Consumer Privacy Act (CCPA) and is standardized by dozens of organizations [8], while the different versions of the TCF are based on the GDPR and are standardized by the Interactive Advertising Bureau (IAB). The P3P standard was retired in 2018 [16]. Currently, only nine companies [2] have publicly declared their support for the Do Not Track (DNT) signal [21], while the NAI system has over 100 AdTech members [13]. Regarding the GPC specification, it is currently still a proposal [9]. In stark contrast to the aforementioned signals, the Transparency and Consent Framework (TCF) has emerged as the dominant privacy preference signal [27], as it was proposed by the same industries that adopted it. The TCF [11] comprises several stakeholders, including publishers, CMPs, advertisers, and vendors. Users visit a publisher's website primarily to consume its content. A publisher may generate income by selling advertising spaces on its website to advertisers, which are companies that intend to display ads to users. Advertisers often collaborate with third-party vendors to help them deliver and optimize their ads. CMPs are responsible for providing consent pop-ups, storing user preferences, and offering an API to allow vendors to access data. The TCF, particularly its "Notice and Choice" paradigm utilized for capturing user signals, presents certain limitations. Firstly, it does not standardize the manner in which user consent is solicited. This has led to the emergence of various methods to obtain consent that can have an impact on the user [29]. It is well known that several CMPs display cookie banners for gathering consent that incorporate design elements intended to encourage users to provide consent [30,32,38]. This type of nudge constitutes a form of dark pattern [36]. Additionally, with the TCF, users are required to express their preferences through cookie banners every time they visit a website. As outlined in [27], it has been estimated that since 2018, users have spent over two thousand years sending TCF consent signals.

In summary, the signals proposed by AdTech (NAI and TCF) collect user preferences through a web page, whereas those suggested by privacy advocates (P3P, DNT/GPC) are collected by a browser. In the latter case, privacy preferences are obtained through a single interaction, and the browser presumes that this decision applies across the entire web. Thus, it is assumed that the user makes a single decision that has long-term effects [27]. Instead, in the former scenario, user choices remain effective until cookies are deleted or a vendor introduces a new one. Therefore, AdTech companies strive to prevent browser settings from having a binding impact.

3   Related Works

The Platform for Privacy Preferences (P3P) was the first attempt to standardize privacy preferences in a machine-readable format [15]. Based on the P3P standard, several user agents have been developed that allow users to avoid reading privacy policies every time they visit a website. One of the most popular user agents was Privacy Bird, which was a browser add-on utilizing P3P to produce a concise privacy report. It examined the P3P policies for each site the user accessed and matched them against the user's privacy preferences. When a user visited a site, the interface displayed whether the site's policies corresponded to the user's privacy preferences, did not match them, or was not P3P-enabled [24]. Another strategy was adopted by the Mozilla Firefox add-on Targeted Advertising Cookie Opt-Out (TACO), which maintained an updated list of opt-out cookies and shared them with thousands of users [20]. However, TACO was a rather drastic tool as it deleted all existing cookies. The P3P protocol quickly became obsolete due to its poor adoption by AdTech vendors. Consequently, all solutions based on the P3P standard are now obsolete. Furthermore, privacy advocates have criticized P3P, as no consequences have been established for false reporting of privacy practices [17]. Since the obsolescence of the P3P standard, privacy-focused browsers such as Mozilla Firefox have integrated alternatives such as DNT. Unfortunately, DNT suffered a similar fate as P3P, as major AdTech vendors explicitly stated that they would ignore DNT signals after Microsoft enabled the DNT signal as a default option in Internet Explorer [5]. As time passed, even pro-privacy browsers such as Firefox removed support for DNT [4]. New browsers such as Brave [7] and add-ons such as Privacy Badger [3] have already enabled the new GPC signal by default. The GPC is a solution that aims to follow the path of DNT. According to [27], there is little reason to be optimistic that AdTech vendors will widely adopt GPC signals. In fact, just as with DNT, it is likely that AdTech providers will claim that an active default signal renders the signal meaningless. However, in this last case, unlike with the DNT signal, privacy advocates can rely on CCPA, which was not available when DNT was first adopted by browsers [27].

The need for websites to comply with GDPR has led them to rely on CMPs. Thus, numerous companies have started providing "Consent as a Service" solutions to help ensure legal compliance. The availability of free solutions, like those offered by Quantcast, has significantly boosted the adoption of the TCF, similar to what Let's Encrypt [12] implemented with the adoption of HTTPS [27]. In this context, users are expected to define their preferences each time they visit a website. To address this issue, academics and industry experts have begun developing Personal Information Management Services (PIMS). PIMSes are tools designed to centralize all of a user's personal data and allow them to manage both incoming and outgoing data from a single location. At present, users typically have access to a limited range of PIMSes, which provide only basic functionality and are mainly focused on managing consent decisions. These tools are available as free browser extensions, primarily for Google Chrome and Mozilla Firefox, that work mainly by blocking cookie banners or automatically responding to requests for permission to process personal data. A significant challenge in implementing automated consent responses is the substantial variance among consent requirements across different cookie banners. Consequently, even if a browser extension is informed of user preferences, it may be unable to adequately address all website specifications [35]. In some cases, adopting harsh approaches such as "reject all" could lead to problems. For example, not granting consent for any data processing activity, such as blocking all cookies, may affect the functionality of certain websites, as the user technically appears with an unresolved request for consent. This issue can be addressed by providing minimal consent, which allows only functional cookies, i.e., first-party cookies vital to the website's operation. In late 2021, a browser extension that gained extensive popularity on various stores was "I don't care about cookies" [10]. It grants consent to either all or only necessary cookies, depending on what is easier to implement technologically for the extension. Currently, the most widely used browser extension is Ghostery [14], which relies on rules that automate interactions with cookie banners, rather than hiding them outright [6]. An alternative approach is presented by the Advanced Data Protection Control (ADPC) technical specification [1]. ADPC allows publishers to request consent using TCF or through specific consent requests while simultaneously enabling users to set general signals, such as "object to all", specific signals, such as consent to a particular request, or a combination of both. Although ADPC is still under development, a prototype is available for Firefox and Chromium-based browsers.

The growing popularity of such browser extensions may suggest that many users prefer not to receive cookie banners while visiting websites and are willing to forego the opportunity to differentiate their authorization preferences [35]. Broadly speaking, such behavior could be characterized as an instance of the Privacy Paradox phenomenon documented in the literature [25]. Many people claim to prize their privacy and express unwillingness to share personal information online. Yet, in practice, they often fail to take sufficient precautions to safeguard their data. Upon examining the history of privacy preference signals, it is unusual for both parties, i.e., websites and AdTech vendors, to embrace a signal. It is expected that investments will continue to be made in TCF signals in the future [27]. We proposed a PIMS to automatically generate rules and respond to any type of cookie banner, with the aim of reducing consent response time and preventing deceptive practices in cookie banners.

4 Methods

As mentioned earlier, one of the challenges for users when browsing online is deciding and responding to each website's initial request for permission, keeping track of all decisions, and updating them if desired. The Transparency and Consent Framework (TCF) is currently the most widely adopted specification, and projections suggest that this trend will continue in the future [27].

Our proposal involves a Personal Information Management Service (PIMS) that enforces a user's privacy policy at the time of website visit. Essentially, the user declares their privacy preferences only once in the PIMS. Afterwards, when the user visits a website, the PIMS automatically responds to consent requests according to the user's policy. A user policy reflects the user's privacy preferences, such as rejecting all cookies. To generate and apply consent rules based on user policies, we utilized a Large Language Model (LLM). A LLM is a type of language model that uses deep learning techniques, such as neural networks, to generate artificial text on a large scale. These models are trained on massive text corpora, consisting of billions of words, and are capable of processing and generating text with high precision and naturalness. The current state-of-the-art for LLMs is GPT (Generative Pre-trained Transformer), developed by OpenAI, which is based on transformer-based architectures [39]. GPT has led to significant advancements in natural language processing, particularly in areas such as common sense reasoning, question answering, and textual entailment [33]. As shown in detail in Sect. 5, we employed ChatGPT for multiple purposes. Firstly, we analysed the content of the web page to identify the cookie banner. Then, we generated rules to interact with the cookie banner based on the user's policy.

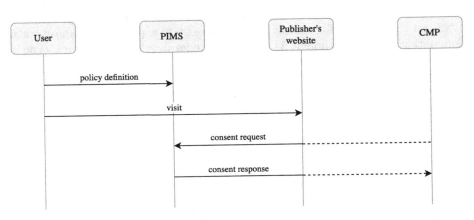

Fig. 1. The diagram illustrates how the proposed PIMS integrates and interacts within the Transparency and Consent Framework. After a user has defined his policy, the PIMS intercepts consent requests from CMPs and responds in a manner consistent with the user's policy.

To illustrate how our proposal fits within the TCF, we provide a concise overview of an eight-step use case. In this scenario, a publisher obtains consent for its specific TCF purposes independently, without partnering with vendors who require user authorization. When user X arrives at the publisher's website (step 1), the publisher contacts its CMP C using a CMP tag, which is a JavaScript tag added to publisher P's website (step 2). The CMP code then runs on the page and checks whether a Transparency and Consent (TC) String corresponding to publisher P exists in user X's local storage (step 3). The TC String is used to store, update, and exchange a user's authorization in a standardized manner. Since this is user X's first visit to publisher P, no such TC String is found. In this case, CMP C displays a cookie banner on the website, similar to the banner shown in Fig. 2 (step 4). Next (step 5), user X makes choices on the cookie banner for each purpose. Then, CMP C creates a TC String for user X-publisher P by encoding the consent information according to the standard (step 6). publisher P stores the TC String locally on user X's device (step 7). Afterward, publisher P can rely on its CMP API to decode the TC String and determine which purpose user X has allowed it to pursue (step 8). The proposed PIMS is implemented as a browser extension and interposes itself between the user and the CMP in steps 4 and 5, as shown in Fig. 1. The PIMS intercepts the CMP request and subsequently responds on behalf of the user according to their established policy. Except for the initial stage where the user defines their own policy within the PIMS, the remaining steps described in the previous use case remain unchanged.

5   Case Study

As a case study, we generated a consent rule and applied it to the Quantcast website [18]. We assumed that the user does not want to accept any cookies. When a user accesses the Quantcast website for the first time, they are presented with the cookie banner shown in Fig. 2. It should be noted that the banner includes a dark pattern that induces the user to click the "Agree" button, highlighted in blue. If the user wishes to reject all cookies, he must first click on the "More options" button. After arriving at the screen shown in Fig. 3, two additional clicks will be required: one on the "Reject all" button, and another on the "Save & exit" button. We prompted ChatGPT to derive consent response rules and identify the location of buttons on the page, generating the necessary code for interaction. Below is an excerpt from the ChatGPT conversation, providing insights into this process. Please note that ellipses have been used to indicate omitted text for brevity.

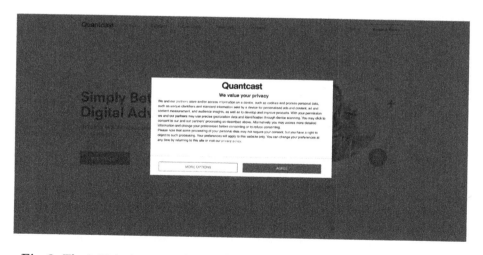

Fig. 2. The initial view of the cookie banner displayed on the Quantcast website.

Rules Generation. With the first question, we establish the context for the entire conversation. We then proceed to discuss the location of the buttons used to indicate the user's choice. Finally, we generate the JavaScript code that interacts with these buttons based on the user's policy.

Question 1. What is a cookie banner and what is its purpose?

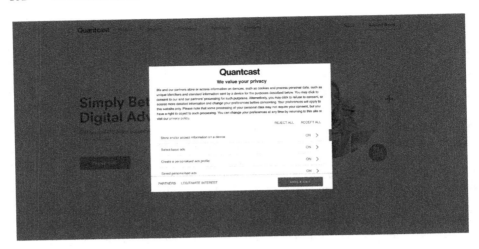

Fig. 3. The display presented upon clicking the "More options" button within the cookie banner on the Quantcast website.

Solution 1. A cookie banner is a message that appears on a website asking for a user's consent to use cookies [...] By giving users the ability to choose which cookies they allow, the banner helps protect user privacy and comply with regulations, such as the GDPR and the CCPA [...].

Question 2. I would like to reject all cookies on this page, does this banner display a button with this option?

```
[...]<div id="qc-cmp2-ui" role="dialog" aria-label="qc-cmp2-ui" aria-modal="true
    " tabindex="0" class="css-6napma"><div class="qc-cmp2-summary-section">
    [...] </div><div class="qc-cmp2-footer_qc-cmp2-footer-overlay_qc-cmp2-footer
    -scrolled"><div class="qc-cmp2-summary-buttons"><button mode="secondary"
    size="large" class="_css-1hy2vtq"><span>MORE OPTIONS</span></button><button
    mode="primary" size="large" class="_css-47sehv"><span>AGREE</span></button><
    /div> </div> </div>[...]
```

Solution 2. Based on the HTML code provided, it does not appear that there is an option to reject all cookies on the page. The only options provided are to "Agree" or to access "More options", which presumably would allow the user to customize their cookie preferences rather than reject all cookies outright. However, without actually interacting with the banner on the live website, it is possible that additional options or information may be available upon further inspection.

Question 3. Please provide me with a JavaScript code to click on the "more" button.

Solution 3. Here is an example of JavaScript code that will simulate a click on the "more" button:

```
const moreButton = document.querySelector('.qc-cmp2-summary-buttons button:first
    -of-type');
moreButton.click();
```

[...] Once the button is clicked, the banner should reveal additional options for managing the cookie preferences.

Question 4. Does this new version of the cookie banner display a button that allows to reject all cookies on this page?

```
[...]<div id="qc-cmp2-ui" role="dialog" aria-label="qc-cmp2-ui" aria-modal="true
" tabindex="0" class="css-1irhpn0"><div class="qc-cmp2-consent-info"><div
class="qc-cmp2-publisher-logo-container">[...]<div>[...]</div><div class="qc
-cmp2-header-links"><button mode="link" size="small" class="_css-8rroe4">
REJECTALL</button><button mode="link" size="small" class="_css-8rroe4">
ACCEPT ALL</button></div></div></div>[...]<div class="qc-cmp2-footer_"><
button class="qc-cmp2-hide-desktop_css-47sehv" mode="primary" size="large">
SAVE &amp; EXIT</button><div class="qc-cmp2-footer-links"><button mode="link
" size="small" class="_css-8rroe4"aria-pressed="false">PARTNERS</button><
button mode="link" size="small" class="_css-8rroe4"aria-pressed="false">
LEGITIMATE INTEREST </button></div><div class="qc-cmp2-buttons-desktop"><
button aria-pressed="false" mode="primary" size="large"class="_css-47sehv">
SAVE &amp; EXIT</button></div></div></div>[...]
```

Solution 4. Yes, this new version of the cookie banner displays a button that allows to reject all cookies on the page. The button with the label "Reject all" can be used to reject all cookies on the page.

Question 5. Please provide me with a JavaScript code to click on the "Reject all" button and close the banner with the preference of rejecting all cookies.

Solution 5. Sure, here's a JavaScript code to click on the "Reject all" button and close the banner with the preference of rejecting all cookies:

```
const rejectAllButton = document.querySelector('.qc-cmp2-header-links_button:
    first-of-type');
rejectAllButton.click();
const saveAndExitButton = document.querySelector('.qc-cmp2-footer_button:first-
    of-type');
saveAndExitButton.click();
```

Note that, this code assumes that the structure of the HTML code for the cookie banner remains the same. If the structure changes, this code may not work as expected.

Browser Extension Setup. We implement our PIMS as a browser extension specifically designed for Mozilla Firefox. The extension consists primarily of two files: the manifest file (shown in Listing 1.1) and the script that executes the auto-consent rule (defined in Listing 1.2). To simplify the execution flow, we include a contextual menu item that allows the user to close the browser extension with a single click, as demonstrated in Listing 1.3. In a real-world scenario, this additional feature would not be necessary, as the code in Listing 1.2 would be invoked directly at the end of the page loading process.

Listing 1.1. manifest.json

```
{
    "manifest_version": 2,
    "name": "Autoconsent",
    "version": "1.0",
    "permissions": [
        "activeTab",
        "contextMenus"
    ],
    "background": {
        "scripts": [
            "background.js"
        ]
    }
}
```

Listing 1.2. autoconsent.js

```
var moreOptionsButton = document.querySelector('.qc-cmp2-summary-buttons_button:
    first-child');
moreOptionsButton.click();

setTimeout(function () {
    const rejectAllButton = document.querySelector('.qc-cmp2-header-links_button
        :first-of-type');
    const saveAndExitButton = document.querySelector('.qc-cmp2-footer_button[
        mode="primary"]');

    if (rejectAllButton && saveAndExitButton) {
        rejectAllButton.click();
        saveAndExitButton.click();
    }
}, 500);
```

Listing 1.3. background.js

```
browser.contextMenus.create({
    id: "autoconsent",
    title: "Autoconsent"
});

browser.contextMenus.onClicked.addListener((info, tab) => {
    if (info.menuItemId === "autoconsent") {
        browser.tabs.executeScript({
            file: "autoconsent.js"
        });
    }
});
```

Rules Execution. After installing the browser extension, the user can apply their policy to all the pages they visit. In this particular use case, the PIMS performs the following actions: it first clicks on the "More options" button, then selects the "Reject all cookies" option from the new screen, and finally closes the banner by clicking the "Save & exit" button. Figure 4 displays the contextual menu item that was introduced in Listing 1.3. It is important to note that this menu item was added solely for demonstration purposes. Its purpose is to highlight the actions of the browser extension and make the presence of the cookie banner noticeable. In an actual scenario, the browser extension would remove the cookie banner quickly after the page has loaded, without the need for user intervention.

Fig. 4. Screenshot demonstrating the automatic invocation of the automated consent response by the browser extension. It is important to note that this action is purely for descriptive purposes, as in reality, it is executed automatically without requiring any user intervention.

6   Discussion and Results

The increasing adoption of GDPR-compliant consent management by websites has led to a de facto standard in the presentation of cookie banners to users. However, despite the existence of standardized frameworks like the TCF, managing and controlling authorizations remains a complex process. It is important to note that the TCF itself does not guarantee GDPR compliance. In many cases, cookie banners are designed to optimize the chances of obtaining user consent [35]. A study conducted by Nouwens et al. [32], which analyzed the top five CMPs on the top 10,000 websites in the UK, revealed the prevalence of dark patterns and implied consent. Only 11.8% of the CMPs met the minimum requirements based on European law.

A limited number of tools are currently available to assist users in making and managing authorization decisions. These tools have certain drawbacks, including increased page loading time, and some even conflict with the website's functionality. The main difference between our proposal and other browser extensions is that our PIMS automates the process of creating and enforcing user policies. This ensures scalability and adaptability to customized cookie banners. A PIMS that interacts with websites, leveraging a signal type that is already widely adopted by AdTech vendors, is a fair compromise between privacy advocates who seek a long-term solution and AdTech vendors who oppose default options incorporated into browsers. In addition, responding automatically to requests for consent, i.e., without requiring direct involvement from users in the consent process, brings several benefits, including circumventing obscure models such as nudges that induce users to accept all cookies, and a considerable reduction in the technical time required to declare one's preferences. In [26], it was estimated that on average, it takes a user at least 30 s to define their preferences on dialog windows and submit them. As we have previously highlighted in our case study, simply choosing to reject all cookies can also require up to three clicks on two different screens.

7   Conclusion and Future Works

In this study, we addressed the issue of managing user consent while visiting a website. We presented a PIMS that generates rules for automatic consent based on a user policy. Our approach eliminates some of the dark patterns found in cookie banners, which frequently encourage users to consent to all cookies. Additionally, it reduces the time spent by users in expressing their preferences on every website they visit. To demonstrate the practicability of our approach, we conducted a case study where we used ChatGPT to create rules based on a user policy. Subsequently, we implemented these rules in a browser extension that enables automatic consent when visiting a website. Our use of the GPT model proved effective in accurately identifying banners and buttons and providing relevant actions aligned with the user's preferences. The proposed browser extension is capable of enforcing policies and closing banners in less than one second from the page's load.

An effective implementation of the proposed PIMS should include a set of rules to address the consent requests received from the primary CMPs. Subsequently, users themselves can contribute to the expansion of a shared database of consent rules by declaring their own policies and browsing the internet. This way, users with similar policies who visit the same website can utilize a rule already available in the shared database. If cookie banners change or a specific rule is absent from the database, the PIMS will generate a new rule and share it with the user in the database. Moreover, this work could be extended in several directions. A more advanced PIMS would track all site authorizations for data processing and periodically propose updates to the user's privacy preferences. Updates made within the PIMS to the user's preferences would be automatically communicated to all other entities processing the user's data. The PIMS could also request information on the data stored by a specific website and request its deletion. Another possible extension would be to develop a user-centric approach that enables the average user to comprehend cookie policies and, based on their preferences, define their own policy. This could be achieved by examining the user's behavior and automatically inferring a policy. Once validated by the user, the PIMS would apply the policy automatically during navigation. Furthermore, in other contexts, a tool similar to our proposal could be useful in identifying and notifying websites that offer non-compliant cookie banners, including those where no banner is displayed on the website.

Acknowledgments. This work was partially supported by project SERICS (PE00000014) under the NRRP MUR program funded by the EU - NGEU.

Conflicts of Interest. The authors declare no conflict of interest.

References

1. Advanced Data Protection Control (ADPC). https://www.dataprotectioncontrol. org/. Accessed 7 May 2023
2. All about Do Not Track. https://allaboutdnt.com/companies/. Accessed 7 May 2023
3. Announcing Global Privacy Control in Privacy Badger. https://www.eff.org/gpc-privacy-badger. Accessed 7 May 2023
4. DNT - HTTP. https://developer.mozilla.org/en-US/docs/Web/HTTP/Headers/ DNT. Accessed 7 May 2023
5. "Do Not Track" set to "on" by default in Internet Explorer 10-IAB response. https://www.iab.com/news/do-not-track-set-to-on-by-default-in-internet-explorer-10iab-response/. Accessed 7 May 2023
6. Ghostery autoconsent. https://github.com/ghostery/autoconsent. Accessed 7 May 2023
7. Global Privacy Control, a new privacy standard proposal by the Brave web standards team. https://brave.com/web-standards-at-brave/4-global-privacy-control/. Accessed 7 May 2023
8. Global Privacy Control (GPC). https://globalprivacycontrol.org/. Accessed 7 May 2023
9. Global Privacy Control (GPC) specification proposal. https://privacycg.github.io/ gpc-spec/. Accessed 7 May 2023
10. I don't care about cookie. https://www.i-dont-care-about-cookies.eu/. Accessed 7 May 2023
11. IAB Europe Transparency & Consent Framework policies. https://iabeurope.eu/ iab-europe-transparency-consent-framework-policies/. Accessed 7 May 2023
12. Let's Encrypt. https://letsencrypt.org/. Accessed 7 May 2023
13. Network Advertising Initiative (NAI). https://thenai.org/. Accessed 7 May 2023
14. Never consent by Ghostery. https://www.ghostery.com/blog/never-consent-by-ghostery. Accessed 7 May 2023
15. The Platform for Privacy Preferences 1.0 (P3P1.0) specification. https://www.w3. org/TR/P3P/. Accessed 7 May 2023
16. The Platform for Privacy Preferences 1.1 (P3P1.1) specification. https://www.w3. org/TR/P3P11/. Accessed 7 May 2023
17. Pretty poor privacy: An assessment of P3P and internet privacy. https://archive. epic.org/reports/prettypoorprivacy.html. Accessed 7 May 2023
18. Quantcast. https://www.quantcast.com/. Accessed 7 May 2023
19. Regulation (EU) 2016/679 of the European Parliament and of the Council of 27 April 2016 on the protection of natural persons with regard to the processing of personal data and on the free movement of such data, and repealing directive 95/46/EC (General Data Protection Regulation). https://eur-lex.europa.eu/eli/ reg/2016/679/oj. Accessed 7 May 2023

20. Targeted Advertising Cookie Opt-out (TACO). https://addons.mozilla.org/en-us/firefox/addon/targeted-advertising-cookie-op/. Offline
21. Tracking Preference Expression (DNT). https://www.w3.org/TR/tracking-dnt. Accessed 7 May 2023
22. Transparency & Consent Framework (TCF). https://iabeurope.eu/transparency-consent-framework/. Accessed 7 May 2023
23. Campanile, L., Iacono, M., Mastroianni, M.: Towards privacy-aware software design in small and medium enterprises. In: 2022 IEEE International Conference on Dependable, Autonomic and Secure Computing, International Conference on Pervasive Intelligence and Computing, International Conference on Cloud and Big Data Computing, International Conference on Cyber Science and Technology Congress (DASC/PiCom/CBDCom/CyberSciTech), pp. 1–8 (2022). https://doi.org/10.1109/DASC/PiCom/CBDCom/Cy55231.2022.9927958
24. Cranor, L.: P3P: making privacy policies more useful. IEEE Secur. Priv. 1(6), 50–55 (2003). https://doi.org/10.1109/MSECP.2003.1253568
25. Gerber, N., Gerber, P., Volkamer, M.: Explaining the privacy paradox: a systematic review of literature investigating privacy attitude and behavior. Comput. Secur. 77, 226–261 (2018). https://doi.org/10.1016/j.cose.2018.04.002, https://www.sciencedirect.com/science/article/pii/S0167404818303031
26. Hils, M., Woods, D.W., Böhme, R.: Measuring the emergence of consent management on the web. In: Proceedings of the ACM Internet Measurement Conference, IMC 2020, pp. 317–332. Association for Computing Machinery, New York (2020). https://doi.org/10.1145/3419394.3423647
27. Hils, M., Woods, D.W., Böhme, R.: Privacy preference signals: past, present and future. Proc. Priv. Enhanc. Technol. 4, 249–269 (2021)
28. Kretschmer, M., Pennekamp, J., Wehrle, K.: Cookie banners and privacy policies: measuring the impact of the GDPR on the web. ACM Trans. Web 15(4) (2021). https://doi.org/10.1145/3466722
29. Machuletz, D., Böhme, R.: Multiple purposes, multiple problems: a user study of consent dialogs after GDPR. Proc. Priv. Enhanc. Technol. 2, 481–498 (2020)
30. Matte, C., Bielova, N., Santos, C.: Do cookie banners respect my choice?: measuring legal compliance of banners from IAB Europe's transparency and consent framework. In: 2020 IEEE Symposium on Security and Privacy (SP), pp. 791–809 (2020). https://doi.org/10.1109/SP40000.2020.00076
31. Mehrnezhad, M., Coopamootoo, K., Toreini, E.: How can and would people protect from online tracking? Proc. Priv. Enhanc. Technol. 1, 105–125 (2022)
32. Nouwens, M., Liccardi, I., Veale, M., Karger, D., Kagal, L.: Dark patterns after the GDPR: scraping consent pop-ups and demonstrating their influence. In: Proceedings of the 2020 CHI Conference on Human Factors in Computing Systems, CHI 2020, pp. 1–13. Association for Computing Machinery, New York (2020). https://doi.org/10.1145/3313831.3376321
33. Radford, A., Narasimhan, K., Salimans, T., Sutskever, I., et al.: Improving language understanding by generative pre-training. https://cdn.openai.com/research-covers/language-unsupervised/language%5Funderstanding%5Fpaper.pdf
34. Schwartz, P.M.: Property, privacy, and personal data. Harv. Law Rev. 117(7), 2056–2128 (2004). http://www.jstor.org/stable/4093335
35. Skiera, B., Miller, K., Jin, Y., Kraft, L., Laub, R., Schmitt, J.: The Impact of the General Data Protection Regulation (GDPR) on the Online Advertising Market. Bernd Skiera (2022)
36. Thaler, R.H.: Nudge, not sludge. Science 361(6401), 431–431 (2018). https://doi.org/10.1126/science.aau9241

37. Trevisan, M., Stefano, T., Bassi, E., Marco, M., et al.: 4 years of EU cookie law: results and lessons learned. Proc. Priv. Enhanc. Technol. **2019**(2), 126–145 (2019)
38. Utz, C., Degeling, M., Fahl, S., Schaub, F., Holz, T.: (Un)informed consent: studying GDPR consent notices in the field. In: Proceedings Of The ACM Conference On Computer And Communications Security, pp. 973–990 (2019)
39. Vaswani, A., et al.: Attention is all you need. Adv. Neural Inf. Process. Syst. **30** (2017)

Secure Mobile Ad Hoc Routing Using Confrontations (SMARUC) and Nodes Communication with CCM (Character Classification Model) - OKE (Optimal Key Exchange) - SSL (Secure Socket Layer) Model

R. M. Krishna Sureddi[1]([✉]), Santosh Kumar Ravva[2], and Ramakrishna Kolikipogu[3]

[1] Department of IT, Chaitanya Bharathi Institute of Technology, Hyderabad, India
`rmkrishnsureddi_it@cbit.ac.in`
[2] Department of CSE, Vasavi College of Engineering, Hyderabad, India
`santosh@staff.vce.ac.in`
[3] Department of IT, Chaitanya Bharathi Institute of Technology(A), Hyderabad, India
`ramakrishna_it@cbit.ac.in`

Abstract. Manet (Mobile Adhoc network) is a dynamic network with no fixed infrastructure. So Data Routing among nodes in a wireless network is pretty complex when compared to traditional centralized network architecture. There is always possibility the nodes vulnerable to all kinds of attacks. Even though cryptography models, key exchange models are there for data exchange but all are struggled with security and all are bound by global time complexities even in message communication among nodes. So we addressed this problem by generating trusted dynamic topology with secure data communication using "SMARUC with CCMOKE" Model. This method which generates exchanges key in minimum time complexity even compared to Diffie-Hellman model. For Crypto, data transmission between nodes done with simple RSC-OKE-SSL crypto model which performs communication in minimum time complexity compared to other cryptography models. By this method of forming dynamic network blocks the doorway of malicious nodes and generates the secured dynamic topology.

Keywords: Cryptography · Keyexchange · SSL · classification · Roughset · encryption · decryption · Hybrid crypto models · entropy · randomness · floating frequency · Crypto tool

1 Introduction

A mobile ad hoc network (MANET) [1] is self configuration autonomous system of mobile nodes. Mobile Nodes are connected by wireless links, the union of which forms a network in the form of a dynamic communication structure. The routers are permitted to move at any speed in any direction and establish themselves indiscriminately. Thus, the network's wireless topology may dynamically vary in an unpredictable manner. There is no fixed arrangement, and information is forwarded in peer-to-peer mode using multi hop routing. MANETs [1–8] are basically peer-to-peer (p2p) multi hop mobile wireless

© The Author(s), under exclusive license to Springer Nature Switzerland AG 2023
O. Gervasi et al. (Eds.): ICCSA 2023 Workshops, LNCS 14105, pp. 160–173, 2023.
https://doi.org/10.1007/978-3-031-37108-0_11

networks where information packets are transferred in a store-and-forward method from source to destination, via intermediate nodes, as shown in Fig. 1. As the nodes move, the resulting change in network topology must be made known to the other nodes so that prior topology information can be updated. Such a network may operate in a stand-alone fashion, or with just a few selected routers communicating with an infrastructure network.

Fig. 1. Illustration of a MANET

a. **Characteristics of MANETs**

- No integrated control and administration is done
- Communication through the various nodes in a network
- Alteration of topology and frequent breakage of links once the connection is proven
- Can be set up anywhere in any situation
- Limited security

b. **Security issues in MANETs**

1) **Easier to hit:** Since the broadcasting is nothing but air, it can be tapped easily.
2) **Quality of Service:** Quality of Service (QoS) guarantee is very much essential for the successful communication of nodes in the network. The different QoS metrics includes throughput, packet loss, delay, and jitter and error rate. The dynamically changing topology, limited bandwidth and quality makes the difficulty in achieving the desired QoS guarantee for the network.
3) **Limited Security:** Easily influenced by all crypto attacks.

1.1 Objective

The main objectives of this paper are

- To generate dynamic secured topology with SMARUC [1,9] Model
- To generate dynamic trusted network in optimized key exchange Model.
- Establish communication among nodes in simple with efficient crypto model.
- To provide secure communication among trusted Nodes through double encryption model.
- Protecting the network from malicious attacks.

1.2 SMARUC² Algorithm Description

Secure Mobile Ad Hoc Routing [4] Confrontations (SMARUC) [2] accomplishes establishment of companion networks in MANETs in the same way as in real life scenarios.

1) Confrontation Your Neighbor

Confrontation is a method to authorize nodes primarily when no stipulation is present. It is a basic test which a node has to complete in order to corroborate its honesty and integrity. Let us assume that the node A confronts its neighbor node B.

Step 1) When a new system is initialized, every node is a foreigner to a different. Thus each node sends its neighbors in the unconfirmed list.
Step 2) The node A picks one of the neighbors, B and performs the usual Share associates Stage.
Step 3) As a reply the neighbor node B either sends its companion directory or the nodes from its unsubstantiated directory if the companion list is empty.
Step 4) On receiving the list, the node A picks up a node which can reach on its own. Let us say that this node is C.
Step 5) Now the node A has two ways to reach the node one through B and another through a route already known to it.
Step 6) The above all 6 steps achieved through - Each node is initialized with a pair of large prime numbers.
Step 7) Node A wants to confront node B. Then it sends one of his random prime numbers as they confront. (Here we send first prime number as the confront i.e. 'a').
Step 8) Here we use public key cryptography algorithm known as RSA.(It uses 2 keys for encryption & Decryption).

2) **Approaches:**

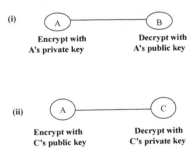

Step 9) Node A send 'a' as they confront to node C.

Step 10) In node C we pertain the RSA algorithm for key.

Generation (public key, private key).

Step 11) Node C sends the public key to node A.

Step 12) Node A encrypts 'a' with the public key of Node C.

Then we get some 'k'. Then node A sends 'k' to node C.

Step 13) Node C receives & decrypts 'k' with C's private key.

Then we get some 'n'.

Step 14) Then node C computes 'c^d mod n' & sends the result to node A. To optimize these computations apply CCM-OKE Model. [Table 1].

Step 15) Now node A sends 'a' as they confront to node B.

Step 16) In node B we apply the RSA algorithm for key generation (public key, private key).

Step 17) Node B sends the public key to node A.

Step 18) Node A encrypts 'a' with the public key of Node B.

Then we get some 'k'. Then node A sends 'k' to node B.

Step 19) Node B receives & decrypts 'k' with B's private key.

Then we get some 'n'.

Step 20) Node B sends 'n' to node C.

Step 21) Node C receives 'n' & computes 'c^d mod n' & sends the result to node A.

Step 22) Since n, c and d are all very large prime numbers, it is unfeasible to determine c and d from the end result of the *mod* function as that is known to be a tough problem.

Step 23) Node A compares both results. If they are equal node B is added to the network. Otherwise discard it [Fig. 3].

In the above SMARUC Algorithm blocks the entrance of malevolent nodes efficiently and the computation of time complexity of a modulo function, reduced with CCM-OKE Model which can be applied to the Diffie-Hellman key exchange algorithm, CRT or RSA key generation. In the above Algorithm from the steps 9 to 21 all the computation time complexity of modular function will be reduced by the following CCM-OKE-Model and then key exchange can be done through Diffie-Hellman key exchange model.

Algorithm for OKE (Optimized Key Exchange) Model to Calculate Pow (w,p) mod n

The Algorithm was modeled based on the binary number system. In which the input parameters are taken in the binary model [10–14].

Steps:

1. Express all the basic input parameters in binary model representation.

P = (pk−1, pk−2, pk−3 .... p2, p1, p0).

Where k represents number of bits to represent X.

W = (wk−1, wk−2, wk−-3, ... w2, w1, w0)

N = (nk−1, nk−2, nk−3 .... n2, n1, n0)

2. Assign the value C to 1.
3. Calculate S = pow(w,3) mod n.
4. i = k−1.
5. If i > = 0 then goto step 6 else goto step 11 6. C = mod(C * C, n).
6. If [(pi ! = 0) & (pi-1 ! = 0)] then goto step 8 otherwise goto step 9
7. C = mod(C * C, n); C = mod(C * S, n); i = i−1.
8. If (pi ! = 0) then C = mod(C * w, n)., i = i−1
9. Goto step 6
10. Return the value of C which is the result of optimizes modular function result.
11. END.

The above algorithm reduces the time complexity of algorithm O(log(k)) by reducing the number of multiplications in modular function evolution. Once the Network is established the data among nodes can be transferred or routing tables of networking nodes protected through CCM-OKE Model which is expanded below.

CCM-OKE Model
Character classification [10, 15,16] Model is one simple, efficient with encrypted secured model which is described as.
   Steps:

1. Consider a secret key of any length, i.e. one character to any number of characters [Table 1].
2. This secret key is stored in a single dimension matrix called key matrix.

   K = [kl, kZ, ." "" ." ." ." ." ." .. , ku.]

3. Perform XOR operation of each key with RSA-key(Z) generated with OKE model in the above algorithm.

   K={k1 XOR Z, K2 XOR Z, ... Kn XOR Z}

   Where Z is a value generated optimized Pow(a,d) mod n.

4. Calculate the encrypted Key from key matrix K using the following formula (Phase 1): Kenc = K1®K2®K3.... ".................... ®CKn where ® iS XOR operator.
5. The random Number for performing shift operations on obtaining kenc key obtained by applying rough sets classification Model on Combined set for Plain Text ASCII values and Secret Key ASCII values.
6. TakeS1 = {Set of ascii values of plain text}

   S2 = {Set of ascii values of secret key}

   S = S1 U S2

   Let us example S={78, 66, 69, 75, 101, 114, 121, 21, 112, 8, 110, 34, 56, 23, 10, 66, 77, 89, 119, 114, 123, 147}

   Then classify the sets [15, 16].

Let us suppose rnd value is 66 which

M1 = { > rnd} = {77,89,119,114 …} or {upper approximation values}

M2 = { < rnd} = {6,8,34,77,75 …} or {lower approximation values}

M3 = {== rnd} = {66} or {equivalent approximates values}

S = MAX(M1, M2, M3).

7. Calculate the encrypted key Kenc, by following way (Phase 2):

   KEnc = KEnc >> S. so S number of times perform shifts.

8. Finding this encrypted key is grounded on ASCII value of each and every character of secret key.
9. Plain text is stored in single dimension matrix called PT.

   For example: PT[] = ABCDEFGHIJKLMNOP........

10. It is grounded on ASCII value of encrypted key.

    C: r[f] = PT[i] Kenc

11. Add both KenC and plain text character by character where i = 1,2, … ,n characters of plain text.
12. Got the Cipher text in matrix CT.
13. That CT sends to the open SSL for double encryption to get two-level encrypted cipher text [Tables 2, 3 and 4].
14. Calculate the reverse process to get back plain text again.

1.3 Open SSL

The open ssl (Secure Socket Layer) unit provides a amalgam multiplicity of commands each of which often has a prosperity of options and wiles (Fig. 2).

The pseudo-commands list-standard-commands, listmessage-digest-commands, and list-cipher-commands output a list of the names of all standard commands, message digest commands, or cipher commands, respectively, that are available in the present open ssl utility.

enc.sh

```
#$1 = filename
Open ssl enc -aes-256-cbc -salt -in $1 -out y.txt -pass
#pass:"sirkrs123"
```

dec.sh

```
Open ssl enc -d -aes-256-cbc -in y.txt -out y.dec -pass
#pass:sirkrs123
```

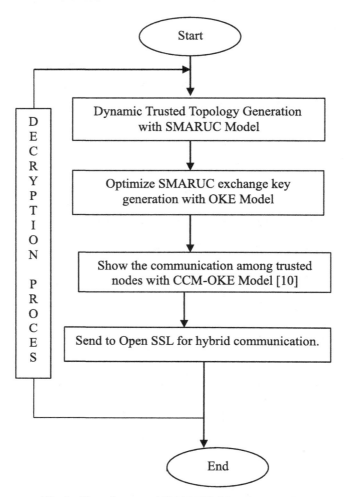

Fig. 2. Flow diagram of SMARUC-CCM-OKE Model

2 Simulation Analysis

The Simulation analysis was performed using NS2 Simulator Package [25].

A. *Simulation Parameters applied on analysis tool are*

- Simulation time: 100 s □ Mobility: Random Way Point.
- Network layer: IP 127.0.0.1
- Source Node: 1
- Destination Node: 2
- Protocol: AODV [3] □ Minimum Speed: 0 m/s □ Maximum Speed: 20 m/s.
- Mac Type: 802.11
- Link Layer Type: LL

- Interface Type: Queue □ Traffic type: CBR
- Packet Size: 28,38,48.

Once the network is established with smaruc model for showing the communication of data from one to another node with CCM-OKE model let us suppose Table [1].

Input data : " Simulator tool "
Secret Key : "RscOkeM"

3   Experimental Results

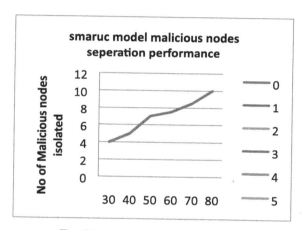

Total No of nodes as X-Coordinator

Fig. 3. Malicious Nodes Separation.

Time Comparison Results Between OKE and Without OKE

Performance Comparison Results of Symmetric classical models with proposed Model
    Where entropy defines the dissimilarity index of cipher text and Floating frequency defines the maximum repeated character Description.
    Performance Results of symmetric Modern Algorithms with proposed Model (Table 5).

Table 1. Characters with its ASCII values

S.NO	Input Text/Secret Key	ASCII
1	S	115
2	I	73
3	M	87
4	U	89
5	L	83
6	A	65
7	T	94
8	O	76
9	R	85
11	T	80
12	O	86
13	L	83

Table 2. CCM-OKE Model Cryptanalysis Values

S.NO	Text Length	Plain Text	Random range	Cypher text	Kenc
1	12	cryptography	10	$%^ww##	30
2	14	Journal paper	20	&&# @We!&67	10
3	8	criticism	15	4rrty6134	20
4	15	Simulation model	10	Qqsr4%%^*	14

Table 3. Analysis of symmetric classical algorithms with proposed Model

S.NO	Encryption Algorithm	Plain Text	Cipher text	Entropy Value	Floating Frequency(MAX)
1	Optimize d CCMOKE Model	Forming encrypted textt	&$et%rtwqwe5!*tuuy	4.42	3
2	Vigenere (B)	Forming encrypted textt	Fptpmsm lvbjbgss jvpmno	3.44	3.84
3	Play Fair (C)	Forming encrypted textt	EPHFKBLFADSWQUMNOLY QQY	3.97	3
4	XOR (D)	Forming encrypted textt	S20Eac/OSA-)1d	0	0
5	Solitaire (E)	Forming encrypted textt	JLBKQMYKRJLLIBUYOWVDT	3.78	

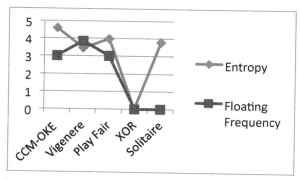

Fig. 4. Quality of cipher in terms of entropy and floating frequency among symmetric classical models

Table 4. Analysis of symmetric Modern algorithms with proposed Model In terms of entropy and frequency

S.NO	Encryption Algorithm	Plain Text	Cipher Text	Entropy Value	Randomness Test
1	Optimized CCMOKE Model	Analysys Of Symmetric Modern algs	$$R%WE2!(gg ©SQcj@#xcvdzSs##&p	5.43	2.56
2	IDEA	Analysys of Symmetric modern algs	x.>.. >..ag ~..u3..[j*c..MlJY	5.12	0.20
3	RC4	Analysys of symmetric modern algs	K!.4..t.F..T.H..o.NTC..j..t*BQ	4.74	0.24
4	DES	Analysys of Symmetric modern algs	..h7.. + l#HJ…w.}.3..k&..Gx… = .	5.22	0.31
5	TRIPPLEDES	Analysys of Symmetric modern algs	H….U..l…m..'..'..l/le..\i.z.2E..1	5.27	1.25
6	AES	Analysys of symmetric modern algs	. < …..{…9'.}..dT{[g..N).p…"(.4	5.41	0.37

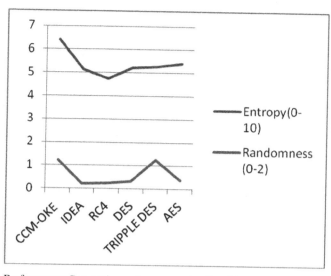

Fig. 5. Performance Comparison of asymmetric Algorithms With proposed Model

Table 5. Analysis of entropy and randomness of Asymmetric Modern algorithms with proposed model.

S.NO	Encryption Algorithm	Plain Text	Cipher text	Entropy Value	Randomness Test
1	Optimized CCM-OKE Model	Analysys of symmetric modern algs	l$@@WQ6!(FF©Sq2j@#xc3erzWs &&y	7.43	1.21
2	RSA	Analysys of symmetric modern algs	.f....Eiv.Y.... =.(< ...?Z...'.H..v!...E ....'R.	5.83	0.19
3	TRIPPLE DES	Analysys of symmetric modern algs	H....U..l...m..'../le..\i.z.2E..l	5.27	1.25

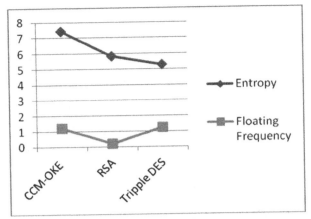

Fig. 6. Analysis of entropy and randomness of Asymmetric Modern algorithms with proposed model.

4   Conclusion

In this paper we have proposed new technique to improve the security in manet in optimizes the modular operation results in terms of both time, space complexities, entropy, Floating frequency [Figs. 4, 5 and 6] and with limited communication cost. The results which we obtained are compared with existed diffie-hellman key exchange, RSA key generation model and various existed crypto algorithms like RSA, DES, Double and tripple DES, AES and so on. The results are verified using crypto tool.

The proposed work specially takes care about initiating the security in MANETs by generating secured dynamic network topology through SMARUC and optimizes the exchange key generation. And it also optimizes the communication cost with reasonable security. The proposed cryptography algorithm developed through user defined dyanamic key . It is observed that which we obtained from the above results, increases the quality of the services among MANETs. In future the above results are comparable with other existed routing protocols and other crypto models for developing better efficient crypto protocol.

References

1. Agrawal, P., Zeng, Q.-A.: Introduction to Wireless and Mobile Systems. Brooks/Cole, Thomson, Pacific Grove, CA (2002)
2. Dhurandher, S.K., Obaidat, M.S.: FACES: friend – based ad hoc routing using challenges to establish security in MANETs systems. IEEE Syst. J. **5**(2), 176–188 (2011)
3. Perkins, C., Royer, E., Das, S.: Ad Hoc on Demand Distance Vector (AODV) Routing. Internet experimental RFC 3561 (2003)
4. Johnson, D.B., Maltz, D.: Dynamic source routing in ad hoc wireless networks. In: Imielinski, T., Korth, H. (eds.) Book Chapter in Mobile Computing, pp. 131–181. Kluwer, Dordrecht, The Netherlands (1996)

5. Jiang, M., Li, J., Tay, Y.C.: Cluster Based Routing Protocol (CBRP) Functional Specification (1998)
6. Sanzgiri, K., Levine, B.N., Shields, C., Dahill, B., Belding-Royer, E.M.: A secure routing protocol for ad hoc networks. In: Proceedings of the 10th IEEE International Conference on Network Protocols (ICNP), Paris, France, pp. 78–89, 12–15 November 2002
7. Hu, Y., Perrig, A., Johnson, D.B.: Ariadne: a secure on-demand routing protocol for ad hoc networks. Wirel. Netw. **11**(1–2), 21–38 (2005)
8. Marti, S., Giuli, T.J., Lai, K., Baker, M.: Mitigating routing misbehavior in mobile ad hoc networks. In: Proceedings of the MobiCom 2000, Boston, MA, pp. 255–265 (2000)
9. Chiang, C.C., et al.: Routing in clustered multihop, mobile wireless networks with fading channel. In: Proceedings of the IEEE SICON'97 (1997)
10. Hasan, A., Sharma, N.: New method towards encryption schemes. In: International Conference on Reliability, Optimization and Information Technology (2014)
11. Vollala, S., Varadhan, V.V.: Efficient modular multiplication algorithms for public key cryptography. In: 2014 IEEE International Advance Computing Conference (IACC)
12. Desmedt, Y.: ElGamal public key encryption. In: Encyclopedia of Cryptography and Security, p. 183. Springer, US (2005)
13. Rivest, R.L., Shamir, A., Adleman, L.: A method for obtaining digital signatures and public-key cryptosystems. Commun. ACM **21**(2), 120126 (1978)
14. Agnew, G.B., Mullin, R.C., Vanstone, S.A.: Fast Exponentiation in GF (2n). In: Advances in Cryptology—EUROCRYPT 1988, pp.225–231. Springer Berlin Heidelberg (1988)
15. Syeda, M., Zbang, Y.Q., Pan, Y.: Parallel granular neural networks for fast credit card fraud detection. In: Proceedings of the IEEE International Conference on Fuzzy Systems 2002, vol.1, pp.572–577 (2002)
16. Polkowski, L., Kacprzyk, J., Skowron, A.: Rough Sets in Knowledge Discovery 2: Applications, Case Studies, and Software Systems. Physica-Verlag, Heidelberg (1998)

An Association Rules-Based Approach for Anomaly Detection on CAN-bus

Gianni D'Angelo[iD], Massimo Ficco[iD], and Antonio Robustelli[(✉)][iD]

Department of Computer Science, University of Salerno, Salerno, Italy
{giadangelo,mficco,arobustelli}@unisa.it

Abstract. With the rapid development of the Internet of Things (IoT) and the Internet of Vehicles (IoV) technologies, smart vehicles have replaced conventional ones by providing more advanced driving-related features. IoV systems typically consist of Intra-Vehicle Networks (IVNs) in which many Electronic Control units (ECUs) directly and indirectly communicate among them through the Controller Area Network (CAN) bus. However, the growth of such vehicles has also increased the number of network and physical attacks focused on exploiting security weaknesses affecting the CAN protocol. Such problems can also endanger the life of the driver and passengers of the vehicle, as well as that of pedestrians. Therefore, to face this security issue, we propose a novel anomaly detector capable of considering the vehicle-related state over time. To accomplish this, we combine different most famous algorithms to consider all possible relationships between CAN messages and arrange them as corresponding associative rules. The presented approach, also compared with the state-of-the-art solutions, can effectively detect different kinds of attacks (DoS, Fuzzy, GEAR and RPM) by only considering CAN messages collected during attack-free operating scenarios.

Keywords: Anomaly detection · CAN-Bus · Association rules · Internet of Vehicles (IoV) · Machine Learning (ML)

1 Introduction

With the rapid development of the Internet of Things (IoT) and the Internet of Vehicles (IoV) technologies, the vehicle industry has evolved drastically over the last decades resulting in extensive automation and replacement of conventional cars. Typically, IoV systems consist of a mesh of sensors and computational units controlled by thousands of Electronic Control Units (ECUs) [1,18]. These ECUs are specifically designed for the optimal management of a wide array of driving-related features ranging from engine control to Anti-lock Braking (ABS) and Advanced Driver-Assistance Systems (ADAS), respectively.

ECUs are distributed all around the vehicle and communicate with each other via Intra-Vehicle Networks (IVNs) using the Controller Area Network (CAN) protocol, which is the de-facto standard for the IoV industry. Indeed, CAN offers

© The Author(s), under exclusive license to Springer Nature Switzerland AG 2023
O. Gervasi et al. (Eds.): ICCSA 2023 Workshops, LNCS 14105, pp. 174–190, 2023.
https://doi.org/10.1007/978-3-031-37108-0_12

many advantages, such as cost-effective wiring, immunity to electrical interference, self-diagnosing, and error correction [2]. However, despite these functional benefits, the rising vehicle communications render the CAN protocol vulnerable to several hostile activities. For instance, airbags and ABS-related attacks may affect the reputation of manufacturers with substantial financial implications (e.g. the vehicles' recalls) [6], while tampering with ECUs (e.g., the odometers of used cars) is another well-known example that may lead to dire consequences for consumers and manufacturers. In addition, IoV-related intrusions may also concern some privacy issues [3,7]. Indeed, since the CAN protocol was designed to operate within a closed network environment, it is affected by the following two weaknesses: the lack of device authentication (that allows impersonation and masquerading attacks) and the usage of unencrypted traffic (that does not guarantee the confidentiality constraint).

Therefore, several Deep Learning (DL) and Machine Learning (ML)-based approaches have been proposed to counteract such hostile activities that, by exploiting the CAN protocol-related weaknesses, can endanger the life of many people, such as drivers, passengers, and pedestrians, respectively. However, most of the supervised DL-based solutions cannot consider new kinds of attacks [11,25], while those semi-supervised not accurately spot some of the well-known attacks (e.g. they present a considerable number of False Positives or False Negatives) [15,28]. On the other hand, ML-based ones do not analyze correlations among multiple CAN messages [7,26,27]. Consequently, they do not consider a complex and real-world operating scenario, namely the vehicle-related state over time. Instead, they perform only a simple message-by-message detection activity.

For this reason, we propose a novel anomaly detector capable of considering the vehicle's state over time. We accomplish this by using a semi-supervised approach based on several famous algorithms. More precisely, we cluster CAN messages into multi-dimensional regions. Then, we match the derived areas in order to consider all possible relationships between different CAN messages. Hence, by employing a sliding temporal window mechanism, we represent the vehicle's state by arranging such correlations as corresponding associative rules. Finally, we demonstrate the effectiveness of our approach, also compared to some notable ML-based solutions, in detecting several kinds of attacks, namely: DoS, Fuzzy, Gear, and RPM, respectively.

Hence, the main contributions of this paper can be summarized as follows:

1. A novel anomaly detection approach is proposed in order to consider only licit CAN messages and represent the vehicle state over time.
2. The effectiveness of the presented detector is evaluated in detecting several attacks and then compared with some notable ML-based solutions.

The remainder of the paper is organized as follows. Section 2 will present the related works on CAN-bus. Section 3 will report the preliminary concepts related to the CAN protocol and the employed algorithms. Section 4 will describe the proposed approach. Finally, Sect. 5 will report the experimental results, while Sect. 6 will show the conclusions and future work.

2   Related Works

The recent growth and popularity of intelligent vehicles have led to an increase in the development of many DL-based models as effective solutions for IoV intrusion detection and security enhancement [9,20,22]. In this section, we report works related to the CAN bus system that, due to its well-known security weaknesses [8,12,17], can be exploited to accomplish several malicious activities and engage the life of drivers, passengers, and pedestrians.

Hossain et al. [11] proposed a Long Short Term Memory (LSTM)-based model to detect and mitigate the CAN bus network attacks. They accomplished this by injecting different attacks (DoS, Fuzzy, and Spoofing) in a dataset related to a real-world vehicle. Then, they used the derived dataset to train and test the proposed model following a Supervised approach. The obtained results, also compared with those derived using other notable datasets, have always shown an average accuracy of 99%. Similarly, Xiao et al. [25] presented SIMATT-SECCU, which leverages an enhanced RNN cell to perform a time-saving anomaly detection. More precisely, they validated their model by comparing the related results and required time effort with several DL-based models (e.g. RNN, GRU, GIDS, and LSTM).

Also, LSTM layers have been employed by Zhu et al. [28] by proposing a Semi-supervised approach. To accomplish this, they considered the literal binary CAN messages instead of revealing the semantics of CAN messages. Then, they employed two LSTM-based models (multi-dimension and multi-task) trained on only attack-free CAN messages collected in various driving conditions, such as parking, acceleration, deceleration, and steering. The achieved results have proven the effectiveness of the proposed models by showing an average accuracy between 96% and 98%. Instead, Lin et al. [15] introduced an anomaly detection framework that leverages Autoencoder and the Ecogeografic-based optimization algorithm (EBO) to learn sequential patterns existing in the CAN traffic. More precisely, they employed a detection model, trained only on attack-free CAN messages, to identify messages related to three famous attacks (DoS, Fuzzy, and Impersonation). The experimental results indicated that the proposed detector outperformed the most notable Machine Learning (ML)-based models by achieving excellent detection rates.

However, most of the supervised DL-based solutions cannot consider new kinds of attacks, while those semi-supervised achieved good detection results but are affected by a considerable quantity of False Positives (FPs) and False Negatives (FNs).

On the other hand, many ML-based solutions have been proposed to improve the detection rates by following a semi-supervised or unsupervised approach [14,19,23]. For the sake of clarity, we report only the contributions that, for their similarity, can help understand the proposed solution.

D'Angelo et al. [7] provided a new data-driven anomaly detection system based on two algorithms. More precisely, they employed the first algorithm (Cluster-based Learning Algorithm - CLA) to learn the behavior of licit messages passing on the CAN bus, while they used the second one (Data-driven Anomaly Detection Algorithm - DADA) to perform a real-time classification. The experimental results, obtained using data related to the CAN bus, have shown the effectiveness of the proposed detector by also outperforming some famous state-of-the-art approaches.

Instead, Yang et al. [27] presented a novel IDS framework to detect various IoV-related attacks. This framework, named Leader Class and Confidence Decision Ensemble (LCCDE), leverages three advanced ML-based algorithms (XGBoost, LightGBM, and CatBoost) to predict the class related to a specific attack. The experimental results, carried out through two public IoV datasets, highlighted an average accuracy of 99% and a low number of FPs and FNs. Similarly, they proposed a multi-tiered hybrid IDS that employs both a signature-based IDS and an anomaly-based IDS to detect known and unknown attacks [26]. Experimental results have proven that the proposed system can detect various known attacks with an average accuracy of 99%, while it achieved good F-Score values for zero-day attack detection.

However, contrary to our approach, these solutions do not analyze licit correlations among multiple CAN bus messages. Consequently, they cannot perform any anomaly detection activity by considering the vehicle-related state over time.

3   Background

In this section, we provide an overview of the preliminary concepts necessary to understand and appreciate the workflow employed by the proposed approach, namely the CAN protocol and some most famous algorithms, respectively.

3.1   CAN Protocol

The Controller Area Network (CAN) is a message-based protocol designed to enable numerous electric components, e.g., microcontrollers, ECUs, sensors, devices, and actuators, to communicate with each other through a single/dual-wire bus (the CAN bus) [17]. It is one of the most famous standards in automotive and industrial applications due to its low cost and flexible design. Indeed, it is mainly employed to provide many advanced driving-related functions, such as auto start/stop, parking assistance, automatic lane detection, and collision avoidance [12]. In detail, CAN is a time-synchronized broadcast protocol, which means all nodes attached to the CAN bus can receive all packets transmitted [7,14]. For this reason, the sent packets do not have any information about the sender and receiver. The CAN frame can be of 4 types: data frame, error frame, overload frame, and remote frame, respectively.

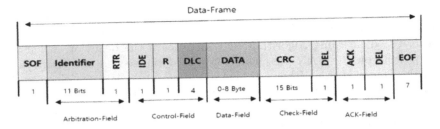

Fig. 1. Structure of the CAN data frame [12].

As shown in Fig. 1, the data frame is composed of seven fields: 1) a Start-of-Frame (SoF) field that denotes the start of a frame; 2) an arbitration field, which contains the identifier of the message and service bits; 3) a control field, which includes the length of the data included in the message and two reserved bits; 4) a data field that contains the transferred data; 5) a CRC field used for error checking; 6) an ACK field employed to acknowledge the receipt of the message; and 7) End-of-Frame (EoF) field that indicates the end of the frame [14].

3.2   K-Nearest Neighbor Algorithm

The K-Nearest Neighbors (KNN) is a supervised learning algorithm used to face both regression and classification tasks. KNN tries to predict the correct class for the test data by calculating the distance between the test data and all the training points. To accomplish this, KNN selects the K number of points closest to the test data. More precisely, the KNN algorithm calculates the probability of the test data belonging to the classes composed of K training data and selects the category holding the highest probability score [10]. Figure 2 shows an iteration of the KNN algorithm using K=5 nearest data points, while its steps can be summarized as follows:

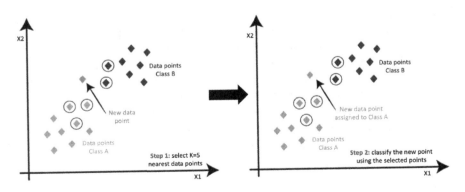

Fig. 2. An iteration of the KNN algorithm with K=5 nearest data points.

1. Select the number K of the neighbors to consider;
2. Derive the distance between each training data point and the new data point.
3. Consider the K nearest neighbors and count the number of the data points in each class.
4. Assign the new data point to that class for which the number of neighbors is maximum.

The success of the KNN algorithm strongly depends on the employed distance and the value K. Typically, the three most famous used distances are Euclidean, Manhattan, and Hamming. Regarding the value of K, it can be chosen randomly or selecting the value that, for instance, gives the minimum error rate [5].

In this study, we employ the KNN algorithm to match the different multi-dimensional regions. Such operation is necessary in order to consider only the licit sequences of CAN messages.

3.3   Apriori Algorithm

The Apriori algorithm, proposed by Agrawal and Srikant in 1994, is one of the most famous and straightforward approaches employed for association rule mining [24]. Apriori is designed to operate on a dataset containing transactions (itemsets) and provide a set of frequent itemsets representing the extracted association rules. To accomplish this, Apriori uses an iterative bottom-up approach and starts by considering every single item in the considered dataset. Then, it generates the itemsets candidates by joining the itemsets generated in the previous step. Finally, the list of candidates is pruned by removing any infrequent itemsets. Apriori repeats this process until no new itemsets can be derived from the previous ones.

The success of the Apriori algorithm strongly depends on the pruning step, in which any itemset that not satisfies a given threshold is pruned. For instance, the support and confidence values represent the most famous threshold values used by the Apriori algorithm. More precisely, given an itemset X, the support is defined as the number of transactions containing X divided by the total number of transactions T.

$$Supp(X) = \frac{count(X)}{T} \tag{1}$$

Instead, given two itemsets X and Y, the confidence is derived as the number of transactions containing X and Y divided by the number of transactions containing X.

$$Conf(X \rightarrow Y) = \frac{count(X\&Y)}{count(X)} \tag{2}$$

Figure 3 shows an execution of the Apriori algorithm using a support value greater than 1.

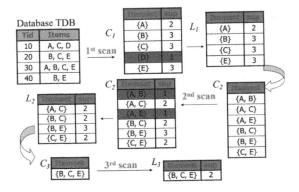

Fig. 3. An execution of the Apriori algorithm [4].

In this study, we employ the Apriori algorithm to mine the association rules as corresponding frequent itemsets. Therefore, we extract only the CAN message sequences useful to represent the vehicle-related state over time.

3.4   Cluster-based Learning Algorithm

The Cluster-based Learning Algorithm (CLA) [7] is an unsupervised approach employed to find a set of behavioral signatures about the CAN bus usage in attack-free scenarios. To this end, CLA follows a multi-step procedure in which the different CAN messages are placed within different subsets and then clustered using the K-Means algorithm. In this way, CLA leads to the definition of multiple centroids (also referred to as gravitational attractors) that individuate, in turn, an admissibility zone. More precisely, such regions represent the CAN commands related to a specific ID within an 8-dimensional space.

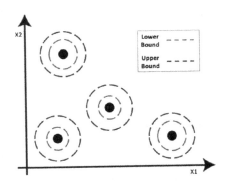

Fig. 4. 2D representation of some centroids and their bounds.

In addition, for each defined cluster, CLA estimates an eligibility area characterized by a lower and an upper bound. Such bounds correspond to the minimum and maximum distance among the points of the considered cluster and its centroid, respectively. Therefore, given an arbitrary CAN ID, this step is fundamental to include the related CAN messages mistakenly excluded by the K-Means algorithm. In a bi-dimensional space, as shown in Fig. 4, this can be represented by two circular crowns around each centroid.

4   The Proposed Approach

This section describes the proposed approach to detect anomalies on CAN-bus by considering the vehicle's state over time. More precisely, since modern cars consist of hundreds of ECUs and sensors, we can define the state as relationships between messages sent in an arbitrary time interval. The following assumption provides the fundaments to perform anomaly detection activities aware of the cooperation between electronic and mechanical components, whose proper functioning is essential to preserve the vehicle's integrity, manufacturers' reputation, and also the people's life [6]. To accomplish this, unlike the most famous ML-based solutions [7,26,27], the proposed approach does not perform a classic message-by-message detection but, instead, follows three main steps, namely: finding the multi-dimensional regions related to each CAN ID, clustering the discovered regions to consider all possible relationships between distinct CAN IDs and extracting the more representative relationships as corresponding association rules, respectively.

Algorithm 1. Training phase

Require: D (attack-free dataset); K (number of clusters related to CLA); N (number of clusters related to KNN); w (size of temporal window); Δ (distance between two temporal windows); $supp$ (value of support).
Ensure: I (frequent itemsets containing the selected association rules); Σ_c (clustered multi-dimensional regions)
1: $\Sigma \leftarrow$ CLA(D,K)
2: $\Sigma_c \leftarrow$ KNN(Σ,N)
3: $t \leftarrow 0$
4: $I \leftarrow \emptyset$
5: **while** $t + w \leq |D|$ **do**
6:     $mess \leftarrow D[t; t + w]$
7:     $rules \leftarrow$ extractRules($mess$,Σ_c)
8:     $I \leftarrow I \cup$ Apriori($rules$,$supp$)
9:     $t \leftarrow t + \Delta$
10: **end while**
11: **return** $\{I, \Sigma_c\}$

As shown in Alg. 1, the training phase begins by considering only CAN messages related to an attack-free scenario. Therefore, given the dataset D, the algorithm finds the multi-dimensional regions by running the Cluster-based Learning Algorithm (CLA) with K clusters. this step provides as output Σ, namely a Map associating each CAN ID to the corresponding region. Notice that, as discussed in Sect. 3.4, the CLA algorithm defines each centroid by providing the related 8-dimensional vector of coordinates and bounds, respectively.

Next, the algorithm clusters the derived regions Σ by running the K-Nearest Neighbor (KNN) with N clusters. This step provides Σ_c, the dataset containing the multi-dimensional coordinates associated with the derived regions. Notice that the KNN algorithm is essential in order to consider all possible relationships between distinct CAN IDs. Indeed, the clustered regions can also be seen as sets related to highly correlated messages sent in the same time interval.

After that, the algorithm runs Apriori and provides I, the dataset of the most frequent itemsets containing the selected associative rules. The algorithm accomplishes this by considering the attack-free messages in D through a sliding temporal window of size w and offset Δ. This step provides the messages ($mess$) representing the vehicle's state in the time interval $[t; t+w]$. Then, the algorithm employs such messages to extract the associative rules ($rules$) from the clustered regions Σ_c. Finally, the algorithm updates the set of frequent itemsets I by performing Apriori with a specific threshold value ($supp$).

Algorithm 2. Testing phase

Require: D_{bus} (messages sent on CAN-bus); I (training frequent itemsets); Σ_c (clustered multi-dimensional regions); w (size of temporal window); Δ (distance between two temporal windows); U (list of licit IDs); $supp$ (value of support).
Ensure: R (detection results dataset).
1: $t \leftarrow 0$
2: $I_{test} \leftarrow \emptyset$
3: $R \leftarrow \emptyset$
4: **while** $t + w \leq |D_{bus}|$ **do**
5:     $mess \leftarrow D_{bus}[t; t+w]$
6:     $\forall \{ID \in mess \mid ID \notin U\} : R \leftarrow R \cup \{(0, 0, 1)\}$
7:     **if** checkDistribution($mess, U$) **then**
8:         $R \leftarrow R \cup \{(0, 0, 1)\}$
9:     **end if**
10:     $rules \leftarrow$ extractRules($mess, \Sigma_c$)
11:     $I_{test} \leftarrow$ Apriori($rules, supp$)
12:     $numRules \leftarrow$ rulesMatcher(I_{test}, I)
13:     **if** $numRules < |I_{test}|$ **then**
14:         $R \leftarrow R \cup \{(|I_{test}|, numRules, 1)\}$
15:     **else**
16:         $R \leftarrow R \cup \{(|I_{test}|, numRules, 0)\}$
17:     **end if**
18:     $t \leftarrow t + \Delta$
19: **end while**
20: **return** R

Subsequently, as shown in Alg. 2, the testing phase begins by considering the messages sent in real-time on the CAN-bus (i.e., when the vehicle is in working). Therefore, given the dataset D_{bus}, the algorithm samples the messages in $[t; t+w]$ using a sliding temporal window of size w and offset Δ.

After that, in order to improve the detection performances, the algorithm considers the following two attack scenarios: 1) For each message, it verifies if the related ID is contained within the list U of known IDs, and 2) it verifies if the messages' distribution (i.e., their frequency) significantly changes respect to a known ID. More precisely, as done by the most famous ML-based detectors [7, 26, 27], the first control (line 6) assumes that an unknown ID is always related to an attack. Instead, the second one (lines 7–9) verifies if several malicious messages are associated with a known ID. Notice that, in both cases, the algorithm updates the detection results R by adding the tuple $(0, 0, 1)$. In detail, the first two values respectively refer to the number of extracted and checked rules, while the third value reports the presence (1) or absence (0) of an attack.

Consequently, only once such tests are passed, the algorithm employs the selected messages ($mess$) to extract the associative rules ($rules$) from the clustered regions Σ_c. Then, the algorithm generates the frequent itemsets I_{test} by performing Apriori with a specific threshold value ($supp$).

Finally, the algorithm checks if the extracted rules (I_{test}) are also present within the training itemsets I. More precisely, the algorithm counts the number of rules ($numRules$) within the training itemsets I. Therefore, if $numRules$ is less than the number of extracted rules $|Itest|$, the algorithm updates R by reporting an attack ($|Itest|, numRules, 1$).

In addition, for the sake of clarity, the training and testing phases are high-level summarized and reported in Fig. 5, respectively.

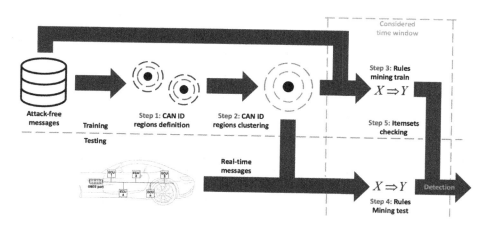

Fig. 5. The high-level workflow.

5 Experimental Results

The goal of the presented experiments is devoted to demonstrating the capabilities of our approach in detecting well-known attacks, namely: DoS, Fuzzy, GEAR and RPM. Also, a comparison with the most famous state-of-the-art solutions is provided in order to remark on the effectiveness of the proposed detector.

5.1 Dataset And Experimental Setting

The experiments have been carried out using the Car-Hacking Dataset provided by the Hacking and Countermeasure Research Lab (HCRL)[1] [20]. More precisely, it consists of five .csv files, that is: 1) attack-free; 2) DoS attack; 3) fuzzy attack; 4) spoofing of the drive GEAR; and 5) spoofing of the RPM gauge, respectively. Each file summarizes around 30–40 minutes of CAN traffic observed from real-world vehicles through the OBD-II port, while the injected messages are performed for 3–5 s for a total of about 300 intrusions. Also, for a DoS attack, the most dominant message (0×000) is injected every 0.3 ms, while random CAN IDs and data values are injected every 0.5 ms in a Fuzzy attack. Finally, for a Spoofing attack (RPM and GEAR), the messages with CAN ID associated with RPM/GEAR are injected every 1 ms. Table 1 provides an overview of the employed dataset.

Table 1. Overview on the involved dataset.

Dataset	Normal mess	Attack mess	Total
GIDS (normal)	988.872	–	988.872
DoS Attack	3.078.250	587.521	3.665.771
Fuzzy Attack	3.347.013	491.847	3.838.860
GEAR Attack	3.845.890	597.252	4.443.142
RPM Attack	3.966.805	654.897	4.612.702
Total	15.226.830	2.331.517	17.558.347

As mentioned earlier, our method makes use of a semi-supervised approach. Accordingly, following the presented Alg. 1, we used only normal messages for training and all traffic (licit and illicit) for testing.

Accordingly, we have run the CLA algorithm with $K = 300$ to find the multi-dimensional regions associated with attack-free CAN messages. Then, we clustered the obtained 8-dimensional regions (centroids), and their bounds, in order to consider all possible relationships between different CAN IDs. To accomplish this, we used the KNN algorithm with $N = 50$. As a result of these steps, the GIDS dataset has been mapped in a new corresponding dataset containing more than 5000 centroids, 1.8 million rows, and 250 columns, respectively.

---

[1] Dataset available at https://ocslab.hksecurity.net/Datasets/car-hacking-dataset.

Next, we employed a sliding temporal window containing 900 CAN messages and offset $= 450$ (i.e., the values respectively of w and Δ). We chose 900 because it represents the number of messages sent on the CAN bus in 0.5 s. However, due to the huge quantity of data, we applied an additional quantization step on centroids and their bounds. More precisely, we accomplished this using the K-Means algorithm [13, 16]. Hence, we mapped about 5000 centroids into 150 corresponding clusters. Then, we quantized the lower and upper bounds by uniquely assigning them into 100 intervals. Consequently, we reduced the number of columns to 75, in which the first 25 columns represent centroids associated only with some specific IDs, while the remaining 50 represent the corresponding bounds.

Subsequently, we used the quantized dataset to extract the most frequent itemsets. To accomplish this, we have run the Apriori algorithm with minimum support $= 0.9$. Finally, we employed the K-Fold Cross Validation algorithm, with $K = 6$, to validate the effectiveness of the mined itemsets and perform a fine-tuning of the considered parameters [21]. More precisely, we have split the training set into six disjointed subsets. Then, the first five partitions have been employed, in turn, as a learning dataset and the remaining one as a testing dataset. The obtained results, shown in Table 2, have proven the effectiveness of such itemsets by achieving all the maximum ratings for each considered metric.

Table 2. Achieved results related to K-Fold cross validation (K=6).

	Acc.	Pre.	Rec.	F1-Mea.
Fold1	1.0000	1.0000	1.0000	1.0000
Fold2	1.0000	1.0000	1.0000	1.0000
Fold3	1.0000	1.0000	1.0000	1.0000
Fold4	1.0000	1.0000	1.0000	1.0000
Fold5	1.0000	1.0000	1.0000	1.0000
Fold6	1.0000	1.0000	1.0000	1.0000

5.2 Evaluation Metrics

To appreciate the effectiveness of the proposed detector, we employed the following evaluation metrics derived from the confusion matrix: Accuracy (Acc.), Precision (Pre.), Recall (Rec.), and F1-Score (F1-Mea.).

$$Accuracy = \frac{TP + TN}{TP + TN + FP + FN} \tag{3}$$

$$Precision = \frac{TP}{TP + FP} \tag{4}$$

$$Recall = \frac{TP}{TP + FN} \tag{5}$$

$$F1 - Score = \frac{2 * Sens * Prec}{Sens + Prec} \tag{6}$$

For each considered category (normal or attack), TPs (True Positives) refer to the CAN messages correctly classified, while TNs (True Negatives) refer to the CAN messages correctly identified in another category. Conversely, FPs (False Positives) represent the CAN messages mistakenly identified as the considered category, while FNs (False Negatives) represent the CAN messages mistakenly identified in another category.

5.3 Achieved Results And Comparison

Next, for the testing, we considered all licit and illicit CAN messages according to the datasets reported in Table 1 (Dos, Fuzzy, Gear, and RPM). More precisely, by following the same procedure described in Alg. 2), we mined the most frequent itemsets. Also, to improve the detection capabilities of our approach, we considered the following two attack scenarios: 1) Verify the presence of an unknown CAN ID in the testing messages, and 2) Verify if the distribution of the messages related to a licit CAN ID significantly changes. Tables 3 and 4 report the achieved results related to normal and attack messages, respectively.

Table 3. Achieved results related to normal CAN messages.

Dataset	Acc.	Pre.	Rec.	F1-Mea.
DoS	1.0000	1.0000	1.0000	1.0000
Fuzzy	0.9971	0.9951	1.0000	0.9975
GEAR	0.9905	1.0000	0.9818	0.9908
RPM	0.9911	1.0000	0.9822	0.9910
Avg	0.9947	0.9988	0.9910	0.9948

Table 4. Achieved results related to attack CAN messages.

Dataset	Acc.	Pre.	Rec.	F1-Mea.
DoS	1.0000	1.0000	1.0000	1.0000
Fuzzy	0.9971	1.0000	0.9930	0.9965
GEAR	0.9905	0.9805	1.0000	0.9902
RPM	0.9911	0.9823	1.0000	0.9911
Avg	0.9947	0.9907	0.9983	0.9945

Finally, we compared our approach with some notable ML-based solutions, namely: the CLA and DADA algorithms proposed by D'Angelo et al. (DA-ALG) and the detectors (LCCDE and MTH-IDS) employed by Yang et al. Table 5 summarizes the comparison between our approach and the considered solutions.

Table 5. Comparison with the most notable ML-based approaches.

Approach	Acc.	Pre.	Rec.	F1-Mea.
Proposed	**0.9947**	**0.9907**	**0.9983**	**0.9945**
DA-ALG	0.9998	0.9986	0.9999	–
LCCDE	0.9999	0.9999	0.9999	0.9999
MTH-IDS	0.9999	0.9999	0.9999	0.9999

As shown in Table 5, our approach has achieved excellent ratings for each derived metric. More precisely, they are very close to those derived by the considered ML-based solutions. Therefore, this might highlight that such detectors are better than the proposed ones because they can better reduce the number of FPs and FNs, respectively. However, contrary to our approach, these solutions do not analyze licit correlations among multiple CAN bus messages. Consequently, they cannot perform any anomaly detection activity by considering the vehicle-related state over time.

6 Conclusions And Future Work

In this paper, we proposed a new anomaly detector to counteract the security issues related to the rapid growth of smart vehicles in the last decades. More precisely, we considered the attacks related to the Controller Area Network (CAN) bus that represents the core communication mechanism used by Electronic Control Units (ECUs) in modern Internet of Vehicle (IoV) systems. However, as is well known, the CAN protocol lacks any built-in security mechanisms that, if exploited for malicious purposes, can endanger the life of many people, such as drivers, passengers, and pedestrians. For this reason, we proposed a novel anomaly detector capable of considering the vehicle's state over time. We accomplished this by using a semi-supervised approach based on several famous algorithms. More precisely, we clustered CAN messages into multi-dimensional regions. Then, we matched the derived areas in order to consider all possible relationships between different CAN messages. Finally, by employing a sliding temporal window mechanism, we represented the vehicle's state by arranging such correlations as corresponding associative rules.

The experimental results, obtained using a famous dataset related to a real vehicle, have shown the capabilities of our approach in detecting different kinds of attacks, namely: DoS, Fuzzy, GEAR, and RPM, respectively. Indeed, the derived performance metrics (Accuracy, Precision, Recall, and F1-Score) have achieved excellent ratings for any considered attack. Finally, we also compared the obtained results with those derived from the state-of-the-art solutions by highlighting, once again, the effectiveness of the proposed approach. Therefore, on the basis of the achieved outcomes, we would like to employ our detector to spot the presence of new anomalies and attacks. More precisely, we intend to use our approach in many other application domains where the correlation among multiple information plays a fundamental role in representing the state of complex systems over time.

Acknowledgments. This work was partially supported by project SERICS (PE00000014) under the NRRP MUR program funded by the EU - NGEU.

CRediT Authorship Contribution Statement

Gianni D'Angelo. Supervision, Methodology, and Reviewing.

Massimo Ficco. Supervision, Methodology, and Reviewing.

Antonio Robustelli. Investigation, Conceptualization, and Writing.

Conflict of interest. The authors declare that they have no conflict of interest.

Availability of Data and Material. The used data is available on https://ocslab. hksecurity.net/Datasets/car-hacking-dataset.

Informed Consent. Informed consent was obtained from all individual participants included in the study.

Ethical Approval. This article does not contain any studies with human participants or animals performed by any of the authors.

References

1. Al-Jarrah, O.Y., Maple, C., Dianati, M., Oxtoby, D., Mouzakitis, A.: Intrusion detection systems for intra-vehicle networks: a review. IEEE Access **7**, 21266–21289 (2019). https://doi.org/10.1109/ACCESS.2019.2894183
2. Bozdal, M., Samie, M., Aslam, S., Jennions, I.: Evaluation of can bus security challenges. Sensors **20**(8) (2020). https://doi.org/10.3390/s20082364, https://www.mdpi.com/1424-8220/20/8/2364
3. Campanile, L., Iacono, M., Levis, A.H., Marulli, F., Mastroianni, M.: Privacy regulations, smart roads, blockchain, and liability insurance: putting technologies to work. IEEE Secur. Priv. **19**(1), 34–43 (2021). https://doi.org/10.1109/MSEC.2020.3012059
4. Chonny: Apriori—association rule mining in-depth explanation and python implementation. https://urlis.net/f2yeu5zt. Accessed 02 Mar 2023
5. Christopher, A.: K-nearest neighbor. https://medium.com/swlh/k-nearest-neighbor-ca2593d7a3c4. Accessed 02 Mar 2023
6. Dürrwang, J., Braun, J., Rumez, M., Kriesten, R.: Security evaluation of an airbag-ECU by reusing threat modeling artefacts. In: 2017 International Conference on Computational Science and Computational Intelligence (CSCI), pp. 37–43 (2017). https://doi.org/10.1109/CSCI.2017.7
7. D'Angelo, G., Castiglione, A., Palmieri, F.: A cluster-based multidimensional approach for detecting attacks on connected vehicles. IEEE Internet of Things J. **8**(16), 12518–12527 (2021). https://doi.org/10.1109/JIOT.2020.3032935
8. EL Madani, S., Motahhir, S., EL Ghzizal, A.: Internet of vehicles: concept, process, security aspects and solutions. Multimedia Tools Appl. **81**(12), 16563–16587 (2022). https://doi.org/10.1007/s11042-022-12386-1

9. Elmasry, W., Akbulut, A., Zaim, A.H.: Evolving deep learning architectures for network intrusion detection using a double PSO metaheuristic. Comput. Netw. **168**, 107042 (2020). https://doi.org/10.1016/j.comnet.2019.107042, https://www. sciencedirect.com/science/article/pii/S138912861930800X

10. Fauzi, M.A., Hanuranto, A.T., Setianingsih, C.: Intrusion detection system using genetic algorithm and k-nn algorithm on dos attack. In: 2020 2nd International Conference on Cybernetics and Intelligent System (ICORIS), pp. 1–6 (2020). https://doi.org/10.1109/ICORIS50180.2020.9320822

11. Hossain, M.D., Inoue, H., Ochiai, H., Fall, D., Kadobayashi, Y.: LSTM-based intrusion detection system for in-vehicle can bus communications. IEEE Access **8**, 185489–185502 (2020). https://doi.org/10.1109/ACCESS.2020.3029307

12. Khatri, N., Shrestha, R., Nam, S.Y.: Security issues with in-vehicle networks, and enhanced countermeasures based on blockchain. Electronics **10**, 893 (2021)

13. Kherbache, M., Espes, D., Amroun, K.: An enhanced approach of the k-means clustering for anomaly-based intrusion detection systems. In: 2021 International Conference on Computing, Computational Modelling and Applications (ICCMA), pp. 78–83 (2021). https://doi.org/10.1109/ICCMA53594.2021.00021

14. Li, X., et al.: Can bus messages abnormal detection using improved SVDD in internet of vehicles. IEEE Internet of Things J. **9**(5), 3359–3371 (2022). https:// doi.org/10.1109/JIOT.2021.3098221

15. Lin, Y., Chen, C., Xiao, F., Avatefipour, O., Alsubhi, K., Yunianta, A.: An evolutionary deep learning anomaly detection framework for in-vehicle networks - can bus. IEEE Trans. Ind. Appl. p. 1 (2020). https://doi.org/10.1109/TIA.2020. 3009906

16. Liu, J., Liang, B., Ji, W.: An anomaly detection approach based on hybrid differential evolution and k-means clustering in crowd intelligence. Int. J. Crowd Sci. **5**(2), 129–142 (2021). https://doi.org/10.1108/IJCS-07-2020-0013

17. Lokman, S.-F., Othman, A.T., Abu-Bakar, M.-H.: Intrusion detection system for automotive controller area network (CAN) bus system: a review. EURASIP J. Wirel. Commun. Netw. **2019**(1), 1–17 (2019). https://doi.org/10.1186/s13638-019-1484-3

18. Markovitz, M., Wool, A.: Field classification, modeling and anomaly detection in unknown can bus networks. Veh. Commun. **9**, 43–52 (2017). https://doi.org/10. 1016/j.vehcom.2017.02.005, https://www.sciencedirect.com/science/article/pii/ S2214209616300869

19. Moore, M.R., Bridges, R.A., Combs, F.L., Starr, M.S., Prowell, S.J.: Modeling inter-signal arrival times for accurate detection of can bus signal injection attacks: a data-driven approach to in-vehicle intrusion detection. In: Proceedings of the 12th Annual Conference on Cyber and Information Security Research. CISRC 2017, Association for Computing Machinery, New York, NY, USA, pp. 1–4 (2017). https://doi.org/10.1145/3064814.3064816

20. Seo, E., Song, H.M., Kim, H.K.: GIDS: GAN based intrusion detection system for in-vehicle network. In: 2018 16th Annual Conference on Privacy, Security and Trust (PST), pp. 1–6 (2018). https://doi.org/10.1109/PST.2018.8514157

21. Shakya, S., Sigdel, S.: An approach to develop a hybrid algorithm based on support vector machine and Naive Bayes for anomaly detection. In: 2017 International Conference on Computing, Communication and Automation (ICCCA), pp. 323–327 (2017). https://doi.org/10.1109/CCAA.2017.8229836

22. Song, H.M., Woo, J., Kim, H.K.: In-vehicle network intrusion detection using deep convolutional neural network. Veh. Commun. **21**, 100198 (2020). https://

doi.org/10.1016/j.vehcom.2019.100198, https://www.sciencedirect.com/science/article/pii/S2214209619302451

23. Taylor, A., Japkowicz, N., Leblanc, S.: Frequency-based anomaly detection for the automotive can bus. In: 2015 World Congress on Industrial Control Systems Security (WCICSS), pp. 45–49 (2015). https://doi.org/10.1109/WCICSS.2015.7420322

24. Utami, M.P., Nurhayati, O.D., Warsito, B.: Hoax information detection system using Apriori algorithm and random forest algorithm in twitter. In: 2020 6th International Conference on Interactive Digital Media (ICIDM), pp. 1–5 (2020). https://doi.org/10.1109/ICIDM51048.2020.9339648

25. Xiao, J., Wu, H., Li, X.: Internet of Things meets vehicles: Sheltering in-vehicle network through lightweight machine learning. Symmetry 11(11) (2019). https://doi.org/10.3390/sym11111388, https://www.mdpi.com/2073-8994/11/11/1388

26. Yang, L., Moubayed, A., Shami, A.: MTH-IDS: a multitiered hybrid intrusion detection system for internet of vehicles. IEEE Internet of Things J. 9(1), 616–632 (2022). https://doi.org/10.1109/JIOT.2021.3084796

27. Yang, L., Shami, A., Stevens, G., de Rusett, S.: LCCDE: a decision-based ensemble framework for intrusion detection in the internet of vehicles. In: GLOBECOM 2022–2022 IEEE Global Communications Conference, pp. 3545–3550 (2022). https://doi.org/10.1109/GLOBECOM48099.2022.10001280

28. Zhu, K., Chen, Z., Peng, Y., Zhang, L.: Mobile edge assisted literal multidimensional anomaly detection of in-vehicle network using LSTM. IEEE Trans. Veh. Technol. 68(5), 4275–4284 (2019). https://doi.org/10.1109/TVT.2019.2907269

Recurrence Plots-Based Network Attack Classification Using CNN-Autoencoders

Gianni D'Angelo🆔, Eslam Farsimadan(✉)🆔, and Francesco Palmieri🆔

Department of Computer Science, Unversity of Salerno, Fisciano, (SA), Italy
{giadangelo,efarsimadan,fpalmieri}@unisa.it
https://www.di.unisa.it

Abstract. The advent of the Internet of Things, with the consequent changes in network architectures and communication dynamics, has affected the security market by introducing further complexity in traffic flow analysis, classification, and detection activities. Consequently, to face these emerging challenges, new empowered strategies are needed to effectively spot anomalous events within legitimate traffic and guarantee the success of early alerting facilities. However, such detection and classification strategies strongly depend on the right choice of employed features, which can be mined from individual or aggregated observations. Therefore, this work explores the theory of dynamic non-linear systems for effectively capturing and understanding the more expressive Internet traffic dynamics arranged as Recurrence Plots. To accomplish this, it leverages the abilities of Convolutional Autoencoders to derive meaningful features from the constructed plots. The achieved results, derived from a real dataset, demonstrate the effectiveness of the presented approach by also outperforming state-of-the-art classifiers.

Keywords: Attack Classification · Recurrence Plots · Autoencoders · Features Extraction · Stacked Networks

1 Introduction

The success of IoT technologies, being the origin of significant changes in communication dynamics (e.g., affecting network layout/architecture, protocols, and interaction patterns), has strongly influenced the nature of Internet traffic introducing new security challenges. In particular, due to the exponential growth of the number of IoT traffic sources and consequent traffic volumes (in terms of a superposition of individual flows on aggregation nodes and interfaces), distinguishing network anomalies became a difficult task, in which randomness and background noise effects are more and more dominant. Also, the evolution from centralized or cloud-based solutions to edge service architectures, with the consequent flattening of infrastructure topologies and the security perimeter dissolution, introduced further complexity in traffic flow collection and interpretation. Such interpretation, implying the understanding of the whole spectrum

© The Author(s), under exclusive license to Springer Nature Switzerland AG 2023
O. Gervasi et al. (Eds.): ICCSA 2023 Workshops, LNCS 14105, pp. 191–209, 2023.
https://doi.org/10.1007/978-3-031-37108-0_13

of the underlying traffic dynamics, requires careful analysis and correlation of the most characterizing traffic features with the final goal of discovering less evident (or often almost hidden) relationships between dynamics that describe the nature of a specific flow (i.e., a legitimate activity or a malicious one). Moreover, such a degree of complexity in the network traffic behavior cannot be effectively described with traditional traffic models, and it has been shown [1] that, given the well-known chaotic nature of Internet traffic, the theory of nonlinear dynamical systems can be very helpful in providing extremely deep insights into traffic flow organization properties by highlighting the existence of periodic structures and recurrence phenomena [2] that are not evident at a glance and are significantly effective in discriminating events that deviate from normality. This is also due to the capability of nonlinear analysis of exploring the system's behavior in the phase space, which is a dimensionally richer representation of the system depicting its evolution pattern simultaneously on multiple time scales. That means, in more detail, reconstructing and studying the system's attractor to appreciate the structure of multi-dimensional curves, also known as trajectories, formed in such space, corresponding to the system's evolution (or motion) over time. Such attractor is highly descriptive of the most significant, intrinsic, and discriminative system dynamics so that it can be used as an invaluable source of features for attack detection and classification.

A Recurrence Plot (RP) [3] is an extremely effective way of representing a system's behavior in phase space and hence visualizing its attractor as a two-dimensional image. Such image is characterized by large-scale or typological patterns that can be homogeneous, periodic, drift and disrupted as well as by the presence of small-scale structures, defining the specific texture, identifying single dots, diagonal, vertical, horizontal, or bowed lines [4,5]. So, the structure of an RP is an effective tool for representing the behavior of a network flow and hence for its classification as normal or anomalous. Unfortunately, while being an extremely effective way of representing the system behavior, the visual interpretation of RPs is extremely difficult and requires much experience. Accordingly, in this work, we exploit the potentialities of a Convolutional Sparse Autoencoders (CNN-SAE)-based neural network in extracting relevant spatial features from the RPs associated with traffic flows. To accomplish this, we start from some elementary statistical features (referred to as basic features) derived by sampling multiple consecutive observations over time and, thus, aggregated within the same temporal window. Then, by leveraging the aforementioned non-linear analysis framework, we arrange them as multiple RPs (one for each basic feature) and hence multi-channel images. After that, a CNN-SAE is employed to derive new spatial features capable of capturing more complex and discriminating dynamics and thus significantly improving the DNNs-based classification process. Therefore, we employ a pipelined architecture by combining the following three main aspects, namely: extracting non-linear characteristics from the basic ones, finding out relevant features from the related RPs processed through the usage of a CNN-SAE, and then performing attack classification tasks by using the classification abilities of a fully-connected softmax DNN, respectively.

In addition, a comprehensive mathematical explanation of the overall workflow is provided to clarify how the proposed approach improves and affects the feature extraction process. Moreover, its effectiveness is investigated in the presence of several unbalanced dataset partitions and finally compared with the most common and widely available state-of-the-art approaches.

Hence, the main contributions of this paper can be summarized as follows:

1. A formal description of the overall workflow is provided to investigate how the proposed approach, from the theoretical point of view, improves and affects the feature extraction process;
2. Non-linear characteristics, arranged as RPs, and the related spatial features extracted using a CNN-SAE are combined to perform attack classification tasks.

The remainder of the paper is organized as follows. Section 2 will report the related works about the most relevant DL-based approaches applied in the attack detection/classification and RP-related classification tasks, respectively. Section 3 will describe the proposed approach by providing a detailed mathematical formalization of the RPs and AEs. Finally, Sect. 4 will report the experimental phase and achieved results, while Sect. 5 will present conclusions and future work.

2   Related Work

Recurrence Plots (RPs) have been applied in many scientific fields for studying and better understanding the behavior of complex systems, including astrophysics, earth sciences, engineering, biology, cardiology, and neuroscience, as extensively surveyed in [4]. In particular DL-based models have been widely employed for extracting non-linear features from RPs calculated on raw data samples [6–8]. For instance, L. Kirichenko et al. [9] have investigated the effectiveness of RPs derived from electroencephalograms (EEG) time series concerning various human conditions. The obtained results, carried out using the Epileptic Seizure Recognition dataset [10], have proven the effectiveness of CNNs in detecting both seizure and no-seizure situations from the related plots with an average accuracy of 98.40%. K. Tziridis et al. [11] have deeply investigated the RPs related to EEG signals by applying to them several noise levels. More precisely, they have perpetuated the input signal by adding, each time, one noise level and then classifying the related RPs through several famous state-of-the-art CNNs, such as AlexNet [12], ResNet18 [13], DenseNet121 [14], and VGG16 [15], respectively. The obtained results have proven, for each considered dataset, the validity of RPs in the presence of several noise levels by achieving an average accuracy between 95% and 97%. Furthermore, RPs have also been investigated in strictly-related Computer Science fields, like Malware classification. In this direction, S. Sartoli et al. [16] have employed a CNN to perform a malware classification task by considering the plots derived from the malware binary images. More precisely, the obtained results carried out from the Microsoft Malware Classification Challenge dataset [17] have proven the effectiveness of the proposed approach with an average accuracy of 96.7% in the presence of nine unbalanced malware families. Internet traffic analysis solutions have also been investigated by using non-linear features arranged as RPs, which offered significant advantages in identifying more complex and unidentified traffic categories [18]. More precisely, since RPs can visualize complex systems' states by representing discriminative and dynamic characteristics [3,19], they might be employed to train a neural network or machine learning mechanism capable of providing good classification performance without being adversely affected by obfuscation techniques. The first anomaly detection experience using non-linear systems theory, and specifically Recurrence Quantification Analysis (RQA), has been described in [20]. Similar techniques have also been employed [21], relying on time-dependent Unthresholded RPs to represent traffic time series, with the goal of extracting non-linear features from them, to be passed in the following to an Extreme Learning Machine-based Auto-Encoder. Convolutional Neural Networks (CNNs), Autoencoders (AEs), and their related combinations are eligible under the umbrella of Deep Neural Networks (DNNs), which have employed to deal with the most disparate classification tasks (e.g., unbalanced dataset, encrypted traffic, attack classification, and anomaly detection) by achieving very promising results [22–25].

Therefore, based on the reported literature contributions and their related results, we combine the abilities of Autoencoders in distilling meaningful and relevant features and the effectiveness of non-linear characteristics in capturing traffic behavior, arranged as RPs, to propose a novel classifier capable of performing attack classification tasks in the presence of different conditions in terms of available training/testing datasets.

3   The Attack Classification Strategy

This section presents the proposed approach for implementing the proposed attack classification strategy capable of exploiting the effectiveness of RPs in capturing traffic flow information. We accomplish this through three main steps, namely: determining new non-linear features from the basic ones (that is, building the RPs), extracting the more representative features from the RPs, and then performing classification using a Stacked Neural Network. More precisely, as shown in Fig. 1, the RPs are built through the traditional delay-coordinate embedding process, whereas the intermediate feature extraction step is performed by employing a CNN-SAE trained on the derived RPs. Then, for implementing the final classification step, we use the AE-related latent space as input to feed a fully-connected softmax neural network. As depicted in Fig. 1, in this way, we combine the effectiveness of RPs in capturing traffic dynamics, the capability of AEs in finding relevant features, and the classification abilities of DNNs. Therefore, in order to better present the proposed workflow's potentialities, we give a detailed description of each step by also providing a mathematical formulation of the involved CNN-SAE to explain how it is able to interpret RPs by

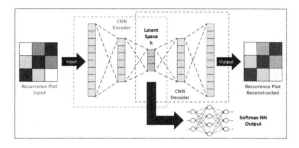

Fig. 1. The proposed workflow.

determining new spatial features that differ from the well-known large-scale or small-scale structures commonly used in human-driven visual inspection.

3.1 Determining Recurrence Plot-Based Features

Understanding the hidden criteria and laws that rule network traffic behavior in certain moments is a very complex task, essentially due to the well-known irregularities and chaotic evolution trends that characterize its evolution. Such complexity is not easily manageable with the traditional event modeling arsenal and can be much better handled by using different concepts, abstractions, and points of view coming from the nonlinear analysis and dynamical system modeling framework.

In order to better understand traffic dynamics under different conditions, we specifically search for redundancies in the observed flows, in terms of a periodic recurrence of specific end-to-end communication patterns, inside traffic data. This is relatively straightforward in typical deterministic systems (e.g., describing an oscillatory phenomenon) where a return to a previously visited state occurs with a specific periodicity. Unfortunately, Internet traffic dynamics are known to be characterizable by using a chaotic system model, which, while deterministic, is aperiodic. In this case, it is not easy to discern temporal dependencies, but considering approximate repetitions of specific events, we can build more complex rules that are able to give a deeper and better representation of the observed behavior. That is, we can still exploit recurrence phenomena to describe the system behavior if we consider the concept of recurrence within a specific threshold, and more specifically, so that we can consider a system state behaving as recurrent when it repeats its behavior after a certain quantity of time, also if not exactly, in a sufficiently close way.

As previously mentioned, RPs allow the visualization of complex systems states, where recurrence is one of the main concepts related to the temporal evolution of their dynamic trajectories. More precisely, as stated by the Takens theorem [5], we can construct a topologically equivalent picture of the behavior of the original multi-dimensional system starting from the time series associated with any individual observable variable. Thus, RPs are an invaluable source of information for understanding the most representative properties of traffic flows. However, their interpretation is extremely complex and prone to errors since it implies a high degree of subjectivity and expertise. Indeed, RPs contain much interesting information about the system of interest concealed in subtle patterns that are not easily ascertained by visual inspection. To overcome this issue, Zbilut and Webber [26] introduced the concept of Recurrence Quantification Analysis (RQA), which is an efficient and deterministic way of non-stationarity features identification in traffic flows. The core of the such analysis is that it uncovers time correlations between data that are not based on linear or non-linear assumptions and cannot be distinguished through the direct study of one-dimensional series of traffic flow volumes [18,27]. However, RQA is able to quantify only an extremely limited part of the information available in an RP, and more effective ways of extracting highly discriminant spatial features from such information are needed.

Therefore, in this section, we employ RPs images to gain significant insights related to network traffic flows by skipping the threshold-related value section issue using a gray scale for distances, in which white and black colors are used to represent short and long distances, respectively. Because network anomalies usually take place within temporal regions of a certain size, they cannot be spotted starting from individual traffic samples. That is, individual observations occurring within a time series can not effectively capture anomalous events if picked one by one or isolated in a completely different context. Instead, the behavior that defines univocally an attack (and consequently the related features) becomes evident only when multiple temporal regions are considered together.

Hence, we do not scrutinize individual traffic flows as a sample at a specific time but consider aggregates of contiguous samples determined through the use of a sliding window scheme, better capturing the traffic behavior over time. This scheme is based on two distinct values: the sliding window size and the related. The offset parameter represents the time distance between two windows. The construction of RPs is performed through delay-coordinate embedding on independent windows of samples of a specific size, taken on the time series resulting from each basic feature, as shown in Fig. 2. The time delay τ and the embedding dimension m used for such purpose have been determined at the training time on the entire set of flows constituting the training set, respectively as the first minimum of average mutual information function [28], and the embedding dimension m, by using the False Nearest Neighbors (FNN) method [29].

Also, we aggregated RPs associated with the different basic features available in sample observations as multi-channel images, in which each channel represents one of the employed features, by improving their descriptive power.

3.2 Using CNN Autoencoders for Extracting Spatial Features from RPs

In this configuration, we suppose that the AE used for processing aggregated RPs, with reference to Fig. 1, includes only three layers, namely: input, hidden, and output, respectively.

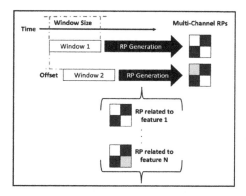

Fig. 2. Schema of the sliding windows for RPs aggregation.

Let $x \in \mathbb{R}^d$ be the input vector of Fig. 1, and let $x^{AE} \in \mathbb{R}^{d'}$ be the input of the considered AE, then $x \equiv x^{AE}$ and $d = d'$.

Indeed, an AE seeks to reconstruct the input by encoding it to a latent space h, which is then decoded to an output $\tilde{x}^{AE}$ defined as follows:

$$\tilde{x}^{AE} = y_{(W',b')}(h_{(W,b)}(x^{AE})) \equiv x^{AE} \tag{1}$$

where (W, b) and (W', b') represent the matrix of the weights and the bias vector of the encoder and decoder respectively, whereas y is the decoder activation function.

Moreover. let n be the number of hidden neurons of AE, then $W \in \mathbb{R}^{n \times d'}$, $b \in \mathbb{R}^n$, and $h_{(W,b)}$ is given by:

$$h_{(W,b)}(x^{AE}) = \sigma(W x^{AE} + b) \tag{2}$$

where σ is the encoder activation function.

Since an Autoencoder is trained by minimizing a loss function $\mathcal{F}$, it is possible to consider additional constraints, also referred to as regularization terms, to give the AE some specific capabilities. For instance, Sparse AEs are often employed to extract meaningful and relevant features from input data and, consequently, to improve the classification results. More precisely, Sparsity can be obtained through different strategies (e.g., L1 regularization and KL regularization) by forcing the involved AE to have only a few simultaneously active nodes (1 in theory) that, as a result, positively affects the learning process [30]. Concerning SAEs, their regularization is accomplished by adding a penalty term to the loss function, that is:

$$\mathcal{F}(x^{AE}, \tilde{x}^{AE})_{Sparse} = \mathcal{F}(x^{AE}, \tilde{x}^{AE}) + \lambda \mathcal{S}(W, b) \tag{3}$$

where λ expresses the degree of regularization, and $\mathcal{S}(W, b)$ represents the sparsity-related term.

Once the training process is completed, the output of the lth hidden neuron h_l can be derived by:

$$h_l = \sigma(\sum_{k=1}^{d'} w_{lk} x_k^{AE} + b_l) \tag{4}$$

Hence, since the input data of a Sparse AE is constrained by $||x^{AE}||^2 \leq 1$, each input data component x_k^{AE} activating the lth neuron is given by:

$$x_k^{AE} = \frac{w_{lk}}{\sum_{m=1}^{d'} (w_{lm})^2}, \; \forall \; k, m = 1 \dots d'. \tag{5}$$

which extracts a feature exactly corresponding to the lth output node. That means that a Sparse AE can learn different sets of characteristics from input data at least equal to the number of considered hidden neurons n.

AEs are frequently coupled with different DNNs flavors to add new functionalities and improve the ability to mine more complex features from input data. Thus, to fully exploit the effectiveness of non-linear characteristics, we use several Convolutional layers to derive relevant relations from the related aggregated RPs that can be considered as spatial features [23].

Let $X \in \mathbb{R}^{N_x \times N_y}$ be the CNN-related input, $RP \in \mathbb{R}^{N \times N}$ be an aggregated RP of Fig. 2, and $C^f \in \mathbb{R}^{a \times b}$ be the fth filter, respectively. Then, $X \equiv RP$ and $N_x \times N_y = d = N \times N$.

On these assumptions, the convolution operation, applied on the CNN-input RP with N_f filters, is defined by:

$$F_{i,j} = \sum_{f=1}^{N_f} \sum_{p=1}^{a} \sum_{q=1}^{b} C_{p,q}^f RP_{i+p-1,j+q-1} \tag{6}$$

with $F_{i,j}$ the components of the filtered input F.

The size of F is defined through its row F_x and column F_y dimensions, by:

$$F_x = \frac{N_x - a + 2P}{S_x} + 1$$
$$F_y = \frac{N_y - b + 2P}{S_y} + 1 \tag{7}$$

where P is the Padding referring to the number of zeros around the border of X, while S_x and S_y are the Strides related to the row and column, which control the shifting of the filter on the input matrix.

Since $d = N_x \times N_y$, it is possible to map any x_k to a point $RP_{i,j}$ into a two-dimensional array. Thus, with abuse of notation, we can assert that:

$$x_k \equiv RP_{i,j} \tag{8}$$

with $k = 1, ..., d$, $i = 1, ..., N_x$, and $j = 1, ..., N_y$.

By substituting $F_{i,j}$ of Eq. 6 into x_k^{AE} of Eq. 4, it yields:

$$h_l = \sigma\left(\sum_{k=1}^{d'} w'_{lk} x_{\phi(k)} + b_l\right) \tag{9}$$

such that $d' = F_x \times F_y$, while

$$w'_{lk} = \sum_{f=1}^{N_f} \sum_{p=1}^{a} \sum_{q=1}^{b} C_{p,q}^f w_{lk} \tag{10}$$

and

$$x_{\phi(k)} \equiv RP_{i+p-1,j+q-1} \tag{11}$$

Analogously to Eq. 4 and Eq. 5, Eq. 9 and Eq. 10 indicate that w'_{lk} (for each l, k) represent the new extracted features that express a more complex knowledge because they are defined as the linear combination of the original w_{lk}. Therefore, the employed CNN-SAE configuration can process non-linear characteristics, arranged as RPs, by providing meaningful features to feed the fully-connected softmax neural network.

4   Performance Evaluation and Results Analysis

The presented experiments and their results are devoted to demonstrating the effectiveness of the proposed approach leveraging RPs for representing network traffic anomalies as multi-channel images and automatically interpreting them through the extraction of highly discriminative spatial classification features. To accomplish this, we employ the learning abilities of CNN Autoencoders trained on a famous dataset, which includes packets generated by different workstations, protocols, and applications.

4.1   Dataset and Basic Features

For the following experiments, we used real-world traffic features available in the Intrusion Detection Evaluation Dataset (CIC-IDS2017)[1] [31], which are composed of several .csv files related to Benign and Attack activities. More precisely, we considered all the Normal traffic captured during Monday 03/07/2017 and Malicious traffic captured from Tuesday 04/07/2017 to Friday 07/07/2017. Table 1 summarizes the traffic nature and related activities for each day and each employed .csv file, respectively.

Since the used dataset provides more than 80 network-related features, we pre-processed it in order to represent each bidirectional flow (summarized as a single dataset entry) as a low-dimensional vector characterized by only the following nine basic features:

---

[1] https://www.unb.ca/cic/datasets/ids-2017.html.

Table 1. Overview on the employed .csv files.

Day/CSV Name	Typology	Description
Monday	Normal	Normal human activities
Tuesday	Attack	Brute Force (FTP/SSH-Patator)
Wednesday	Attack	DoS/DDoS
Thursday	Attack	Brute Force (FTP/SSH-Patator)
Friday1	Attack	Port Scan
Friday2	Attack	DDoS

– *Total Fwd Packets*: number of sent packets from Sender;
– *Total Bwd Packets*: number of sent packets from Receiver;
– *Flow Bytes/s*: flow of bytes for second;
– *Flow Packets/s*: flow of exchanged packets for second;
– *Average Packet Size*: average number of sent packets;
– *Packet Length Mean*: mean length of the exchanged packet;
– *Down/Up Ration*: the Down/Up ratio estimated for the considered flow;
– *SYN Flag Count*: number of set SYN Flags;
– *ACK Flag Count*: number of set ACK Flags.

Then, we used the related ground-truth to associate each flow with its corresponding typology (normal or each type of attack), thus adding the supervisory signal. Finally, following the achieved results, we rescaled each .csv file employing a standard normal distribution, with zero mean and standard deviation equal to 1 ($\mu = 0$, $\sigma = 1$).

4.2   Experimental Setting

Once the basic features have been selected and scaled, we merged all related .csv files as a whole dataset in order to estimate the embedding dimension m and the time_delay τ. More precisely, for each feature-related column, we performed the False Nearest Neighbors (FNN) Algorithm [29] and derived the Average Mutual Information (AMI) using the Non-Linear Time Series Analysis (NoLiTSA) Python framework [32]. Therefore, we set the minimum value $m = 3$ and $\tau = 1$ because they were the common values capable of minimizing the false neighbors and the AMI, respectively. Then, we split the employed dataset into two mutually-exclusive sets using, for each .csv file, the 70% of vectors for training and the remaining 30% for testing. The resulting .csv files were aggregated to form the overall training and testing datasets, respectively. Note that the temporal order was conserved during such a splitting process. Next, by following the schema proposed in Fig. 2, several sliding windows characterized by having different dimensions and offsets have been considered, as reported below:

– winDim: dimension for each window (8, 16, 32, 64, 128);
– offset: distance between two windows (1 - Consecutive, winDim/2 - semi-overlapped, winDim - non-overlapped).

More precisely, for each set of flows (each characterized by the 9 basic features mentioned above) falling within a specific sliding window, the related RPs as $(winDim - (m-1)\tau) \times (winDim - (m-1)\tau)$ matrices for each considered basic feature were first generated. Then, the resulting RPs (one for each basic feature) were aggregated to form a single multi-channel (9-channels) RP image, which characterizes the set of traffic flows falling within the considered time window.

Although many experiments were carried out by using different combinations of $winDim/offset$, $winDim = 16$ showed to get best results. Therefore, in all experiments, we used this dimension for the time window. Table 2, Table 3, and Table 4 show the details of the training and testing sets derived by using a time window of size 16 and offset values 1, 8, and 16, respectively.

Table 2. Dataset division with winDim = 16 and offset = 1.

Category	Training	Testing	Total
DDoS	89601	38385	127986
DoS	172275	73795	246070
FTP-Patator	5537	2353	7890
Port Scan	111137	47617	158754
SSH-Patator	4097	1745	5842
Normal	370609	158817	529426
Total	753256	322712	1075968

Table 3. Dataset division with winDim = 16 and offset = 8.

Category	Training	Testing	Total
DDoS	11201	4799	16000
DoS	21537	9227	30764
FTP-Patator	693	295	988
Port Scan	13893	5953	19846
SSH-Patator	513	219	732
Normal	46327	19853	66180
Total	94164	40346	134510

Table 4. Dataset division with winDim = 16 and offset = 16.

Category	Training	Testing	Total
DDoS	5601	2400	8001
DoS	10770	4615	15385
FTP-Patator	347	148	495
Port Scan	6947	2977	9924
SSH-Patator	257	110	367
Normal	23164	9927	33091
Total	47086	20177	67263

Finally, the dataset pre-processing phase, the related RPs extraction, and all the experiments have been conducted with an iMac Desktop equipped with an Intel 6-core $i7$ CPU @ 3.2 GHz and 16 GB RAM.

4.3   Evaluation Metrics

To assess the classification effectiveness of the presented scheme, we considered the traditional evaluation metrics that can be extracted from the confusion matrix: Accuracy (Acc.), Sensitivity (Sens.), Specificity (Spec.), Precision (Prec.), F-Measure (F-Mea.), and Area Under the ROC Curve (AUC), as defined below.

$$Accuracy = \frac{TP + TN}{TP + TN + FP + FN} \tag{12}$$

$$Sensitivity = \frac{TP}{TP + FN} \tag{13}$$

$$Specificity = \frac{TN}{TN + FP} \tag{14}$$

$$Precision = \frac{TP}{TP + FP} \tag{15}$$

$$F - Measure = \frac{2 * Sens * Prec}{Sens + Prec} \tag{16}$$

$$AUC = \frac{Sens + Spec}{2} \tag{17}$$

where for each category, TPs (True Positives) are the flows correctly classified, FPs (False Positives) are the flows incorrectly classified, FNs (False Negatives) are the flows incorrectly rejected, and TNs (True Negatives) are the flows correctly rejected.

4.4   Model Description and Results

As mentioned earlier, we used a CNN-SAE for interpreting RPs. Accordingly, in this Section, the implementation details are first reported, and then the experimental results are shown.

Figure 3 shows the high-level organization of the CNN layers employed for the encoder side. As depicted, it includes a sequence of three Conv2D layers with kernel_size=$(2, 2)$, activation=relu, and padding=same, characterized by having 18, 8, and 4 filters, respectively. After that, a Flatten layer is employed to map the extracted features as one-dimensional latent vectors. Hence, after having built the decoder side using the inverse sequence of the encoding layers, we trained the CNN-SAE configuration by using Adam optimizer as well as the Mean Absolute Error (MAE) as loss function for 50 epochs and batch_size = 64.

Next, we fed a fully-connected softmax neural network comprising two Dense layers with 512 neurons for each layer, activation=relu for both layers and dropout=$0.5, 0.4$, respectively. Also, to obtain the classification results as probability distributions, we used a third dense layer with 6 neurons and activation=softmax as the output layer. Then, we trained the whole network with Adam optimizer and SparseCategoricalFocalLoss loss function for 20 epochs and batch_size = 256.

Many experiments were carried out by varying the following hyperparameters:

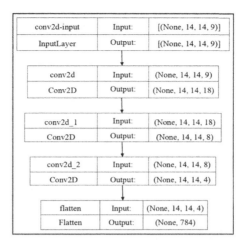

Fig. 3. CNN layers high-level organization.

- numConvLayers: the number of Conv2D layers considered (1, 2, 3);
- numFilters: the number of filters considered for each Conv2D layer (1, 2, 4, 8, 12, 14, 16, 18, 28, 36);
- strides: the stride length and combinations for each Conv2D layer ((1, 1), (1, 2), (2, 1), (2, 2));
- numDenseLayers: the number of Dense layers considered (1, 2, 3, 4);
- numNeurons: the number of neurons considered for each Dense layer (16, 24, 28, 32, 64, 96, 128, 256, 512, 1024);
- dropout: dropout values for each Dense layer (0.05, 0.1, 0.2, 0.3, 0.4, 0.5);
- activation: activation functions employed (relu, softmax, sigmoid);
- batch_size: considered batch_size values (32, 64, 128, 256, 512, 1024, 2048);
- loss: loss functions used (Mean Squared Error (MSE), Mean Absolute Error (MAE), SparseCategoricalCrossentropy, SparseCategoricalFocalLoss).

Note that only the configurations that achieved the best results were reported in this Sect. Table 5, Table 6, and Table 7 report the derived Confusion Matrices, while Table 8, Table 9, and Table 10 summarize the corresponding classification metrics derived by fine-tuning the whole CNN-SAE-NN stacked network for 20 additional epochs.

Table 5. Confusion Matrix (offset = 1).

	DDoS	DoS	FTP-Patator	Port Scan	SSH-Patator	Normal
DDoS	38149	215	0	14	0	7
DoS	1992	70734	0	661	0	408
FTP-Patator	0	0	2331	0	4	18
Port Scan	90	122	0	47303	0	102
SSH-Patator	0	0	0	0	1745	0
Normal	6	52	0	0	0	158759

Table 6. Confusion Matrix (offset = 8).

	DDoS	DoS	FTP-Patator	Port Scan	SSH-Patator	Normal
DDoS	4761	30	0	3	0	5
DoS	351	8712	0	97	0	67
FTP-Patator	0	0	291	0	0	4
Port Scan	2	13	0	5925	0	13
SSH-Patator	0	0	0	0	219	0
Normal	0	10	0	0	0	19843

Table 7. Confusion Matrix (offset = 16).

	DDoS	DoS	FTP-Patator	Port Scan	SSH-Patator	Normal
DDoS	2365	21	0	5	0	9
DoS	118	4251	0	103	1	142
FTP-Patator	0	0	145	0	0	3
Port Scan	3	5	0	2962	0	7
SSH-Patator	0	0	0	0	109	1
Normal	0	2	0	0	0	9925

Table 8. Statistic Metrics related to dataset with offset = 1.

Category	Acc.	Spec.	Prec.	Sens.	F-Mea.	AUC
DDoS	0.9928	0.9927	0.9481	0.9939	0.9704	0.9933
DoS	0.9893	0.9984	0.9945	0.9585	0.9762	0.9785
FTP-Patator	0.9999	1.0000	1.0000	0.9907	0.9953	0.9953
Port Scan	0.9969	0.9975	0.9859	0.9934	0.9897	0.9955
SSH-Patator	1.0000	1.0000	0.9977	1.0000	0.9989	1.0000
Normal	0.9982	0.9967	0.9966	0.9996	0.9981	0.9982
Avg.	0.9962	0.9976	0.9872	0.9893	0.9881	0.9935

4.5 Comparison and Discussion

Table 11 summarizes the averages of the performance metrics related to the employed CNN-SAE-NN configuration for each considered offset.

To better demonstrate the effectiveness of the proposed classification framework, we compare its obtained results with those derived by using the most famous state-of-the-art ML-based classifiers, such as Naive Bayes-based classifier (NB), Logistic classifier (LOG), Support Vector Machine classifier (SVM), J48 decision-tree classifier (J48), and Multilayer Perceptron classifier (MLP), specifically arranged for attack detection and classification, where all the experiments were carried out using WEKA [33]. Moreover, in order to compare the proposed method with another model based on DL, we examined several CNN and convolutional sparse autoencoder architectures that are very effective in image processing. In this section, we report just the results achieved from the best architecture (in terms of performance metrics) [34]. More precisely, we have evaluated their classification capabilities in comparison with our method by considering non-overlapped time windows with offset = 16, which is the worstscenario of our approach (see table Table 10). Table 12 reports this comparison between the average results of our proposed neural network configuration and the average results of these classifiers.

Table 9. Statistic Metrics related to dataset with offset = 8.

Category	Acc.	Spec.	Prec.	Sens.	F-Mea.	AUC
DDoS	0.9903	0.9901	0.9310	0.9921	0.9606	0.9911
DoS	0.9859	0.9983	0.9940	0.9442	0.9684	0.9712
FTP-Patator	0.9999	1.0000	1.0000	0.9864	0.9932	0.9932
Port Scan	0.9968	0.9971	0.9834	0.9953	0.9893	0.9962
SSH-Patator	1.0000	1.0000	1.0000	1.0000	1.0000	1.0000
Normal	0.9975	0.9957	0.9955	0.9995	0.9975	0.9976
Avg.	0.9951	0.9969	0.9840	0.9863	0.9848	0.9916

Table 10. Statistic Metrics related to dataset with offset = 16.

Category	Acc.	Spec.	Prec.	Sens.	F-Mea.	AUC
DDoS	0.9923	0.9932	0.9513	0.9854	0.9606	0.9893
DoS	0.9806	0.9982	0.9935	0.9211	0.9684	0.9597
FTP-Patator	0.9999	1.0000	1.0000	0.9898	0.9932	0.9899
Port Scan	0.9939	0.9937	0.9648	0.9797	0.9893	0.9943
SSH-Patator	0.9999	1.0000	0.9909	0.9909	1.0000	0.9954
Normal	0.9919	0.9842	0.9839	0.9998	0.9918	0.9920
Avg.	0.9931	0.9949	0.9807	0.9787	0.9794	0.9868

Table 11. Avg. Statistic Metrics comparison related to each considered offset value.

Offset	Acc.	Spec.	Prec.	Sens.	F-Mea.	AUC
offset = 1	0.9962	0.9976	0.9872	0.9893	0.9881	0.9935
offset = 8	0.9951	0.9969	0.9840	0.9863	0.9848	0.9916
offset = 16	0.9931	0.9949	0.9807	0.9787	0.9794	0.9868

As shown in Table 12, the proposed CNN-SAE network drastically outperforms other ML-based methods by significantly improving the average of all evaluation metrics, specifically F-Measure. It proves, once again, the effectiveness of the proposed approach and the abilities of Autoencoders that, in any application scenario (e.g., dataset partitions), are capable of deriving meaningful features from traffic dynamics arranged as RPs and thus achieve excellent classification results.

Table 12. Comparison between the proposed configuration and ML-based approaches.

Method	Acc.	Spec.	Prec.	Sens.	F-Mea.	AUC
NB	0.7604	0.8716	0.4506	0.5448	0.2657	0.7082
LOG	0.9657	0.9731	0.6175	0.6005	0.6020	0.7868
SVM	0.9369	0.9446	0.6295	0.4873	0.4999	0.7160
J48	0.9926	0.9937	0.9868	0.8929	0.9243	0.9434
MLP	0.9499	0.9533	0.7759	0.6034	0.6546	0.7783
CNN	0.9919	0.9942	0.9733	0.9376	0.9539	0.9659
Proposed	0.9931	0.9949	0.9807	0.9787	0.9794	0.9868

5   Conclusion and Future Work

In this paper, we proposed a novel IoT-related network attacks classifier by combining the capabilities of AEs in automatically finding relevant features and the effectiveness of characteristics coming from non-linear analysis theory arranged as RPs. More precisely, we considered statistical information related to benign and malicious traffic-related activities available in the CIC-IDS2017 dataset as raw input data. Then, we employed the corresponding multi-channel image representation of RPs and a Convolutional Sparse Autoencoder (CNN-SAE) to perform the automatic interpretation of RP images, aimed at using the reliable discriminating power of such non-linear structures in attack classification tasks. The achieved results, derived as statistic metrics from the multi-class confusion matrix, have proven the effectiveness of the proposed classifier in the presence of several unbalanced datasets partitions by obtaining an average F-Measure of more than 98%. Finally, we have evaluated the proposed approach by comparing it with the most famous state-of-the-art ML-based attack classification techniques. The proposed approach outperformed all considered approaches with significant improvements in all evaluation metrics.

Therefore, based on the derived outcomes, we would like to propose two possible future works. The first one can be investigating the effectiveness of RPs and CNN-SAEs for multiple hostile traffic flow detection and classification in federated organizations. A possible starting point can be analyzing some of the existing effective federated approaches in this direction, such as [35]. The second one is exploring the abilities of Autoencoders in deriving relevant traffic features by considering the combination of several non-linear extraction methods. More precisely, the following studies might improve the effectiveness of real-time attack detectors and classifiers by reducing the impact of Distributed Denial of Services (DDoS) attacks and the required time for their detection, classification, and mitigation, respectively.

Acknowledgements. This work was partially supported by project SERICS (PE00000014) under the NRRP MUR program funded by the EU - NGEU.

References

1. Palmieri, F.: Network anomaly detection based on logistic regression of nonlinear chaotic invariants. J. Netw. Comput. Appl. **148**, 102460 (2019). ISSN 1084–8045. https://doi.org/10.1016/j.jnca.2019.102460
2. Poincaré, H.: Sur le problème des trois corps et les équations de la dynamique. Acta mathematica **13**(1), A3–A270 (1890)
3. Eckmann, J.-P., Kamphorst, S.O., Ruelle, D.: Europhysics Letters (EPL). https://doi.org/10.1209/0295-5075/4/9/004 (1987)
4. Marwan, N., Carmen Romano, M., Thiel, M., Kurths, J.: Recurrence plots for the analysis of complex systems. Phys. Rep. **438**(5), 237–329 (2007). ISSN 0370–1573. https://doi.org/10.1016/j.physrep.2006.11.001
5. Takens, F.: Detecting strange attractors in turbulence. In: David, R., Young, L.S., (eds.) Dynamical Systems and Turbulence, Warwick 1980, pp. 366–381, Berlin, Heidelberg, 1981. Springer, Berlin Heidelberg (1980). ISBN 978-3-540-38945-3
6. Garcia-Ceja, E., Uddin, M.Z., Torresen, J.: Classification of recurrence pots distance matrices with a convolutional neural network for activity recognition. Procedia Comput. Sci. **130**, 157–163 (2018)
7. Menini, N., et al.: A soft computing framework for image classification based on recurrence plots. IEEE Geosci. Rem. Sens. Lett. **16**(2), 320–324 (2019). https://doi.org/10.1109/LGRS.2018.2872132
8. Patil, M.S., Loka, R., Parimi, A.M.: Application of ARIMA and 2d-CNNNS using recurrence plots for medium-term load forecasting. In: 2021 IEEE 2nd China International Youth Conference on Electrical Engineering (CIYCEE), pp. 1–5 (2021). https://doi.org/10.1109/CIYCEE53554.2021.9676838
9. Kirichenko, L., Radivilova, T., Bulakh, V., Zinchenko, P., Saif Alghawli, A.: Two approaches to machine learning classification of time series based on recurrence plots. In: 2020 IEEE Third International Conference on Data Stream Mining & Processing (DSMP), pp. 84–89 (2020). https://doi.org/10.1109/DSMP47368.2020.9204021
10. Andrzejak, R.G., et al.: Indications of nonlinear deterministic and finite-dimensional structures in time series of brain electrical activity: dependence on recording region and brain state. Phys. Rev. E **64**, 061907 (2001)
11. Tziridis, K., Kalampokas, T., Papakostas, G.A.: EEG signal analysis for seizure detection using recurrence plots and tchebichef moments. In: 2021 IEEE 11th Annual Computing and Communication Workshop and Conference (CCWC), pp. 0184–0190 (2021). https://doi.org/10.1109/CCWC51732.2021.9376134
12. Krizhevsky, A., Sutskever, I., Hinton, G.E.: Imagenet classification with deep convolutional neural networks. In: Pereira, F., Burges, C.J., Bottou, L., Weinberger, K.Q., (eds.), Advances in Neural Information Processing Systems. Curran Associates Inc
13. He, K., Zhang, X., Ren, S., Sun, J.: Deep residual learning for image recognition. In: Proceedings of the IEEE Conference on Computer Vision and Pattern Recognition(2015). https://arxiv.org/abs/1512.03385
14. Huang, G., Liu, Z., van der Maaten, L., Weinberger, K.Q.: Densely connected convolutional networks. In: Proceedings of the IEEE Conference on Computer Vision and Pattern Recognition, pp. 4700–4708 (2016). https://arxiv.org/abs/1608.06993
15. Simonyan, K., Zisserman, A.: Very deep convolutional networks for large-scale image recognition (2014). https://arxiv.org/abs/1409.1556

16. Sartoli, S., Wei, Y., Hampton, S.: Malware classification using recurrence plots and deep neural network. In: 2020 19th IEEE International Conference on Machine Learning and Applications (ICMLA), pp. 901–906 (2020).https://doi.org/10.1109/ICMLA51294.2020.00147
17. Ronen, R., Radu, M., Feuerstein, C., Yom-Tov, E., Ahmadi, M.: Microsoft malware classification challenge (2018). https://arxiv.org/abs/1802.10135
18. Palmieri, F., Fiore, U.: A nonlinear, recurrence-based approach to traffic classification. Comput. Netw. **53**(6), 761–773 (2009). https://doi.org/10.1016/j.comnet.2008.12.015
19. Hirata, Y.: Recurrence plots for characterizing random dynamical systems. Commun. Nonlinear Sci. Numer. Simul. **94**, 105552 (2021). https://doi.org/10.1016/j.cnsns.2020.105552. ISSN 1007–5704
20. Palmieri, F., Fiore, U.: Network anomaly detection through nonlinear analysis. Comp. Secur. **29**(7), 737–755 (2010)
21. Hu, Min, Feng, Xiaowei, Zhou, Shengchen, Xu, Wei: Anomaly detection in time series data based on unthresholded recurrence plots. In: Abawajy, Jemal, Choo, Kim-Kwang Raymond., Islam, Rafiqul, Xu, Zheng, Atiquzzaman, Mohammed (eds.) ATCI 2018. AISC, vol. 842, pp. 477–484. Springer, Cham (2019). https://doi.org/10.1007/978-3-319-98776-7_52
22. Wang, P., Ye, F., Chen, X., Qian, Y.: Datanet: deep learning based encrypted network traffic classification in SDN home gateway. IEEE Access **6**, 55380–55391 (2018). https://doi.org/10.1109/ACCESS.2018.2872430
23. D'Angelo, G., Palmieri, F.: Network traffic classification using deep convolutional recurrent autoencoder neural networks for spatial–temporal features extraction. J. Netw. Comput. Appl. **173**, 102890 (2021). https://doi.org/10.1016/j.jnca.2020.102890. ISSN 1084–8045
24. Lopez-Martin, M., Carro, B., Sanchez-Esguevillas, A., Lloret, J.: Network traffic classifier with convolutional and recurrent neural networks for internet of things. IEEE Access **5**, 18042–18050 (2017)
25. Lotfollahi, M., Jafari Siavoshani, M., Shirali Hossein Zade, R., Saberian, M.: Deep packet: a novel approach for encrypted traffic classification using deep learning. Soft Comput. **24**(3), 1999–2012 (2020). https://doi.org/10.48550/arXiv.1709.02656
26. Zbilut, J.P., Webber, C.L.: Embeddings and delays as derived from quantification of recurrence plots. Phys. Lett. A **3**, 199–203 (1992). https://doi.org/10.1016/0375-9601(92)90426-M. ISSN 0375–9601
27. Almeida-Ñauñay, A.F., Benito, R.M., Quemada, M., Losada, J.C., Tarquis, A.M.: Recurrence plots for quantifying the vegetation indices dynamics in a semi-arid grassland. Geoderma **406**, 115488 (2022). https://doi.org/10.1016/j.geoderma.2021.115488. ISSN 0016–7061
28. Hegger, R., Kantz, H., Schreiber, T.: Practical implementation of nonlinear time series methods: the tisean package. Chaos Interdisc. J. Nonlinear Sci. **9**(2), 413–435 (1999)
29. Kennel, M.B., Brown, R., Abarbanel, H.D.I.: Determining embedding dimension for phase-space reconstruction using a geometrical construction. Phys. Rev. A **45**, 3403–3411 (1992)
30. Makhzani, A., Frey, B.: k-sparse autoencoders (2014). arXiv: 1312.5663 [cs.LG]
31. Sharafaldin, I., Lashkari, A.H., Ghorbani, A.A.: Toward generating a new intrusion detection dataset and intrusion traffic characterization. In: ICISSP, vol. 1, pp. 108–116 (2018)
32. Mannattil, M.: NoLiTSA - NonLinear Time Series Analysis (2022). https://github.com/manu-mannattil/nolitsa. Accessed 26 July 2022

33. Witten, I.H., Frank, E., Hall, M.A., Pal, C.J.: Data Mining, Fourth Edition: Practical Machine Learning Tools and Techniques 4th. isbn: 0128042915 (Morgan Kaufmann Publishers Inc., San Francisco, CA, USA, 2016)
34. Luo, W., Li, J., Yang, J., Xu, W., Zhang, J.: Convolutional sparse autoencoders for image classification. IEEE Trans. Neural Netw. Learn. Syst. **29**(7), 3289–3294 (2018). https://doi.org/10.1109/TNNLS.2017.2712793
35. Marulli, F., Balzanella, A., Campanile, L., Iacono, M., Mastroianni, M.: Exploring a federated learning approach to enhance authorship attribution of misleading information from heterogeneous sources. In: 2021 International Joint Conference on Neural Networks (IJCNN), pp. 1–8 (2021). https://doi.org/10.1109/IJCNN52387.2021.9534377

Conversations South-North on Climate Change Adaptation Towards Smarter and More Sustainable Cities (CLAPS 2023)

An Integrated Approach for the Co-governance of Sustainable and Resilient Cities: A Focus on Green Infrastructures and Transport Mobility in Catania (Italy)

Luisa Sturiale[1]([⊠]), Matteo Ignaccolo[1], Vincenza Torrisi[2]([⊠]), and Alessandro Scuderi[3]

[1] Department of Civil Engineering and Architecture, University of Catania, Viale Andrea Doria, 6, 95125 Catania, Italy
luisa.sturiale@unict.it

[2] Department of Electrical, Electronic and Computer Engineering, University of Catania, Viale Andrea Doria, 6, 95125 Catania, Italy
vincenza.torrisi@unict.it

[3] Agriculture Food and Environment Department (D3A), University of Catania, Viale Andrea Doria, 95127 Catania, Italy

Abstract. Among the Sustainable Development Goals in the UN Agenda 2030, Goals 11 "Sustainable Cities and Communities" aims to *"make cities and human settlements inclusive, safe, resilient and sustainable"*. Among the different targets it aims to promote a participatory and integrated transport-land planning; to guarantee accessibility to green areas and safe and inclusive public spaces, especially to vulnerable users; to ensure access to safe and economic living spaces and transport systems. This work presents an integrated approach to consider the role of Green Infrastructures (GIs) and Transport Mobility (TM) as key components in the transition towards a model of sustainable and resilient cities. The analysis of these two components of the urban system, especially in cities with high rates of motorisation and traffic congestion, on the one hand, and with a non-widespread presence of green areas, on the other, becomes strategic for implementing actions aimed at making cities more sustainable.

The analyzed case study focuses on Catania (Italy) at different territorial levels, considering both the urban area and the neighboring municipalities.

The study consists of two steps: (i) first, an interview-based methodology has been implemented to analyze citizen's perception of GIs to tackle climate change and the willingness to pay to sustain the maintenance of these infrastructures; (ii) on the other hand, an extended survey will be performed to evaluate the propensity of users towards innovative shared transport systems and also the willingness to pay for the service. The obtained results from the first round of interviews highlighted the citizens point of view linked to GIs and their interest in the co-management. Research findings will constitute a decision support for administration and stakeholder to guide public investments and achieve awareness among citizens in order to promote co-governance actions and develop climate adaptation strategies and improve the quality of life in urban areas.

Keywords: Climate Change · Urban Green Areas · Transport Mobility · Urban areas · Survey · Citizens' Perception

© The Author(s), under exclusive license to Springer Nature Switzerland AG 2023
O. Gervasi et al. (Eds.): ICCSA 2023 Workshops, LNCS 14105, pp. 213–230, 2023.
https://doi.org/10.1007/978-3-031-37108-0_14

1 Introduction

It is possible to reduce the effects of climate change on society and the environment through specific actions, which can be oriented in two directions: mitigation, which aims to progressively reduce emissions of gases responsible for global warming, and adaptation, which aims to reduce the vulnerability of environmental, social and economic systems and increase their resilience to climate. Clearly, no one option is sufficient on its own, but adaptation and mitigation actions need to be coordinated in order to pursue effective results over time. This can be achieved through governance policies and cooperation between different stakeholders and could be enhanced by integrated responses that link mitigation and adaptation with other societal goals [1].

Assessing the integrated effects of planning and programming choices aimed at reducing climate-changing emissions is a priority theme of the document *"Transforming our world: The 2030 Agenda for Sustainable Development"* The 2030 Agenda sets 17 Sustainable Development Goals (SDGs) and 169 targets to be achieved over the next 15 years. Goal 11, *"Sustainable Cities and Communities"*, is specifically dedicated to urban systems, with the goal of *"making cities and human settlements inclusive, safe, resilient and sustainable"* [2].

Cities will play an important role in combating climate change and will be called upon to adopt innovative solutions and rethink urban management and planning [3].

All the targets in Goal 11 are important and complementary to each other in order to achieve the 2030 objective, but it is clear that the related actions must be developed according to the characteristics of the area in question. In particular, in urban realities in which there is a criticality in mobility-related aspects, extreme climate change events are more frequent and there are problems with the use of public green spaces, Targets 11.2, 11.3 and 11.7 will be considered with more attention (Fig. 1).

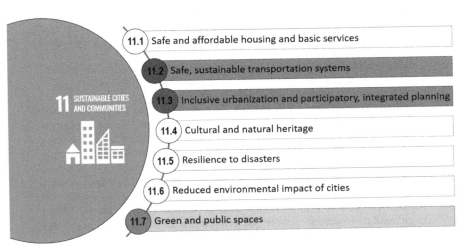

Fig. 1. Targets within Goal 11 "Sustainable Cities and Communities" (author elaboration)

In particular, the Target 11.2. Provides: "By 2030, provide access to safe, affordable, accessible and sustainable transport systems for all, improving road safety, notably by expanding public transport, with special attention to the needs of those in vulnerable situations, women, children, persons with disabilities and older persons". Target 11.3 provides: "By 2030, enhance inclusive and sustainable urbanization and capacity for participatory, integrated and sustainable human settlement planning and management in all countries". And the Target 11.7 provides: "By 2030, provide universal access to safe, inclusive and accessible, green and public spaces, in particular for women and children, older persons and persons with disabilities".

According to the Targets 11.2 and 11.3, it is fundamental to promote an integrated planning approach to foster multi-level sustainability, i.e. environmental, social and economic [4]. Consistent with the three pillars of sustainability, the externalities mainly considered associated with the transport sector concern air pollution (environmental), fuel consuption (economic), traffic congestion and road accidents (social). More widely, the transport sector gives rise to both positive and negative production and consumption externalities [5–7].

Examples of positive externalities can be found among those that increase the commercial or residential value of areas within which a new transport service is implemented (e.g. a commercial activity or a residential building served by a new metro stop) [8, 9]. However, if safe, inclusive and sustainable transport systems are not designed, the associated negative externalities outnumber.

A first category of negative externalities consists of those limited to producers or consumers of a specific transport service; these externalities correspond to external costs expressed in monetary terms, since the main components of these costs are subject to market transactions. These external costs include, for example, the greater consumption of fuel inducted by *traffic congestion* [10] among the components that are difficult to estimate there is the *value of time*, included in the calculation of the generalized cost for passengers [11]. A second category of negative externalities caused by traffic includes those for which it is possible to easily estimate the times and costs of the interventions to eliminate their negative effects; these externalities can also be expressed in monetary terms and correspond to external costs. This category includes, for example, *traffic noise, environmental pollution* and *road accidents* [12, 13]. A third category bring in externalities for which both the identification of the effects and the evaluation in monetary terms are subjective. This category includes, for example, the effects of road accidents in terms of deaths and injuries and, even more, the monetary assessments of the catastrophic effects resulting from *climate change* [14].

Within this context, decision support models for the transport system choices are fundamental and the problem must be framed with a multi-criteria approach [15, 16]. A system of models needs to be developed, integrating models of land use (strategic/long term) [17–19], agent-based passenger and freight transport demand models (tactical/medium term) [20, 21], and multimodal network (operational/short term) [22], in order to cover and integrate different levels of analysis. All this must be supported by transport and territorial planning strategies within the Sustainable Urban Mobility Plans (SUMPs) [23, 24], to face the transition of the mobility system towards decarbonization. Among these strategies, it is possible to identify new services and technologies for passengers mobility and transport of goods at an urban, sub-urban and regional level, analyzing their characteristics and requirements [25, 26]. Innovative solutions for sustainable mobility in weak-demand areas are Demand Responsive Transport (DRT) services, integrating Local Public Transport (LPT) and characterized by flexible routes and timetables in order to match the users' requests [27].

In line to the Target 11.7, the Green Infrastructure (GIs), are progressively being included in cities' green plans as part of climate adaptation measures [28–33]. According to the European Union (E.U.), the GIs "... *Are networks of natural and semi-natural areas planned at strategic level with other environmental elements, designed and managed in such a way as to provide a wide spectrum of ecosystem services. This includes green (or blue, in the case of aquatic ecosystems) and other physical elements in areas on land (including coastal areas) and marine areas. On the mainland, green infrastructures are present in a rural and urban context*" [34]. Forms of GIs include green roofs, green walls, urban forests, urban green spaces, urban trees, bioswales, rain gardens, urban agriculture (urban gardens; community gardening; community greening; peri-urban agriculture, agricultural parks), river parks, local produce markets, constructed wetland areas, alternative energy farms, and nature conservation areas, among the most common [35–38].

The growing importance of GIs in the urban context for a new model of resilient and sustainable urban development is acknowledged at a political level and there are many research and studies in the literature [39–42].

This work presents an integrated approach to consider the role of Green Infrastructures (GIs) and Transport Mobility (TM) as key components in the transition towards a model of sustainable and resilient cities. The analysis of these two components of the urban system, especially in cities with high rates of motorisation and traffic congestion, on the one hand, and with a non-widespread presence of green areas, on the other, becomes strategic for implementing actions aimed at making cities more sustainable.

The research presents a co-governance approach that could be a useful tool for carrying out strategic actions to make cities sustainable and resilient. The integrated approach was applied on Catania (Italy), a city characterised by a high rate of motorisation and a low availability of green space per inhabitant. After briefly illustrating the case study from the aspect of the two components considered (GIs and mobility) in Sect. 2, Sect. 3 describes the adopted methodology characterized by an integrated approach and Sect. 4 reports the main results already obtained for the GIs investigation, instead the research related to TM is in progress and the results will be provided in next contribution; finally, Sect. 5 concludes the paper. Research findings will constitute a decision support for administration and stakeholder to guide public investments and achieve awareness among citizens in order to promote co-governance actions and develop climate adaptation strategies and improve the quality of life in urban areas.

2 Case Study

The selected case study coincides with the city of Catania, located in the southeast coast of Sicily (Italy). Is has a territorial extension of 180,000 m^2 and a population of about 300,000 inhabitants [43].

The city of Catania is densely populated in its northern part, while the southern part (corresponding to the VI municipality) is mainly an industrial, airport and commercial area. However, it is necessary to highlight that some populous suburban neighborhoods administratively belong to neighboring municipalities as fractions: this is the case of Canalicchio (Tremestieri Etneo), of Fasano (Gravina di Catania), of Lineri (Misterbianco) and others. There are ten first-crown municipalities which, through urban sprawl processes, have been characterized by a strong increase in population to the detriment of the municipality of Catania, which has gone from over 400,000 residents in the early seventies to around 300,000 nowdays: Aci Castello, Aci Catena, Gravina di Catania, Mascalucia, Pedara, Trecastagni, Misterbianco, San Giovanni la Punta, San Gregorio di Catania, San Pietro Clarenza, Sant'Agata li Battiati, Tremestieri Etneo and Valverde (Fig. 2).

This regional development involves a high commuting phenomenon by users who daily gravitate to the city of Catania for various travel reasons (i.e. study, work and leisure). Therefore, the centrifugal movements of the population have changed the relationship between the city of Catania and the Etna municipalities, which have grown completely spontaneously, which have developed without control and the support of adequate urban planning tools, damaging the landscape and generating an extremely chaotic territory difficult to manage.

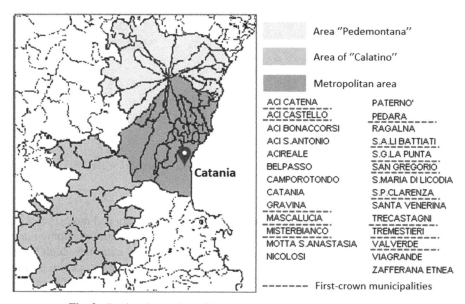

Fig. 2. Regional planning of Catania (Author elaboration from [44])

The functional imbalance, the "disorderly" distribution of the population over a vast and uneven territory, and often the lack of adequate transport systems, also cause serious livability issues. In fact, the municipality of Catania occupies the 91st position out of 107 in the annual ranking on the quality of life drawn up by the "Sole 24 Ore" and the worst index is reserved for the urban ecosystem, within which the urban transport is considered [45].

Data provided from the National Institute of Statistics (ISTAT) allow to have an overview about the situation of transport sector in Italy, with particular reference to circulating cars and motorcycles in Italian municipalities, and also their emission characteristics (in accordance with the "Euro" categories and types of fuel used). These "numbers" determine the " pressure" on the urban environment, in terms of polluting emissions and noise, as well as traffic congestion and, therefore, the "state" of air quality and the "impact" on people's health.

The map shown in Fig. 3 represents the data relating to circulating cars and motorcycles in Italy, at the provincial level. The national average is 660 cars and 128 motorcycles (for a total of 788) circulating for every thousand inhabitants [46].

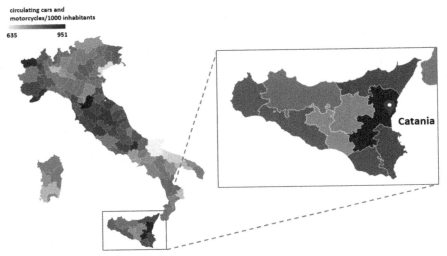

Fig. 3. Density of circulating cars and motorcycles in Italy in 2019 (Author elaboration from data provided by [46])

In particular, Fig. 4 shows the data relating to circulating cars and motorcycles per 1,000 inhabitants, in some major Italian cities. It is evident that the phenomenon of private mobility centrality in our lives and in cities has reached extremely high levels. In Catania there are 1,001 cars and motorcycles per 1,000 inhabitants, i.e. on average each person has a vehicle (including infants and the elderly over 80 years of age) [47].

Furthermore, observing the characteristics of these vehicles, it can be seen that the share of low-emission vehicles is still just over 10% of the total. More in detail, even more than 30% of them have an emission class equal to Euro 3 or less and over 54% is equal to Euro 4 (mandatory for new cars registered since January 2006) or less. The share of zero emission vehicles is equal to 0.2% (Fig. 5) [48]. This evidently means that there is an enormous quantity of motor vehicles which generate very high levels of pollutants and thus the transport decarbonisation is really challenging. Within this

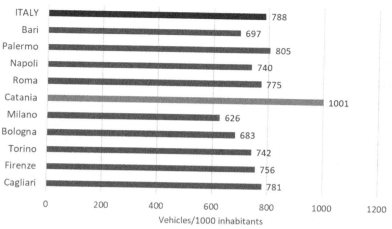

Fig. 4. Circulating cars and motorcycles per 1,000 inhabitants in some major Italian cities in 2019 (Author elaboration from data provided by [47])

context, especially for weak-demand areas and where the LPT is not efficient (cities in Southern Italy often have high motorization rates for this reasons), the implementation of DRT services can be a succeeding strategy.

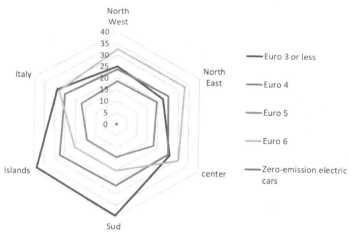

Fig. 5. Vehicles circulating by emission class in Italy in 2020. (Author elaboration from data provided by [48])

The city of Catania has been chosen as a case study both for the high motorization rates, but also for the reduced presence of GIs. Furthermore, in Catania the green areas have represented a sensitive issue in the last thirty years for their maintenance, cleaning and livability. Table 1 reports the GIs in the city of Catania, categorized by type:

Table 1. The Green Infrastructures of Catania (author elaboration from data provided by [49])

Green Typology	Mq
Urban Parks (>8,000 sqm)	513,577
Green Equipment. (<8,000 sqm)	431,270
Urban Design Areas	715,500
Urban Forestation	–
School gardens	350,000
Botanical Gardens and Vivai	20,000
Zoological Gardens	–
Cemetery	50,000
Urban Gardens (mainly managed by families)	2,500
Sports areas/Outdoor play	100,000
Bosch areas (>5000 sqm)	972,769
Uncultivated Green	1,688,044
Total Urban Green	**4,843,660**

The public green is made up of the parks located within the city. There are six characterized by size and relevance shown in Fig. 6.

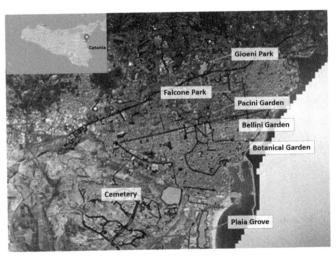

Fig. 6. The GIs in Catania (the green zones in the picture) (our elaborations).

The Bellini Garden or Villa Bellini, called 'a Villa, which is dedicated to the musician Vincenzo Bellini; the Pacini Garden or Villa Pacini, named Villa 'e varagghi (ie "of the yawns") dedicated to the musician Giovanni Pacini; among the most extensive there is the Gioieni Park (located north of the Borgo district); the Falcone and Borsellino Park (north of Corso Italia), dedicated to the homonymous magistrates; and the Plaia Grove (the largest by extension, in the area between the south of the city and the Vincenzo Bellini airport, the former Municipal Fruit and Vegetable Market and the Plaia district). Due to its historical importance and for the conservation of biodiversity, the Botanical Garden of Catania in the Mercede district should be mentioned. As evident from the image shown above, the GIs in Catania have a reduced extension (4,843,660 Kmq) compared to the entire city (183 Kmq), with an availability of urban green per inhabitant equal to 18.1 Mq/inhabitants (Fig. 7) [50]. However, considering the availability of "effectively usable" urban green areas, in the city of Catania the available square meters per inhabitant are reduced by more than 50%, with a value equal to 8,2 Mq/inhabitants, significantly lower than the minimum threshold indicated by the World Health Organization (WHO) equal to 9 Mq/inhabitants [51].

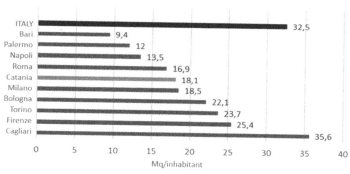

Fig. 7. Availability of urban green within Italian Municipalities in 2021 (Author elaboration from data provided by [50])

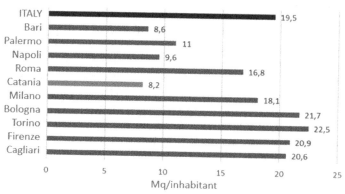

Fig. 8. Availability of "effective usable" urban green within Italian Municipalities in 2021 (Author elaboration from data provided by [50])

3 Materials and Methods

3.1 Methodological Framework

The main goal of the research focuses on the topic of sustainable and resilient cities, presenting an integrated approach characterized by an interview-based methodology, which consists of two step analysis: (i) first, a questionnaire has been implemented to analyze citizen's perception of GIs to tackle climate change and the willingness to pay to sustain the maintenance of these infrastructures; (ii) on the other hand, an extended survey will be performed to evaluate the propensity of users towards innovative shared transport systems and also the willingness to pay for the service. This methodological approach is applied to the case study of Catania, described in the previous section, and the obtained data from the interview are processed through statistical and cluster analysis in order to obtain a meaningful interpretation (Fig. 9).

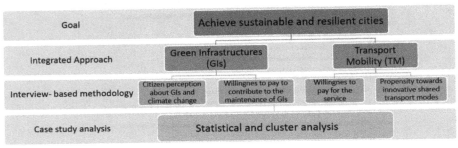

Fig. 9. Methodological framework

3.2 Interview-Based Survey

The questionnaire carried out to investigate the degree of perception of GIs and the impacts on climate change involved a sample of 500 citizens of Catania. The sample size has been fixed a priori for some significant variables (e.g. gender and age), according to the non-probabilistic sampling method, which allows more flexibility [42, 52, 53]. The structure of the questionnaire consisted of an introductory part to shortly introduce the research objective and five following sections. It envisaged no. 20 questions and a section with pictures to be evaluated. The questionnaire allowed to obtain mixed survey data, both from online GoogleDocs and face-to-face interviews and provided quantitative and qualitative information on:

- socio-demographics characteristics;
- behaviour towards GIs;
- level of knowledge and perception of quality of life;
- willingness to pay for GIs;

– perception of climate change problem.

As for the TM investigation, the main aim is to investigate the propensity to use DRT services in Catania. Therefore, two work phases will be envisaged: a *Desk Work* for the analysis of citizens' transport supply and demand and the study of the segmentation of mobility behaviors and a *Field Work* for the detection of the knowledge degree and potential use of DRT services in Catania and neighboring municipalities. More specifically, a structured questionnaire will be implemented on a sample reasoned using Computer Assisted Telephone Interviewing (CATI) and Computer Assisted Web Interviewing (CAWI) techniques to detect the following quantitative and qualitative information on:

– Socio-economic characteristics of the sample;
– Degree of knowledge and propensity to use DRT;
– Willingness to pay for the DRT service;
– Choice experiments.

The choice experiments will be based on travel costs and times values, analyzing short and medium distance scenarios and comparing the DRT with other transport alternatives (e.g. car; metro; bus).

4   Results and Discussion

This section reports the main results related to the performed research on GIs [42], as already mentioned in the reminder of the paper. The analysis of the socio-demographic structure through the performed questionnaire allowed to obtain the composition of the interviewed sample according to these characteristics: gender, age, residence, educational qualification, working sector. The results are summarized in Table 2: the sample is mainly made up of women; the prevailing age is over 51 years, while the remaining part of the sample is equally distributed among the other age groups. Consistent with the research aim, most of the sample has their residence within the Municipality of Catania. All respondents have a High School Diploma, and among these over 70% have a bachelor's or master's degree. As regards the employment, over half of the sample is employed by the Public Administration (PA); another part belongs to the service sector; and even if in a small percentage, the preferences of employees in the industrial sector, students, health care, etc. are also detected.

This paper reports the results relating to two significant aspects emerging from the analysis carried out, respectively relating to: (a) adaptation measures to climate change through urban GIs; (b) use of urban green areas.

For the first one it has been investigated Q1: *"What types of measures/actions to be primarily implemented in Catania or in the neighborhood to face climate change through urban GIs (evaluation based on provided pictures)"*. Figure 10 summarized the obtained results according to which the emerging measure/action is represented by the *increasing green spaces in areas of public use* (i.e. 33%), followed by the *improvement of the maintenance of existing GIs* (i.e. 27%), and finally, comparable in the evaluation by the interviewees, the *design of usable green areas* and the *greater protection and care of green spaces* (i.e. both 20%).

Table 2. Socio-demographic structure of the interviewed sample relating to GIs

Gender		Working sector	
Male	26%	Agriculture	3%
Female	74%	Industry	10%
Age		Public Administration (PA)	53%
18–25 years	20%	Services	20%
26–35 years	17%	Students	6%
36–50 years	23%	Health	6%
Over 51 years	40%	Associations	2%
Residence		**Educational classification**	
Catania	83%	High School	23%
Outside Catania	17%	Bachelor	47%
		Master	30%

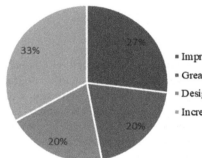

- Improved maintenance (street furniture fountains, etc.).
- Greater protection and care of green spaces
- Design of usable green area
- Increasing green spaces in areas of public use

Fig. 10. Percentage evaluation of initiatives proposed by citizens to implement GIs

For the second aspect it has been investigated Q2: *"Motivation and frequency degree of urban green areas; recognized benefits to urban green spaces"*. Figure 11 represents through a bar diagram the subjective assessments provided by the interviewees, reported to a numerical value ranging from 1 to 5 using the Likert scale.

There is a general attention from users to the benefits given by GIs. In fact, for none of the considered benefits there are answers "not at all important", except for the benefit *increase in property value*. The main benefits recognized to GIs are the *temperature control* and the *carbon dioxide uptake*, considered as a much important benefits by more than 70% of the sample, followed by the *promotion of physical and mental wellbeing* much important for about 67% of the sample and by the *use for leisure activities* for about the 65% of the sample. On the other hand, the benefits considered less influential are the *increase in property value*, the *rainwater regulation* and the *noise reduction*, all considered much more important benefits for more or less 40% of the interviewees.

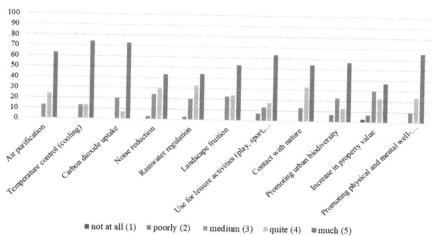

Fig. 11. Recognized benefits to urban green spaces

The graph represented in Fig. 12 compare the willingness to pay for GIs by citizens in two different situations: (i) without tax reduction and (ii) with tax reduction. The first one considers the willingness of citizens to contribute for maintaining GIs with no boundary condition; in this case a high percentage of citizens is not willing to pay anything (i.e. 26% of citizens answered 0 €) or a very low amount (26% of citizens answered 1–10 €), instead only 7% of citizens are willing to pay more than 100 €. This last percentage increases in the second considered situation (the number of citizens triples from 7% to 22%) for which citizens are given the opportunity to contribute to the maintenance of the GIs by considering a municipal tax reduction thanks to a crowdfunding among neighborhood residents. In this case, the percentage of citizens willing to pay for GIs rises from 74% to 86% of the interviewees.

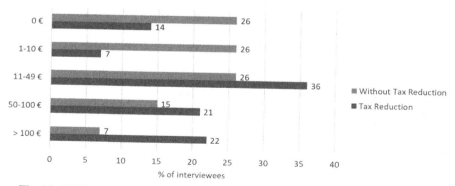

Fig. 12. Willingness to pay for the maintenance of GIs with and without tax reduction

The cluster analysis highlighted the predominant one for 40% of the sample is made up of users belonging to the middle class, who use green spaces only for socialization and not for other benefits (above mentioned). Therefore, it follows that these users are not willing to pay for the maintenance of GIs, but the fundamental element is their free use. These results match those relating to the willingness to pay, which is almost equal to zero. However, if it is possible a tax reduction of the costs for the maintenance of the GIs, then users are more positively predisposed to the willingness to pay for GIs. This demonstrates that individuals respond to the proposed incentives and from a co-governance perspective, this research allows administrations to know what to do.

5   Conclusions

This paper provided the main results obtained from the first step of a wider research dealing with GIs and TM to gather useful information for supporting stakeholders and local authorities to develop shared strategic actions in order achieve climate change reduction and promote sustainable and resilient cities in accordance with the SDG 11 "Sustainable Cities and Communities".

The expected impacts of climate change in urban settlements are very different: impacts on health and quality of life (in particular for vulnerable users), impacts on the buildings, on water, energy and transport infrastructures, on cultural heritage (due to landslides, floods and heatwaves), impacts on energy production and supply. Thus, to deal effectively with these impacts, it is fundamental the coordination of a very broad institutional network (i.e. multilevel governance) [54–56]. Therefore, the research highlighted the usefulness of involving citizens in the implementation of strategies and actions to reduce climate change.

The research, although in process, provided preliminary information on the importance attributed to urban GIs by citizens and their relationship with climate change. A key element for future co-governance actions has been the surveying of citizens' willingness to pay to contribute for the management of urban GIs, both in terms of participatory planning and monetary contribution (one-time or in the form of crowdfunding). The research also made it possible to highlight the need to promote awareness-raising actions on benefits that GIs offers on climate change. Thus, it is important to promote collaboration with citizens to support long-term actions towards climate adaptation and to obtain information about the perception of urban green, which is strategic for urban policies.

Future research developments will focus on integrating the results with the ongoing TM survey, which will certainly be useful in building a comprehensive framework on the strengths and weaknesses on which local governments will need to act in order to promote sustainable and resilient cities.

Author Contributions. This paper is the result of the joint work of the authors. 'Abstract', and 'Conclusions' were written jointly by the authors. LS and VT wrote the 'Introduction', 'Case Study', "Materials and Methods"; LS, VT and AS wrote "Results and discussion"; LS, VT and MI coordinated and supervised the paper.

Acknowledgements. This work is financed by the MIUR (Ministry of Education, Universities and Research [Italy]) through a project entitled WEAKI TRANSIT: WEAK-demand areas

Innovative TRANsport Shared services for Italian Towns (Project code: 20174ARRHT, CUP: E44I17000050001), financed with the PRIN 2017 (Research Projects of National Relevance) programme. We authorise the MIUR to reproduce and distribute reprints for Governmental purposes, not with standing any copyright notations there on. Any opinions, findings and conclusions or recommendations expressed in this material are those of the authors, and do not necessarily reflect the views of the MIUR. The work of V. Torrisi was supported by European Union (NextGeneration EU), through the MUR-PNRR project SAMOTHRACE (ECS00000022).

References

1. Intergovernmental Panel on Climate Change (IPCC). Climate Change 2014; Contribution of Working Groups I, II and III to the Fifth Assessment Report of the Intergovernmental Panel on Climate Change[Core Writing Team, R.K. Pachauri and L.A. Meyer (eds.)]. IPCC, Geneva, Switzerland, 151 (2014)
2. United Nations. Transforming our World: The 2030 Agenda for Sustainable Development; United Nations: New York, NY, USA (2015)
3. United Nations. Revision of the World Urbanization Prospects; United Nations: New York, NY, USA (2018)
4. Purvis, B., Mao, Y., Robinson, D.: Three pillars of sustainability: in search of conceptual origins. Sustain. Sci. **14**, 681–695 (2019)
5. Santos, G., Behrendt, H., Maconi, L., Shirvani, T., Teytelboym, A.: Part I: externalities and economic policies in road transport. Res. Transp. Econ. **28**(1), 2–45 (2010)
6. Sovacool, B.K., Kim, J., Yang, M.: The hidden costs of energy and mobility: a global meta-analysis and research synthesis of electricity and transport externalities. Energy Res. Soc. Sci. **72**, 101885 (2021)
7. Chatziioannou, I., Alvarez-Icaza, L., Bakogiannis, E., Kyriakidis, C., Chias-Becerril, L.: A structural analysis for the categorization of the negative externalities of transport and the hierarchical organization of sustainable mobility's strategies. Sustainability **12**(15), 6011 (2020)
8. Banerjee, A., Duflo, E., Qian, N.: On the road: access to transportation infrastructure and economic growth in China. J. Dev. Econ. **145**, 102442 (2020)
9. Kelobonye, K., Zhou, H., McCarney, G., Xia, J.C.: Measuring the accessibility and spatial equity of urban services under competition using the cumulative opportunities measure. J. Transp. Geogr. **85**, 102706 (2020)
10. Afrin, T., Yodo, N.: A survey of road traffic congestion measures towards a sustainable and resilient transportation system. Sustainability **12**(11), 4660 (2020)
11. Litman, T.: Measuring transportation. traffic, mobility and accessibility. ITE J. **73**(10), 28–32 (2003)
12. Marques, J., Batista, S.F.A., Menendez, M., Macedo, E., Coelho, M.C.: From aggregated traffic models to emissions quantification: connecting the missing dots. Transp. Res. Procedia **69**, 568–575 (2023)
13. Cabrera-Arnau, C., Prieto Curiel, R., Bishop, S.R.: Uncovering the behaviour of road accidents in urban areas. R. Soc. Open Sci. **7**(4), 191739 (2020)
14. Albuquerque, F.D., Maraqa, M.A., Chowdhury, R., Mauga, T., Alzard, M.: Greenhouse gas emissions associated with road transport projects: current status, benchmarking, and assessment tools. Transp. Res. Procedia **48**, 2018–2030 (2020)
15. Ortega, J., Moslem, S., Palaguachi, J., Ortega, M., Campisi, T., Torrisi, V.: An integrated multi criteria decision making model for evaluating park-and-ride facility location issue: a case study for Cuenca City in ecuador. Sustainability **13**(13), 7461 (2021). https://doi.org/10.3390/su13137461

16. Garau, C., Annunziata, A., Yamu, C.: A walkability assessment tool coupling multi-criteria analysis and space syntax: the case study of Iglesias, Italy. Euro. Planning Stud. 1–23 (2020)
17. Levine, J., Grengs, J., Merlin, L.A.: From Mobility to Accessibility: Transforming Urban Transportation and Land-use Planning. Cornell University Press (2019)
18. Annunziata, A., Desogus, G., Mighela, F., Garau, C.: Health and mobility in the post-pandemic scenario. an analysis of the adaptation of sustainable urban mobility plans in key contexts of Italy. In: Computational Science and Its Applications ICCSA 2022 Workshops: Malaga, Spain, July 4/7, 2022, Proceedings, Part VI, pp. 439–456. Cham: Springer International Publishing (2022). https://doi.org/10.1007/978-3-031-10592-0_32
19. Garau, C., Desogus, G., Maltinti, F., Olivo, A., Peretti, L., Coni, M.: Practices for an integrated planning between urban planning and green infrastructures for the development of the municipal urban plan (MUP) of Cagliari (Italy). In: Gervasi, O., et al. (eds.) ICCSA 2021. LNCS, vol. 12958, pp. 3–18. Springer, Cham (2021). https://doi.org/10.1007/978-3-030-870 16-4_1
20. Calabrò, G., Torrisi, V., Ignaccolo, M., Inturri, G.: Improving inbound logistic planning for large-scale real-word routing problems: a novel ant-colony simulation-based optimization. Eur. Transp. Res. Rev. **12** (2020). https://doi.org/10.1186/s12544-020-00409-7. ISSN: 1867–0717
21. Torrisi, V., Ignaccolo, M., Inturri, G.: The microsimulation modeling as a tool for transport policies assessment: an application to a real case study. In: AIP Conference Proceedings, vol. 2611, no. 1, p. 060006. AIP Publishing LLC (2022 November)
22. Elbert, R., Müller, J.P., Rentschler, J.: Tactical network planning and design in multimodal transportation–a systematic literature review. Res. Transp. Bus. Manag. **35**, 100462 (2020)
23. Torrisi, V., Garau, C., Inturri, G., Ignaccolo, M.: Strategies and actions to-wards sustainability: encouraging good ITS practices in the SUMP vision. In: AIP Conference Proceedings, vol. 2343, no. 1, p. 090008. AIP Publishing LLC (2021 March). https://doi.org/10.1063/5.004 7897
24. Torrisi, V., Garau, C., Ignaccolo, M., Inturri, G.: Sustainable urban mobility plans: key concepts and a critical revision on SUMPs guidelines. In: Gervasi, O., et al. (eds.) ICCSA 2020. LNCS, vol. 12255, pp. 613–628. Springer, Cham (2020). https://doi.org/10.1007/978-3-030-58820-5_45
25. Torrisi, V., Ignaccolo, M., Inturri, G.: Innovative transport systems to promote sustainable mobility: developing the model architecture of a traffic control and supervisor system. In: Gervasi, O., et al. (eds.) ICCSA 2018. LNCS, vol. 10962, pp. 622–638. Springer, Cham (2018). https://doi.org/10.1007/978-3-319-95168-3_42
26. Campisi, T., Cocuzza, E., Ignaccolo, M., Inturri, G., Torrisi, V.: Exploring the factors that encourage the spread of EV-DRT into the sustainable urban mobility plans. In: Gervasi, O., et al. (eds.) ICCSA 2021. LNCS, vol. 12953, pp. 699–714. Springer, Cham (2021). https://doi.org/10.1007/978-3-030-86976-2_48
27. Zhao, J., Sun, S., Cats, O.: Joint optimisation of regular and demand-responsive transit services. Transportmetrica Transp. Sci. **19**(2), 1987580 (2023)
28. EC. Towards an EU research and innovation policy agenda for nature-based solutions & renaturing cities. 2015. Towards an EU research and innovation policy agenda for nature-based solutions & renaturing cities - Publications Office of the EU (europa.eu). Accessed 28 Jan 2022
29. Economides, C.: Green Infrastructure: Sustainable Solutions in 11 Cities across the United States. Columbia University Water, New York, NY, USA (2014)
30. EEA. Nature-based solutions in Europe: Policy, knowledge and practice for climate change adaptation and disaster risk reduction. EEA Report 01/2021. Luxembourg: Publications Office of the European Union (2021)

31. Carrus, G., et al.: Go greener, feel better? The positive effects of bio-diversity on the well-being of individuals visiting urban and peri-urban green areas. Landsc. Urban Plan. **134**, 221–228 (2015)
32. EC. Nature-based solutions (2020). (https://ec.europa.eu/info/research-and-innovation/research-area/environment/naturebased-solutions_en). Accessed 13 Sept 2022
33. Wei, J., Qian, J., Tao, Y., Hu, F., Ou, W.: Evaluating spatial priority of urban green infrastructure for urban sustainability in areas of rapid urbanization: a case study of Pukouin China. Sustainability **10**, 327 (2018)
34. Environment Directorate (ED)-General for the Environment. Communication from the commission to the European Parliament, the Council, the European Economic and Social Committee and the Committee of the Regions Green Infrastructure (GI)—Enhancing Europe's Natural Capital; Environment Directorate-General for the Environment. Bruxelles, Belgium (2013)
35. Escobedo, F.J., Giannico, V., Jim, C.Y., Sanesi, G., Lafortezza, R.: Urban forestry & urban greening urban forests, ecosystem services, green infrastructure and nature-based solutions: nexus or evolving metaphors ? Urban For. Urban Green. **37**, 3–12 (2019)
36. Sturiale, L., Scuderi, A.: The role of green infrastructures in urban planning for climate change adaptation. Climate **7**, 119 (2019)
37. Scuderi, A., La Via, G., Timpanaro, G., Sturiale, L.: The digital applications of Agriculture 4.0: strategic opportunity for the development of the Italian citrus chain. Agriculture **12**(3), 400 (2022)
38. Sturiale, L., Scuderi, A.: Information and communication technology (ICT) and adjustment of the marketing strategy in the agrifood system in Italy. In: HAICTA, pp. 77–87 (September 2011)
39. Bayulken, B., Huisingh, D., Fisher, P.M.J.: How are nature based solutions helping in the greening of cities in the context of crises such as climate change and pandemics ? a comprehensive review. J. Clean. Prod. **288**, 125569 (2021)
40. Brink, E., Wamsler, C.: Collaborative governance for climate change adaptation: mapping citizen-municipality interactions. Environ. Policy Gov. **28**, 82–97 (2018)
41. Sturiale, L., Scuderi, A., Timpanaro, G.: A Multicriteria decision-making approach of tree meaning in the new urban context. Sustainability **14**(5), 2902 (2022)
42. Sturiale, L., Scuderi, A., Timpanaro, G.: Citizens' perception of the role of urban nature-based solutions and green infrastructures towards climate change in Italy. Front. Environ. Sci. **11**, 1105446 (2023). https://doi.org/10.3389/fenvs.2023.1105446
43. National Institute of Statistics (ISTAT). Bilancio demografico mensile anno 2023 (dati provvisori), su demo.istat.it, ISTAT, 7 aprile 2023 (2023)
44. Regional Province of Catania. Ufficio Pianificazione Del Territorio - Sistemi Informativi - Web Gis E Cartografia - E-Government (2003). https://public.cittametropolitana.ct.it/cartografia/index.asp
45. 33rd Quality of Life Survey from Il Sole 24 ore (2022). https://www.cataniatoday.it/cronaca/classifica-sole-24-ore-qualita-vita-catania.html
46. National Institute of Statistics (ISTAT). Density of cars and motorcycles circulating by municipalities (2019). https://www.istat.it/it/archivio/254037
47. National Institute of Statistics (ISTAT). Tavole di dati, Mobilità urbana (2019). https://www.istat.it/it/archivio/254037
48. Ambiente e non solo. Vehicles circulating by emission class in Italy in 2020 (2020). https://ambientenonsolo.com/la-mobilita-nei-109-comuni-capoluogo/
49. Municipality of Catania for Environmental and Green Policies and Energy Management of the Autoparco - Service for the Protection and Management of Public Green, Giardino Bellini and Parchi (2017)

50. National Institute of Statistics (ISTAT). Verde urbano (2022). https://www.istat.it/it/archivio/254037
51. World Health Organization (WHO). Urban green spaces and health (2016). https://apps.who.int/iris/handle/10665/345751
52. Wooldridge, J.M.: Econometric Analysis of Cross Section and Panel Data. MIT Press, Cambridge, MA (2002)
53. Gujarati, D.: Basic Econometrics. 4. New York, NY, USA: McGraw Hill (2003)
54. Wicki, S., Schwaab, J., Perhac, J., Grêt-Regamey, A.: Participatory multi-objective optimization for planning dense and green cities. J. Environ. Plan. Manag. **64**, 2532–2551 (2021)
55. Scuderi, A., Sturiale, L.: Evaluations of social media strategy for green urban planning in metropolitan cities. In: Calabrò, F., Della Spina, L., Bevilacqua, C. (eds.) ISHT 2018. SIST, vol. 100, pp. 76–84. Springer, Cham (2019). https://doi.org/10.1007/978-3-319-92099-3_10
56. Sturiale, L., Scuderi, A., Timpanaro, G., Foti, V.T., Stella, G.: Social and inclusive value generation in metropolitan area with the urban gardens planning. Green Energy Technol. 285–302 (2020)

Comparison of the Environmental Benefits of Cold Mix Asphalt and Its Application in Pavement Layers

Francesco Grazietti$^{(\boxtimes)}$ (iD), James Rombi (iD), Francesca Maltinti (iD), and Mauro Coni (iD)

Università degli Studi di Cagliari, via Marengo 2, 09123 Cagliari, Italy
francesco.grazietti@unica.it

Abstract. Increasing CO_2 emissions and the importance of reducing the carbon footprint in transportation infrastructure are topics of growing interest in civil engineering. This paper examines the use of asphalt mix designs alternative to classic Hot Mix Asphalt (HMA) such as Warm Mix Asphalt (WMA) and Cold Mix Asphalt CMA) as sustainable solutions to mitigate environmental impacts and promote material reuse. The introduction stresses the importance of use in the transportation sector and highlights the potential for reducing CO_2 emissions and energy consumption by lowering processing temperatures [10]. The following paper analyzes asphalt technologies, exploring the merits and demerits of different solutions and assessing the suitability of recycled materials. It proceeds by quantifying the use of HMA, WMA and CMA at global, European, and Italian levels, highlighting the evolution of production techniques and their diffusion in different contexts.

In the conclusions, considerations are made on the environmental benefits and technical feasibility of WMA and CMA, emphasizing the importance of promoting the adoption of these solutions in transportation infrastructure for sustainable resource management and climate impact reduction.

The paper contributes to the debate on the use of sustainable materials in the construction industry by encouraging research and innovation in the design and implementation of greener transportation infrastructure.

Keywords: Warm Mix Asphalt (WMA) · Cold Mix Asphalt (CMA) ·
Transportation infrastructure · Environmental impact

1 Introduction

Road networks are the backbone of transportation infrastructure in most countries, allowing for the movement of goods and people across vast distances. In the UK, for example, road transport accounts for a staggering 91% of passenger travel and 67% of goods transport. Similarly, the figures for the European Union and the US are equally impressive, with 92% and 88% of passenger travel, respectively, and up to 48% of goods transport being conducted on roads [1]. It's clear that road transport is a vital component of the global economy, providing an essential link between producers, consumers, and

© The Author(s), under exclusive license to Springer Nature Switzerland AG 2023
O. Gervasi et al. (Eds.): ICCSA 2023 Workshops, LNCS 14105, pp. 231–245, 2023.
https://doi.org/10.1007/978-3-031-37108-0_15

suppliers. However, the environmental impact of road infrastructure is also significant, as green-house gas emissions and energy consumption associated with construction, maintenance, and use of roads contribute to climate change. In Italy, the situation is not different. In 2020, total passenger traffic amounted to 614.6 billion passenger-kilometers, representing a 36.4% decrease from the previous year. Of this total, an overwhelming 94.3% of passenger travel was conducted on roads, with only 4.2% taking place on rail, 1% by air, and 0.4% by sea. Private transportation, such as cars and motorcycles, accounted for most of the travel, growing from 79.8% in 2019 to 84.9% in 2020. In contrast, rail transport decreased from 5.9% in 2019 to 3.5% in 2020, while collective urban and extra-urban transport decreased from 11.5% to 10.1%, and air transport decreased from 2.3% to 1% [2]. Given the predominance of road transport in Italy and the significant environmental impact associated with it, it is critical to address these challenges by adopting innovative solutions that can reduce the carbon footprint and promote sustainability. One area of focus is the development of new technologies for asphalt mixes, such as Cold Mix Asphalt (CMA) and Warm Mix Asphalt (WMA), which can significantly reduce energy consumption and partially reduce greenhouse gas emissions compared to traditional asphalt.

Asphalt is a material widely used in the construction of transportation infrastructure such as roads, highways and airport runways. Its versatility, durability and strength make it an ideal choice for paving. How- ever, asphalt production and paving also have a significant impact on the environment, mainly due to greenhouse gas emissions and energy consumption associated with the extraction, processing and transportation of the materials. In the current global scenario of growing concern about climate change and resource sustainability, the construction industry is faced with the challenge of identifying and adopting innovative solutions to reduce the environmental impact associated with asphalt production and application. In this context, the research and development of new asphalt mix technologies that promote a more efficient use of resources and a reduction in pollutant emissions is a crucial challenge for the industry. The most used types of asphalt mixes are Hot mix asphalt (HMA), Warm mix asphalt (WMA), Cold Mix Asphalt (CMA). This article aims to analyze the different asphalt mix technologies currently available, highlighting their advantages and disadvantages, especially from an environmental perspective. In addition, the potential applications and implications of these technologies in the Italian context will be discussed.

2   HWA, WMA, CMA - Definition, Disadvantages and Advantages

Asphalt production technologies are mainly divided into three categories: Hot Mix Asphalt (HMA), Warm Mix Asphalt (WMA) and Cold Mix Asphalt (CMA). These types differ in composition, chemical and physical characteristics and processing temperatures. The following will provide a general overview of the components and production and laying temperatures of each of these asphalt technologies.

HMA is the traditional and still the most widely used type of asphalt mix; it is composed mainly of aggregates, bituminous binders and occasionally additives. Aggregates, which make up 80–90% of the weight of HMA, are generally composed of crushed rock, gravel, sand, and mineral powders. The bituminous binder acts as a bonding agent for the aggregates, imparting strength and durability to the mixture. Sometimes, additives are introduced into HMA to improve mechanical properties, such as wear resistance and moisture resistance, or to reduce the viscosity of the bitumen, improving its workability during production and laying. Temperatures used in the production of HMA vary between 150 and 180 °C for aggregates and 160–175 °C for bitumen [4]. Various mixtures have been made of this type that are capable of giving the material superior or specific performance characteristics, as in the case of drainage or sound-absorbing asphalt mixes.

WMA has a similar composition to HMA, consisting mainly of aggregates, bituminous binders and additives. The main difference lies in the use of specific additives or modifications to the production process to allow processing at lower temperatures (between 100 and 140 °C). These additives, called viscosity-lowering agents, can be chemical compounds, organic or inorganic, that reduce the viscosity of the bitumen, allowing better workability of the material at lower temperatures. WMAs also include half-warm asphalt (HWMA), that is, when the maximum production temperature is below 100 °C (212 °F). There are various processes and products to achieve this reduction, but generally WMA technologies fall into four categories:

1. Water-based, nonadditive-based, and foam-based processes. Bitumen foam is formed by spraying water into heated bitumen or adding wet sand into the asphalt mixture.
2. Water-containing additives such as natural and synthetic zeolites, also based on foaming. Foam is formed by adding zeolite to the asphalt mixture during production;
3. Organic additives such as waxes and fatty acid amides. These organic waxes have longer chemical chains and a melting point of about 100 °C, reducing the viscosity of the binder and allowing the asphalt production and laying temperature to be lowered by 20–30 °C.
4. Chemical additives change the structure of the asphalt binder and reduce viscosity, allowing asphalt production and laying temperatures to be lowered by about 40 °C [3].

CMA is composed mainly of aggregates, such as crushed rock, slag and gravel, and binder materials such as bitumen emulsions or fluidized bitumen. The material is currently used for small repair and construction work, as it does not require a large investment in equipment. Unlike HMA and WMA, CMA uses water and solvents as additional components. Bitumen emulsion, containing about 60% bitumen and 40% water, is the most common binder in CMA, due to the use of an emulsifier that keeps the bitumen suspended in an aqueous medium. Cationic emulsions are the most used in road construction and maintenance. Aggregates in CMA are subjected to the same tests and limit values as those used in HMA. During the production of CMA, potable water is added to the mix to lubricate the aggregates and improve the workability and coverage of the aggregates.

2.1 Advantages and Disadvantages

- HMA is widely used around the world because of its many advantages, although it also has some disadvantages. HMA is valued for its high strength and durability, which make it suitable for withstanding heavy traffic and weather conditions. In addition, the laying process of HMA is quite rapid and the material can be produced in large quantities, allowing for a reduction in construction time and related costs. The spread of production facilities and the now-important knowledge about the material still make it the most chosen solution worldwide for road superstructures.

- However, the use of HMA also has disadvantages. Manufacturing and laying the material requires high temperatures, leading to significant energy consumption and higher greenhouse gas emissions. Work safety is a central issue these years; high temperatures pose significant risks to paving operators. In addition, except in the case of drainage asphalt, HMA is relatively impermeable and therefore capable of causing storm water drainage problems and increasing the risk of flooding in urban areas. Despite these drawbacks, HMA continues to be widely used worldwide for its reliability and performance in terms of strength and durability.

- The main advantages of Warm Mix Asphalt (WMA) include energy savings due to lower working temperatures, reduced emissions, reduced viscosity of the asphalt mix, resulting in better processability and lower cooling rate. In addition, at the plant level, it does not require major modifications to existing HMA production facilities [3]. The advantages of WMA undoubtedly include the ability to perform paving work in colder weather conditions, as the temperature of the newly produced mix is closer to that of the outdoor environment. This leads to an extension of the working season and an increase in material transport distance. Also due to the lower temperatures, the opening of traffic lanes can take place in a shorter time due to the shorter cooling period after the work is done, which can be particularly advantageous for work on roads with high traffic volume. The use of reduced temperatures in WMA compared to HMA can positively affect air quality on construction sites and reduce the risk of burns to operators.

- However, there are disadvantages related to the scarcity of research and the short service life of WMA. The physical and mechanical characteristics of WMA are worse than hot mix asphalt and vary depending on the technology used. In addition, the use of additives to improve the cohesive properties between the mineral materials and the bitumen results in increased costs and, in some cases, an extension of the asphalt mixing cycle.

- CMA, due to its low production and compaction temperature, offers many advantages, greater emission reduction than WMA, lower fuel consumption and better working conditions. The cold asphalt recycling process is energy efficient and particularly suitable on smoggy days. Compared with HMA, CMA reduces energy consumption by 60% and generates lower CO_2 emissions, with 53.6 kg for HMA and 36.1 kg for CMA per ton produced. However, the possible addition of cement to CMA to increase its strength significantly increases CO_2 emissions, which become comparable to those of HMA without cement. The economic benefits of CMA depend on the type of energy used, its cost, and potential pollution. Paving with CMA allows workability at lower temperatures, reducing road construction time.

- However, CMA with the technologies currently in use has some limitations: it does not achieve the required strength and stability, which limits its use mainly to rural roads with low traffic density and low axle loads. Moisture damage is a major problem, as water used in preparation reduces the adhesion between binder and aggregates, causing deformation and cracking. In addition, CMA requires a longer curing time to reach full strength, putting it at a disadvantage compared to HMA and WMA (Fig. 1 and Table 1).

Table 1. Comparative table of asphalt mixes: design, production temperature, advantages and vanishing points of Hot Mix Asphalt (HMA), Warm Mix Asphalt (WMA) and Cold Mix Asphalt (CMA)

Mix Design	Production Temperature	Advantages	Disadvantages
HMA	150° - 180° C	• Superior mixture performance • Lower initial cost • Dedicated and widespread production facilities	• High production temperature • High emissions • High energy consumption
WMA	90° - 140° C	• Low production temperature • Energy savings • Better working conditions • Longer transport distance • Less plant wear and deterioration • Less binder aging	• Lower mixture performance than HMA • Higher initial cost due to the use of additives • Poor aggregate coating and bonding • Absence of regulations on use in several countries
CMA	10° - 40° C	• Lower fuel consumption • Production at room temperature • Reduced energy consumption • Low emissions • Longer transport distance	• Lower strength and stability • Limited mainly to rural roads • Moisture and adhesion problems • Slower curing • Absence of regulations on use in several countries

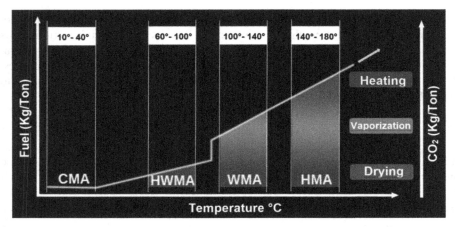

Fig. 1. Type of mixes with their manufacture temperature and fuel consumption per ton.

According to a study by Chehovits and Galehouse (2010), the production of HMA requires 275 MJ/t (megajoules per ton) of energy, while WMA consumes 234 MJ/t, or 15% less than HMA. In the case of CMA, no aggregate heating is required, so energy consumption is reduced to only 14 MJ/t, making it about 95% more efficient than HMA and WMA [4].

Regarding energy consumption per ton of installed material, CMA and the cold in-situ recycling process are more efficient than HMA and hot in-situ recycling. The cold in-situ recycling method is the most energy efficient because it requires less binder and the aggregates are recovered directly on site. To produce one ton of installed material, HMA requires 680 MJ of energy, while CMA and cold in-situ recycling consume 2/3 and 1/5, respectively [5]. This indicates that CMA is more efficient than HMA. The total energy consumption in making the different types of asphalt mixes varies according to the techniques used and the individual components involved (Fig. 2).

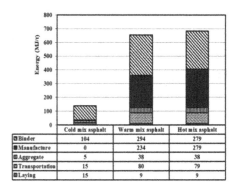
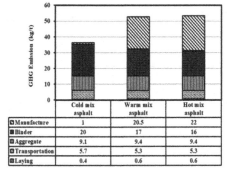

Fig. 2. Total energy and GHG emissions use for different asphalt mixes.

The table highlights important differences in the energy required to produce CMA, WMA, and HMA. Regarding the binder, CMA requires significantly less energy (104 MJ/t) than WMA (294 MJ/t) and HMA (279 MJ/t). In addition, CMA requires no additional energy for production, whereas WMA and HMA require 234 and 279 MJ/t, respectively.

For transportation, CMA is more energy efficient, requiring only 15 MJ/t, compared to WMA (80 MJ/t) and HMA (79 MJ/t).

Examining the emission data, the authors see that the most significant difference is found in the production stage. CMA has significantly lower emissions than WMA and HMA in the production phase (1 kg/t for CMA, 20.5 kg/t for WMA, and 22 kg/t for HMA). However, at the transport stage, emissions are slightly higher for CMA (5.7 kg/t) than for WMA (5.3 kg/t) and HMA (5.3 kg/t). In the laying phase, the differences between the three materials are minimal, with values ranging from 0.4 kg/t to 0.6 kg/t. This higher emission related to transport may be because CMA is produced at lower temperatures than WMA and HMA and can be transported more easily via properly packed bags over a longer distance while maintaining the proper temperature and ensuring proper laying. In addition, the availability of CMA production facilities of good mechanical properties could be limited locally, requiring the material to be transported from more distant facilities. This results in increased transportation distances and, consequently, emissions.

3 Trends in Asphalt Production in Europe and the United States from 2011 to 2021

In a recent study conducted based on data collected through 2021, the European asphalt industry was analyzed, looking at aspects such as production, asphalt types, applications, binders, reuse and recycling rates, number of companies, and production sites (Fig. 3).

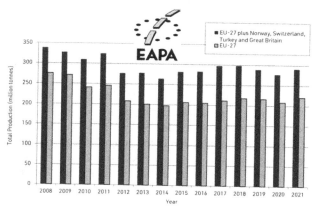

Fig. 3. Total production of HMA and WMA from 2011 to 2021 (Million tons) [5]

This information was obtained through input from members of the European Asphalt Pavement Association (EAPA) and represents the most reliable and up-to-date figures available for the asphalt industry.

In some cases, data from some countries were not available ("no data" - //) and considered zero in the calculation of the totals. In other situations, some countries did not provide data for a particular year, but it was possible to estimate them based on time series of data provided in previous years.

Table 2. Total production of HMA and WMA from 2011 to 2021 (Million tons) [6]

Country	2011	2012	2013	2014	2015	2016	2017	2018	2019	2020	2021
EU-27	246.1	208.2	200.5	197.1	206.0	204.9	211.2	217.6	216.2	208.3	220.7
Europe	324.3	276.4	277.3	263.7	280.9	282.5	296.7	297.9	288.9	276.9	290.6
USA	332.0	326.9	318.1	319.0	331.0	340.0	344.0	353.0	382.0	370.0	392.0
South Africa	5.7	5.7	5.5	5.4	4.8	4.8	4.1	4.2	4.1	2.3	2.8

The Table n. 2 shows the total production of HMA and WMA in millions of tons from 2011 to 2021 in four different geographic areas: the 27-country European Union (EU-27), Europe including Britain, Norway, Switzerland, and Turkey, the United States of America (U.S.), and South Africa. Analyzing the data, some trends and variations over time can be seen for each geographic area. In the EU-27, total asphalt production increased from 246.1 million tons in 2011 to 220.7 million tons in 2021. An initial decline is observed until 2014, followed by a recovery between 2015 and 2018 and a slight decrease in 2019 and 2020. In 2021, production increased from the previous year, but remains below the 2011 level. As for Europe including the above-mentioned countries, production decreased from 324.3 million tons in 2011 to 290.6 million tons in 2021. The trend is similar to that of the EU-27, with an initial decline until 2014, a recovery between 2015 and 2018, and a decline in 2019 and 2020. Again, there is an increase in production in 2021, but we are still below 2011 levels.

In the United States, asphalt production has increased overall over the time interval under consideration, from 332 million tons in 2011 to 392 million tons in 2021. Growth has not been steady, with a decline between 2011 and 2013, followed by a substantial increase between 2014 and 2019. There was a slight decline in 2020, but production increased in 2021, reaching its peak over the entire period.

The decline was particularly noticeable between 2019 and 2020, with a decrease of nearly 50%. HMA and WMA production in the geographic areas that were involved in the study showed different trends over the period 2011–2021, with an overall decrease in Europe and South Africa and an increase in the United States. Tied to these variations is economic, political, and infrastructural factors that may have changed asphalt demand and subsequent production in these years.

Over the period 2011–2021, the factors behind these fluctuations can certainly be attributed to various reasons of which the first is related to the global economic crisis of 2008, capable of having a significant impact on the world economy for several years.

The decline in asphalt production in Europe between 2011 and 2014 may be due in part to the austerity policies adopted in many European countries, with reduced investment in public infrastructure. In the United States, the economy recovered faster after the 2008 crisis than in Europe, which may have led to increased demand for asphalt for new superstructure, explaining the increase in production between 2014 and 2019. From 2019 onward, it is evident how any change is due to the influence of the COVID-19 epidemic on the entire global economy and industrial production. With the restrictive measures imposed, disruptions in supply chains were inevitable, resulting in a reduction of asphalt produced.

The data show that, especially in South Africa, there was a significant decline. Political instability and resulting conflicts have slowed the post-pandemic economic recovery, which will be reflected in future data. As a final but main point of interest in the paper, it is evident that in recent years there has been an increasing focus on environmental sustainability and the use of environmentally friendly as well as reusable materials and technologies in the construction sector, particularly in road paving. The study and subsequent use of mix designs including Reclaimed Asphalt Pavement (RAP) and waste products from other processes to improve the performance and mechanical properties of recycled materials has allowed for less use of virgin and newly produced material. Particularly in Europe, where many countries are investing in green infrastructure projects and using alternative materials (Table 3).

Table 3. Total production of HMA and WMA from 2011 to 2021 (in million tonnes) – Europe

Country	2011	2012	2013	2014	2015	2016	2017	2018	2019	2020	2021
Austria	8.0	7.2	7.0	7.2	7.2	7.4	7.4	7.5	7.5	7.4	7.3
Czech R	5.8	5.6	5.4	6.4	8.0	6.7	7.4	7.9	6.8	6.7	7.2
Finland	5.0	4.5	4.5	4.7	5.4	5.9	6.4	6.1	5.5	7.6	6.1
France	39.2	35.3	35.4	31.9	31.5	33.6	33.7	35.0	35.8	31.9	34.7
Germany	50.0	41.0	41.0	39.0	39.0	41.0	42.0	41.0	40.0	38.0	38.0
Great Britain	22.4	18.5	19.2	20.6	21.9	22.0	22.7	22.9	25.2	23.0	25.7
Greece	2.3	1.6	2.7	2.7*	2.5*	2.3*	2.3*	2.3*	2.3*	2.3*	2.3*
Hungary	2.3	2.5	2.7	3.8	3.9	2.8	2.6	4.7	5.0	4.8	4.9
Italy	28.0	23.2	22.3	22.3	23.1	23.1	23.7	26.0	30.1	30.1*	37.6
Netherlands	9.6	9.2	9.7	9.0	8.0	8.2	8.1	7.9	7.7	7.1	7.2
Norway	6.7	6.3	6.4	7.0	6.9	7.2	7.8	7.5	7.7	6.9	6.9
Poland	26.5	21.1	18.2	16.5	18.5	19.0*	19.0*	19.0*	19.0*	19.0*	19.0*
Portugal	6.4	6.4*	6.4*	6.4*	6.4*	6.2*	6.2*	6.2*	3.1	3.4	4.0
Romania	3.6	3.2	4.1	4.5	4.5*	4.5*	4.5*	4.5*	1.7	1.0	1.0*
Spain	29.3	19.5	13.2	14.5	16.4	13.1	15.2	16.0	18.8	17.1	18.9

(continued)

Table 3. (*continued*)

Country	2011	2012	2013	2014	2015	2016	2017	2018	2019	2020	2021
Sweden	8.1	7.7	7.6	8.5	8.2	8.2*	8.2*	8.2*	8.2*	8.2*	8.2*
Turkey	43.5	38.4	46.2	30.9	37.9	40.4	46.9	41.7	32.7	31.7	30.3

The data presented show the total production in millions of tons of asphalt mix for various European countries from 2011 to 2021.

Focusing on Italy, production increased from 28.0 million tons in 2011 to 37.6 million tons in 2021, showing significant growth. Between 2011 and 2016, Italian production was rather stable, hovering around 22–23 million tons. However, from 2017 onward, there has been a gradual increase, culminating in the highest value in 2021.

Comparing Italy with other major European countries such as France, Germany, Spain and Great Britain, we see that Germany maintained the highest production during the period analyzed, fluctuating between 38 and 50 million tons. France, after an initial decline, showed some stability between 31.5 and 35.8 million tons, while Spain saw a substantial decrease in production, from 29.3 million tons in 2011 to 18.9 in 2021. Great Britain, on the other hand, showed growth in production, rising from 22.4 million tons in 2011 to 25.7 in 2021.

In summary, Italy showed significant growth in asphalt production between 2011 and 2021, while other major European countries such as France and Britain showed some stability or moderate growth. Germany remained the largest producer among the listed countries, while Spain showed a considerable decline in production over the years.

Taking an example in relation to the French case, in terms of the road network, excluding vicinities (chemins ruraux) France has 1,028,260 km of roads (61.27% urban and 38.73% suburban)[7] compared to 167,565 km of Italian roads.[8].

Between 1990 and 2019, about 15,000 km of new roads were built in Italy,[9] a number that is not particularly large; several possible reasons can be hypothesized for greater asphalt production than in France, despite the fact that the French road network is much more extensive. One possible reason could be related to the need for maintenance of existing roads and the possible poor quality of materials and construction techniques used in the past. If Italy's infrastructure requires more frequent maintenance due to age, deterioration, or poor quality of materials and/or placements, this could explain the higher production of asphalt mix in the country, even though the road network is less extensive than in France. It should also be considered that other countries such as France may have adopted alternative materials for road paving than asphalt, making more extensive use of different solutions, such as cementitious conglomerate for rigid pavements not widespread in Italy except in some northern regions.

In Italy, 90% of the asphalt used is asphalt concrete (asphalt concrete EN 13108–1), while 1% is stone mastic asphalt EN 13108–5 and 9% is porous asphalt EN 13108–7. The data shows that Italy makes extensive use of stone mastic asphalt (asphalt concrete), the most common and widely used type of asphalt throughout the world capable of adapting to temperature variations and traffic stresses without significant damage. However, the use of modified asphalt mixes shows that Italy is also adopting alternative solutions to improve road pavement characteristics. The former allows greater resistance to wear and deformation, and the latter is used to improve road safety due to its permeable structure that allows better water drainage.

Table 4. Total production WMA from 2013 to 2021 (in million tonnes)

Paese	2013	2014	2015	2016	2017	2018	2019	2020	2021
Croatia	0	0,04	0,06	0,06	–	–	–	0,075	0,08
France	3,55	4,023	4,552	4,324	3,824	3,728	4,305	4,058	6,52
Great Britain	1	<1,000	<1,000	–	<0,300	<1,000	<1,000	>1,000	1,000*
Hungary	0,02	0,038	0,07	0,208	0,21	0	0,18	0,35	0
Netherlands	0,06	0,133	0,1	0,100*	0,06	–	–	–	–
Norway	0,38	0,54	0,592	0,502	0,869	1,339	1,74	1,851	1,754
Spain	0,086	0,14	0,14	0,06	0,2	0,18	0,38	0,5	0,65
Switzerland	0,87	0,388	//	//	//	//	0,5	//	//
USA	69	103	109	106	133	143	150	169	85

The previous Table n. 4 shows WMA production in different countries from 2013 to 2021, in millions of tons. France shows a significant increase in WMA production, rising from 3.55 million tons in 2013 to 6.52 million tons in 2021, highlighting the country's growing commitment to promoting more sustainable materials and solutions for road infrastructure.

The United States had considerable warm mix asphalt production, increasing from 69 million tons in 2013 to 85 million tons in 2021, although a decrease from the peak of 169 million tons in 2020 is noted likely because of Covid19 and the recovering economy.

WMA production in Italy is not included in the table to underscore how its use is more than rare, making it necessary to emphasize how the adoption of this more sustainable technology could help reduce the environmental impact of Italy's road infrastructure.[8] The table shows that several countries are increasing WMA production, signaling a growing focus on sustainability in the road paving sector. The uptake of this technology varies widely among countries, suggesting the need for further efforts to promote greener solutions globally.

Regarding the production of CMA, EAPA's data in Europe shows considerable variation between countries and over time. France is the largest producer, peaking at 2,220,000 tons in 2021 [7]. Spain saw a decrease in production, from 200,000 tons in 2011 to 83,000 tons in 2021. On Italy there is no data, highlighting how the technology is used only for partial repairs of wear layers. It is important to evaluate and continue studying CMAs as solutions for the future, as they can generate less environmental impact than traditional bituminous mixtures.

4 Asphalt Production Scenarios in Italy: Energy Analysis and CO2 Emission Reduction

Different scenarios related to asphalt production in Italy will be analyzed below. The table presents five scenarios with different percentages of HMA, WMA and CMA, showing the total energy consumption and energy savings compared to the exclusive use of HMA from total asphalt production data in 2021 and on the energy consumption values for each type (Table 5).

Table 5. Five scenarios with different percentages of HMA, WMA, CMA - Energy

Values	Description	Unit
37,6	Total production 2021	Million tonnes
275	Energy for HMA	MJ/t
234	Energy for WMA	MJ/t
14	Energy for CMA	MJ/t

	% HMA	% WMA	% CMA	HMA (MJ)	WMA (MJ)	CMA (MJ)	Total (MJ)	Saving (MJ)
1	100%	0%	0%	10.340.000.000	-	-	10.340.000.000	-
2	70%	30%	0%	7.238.000.000	2.639.520.000	-	9.877.520.000	462.480.000
3	50%	30%	20%	5.170.000.000	2.639.520.000	105.280.000	7.914.800.000	2.425.200.000
4	40%	40%	20%	4.136.000.000	3.519.360.000	105.280.000	7.760.640.000	2.579.360.000
5	30%	50%	20%	3.102.000.000	4.399.200.000	105.280.000	7.606.480.000	2.733.520.000

The data in the table show the energy consumption to produce HMA, WMA and CMA by combining the percentage use of the various technologies in different scenarios. The first is the current figure with only HMA, the total energy consumption is 10,340,000,000 MJ. In the third scenario, combining 50% HMA, 30% WMA and 20% CMA, the total energy consumption drops to 7,914,800,000 MJ, a saving of 2,425,200,000 MJ compared to the first scenario. The adoption of WMA and CMA can lead to significant reductions in energy consumption compared with the exclusive use of HMA.

Regarding CO_2 emissions, according to the data provided, the production of 1 ton of HMA and CMA results in emissions of 53.6 and 36.1 kg of CO_2, respectively. However, the addition of cement to CMA can significantly increase CO_2 emissions. The addition of 2% cement in CMA results in CO_2 emissions like those of HMA without cement (Table 6).

Table 6. Four scenarios with different percentages of HMA, WMA, CMA – GHG emissions

Emissions CO_2 HMA (kg/t)	Emissions CO_2 WMA (kg/t)	Emissions CO_2 CMA (kg/t)
53,6	52,8	36,1

	% HMA	% WMA	% CMA	Emissions CO_2 HMA (kg/t)	Emissions CO2 WMA (kg/t)	Emissions CO_2 CMA (kg/t)	Emission CO_2 Total (kg/t)
1	70%	20%	10%	37,52	10,56	3,61	**51,69**
2	60%	25%	15%	32,16	13,2	5,415	**50,775**
3	50%	30%	20%	26,8	15,84	7,22	**49,86**
4	40%	35%	25%	21,44	18,48	9,025	**48,945**

The table shows a gradual reduction in CO2 emissions as the percentages of WMA and CMA increase relative to HMA. However, the reduction in emissions is not significant, from 51.69 kg/t in the first scenario to 48.945 kg/t in the fourth scenario. The explanation lies in the limited impact of WMA technologies in particular and CMA on overall emissions. The production process of WMA requires less thermal energy than HMA, but maintains similar orders of magnitude so that replacing HMA with WMA may only partially reduce emissions; the use of CMA may not offer the same performance in terms of durability and mechanical strength as HMA and WMA, limiting its adoption in some applications; and finally, the possible addition of cement or additives to the latter may cause an increase in CO2 emissions.

5   Conclusions

Different alternatives to the production of classic HMA were analyzed in terms of environmental impact and energy efficiency. From the results obtained, the use of WMA and CMA with the technologies considered was shown to generate significant energy savings compared to the exclusive use of HMA. However, in terms of CO2 emission reduction, the changes were not of a significant order of magnitude. The push on the study and subsequent use of more sustainable production technologies remains critical to responsible and sustainable resource management and the reduction of atmospheric emissions and thus climate impact. The use of technical solutions such as WMA and CMA are just one step in the right direction to reduce the environmental impact of the asphalt industry.

Research and innovation are essential for a sustainable future and a more environmentally friendly asphalt industry. So, efforts related to research and development of increasingly less impactful materials must be constant, particularly in relation to those capable of improving performance characteristics over traditional ones by focusing on the recovery of waste materials from other production processes.

Author Contributions. Concept and methodology, Grazietti F., Rombi, J., and Coni, M.; analysis, Grazietti F., Rombi, J., and Coni M., writing, review and editing, Grazietti F., Rombi, J., Maltinti F., and Coni M.. All authors have read and agreed to the published version of the manuscript.

References

1. Jain, S., Singh, B.: Cold mix asphalt: an overview. J. Clean. Prod. **280** 124378 (2021). https://doi.org/10.1016/j.jclepro.2020.124378
2. Gibbons, S., Lyytikäinen, T., Overman, H.G., Sanchis-Guarner, R.: New road infrastructure: the effects on firms. J. Urban Econ. **110,** 35–50 (2019). https://doi.org/10.1016/j.jue.2019.01.002
3. Dossier ANFIA.pdf
4. Quaderni tecnici volume 5 - Anas
5. Vaitkus, A., Čygas, D., Laurinavičius, A., Vorobjovas, V., Per-veneckas, Z.: Influence of warm mix asphalt technology on asphalt physical and mechanical properties. Constr. Build. Mater. **112,** 800–806 (2016)
6. Chehovits, J., Galehouse, L.: Energy usage and greenhouse gas emissions of pavement preservation processes for asphalt concrete pavements. In: Proceedings on the 1st International Conference of Pavement Preservation, pp. 27–42 (2010)
7. Brown, S., Needham, D.: A study of cement modified bitumen emulsion mixtures. Asphalt Paving Technol. **69,** 92–121 (2000)
8. Asphalt in figures 2021 - EAPA European Asphalt Pavement Association
9. SeA, R.: La rete stradale in Europa e nel mondo: confronti Italia-Francia, Strade & Autostrade. https://www.stradeeautostrade.it/traffico-smart-mobility/la-rete-stradale-in-europa-e-nel-mondo-confronti-italia-francia/
10. Documento strategico mobilità stradale 2022–2026 - MIT.pdf. https://www.mit.gov.it/nfsmit gov/files/media/notizia/2022-07/Documento_strategico_mobilit%C3%A0_stradale.pdf
11. Mashaan, N.S., Chegenizadeh, A., Nikraz, H., Rezagholilou, A.: Investigating the engineering properties of asphalt binder modified with waste plastic polymer. Ain Shams Eng. J. **12**(2), 1569-1574 (2021)
12. Cheraghian, G., et al.: Warm mix asphalt technology: an up to date review. J. Clean. Prod. **268,** 122128, set (2020). https://doi.org/10.1016/j.jclepro.2020.122128
13. Catani, A.: Siteb: MERCATO BITUME ITALIA 2021. https://www.siteb.it/sitebNew/siteb-mercato-bitume-italia-2021/
14. Asi, I., Assa'ad, A.: Effect of Jordanian oil shale fly ash on asphalt mixes. J. Mater. Civ. Eng. **17**(5), 553–559 (2005)

15. Chegenizadeh, A., Tufilli, A., Arumdani, I.S., Budihardjo, M.A., Dadras, E., Nikraz, E.H.: Mechanical Properties of cold mix asphalt (CMA) mixed with recycled asphalt pavement. Infrastructures, **7**(4), 4 (2022). https://doi.org/10.3390/infrastructures7040045

16. Milad, A., et al.: A comparative review of hot and warm mix asphalt technologies from environmental and economic perspectives: towards a sustainable asphalt pavement. Int. J. Environ. Res. Public. Health, **19**(22), fasc, 14863 (2022). https://doi.org/10.3390/ijerph192 214863

A Theoretical Framework for Climate Change Adaptation Participatory Planning in Vulnerable Coastal Zones

Chiara Garau[1]([⊠]) [iD], Giulia Desogus[1] [iD], Erika Orrù[1], and Claudia Loggia[2] [iD]

[1] Department of Civil and Environmental Engineering and Architecture (DICAAR), University of Cagliari, Via Marengo 2, 09123 Cagliari, Italy
cgarau@unica.it
[2] School of Built Environment and Development Studies (SoBEDS), University of KwaZulu-Natal, Howard College Campus, Durban 4041, South Africa

Abstract. Coastal zones are vulnerable climatic ecosystems. This is due to anthropogenic factors such as population growing and increase in settlement density, as well as geographical and natural pressures, including coastal danger, sea level rise, and biodiversity loss. Managing these problems and their interdependencies requires a bottom-up approach which can involve coastal communities in the climate change adaptation processes and encourage citizen participation towards a more sustainable resource management. This paper seeks to propose a set of guidelines on climate change adaptation through participatory planning for the assessment of the vulnerability of highly problematic areas such as coastal ones. To achieve this goal, a holistic approach based on systematic and transversal assessment of participatory best practices was applied and a theoretical framework was developed specifically for coastal areas. The proposed guidelines will facilitate (ii) a broader understanding of climate change concerns by the public and coastal tourism, (ii) the incorporation of stakeholders' requirements into local climate change policies, and (iii) local empowerment of coastal communities in accordance with sustainability principles.

Keywords: Sustainable Development · Participatory Planning · Climate Change · Coastal Zones · Bottom-Up Urban Planning · Urban Strategies

1 Introduction

Coastal ecosystems are among the most vulnerable to the effects of climate change because of human and natural pressures. Millions of people depend on these ecosystems for sustenance, recreation, and coastal tourism, even though climate change is affecting their stability [1]. The loss of these ecosystems can have severe repercussions for coastal communities, including loss of livelihoods and intensified vulnerability to natural disasters. Indeed, the effects of climate change, such as sea level rise, coastal hazards, and biodiversity loss, present significant obstacles for coastal communities. Addressing

© The Author(s), under exclusive license to Springer Nature Switzerland AG 2023
O. Gervasi et al. (Eds.): ICCSA 2023 Workshops, LNCS 14105, pp. 246–268, 2023.
https://doi.org/10.1007/978-3-031-37108-0_16

these challenges requires employing a bottom-up strategy which includes citizen participation and participatory planning [2] and promotes a broader public understanding of issues related to climate change. Indeed, participatory planning is an effective response to the urban complexities presented by top-down forms of urban planning [3, 4]. Adaptation to climate change presents the most compelling specific instance for participatory practices to resolve "structural vulnerabilities in relation to service provision, economic inequalities and access to policy making" [5, p.2]. This relates to the effectiveness of integrating a spatial approach into participatory practices. Indeed, a spatial approach to participatory practices requires mapping exercises, which make conflicts and compatibilities of human use spatially clear and, thus, presumably controllable [6]. This type of cartography encompasses ecosystems, their characteristics, and the human activities that impact these ecosystems [7]. Participatory urban planning is a bottom-up approach in which citizens actively participate in decision-making processes. Citizens can take responsibility for the procedures in which they are involved and can contribute, with their knowledge and experience, to the development of sustainable policies. Integration of stakeholder requirements into local policies is crucial for effective climate change adaptation and mitigation [8]. This process allows stakeholders to contribute with their knowledge and experience to the development of policies that are customised to fulfil their requirements and interests. Moreover, this system ensures that policies are developed in dialogue with the communities they will affect, allowing them to take part in the process, feeling more engaged in the results and successfully implementing them. In climate-vulnerable coastal ecosystems, the inclusion of stakeholder requirements is crucial because it enables the development of policies adapted to the specific needs of coastal communities. According to Kearney et al. (2007), most of the coastal community criticism comes from the sea-land relationship. In addition to the problems of the mainland (environmental changes and competing land uses) and those of the sea (jurisdictional challenges), coastal communities must also deal with erosion, inundations, pollution from agricultural runoff, and access challenges [9]. Furthermore, coastal communities have a deep understanding of their local environments, and their inclusion is important for assessing the vulnerability of these areas and developing policies perfectly suited to their requirements. Vulnerability assessment is the first step towards effective adaptation to climate change [10, 11]. It is essential to identify the factors that contribute to vulnerability, including both natural and anthropogenic pressures. The assessment should consider all aspects of vulnerability, including social, economic, and environmental factors, and also "biophysical orientations (i.e., bridging contextual/bottom-up and climate-driven/top-down approaches)" [12, p.134]. In the context of vulnerable coastal ecosystems, the assessment should consider the impacts of climate change on coastal infrastructure, settlement trends and biodiversity loss. Involving coastal communities improves the probability that developed policies will be effectively implemented and accepted. Considering these premises, this paper explores the role of participatory urban planning as a model that enables local communities to address the impacts of climate change on climate-vulnerable ecosystems in coastal zones. The main goal is to propose guidelines on the participatory practices of coastal communities, with particular attention to the coastal areas. This study aims to answer the questions: (i) what concerns do coastal communities have regarding climate change? (ii) what type of mechanisms are in place between the requirements of the local population and those of decision-makers in the context of environmental problem-solving decisions?

To achieve this, the paper starts by focusing on vulnerable coastal zones in relation to adaptation to climate change (Sect. 2). Subsequently, Sect. 3 proposes a theoretical framework with various participatory planning methods and tools to identify guidelines for participatory planning for climate change adaptation in vulnerable coastal zones. Finally, the results and future directions are discussed (Sect. 4).

2   Climate Change and Participatory Practices: Why Coastal Zones?

Coastal zones are the world's most diversified and productive ecosystems where land and sea merge and interact. These ecosystems are extraordinarily complex due to the intersection of a wide range of geomorphological, socioeconomic, and ecological conditions with human activities associated with urbanisation, port activity, industrialisation, and tourism. Indeed, these areas provide a variety of vital services for both humans and animals. Nevertheless, many coastal regions are vulnerable to the effects of climate change, such as sea level rise, storm surges, and erosion. In addition, coastal areas are home to millions of people and support a variety of ecosystems, making them extremely vulnerable to climate change. These concerns have significant repercussions for the environment and for the communities that depend on these areas for their livelihoods. In these areas, climate change represents one of the most critical environmental challenges the planet currently faces [13, 14].

According to Laignel et al. (2023), the future sustainability of coastal zones is entirely dependent on being capable of using systematic monitoring with an emphasis on: (1) anthropogenic factors affecting "coastal zones at different spatiotemporal scales (sea level rise, winds and waves, offshore and coastal currents, tides, storm surges, river runoff in estuaries and deltas, sediment supply and transport, vertical land motions and land use); (2) morphological response (e.g., shoreline migration, topographical changes)" [15, p.1].

Coastal zones can be protected from the effects of climate change through a variety of practical measures. This can be accomplished by adopting policies and regulations aimed at reducing carbon emissions and encouraging the use of renewable energy sources. Adaptations can also be made to coastal infrastructure and management practices to mitigate the effects of climate change. Developing coastal defences, restoring natural habitats, and instituting coastal zone management plans can assist in erosion control and runoff management. Lastly, the development of adaptive strategies is essential for mitigating the effects of climate change that are already happening. To achieve climate goals, these strategies may involve relocating infrastructure at risk from rising sea levels and providing early warning systems, but it is necessary to develop climate-resilient communities that are aware of it and actively participate in climate actions. For instance, applying a more inclusive, people-centred disaster approach is fundamental to empower local communities affected by natural disasters [16]. Resilience can start from awareness and local governments should support and empower communities for a more effective disaster response.

In the context of climate change, participatory practices include individuals, communities, and/or groups in the identification, planning, and implementation of initiatives that can mitigate the effects of climate change. Participatory practices are based on the concept that everyone has an individual perspective and can contribute to a global strategy for addressing the challenges presented by climate change. Participatory practices can stimulate more inclusive and effective responses to climate change through the integration of diverse perspectives. Community-led initiatives are an example of participatory practices that can be employed in climate change mitigation. For instance, community initiatives can assist in identifying climate-vulnerable areas, such as coastal zones and surrounded by water regions. Participatory spatial mapping has been applied to several fields such as socioeconomics, education, health, mobility, service allocation, prevention of crime and monitoring. The underpinning idea is that local people can design their own maps that might be more accurate than the ones produced by professionals [17]. Community-based mapping has been used to produce indigenous maps for claims on ancestral lands [18] and to ensure access to and the ownership of information [19]. In the 2000s, innovative participatory techniques emerged as increasingly popular to assist communities in assessing the causes and effects of climate change, integrating scientific and local knowledge of the issue, and developing adaptation strategies [20]. The literature of those years suggested the need for effective methods to engage or activate communities and to support community roles, as well as systemic approaches to understanding climate change and adaptation needs [21]. Ross et al. (2015) state that local communities may be at the forefront of climate change's negative effects because inhabitants and organisations are integrally connected to and familiar with the region's unique social, historical, and political contexts. This has both social justice and practical implications [20]. The concept of local knowledge for preventing climate change was reaffirmed in 2007 by the IPCC's Fourth Assessment Report on Climate Change, which states that scientific and political consensus helps community's understanding of complicated problems such as climate change. "In the case of climate change, participatory processes encourage local practitioners from climate-sensitive endeavours to become engaged so that past experiences can be included in the study of (and the planning for) future climate change and development pressures" [13, p.1]. Subsequently, policymakers have increasingly planned for future local and regional climate-related impacts. The importance of involving stakeholders in such decision-making processes is debated, but more evidence is required to persuade institutions to involve stakeholders to make sensible decisions [22]. Although community engagement in climate change adaptation initiatives has been encouraged for some time, their implementation in decision-making processes is still lacking [23–25]. Currently, the Report Committee on Political Affairs and Democracy of the EU (2021) asserts "tackling climate change is a momentous challenge which requires not only clear political engagement from the authorities but also the active involvement of citizens. Combining a top-down and a bottom-up approach would enhance citizens' trust in public decision-making as well its legitimacy, transparency, inclusiveness, and responsiveness. It would also result in greater support for public action." [13, p.1]. Based on these premises, the authors note that the literature has not yet explored the most effective participatory approaches in the context of coastal zone climate management, where participatory practice can take many forms, such as community-based planning, stakeholder involvement, and management agreements.

This paper, seeks to demonstrate the potential advantages of such bottom-up approaches, through the development of an inventory of participatory practices which will serve as a basis for designing a specific climate change adaptation strategy in vulnerable Coastal Zones.

3 Methodological Approach for Vulnerable Coastal Zones

In recent years, the vulnerability of coastal zones has become even more evident because climate change impacts pose significant threats to populations and environments. Understanding, evaluating, and mitigating these risks requires a bespoke methodological strategy that takes into consideration the dynamicity and complexity of coastal zones. This section aims at providing a comprehensive outline of participatory practices and how these methodologies can (i) help in decision-making, (ii) involve the population and (iii) improve the resilience of these areas and reduce risks.

3.1 Comparison Between Participatory Planning Best Practices

Based on the aforementioned considerations and motivations, participatory practices can be divided into the following categories: a) general models analysing participatory planning involving a wide range of citizens and organisations; b) models analysing decision-making and engagement processes that involve citizens in making specific decisions and include online surveys, public meetings, and focus groups; c) models analysing online participatory planning that allow citizens to participate without being physically present; and d) models analysing the various methods of participatory planning in behavioural processes. Below they are described in detail.

a) *Analytical models of participatory planning in general.* Participatory planning consists in involving community members in in decisions making processes that impact their environment and future. It is based on active collaboration and gives community members a direct role in planning and implementing policies affecting their well-being. The primary goal of participatory planning is to create more sustainable, conscientious, and responsible communities. In this regard, the White's model "typology of participation" [26] distinguishes four types of participation and asserts that the actors of each typology ('at the top'; more powerful actors; 'at the grass roots'; and less powerful actors) have different perceptions and interests.

The typologies of participation are: (i) nominal, used by more powerful actors to give legitimacy to development objectives; (ii) structural, used by the community to a specific end; (ii) representative, involves giving community members a voice in decision making and project implementation, and (iv) transformative, resulted in the empowerment of those involved [25, 27].

The CLEAR Participation model developed by Lawndes and Pratchett (2006) correlates barriers to empowerment with policy responses and requirements. This model identified five factors behind citizen participation responses: "Can do—have the resources and knowledge to participate; Like to—have a sense of attachment that reinforces participation; Enabled to—are provided with the opportunity for participation; Asked to—are mobilized through public agencies and civic channels; Responded to—see evidence that their views have been considered" [28, p.22].

The Behaviour Grid model by BJ Fogg (2010) [29] describes 15 ways in which a community or an individual's behaviour can be influenced through psychological strategies and persuasive techniques.

In conclusion, these models are useful tools for comprehending participatory planning and assisting administrators and community members in the development of more effective and inclusive participatory decision-making processes. Adopting such models can facilitate the development of more sustainable and equitable communities, but it is important that they be applied in a manner that considers the actual needs of the community in consideration.

b) *Analytical models of decision-making and participation processes.* Individually or collectively, the decision-making process consists of a series of actions and decisions that lead to a decision. Numerous factors, including emotions, opinions, available information, social pressure, and long-term objectives, can influence this process. On the other hand, Involvement is the process of motivating people to actively participate in a decision-making process or of fostering a sense of belonging and responsibility towards a common objective. Involvement can be an effective strategy for improving the effectiveness and efficacy of decisions, as well as for fostering feelings of trust and collaboration among group members. "Levels, spaces, and Forms of Power" by John Gaventa (2006), "Varieties of Participation" by Archon Fung (2006), "Spectrum of public participation IAP2" (2007), and Engagement in the policy cycle by Diane Warburton (2007) are among the most significant recent models. The first one "Levels, spaces, and Forms of Power" examines levels, spaces, and shapes through a "power cube" that investigates how their intersection defines various dimensions of power. The "forms" dimension refers to the visible, hidden, and invisible manifestations of power, "spaces" refers to the potential spaces for action and participation, and "levels" refers to the process of decision-making at the local, national, and global levels [30, 23]. The Spectrum of public participation IAP2 [31] depicts various levels of participation and was created to aid in the selection of the level of participation that defines the public's role in any kind of public participation process [32]. Engagement in the policy cycle [33] evaluates public participation by emphasising that there are times when public expectations should not be expressed (for instance, when a decision has already been made or when a delaying stratagem is employed because it is too difficult to decide immediately). However, participation is a prerequisite when social and political change is still possible [31]. Finally, Varieties of Participation by Archon Fung emphasises the various ways the public can participate in government policy and decision-making [34]. This model consists of (1) the methods of participatory selection; (2) the modes of communication and decision-making provided to the public, and (3) the degrees of power and authority granted to public participants. These three factors are examined using a three-dimensional model known as the democracy cube, which identifies various participatory mechanisms suitable for addressing government problems [33].

c) *Analytical models of online Participatory Planning.* Online participatory planning refers to the process of involving a diverse group of stakeholders, including citizens, community organizations, and government officials, in the planning of a project's development using digital platforms. In the early 2000s, online tools, such as surveys and interactive maps, were used to collect feedback and monitor community preferences [27, 35–37]. Since then, digital technologies associated with participatory planning have evolved, along with the development of new tools, approaches, and techniques. The city dashboards and connected applications provide public administrators with real-time data provided by citizens regarding the various requirements, challenges, and opportunities of the urban context under analysis. Smart Specialisation Platforms (SSPs) are digital platforms that facilitate collaboration and knowledge exchange between companies, research institutions, and government agencies within specific sectors or regions) [38–41, 41]. More in particular:

(i) Among their many functions, city dashboards enable citizens to access an extensive range of data quickly and easily about the city via the web or mobile applications. These data can be related to a variety of topics, including mobility, air quality, energy consumption, differentiated waste collection, local economic trend, etc. [42, 43] Citizens can therefore become co-producers of information using city dashboards, thereby enhancing the transparency of the public administration, and fostering a heightened awareness for the management and development of the city [40].

(ii) SSPs present an opportunity to strengthen local governance in the planning and implementation of urban policies. SSPs are collaborative big data platforms that bring together public authorities, businesses, universities, and other local actors to define a smart specialisation strategy for urban or regional development.

Among the most authoritative examples of city dashboards and SSPs are: (i) The Amsterdam Smart City programme (ASC), a public-private initiative that acts as an information connector, facilitating cooperation and the exchange of ideas and opportunities between partner; (ii) Helsinki Smart Region (HSR), a regional smart specialisation strategy aimed at enhancing regional innovation potential and developing international collaborations by employing the region's economic, environmental, and social resources effectively; (iii) Copenhagen Smart City (CSC) uses smart data to create a sustainable city and a more favourable business climate. The city's strategy includes three goals: achieving carbon neutrality, creating a greener and more sustainable city, and fostering economic growth; and (iv) Snap4City - Florence Smart City (FSC) is based on two key factors: collaboration with public authorities, businesses, universities, and other local actors and a holistic approach.

d) *Analytical models of different methods of participation in behavioural processes.* Below some of these models.

i. Shared Space Café - a facilitated dialogue process that encourages conversations among participants, designed to increase mutual understanding and collaboration [44].

ii. World Café - a structured process for small and large group conversations, designed to foster open dialogue, creativity and innovation [45].

(iii) Open Space Technology – a self-organizing approach to facilitating interactive and participatory meetings and events, allowing participants to designate their own issues and discussion priorities [45]. In an Open Space environment, participants meet and organise themselves based on the issues that arise during discussions. The objective is to collect ideas and recommendations in a collaborative and innovative setting. A practical approach to Open Space Technology are the Living labs. These are intended to encourage end-user participation in the development of innovative solutions. In this scenario, the main goal is to generate productive and feasible solutions, using user experience and knowledge to improve effectiveness and efficiency.

(iv) Appreciative Inquiry - a method of inquiry that emphasises on identifying, understanding, and celebrating an organization's strengths and successes to promote effective and positive change [45].

(v) Public Participation Geographic Information Systems (PPGIS)- an approach for involving citizens, stakeholders, and decision makers in the development and use of geospatial technologies to facilitate decision-making process [7]. With the evolution of ICTs, PPGIS have been combined with extensions to more established programs, innovative tools, apps and combined to big data platforms. All of this is aimed at offering a variety of interactive functions that enable users to access real-time geospatial data and participate in the process of defining environmental and territorial policies. Moreover, it allows users to share information, interact with other users, create customised maps. These modalities and approaches promote greater transparency and accountability in environmental and land-use policies and improve durability and democracy in urban planning.

(vi) Participatory Rural Assessment (PRA)/Participatory Learning and Action (PLA) - approaches and methodologies used to support planning, decision-making, and community action, particularly in rural and resource-poor regions [46, 47];

(vii) Local knowledge mapping (LKM) supports community-based development and sustainable resource management by producing, capturing, and disseminating local knowledge, especially among marginalised or disadvantaged groups [48].

(viii) Metaverse and Performance Modelling - In recent years, the use of technology in behavioural processes is increasing popularity [49–55]. This trend has been driven by the demand for more efficient and successful approaches to comprehending human behaviour and enhancing decision-making. A key component of these patterns is the capacity to identify emotions accurately. This resulted in the creation of specific tools od apps, which use facial expressions to identify emotions.

The development of learning-based performance models is another area of emphasis in behavioural processes. This means utilising data to predict performance outcomes and identify improvement opportunities. This approach allows more targeted interventions and can result in improved decision-making outcomes. In the field of behavioural processes, digital twin technology is another emerging field. These are virtual replicas used to simulate and predict behaviour in a variety of scenarios. This technology facilitates a deeper comprehension of complex systems and can guide decision-making in real-world situations.

3.2 Results

By applying high- or low-technological approaches and tools, the bottom-up models described in the previous section can be used to actively engage citizens. Nonetheless, it must be kept in mind that each model has its limitations, and that the selection of the most appropriate model depends on the specific requirements of the case study, particularly if the context is in a coastal area with unique characteristics. Table 1 provides an overview of the proposed approaches and highlights their key principles. Active involvement typically implies the participation of all stakeholders, including citizens, NGOs, and local government officials. This approach is particularly relevant in coastal areas, where the impacts of climate change are increasing the vulnerability of communities. The process of raising awareness is long and complex, and awareness activities are crucial because they serve to identify potential risks and vulnerabilities during the long-term planning stage. Climate change refers to long-term changes in the environment, particularly those associated with rising temperatures, rising sea levels, acidification of the ocean, and the occurrence of extreme weather events. Due to their location and susceptibility to natural disasters and sea level rise, these changes have significant implications for coastal zone planning and management. It is expected that coastal cities will face great challenges in managing the significant growth in exposure as a consequence of both human and environmental influences, including climate change [56]. In addition, the global rise in sea level significantly impacts Africa's coastal cities due to the socio-economic vulnerability of urban poor. In this context, spatial approaches in their various forms that integrate ICTs and participatory practices have shown to be significantly effective for developing a shared understanding of the territory and bringing inclusive and democratic participatory processes into practice. For instance, the spatial approach can be utilised to create a virtual map of the territory on which citizens can investigate and experiment with various development options. The generated maps can be incorporated into databases, SSPs, or dashboards, and are always usable, consultable, and integrable in real-time. Indeed, these cutting-edge tools (i) identify common challenges and opportunities and co-produce solutions; (ii) allow cities to collect, analyse, and visualise data on various aspects of urban life, such as transport, energy consumption, air quality and public services; (iii) support city leaders in monitoring and optimising city performance, enhancing citizen engagement, and facilitating evidence-based decision making. Using these platforms within a participatory planning process has numerous advantages. Firstly, the data processed are readily accessible and comprehensible, forming an effective tool for citizen empowerment. Secondly, the adoption of these cutting-edge techniques increases data collection and analysis efficiency. Lastly, city displays can be used to identify problems and monitor the adopted solutions, thereby increasing the transparency of the decision-making process and citizen participation in urban planning also via a spatial approach.

It should be noted that for the spatial approach (but in general for all participatory approaches considered) to function optimally, the most technologically advanced tool is not always the most effective if it is not completely understood in the context analysed. All these assessments conducted seek to determine the most effective methods of involvement and participation for each phase of the decision-making process. Therefore, the use of the best participatory practice combined with i) the active participation of all

Table 1. Key principles of participatory planning models

Models and approaches	KeyPrinciples
Analytical models of participatory planning in general	
Typology of participation	1) Nominal participation; 2) Instrumental participation; 3) Representative participation 4) Transformative participation
CLEAR Participation	Each user can design his/her method to satisfy local demands. Nevertheless, during the implementation of the instrument, users should be aware on these points: 1) Existing data sources 2) Internal or counselling activities 3) Quantitative or qualitative information 4) Range of stakeholders involved 5) Analysis level 6) Sequences: organizations might not be interested in collecting all the information at the same time. Organizations might want, as a first step, to do an initial internal diagnosis using a small team of elected politicians or public administrators before extending the process to other stakeholders or focusing on specific geographical communities or communities of interest
Behaviour Grid	1) Clear expectations: the behaviour grid gives guidelines and clear expectations to the behaviour in a particular contest 2) Coherence: the behaviour grid promotes coherence in the behavioural management, ensuring that all the individuals are treated with equality and coherence 3) Positive enhancement: the behaviour grid encourages a positive behaviour rewarding individuals to achieve the desired results 4) Based on consequences: the behaviour grid includes also the consequences of negative behaviour; it gives a clear understanding of repercussions if predetermined expectations are missed 5) Efficient communication: the behaviour grid facilitates an efficient communication between the individuals, it ensures that everyone is aware of expectations and consequences 6) Flexibility: the behaviour grid can be adapted to be used with specific situations and specific individuals. It becomes, indeed, a useful instrument for various contexts 7) Proactive approach: the behaviour grid promotes a proactive approach in the behavioural management, it focuses on prevention of negative behaviour before it will happen 8) Responsibility: the behaviour grid encourages responsibility, it ensures that individuals are considered responsible of their actions, both positive and negative ones 9) Objective oriented: the behaviour grid is objective oriented; it gives a clear framework to the people about what to work on to achieve specific results 10) Continuous improvement: the behaviour grid promotes continuous improvement to give to people feedback about their behaviour and encouraging them to support positive changes

(*continued*)

Table 1. (*continued*)

Models and approaches	KeyPrinciples
Analytical models of decision-making and participation processes	
Levels, spaces and forms of power	1) Power is not equally distributed in society: power is detained by specific individuals or groups that are able to exercise control on other people 2) Power can be obvious or hidden: obvious power is clear and can be easily detected, whereas hidden power, as it says, it is hidden and therefore more difficult to detect 3) Power can be used through various shapes, some of them include economic, political, legal social, cultural, and even psychological means 4) Power can be contested and negotiated: people can challenge power and try to negotiate it for a more equal distribution of power 5) Power relationships are not fixed: they can change during the time when circumstances between people change and if social, economic, and political conditions change 6) Power is relational: it exists in dynamic interactions between individuals or groups of people, more than being an intrinsic characteristic of an individual or a group of people 7) Power can be legitimate or illegitimate: it depends on the rules, the values and the laws of a society, power can be considered legitimate or illegitimate 8) Power can be strengthening or weakening: whereas power can allow individuals or groups achieve their goals, it can also limit their ability to do it 9) Power affects people in different ways: depending on some factors, as sex, race, class and other identity indicators, power can have different effects and it can be perceived in different ways by individuals or groups 10) Resistance to power can be a form of power: when people challenge or resist power, they are expressing their form of power and raising their voice
Varieties of Participation	1) public participation in governmental policy-making and decision-making; 2) national level application; 3) functioning of local (e.g., municipal or educational) governments and institutions; 4) there is no canonical form of direct participation in modern democratic governance; 5) public participation advances multiple purposes and values in contemporary governance; 3) mechanisms of direct participation are not a strict alternative to political representation but instead complement them

(*continued*)

Table 1. (*continued*)

Models and approaches	KeyPrinciples
Spectrum of public participation IAP2	1) Inform: to give to the public balanced and objective information to help it in understanding the problem, the alternatives, the opportunities and/or the solutions 2) Consult: to obtain public feedback on analysis, alternatives and/or decisions 3) Involve: working directly with the public during the decisional process to guarantee that concerns and aspirations of the public are constantly understood, taken care of and combined in the final decision 4) Collaborate: to collaborate with the public in every aspect of the decisional process, including the development of alternatives and the identification of the favourite solution 5) Empower: giving to the public the responsibility and the authority to take joint decisions with the policy makers
Engagement in the policy cycle	1) Inclusion: the policy cycle should involve all the interested parties that can be influenced or that can have an interest in the policy. Their perspectives should be taken into consideration 2) Transparency: the policy cycle should be conducted open to checks and it should include a clear communication about process, results, and recommendations 3) Reactivity: the policy cycle should respond to environmental changes, and it should include the feedback of stakeholders in order to improve the policy results 4) Based on proofs: the policy cycle should be informed by reliable proofs and analysis to guarantee that the political measure is based on reality, therefore, it would have better chances of succeed 5) Continuous improvement: the cycle of policy should allow a continuous supervision and valuation to evaluate the efficacy of the policy and to identify the opportunities to perfect it or improve it 6)Responsibility: the policy cycle should plan clear mechanism of responsibility in order to ensure that all the involved actors would be considered responsible of their actions and decisions 7) Participation: the policy cycle should give priority to active participation of all the interested parties in policy process to guarantee that their voices will be heard, and their needs satisfied 8) Coherence: the policy cycle should guarantee that policies are coherent and aligned with the framework, the goals and priorities at regional and national level

(*continued*)

Table 1. (*continued*)

Models and approaches	KeyPrinciples
Analytical models of online Participatory Planning	
City Dashboards	1) It improves citizens participation: the connection between participative practices and city dashboard can increase citizens participation in the city management. The instruments of information visualization give to citizens an opportunity to better understand the city issues and to have a clear idea of the general trend 2) It increases transparency: the connection between participative practices and city dashboards can improve transparency in the city management. Open data and information access can give citizens the possibility to evaluate city choices and to give more significative feedback 3) Real time monitoring: city dashboards can give real time monitoring of the condition of the city, such as quality of the air, of the services, traffic gridlock, levels of acoustic pollution and more others. This can help citizens to actively participate and to take informed decision about the city services 4) It enhances collaboration between citizens and authorities: the connection between participative practices and city dashboards helps governmental authorities to understand better the needs of the city and of its citizens. This can encourage a better collaboration between authorities and citizens who can work together to solve city issues and improve the quality of life 5) Support to decisions based on data: the connection between participative practices and city dashboards allows governments to take decisions based on data and on evaluation of city needs. This can improve the efficiency of public policy and to achieve a better operative efficiency 6) It enhances efficiency in city management: the connection between participative practices and city dashboards can improve efficiency in city management. This can allow governmental authorities to answer in a faster and more efficiently to the demands of the city and of its citizens
Smart Specialisation Platforms (SSPs)	1) More inclusion and representativeness of the parties involved: involving citizens and stakeholders in defining clever specialization strategies can guarantee more inclusion and representativeness of local interests in public policy 2) More legitimation and sustainability of the strategy: activating participative practices can increase the legitimacy of the clever specialization strategy on behalf of the local population, it makes it more sustainable and long lasting 3) More capacity of innovation and adaptation: involving a wide range of stakeholders can lead to a major capacity of innovation and adaptation of volatile demands of the market

(*continued*)

Table 1. (*continued*)

Models and approaches	KeyPrinciples
Analytical models of different methods of participation in behavioural processes	
Shared Space Café	1) In the space, everyone has the same opportunities and duties, regardless of his/her ethnic group, culture, language, education, gender, or social condition
	2) Individuals are respected for their opinions, beliefs and personalities without being undergone to any form of discrimination
	3) Communication is encouraged and resources and ideas are shared openly in the space
	4) Every person is responsible of his/her security and of the one of the others. Before taking any action, a notice is communicated
	5) The environment is planned to support diversity, in this environment people from different extractions can collaborate freely
	6) Participants in the shared space can see above their differences and they can work together towards shared visions and goals, this creates a sense of community
	7) Creativity and innovation are encouraged and people have the power to grow and develop throughout tutoring, sharing knowledges and developing competences
Open Space Technology (OST)	1) Whoever comes is the right people: there is no need to invite specific individuals, on the contrary, it is trusted that whoever is present it is the right group of people to address the issue
	2) Whatever happens is the only thing that could have: the group should not lose time in lingering on what could have been or what should have been, instead, it should focus on what is happening in the very moment
	3) Whenever it starts is the right time: instead of trying to strictly manage the opening times or the session times, it should be allowed to the session to start when the group is ready and enthusiastic
	4) When it is over, it is over: it is better to leave the session to finish when it is naturally done instead of imposing arbitrary limits of time
	5) The law of two feet: every individual is encouraged to assume the responsibility of his/her learning process and of his/her participation and to undertake all the necessary actions to maximize his/her learning and contribution. This includes the possibility to leave or attend to the sessions as desired
	6) The importance of offering: encouraging participants to offer suggestions or ideas, but also to be open to suggestions and ideas of other people
	7) The research of the passion: allowing people to deepen topics for which they have a specific passion instead of trying to cover all the topics in a superficial way
	8) The power of participation: encouraging participation of as many people as possible, this includes people that traditionally could not talk in formal contexts

(*continued*)

Table 1. (*continued*)

Models and approaches	KeyPrinciples
World Café	1) Create hospitable space in which participants can feel themselves welcomed and at ease in sharing their ideas 2) Encourage everyone's participation and dedication, independently from his/her role or position 3) Focus on conversations instead of on presentations or conferences 4) Plan questions that inspire creative thinking and open dialogue 5) Facilitate discussions in small groups that allow focused and more intimate conversations 6) Encourage participants to contribute with their prospectives and experiences to the conversation 7) Encourage participants to actively listen and to build on other people's ideas 8) Use of visual instruments to increase communication and comprehension 9) Co-create significate and comprehension throughout thoughts and synthesis 10) Encourage participants to act at the base of intuitions and ideas generated through the World Cafè process
Appreciative Inquiry	1) Based on investigation: the Appreciative Inquiry (AI) is based on a participated and collaborative process of investigation. The process is focused on the exploration of the best of people, of their organization and other areas of interests 2) Based on strength points: the process is projected to identify strength points of individuals and of organization and to use them to obtain better results 3) Appreciation: the process is gratefully driven and encourages people to evaluate and recognise other's strength points 4) Collaborative: Appreciative Inquiry is a collaborative process that encourages all the interested parties to participate and co-create solutions 5) Indefinitely timing: it is an indeterminate approach, this means that it doesn't exist a pre-determined result. On the contrary, the goal is to explore and discover new possibilities 6) Engagement: Appreciative Inquiry encourages active participation and engagement from all the interested parties, this creates a sense of involvement and belonging 7) Development: Appreciative Inquiry is an approach to development, focused on building what works well to create a better future both for individuals and organizations 8) Action oriented: Appreciative Inquiry underlines actions towards the achievement of positive results, combining strategic planification and implementation 9)Sustainable: the approach is built to be sustainable, with a focus on long-term benefits more than only towards to short-term gains

(*continued*)

Table 1. (*continued*)

Models and approaches	KeyPrinciples
Participatory rural appraisal (PRA)	1) Participation: PRA is a participative methodology that involves all the members of the community, included farmers, women, youngsters, and disadvantaged people 2) Approach based on local knowledge: PRA recognises that people who live and work in rural areas have a deep knowledge of their natural resources, of the wild fauna, of the plants and the earth condition 3) Collaboration and partnership: PRA encourages collaboration between members of the community, not governmental organization (NGOs), government and other partners 4) Use of visual and interactive methods: PRA uses visual and interactive methods, as maps, diagrams, approach walk, and other participative techniques to promote collective discussion and comprehension 5) Respecting and valuing community members' rights: PRA must respect and enhance community members' rights, including the ones of women, youngsters, disadvantaged people, and elderly 6) Sharing knowledge and information: PRA is based on sharing knowledges and information between community members, partners, and other interested parties 7) Action oriented approach: PRA is focused on an action-oriented approach, promoting the use of pragmatic and sustainable solutions to solve local issues 8) Respect for the environment and the culture: PRA takes in account cultural and environmental aspects of the community. It promotes conservation and sustainable use of natural resources
Public Participation Geographic Information Systems	1) Online mapping platforms that allow individuals and communities to actively participate to collect, analyse and share spatial data 2) It integrates GIS and participative methods to consent to locals, planners and decision makers to collaborate and take informed decisions about the use of soil, environmental issues and infrastructure development 3) PPGIS technologies allow people to collect and share data about natural characteristics and the artificial ones, as the position of important reference points or cultural sites, areas that need reactivation or environmental protection and critical points for the traffic congestion or public security issues 4) The PPGIS instruments offer different modes for users to interact and visualize data, as the creation of maps, the generation of reports or the creation of scenarios that show the potential impact of different decisions 5) PPGIS applications have been used in various contexts as urban planification, environmental management, disaster response and community development 6) PPGIS allows citizens to be involved in decisional processes about issues that would interfere with their everyday life; in this way it would contribute to create a more participative and democratic society

(*continued*)

Table 1. (*continued*)

Models and approaches	KeyPrinciples
Participatory Leaning and Action (PLA)	1) Collaborative and inclusive: PLA underlines the importance of involving all the interested parts in learning and decisional process, including the ones that are traditionally emarginated or excluded 2) Contextualized: PLA recognises that learning and action must be eradicated in specific cultural, social, economic, and political contexts of the community and the organization 3) Experiential: PLA encourages active and practical learning through practical experiences that promote considerations and critical thinking 4) Empowering: PLA aims to increase capacities of individuals and communities to act for themselves and to influence decisional processes 5) Continuous: PLA recognises that learning and action are ongoing and they should be continuously evaluated, reviewed and improved 6) Reflective: PLA underlines the importance of thoughts and self-consciousness in the process of learning and action, including recognition and challenging dynamics of power and prejudices 7) Action oriented: PLA gives priority to development and implementation of the action and concrete strategies to face issues and objectives of the community and the organization 8) Adaptive: PLA recognises that learning and action must be flexible and sensitive to changing circumstances and new information
Local knowledge mapping (LKM)	1) Collaboration: LKM is a collaborative process which plans involvement of different interested parts to identify sources and gaps of knowledge 2) Participation: LKM promotes participation involving local communities in the mapping process and allowing them to have easy access to information 3) Local property: LKM is focused on building local property of knowledge, ensuring that it is relevant and useful for local communities 4) Contextualization: LKM requires contextualization of knowledge taking into account of the social, cultural and environmental contexts that shape it 5) Diversity: LKM recognises diversity of knowledge and perspectives sources. It recognises that knowledge is not limited to experts and academics 6) Interdisciplinary approach: LKM reunites different disciplines such as anthropology, geography, and ecology, in order to create a holistic understanding of local knowledge 7) Ethical considerations: LKM follows ethical guidelines to collect, analyse and disseminate local knowledges. It guarantees the respect of confidentiality and informed consent 8) Sustainability: LKM aims to create sustainable and long-lasting knowledge nets that can be adapted and improved through time

(*continued*)

Table 1. (*continued*)

Models and approaches	KeyPrinciples
Metaverse and Performance Modelling	1) Expanding participative experience: it allows to create a virtual simulation in which participants can interact in a more dynamic and involving way than traditional participative practices 2) Communication improvement: models and visual representation can help participants to better understand the information and to communicate more effectively during participative practices 3) Building future scenarios: to create virtual models can allow participants to visualize and experiment possible future scenarios in more concrete way; it would give a support to decisional processes 4) More collaboration during practices means to involve competences and knowledge of professionals coming from different education fields. This kind of multidisciplinary collaboration can lead to major consciousness and understanding of complex issues that are faced 5) Cost reduction: use of virtual modes can reduce costs such as time, money and resources needed for traditional participative practices, it will increase decisional process efficiency and improve citizen participation

citizens as effectively as possible, ii) the consideration of the particular spatial context and the best innovative techniques and technologies for that specific spatial and cultural reality, represent key decisions for achieving a conscious development. Figure 1 shows these relationships also considering climate change in highly vulnerable areas such as coastal zones.

4 Discussions and Conclusions

Local communities and other stakeholders (e.g., governments, academic institutions, community-based organisations, etc.) should be actively involved in coastal zone climate management decision-making processes to ensure that their concerns and specific requirements are represented in planning and implementation phases. The above mentioned bottom-up approaches recognise the complex interrelationships between the environment, economy, and society and aim (i) to create a collaborative and inclusive approach to coastal zone management, (ii) to assist planners (and other professionals) and policy makers understand the social, economic, and ecological context of coastal areas, (iii) to help identify potential trade-offs and conflicts that must be addressed in the management of these areas, and (iv) to develop a standard methodology for high-resolution coastal zone assessments.

Participatory practices can also contribute to the development of social capital and community resilience in the face of climate change's effects. Collaborative decision-making can facilitate cooperation and problem-solving by fostering trust and mutual understanding among stakeholders. This enables the development of self-organisation and social networks that can be mobilised to respond to the effects of climate change, such as adapting to changes in managing sea level rise, storm surges and erosion.

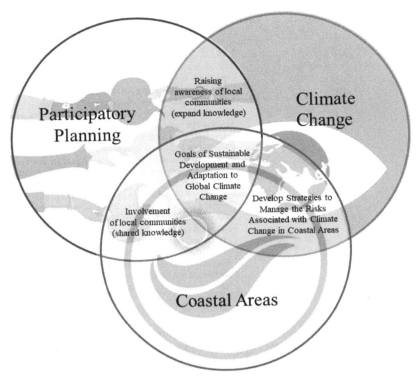

Fig. 1. Relationships between Climate Change, Coastal Zones, and Participatory Planning

In African cities, such bottom-up practices allow to involve previously marginalized communities by integrating their local knowledge and perceptions, which is essential for improving quality of life and reducing risk in unplanned and spontaneous settlements. Participatory practices in the context of coastal zones and climate change can also contribute to more equitable outcomes for all stakeholders. Planners, policymakers, community-based organisations and research institutions can ensure that the requirements and concerns of marginalised groups are taken into consideration by involving a diverse range of voices and perspectives in the decision-making process. The success of technology-based participatory practices is closely tied to the selection of the most appropriate technology for the context under investigation, as well as an involvement that does not manipulate the citizens involved. Participatory practices stimulate collaboration and inclusiveness in decision-making processes and have proven to be a valuable aid in coastal zone management. All these bottom-up approaches acknowledge that all individuals with diverse perspectives and experiences (including the marginalised population) can provide valuable insights and contribute to co-produce practical solutions to complex problems. This study emphasises the significance of openness, responsibility, and equity in decision-making processes. Participatory planning approaches are crucial tools for coastal communities to address the effects of climate change on climate-vulnerable ecosystems in coastal zones. Integrating stakeholder needs and expectations into local climate change policies and involving coastal communities are key to the success of these approaches. Coastal communities can take charge of their future and devise strategies to adapt to the effects of climate change while safeguarding vital ecosystems through participatory planning. By doing so, they can reach community resilience and contributing to sustainable development.

Future studies will look at the application of the proposed theoretical framework to various case studies in vulnerable coastal areas in different continents and with unique morphologic characteristics.

Authors' Contributions. This paper is the result of the joint work of the authors. 'Abstract', 'Methodological Approach for Vulnerable Coastal Zones', and 'Comparison Between Participatory Planning Best Practices' were written jointly by the authors. GD wrote 'Results'. CG wrote the 'Introduction'. CL wrote 'Discussion and Conclusions'. EO wrote 'Climate Change and Participatory Practices: Why coastal zones?'. CL wrote 'Discussion and Conclusions'. CG coordinated and supervised the paper.

Acknowledgements. This study was supported by the project "ISL - Forming interdisciplinary Island Communities of Practice operating for sustainable cultural tourIsm models", small scale Erasmus+ project (KA210-ADU-6B12071A), DE02 - Nationale Agentur Bildung für Europa beim Bundesinstitut für Berufsbildung. This study was also supported by the project "ISL+, People-oriented, place-based and locally driven planning approach supporting island cultural tourism development", Erasmus+ project (KA220-ADU - Cooperation partnerships in adult education), DE02 - Nationale Agentur Bildung für Europa beim Bundesinstitut für Berufsbildung (Project under evaluation). This study was also supported by the technical-scientific collaboration agreement "PON METRO 2014–2020 AXIS 6 - Action CA6.1.1.b - Cagliari smart city: Integration of urban governance with the mitigation of urban heat islands (CA_UHI)" signed between the Municipality of Cagliari and the University of Cagliari (DICAAR - Department of Civil and Environmental Engineering and Architecture). This study was carried out within the RETURN Extended Partnership and received funding from the European Union Next-GenerationEU (National Recovery and Resilience Plan – NRRP, Mission 4, Component 2, Investment 1.3 – D.D. 1243 2/8/2022, PE0000005).

References and Notes

1. United Nations Framework Convention on Climate Change (2022). https://www.sciencedi rect.com/topics/earth-and-planetary-sciences/united-nations-framework-convention-on-cli mate-change. Accessed 17 Apr 2023
2. Participatory Urban Planning for Climate Change Adaptation. https://unfccc.int/files/bodies/ awg/application/pdf/05_vanessa_castan-broto.pdf. Accessed 17 Apr 2023
3. Garau, C.: Citizen participation in public planning: a literature review. Int. J. Sci. 1(12), 21–44 (2012)
4. Garau, C.: Processi di piano e partecipazione. Gangemi Editore Spa (2013)
5. Castán Broto, V., Boyd, E., Ensor, J.: Participatory urban planning for climate change adaptation in coastal cities: lessons from a pilot experience in Maputo, Mozambique, current opinion. Environ. Sustain. **13**, 11–18 (2015). https://doi.org/10.1016/j.cosust.2014.12.005
6. Loggia, C., Govender, V.: A Hybrid methodology to map informal settlements in Durban, South Africa. In: Proceedings of the Institution of Civil Engineers - Engineering Sustainability, vol. 173, no. 5, pp. 257-268 (2020).https://doi.org/10.1680/jensu.19.00005

7. Moore, S.A., Brown, G., Kobryn, H., Strickland-Munro, J.: Identifying conflict potential in a coastal and marine environment using participatory mapping. J. Environ. Manage. **197**, 706–718 (2017). https://doi.org/10.1016/j.jenvman.2016.12.026

8. Different Models and Concepts of (Youth) Participation (2011). https://www.academia.edu/2548314/Different_Models_and_Concepts_of_Youth_Participation. Accessed 17 Apr 2023

9. Kearney, J., Berkes, F., Charles, A., Pinkerton, E., Wiber, M.: The role of participatory governance and community-based management in integrated coastal and Ocean management in Canada. Plan. Theory Pract. **79–104** (2006). https://doi.org/10.1080/10.1080/08920750600970511

10. AR5 Climate Change 2014: Impacts, Adaptation, and Vulnerability. https://www.ipcc.ch/report/ar5/wg2/. Accessed 17 Apr 2023

11. Forum on Cities and Subnationals (henceforth the Forum) at the UNFCCC Warsaw COP in November 2013. https://unfccc.int/event/forum-on-experiences-and-best-practices-of-cities-and-subnational-authorities-in-relation-to. Accessed 17 Apr 2023

12. Climate Change 2022: Impacts, Adaptation and Vulnerability (2022). https://report.ipcc.ch/ar6/wg2/IPCC_AR6_WGII_FullReport.pdf. Accessed 17 Apr 2023

13. Climate Change 2007: Working Group II: Impacts, Adaptation and Vulnerability (2022). https://archive.ipcc.ch/publications_and_data/ar4/wg2/en/ch20s20-8-2.html. Accessed 17 Apr 2023

14. More participatory democracy to tackle climate change (2021). https://assembly.coe.int/LifeRay/POL/Pdf/TextesProvisoires/2021/20210622-ClimateDemocracy-EN.pdf. Accessed 17 Apr 2023

15. Laignel, B., Vignudelli, S., Almar, R., et al.: Observation of the coastal areas, Estuaries and Deltas from space. Surv. Geophys. (2023). https://doi.org/10.1007/s10712-022-09757-6

16. Williams, D.S., et al.: Vulnerability of informal settlements in the context of rapid urbanization and climate change. Environ. Urban. **31**(1), 157–176 (2019)

17. Chambers, R.: Participatory mapping and geographic information systems: whose map? who is empowered and who disempowered? who gains and who loses? Electron. J. Inf. Syst. Dev. Countries **25**(1), 1–11 (2006). https://doi.org/10.1002/j.1681-4835.2006.tb00163.x

18. Massey, D., Jess, P.M.: A Place in the World? Places. Oxford University Press, Oxford, UK, Cultures and Globalization (1995)

19. Elwood, S.: Negotiating knowledge production: the everyday inclusions, exclusions, and contradictions of participatory GIS research. Prof. Geogr. **58**(2), 197–208 (2006). https://doi.org/10.1111/j.1467-9272.2006.00526.x

20. 60 participatory learning and action Community-based adaptation to climate change. https://www.iied.org/sites/default/files/pdfs/migrate/14573IIED.pdf. Accessed 17 Apr 2023

21. Ross, H., et al.: A participatory systems approach to understanding climate adaptation needs. Clim. Change **129**(1–2), 27–42 (2015). https://doi.org/10.1007/s10584-014-1318-6

22. Contestabile, M.: Participatory planning. Nat. **3**, 861 (2013). https://doi.org/10.1038/nclimate2021

23. Samaddar, S., et al.: Successful community participation in climate change adaptation programs: on whose terms? Environ. Manage. **67**(4), 747–762 (2021). https://doi.org/10.1007/s00267-020-01421-2

24. Salazar, V.: From practices to praxis: ASEAN's transnational climate governance networks as communities of practice. J. Curr. Southeast Asian Aff. (2023). https://doi.org/10.1177/18681034231167443

25. Swanson, K.: Centering equity and justice in participatory climate action planning: guidance for urban governance actors. Plan. Theory Pract. (2023). https://doi.org/10.1080/14649357.2023.2189288

26. White, S.C.: Depoliticising development: the uses and abuses of participation (La dépolitisation du développement: usages et abus de la participation / Despolitisando o desenvolvimento: participação: usos e abusos/Despolitizando el desarrollo: los usos y abusos de la participación). Dev. Pract. **6**(1), 6–15 (1996). http://www.jstor.org/stable/4029350
27. People working together around the world to generate ideas and action for social change. https://www.participatorymethods.org/method/levels-participation. Accessed 17 Apr 2023
28. Participation Models A chase through the maze Citizens, Youth, Online. https://www.nonfor mality.org/wp-content/uploads/2012/11/Participation_Models_20121118.pdf. Accessed 17 Apr 2023
29. Behavior Wizard (2022). https://behaviordesign.stanford.edu/resources/behavior-wizard. Accessed 17 Apr 2023
30. Gaventa, J.: Finding the Spaces for Change: A Power Analysis. https://www.powercube.net/ wp-content/uploads/2009/12/finding_spaces_for_change.pdf. Accessed 17 Apr 2023
31. Core Values, Ethics, Spectrum – The 3 Pillars of Public Participation. https://www.iap2.org/ page/pillars. Accessed 17 Apr 2023
32. A potpourri of participation models. https://www.nonformality.org/2011/07/participation-pot pourri/. Accessed 17 Apr 2023
33. Making a Difference: A guide to Evaluating public participation in central government. http://www.sp.gov.tr/upload/Sayfa/47/files/Making_a_Differece_-_A_guide_to_e valuating_public_participation_in_centralgovernment.pdf. Accessed 17 Apr 2023
34. Varieties of Participation. https://organizingengagement.org/models/varieties-of-participa tion/. Accessed 17 Apr 2023
35. Participation Online – The Four C's. https://participationpool.eu/resource/participation-onl ine-the-four-cs/. Accessed 17 April 2023
36. Garau, C., Annunziata, A.: Smart city governance and children's agency: an assessment of the green infrastructure impact on children's activities in Cagliari (Italy) with the tool opportunities for children in urban spaces (OCUS). Sustainability **11**(18), 4848 (2019)
37. Fogg, B.J., Eckles, D.: The behavior chain for online participation: how successful web services structure persuasion. In: de Kort, Y., IJsselsteijn, W., Midden, C., Eggen, B., Fogg, B.J. (eds.) PERSUASIVE 2007. LNCS, vol. 4744, pp. 199–209. Springer, Heidelberg (2007). https://doi.org/10.1007/978-3-540-77006-0_25
38. Chiordi, S., Desogus, G., Garau, C., Nesi, P., Zamperlin, P.: A preliminary survey on smart specialization platforms: evaluation of European best practices. In: Gervasi, O., et al. (eds.) Computational Science and Its Applications – ICCSA 2022 Workshops. ICCSA 2022. Lecture Notes in Computer Science, vol. 13382. Springer, Cham (2022). https://doi.org/10.1007/978-3-031-10592-0_7
39. Garau, C., Nesi, P., Paoli, I., Paolucci, M., Zamperlin, P.: A big data platform for smart and sustainable cities: environmental monitoring case studies in Europe. In: Gervasi, O., et al. (eds.) ICCSA 2020. LNCS, vol. 12255, pp. 393–406. Springer, Cham (2020). https://doi.org/ 10.1007/978-3-030-58820-5_30
40. Azzari, M., Garau, C., Nesi, P., Paolucci, M., Zamperlin, P.: Smart city governance strategies to better move towards a smart urbanism. In: Gervasi, O., et al. (eds.) ICCSA 2018. LNCS, vol. 10962, pp. 639–653. Springer, Cham (2018). https://doi.org/10.1007/978-3-319-95168-3_43
41. Mannaro, K., Baralla, G., Garau, C.: A goal-oriented framework for analyzing and modeling city dashboards in smart cities. In: Bisello, A., Vettorato, D., Laconte, P., Costa, S. (eds.) SSPCR 2017. GET, pp. 179–195. Springer, Cham (2018). https://doi.org/10.1007/978-3-319-75774-2_13
42. Mannaro, K., et al.: Towards a smart region: the case study of a teledermatology platform in Sardinian region (Italy). In: 2017 IEEE 13th International Conference on Wireless and Mobile Computing, Networking and Communications (WiMob), pp. 370–377. IEEE (2017)

43. Rashid, A., et al.: RES-Q an ongoing project on municipal solid waste management program for the protection of the Saniq River basin in Southern Lebanon. In: Gervasi, O., et al. (eds.) ICCSA 2021. LNCS, vol. 12956, pp. 536–550. Springer, Cham (2021). https://doi.org/10. 1007/978-3-030-87010-2_40

44. Shared Space Café. https://organizingengagement.org/models/shared-space-cafe/. Accessed 17 Apr 2023

45. Metodologie Participative. https://www.format.bo.it/metodologie-partecipative/ Accessed April 17, 2023

46. Introducing Participatory Approaches, Methods and Tools. https://www.fao.org/3/ad424e/ ad424e03.htm. Accessed 17 Apr 2023

47. Mayoux, L. Participatory Methods. https://watsanmissionassistant.org/wpcontent/uploads/ 2018/08/participatory-methods-_linda-mayoux.pdf. Accessed 17 Apr 2023

48. Hemmerling, S.A., et al.: Elevating local knowledge through participatory modeling: active community engagement in restoration planning in coastal Louisiana. J. Geogr. Syst. **22**(2), 241–266 (2019). https://doi.org/10.1007/s10109-019-00313-2

49. Mariotti, M., Gervasi, O., Vella, F., Cuzzocrea, A., Costantini, A.: Strategies and systems towards grids and clouds integration: a DBMS-based solution. Futur. Gener. Comput. Syst. **88**, 718–729 (2018). https://doi.org/10.1016/j.future.2017.02.047

50. Biondi, G., Franzoni, V., Gervasi, O., Perri, D.: An approach for improving automatic mouth emotion recognition. In: Misra, S., et al. (eds.) ICCSA 2019. LNCS, vol. 11619, pp. 649–664. Springer, Cham (2019). https://doi.org/10.1007/978-3-030-24289-3_48

51. Vella, F., Neri, I., Gervasi, O., Tasso, S.: A Simulation framework for scheduling performance evaluation on CPU-GPU heterogeneous system. In: Murgante, B., et al. (eds.) ICCSA 2012. LNCS, vol. 7336, pp. 457–469. Springer, Heidelberg (2012). https://doi.org/10.1007/978-3-642-31128-4_34

52. Riganelli, M., Franzoni, V., Gervasi, O., Tasso, S.: EmEx, a tool for automated emotive face recognition using convolutional neural networks. In: Gervasi, O., et al. (eds.) ICCSA 2017. LNCS, vol. 10406, pp. 692–704. Springer, Cham (2017). https://doi.org/10.1007/978-3-319-62398-6_49

53. Perri, D., Sylos Labini, P., Gervasi, O., Tasso, S., Vella, F.: Towards a learning-based performance modeling for accelerating deep neural networks. In: Misra, S., et al. (eds.) ICCSA 2019. LNCS, vol. 11619, pp. 665–676. Springer, Cham (2019). https://doi.org/10.1007/978-3-030-24289-3_49

54. Laganà, A., Gervasi, O., Tasso, S., Perri, D., Franciosa, F.: The ECTN virtual education community prosumer model for promoting and assessing chemical knowledge. In: Gervasi, O., et al. (eds.) ICCSA 2018. LNCS, vol. 10964, pp. 533–548. Springer, Cham (2018). https:// doi.org/10.1007/978-3-319-95174-4_42

55. Simonetti, M., Perri, D., Amato, N., Gervasi, O.: Teaching math with the help of virtual reality. In: Gervasi, O., et al. (eds.) ICCSA 2020. LNCS, vol. 12255, pp. 799–809. Springer, Cham (2020). https://doi.org/10.1007/978-3-030-58820-5_57

56. Nicholls, R.J., et al.: Ranking port cities with high exposure and vulnerability to climate extremes: exposure estimates (2008). https://doi.org/10.1787/011766488208

Legal Protection Issues for Sustainable Waterfront Development: The Athenian Riviera, Greece

Foteini Bageri[✉]

Judge (Associate Councilor) of the Hellenic Council of State, Athens, Greece
fotini.bageri@gmail.com

Abstract. The Greek coastal territory, having a coastline length of 15,000 km, constitutes a major natural resource and, at the same time, a sensitive ecosystem that needs increased protection, in order to preserve its natural capital and its landscape, but also to ensure the citizens' free access to the sea. Its management, as a transitional zone between land and sea, is directly related to maritime spatial planning and the principle of sustainability. The research attempts to highlight critical issues of the coastal area's legal protection, during its exploitation and planning, choosing as a case study the part of Athens sea front, from the Faliron Bay to the area of the former "Hellinikon Airport" which forms the main "openness" of Athens to the sea. The selection of the research's subject and study area was due to the great urban regenerations that were and are being elaborated in it, as a result of the state's and individuals' interest for its investment, exploitation and utilization. The research methodologically approaches the issues from the point of view of the coastal area's legal protection provided by the institutional framework and its implementation by the Hellenic Council of State.

Keywords: coastal cities · sustainable waterfront development · maritime spatial planning · integrated coastal zone management · sustainability and climate adaptation

1 Introduction

The Greek coastal area, with a coastline of 15,000 km, is a dominant feature of the Greek territory, an extremely important national resource and a significant comparative national advantage at the level of the European Union [1, 2]. At the same time, however, it is a sensitive ecosystem that requires increased protection, due to the scope and intensity of the economic and manmade activities that are developed in it, which burden its carrying capacity. The management of coastal zones, which constitute the transition zone between land and sea, is directly linked to maritime spatial planning [3], which aims to ensure that all activities organised in maritime areas are rationally managed so that they are within the framework of the principle of sustainability [4].

   The research attempts, in essence, to highlight the legal protection issues of the coastal area and, in particular, the part of the coastal front of Attica, from the Faliron

© The Author(s), under exclusive license to Springer Nature Switzerland AG 2023
O. Gervasi et al. (Eds.): ICCSA 2023 Workshops, LNCS 14105, pp. 269–287, 2023.
https://doi.org/10.1007/978-3-031-37108-0_17

Bay to the area of the former "Hellinikon airport", which constitutes the main opening of the city of Athens to the sea. The reason for the selection of this particular area was the fact that, in recent decades, the development and investment interest of the state and private investors has focused on the spatial configuration, exploitation and use of this part of the coastal area of Attica, resulting in the intensification of uses and pressures and the formation of an environmentally and spatially burdened coastal area. Particularly decisive for that selection was, on the one hand, the choice of the state to proceed, about a decade ago, with the redevelopment of the Faliron Bay and on the other hand, the decision of the state to proceed, during approximately the same period of time, with the investment and development exploitation of the single property of the area of the former "Hellinikon airport".

The basic axis of reference which governs the examination of all the individual vision perspective of the study is the basic jurisprudential principle that has been formulated by the country's Supreme Administrative Court (namely the Hellenic Council of State - 'Symvoulio tis Epikrateias'- hereinafter CoS or the Court) that the coasts, which are vulnerable ecosystems within the meaning of Article 24 of the Greek Constitution (hereinafter Constitution), must be subject to a special regime of soft management, in harmony with the constitutionally enshrined principle of sustainable development. This regime is usually the subject of a specific law but in any event, in the absence of a specific legislative protection regime, the coast is directly subject to the protection imposed by Art. 24 of the Constitution and Article 130P of the Maastricht Treaty.

The above-mentioned constitutional protection of the coast requires, first and foremost, the drawing up of the relevant spatial plans [5], which has unfortunately not yet taken place, despite the fact that attempts have been made to regulate the spatial planning of the coastal zone with the draft Special Spatial Planning and Sustainable Development Frameworks for the Coastal Area of 2003 (Ministry of Environment and Spatial Planning) and 2009 (Ministry of Environment and Spatial Planning), which were never approved [3]. The protection of the coastal area and the planning of activities in the marine area is one of the most important issues that are in the focus of interest both in Greece, the European Union and third countries and, at the same time, a challenge for the Greek public administration and the sciences related to the areas' planning [6].

2   Methodology and Sources

Place of Reference: The paper approaches the issue methodologically from the point of view of the protection of the coastal area provided by the institutional texts and their interpretation and implementation by the Court and focuses its interest, spatially and temporally, on the two most important - due to their spatial consequences - urban interventions, namely the redevelopment of the Faliron Bay and the development of the area of the former "Hellinikon airport" (Fig. 1).

Research Process-Sources: Methodologically, the research was based, first of all, on the search and study of secondary sources, namely, the protection of the coastal area provided by the institutional texts (national, EU and international legislation) and their implementation by the Court (case law), with emphasis on the study area, as well as the relevant scientific articles and literature on the subject. In addition, for a better understanding of the specific area's spatial particularities, as well as its environmental dimensions and for the adequate support of secondary sources, a field survey was carried out in the area, which demonstrated the legal protection issues and problems of the coastal area in question. In particular, the fieldwork helped to identify and shed light on many and varied economic activities and uses currently taking place in the area and to shed light on the emerging conflicts between them, as well as the interrelationship and dynamics that are developing between them and the adjacent land area.

3   The Coastal Zone from the Faliron Bay to the Former "Hellinikon Airport": Characteristics and Peculiarities

The development of the urban complex of Athens has evolved rapidly and in such a way that, as has been vividly observed, 'the city seems to be turning its back on the sea' [7]. The shores of the Saronic Gulf have also been at the centre of development and investment pressures over the last twenty years and a number of fragmentary zoning schemes for public and private uses have fragmented its coastline. Today, the coastal front of Attica from the Faliron Bay to the coastal zone of the former "Hellinikon airport", which is mostly occupied by the sports and Olympic facilities of Ag. Kosmas, brings together a complex network of supra-local uses of tourism, sports, nautical facilities, recreational infrastructure, transport, marinas, catering (restaurants, bars, cafes), shops, having as the dominant use that of the marina (tourist port). It is characteristic that in the specific area five (5) marinas (Athens Marina, Kallithea Delta Marina, Flisvos Marina, Alimos Marina and Ag. Kosmas Marina) have been located and are in service.

The consequence of the fragmentation of uses, the concentration and densification of all these activities and land uses on this coastal area is, first of all, that the accessible part of the coastal area, especially the seashore and the beach, is reduced, making it difficult and, in some cases, impossible for citizens to access the sea. Given the fact that redevelopment projects are under way in the wider area of the Faliron Bay, which makes access to the coast difficult and dangerous, it is characteristic that very few open parts of the seashore and beach remain for the common use and enjoyment of citizens. The coastal section from the Peace and Friendship Stadium to Agia Marina of Kropia is protected, in principle, by the Presidential Decree of 1.3/5.3.2004 on the determination of protection zones, land use and building conditions from the Faliron Bay to Agia Marina Kropia, a particularly useful institutional tool for the protection of the coast, the control of supra-local uses and inter-municipal cooperation in coastal management.

The coastal front of the area under consideration (Fig. 1) belongs administratively to the Regional Unit of the South Sector of Athens, is located in a position of central importance for the city and constitutes the natural outlet to the sea for the city of Athens. It is approximately 12 km long and consists of the coastal areas of the municipalities of Moschato-Tavros, Kallithea, Paleo Faliron, Alimos and Elliniko – Argyroupolis. Particularly, the coastal zone of the Faliron Bay, 2 km long, ranging in width from 25 to 900 m, is historically the natural outlet of the Athens Basin area to the Saronic Sea and covers an area of 800 acres along the coastline, including the coastal zone around the urban areas of Moschato, Kallithea and Paleo Faliron, from the mouth of the Kifissos River to the Municipal Sports Centre of the municipality of Paleo Faliron. Within the

Fig. 1. The place of reference: From Faliron Bay to the former Hellinikon airport [11–14]

Faliron Bay to the left of the Peace and Friendship Stadium and the adjacent Marina, one of the most important spatial interventions that have ever taken place in the coastal area of Attica is underway but these projects have come to a standstill.

On the other hand, the development and utilisation of the former "Hellinikon airport" has followed its own parallel fifty-year course of successes and failures, from 1978, the year in which it was decided by law that this land would be commercially exploited to finance the construction of a new airport in Spata. During this period many studies have been carried out but, as Professor L. Wassenhoven has aptly underlined, the case of the former "Hellinikon airport" is a typical example of the chronic inability of the state (central, regional) and local government to respond to spatial planning on such a scale [8]. The area of the Metropolitan Pole of Hellinikon-Ag. Kosmas of the Region of Attica is administratively integrated within the boundaries of the Municipalities of the former "Hellinikon airport"- Argyroupolis, Alimos and Glyfada. Along its western boundary (towards the beach side of Ag. Kosmas) it is bounded by the coastal Poseidonos Avenue and the residential area of the lower former "Hellinikon airport". On the eastern boundary is Vouliagmeni Avenue. It has an area of approximately 6,008 acres. It is about 10 km from the centre of Athens and the Acropolis and it consists of three individual properties: the former "Hellinikon airport", with a surface area of 5.249.873 sq.m., the former Olympic Sailing Centre of Agios Kosmas and the National Youth Sports Centre. The last two constitute the coastal front of the Metropolitan Pole of Hellinikon-Ag. Kosmas, and, after deducting the areas occupied by the seashore and the beach (197.600 sq.m.), have a total surface area of 758.203 sq.m.

The area of the former "Hellinikon airport", after the Olympic Games and the transfer of the airport to Spata, took on the form of an "urban void", the spatial status of which was the subject of only fragmentary regulations in the post-Olympic period. However, although this property has been of great interest to the legislator since 2011, it has not since then acquired a spatial identity in its entirety. With the approval of the Integrated Development Plan of the Metropolitan Pole of Hellinikon-Agios Kosmas of the Region of Attica by the Presidential Decree of 28.2.2018 (Government Gazette A.A.P. 35), an attempt is made to implement the overriding, strategically important planning contained in the new Athens Regulatory Plan (Law 4277/2014), which elevates the Metropolitan Pole of Hellinikon-Agios Kosmas not only to a metropolitan, but also to a national and international pole of national and international scope. On the other hand, due to the intensity and extent of the environmental impacts [9, 10], but also the spatial and social footprint that the planned project would have, serious reservations were raised about its construction and implementation by various collective representative bodies and citizens, but also in the context of public discourse [11–14], in view of the fact that the exploitation of the area in question was promoted in the context of the country's memorandum obligations and the need for rapid economic growth.

4 Legal Protection Issues: Priorities for Coastal Sustainability and Resilience

4.1 Exceeding Carrying Capacity

Coasts as fragile ecosystems are directly subject to the protection imposed by Article 24 of the Constitution (CoS 3944/2015, 2713/2013, 4542/2009, 2506/2002, 3346/1999) and must be subject to a special regime of soft management and development, in line with the constitutionally enshrined principle of sustainable development. The over-concentration of marina, fishing, tourism and catering uses in the coastal area of the region, in view of the fragile nature of coastal ecosystems, raises a major issue of legal protection of the carrying capacity of the coastal area, which is exceeded by the exploitation of those uses, in breach both of Article 24 of the Constitution and of the Protocol on Integrated Coastal Zone Management in the Mediterranean, which is an integral part of the International Convention for the Protection of the Marine Environment and the Coastal Region of the Mediterranean and at the same time part of European Union law.

4.2 Failure to Adopt the Special Framework for Spatial Planning and the Coastal Zone's Sustainable Development

The issues of the coastal area's legal protection highlight the need for a comprehensive planning of activities developed in the marine and terrestrial space, which requires a comprehensive understanding of local conditions and particularities. The sustainable coexistence of land uses and activities, as well as their appropriate and rational location in the marine and coastal area, requires an integrated planning and management approach through the field of maritime spatial planning and, in particular, Integrated Coastal Zone Management (ICZM). While the spatial planning system in Greece has a sufficient number of tools for the strategic management of spatial issues arising at national and regional level, the coastal area has not been addressed in total. The elaboration of the Spatial Planning and Sustainable Development for the Coastal Area Special Framework is intended to cover the coastal protection deficit, in accordance with Law 4546/2018, with which the important Directive 2014/89/EU was incorporated into the national legal order.

4.3 Compatibility of Existing Uses and Building Conditions - Restrictions by the Presidential Decree of 1/5.3.2004

Reservations are expressed as to whether the presidential decree of 1/5.3.2004 has been observed by the Planning that has been prepared and implemented, and is still being observed in practice, in the development of all man-made activities and uses within the critical coastal area. It would therefore be an interesting subject for another study, which would aim to investigate whether the existing or ongoing planning is in line with the provisions of the 2004 decree for the coastal zone (from Faliron Bay to Ag. Marina Kropia). It is therefore very important that state control and supervision is carried out in order to ensure that existing and new uses and activities comply with this institutional framework.

4.4 Violation of Beach and Shore's Public Character and Legislation

The field survey revealed, among other things, a generalised process of granting to municipalities or private individuals the exclusive use of the seashore and the beach of the area concerned, resulting in the violation of the public nature of the seashore and the beach. The coast is not only a source of income for the State, local authorities or private individuals, but, above all, a place where the State and the local authorities should carry out environmental restoration and improvement projects from the contributory fees collected. On the contrary, in parts of the area concerned, the field survey found out that private enterprises are operating on the seashore and the beach under exclusive concession contracts that negate their public nature, in violation of the provisions of Law 2971/2001, the latter of which only allows simple and not exclusive use and require the demolition of any arbitrary structure built within them. It is therefore appropriate to establish a state mechanism for monitoring the terms and conditions of concession agreements and the demolition of unauthorised constructions on the seashore and the beach.

4.5 Lack of Accessibility

The spatial planning which has taken place over the past decades in the coastal area concerned has resulted in the virtual disconnection of the urban complex from the coastal zone. One of the factors contributing to this was the fact that Poseidonos Avenue divided the city in two and in some places completely cut off the view of the sea, erecting a wall between it and the urban complex. This was due to the fact that spatial planning was not sufficiently combined with sectoral planning (e.g. transport), having as a direct consequence that the roads' layout and transport traffic contributed even more to the spatial exclusion of the sea from the urban complex. In the light of the provisions of Law 4546/2018 and the Protocol on the Integrated Coastal Zone Management and in conjunction with the state's obligation, under Art. 2 of Law 2971/2001 for the protection of the coastal zone ecosystem, the provisions of Art. 13 and 15 of Law 2971/2001 must be interpreted as having the concept that only the concession to primary local authorities of non exclusive rights over the seashore and the beach for the exercise of - mild and compatible with the designation of those elements as common property - activities is permitted. Consequently, activities such as bar-restaurants are activities, which are not compatible with the character and purpose of the seashore as a natural asset in common use, are not permitted by law.

4.6 Violation of Coastal Ecosystems, Landscape Aesthetics and Coastal Zones' Geomorphology Integrity, in View of Climate Change and the European Green Agreement

The Climate change and environmental degradation threaten coastal zones, as well as the very existence of Europe and the world. Extensive intervention in the coastal area concerned has resulted in the degradation of the natural environment, adversely affecting and altering its geomorphology and aesthetics. Within the level of legal protection provided by the European legislation, the Community Directive 2001/42 "on the assessment of the environmental effects of certain plans and programmes", which was incorporated into the Greek legal order by the Ministerial Decision 107017/2006 (Government Gazette B1225/5.9.2006), establishes the obligation to assess the environmental impact of plans and programmes of national, regional, prefectural or local character. Projects and activities developed in coastal zones definitely fall within the scope of the aforementioned Directive.

5 The Judicial Dimension in Coastal Areas' Legal Protection

A. General issues

Although the wording and terminology of Article 24 par. 2 of the Constitution refer to land spatial planning, since the activities described take place by definition on land (town planning, development, shaping, development and expansion of towns and residential areas, ensuring the best possible living conditions), however, the case-law of the Court has given the concept of spatial restructuring of the country an integral dimension, so as to include maritime spatial planning [15].

5.1 Coasts

According to the established case law of the Court, the two obligations imposed, by Article 24 of the Constitution, on the State, namely the obligation to protect the natural and cultural environment and the spatial planning of the country "are obviously interdependent, so that there can be no protection of the environment without spatial planning and vice versa" (CoS 1243/2016, 670/2020, 4542/2009 7 m., 2506/2002 7 m. etc.). Within this framework, the ecosystems of the country's coasts are treated as part of the natural environment, indeed vulnerable (CoS 978/2005) and as such need increased protection (CoS 1500/2000). In particular, the coasts must, in the sense of the above constitutional requirement, be under a special regime of soft management and development, which alone is sustainable, i.e. in line with the constitutionally enshrined principle of sustainable development (CoS 3944/2015, 2713/2013, 4542/2009, 2506/2002, 3346/1999). Moreover, the protection of the coast is also ensured at supranational level by the Protocol of the Integrated Coastal Zone Management of the Mediterranean, which is an integral part of the international Convention for the Protection of the Marine Environment and the Coastal Region of the Mediterranean, i.e. the Barcelona Convention, ratified by Law 855/1978 and forms part of EU law (CoS 3977/2010, 2752/2013, see also judgment of the ECJ of 7.10.2004, Commission v France C-239/03 on the protection of Lake Berre). The above-mentioned constitutional protection of the coastline presupposes, first and foremost, the preparation of the relevant spatial plans, which must include for example all types of port works, which constitute substantial technical interventions and alterations to coastal ecosystems (CoS 1343/2016, 2430/2010, 3940/2008, 2266/2007, 1340/2007, 978/2005, 2506/2002, 1507/2000, 1434/1998, 4634/1997, etc.).

5.2 Seashore and Beach _ Arbitrary Construction

Moreover, the Court has consistently ruled (CoS 76/2020, 4442, 2245, 1229/2014 etc.) Law 2971/2001 establishes an administrative procedure for the determination of the boundary line of the seashore as a natural phenomenon, i.e. the maximum normal wave height in a given land zone. Law 2971/2001 regulates and protects, in principle, only certain zones of the coastal area, namely the coastal zone, the beach, the coastal zone up to 100 m from the coastline and the ports. According to the case law of the Court, arbitrary buildings erected wholly or partly within the sea or the sea are subject to compulsory demolition. In addition, the Court ruled that Article 970 of the Civil Code lays down a basic rule of public law according to which the assignment by the administrative authority to natural or legal persons of special rights to common property is lawful only if and in so far as, even after the assignment of those rights, the common use of the property continues to be served or at least is not negated (CoS in plenary session 394/1963, 1377/1971, 2799/1972, 61/1974, 1467/1990, 891 - 895/2008, 2685/2010 7 m.). This rule is repeated, in the case of the seashore, in the relevant special administrative legislation (Law 2971/2001, Articles 2, 13, 14 and 15).

5.3 Direct Concession of the Right of Beach and Seashore's Simple Use to a Local Government Organization

With regard to the status of direct concessions to primary local authorities issue in exchange for the right of simple use of the beach and the bank and riparian zone of large lakes and navigable rivers, the Court has repeatedly accepted (CoS 1630/2016, 646/2015, 3944/2015 7 m. etc.) that the provisions of Articles 13 and 15 of Law 2971/2001, interpreted in the light of Article 24 of the Constitution, but also of the Protocol on Integrated Coastal Zone Management in the Mediterranean, must be interpreted as having the meaning that the concession of the right of beach and seashore's simple use to primary local authorities for the exercise of mild activities must be carried out individually and on a case-by-case basis, following an individual assessment by the administration, accompanied by the necessary diagrams in order to ensure its intended use as a public asset.

5.4 Sustainable Development

Within this framework, as has been ruled by several Court decisions, Art. 24 par. 1 and 6, elevates the natural and cultural environment to an independently protected asset. The competent organs of the State are required to take positive action for the effective safeguarding of this asset and, in particular, to take the necessary legislative and administrative, preventive and repressive, measures, intervening to the extent necessary, in economic or other individual or collective activity. In taking those measures, the legislative and executive bodies must take into account other factors relating to the general national and public interest, but the pursuit of those objectives and the balancing of the respective legal interests to be protected must go hand in hand with the State's obligation to protect the environment in such a way as to ensure sustainable development for the benefit of future generations. Furthermore, from the provisions of Art. 24 par. 1 and 2, 79 par. 8 and 106 par. 1 of the Constitution, it follows that spatial planning, which is the spatial expression of economic and social development programmes, is the responsibility of the State, which is obliged, in accordance with the principles and findings of the science of spatial planning, to take the measures necessary for rational spatial planning in order to ensure the protection of the environment, the best possible living conditions for the population and economic development in accordance with the principle of sustainability. Within this framework, an essential factor for sustainable development and the protection of sensitive ecosystems are the spatial plans, which set the long-term objectives of economic and social development and regulate, inter alia, the framework for the development of residential areas (CoS in plenary session 3632/2015, in plenary session

3920/2010, 4189, 4966/2014, 1421, 1422, 4784, 4785/2013, 3396–7/2010, 3037/2008, 705/2006, 1569/2005 etc.).

In particular, in the exercise of the annulment of an administrative act, the judge examines, inter alia, whether the environmental impact assessment, which is the basic instrument for applying the prevention and precautionary principle, meets the requirements of the law and whether its content is sufficient to enable the competent administrative bodies to assess and evaluate the risks and consequences of the project or activity and to assess whether the realisation of the project or activity is likely to lead to a significant reduction in the environmental impact of the project or activity.

B. Particular Issues

Related to the area from the Faliron Bay to the former "Hellinikon airport"

5.5 Opinion 55/2002 _ Approval of the Olympic Facilities Area and the Redevelopment of the Faliron Bay E.S.O.A.P.

The Court accepted that since, under Law 2730/1999, the development of the pole of the Faliron Bay is post-Olympic and is simply linked to the Olympic works, its creation is intended, inter alia, to improve the general development of its area and, therefore, to solve its problems and indeed its fundamental problems. The designation of the Faliron Bay and its wider area as a supra-local pole of activities (tourism, recreation, social services and culture), linked to the Olympic works, but without the large-scale development previously envisaged, means that the legislator, respecting the protection of the coastline imposed by Article 24 of the Constitution, does not tolerate the use of land siltation as a method of increasing the area of the pole to serve all the activities developing in the pole, except to the extent that it is necessary for the creation of the Olympic facilities and the solution of the basic problems of the wider area. On this basis, the Court held that the measures provided for by the draft presidential decree.

5.6 CoS 2173/2002 _ TRAM Project

The Court held that the Athens Regulatory Plan Law (R.S.A.) was adopted in compliance with Art. 24 paragraph 1 and 2 of the Constitution. The provisions of Law 1515/1985 provide for guidelines, programmes and measures for the upgrading of the natural and man-made environment, which bind the Administration in the exercise of its regulatory power or the adoption of individual acts. Within the meaning of those provisions and in particular Art. 15A paragrah 2, the areas of the supra-local poles, including the Faliron Bay, must be accessible to the inhabitants of Attica, and indeed with the desired creation of a single network of connections to serve their recreational, sporting and cultural needs. The legislator, in order to draw up the Athens regulatory plan, specifically weighed the need to protect the environment of the wider Athens area and, in the context of this protection, provided, among other things, for a fixed-track system of public transport as a high level of service. Therefore, the provision in itself of the project at issue (Law 1515/1985) is not contrary to Art. 24 paragraphs 1 and 2 of the Constitution.

5.7   Opinion 371/2003 _ Definition of Protection Zones, Land Uses and Building Conditions and Restrictions from the Faliron Bay to Agia Marina Kropias

The Court observed that the execution of a technical project on the coast, such as the creation of an artificial sandy beach, is allowed only for reasons of public interest and provided that it is compatible with the ecosystem concerned. Consequently, a provision of the plan authorising the creation of new bathing beaches, and indeed indiscriminately in any part of the regulated coastal zone, was not lawful because it did not appear that there were reasons in the public interest requiring such an intervention, which was not compatible with the natural function and aesthetics of coastal ecosystems.

5.8   Opinion 132/2013 _ Approval of Faliron Bay's Integrated Regeneration Programme

The Court accepted that Art. 1 paragraph 2(c) of Law 2730/1999, which added to the category of supra-local recreational, sports and cultural poles originally, provided for by Law 1515/1985, the category of tourism-recreation and social services use, does not contradict Art. 24 of the Constitution. Furthermore, the Court ruled that the activities authorised by Art. 11 of Law 3843/2010 in the redevelopment area of Faliron Bay and consequently the other provisions of that article on the conditions for the structure of the area redevelopment zones (structure and coverage factors), as amended by par. 4 of Art. 51 of Law 4042/2012 do not constitute a deterioration of the residential environment and the living conditions of the residents and do not contravene Art. 24 of the Constitution in force, since they involve a mild intervention in the artificially shaped coast of the Faliron Bay, which improves the existing situation and highlights the character of the area as a supra-regional pole of sport, tourism, recreation, social services and culture, in view of the judicial marginal control.

5.9   Opinion 93/2018 _ Approval of Alimos Marina Master Plan

The Court held that since the plan, in accordance with the Strategic Environmental Impact Assessment and the other elements accompanying it, is consistent with the objectives and guidelines of the new Athens Regulatory Plan, Articles 2 and 3 of the draft presidential decree lawfully modify the existing regulations for the land area of the marina. The Court held that even if ports and tourist ports contribute to the local development of an island or non-island area, the ownership, as well as the choice of how to use, administer, manage and exploit them, belongs in principle to the state, and the legislator has the discretion to choose the most appropriate way to use ports and tourist ports without being obliged to grant their management exclusively to the relevant local authority or to maintain any management granted to a local authority. Therefore, the legislator is not prevented from transferring to the Hellenic Property Fund the right to grant to third parties the rights of use, administration, management and operation of ports and tourist ports, even if the management has been granted to Local Government Organisations (CoS 1155/2016 in plenary session).

Related to the area of the former "Hellinikon airport"

5.10   Opinion in Plenary Session 29/2018 _ SOA "Former Hellinikon Airport"

The Council of State in plenary session (PE 29/2018) gave an opinion that: (a) mild interventions on the coast, the upgrading of the beach and the possibility of constructing an aquarium are legally provided for, in conjunction with the wider redevelopment of the Faliron bay that has been approved by the Court (Opinion 132/2013), (b) the Integrated Development Plan partially modifies the provisions of the Plan of 1.3.2004 Presidential Decree because it provides for the possibility of pure residential and tourism-recreational uses on the coastal front of the Metropolitan Pole Ellinikon - Ag.Kosmas, (c) Only limited coverage (15%) is allowed on the coastal front, which is consistent with the character and physiognomy of the entire property and in order to facilitate the exits of the Park to the sea, (d) The provisions of the draft presidential decree, which establishes residential, urban centre, tourism-recreation, etc. land uses in the area, firstly, or by modifying those already provided for, are in accordance with Article 24 of the Constitution.

5.11   CoS in Plenary Session 1305/2019 _ Legality of the Former "Hellinikon Airport" Integrated Development Plan

The Court ruled that the constitutional (Art. 24(1) and (2)) purpose of protecting the environment and ensuring the best possible living conditions for the population is, in principle, achievable, by linking environmental protection with economic development, also inspired by the Constitution, which, according to the letter of the relevant constitutional provision (Art. 106 (1) and (2)), is, in the first place, achievable through the link between environmental protection and economic development. This is because respect for the environment as a collective good and the preservation of its quality not only do not exclude but also presuppose and are facilitated by the economic development. Conversely, however, economic development, which is achieved, inter alia, through the exploitation of natural resources, may not be pursued without the competent legislative and administrative bodies taking care to protect and preserve the environment, so that economic development may become sustainable, defined by the principle of sustainability, as required by the Constitution. Furthermore, the spatial status of the area was fragmentary and discontinuous, so that any subsequent complete planning of the area and the imposition of new uses and building conditions cannot be understood as a degradation or deterioration of the environment and the living conditions of neighboring areas.

On the contrary, a dissenting opinion of 10 out of 30 judges supported that as far as coastal areas are concerned, the contested presidential decree allows for its urbanisation, with a 40% coverage rate and a predominant use of housing, as well as the construction of a high-rise building, without there being any spatial and/or urban planning necessity for that residential development, but with a view to the most advantageous use of the wider property, the project is based on rules which are not compatible with Art. 24 of the Constitution, in conjunction with Art. 106 thereof, which brings about an unacceptable deterioration of the natural and residential environment of Attica in relation to the previous special planning of the area, and is therefore unlawful.

5.12   CoS in Plenary Session 1761/2019 _ Legality of the Integrated Development Plan of the Former "Hellinikon Airport" and Environmental Impact Study

The Court, reiterating its 1305/2019 decision, held that a) under Directive 2001/42/EC "on the assessment of the effects of certain plans and programmes on the environment", there was no obligation to prepare a Strategic Environmental Impact Assessment before the adoption of the relevant Law 4062/2012, issued after the Medium-Term Fiscal Management Programme, or the Law 4422/2016, b) the consultation procedure followed was not contrary to either Directive 2001/42/EC or the Aarhus Convention, c) the examination of the compatibility of the integrated development plan with the "Attica landscape" does not fall within the competence of the archaeological service and that the provision of tall buildings does not violate the cultural environment and, therefore, does not constitute a violation of Art. 24 par. 1 and 6 of the Constitution and d) the integrated development plan does not constitute an impermissible deterioration of the environment and a deterioration of the residential conditions in relation to the previous status of the area, which constituted an "urban void" and was characterised by discontinuity.

5.13   CoS in Plenary Session 2776/2020 _ Ownership of the Former "Hellinikon Airport's" Public Spaces

The Court found that State owns 70% of the land of the Metropolitan Pole and the investor will receive 30% of the land on an undivided basis under the purchase and sale agreement concluded. However, before this happens, the property will be divided into areas of exclusive ownership of the State (70% of the land) and, prospectively, of the investor (30%), thus creating two portions of exclusive ownership, the first of the State and the second of the investor. However, there is no indication that the common areas will be included in the investor's share. On the contrary, it is clear from the content of the purchase contract and the legislation that the State and not the investor will control, through regulations and the adoption of standards, the public spaces of the Metropolitan Pole.

5.14   CoS 895/2021 _ Legality of the Spatial Organisation of Development Zones PM-A1 and PM-A2 St. Kosmas Marina Neighbourhood and St. Kosmas Aquarium Neighbourhood

The Court's decision 895/2021 ruled that the approval of the spatial organization of the Development Zones PM-A1 Agios Kosmas Marina Neighborhood and PM-A2 Agios Kosmas Aquarium Neighborhood of the Metropolitan Pole of Hellenic area - Agios Kosmas and the environmental conditions thereof was legal.

6   Conclusions and Discussion

During the last twenty years, the area from the Faliron Bay to the former "Hellinikon airport" has been at the centre of the economic commitments of the Greek state, but also of the state's objective change for the development of Attica's coastal front. The plans for the Olympic projects further aggravated Athens relationship with the sea, as they did not seem to facilitate the city's connection to it, taking into account the fact that the Olympic facilities both in Faliron Bay and former "Hellinikon airport" remained largely unused, devalued and closed.

6.1 Regarding Legislation: The Spatial Legislation as a Result of the Changing Needs of the Greek State

The study of the evolution of spatial planning legislation for the area concerned allows, in my opinion, to draw some conclusions in relation to the spatial implications of the legislative production as regards the coastal area. First of all, the relevant legislative production did not take place by chance or occasionally, but it was the consequence of the alterations of the Greek State's economic, social, developmental and spatial needs and priorities over time. Furthermore, the increase in legislative production for the area concerned during the last two decades, initially for the redevelopment of the Faliron Bay and later for the Hellinikon, is part of the change of the legislator's targeting under the pressure of the economic crisis and the need of the Greek state to repay its public debt and to create appropriate conditions for attracting investment and development, creating jobs and exploiting the privileged competitive advantage of Attica's coastal area.

6.2 Regarding the Field Research _ The Spatial Footprint of the Legislation

While the area of the Faliron Bay seemed to acquire a new form and potential for the overall upgrading of the metropolitan complex, through the plans of the Olympic Games, nevertheless, a significant part of the Integrated Redevelopment Plan carried out in the context of the Olympic preparations remained unused and was gradually discredited, while the remaining part of the infrastructure and redevelopment projects was never implemented, due to the time constraints and financial limitations at the time. As a result, the resolution of major environmental and operational problems of the capital associated with these projects suspended the city's dynamism and devalued the completed Olympic Games projects. On the other side of the coastal front, the area of the former "Hellinikon airport", after the Olympic Games and the transfer of the airport to Spata, assumed the form of an "urban void" and it had not acquired a spatial identity in its entirety. Appeals for annulment brought by citizens and collective bodies representing them in the Hellenic Court of State were rejected by the aforementioned decisions of the Court.

   Despite the broad legislative production of spatial planning regulations for the area concerned, the intense state's interest for the regulation of the area, as well as the special institutional tools that had already been established by the legislator since 2002, from which one would expect the implementation of the urban planning and the improvement of the residents' living conditions, as well as the coastal area in general, however, the urban planning did not have the expected results. As the field research has shown, large parts of the study area from the Faliron Bay to the former "Hellinikon airport" showed a picture of abandonment, degradation or poor maintenance. It remains to be seen in practice what the new regenerations spatial impact on both sides of the area will be, when they will have been completed.

Furthermore, the control of land use in the coastal area, which was attempted especially with the decree of 1/5.3.2004, was not accompanied by the corresponding control of residential development in the land zone in the immediate vicinity of the coastal front. Another major problem identified during the field survey is the coverage of large parts of the seashore and beach by the extensive concession of the right to use the beach and the seashore, which results in the annulment of their public nature, in apparent violation of the relevant legislation, as well as their constitutional protection status. It is therefore necessary to revise that regime, to monitor its lawful operation and, in certain cases, to reduce the number of concessions which have led to the de facto occupation of the whole part of the seashore and the beach.

In my opinion, the unbalanced development and institutionalization of the various uses and activities in the wider coastal zone under consideration undermines the objectives of the spatial planning and the project of Attica's coastal front spatial planning itself. In other words, it seems that what the legislator of the presidential decree of 1/5.3.2004 attempted to do in the coastal front of the area is in practice annulled by the legislator's fragmentary attempt to regulate individual parts of the coastal area. The reference to the critical legislative framework and the case law examples demonstrate, in my opinion, that the management of the coastal zone in Greece is characterised by a diffusion of responsibilities and a lack of coordination at the level of planning and control of natural and man-made activities. The lack of coordination at the planning level is partly due to the unavoidable fact that urban planning is different in time and therefore fragmented and when it is carried out, it responds to the alterations of state's local authorities' or private parties' social, economic and development needs.

Inevitably, the study puts at the heart of the search of the causes, which have contributed to the current poor state of the critical coastal area, the issue of its sustainability and sustainable development, which is the great challenge of spatial planning and urban design. It can be seen that while the debate in Europe on integrated coastal zone management has been underway since the early 2000s (signing of the Madrid Protocol of 21.1.2008 on integrated coastal zone management in the Mediterranean), Greece is still too late to incorporate the parameter of maritime spatial planning and integrated coastal zone management into its legislation and policies. Only in 2018, Law 4546/2018 incorporated into the Greek legislation the Directive 2014/89/EU for the marine spatial planning. Before that, Law 3983/2011 had already incorporated the Framework Directive 2008/56/EC on Marine Strategy, but it had not any tangible effects on the protection of the coastal area. The importance of marine spatial planning is demonstrated by the fact that it is the process by which the competent authority analyses and organises human activities in marine and coastal areas in order to achieve the synthesis of ecological, environmental, economic, social and cultural aspects with the aim of promoting sustainable development.

However, the sustainable coexistence of uses and activities and their appropriate and rational land use planning in the marine and coastal area requires an integrated planning and management approach through the field of marine spatial planning, which is a bracket of the Integrated Coastal Zone Management. The lack of integrated management of Attica's coastal zone is, in my opinion, responsible - to a large extent - for the problems it is currently experiencing. The challenges for the country are expected to be of great importance, if one considers that already Law 3851/2010 on the development of Renewable Energy Sources, and earlier, Law 3468/2006, allowed the installation of floating wind parks within the national maritime space [16].

6.3 Legal Protection Issues

The legal protection issues, which have been raised by the adoption of "zoning" legislation for the coastal area concerned and by the practice of the administration and private parties, have at their core the degradation of the marine and coastal space and the excess of its carrying capacity by the over-concentration of incompatible land uses and the violation of the integrity and quality of the marine ecosystem. Furthermore, a question arises as to the compatibility of the existing land uses with the Presidential Decree of 1/5.3.2004.

Moreover, the violation of the seashore's public nature and protective legislation through the extensive concessions of the right to use the beach and the seashore, makes it impossible for citizens to access the coastal area and cancels their public nature. The lack of approval of the Special Framework for Spatial Planning and Sustainable Development of the Coastal Area and Tourism is therefore of particular importance and should become a priority of the Greek state in order to address the legal protection problems, as well as the spatial problems which the survey highlighted, because it will help address and solve the contradictions, discontinuities and incompatibilities between the various sectoral uses (transport, tourism, housing, recreation, marinas, etc.).

6.4 Relevant Hellenic Council of State's Case Law

With regard to the jurisprudential treatment by the Hellenic Council of State of the coastal area's legal protection issues, the Court has consistently accepted that Article 24 of the Constitution imposes on the State, on the one hand, the obligation to protect the natural and cultural environment, and on the other hand, it imposes the spatial organization of the country, which is entrusted to the State. Those two obligations are clearly interdependent, so that there can be no protection of the environment without spatial planning and vice versa. Through its case-law, the Court has made a decisive contribution to the protection of the coast, the foreshore and the beach and the coastal ecosystems in general.

Moreover, the Court held, in essence, that the investment and development of the area of the former "Hellinikon airport" is lawful, while preserving the public character of the coastal front of the Metropolitan Pole and the Metropolitan Green Park, based on the consideration that the objective of protecting the environment and ensuring the best possible living conditions for the population, as enshrined in Art. 24 of the Constitution, can be achieved by linking the environment to economic development and, conversely, economic development can be sustainable when it is defined by respect for the protection of the environment. In any event, although the Court held that the Presidential Decree which established the Integrated Development Plan of the Ellinikon, in so far as it was challenged, did not infringe Art. 24 on the environmental protection, it nevertheless reiterated its case-law that, in any event, a deterioration of the inhabitants' living conditions and the land uses is tolerable, if it is necessitated by exceptional reasons of public interest, following a balancing exercise by the formal or regulatory legislature, which is subject to marginal judicial review.

Apart from that, the projects for the development of the former "Hellinikon airport" and the regeneration of the Faliron Bay constitute, in my opinion, fundamental political choices which belonged from the beginning to the legislature and the state's administration. Therefore, the judicial review of related acts is "marginal" and it cannot reach the correctness and feasibility of these choices, as the Court repeated on the occasion of the Hellinikon case and the judge's intervention is limited to a narrow review of the extreme limits of the administration's discretion, that is, the search for manifest errors in the weighing of development prospects against environmental risks [17, 18].

The concept of sustainability and sustainable development is a legal concept and a general principle of international environmental law, as well as of the Greek Constitution [19–21], the violation of which is marginally controlled by the judge. In particular, as the Hellenic Council of State has held, in the exercise of the judicial review, which also includes the error of fact, the judge examines, inter alia, whether the environmental impact study, which is the basic instrument for applying the precautionary principle, meets the requirements of the law and whether its content is sufficient to enable the competent administrative bodies to discern and assess the consequences of the project or activity and to assess whether its implementation complies with the provisions of the relevant legislation, as well as with the constitutional requirements and the definitions of the EU Treaty.

However, the direct assessment by the court of the consequences of a project or activity and the assessment of whether its implementation is contrary to the principle of sustainable development are beyond the scope of the judicial review, because they require an examination of technical issues and a substantive assessment of the factual circumstances. It is certain that the Hellenic Council of State, following the evolution and transformations of the Greek state, the economy and society, will be confronted, in the coming years, with important issues of coastal protection.

In conclusion, coastal areas should not only be seen as recreational areas or transport routes with unlimited potential in terms of building and residential activity, recreation, tourism and navigation, but also as sensitive and finite ecosystems. Major urban redevelopments such as those of the Faliron Bay and the former "Hellinikon airport" demonstrate, in my opinion, that it is necessary to seek synergies between the public and private sectors in order to satisfy public interest objectives, one of which is the enjoyment of the coastal area by citizens. The need to make use of public property and the sustainable development of public property leads to the search for the point of optimum balance, where the combination of public and private interests, environmental protection, social welfare, preservation of cultural capital and economic development is achieved. It remains to be proven in the future and in practice the feasibility of the realisation of the gigantic investment of the former "Hellinikon airport" and the Faliron Bay and their sustainability, in case they are finally materialized.

Acknowledgements. This research is the subject of the author's post-graduate thesis in the framework of the Master's Programme 'Urban and Spatial Planning' under the supervision of Associate Professor Yiota Theodora [National Technical University of Athens (N.T.U.A.), School of Architecture, October, 2021].

References

1. Coccossis, H.: Presentation of the results of a study-research of coastal area and islands in YPEXODE (2001). (in Greek)
2. Coccossis, H.: Coastal and Island area. In: Proceedings of a Conference, pp. 35–41. Zappeion Hall (1999). (in Greek)
3. Wassenhoven, L.: Marine Spatial Planning, pp. 126–289, University Publications of Crete (2017). (in Greek)
4. Coccossis, H., Papatheochari, T.H.: Linking marine spatial planning & integrated coastal zone management. In: Proceedings of the 4th Panhellenic Conference on Urban Planning, Spatial Planning & Regional Development, Volos, University of Thessaly (2015). (in Greek)
5. Sakellaropoulou, K.: The case law of the Hellenic Council of State on the planning and management of the marine and coastal area. In: Serraos, K., Melissas, D. (eds.), Marine Spatial Planning, NTUA, scientific symposium organized by the Department of Urban Planning Research of NTUA, The Hellenic Society for Environment and Culture and the Scientific Society of Urban and Spatial Planning Law, vol. 40, p. VII, Sakkoulas Publications, Athens-Thessaloniki (2018). (in Greek)
6. Serraos, K., Melissas, D.: Marine Spatial Planning, see above, p. VII, Sakkoulas Publications, Athens-Thessaloniki (2018). (in Greek)
7. Polyzos, Y.: Recovering the coastal front of Athens. In: Ecotribes (2015). https://ypodomes.com/y-vvnc-o-oc-avak-v-ac-o-apa-ak-m-w-o-nc-ao-vac
8. Wassenhoven, L.: HELLENIC...Passion: The Development of the Former Hellinikon Airport, p. 361. Sakkoulas Publications, Athens-Thessaloniki (2018). (in Greek)
9. Theodora, Y., Spanogianni, E.: Assessing coastal urban sprawl in the Athens' southern waterfront for reaching sustainability and resilience objectives. Ocean Coast. Manag. 222(6), 106090. https://doi.org/10.1016/j.ocecoaman.2022.106090
10. Theodora, Y., Spanogianni, E.: Athens waterfront development: the public space as a means for sustainable regeneration. In: Passerini, G., Ricci, S. (eds.), The Sustainable City XIV, WIT Transactions on Ecology and the Environment, vol. 249, pp. 219–231. WIT Press (2020). https://doi.org/10.2495/sc200191
11. Wassenhoven, L., Pagonis, T.H., Manos, S.T.: The dialogue for former Hellinikon airport is open (2019). https://www.kathimerini.gr/society/1047891/anoigei-o-dialogos-gia-to-former Hellinikonairport/
12. Newsroom: The former Hellinikon airport will never become the Hide Park of Europe (2010). https://www.kathimerini.gr/society/381518/to-elliniko-den-tha-ginei-pote-to-chaint-park-tis-eyropis/
13. Mpellos, I.: A new town of 10.800 houses in former Hellinikon airport (2019). https://www.kathimerini.gr/economy/local/1053649/mia-nea-poli-10-800-katoikion-sto-elliniko/
14. Mpellos, I.: The way is opened for bulldozers to enter former Hellinikon airport, (2019). https://www.kathimerini.gr/economy/local/1057363/anoigei-o-dromos-gia-na-mpoyn-mpoylntozes-sto-elliniko/
15. Menoudakos, K.: Reflections on the book Marine Spatial Planning by Professor L. Wassenhoven, in Serraos, K., Melissas, D., Marine Spatial Planning, see above (2018). (in Greek)
16. Melissas, D.: Floating wind parks, proposal for an institutional framework for safe investments with minimal public costs. Sakkoulas Publications, Athens-Thessaloniki (2021). 27 and p. III of the Preface
17. Sakellaropoulou, K.: Environment and Development: adjustments and judicial control, Law and Nature (2016). https://nomosphysis.org.gr/13189/perivallon-kai-anaptyksi-stathmiseis-kai-dikastikos-elegxos/

18. Dellis, G.: From the carnage of Pylos to Kassandra's mine. "Sustainable development", between jurisprudence of the judge and fiction of theory, Honorary Volume of the Council of State - 75 years, p.1057 (2004). et seq
19. Decleris, M.: Introduction to Sustainable Citizenship, Guide to 21st Century Policy, Chamber of Environment and Sustainability, p. 226. Sustainable World Publications (2005)
20. Decleris, M.: The Law of Sustainable Development, General Principles, Ant. N. Sakkoulas Publications (2000). (in Greek)
21. Decleris M.: The law of sustainable development, A report produced for the European Commission, Office for Official Publications of the European Communities (2000). https://www.pik-potsdam.de/avec/peyresq2003/talks/0917/sillence/background_literature/sustlaw.pdf

Computational Mathematics, Statistics and Information Management (CMSIM 2023)

Relating Student's Performance with Individual Characteristics

M. Filomena Teodoro[1,2(✉)] ⓘ, Alcindo Delgado[1], and J. M. Martins[1]

[1] CINAV, Center of Naval Research, Portuguese Naval Academy, University Military Institute, 2810-001 Almada, Portugal
mteodoro64@gmail.com
[2] CEMAT, Center for Computational and Stochastic Mathematics, Instituto Superior Técnico, Lisbon University, 1048-001 Lisbon, Portugal
maria.teodoro@tecnico.ulisboa.pt

Abstract. A Portuguese Military Academy has a significant failure rate, losing about half of the admitted individuals during the course. This work aims to understand the causes associated to low income, through the analysis of the data of the individuals from the application to the end of the course, in order to identify the characteristics of individuals with greater and less likely to succeed in the Military Academy. This work was started in [1]. In an initial phase, some techniques of descriptive statistics of data analysis were used. The first step of this analysis, the candidates are analyzed independently, and the admitted and the finalists are analyzed together comparing the variables at the beginning and at the end of the courses. Simple statistical inference techniques were used [30], namely confidence intervals, parametric tests, contingency tables. Such analysis was completed in [31] using intermediate level inference techniques, namely analysis of variance (ANOVA). In the present manuscript we intend to complete this approach using a general linear models approach [20,32] after the selection of factors by factorial analysis [2,3,8,9]. The study evidences greater success for individuals entering in NA with better grades and for individuals taking notice of the application competition over the internet.

Keywords: Indicators of Academic Success · Academic Performance · Optimization of Education · General Linear Models · Factorial Analysis

1 Introduction

The Portuguese Naval Academy has an academic failure rate of around 64%.

More than half of the admitted students do not finish the course. This project arises in order to understand the causes associated to the low performance.

For the NA, a public military university, very restricted for budgetary reasons, there is a need to understand the reasons for failure, that would diminish internal attrition.

Common qualified staff, with the means available to carry out studies of this nature, and a commitment to continuous improvement of the quality of it is a challenge to know the predictors of success.

ⓒ The Author(s), under exclusive license to Springer Nature Switzerland AG 2023
O. Gervasi et al. (Eds.): ICCSA 2023 Workshops, LNCS 14105, pp. 291–302, 2023.
https://doi.org/10.1007/978-3-031-37108-0_18

The institution needs to be able to identify the performance, and be awake to possible irregularities during the process of individuals formation or destructive phenomena of the good performance of the collective and/or individual.

It is mandatory to perform a statistical analysis of individuals from the beginning to the end of the course, to identify the characteristics (denominated variables) of individuals with higher and lower probability to contribute to academic success at the Naval Academy.

The outline of this work consists in five sections. Section 2 describes the motivation and objectives. The statistical models are described in Sect. 3. Section 4 displays some details about the empirical application. In Sect. 5, we present some results and do some discussion. In Sect. 6 we get some conclusions.

2   Preliminaries

2.1   Some Related Studies

In [22] the authors aimed to identify the factors which are able to explain academic success and drop out of IT Croatian students, allowing to explore differences in perception of current students and alumni and to explore differences between genders. A similar study can be found in [19] where three personality factors and stress are evaluated in the sense of explain academic sussec of medicine students. Only two factors and stress were considered significant. In [33] was required to some Japanese accounting students to define success, and to identify five the Factors that affect their success and five factors that affect failure. The work presented in [4] evaluated the influence of personality traits on university performance using a sample of Italian freshmen students. In [7] Furnham considers personality, cognitive ability, and beliefs about intelligence as predictors of academic performance. The studyi ntroduced in [28] assessed the influence of individual characteristics, including personality traits and socio-demographic characteristics, on voluntary engagement in scientific research of undergraduate medical students. In Brazil, considering a sample of students from a small private college and a large public university, the authors of [16] investigate the effects of personality traits, measured by the Big Five (neuroticism, extroversion, openness to experience, agreeableness, and conscientiousness), Core Self-evaluation (locus of control, neuroticism, self-eficacy, and self-esteem), and Grit (loosely defined as enthusiasm and resilience), on academic performance. The results suggest results suggest that investing in some specifc personality traits, such as Grit and conscientiousness can have signifcant payoffs in terms of academic performance. In [10], is done a meta-analyses about visible learning. The authors of [11] perform a meta-analytic review where personality is related with performance motivation. Outhers interesting studies relating personality factors with academic sussecc can be found in literature, for example, in [5, 6, 12–14, 24–27, 34, 35].

2.2   The Institution Details

This work is a case study, that deliberately addresses the Naval Academy of the Portuguese Navy.

The NA, an academy with singular characteristics, is also characterized by its conditions, which shape not only the universe of candidates, but also the success during course attendance.

When competing in NA, the candidate has to face constraints that are not observed in the remaining students in other higher education institutions, detailing:

1. Tests of admission with great physical exigency;
2. Mandatory to wear uniforms on journeys;
3. Freedom inhibition to leave daily;
4. Freedom inhibition to leave if you do not comply with the military regulations;
5. Military discipline, both among peers and with the surrounding environment;
6. Loss the school year if the student fails in a single curricular unit;
7. It is possible to fail a year but its repetition lacks approval and it can only be achieved with exemplary military behavior;
8. Mandatory to spend annually about two months boarded on warships;
9. Accumulates the frequency of an integrated master's degree course with physical preparation, military and naval training, training leadership-oriented behavioral and scientific research in areas linked to the sea;
10. Does not have daily available time for rest or well-being, due to the great time requirements for the studies and for the component as well as for naval military training.

The aim of this study is to analyze the data of the candidates for EN in the sense to relate the academic success or failure of individuals who are admitted to this educational institution, with socio-economic, cultural and performance details.

Although many variables considered for this study could be equally useful for studies of this nature applied to other institutions, any conclusions taken from this study can not be applied to students who integrate different realities from those of the NA.

This institution presents a singular physical environment in the daily life of those who attend.

In order to carry out this project, it was taken into account of certain issues to evaluate, such as:

– The stereotype of the heterogeneity of social classes, and the gender associated with curricular units (or area of knowledge), known as bipolarization of knowledge;
– The phenomenon of increasing female participation in services;
– The functionalist perspective of education.

The dedication of any individual in a common context is seen as a predictor of success, however, because it is a very specific context and other factors, such as low rest level and adaptations to hourly demands, inter alia, overlap with the capabilities of the individual, leading to academic failure.

An oscillation of the variables, from year to year or in the same year, between the group of those admitted and the group of finalists is natural, however, a significant or persistent variation of a variable tends to express some phenomenon or event, especially of a social nature, which is a way of influencing the group or generation, motivation, focus or other levels, which goes against the predisposition of students to academic success in the NA. The main phenomenon targeted by this study is the transition of individuals who entering the NA, from the 1st to the 5th year, and the consequent reduction in the number of individuals who were admitted during this five-year period.

Based on data from the admission years from 2007 to 2011, the NA presents a very high academic failure rate, with a success rate always below 50%, even knowing that individuals who complete their studies have a guaranteed job in the Navy.

To characterize the success profiles in the NA we consider the group of admitted individuals, and within the group of individuals who finish the course successfully.

The data analysis is made in order to identify the predictive variables of success and the information available for the accomplishment of this study.

3   Methodology

3.1   General Linear Models

In the classical linear model, a vector X with p explanatory variables $X = (X_1, X_2, \ldots, X_p)$ can explain the variability of the variable of interest Y (response variable), where

$$Y = Z\beta + \varepsilon \tag{1}$$

and Z is a specification matrix with size $n \times p$ (usually $Z = X$, considering an unitary vector in first column), β a parameter vector and ε a vector of random errors ε_i, independent and identical distributed to a reduced Gaussian.

The data are in the form (y_i, x_i), $i = 1, \ldots, n$, as result of observation of (Y, X) n times. The response variable Y has expected value

$$E[Y|Z] = \mu. \tag{2}$$

GLM is an extension of classical model where the response variable, following an exponential family distribution [32], do not need to be Gaussian. Another extension from the classical model is that the function which relates the expected value and the explanatory variables can be any differentiable function. Y_i has expected value

$$E[Y_i|x_i] = \mu_i = b'(\theta_i), \quad i = 1, \ldots, n. \tag{3}$$

It is also defined a differentiable and monotone link function g which relates the random component with the systematic component of response variable. The expected value μ_i is related with the linear predictor $\eta_i = z_i^T \beta_i$ using the relation

$$\mu_i = h(\eta_i) = h(z_i^T \beta_i), \qquad \eta_i = g(\mu_i) \tag{4}$$

where h is a differentiable function; $g = h^{-1}$ is the link function; β is a vector of parameter with size p (the same size of the number of explanatory variables); Z is a specification vector with size p.

There are different link functions in GLM. When the random component of response variable has a Poisson distribution, the link function is logarithmic and the model is log-linear.

In particular, when the linear predictor $\eta_i = z_i^T \beta_i$ coincides with the canonical parameter θ_i, $\theta_i = \eta_i$, which implies $\theta_i = z_i^T \beta_i$, the link function is denominated as canonical link function.

Sometimes, the link function is unknown being estimated simultaneously with the linear component of the semi-parametric model, for example, for electricity spot prices.

A detailed description of GLM methodology can be found in several references such as [20,32].

3.2 Factorial Analysis

Factor analysis (FA) is technique often used to reduce data. The purpose is to get a reduced number of variables from an initial big set of variables and get easier interpretations [9,17]. The FA computes indexes with variables that measures similar things. There are two types of factor analysis: exploratory factorial analysis (EFA) and confirmatory factorial analysis (CFA) [36]. It is called EFA when there is no idea about the structure or the dimension of the set of variables. When we test some specific structure or dimension number of certain data set we name this technique the CFA.

There are various extraction algorithms such as principal axis factors, principal components analysis or maximum likelihood (see [3,29] for example). There are numerous criteria to decide about the number of factors and theirs significance. For example, the Kaiser criterion proposes to keep the factors that correspond to eigenvalues greater or equal to one.

In the classical model, the original set contains p variables $(X_1, X_2, \ldots, X_p)$ and m factors $(F_1, F_2, \ldots, F_m)$ are obtained. Each observable variable X_j, $j = 1, \ldots, p$ is a linear combination of these factors:

$$X_j = \alpha_{j1} F_1 + \alpha_{j2} F_2 + \cdots + \alpha_{jm} F_m + e_j, \ j = 1, \ldots, p, \tag{5}$$

where e_j is the residual. The factor loading α_{jk} provides an idea of the contribution of the variable X_j, $j = 1, \ldots, p$, contributes to the factor F_k, $k = 1, \ldots, m$. The factor loadings represents the measure of association between the variable and the factor [9, 36].

FA uses variances to get the communalities between variables. Mainly, the extraction issue is to remove the largest possible amount of variance in the first factor. The variance in observed variables X_j which contribute to a common factor is defined by communality h_j^2 and is given by

$$h_j^2 = \alpha_{j1}^2 + \alpha_{j2}^2 + \cdots + \alpha_{jm}^2, \qquad j = 1, \ldots, p. \tag{6}$$

According with the author of [15], the observable variables with low communalities are often dropped off once the basic idea of FA is to explain the variance by the common factors. The theoretical common factor model assumes that observables depend on the common factors and the unique factors being mandatory to determine the correlation patterns. With such objective the factors/components are successively extracted until a large quantity of variance is explained. After the extraction technique be applied, it is needed to proceed with the rotation of factors/components maximizing the number of high loadings on each observable variable and minimizing the number of factors. In this way, there is a bigger probability of an easier interpretation of factors 'meaning'.

4   Empirical Application

4.1   Sample Characterization

This study is applied to a universe of 3091 candidates, of which 295 were admitted, and 103 of these successfully completed the course.

Treatment and cleaning of the information was performed, after which analysis of the data concerning the candidates and the individuals who were during the period under study was completed.

The concept of "transition", often used throughout this work, means the passage from the group of admitted to the success group (finalists) to the over the five-year period that completes the training cycle for officers in the NA.

The decrease of individuals is justified by factors such as disapproval, withdrawal, expulsion, among others.

The simple analysis of collected data conduced to:

– Generally, the age group is between 17 and 26 years;
– Occasionally, individuals with a maximum of 29 years, with no experience except in particular cases, financially dependent;
– They come from public education with daily return to the family home;
– Their origin from all parts of the country and from different social environment;
– Without any kind of preparation for the five years of military education;
– Great attrition during the five year course.

The variables studied in detail were:

– Success (1 - success, 0 failure)
– Gender (1 - Men, 0 - Female)
– Distance to NA (distance between the student's residence and the NA)
– Grade at Entry (note of admission of the student in the NA)
– Higher Education Attendance (1 - attended higher education before entering Naval Academy, 0 - otherwise)
– Knowledge of Contest in Internet (1 - was aware of the internet contest, 0 - otherwise)
– Knowledge of Contest through Family (1 - had knowledge of the contest through relatives, 0 - otherwise)
– Know. Contest Visit EN (1 - had knowledge of the contest through a visit to the Naval School, 0 - otherwise)
– Acc. Higher Educat. (1 - went to higher education beyond the Naval School, 0 - otherwise)
– Parent or Mother Active (1 - If the parents get some income: salary/pension, 0 - otherwise)
– Military/Military Parents (1 - If the parents are/were military/militarized, 0 - otherwise))

In [1, 31] was performed a preliminary analysis, the data was organized using descriptive and some simple inference techniques, namely parametric and nonparametric tests, contingency tables, ANOVA Approach (parametric, nonparametric). In present work we have applied logistic modeling, factorial analysis and discriminant analysis.

5 Results and Discussion

The results described in [1, 31] were confirmed by the logistic model which is still being improved.

From the analysis applied to the variables after the end of the course to characterize the transition phase after five years, we can evidence that success rate is better for groups with smaller number of admitted individuals.

Although of the adversities of integrating women into top-class of the armed forces and certain determinations that defend the stereotype of the gender associated with the discipline, there is significant evidence of no prevalence of gender in relation to performance.

No despite the adversities that the NA presents inherent to a Military life, individuals who fail to complete the course are the ones that have worse entry grade. As a rule, individuals who have better grades can be succeeded.

Although of a greater academic experience, students who already had some experience in higher education previously to their ingress in the NA, their level of the performance does not stand out.

The internet is an excellent way of disseminating NA. Individuals who take notice of the competition through the internet tend to have good performance. Although the family members represent the greater form of disclosure of the NA, this disclosure is not conducive to success. Visits to the NA, despite being programmed with the specific purpose of the competition and the Navy, have proved to be a form of unfavorable disclosure.

Both parents in the active is unfavorable factor to the success of individuals in the NA. This fact may be justified by the possible financial stability that fuels the intolerance of fatigue, the effort and the spirit of sacrifice inherent in military life. To be son of military or militarized parents is unfavorable to success of individuals in the NA. This may be justified by greater willingness on the part of the parents than on the individual about a career as Navy Officer.

The next step of process applies a FA. Considering the factor analysis approach, we summarize the results in Table 1. We estimated the communality for the factors, analyzed the significance of R-matrix (test about the multicollinearity or singularity). The Bartlett's sphericity test provided a strongly significant level p, so we confirmed the existence of patterned relationships. Also, the Kaiser-Meyer-Olkin measure (KMO) of sampling adequacy revealed that the data is appropriate to apply an EFA.

Table 1. Total variance accounted for each factor and component matrix details.

Total Variance Explained[a]

Component	Extraction ... Cumulative %	Rotation Sums of Squared Loadings Total	% of Variance	Cumulative %
1	22,560	1,954	21,706	21,706
2	37,752	1,327	14,742	36,448
3	51,004	1,272	14,137	50,585
4	63,764	1,186	13,179	63,764
5				

Table 2. Rotate component matrix details.

Rotated Component Matrix[a,b]

	Component			
	1	2	3	4
Distance	,155		,258	-,756
Grade	,386	,529	-,344	
Attendance	-,120		,625	
Knowledge Internet	,925			
Knowledge Family	-,903	,251		
Knowledge Visit		-,617	-,399	
Apply Higher	,135		,662	
MotherFather Employed	-,258	,763		,125
MotherFather_Militar			,287	,755

In Table 1 is presented the total variance associated to the eigenvalues accounted by each factor by descendent order. The ith line corresponds to cumulative variance percentage explained by the first i factors after extraction and after rotation. Notice that Table 1 also contains information about rotated component matrix and component score component matrix (Tables 2 and 3).

If we consider the Kaiser criterion for simplicity, we retain the first 4 factors (eigenvalues great or equal to one). Other criteria may be applied, for example using the scree plot or using the average of extracted communalities to determine the eigenvalue cutt-off. The varimax algorithm which produces orthogonal factors was applied after the extraction process. This technique is adequate when we want to identify variables to create indexes or new variables without inter-correlated components. In the present case, we could get the 'meaning' of each factor. Namely each factor is related with:

Table 3. Component score coefficient matrix.

Component Score Coefficient Matrix[a]

	Component			
	1	2	3	4
Distance	,030	,041	,203	-,635
Grade	,226	,448	-,299	-,026
Attendance	-,054	-,085	,496	,073
Knowledge Internet	,486	,089	,076	,044
Knowledge Family	-,455	,133	,038	-,045
Knowledge Visit	-,019	-,448	-,280	,081
Apply Higher	,075	,032	,520	-,061
MotherFather Employed	-,081	,571	-,094	,082
MotherFather_Militar	,114	,047	,222	,651

F1- How took knowledge of admission contest; **F2**- Economic level of family; **F3**- Previous attendance of higher education; **F4**- Combines distance of family residence and knowledge of military environment.

6 Conclusion

In present work it is performed a statistical analysis of individuals from the beginning to the end of the course, to identify the characteristics (denominated variables) of individuals with higher and lower probability to contribute to academic success at the Naval Academy. The data collection corresponds to the time interval 2007–2011, it is not complete, more "5 years" data set shall be considered to be analyzed statistically so we can get a more detailed analysis.

This sample can be considered to get some results as an alert to the need and value of ongoing study to a larger horizon.

By first it was performed a descriptive analysis and applied an analysis of variance [1,31].

In a second stage it is on going the analysis of results from logistic model approach simultaneously with the results from Factorial Analysis.

The statistical approach, estimating a model with relevant information using more elaborate techniques such as generalized linear models was performed. The model improvement and validation is still going on. The statistical process was explained, but not detailed. It is still going on the naming of selected factors, the obtained results and factors scores will be described in detail on an extended version of this article. Relationships between socio-demographic variables and success are being evaluated.

Some important issues about academic success in NA were obtained, reinforcing the importance and need of prevention measures implementation. For improved success and quality of performance of the candidates is necessary an early diagnosis and an early and appropriate intervention. Prevention is possible by controlling known and modifiable risk factors.

Prevention requires a higher degree of awareness and possibly the implementation of awareness campaigns promoting regular assessment of the individual performance. Another line of study is to take into consideration similar studies [5, 6, 12–14, 23–27], using the big five personality traits related with academic success. In the present worK was applied an Experimental FA, in future, we will apply a confirmatory FA with five factors.

Acknowledgements. This work was supported by Portuguese funds through the Center of Naval Research (CINAV), Portuguese Naval Academy, Portugal and The Portuguese Foundation for Science and Technology (FCT), through the Center for Computational and Stochastic Mathematics (CEMAT), University of Lisbon, Portugal, project UID/Multi/04621/2019.

References

1. Gomes, A.D.: Rentabilização de Capital Humano. Master Thesis, Escola Naval, Almada (2016)
2. Anderson, T.W.: An Introduction to Multivariate Analysis. Wiley, New York (2003)
3. Child, D.: The Essentials of Factor Analysis. Continuum International Pub. Group, New York (2006)
4. Corazzini, L., D'Arrigo, S., Millemaci, E., Navarra, P.: The influence of personality traits on university performance: evidence from Italian freshmen students. PLoS ONE **16**(11), e0258586 (2021). https://doi.org/10.1371/journal.pone.0258586
5. McCrae, R.R., Costa, P.T.: Personality in Adulthood: A Five-Factor Theory Perspective. Guilford Press, New York (2003)
6. De Feyter, T., Caers, R., Vigna, C., Berings, D.: Unraveling the impact of the Big Five personality traits on academic performance: the moderating and mediating effects of self-efficacy and academic motivation. Learn. Individ. Differ. **22**(4), 439–448 (2012). https://doi.org/10.1016/j.lindif.2012.03.013
7. Furnham, A., Chamorro-Premuzic, T., McDougall, F.: Personality, cognitive ability, and beliefs about intelligence as predictors of academic performance. Learn. Individ. Differ. **14**, 49–66 (2003)
8. Hair, J.F., Anderson, R.E., Tatham, R.L., Black, W.C.: Multivariate Data Analysis, 4th edn. Prentice Hall, New Jersey (1998)
9. Harman, H.H.: Modern factor analysis. Univ. of Chicago Press, Chicago, IL (1976)
10. Hattie, J.A.: Visible Learning: A Synthesis of Over 800 Meta-Analyses Relating to Achievement. Routledge, Oxon (2009)
11. Judge, T.A., Ilies, R.: Relationship of personality to performance motivation: a meta-analytic review. J. Appl. Psychol. **87**(4), 797–807 (2002). https://doi.org/10.1037/0021-9010.87.4.797
12. Komarraju, M., Karau, S.J.: The relationship between the big five personality traits and academic motivation. Pers. Individ. Differ. **39**(3), 557–567 (2005). https://doi.org/10.1016/j.paid.2005.02.013

13. Komarraju, M., Karau, S.J., Schmeck, R.R.: Role of the big five personality traits in predicting college students' academic motivation and achievement. Learn. Individ. Differ. **19**(1), 47–52 (2009). https://doi.org/10.1016/j.lindif.2008.07.001

14. Komarraju, M., Karau, S.J., Schmeck, R.R., Avdic, A.: The Big Five personality traits, learning styles, and academic achievement. Pers. Individ. Differ. **51**(4), 472–477 (2011). https://doi.org/10.1016/j.paid.2011.04.019

15. Marôco, J.: Análise Estatística com o SPSS Statistics. Report Number, Pêro Pinheiro (2014)

16. Mello, M.A., Coelho, C.A., Oliveira, L.A.: Personality traits and academic performance: evidence from college students in Brazil. R. Bras. Eco. de Emp. RBEE **22**(1), 5–20 (2022)

17. Mood, A.: Introduction to the Theory of Statistics. McGraw-Hill Inc., Auckland (1984)

18. Moreira, P., Pedras, S., Pombo, P.: Students' personality contributes more to academic performance than well-being and learning approach–implications for sustainable development and education. Eur. J. Investig. Health Psychol. Educ. **10**(4), 61132–1149 (2020). https://doi.org/10.3390/ejihpe10040079

19. Nechita, F., Alexandru, D.O., Turcu-Ştiolică, R., Nechita, D.: The influence of personality factors and stress on academic performance. Curr. Health Sci. J. **41**(1), 47 (2015). https://doi.org/10.12865/CHSJ.41.01.07

20. McCullagh, P., Nelder, J.A.: Generalized Linear Models. Chapman & Hall, Londres (1989)

21. Noftle, E.E., Robins, R.W.: Personality predictors of academic outcomes: big five correlates of GPA and SAT scores. J. Pers. Soc. Psychol. **93**, 116–130 (2007)

22. Oreški, D., Hajdin, G., Kliček, B.: Role of personal factors in academic success and dropout of IT students: evidence from students and alumni. TEM J. 5(3), 371–378 (2016). https://doi.org/10.18421/TEM53-18

23. Paunonen, S.V., Ashton, M.C.: Big five predictors of academic achievement. J. Res. Pers. **35**(1), 78–90 (2001)

24. Poropat, A.E.: An examination of the relationship between personality and citizenship performance in academic and workplace settings. Doctoral Dissertation, Griffith University, Brisbane, QLD (2005)

25. Poropat, A.E.: A meta-analysis of the five-factor model of personality and academic performance. Psychol. Bull. **135**(2), 322–338 (2009). https://doi.org/10.1037/a0014996

26. Poropat, A.E.: The Eysenckian personality factors and their correlations with academic performance. Br. J. Educ. Psychol. **81**(1), 41–58 (2011). https://doi.org/10.1348/000709910X497671

27. Poropat, A.E.: Other-rated personality and academic performance: evidence and implications. Learn. Individ. Differ. **34**, 24–32 (2014). https://doi.org/10.1016/j.lindif.2014.05.013

28. Salgueira, A., et al.: Individual characteristics and student's engagement in scientific research: a cross-sectional study. BMC Med. Educ. **12**, 95 (2012). http://www.biomedcentral.com/1472-6920/12/95

29. Sharma, S.: Applied Multivariate Techniques. Wiley, New York (1996)

30. Tamhane, A.C., Dunlop, D.D.: Statistics and Data Analysis: From Elementary to Intermediate. Prentice Hall, New Jersey (2000)

31. Teodoro, M.F., Delgado, A.D., Martins, J.M.: Academic success and personal characteristics analysis by ANOVA approach. Under evaluation

32. Turkman, M.A., Silva, G.: Modelos Lineares Generalizados da teoria à prática. Sociedade Portuguesa de Estatística, Lisbon (2000)

33. Sugahara, S., Boland, G.: How accounting students define success, and the factors affecting their success and failure, while studying in the accounting schools of Japan. Procedia. Soc. Behav. Sci. **141**, 64–69 (2014). https://doi.org/10.1016/j.sbspro.2014.05.012

34. Vedel, A., Poropat, A.E.: Personality and academic performance. In: Zeigler-Hill, V., Shackelford, T. (eds.) Encyclopedia of Personality and Individual Differences. Springer, Cham (2017). https://doi.org/10.1007/978-3-319-28099-8_989-1

35. Vinciguerra, A., Réveillère, C., Potard, C., Lyant, B., Cornu, L., Courtois, R.: Personality profiles of students at risk of dropping out: resilients. Overcontrollers and Undercontrollers, Encephale **45**(2), 152–161 (2019). https://doi.org/10.1016/j.encep.2018.07.002
36. Young, A.G., Pearce, S.: A beginner's guide to factor analysis: focusing on exploratory factor analysis. Tutor. Quant. Methods Psychol. **9**(2), 79–94 (2013)

Black Scabbardfish Species Distribution: Geostatistical Inference Under Preferential Sampling

Paula Simões[1,2]([✉]) [ID], M. Lucília Carvalho[3] [ID], Ivone Figueiredo[3,4] [ID],
Andreia Monteiro[1] [ID], and Isabel Natário[1,5] [ID]

[1] NOVA MATH - Center for Mathematics and Applications, NOVA University
of Lisbon, Lisbon, Portugal
`pc.simoes@campus.fct.unl.pt`
[2] Military Academy Research Center - Military University Institute (CINAMIL),
Lisbon, Portugal
[3] Centre of Statistics and its Applications (CEAUL), Faculty of Sciences of the
University of Lisbon, Lisbon, Portugal
[4] Portuguese Institute for Sea and Atmosphere (IPMA), Lisbon, Portugal
[5] Department of Mathematics, Faculty of Science and Technology,
NOVA University of Lisbon, Caparica, Portugal

Abstract. Black Scabbardfish (BSF) is a highly prized deep-sea species
that occurs in continental waters at depths greater than 800 m. It has
been recognized that improving knowledge of its biodiversity and abundance along the Portuguese coast of BSF species is a scientifically and
socially relevant issue, mainly due to the fact of absence of dedicated
deep-water research surveys in this area, the spatial distribution of its
abundance is mainly inferred from commercial deep-water longline fishery that operates along the continental slope. Black Scabbardfish (BSF)
captures are modelled using a geostatistical analysis combined with a
preferential sampling technique which enables to better capture the
variability of the BSF captures providing a more realistic pattern of
BSF distribution. This approach allows a better knowledge os BSF spatial distribution assuming that the selection of the sampling locations
depends on the values of the observed variable of interest. BSF captures are jointly modeled with their locations, using a Bayesian approach and INLA methodology, considering stochastic partial differential
equations (SPDE) in the geostatistical model and in the Log-Cox point
process model for the locations. Several different covariates and random
effects were considered. The best two fits are presented, the first including
covariate depth in the intensity of the point process besides the shared
spatial effect with the response, and the second fit having covariate vessel
tonnage in the response adding to the shared spatial effect and covariate
depth again included in the point process intensity.

Supported by national funds through the FCT - Fundação para a Ciência e a
Tecnologia, I.P., under the scope of the projects PREFERENTIAL, PTDC/MAT-
STA/28243/2017, UIDP/00297/2020 (Center for Mathematics and Applications) and
UIDB/00006/2020(CEAUL)x.

© The Author(s), under exclusive license to Springer Nature Switzerland AG 2023
O. Gervasi et al. (Eds.): ICCSA 2023 Workshops, LNCS 14105, pp. 303–314, 2023.
https://doi.org/10.1007/978-3-031-37108-0_19

Keywords: Preferential sampling · Geostatistics · Point process · SPDE · INLA

1 Introduction

Black Scabbardfish (BSF) is a deep-water species that occurs in continental waters at depths greater than 800 m. On the portuguese coast BSF constitutes an important commercial resource. In the absence of dedicated deep-water research surveys in this area, the spatial distribution of its abundance is mainly inferred from commercial deep-water longline fishery operating along the continental slope.

The Portuguese Institute of Sea and Atmosphere (IPMA) provided georeferenced data on the location of the fishing hauls and the corresponding captures for a number of differently sized vessels belonging to the Black Scabbardfish (BSF) fishing fleet. The commercial longline fishing that operates along the continental slope is the main contributor to the information obtained on the spatial distribution of the abundance of this species, as dedicated deep-water research surveys in this area are scarce. This information, understood as preferentially sampled data, is used here combined with environmental covariates, to predict where the species is likely to exist, also in unsampled locations, for management and conservation purposes, in order to ensure the sustainability of commercial fisheries and protect the biodiversity of species that are of high interest for consumption.

A classical geostatistical approach was considered in a preliminary study of this species [1], using different regression models with covariates, structured and unstructured random effects, under a Bayesian approach. However, the information on the capture sites of the species should have been accounted for in the modelling process due to the preferential nature of the data, as classical geostatistical techniques may have produced biased results [5,10,15].

The objective of this research work is two-folded. In one hand, to perform species distribution modelling of the BSF data by using a geostatistical model-based method that takes preferentiability into account. Under a Bayesian approach and resorting to INLA methodology [11], using the stochastic partial differential equations (SPDE) approach to model the spatial effects that are shared by a geostatistical model for the captures and a Log-Cox point process model (LGCP) for the locations [7], BSF captures can be analysed considering several different covariates and random effects [5,10]. On the other hand, considering the present modelling of the BSF captures, predictions can be made at several potential sampling locations (unobserved locations) in order to be able to construct a survey design to improve the BSF abundance estimates in Portuguese waters. The present study contributes to the first part of the analysis, to perform species distribution modelling. This analysis is used in the second part of the work, to construct a survey design to improve the BSF abundance estimates, as in [3,13].

Considering the referred Bayesian framework, using INLA and SPDE for estimating jointly the geostatistical model for captures and the Log-Cox point process model for the locations, BSF captures are estimated using different models. From these, both in terms of a classical geostatistical approach and further taking preferentiability into account, the two best models are presented. Within the latter models, first it is considered the inclusion of covariate depth in the intensity of the point process and of a spatial effect in the response, and for the second one the covariate group of tonnage is also incorporated in the response.

2   Species Distribution Modelling for the Black Scabbardfish

2.1   Black Scabbardfish Data

A set of 15 vessels belonging to the BSF fishing fleet, with different sizes, contributes through the Portuguese Institute of Sea and Atmosphere (IPMA) in providing georeferenced data corresponding to the BSF catches (in Kg) and respective fishing haul locations. The database also includes information in terms of tonnage and vessel identification, speed and depth at which the catch was made. The time period covers the years 2002 to 2013, however a subset of the original data was taken for this data analysis: it comprehends the years between 2009 to 2013, catches that took place from September to February on the southern fishing zone that corresponds to a latitude below than 39.3. This subset of the original data includes 733 observations. Figure 1 shows the spatial distribution of the capture points of the considered data subset. In addition to the available variables, it is also intended to consider environmental factors as covariates to perform species distribution modelling. For the present analysis the covariates depth revealed to be significant.

The original data displays skewness, with a Gamma distribution possibly being a good fit for the observed captures. In order to have an approximately Normal distribution of the response, a Box-Cox transformation of BSF captures data (Y) was carried out. The new transformed response (Y^*) as been defined according with the expression $Y^* = \frac{Y^\lambda - 1}{\lambda}$, with $\lambda = \frac{1}{2}$.

The vessel tonnage is classified as low tonnage (less than 26 tonnes) and medium Tonnage (higher than 26). 484 of observations are from the vessels are registered as low tonnage, and the remaining 249 observations are registered as medium tonnage. Depth variable has a minimum value of -1997.4 m, median value of -1298.3 m and a interquartile range of 214.0 m with a maximum value of -770.8 m.

2.2   Geostatistical Classical Model Versus Preferential Sampling Model

Let Y_i denote the georeferenced species captures for site i, $i = 1, \ldots, n$, assuming the following distribution for the observations, $Y_i \sim N(\mu_i, \sigma_o^2)$ where n is the

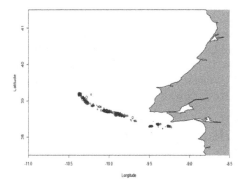

Fig. 1. Black Scabbardfish data locations.

total number of fishing hauls, σ_o^2 is the nugget effect, μ_i is the response mean. The classical geostatistical model is given by:

$$Y_i|(S, \boldsymbol{X} = \boldsymbol{x})] = \mu_i + e_i = \beta_0 + \sum_{m=1}^{M} \beta_m C_{mi} + S(x_i) + e_i,$$

$$e \sim N(\mathbf{0}, \sigma_o^2),$$

(1)

where $\boldsymbol{C} = (C_1, \ldots, C_M)$ corresponds to the considered covariates in the study, $\boldsymbol{\beta}$ is the corresponding fixed effects, essentially environmental factors and available information about the vessels. The spatial effect of the model is given by S, modelled as Latent Gaussian Field (GF), a stationary Gaussian Process with mean zero, variance σ^2, and a Matérn correlation function, with correlation shape parameter fixed $k = 1.5$, correlation range ϕ and nugget variance τ^2, [2,7].

The spatial effects are approximated by the SPDE approach, $S(x) = \sum_{g=1}^{G} A_{ig} \widetilde{S}_g$. $\widetilde{S}_g$ are zero mean Gaussian distributed weights; A_{ig} is the generic element of the sparse $n \times G$ matrix A that maps the Gaussian Markov Random Field (GMRF), projecting the $\widetilde{S}$ defined on the G vertices of a triangulation of the area under study (forming a mesh) to the n locations $(x_1, ..., x_n)$ [1,2].

For β_m Normal non informative priors are assumed, $\beta_m \sim N(0, 0.001^{-1})$. In terms of the marginal standard deviation σ and the range r of the Matérn field, the penalise complexity priors (PC prior) are considered here. Based on the work of Fuglstad (2019) [6], that extends the work of Simpson (2017) [12], a joint prior for the range and for marginal variance of one-dimensional, two-dimensional or three-dimensional Matérn Gaussian Random Field with fixed smoothness was developed. Essentially it corresponds to the construction of a prior for the Matérn covariance function of a considered GMRF that is independent of the observation process. The prior distribution is weakly informative and penalizes complexity by reducing the range to infinity and the marginal variance towards zero [6]. This approach stands out by the fact that is a way to overcome the problem of overfitting, featuring that the prior distribution do not depend on the spatial design, improving predictive performance [6]. In this work, the hyperparameters are select in order to satisfy:

PC prior for the range: $P[r < r_0] = \alpha_1 \rightarrow P[r < 30] = 0.2$;

PC prior for the standard deviation: $P[\sigma > \sigma_0] = \alpha_2 \rightarrow P[\sigma > 10] = 0.01$.

With these prior distributions a standard deviation greater than 10 is considered as well as a range less than 30.

The presented spatial model (1) corresponds to a classical geostatistical model considered under a Bayesian approach. In order to take into consideration the preferential nature of these data, it is also needed to consider the fishing sites of the data in the modelling process. That is a preferential sampling model should be considered, wherein captures of a species of interest are jointly modeled with their locations. The observed locations $(x_1, ..., x_n)$, are assumed to form a non-homogeneous Poisson process. Log-Gaussian Cox Process (LGCP) are a specific class of Cox processes in which the logarithm of the intensity surface is a Gaussian Random field. Through the underlying spatial field, S, defined as before, the observed captures $Y = (Y_1, ..., Y_n)$ are related to the intensity of the point process. Based on a trend function that may depend on covariates, the species distribution model is described. This preferentially sampling model share information in what concerns to the mean captures and sampling intensity (the number of points per unit area), on the observed species captures and on the point process [7,9,10].

$$\begin{aligned}
Y_i|(S, \boldsymbol{X} = \boldsymbol{x})] &= \beta_0^y + \beta^y S(x_i) + e_i \\
e &\sim N(0, \sigma_o^2) \\
\boldsymbol{X}|S &\sim P(\lambda) \\
\lambda_i|S &= \exp(\beta_0^{pp} + S(x_i))
\end{aligned} \tag{2}$$

where β_0^y is the intercept for the model of the captures, β_0^{pp} is the intercept for the intensity of the LGCP, β^y is a weight on the shared spatial random field effect. If more observation sites correspond to higher captures, a value of $\beta^y > 0$ is expected; when $\beta^y = 0$ the model has no preferential sampling; when there are more observation sites for lower captures a value of $\beta^y < 0$ is estimated.

Inference in made considering the SPDE approach for geostatistical data and Integrated Nested Laplace Approximation (INLA) methodology. An approximate stochastic weak solution of a Stochastic Partial Differential Equation is used, that is a continuous Gaussian field with a Matérn covariance structure, [8,11]. The triangulation of the considered spatial domains, through the constrained refined Delaunay triagulation, is required in the first stage. A mesh that covers the study region is built, see Fig. 2. It was also considered penalized complexity priors (PC Priors) for the model parameters, range r and marginal standard deviation σ, of the spatial effect, $(P[r < 30] = 0.2, P[\sigma > 10] = 0.01)$ for the SPDE approach [6,13].

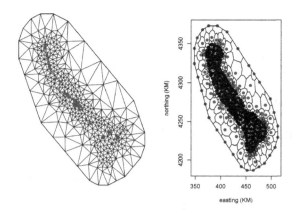

Fig. 2. Mesh constructed for BSF Data (left) and Voronoy polygons used to make inference for LGCP (right).

3   Geostatistical Inference Under Preferential Sampling

The BSF captures are analysed, considering different models, both for the classic geostatistical approach and considering the joint model of the geostatistical data and the points location [2,7]. The two best fits, both for the classical geostatistical point of view and considering the preferential sampling approach, are presented. Several different covariates and random effects were considered. The first model presented includes covariate depth in the intensity of the point process along with the shared spatial effect with the response, and the second model includes covariate vessel tonnage in the response along with the shared spatial effect and covariate depth again included in the point process intensity.

Inference is made mainly through the package R-INLA [8,11].

3.1   Classical Models

Model 1C: Including Covariate D Depth (Fixed Effect) and a Spatial Random Effect for Modelling Captures

$$Y_i|(S, \boldsymbol{X} = \boldsymbol{x})] = \beta_0 + \beta_1 D_i + S(x_i) + e_i,$$

$$e \sim N(0, \sigma_o^2),$$

(3)

where β_0 is the intercept, β_1 is the depth fixed effect and S is the random spatial effect.

Figure 3 shows the posteriori predicted mean of the spatial random effect and the corresponding standard deviation for model 1C, as well as the Box-Cox transformation of the BSF captures data observations.

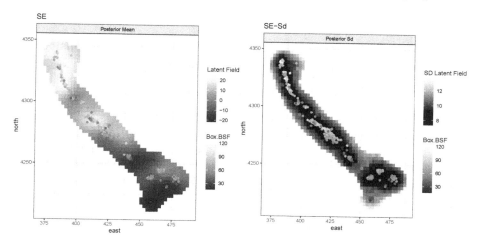

Fig. 3. Posterior predicted mean and standard deviation of the spatial effect, model 1C, and the Box-Cox transformation of the BSF captures data observations.

Model 2C: Including Covariate Group of Tonnage, *PRT* (Fixed Effects) and a Spatial Random Effect for Modelling Captures

$$Y_i|(S, \boldsymbol{X} = \boldsymbol{x})] = \beta_0 + \sum_{m=2}^{M} \beta_m PRT_{mi} + S(x_i) + e_i,$$
$$e \sim N(0, \sigma_o^2), \tag{4}$$

where β_0 is the intercept, β_m are the group tonnage fixed effects and S is the spatial random effect.

For model 2C the posteriori predicted mean of the spatial random effect and the corresponding standard deviation, as well as the Box-Cox transformation of BSF captures data observations can de seen in Fig. 4.

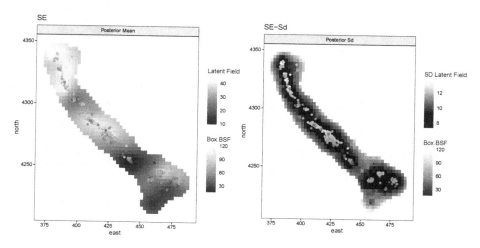

Fig. 4. Posterior predicted mean and standard deviation of the spatial effect, model 2C, and the Box-Cox transformation of BSF captures data observations.

3.2   Preferential Models

Model 1P: Point Process with Covariate Depth (D) on Intensity and Sharing a Random Spatial Effect with Captures

$$
\begin{aligned}
Y_i|(S, \boldsymbol{X} = \boldsymbol{x})] &= \beta_0^y + \beta^y S(x_i) + e_i, \\
e &\sim N(0, \sigma_o^2), \\
\lambda_i|S &= \exp(\beta_0^{pp} + \beta_1^{pp} D_i + S(x_i)),
\end{aligned}
\tag{5}
$$

where β_0 is the captures model intercept, β_0^{pp} is the point process intercept, β_1 is the depth fixed effect and S is the shared spatial random effect. The observed locations are modelled by a Log-Gaussian Cox Process (LGCP), $X|S$.

Figure 5 shows the posteriori predicted mean of the spatial random effect and the corresponding standard deviation, as well as the Box-Cox transformation of BSF captures data observations for model 1P. This model has an estimated value of β^y of **1.237**, greater than 0, meaning that the BSF captures, are **higher** where there are **more** observation locations.

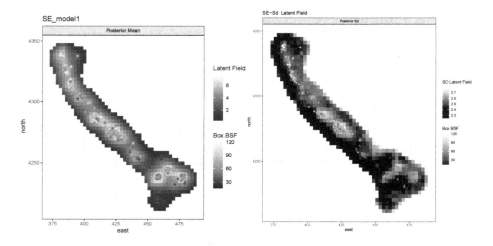

Fig. 5. Posterior predicted mean and standard deviation of the spatial effect, model 1P, and the Box-Cox transformation of BSF captures data observations.

Model 2P: Including Covariate *PRT*, Group of Tonnage (Fixed Effect), Point Process with Covariate Depth (D) on Intensity and Sharing a Random Spatial Effect with the Captures

$$
\begin{aligned}
Y_i|(S, \boldsymbol{X} = \boldsymbol{x})] &= \beta_0^y + \beta_1^y PRT_i + \beta^y S(x_i) + e_i, \\
e &\sim N(0, \sigma_o^2), \\
\lambda_i|S &= \exp(\beta_0^{pp} + \beta_1^{pp} D_i + S(x_i))
\end{aligned}
\tag{6}
$$

where β_0 is the intercept for the model of the captures, β_0^{pp} is the point process intercept, β_1 is the depth fixed effect and S is the shared spatial random effect. The observed locations are modelled by a LGCP, $X|S$.

For model 2P the posteriori predicted mean of the spatial random effect and the corresponding standard deviation, as well as the Box-Cox transformation of the BSF captures data observations can de seen in Fig. 6. This model has an estimated value of β^y of **0.228**, greater than 0, meaning that the response values are **higher** where there are **more** observation locations.

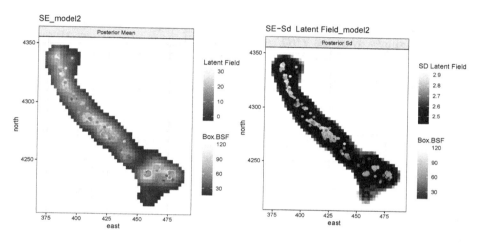

Fig. 6. Posterior predicted mean and standard deviation of the spatial random effect, model 2P, and the Box-Cox transformation of BSF captures data observations.

3.3   Conclusion

Parameter estimates for two selected models, both in terms of the classical and preferential approaches, are summarized in Tables 1 and 2, respectively. Using the Deviance Information Criterion (DIC) and the Watanabe-Akaike Information Criterion (WAIC), well-known Bayesian model choice criterion for comparing models, these models were selected, from several other fits, through their predictive accuracy [14].

Table 1. Parameter estimates for the classical approach, model 1C and model 2C.

Model	β_0^y	D	PRT medium	r (range)	σ (StDev)	τ_o (Prec Gaussian)	DIC	WAIC
Model 1C	62.432	−0.001	-	37.791	14.448	0.006	5893.07	5898.09
Model 2C	29.654	-	14.761	38.381	12.579	0.006	5866.95	5871.39

Table 2. Parameter estimates for the preferential approach, model 1C and model 2C.

Model	β_0^{pp}	D	β_0^y	PRT medium	r (range)	σ (StDev)	τ_o (Prec Gaussian)	β^y	DIC	WAIC
Model 1P	−10.710	−0.002	62.253	-	39,128	3.784	0.003	1.237	7459,92	8850.97
Model 1P	−6.680	0.001	32.914	24.304	25,573	11.999	0.005	0.228	7269,67	8650.00

The values for DIC and WAIC in each approach (classical and preferential) are very similar. In spite of this, for the classical approach, the model including covariates PRT and group of tonnage (fixed effect) and a spatial random effect for modelling captures has the lowest values. For the preferential approach, the model including covariates PRT and group of tonnage (fixed effect) for the captures, and covariate depth (D) for the point process intensity, sharing with captures the random spatial effect seems to be the best model to fit the data.

4   Discussion

BSF captures were modelled considering several different covariates and spatial random effects, considering a joint model of the geostatistical data and the points location and also via a classical geostatistical model, taken under a Bayesian approach. The preferential sampling model better captures the variability of the BSF captures providing a more realistic pattern of the BSF distribution. In the presence of preferentially of the sampled data (the sampling locations depends on the values of the observed variable of interest) this approach allows a better understanding of the spatial distribution of BSF. This information combined with environmental covariates, can now be used to predict where the species is likely to exist, also in unsampled locations, for management and conservation purposes, in order to ensure the sustainability of commercial fisheries and protect the biodiversity of this species that is of high interest for consumption. The study could be more broadly extended in such a way as to include important ecological factors, which may be important in the estimation, or by allowing a term for the time effects, in terms of a spatio-temporal approach [2,9].

Taking into account the present modelling of the BSF captures, predictions can be made at several potential sampling locations (unobserved locations) in order to construct a survey design to improve the BSF abundance estimates, which represents the second part of the work [13]. These locations can be obtained through the triangulation of the considered spatial domain, taking into account the chosen mesh. The estimated values for BSF captures in their spatial prediction coordinates can be obtained considering both approaches (classical vs preferential), what might constitute an important issue, for future approach, in order to be able to analyse the effect of preferentiality on the choice of new sampling locations, for sampling design purposes, and its influence in the sampling design choice.

In terms of future work, the aim is thus to implement geostatistical sampling design strategies for preferentially sampled data, addressing the problem of designing for spatial prediction purposes when the covariance function is not known and has to be estimated from the same data. Within this approach, different design classes could be investigated, namely random, simple inhibitory and adaptive geostatistical samplig designs [3,4], in order to reach an optimal survey BSF design. Another important issue to be further considered is the development of a new sampling design without transforming the captures BSF, that also enables a realistic pattern of BSF captures distribution estimates. This will require that the Geostatistical preferential model to be considered for the BSF captures assumes a Gamma distribution instead, as well as the follow up with suitable design strategies for BSF captures under preferential sampling with this Gamma distribution.

These latter issues are considered pertinent to the ongoing mission of improving knowledge about the abundance of certain fish species (BSF or others), which is a extremely determining factor to support, from a national as well as international perspective, the sustainability of commercial fisheries and safeguard the biodiversity of species of significant consumption interest.

Acknowledgments. This work is funded by national funds through the FCT - Fundação para a Ciência e a Tecnologia, I.P., under the scope of the projects PREFERENTIAL, PTDC/MAT-STA/28243/2017, UIDP/00297/2020 (Center for Mathematics and Applications) and UIDB/00006/2020(CEAUL).

References

1. André, L.M., Figueiredo, I., Carvalho, M.L., Simões, P., Natário, I.: Spatial modelling of black scabbardfish fishery off the Portuguese coast. In: Gervasi, O., et al. (eds.) ICCSA 2020. LNCS, vol. 12249, pp. 332–344. Springer, Cham (2020). https://doi.org/10.1007/978-3-030-58799-4_25
2. Blangiardo, M., Cameletti, M., Baio, G., Rue, H.: Spatial and spatio-temporal models with R-INLA. Spat. Spatio-Temporal Epidemiol. **4**, 33–49 (2013)
3. Chipeta, M., Terlouw, D., Phiri, K., Diggle, P.: Adaptive geostatistical design and analysis for prevalence surveys. Spat. Stat. **15**, 70–84 (2016)
4. Chipeta, M., et al.: Inhibitory geostatistical designs for spatial prediction taking account of uncertain covariance structure. Environmetrics **28**(1), e2425 (2017)
5. Diggle, P., Menezes, R., Su, T.: Geostatistical inference under preferential sampling. J. Roy. Stat. Soc.: Ser. C (Appl. Stat.) **59**(2), 191–232 (2010)
6. Fuglstad, G.A., Simpson, D., Lindgren, F., Rue, H.: Constructing priors that penalize the complexity of Gaussian random fields. J. Am. Stat. Assoc. **114**(525), 445–452 (2019)
7. Krainski, E.T., et al.: Advanced Spatial Modeling with Stochastic Partial Differential Equations Using R and INLA. CRC Press, Boca Raton (2018)
8. Lindgren, F., Lindström, J., Rue, H.: An explicit link between Gaussian fields and Gaussian Markov random fields: the SPDE approach. Centre for Mathematical Sciences, Faculty of Engineering, Lund University, Mathematical Statistics (2010)
9. Martínez-Minaya, J., Cameletti, M., Conesa, D., Pennino, M.G.: Species distribution modeling: a statistical review with focus in spatio-temporal issues. Stoch. Env. Res. Risk Assess. **32**(11), 3227–3244 (2018). https://doi.org/10.1007/s00477-018-1548-7

10. Pennino, M., et al.: Accounting for preferential sampling in species distribution models. Ecol. Evol. **9**(1), 653–663 (2019)
11. Rue, H., Martino, S., Chopin, N.: Approximate Bayesian inference for latent Gaussian models by using integrated nested Laplace approximations. J. R. Stat. Soc.: Ser. b (Stat. Methodol.) **71**(2), 319–392 (2009)
12. Simpson, D., Rue, H., Riebler, A., Martins, T.G., Sorbye, S.H.: Penalising model component complexity: a principled, practical approach to constructing priors. Stat. Sci. **32**(1), 1–28 (2017)
13. Simões, P., Carvalho, M.L., Figueiredo, I., Monteiro, A., Natário, I.: Geostatistical sampling designs under preferential sampling for black scabbardfish. In: Bispo, R., Henriques-Rodrigues, L., Alpizar-Jara, R., de Carvalho, M. (eds.) SPE 2021. Springer Proceedings in Mathematics and Statistics, vol. 398, pp. 137–151. Springer, Cham (2022). https://doi.org/10.1007/978-3-031-12766-3_11
14. Spiegelhalter, D., Best, G., Carlin, P., Van Der Linde, A.: Bayesian measures of model complexity and fit. J. R. Stat. Soc.: Ser. b (Stat. Methodol.) **64**(4), 583–639 (2002)
15. Watson, J., Zidek, J.V., Shaddick, G.: A general theory for preferential sampling in environmental networks. Ann. Appl. Stat. **13**(4), 2662–2700 (2019)

Zika: A Case Study

M. Filomena Teodoro[1,2(✉)] (iD) and João Faria[2,3]

[1] CEMAT - Center for Computational and Stochastic Mathematics, Instituto Superior Técnico, Lisbon University, Lisbon, Portugal
mteodoro64@gmail.com

[2] CINAV - Center for Naval Research, Portuguese Naval Academy, Military University Institute, Portuguese Navy, Almada, Portugal

[3] IHMT, Institute of Hygiene and Tropical Medicine, New University of Lisbon, Lisbon, Portugal

Abstract. This manuscript analyzes Zika virus infection KAP among the fleet of Portuguese Navy ships. We developed a statistical ana those who have travelled in ZIKV endemic areas lysis, a cross-sectional study, that divided the study group into distinct groups traveling in ZIKV those travelling in ZIKV endemic areas endemic areas, and those traveling in non-ZIKV endemic areas. The present study evaluates the correct/incorrect answers off a questionnaire about knowledge, attitudes and practices related to Zika infection applied to those who travel to endemic areas of the Zika virus. The level of knowledge about ZIKV shows significant differences between different groups. Preliminary results are similar to other studies showing the need to implement a health education program on Zika infection in advance of possible future Zika virus outbreaks.

Keywords: Literacy · Questionnaire · Statistical Approach · Zika Virus · Infection

1 Introduction

During th fourth decade of the last century, when studying yellow fever in the Zika forest of Uganda, the Zika virus was identified in a rhesus monkey. The Zika virus belongs to the Flaviviridae family, genus Flavivirus (Sharma, 2020). In 1952, a human case of Zika infection was reported in Uganda (Dick, 1952)after three more cases of human infection during a jaundice epidemic in Nigeria (MacNamara, 1954).Between the 1960s and 1980s, cases of ZIKV infection were identified. With the large number of transcontinental flows that have occurred in recent decades, the spread of Zika grows exponentially. The authors (Zanluca, 2015) (Walddell L, 2016) prove that the increased dissemination of Zika contributes to a greater probability of genetic mutations and promotes the existence of a more resistant and epidemic potential. The spread of infection increases the possibility of genetic mutation in some pathogenic microorganisms. Authors (ECDC, 2016) (Cao-Lormeau, 2016). Evidence that the presence of ZIKV in distant local populations, combined with high migration rates, may result in longer

© The Author(s), under exclusive license to Springer Nature Switzerland AG 2023

O. Gervasi et al. (Eds.): ICCSA 2023 Workshops, LNCS 14105, pp. 315–326, 2023.
https://doi.org/10.1007/978-3-031-37108-0_20

viremia and more persistent virus in some body fluids. On mission, military navigators can become infected when visiting native locations. Under this potential problem, prevention policy is important, when military personnel need to visit ZIKV endemic sites where exposure to the virus may occur, disease prevention and health education are necessary. Knowledge, Attitudes and Practices (KAP) need to be evaluated in relation to this issue to develop intervention strategies through health education measures, correct attitude and preventive actions. Statistical analysis was carried out, first using some descriptive techniques, secondly using some traditional comparison tests, finally using generalized linear models to obtain predictive models), a cross-sectional study that, in addition to describing knowledge, attitudes and actions allow us. In the case of ZIKV, it allows comparing different study groups: those moving to Zika endemic areas, those who had travelled to Zika endemic areas. A questionnaire was used for these groups. The preliminary results are in line with similar studies that have been done before.

2 Preliminaries

2.1 Historical Note

Until 1977, cases of human infection with Zika were confined to tropical Africa. In India, Indonesia, Malaysia and Pakistan, spread of ZIKV has occurred, but without severity. Due to low severity, Zika infection is rarely reported in Asia (Kindhauser A, 2016) (Olson J, 1981). Outside of Africa and Asia, in Micronesia, the first reported human outbreak occurred in 2007, but without hospitalization. Until 2008, it was accepted that the infection was transmitted exclusively by the mosquito *Aedes aegypti* (Kindhauser A, 2016), but the first sexual transmission was reported in Micronesia in 2008. This was accompanied by rash, conjunctivitis, and arthralgia, but without hospitalization. As the authors point out (Kindhauser A, 2016) until this event, no human outbreak had been recorded and only 14 cases were isolated. Later, during 2013, a strong rate of infection occurred in about 70% of the population of French Polynesia, with neurological manifestations in infants (microcephaly) and adults (Guillain Barre syndrome [GBS]).

Later, in 2015, successive Zika outbreaks were reported in Brazil, first without associated complications and finally with cases related to GBS and a greater number of babies born with microcephaly. In the same year, an outbreak of Zika occurred in Cape Verde with no recorded neurological complications (Walddell L, 2016), (WHO/Europe, 2016), (Kindhauser A, 2016), (Olson J, 1981), (Sampathkumar P S. J., 2016), (Rabaan A, 2017).

Due to the number of confirmed Zika cases associated with microcephaly and neurological disorders, WHO declared Zika infection as a public health emergency of international concern (Sampathkumar P S. J., 2016), (Rabaan A, 2017), but later that year, warning has been removed. Almost simultaneously, the emergency committee proposed the following lines of action: surveillance of Zika virus transmission, long-term measures, travel-related measures, and information sharing (Who, 2016a).

Several studies have been conducted on knowledge, attitudes and practices regarding Zika infection. In (Pergolizzi, 2020), the results show that comprehensive national preventive health education programs are needed.

In (Darrow, 2018), a high level of awareness about the risk of Zika infection was evident, and most students reported taking steps to prevent exposure to the Zika virus. The results of the questionnaire are consistent with the fact that in 2016, the southern states of the United States reported outbreaks of the Zika virus (Sharma, 2020), (CDC, 2019), (Services, 2016).

We can easily find more similar studies from different places and authors: (Plaster, 2018), (Gregorio Jr., 2019), (Wishner, 2020), (Lim, 2020), (Rosalino, 2016).

2.2 Sample

The Portuguese Navy has 17 ships and two submarines, all capable of conducting international operations. To effectively carry out assigned missions while traveling outside Portugal, officers on board are exposed to many infectious agents and contribute to improving their health. This can be seen in Table 1 which shows several NRP ship destinations. In Fig. 1, you can see a map with some of the ports identified as particularly vulnerable to Zika transmission (PAHO/WHO, 2016). In this study, the NRP ship during the mission identified several ports with a history of Zika transmission in several countries such as Angola, Cameroon, Cape Verde, Gabon, Guinea-Bissau, Ivory Coast, Nigeria, Senegal, Indonesia, Thailand, etc. Some of the countries identified as ports of entry for NRP vessels (NRP - Navio da República Portuguesa (Ship from Portuguese Republic)) in this study were identified as countries with local Zika infection records in their missions: Angola, Cameroon, Cape Verde, Gabon, Guinea-Bissau, Ivory Coast, Nigeria, Senegal, Indonesia, Thailand.

Questionnaires are created, tested, modified, and used later. A pre-questionnaire was implemented to staff of Portuguese Navy frigate NRP Court-Real (the ship was docked at the naval base of Lisbon during preliminary trial) so we could confirm that questionnaires 1 and 2 were clear for prospective participants. Also relevance, placement and order of questions were evaluated. It was evaluated the relevance, position and order of the questions. After using this questionnaire trial, after the necessary corrections, the final version was ready. The target population selected to answer the questionnaires 1/2 is the embarked staff of selected ships described in Table 1.

Table 1. NRP Ships chosen to the study.

1. Questionnaire to whom is going to navigate in endemic zones
NRP D. Carlos I
NRP Figueira da Foz
NRP D. Francisco de Almeida
NRP Viana do Castelo
2. Questionnaire to whom had navigated in endemic zones
NRP Vasco da Gama
NRP Almirante Gago Coutinho
NRP Sagres

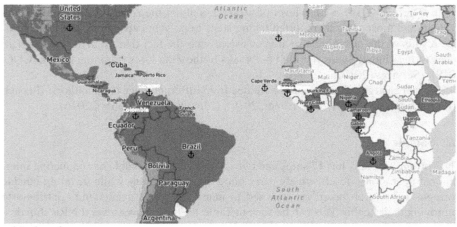

Map legend

 Mooring Points

Countries or territories with reported cases of Zika (past or present)**

Zone with low probability of infection with Zika by high elevation (>2000 meters)

Countries with mosquito, but no cases of Zika registered **

Countries or territories without mosquitoes that propagate Zika *

* *Aedes aegypti*
** Zika's autochthonous cases

Fig. 1. Mooring ports of NRP ships considered in the study (map adapted from (PAHO/WHO, 2016)).

3   Empirical Application

It was given the approval to apply an adapted questionnaire available (WHO, 2016) and validated by the authors of (Rosalino, 2016). Some of these ships had returned from mission overseas, others were moored in preparation for departure on mission.

After the verification that questionnaires 1 and 2 were correctly understood by potential participants, a questionnaire was applied to each navigator from ship staff. Data collection is still being organized and analyzed. The present work is the continuation of (Faria J., 2019), (Faria J. T., 2019), (Teodoro, 2023) where some important results and a detailed discussion with the application of a factorial analyses to reduce the dimensionality of the problem can be already found. Here we analyze with detail some detail the sociodemographic information contained in questionnaire – part 1. Also, we analyze some questions from part 2 of questionnaire.

3.1   Socio-demographic Characterization (Questionnaire – Part 1)

Age
The population selected to respond to the questionnaires concerns the military belonging to the crews of some of these ships, with a total of 256 elements participating. This is

a relatively young population, with the majority between 20 and 39 years old, around 85.5%. The average age is 31 years old, with a standard deviation of 6.8, with 20 years old as a minimum and 49 years old as a maximum. As Fig. 2. Displays, the ages of the participants were stratified into three different classes.

Fig. 2. Distribution of participants by age groups.

Gender

With regard to gender, there is a clear disparity between the participants, the majority being male (83.9%) – see Fig. 3. This disproportion between the two genders is a trend that has gradually been changing, given the will of military leaders in facilitating and promoting the inclusion of women in the Armed Forces. However, the fact that there is a large population of male elements, makes us aware of the need to develop more informative sessions on the disease, which focus on the practice of protected sexual relations after returning from missions in countries endemic for Zika.

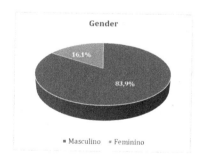

Fig. 3. Distribution of participants by gender.

Relativelly to participants' level of education, the majority (n = 161/63.1%) reported having completed the 12th year of schooling, followed by the 9th year (n = 38), Master's (n = 34) and degree (n = 22) (see Fig. 4).

Military Specialty

"Military specialty" refers to the area of knowledge to which each military member belongs, and consequently a series of specific normative functions are foreseen for each of them. Military personnel from 28 different specialties partic-ipated in the study The four with the greatest participation were Navy/Maneuver (M), Marine (FZ), Electromechanical (EM) and Communications (C). The specialties participating in the study are displayed in Fig. 5.

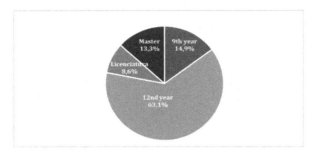

Fig. 4. Distribution of participants by level of education.

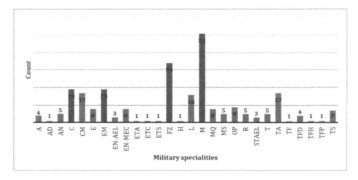

Fig. 5. Distribution of participants by military specialties.

The Navy/Maneuver classes are the ones with the highest number of individuals, possibly because the questionnaires were applied on the NRP Sagres, a sailing ship that only has men in its crew, and also because it is a sailing ship, the amount of elements of the Maneuver class is considerably higher than the rest.

3.2 Questionnaire – Part 2

Fever Causes

At the beginning of the second part of the questionnaire, participants were asked which of the following response options *"Zika/Dengue/Chikungunya"*, *"Malaria"*, *"Flu"* and *"Other"*, could be the cause of an episode of fever during the course of of your missions. Only one participant belonging to the Pre-mission group filled in the *"Other"* field, having answered *"Yellow Fever"*. Regarding the other answers to this question, about half of the participants in the Post-mission group answered the first two options wrongly, not attributing a possible episode of fever to any of the mentioned arboviruses (*Zika/Dengue/Chikungunya* – 49.6%, n = 58 and *Malaria* – 46.2%, n = 54). Still in this group, only a small number of people (15.5%, n = 18) attributed a possible cause of fever to "*Zika/Dengue/Chikungunya*", similarly to the Pre-mission group, despite presenting a higher number, also had a small number of participants (35.5%, n = 49) putting these three diseases as a hypothesis for the cause of fever (see Fig. 6 And Fig. 7).

Fig. 6. Perception of the causes of fever during the mission (Pre-mission on left, Post-mission on right). (Color figure online)

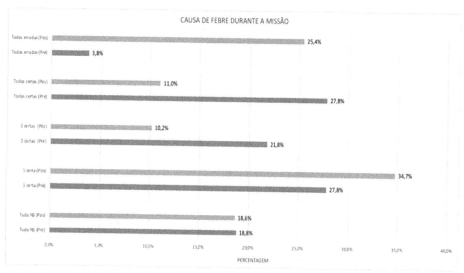

Fig. 7. Percentage of correct and incorrect answers for the fever causes questions (blue-pos-mission, green-pre-mission). (Color figure online)

Zika Knowledge

In question no. 2 of the second part of the questionnaire, the aim was to find out whether "Zika" was a familiar term for the participants, and if not, they should terminate their participation and hand the questionnaire over to the researcher. The next question aimed to find out which are the main sources of knowledge used to obtain information about

Zika, with five options being given with the possibility of answering "Yes" or "No" in each of them.

In the Pre-mission group, of the 138 participants, 65.9% reported having heard about Zika, with the majority (89%) obtaining information on the subject through TV, radio, newspapers and posters, placing the contribution of professionals health in third place, with 30.8%. As described in the articles by (Ricamonte B, 2018), (Binsaad Y, 2017), (Mouchtouri V, 2017), (Michael G, 2017) and (Gupta N, 2016), the participants in their studies also considered TV and radio as the main ways of obtaining information on Zika (79), (Ricamonte B, 2018), (Binsaad Y, 2017), (Mouchtouri V, 2017), (Gupta N, 2016) (Fig. 8).

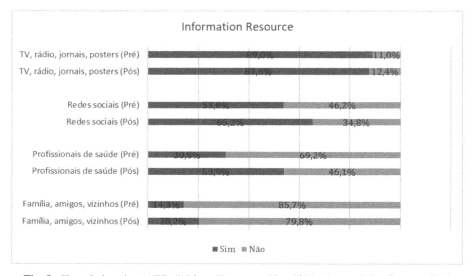

Fig. 8. Knowledge about "Zika" (blue -Yes, green-No). If Yes, how. (Color figure online)

The author of (Ricamonte B, 2018) even refers to the meager contribution of health professionals (8.8%) in terms of improving the knowledge of pregnant women in the Philippines, indicating the media (93.1%) as the main way of obtaining knowledge about the theme, suggesting in its conclusions the need for greater efforts on the part of health organizations in ord er to increase the awareness of the population and fill these gaps in knowledge, in order to promote favorable attitudes towards the infection.

In the Pre-mission group, of the 138 participants, 65.9% reported having heard about Zika, with the majority (89%) obtaining information on the subject through TV, radio, newspapers and posters, placing the contribution of professionals of health in third place, with 30.8%. As described in the article by (Ricamonte B, 2018), (CDC, 2019) (Binsaad Y, 2017), (Mouchtouri V, 2017), (Michael G, 2017) and (Gupta N, 2016), the participants in their studies also considered TV and radio as the main ways of obtaining information on Zika (79) (Ricamonte B, 2018), (Binsaad Y, 2017), (Mouchtouri V, 2017), (Michael G, 2017). The author of (Ricamonte B, 2018) even refers to the meager contribution of health professionals (8.8%) in terms of improving the knowledge of pregnant women in the Philippines, indicating the media (93.1%) as the main way of obtaining knowledge about the theme, suggesting in its conclusions the need for greater efforts on the part of health organizations in order to increase the awareness of the population and fill these gaps in knowledge, in order to promote favorable attitudes towards the infection.

Regarding the Post-mission group, out of 118 participants, 75.4% reported having heard about "Zika", with the vast majority (87.6%) selecting the answer "TV, radio, newspapers and posters" as the answer. Main source of obtaining information about Zika, having selected health professionals in third place, with 53.9%.

With regard to health professionals, it is considered that the difference between the "pre" and "post" group may be related to the period of readiness that precedes the missions, which generally include lectures given by the nurse or doctor on board, lectures these that address issues such as health prevention, traveler's health and infectious diseases. We believe that this is a low percentage, with the need to improve the communication strategies used by these professionals.

The use of social networks (internet) is indicated by (Huang Y, 2017), (Ibrahim N, 2018), (Harapan H, 2018) and (Arief M, 2017) as being the preferred source of information for the interviewed populations, seen as a good vehicle of information, thus resembling the results obtained in the two groups of our investigation (Harapan H, 2017), (Huang Y, 2017), (Ibrahim N, 2018) and (Arief M, 2017). In the study by (Ibrahim, 2017), aimed at medical students in Saudi Arabia, 56.1% indicated Facebook as the most common source for obtaining information about ZIKV, followed by other internet sources (Ibrahim N, 2018), (Ricamonte B, 2018).

4 Conclusion

People that spend long periods of time navigating, often with mooring ports that involve contact with Zika virus. Considering this fact, it is mandatory to evaluate the level of knowledge about Zika infection. In the present work we analyze some questions of the applied questionnaire, namely, if Zika infection could induce fever, if the participants in the study knew Zika infection, and if yes, how they did that. We have considered the data pre-mission ans post-mission group. We could stablish that almost 25% and 35% (respectively pre mission and pos mission) of staff did not know the existence of ZIKA virus. Between the staff that knew the existence of Zika, the majority took acknowledge of Zika virus by the media, Only about one third took acknowledge by the health profissionals. Our study that the results suggest that a comprehensive navigator preventive healthcare educational program is mandatory before some emergent outbreak occurs again.

Acknowledgments. This work was supported by Portuguese funds through *the Center for Compu-tational and Stochastic Mathematics* (CEMAT), *The Portuguese Foundation for Science and Technology* (FCT), University of Lisbon, Portugal, project UID/Multi/04621/2019, and Center of Naval Research (CINAV), Naval Academy, Portuguese Navy, Portugal.

References

Arief, M., et al.: A Cross-sectional survey on the knowledge and attitudes towards Zika virus and its prevention among residents of Selangor. Malaysia. J. Pharm. Pract. Commun. Med. **3**(2), b1-88 (2017)

Binsaad, Y.: Public knowledge, attitudes and behavior towards Zika virus in Saudi Arabia. Int. J. Adv. Res. **5**(1), 2898–2903 (2017)

Cao-Lormeau, V.M., et al.: Guillain Barré syndrome outbreak associated with Zika virus infection in French Polynesia: a case control study. Lancet **387**(10027), 1531–1539 (2016)

CDC. (2019). Zika in the US. Obtido de https://www.cdc.gov/zika/geo/index.html

Darrow, W., Bhatt, C., Rene, C., Thomas, L.: Zika virus awareness and prevention practices among university students in Miami: fall 2016. Health Educ. Behav. **11**, 967–976 (2018). https://doi.org/10.1177/1090198118760687

Dick, G.W., Kitchen, S.F., Haddow, A.J.: Zika virus (I). Isolations and serological specificity. Trans. R. Soc. Tropic. Med. Hyg. **46**(5), 509–520 (1952). https://doi.org/10.1016/0035-9203(52)90042-4

ECDC. Factsheet about Zika virus disease. Obtido em 2023 de March de 23, de (2016). http://ecdc.europa.eu/en/zika-virus-infection/facts/factsheet

Faria, J.: Conhecimentos, atitudes e práticas de prevenção sobre Zika da população embarcada em navios da Marinha Portuguesa. *Master Thesis*. Lisboa: Instituto de Higiene e Medicina Tropical, Universidade Nova de Lisboa (2019)

Faria, J., Teodósio, R., Teodoro, M.F.: Knowledge of the boarded population about Zika virus. In: Misra, S., et al. (eds.) Computational Science and Its Applications – ICCSA 2019. Lecture Notes in Computer Science, vol. 11621, pp. 97–110. Springer, Cham (2019). https://doi.org/10.1007/978-3-030-24302-9_8

Gregorio, E.R., Jr., et al.: Knowledge, attitudes, and practices of public secondary school teachers on Zika virus disease: a basis for the development of evidence-based Zika educational materials for schools in the Philippine. PLoS ONE **14**, e0214 (2019). https://doi.org/10.1371/journal.pone.0214515

Gupta, N., Randhawa, R., Thakar, S., Bansal, M., Gupta, P., Arora, V.: Knowledge regarding Zika virus infection among dental practitioners of tricity area (Chandigarh, Panchkula and Mohali) India. Niger. Postgrad. Med. J. **23**(1), 33–37 (2016)

Harapan, H., et al.: Healthcare workers' knowledge towards Zika virus infection in Indonesia: a survey in Aceh. Asian Pac. J. Trop. Med. **10**(2), 189–194 (2017)

Harapan, H., et al.: Attitudes towards Zika virus infection among medical doctors in Aceh province, Indonesia. J. Infect. Public Health **11**(1), 99–104 (2018)

Huang, Y., et al.: Knowledge, attitudes, and practices regarding Zika: paper- and internet-based survey in Zhejiang. China. JMIR Pub. Health Surveill. **3**(4), e7663 (2017)

Ibrahim, N.K., Moshref, R.H., Moshref, L.H., Walid, J.B., Alsati, H.S.: Knowledge and attitudes towards Zika virus among medical students in King Abdulaziz university, Jeddah, Saudi Arabia. J. Infect. Pub. Health **11**, 18–23 (2018)

Khan, M.U., Ahmad, A., Arief, M., Saleem, F., Hassali, M.A., Bhagavathula, A.S.: Public knowledge and attitudes towards Zika Virus and its prevention in Malaysia. Value Health **19**(7), A423–A424 (2016)

Kindhauser, M.K., Allen, T., Frank, V., Santhana, R.S., Dye, C.: Zika: the origin and spread of a mosquito-borne virus. Bull. World Health Organ. **94**(6), 675–686 (2016)

Lim, K.Y., Tham, H.W.: Knowledge, awareness, and perception of community pharmacists to Zika virus infection in Klang valley Malays. Health Serv. Insights **13** 1–112020). https://doi.org/10.1177/1178632920921425

MacNamara, F.: A report on three cases of human infection during an epidemic of jaundice in Nigeria. Trans. R. Soc. Trop. Med. Hyg. **48**, 139–145 (1954). https://doi.org/10.1016/0035-9203(52)90042-4

Maroco, J.A.: Anáalise Estatfística com o SPSS Statistics. Pero Pinheiro: Report Number (2014)

Michael, G.C., Aliyu, I., Grema, B.A., Ashimi, A.O.: Knowledge of Zika virus disease among reproductive-age women attending a general outpatient clinic in northern Nigeria. South Afr. Fam. Pract. **1**(1), 1–6 (2017)

Mouchtouri V.P.D.: Int. J. Environ. Res. Public Health. Knowledge, Attitudes, and Practices about the Prevention of Mosquito Bites and Zika Virus Disease in Pregnant Women in Greece, **14**(367) (2017)

Olson, J.G., Ksiazek, T.G.: Zika virus, a cause of fever in Central Java, Indonesia. Trans R Soc Trop Med Hyg. **75**(3), 389–393 (1981)

PAHO/WHO. (2016). Timeline of Emergence of Zika virus in the Americas. Obtido em 8 de April de 2023, de www.PAHO.org

Pergolizzi, J.V., Quang, J.A.L., Taylor, R., Magnusson, P., Nalamachu, M., Pergolizzi, C., Raffa, R.B.: Survey of students regarding Zika infection: is the next generation aware of the dangers? Pharmacol. Pharm. **11**(11), 306–315 (2020). https://doi.org/10.4236/pp.2020.1111025

Plaster, A.N., Painter, J.E., Tjersland, D.H., Jacobsen, K.H.: University students' knowledge, attitudes, and sources of information About Zika virus. J. Community Health **43**(4), 647–655 (2018). https://doi.org/10.1007/s10900-017-0463-z

Rabaan, A.A., Bazzi, A.M., Al-Ahmed, S.H., Al-Ghaith, M.H., Al-Tawfiq, J.A.: Overview of Zika infection, epidemiology, transmission and control measures. J. Infect. Pub. Health **10**(2), 141–149 (2017)

Oducado, R.M., Ricamonte, B.T., Jover, C.C., Ngitngit, E.J., Hiponia, A.Y., Macables, G.H.: Knowledge and attitude toward Zika virus disease among pregnant women in Iloilo city Philippines. Pub. Health Res. **8**(5), 115–120 (2018)

Rosalino, C.: Conhecimentos, atitudes e práticas sobre Zika de viajantes visitando o Rio de Janeiro, Brasil, durante os Jogos Olimpicos e Paraolmpicos de 2016: Inquuérito no Aeroporto Internacional António Carlos. Obtido em 1 de May de 2019, de (2016). http://aplicacao.saude.gov.br/plataformabrasil/login.jsf

Roundy, C.M., et al.: Lack of evidence for Zika virus transmission by Culex mosquitoes. Emerg. Microbes Infect. **6**(e90), 1–2 (2017)

Sampathkumar, P., Sanchez, J.L.: Zika virus in the Americas: a review for clinicians. Mayo Clin. Proc. **91**(4), 514–521 (2016)

Services, U.D.: Operational risk communication and community engagement plan responding to local mosquito-borne transmission of Zika virus. Retrieved from. Obtido de (2016). https://www.cdc.gov/zika/pdfs/z-cart-plan.pdf

Sharma, V., Sharma, M., Dhull, D., Sharma, Y., Kaushik, S., Kaushik, S.: Zika virus: an emerging challenge to public health worldwide. Can. J. Microbiol. **66**(2), 87–98 (2020). https://doi.org/10.1139/cjm-2019-0331

Teodoro, M.F.: Navigators' about Zika infection. Biomedial Bioestatics Imternacional J. **12**(2), 34–38 (2023). https://doi.org/10.15406/bbij.2023.12.00380

Waddell, L.A., Greig, J.D.: Scoping review of the Zika virus literature. PloS one **11**(5), e0156376 (2016)

WHO. (2016). Inquéritos sobre Conhecimentos, Atitudes e Práticas. Doença do Vfírus Zika e Potenciais Complicações- Pacote de recursos. WHO. Obtido em 05 de February de 2018, de https://apps.who.int/iris/bitstream/handle/10665/204689/WHO_ZIKV_RCCE_16.2_por.pdf?sequence=5

Who. Zika—Strategic response framework and joint operations plan: January-June 2016 (WHO/ZIKV/SRF/16.1). WHO. Obtido em 23 de March de 2023, de (2016a). http://apps.who.int/iris/bitstream/10665/204420/1/ZikaResponseFramework_JanJun16_eng.pdf?ua=1

WHO/Europe. (2016). Zika virus Technical report. Interim Risk Assessment - WHO European. WHO. Obtido em 23 de March de 2023, de http://www.euro.who.int/__data/assets/pdf_file/0003/309981/Zika-Virus-Technical-report.pdf?ua=1

Willison, H.J., Jacobs, B.C., van Doorn, P.A.: Guillain-barre syndrome. Lancet **388**, 717–727 (2016)

Wishner, C., Taylor, C., Leigh, L., Williams, M., Bell, M.A., Luebke, S.: Physician assistant students' knowledge of Zika virus: a pilot study. Infect. Dis. Res. Treat. **13**, 1–11 (2020). https://doi.org/10.1177/1178633720909158

Zanluca, C., Melo, V.C.A.D., Mosimann, A.L.P., Santos, G.I.V.D., Santos, C.N.D.D., Luz, K.: First report of autochthonous transmission of Zika virus in Brazil. Memórias do Instituto Oswaldo Cruz **110**(4), 569–572 (2015)

Mathematical Analysis of Autonomous and Nonautonomous Hepatitis B Virus Transmission Models

Abdallah Alsammani[✉]

Department of Mathematics, Jacksonville University, Jacksonville, FL 32211, USA
aalsamm@ju.edu

Abstract. This study presents an improved mathematical model for Hepatitis B Virus (HBV) transmission dynamics by investigating autonomous and nonautonomous cases. The novel model incorporates the effects of medical treatment, allowing for a more comprehensive understanding of HBV transmission and potential control measures. Our analysis involves verifying unique solutions' existence, ensuring solutions' positivity over time, and conducting a stability analysis at the equilibrium points. Both local and global stability are discussed; for local stability, we use the Jacobian matrix and the basic reproduction number, R_0. For global stability, we construct a Lyapunov function and derive necessary and sufficient conditions for stability in our models, establishing a connection between these conditions and R_0. Numerical simulations substantiate our analytical findings, offering valuable insights into HBV transmission dynamics and the effectiveness of different interventions. This study advances our understanding of Hepatitis B Virus (HBV) transmission dynamics by presenting an enhanced mathematical model that considers both autonomous and nonautonomous cases.

Keywords: HBV model · Nonautonomous · stability analysis · DFE · epidemic equilibrium · numerical simulations

1 Introduction

Hepatitis B Virus (HBV) is a significant global health concern, affecting millions of people worldwide and posing a considerable burden on public health systems [1]. The transmission dynamics of HBV are complex, involving multiple interacting factors such as the rates of infection, recovery, and medical treatment. Understanding these dynamics is essential for devising effective prevention and control strategies [14].

Mathematical models have been widely employed to study the transmission dynamics of infectious diseases, including HBV [8, 15]. Early HBV models primarily focused on autonomous systems, assuming constant parameters over time [16, 17]. However, more recent models have considered nonautonomous systems, taking into account time-varying parameters and seasonal fluctuations [9, 13]. These models provide a more realistic representation of the disease transmission process.

In this study, we present an improved mathematical model for HBV transmission dynamics by investigating both autonomous and nonautonomous cases. The model

© The Author(s), under exclusive license to Springer Nature Switzerland AG 2023
O. Gervasi et al. (Eds.): ICCSA 2023 Workshops, LNCS 14105, pp. 327–343, 2023.
https://doi.org/10.1007/978-3-031-37108-0_21

incorporates the effects of medical treatment, allowing for a more comprehensive understanding of HBV transmission and potential control measures. The analysis includes verifying the existence of unique solutions, ensuring the positivity of solutions over time, and conducting a stability analysis at the equilibrium points [6, 12].

We discuss both local and global stability. For local stability, we use the Jacobian matrix and the basic reproduction number, R_0 [7]. For global stability, we construct a Lyapunov function and derive necessary and sufficient conditions for stability in our models, establishing a connection between these conditions and R_0 [4, 11].

Numerical simulations substantiate our analytical findings, offering valuable insights into HBV transmission dynamics and the effectiveness of different interventions. The results of this study contribute to the growing body of literature on HBV mathematical modeling and provide a basis for further research and policy development.

2   Model Formulation

A nonlinear differential equation model was developed to study HBV transmission, considering medical treatment effects and various rates [2, 3, 15, 16, 18]. The model is defined as:

$$\begin{cases} \frac{dx}{dt} &= \Lambda - \mu_1 x - (1-\eta)\beta xz + qy \\ \frac{dy}{dt} &= (1-\eta)\beta xz - \mu_2 y - qy \\ \frac{dz}{dt} &= (1-\epsilon)py - \mu_3 z \end{cases} \tag{1}$$

Here, the variables and parameters represent the following

- $x(t)$: The number of uninfected cells (target cells) at time t.
- $y(t)$: The number of infected cells at time t.
- $z(t)$: The number of free virus particles at time t.

Table 1 summarizes the description of the parameters in the system (1).

Table 1. Parameters descriptions

Parameter	Description
Λ	*Production rate of uninfected cells x*
μ_1	*Death rate of x-cells*
μ_2	*Death rate of y-cells*
μ_3	*Free virus cleared rate*
η	*Fraction that reduced infected rate after treatment with the antiviral drug*
ϵ	*Fraction that reduced free virus rate after treatment with the antiviral drug*
p	*Free virus production rate y-cells*
β	*Infection rate of x-cells by free virus z*
q	*Spontaneous cure rate of y-cells by non-cytolytic process*

Notice that η and ϵ are small positive fractions between 0 and 1, then $(1 - \eta) > 0$ and $(1 - \epsilon) > 0$, also all other parameters $\beta, q, p, \mu_1, \mu_2$ and μ_3 are positive.

Notations: Throughout this paper, we will consider the following.

- $\mathbb{R}^3 = \{(x, y, z)| (x, y, z) \in \mathbb{R}\}$, and $\mathbb{R}^3_+ = \{(x, y, z) \in \mathbb{R}^3| x \geq 0, y \geq 0, z \geq 0\}$.
- If $\mathbf{u} = (x, y, z)^T \in \mathbb{R}^3$ then the system (1) can be written as

$$\frac{d\mathbf{u}(t)}{dt} = f(\mathbf{u}(t)) \tag{2}$$

where

$$f(\mathbf{u}(t)) = f(x(t), y(t), z(t)) = \begin{pmatrix} \Lambda - \mu_1 x - (1 - \eta)\beta xz + qy \\ (1 - \eta)\beta xz - \mu_2 y - qy \\ (1 - \epsilon)py - \mu_3 z \end{pmatrix} \tag{3}$$

and $u_0 = u(t_0) = (x(t_0), y(t_0), z(t_0)) = (x_0, y_0, z_0)$.

2.1 Properties of Solutions

We discuss the basic properties of the HBV model, including solution existence, uniqueness, and positivity. Existence is ensured by Lipschitz continuity, uniqueness through the Picard-Lindelof or Banach's fixed-point theorems, and positivity by analyzing the model equations.

Theorem 1 (Local Existence).
For any given $t_0 \in \mathbb{R}$ and $u_0 = (x_0, y_0, z_0) \in \mathbb{R}^3_+$ there exists $T_{max} = T_{max}(t_0, u_0)$ such that the system from (1) has a solution $(x(t; u_0), y(t; t_0, u_0), z(t; t_0, u_0))$ on $[t_0, t_0 + T_{max})$. Furthermore, If $T_{max} < \infty$ then the solution will blow up, i.e.,

$$\limsup_{t \to T_{max}} (|x(t_0 + t; t_0, u_0)| + |y(t_0 + t; t_0, u_0)| + |z(t_0 + t; t_0, u_0)|) = +\infty$$

Proof. It is clear that this function $f(u(t))$ in Eq. 3 is continuous, and its derivatives with respect to x, y, and z are also continuous. Therefore, the system (1) has a unique local solution.

It is well known that solutions of ordinary differential equations may blow up in finite time.

Since the system 1 is a population system, it is very important to ensure that the solution is always positive.

Lemma 1. *suppose $(x(t_0), y(t_0), z(t_0)) \in \mathbb{R}^3_+$ is the initial value of the system 1, then the solution $(x(t), y(t), z(t))$ is positive for all $t \in [t_0, t_0 + T_{max})$.*

Proof. Notice that $z(t)$ has an explicit solution that depends on $y(t)$. Thus, if $y(t)$ is positive, that implies $z(t)$ is also positive for all $t \geq t_0$.

Then, it is enough to show the positiveness for x and y. By contradiction suppose not, then there exists $\tau \in [t_0, t_0 + T_{max})$ such that $x(t) > 0, y(t) > 0$ and $z(t) > 0$ on $[t_0, \tau)$ this implies one of the following cases

(i) $x(\tau) = 0$ and $y(\tau) > 0$
(ii) $x(\tau) > 0$ and $y(\tau) = 0$
(iii) $x(\tau) = 0$ and $y(\tau) = 0$

Now we will show that none of the above cases is possible.

Claim. Case (i) is not possible.

Proof. From the basic definition of the derivative, we have.

$$\frac{dx}{dt}(\tau) = \lim_{t \to \tau} \frac{x(t) - x(\tau)}{t - \tau} = \lim_{t \to \tau} \frac{x(t)}{t - \tau} \le 0 \qquad \to \quad (1)$$

from the first equation in 1 we have

$$\frac{dx}{dt}(\tau) = \Lambda - \mu_1 x(\tau) - (1 - \eta)\beta x(\tau)v(\tau) + qy(\tau)$$
$$= \Lambda + qy(\tau) \ge py(\tau) > 0 \qquad \to \quad (2)$$

That is a contradiction. Therefore, case(1) is not possible.

Claim. Case (ii) is not possible.

Proof. We know that

$$\frac{dy}{dt}(\tau) = \lim_{t \to \tau} \frac{y(t) - y(\tau)}{t - \tau} = \lim_{t \to \tau} \frac{y(t)}{t - \tau} \le 0 \qquad \to \quad (3)$$

from the second equation in 1 we have

$$\frac{dy}{dt}(\tau) = (1 - \eta)\beta v(\tau)x(\tau) > 0 \qquad \to \quad (4)$$

from (3) and (4) we have a contradiction, thus, case(2) is not possible.

Similarly, case(iii) is also not possible.
    Therefore, the statement in the lemma is correct.
    Now we show the global existence of the solution, which is enough to show that the solution of the system 1 is bounded.

Theorem 2 (Global Existence "Boundedness"). *For given* $t_0 \in \mathbb{R}$ *and* $(x_0, y_0, z_0) \in \mathbb{R}_+^3$, *the solution* $(x(t), y(t), z(t))$ *exists for all* $t \ge t_0$ *and moreover,*

$$0 \le x(t) + y(t) \le M \qquad \text{and} \quad 0 \le z(t) \le e^{\mu_3(t-t_0)}z_0 + (1 - \epsilon) M \left(\frac{1 - e^{-\mu_3(t-t_0)}}{\mu_3} \right)$$

where $M = Max \left\{ x_0 + y_0, \ \frac{\Lambda}{min(\mu_1, \mu_2)} \right\}$

Proof.

It is enough to show that $|x(t)| + |y(t)| < \infty$ on $(t_0, t_0 + T_{max})$.

By adding the first two equations in 1 we get

$$\frac{dx}{dt} + \frac{dy}{dt} = \Lambda - \mu_1 x - \mu_2 y \tag{4}$$

$$\leq \Lambda - min\{\mu_1, \mu_2\}[x(t) + y(t)]. \tag{5}$$

Let $v(t) = x(t) + y(t)$ the Eq. 4 becomes

$$v(t) \leq \Lambda - min\{\mu_1, \mu_2\}\, v(t).$$

By the ODE comparison principle, we have

$$v(t) \leq Max\left\{v_0, \ \frac{\Lambda}{min(\mu_1, \mu_2)}\right\}$$

which implies $T_{max} = +\infty$.

It is clear that for t large, we have

$$v(t) \leq \frac{\Lambda}{min\{\mu_1, \mu_2\}}$$

Which means both $x(t)$ and $y(t)$ are bounded. It is clear that $z(t)$ is also bounded directly by solving the third equation in system 1.

In summary, the system of differential equations (1) has a unique and positive solution for any set of initial values, which is essential for the model's physical interpretation. These properties provide a solid foundation for further analysis of the system's dynamics and stability.

3 Stability Analysis

Stability analysis is an essential aspect of mathematical modeling as it allows us to investigate the behavior of the system of differential equations (1) over time and identify conditions for the system to reach an equilibrium state. In this section, we will perform a stability analysis of the system's equilibrium points.

3.1 Equilibrium Solutions

The equilibria of the system 1 are all the points in $\mathbb{R}^3$ such that $\dot{x} = \dot{y} = \dot{z} = 0$. The system 1 has only two two equilibrium points which are

1. Disease-free equilibrium $(\bar{x}_0, \bar{y}_0, \bar{z}_0) = \left(\frac{\Lambda}{\mu_1}, 0, 0\right)$ and
2. Endemic equilibrium

$$(\bar{x}, \bar{y}, \bar{z}) = \left(\frac{\mu_1\mu_3(\mu_2 + p)}{q\beta\mu_2(1 - \eta)(1 - \epsilon)}, \frac{\Lambda}{\mu_2} - \frac{\mu_1\mu_3(\mu_2 + p)}{q\beta\mu_2(1 - \eta)(1 - \epsilon)}, \frac{q\Lambda(1 - \epsilon)}{\mu_2\mu_3} - \frac{\mu_1(\mu_2 + p)}{\beta\mu_2(1 - \eta)}\right)$$

The endemic equilibrium $(\bar{x}, \bar{y}, \bar{z})$ represents a state in which the infection persists in the population. Analyzing the stability of this equilibrium helps us understand the long-term behavior of the infection dynamics and informs public health interventions to control the disease.

3.2 Local Stability

The Jacobian matrix $J(x, y, z)$ represents the linearization of the system of ODEs around a particular point (x, y, z). It is used to analyze the stability of equilibrium points in the system. The Jacobian matrix $J(x, y, z)$ of the system 1 is a 3×3 matrix containing the partial derivatives of the system's equations with respect to the state variables x, y, and z. It is given by

$$J(x, y, z) = \begin{bmatrix} -\mu_1 - (1-\eta)\beta z & q & -(1-\eta)\beta x \\ (1-\eta)\beta z & -(\mu_2 + q) & (1-\eta)\beta x \\ 0 & (1-\epsilon)p & -\mu_3 \end{bmatrix} \tag{6}$$

The Jacobian matrix $J(x, y, z)$ is used to analyze the local stability of the equilibrium points in the system by evaluating it at those points and computing the eigenvalues. The eigenvalues determine the nature of the equilibrium points (stable, unstable, or saddle).

3.2.1 Local Stability of Infection-Free Equilibrium

The local stability of the equilibrium points can be analyzed using linearization techniques. By evaluating the Jacobian matrix at the equilibrium points and examining its eigenvalues, we can determine the local stability characteristics of the system.

Computing the Jacobian at diseases-free equilibrium gives

$$J(x_0, y_0, z_0) = \begin{bmatrix} -\mu_1 & q & 0 \\ 0 & -(\mu_2 + q) & 0 \\ 0 & (1-\epsilon)p & -\mu_3 \end{bmatrix} \tag{7}$$

Therefore, the reproduction number R_0 is given by

$$R_0 = \frac{(1-\eta)\beta \frac{\Lambda}{\mu_1}}{\mu_2 + q} \tag{8}$$

Notice that, $R_0 < 1$ implies both conditions ($Tr(J_1) < 0$ and $Det(J_1) > 0$). Therefore, if $R_0 < 1$, then the disease-free equilibrium is locally asymptotically stable. If $R_0 > 1$, then the disease-free is unstable.

3.3 Global Stability

To investigate the global stability of the equilibrium points, we can use Lyapunov functions or comparison theorems. By constructing an appropriate Lyapunov function and showing that it satisfies certain properties, we can prove the global stability of the system.

Lemma 2. *The system 1 is exponentially stable at its equilibrium points* $(\bar{x}, \bar{y}, \bar{z})$ *if the following conditions hold*

$$\begin{cases} 2\mu_1 + (1-\eta)\beta\bar{z} & > & (1-\eta)\beta\frac{\Lambda}{min(\mu_1, \mu_2)} + q \\ 2\mu_2 + q & > & (1-\eta)\beta\left(\bar{z} + \frac{\Lambda}{min(\mu_1, \mu_2)}\right) + (1-\epsilon)p \\ 2\mu_3 & > & (1-\epsilon)p + \frac{(1-\eta)\Lambda\beta}{min(\mu_1, \mu_2)} \end{cases} \tag{9}$$

Proof. In fact, it is enough to show that

$$|x - \bar{x}| \to 0, \quad |y - \bar{y}| \to 0, \quad and \quad |z - \bar{z}| \to 0, \quad as \quad t \to \infty \qquad (10)$$

Since $x - \bar{x}$, $y - \bar{y}$, and $z - \bar{z}$ satisfies the system 1. From system 1 we have

$$\begin{cases} \frac{d}{dt}(x - \bar{x}) = -(\mu_1 + (1 - \eta)\beta\bar{z})(x - \bar{x}) + q(y - \bar{y}) - (1 - \eta)\beta x(z - \bar{z}) \\ \frac{d}{dt}(y - \bar{y}) = (1 - \eta)\beta\bar{z}(x - \bar{x}) - (q + \mu_2)(y - \bar{y}) + (1 - \eta)\beta x(z - \bar{z}) \\ \frac{d}{dt}(z - \bar{z}) = (1 - \epsilon)p(y - \bar{y}) - \mu_3(z - \bar{z}) \end{cases} \qquad (11)$$

Now, let $X = x - \bar{x}$, $Y = y - \bar{y}$ and $Z = z - \bar{z}$ then system 11 becomes

$$\frac{dX}{dt} = -(\mu_1 + (1 - \eta)\beta\bar{z})X + qY - (1 - \eta)\beta x Z \qquad (12)$$

$$\frac{dY}{dt} = (1 - \eta)\beta\bar{z}X - (q + \mu_2)Y + (1 - \eta)\beta x Z \qquad (13)$$

$$\frac{dZ}{dt} = (1 - \epsilon)pY - \mu_3 Z \qquad (14)$$

Now, since $X = X_+ - X_-$, where X_+ and X_- are the positive and negative parts of the function X, and also we have

$$XX_+ = (X_+ - X_-)X_+ = X_+^2$$

$$-XX_- = -(X_+ - X_-)X_- = X_-^2$$

$$(X_+ \pm X_-)^2 = X_+^2 + X_-^2 = |X|^2$$

This implies that

$$\dot{X}X_+ = \frac{1}{2}\frac{d}{dt}X_+^2 \qquad and \qquad -\dot{X}X_- = \frac{1}{2}\frac{d}{dt}X_-^2$$

Now multiplying Eq. 12 by X_+ gives

$$\dot{X}X_+ = -[\mu_1 + (1 - \eta)\beta\bar{z}]XX_+ + qYX_+ - (1 - \eta)\beta x Z X_+$$

$$\frac{1}{2}\frac{d}{dt}X_+^2 = -[\mu_1 + (1 - \eta)\beta\bar{z}]X_+^2 + qYX_+ - (1 - \eta)\beta x Z X_+ \qquad (15)$$

If we multiply Eq. 12 by X_- we get

$$\frac{1}{2}\frac{d}{dt}X_-^2 = -[\mu_1 + (1 - \eta)\beta\bar{z}]X_-^2 + qYX_- + (1 - \eta)\beta x Z X_- \qquad (16)$$

adding Eq. 15 and Eq. 16 we get

$$\frac{1}{2}\frac{d}{dt}(X_+^2 + X_-^2) = -[\mu_1 + (1 - \eta)\beta\bar{z}](X_+^2 + X_-^2) + qY(X_+ - X_-) + (1 - \eta)\beta x Z(X_+ - X_-)$$

$$\frac{1}{2}\frac{d}{dt}|X|^2 = -[\mu_1 + (1-\eta)\beta\bar{z}]|X|^2 + q(Y_+ - Y_-)(X_+ - X_-) + (1-\eta)\beta x(Z_+ - Z_-)(X_+ - X_-)$$

$$= -[\mu_1 + (1-\eta)\beta\bar{z}]|X|^2 + q(Y_+X_+ + Y_-X_- - Y_-X_+ - Y_+X_-)$$
$$+ (1-\eta)\beta x(X_+Z_- + X_-Z_+ - X_+Z_+ - X_-Z_-)$$

$$\leq -[\mu_1 + (1-\eta)\beta\bar{z}]|X|^2 + \frac{1}{2}qY_+^2 + \frac{1}{2}qX_+^2 + \frac{1}{2}qY_-^2 + \frac{1}{2}X_-^2 - q(Y_-X_+ + Y_+X_-)$$
$$+ \frac{1}{2}(1-\eta)\beta x(X_+^2 + Z_-^2 + X_-^2 + Z_+^2) - (1-\eta)\beta x(X_+Z_+ + X_-Z_-)$$

$$\leq -[\mu_1 + (1-\eta)\beta\bar{z}]|X|^2 + \frac{1}{2}q|Y|^2 + \frac{1}{2}(1-\eta)\beta x|X|^2 + \frac{1}{2}q|X|^2 + \frac{1}{2}(1-\eta)\beta x|Z|^2$$
$$- q(Y_-X_+ + Y_+X_-) - (1-\eta)\beta x(X_+Z_+ - X_-Z_-)$$

Thus,

$$\frac{1}{2}\frac{d}{dt}|X|^2 \leq -\left[\mu_1 + (1-\eta)\beta\bar{z} - \frac{1}{2}q - \frac{1}{2}(1-\eta)\beta x\right]|X|^2 + \frac{1}{2}q|Y|^2 + \frac{1}{2}(1-\eta)\beta x|Z|^2$$
$$- q(Y_-X_+ + Y_+X_-) - (1-\eta)\beta x(X_+Z_+ - X_-Z_-) \tag{17}$$

Similarly, by using the same computational technique, we got

$$\frac{1}{2}\frac{d}{dt}|Y|^2 \leq \frac{1}{2}(1-\eta)\beta\bar{z}|X|^2 - \left[(q+\mu_2) - \frac{1}{2}(1-\eta)\beta\bar{z} - \frac{1}{2}(1-\eta)\beta x\right]|Y|^2 + \frac{1}{2}(1-\eta)\beta x|Z|^2$$
$$- (1-\eta)\beta\bar{z}(X_+Y_- + X_-Y_+) - (1-\eta)\beta x(Z_+Y_- + Z_-Y_+) \tag{18}$$

and

$$\frac{1}{2}\frac{d}{dt}|Z|^2 \leq -[\mu_3 - \frac{1}{2}(1-\epsilon)]|Z|^2 + \frac{1}{2}(1-\epsilon)p|Y|^2 - (1-\epsilon)p(Y_+Z_- + Y_-Z_+) \tag{19}$$

Now, by adding 17 , 18 and 19 we get

$$\frac{1}{2}\frac{d}{dt}\left(|X|^2 + |Y|^2 + |Z|^2\right) \leq -\left[\mu_1 + \frac{1}{2}(1-\eta)\beta\bar{z} - \frac{1}{2}q - \frac{1}{2}(1-\eta)\beta x\right]|X|^2$$
$$- \left[\mu_2 + \frac{1}{2}q - \frac{1}{2}(1-\eta)\beta\bar{z} - \frac{1}{2}(1-\eta)\beta x - (1-\epsilon)p\right]|Y|^2$$
$$- \left[\mu_3 - \frac{1}{2}(1-\epsilon)p - (1-\eta)\beta x\right]|Z|^2 - [q(Y_+X_- + Y_-X_+)$$
$$+ (1-\eta)\beta x(X_+Z_+ + X_-Z_-) + (1-\eta)(X_+Y_- + X_-Y_+)$$
$$(1-\eta)\beta x(Z_+Y_- Z_-Y_+) + (1-\epsilon)p(Y_+Z_- + Y_-Z_+)] \tag{20}$$

Therefore,

$$\frac{d}{dt}\left(|X|^2 + |Y|^2 + |Z|^2\right) \leq -\nu_1|X|^2 - \nu_2|Y|^2 - \nu_3|Z|^2 - W \tag{21}$$

where

$$\nu_1 = 2\mu_1 + (1-\eta)\beta\bar{z} - (1-\eta)\beta x - q$$
$$\nu_2 = \mu_2 + q - (1-\eta)\beta\bar{z} - (1-\eta)\beta x - (1-\epsilon)p$$
$$\nu_3 = 2\mu_3 - (1-\epsilon)p - (1-\eta)\beta x$$
$$W = q(Y_+X_- + Y_-X_+) + (1-\eta)\beta x(X_+Z_+ + X_-Z_-) + (1-\eta)(X_+Y_- + X_-Y_+)$$
$$+ (1-\eta)\beta x(Z_+Y_- Z_-Y_+) + (1-\epsilon)p(Y_+Z_- + Y_-Z_+)$$

Condition 23 guaranteed that ν_1, ν_2, an ν_3 are always positive. Since $W \geq 0$, then the inequity 21 still holds after removing W.

Now Let $k = \min n \{\nu_1, \nu_2, \nu_3\}$ and let $V(t) = |X(t)|^2 + |Y(t)|^2 + |Z(t)|^2$ then the inequality 21 becomes

$$\frac{dV(t)}{dt} \leq -kV(t)$$

$$0 \leq V(t) \leq V_0 e^{-kt} \longrightarrow 0 \quad \text{as} \quad t \to \infty \tag{22}$$

3.4 Stability at Disease-Free Equilibrium

Substituting $(\bar{x}, \bar{y}, \bar{z}) = (\Lambda/\mu_1, 0, 0)$ in condition 9 we get the following conditions

$$\begin{cases} 2\mu_1 & > & (1-\eta)\beta\frac{\Lambda}{\mu^*} + q \\ 2\mu_2 + q & > & (1-\eta)\beta\frac{\Lambda}{\mu^*} + (1-\epsilon)p \\ 2\mu_3 & > & (1-\epsilon)p + \frac{(1-\eta)\Lambda\beta}{\mu^*} \end{cases} \tag{23}$$

where $\mu^* = min(\mu_1, \mu_2)$, and basic productive number $R_0 = \frac{\Lambda\beta p(1-\epsilon)(1-\eta)}{\mu_1\mu_2(\mu_1+(1-\epsilon)p)}$.

Theorem 3. *The autonomous dynamic systems 1 is exponentially stable if $R_0 < 1$ and conditions 23 are satisfied.*

Proof. Consider the Lyapunov function

$$V(x, y, z) = \frac{1}{2}[(x - \Lambda/\mu_1)^2 + y^2 + z^2]$$

which is clearly positive, and by following some computations in the proof of Lemma 2 we get $V' \leq 0$. That completed the proof.

3.5 Stability at the Endemic Equilibrium

Substituting the endemic equilibrium $((\bar{x}, \bar{y}, \bar{z}))$ where

$$\begin{cases} \bar{x} & = & \frac{\mu_1\mu_3(\mu_2+p)}{q\beta\mu_2(1-\eta)(1-\epsilon)}, \\ \bar{y} & = & \frac{\Lambda}{\mu_2} - \frac{\mu_1\mu_3(\mu_2+p)}{q\beta\mu_2(1-\eta)(1-\epsilon)}, \\ \bar{z} & = & \frac{q\Lambda(1-\epsilon)}{\mu_2\mu_3} - \frac{\mu_1(\mu_2+p)}{\beta\mu_2(1-\eta)} \end{cases} \tag{24}$$

in condition 9 we get the following conditions

$$\begin{cases} \mu_1\mu_2\mu_3 + (1-\epsilon)(1-\eta)\Lambda\beta q & > & \frac{(1-\eta)\Lambda\beta\mu_2\mu_3}{min(\mu_1,\mu_2)} + q\mu_2\mu_3 + p\mu_1\mu_3 \\ 2\mu_2^2 + \mu_1\mu_2 + p\mu_1 + q & > & \frac{(1-\eta)(1-\epsilon)\beta\Lambda q}{\mu_3} + \frac{(1-\eta)\Lambda\beta}{min \mu_1,\mu_2} \\ 2\mu_3 & > & (1-\epsilon)p + \frac{(1-\eta)\Lambda\beta}{min(\mu_1,\mu_2)} \end{cases} \tag{25}$$

Theorem 4. *The solution of system 1 is exponentially stable at the endemic equilibrium 24 if conditions 25.*

.

Proof. The proof follows by Lemma 2.

4 Nonautonomous HBV Model

In this section, we will discuss the nonautonomous HBV infection model where the production number Λ is time-dependent. We will provide a brief introduction to nonautonomous dynamical systems, followed by a stability analysis of the nonautonomous HBV model.

4.1 Preliminaries of Nonautonomous Dynamical Systems

Before we start analyzing our nonautonomous model, we provide an overview of the preliminaries of nonautonomous dynamical systems. Nonautonomous systems differ from autonomous systems in that they depend on the actual time t and the initial time t_0 rather than just their difference. We will introduce some basic concepts and theorems that are essential for understanding nonautonomous systems.

1. **Process Formulation:** A common way to represent nonautonomous dynamical systems is through process formulation. In this representation, a process is a continuous mapping $\phi(t, t_0, \cdot) : \mathbb{R}^n \to \mathbb{R}^n$ that satisfies the initial and evolution properties:
   (a) $\phi(t_0, t_0, u_0) = u_0$ for all $u_0 \in \mathbb{R}^n$.
   (b) $\phi(t_2, t_0, u) = \phi(t_2, t_1, \phi(t_1, t_0, u))$. for all $t_0 \leq t_1 \leq t_2$ and $u_0 \in \mathbb{R}^n$.
2. **Invariant Families:** A family $\mathcal{A} = \{A(t) :, t \in \mathbb{R}\}$ of nonempty subsets of $\mathbb{R}^n$ is said to be:
   (a) Invariant with respect to ϕ, or ϕ-invariant if

   $$\phi(t, t_0, A(t_0)) = A(t) \qquad \text{for all} \quad t >\geq t_0.$$

   (b) Positive Invariant, or ϕ-Positive invariant if

   $$\phi(t, t_0, A(t_0)) \subset A(t) \qquad \text{for all} \quad t >\geq t_0.$$

   (c) Negative Invariant, or ϕ- negative

   $$\phi(t, t_0, A(t_0)) \supset A(t) \qquad \text{for all} \quad t >\geq t_0.$$

3. **Nonautonomous Attractivity:** A nonempty, compact subset $\mathcal{A}$ of $\mathbb{R}^n$ is said to be
   i. Forward attracting if

   $$\lim_{t \to \infty} dist(\phi(t, t_0, u_0), A(t)) = 0 \qquad \text{for all } u_0 \in \mathbb{R}^n \text{ and } t_0 \in \mathbb{R},$$

   ii. Pullback attracting if

   $$\lim_{t \to -\infty} dist(\phi(t, t_0, u_0), A(t)) = 0 \qquad \text{for all } u_0 \in \mathbb{R}^n \text{ and } t_0 \in \mathbb{R}.$$

4. **Uniform Strictly Contracting Property:** A nonautonomous dynamical system ϕ satisfies the uniform strictly contracting property if for each $R > 0$, there exist positive constants K and α such that

   $$|\phi(t, t_0, x_0) - \phi(t, t_0, y_0)|^2 \leq K e^{-\alpha(t - t_0)} |x_0 - y_0|^2 \tag{26}$$

   for all $(t, t_0) \in \mathbb{R}^2_\geq$ and $(x_0, y_0) \in \bar{\mathbb{B}}(0; R)$, where $\bar{\mathbb{B}}$ is a closed ball centered at the origin with radius $R > 0$.

Remark: The uniform strictly contracting property, together with the existence of a pullback absorbing, implies the existence of a global attractor that consists of a single entire solution.

These preliminaries provide a foundation for understanding nonautonomous dynamical systems, which is essential when analyzing models such as the nonautonomous HBV infection model. With these concepts in hand, one can analyze the stability of such systems and investigate the behavior of solutions over time [5, 10].

4.2 Model Formulation

When the productive number Λ in 1 is time-dependent $\Lambda(t)$, that changes the system from autonomous to a nonautonomous model represented as follows

$$\begin{cases} \frac{dx}{dt} &= \Lambda(t) - \mu_1 x - (1-\eta)\beta xz + qy \\ \frac{dy}{dt} &= (1-\eta)\beta xz - \mu_2 y - qy \\ \frac{dz}{dt} &= (1-\epsilon)py - \mu_3 z \end{cases} \tag{27}$$

which can be written as

$$\frac{du(t)}{dt} = f(t, u(t)), \quad where \quad u(t) = (x(t), y(t), z(t))^T \in \mathbb{R}^3, \quad and \quad t \in \mathbb{R}.$$

with initial condition $u_0 = (x_0, y_0, z_0)^T$

4.3 Solution Properties

The existence of a local solution follows from the fact that $f(t, u(t))$ is continuous, and its derivative is also continuous. The following Lemma proves the positiveness

Lemma 3. *Let $\Lambda : \mathbb{R} \to [\Lambda_m, \Lambda_M]$, then for any $(x_0, y_0, z_0) \in \mathbb{R}_+^3 := \{(x, y, z) \in \mathbb{R}^3 : x \geq 0, y \geq 0, z \geq 0\}$ all the solutions of the system (27–27) corresponding to the initial point are:*

  i. *Non-negative for all*
 ii. *Uniformly bounded.*

Proof. i. The proof is similar to the positiveness of the autonomous case that was introduced earlier.

 ii. Set $\|X(t)\|_1 = x(t) + y(t) + z(t)$, if we combine the three equations in (27–27) we get:

$$\dot{x}(t) + \dot{y}(t) + \dot{z}(t) = \Lambda(t) - \mu_1 x - (\mu_2 - (1-\epsilon)p)y - \mu_3 z \tag{28}$$

assume $\mu_2 > (1-\epsilon)p$ and let $\alpha = min\mu_1, \mu_2 - (1-\epsilon)p, \mu_3$, then we get

$$\frac{d}{dt}\|X(t)\|_1 \leq \Lambda_M - \alpha\|X(t)\|_1 \tag{29}$$

this implies that

$$\|X(t)\|_1 \leq max\{x_0 + y_0 + z_0, \frac{\Lambda_M}{\alpha}\} \tag{30}$$

Thus, the set $B_\epsilon = \{(x, y, z) \in \mathbb{R}_+^3 : \epsilon \leq x(t) + y(t) + z(t) \leq \frac{\Lambda_M}{\alpha} + \epsilon\}$ is positively invariant and absorbing in $\mathbb{R}_+^3$.

4.4   Stability Analysis

This section discusses the stability analysis of the systems 27; first, we show the uniform strictly contracting property and then prove that the system has a positively absorbing set. Then, we provide sufficient conditions that stabilize the system 27.

Theorem 5. *The nonautonomous system (27–27) satisfies a uniform strictly contracting property, if $\mu_2 > (1 - \epsilon)p$.*

Proof. Let

$$
\begin{cases}
(x_1, y_1, z_1) & = & (x(t, t_0, x_0^1), y(t, t_0, y_0^1), z(t, t_0, z_0^1)) \\
\text{and } (x_2, y_2, z_2) & = & (x(t, t_0, x_0^2), y(t, t_0, y_0^2), z(t, t_0, z_0^2))
\end{cases} \tag{31}
$$

and are two solutions of the system (27–27) by similar computational in autonomous case we get

$$
\begin{cases}
\frac{d}{dt}(x_1 - x_2) = -(\mu_1 + (1 - \eta)\beta z_1))(x_1 - x_2) + q(y_1 - y_2) - (1 - \eta)\beta x_2(z_1 - z_2) \\
\frac{d}{dt}(y_1 - y_2) = (1 - \eta)\beta z_1(x_1 - x_2) - (q + \mu_2)(y_1 - y_2) + (1 - \eta)\beta x(z_1 - z_2) \\
\frac{d}{dt}(z_1 - z_2) = (1 - \epsilon)p(y_1 - y_2) - \mu_3(z_1 - z_2)
\end{cases} \tag{32}
$$

Now, let $X = x_1 - x_2$, $Y = y_1 - y_2$ and $Z = z_1 - z_2$ then system 32 becomes

$$
\frac{dX}{dt} = -(\mu_1 + (1 - \eta)\beta z_1)X + qY - (1 - \eta)\beta x_2 Z \tag{33}
$$

$$
\frac{dY}{dt} = (1 - \eta)\beta z_1 X - (q + \mu_2)Y + (1 - \eta)\beta x_2 Z \tag{34}
$$

$$
\frac{dZ}{dt} = (1 - \epsilon)pY - \mu_3 Z \tag{35}
$$

This implies that

$$
\begin{aligned}
\frac{1}{2}\frac{d}{dt}|X|^2 \leq & -[\mu_1 + (1 - \eta)\beta z_1 - \tfrac{1}{2}q - \tfrac{1}{2}(1 - \eta)\beta x_2]|X|^2 + \tfrac{1}{2}q|Y|^2 + \tfrac{1}{2}(1 - \eta)\beta x_2|Z|^2 \\
& - q(Y_- X_+ + Y_+ X_-) - (1 - \eta)\beta x(X_+ Z_+ - X_- Z_-)
\end{aligned} \tag{36}
$$

Similarly, by using the same computational technique, we got

$$
\begin{aligned}
\frac{1}{2}\frac{d}{dt}|Y|^2 \leq & \tfrac{1}{2}(1 - \eta)\beta z_1|X|^2 - [(q + \mu_2) - \tfrac{1}{2}(1 - \eta)\beta \bar{z} - \tfrac{1}{2}(1 - \eta)\beta x_2]|Y|^2 + \tfrac{1}{2}(1 - \eta)\beta x_2|Z|^2 \\
& - (1 - \eta)\beta z - 1(X_+ Y_- + X_- Y_+) - (1 - \eta)\beta x(Z_+ Y_- + Z_- Y_+)
\end{aligned} \tag{37}
$$

and

$$
\frac{1}{2}\frac{d}{dt}|Z|^2 \leq -[\mu_3 - \tfrac{1}{2}(1 - \epsilon)]|Z|^2 + \tfrac{1}{2}(1 - \epsilon)p|Y|^2 - (1 - \epsilon)p(Y_+ Z_- + Y_- Z_+) \tag{38}
$$

Now, by adding 17 , 18 and 19 we get

$$\frac{1}{2}\frac{d}{dt}\left(|X|^2 + |Y|^2 + |Z|^2\right) \leq -\left[\mu_1 + \frac{1}{2}(1-\eta)\beta z_1 - \frac{1}{2}q - \frac{1}{2}(1-\eta)\beta x_2\right]|X|^2$$
$$-\left[\mu_2 + \frac{1}{2}q - \frac{1}{2}(1-\eta)\beta z_1 - \frac{1}{2}(1-\eta)\beta x_2 - (1-\epsilon)p\right]|Y|^2$$
$$-\left[\mu_3 - \frac{1}{2}(1-\epsilon)p - (1-\eta)\beta x\right]|Z|^2 - [q(Y_+X_- + Y_-X_+)$$
$$+ (1-\eta)\beta x(X_+Z_+ + X_-Z_-) + (1-\eta)(X_+Y_- + X_-Y_+)$$
$$(1-\eta)\beta x_2(Z_+Y_- Z_-Y_+) + (1-\epsilon)p(Y_+Z_- + Y_-Z_+)]$$
$$(39)$$

Since x_2 and z_1 are bounded, assume that $\gamma_2 = max\{x_2\}$ and $\gamma_1 = max\{z_1\}$. Therefore,

$$\frac{d}{dt}\left(|X|^2 + |Y|^2 + |Z|^2\right) \leq -\nu_1|X|^2 - \nu_2|Y|^2 - \nu_3|Z|^2 - W \qquad (40)$$

where

$$\nu_1 = 2\mu_1 + (1-\eta)\beta\gamma_1 - (1-\eta)\beta\gamma_2 - q$$
$$\nu_2 = \mu_2 + q - (1-\eta)\beta\gamma_1 - (1-\eta)\beta\gamma_2 - (1-\epsilon)p$$
$$\nu_3 = 2\mu_3 - (1-\epsilon)p - (1-\eta)\beta\gamma_2$$
$$W = q(Y_+X_- + Y_-X_+) + (1-\eta)\beta x(X_+Z_+ + X_-Z_-) + (1-\eta)(X_+Y_- + X_-Y_+)$$
$$+ (1-\eta)\beta x(Z_+Y_- Z_-Y_+) + (1-\epsilon)p(Y_+Z_- + Y_-Z_+)$$

Let $\alpha = min\{\nu_1, \nu_2\nu_3\}$, then Eq. 40 becomes

$$\frac{d}{dt}\left(|X|^2 + |Y|^2 + |Z|^2\right) \leq -\alpha(|X|^2 + |Y|^2 + |Z|^2) - W \qquad (41)$$

Which has a solution

$$|X|^2 + |Y|^2 + |Z|^2 \leq Ke^{-\alpha(t-t_0)}(|X_0|^2 + |Y_0|^2 + |Z_0|^2) \qquad (42)$$

Notice that, for ν_1, ν_2, ν_3 to following positive conditions must hold.

$$2\mu_1 + (1-\eta)\beta b_1 > (1-\eta)\beta\frac{\Lambda_M}{min(\mu_1,\mu_2)} + q \qquad (43)$$

$$2\mu_2 + q > (1-\eta)\beta\left(b_1 + \frac{\Lambda_M}{min(\mu_1,\mu_2)}\right) + (1-\epsilon)p \qquad (44)$$

$$2\mu_3 > (1-\epsilon)p + \frac{(1-\eta)\beta\Lambda_M}{min(\mu_1,\mu_2)} \qquad (45)$$

Theorem 6. *Suppose $\Lambda : \mathbb{R} \to [\Lambda_m, \Lambda_M]$, where $0 < \Lambda_m < \Lambda - M < \infty$, is continuous, then the system (27–27) has a pullback attractor $\mathcal{A} = \{A(t) : t \in \mathbb{R}\}$ inside $\mathbb{R}_+^3$. Moreover, if $\mu_2 > (1-\epsilon)p$, and the conditions (43–45) hold, then the solution of the system is exponentially stable.*

Proof. The proof follows the previous proofs.

5   Numerical Results

To perform numerical simulations, we use numerical solvers to integrate the system of ordinary differential equations (ODEs) over time. In this case, we will use MATLAB to perform the simulations.

At the disease-free equilibrium point $(\frac{\Lambda}{\mu_1}, 0, 0)$, parameters have to satisfy condition (23). We will use the parameters from Table 2 that satisfy this condition and present the results as follows (Fig. 1 and Table 3):

Table 2. List of parameters that satisfied conditions 23

parameters	Λ	μ_1	μ_2	μ_3	β	η	ϵ	p	q
values	9.8135	2	3	7	0.2	0.2	0.5	0.01	5

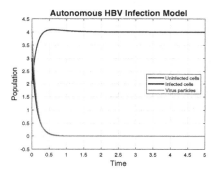

Fig. 1. The Solution of the model 1 around Diseases-free equilibrium.

Table 3. List of parameters that satisfied conditions 25

parameters	Λ	μ_1	μ_2	μ_3	β	η	ϵ	p	q
values	100	5	7	2	0.7	0.2	0.2	2	6

5.1   Nonautonomous Case

Figure 3 shows the solutions of the system 27 using an appropriate set of parameters that satisfied the necessary conditions. We approximate the healthy cells' productive function by $\Lambda(t) = cos(2t + \pi/3) + 10$, which is a positive and bounded function. On the interval $[0, 5]$ for the other parameters in the Table 4 (Figs. 2, 4 and 5).

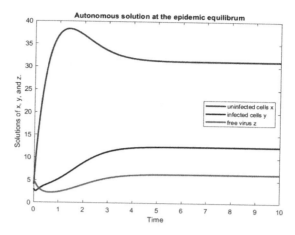

Fig. 2. Numerical simulation of the autonomous HBV infection model at the epidemic equilibrium.

Table 4. Set of parameters that satisfy the required conditions

μ_1	μ_2	μ_3	β	η	ϵ	p	q	Λ
2	3	7	0.2	0.2	0.5	0.01	5	12

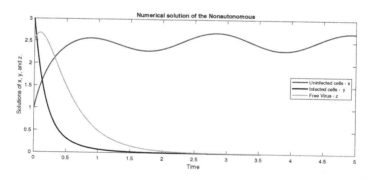

Fig. 3. Numerical simulations of the nonautonomous HBV infection model at the disease-free equilibrium (DFE).

Table 5. This set of parameters satisfy both Auto/nonautonomous conditions

μ_1	μ_2	μ_3	β	η	ϵ	p	q	Λ
6	7	0.1	0.3	0.5	0.1	5	10	20

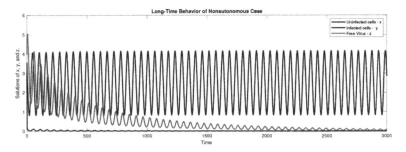

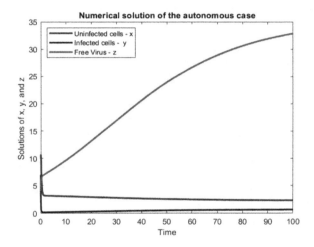

Fig. 4. Numerical simulations of the nonautonomous HBV infection model (Eqs. 27, 27, and 27) with time-dependent production number $\Lambda(t)$.

For the same set of parameters 5, the autonomous model blowup.

Fig. 5. The free virus solution $z(t)$ blowup, for the same set of parameters that is used on the nonautonomous case.

6 Conclusion

This study presents an enhanced model for Hepatitis B Virus (HBV) transmission, including autonomous and nonautonomous cases and medical treatment impacts. It validates unique solutions and assesses their positivity over time, with a detailed stability analysis at the equilibrium points. Local and global stability are explored using the Jacobian matrix, R_0, and a Lyapunov function, respectively, linking stability conditions to R_0. Numerical simulations demonstrate the disease-free equilibrium's stability and provide insights into HBV dynamics and intervention effectiveness. Nonautonomous systems can better represent HBV transmission dynamics by including time-dependent factors, while autonomous systems assume constant parameters. Choosing between the two depends on the research question or application, but nonautonomous models may offer more accurate insights into real-world situations and control strategies.

References

1. The World Health Organization - hepatitis B. https://www.who.int/news-room/fact-sheets/detail/hepatitis-b. Accessed 24 June 2022
2. Abdulrashid, I., Alsammani, A.A., Han, X.: Stability analysis of a chemotherapy model with delays. Discrete Continuous Dyn. Syst.-Ser. B **24**(3) (2019)
3. Alsammani, A.A.M.: Dynamical behavior of nonautonomous and stochastic HBV infection model (2020)
4. Cao, J., Wang, Y., Alofi, A., Al-Mazrooei, A., Elaiw, A.: Global stability of an epidemic model with carrier state in heterogeneous networks. IMA J. Appl. Math. **80**(4), 1025–1048 (2015)
5. Caraballo, T., Han, X.: Applied Nonautonomous and Random Dynamical Systems: Applied Dynamical Systems. Springer, Cham (2017). https://doi.org/10.1007/978-3-319-49247-6
6. Diekmann, O., Heesterbeek, J.A.P., Metz, J.A.: On the definition and the computation of the basic reproduction ratio r 0 in models for infectious diseases in heterogeneous populations. J. Math. Biol. **28**, 365–382 (1990)
7. Van den Driessche, P., Watmough, J.: Reproduction numbers and sub-threshold endemic equilibria for compartmental models of disease transmission. Math. Biosci. **180**(1–2), 29–48 (2002)
8. Hethcote, H.W.: The mathematics of infectious diseases. SIAM Rev. **42**(4), 599–653 (2000)
9. Khatun, Z., Islam, M.S., Ghosh, U.: Mathematical modeling of hepatitis b virus infection incorporating immune responses. Sens. Int. **1**, 100017 (2020)
10. Kloeden, P.E., Rasmussen, M.: Nonautonomous Dynamical Systems. No. 176, American Mathematical Society (2011)
11. Korobeinikov, A., Maini, P.K.: A Lyapunov function and global properties for SIR and SEIR epidemiological models with nonlinear incidence (2004)
12. Li, M.Y., Muldowney, J.S.: Global stability for the SEIR model in epidemiology. Math. Biosci. **125**(2), 155–164 (1995)
13. Ma, Z.: Dynamical Modeling and Analysis of Epidemics. World Scientific, Singapore (2009)
14. McMahon, B.J.: The natural history of chronic hepatitis B virus infection. Hepatology **49**(S5), S45–S55 (2009)
15. Nowak, M., May, R.M.: Virus Dynamics: Mathematical Principles of Immunology and Virology: Mathematical Principles of Immunology and Virology. Oxford University Press, UK (2000)
16. Nowak, M.A., Bonhoeffer, S., Hill, A.M., Boehme, R., Thomas, H.C., McDade, H.: Viral dynamics in hepatitis B virus infection. Proc. Natl. Acad. Sci. **93**(9), 4398–4402 (1996)
17. Perelson, A.S.: Modelling viral and immune system dynamics. Nat. Rev. Immunol. **2**(1), 28–36 (2002)
18. Perelson, A.S., Neumann, A.U., Markowitz, M., Leonard, J.M., Ho, D.D.: HIV-1 dynamics in vivo: virion clearance rate, infected cell life-span, and viral generation time. Science **271**(5255), 1582–1586 (1996)

Modelling the Fuel Consumption of a NRP Ship Using a Kalman Filter Approach

M. Filomena Teodoro[1,2(✉)] ⓘ, Pedro Carvalho[2], and Ana Trindade[2]

[1] CEMAT, Center for Computational and Stochastic Mathematics, Instituto Superior Técnico, Lisbon University, 1048-001 Lisbon, Portugal
maria.teodoro@tecnico.ulisboa.pt

[2] CINAV, Center of Naval Research, Naval Academy, Military University, 2810-001 Almada, Portugal

Abstract. The Kalman filter can be applied in the most diverse areas of knowledge, for example, medicine, agriculture, social sciences, computing, etc. The Kalman filter is a recursive tool that can be used under the aim of Navigation and Integration Systems. We make a brief approach to the derivation of a Kalman filter dividing the work into two parts. By first, a Kalman filter is used to simulate different situations analyzing the "response" of the filter considering distinct cases for distinct states of the shop motor; at second, a specific Kalman filter is built to filter the fuel consumption data collected directly from the on-board records of a ship from Portuguese Republic.

Keywords: Kalman Filter · Fuel Consumption Modeling · Computational Algorithms

1 Introduction

In 1960, the engineer Rudolf Kalman published an article (Kalman, A new approach to linear filtering and prediction problems 1960), (Kalman, New methods in wiener filter theory 1963) in which he presented a new method of linear filtration. This method uses measurements of independent variables and the associated noise to filter the system signal and predict its next state using statistical techniques. This new method introduced by Kalman in early sixties decade came to be known as Kalman Filter (KF) and had its first use aboard the spacecraft navigation computers of the APOLLO project.

The KF is one of the most applied methods for tracking and estimation due to its simplicity, optimality, tractability and robustness (Uhlmann 1997).

Accordingly with the authors of (Sorenson 1985), (R. G. Brown 2012) the KF can be seen as a sequential minimum mean square error (MMSE) estimator of a signal with noise. This signal is described by a state (or dynamical) model. When the errors are Gaussian distributed, the KF conduces to an optimal MMSE estimator; if the errors are not Gaussian distributed, the estimator still is a linear MMSE estimator. In (G. Welch 2006) is illustrated in a simple way the basic concepts of FK.

© The Author(s), under exclusive license to Springer Nature Switzerland AG 2023
O. Gervasi et al. (Eds.): ICCSA 2023 Workshops, LNCS 14105, pp. 344–361, 2023.
https://doi.org/10.1007/978-3-031-37108-0_22

This work presents a brief approach to the derivation of a KF when the input is a scalar quantity. It was considered a KF to estimate a first order system. Several simulations were carried out with these models and the results of applying the filter in different situations were analyzed.

It ended with the analysis of a KF model, built specifically to filter NRP Douro consumption data.

The approach that was made in this work considered only the discrete KF, once, in practice, observations and controls were carried out in discrete case.

The KF was used in the form of a linear system to obtain the best estimate of the state vector conditional to past observations. The estimate was calculated using the reconstruction of the state vector using the previous state vector estimate, the known inputs and measured outputs. The observed consumption value was registered hourly in NRP Douro, with AV3 machine regime, using a one-dimensional KF considering white random noise in the measure equation. It was possible to verify that the applied KF was effective and conduced to good measures of estimation and prevision.

2 Preliminaries

In statistics, the Kalman filter is a mathematical method created by Rudolf Kalman, with the objective of using measurements of magnitudes carried out over time (contaminated with noise and other uncertainties) and generating results that tend to approximate the real values of the measured quantities and associated values.

In theoretical terms, the Kalman filter is an algorithm that produces estimates of the state of a system using noisy measurements observed over time. The filter operates recursively, that is, it only needs the measurement at the current instant and the calculation of the state of the previous instant. Furthermore, it is not always possible or desirable to measure some variables of interest for a given purpose (such as, for example, control systems) and the Kalman filter can be used to infer these variables through indirect measurements.

The easy implementation in digital computers due to its recursion, the possibility of being used without knowing exactly its "internal" functioning and the fact that it uses a representation in state space, are some of the reasons that make this filter so popular.

The Kalman filter can be applied in the most diverse areas of knowledge, including medicine, agriculture, social sciences, computing, etc. With numerous applications, the Kalman filter is one of the most recurrent topics in the academic world and serves as the theme of this work, developed within the curricular unit Navigation and Integration Systems, with the objective of applying the theory of signal filtering to a case practical, solidifying students' learning.

In this work we intend to make a brief approach to the derivation of a Kalman filter when the input is a scalar quantity. To meet the defined objectives, the work was divided into two parts. A first part, in which a Kalman filter is used, using MATLAB code to simulate different situations and analyze the "response" of the filter. In the second part, a specific Kalman filter is built to filter NRP Douro consumption data and analyze the results. The data used were collected directly from the on-board records and only a sample of these data was selected for filtering.

3 Kalman Filter

Kalman filters are based on discretized linear dynamical systems in the time domain. The state of the system is represented as a vector of real numbers. At each time step, a linear operator is applied to the state to generate the next state, with added noise and, optionally, some information about the control inputs if they are known. Later, another linear operator with more addition of noise generates the real state observations.

In order to use the Kalman filter to estimate the complete state of a process given only a sequence of noisy observations, it is necessary to model the process according to the structure of the Kalman filter. This means specifying the following matrices: a_j, the state transition model; h_j, the observation model; Q_j, the process noise covariance; R_j, the covariance of the observation noise; and, occasionally, b_j, the model of the control inputs, for each time step j, as described below.

Discrete-time linear systems are often represented in a state variable format given by the following equation:

$$x_j = ax_{j-1} + bu_j \tag{1}$$

where, in this case, the state variable, x_j, and the input value, u_j, are scalars, a and b are constants, and j represents the time variable. Equation 1 shows that the current value of the state variable at time j (x_j) is equal to its value at the previous time (x_{j-1}) multiplied by a constant (a) plus the current input value (u_j) multiplied by another constant (b). In Fig. 1, diagram 1 schematically represents Eq. 1, where the block with T represents a time delay (input is x_j, output is x_{j-1}).

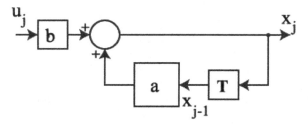

Fig. 1. Diagram 1.

If you add some noise to the process, you have the Eq. 2:

$$x_j = ax_{j-1} + bu_j + w_j. \tag{2}$$

The noise, w, is a source of white noise with zero mean and covariance Q and is uncorrelated with the input value. In Fig. 2, diagrama 2 schematically represents Eq. 2. In this situation, it is possible to filter the signal x so that the effects of noise w are minimized.

Assuming that it is not possible to directly measure the signal x, and instead, z is measured, which is x multiplied by a gain (h) with introduced noise (v) we consider Eq. 3.

$$z_j = hx_j + v_j. \tag{3}$$

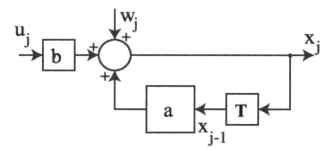

Fig. 2. Diagram 2.

The measured value, z, depends on the current value of x, as determined by the gain, h. Furthermore, the measurement has its own associated noise, v. The measurement noise, v, is a source of white noise with zero mean and covariance R and is uncorrelated with the input value or the noise w. The two noise sources are independent of each other and independent of the input value (Fig. 3).

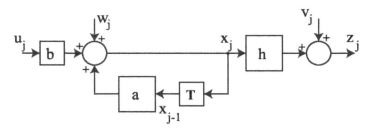

Fig. 3. Diagram 3.

Applying the Kalman filter to the previous system, it is possible to filter z and estimate the variable x while minimizing the effects of w and v. For this, it might seem reasonable to obtain an estimate of the state variable (and the output value) simply by reproducing the system architecture. This simple (and ultimately useless) way of getting an estimate of x_j (which we'll call $\hat{x}_j$) would be schematized as follows (see Diagram 4 displayed in Fig. 4). This model is very similar to the previous one. The first difference noted is that the original estimate of x_j is now designated $\hat{x}_j$; which is designated as a priori estimate:

$$\hat{x}_{\bar{j}} = a\hat{x}_{j-1} + bu_j. \tag{4}$$

This model is very similar to the previous one. The first difference noted is that the original estimate of xj is now designated $\hat{x}_j$; which is called a priori estimation (Eq. 4). However, this approach has two glaring weaknesses. The first is that there is no correction (update), if the exact quantities a, b or h (or the initial value x_0) are not known, the estimate will not allow to determine the exact value of x. And the second, does not compensate for the introduction of noise sources (w and v).

Diagram 5 (Fig. 5) presents a solution that allows overcoming the two problems presented.

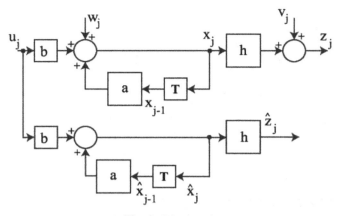

Fig. 4. Diagram 4.

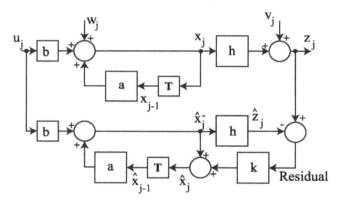

Fig. 5. Diagram 5.

This *a priori* estimate is used to predict an estimate for the output value, $\hat{z}_j$. The difference between this estimated value and the actual value is called the residual, or innovation (Eq. 5).

$$Residual = z_j - \hat{z}_{\bar{j}} = z_j - h\hat{x}_{\bar{j}} \tag{5}$$

If this residual difference is small, it usually means you have a good estimate; if it is large, the estimate is not so good. We can use this information to refine the initial guess of x_j; this new estimate is called the *a posteriori* estimate, $\hat{x}_j$. If the residual value is small, so will the correction of the estimate. As the residual value grows, so does the correction. A relevant equation will be Eq. 6:

$$\hat{x}_j = \hat{x}_{\bar{j}} + k(Residual) = \hat{x}_{\bar{j}} + k\left(z_{\bar{j}} - h\hat{x}_{\bar{j}}\right). \tag{6}$$

Nesta fase, o filtro de *Kalman* é utilizado para determinar a quantidade k (designada por Ganho de *Kalman*) que é usada para refinar a estimativa inicial. E é este processo que está no coração da filtragem de *Kalman*.

Note: The aim is to try to find an ideal estimator and, so far, we have only been able to optimize the gain value, k. However, assuming that a copy of the original system (that is, the gains a, b and h were defined as shown) should be used to form the estimator. It can then be assumed that the estimator, shown above, is the ideal (optimal) linear estimator.

3.1 Kalman Gain

To determine the *Kalman gain*, k, we define the errors of initial estimate: the *a priori* error $e_{\bar{j}}$, and the *a posteriori error*, e_j. Each one is defined as the difference between the real value x_j and its estimate (respectively *a priori* and a posteriori) as we can find in Eq. 7:

$$\begin{aligned} e_{\bar{j}} &= x_j - \hat{x}_{\bar{j}} \\ e_j &= x_j - \hat{x}_j \end{aligned}. \tag{7}$$

The variance of the errors defined by Eq. 7 are given by Eq. 8

$$\begin{aligned} p_{\bar{j}} &= \mathrm{E}\left\{ \left(e_{\bar{j}}\right)^2 \right\} \\ p_j &= \mathrm{E}\left\{ \left(e_j\right)^2 \right\} \end{aligned}, \tag{8}$$

where the $E\{\}$ operator represents the expected or average value. These definitions will be used in the calculation of the quantity k.

A Kalman filter minimizes the *a posteriori* variance, p_j, by appropriately choosing the value of k. Substituting Eq. 7 in Eq. 8 and then substituting in Eq. 6, we obtain:

$$\begin{aligned} p_j &= \mathrm{E}\left\{ \left(x_j - \hat{x}_j\right)^2 \right\} \\ p_j &= E\left\{ \left(x_j - \hat{x}_{\bar{j}} - k\left(z_j - h\hat{x}_{\bar{j}}\right)\right)^2 \right\} \end{aligned}. \tag{9}$$

To determine the value of k that minimizes the variance, we solve the equation $\frac{\partial p_j}{\partial k} = 0$.

$$\begin{aligned} \frac{\partial p_j}{\partial k} = 0 &= \frac{\partial E\left\{ \left(x_j - \hat{x}_{\bar{j}} - k\left(z_j - h\hat{x}_{\bar{j}}\right)\right)^2 \right\}}{\partial k} \\ &= 2E\left\{ \left(x_j - \hat{x}_{\bar{j}} - k\left(z_j - h\hat{x}_{\bar{j}}\right)\right)\left(z_j - h\hat{x}_{\bar{j}}\right) \right\} \\ &= 2E\left\{ x_j z_j - \hat{x}_{\bar{j}} z_j - k z_j^2 + kh\hat{x}_{\bar{j}} z_j - h x_j \hat{x}_{\bar{j}} + h\left(\hat{x}_{\bar{j}}\right)^2 + khz_j \hat{x}_{\bar{j}} - kh^2\left(\hat{x}_{\bar{j}}\right)^2 \right\} \\ &= 2E\left\{ x_j z_j - \hat{x}_{\bar{j}} z_j - h x_j \hat{x}_{\bar{j}} + h\left(\hat{x}_{\bar{j}}\right)^2 \right\} - 2kE\left\{ z_j^2 - 2h\hat{x}_{\bar{j}} z_j + h^2\left(\hat{x}_{\bar{j}}\right)^2 \right\} \end{aligned} \tag{10}$$

Solving equality (10) we obtain the Kalman gain expression given by Eq. 11.

$$k = \frac{E\left\{ x_j z_j - \hat{x}_{\bar{j}} z_j - h x_j \hat{x}_{\bar{j}} + h\left(\hat{x}_{\bar{j}}\right)^2 \right\}}{E\left\{ z_j^2 - 2h\hat{x}_{\bar{j}} z_j + h^2\left(\hat{x}_{\bar{j}}\right)^2 \right\}}. \tag{11}$$

Rewriting expression (11) we obtain a simplified formua for the Kalman gain, given by expression (12)

$$k = \frac{h p_{\bar{j}}}{h^2 p_{\bar{j}} + R}. \tag{12}$$

The expression (12) needs a value for the *a priori* covariance which, in turn, requires knowledge of the state variable x_j. Therefore, it will be necessary to determine an estimate for the *a priori* covariance. Before that, it is important to analyze this equation in detail. First note, the "constant", k (gain), changes with each iteration. For that reason, it should actually be written with an index (ie k_j). Next, and more significantly, one can analyze what happens when each of the three terms of Eq. (12) is changed.

If the *a priori* error is very small, the corresponding k will be very small, so the correction (update) will also be very small. In other words, you can ignore the current measurement and simply use the previous estimates to form the new estimate. This would be expected: if the first (*a priori*) estimate is good (that is, with a small error), there is very little need to correct it.

If the *a priori* error is very large (so that the measurement noise term, R, in the denominator is not important), then $k = 1/h$. In effect, this shows that one can disregard the *a priori* estimate and use the current (measured) output value to estimate the value of the state variable. This is clear from its substitution in Eq. (6). Again, this would be expected: if the *a priori* error is large, one should disregard the *a priori* estimate and instead use the current measurement of the output value to form the new estimate of the state variable.

$$\hat{x}_j = \hat{x}_{\bar{j}} + k(Residual) = \hat{x}_{\bar{j}} + k\left(z_j - h\hat{x}_{\bar{j}}\right) = \hat{x}_{\bar{j}} + \frac{1}{h}\left(z_j - h\hat{x}_{\bar{j}}\right) = \frac{z_j}{h} \tag{13}$$

If the measurement noise, R, is too large, k will again be too small, and the current measurement is again neglected in forming the new estimate. This would be expected: if the measurement noise is large, there is little confidence in the measurement and the new estimate will depend more on the previous estimates.

3.2 A Priori Covariance

To determine the a *priori* variance we consider its definition

$$
\begin{aligned}
p_{\bar{j}} &= \mathrm{E}\left\{ \left(x_j - \hat{x}_{\bar{j}}\right)^2 \right\} \\
&= \mathrm{E}\left\{ \left(ax_{j-1} + bu_j - w_j - \left(a\hat{x}_{j-1} + bu_j\right)\right)^2 \right\} \\
&= \mathrm{E}\left\{ \left(a\left(x_{j-1} - \hat{x}_{j-1}\right) + w_j\right)^2 \right\} \\
&= \mathrm{E}\left\{ a^2\left(x_{j-1} - \hat{x}_{j-1}\right)^2 + 2aw_j\left(x_{j-1} - \hat{x}_{j-1}\right) + w_j^2 \right\}
\end{aligned}
\tag{14}
$$

and the Eq. (15)

$$
\mathrm{E}\left\{ 2aw_j\left(x_{j-1} - \hat{x}_{j-1}\right) \right\} = 2a\mathrm{E}\left\{ w_j e_{j-1} \right\} = 0
\tag{15}
$$

obtaining a simpler expression of $p_{\bar{j}}$:

$$
p_{\bar{j}} = a^2\mathrm{E}\left\{ \left(x_{j-1} - \hat{x}_{j-1}\right)^2 \right\} + E\left\{ w_j^2 \right\} = a^2 p_{j-1} + Q.
\tag{16}
$$

3.3 A Posteriori Covariance

Similarly to the computation of the variance a *priori*, the computation of the variance *a posteriori* start with its definition following some simplifications.

$$
\begin{aligned}
p_j &= \mathrm{E}\left\{ \left(x_j - \hat{x}_j\right)^2 \right\} \\
&= \mathrm{E}\left\{ \left(x_j - \left(\hat{x}_{\bar{j}} - hk\hat{x}_{\bar{j}} + kz_j\right)\right)^2 \right\} \\
&= \mathrm{E}\left\{ \left(x_j - \left(\hat{x}_{\bar{j}} - hk\hat{x}_{\bar{j}} + k\left(hx_j + v_j\right)\right)\right)^2 \right\} = \mathrm{E}\left\{ \left(\left(x_j - \hat{x}_j\right)(1 - hk) - kv_j\right)^2 \right\} \\
&= \mathrm{E}\left\{ \left(x_j - \hat{x}_j\right)^2(1 - hk)^2 - 2kv_j\left(x_j - \hat{x}_j\right)(1 - hk) + k^2 v_j^2 \right\} = \ldots \\
&= \mathrm{E}\left\{ \left(x_j - \hat{x}_j\right)^2 \right\} + k^2\mathrm{E}\left\{ v_j^2 \right\} = (1 - hk)^2 p_{\bar{j}} + k^2 R
\end{aligned}
\tag{17}
$$

Reorganizing formula (17) obtain (18):

$$
R = \frac{p_{\bar{j}}\left(h - h^2 k\right)}{k}.
\tag{18}
$$

Including formula (18) in expression (17) we get

$$
p_j = (1 - hk)^2 p_{\bar{j}} + k^2 \frac{p_{\bar{j}}\left(h - h^2 k\right)}{k} = p_{\bar{j}}\left(1 - 2hk + h^2 k^2 + kh - h^2 k^2\right) = p_{\bar{j}}(1 - hk).
\tag{19}
$$

3.4   Iterative Process Summary

The *Kalman* filter process starts with a system descrition in terms of a, b e h. The state variable is x, u and z are respectively the input and output of the system. The index of time is j. The equations of transition and the measure rule all system:

$$x_j = ax_{j-1} + bu_j + w_j$$
$$z_j = hx_j + v_j.$$

The process comprises two steps, a prediction step (which calculates the next state estimate based only on past measurements of the output values) and a correction step (which uses the current estimate value to refine the result provided by the output).

Prediction Step
The a priori state estimate is formed based on the previous state estimate and the current value of the input.

$$\hat{x}_{\bar{j}} = a\hat{x}_{j-1} + bu_j$$

To calculate the a priori covariance:

$$p_{\bar{j}} = a^2 p_{j-1} + Q$$

It is possible to observe that these two equations use previous values of the estimate and posterior state covariance. Therefore, the first iteration of a Kalman filter requires estimates (which are usually just guesses) of these two variables. The exact estimate is usually not important as the values converge to the correct value over time; an ill-defined initial guess just takes more iterations to converge.

Correction Step (Update)
To correct (update) the prior estimate, we need the Kalman filter gain, K.

$$K = \frac{hp_{\bar{j}}}{h^2 p_{\bar{j}} + R}$$

This gain is used to correct (update) the prior estimate and thus obtain the posterior estimates.

$$\hat{x}_j = \hat{x}_{\bar{j}} + K\left(z_{\bar{j}} - h\hat{x}_{\bar{j}}\right)$$

And finally calculate the covariance *a posteriori*.

$$p_j = p_{\bar{j}}(1 - hK_j)$$

Notation
The used notation is displayed in Table 1.

The notation $\hat{x}(k|k)$ can be red as the estimate the x knowing the information in time $k-1$, meaning a priori estimate. $\hat{x}(k|k)$ is red as as the estimate the x knowing the information in time k, meaning a posteriori estimate.

Table 1. Notation meaning

Variable	Notation
time	j
state	x_j
System gains	a, b, h
input	u_j
result	z_j
gain	k_j
a priori estimate	$\hat{x}_j^-$
a posteriori estimate	$\hat{x}_j$
a priori covariance	$p_j^- = p(j|j-1)$
a posteriori covariance	$p_j = p(j|j)$

4   Empirical Approach

The next examples of the Kalman filter application, include two that are based on a model that uses the Kalman filter to estimate a constant and, with some few changes, and a a first order system, both in simulated environment. By last it was considered a model constructed with the specific purpose of estimating the consumption of NRP Douro.

4.1   Example: Estimating a Constant

The use of a Kalman filter is analyzed to estimate the value of a system with a gain a K = 1. If there is no noise in the system (w), the system output is a constant. This is shown in Fig. 6. The output gain, h, is set to 3; h = 3. The measurement noise covariance (v), R, is set to 1; R = 1. The initial estimate of the state is 1.5 and the initial estimate of the posterior covariance is 1. In Fig. 6 the upper left graph shows the actual state (red), the prior estimate (blue - the prediction step) and the a posteriori estimation (green - the corrected (updated) step). The lower left graph shows the actual error between the estimates and the actual state. The graph in the upper right corner shows the calculated covariances and the graph in the lower right corner shows the gain of the Kalman filter.

As expected, the posterior estimate is closer to the exact value at each step than the prior estimate. Error covariances start out large but decrease quickly. The Kalman filter gain decreases as confidence in the prior estimate increases. The graphs in Fig. 7 show when process noise is introduced (Q = 0.01) so the state does not remain constant. The remaining parameters are kept the same. Again, the a posteriori estimate is closer to the exact value at each step than the a priori estimate. Error covariances start out large but decrease quickly. Again, the a posteriori estimate is closer to the exact value at each step than the a priori estimate. Error covariances start out large but decrease quickly. The Kalman filter gain decreases as the confidence in the prior estimate increases, but it does not decrease as sharply as in the first case (without process noise).

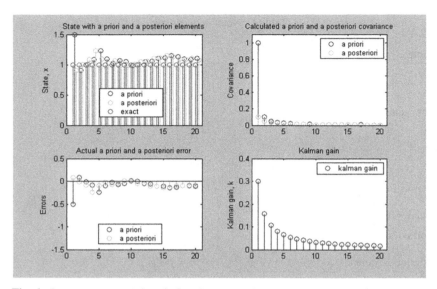

Fig. 6. Parameters: a = 1, h = 3, Q = 0, R = 1; x0 = 1,5, p0 = 1 (Color figure online)

This indicates that a larger correction is needed at each step – which is to be expected since noise is being introduced to the state itself at each step.

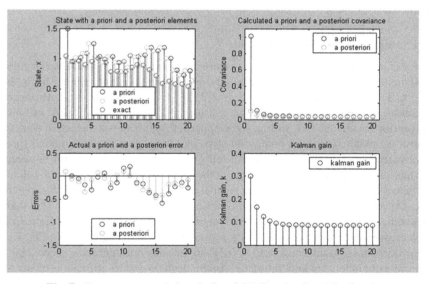

Fig. 7. Parameters: a = 1, h = 3, Q = 0,01, R = 1; x0 = 1,5, p0 = 1.

The Fig. 8 present graphs that are similar to previous case (above), only the process noise has increased (Q = 0.1). Again, at each iterate, the posterior estimate is closer to the exact value than the prior estimate. Error covariances start out large but decrease quickly. The Kalman filter gain decreases as the a priori estimate becomes more reliable, however it does not reach values as low as in the first case (without process noise) or in the second case *(Q = 0.1)*. This indicates that a larger correction is needed at each step – which is again expected, since the increase in the noise value of the measurement at each step makes the a priori estimate less good.

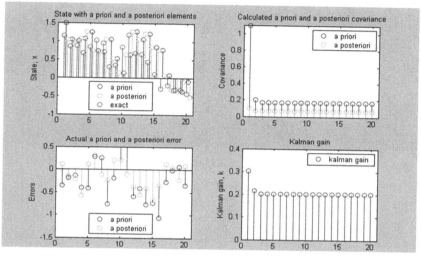

Fig. 8. Parameters: a = 1, h = 3, Q = 0,1, R = 1; x0 = 1,5, p0 = 1.

The graphs in Fig. 9 are similar to the ones presented in Fig. 7. Here only the measure error is increased *(R = 2)*.

Again, the a posteriori estimate is closer to the exact value at each step than the a priori estimate. Error covariances start out large but decrease quickly. The Kalman filter gain decreases as confidence in the prior estimate increases. Although it does not decrease as much as in the first case (without process noise), it reaches lower values than in the second case *(Q = 0.1)*. This means that, in relation to these two cases, one can rely more on the a priori estimate and less on the measurement, as the measurement noise is higher. Similar work was developed considering first order systems. By a question of space in article, it is not described in the manuscript. Follows a model constructed with the specific purpose of estimating the consumption of NRP Douro.

4.2   Estimating the Consumption of NRP Douro

This model is considered to estimate the consumption of the NRP Douro, with an AV3 machine regime (Fig. 10).

Assuming that the consumption at a stable machine speed is constant, that is, if the machine speed is not changed, the hourly consumption value is constant. However, from

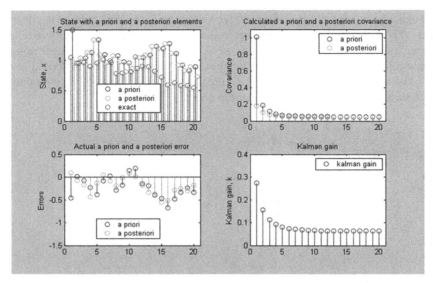

Fig. 9. Parameters: a = 1, h = 3, Q = 0,01, R = 2; x0 = 1,5, p0 = 1

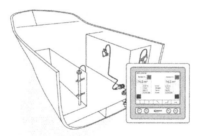

Fig. 10. Example of a fuel tank with an electronic sensor.

experience it is known that the true value of consumption suffers from fluctuations. Thus, one can describe the dynamics of the system through the following equation:

$$x_j = c + w_j \tag{20}$$

where c is the constant consumption rate and w_j is isa random noise value, which corresponds to a covariance Q.

The following assumptions were considered:

1. The consumption of the NRP Douro, with AV3 machines, is 200 L/hour.
2. Assuming the model is accurate, the noise variance value w, Q, is 0.5.
3. The range of error associated with the measurements is 64 L.
4. The range of error associated with the initial estimate is 400 L.
5. Measurements are taken hourly.
6. The measured consumption values correspond to a sample of 150 measurements.

7. The actual consumption values corresponding to each measurement with a random noise w introduced.

4.3 Kalman Filter Construction

ITERATION ZERO
Before first iteration, we need to initilize the Kalmen filter and estimate the next state.
INICIALIZATION
No body knows the real consumption of NRP Douro. It was assumed that is 200 L per hour (lts/h).

$$\hat{x}_{0,0} = 200 l/h$$

Considering that this assumption is very inaccurate, we define the initialization estimation error σ as 20 l/h. The estimated initialization uncertainty is the error variance ($\sigma2$):

$$p_{0,0} = 20^2 = 400$$

This variation is very high. If initialized with a more significant value, faster convergence of the Kalman filter is obtained.
PREDICTION
It is possible to predict the next state based on initialization values. As this dynamic model is a constant, the posterior estimate is equal to the prior estimate:

$$\hat{x}_{1,0} = 200 \, l/h$$

The extrapolated estimated uncertainty (variance):

$$p_{1,0} = p_{0,0} + Q = 400 + 0,25 = 400,25$$

FIRST ITERATE
STAGE 1-MEASUREMENT
The measured value:

$$z_1 = 200 \, l/h$$

The measurent error is 8 (σ), tthe variance ir given by ($\sigma2$) é 64, so:
$R_1 = 64$.
STAGE 2 - CORRECTION (UPDATE)
Computing the Kalman gain:

$$k_1 = p_{1,0} \div \left(p_{1,0} + R_1\right) = 400,25 \div (400,25 + 64) = 0,86214324$$

The Kalman gain is almost 1, which shows that the estimation error is much larger than the measurement error.
Estimating the actual state:

$$\hat{x}_{1,1} = \hat{x}_{1,0} + k_1\left(z_1 - \hat{x}_{1,0}\right) = 200 + 0,86214324 \times (200 - 200) = 200$$

Evaluating the variance of the actual state:

$$p_{1,1} = (1 - k_1) \times p_{1,0} = (1 - 0,86214324) \times 400,25 = 55,1771682$$

STAGE 3- PREDICTION
As the Dynamic Model of the system in use is constant, that is, the consumption value per hour does not change, then:

$$\hat{x}_{2,1} = \hat{x}_{1,1} = 200$$

The predict variance is:

$$p_{2,1} = p_{1,1} + Q = 55,537188 + 20 = 75,537188$$

REMAINING ITERATES
The remaining iterative process is just the repetition of the scheme.

5   Results and Discussion

In Fig. 11 is displayed actual value (green), measured value (red) and estimated value (blue) of consumption hourly rate. The analysis of the graph, it is verified that the estimated value converges to the real value. Graph 2 shows the uncertainty in the estimate.

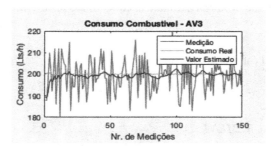

Fig. 11.   KF simulation.

Figure 12 shows the uncertainty in the estimate. The value of the estimate uncertainty decreases rapidly. After 150 measurements, the value of the uncertainty in the estimate is 1.403, that is, the standard deviation of the uncertainty in the estimate is 1.969 lts/h. It can thus be said that the estimated consumption is 200.167 ± 1969 lts/h.

Figure 13 displays the Kalman gain.

From the analysis of Fig. 13, it is verified that the Kalman gain value decreases rapidly. The Kalman filter gain decreases as confidence in the prior estimate increases, making the measurement weight smaller and smaller.

Figure 14 shows the actual error between the estimates and the actual state. From the analysis of the graph, it can be seen that the error value starts out large, but decreases quickly. The error decreases as the estimated value approaches the actual value.

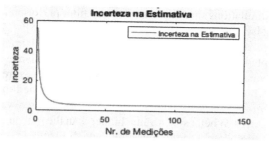

Fig. 12. Uncertainty of the estimate.

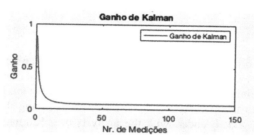

Fig. 13. Kalman gain.

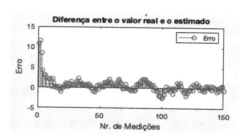

Fig. 14. Error between estimates and actual state.

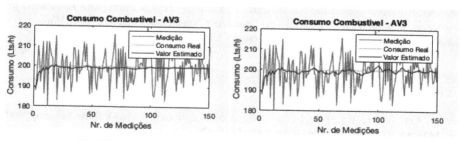

Fig. 15. KF Simulation. On right $Q = (5)^2$. On left $Q = (0.5)^2$.

The following simulations show how the Kalman filter performance is influenced by the measurement noise parameter, when, $Q = (0,5)^2$ and $Q = (5)^2$ (Fig. 15).

In this case, the constant, c, consumption, was observed 150 times, where the observations were corrupted by white noise with zero mean and variance 0.52. The Kalman filter estimated the value of the constant across the 150 noisy measurements. In the filter simulations, in which the variance value is changed, it is verified that the best performance among the simulations performed is the one that uses the real value of the variance of the measurement error. When using a value higher than the real one, it is observed that the filter responds more slowly to the measures, which results in a reduced estimated variance, but a slower convergence. When using a value lower than the real one, the filter responds more quickly to the measurements, which increases the estimated variance.

6 Conclusions

This work presents a brief approach to the derivation of a Kalman filter when the input is a scalar quantity. This was followed by the analysis of a Kalman filter model to estimate a constant and, of a similar model, to estimate a first-order system. Several simulations were carried out with these models and the results of applying the filter in different situations were analyzed. It ended with the analysis of a Kalman filter model, built specifically to filter NRP Douro consumption data.

The approach that was taken to the Kalman filter in this work was dedicated only to the discrete case, since in practical situations observations and controls are carried out in discrete time.

The Kalman filter was used in a linear system to obtain the best estimate of the state vector conditioned to the observations. This estimate was calculated by reconstructing the state vector using the previous state vector estimate, the known inputs, and the measured outputs.

In the consumption model presented, the hourly consumption value of the NRP Douro was estimated, with AV3 machine regime, using a one-dimensional Kalman filter. Despite having used a random noise value for the measurements, it was possible to verify that the applied Kalman filter was effective and presented a good estimate.

Acknowledgements. This work was supported by Portuguese funds through the Center of Naval Research (CINAV), Portuguese Naval Academy, Portugal and *The Portuguese Foundation for Science and Technology* (FCT), through the Center for *Computational and Stochastic Mathematics* (CEMAT), University of Lisbon, Portugal, project UID/Multi/04621/2019.

References

Brown, R.G., Hwang, P.Y.: Introduction to Random Signals and Applied Kalman Filtering: with MATLAB Exercises, 4th edn. Wiley, New Jersey (2012)

Julier, S.J., Uhlmann, J.K.: New extension of the Kalman filter to nonlinear systems. In: Signal Processing, Sensor Fusion, and Target Recognition VI, vol. 3068, pp. 182–193. SPIE (1997)

Kalman, R.E.: A new approach to linear filtering and prediction problems. J. Basic Eng. **82**(1), 35–45 (1960)

Kalman, R.E.: New methods in wiener filter theory. In: Bogdanoff, J.L., Kozin, F. (eds.) Proceedings of the First Symposium on Engineering Application of Random Function Theory and Probability, Wiley, New York (1963)

Sorenson, H.W.: Kalman Filtering: Theory and Application. IEEE Press, New Jersey (1985)

Welch, G., Bishop, G.: An introduction to Kalman filter (2006). Technical Report TR 95-041

A Portuguese Case Study About Barotrauma

M. Filomena Teodoro[1,2]([envelope]) [iD] and Marina A. P. Andrade[3] [iD]

[1] CINAV, Naval Academy, Military Universitary Institute, 2810-001 Almada, Portugal
mteodoro64@gmail.com
[2] CEMAT - Center for Computational and Stochastic Mathematics, Instituto Superior Técnico, Lisbon University, 1048-001 Lisbon, Portugal
[3] Centro de Investigação em Ciências da Informação, Tecnologias e Arquitetura, Instituto Universitário de Lisboa (ISCTE-IUL), Lisbon, Portugal
maria.teodoro@tecnico.ulisboa.pt, marina.andrade@iscte-iul.pt

Abstract. This work aimed to (Fijen 2016) determine the incidence and severity of barotrauma and identify the possibility of middle ear barotrauma in a high number of patients undergoing regular hyperbaric oxygen therapy. To explore and clarify this issue in terms of incident, seriousness and recurrence, age, gender, clinical signs, the specific history of chronic rhinitis, and symptoms of nasal obstruction during the occurrence were registered.

A first approach was performed by the authors where a descriptive statistical analysis and some elementary and intermediate statistical techniques such as variance analysis were performed. In the actual manuscript, a Logit model is built allowing us to relate the occurrence of barotrauma with the clinical profile of patients. We could conclude that Hyperbaric Oxygen Therapy is safe.

Keywords: Hyperbaric Oxygen Therapy · Logit Approach · Barotraumatism Occurrence · Middle Ear · Risk Factors

1 Introduction

Hyperbaric Oxygen Therapy (HBOT) is a treatment in which 100% oxygen (O2) is administered periodically in a chamber at a pressure above sea level. This growing intensity of O2 flow in the tissues allows the improvement of the treatment of ischemia and infection by reducing edema and tissue hypoxia (Acott 1999), (Mathieu 2006). Middle ear barotrauma (BTOM) is the most common complication. However, the incidence, risk factors, and severity are not fully understood. This work began with the collection of clinical characteristics of 1732 patients treated at the Portuguese Navy's Underwater and Hyperbaric Medicine Center (HMCS) from 2012 to 2016 presented in (Teles 2017), (M. F. Teodoro 2018), and (M. F. Teodoro 2018a). The socio-demographic details, frequency, severity, and recurrence were registered. This work focused in identify possible risk factors such as age, gender, clinical indications for HBOT, and history of allergic rhinitis. A statistical model was constructed to analyze the effect of gender and personal history of early-stage nasal obstruction on the probability of BTOM.

© The Author(s), under exclusive license to Springer Nature Switzerland AG 2023
O. Gervasi et al. (Eds.): ICCSA 2023 Workshops, LNCS 14105, pp. 362–373, 2023.
https://doi.org/10.1007/978-3-031-37108-0_23

Some risk factors are also identified in this section. Generalized least squares (GLM) methods (Nelder 1972), (Turkman 2000) were used to estimate the model. Some results are discussed in the present manuscript.

The structure of the work consists of 6 sections. Section 2 describes some of the adopted methods. Section 3 explains the principles of data collection. In Sect. 4, we recruited groups of 142 and 150 patients (without BTOM) from hyperbaric therapy patients using the study group (with BTOM) and control statistical methods. The first part uses basic techniques. An approximate model is also presented in Sect. 4. In the last section, we will discuss and reach some conclusions.

2 Preliminaries

2.1 HBOT

Hyperbaric oxygen therapy is a treatment used to accelerate recovery from carbon monoxide poisoning, gangrene, wounds that do not heal, and infections that require oxygen. For this treatment, we enter a special chamber to breathe pure oxygen at air pressure levels of 1.5 to 3 times above the media. The objective is to fill the blood with sufficient oxygen to repair the tissues and restore the body's normal function. HBOT helps wound healing by bringing oxygen-rich plasma to oxygen-depleted tissues (Hyperoxia). The sores cause damage to the body's blood vessels, which release fluid that leaks into the tissues and causes swelling. This swelling deprives the damaged cells of oxygen, and the tissue begins to die. HBOT reduces swelling while oxygenating tissues. More pressure in the chamber increases the amount of oxygen in the blood (Hyperoxemia). The goal of HBOT is to break the cycle of swelling, lack of oxygen, and tissue death. HBOT prevents "reperfusion injury". This is serious tissue damage that occurs when the blood returns to tissues after they have been deprived. For example, when blood flow is disrupted due to a crush injury, a series of events within damaged cells release harmful oxygen radicals. These molecules can cause irreversible tissue damage. They cause blood vessels to close and blood flow to stop. HBOT encourages the body's oxygen radical scavengers to seek out the problem molecules and allow healing to continue. HBOT helps to inhibit the action of harmful bacteria and strengthens the body's immune system. HBOT can inactivate toxins from certain bacteria. It also increases the concentration of oxygen in the tissues. This helps them to resist infection. In addition, this treatment improves the ability of white blood cells to find and destroy invaders. HBOT stimulates the formation of new collagen and new skin cells. It does this by stimulating the growth of new blood vessels. It also stimulates cells to produce certain substances, such as vascular endothelial growth factors. These attract and stimulate the endothelial cells needed for healing.

2.2 General Linear Models

In the classical linear model, a vector X with p explanatory variables $X = (X_1, X_2,..., X_p)$ can explain the variability of the variable of interest Y (response variable), where $Y = Z\beta + \varepsilon$, where Z is some specification matrix, β a parameter vector and ε a random vector of errors.

The data are in the form (y_i, x_i), $i = 1,..., n$, as a result of observation of (Y, X) n times. The response variable Y has an expected value $E[Y|Z] = \mu$.

Generalized linear models (GLM) formulation is an extension of the classical model where the response variable, follows an exponential family distribution (Turkman 2000) where the structure of the error does not need to have Gaussian distribution. Another extension from the classical model is that the function which relates the expected value and the explanatory variables can be any differentiable function b. Y_i has expected value

$$E[Y_i \backslash x_i] = \mu_i = b'(\theta_i), \ i = 1, \cdots, n.$$

It is also defined as a differentiable and monotone link function g which relates the random component with the systematic component of the response variable. The expected value μ_i is related to the linear predictor using the relation

$$\mu_i = h(\eta_i) = h(z_i^T \beta_i), \ \eta_i = g(\mu_i) \tag{1}$$

where h is a differentiable function and $g = h^{-1}$ is the link function; β is a vector of parameters with size p (the same size of the number of explanatory variables); z is a specification vector with size $p + 1$. A more detailed description of GLM can be found in (Turkman 2000). There are different link functions in GLM. When the random component of the response variable has a Poisson distribution, the link function is *logarithmic*, and the model is *log-linear*. Sometimes, the link function is unknown being estimated simultaneously with the linear component of the semi-parametric models. A detailed description of GLM methodology can be found in several references such as (Nelder 1972), (Turkman 2000).

3 Empirical Application

3.1 Sample

This study is a collaboration between the Medical Faculty of the University of Lisbon and the Center for Underwater and Hyperbaric Medicine of the Portuguese Navy. This study was a retrospective observational study designed in patients receiving routine hyperbaric oxygen therapy from January 1, 2012 to December 31, 2016.

All patients had an otolaryngologic (ORL) evaluation and tympanic examination prior to initiation of treatment. HBOT-trained volunteers who learned how to use Valsalva and Toynbee. Alerts you to warning signs and symptoms of complications. Only one patient with a type A tympanogram of the Jerger system was performed. (Audiologyonline 2023), (Jerger 1970), (Feldman 1976).

All tympanograms with maximum intratympanic pressure between -99 daPa and $+$ 99 daPa and type A tympanograms according to Jerger's classification were considered "normal" (see Figures 1 and 2), the remaining tympanograms were "abnormal". An HBOT specialist nurse is always on hand to help patients with balance issues (equalizing difficulty).

If the patient reported otologic symptoms, the incident was recorded in the nurse's log, and the patient again underwent to perform a tympanogram and an otolaryngologic evaluation.

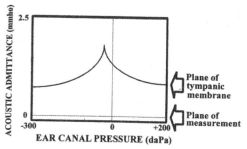

Fig. 1. A normal tympanogram. Peak with a small displacement from atmospheric pressure. Plan of measurement and plane of tympanic membrane. Adapted from (Feldman 1976).

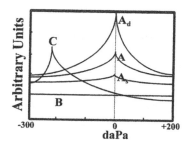

Fig. 2. Jerger classification illustration. Type A: peak near atmosphere pressure; Type Ad: high peak; Type As: smaller peak, Type B: flat; Type C: negative pressure. Adapted from (Feldman 1976).

The patients were included in a therapeutic protocol consisting of daily HBOT sessions, each session lasting 100 min, during which the patient was exposed to a pressure of 2.5 ata. The session begins with a 10-min compression phase followed by a 75-min treatment phase and a 15-min decompression phase. The treatment phase is divided into two consecutive 35-min breaks with 5-min breaks where the patient breathes air. During the compression and decompression phase, the patient breathes air.

Clinical records of all patients with symptoms consistent with BTOM (hearing discomfort, otalgia, numbness of the cephalic pinna, hearing loss, tinnitus and otorrhagia) were analyzed and clinical data were recorded: age, gender and clinical indications for HBOT (sudden deafness, sonotrauma, otitis externa, diabetic ischemia, chronic arterial disease, mandibular osteoradionecrosis, etc.). Symptoms of acute nasal obstruction at the time of onset may block the lumen of the tube and lead to tubal dysfunction (Fijen 2016).

An individual's medical history, including a previous diagnosis of allergic rhinitis and several commonly used medications associated with an increased risk of drug-induced non-allergic rhinitis, is considered at risk for chronic non-obstruction. For BTOM, location (right, left, or both ears), extent of lesion, frequency of recurrence, and post-BTOM middle ear pressure (high post-BTOM) were analyzed. A group of *150* patients were randomly selected in the control population who did not experience BTOM during treatment. Statistical analysis was performed to compare clinical characteristics and confirm risk factors between the two groups. BTOM levels can be determined using a modified Teed classification (Teed 1944), first proposed by Wallace Teed (US Diver in World War II) and modified by Haines and Harris (Haines 1946). On a 6-step scale from 0° to 5°, the levels are shown in Table 1 and shown in the Fig. 3.

Table 1. Modified Teed classification: gravity of BTOM.

Modified Teed classification[a]	
Scale Level	Description
0	Symptomatology without otological signs
1	Diffuse hyperemia and tympanic membrane retention
2	Light hemorrhage within the tympanic membrane
3	Significant hemorrhage within the tympanic membrane
4	Outstanding and dark tympanic membrane
5	Free haemorrhage in the middle ear, with tympanic perforation, bleeding visible inside or outside the external auditory canal

a. A simpler description of the scale classification can be found in (), (Davis 2011).

3.2 Sample Characterization

To classify the data, firstly a study and control groups of *142* and *150* subjects were selected, respectively. In the first step, were calculated some simple measures using descriptive statistical techniques, and run some intermediate-level techniques (eg, tests of proportions, tests of independence, tests of comparison, others) (Tamhane 2000).

Given the non-quantitative nature of the relevant variables in the initial analysis of the data, measures of association, non-parametric Spearman correlation coefficients and non-parametric Friedman paired-sample tests were calculated. Figure 3 displays the classification of age in classes for the control and study groups. Age of the selected group of *178* patients who received HBOT. Control patients did not suffer from BTOM and all patients in the study group had BTOM during the treatment session. The minimum age of the control and study groups was *10* years, the maximum age was *83* years and the mean age was *55.05* and *55.36* years respectively. There was no evidence of differences between age distributions (*p-value* = *0.80*). The study group consisted of *70* men and *72* women, and the control group consisted of 94 men and *56* women. Distribution by gender and group differed statistically (*p-value* = *0.025*).

There exist several reasons that conduce to clinical indication for hyperbaric oxygen therapy. The diseases that implied the HBOT indication versus number of occurrences are shown in Fig. 4.

The most common clinical signs in the two groups were sudden deafness (*45%* and *57%* in the study and control groups, respectively), *radicular complications* (*31.47%* and

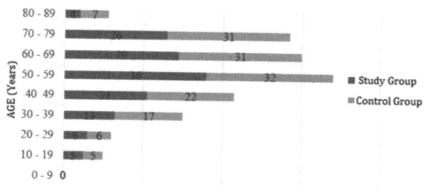

Fig. 3. Classification of age relatively to Control group e and Study group.

18%, respectively) and *diabetic ischaemia (10%* in each group)). Of the *radiographic problems, radicular cystitis* was the most common in both groups *(13.2% and 11%).* *Osteonecrosis of the lower jaw* in the study group *(9.8%)* and the control group *(2%)* were distinct. The prevalence of *rheumatoid arthritis* in each group was similar (approximately 4% in each group).

Evaluating *sudden deafness* (more in the control group, *p = 0.025)* and *osteonecrosis of the jaw* (more in the study group, *p = 0.028)* were statistically significant between the two groups. The difference in the rates of diagnoses of *rickettsial cystitis* and *radial proctitis* between the two groups was not statistically significant.

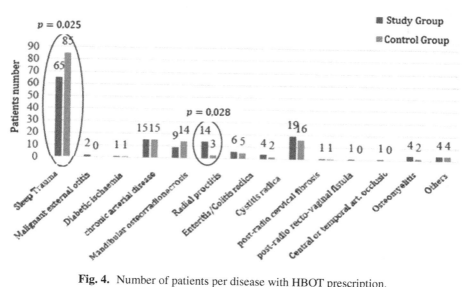

Fig. 4. Number of patients per disease with HBOT prescription.

The characteristics of BTOM in patients are shown in Table 2. Table 2 considers the frequency and number of treatment sessions until BTOM develops. Between 1732 patients, 143 had BTOM, and the incidence of patients with BTOM was approximately 8.3%. Only 41% of patients had complete information recorded during the clinical process. From the data collected (see Table 2), BTOM occurred in 36% of cases in the first 3 sessions (19% in the first session) and in 44% of cases up to 5 sessions. The incidence of BTOM in patients was 8.3%, with the majority of cases being unilateral in 62% and the remaining 21% cases being bilateral. The recurrence rate was 28%.

Among patients with middle ear injuries, most patients (62%) had unilateral BTOM (mostly in the right ear). A significant proportion (21%) suffered BTOM in both ears during the same session. The results obtained were 34% BTOM in the right ear, 28% in the left ear and 21% in both ears. As shown in Table 3 and Fig. 5, the BTOM gravity, considering the number of unilateral and bilateral recurrent BTOMs, totals 208 BTOMs per ear.

Most were rated with level 1 of Teed classification (30%). Approximately 20% of analyzed ears scored 3 or higher in this classification. The number of BTOM ears (reference) in each category are shown in Table 3. About 50% of BTOM ears are classified in the first four levels, and almost 20% of BTOM ears are more severe (classified as 4 or 5). In 57 cases (27%), BTOM was not documented in the process (physician not registered or patient did not choose to see a specialist other than his own specialist out of CMSH) and could not be classified.

Table 2. Number of sessions at the time of BTOM occurrence per number of patients.

Number of sessions	Number of patients
0–3	21
4–5	25
6–9	9
10–14	5
15–19	3
20–99	6
29–49	3
50–69	5
70–99	1
>100	1

Table 3. Percentage of BTOM ears per gravity level (considering modified Teed classification).

BTOM gravity Modified Teed classification	
Scale Level	Percentage of BTOM ears
0	5.77
1	30.00
2	17.00
3	9.13
4	9.61
5	1.44

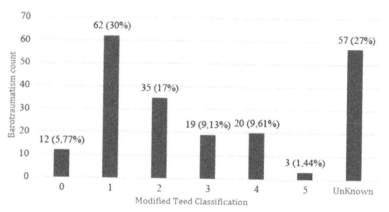

Fig. 5. Gravity of BTOM. Teed modified classification.

4 The Model

In this section are presented some models after the process of estimation by GLM, validation and selection of the models, and testing some distinct link functions g to estimate adequate models. The *log-log*, *logistic*, and *probit* regression were taken into consideration. To get the "'best" explanatory variables in each case, was used the stepwise selection.

Once we have dichotomous data, discrete models were preferably estimated by logistic and probit regression. Almost all estimated and selected models have validation tests with *p-values* between 0.001 and 0.08. In the estimation process, we did not take into consideration some potential variables due the fact that the patient's medical register had a lot of miss information. The residential area and race, once there were few individuals had a complete register. The description and codification of considered variables are in Table 4.

The logistic model relative to the dependent variable Y1, was obtained in several steps. Initially, the selection of the best set of covariates that conduces to the "best" model, was done by stepwise, based on the p-values from Wilks test likelihood ratio relative to inclusion/exclusion of covariates. The impact of a covariate in the occurrence of barotraumatism is measured by the obtained *p-value*: a small *p-value* means a significant influence. First are selected the principal effects, and last, the second-order interaction. Female gender, diagnosis of osteoradionecrosis of the mandible, and personal history of allergic rhinitis were identified (statistically significant) as risk factors. No significant relationships were found between age, remaining clinical indications, risk medication, and changes in tympanogram performed prior to initiation of treatment when we consider models without interaction. When the models are estimated with interaction, we have significance with gender, allergic rhinitis, and corticoid therapeutic, another significant interaction was obtained with number of sessions and osteoradionecrosis when we consider the barotrauma classification as dependent variable.

Table 4. Codification of considered variables.

Variables	Description	Codification
Y_1	BTOM occurence	1 = Yes 0 = No
Y_2	Teed Classification level	0 = (0, 1, 2) low 1 = (3, 4, 5) high
Y_3	Type of BTOM	0 = no occurrence 1 = unilateral 2 = bilateral
X_1	Number of sessions	1, ...9 = 1.....9 10 = greater than 9
X_2	diagnosis of osteoradionecrosis	1 = Yes 0 = No
X_3	history of allergic rhinitis	1 = Yes 0 = No
X_4	Cortcoid therapeutic	1 = Yes 0 = No
X_5	tympanogram	1 = Yes 0 = No
X_6	age	'1' = (<18) '2' = ([18. 29]) '3' = ([30.49]) '4' = ($\geq$50)
X_7	Gender	0 = Female 1 = Male

Relatively to BTOM occurrence (the aim of study), the obtained model considering principal effects (gender, allergic rhinitis, diagnosis of osteoradionecrosis) is given by structural form (2). We also found some significant interactions between the diagnosis of osteoradionecrosis and allergic rhinitis in females. The estimated model for barotrauma classification (high/low) as the dependent variable, considering principal and second and third-order effects, is summarized in structural Eq. (3).

$$\ln\left[\frac{\pi_i}{1 - \pi_i}\right] = \beta_0 + \sum_{j=1}^{3} \beta_j x_{ij} \tag{2}$$

$$\ln\left[\frac{\pi_i}{1 - \pi_i}\right] = \alpha_0 + \sum_{j=1}^{2} \alpha_j x_{ij} + \alpha_3 x_{i1} x_{i2} + \alpha_4 x_{i7} x_{i3} x_{i4} \tag{3}$$

The significant explanatory variables and parameters p-value of models (2) and (3) are displayed in Table 5 and include some significant interactions. Model (2) has a deviance global test with *p-value = 0,010*, by other hand, model (3) conduces to *p-value = 0.015*. Another evaluation of models is done by residual analysis.

When all validation and selection techniques are completed, we need to be able to choose correctly between different models with close explanatory performance. The best models with similar performance conduce to estimates which are combined using a weighted mean using the p-values of the global test.

Table 5. Models parameters. Model (2) without interaction; Model (3) with interaction.

Effect	Parameter Model (2)	P-value Model (2)	Parameter Model (3)	P-value Model (3)
Intercept	$\hat{\beta}_0$	0.001	$\hat{\alpha}_0$	0.002
(x_2)	$\hat{\beta}_1$	0.004	$\hat{\alpha}_1$	0.005
(x_3)	$\hat{\beta}_2$	0.005		
(x_7)	$\hat{\beta}_3$	0.004		
$(x_7.x_2.x_3)$	$\hat{\beta}_4$	0.05	$\hat{\alpha}_3$	0.004
$(x_1.x_2)$			$\hat{\alpha}_4$	0.06
$(x_7.x_3.x_4)$			$\hat{\alpha}_4$	0.004

We are interested in the comparison of odd ratios for different values of explanatory variables. The odd ratios for the two identified models A (without and with interactions) and B (with interactions) are given by formulae (4) and (5) respectively.

$$\Psi = \left[\frac{\pi_i}{1 - \pi_i}\right] = \exp\left[\beta_0 + \sum_{j=1}^{3} \beta_j x_{ij}\right] \tag{4}$$

$$\Psi = \left[\frac{\pi_i}{1 - \pi_i}\right] = \exp\left[\alpha_0 + \sum_{j=1}^{2} \alpha_j x_{ij} + \alpha_3 x_{i1} x_{i2} + \alpha_4 x_{i7} x_{i3} x_{i4}\right] \tag{5}$$

5   Discussion

The evaluation about the possibility of occurrence of BTOM and the establishment of some association with some the individual characteristics/clinical profile of patients can be done. From formulae (4) and (5) we can estimate the odds ratio for some values of explanatory variables. For example, the odd ratio (Higher/Lower) for two females with historical allergic rhinitis with and without therapeutic, the value of the odd ratio is lower than one, supposing that they have similar remaining characteristics. It means that the probability of a higher Teed classification is less than the probability of a lower Teed classification (using model (5)).

Using the model (4) for the same gender, considering two patients with allergic rhinitis, we have the odd ratio greater than one, if only one of both patients has osteoradionecrosis and considering the same values of remaining explanatory variables. This means that the probability of BTOM increases relatively to a patient with osteoradionecrosis comparatively with another patient without osteoradionecrosis. Other relations and a detailed analysis can be performed in detail and it is planned for the future.

6   Conclusion

HBOT is an effective and safe medical therapy. Proper teaching of the active leveling maneuver and careful monitoring during the first session can significantly reduce the incidence of BTOM. The CMSH of the Portuguese Navy has 8:3% BTOM, mainly in low gravity. The risk of recurrence needs to be assessed, consequently some patients need to take prophylactic medication during the treatment period. The aim of the study was to determine the incidence and severity, also to detect risk factors for middle ear barotrauma in a population of patients attending hyperbaric oxygen therapy.

Several general linear models were computed allowing to get a set of explanatory variables, some of them were identified as risk variables. In a model without interaction, male gender, diagnosis of osteoradionecrosis of the jaw, and history of allergic rhinitis were statistically significant. There was no significant relationship between age, other clinical indications, treatment risk and tympanogram changes made before HBOT.

Acknowledgments. The first author was supported by Portuguese funds through the Center for Computational and Stochastic Mathematics (CEMAT), The Portuguese Foundation for Science and Technology (FCT), University of Lisbon, Portugal, project UID/Multi/04621/2019, and Center of Naval Research (CINAV), Naval Academy, Portuguese Navy, Portugal. The second author, this work was partially supported by Fundação para a Ciência e a Tecnologia, I.P. (FCT) [ISTAR Projects: UIDB/04466/2020 and UIDP/04466/2020].

References

Acott, C.: A brief history of diving and decompression illness. SPUMS J. **29**(98–109), 31 (1999)

Audiologyonline. https://www.audiologyonline.com/ask-the-experts/common-types-of-tympanograms-361. Accessed 23 Apr 2023

Beuerlein, M., Nelson, R.N., Welling, D.B.: Inner and middle ear hyperbaric oxygen-induced barotrauma. Laryngoscope **107**(10), 1350–1356 (1997)

Davis, E.: The foundations for today's future. Diving Hyperb. Med. J. **41**(3), 118–120 (2011)

Feldman, A.S.: Tympanometry: application and interpretation. Ann. Otol. Rhinol. Laryngol. **85**(2), 202–208 (1976)

Fijen, V.A., Westerweel, P.E., Jan, P., Van Ooij, A.M., Van Hulst, R.A.: Tympanic membrane bleeding complications during hyperbaric oxygen treatment in patients with or without antiplatelet and anticoagulant drug treatment. Diving Hyperb. Med. J. **46**(1), 22–25 (2016)

Haines, H.L., Harris, J.D.: Aerotitis media in submariners. Ann. Otol. Rhinol. Laryngol. **55**, 347–371 (1946)

Jerger, J.F.: Clinical experience with impedance audiometry. Arch. Otolaryngol. **92**(4), 311–324 (1970)

Mathieu, D. (ed.): Handbook on Hyperbaric Medicine. Springer, Netherlands, Dordrecht, Dordrecht (2006)

Nelder, J.A., Wedderburn, R.W.: Linear models. J. R. Stat. Soc. Ser. A (General) **135**(3), 370–384 (1972)

Tamhane, A.C., Dunlop, D.D.: Statistics and Data Analysis: from Elementary to Intermediate. Prentice Hall, New Jersey (2000)

Teed, R.: Factors producing obstruction of the auditory tube in submarine personnel. US Navy Med. Bull. **42**, 293–306 (1944)

Teles, S.: O Barotraumatismo do Ouvido Médio em Doentes a Fazer Oxigenoterapia Hiperbárica. Medical Faculty, Lisbon University, Lisbon (2017)

Teodoro, M.F., Teles, S.S., Marques, M.C., Guerreiro, F.G.: Barotraumatism occurrence and hyperbaric oxygen therapy, a preliminary analysis. In: AIP Conference Proceedings, pp. 460007–460010 (2018)

Teodoro, M.F., Teles, S.S., Marques, M.C., Guerreiro, F.G.: Relating hyperbaric oxygen therapy and barotraumatism occurrence: a linear model approach. In: Gervasi, O., et al. (eds.) ICCSA 2018. LNCS, vol. 10961, pp. 485–495. Springer, Cham (2018). https://doi.org/10.1007/978-3-319-95165-2_34

Turkman, M.A. Silva, G.: Modelos Lineares Generalizados da teoria à prática. Lisboa: Sociedade Portuguesa de Estatística (2000)

A Study on the Maintenance of Distributed Lag Model in Time Series Prediction Model

Jung-Ho Choo⬤, Yu-Jin Kim⬤, and Jung-Ho Eom$^{(\boxtimes)}$ ⬤

Daejeon University, 62 Daehakro, Dong-Gu, Daejeon 300-716, Republic of Korea
eomhun@gmail.com

Abstract. An ambiguity in time series prediction analysis is that the distributed lag model can be transformed due to AR, differencing, MA, and seasonality adjustment. This means that the time series prediction model can make predictions without considering distributed lag model, which is a characteristic of time series. This study is to confirm whether the time series prediction model maintains the distributed lag model. Analysis tools were used cross-correlation and Granger causality test. Time series forecast models were used statistics-based ARIMA model and RNN-based LSTM model. And we used monthly terror attack data and monthly time series data of international oil prices from 1996 to 2020. The research method is four stages. First, we performed cross-correlation and Granger causality tests. Second, the ARIMA model and LSTM model were applied to the time series. Thirdly, we reperformed cross-correlation and Granger causality tests on the predicted results. Fourth, in the conclusion, the first and third steps results were compared to confirm whether the prediction model maintained distributed lag model. As a result of this research method, the ARIMA model maintained the distributed lag model in the cross-correlation, and the LSTM model maintained the distributed lag model in the Granger causality test.

Keywords: Distributed lags model · ARIMA · LSTM · Cross-correlation · Granger causality

1 Introduction

This study is to confirm whether the forecasting model maintains the distributed lag model. Time series prediction analysis may not maintain the distributed lag model due to AR, differencing, MA, and seasonality adjustments. This means that time series prediction results may differ from original time series the distributed lag model. Differencing adjusts the trend of the time series and make it stationary. Therefore, the original time series and the Undifferentiated time series are different from each other. However, in the ARIMA model, the differencing equalizes average and dispersion in the time series so that the time series has stationarity. Differencing in LSTM (Long-Short-Term-Memory) models improve predictive accuracy. MA (Moving Average) or SMA (Seasonal Moving Average) can change the characteristics of distributed lag model. The SMA has a good effect of seasonality adjustment. However, if this is applied excessively, it is different from the appearance of the original time series. MA represents the current data as a

© The Author(s), under exclusive license to Springer Nature Switzerland AG 2023
O. Gervasi et al. (Eds.): ICCSA 2023 Workshops, LNCS 14105, pp. 374–391, 2023.
https://doi.org/10.1007/978-3-031-37108-0_24

combination of white noise. This characteristic of MA allows effective analysis by mitigating non-uniform delay of time series data. However, this characteristic of MA broke the relationship if there was a causal relationship between other time series.

Therefore, we applied the ARIMA model and the LSTM model to the time series data of the current society, and confirmed whether the forecasting model maintains the distributed lag model. We selected Cross-correlation and Granger causality test as methods to determine whether the distributed lag model is maintained. We used the time series by monthly terror attack and international oil prices by month from 1996 to 2020. We empirically analyze the hypothesis that the time series prediction model maintains the distributed lag model using real society time series data. Under this hypothesis Sect. 2 reviews the related work to this study and explains the analysis tools and order of the study. In Sect. 3, time series data are analyzed in the order of research set in Sect. 2. Finally, the research hypothesis is evaluated with the results of Sect. 3.

2 Related Work and Method

2.1 Related Work

In Kim's paper [2], compensated the Granger causality test of the index according to economic policy with stock returns and gold futures. And this paper predicted the closing price of asset prices with a deep learning LSTM model. Through the Granger causality test, this paper was analyzed the impact of the economic policy index on the rate of return and money in bitcoin, predicted the public with an LSTM model, and analyzed the model's cooperation. As a result, it was confirmed that there is a significant relationship between the indicator and the increase in Bitcoin price. In addition, in the shock response function analysis, there was a supportive response to the economic policy index in future assets and finally, in the LSTM analysis, the digital self-prediction index was not repeated. The time series recording the KOSPI index represents an excellent predictor of economic policy indicators [2].

In Sun's paper [3], applied ARIMA and VAR models to portal and Internet information media service industries, information service industries, and online delivery industries. When being apply the information service industry to the ARIMA model, the most appropriate models are ARIMA $(1, 1, 1)(0, 1, 1)_{12}$ and ARIMA $(2, 1, 0)(1, 1, 0)_{12}$, it respectively showed an accuracy of 5.226% and 5.044%. The Granger causality test between the production index of database online providers and the portal and information-media service industries showed a significant result of 5%, and database online providers and portal and Internet information-media services had a significant effect on the wholesale and retail industries [3].

In Lee's papers [4], analyzed the causal relationship between two variables of housing price and transaction volume using the VEC model and compared the predictive power with the VAR model the VEC model and the AR model. For the forecast of time series, the out-of-sample prediction, dynamic, recursive forecast model method was applied to the time τ and then the prediction was made by increasing the period by 1 to the total $\tau + h$, and the accuracy was using Clark and McCracken's MES-F test and boot simulation. As a result of the study, there was a long-term positive correlation between transaction volume and housing price in the VEC model. But the causality from transaction volume to price was low. In the comparison of forecast power was high in the order of the VEC model, VAR model and AR model [4].

According to Kim's research method, the Granger causality test between time series was performed and then prediction was made with the LSTM model, so it cannot be confirmed whether the causal relationship between time series after forecasting with the LSTM model is the same as before prediction. Sun's research method was to make time series predictions with an ARIMA model and then to confirm the causal relationship between time series. That is, it cannot be confirmed whether the causal relationship before applying the ARIMA model to the time series is the same as after forecasting. Lastly, Lee's research method is identified the causal relationship between time series with the VEC model, and then compared the predictive accuracy by predicting with the VAR model and the AR model. This research method confirmed the causal relationship between time series and then predicted. It is not possible to compare whether the causal relationship before and after the prediction is the same. What the three related work have in common is that they did not identify the causal relationship before and after prediction. In other words, they did not check whether the distributed lag model before and after the prediction was maintained [2–4].

2.2 Method

As mentioned earlier, the purpose of this study is to check whether the distributed lags model is maintained when applying prediction models to time series data. The source of the data was used GTD (Global Terrorism Database) [5] for terror attack time series data, and Korea National Oil Corporation (Petronet) [6] for international oil price time series data. And the program was used R version 4.2.1. The reason for using the terror attack time series is that it has seasonality. In other words, terror attack occurs uncertainly, so it may be disadvantages using time series analysis data. However, since there is a seasonality that occurs in a similar pattern every year, it can be used for time series analysis.

Standard analysis was performed using the Box-Jenkins method for ARIMA model analysis. As shown Fig. 1, the Box-Jenkins method proceeds in the order of identify model, parameter estimation, diagnostic model, model adoption and forecasting.

Fig. 1. Box-Jenkins method [7].

The ARIMA model consists of AR (Autoregressive), I (differencing) and MA (Moving average). The distinction between the ARIMA model and the ARMA model is the presence or absence of an I (differencing), which means that the ARIMA model can analyze time series data are non-stationary. The expression of AR is as follows.

$$y_t = \delta + \theta_1 y_{t-1} + \theta_2 y_{t-2} + \cdots + \theta_p y_{t-p} + e_t \tag{1}$$

The expression of I (differencing) is as follows.

$$1^{\text{st}}\text{differencing}: y_t' = y_t - y_{t-1} \tag{2}$$

$$2^{\text{nd}}\text{differencing}: y_t'' = y_t' - y_{t-1}' \tag{3}$$

The expression of MA is as follows.

$$MA_t = \frac{1}{2k+1}\sum_{i=-k}^{k} Y_{t+k} \tag{4}$$

The LSTM model works as shown in Fig. 2. As noted earlier, the LSTM model is a deep learning analysis model that has improved RNN (Recurrent Neural Network). As shown in Fig. 2, we show that the problem of RNN, such as the slope loss problem, is improved by adding hidden layers and cell states to the LSTM model. In other words, the predictive power has improved as the partial learning information can be memorized and reflected in new learning.

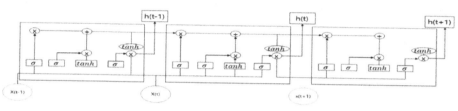

Fig. 2. LSTM architecture [8].

The LSTM model prevents the slope lose and effectively allows the slope to flow through three gates to protect and control the cell state the forget gate (f_t), input gate (i_t) and output gate. The forget gate (f_t) is a gate for forgetting past information. The output gate (0_t) of the sigmoid function is 0 to 1, if the value is 0, the information in the previous state is forgotten, and if the value is 1, the information in the previous state is completely remembered [9]. It remembers and receives input and cycles, takes s sigmoid, and sends it out [10]. The input gate (i_t) is a gate for storing flow information, and its sigmoid value is between 0 and 1 [9]. However, since $\tilde{c}_t$ is a Hadamard product and is the result of the hyperbolic tangent, its value is -1 to 1. That is, the value of sigmoid above may be -1 to 1, and the result may be a negative number [10]. Finally, the output gate (0_t) is the gate for the final results h_t, and the value obtained by Hadamard product of the hyperbolic tangent of the cell state is the final result of the LSTM. The formula for the LSTM cell is as follows [9].

$$f_t = \sigma_g\left(W_f x_t + U_f h_{t-1} + b_f\right) \tag{5}$$

$$i_t = \sigma_g\left(W_i x_t + U_i h_{t-1} + b_i\right) \tag{6}$$

$$0_t = \sigma_g\left(W_o x_t + U_o h_{t-1} + b_o\right) \tag{7}$$

$$c_t = f_t \odot c_{t-1} + i_t \odot \sigma_c (W_c x_t + U_c h_{t-1} + b_c) \tag{8}$$

$$h_t = o_t \odot \sigma_h (c_t) \tag{9}$$

Cross-correlation is a way to check the similarity of two-time series [11]. This correlation analysis method is the correlation of time series observations through the delay between two-time series. Looking at the cross-correlation formula, we can see the similarity through the observations between the two-time series. The formula for the LSTM cell is as follows [11].

$$r_k = \frac{\sum_{t=1}^{N-k}(x_t - \bar{x})(y_{k+k} - \bar{y})}{\sum_{t=1}^{N}(x_t - \bar{x})^2 \sum_{t=1}^{N}(y_t - \bar{y})^2} \tag{10}$$

Granger causality test for time series the standard causal relationship test method is different from correlation analysis because it identifies the causal relationship through a distributed lags model between time series. Therefore, this test method can be confirmed the direction of the causal relationship between time series. The formula for the Granger causality test is as follows [12].

$$Y_t = \sum_{i=0}^{m} \alpha_i X_{t-i} + \sum_{j=0}^{m} \beta_j Y_{t-j} + \epsilon_{1t} \tag{11}$$

$$X_t = \sum_{i=0}^{m} \lambda_i X_{t-k} + \sum_{j=0}^{m} \delta_j Y_{t-j} + v_{2t} \tag{12}$$

$$F = \frac{(SSE_R - SSE_{UR})/q}{(SSE_{UR})/(n-k)} \tag{13}$$

In the above F Eq. (13), SSE_R and SSE_{UR} are obtained as a sum of the two Eqs. (13). Subsequently the SSE is obtained when the constraint $\alpha_i = 0$, are given in (11) and $\delta_j = 0$ in (12) and when they are not. After that, if the value of the test statistics is greater than the threshold, the null hypothesis $H_0 : \alpha_i = 0$ or $H_0 : \delta_j = 0$ is rejected as the influence of the given condition is large.

This study is used to ARIMA, LSTM, cross-correlation, and Granger causality establish the hypothesis, method, and sequence of the study as follows.

H_o: Even if the prediction model is applied to time series data, the distributed lags model is maintained.

1. Granger causality test and Cross correlation of monthly terror attacks and international oil price from 1996 to 2020.
2. By forecasting three years of terror attacks and international oil price time series using the ARIMA model and LSTM model and generate time series data reflecting the forecast results.
3. Using two-time series data reflecting the forecasting results, the Granger causality test and Cross correlation before the prediction was performed.
4. Analyze the first and third results to evaluate the research hypothesis.

3   Analysis Result

3.1   Checking the Distributed Lag Model of the Original Time Series

The research method of the Granger causality test followed two steps. First, it is determined whether the first time series data is a stationary time series. The reason why time series data is determined to be stationary is that the variance of the mean increases with time lag in the case of non-stationary time series. If the Granger causality test is performed with a time series that does not have stationarity, may occur spurious regression results. To prevent this, an ACF (Auto-correlation function), PACF (Partial Auto-correlation function) and ADF (Augmented Dickey-Fuller) test was performed.

Second, it is to confirm the lag of the appropriate Granger causality test. The result of the Granger causality test is sensitive to the length of the selected lag. Therefore, in order to proceed smoothly with the Granger causal relationship, an appropriate number of lags must be determined. Since the data used are monthly terror attack and international oil price time series data, 1, 4, 6, 12, 18, 24… were set to reflect the level of interest by quarter and year.

Before proceeding with the Cross-correlation and Granger causality test between monthly terror attack and international oil prices from 1996 to 2020, it is necessary to determine whether the time series has stationarity. Figure 3 is a graph visualized to intuitively analyze the two-time series.

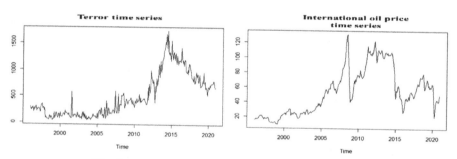

Fig. 3. Terror and international oil price General graphs

At the Fig. 3 of monthly terror attack and international oil prices from 1996 to 2020, both time series have points of sharp rise and fall, so we can suspect that the average may not be constant.

In addition, looking at the ACF (Autocorrelation Function) and PACF (Partial Autocorrelation Function) of terror attack and international oil prices in Fig. 4, there is a strong trend with a fast decrease as the time lag increases. That is, we assumed a time series non-stationarity.

It is necessary to check whether the two-time series data are stationary time series through the ADF test, which is a traditional stationarity confirmation method. ADF test results-Name of the terror attack time series is tr, and the international oil price is abbreviated to di-are shown in Table 1.

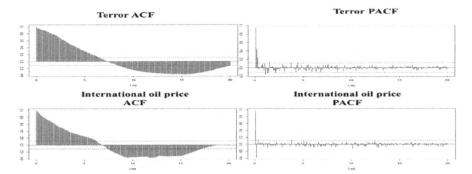

Fig. 4. ACF and PACF of terror attack and international oil prices time series.

Table 1. Result of ADF test.

ADF test	Dickey-Fuller	Lag order	p-value
tr	−1.7251	6	0.6926
tr, $d = 1$	−7.6349	6	0.01*
di	−1.8071	6	0.6576
di, $d = 1$	−7.103	6	0.01*

* in Table 1 is statistically significant as lower than 0.01. According to the ADF test results when the original time series and the 1st differencing of two-time series are performed, it can be seen that 1st differencing between the two-time series is required to become stationary time series data. So according to the results of the ADF test, the Granger causality test was used time series with the 1st differencing, and the graph of the series to which the 1st differencing was applied is shown in Fig. 5.

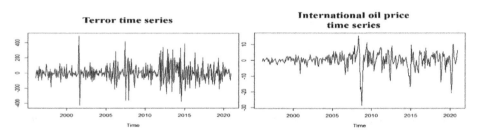

Fig. 5. General graph with 1st differencing applied two-time series.

Prior to the Granger causality test of the two-time series, cross-correlation analysis was performed to confirm the similarity between the time series. The reason for performing the cross-correlation analysis is that it analyzes the correlation between different time series between −1 and +1, so that the distributed lags models between time series can be compared simultaneously. Looking at Fig. 6, the highest cross-correlation is −

18 lag. So, we assumed that the terror attack time series can affect the international oil price time series with an 18 month frequency.

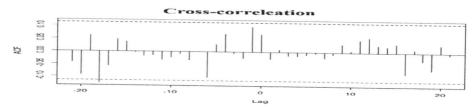

Fig. 6. Result of cross-correlation.

Cross-correlation used a distributed lag model between time series. In other words, cross-correlation is more difficult to confirm a clear causal relationship than Granger causality test. Therefore, in order to identify a clear causal relationship, a Granger causality test was performed between the two-time series, and the results are shown in Table 2.

Table 2. Result of Granger causality test.

Lag	tr → di		di → tr	
	F-statistic	P-value	F-statistic	P-value
24	1.4323	0.0935[*]	0.8374	0.6868
30	1.4002	0.098085*	1.0303	0.4297
84	0.7928	0.8228	1.6049	0.4064*

[*] in Table 2 is statistically significant as lower than 0.05. Table 2 shows the results of the Granger causality test between terror attack and international oil price time series. In the causal relationship direction of terror attack in international oil prices, it can be confirmed that there is a causal relationship with a significant probability of less than 5% of in the lag of 24 and 30. Conversely in the causal relationship from international oil prices to terror attack, it was confirmed that there was a significant causal relationship with a probability of less than 5% of in the lag of 84. Now we have performed cross-correlation and Granger causality test as time series of the original state. Therefore, after forecasting three years with the ARIMA model and LSTM model and then cross-correlation and Granger causality test should be performed again.

3.2 ARIMA Model

Before forecasting a time series with an ARIMA model, we verified that original time series are not stationary in previous Sect. 3.1. Therefore, in the ARIMA model analysis, we did beyond the process of identify model and proceed with the method of parameters estimation of Box-Jenkins method.

In the parameters estimation stage, ARIMA $(0, 1, 1)(0, 0, 2)_{12}$ was selected as an appropriate ARIMA model for time series in the case of terror attack. And ARIMA

$(0, 1, 1)(0, 0, 2)_{12}$ reflecting the seasonality existing in the terror attack time series is analyzed as the SARIMA model. In the case of international oil prices, seasonality did not exist. So it was analyzed as an ARIMA model, and ARIMA(0,1,2) was selected as an appropriate model. And the results and model values of these two models are shown in Table 3.

Table 3. ARIMA model values.

Model	ARIMA $(0, 1, 1)(0, 0, 2)_{12}$	ARIMA(0,1,2)
AIC	3607.59	1751.34
σ^2	9873	20.05
Ljung-box test	Pass	Pass

When forecasting three years with the ARIMA $(0, 1, 1)(0, 0, 2)_{12}$ model and the ARIMA(0,1,2) model the diagnostic values in Table 4. The forecasted graph in Fig. 7 are shown.

Table 4. ARIMA model forecast diagnostic values.

Diagnostic	ARIMA $(0, 1, 1)(0, 0, 2)_{12}$	ARIMA(0,1,2)
MAPE	24.89029	6.702753
RMSE	99.19756	4.470594

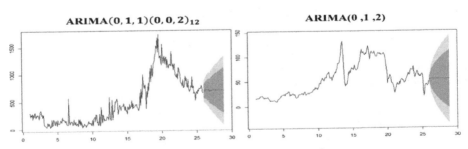

Fig. 7. ARIMA model Forecast graph.

Table 4 shows the diagnostic values of the ARIMA model. In the case of terror attack, seasonality exists, so it is assumed that MAPE (Mean Absolute Percentage Error) and RMSE (Root Mean Squared Error) values tend to be high. In the case of international oil prices, it was assumed that the values of MAPE and RMSE tended to be low because there was no seasonality.

3.3 LSTM Model

The LSTM model analysis will follow the operation of Fig. 2. And before applying the time series as the LSTM model, we willperform a 1st differencing to improve the model forecast performance and adjust with a stationary time series. Since the 1st differencing was made between the two-time series in the Granger causality test, the time series with the 1st differencing can be referred to Fig. 5.

As previous noted, the LSTM model is a technique for forecasting the future by learning the time series. So, when we analysis the time series with the LSTM model, there is something to be careful. It is to set the model learning rate and the layer dropout. In this study, we set the learning rate of 80% for both time series so that it can be forecasted after sufficient learning.

And the value of layer dropout with a learning rate of 80% was predicted for 3 years with the value when the lowest over fitting was confirmed. The above verification method confirmed the prediction accuracy by RMSE.

Table 5. LSTM model diagnostic values.

Diagnostic	terror attack	International oil prices
RMSE	95.21628	5.159664

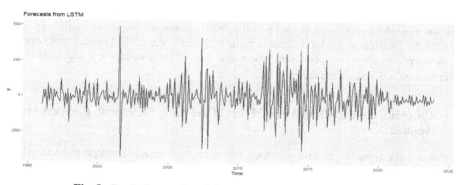

Fig. 8. Prediction results of the terror attack using LSTM model.

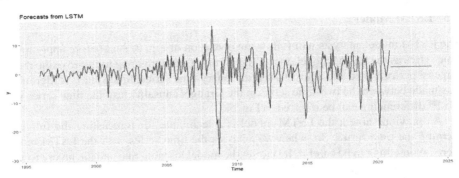

Fig. 9. Prediction results of the international oil prices using LSTM model.

Table 5, Fig. 8, and Fig. 9 show the RMSE and forecasting result when 80% of the learning rate and the layer dropout value to minimize overfitting are applied to each time series. In the case of terror attack, when the learning rate was 80% the layer dropout to minimize overfitting was 0.4% and the RMSE at this rate was 95.21628. In the case of international oil prices, the value of layer dropout, which minimizes overfitting was 0.1 and the value of RMSE was 5.159664.

An interesting point in the LSTM model analysis of terror attack and international oil prices is that, like the ARIMA model analysis, in the case of international oil without seasonality, the predicted values are static. In addition, the LSTM model was superior in the prediction model diagnosis value of RMSE, the terror attack time series prediction, and the ARIMA model was superior in the international oil price time series. In addition, in the prediction model diagnosis value of RMSE, the LSTM model was superior in the terror attack time series prediction and the ARIMA model was superior in the international oil price time series.

3.4 Checking the Distributed Lag Model of the Time Series with Forecast Model Applied

We obtain the time series data to which the prediction results through the analysis of the ARIMA model and the LSTM model. So, we could confirm whether the time series to which the prediction results are applied maintains the distributed lag model of the original time series. In this table of contents, we performed the Granger causality test by confirming the quality of the time series and applying the differencing according to the stationary of the time series, like the previous research method of the Granger causality test. We set the lag of the Granger causality test to 1, 4, 6, 12, 24…, and the cross-correlation to a lag of −21 to 21 for the original time series. The time series with predictive model applied had more observations.

Before analyzing cross-correlation and the Granger causality test, we confirmed the stationary of the time series to which the forecasted results of the ARIMA model and the LSTM model were used by the ACF, PACF, ADF test. It was shown in Fig. 10, Fig. 11, and Table 6.

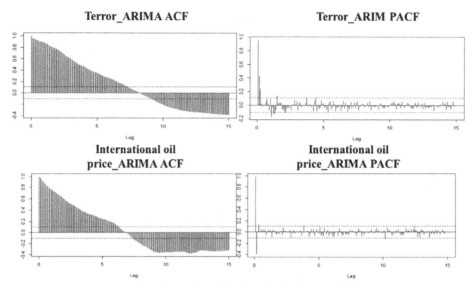

Fig. 10. ACF and PACF of ARIMA model.

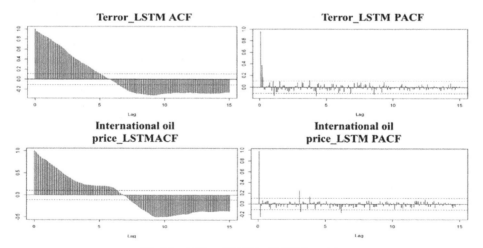

Fig.11. ACF and PACF of LSTM model.

Looking at Fig. 10 and 11, the ACF and PACF of both models decrease rapidly with time. This phenomenon is that both the ARIMA model and the LSTM applied time series have a strong trend, so they can't be time series that do have stationarity. That is, it is necessary to determine whether the time series is stationary through the ADF test.

Table 6. ADF test of applied time series with prediction results.

ADF test	Dickey-Fuller	Lag order	P-value
tr_ARIMA	−1.6464	6	0.7528
di_ARIMA	−1.91	6	0.6146
tr_ARIMA, $d = 1$	−8.1436	6	0.01*
di_ARIMA, $d = 1$	−7.5691	6	0.01*
tr_LSTM	−0.94363	6	0.9467
di_LSTM	−1.2007	6	0.9053
tr_LSTM, $d = 1$	−7.7046	6	0.01*
di_LSTM, $d = 1$	−8.1432	6	0.01*

* in Table 6 is statistically significant as lower than 0.01. We confirmed the stationary of the time series with the ARIMA model and LSTM model applied were judged to be times series without non-stationary when $d = 0$. Therefore, in order to analyze in a time series having stationary, the first order differencing had to be applied. Figure 12 shows the general graph of the time series in which the time series with stationary was found by the ADF test.

Prior to the Granger causality test, the distributed lags model of the times series was identified through cross-correlation analysis that can find out the similarity between the two-time series. In the case of the time series with the ARIMA model applied on the left of Fig. 13, the two-time series are similar with a lag of −18, and then similar with a lag of −1. In the case of the time series with the LSTM model applied on the right side of Fig. 13, the highest similarity was observed at −20 lag, followed by the highest similarity at 0 lag. We compared the cross-correlation function of the original time series data shown in Fig. 6 with the cross-correlation function of the time series with the prediction model applied. In the case of the ARIMA model, the two-time series at −18 lag, the same lag as the original time series, and −1, the next similar lag. The result is similar, so that the distributed lags model was considered when the ARIMA model performed the prediction, and the difference in cross-correlation values with the original time series was an average of 1.1%. So, in the case of ARIMA model we can support the research hypothesis H_0 that we established earlier.

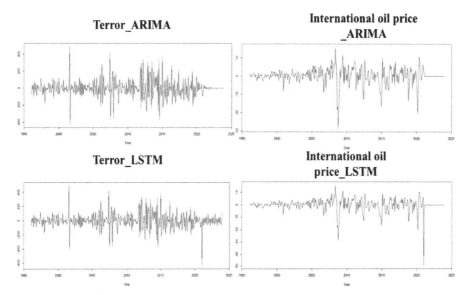

Fig. 12. 1st differencing graph of time series data with forecast results applied.

On the other hand, in the case of the time series with the LSTM model applied, it hasn't a similar distributed lags model to the original time series because it shows high similarity at lags of -20 and 0. And the difference in cross-correlation values has a large difference of about 20% on average. According to the result of the cross-correlation function, the ARIMA model performs prediction considering the distributed lags model of the original time series, and it is insufficient to support H_0 in the cross-correlation of the LSTM model prediction.

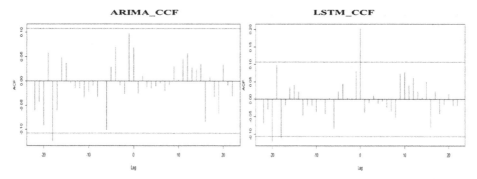

Fig. 13. Applied cross-correlation of ARIM model and LSTM model.

When the Granger causality test of the time series data to which the prediction results of the ARIMA model are applied is performed, the results shown in Table 7. * in Table 7 is statistically significant as lower than 0.01.

Table 7. Granger causality test results of ARIMA model applied time series.

Lag	tr_ARIMA → di_ARIMA		di_ARIMA → tr_ARIMA	
	F-statistic	P-value	F-statistic	P-value
6	0.1823	0.9816*	2.1657	0.04608*
18	0.4958	0.9589*	1.4844	0.09441*
24	0.9087	0.5903	1.5805	0.04493*
30	1.1389	0.29	1.4857	0.05595*
36	1.259	0.1607	1.3784	0.08508*
48	1.3495	0.0819*	1.116	0.2981
54	1.4906	0.02851*	0.9013	0.6653
60	1.3581	0.0694*	0.9827	0.5195
72	1.3488	0.07457*	0.9058	0.6727
78	1.4165	0.05065*	0.9267	0.6352
84	1.6718	0.01022*	0.8987	0.6865
90	1.4826	0.0484*	1.1459	0.2838

* in Table 7 is statistically significant as lower than 0.05. Looking at the results of the Granger causality test of the time series with the ARIMA model applied in Table 7, the results contradicted the results of the Granger causality test of the original time series data. In the Granger causality test of the original time series data, the terror attack variable affects the international oil price at lags of 24 and 30, and that the international oil price affects terror attack at the lag of 84. However, the Granger causality test results of the time series to which the prediction results of the ARIMA model were applied showed that terror attack affects international oil prices at lags of 48, 54, 60, 72, 78, 84, and 90. International oil prices were found to have an effect on terror attack at time lags of 6, 18, 24, 30 and 36. In other words, the causality of the two-time series changed by being apply the ARIMA model. This can be said that the causality of the original time series to which the prediction results of the ARIMA model are applied has changed, and unlike the cross-correlation results, it is difficult to support H_0.

Table 8. Granger causality test results of LSTM model applied time series.

Lag	tr_LSTM → di_LSTM		di_LSTM → tr_LSTM	
	F-statistic	P-value	F-statistic	P-value
78	1.3152	0.09803[*]	1.0123	0.4736
84	1.4893	0.03588*	0.9293	0.46308
102	1.3615	0.176	1.6516	0.06452*

[*] in Table 8 is statistically significant as lower than 0.05. The Granger causality test result of the time series to which the prediction result of the LSTM model is applied, it is similar to the Granger causality test of the original time series. According to Table 7, in the causal direction of international oil prices in terror attack, causality exists at lags of 78 and 84. Conversely, in the causal direction of terror attack in international oil prices, causality exists at a lag of 102. It can be judged that the LSTM model maintained the distributed lag model. Because the lag occurred at an interval of 6 in the causal direction of the international oil price in the original time series terror attack. Also, in the causal direction of terrorism in international oil prices, causality appeared at a lag of 84 in the original time series, and a time series was formed at 102 in the time series to which the LSTM model was applied. These results it that predicting the LSTM model considers the distributed lag model of the time series used for prediction. Because there is the characteristic that the Granger causal test uses the distributed lag model. That is, in the cross-correlation function analysis, the ARIMA model considers the lag distribution model when making predictions, and in the Granger causal test, the LSTM model considers the lag distribution model when making predictions, and the H_O hypothesis can be supported.

4 Conclusion

In this study, terror attack and international oil price time series data were used with ARIMA, a statistical prediction model, and LSTM, a deep learning prediction model. We confirmed whether these models maintain the distributed lag model when these models predict through cross-correlation and Granger causality tests. The results of the Granger causality test when the prediction model was not applied had causality at 24 lags and 30 lags in the causal direction of international oil prices in terror attack. In the causal direction of terror attack in international oil prices, causality was confirmed at 84 lags. When the ARIMA model was analyzed through the Box-Jenkins method, the terror attack time series data that is reflected the seasonality was judged to be suitable the SARIMA model of ARIMA $(0, 1, 1)(0, 0, 2)_{12}$ as MAPE 24.89029 and RMSE 99.19756. Since the ARIMA analysis of international oil prices has no seasonality, ARIMA $(0,1,2)$ was judged to be an appropriate model with MAPE 6.702753 and RMSE 4.470594. When the LSTM model was analyzed with a learning rate amount of 80%, the appropriate layer dropout value for the terror attack time series data was 0.4, and the RMSE at this time was 95.21628. The appropriate layer dropout for international oil prices was 0.1, at which time the RMSE was 5.159664. When the prediction results obtained by the ARIMA model and the LSTM model were applied to the original time series, we reperformed the cross-correlation analysis and the Granger causality test. The results is: in the case of the ARIMA model, the two-time series were most similar at −18 lag which is a very similar result to the cross-correlation analysis of the original time series, and then similar at -1 lag. In addition, it was judged that the accuracy of the average value of cross-correlation differed by about 1.1%, it was predicted similarly to the lag distribution model of the original time series. Conversely, the cross-correlation analysis of the LSTM prediction model showed that the two-time series were most similar at -20 lag, followed by 0 lag. Numerically, there was a difference of about 20.8% from the original time series. It was judged that the ARIMA model maintains the distributed lag model and forecasts rather than the LSTM model, even considering that the result of the cross-correlation increases the observed value when the forecasting model is applied to the time series.

On the contrary, in the Granger causality test, causality was confirmed at lags of 48, 54, 60, 72, 78, 84, and 90 in the causal direction of international oil prices in terror attack in the predicted time series data of the ARIMA model. In the causal direction of terror attack in international oil prices, causality was confirmed at lags of 6, 18, 24, and 30, which is quite different from previous causal relationship tests between existing time series. As a result of the prediction of the LSTM model, time series data was confirmed causality at lags of 78 and 84 in the causal direction of international oil prices in terror attack. In the causal direction of terror attack in international oil prices, causality was confirmed at a lag of 102. We compared the Granger causality test results of the original time series and the test results of the time series to which the forecasting model was applied. Considering that the observed increased by applying the forecasting model, the result of the causal direction of international oil prices in terror attack was 78, 84 lags. It was the same as that at an interval of 6, like the original time series. In the causal direction of terror attack in international oil prices, it can be judged that only one causality was confirmed, such as 84 and 102, respectively, maintaining the distributed lag model of the original time series data. In other words, in the cross-correlation analysis, the ARIMA model originally maintained the distributed lag model of the time series data, and in the Granger causal test, the LSTM model maintained the original distributed lag model of the time series data.

As mentioned above, the purpose of this study was to confirm whether the forecasting model maintains the distributed lag model when making predictions. The analysis tools used to confirm this were the Granger causality test, which confirms causality between time series with a distributed lag model, and the cross-correlation, which confirms the similarity of two-time series through lag. Since the Granger causal test and cross-correlation both use the distributed lag model, the distributed lag model of the time series to which the original time series and forecasting model was applied was confirmed. But there is a limitation that it was not compared with an accurate distributed lag model of the time series. In future research, we will devise a research method that can accurately observe this distributed lag model so that we can get closer to the essence of the predictive model. In addition, this study applied ARIMA model and LSTM model to specific time series, such as terror attack and international oil prices, it is unknown whether the distributed lag model is maintained when the forecasting model is applied to other time series. In the next study, we will try to devise whether other prediction models other than the ARIMA model and the LSTM model maintain the distributed lag model, and how the forecasting model can effectively maintain the distributed lag model.

Acknowledgement. This work was supported by the Ministry of Education of the Republic of Korea and the National Research Foundation of Korea (NRF-2022S1A5C2A03093531).

References

1. Choi, Y.W.: Accuracy improvement technique for the prediction of future living population based on the Diff LSTM algorithm. Graduate School of Information and Communications of Sungkyunkwan University, pp. 1–50 (2022)
2. Kim, S.W.: Prediction performance of LSTM-based economic policy uncertainty index on asset prices: traditional asset vs digital asset. J. Digit. Contents Soc. **23**(6), 1105–1113 (2022)
3. Sun, I.-S., Park, S.H.: Prediction of information service industry & analysis of its causal relation with wholesale & retail industries using time series analysis. e-Bus. Stud. **15**(6), 101–120 (2014)
4. Lee, Y.S., Lee, J.P.: Causality and predictability of price-volume in housing market-evidence from Seoul and Busan housing markets. SH Urban Res. Insight **8**(3), 51–67 (2018)
5. GTD Hompage. https://www.start.umd.edu/gtd/. Accessed 09 Jan 2023
6. Petronet Homepage. https://www.petronet.co.kr/v3/index.jsp. Accessed 09 Jan 2023
7. Tang, Z., De Almeida, C., Fishwick, P.A.: Time series forecasting using neural networks vs. Box-Jenkins methodology. SIMULATION **57**(5), 303–310 (1991)
8. Dudek, G., Pełka, P., Smyl, S.: A hybrid residual dilated LSTM and exponential smoothing model for midterm electric load forecasting. IEEE Trans. Neural Netw. Learn. Syst. **33**(7), 2879–2891 (2021)
9. Hochreiter, S., Schmidhuber, J.: Long short-term memory. Neural Comput. **9**(8), 1735–1780 (1997)
10. Nifa, K., Boudhar, A., Ouatiki, H., Elyoussfi, H., Bargam, B., Chehbouni, A.: Deep learning approach with LSTM for daily streamflow prediction in a semi-arid area: a case study of Oum Er-Rbia river basin, Morocco. Water **15**(2), 262 (2023)
11. Bourke, P.: Cross correlation. In: Cross Correlation, Auto Correlation—2D Pattern Identification (1996)
12. Hur, Y.K., Jang, K.S., Kim, S.J., Kim, H.M.: The granger casuality analysis between prices and trading volume in the housing market-focused on apartment property markets in Seoul. Hous. Stud. Rev. **16**(4), 49–70 (2008)

The Possible Equivalent Value Set for Incomplete Data Set

Rabiei Mamat[1]($\boxtimes$)(iD), Asma' Mustafa[1], Ahmad Shukri Mohd Nor[1], and Tutut Herawan[2,3,4]

[1] Faculty of Ocean Engineering Technology and Informatics, Universiti Malaysia Terengganu, Kuala Nerus Terengganu, Malaysia
`rab@umt.ed.my, ashukri@umt.edu.my`
[2] Sekolah Tinggi Pariwisata Ambarrukmo Yogyakarta, Jalan Ringroad Timur No. 52, Bantul, Daerah Istimewa Yogyakarta, Indonesia 55198
`tutut@stipram.ac.id`
[3] AMCS Research Center, Jalan Griya Taman Asri, 55512 Yogyakarta, Indonesia
[4] Institute for Big Data Analytics and Artificial Intelligence, UiTM Shah Alam, 40450 Shah Alam, Selangor Darul Ehsan, Malaysia

Abstract. Incomplete or missing data is a significant challenge in real-world information systems that can lead to flawed decision-making. The rough set theory has limitations when dealing with incomplete information systems, and researchers have proposed alternative approaches. This paper proposes a new similarity relation that utilises probable equivalent value sets to improve the accuracy of incomplete information systems. The approach enhances the quality of decision-making and provides reliable results. Experiments conducted on various datasets with different levels of missing data show that the approach can improve the accuracy of incomplete information processing by up to 90%. Compared to existing methods, the proposed approach can handle both categorical and continuous attributes, address problems of non-uniqueness and redundancy of probable equivalent value sets, and is not dependent on any specific data distribution. In conclusion, the proposed technique provides an effective solution to the challenges of incomplete information systems. By using probable equivalent value sets, the approach improves the accuracy of incomplete information processing and enhances the quality of decision-making. It has potential for applications in data science and related areas, and further research is needed to explore its limitations and applicability to real-world problems.

Keywords: Incomplete Information System · Rough set theory · Similarity Relation

1 Introduction

An incomplete information system is a type of data that can create challenges in decision-making applications. It arises when one or more attributes lack a value

© The Author(s), under exclusive license to Springer Nature Switzerland AG 2023
O. Gervasi et al. (Eds.): ICCSA 2023 Workshops, LNCS 14105, pp. 392–403, 2023.
https://doi.org/10.1007/978-3-031-37108-0_25

or have an unknown value, leaving gaps in the information that is necessary for accurate decision-making. Incomplete information systems can result in flawed decision-making, as queries may receive incorrect or insufficient responses. This issue has led researchers to develop various approaches to tackle the difficulties of incomplete information systems. Some methods involve transforming incomplete information into complete information by using specific rules or techniques, such as probability statistics. However, this indirect approach can alter the original "nugget" of information and may cause the loss of important "intents" that were present in the original information system [18,19]. As a result, it is crucial to develop alternative methods that can enhance decision-making accuracy while preserving the integrity of the original information system.

Rough set theory has proven to be a powerful tool in addressing various decision-making challenges in real-world scenarios [1,2,4,7,13,14,16,17,21–25]. This theory relies on indiscernibility relations, which enable the identification of two items as being identical if their attribute values are the same. By using these relations, rough set theory has demonstrated its ability to effectively extract valuable knowledge from data, allowing for automatic analysis without requiring prior knowledge [20]. This approach has proven to be highly effective in numerous fields, including medicine, finance, and engineering, among others. Despite its success, rough set theory has limitations when dealing with imperfect information systems [10]. The indiscernibility relation may not be able to handle incomplete or ambiguous data, which is common in real-world scenarios. As a result, researchers have proposed alternative approaches that aim to address these challenges. These methods leverage advanced mathematical techniques, such as probabilistic reasoning and fuzzy logic, to improve the accuracy and reliability of rough set theory. The combination of these methods with rough set theory has proven to be highly effective in dealing with imperfect information systems and has led to significant advancements in decision-making and knowledge discovery.

Researchers have made several attempts to develop new rough set relationships that can effectively handle incomplete information systems. For instance, Kryszkiewicz [6] proposed an indiscernibility relation that relied on a tolerance relation. This approach aimed to improve the accuracy of rough set theory when dealing with incomplete information systems. Another proposed method was presented by Stefanowski and Tsoukias [15], who introduced a similarity relation to refine the results obtained from the tolerance relation. However, despite these advancements, the precision of the approximations produced by these approaches is still questionable as demonstrated by Wang [18,19] and Nguyen [11], and further research is needed to refine their efficacy.

Researchers have also explored the use of possible-world semantics to represent missing attribute values in incomplete information systems. This approach involves defining a subset of values within a domain to represent missing values accurately [8,9]. By using this approach, researchers can develop accurate approximations that account for the uncertainty associated with missing data. Furthermore, possible-world semantics can be applied to a range of domains, making it a versatile tool for handling incomplete information systems in various fields, including medicine, finance, and engineering.

In this paper, a new similarity relation of rough set to improved the approximation accuracy of incompleted information system is introduced. In this new approach, a new definition of possible equivalent value-set is derived and then the similarity relation is measured using the similarity precision. The rest of the paper is organized as follows. In Sect. 2, an overview of rough set theory and its relation to incomplete information system is given. Also in the same section, a review on rough-set based tolerance relation where their weakness in handling incomplete information system is discussed.

In Sect. 3, the concept of possible equivalent value set is explains followed by Sect. 4 which give a review on rough-set based similarity relation. In Sect. 5, an example of the implementations of proposed approach is described with some example data. Next, in Sect. 6, the result and discussion of implementations uisng some benchmark data is given. Finally, the conclusions is given in Sect. 7.

2   Rough Set Theory and Incomplete Information System

2.1   Rough Set Theory

An information system $\mathcal{IS}$ is a quadruple, $\{\mathcal{O}, \mathcal{A}, \mathcal{V}, \delta\}$ where $\mathcal{O}$ is a non-empty finite set of objects and $\mathcal{A}$ is non-empty finite set of attributes. $\mathcal{V} = \bigcup_{\alpha \in \mathcal{A}} \mathcal{V}_\alpha$ is a finite non - empty set of values of $\alpha \in \mathcal{A}$ where $\mathcal{V}_\alpha$ is a value set of attribute α. δ is a total function $\delta : \mathcal{U} \times \mathcal{A} \to \mathcal{V}$ such that $\delta(u, \alpha) \in \mathcal{V}_\alpha$ for every $(u, \alpha) \in U \times A$ [5]. Two objects in an information system are called indiscernible (indistinguishable or similar) if they have the same feature.

Definition 1: [12] Given a set of attributes $\mathcal{B} \subseteq \mathcal{A}$ in $\mathcal{IS}$ and $x, y \in \mathcal{O}$. Objects x and y are said to be $\mathcal{B}$-indiscernible if and only if $\delta(x, b) = \delta(y, b)$ for every $b \in \mathcal{B}$.

Obviously, each subset of $\mathcal{A}$ inherently produces a different indiscernibility relation. An indescernibility relation produces by the set of attribute $\mathcal{B}$ is denoted as $IND(\mathcal{B})$ and it is equivalence relation. The partition of $\mathcal{O}$ produced by $IND(\mathcal{B})$ is denoted by $\mathcal{O}/\mathcal{B}$ while the equivalence class in the partition $\mathcal{O}/\mathcal{B}$ containing $x \in \mathcal{O}$ is denoted by $[x]_\mathcal{B}$. Thus, the notions of lower and upper approximations of a set is defined as follows.

Definition 2: [12] Given $\Gamma \subseteq \mathcal{O}$ and the equivalence class $[x]_\mathcal{B}$, the $\mathcal{B}$-lower approximation of Γ, denoted by $\underline{\mathcal{B}}(\Gamma)$ and $\mathcal{B}$-upper approximation denoted by $\overline{\mathcal{B}}(\Gamma)$ are defined by $\underline{\mathcal{B}}(\Gamma) = \{x \in \mathcal{O} | [x]_\mathcal{B} \subseteq \Gamma\}$ and $\overline{\mathcal{B}}(\Gamma) = \{x \in \mathcal{O} | [x]_\mathcal{B} \cap \Gamma \neq \emptyset\}$, respectively.

An information system $\mathcal{IS}$ is called complete information system if the total function returned not null value such that $\delta_\alpha(o) \neq \emptyset$ for all $\alpha \in \mathcal{A}$ and for all $o \in \mathcal{O}$. Otherwise, if exist any $o \in \mathcal{O}$ such that $\delta_\alpha(o) = \emptyset$ for any $\alpha \in \mathcal{A}$, the information system is known as incomplete information. Usually, the unknown or missing value in incomplete information system is denoted by '*' and the incomplete information system is denoted by $\mathcal{IIS} = \{\mathcal{O}, \mathcal{A}, \mathcal{V} \cup \{*\}, \delta\}$. Unfortunately, operation of the original indiscernibility relation on this incomplete information system returned irrelevant outcomes.

2.2   The Tolerance Relation

[6] proposed the tolerance relation which tolerated the * with any real value from the same missing value attribute in the incompleted information system.

Definition 3: [6] If given an incomplete information system $\mathcal{IIS}$ as denoted above, for any subset of attribute $\Lambda \subseteq \mathcal{A}$, a tolerance relation $\mathcal{T}$ is defined as below.

$$\forall_{x,y \in \mathcal{O}}(\mathcal{T}_\Lambda(x,y) \Leftrightarrow \forall_{c_j \in \Lambda} c_j(x) = c_j(y) \vee c_j(x) = * \vee c_j(y) = *)) \tag{1}$$

Obviously, $\mathcal{T}$ is reflexive and symmetric, but not transitive. From this perspective, an object x that have the missing value, which is currently replaced by '*', can be compared with an object y using any possible known attribute values from the corresponding attribute. The tolerance class of an object x with reference to an attribute set Λ which is denoted as $\mathcal{I}_\Lambda^\mathcal{T}$ is defined as :

$$\mathcal{I}_\Lambda^\mathcal{T}(x) = \{y | y \in \mathcal{O} \wedge \mathcal{T}_\Lambda(x,y)\}. \tag{2}$$

Thus, based on the tolerance relation, the upper and lower approximation of an object X can further be defined as in Definition 4 and Definition 5.

Definition 4: The lower approximation of an object set X with reference to an attribute set $\Lambda \in \mathcal{A}$ denoted by $X_\Lambda^\mathcal{T}$ is defined as:

$$X_\Lambda^\mathcal{T} = \{x | x \in \mathcal{O} \wedge \mathcal{I}_\mathcal{B}^\mathcal{T}(x) \subseteq X\}. \tag{3}$$

Definition 5: The lower approximation of an object set X with reference to an attribute set $\Lambda \in \mathcal{A}$ denoted by $X_\mathcal{T}^\Lambda$ is defined as:

$$X_\mathcal{T}^\Lambda = \{x | x \in \mathcal{O} \wedge \mathcal{I}_\mathcal{B}^\mathcal{T}(x) \cap X \neq \emptyset\}. \tag{4}$$

Definition 6: The approximation accuracy of object set X with reference to set B is defined as

$$Accuracy = \frac{X_\Lambda^\mathcal{T}}{X_\mathcal{T}^\Lambda}. \tag{5}$$

In the tolerance relations, objects with no shared values are considered indistinguisable. This is irrational situation that clearly exposes the tolerance relation's limitation. In order to overcome such drawback, Wang [18,19] introduced limited tolerance relation.

Definition 7: Given an $\mathcal{IIS}$ as defined above. By taking $P_\mathcal{B}(x) = \{b|b \in \mathcal{B} \wedge$ $b(x) \neq *\}$, and if $(P_\mathcal{B}(x) \cap P_\mathcal{B}(y) \neq \emptyset)$ denoted by α and $(b(x) \neq *) \wedge (b(y) \neq *)$ denoted by β, for all $x, y \in \mathcal{O} \times \mathcal{O}$ and $b \in \mathcal{B}$, then the limited tolerance relation denoted by $\mathcal{LT}$ on $\mathcal{O}$ and attribute set $B \subseteq A$ is defined as follows.

$$(\mathcal{LT}_\mathcal{B}(x, y) \Leftrightarrow (b(x) = b(y) = *) \vee (\alpha \wedge \beta) \rightarrow (b(x) = b(y))) \tag{6}$$

Obviously, the limited tolerance relation is also symmectric, reflexive but not transitive. The limited tolerance relation improved the tolerance relation by taking the similarity of at least one known attribute value of the two objects into consideration for the corresponding attribute. On the other hand, the drawback of limited tolerance relationships is that they are unable to distinguish between two types of unknown attribute values. In other words, the precision of the approximation is still up for debate.

3   Possible Equivalent Value Set

One technique to increase approximate correctness is to replace the missing value in the information system with prospective values that have already been established in the domain, as described in [8, 9]. In this paper, a possible equivalent value set with three semantics is proposed. In this case, as usual, the incomplete information system is categorised into either "has value" or "without value", but the semantics for both categories is broken into three, which are defined as follows:

(Y) for "any value" denoted by "*": For $\delta_a(x) = *$, where * can be replaced by any value in $\mathcal{V}_a$.
(M) for "Maybe value" denoted by "λ": For $\delta_a(x) = \lambda$, where λ is one of the value in $M_a(x) \subseteq \mathcal{V}_a$ and $|M_a(x) > 1|$

The semantics for "without value" is defined as follows:

(N) for "not applicable value" denoted by "∞": For $\delta_a(x) = \infty$, where $\forall x \in \mathcal{O}$ and $\forall a \in \mathcal{A}$, the value is not exists.
Based on the different semantics above, if $P_a(x)$ is the set of possible value of object x with respect to attribute a, the value set information function is defined as follows.

$$P_a(x) = \begin{cases} \{\delta_a(x)\}, & \text{if } \delta_a(x) \in \{V\}_a, \\ \mathcal{V}_a, & \text{if } \delta_a(x) = *, \\ M_a, & \text{if } \delta_a(x) = \lambda \text{ and } M_a \in \mathcal{V}_a, \\ \infty, & \text{if } \delta_a(x) = \infty, \end{cases} \tag{7}$$

Based on the newly proposed semantics of possible values, $\mathcal{V}$ components of the $\mathcal{IIS}$ for any $a \in \mathcal{A}$ can be defined as

$$\mathcal{V}' = \mathcal{V} \cup \{*\} \cup \{\lambda\} \cup \{\infty\} \tag{8}$$

where $\mathcal{V} = \bigcup_{a \in \mathcal{A}} \mathcal{V}_a$ and $\mathcal{V}_a$ is a domain of attribute a. The $*, \lambda$ and ∞ is a special symbols of $any - value$, $maybe - value$ and $not - applicable - value$ respectively.

The information function $\delta_a : \mathcal{O} \rightarrow \mathcal{V}'$ is defined such that $\delta_a(x) \in \mathcal{V}'_a, x \in \mathcal{O}$, $\mathcal{V}'_a = \mathcal{V}_a \cup \{*\} \cup \{\lambda\} \cup \{\infty\}$.

Obviously, it does not change the original content of incomplete information system.

4   Similarity Relation

In this section, a review about a rough-set based similarity relation concept in an incompleted information system is given.

Definition 8: Given an incomplete information system as defined above with $\mathcal{V}$ as in equation (6) and let $\mathcal{B} \subseteq \mathcal{A}$. For all $x, y \in \mathcal{U}$ and for all $a \in \mathcal{B}$, the similarity relation with possible equivalent value set is defined as:

$$Sim_\mathcal{B}(x, y) \Leftrightarrow (f_a(x) = f_a(y) \vee P_a(x) \cap P_a(y) \neq 0), \tag{9}$$

Based on the Definition 8, the similarity class can be defined as in Definition 9.

Definition 9: The similarity class $S_\mathcal{B}(x)$, of object $x \in \mathcal{U}$ with reference to set $\mathcal{B}$ is defines as:

$$S_\mathcal{B}(x) = \{y \in \mathcal{U} | Sim_\mathcal{B}(y, x)\} \tag{10}$$

$$S_\mathcal{B}^{-1}(x) = \{y \in \mathcal{U} | Sim_\mathcal{B}(x, y)\}. \tag{11}$$

Definition 10: The lower approximation and upper approximation of X denoted by $\underline{S_\mathcal{B}}(x)$ and $\overline{S_\mathcal{B}}(x)$ respectively can be defined as follows:

$$\underline{S_\mathcal{B}}(x) = \{x \in \mathcal{U} | S_\mathcal{B}^{-1} \subseteq X\} \tag{12}$$

$$\overline{S_\mathcal{B}}(x) = \cup \{S_\mathcal{B}(x) | x \in X\} \tag{13}$$

5   Implementations

Consider the following example on how to compute the similarity class for an incomplete information system with a possible equivalent value set. Let Table 1 is a list of students who apply for the scholarship. The decision $\{d\}$ for Table 1 is based on four criteria: the ability to do analysis (C_1), studying BSc in Mathematics (C_2), the communication skills (C_3) and ability to speak in English (C_4). The value for attribute C_1 and C_2 is based on three different levels: 1-poor, 2-moderate and 3-good. Attribute value for C_3 and C_4 are based on other three different levels: 1-not fluent, 2-moderate and 3-fluent. As seen in Table 1, the unknown or missing value objects for attribute is denoted by $*$. The decision $\{d\}$ has two different class which are *accept* and *reject*. The initial stage in the procedure is to find a suitable information function for each piece of missing data. It's done by looking at each piece of information and mapping it to Eq. 7.

Table 1. An Incomplete information table

Students	C_1	C_2	C_3	C_4	Decision(d)
s_1	3	3	3	*	accept
s_2	1	*	3	3	accept
s_3	*	*	3	3	reject
s_4	3	*	3	3	accept
s_5	3	*	3	3	accept
s_6	*	3	*	3	reject
s_7	1	3	3	*	accept
s_8	1	*	3	*	accept
s_9	*	3	*	*	reject
s_{10}	3	3	3	3	accept

Table 2 depicts the outcome, with each missing element being substituted by the appropriate information function for different semantics. In this example, the used information function is $f_a(x) = *, f_a(x) = \lambda_{c_i}^{s_j}$ and $f_a(x) = \infty$.

Table 2. An Incomplete information table with different semantics

Students	C_1	C_2	C_3	C_4	Decision(d)
s_1	3	3	3	λ_{c4}^{s1}	accept
s_2	1	λ_{c2}^{s2}	3	3	accept
s_3	λ_{c1}^{s3}	∞	3	3	reject
s_4	3	λ_{c2}^{s4}	3	3	accept
s_5	3	λ_{c2}^{s5}	3	3	accept
s_6	λ_{c1}^{s6}	3	*	3	reject
s_7	1	3	3	λ_{c4}^{s7}	accept
s_8	1	λ_{c2}^{s8}	3	λ_{c4}^{s8}	accept
s_9	∞	3	*	λ_{c4}^{s9}	reject
s_{10}	3	3	3	3	accept

Next, Table 2 can be equivalently interpreted by a value-set as shown in Table 3. Obviously, a value that is depicted by a different semantics in previouse step is replace by a value to represent a singleton set for a known value. It can be seen in Table 3 that the possible value of $F_a(x) = *$ is $\{1, 2, 3\}$, the possible value for $\lambda_{c4}^{s1} = \lambda_{c2}^{s2} = \lambda_{c1}^{s3} = \lambda_{c2}^{s4} = \lambda_{c4}^{s7} = \lambda_{c4}^{s9} = \{1, 2\}$ and the possible value for $= \lambda_{c2}^{s5} = \lambda_{c1}^{s6} = \lambda_{c2}^{s8} = \lambda_{c4}^{s8} = \{2, 3\}$.

Finally, the accuracy of approximation can be measured using Definition 5. The similarity class for newly defined incomplete information system with

Table 3. Incomplete information system with Equivalent value-set

Students	C_1	C_2	C_3	C_4	Decision(d)
s_1	3	3	3	1, 2	accept
s_2	1	1, 2	3	3	accept
s_3	1, 2	∞	3	3	reject
s_4	3	1, 2	3	3	accept
s_5	3	2, 3	3	3	accept
s_6	2, 3	3	1, 2, 3	3	reject
s_7	1	3	3	1, 2	accept
s_8	1	2, 3	3	2, 3	accept
s_9	∞	3	1, 2, 3	1, 2	reject
s_{10}	3	3	3	3	accept

possible equivalent set as in Table 3 is computed using Definition 9. The final similarity class are:

$$S_C(S_1) = \{S_1\},$$
$$S_C(S_2) = \{S_2, S_8\},$$
$$S_C(S_3) = \{S_3\},$$
$$S_C(S_4) = \{S_4, S_5\},$$
$$S_C(S_5) = \{S_4, S_5, S_{10}\},$$
$$S_C(S_6) = \{S_5, S_6, S_{10}\},$$
$$S_C(S_7) = \{S_7, S_8\},$$
$$S_C(S_8) = \{S_2, S_7, S_8\},$$
$$S_C(S_9) = \{S_9\},$$
$$S_C(S_{10}) = \{S_5, S_6, S_{10}\}.$$

The indiscernibility relation on decision attribute $\{d\}$ is as follow:

$$O/IND(d) = \{\{S_1, S_2, S_4, S_5, S_7, S_8, S_{10}\}, \{S_3, S_6, S_9\}\}.$$

Thus, the lower and upper approximation for decision attribute $\{d\}$ are:

$$\underline{S_C}(accept) = \{S_1, S_2, S_4, S_5, S_7, S_8\},$$
$$\underline{S_C}(reject) = \{S_3, S_9\},$$

$$\overline{S_C}(accept) = \{S_1, S_2, S_4, S_5, S_6, S_7, S_8, S_{10}\},$$
$$\overline{S_C}(reject) = \{S_3, S_6, S_9, S_{10}\}.$$

By using the equation in Definition 5, the accuracy of the proposed method is calculated as follows:

$$Accuracy_{accept} = \frac{|\underline{S_C}(accept)|}{|\overline{S_C}(accept)|} = \frac{6}{8} = 0.75,$$
$$Accuracy_{reject} = \frac{|\underline{S_C}(reject)|}{|\overline{S_C}(reject)|} = \frac{2}{4} = 0.5.$$

Hence, the accuracy average is: $\frac{0.75+0.5}{2} = 0.625$. Indirectly, it shown that the proposed similarity relation with possible equivalent value-set has better accuracy as compared to limited relation approach. The results of the comparison using various datasets will be presented in the next section.

6   Result and Discussion

Four different datasets were obtained from the benchmark UCI Machine Learning Repository [3]. The accuracy of approximation is calculated as explained in the Sect. 5. The description of the datasets is presented in Table 4.

Table 4. Datasets Descriptions

Dataset Name	Number of Attributes	Number of Objects	Number of Classes
Soybean	7	20	2
Monk	6	25	2
TicTacToe	5	30	2
Car	6	40	4

It consists of one incompleted dataset i.e.: the soybean dataset and three complete datasets i.e.: monk, tic tac toe and car. For the purpose of providing incomplete dataset, 10% of known value is removed from complete datasets. The result of the analysis is shown in Table 5 while graphical comparisons is shown in Fig. 1.

Table 5. Accuracy data of Similarity Relation with Possible Equivalent Value-Set (SR-PEVS) Compared To Limited Tolerance Relation(LTR)

Dataset Name	LTR	SR − PEVS	Improvement
Soybean	0.3131	0.5993	91.41%
Monk	0.5458	0.8607	57.70%
TicTacToe	0.4885	0.7122	45.79%
Car	0.3657	0.5570	52.17%

From Table 5 and Fig. 1, the result obviusly show that the proposed approach have better accuracy as compared to limited tolerance relation approach. For original incomplete soybean datasets, LTR has shows of 0.3131 accuracy while SR-PEVS has shows of 0.5993 accuracy which improve the accuracy by 90%.

Meanwhile, the LTR approach achieves accuracy of 0.5458, 0.4885, and 0.3657, respectively, when using datasets with a 10% modification: monk, tic-tac-toe, and car. SR-PEVS, on the other hand, exhibited greater accuracy with 0.8607, 0.7122, and 0.5570, respectively, using the same datasets. However, in overall, SR-PEVS, shows a 57%, 45%, and 52% improvement in accuracy.

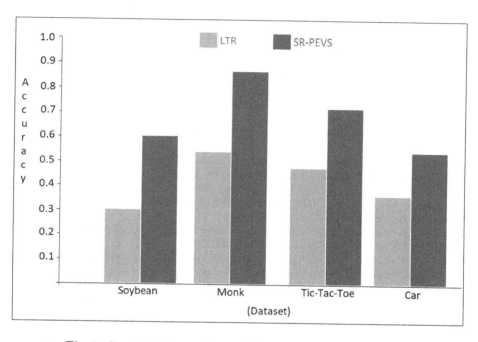

Fig. 1. Graphical Comparisons of LTR and SR-PEVS Accuracy.

7   Conclusions

In this paper, a new extension of rough set theory for improving the accuracy of incomplete information systems is investigated. A new approach called Possible Equivalent Value-Set is introduced to work with a new proposal of rough set similarity relation. A comparisons with previously known method Limited Tolerance Relation is made using four datasets from UCI repository for benchmark. The findings suggest that with the recommended technique, an imperfect information system's accuracy can be boosted by up to 90%. The proposed method can improved the accuracy of incomplete information system up to 90%.

Acknowlegements. The work of Rabiei Mamat, Asma' Mustafa, and Ahmad Shukri Mohd Nor is supported by RMIC, Universiti Malaysia Terengganu. The work of Tutut Herawan is supported by AMCS Research Center.

References

1. Akram, M., Shumaiza, Arshad, M.: A new approach based on fuzzy rough digraphs for decision-making. J. Intell. Fuzzy Syst. **35**, 2105–2121 (2018). https://doi.org/10.3233/JIFS-172069
2. Du, M.L., Tung, T.H., Tao, P., Chien, C.W., Chuang, Y.C.: Application of rough set theory to improve outpatient medical service quality in public hospitals based on the patient perspective. Front. Public Health **9**, 739119 (2021). https://doi.org/10.3389/fpubh.2021.739119
3. Dua, D., Graff, C.: UCI machine learning repository (2017). http://archive.ics.uci.edu/ml
4. Fan, J., et al.: A novel hybrid decision-making model for team building in cloud service environment. Int. J. Comput. Integr. Manufact. **32**, 1134–1153 (2019). https://doi.org/10.1080/0951192X.2019.1686172
5. Herawan, T., Deris, M.M., Abawajy, J.H.: A rough set approach for selecting clustering attribute. Knowl.-Based Syst. **23**, 220–231 (2010). https://doi.org/10.1016/j.knosys.2009.12.003
6. Kryszkiewicz, M.: Rough set approach to incomplete information systems (1998). https://doi.org/10.1016/S0020-0255(98)10019-1
7. Li, J., Fang, H., Song, W.: Failure mode and effects analysis using variable precision rough set theory and TODIM method. IEEE Trans. Reliab. **68**, 1242–1256 (2019). https://doi.org/10.1109/TR.2019.2927654
8. Lipski, W.: On databases with incomplete information. J. ACM (JACM) **28**, 41–70 (1981). https://doi.org/10.1145/322234.322239
9. Luo, J., Fujita, H., Yao, Y., Qin, K.: On modeling similarity and three-way decision under incomplete information in rough set theory. Knowl.-Based Syst. **191**, 105251 (2020). https://doi.org/10.1016/j.knosys.2019.105251
10. Luo, J., Qin, K., Zhang, Y., Zhao, X.R.: Incrementally updating approximations based on the graded tolerance relation in incomplete information tables. Soft Comput. **24**(12), 8655–8671 (2020). https://doi.org/10.1007/s00500-020-04838-3
11. Nguyen, D.V., Yamada, K., Unehara, M.: Extended tolerance relation to define a new rough set model in incomplete information systems. Adv. Fuzzy Syst. 9 (2013). https://doi.org/10.1155/2013/372091
12. Pawlak, Z., Skowron, A.: Rudiments of rough sets. Inf. Sci. **177**, 3–27 (2007). https://doi.org/10.1016/j.ins.2006.06.003
13. Praba, B., Gomathi, G.: Hypergraphs and rough sets with their applications in decision-making problems. New Math. Nat. Comput. **18**, 293–311 (2022). https://doi.org/10.1142/S1793005722500156
14. Riaz, M., Dayyaz, B., Firdous, A., Fakhar, A.: Novel concepts of soft rough set topology with applications. J. Intell. Fuzzy Syst. **36**(4), 3579–3590 (2019). https://doi.org/10.3233/JIFS-181648
15. Stefanowski, J., Tsoukìas, A.: Incomplete information tables and rough classification (2001). https://doi.org/10.1111/0824-7935.00162
16. Sun, B., Chen, X., Zhang, L., Ma, W.: Three-way decision making approach to conflict analysis and resolution using probabilistic rough set over two universes. Inf. Sci. **507**, 809–822 (2020). https://doi.org/10.1016/j.ins.2019.05.080
17. Sun, L., Wang, W., Xu, J., Zhang, S.: Improved LLE and neighborhood rough sets-based gene selection using lebesgue measure for cancer classification on gene expression data. J. Intell. Fuzzy Syst. **37**, 1–12 (2019). https://doi.org/10.3233/JIFS-181904

18. Wang, G.: Extension of rough set under incomplete information systems. In: 2002 IEEE World Congress on Computational Intelligence. 2002 IEEE International Conference on Fuzzy Systems. FUZZ-IEEE'02. Proceedings (Cat. No. 02CH37291), vol. 2 (2002). https://doi.org/10.1109/fuzz.2002.1006657
19. Wang, G., Guan, L., Hu, F.: Rough set extensions in incomplete information systems. Front. Electr. Electr. Eng. China **3**, 399–405 (2008). https://doi.org/10.1007/s11460-008-0070-y
20. Yan, T., Han, C.: A novel approach of rough conditional entropy-based attribute selection for incomplete decision system. Math. Prob. Eng. **2014**, 1–28 (2014). https://doi.org/10.1155/2014/728923
21. Yang, Q., Du, P.A., Wang, Y., Liang, B.: A rough set approach for determining weights of decision makers in group decision making. PLoS One **12**, 1–16 (2017). https://doi.org/10.1371/journal.pone.0172679
22. Zhang, H., He, Y.: A rough set-based method for dual hesitant fuzzy soft sets based on decision making. J. Intell. Fuzzy Syst. **35**, 3437–3450 (2018). https://doi.org/10.3233/JIFS-17456
23. Zhang, K., Zhan, J., Wu, W.Z.: Novel fuzzy rough set models and corresponding applications to multi-criteria decision-making. Fuzzy Sets Syst. **383**, 92–126 (2020). https://doi.org/10.1016/j.fss.2019.06.019
24. Zhang, L., Xue, X.: Study on decision-making of soccer robot based on rough set theory. Inter. Stud. Soc. Behav. Commun. Biolog. Artif. Syst. **20**(1), 61–77 (2019). https://doi.org/10.1075/is.18020.zha
25. Zhang, L., Zhan, J., Xu, Z.: Covering-based generalized if rough sets with applications to multi-attribute decision-making. Inf. Sci. **478**, 275–302 (2019). https://doi.org/10.1016/j.ins.2018.11.033

Computational Optimization and Applications (COA 2023)

An Exact Optimization Approach for Personnel Scheduling Problems in the Call Center Industry

Rita Martins[1] , Telmo Pinto[1,2(✉)] , and Cláudio Alves[1]

[1] Centro ALGORITMI, University of Minho, Braga, Portugal
claudio@dps.uminho.pt
[2] CEMMPRE, University of Coimbra, Coimbra, Portugal
telmo.pinto@dem.uc.pt

Abstract. Nowadays, the importance of the call center industry is increasing because they are a major means of communication between organizations and their customers. So, ensuring optimized personnel schedules in call centers has several advantages, such as reduced total labor costs, overstaffing, increased employee satisfaction, and acceptable waiting times. In this paper, we address the personnel scheduling problem in a 24/7 call center where the scheduling process is done manually. So, the main goal is to explore exact solution approaches to achieve better solutions while reducing the processing time. The proposed optimization model is an Integer Programming model to assign shifts to workers while minimizing the total penalization associated with employees' time preferences. The model is tested with several instances, including randomly generated and real-world data instances. The quality of the model is assessed through a computational study of its linear relaxation, concluding that the model presents null integrality gaps in all the tested instances. Additionally, to evaluate the performance of the model when running large instances, several randomly generated instances were tested, achieving good computational results.

Keywords: personnel scheduling · call centers · optimization · integer programming

1 Introduction

Over the last few years, the importance of studying personnel scheduling problems increased considerably. This is due to the impact of the labor cost on companies' costs [7]. Therefore, reducing this cost, even just a little, can be very advantageous and worthwhile. According to Bard et al. [4], weak personnel schedules can lead to an oversupply of workers with too much idle time, or an undersupply with an attendant loss of business. Thompson [18] reports three reasons for paying particular attention to staff scheduling. The first consists of the employee's preferences since a work schedule that comes reasonably close

© The Author(s), under exclusive license to Springer Nature Switzerland AG 2023
O. Gervasi et al. (Eds.): ICCSA 2023 Workshops, LNCS 14105, pp. 407–424, 2023.
https://doi.org/10.1007/978-3-031-37108-0_26

to meeting them can improve customer service. The second reason is related to the real-time spent on developing a labor schedule, which can leave less time for the scheduler to manage the employees and interact with customers. Finally, the third reason is profitability and effectiveness since short-term overstaffing and long-term understaffing can be reduced.

One of the main goals of an organization is to satisfy the customer and also the employees in a cost-effective manner. There are many concerns to consider, such as shift equity, staff preferences, flexible workplace agreements, and part-time work. Thus, decision support systems must be carefully implemented to achieve optimized staff schedules. Personnel scheduling consists of assigning workers shifts and days off so that each has a line of work. This process can be complex because schedulers must assign employees to shifts and tasks while accounting for different rules and regulations and workers' availability. In the first phase of this process, it is necessary to have an idea of the number of staff needed to meet the service demand and also to know the particular skills of all individuals so that they can be allocated to shifts whose tasks meet their skills.

As time goes by, the relative importance of satisfying the needs of employees in staffing and scheduling decisions has increased. Nowadays, organizations want to offer some conditions to their employees that were not a concern in the past. Consequently, and as referred to above, organizations create work schedules considering employee preferences [5] and trying to offer part-time contracts or flexible work hours [4]. Mohan [15] considers a staff scheduling problem consisting entirely of part-time workers and also considers their shifts' preferences.

Several personnel scheduling problems with different characteristics can be found in the literature. This fact can be explained since, as can be expected, different work environments imply different requirements. Therefore, some features receive particular attention, such as workforce characteristics, shift flexibility, the type of constraints and objective function used to model the problem, and the selection of the solution method to solve the problem. These features will be presented below.

Several classification methods for personnel scheduling problems can be found, providing a general framework for classifying the contributions carried out in this area. Baker [3] proposed the first one, which is commonly studied in the literature for general labor scheduling [6].

Van den Bergh et al. [7] proposed a classification method that organizes the literature review using different perspectives. Therefore, the classification fields are the following: personnel characteristics, decision delineation, shift definition; constraints, performance measures, and flexibility; solution method and uncertainty incorporation; and application area and applicability of research. Each field is described in detail as follows.

1.1 Personnel Characteristics, Decision Delineation and Shifts Definition

In order to classify personnel members, one can look at their labor contracts. In this way, it is possible to distinguish two categories: full-time and part-time workers. Mohan [15] considered a scheduling problem where the workforce is composed entirely of part-time workers, claiming that more people are opting to work part-time due to the flexibility it offers. Bard et al. [4] considered both full-time and part-time workers. In some cases, casual workers, such as workers from another company division, are also considered to deal with the lack of a regular workforce. Another existing classification is based on the grouping of employees, where the workers are categorized into individual or crew entities. Usually, this last one can be found in scheduling problems in the transportation area. Besides that, one must remember that different employees have different availability and also different individual personal preferences, which are both important since one of the main goals of an organization is to satisfy the employees.

According to Felici and Gentile [13], a shift is a work duty characterized by a starting time and a duration. Shifts can be fixed or variable in terms of starting-time or length for each employee and each day. In personnel shift scheduling, shifts and days-off are assigned to each worker so that every employee has a line of work while considering some existing conditions or requirements.

As expected, in personnel scheduling problems, making some decisions is imperative and inevitable. The main ones are related to the assignment of tasks (e.g., a given employee is assigned to a certain task) and shift sequences (e.g., a given employee works on day 1 in the morning, but he/she does not work on day 2 and works on day 3 in the morning). The task assignment methods depend on whether tasks times are fixed or movable, breaks exist in shifts, overtime is allowed, or specific skills or qualifications are required to perform certain tasks. According to Smet et al. [17], tasks should be incorporated in the construction of rosters for employees to reduce operational expenses while preserving a high quality of service. Maenhout and Vanhoucke [14] claimed that when the scheduler integrates personnel shift scheduling and personnel task scheduling, the obtained personnel roster is improved.

1.2   Application Area: Scheduling in Call Centers

According to Ernst et al. [11], staff scheduling methods have been applied to transportation systems such as airlines and railways, health care systems, emergency services such as police, ambulance, and fire brigade, call centers, and many other service organizations such as hotels, restaurants, and retail stores. Van den Bergh et al. [7] add other application areas like military, supermarkets, festivals, and parking lots personnel scheduling problems. Even so, there are two applications of staff scheduling and rostering that stand out from the other: transportation services, particularly airline crew scheduling, and rostering because of its economic scale and impact, and nurse scheduling since it is unacceptable not to fully support patient care needs.

Since the case study to be considered concerns personnel scheduling in a call center environment, a brief literature review of this application area will be presented.

The importance of call centers for companies is widely increasing because, although they are not the only ones, they are a vital channel for companies to communicate with their customers [12], having a crucial role in customer acquisition and retention [1]. Consequently, having a good scheduling system is fundamental because an inadequate number of agents for each shift affects customer satisfaction, for instance, because of long waiting times and labor-related costs. According to Cordone et al. [10], a major part of the call center's operational costs are related to labor costs. That is why the staff scheduling problem became the main problem in call center operations. However, it is not easy to solve due to the uncertainty of the number of tasks that are needed to be performed.

According to Robbins and Harrison [16], some OR methodologies, such as queuing theory, optimization, and simulation, can be found in the literature on call centers' problems. Usually, solving shift scheduling problems in a call center can be divided into two phases. In the first one, the goal is to determine the number of required agents for each period, considering some customer service measures like customer waiting times or abandonment rates. For this task, some authors use queuing and simulation models to obtain the correct numbers, as can be seen in [12] and [9]. The second phase is defined by the scheduling algorithm, where the goal is to allocate employees to the shifts, considering a particular objective function, as seen before.

Bhulai, Koole, and Pot [8] propose an integer programming model for the shift scheduling problem in a call center, where they considered a multiskill workforce, and their objective is to obtain a good service-level against minimal costs. In this sense, the presented method is divided into two phases: determination of the required number of agents for each period, considering service-level constraints, and determination of an optimal set of shifts, minimizing costs while satisfying the required workforce calculated in the first step. The service-level constraints studied include a minimum bound of calls with a waiting time of less than 20 s. Considering a workforce with two distinct skills, shifts of five and six hours, and satisfying the service-level constraint for 80% of the calls, the optimal number of shifts is 167. The authors checked the optimality of the methods from both steps and concluded that the solution obtained is less than 3% from the optimal objective value. In conclusion, the authors highlighted the short computation time required and easy implementation, as also referred that, although the method was developed for call centers, it can be used for other service systems that involve multiple distinguished skills, agents working on different tasks, and employees with identical productivity within the same skill group.

Alfares [2] presented a two-step solution method to minimize the labor cost in a call center by determining the optimum number of agents and their schedules to meet demand. In the first step, queuing theory converts extensive data into demand values for a typical workweek. Then, an integer programming model is built to construct detailed weekly schedules. These schedules include each agent's work hours, meal breaks, and off days. The problem approached considers a call center that operates 24 h a day, 7 days of week. The 47 agents working there are divided into three groups, having different pay scales and work schedules. There are two problems in this organization to be tackled: customers are not completely satisfied because they are placed on hold for several minutes during peak periods, and the 1-hour breaks the workers are entitled to are unscheduled. Before the study of the solution method proposed, using no scientific methods but based on the management's observations, a schedule for each worker was built. Then, two instances were solved using LINDO optimization software, differing in the minimum number of employees required in the considered hours. The solutions obtained and the *a priori* solution were compared. Although both of the solutions given by the integer programming model were better than the *a priori* schedule, since the workforce size is reduced, the workforce utilization is increased, and the labor cost decreased, the management chose one of them because it was the one that minimizes most the waiting time.

The purpose of the work presented in this paper is to create timetables faster and with higher quality than those currently created manually, using exact approaches to solve personnel scheduling issues at call centers. This paper is organized as follows. Section 2 concerns the problem's main characteristics and the description of an example of an instance. In Sect. 3, the developed Integer Programming model is presented and described. In Sect. 4, the computational experiments are described and discussed. Finally, Sect. 5 summarizes the principal findings, resulting conclusions, and suggestions for future work.

2   Problem Definition

The call center considered in this work operates 24 h a day and 7 days a week, having a new shift starting every 30 min (the company discretizes the demand of the workforce for each interval of 30 min). This means that, in a day, there are 48 different shifts: the first shift starts at 00 h 00, and the last shift starts at 23 h 30. Each shift has a fixed duration of 9 h and some mandatory breaks that are informally managed within the team. The planning horizon of the problem is one month, divided into periods of 30 min that constitute set H. So, for example, considering a planning horizon of a single day, set H is formed by 48 elements, as can be seen in Fig. 1.

hours	00:00:00	00:30:00	01:00:00	01:30:00	02:00:00	02:30:00	03:00:00	03:30:00	04:00:00	04:30:00	05:00:00	05:30:00
H	0	1	2	3	4	5	6	7	8	9	10	11

hours	06:00:00	06:30:00	07:00:00	07:30:00	08:00:00	08:30:00	09:00:00	09:30:00	10:00:00	10:30:00	11:00:00	11:30:00
H	12	13	14	15	16	17	18	19	20	21	22	23

hours	12:00:00	12:30:00	13:00:00	13:30:00	14:00:00	14:30:00	15:00:00	15:30:00	16:00:00	16:30:00	17:00:00	17:30:00
H	24	25	26	27	28	29	30	31	32	33	34	35

hours	18:00:00	18:30:00	19:00:00	19:30:00	20:00:00	20:30:00	21:00:00	21:30:00	22:00:00	22:30:00	23:00:00	23:30:00
H	36	37	38	39	40	41	42	43	44	45	46	47

Fig. 1. Example: set of time periods with a planning horizon of a day

Each worker cannot work more than 5 consecutive working days every 7 days and can only be on one shift per day. Additionally, between two consecutive shifts, each worker must stop for at least 11 h. Ideally, one worker has the same shift for a maximum of 2 weeks, creating a stable route for each one to provide a comfortable schedule for the workers. However, the company intended a maximum of 2 weeks since shifts could be changed to ensure the same workers were not assigned to the same shifts considered less attractive.

The workforce is divided geographically between two industrial centers, where the workers are also divided into teams according to their language and team skills. This means that each worker w will have a corresponding skill set K_w, composed by the different teams that he/she can be assigned because he/she has the required skills. To guarantee workers' satisfaction, their time preferences are considered using a penalization system: the exact preferred time has a minimum penalization associated, *i.e.* 1, which increases exponentially as the considered time gets away from the preferred time.

The scheduling goal is to assign workers to teams and shifts, minimizing the total penalization when considering workers' preferences and ensuring that the workforce requirements r^{kh} for certain team k at a certain time period h are covered. In this organization, a monthly personnel scheduling is carried out, and this process is done manually by a scheduler. So, the current process time is larger than expected, having a duration of some days. Figures 2 and 3 represent the schedules obtained by this process referring to two different teams of the considered call center.

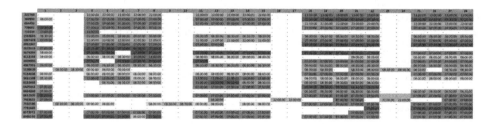

Fig. 2. Schedule of team 1 obtained manually

The following notation is used in the development of the model:

Indices and Sets

k: index for the set of teams K;
h: index for the set of time periods H;
w: index for the set of workers W;
H: set of time periods;
K: set of teams;
W: set of workers

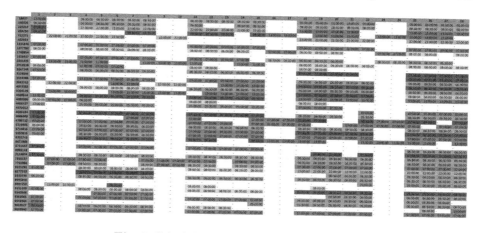

Fig. 3. Schedule of team 2 obtained manually

Parameters

K_w: set of teams to which a worker w $(w \in W)$ can be assigned because he/she has the required skills;

p_w^h: penalization of assigning worker w on time period h;

r^{kh}: number of workers that are needed at team k and time period h;

2.1 Example of an Instance

An instance of this problem is defined based on the notation presented in the previous section. In this section, an example of an instance will be described.

Consider a scenario where the planning horizon is one day. There is only 1 working team composed of 3 different workers. Table 1 shows the data referring to four parameters: teams, time periods, workers, and the sets associated with each worker that gives the list of teams where he/she can work in. Note that all the workers are identified by an ID number composed only of integer numbers (Table 2).

Table 1. Instance example: teams, time periods and workers

$K = \{1\}$
$H = \{0, ..., 47\}$
$W = \{1, 2, 3\}$

In this particular case, only one worker is required to work the shift starting at 8 h 00. Concerning the preference's penalizations, one has three different situations: worker 1 prefers to work on 17 h 30 shift, which means that, in that hour, the associated penalization will be minimum (*i.e.*, equals to 1); worker 2 prefers to work on 07 h 00 shift, which means that a penalization of 1 is associated to

Table 2. Instance example: set of teams to which a worker w can be assigned

w	K_w
1	$\{1\}$
2	$\{1\}$
3	$\{1\}$

that hour; and worker 3 prefers to work on 14 h 30 shift, which means that, in that hour, the associated penalization will also be minimum. The considered values of both necessities and preference's penalizations can be seen in Table 3 and Table 4.

Table 3. Instance example: workforce requirements

period time	team 1	period time	team 1	period time	team 1
0	0	16	1	32	1
1	0	17	1	33	1
2	0	18	1	34	0
3	0	19	1	35	0
4	0	20	1	36	0
5	0	21	1	37	0
6	0	22	1	38	0
7	0	23	1	39	0
8	0	24	1	40	0
9	0	25	1	41	0
10	0	26	1	42	0
11	0	27	1	43	0
12	0	28	1	44	0
13	0	29	1	45	0
14	0	30	1	46	0
15	0	31	1	47	0

3   An Integer Programming Model

This work aims to develop an efficient exact solution method to solve personnel scheduling problems at call centers providing automatic schedules instead of manual ones. Thus, considering the problem described in Sect. 2, the following integer programming (IP) model was developed.

Decision Variables

$$x_w^{kh} = \begin{cases} 1, \text{ if worker } w \text{ is assigned to team } k, \text{ and to the shift } h, \\ 0, \text{ otherwise.} \end{cases} \tag{1}$$

Table 4. Instance example: preferences' penalizations

period time	worker 1	worker 2	worker 3
0	64	128	512
1	64	64	512
2	128	64	1024
3	128	32	1024
4	256	32	2048
5	256	16	2048
6	512	16	2048
7	512	8	1024
8	1024	8	1024
9	1024	4	512
10	2048	4	512
11	2048	2	256
12	2048	2	256
13	1024	1	128
14	1024	1	128
15	512	1	64
16	512	1	64
17	256	1	32
18	256	2	32
19	128	2	16
20	128	4	16
21	64	4	8
22	64	8	8
23	32	8	4
24	32	16	4
25	16	16	2
26	16	32	2
27	8	32	1
28	8	64	1
29	4	64	1
30	4	128	1
31	2	128	1
32	2	256	2
33	1	256	2
34	1	512	4
35	1	512	4
36	1	1024	8
37	1	1024	8
38	2	2048	16
39	2	2048	16
40	4	2048	32
41	4	1024	32
42	8	1024	64
43	8	512	64
44	16	512	128
45	16	256	128
46	32	256	256
47	32	128	256

IP Model

$$\min. \sum_{w \in W} \sum_{k \in K_w} \sum_{h \in H} p_w^h x_w^{kh} \tag{2}$$

s.t.

$$\sum_{h=i}^{min(|H|-1,i+335)} \sum_{k \in K_w} x_w^{kh} \leq 5, \ \forall w \in W, \ \forall i \in I = \{h \in H : h \bmod 336 = 0\}, \tag{3}$$

$$\sum_{h=f}^{f+47} \sum_{k \in K_w} x_w^{kh} \leq 1, \ \forall w \in W, \ \forall f \in F = \{h \in H : h \bmod 48 = 0\}, \tag{4}$$

$$\sum_{\{w \in W : k \in K_w\}} \sum_{h=\max\{0,b-17\}}^{b} x_w^{kh} \geq r^{kb}, \ b \in H, \ \forall k \in K, \tag{5}$$

$$\sum_{k \in K_w} \sum_{h=i}^{i+39} x_w^{kh} \leq 1, \forall w \in W, i \in J = \{h \in H : h \leq |H| - 40\}. \tag{6}$$

$$x_w^{kh} \in \{0,1\}, \forall w \in W, \forall k \in K_w, \forall h \in H \tag{7}$$

The purpose of this IP model is to assign workers to teams and shifts. To formulate the problem, a set of decision variables (1) is used to indicate if a worker is assigned to a certain team and to the shift starting at a certain period of time. The objective function (2) is to minimize the total penalization when considering workers' preferences.

Constraints (3) and (4) ensure that each worker cannot work more than 5 days per week and can only be in one shift per working day, respectively. In (3), the set $I = \{h \in H : h \bmod 336 = 0\}$ is composed by all the time periods $h \in H$ that are divisors of 336. In practice, all the time periods that belong to this set are the first period of time of every 7-day week because 336 time periods of 30 min correspond to a whole week, starting at 00 h 00 of day 1 to 23 h 30 of day 7. So, to ensure that each worker only works a maximum of 5 days per week, the set I guarantees that the summed shifts correspond to only a week. Additionally, the upper bound of the summation in I is given by $min(|H| - 1, i + 335)$, where $i \in I$, because of the possibility of the month finishing in the middle of a week. If the considered month does not include the whole week, then the upper bound of the summation will be $|H| - 1$. Otherwise, the upper bound will be $i + 335$, where $i \in I$. In (4), the logic is the same, but the time horizon is only a day, that is, 48 time periods of 30 min. Therefore, the set $F = \{h \in H : h \bmod 48 = 0\}$ is composed by all the time periods $h \in H$ that are divisors of 48, that is, all the time periods that belong to this set are the first period of time of every day. In this case, the upper bound of the summation in F is only given by $f + 47$, where $f \in F$, because all the days considered are complete.

Constraints (5) force the number of allocated workers to a certain shift in a certain period of time and team to be at least equal to the number of required workforce in that same period of time and team. In this constraint, the lower and upper bounds of the summation in H are, respectively, $\max\{0, b - 17\}$ and b, where $b \in H$. This is because, in order to know if the required number of workers in a certain time period is covered, it is necessary to sum all the workers that started working a maximum of 08 h 30, *i.e.* 17 time periods, before the time period considered until the ones that start working in the exact time period considered. In the beginning of every month, until the considered time period is less than 17, the sum is done from the time period 0, not considering the data of the previous month.

Constraints (5) force the number of allocated workers to a certain shift in a certain period of time and team to be at least equal to the number of required workforce in that same period of time and team. In this constraint, the lower and upper bounds of the summation in H are, respectively, $\max\{0, b - 17\}$ and b, where $b \in H$. This is because, to know if the required number of workers in a certain time period is covered, it is necessary to sum all the workers that started working a maximum of 08 h 30, *i.e.* 17 time periods, before the time period considered until the ones that start working in the exact time period considered. At the beginning of every month, until the considered time period is less than 17, the sum is done from the time period 0, not considering the data of the previous month.

Constraints (6) establish, for each worker, a mandatory break of at least 11 h between two consecutive shifts. To ensure that, a time interval of 40 time periods is considered. This interval comprises 18 time periods corresponding to a 9-hour shift plus 22 time periods corresponding to an 11-hour break. To deal with the end of the month, the set $J = \{h \in H : h \leq |H| - 40\}$ is used, guaranteeing that the limit is not overpast.

To include workers' preferences, and based on the quantification of preference violations proposed by Bard and Purnomo [5], a penalization system was built. Let p be the time preference of a worker. Considering that $h \in \{0, ..., 47\}$ represents the $(h + 1)$th 30-min time period of a day, a penalty point v is fixed to calculate a penalization value 2^{v-1}, according to the difference between h and p, as seen in Table 5.

Table 5. Penalization System

violation	penalty points v	penalization 2^{v-1}
$0 < \|h - p\| \leq 2 \vee \|h - p\| > 45$	1	1
$2 < \|h - p\| \leq 4 \vee 43 < \|h - p\| \leq 45$	2	2
$4 < \|h - p\| \leq 6 \vee 41 < \|h - p\| \leq 43$	3	4
$6 < \|h - p\| \leq 8 \vee 39 < \|h - p\| \leq 41$	4	8
$8 < \|h - p\| \leq 10 \vee 37 < \|h - p\| \leq 39$	5	16
$10 < \|h - p\| \leq 12 \vee 35 < \|h - p\| \leq 37$	6	32
$12 < \|h - p\| \leq 14 \vee 33 < \|h - p\| \leq 35$	7	64
$14 < \|h - p\| \leq 16 \vee 31 < \|h - p\| \leq 33$	8	128
$16 < \|h - p\| \leq 18 \vee 29 < \|h - p\| \leq 31$	9	256
$18 < \|h - p\| \leq 20 \vee 27 < \|h - p\| \leq 29$	10	512
$20 < \|h - p\| \leq 22 \vee 25 < \|h - p\| \leq 27$	11	1024
$22 < \|h - p\| \leq 25$	12	2048

4   Computational Experiments and Analysis

Several computational experiments were executed to evaluate and analyze the performance of the model. The code is implemented in IBM ILOG CPLEX Optimization Studio 12.7.0.0, and the tests are carried out on an Intel Core i7-6500U processor and 8 GB of memory RAM, with Windows 10 operating system.

A way to obtain information about the IP problem is through the solution of its linear relaxation. The linear programming (LP) relaxation of an integer programming model is the problem that arises when the integrality constraints are relaxed, which means that all variables are allowed to take non-integer values. Hence, the optimal solution to the LP is not necessarily integer. However, since the feasible region of the LP is larger than the feasible region of the IP, the optimal value of the former is no worse than the optimal value of the latter. This implies that the optimal value to the LP is a lower bound on the optimal value for the problem we started with. The gap between the optimal LP value and the optimal integral solution is called the integrality gap of the linear program, and it is given by

$$IG = \frac{OPT_{int}}{OPT_{frac}}, \tag{8}$$

where OPT_{int} is the optimal value of the IP and OPT_{frac} is the optimal value of the LP.

In order to analyze the integrality gap of the linear program and to evaluate the quality of the IP model, a set of 55 randomly generated instances and a set of 3 real-data instances were tested, in which the planning horizon is a 28-day month or a 31-day month. While the number of workers in the first set varies between 30, 50, 75, 100, and 150, in the second set it only varies between 55 and 71 workers. More information about which one of the instances, including the number of teams, number of workers required, and values of penalizations are described in Table 6.

The results are given in Table 7. Column OPT_{int} and OPT_{frac} give the optimal value of the IP model and the optimal value of the LP relaxation, respectively. Assuming the same thinking, column CPU_{int} time gives the processing time (minutes) for each one of the instances executed with the IP model, and column CPU_{frac} time the processing time (minutes) for each one of the instances executed with the LP relaxation. At last, the last column *LP solution is integer?* tells us if the obtained solution of LP relaxation allows non-integer variables or not. In all instances, the optimal value of both models is the same, which means that the integrality gap is 1, that is, the null integrality gap. We can not state that the model has a null integrality gap but that the model has a null integrality gap for a large set of instances. Additionally, in some cases, the optimal solution allows non-integer variables. So, this means that, although the LP relaxation gave us good approximation solutions of the IP model, the solution may turn out to be integer infeasible, and if we round it, the solution may not be the optimal integer solution.

Table 6. Computational experiments 1 - instances' data

instance	planning horizon	number of workers	number of teams	workforce requirements	preferences' penalizations
1	31 days	30	1	req0	pref0
2	31 days	30	1	req1	pref0
3	31 days	30	1	req2	pref0
4	31 days	30	1	req3	pref0
5	31 days	30	1	req4	pref0
6	31 days	30	1	req5	pref0
7	31 days	30	1	req6	pref0
8	31 days	30	1	req7	pref0
9	31 days	30	1	req8	pref0
10	31 days	30	1	req9	pref0
11	31 days	30	1	req10	pref0
12	31 days	50	1	req0	pref1
13	31 days	50	1	req1	pref1
14	31 days	50	1	req2	pref1
15	31 days	50	1	req3	pref1
16	31 days	50	1	req4	pref1
17	31 days	50	1	req5	pref1
18	31 days	50	1	req6	pref1
19	31 days	50	1	req7	pref1
20	31 days	50	1	req8	pref1
21	31 days	50	1	req9	pref1
22	31 days	50	1	req10	pref1
23	31 days	75	1	req0	pref2
24	31 days	75	1	req1	pref2
25	31 days	75	1	req2	pref2
26	31 days	75	1	req3	pref2
27	31 days	75	1	req4	pref2
28	31 days	75	1	req5	pref2
29	31 days	75	1	req6	pref2
30	31 days	75	1	req7	pref2
31	31 days	75	1	req8	pref2
32	31 days	75	1	req9	pref2
33	31 days	75	1	req10	pref2
34	31 days	100	1	req0	pref3
35	31 days	100	1	req1	pref3
36	31 days	100	1	req2	pref3
37	31 days	100	1	req3	pref3
38	31 days	100	1	req4	pref3
39	31 days	100	1	req5	pref3
40	31 days	100	1	req6	pref3
41	31 days	100	1	req7	pref3
42	31 days	100	1	req8	pref3
43	31 days	100	1	req9	pref3
44	31 days	100	1	req10	pref3
45	31 days	150	1	req0	pref4
46	31 days	150	1	req1	pref4
47	31 days	150	1	req2	pref4
48	31 days	150	1	req3	pref4
49	31 days	150	1	req4	pref4
50	31 days	150	1	req5	pref4
51	31 days	150	1	req6	pref4
52	31 days	150	1	req7	pref4
53	31 days	150	1	req8	pref4
54	31 days	150	1	req9	pref4
55	31 days	150	1	req10	pref4
56	28 days	71	2	$req11_{team1}$ $req11_{team2}$	pref5
57	31 days	71	2	$req12_{team1}$ $req12_{team2}$	pref5
58	28 days	55	5	$req13_{team1}$ $req13_{team2}$ $req13_{team3}$ $req13_{team4}$ $req13_{team5}$	pref6

Table 7. Computational experiments 1 - results

instance	OPT_{int}	CPU$_{int}$ time	OPT_{frac}	CPU$_{frac}$ time	LP solution is integer?
1	329	00:26:93	329	00:20:20	yes
2	329	00:24:73	329	00:19:85	yes
3	322	00:24:49	322	00:20:07	yes
4	322	00:26:89	322	00:19:94	yes
5	366	00:27:25	366	00:19:98	yes
6	366	00:26:85	366	00:19:96	yes
7	364	00:26:03	364	00:19:65	yes
8	366	00:25:02	366	00:20:23	yes
9	343	00:24:27	343	00:19:98	yes
10	343	00:24:05	343	00:20:00	yes
11	345	00:24:24	345	00:19:72	yes
12	293	00:37:94	293	00:29:80	yes
13	293	00:36:71	293	00:29:91	yes
14	296	00:37:35	296	00:30:32	yes
15	296	00:37:19	296	00:29:93	yes
16	295	00:36:98	295	00:30:86	yes
17	295	00:37:15	295	00:30:08	yes
18	294	00:39:91	294	00:30:50	yes
19	295	00:37:92	295	00:30:36	yes
20	292	00:37:56	292	00:30:52	yes
21	292	00:36:93	292	00:29:69	yes
22	294	00:36:84	294	00:30:21	yes
23	293	00:55:72	293	00:43:96	yes
24	293	00:52:93	293	00:43:37	yes
25	296	00:54:84	296	00:43:01	yes
26	296	00:54:95	296	00:43:60	yes
27	295	00:52:90	295	00:43:57	yes
28	295	00:56:06	295	00:43:16	yes
29	294	00:51:29	294	00:43:53	yes
30	295	00:50:51	295	00:43:50	yes
31	292	00:52:37	292	00:46:89	yes
32	292	00:53:94	292	00:42:89	yes
33	294	00:52:32	294	00:43:26	yes
34	293	01:13:05	293	00:57:15	yes
35	293	01:14:72	293	00:57:05	yes
36	296	01:07:53	296	00:57:31	yes
37	296	01:07:97	296	00:56:66	yes
38	295	01:44:39	295	00:56:94	yes
39	295	01:57:52	295	00:56:92	yes
40	294	01:55:99	294	00:57:16	yes
41	295	01:58:96	295	00:57:46	yes
42	292	01:56:45	292	00:57:71	yes
43	292	01:57:10	292	00:57:74	yes
44	294	01:43:72	294	00:57:75	yes
45	293	02:19:79	293	01:27:43	yes
46	293	01:51:79	293	01:26:88	yes
47	296	02:00:22	296	01:28:97	yes
48	296	01:56:59	296	01:26:70	yes
49	295	02:04:18	295	01:26:19	yes
50	295	02:03:17	295	01:27:55	yes
51	294	02:02:82	294	01:26:52	yes
52	295	01:39:51	295	01:26:30	yes
53	292	02:01:27	292	01:27:11	yes
54	292	02:00:58	292	01:31:75	yes
55	294	02:00:58	294	01:31:95	yes
56	1107	00:53:23	1107	00:45:66	yes
57	1077	1:21:57	1077	00:59:21	no
58	1099	00:46:48	1099	00:38:67	yes

To evaluate the performance of the model with large instances, 15 randomly generated instances were tested, considering the planning horizon, the number of workers, and the preferences' penalizations equal in all cases, varying only the workforce's requirements. So, all instances have a planning horizon of a 31-day month and 500 workers organized in a single team. The preferences' penalizations follow the same logic mentioned above but are applied to 500 workers. Regarding workforce requirements, they were randomly generated between 0 and 50 or between 0 and 100, as can be seen in Table 8.

Table 8. Computational experiments 2 - instances' data

instance	planning horizon	number of workers	number of teams	workforce requirements
59	31 days	500	1	randbetween(0,50)
60	31 days	500	1	randbetween(0,50)
61	31 days	500	1	randbetween(0,50)
62	31 days	500	1	randbetween(0,50)
63	31 days	500	1	randbetween(0,50)
64	31 days	500	1	randbetween(0,50)
65	31 days	500	1	randbetween(0,50)
66	31 days	500	1	randbetween(0,50)
67	31 days	500	1	randbetween(0,50)
68	31 days	500	1	randbetween(0,50)
69	31 days	500	1	randbetween(0,100)
70	31 days	500	1	randbetween(0,100)
71	31 days	500	1	randbetween(0,100)
72	31 days	500	1	randbetween(0,100)
73	31 days	500	1	randbetween(0,100)

The combination of the memory RAM of the computer used in the computational experiments and the version of the IBM ILOG CPLEX Optimization Studio initially used, *i.e.* 12.7.0.0, makes it impossible to achieve any results when testing instances of Table 8, forcing a software version update. So, to test these 15 instances, the code is implemented in IBM ILOG CPLEX Optimization Studio 12.10.0.0.

The results are given in Table 9. Column OPT gives the optimal value of the IP model, followed by column $CPU\ time$ that provides the process with time (minutes) for each one of the instances executed. In instance 65, the highest CPU time is achieved, having 744000 variables and 743988 constraints. So, considering the tested instances' size, the model presents a good performance, achieving good computational results.

Table 9. Computational experiments 2 - results

instance	OPT	CPU time
59	3414	06:47:00
60	3374	06:49:45
61	3438	06:32:41
62	3405	06:55:49
63	3360	07:01:94
64	3374	06:53:62
65	3387	07:12:48
66	3465	07:12:06
67	3348	06:56:46
68	3382	06:36:81
69	6772	06:51:57
70	6757	06:34:06
71	6770	06:26:12
72	6868	07:03:08
73	6768	06:31:35

Considering the solution given when executing real-data instance 56 and using Excel's tools, Figs. 4 and 5 illustrate the final schedule of team 1 and team 2, respectively. The CPU time in this scenario is lower than 1 min, having 190848 variables and 97615 constraints. The goal of reducing the processing time was obviously achieved.

When compared to schedules represented in Figs. 2 and 3, schedules of Figs. 4 and 5 appear to have less stability than the former. However, the penalization systems used to obtain them are different: the one used in the proposed method is more relaxed. So, consider, for example, a worker that prefers to work in the 07 h 00 shift. In the IP developed model, assigning this worker to the 07 h 00 shift or assigning the same worker to the 08 h 00 shift is identical because the penalization associated with these two time periods is the same.

Fig. 4. Schedule of team 1 - IP solution

Fig. 5. Schedule of team 2 - IP solution

5 Conclusions

The personnel scheduling problem is a critical problem in the call center industry since call centers ensure communication between companies and customers.
So, it is important for call centers to be staffed so that the waiting times experienced by customers are acceptable. In general, good and optimized schedules are
advantageous for companies because they can avoid overstaffing, minimizing the
total labor costs. To automate a manual scheduling process done in companies
and, therefore, reduce the processing time, the main goal of this project was to
contribute with a new solution approach that relies on exact methods. In this
sense, an integer programming model for assigning work shifts to each employee
in a 24/7 call center while considering their time preferences is proposed and
implemented on IBM ILOG CPLEX Optimization Studio 12.7.0.0.

The model and its linear relaxation were tested to analyze the quality of the
original model with both randomly generated and real-world instances. The integer programming model was proven to have a null integrality gap in all instances
tested, which means that its formulation is strong. So, the proposed model is
a good quality model. To evaluate the performance of the model when running
large instances, more instances were tested, using a more updated version (version 12.10.0.0) of the chosen software since the older one was not able to run
such large instances with the proposed method. The model was proven to have
a good performance, achieving low CPU times considering the size of the tested
instances.

An advantage of the developed model is that it can be applied to scheduling
problems in other areas. It would be interesting to add more constraints in the
proposed IP model for future work, such as scheduling of days-off and breaks
and the possibility of workers changing shifts between them. It would also be
interesting to implement the suggested solution method in an organization to

analyze some performance measures, like attendance and reactivity percentage. These topics can be seen as limitations of the proposed approach.

Funding. This work has been supported by FCT - Fundação para a Ciência e a Tecnologia within the R&D Units Project Scope UIDB/00319/2020.

References

1. Aksin, Z., Armony, M., Mehrotra, V.: The modern call center: a multi-disciplinary perspective on operations management research. Prod. Oper. Manag. **16**(6), 665–688 (2007)
2. Alfares, H.: Operator staffing and scheduling for an it-help call centre. Eur. J. Ind. Eng. **1**, 414–430 (2007)
3. Baker, K.R.: Workforce allocation in cyclical scheduling problems: a survey. J. Oper. Res. Soc. **27**(1), 155–167 (1976)
4. Bard, J.F., Binici, C., deSilva, A.H.: Staff scheduling at the united states postal service. Comput. Oper. Res. **30**(5), 745–771 (2003)
5. Bard, J.F., Purnomo, H.W.: Preference scheduling for nurses using column generation. Eur. J. Oper. Res. **164**(2), 510–534 (2005)
6. Bechtold, S.E., Brusco, M.J., Showalter, M.J.: A comparative evaluation of labor tour scheduling methods. Decis. Sci. **22**(4), 683–699 (1991)
7. den Bergh, J.V., Beliën, J., Bruecker, P.D., Demeulemeester, E., Boeck, L.D.: Personnel scheduling: a literature review. Eur. J. Oper. Res. **226**(3), 367–385 (2013)
8. Bhulai, S., Koole, G., Pot, A.: Simple methods for shift scheduling in multiskill call centers. Manuf. Serv. Oper. Manag. **10**, 411–420 (2008)
9. Cezik, M.T., L'Ecuyer, P.: Staffing multiskill call centers via linear programming and simulation. Manag. Sci. **54**(2), 310–323 (2008)
10. Cordone, R., Piselli, A., Ravizza, P., Righini, G.: Optimization of multi-skill call centers contracts and work-shifts. Serv. Sci. **3**, 67–81 (2011)
11. Ernst, A., Jiang, H., Krishnamoorthy, M., Sier, D.: Staff scheduling and rostering: a review of applications, methods and models. Eur. J. Oper. Res. **153**(1), 3–27 (2004). Timetabling and Rostering
12. Ertogral, K., Bamuqabel, B.: Developing staff schedules for a bilingual telecommunication call center with flexible workers. Comput. Ind. Eng. **54**(1), 118–127 (2008)
13. Felici, G., Gentile, C.: A polyhedral approach for the staff rostering problem. Manag. Sci. **50**(3), 381–393 (2004)
14. Maenhout, B., Vanhoucke, M.: A perturbation matheuristic for the integrated personnel shift and task re-scheduling problem. Eur. J. Oper. Res. **269**(3), 806–823 (2018)
15. Mohan, S.: Scheduling part-time personnel with availability restrictions and preferences to maximize employee satisfaction. Math. Comput. Model. **48**(11), 1806–1813 (2008)
16. Robbins, T.R., Harrison, T.P.: A stochastic programming model for scheduling call centers with global service level agreements. Eur. J. Oper. Res. **207**(3), 1608–1619 (2010)
17. Smet, P., Wauters, T., Mihaylov, M., Berghe, G.V.: The shift minimisation personnel task scheduling problem: a new hybrid approach and computational insights. Omega **46**, 64–73 (2014)
18. Thompson, G.M.: Labor scheduling: a commentary. Cornell Hotel Restaur. Adm. Q. **44**(5), 149–155 (2003)

A Bi-objective Optimization Approach for Wildfire Detection

Filipe Alvelos[1]([envelope]) [iD], Sarah Moura[2] [iD], António Vieira[2] [iD],
and António Bento-Gonçalves[2] [iD]

[1] ALGORITMI Research Center/LASI, University of Minho, Braga, Portugal
`falvelos@dps.uminho.pt`
[2] Centro de Estudos de Comunicacão e Sociedade/Departamento de Geografia,
University of Minho, Braga, Portugal
`{vieira,bento}@geografia.uminho.pt`

Abstract. We consider the problem of buying and locating equipment for covering a (discretized) region. We propose two approaches, based on mathematical programming modelling and the epsilon-constraint method, that allow obtaining the efficient frontier of a bi-objective optimization problem. In the first approach, the objectives are maximizing coverage and minimizing cost. In the second approach, lexicographic optimization is used to incorporate additional objectives - maximizing double coverage and minimizing the maximum fire rate of spread of uncovered points. The latter objective comes from the specific application that motivated this work: wildfire detection. We present results from a case study in a portuguese landscape, as an example of the potential of optimization models and methods to support decision making in such a relevant field.

Keywords: Location · Multi-objective optimization · Wildfire detection

1 Location Problems and Wildfire

In this paper, we consider the problem of buying and locating equipment for covering a given region represented as a set of points.

Location problems have their modern roots in the 1960s. Nowadays, the existing body of work on models, methods and location applications is quite extensive. For a comprehensive work on location problems, we refer the reader to the book edited by Laporte et al. [10].

The problem we address in this paper can be seen as a variation of the well known maximal coverage problem [3]. The basic version of this problem can be stated as to decide which sites should be chosen (from a discrete set of potential sites) to install facilities to maximize the number of clients covered (e.g. within a given ray of a facility). In [12] an overview of more recent work in the maximal covering problems is provided, including applications, solution methods and variants.

© The Author(s), under exclusive license to Springer Nature Switzerland AG 2023
O. Gervasi et al. (Eds.): ICCSA 2023 Workshops, LNCS 14105, pp. 425–436, 2023.
https://doi.org/10.1007/978-3-031-37108-0_27

The covering problem addressed in this paper extends the maximal coverage problem in two ways: firstly, it includes a budget for the equipment cost that is not known *a priori*; secondly, the coverage objective is addressed as a set of hierarchically related objectives. These extensions result on a bi-objective problem (cost vs. coverage) with a coverage objective function resulting from lexicographic optimization.

The motivation for this problem comes from the desire to improve wildfire detection in a Portuguese municipality. Optimization has been used in wildfire detection. In particular, [4] use the maximal covering problem in wildfire detection. We extend that work by using a bi-objective approach and consider additional objectives, namely to maximize double coverage (as defined in, e.g., [8]) and to minimize the potential of fire spread. We show how these objectives can be integrated (through using lexicographic optimization in the epsilon-constraint method) to provide the efficient frontier to a decision maker. We refer the reader to [11] and [6] for surveys on optimization and fire.

We describe a practical application of the models and methods proposed which consists in the use of drones (unmanned aerial vehicles - UAV) in fire detection. Fire detection comprises find and gathering information about ignitions. When an ignition alarm appears, a drone may be sent to the (approximate) location of the ignition to collect information about if the ignition is real or just resulting from a false alarm, the current status of the fire (e.g. perimeter and intensity) and its potential for spreading. This information may improve the decisions to be made about the initial attack resources and fire suppression tactics to be employed.

The paper is organized as follows: In Sect. 2 we define the problem, introduce the base model and describe the method to solve it. Section 3 addresses the additional objectives and how they are incorporated through lexicographic optimization in the solution approach described previously. Section 4 described the practical application of proposed methods. The conclusions of this works are drawn in Sect. 5.

2   Bi-objective Optimization for Buying and Locating Equipment

2.1   Problem Definition

We consider the problem of deciding which resources to buy and where to locate them in order to cover a given region. The available locations and the areas to be covered are discrete, i.e. they are set points. Discretization has the clear advantage of turning the problem into a linear one (distances become constants), allowing the use of linear (integer) programming models that have been proved to be particularly successful [10].

We characterize each type of resource by a unit cost and by the set of points it covers in each potential location. In the base version of the approach, we consider two conflicting objectives: to maximize the coverage and to minimize the cost.

The motivation for addressing this problem comes from its applicability in wildfire detection, where demands are associated with potential fire ignitions. With small adjustments, the proposed model is suitable for supporting decisions about, for example, locating vigilance towers, activating water sources, buy and positioning drones, pre-positioning fire fighting resources, buy and locating cameras and sensors.

2.2   Model

The mathematical notation to be used in the following models is:

- J set of demand points;
- K set of types of resources;
- I^k set of potential locations for resources k, $k \in K$;
- J^{ki} set of demand points covered by a resource of type k, $k \in K$, located at i, $i \in I^k$; $J^{ki} \subseteq J$;
- KI^j set of pairs (k, i) of a resource of type k, $k \in K$, and a location i, $i \in I^k$, that cover demand j;
- c_k cost of one unit of the resource of type k.

We note that the coverage relation is represented explicitly by the set of covered points for each pair type of resource - location through the sets J^{ki} and KI^j. This allows flexibility in the type of resources to be included in the model. Although elementary coverage rules, as defining the demand points covered as the ones that are inside a circle centered in the location with the ray characterized by the type of equipment, can still be used, virtually any function can be used. For example, we may use nonlinear functions of the distance for sensors or explicitly enumerate points that are not covered by vigilance towers because they stand in a valley.

If the single objective is minimizing cost, the well known set covering model can be used directly. We define the decision variables:

$$
y_{ki} = \begin{cases} 1, & \text{if an equipment of type } k \text{ is located at point } i \\ 0, & \text{otherwise} \end{cases} \quad k \in K, i \in I^k.
$$

The model is:

$$
\text{Minimize} \quad \sum_{k \in K, i \in I^{ki}} c_k y_{ki} \tag{1}
$$

Subject to:

$$
\sum_{(k,i) \in KI^j} y_{ki} \geq 1 \qquad\qquad j \in J \tag{2}
$$

$$
y_{ki} \in \{0, 1\} \qquad\qquad k \in K, i \in I^k \tag{3}
$$

The objective function (1) minimizes the cost of the equipment to buy and locate. Constraints (2) assure each demand is satisfied and constraints (3) define the domain of the decision variables.

This model is infeasible if there are demands that cannot be covered, even if all resources are used. Therefore, to avoid that, but also to increase the flexibility to the more elaborated models to be proposed next, we consider the inclusion of decision variables x_j related to the demand being satisfied or not:

$$x_j = \begin{cases} 1, & \text{if demand point } j \text{ is covered} \\ 0, & \text{otherwise} \end{cases} \qquad j \in J$$

A model to maximize coverage is then:

$$\text{Maximize} \sum_{j \in J} x_j \tag{4}$$

Subject to:

$$x_j \le \sum_{(k,i) \in KI^j} y_{ki} \qquad\qquad j \in J \tag{5}$$

$$y_{ki} \in \{0, 1\} \qquad\qquad k \in K, i \in I^k \tag{6}$$

$$x_j \in \{0, 1\} \qquad\qquad j \in J \tag{7}$$

The objective function (4) maximizes the coverage, while constraints (5) state that for a demand to be counted as covered it must effectively be covered, at least, by a resource location pair. The domains of the variables are given by (6) and (7).

In practice, both objectives, to minimize cost and to maximize coverage, are relevant and therefore we model the problem as a bi-objective problem:

$$\text{Minimize} \sum_{k \in K, i \in I^{ki}} c_k y_{ki} \tag{8}$$

$$\text{Maximize} \sum_{j \in J} x_j \tag{9}$$

Subject to:

$$x_j \le \sum_{(k,i) \in KI^j} y_{ki} \qquad\qquad j \in J \tag{10}$$

$$y_{ki} \in \{0, 1\} \qquad\qquad k \in K, i \in I^k \tag{11}$$

$$x_j \in \{0, 1\} \qquad\qquad j \in J \tag{12}$$

2.3   Solution Method

Given the power of current state of the art mixed integer programming solvers and the relatively small size of the model for typical real world instances, we use the epsilon-constraint method [2], to obtain efficient solutions. We note that, with this method, the full efficient frontier can be obtained (including non-supported solutions) in opposition with weight-based approaches. We keep the coverage as an objective and address the cost as a constraint resulting in the following mixed integer programming model, termed $MIP(b)$:

The $MIP(b)$ model is:

$$\text{Maximize } \sum_{j \in J} x_j$$

Subject to:

$$x_j \leq \sum_{(k,i) \in KI^j} y_{ki} \qquad\qquad j \in J$$

$$\sum_{k \in K, i \in I^{ki}} c_k y_{ki} \leq b \qquad\qquad\qquad (13)$$

$$y_{ki} \in \{0,1\} \qquad\qquad k \in K, i \in I^k$$
$$x_j \in \{0,1\} \qquad\qquad\qquad j \in J$$

Constraint (13) comes from the first objective of (8–12). For different values of the budget b, a solution that maximizes the coverage is obtained. If the b values are chosen systematically and with sufficiently small variations, the efficient frontier is obtained.

Algorihtm 1 corresponds to this approach and uses the notation:

- b current budget;
- z proportion of covered demands;
- x optimal solution of the current MIP;
- S set of efficient solutions;
- Δ step of the epsilon-constraint method (budget increment from one iteration to the next);
- $MIP(b)$ MIP model with b as the right hand side of the budget constraint.

After the initialization, at each iteration, the epsilon-constraint method solves the mixed integer programming model, $MIP(b)$, with a fixed budget. If the optimal solution of $MIP(b)$ was not found before, the optimal solution is added to the set of the efficient solutions. The iteration ends with the updating of the coverage and the budget. The algorithm ends when a 100% coverage is obtained.

3 Addressing Additional Objectives

3.1 Modeling Double Coverage and Min Max Uncovered Demand

Besides the objectives previously introduced, we consider two other objectives, both related with coverage. The first one is motivated by the potential need to satisfy different demands in the same time interval - solutions with better double coverage (i.e. with more points covered by, at least, two resources) are preferable. This is a straightforward way of addressing dynamic (time evolving) aspects of the problem: if a resource is busy, a demand can be satisfied by another one.

Algorithm 1. Epsilon-constraint method

$S \leftarrow \emptyset$
$b \leftarrow 0$
$z \leftarrow 0$
while $z < 1$ **do**
  Solve $MIP(b)$
  $S \leftarrow S \cup \{x\}$
  $z \leftarrow \frac{\sum_{j \in J} x_j}{|J|}$
  $b \leftarrow b + \Delta$
end while

The model below maximizes double coverage and relies on the definition of the decision variables

$$w_j = \begin{cases} 1, & \text{if demand point } j \text{ is covered at least twice} \\ 0, & \text{otherwise} \end{cases} \qquad j \in J$$

$$\text{Maximize} \sum_{j \in J} w_j \qquad\qquad\qquad (14)$$

Subject to:

$$2w_j \leq \sum_{(k,i) \in KI^j} y_{ki} \qquad\qquad j \in J \qquad (15)$$

$$\sum_{k \in K, i \in I^{ki}} c_k y_{ki} \leq b \qquad\qquad\qquad (16)$$

$$y_{ki} \in \{0, 1\} \qquad\qquad k \in K, i \in I^k \qquad (17)$$

$$w_j \in \{0, 1\} \qquad\qquad j \in J \qquad (18)$$

The objective function (14) maximizes the double coverage. Constraints (15) relate the double coverage variables with the resource location variables, not allowing that a non covered twice demand to be counted as covered. The domain of the variables are defined by (18).

In the second additional objective, weights are associated with demand points. The objective is to minimize the weight of the uncovered demand with higher weight. The additional parameters and decision variables, and the model are presented below.

- parameters r_j - weight of demand point j, $j \in J$;
- decision variable z - weight of the uncovered demand point with higher weight.

$$\text{Minimize } z \tag{19}$$

Subject to:

$$z \geq r_j(1 - x_j) \qquad\qquad j \in J \tag{20}$$

$$x_j \leq \sum_{(k,i) \in KI^j} y_{ki} \qquad\qquad j \in J \tag{21}$$

$$\sum_{k \in K, i \in I^{ki}} c_k y_{ki} \leq b \tag{22}$$

$$x_{ki} \in \{0, 1\} \qquad\qquad k \in K, i \in I^k \tag{23}$$

$$z \geq 0 \qquad\qquad j \in J \tag{24}$$

Objective (19) and constraints (20) translate the well known linearization of minmax functions. The domain of the decision variable z is defined by (24). If all demands are covered, then $z = 0$.

3.2 Lexicographic Optimization

Taking into account the motivation of this work, we consider the three coverage objectives hierarchically. Given the high importance of early detection of ignitions in the success of initial attacks (e.g. [9]), the first objective is to maximize the (single) coverage. Among solutions with the same coverage, a solution with double coverage is preferred. Among solutions with the same double coverage, a solution with the maximum uncovered demand as small as possible is chosen.

In algorithmic terms, for a fixed budget (b), problem $MIP(b)$ is first solved. Let f_1 be the value of its optimal solution (i.e. the optimal single coverage value). This value is used in a constraint (constraint (25) in the model below) that does not allow the single coverage to be deteriorated when the double coverage is maximized. The second problem to be solved is then:

$$\text{Maximize } \sum_{j \in J} w_j$$

Subject to:

$$\sum_{j \in J} x_j = f_1 \tag{25}$$

$$x_j \leq \sum_{(k,i) \in KI^j} y_{ki} \qquad\qquad j \in J$$

$$2w_j \leq \sum_{(k,i) \in KI^j} y_{ki} \qquad\qquad j \in J$$

$$\sum_{k \in K, i \in I^{ki}} c_k y_{ki} \leq b$$

$$y_{ki} \in \{0, 1\} \qquad\qquad k \in K, i \in I^k$$

$$x_{ki} \in \{0, 1\} \qquad\qquad k \in K, i \in I^k$$

$$w_j \in \{0, 1\} \qquad\qquad j \in J$$

Let f_2 be the value of the optimal solution of this second problem (i.e. the optimal double coverage value with a constraint on the optimal coverage value). The last problem to be solved is:

Minimize z

Subject to:

$$z \geq r_j(1 - x_j) \qquad\qquad\qquad j \in J$$

$$\sum_{j \in J} x_j = f_1 \qquad\qquad\qquad\qquad (26)$$

$$\sum_{j \in J} w_j = f_2 \qquad\qquad\qquad\qquad (27)$$

$$x_j \leq \sum_{(k,i) \in KI^j} y_{ki} \qquad\qquad j \in J$$

$$2w_j \leq \sum_{(k,i) \in KI^j} y_{ki} \qquad\qquad j \in J$$

$$\sum_{k \in K, i \in I^{ki}} c_k y_{ki} \leq b$$

$$x_{ki} \in \{0, 1\} \qquad\qquad k \in K, i \in I^k$$

$$y_{ki} \in \{0, 1\} \qquad\qquad k \in K, i \in I^k$$

$$w_j \in \{0, 1\} \qquad\qquad\qquad j \in J$$

$$z \geq 0 \qquad\qquad\qquad\qquad j \in J$$

Constraints (26) and (27) forbid the deterioration of the single and double coverages.

An interesting variation of this approach is to assign weights to the demands in the coverage objective(s) to take into account fire danger and/or fire spread potential (through fire rate of spread estimates as used in the unconvered demand objective). Another interesting variation is to consider the uncovered demand objective as the second most important when single coverage is not total (keeping double coverage as the second objective when coverage is total).

4   Practical Application

4.1   Description

We applied the proposed method in a landscape that includes Baião, a municipality in the north of Portugal, in the problem of buying drones and establishing their base for wildfire detection. The local authorities provided six potential location for drones (e.g. firefighters headquarters) and defined a landscape of 217.7 km^2 centered in the municipality.

We characterized the demand through land use data, publicly available [5]. From the nine existing categories of land use (in the first categorization level), we selected forest and bushes (the flammable ones) as demand points (around 75% of the total number of nodes).

Land use was also used to determine the fuel category associated with each demand point (through a correspondence between the land use level 4 and the portuguese fuel models [7]). Based on the fuel models, slopes and (upslope) wind, a fire rate of spread was obtained with BehavePlus6 [1] corresponding to a worst-case value for each demand point.

We considered three types of drones characterized by a unit cost (1.5 k€, 2 k€, 15 k€) and a range (4 km, 6 km and 11 km, in the same order as the cost).

4.2   Cost vs. Single Coverage

By applying the method described in Sect. 2.3, we obtained the values of (all) efficient solutions displayed in Table 1.

Table 1. Values of the efficient solutions.

Budget (k€)	Coverage (%)
0	0.0
1.5	25.0
2	53.2
3.5	71.7
4	87.9
5.5	91.6
6	93.2
7.5	94.4
8	94.5
16.5	94.7
17	99.2
18.5	99.9
30	100.0

For example, with a budget of 4 k€ (two drones of the second type with the bases displayed in Fig. 1) is enough to cover almost 90% of the landscape. A budget of 17 k€ allows covering 99 % of the landscape (Fig. 2): the optimal solution consists in buying one drone with a range of 11 km and one with a range of 6 km) and locating them in the bases signaled with a blue and a green cross, respectively.

4.3   Cost vs. Coverage with Lexicographic Optimization

The major results of the application of the methods described in this paper to the case study are displayed in Fig. 3. The data series 'coverage' is the single

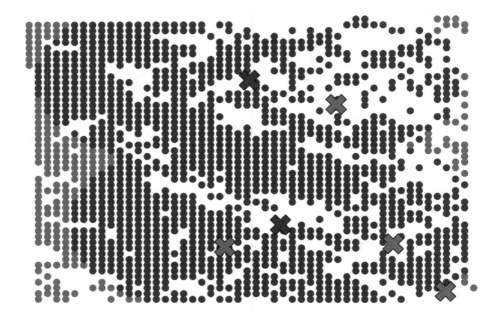

Fig. 1. Optimal solution for a budget of 4 k€.

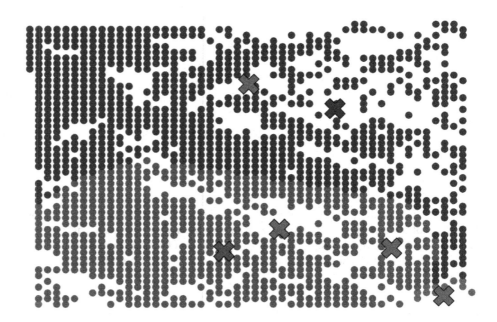

Fig. 2. Optimal solution for a budget of 17 k€.

coverage for each budget (the values of Table 1). Data series 'lex: double coverage' and 'lex: min max ros' refer to the values of the objective functions described in Sect. 3, while 'max coverage: double coverage' refers to the values of double coverage when only single coverage is optimized. The arrows signal particularly significant increases of the double coverage when the lexicographic optimization approach is used.

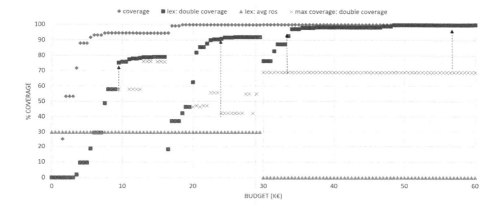

Fig. 3. Results for different approaches for buying and locating drones

5 Conclusions

In this paper we addressed the problem of buying and locating equipment for covering a given spatial region. Our motivation came from the potential of optimization in practical wildfire detection. Using a combination of well-known models and methods (mixed integer programming, covering models, epsilon-constraint, lexicographic optimization) we proposed a general way of approaching this type of problems. We presented results on a case study where it was intended to buy drones and locate them to cover a landscape around a municipality. All the efficient solutions of the bi-objective problem (cost vs. coverage) with lexicographic coverage optimization (double coverage and min max uncovered fire rate of spread are also optimized) were obtained, allowing the municipality to make an informed choice between the different alternatives.

Acknowledgements. This research was supported by FCT - Fundação para a Ciência e Tecnologia, within the scope of project "O3F - An Optimization Framework to reduce Forest Fire" - PCIF/GRF/0141/2019. We also acknowledge the Municipality of Baião and the Volunteer Firefighters of Baião and Sta. Marinha do Zêzere for the constant support and for accompanying in the technical and field visits to Baião.

References

1. Andrews, P.L.: Current status and future needs of the BehavePlus fire modeling system. Int. J. Wildland Fire **23**(1), 21–33 (2014)
2. Chankong, V., Haimes, Y.Y.: Multiobjective Decision Making Theory and Methodology. Elsevier, New York (1983)
3. Church, R., ReVelle, C.: The maximal covering location problem. Pap. Regional Sci. Assoc. **32**(1), 101–118 (1974). https://doi.org/10.1007/BF01942293
4. Dimopoulou, M., Giannikos, I.: Spatial optimization of resources deployment for forest-fire management. Int. Trans. Oper. Res. **8**(5), 523–534 (2001)
5. Direção-Geral do Território. https://www.dgterritorio.gov.pt. Accessed 18 Apr 2023
6. Duff, T.J., Tolhurst, K.G.: Operational wildfire suppression modelling: a review evaluating development, state of the art and future directions. Int. J. Wildland Fire **24**(6), 735–748 (2015)
7. Fernandes, P., et al.: Modelos de combustível florestal para Portugal. In: Actas do 6o Congresso Florestal Nacional, Lisboa, Portugal, pp. 348–354. SPCF (2009)
8. Gendreau, M., Laporte, G., Semet, F.: Solving an ambulance location model by tabu search. Locat. Sci. **5**, 75–88 (1997)
9. Rodrigues, M., Alcasena, F., Vega-García, C.: Modeling initial attack success of wildfire suppression in Catalonia, Spain. Sci. Total Environ. **666**, 915–927 (2019)
10. Laporte, G., Nickel, S., Saldanha-da-Gama, F. (eds.): Location Science. Springer, Cham (2019). https://doi.org/10.1007/978-3-030-32177-2
11. Minas, J.P., Hearne, J.W., Handmer, J.W.: A review of operations research methods applicable to wildfire management. Int. J. Wildland Fire **21**(3), 189–196 (2012)
12. Murray, A.T.: Maximal coverage location problem: impacts, significance, and evolution. Int. Reg. Sci. Rev. **39**(1), 5–27 (2016)

Resource Dispatch Optimization for Firefighting Based on Genetic Algorithm

Marina A. Matos[ID], Ana Maria A. C. Rocha[(✉)][ID], Lino A. Costa[ID],
and Filipe Alvelos[ID]

ALGORITMI Research Centre/LASI, University of Minho, Campus de Gualtar,
4710-057 Braga, Portugal
mmatos@algoritmi.uminho.pt, {arocha,lac,falvelos}@dps.uminho.pt

Abstract. The number of forest fires has increased in recent years. Rising ambient temperatures and rising demographics are the main drivers of these disasters. Optimization has been widely applied in forest firefighting problems, allowing improvements in the effectiveness and speed of firefighters actions. In this work, a resource dispatch problem for forest firefighting (involving 7 resources to extinguish 20 ignitions) is presented. The main goal is to minimize the total burned area caused by the ignitions. To solve this work, a genetic algorithm (GA) adapted to this problem was used. Furthermore, a statistical analysis was carried out among several GA operators, crossover, mutation and selection, to verify which operators obtain the best results for this problem.

Keywords: Forest Fires · Single-objective Optimization · Dispatching Problem · Genetic Algorithm

1   Introduction

Over the years, the number of forest fires on our planet has been very high, proving to be quite worrying, as they represent high-risk situations for the health of living beings and forests. Wildfires damage wildlife and the atmosphere, bringing serious environmental problems. In recent years, the causes of fires have been due to climate change, such as the increase in ambient temperature and due to the criminal hand. For example, between 2019 and early 2020, Australia was devastated by several forest fires caused by unprecedented high temperatures [6].

Every year, around 4 million square kilometers of land (roughly the size of the European Union) are burned worldwide [17]. In Europe, more than five thousand five hundred square kilometers of land burned in 2021, with one thousand square kilometers belonging to protected areas in the European Union [18]. In 2017,

This work has been supported by FCT Fundação para a Ciência e Tecnologia within the R&D Units Project Scope UIDB/00319/2020 and PCIF/GRF/0141/2019: "O3F - An Optimization Framework to reduce Forest Fire" and the PhD grant reference UI/BD/150936/2021.

ⓒ The Author(s), under exclusive license to Springer Nature Switzerland AG 2023
O. Gervasi et al. (Eds.): ICCSA 2023 Workshops, LNCS 14105, pp. 437–453, 2023.
https://doi.org/10.1007/978-3-031-37108-0_28

Portugal faced several forest fires, being a record year for the number of fires that occurred. The main causes were high temperatures and dry thunderstorms [7].

Firefighting is a very important and studied area in the literature. It is necessary to protect and avoid catastrophes, such as forest fires, and for this purpose studies are carried out to support the decisions of professionals in forest firefighting (firefighters, civil protection, etc.). The number, skills and level of preparation of firefighting teams are very important factors in fighting fires [1]. The better and faster the performance of the firefighting team, the less damage will be caused. The gradual increase in forest fires has been a worrying factor for society and for the planet Earth, since they cause deaths, pollution, damage to infrastructures, among other negative aspects. The management of the suppression of forest fires implies knowing how many and which combat resources must be dispatched for each forest fire, in order to extinguish the fire in the best way and quickly. For example, in the paper by Zeferino et al. [19] a mathematical optimization model was developed to find the best location solution for different aircraft that maximizes the coverage of risk areas. Its application was used in a case study in Portugal. In engineering, some optimization strategies have been used to solve problems associated with fire suppression aiming to find the optimal trajectory and location of combat vehicles, obtaining the shortest route, determining the number and which resources to dispatch, among others. In the work by Chan et al. [8] the Firefly algorithm was proposed to dispatch a limited amount of drones and firefighters between several zones. The performance of Firefly algorithm was evaluated in a wide variety of configurations, showing that when a relatively small number of drones are used (for example, 10–20% of the total number of zones) the algorithm can reach up to 80–95% of the optimal performance in most cases. A mathematical model was formulated in [10] for firefighting and rescue service dispatch problem. This problem aims to determine the allocation of firefighters to vehicles and how the vehicles should be dispatched for an emergency. The model was solved exactly and heuristically using data from Skåne, in Sweden. The results showed that the exact solution method is very time consuming in some cases, and that, in most cases, the heuristic finds an optimal solution.

Other studies were developed to determine how many and which resources are available and where and when to act in a given forest fire. In order to reduce forest fires, it is necessary to contribute with studies and develop support systems for forest management, using modern techniques for monitoring, detection and control [1]. Planning how many and which forest firefighting resources are needed to extinguish a given fire is a very relevant area of study that can lead to damage reduction and support decision makers in combat actions. A resource dispatch problem is defined as a problem that simulates where, when and what resources will act on the ground. This problem when applied to forest firefighting, is based on knowing which means of combat should be sent for a given fire and when to send them [2]. The genetic algorithm (GA) is one of the most used metaheuristics in this type of problem. Several works have been presented, applying the genetic algorithm to forest firefighting associated problems. A problem using a resource for multiple simultaneous ignitions was introduced by [14]. The objective was to find the optimal sequence of actions in firefighting, minimizing the total fire damage in the burned areas. They proposed a stochastic formulation to solve the problem concluding that the approach was effective and efficient.

Baisravan et al. [13] proposed several decision support strategies to minimize the total burned area. For this, the GA was applied to find the best strategy in order to reach the objective, using a certain number of resources. The GA builds an optimal line of fire to reduce the total area burned and provides the attacking teams with suitable locations for the line of fire to be built before the fire escapes. A significant decrease in the damage caused was verified. Later, Baisravan et al. [12] presented a GA-based approach for the development of efficient strategies in fire building lines, using intelligent dispatch of resources to minimize total damage to wild areas caused by fires. The approach used a simulation optimization technique where the GA uses advanced wildfire propagation models based on Huygens principles to evaluate the cost index. Homogeneous and heterogeneous environmental conditions were considered with uncertainty in meteorological conditions. Monte-Carlo simulations were used to develop robust strategies under uncertain conditions. With this approach it was possible to verify its effectiveness in the dispatch of resources to combat complex forest fires in uncertain and dynamic conditions. The work developed by Matos et al. [16] aimed to find an optimal scheduling of a forest firefighting resource in the combat of multiple ignitions. The goal was to minimize the total burned area, using GA in a problem with 10 forest fire ignitions located.

This work aims to study a resource dispatch problem for forest firefighting. It is intended to assign 7 resources of forest firefighting to combat 20 ignitions of a forest fire. An adapted GA, implemented in *Python* language, was used to minimize the total burned area of the ignitions. Furthermore, several GA operators, crossover, mutation and selection were tested, and a statistical analysis was carried out to verify which operators to apply in order to obtain the best results in this problem.

This paper is organized as follows. The genetic algorithm is described in Sect. 2, which is used to solve the problem presented in Sect. 3. The experimental results are shown in Sect. 4, where the statistical analysis of the results is also presented. Finally, the conclusions of this study and future work are exposed in Sect. 5.

2   Genetic Algorithm

Genetic Algorithms are well-known and commonly used optimization algorithms, originally proposed by John Holland in 1975 [11]. The genetic algorithm is a stochastic global optimization algorithm inspired by the evolutionary theory of species, namely natural selection, survival of the fittest and the inheritance of traits from parents to offspring by reproduction. The main components of a GA are the chromosome population, the operators (selection, crossover and mutation), the fitness function and the algorithm termination [15].

The GA can be described by the following pseudo-code:

1. Randomly initialize the population of individuals (chromosomes).
2. Compute the fitness function of each individual in the population.
3. Select individuals based on their fitness to serve as parents to form a new population.
4. Perform crossover and mutation on parents to create offspring to form a new population.
5. Copy the best individual to the new population (elitism).
6. Repeat steps 2–5 until termination condition is satisfied.

Initialization

GA is particularly suitable for exploring the search space of a combinatorial optimization problem, for example through a permutation representation of the individuals in population [4]. In this paper, a permutation representation was adopted to represent a possible solution to the problem of dispatching forest firefighting resources. In this representation, each chromosome is a sequence of integer values that can only appear once, that is, each combat resource can fight a certain number of ignitions at different instants of time, following a certain order of priority, which represents each chromosome [3]. The number of elements in the chromosome is given by multiplying the number of resources by the number of ignitions. An example representation of the permutation with 3 resources (R_1, R_2, R_3) and 4 ignitions (I_1, I_2, I_3, I_4), for each instant of time t, is presented in Table 1, where the chromosome length is 12. The permutation representation indicates the order of action of each resource, where the first four elements of the chromosome show the order of action of resource R_1, then from the 5th to the 8th element gives the order of action of resource R_2 and the last four elements give the order of action of resource R_3 in each ignition. Thus, at the initial instant of time, the chromosome in Table 1 indicates that the resource R_1 goes to ignition I_2, the resource R_2 goes to ignition I_1 and the resource R_3 goes to ignition I_3. Afterwards, R_1 goes to ignition I_3, the resource R_2 goes to ignition I_2 and the resource R_3 goes to ignition I_1 and so on.

Table 1. Permutation representation (example)

Resource	R1				R2				R3			
Chromossome	4	5	2	8	1	9	10	11	7	3	12	6
Ignitions Order	I_2	I_3	I_1	I_4	I_1	I_2	I_3	I_4	I_3	I_1	I_4	I_2

Fitness Function

The fitness function measures the quality of the chromosome (in terms of solution) and is related to the objective function. In each generation, the fittest chromosomes in the population are more likely to be selected to generate offspring through crossover and mutation genetic operators.

Operators

The genetic material from the chromosomes is combined to ensure that promising new regions of the search space are explored. However, genetic operators must ensure that feasible permutations are maintained during the search. Several specialized genetic operators have been developed to meet this requirement [4]. Thus, the genetic operators that will be explored and tested for the resource dispatch problem for forest firefighting are shown in Table 2.

Table 2. GA operators explored this work

Crossover	Mutation	Selection
Edge recombination (ER)	Inverse (IM)	Tournament (TS)
Exponential (ExpC)	Bitflip (BM)	Random (RS)
Order-based (OR)	Polynomial (PM)	
Simulated Binary (SBX)		
Uniform (UC)		

Edge recombination crossover is a permutation (ordered) chromosome crossover operator aiming to introduce as few paths as possible between the various elements. In other words, edge recombination uses an adjacency matrix where there is a list of neighbors of each element of the parent chromosomes (see example in Fig. 1).

Fig. 1. Edge recombination crossover

The exponential crossover is similar to the one-point crossover or the two-points crossover. First, a chromosome position is chosen at random. Then a given number of consecutive positions are swapped between parents according to a decreasing exponential distribution [20], as can be seen in Fig. 2.

The order-based crossover is an operator used for permutation representations with the intention of transmitting information about the relative ordering to the offprints. An example of application of the order-based crossover can be visualized in Fig. 3.

The simulated binary crossover operator uses two parent vectors that give rise to two offspring solutions (see Fig. 4). This involves a parameter, called a distribution index that is held fixed in a positive value throughout a simulation.

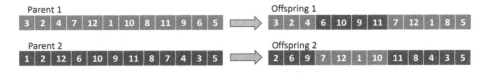

Fig. 2. Exponential crossover

Fig. 3. Order-based crossover

If the distribution index value is large, then the resulting top-down solutions are close to the parent solutions. On the other hand, if the value of the distribution index is a small value, it is likely that the solutions are far from the parents [9].

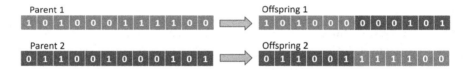

Fig. 4. Simulated binary crossover

The uniform crossover treats each gene on the chromosome individually, as can be seen in Fig. 5. In other words, you basically toss a coin to each gene and decide whether or not it will be included in the offspring.

Fig. 5. Uniform crossover

The inversion mutation randomly selects some positions within a chromosome and inverts the genes on the subchromosome between those positions (see an example in Fig. 6).

Fig. 6. Inversion mutation

The bitflip mutation operator randomly selects a gene from the parent chromosome, with binary encoding, and transforms it from 0 to 1 or vice versa, as shown in Fig. 7.

Fig. 7. Bitflip mutation

The polynomial mutation is similar to what occurs in SBX (Fig. 8), that is, a gene from the parent chromosome is selected and this is transformed into a random value (among the maximum number of genes on the chromosome) in the child chromosome.

Fig. 8. Polynomial mutation

In random selection, only two chromosomes (parents) are selected to participate in mating and they cannot mate more than once, giving rise to offspring. So, successively, pairs of parents are selected at random without reposition from the population to generate offspring by the application of crossover and mutation.

Tournament selection, successively, selects at random two or more parent chromosomes and the one with the highest fitness function value is selected to generate offspring.

Termination

Termination is the final step of a GA, where the algorithm ends if it reaches some defined stopping criterion close to the optimal solution. For example, it ends when there are no improvements in the solution (the value of the objective function stagnates), when the maximum number of iterations is reached or when the objective function value reaches a certain predefined value. If the algorithm does not end, a new generation is performed where the GA operators (selection, crossover and mutation) are used to generate a new chromosome. This cycle is repeated until a certain stopping criterion is satisfied.

3   Problem Description

This work presents a resource dispatch problem for forest firefighting aiming to know which means of combat and when to send them to fight a fire. The objective is to minimize the total burned area, assigning 7 combat resources to suppress 20 ignitions of a wildfire. Thus, the goal is to determine, for each instant of time, which combat resource should go to each ignition, reducing the damage caused (total burned area).

For solving this problem, some assumptions are considered.

Ignition Assumptions:

- Each ignition can only be extinguished once.
- Each ignition can be extinguished by one or more resources.
- The water required to extinguish a given ignition varies over time.
- For each ignition, the fire spreads and therefore the burned area varies over time.
- The distance between the base and each ignition, and between ignitions is known.
- Whenever the water capacity of the resources assigned to a given ignition is sufficient to extinguish it, it is extinguished instantly.

Resource Assumptions:

- All resources, in the initial instant of time, are located in the base.
- Each resource has a maximum tank water capacity, that cannot be refilled when it is empty.
- At the initial instant of time, all resources have full tank water capacity.
- Each resource can only be assigned to one ignition at each instant of time.
- The resources velocity is considered constant.
- The travel time between the base and each ignition and between ignitions is the same for all resources.

The resource dispatch problem for forest firefighting is described as follows. The goal of this problem is to minimize the total burned area (TBA), using 7 resources (A, B, C, D, E, F and G) to extinguish 20 ignitions (I_i, $i = 1, \ldots, 20$) of a fire considering several instants of time. The data used in this work was generated to simulate a real situation. The resources are vehicles consisting of water tanks totaling 9000 l of available water, whose capacity (in liters (l)) of each resource is listed in Table 3.

Table 3. Resource capacity

Resource	A	B	C	D	E	F	G
Capacity	500	1000	3000	1500	1000	500	1500

Table 4 shows the travel times (in minutes) between the location of each ignition and travel time from the base (Base) to each ignition. That is, it corresponds to the travel time from location where the 7 firefighting means are located at the beginning (in the Base), and each of the 20 ignitions and between each ignition (I_i). Travel times range between 10 and 100 min, with intervals of every 10 min $t = \{10, 20, 30, 40, 50, 60, 70, 80, 90, 100\}$.

Table 4. Travel time between ignition locations

I_i	Base	1	2	3	4	5	6	7	8	9	10	11	12	13	14	15	16	17	18	19	20
Base	0	20	20	20	20	20	20	10	20	10	20	30	30	30	20	20	30	20	30	30	20
1	20	0	20	10	20	20	10	10	10	30	30	20	20	20	30	20	20	10	30	30	30
2	20	20	0	20	10	20	20	20	10	20	10	20	30	10	10	10	30	30	30	20	30
3	20	10	20	0	20	30	30	20	30	30	20	10	20	10	20	30	20	20	30	30	20
4	20	20	10	20	0	20	30	10	20	20	10	20	30	30	30	30	30	20	20	10	20
5	20	20	20	30	20	0	20	10	10	30	20	20	10	10	30	20	20	20	10	10	20
6	20	10	20	30	30	20	0	20	20	10	30	30	10	20	20	20	20	30	10	30	10
7	10	10	20	20	10	10	20	0	20	20	20	30	10	30	20	30	10	30	20	10	20
8	20	10	10	30	20	10	20	20	0	10	10	30	20	20	10	20	20	30	20	20	20
9	10	30	20	30	20	30	10	20	10	0	10	20	20	20	30	20	30	20	20	20	30
10	20	30	10	20	10	20	30	20	10	10	0	10	30	20	20	10	10	20	20	10	10
11	30	20	20	10	20	20	30	30	30	20	10	0	20	20	20	30	10	10	20	10	20
12	30	20	30	20	30	10	10	10	20	20	30	20	0	10	20	20	20	10	10	20	20
13	30	20	10	10	30	10	20	30	20	20	20	20	10	0	10	30	10	20	20	30	20
14	20	30	10	20	30	30	20	20	10	30	20	20	20	10	0	10	20	10	30	20	30
15	20	20	10	30	30	20	20	30	20	20	10	30	20	30	10	0	30	30	10	10	30
16	30	20	30	20	30	20	20	10	20	30	10	10	20	10	20	30	0	10	20	10	30
17	20	10	30	20	20	20	30	30	30	20	20	10	10	20	10	30	10	0	10	20	20
18	30	30	30	30	20	10	10	20	20	20	20	20	10	20	30	10	20	10	0	20	30
19	30	30	20	30	10	10	30	10	20	20	10	10	20	30	20	10	10	20	20	0	20
20	20	30	30	20	20	20	10	20	20	30	10	20	20	20	30	30	30	20	30	20	0

The burned area (in ha) of each ignition for each instant of time is shown in Table 5. The rows refer to each ignition I_i and the columns correspond to the instant of time t (in minutes). In each ignition, over time, the burned area increases, and for some ignitions the growth rate is lower than in others.

Table 5. Burned area for each ignition i at each instant of time t

I_i	t									
	10	20	30	40	50	60	70	80	90	100
1	5.0	7.4	10.1	13.1	16.4	20.1	24.1	28.5	33.5	38.9
2	10.0	12.4	15.1	18.1	21.4	25.1	29.1	33.5	38.5	43.9
3	7.0	8.4	10.6	14.3	20.4	30.4	47.0	74.3	119.3	193.5
4	11.0	14.9	20.3	27.9	38.5	53.3	73.9	102.7	142.9	198.9
5	9.0	11.7	16.2	23.6	35.8	55.9	89.0	143.6	233.6	382.0
6	60.0	62.7	67.2	74.6	86.8	106.9	140.0	194.6	284.6	433.0
7	20.0	27.5	36.6	47.7	61.3	77.9	98.2	122.9	153.2	190.1
8	50.0	57.5	66.6	77.7	91.3	107.9	128.2	152.9	183.2	220.1
9	80.0	82.7	87.2	94.6	106.8	126.9	160.0	214.6	304.6	453.0
10	100.0	102.2	105.5	110.5	117.9	128.9	145.4	169.9	206.5	261.1
11	46.0	53.5	62.6	73.7	87.3	103.9	124.2	148.9	179.2	216.1
12	20.0	20.4	21.1	22.6	25.4	30.8	41.5	62.2	102.5	181.1
13	40.0	41.2	42.6	44.5	47.0	50.1	54.1	59.3	66.0	74.5
14	30.0	32.2	35.5	40.5	47.9	58.9	75.4	99.9	136.5	191.1
15	180.0	187.0	195.2	205.0	216.5	230.1	246.1	265.1	287.5	314.0
16	170.0	172.7	177.2	184.6	196.8	216.9	250.0	304.6	394.6	543.0
17	40.0	43.1	47.5	53.5	62.0	73.8	90.3	113.4	145.5	190.3
18	90.0	92.3	95.6	100.2	106.5	115.4	127.7	145.0	169.1	202.8
19	35.0	38.3	43.5	51.5	63.8	82.8	112.2	157.5	227.6	335.8
20	50.0	52.2	55.3	60.0	66.8	76.9	91.6	113.3	145.2	192.0

The amount of water (in liters) required to extinguish each ignition I_i at each instant of time t is shown in Table 6. For each instant of time, the larger the burned area, the greater the amount of water needed to extinguish a given ignition.

4   Experimental Results

In this work, GA is implemented in the *Python* language, after being adapted from the *pymoo* framework: Single-objective Optimization in Python [5]. First, a permutation representation is used so that the solution to the problem takes the form of the order in which a sequence of events should occur, as described in Sect. 2. The permutations represent solutions of the problem, where an array with size equal to the number of resources times the number of ignitions was generated. Then the array is ranked in descending order of combat priority of ignitions for each resource. Finally, a reordering was applied to the resources that still have sufficient capacity to extinguish ignitions. Then, some GA operators are tested to determine the configuration that best performed in solving the problem

Table 6. Water required for extinguish each ignition I_i at each instant of time t

I_i	t									
	10	20	30	40	50	60	70	80	90	100
1	79.3	96.7	112.9	128.4	143.7	158.8	174.0	189.4	205.1	221.1
2	112.1	125.0	137.9	150.9	164.1	177.5	191.2	205.3	219.9	234.9
3	93.8	102.5	115.4	134.0	160.1	195.5	243.0	305.5	387.2	493.1
4	117.6	136.8	159.8	187.3	220.0	258.8	304.8	359.2	423.7	500.0
5	106.3	121.3	142.7	172.2	212.0	264.9	334.4	424.8	541.8	692.8
6	274.6	280.7	290.6	306.2	330.2	366.4	419.4	494.5	598.0	737.6
7	158.5	185.8	214.4	244.8	277.5	312.9	351.2	393.0	438.7	488.8
8	250.7	268.7	289.2	312.5	338.7	368.2	401.3	438.4	479.8	525.9
9	317.1	322.4	331.0	344.8	366.3	399.3	448.4	519.3	618.7	754.5
10	354.5	358.4	364.2	372.6	384.9	402.5	427.4	462.0	509.4	572.8
11	240.4	259.2	280.4	304.3	331.2	361.3	395.0	432.6	474.5	521.1
12	158.5	160.0	162.9	168.4	178.5	196.8	228.2	279.5	358.9	477.0
13	224.2	227.4	231.5	236.6	243.0	251.0	260.9	273.0	287.9	306.0
14	194.2	201.2	211.3	225.6	245.3	272.1	307.7	354.3	414.1	490.0
15	475.6	484.7	495.3	507.5	521.6	537.7	556.1	577.2	601.1	628.1
16	462.2	465.9	471.9	481.6	497.3	522.0	560.5	618.7	704.2	826.0
17	224.2	232.8	244.2	259.4	279.1	304.6	336.9	377.4	427.6	489.1
18	336.3	340.6	346.6	354.8	365.8	380.8	400.7	426.9	461.0	504.8
19	209.7	219.5	233.8	254.3	283.1	322.6	375.4	444.9	534.8	649.6
20	250.7	256.0	263.7	274.6	289.8	310.8	339.4	377.4	427.2	491.2

of dispatching forest firefighting resources. Finally, a statistical analysis is carried out between the different tests of the GA operators (crossover, mutation and selection) to support the decision of which are the best operators to use to obtain the best solution for this problem. At the end, a discussion will be held on the results obtained.

Regarding the parameters used by GA, the population size was set to 20, and the GA default values for the maximum number of generations and the maximum number of function evaluations were 1000 and 100000, respectively. As GA is a stochastic algorithm, 30 independent runs were performed in order to statistically analyze its performance.

The numerical experiments were carried out on a PC 11th Gen Intel(R) Core(TM) i7-1165G7 @ 2.80GHz, 2803 Mhz, 4 Nucleus(s), 8 Processor(s) Logic(s), 16 Gb RAM. The code was implemented in *python* (version 3.9.13) using *VScode* (Version 1.77).

4.1 Testing GA Operators

The strategy used for testing the GA operators presented in Table 2 was as follows. First, keeping the default selection and mutation operators of the *pymoo* framework (Tournament Selection and Inverse Mutation), the crossover operator was varied. Then, for the crossover operator that obtained the best performance in terms of total burned area, the Tournament Selection was maintained and the mutation operator was varied. Finally, for the crossover and mutation operator that obtained the best result, the other selection operator (Random Selection) was tested.

Table 7 shows the average solution values, among the 30 runs, for the total burned area (TBA_{av}), the number of objective function evaluations (nfe_{av}), the total remaining water (RW_{av}), the total water used (UW_{av}) and the execution time ($Time_{av}$), in seconds. In addition, the standard deviation (St dev) is also reported. The solution with the smallest average value of the total burned area found is marked in bold.

Table 7. Average solution values for different crossover, mutation and selection operators

Selection	Crossover	Mutation	TBA_{av}	RW_{av}	UW_{av}	St dev	nfe_{av}	$Time_{av}$
TS	ER	IM	1322.1	2781.2	6218.8	26.8	620.0	11.1
TS	ExpC	IM	1277.4	2847.9	6152.1	27.1	620.0	6.7
TS	OR	IM	1306.8	2718.6	6281.4	24.1	620.0	5.4
TS	SBX	IM	1306.5	2786.7	6213.3	30.0	620.0	4.1
TS	UC	IM	1303.9	2992.0	6008.0	27.1	620.0	3.6
TS	ExpC	BM	1272.4	3065.0	5935.0	35.4	628.7	5.3
TS	**ExpC**	**PM**	**1249.9**	**3108.8**	**5891.2**	**36.2**	**1584.7**	**16.1**
RS	ExpC	PM	1251.8	3027.4	5972.6	30.6	1540.7	21.1

In a first approach, a statistical analysis was performed among the GA crossover operators. Thus, the crossover operator, with the lowest value of the total burned area, was chosen (Exponential, ExpC). Then, the GA mutation operators IM and PM were tested. Finally, the best mutation operator was chosen (Polynomial, PM), and GA selection operator RM was also tested. For the statistical analysis, a one-tailed paired sample t-student test was used, where the p-values and the differences between the TBA values of each operator are presented in the next tables. In all tests, a significance level of 5% was considered.

Testing Crossover

As mentioned earlier, the several GA crossover operators were tested by setting the default operators of *pymoo* for selection and mutation (TS and IM). Table 8 shows the p-values, in the lower triangular part of the table, and average differences between the TBA values of the crossover operators, in the upper triangular part of the table.

Table 8. Statistical analysis for crossover operator

	ExpC	ER	OR	SBX	UC
ExpC	–	**−44.789**	**−29.446**	**−29.169**	**−26.561**
ER	<0.001	–	**15.343**	**15.620**	**18.228**
OR	<0.001	0.012	–	0.277	2.886
SBX	<0.001	0.019	0.484	–	2.608
UC	<0.001	0.006	0.332	0.363	–

With the crossover operator ExpC, the best result was obtained, when compared to all other crossover operators, since the TBA values were negative. On the other hand, the ER was the worst operator compared to the others (OR, SBX and UC crossovers), where the difference between the TBA values of the various operators was positive. The statistical analysis showed that there were significant differences between the crossover operator ExpC and the others, since the p-value was less than 0.05. When comparing the p-values of the ER crossover with those OR, SBX and UC, the statistical analysis indicates that the differences are significant, since p-values are less than 0.05. Finally, comparing the crossovers OR with SBX, OR with UC and SBX with UC, it is possible to notice that there were no significant differences between these operators, as the p-values were greater than 0.05. Therefore, the best operator was ExpC.

Testing Mutation

Then, the previously chosen crossover operator (ExpC) was fixed and the TS was maintained, a statistical analysis was performed between the GA mutation operators. As can be seen in Table 9 there were no significant differences between IM and BM operators, as the p-value is greater than the 0.05. In addition, it was also possible to observe that the PM operator stood out from the IM and BM operators, since the p-value was less than 0.05, showing significant differences between them. Thus, it was possible to conclude that the best GA mutation operator was the PM.

Table 9. Statistical analysis for mutation operator

	IM	BM	PM
IM	–	4.962	**27.413**
BM	0.272	–	**22.451**
PM	<0.001	0.009	–

Testing Selection

Finally, after the best crossover and mutation operators had been previously chosen (ExpC and PM), a statistical analysis was performed between the RS and TS operators. In Table 10, it can be seen that there were no significant differences (p-value greater than 0.05), which means that it is indifferent to use RS or TS.

Table 10. Statistical analysis for selection operator

	RS	TS
RS	–	1.905
TS	0.413	–

After the statistical analysis, it was found that the best operators for this problem were ExpC and PM. Concerning the selection operator, the TS operator was selected due to the lowest average value of TBA (marked in bold in Table 7).

4.2   Best Result Analysis

The best solution found by GA, among the 30 runs, when using the best operators previously chosen, ExpC, PM and TS, is presented in Table 11. It shows the optimal value obtained for TBA, the number of function evaluations (nfe) and the execution time (Time). The table also shows the values of the remaining water (RW) and the used water (UW) in that best solution.

Table 11. Best solution found using ExpC, PM and TS operators

	TBA	RW	UW	nfe	Time
Best Solution	1236.2	3976.0	5024.0	1900.0	19.5

Table 12 shows the best solution found by GA in terms of the instant of time each resource is assigned to each ignition. The symbol → represents that the resource of combat is traveling.

Table 12. Best solution found by GA for TBA = 1236.2 ha

R	t					
		10	20	30	40	50
A	Base	$\rightarrow$	I_4	I_{19}		
B	Base	$\rightarrow$	I_3	I_{11}	$\rightarrow$	I_{20}
C	Base	I_9	$\rightarrow$	I_{15}	I_2	I_{13}
D	Base	I_7	I_1	I_6	I_{18}	I_{12}
E	Base	I_7	I_{16}	I_5	$\rightarrow$	
F	Base	$\rightarrow$	I_8	$\rightarrow$	I_{20}	
G	Base	$\rightarrow$	I_{14}	I_{17}		

In the beginning, all the resources are at the Base. At $t = 10$, resources C and D are assigned to ignitions I_9 and I_7 respectively. At $t = 20$ resources A, B, D, E, F and G are assigned to extinguish ignitions I_4, I_3, I_1, I_{16}, I_8 and I_{14}, respectively. In addition, resource C is assigned to ignition I_{15}, but the trip from I_9 to I_{15} takes 20 min (see Table 4), so at $t = 20$ it is traveling. The ignitions I_{19}, I_{11}, I_{15}, I_6, I_5 and I_{17} are extinguished in the instant of time $t = 30$. At this instant of time, resource A is not assigned to any further ignitions, as it does not have enough water capacity to extinguish any still active ignition (remain water of resource A is 129.4 l). At the instant of time $t = 40$, resources C, D and E are dispatched to ignitions I_2, I_{18} and I_{10}, respectively, extinguishing them. Resource F is assigned to ignition I_{20}, but does not have enough water to extinguish this ignition by itself, running out of water. At this time ($t = 40$) the ignition I_{20} requires 274.6 l of water (see Table 6), but resource F only has 231.3 l of water. Since resource F cannot extinguish I_{20} alone, resource B is assigned to support extinguishing this ignition at time $t = 50$. At this time, I_{13} and I_{12} are extinguished by resources C and D, respectively. Note that resource F has used all of its water tank capacity. Although some resources were low on water, or even without water, a total 3976.0 l of water still remained. Thus, at time $t = 50$ all ignitions were extinguished and the total water used was 5024.0 l.

5   Conclusions and Future Work

The occurrence of forest fires has increased in recent years and is essentially due to natural or human factors. Therefore, it is necessary to look for solutions that can manage fire suppression, such as optimizing firefighting actions.

In this work, a resource dispatch problem for forest firefighting was addressed. The problem was based on 7 resources that would have to be assigned to 20 ignitions in order to extinguish them, minimizing the total burned area. For this, the metaheuristic GA from the *pymoo* framework was used, and adapted with permutation representation to obtain the optimal solution of the problem. Furthermore, several GA operators, crossover, mutation and selection were tested, and a statistical analysis was carried out to verify which operators to apply in order to obtain the best results in this problem. After this analysis, it was found that the best operators were ExpC crossover, PM mutation and TS selection. Then, the optimal solution found in terms of total burned area was TBA = 1236.2 ha using the best GA operators. By analyzing this solution, it was possible to identify at what instant of time each resource goes to each ignition. With this approach it was possible to realize that the strategy was effective and fast.

In the future, it is intended to deal with this problem but using real data. A multi-objective approach can also be applied to the resource dispatch problem for forest firefighting, minimizing simultaneously the total burned area and the used water.

References

1. Attri, V., Dhiman, R., Sarvade, S.: A review on status, implications and recent trends of forest fire management. Arch. Agric. Environ. Sci. **5**(4), 592–602 (2020)
2. Bélanger, V., Lanzarone, E., Nicoletta, V., Ruiz, A., Soriano, P.: A recursive simulation-optimization framework for the ambulance location and dispatching problem. Eur. J. Oper. Res. **286**(2), 713–725 (2020)
3. Bessedik, M., Benbouzid-Si Tayeb, F., Cheurfi, H., Blizak, A.: An immunity-based hybrid genetic algorithms for permutation flowshop scheduling problems. Int. J. Adv. Manuf. Technol. **85**, 2459–2469 (2016)
4. Bierwirth, C., Mattfeld, D.C., Kopfer, H.: On permutation representations for scheduling problems. In: Voigt, H.-M., Ebeling, W., Rechenberg, I., Schwefel, H.-P. (eds.) PPSN 1996. LNCS, vol. 1141, pp. 310–318. Springer, Heidelberg (1996). https://doi.org/10.1007/3-540-61723-X_995
5. Blank, J., Deb, K.: Pymoo: multi-objective optimization in Python. IEEE Access **8**, 89497–89509 (2020)
6. Boer, M.M., de Dios, V.R., Bradstock, R.A.: Unprecedented burn area of Australian mega forest fires. Nat. Clim. Chang. **10**(3), 171–172 (2020)
7. Carmo, I.I.V.: O papel dos Instrumentos de Gestão Territorial na prevenção e mitigação dos incêndios florestais: o caso do incêndio de Pedrogão Grande (2017) (in Portuguese). Ph.D. thesis (2021)
8. Chan, H., Tran-Thanh, L., Viswanathan, V.: Fighting wildfires under uncertainty: a sequential resource allocation approach. In: Proceedings of the Twenty-Ninth International Conference on International Joint Conferences on Artificial Intelligence, pp. 4322–4329 (2021)
9. Deb, K., Sindhya, K., Okabe, T.: Self-adaptive simulated binary crossover for real-parameter optimization. In: Proceedings of the 9th Annual Conference on Genetic and Evolutionary Computation, pp. 1187–1194 (2007)
10. Granberg, T.A.: Optimized dispatch of fire and rescue resources. In: Computational Logistics: 13th International Conference (ICCL 2022), Barcelona, Spain, 21–23 September 2022, Proceedings, pp. 132–146. Springer, Cham (2022). https://doi.org/10.1007/978-3-031-16579-5_10
11. Holland, J.H.: Adaptation in Natural and Artificial Systems. MIT Press, Cambridge, MA (1975)
12. HomChaudhuri, B., Kumar, M., Cohen, K.: Genetic algorithm based simulation-optimization for fighting wildfires. Int. J. Comput. Methods **10**(06), 1350035 (2013)

13. HomChaudhuri, B., Zhao, S., Cohen, K., Kumar, M.: Generation of optimal fireline for fighting wildland fires using genetic algorithms. In: Dynamic Systems and Control Conference, vol. 48920, pp. 111–118 (2009)

14. Kali, A.: Stochastic scheduling of single forest firefighting processor. Can. J. For. Res. **46**(3), 370–375 (2016)

15. Lambora, A., Gupta, K., Chopra, K.: Genetic algorithm - a literature review. In: 2019 International Conference on Machine Learning, Big Data, Cloud and Parallel Computing (COMITCon), pp. 380–384 (2019). https://doi.org/10.1109/COMITCon.2019.8862255

16. Matos, M.A., Rocha, A.M.A.C., Costa, L.A., Alvelos, F.: A genetic algorithm for forest firefighting optimization. In: Gervasi, O., Murgante, B., Misra, S., Rocha, A.M.A.C., Garau, C. (eds.) Computational Science and Its Applications – ICCSA 2022 Workshops (ICCSA 2022). LNCS, vol. 13378, pp. 55–67. Springer, Cham (2022). https://doi.org/10.1007/978-3-031-10562-3_5

17. Naderpour, M., Rizeei, H.M., Khakzad, N., Pradhan, B.: Forest fire induced Natech risk assessment: a survey of geospatial technologies. Reliab. Eng. Syst. Saf. **191**, 106558 (2019)

18. San-Miguel-Ayanz, J., et al.: Forest fires in Europe, Middle East and North Africa 2021 (KJ-NA-31-269-EN-N (online), KJ-NA-31-269-EN-C (print)) (2022). https://doi.org/10.2760/34094

19. Zeferino, J.A.: Optimizing the location of aerial resources to combat wildfires: a case study of Portugal. Nat. Hazards **100**(3), 1195–1213 (2020). https://doi.org/10.1007/s11069-020-03856-6

20. Zhao, S.Z., Suganthan, P.N.: Empirical investigations into the exponential crossover of differential evolutions. Swarm Evol. Comput. **9**, 27–36 (2013)

OR in Hospital Admission Systems: An Overview of the 20th Century

M. J. F. De Oliveira[1] and Ana Teixeira[2,3](✉)

[1] Alberto Luiz Coimbra Institute of Post-Graduation and Research in Engineering, Federal University of Rio de Janeiro, Rio de Janeiro, Brazil
mario_jo@pep.ufrj.br
[2] University of Trás-os-Montes e Alto Douro, Quinta de Prados, Vila Real, Portugal
ateixeir@utad.pt
[3] Mathematics Centre, University of Minho - Pole CMAT - UTAD, Braga, Portugal

Abstract. In this article a review of Hospital Admission Systems based upon articles published during the 20th century is presented. The past history of Operations Research as applied to the admission of patients to hospital in this period is examined and the major contributions, mainly in Great Britain and the United States, are reviewed. The usual procedure for admitting patients is highlighted and the main administrative problems associated with the admission and hospitalization of patients is identified. The sources, elements and methods employed by previous research are examined and a practical application geared by the use of the available information is described. It is hoped that this material can help the reader understand the evolution of this field over the 20th century and take a broad view on the subject. Additionally, a characterization of the documents analyzed in this paper in accordance with specific key elements is proposed.

Keywords: Operations Research · Hospital Admission Systems · Health Services · 20th century · Overview

1 Introduction

Operations Research (OR) is an exciting ground providing tools, perspectives and new ways to structure and think about theory and practice. The roots of OR in hospitals may be traced to Great Britain in the late 1940's and are related to the development of the National Health Services. The Nuffield Provincial Hospitals Trust in 1949 established a research group under the direction of L. Davies [43]. Within this activity a set of OR studies were made, frequently motivated by the need for a basis for architectural decisions – the nation faced a large hospital building program. Their first publication appeared in 1955; other pioneering studies were published by Bailey [1, 2], Welch [60] and others. It is interesting to note the influence that the organization of the nation in regions, each with its hospital board, had on research. Topics such as "Regional Planning", "Estimation of Regional Needs" and "Internal Hospital Activities" have formed branches of research.

The closest counterpart to British developments has been the passage of the Hill-Burton Act of 1954 in the United States of America. The purpose of this Act was to

© The Author(s), under exclusive license to Springer Nature Switzerland AG 2023
O. Gervasi et al. (Eds.): ICCSA 2023 Workshops, LNCS 14105, pp. 454–466, 2023.
https://doi.org/10.1007/978-3-031-37108-0_29

assist in the developing and carrying out comprehensive state-wide and local plans for the development of hospitals and health related facilities. The Act required States to create a planning program that would survey existing facilities and promote hospital construction plans. Hill-Burton funds have been the principal source of support for research on the organization of the health services in the United States. Research topics such as "Statistical Patterns of demand for hospital services", "Hospital facilities utilization" and "Economics of automating selected hospital activities" have formed branches of activities [33].

The first published papers are related to demand for Health Services and utilization of facilities in both the United Kingdom (UK) and the United States of America (USA). An examination of the early OR studies in Hospital Admission Systems (HAS) allows a classification of efforts according to problem areas. There is a set of problems relating to demand and utilization of facilities, from which one can trace the origin of some of the problem areas discussed in this paper. One is particularly concerned with the incidence of illness, accidents, intensity of medical care and the length of stay in hospitals. Such problems have attracted the attention of operational researchers such as Newell [40], Bailey [1], Balintfy [3], Thompson [69], Connor [16], Blumberg [11, 12] and Young [63]. To summarize, most of the early studies in Britain and the United States would be classed as queuing and flow studies and it is interesting to note that they arise from the branches of activities originated in both countries. Complex problems of probabilistic nature, sometimes dominated by systematic factors such as seasonal variation, scheduling rules and other mathematical features, have also attracted the attention of researchers.

It is possible to draw the growing interest in hospital admission systems or at least in their components from the late 1940s. One can find valuable feedback, namely the papers produced by Milsun et al. [40], Boldy [10], Stimson, [56] Murchie [41], Fries [27] and Lagergren [37]. One can also find many publications in the OR field for managing emergency services. Most of the earlier studies concentrate on management considerations and administrative issues such as the demand for services [32], service capacity [55], evacuation planning [22], and positioning of emergency vehicles [14]. Other interesting OR approaches arise from the literature. It is noticeable the appearance of soft models [48], hybrid models [64], expert systems [38] 3D data visualization [20] and interactive models [62]. Additionally, some studies have been carried out by an existing research group at the Federal University of Rio de Janeiro, most of which unknown. Among the research topics one can point out some specific issues such patient-oriented modeling of emergency admission systems [21] and 3D Visual simulation [20].

From what has already been mentioned, it can be perceived that there is a large amount of information concerning the topic. Thus, an evaluation of all these pieces of work points to the need to put together these initiatives into an integrated model. Therefore, it justifies to aggregate the information contained in all the works related to this topic and catalog it in accordance with specific key elements previously chosen.

This paper is organized as follows: In Sect. 2 the methodology of the study is presented. In Sect. 3 the results of the overview are presented and analyzed. A characterization of the analyzed manuscripts in terms of previously chosen key factors is proposed in Sect. 4 and, finally, in Sect. 5, the main conclusions are presented.

2 Methodology

The aim of this study is to analyze the main features on the concept of Hospital Admission Systems (HAS) from a series of relevant manuscripts that have been disseminated in some of the most prestigious publications during the 20th century and characterize and aggregate the information contained in these works according to pre-specified issue. One is only interested in those manuscripts that can be considered essential references in the HAS field. Therefore, a set of relevant databases and web search engines is selected, namely: Web of Science, Current Contents Connect, Inspec, and PubMed as well as Academic Research Microsoft, Periódicos CAPES and Scholar Google. Additionally, in order to increase the reading, most of the considered manuscripts in the database are written in English, being only a very small portion of them written in French and Portuguese. The sources of information required for the present research consist of a group of specialized manuscripts in the OR and Health field. It is necessary to analyze works of good quality, so that our findings will be based on research and innovation developments that are observing good value criteria.

The analysis proposed here contains publications collected in two different moments. The first moment comprises the period until 1980 and is based upon an extensive unpublished review provided by one of the authors [18]. This bibliography covers most of the published papers in the United Kingdom and United States, as well as works developed by a research group at the Federal University of Rio de Janeiro. Theoretical text books as a class have been excluded, but those closely related with HAS have been considered. The bibliography was prepared by means of a card index and about 46 contemporary periodicals were scanned for relevant articles using inter library loan services.

The second moment comprises the period 1981–1999 and encompasses references taken from scientific databases of renowned prestige, completing the selection of manuscripts with the examination at important web search engines. We opted to work with the most prestigious catalogues in the area of OR applied to Health Services, complementing them with well-known search engines.

Here, the focus goes essentially to the articles present in the databases: Web of Science, Current Contents Connect, Inspec, and PubMed as well as in the web search engines: Academic Research Microsoft, Periódicos CAPES and Scholar Google, since they contain a wide range of top journals that report research findings. We have also included some MSc and Ph.D. thesis, Journals, Conference Proceedings from Operational Research Applied to Health Services (ORAHS) meetings and few working papers; in the understanding that some quality unpublished works tend to be in this type of manuscripts.

To search for works in the context of this research, the keywords "Hospital", "Admission" and "systems" were used. Initially, a search using these keywords in the title, abstract or keywords of manuscripts was performed. A manual search was also accomplished to detect synonyms of the above words. In the next phase, the references cited in the manuscripts obtained, as well as other items listed in the search engines, were also examined and, when appropriate, included in the platform.

After the selection of manuscripts, key issues related with the main features of HAS were assessed in all the publications. The manuscripts were carefully cataloged in a database specially designed for this purpose. During this process, the authors individually examined the information contained in each article and the most important elements were identified. If a discrepancy in the categorization of any reviewed article was noticed reassessment was performed until a consensus was reached.

3 An Overview

According to the bibliographic study carried out by De Oliveira [18] it is possible to trace by the 1950's the growing interest in the Hospital admission problem or at least in the components of it. Sufficient interest and activity existed to justify the first Conference on OR applied to Health Services [26]. Perhaps because of the regional organization of the British Health Services the predominant topic under discussion was the estimation of regional requirement and the corresponding need for medical facilities and personnel. General discussion centered on problems of estimating hospital capacity requirements, which in turn depend upon measures of incidence of illness and hospital length of stay. With this in mind, Balintfy [3–5] considered a ward census predictor model in close correspondence to real-system behavior by formulating the problem as a Markov Process. Singer [53] developed a stochastic model of the variation of state of health of patients within a hospital.

Because of the probabilistic nature of transitions of patients from one category to another, the composition of the inpatient population displays a high degree of variability which results in corresponding fluctuations in demand on human and material resources. Using the classification scheme provided by Connor [16] an index was developed to indicate the total amount of time required for bed-site care by which nursing personnel are allocated among the hospital wards. Newell [42] analyzed the number of hospital beds to be reserved for emergency. A simple mathematical model of the demand pattern is suggested and tested against data from a hospital of London. It concluded that any emergency beds provision should take into account constant weekly and/or seasonal differences. Moreover, Gue [30] suggested a method of distributing nursing workload to the ward nursing staff. He has studied the random variation of nursing care and predicted the effect of this variation on the waiting time between each patient's care, whereas Connors [17] provided a stochastic elective admission scheduling algorithm which uses empirical data in order to measure both patient's satisfaction and hospital efficiency. Bithell [8] has studied stochastic models to evaluate the variability of the utilization of hospital resources - especially of beds, as measured by the bed occupancy. It is shown how this extended theory can be used to compute transition matrices of complicated chains and to build models accommodating daily variations which are commonly observed throughout the week.

Kolesar [36] suggests a Markovian decision model for modeling a hospital admission scheduling system which allows a great deal of flexibility in the type of service and arrival distributions used. The model aims to exercise control over the hospital census and deals with the number of scheduled admission. It enables one to obtain good decision rules which are imbedded in a linear programming formulation. Shonick [50] considers a stochastic model for the distribution of a distinctive patient facility. Related waiting list size and waiting times are also discussed. This work is extended by Shonick and Jackson [51]. Offensend [44] presents a discrete time, discrete state stochastic model to describe the dynamics of admission systems based on patient census and on nursing workload.

Thompson, Avant and Spiker [58] have studied the problem of occupancy of the maternity suite. The queuing model is constructed from analogies with previous results obtained by Bailey [1], Welsh and Bailey [61], and by Flagle [25] for intensive care units. Young [63] treats the hospital as an information servo-control system, with input and output given by the flow of patients and the state of the system given by the bed occupancy. His study recognizes the existence of both chance and controllable deterministic factors in the environment, and deals with these simultaneously in order to provide meaningful decision rules for the hospital administration.

Resh [45] has studied the problem of scheduling patients for admission to surgery and used a two stage sequence of linear and non-linear mathematical programming models with stochastic constraints and integer solutions. The first stage is concerned with the optimal kind and number of patients to admit during the scheduled horizon. The second stage is concerned with daily optimal allocation of inpatients to operating rooms. Fetter and Thompson [23] proposed a tentative two stage model of an entire general hospital involving simulation followed by linear programming. The basic data consists of the frequencies and conditional probabilities for each route followed by patients through the hospital and the time spent in the various care zones. The linear programming model then maximizes overall bed utilization, subject to cost constraints.

Kolesar [36] discussing the problem of pre-scheduling elective admissions suggests a Markovian decision model followed by linear programming. Each of the suggested problems involves the optimization over all possible stationary decision rules of a linear function of the long run state probabilities, subject to linear constraints obtained from the steady state equations of the Markov chain. A general review of this model is examined by De Oliveira [19]. This model is restricted in the planning horizon because of its Markovian assumption. Within this restriction its use is demonstrated in deriving decision rules which, via the Linear Programming component of the model, can be devised either to maximize average census level or to minimize probability of overflow.

Finarelli [24] proposes a heuristic scheduling system designed to maximize the utilization of surgical beds, while satisfying constraints on (i) the number of patients not admitted as scheduled, (ii) the utilization of the surgical suite, and (iii) the overtime and/or cancellations associated with the operation theatre. Barber [6] uses chance-constrained mathematical programming to obtain the maximum number of new elective admissions that can be scheduled for a particular day, in order to provide global long term optimization of the hospital census. Swain et al. [57] use a heuristic scheduling system to control the pattern of additional elective admissions for a certain day, which will maximize the predicted patient days in the hospital over the intervenient days, subject to a constraint on the probability that the occupancy is greater than the number of available beds.

Thompson and Fetter [59] described the use of a simulation model of the maternity suite to predict the facility requirements for any patient loads and any desired service level. A new version of this simulation appears later in the literature. It includes an out-patient clinic, a surgical pavilion and a clinical laboratory. Smith and Solomon [55] analyzes admission policies for a large specialized hospital. The objective is to select the best policy which allows the stabilization of admission rate and hospital census. Handyside and Morris [32] describe a method were data relating the length of stay and mean admission rate can be used to simulate the admission of Emergency patients, and to predict the effect upon bed occupancy of various rotational admission policies.

Robinson, Wing and Davis [47] examine six alternative methods of scheduling elective patients taking into consideration attributes such as the desired admission dates and its flexibility, the potential length of stay in the hospital, and the demand for services. Barnoon and Wolfe [7] describe a practical method of predicting discharges and scheduling admissions in a surgical unit having almost exclusively elective patients. They examine measures such as the utilization of the unit, the idle time of the medical staff and operating theatre in periods of high demand.

Goldman and Knappenberger [29] investigate alternative priority disciplines to deal with elective surgery cases in order to obtain maximum effectiveness in the operating suite. Rikkers [46] simulates the bed utilization in a hospital with flexible boundaries between units. Blewet et al. [9] simulate the use of sharing resources between specialties. Patients are categorized according to consultant, sex and diagnosis. Hancock et al. [31] use simulation to investigate the effects of the number of beds, percentage of emergency cases and the length of stay in the performance of the admission system. A practical method is developed for predicting the current size of hospital facilities, given the expected demand.

Since it is extremely difficult to examine the admission system in all its complexity by means of analytical methods alone, an integrated model was planned by De Oliveira [19]. The aim of this model is tree-fold. Firstly, it attempts to analyse alternative scheduling policies with a more flexible lead time. Secondly, it seeks to examine possible ways of reducing the variability of the census. Thirdly, it allows examination of the response of the system to the introduction of control over variables of the model. It is shown how even partial information about patients can improve the appointment system and waiting line management. Each of these models can account for different, yet only partial features of the HAS. Nonetheless, each one sheds light into different points and complementary aspects of the admission system. An integrated information support system, which may be looked upon as a model in its own right is recommended. This system utilizes fully the information available in the data base and allows the hospital administration to benefit as much as possible from such information.

Jun et al. [35] published a survey that focus on the application of discrete event simulation to single or multi-facility health care clinics and systems of clinics. It showed that a large amount of research has been conducted concerning both patient flow and resource allocation and that simulation is particularly appropriate to approach the difficulties in this area. Smith-Daniels et al. [54] published a review of the literature on demand management strategies and capacity services until 1986. They also take a look at the applications and in healthcare. It is argued that the creation of Healthcare Organizations means that decisions about the capacity and resources are better defined, due to the clear objectives of these organizations. This review was later extended by Jack et al. [34] covering the remaining period of the 20th century. The main contribution is to synthesize research on demand management, capacity management and performance. However, there are limitations of this study because, among others, several conference papers and unpublished dissertations that are also worth to be revised are not included in the study.

Many publications in the OR field for managing emergency services can be found. Most of the earlier studies concentrate on management considerations and administrative issues such as the demand for services [32], service capacity [55], evacuation planning [22], and positioning of emergency vehicles [15]. Other interesting OR approaches also arise from the literature. It is noticeable the appearance of soft models [48], hybrid models [64], expert systems [38] 3D data visualization [20] and interactive models [62]. At the Federal University of Rio de Janeiro research involving patient-oriented modeling of emergency admission systems [21] and 3D Visual simulation [20], among others, was accomplished. Features common to these studies are long waiting times, bottlenecks in attendance, flow problems and configuration of human and material resources. The necessity of conciliate all these facets leads to the need to assemble them in an integrated model.

4 A Characterization

A model of an admission system is generally composed of a structured set of components connected together and to the environment for a particular purpose. The system boundaries are usually defined arbitrarily. The model described is, therefore, a part of reality. The model describes how the parts are organized. The dynamics describes how the parts interact. The interaction is usually performed by a method. The method generally requires quality, effectiveness and efficiency.

The system status indicates the situation in a certain instant. The most important aspects of this state should be monitored. As the system state is modified over time, these should be described in detail, including the respective statistics of the changes. The changes produced in the state of a system is generally controlled statistical pattern (historical or estimated), from which samples are taken. These patterns can be adjusted to theoretical or empirical distributions that will operate a model.

The elements to be used in the model are all those which are involved in a real system. These are the material and human resources and infrastructure. Each element has its own features, called attributes, which are fixed or variable values associated with an element along the simulation. An element can have one or more attributes. Attributes may be correlated to each other. The difference found in the attribute value can cause a change in the system state and contribute to the efficiency of the model. The time elapsed between a stimulus and a significant change of state is one of the important variables to assess the response of the model. The attribute can possibly be described numerically.

Entities are objects or people involved in the real system. Although entities are individually identifiable, they can be grouped into classes. An entity is said to be permanent when it is always present in the system. On the other hand, it is said temporary and its permanence is restricted to only part of the simulated period. Activity is a function within the system where entities remain, alone or with others, for some time causing a change in the system state. Thus, the activities can be considered as operations and/or procedures that have duration of time and require the availability of entities necessary for its development. Activity defines an active state during which one or more entities work together for a predetermined period of time. The duration of an activity is generally defined as a random variable described by a probability distribution. Specific duration of

Table 1. Percentage of articles in terms of the key elements

Key elements	Percentage		
Entities	patients 75%	nurses 12%	
Activities	admit 30%	manage 10%	
Resources	Beds 43%	Financial 10%	Surgery room 10%
Services	Emergency 45,40%	Surgery 25%	
Planning level	Regional 45%	National 41%	
Hospital Type	Acute 31%	Teaching 31%	Emergency 19%
Patient Type	Inpatient 45%	Elective 30%	Booked 16%
Performance	care 10%	capacity 10%	demand 10%
Model Type	Stochastic 20%	Discrete 20%	Decision 15%
Mathematical	Simulation 34%	Statistics 24%	Optimization 18%
Theory vs. Practice	Theoretical 86%	Practical 12%	

an activity is determined by a sampling process. By integrating research findings from across a number of different studies, this research synthesis comprehensively examines the main features on the concept of HAS addressed in all the analyzed works and making possible their characterization in accordance with the following eleven key elements.

- Entities: actors involved, namely: administrators, auxiliary personnel, doctors, nurses, patients, psychologists and technicians.
- Activities: type of actions performed, such as: admit, discharge, transfer, allocate, control, evaluate, inform, manage, monitor, plan, schedule and predict.
- Resources: like units, services, rooms, wards, beds, financial, surgery room and equipment.
- Services: such as ambulatory, emergency, surgery, intensive care, pharmacy, blood bank, radiology, tomography, laundry and X-ray.
- Planning level: political and/or geographic scope: tactical or strategic, municipal, national, regional.
- Type of Hospital: public, private, general, acute, emergency, outpatient and teaching.
- Type of Patient: booked, emergency, elective, inpatient and outpatient.
- Performance measures: accessibility, quality of care, efficiency, satisfaction, capacity, demand, work load, length of stay, utilization rate and waiting time, among others.
- Type of model: for example, stochastic, deterministic, decision, continuous, and discrete.

- OR methodology applied: for instance, Simulation, Mathematical Programming, Optimization, Queuing Theory, Stochastic Process, Statistics, and Visualization.
- Theory versus practice: Comments on theoretical and/or practical implementation of the results.

The number of references over the period in study is quite large and it had to be delimited, so that the quantity and diversity of data did not prevent to achieve one's purposes. A set of 139 publications was considered; more than 84% of the sample are articles published in scientific journals, being the PhD thesis slightly more than 9%.

All the analyzed works were gathered in a database and cataloged in accordance with the eleven attributes previously listed and described. It is interesting and important to be aware of which are the key elements and correspondent classes more referenced in the literature. Table 1 contains information concerning the most references classes for each key element. In this table, one can see that the most cited *entities* are *patients* and *nurses* (as for example in the works of [13, 15, 49, 52]), while *admission* and *management* are the two most frequent *activities* (in particular [13, 15, 28, 52]); *beds, financial* and *surgery room* are most referenced *resources* (like in [15, 37, 49, 52]), while *emergency* and *surgery* are the most used *services* (for instance in [13]). Most of the *planning decisions* are either *regional* or *national* (as illustrated in [49]), while *acute, emergency* and *teaching* hospitals are the most frequent *types of hospital* (as in [28, 39, 60]). The most mentioned *performance measures* are *care, capacity* and *demand* (as the case of [13, 15, 52]) being *stochastic, discrete* and *decision* the most used *models* in the reviewed literature (like in [19]).

Additionally, one observe that, for every ten analyzed articles, it can be found approximately thirty-five references on *performance measures*, twenty on *activities*, nine on *entities*, eight on *resources* and *services*, six on *mathematical technics*, four on the *type of patients*, three on the *type of models* and on its *possible applicability* and one on *planning level* and *hospital type*.

5   Conclusions

From this work, we can conclude that the application of OR methods to HAS has been a subject of study for many years. The first published works attempting to apply such methods to the admission problem stem from the development of the Health Services both in Britain and the United States, when a series of problems relating demand and utilization of hospital facilities were defined. The original approaches to these problems arose from analogies with similar processes occurring in industry and related areas. At first, progress was made towards a better understanding of the nature of the system, more so in identifying the best decisions. Whenever OR made a contribution it was to reveal to the hospital administration and planners the predominantly stochastic and variable nature of the admission problem.

It appears that the most suitable variable for developing the first OR models of the admission system, has been the hospital census upon which the models are based. The organization of inpatient facilities, however, is complex; it varies from hospital to hospital and involves a series of factors and additional variables, which means that the admission problems of particular hospital should often have features of their own. Thus, although approaches have many theoretical grounds in common, they often vary since the particular circumstances of the hospital studied differ.

Most studies focus on, at least, one of three main features of the census upon which the admission policies rest, i.e. variability, prediction and census control. The stochastic models have been used mostly to study census variability and prediction. The optimization models have been used chiefly for designing admission policies and to exercise control over the census. Complex problems which may not be treated analytically have been studied experimentally through the use of simulation.

It can also be concluded that one of the biggest concerns stated in the literature is related to the performance measures and is similarly distributed mainly by the quality of care, capacity and demand. It can be perceived that activities also assume a prominent role in the literature, with the admission of patients being addressed in almost a third of all the studies, followed by management. Entities take the third place, representing approximately 10% of the total number of articles, with patients being the focus of three quarters of these manuscripts.

Because of the limited scope of the studies during the period in analysis and the complexity of the hospital environment it is noticeable that, while many models have been proposed, they appear to have had little success in their practical implementation. The authors also observe that they continue to study this issue.

Acknowledgments. The research was partially financed by the Portuguese Funds through FCT (Fundação para a Ciência e a Tecnologia), within the Projects UIDB/00013/2020 and UIDP/00013/2020.

References

1. Bailey, N.T.J.: Queuing for medical care. Appl. Stat. **3**, 137–145 (1954)
2. Bailey, N.T.J.: Statistics in hospital planning and design. Appl. Stat. **5**, 146 (1956)
3. Balintfy, J.L.: A stochastic model for the analysis and prediction of admission and discharges in hospitals. Manag. Sci.: Models Tech. **2**, 288–299 (1960)
4. Balintfy, J.L.: Mathematical models and analysis of certain stochastic processes in general hospitals. Doctoral dissertation. The Johns Hopkins University (1962)
5. Balintfy, J.L.: A hospital census-predictor model. In: Smalley and Freeman. Hospital Industry Engineering, pp. 312–316. Reinhold Publishing Corp, New York (1966)
6. Barber, R.W.: Optimal control of the hospital inpatient census. Doctoral dissertation. Department of Environmental Engineering. Harvard University (1975)
7. Barnoon, S., Wolfe, H.: Scheduling a multiple Operating room system: a simulation approach. Health Serv. Res. **3**, 272–285 (1968)
8. Bithell, J.F.: The rationalization and control of hospital admission systems. D.Phil thesis. Oxford University (1969)
9. Blewett, F., et al.: Computer simulation models in a multi- specialty ward. Oper. Res. Q. **23**, 139–149 (1972)
10. Boldy, D.: A review of the application of mathematical programming to tactical and strategic health and social service problems. Oper. Res. Q. **27**(2), 439–448 (1976)
11. Blumberg, M.S.: DPF concept helps predict bed needs. Mod. Hosp. **97**, 75–81 (1961)
12. Blumberg, M.S.: Hospital automation: the needs and the prospects. Hospitals **35**(15) (1961)

13. Brillman, J.C., et al.: Triage: limitations in predicting need for emergent care and hospital admission. Ann. Emerg. Med. **27**, 493–500 (1996)
14. Chaiken, J., Larson, R.: Methods for allocating urban emergency units: a survey. Manag. Sci. **19**, 110–130 (1998)
15. Chauny, F., et al.: Nursing care demand prediction based on a decomposed semi-Markov population model. Oper. Res. Lett. **2**(6), 279–284 (1984)
16. Connor, R.J.: A hospital inpatient classification system. Doctoral dissertation. The Johns Hopkins University (1960)
17. Connors, M.M.: A stochastic elective admissions scheduling algorithm. IBM DP Center, pp. 320–334 (1968)
18. De Oliveira, M.J.F.: A bibliographic review in the admission scheduling problem. Health Services Operation Research Unit. Strathclyde University (1978)
19. De Oliveira, M.J.F.: The use of information in planning hospital admission with special reference to Glasgow Western Infirmary 1977–79. Doctoral dissertation. Strathclyde University (1982)
20. De Oliveira, M.J.F.: 3D visual simulation platform for the project of a new hospital facility. In: de Angelis, V., Ricciardi, N., Storchi, G. (eds.) Monitoring, Evaluating, Planning Health Services, pp. 39–52. World Scientific Publishing Co., Pte., Ltd., Singapore (1999)
21. De Oliveira, M.J.F.: A patient-oriented modeling of emergency admission system of a Brasilian hospital. EURO XIII, Glasgow, pp. 19–22 (1994)
22. De Silva, F.N., Pidd, M., Eglese, R.W.: A simulation model for emergency evacuation. Eur. J. Oper. Res. **90**(3), 413–419 (1996)
23. Fetter, R.B., Thompson, J.D.: A decision model for the design and operations of a progressive patient care hospital. Med. Care **7**, 450–462 (1969)
24. Finarelli, H.: An algorithm for scheduling the hospital admissions of elective surgical patients. Doctoral dissertation. College of Engineering. University of Pensilvania (1971)
25. Flagle, C.D.: The problem of organization for hospital inpatient care. Manag. Sci.: Models Tech. **2**, 275–287 (1960)
26. Flagle, C.D.: Letter to the editor—conference on operational research in the health services of Great Britain. Oper. Res. **9**(3), 417–418 (1961). https://doi.org/10.1287/opre.9.3.417
27. Fries, B.E.: Bibliography of operational research in health care systems. Oper. Res. Int. J. **24**, 801–814 (1976)
28. Gemmel, P., Dierdonck, R.: Admission scheduling in acute care hospitals: does the practice fit with the theory? Int. J. Oper. Prod. Manag. **19**(9), 863–878 (1999)
29. Goldman, J., Knappenberger, H.A., Moore, E.W.: Evaluation of operating room scheduling policies. Hosp. Manag. **107**, 40–51 (1969)
30. Gue, R.L.: A stochastic description of direct patient care and its relation to communication in a hospital. Doctoral dissertation. Johns Hopkins University (1964)
31. Hancock, W.M., et al.: Parameters affecting hospital occupancy and its implications for facility sizing. Health Serv. Res. **13**(3) (1978)
32. Handyside, A.J., Morris, D.: Simulation of emergency bed occupancy. Health Serv. Res. **2**, 287–298 (1967)
33. Hill-Burton Act PL 79-725. Publication of the American Hospital Association PHS-855b (1961). Area-wide planning for hospitals and related health facilities. Washington DC (1946)
34. Jack, E.P., Powers, T.L.: A review and synthesis of demand management, capacity management and performance in health-care services. Int. J. Manag. Rev. **11**(2), 149–174 (2009)
35. Jun, J.B., Jacobson, S.H., Swisher, J.R.: Applications of discrete event simulation in health care clinics: a survey. J. Oper. Res. Soc. **50**, 109–123 (1999)
36. Kolesar, P.: A Markovian model for hospital admission scheduling. Manag. Sci. **16**, B384–B396 (1970)

37. Kuzdrall, P., et al.: Simulating space requirements and scheduling policies in a hospital surgical suite. Simulation **36**(5), 163–171 (1981)
38. Lagergren, M.: What is the role and contribution of models to management and research in the health services? Eur. J. Oper. Res. **105**(2), 257–266 (1998)
39. Lane, D., Husemann, E.: System dynamics mapping of acute patient flows. J. Oper. Res. Soc. **59**, 213–224 (2008)
40. Milsun, J.H., Turban, E., Vertinsky, I.: Hospital admission systems: their evaluation and management. Manag. Sci. **19**, 646–666 (1973)
41. Murchie, M.D.: Analysis of hospital admission systems. B.Sc. dissertation. Department of Mathematics. University of Strathclyde (1976)
42. Newell, D.J.U.: Immediate admissions to hospital. Brit. J. Prev. Soc. Med. **8**, 77–80 (1954)
43. Trust, N.P.H.: Studies in the Functions and Design of Hospitals. Oxford University Press, London (1955)
44. Offensend, F.L.: A hospital admission system based on nursing work load. Manag. Sci. **19**, 131–138 (1972)
45. Resh, M.: Mathematical programming of admissions scheduling in hospitals. Ph.D. dissertation. The John Hopkins University, Baltimore (1967)
46. Rikkers, R.F.: Effect of spoke design on occupancy: a simulation model. Health Serv. Res. **5**, 233–247 (1970)
47. Robinson, G.H., Wing, P., Davies, L.E.: Computer simulation of hospital scheduling systems. Health Serv. Res. **3**, 130–141 (1968)
48. Rosenhead, J.: Emergency but no accident. J. Oper. Res. Soc. **66**(2), 1–5 (1988)
49. Ruth, R.: A mixed integer programming model for regional planning of a hospital inpatient service. Manag. Sci. **27**(5), 521–533 (1981)
50. Shonick, W.: A stochastic model for occupancy-related random variables in general-acute hospitals. J. Am. Stat. Assoc. **65**(332), 1474–1500 (1970). https://doi.org/10.1080/01621459.1970.10481178
51. Shonick, W., Jackson, J.R.: An improved stochastic model in occupancy- related random variables in general acute hospitals. Oper. Res. **21**, 952–965 (1973)
52. Shuman, L., et al.: Location of ambulatory care centers in a metropolitan area. Health Serv. Res. Summer **8**(2), 121–138 (1973)
53. Singer, S.: A stochastic model of variation of categories of patients within a hospital. Doctoral dissertation. The Johns Hopkins University (1961)
54. Smith-Daniels, V.L., Schweikhart, S.B., Smith-Daniels, D.E.: Capacity management in health care services: review and future research directions. Dec. Sci. **19**(4), 889–919 (1988). https://doi.org/10.1111/j.1540-5915.1988.tb00310.x
55. Smith, W.G., Solomon, M.B.: A simulation of hospital admission policy. Commun. ACM **9**(5), 362–365 (1966)
56. Stimson, D., Stimson, R.: Operations Research in Hospitals. Chicago Hospital and Research Trust (1972)
57. Swain, R.W., et al.: Implementation of a model for census prediction and control. Health Serv. Res. **12** (1977)
58. Thompson, J.D., Avant, D.W., Spiker, E.D.: How queuing theory works in the hospital. Mod. Hosp. **94**, 75–78 (1960)
59. Thompson, J.D., Fetter, R.B.: Economics of occupancy with varying mixes of private and other patient (1969)
60. Vogel, L.: Special feature: Issues in patient care scheduling at a large teaching hospital. J. Ambul. Care Manag. **12**(4), 61–69 (1989)
61. Welsh, J.D., Bailey, N.T.J.: Appointment systems in hospital outpatient departments. Lancet **1**, 1105 (1952)

62. Weng, M.L., Houshmand, A.A.: Health care simulation: a case study at a local clinic. In: Winter Simulation Conference, Phoenix, AZ (1999)
63. Young, J.P.: A queuing theory approach to the control of Hospital Inpatient census. Doctoral dissertation. The Johns Hopkins University (1962)
64. Zaki, A.S., Cheng, H.K., Parker, B.R.: A simulation model for the analysis and management of an emergency service system. Socio-Econ. Plann. Sci. **31**(3), 173–189 (1997)

Comparison of Hybrid Direct-Search Approaches for Beam Angle Optimization in Intensity-Modulated Proton Therapy

Humberto Rocha[1,2]([✉]) and Joana Dias[1,2]

[1] University of Coimbra, FEUC, CeBER, 3004-512 Coimbra, Portugal
{hrocha,joana}@fe.uc.pt
[2] University of Coimbra, INESC-Coimbra, 3030-290 Coimbra, Portugal

Abstract. Directional direct-search methods are derivative-free optimization methods that have been used with great success in different types of real-world problems, in particular nonconvex problems with many local minima, regardless of whether derivatives are available or not. In particular, directional direct-search approaches have proven to be a good alternative to address the Beam Angle Optimization (BAO) problem – optimal selection of beam directions – in Intensity-Modulated Proton Therapy (IMPT). BAO is a highly nonconvex optimization problem that requires long computational execution times. Efficiency at this level becomes more pressing when considering protons (instead of standard photons) given the extra degrees of freedom provided by different levels of energy and the existence of different scenarios for robust IMPT plans. Despite the good performance reported in the literature when using a reduced number of random poll directions in directional direct-search methods, for the BAO problem these probabilistic (descent direction exists with a given probability) approximations showed competitive mean results against the deterministic counterpart but presented outliers, i.e., for some runs of the randomized approximation the quality of the solutions is clearly inferior. In this study we compare two hybrid strategies that combine deterministic and probabilistic directional direct-search approaches aiming at obtaining the best out of each approach: consistent quality of results and enhanced computational times, respectively. For the head-and-neck cancer case used in the computational tests, hybrid approaches obtained enhanced computational times compared to the deterministic approach with competitive results in terms of quality of the solutions obtained. In future work, hybrid directional direct-search approaches performance needs to be assessed for a set of benchmark optimization problems.

Keywords: derivative-free optimization · directional direct-search · deterministic · probabilistic · beam angle optimization · protons

© The Author(s), under exclusive license to Springer Nature Switzerland AG 2023
O. Gervasi et al. (Eds.): ICCSA 2023 Workshops, LNCS 14105, pp. 467–478, 2023.
https://doi.org/10.1007/978-3-031-37108-0_30

1   Introduction

Directional direct-search methods are a class of algorithms that do not use derivatives (derivative-free) making use of a set of (polling) directions to evaluate the objective function on a finite number of points. These methods have been used with great success in different types of real-world problems, in particular non-convex problems with many local minima, regardless of whether derivatives are available or not. Their advantage in these types of problems comes from the fact that they do not use derivatives and thus mitigate the issue of local entrapment. However, for an $n-$dimensional optimization problem, to ensure (deterministic version) that at least one polling direction is a descent direction, at least $n + 1$ directions of a positive spanning set – a set of vectors (directions) that positively spans the search space – are required [1]. This minimum threshold on the number of function evaluations at each iteration guarantees frameworks with deterministic convergence at the cost of computational time efficiency particularly for functions that are expensive to evaluate. Alternatively, versions of directional direct-search algorithms that use a number of random directions smaller than n+1 (as small as two random polling directions) have been proposed in the literature, presenting good numerical results [6]. These frameworks with probabilistic convergence have computational time efficiency as their main feature.

Deterministic directional direct-search approaches have proven to be a good alternative to address the Beam Angle Optimization (BAO) problem – optimal selection of beam directions – in radiation therapy treatment planning [4,8–14]. The BAO problem is a difficult highly nonconvex optimization problem that is commonly formulated as an expensive multi-modal black-box optimization problem which results in lengthy computationally time procedures [8]. Efficiency at this level becomes more pressing when considering protons (instead of standard photons) given the extra degrees of freedom provided by different levels of energy and the existence of different scenarios for robust IMPT plans.

Despite the good performance reported in the literature when using a reduced number of random poll directions in directional direct-search methods [5,6], for the BAO problem these probabilistic (descent direction exists with a given probability) approximations showed competitive mean results against the deterministic counterpart but presented outliers, i.e., for some runs of the randomized approximation the quality of the solutions is clearly inferior [13]. Solutions for healthcare problems are required to be of high-quality every time, which explains why the conclusions in Rocha and Dias [13] are not fully aligned with those previously reported.

In this study we compare two hybrid strategies that combine deterministic and probabilistic directional direct-search approaches aiming at obtaining the best out of each approach: consistent quality of results and enhanced computational times, respectively. For the head-and-neck cancer case used in the computational tests, hybrid approaches obtained enhanced computational times compared to the deterministic approach with competitive results in terms of the quality of the solutions obtained.

The remaining of the paper is organized as follows. Next section presents the main features of directional direct-search methods. Section 3 describes IMPT treatment planning for a head-and-neck cancer case. Computational results are presented in Sect. 4 and conclusions are drawn in the last section.

2   Directional Direct-Search Methods

Directional direct-search methods make use of polling directions to generate, at each iteration k, trial points that are neighbors of the current iterate (best solution do far) $\mathbf{x}^k$. Trial points $\mathbf{x}^{k+1}$, also called poll points, are calculated as

$$\mathbf{x}^{k+1} = \mathbf{x}^k + \alpha_k \mathbf{d},$$

where vector $\mathbf{d}$ is a polling direction selected from a set of directions $\mathbf{D_k}$ and α_k is the step size. After the objective function $f : \mathbb{R}^n \to \mathbb{R}$ being evaluated at a finite number of poll points, the next iterate $\mathbf{x}^{k+1}$ is set to one poll point that improves (decreases in a minimization problem) f. The next iterate $\mathbf{x}^{k+1}$ will remain the same as the current iterate $\mathbf{x}^k$ when no poll point improves f and in this case the step size is decreased. This iterative procedure generates a sequence of non-increasing iterates $\{\mathbf{x}^k\}$. Set $\mathbf{D_k}$ might be updated to obtain $\mathbf{D_{k+1}}$.

Directional direct-search methods are typically organized around two steps at each iteration. In the first step, called search step, a finite number of trial points $\mathbf{S_k}$ can be tested using any (rules-free) strategy or a priori knowledge of the problem. This step can provide a more global character to the method but is optional and can be left empty ($\mathbf{S_k} = \emptyset$). The second step, called poll step, uses polling directions to move towards regions where iteratively the objective function value is improved. Algorithm 1 depicts a direct-search method.

2.1   Deterministic Directional Direct-Search

In Algorithm 1, when considering a set of directions $\mathbf{D_k}$ that corresponds to a positive spanning set, the strict rules of the poll step ensures the (deterministic) convergence of directional direct-search methods. A positive spanning set for $\mathbb{R}^n$ can be defined as a set of nonzero vectors of $\mathbb{R}^n$ whose positive combinations span $\mathbb{R}^n$. A positive basis is a positive spanning set with no proper set that positively spans $\mathbb{R}^n$. It can be shown that a positive basis for $\mathbb{R}^n$ contains at least $n + 1$ vectors (minimal positive basis) and cannot contain more than $2n$ (maximal positive basis) [1]. Let $\mathbf{D_k}$ denote an $n \times p$ matrix whose p $(\geq n + 1)$ columns form a positive spanning set. One of the main features of $\mathbf{D_k}$, for optimization purposes, is that, unless the current iterate is at a stationary point, there is always a vector $\mathbf{v} \in \mathbf{D_k}$ that is a descent direction, i.e., there is an $\alpha_k > 0$ such that $f(\mathbf{x}^k + \alpha_k \mathbf{v}) < f(\mathbf{x}^k)$. Selection of the set of poll directions, $\mathbf{D_k}$, is one of the distinguishing features of a directional direct-search algorithm. When all directions of $\mathbf{D_k}$ are explored at each iteration, polling is called complete. Polling is called opportunistic when the first poll direction leading to descent is taken. In this case, the order of the poll directions may influence the computational performance of the method [2].

Algorithm 1. Directional direct-search method
___
Initialization:

  - Set $k = 0$.
  - Choose initial point $\mathbf{x}^0 \in \mathbb{R}^n$.
  - Choose initial step size $\alpha_0 > 0$.
  - Choose minimum step size $\alpha_{min} > 0$.

While $\alpha_k \geq \alpha_{min}$ **do**

  1. Search step:
     Evaluate f at a finite number of points, $\mathbf{S_k}$.
     If $\exists\, \mathbf{x}^{k+1} \in \mathbf{S_k}$: $f(\mathbf{x}^{k+1}) < f(\mathbf{x}^k)$, select $\mathbf{x}^{k+1}$ and go to step 4.
     Otherwise, go to step 2.
  2. Poll step:
     Choose a set of poll directions, $\mathbf{D_k}$.
     If $f(\mathbf{x}^k) \leq f(\mathbf{x})$, $\forall \mathbf{x} \in \{\mathbf{x}^k + \alpha_k \mathbf{d_i} : \mathbf{d_i} \in \mathbf{D_k}\}$, $\mathbf{x}^{k+1} = \mathbf{x}^k$ and go to step 3.
     Otherwise, choose $\mathbf{x}^{k+1} = \mathbf{x}^k + \alpha_k \mathbf{d_i} : f(\mathbf{x}^{k+1}) < f(\mathbf{x}^k)$ and go to step 4.
  3. $\alpha_{k+1} = \frac{1}{2} \times \alpha_k$.
  4. $\alpha_{k+1} = \alpha_k$.
  5. $k = k + 1$.

2.2 Probabilistic Directional Direct-Search

Randomization proved to be a winning strategy for different types of algorithms, including for deterministic directional direct-search [2]. However, when a reduced number of directions ($< n + 1$) is considered to enhance competitiveness in terms of computational time, in particular for expensive functions to evaluate, the question is no longer how to randomly choose a direction from a (positive spanning) set where a descent direction exists but rather whether a descent direction is obtained often enough. Probabilistic directional direct-search methods consider polling directions randomly generated not necessarily fulfilling the positive spanning property. Deterministic directional direct-search methods were extended by assuming that the set of polling directions $\mathbf{D_k}$ includes only a descent direction with a certain probability [6]. Nevertheless, that probabilistic approach enjoys almost-sure global convergence (convergent with probability almost one) provided the polling directions $\mathbf{D_k}$ are uniformly distributed on the unit ball [6]. Furthermore, probabilistic approaches testing a reduced number (as low as two) of random poll directions at each iteration reported excellent numerical results [5,6]. However, the results reported are typically the best value obtained after a few runs or at best mean results. When looking at the results for all the runs, there may be some that are not of high-quality which is not acceptable in a healthcare context [13].

2.3   Hybrid Directional Direct-Search

Algorithm 1 can describe both deterministic and probabilistic directional direct-search approaches. The only difference is the choice, in the poll step, of the set of polling directions, $\mathbf{D_k}$, at each iteration. While the deterministic version considers $\mathbf{D_k}$ as a positive spanning set, the probabilistic version considers $\mathbf{D_k}$ as set of random directions not necessarily fulfilling the positive spanning property. The advantage of the former is that they manage to consistently obtain good results (it is a deterministic method where in two consecutive runs the same results are obtained) while the advantage of the latter is to obtain results with best efficiency in terms of computational time, in particular when the number of polling directions considered is as small as two.

One of the numerical characteristics of (deterministic) directional direct-search methods is that they typically produce most of the improvement in the objective function value in the first iterations but then take a long time to terminate with small improvements in the objective function value. Figure 1, adapted from Rocha et al. [10], illustrates this behavior considering the history of BAO procedures for four head-and-neck cancer cases. To take advantage of these characteristics, one can think of considering a hybrid method where, in the first iterations $\mathbf{D_k}$ is a positive spanning set (deterministic descent) and in the final iterations, in order to accelerate termination, a small number (two) of random polling directions is considered (probabilistic descent). This deterministic-probabilistic hybrid version has only the guarantee of convergence with probability almost one to a local minimum [6]. One could also think of an inverse hybrid version, where in the first iterations a small number (two) of random polling directions is considered (probabilistic descent) followed by iterations where $\mathbf{D_k}$ is a positive spanning set (deterministic descent). This probabilistic-deterministic hybrid version has the guarantee of convergence to a local minimum [1].

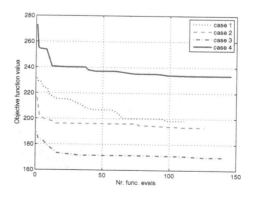

Fig. 1. Objective function value history of BAO procedures for four head-and-neck cancer cases.

3   IMPT for a Head-and-Neck Cancer Case

The different approaches are tested using a head-and-neck cancer case that is provided by matRad [16], a non-clinical radiation therapy (RT) treatment planning system written in MATLAB. Prescribed and tolerance doses for tumor volume (PTV) and organs-at-risk (OARs) considered are displayed in Table 1.

Table 1. Prescribed doses for the PTV and tolerance doses for the OARs considered.

Structure	Prescribed dose	Tolerance Dose	
		Mean	Max
PTV	70 Gy	–	–
Parotids	–	26 Gy	–
Brainstem	–	–	54 Gy
Spinal Cord	–	–	45 Gy
Skin	–	–	75 Gy

IMPT is a sophisticated RT technique, first introduced in the late 1990s by Lomax [7], where proton beams are discretized into a large number of beamlets, i.e. narrow pencil beams, with a sequence of appropriate energies. The intensities of all beamlets are jointly optimized in a large-scale optimization problem called fluence map optimization (FMO). The optimal FMO value can be obtained by matRad, for a given set of beam directions, by selecting the appropriate options as displayed in Fig. 2. A common beam angle configuration for head-and-neck corresponds to coplanar equispaced beams, typically used in clinical practice. A treatment plan with five coplanar equispaced beams, as illustrated in Fig. 2, is used as clinical benchmark.

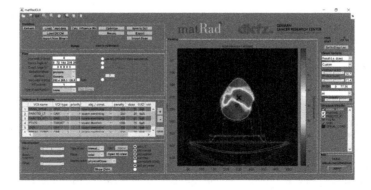

Fig. 2. IMPT for the head-and-neck case from matRad package [16].

IMPT considers a smaller number of beams than RT treatments with photons, making appropriate selection of incidence directions even more important [3]. IMPT BAO is a very difficult non-convex optimization problem, even for finding optimal sets of five beams, as is the case. Figure 3 illustrates a proton beam exiting the head of a gantry rotating around the treatment couch where the patient lies during treatment. If the couch is fixed at zero degrees, as in Fig. 3, all beams are coplanar as they lay in the plane of rotation of the gantry. When the couch rotates, noncoplanar irradiation directions are possible.

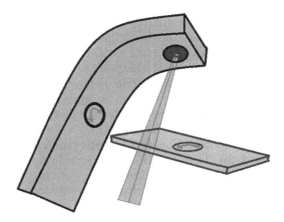

Fig. 3. Illustration of a gantry rotating around the treatment couch that can also rotate.

The IMPT BAO problem for a five-beam ensemble can be formulated as follows:

$$\min f(\theta_1, \theta_2, \theta_3, \theta_4, \theta_5, \phi_1, \phi_2, \phi_3, \phi_4, \phi_5)$$

$$\text{s.t. } (\theta_1, \theta_2, \theta_3, \theta_4, \theta_5, \phi_1, \phi_2, \phi_3, \phi_4, \phi_5) \in \mathbb{R}^{10},$$

where θ are the gantry angles, ϕ are the couch angles and f is the optimal FMO value obtained by matRad that measures the quality of the beam angle ensemble $(\theta_1, \theta_2, \theta_3, \theta_4, \theta_5, \phi_1, \phi_2, \phi_3, \phi_4, \phi_5)$. For each beam ensemble, obtaining the optimal value of the FMO problem resorting to matRad takes two to five minutes for a head-and-neck cancer case. Thus, BAO can be simply seen as the optimization of an expensive multi-modal black-box function, f.

4   Computational Results

A laptop running an Intel i7-6700 processor @ 2.60 GHz with MATLAB R2023a version was used for the computational tests. The matRad package was used to obtain the optimal FMO value for the head-and-neck case considering five-beam ensembles. Two deterministic approaches with opportunistic polling were tested considering a minimal – $n + 1$ polling directions – and a maximal – $2n$ polling directions – positive basis, $[e_1 \ldots e_n \ - e]$ and $[e_1 \ldots e_n \ - e_1 \ldots - e_n]$, respectively, where e_i is the ith column of the identity matrix in $\mathbb{R}^n$ and $e = [1 \ldots 1]^\top$. Deterministic directional direct-search approaches can be seen as a benchmark for the results obtained by other approaches as they have already proved to consistently obtain solutions of high-quality [15]. Probabilistic approaches were tested for a maximum (opportunistic approach) of $2n$, $n + 1$, $n/2$, 2 and 2 symmetric (2sim) directions at each iteration, considering $\mathbf{D_k}$ constituted by random polling directions uniformly distributed on the unit ball [6]. Two hybrid approaches were also tested and compared. The first approach considers in the first iterations $\mathbf{D_k} = [e_1 \ldots e_n \ - e_1 \ldots - e_n]$, a maximal positive basis with $2n$ polling directions, and in the final iterations two random polling directions uniformly distributed on the unit ball. This deterministic-probabilistic hybrid version is denominated **Hyb_2n_2**. The second approach considers in the first iterations two random polling directions uniformly distributed on the unit ball, and in the final iterations $\mathbf{D_k} = [e_1 \ldots e_n \ - e_1 \ldots - e_n]$, a maximal positive basis with $2n$ polling directions. This probabilistic-deterministic hybrid version is denominated **Hyb_2_2n**. The transition in these hybrid versions is performed when the step size α_k is closer to the minimum step size α_{min} than the initial step size α_0. All approaches only perform the poll step without performing search step, i.e., $S_k = \emptyset$. Results from all approaches were compared with the five-beam clinical benchmark ensemble (denominated **Benchmark**). The deterministic approaches (denominated **Det**) only need to be run once, since they will always lead to the same result. However, due to the random behavior of the probabilistic (denominated **Unif**) and hybrid approaches, these should be run more than once since different runs can lead to different results. If the values of the objective function span over a wide interval this can be seen as a serious disadvantage for the optimization algorithm since, in real practice, most of the time the algorithm will be run only once. All randomized approaches were run twenty times.

The results of all the different approaches, including the clinical benchmark, are depicted in Fig. 4. Figure 4(a) shows that all different approaches, deterministic, probabilistic, and hybrid, improve the clinical benchmark solution which is automatically a very good result. However, only **Hyb_2n_2** approach manage to obtain consistently high-quality results competitive with the best deterministic approach, **Det_2n**. Moreover, computational times of **Hyb_2n_2** approach clearly improve the computational time of **Det_2n** (see Fig. 4(b)). The remaining randomized approaches, all the probabilistic ones and the probabilistic-deterministic hybrid approach, perform worst in terms of quality of solutions, with some runs that scarcely improve the clinical benchmark. However, in terms of computational time, larger gains are observed for the probabilistic approaches, in particular when using a reduced number of polling directions. Many strategies can be devised to take advantage of this computational time gap. A naïve

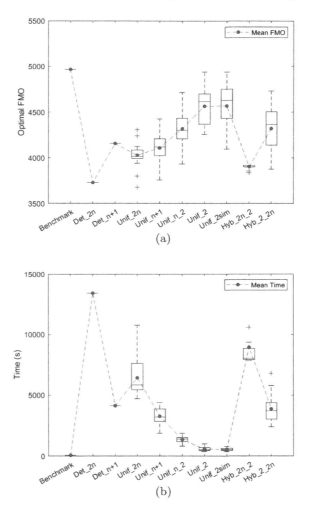

Fig. 4. Optimal FMO obtained by the different approaches – (a) and the corresponding computational times in seconds – (b).

approach would be to simply run several times the probabilistic approaches considering as starting point the best point of the last run. Figure 5 display the results when the probabilistic approaches were run ten times sequentially. While the computational time is still competitive (see Fig. 5(b)) the quality of the results improved but still fall short of the required (see Fig. 5(a)).

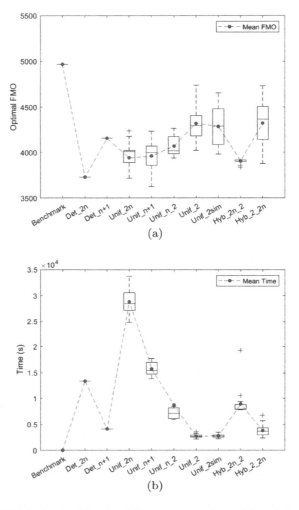

Fig. 5. Optimal FMO obtained by the different approaches – (a) and the corresponding computational times in seconds – (b).

5   Conclusions

The optimal selection of beam directions in radiation therapy is a very difficult highly nonconvex optimization problem. Deterministic directional direct-search approaches have been successfully used to address this problem. Despite the different strategies developed to accelerate these approaches, further efficiency in terms of computational time is still required for proton radiotherapy. The excellent computational performance reported by directional direct-search approaches when using a reduced number of random polling directions, showed competitive mean results for the BAO problem against the deterministic counterpart but presented outliers, i.e., for some runs of the randomized approximation the quality of the solutions is clearly inferior. In this study we compared two hybrid strategies that combine deterministic and probabilistic directional direct-search approaches aiming at obtaining the best out of each approach: consistent quality of results and enhanced computational times, respectively. The deterministic-probabilistic approach proved to be a competitive approach both in terms of consistency of quality of solutions and in terms of computational time. The main reason for the success of this approach may be related to the fact that it takes advantage of the numerical characteristics of deterministic directional direct-search methods that typically produce most of the improvement in the objective function value in the first iterations but then take a long time to terminate with small improvements in the objective function value. To see if this holds in general, or if it holds only for this problem, in future work, hybrid directional direct-search approaches performance need to be assessed for a set of benchmark optimization problems.

Acknowledgments. This work has been supported by Compete 2020 and Lisboa 2020 under project grant POCI-01-0247-FEDER-047222 and by the Fundação para a Ciência e a Tecnologia (FCT) under project grants UIDB/05037/2020 and UIDB/00308/2020.

References

1. Alberto, P., Nogueira, F., Rocha, H., Vicente, L.N.: Pattern search methods for user-provided points: application to molecular geometry problems. SIAM J. Optim. **14**, 1216–1236 (2004)
2. Audet, C., Dennis, J.E., Jr.: Mesh adaptive direct search algorithms for constrained optimization. SIAM J. Optim. **17**, 188–217 (2006)
3. Cao, W., et al.: Reflections on beam configuration optimization for intensity-modulated proton therapy. Phys. Med. Biol. **67**, 13TR01 (2022)
4. Carrasqueira, P., Rocha, H., Dias, J., Ventura, T., Ferreira, B., Lopes, M.C.: An automated treatment planning strategy for highly noncoplanar radiotherapy arc trajectories. Int. Trans. Oper. Res. **30**, 206–223 (2023)
5. Gratton, S., Vicente, L.N.: A merit function approach for direct search. SIAM J. Optim. **24**, 1980–1998 (2014)
6. Gratton, S., Royer, C.W., Vicente, L.N., Zhang, Z.: Direct search based on probabilistic descent. SIAM J. Optim. **25**, 1515–1541 (2015)
7. Lomax, A.: Intensity modulation methods for proton radiotherapy. Phys. Med. Biol. **44**, 185–205 (1999)
8. Rocha, H., Dias, J., Ferreira, B.C., Lopes, M.C.: Selection of intensity modulated radiation therapy treatment beam directions using radial basis functions within a pattern search methods framework. J. Glob. Optim. **57**, 1065–1089 (2013)
9. Rocha, H., Dias, J., Ferreira, B.C., Lopes, M.C.: Beam angle optimization for intensity-modulated radiation therapy using a guided pattern search method. Phys. Med. Biol. **58**, 2939–2953 (2013)
10. Rocha, H., Dias, J., Ferreira, B.C., Lopes, M.C.: Pattern search methods framework for beam angle optimization in radiotherapy design. Appl. Math. Comput. **219**, 10853–10865 (2013)

11. Rocha, H., Dias, J., Ferreira, B.C., Lopes, M.C.: Noncoplanar beam angle optimization in IMRT treatment planning using pattern search methods. J. Phys. Conf. Ser. **616**, 012014 (2015)

12. Rocha, H., Dias, J., Ventura, T., Ferreira, B.C., Lopes, M.C.: A derivative-free multistart framework for an automated noncoplanar beam angle optimization in IMRT. Med. Phys. **43**, 5514–5526 (2016)

13. Rocha, H., Dias, J.: A randomized direct-search approach for beam angle optimization in intensity-modulated proton therapy. In: Gervasi, O., et al. (eds.) ICCSA 2021. LNCS, vol. 12953, pp. 320–332. Springer, Cham (2021). https://doi.org/10.1007/978-3-030-86976-2_22

14. Rocha, H., Dias, J., Ventura, T., Ferreira, B.C., Lopes, M.C.: Beam angle optimization in IMRT: are we really optimizing what matters? Int. Trans. Oper. Res. **26**, 908–928 (2019)

15. Ventura, T., Rocha, H., Ferreira, B., Dias, J., Lopes, M.C.: Comparison of two beam angular optimization algorithms guided by automated multicriterial IMRT. Phys. Med. **64**, 210–221 (2019)

16. Wieser, H.-P., et al.: Development of the open-source dose calculation and optimization toolkit matRad. Med. Phys. **44**, 2556–2568 (2017)

A Hybrid Genetic Algorithm for Optimal Active Power Curtailment Considering Renewable Energy Generation

André Pedroso[1,3], Yahia Amoura[1,2], Ana I. Pereira[1],
and Ângela Ferreira[1(✉)]

[1] Research Centre in Digitalization and Intelligent Robotics (CeDRI),
Instituto Politécnico de Bragança, Bragança, Portugal
{andre.pedroso,yahia,apereira,apf}@ipb.pt
[2] University of la Laguna, Santa Cruz de Tenerife, Spain
[3] Federal University of Technology - Paraná, Curitiba, Brazil

Abstract. This paper analyzes the application of a population-based algorithm and its improvement in solving an optimal power flow problem. Simulations were performed on a 14-bus IEEE network modified to include renewable energy sources-based power plants: a wind park and two photovoltaic solar parks. In this scenario, the high penetration of intermittent energy sources in the grid makes it necessary to curtail active power during peak generation to maintain the balance between load and generation. However, European energy market regulations limit the annual curtailment of RES generators and penalize discriminatory curtailment actions between generators. This work exploits the minimization of transmission active loss while respecting its security constraints. Additionally, constraints were introduced in the optimal power flow problem to mitigate active power curtailment of the renewable source generators and to secure a non-discriminatory characteristic in curtailment decisions. The non-convex nature of the problem, intensified by the introduction of non-linear constraints, suggests the exploitation of heuristic algorithms to locate the optimal global solution. The obtained results demonstrate that a hybrid GA algorithm can improve convergence speed, and it is useful in determining the problem solution in cases where deterministic algorithms are unable to converge.

Keywords: Energy curtailment · Optimal power flow · Genetic algorithm · Interior point · Active-set

1 Introduction

The optimal settings of control variables within an electrical power network in order to minimize the operating cost of the system while ensuring its stable and reliable operation are performed through an Optimal Power Flow (OPF) [1]. The method is used to expedite accessible generation plants in a way that minimizes a

© The Author(s), under exclusive license to Springer Nature Switzerland AG 2023
O. Gervasi et al. (Eds.): ICCSA 2023 Workshops, LNCS 14105, pp. 479–494, 2023.
https://doi.org/10.1007/978-3-031-37108-0_31

specific objective function. OPF can completely represent the network conditions and nodal control balance [2]. It also keeps up limits on transport voltage, branch power flows, and generator yields. Standard OPF definitions incorporate minimizing operating costs, optimizing the allocation of resources, and minimizing network losses [3]. Other objectives have been introduced, for instance, to reduce the environmental impact of power generation [4] and maximize renewable penetration in the distribution grid [5]. The contribution of the work presented in this paper tackles the optimization of active power curtailments. The algorithms used to solve OPF issues include both numerical programming procedures and heuristic optimization.

Since it was first presented by Carpendier in 1962 [6], OPF methods have been widely studied and applied within the power systems field, especially due to their capacity to achieve economic efficiency and maintain a safe and robust power system operation. Additionally, the current deregulation of the energy market and the introduction of new technologies, such as Flexible AC Transmission Systems (FACTS), are impacting the behavior of the grid, making necessary fast and reliable methods to estimate the future state of the system and define the best operational decisions, for instance, in the day ahead OPF methods, which makes OPF even more relevant nowadays [7].

Commonly, the OPF is defined as a non-convex optimization problem, from which the optimal solution can be trapped by local minima. According to several purposes that may be used to solve an application by the standard OPF, which majority include nonlinear constraints, achieving global optimality is the main goal, which requires robust optimization algorithms [8].

To simplify the problem and achieve a globally optimal solution, some solvers implement the DC-OPF, which neglects the transmission losses, and considering the magnitudes of the voltages constant, the reactive power flow is neglected, and only the active power flow is considered. In this way, the number of variables that need to be optimized is reduced, and the problem becomes linear and can be solved by linear programming solvers [9].

The available approaches that have been applied to the purpose of optimizing the OPF consist mainly of two categories, including the deterministic and/or evolutionary algorithms [10]. Deterministic optimization algorithms consist of quadratic programming (QP), Non-Linear Programming (NLP), and the interior point (IP) method, among others. However, these methods may have trouble dealing with multiple local minima, given the non-convexity of the OPF problems. As a consequence of the limitations of deterministic methods, evolutionary approaches like the Genetic Algorithm (GA) and Particle Swarm Optimisation (PSO) are being proposed as suitable candidates for addressing the OPF problem. Genetic algorithms represent a robust approach for solving these types of optimization problems since their global search mechanisms are more consistent in converging to the global solution. Additionally, the GA does not need to assume that the search space is discrete or continuous because it evaluates multiple points in the entire parameter space simultaneously, strictly based on the objective function.

The optimization approaches proposed above have been widely used. However, in [11], an effective Mixed-Integer Genetic Algorithm (MIGA) was presented to solve non-convex OPF problems with security limitations. Concurring with the numerical studies on 26-bus and the IEEE 57-bus systems, the MIGA performs better than the single evolutionary approach based on the GA. A novel hybrid method integrating a GA with a nonlinear Interior Point Method (IPM) was used for solving the OPF problem in [12]. In the hybrid approach, GA is responsible for solving the discrete optimization with the continuous variables, and the IPM is responsible for solving the continuous optimization with the discrete variables. Numerical computations were implemented on IEEE 30-bus, IEEE 118-bus, and realistic Chongqing 161-bus test systems. In [13], the Newton-Raphson algorithm for the minimization of the mismatch of the power flow equations was integrated into the PSO algorithm. PSO was applied for the transient-stability-constrained OPF problem modeled as an extended OPF with additional rotor angle inequality constraints. A hybrid Tabu Search and Simulated Annealing (TSSA) approach was proposed in [14] to deal with OPF control with FACTS devices. The results from an IEEE 30-bus system demonstrate that the proposed hybrid TSSA approach can perform better than GA, SA, or TS alone. Differential Evolution (DE) based approach was used to solve the OPF problem with multiple and competing objectives in [15]. The OPF problem was divided into two sub-problems, including active power dispatch and reactive power dispatch.

Furthermore, the high penetration of renewable energy sources (RES) power generation in the electric grid, predominantly photovoltaic and wind power plants, is affecting the OPF problem complexity. The non-dispatchable nature of these generators is impacting the grid generation profile, causing network congestion and jeopardizing grid stability and operation planning [16].

In moments of high energy production and low consumption, operators may have to curtail part of the generation in order to achieve the energy balance or even to maintain grid stability. To avoid large values of RES curtailment, which can be considered energy waste and may discourage new investors in the renewable energy field, European market regulation specified that the maximum annual RES energy curtailment should not exceed 5% of the generator's annual maximum production and it is determined that curtailment must be non-discriminatory between the generators [21].

Many approaches were proposed to mitigate the occurrence of these events, especially in countries that encouraged the high implementation of RES generation, for instance, deploying demand response programs to incentivize consumers to reduce their energy usage during periods of high demand or resort storage systems. One of the most efficient approaches is the use of pumped hydro energy storage when there is an excess of RES-based electricity. In this way, the water is stored in an upper reservoir until load peak hours, at which point the potential energy of water is converted into electrical energy. However, given the necessary infrastructure, pumped hydro storage can have a considerable environmental impact and be expensive. Hence, well-planned energy curtailment can avoid unnecessary system expansion, which is usually an expensive and long-term project [20].

The non-discriminatory curtailment behavior among the generators is addressed in this work by introducing a new nonlinear constraint into the OPF problem. The results indicate that this constraint increases the complexity of the problem, and a deterministic algorithm becomes less efficient and has problems converging to a solution when the additional constraint is active. By applying a GA hybrid algorithm, the speed of response and the convergence rate of the algorithm are improved.

This section introduced the state of the art regarding the OPF problem and defined the contribution of the work developed in this paper. Section 2 details the OPF problem formulation: first, the standard formulation is defined, followed by the modified version, which includes the additional constraint. Section 3 shows the case study built to test the paper's proposition. Section 4 presents the optimization approaches used in the work. Section 5 presents and discusses the achieved results. Finally, Sect. 6 concludes the study and proposes a guideline for future works.

2   Optimal Power Flow

The Optimal Power Flow (OPF) topic is an extension of the Power Flow (PF) circumstance, where system variables, including bus parameters, are used to assess the conditions of an electric grid. To build an optimal power flow system, the context is formulated as a minimization optimization problem in which the constraints are subject to equality and inequality restrictions that make the problem more complex to solve by applying conventional power flow solutions. The constraints characterize the bus parameters such as voltage, magnitude, and active and reactive power. The optimization process aims to minimize power system-related issues, including total network losses, voltage deviation, and generation cost, among others. This study aims to minimize network losses. The computational optimization problem and the corresponding constraints are defined hereinafter.

2.1   Standard OPF

The standard optimal power flow can be formulated as a uni-objective optimization problem with a minimization purpose, as follows:

$$\min \quad f(x) \tag{1}$$
$$s.t \quad g(x) = 0 \tag{2}$$
$$h(x) \leq 0 \tag{3}$$

where $f(x)$, $g(x)$, and $h(x)$ represent the objective function that must be minimized, equality constraints, and inequalities constraints, respectively. Vector x

is defined by the standard power flow problem's variables, i.e., bus voltage magnitudes and phases, active and reactive injected power in the slack bus, and the latter also for the PV bus.

Equality Constraints. As mentioned, the nonlinear equality constraints are the cause of the complexity of solving the OPF problem. Its standard formulation is represented as:

$$P_i = \sum_{k=1}^{N} |V_i||V_k||Y_{ik}|cos(\theta_i - \theta_k - \delta_{ik}) \tag{4}$$

$$Q_i = \sum_{k=1}^{N} |V_i||V_k||Y_{ik}|sin(\theta_i - \theta_k - \delta_{ik}) \tag{5}$$

where P_i and Q_i are the results in active and reactive power injected at the bus i, $|V_i|$, $|V_k|$, θ_i and θ_k, are the voltage magnitude at buses i and k and their angles, $|Y_{ik}|$ and δ_{ik} are the admittance's magnitude and angle of the branch ik and N is the number of generation buses [9].

These equations are known as the polar form of alternating current power flow (AC-PF) equations. In some cases, they are represented by their algebraic version or DC form. The latter has the great benefit of being linear and, therefore, can easily converge to the optimal solution of the problem because it makes the optimization system convex. However, this method may not fully represent the power system dynamics since it is a simplification of the AC version and cannot address the problem of minimizing network losses.

Inequalities Constraints. The capacity to formulate and solve a problem considering its limitations is one of the great advantages of using optimization. In the OPF problem, these limits are embedded in the inequalities constraints. These limits represent the security operating values that the variables can achieve without damaging the grid or undermining its stability. OPF standard inequalities constraints are:

$$\theta_{min} \leq \theta_i \leq \theta_{max} \tag{6}$$
$$V_{min} \leq V_i \leq V_{max} \tag{7}$$
$$P_{min} \leq P_i \leq P_{max} \tag{8}$$
$$Q_{min} \leq Q_i \leq Q_{max} \tag{9}$$
$$S_{min} \leq S_{ik} \leq S_{max} \tag{10}$$

where S_{ik} represents the apparent power flow through the line between the bars i and k, computed as $|V_i Y_{ii}|e^{j(-\delta_{ii})} + |V_i V_k Y_{ik}|e^{j(\theta_i + \theta_k - \delta_{ik})}$, in which $j = \sqrt{-1}$.

2.2 Active Power Curtailment

To evaluate active power curtailment, different procedures have already been used in the literature. In [18], the operation problem of mitigating active power curtailment was managed by forecasting the curtailment and defining the buses with a higher impact in this aspect within the system. Regarding the discriminatory nature of curtailment, the work performed in [17] added penalizing terms to generators with high energy curtailment, and authors in [19] used power distribution factors in the OPF problem. In both methods, DC-OPF was employed, which ensures a solution to the problem.

In this paper, the renewable energy curtailment is represented by the value of energy that is not being used concerning the maximum energy available for dispatch in the generator at the moment. This is formulated as:

$$C_s = \frac{P_s^{max} - P_s}{P_s^{max}} \tag{11}$$

in which P_s is the vector containing the generation power of the RES plants, P_s^{max} the maximum available power at the generator, being s the bus number in which the renewable energy generation parks are located. Since the European regulation limits the curtailment to 5% of the annual production of the generator, the following inequality is added to the OPF problem:

$$C_s \leq 0.05 \tag{12}$$

The active power curtailment discrimination can be formulated by the standard deviation of the total energy curtailed at each RES generator:

$$D = \sqrt{\frac{\sum_{i \in s}(E_i - M_c)^2}{N_s}} \tag{13}$$

where E_i is the total energy curtailed from generator i, computed as:

$$E_i = \frac{\sum_{k=0}^{T}(P_s^{max}(k) - P_s(k))}{\sum_{k=0}^{T} P_s^{max}(k)} \tag{14}$$

M_c is the mean value of the vector E_s, N_s is the number of RES generators connected to the grid, and T is the number of time steps for which the OPF problem was evaluated.

3   Case Study

The electric grid used to test the proposed algorithms is the IEEE 14-bus example grid, illustrated in Fig. 1. The grid is an approximation of the American electric power system as of February 1962 [22]. IEEE 14-bus contains 5 generator buses and 11 load buses. In order to include RES generation in the model, three generators, represented in the figure as Gen 3, Gen 6, and Gen 8, were replaced by non-dispatchable energy sources. Gen 3 is a 100 MW wind park, and the latter are solar parks with capacities of 70 MW and 100 MW, respectively.

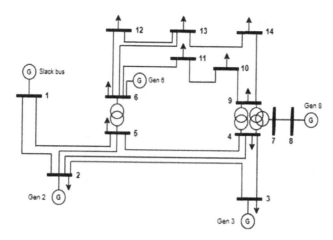

Fig. 1. IEEE 14-bus grid model representation.

3.1 Load and Generation Profiles

In order to simulate the curtailment over a whole year, four case scenarios, representing typical day conditions of a season, were designed to model the load and generation at different moments of the year.

The load at each bus was defined by using a dataset of real residential and industrial site load profiles [23]. The values of the data set were scaled to fit the original 14-bus model's load magnitude.

Solar and wind power generation is predominantly dependent on weather conditions; therefore, to estimate these values, it was used 20-year weather data from the city of Bragança in Portugal, available in [24]. The data set includes wind speed, solar irradiance, and temperature, which are the most influential variables in terms of forecasting or estimating solar and wind power generation.

An hourly data vector for one year was created by calculating the average value of the variables in the dataset. Four case scenarios were selected from this vector to represent a typical day for a specific period of the year. The year is divided as follows:

1. November, December and January;
2. February, March and April;
3. May, June and July;
4. August, September and October.

After defining the benchmark cases, the power at each RES generator was calculated by the mathematical model of the wind and solar park generation. The power supplied by the solar parks is computed as follows:

$$P_{pv}(G) = \eta \cdot S \cdot G \tag{15}$$

where P_{pv} is the individual cell dispatched power, η is the efficiency coefficient of each cell, S is the surface of the photovoltaic module and G the irradiation value at that moment.

The wind park's hourly power production can be represented as follows:

$$\begin{cases} P_{wd} = 0, & v \leq v_d \text{ or } v \geq v_c \\ P_{wd}(v) = P_n(\dfrac{v - v_d}{v_n - v_d}), & v_d \leq v \leq v_n \\ P_{wd} = P_n, & v_n \leq v \leq v_c \end{cases} \tag{16}$$

in which P_{wt} is the power delivered by the turbine, v_d the cut-in velocity, v_c the cut-out velocity, v_n the rated velocity and P_n the turbine rated power [25].

In order to scale the production with acceptable values by the system operation,

$$P_{pv}^{park} = N_{cell} P_{pv} \tag{17}$$

$$P_{wd}^{park} = N_{turbine} P_{wd} \tag{18}$$

where P_{pv}^{park} and P_{wd}^{park} are the solar and wind park power generation and N_{cell} and $N_{turbine}$ are the number of PV modules and the number of wind turbines, respectively.

To demonstrate that the curtailment is present in the designed cases, the total load and RES generation of the first case scenario is displayed in Fig. 2. The excess generation between 9:00 and 15:00 will activate the constraints related to active curtailment, represented in Eqs. (12) and (13).

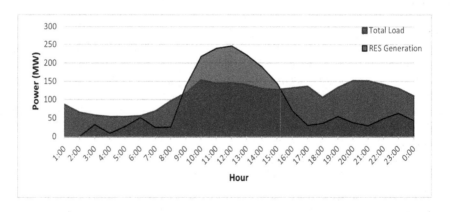

Fig. 2. First case scenario total load and generation values through the day.

3.2 Objective Function

The objective function is specified in (1) by the function $f(x)$, which will guide the algorithm's decisions. As mentioned, the main objective of the OPF problem defined in this paper is to minimize network active losses while considering standard constraints and the limits on active power curtailment. This objective function is well-suited to the case scenario since the limitation on active curtailment is detrimental to grid efficiency. Therefore, the system should operate as close as possible to the constraint limits in order to mitigate active losses. Since no flexible load is connected to the grid, the total active losses are equal to the sum of the active injected power at all buses [26]. In this case, the objective function can be defined as,

$$f(x) = \sum_{i=1}^{N} P_i \tag{19}$$

The limit values for the inequality constraints applied to the OPF problem are defined in Table 1, considering that the base value of apparent power in the case study is equal to 100 MVA.

Table 1. Values of OPF inequality constraints.

Variables	Lower bounds	Upper bounds
V_i (p.u)	0.95	1.05
θ_i (°)	-60	60
S_{ik} (p.u)	–	1.0
P_2 (p.u)	0.4	0.4
Q_2 (p.u)	-0.4	0.5
P_s (p.u)	0	P_s^{max}
D	–	0.01

4   Optimization Approaches

Three optimization approaches have been used to optimize the active power curtailment, two of them using deterministic algorithms and the third one exploiting a hybrid optimization procedure.

4.1   Deterministic Optimization Method Based on Interior Point Algorithm

The interior point method (IPM) is used to find the optimal solution to an optimization problem by moving from one point on the objective function to another point in the interior of the feasible region. The application of the IPM is employed to obtain the solution to the nonlinear optimal power flow (OPF) problem [27]. These types of methods combine simplicity in the treatment of inequality constraints with efficient computational performance. These characteristics have been the subject of extensive theoretical research. Several strategies were proposed for an OPF with active power dispatching and voltage security using an IPM that proved to be robust, especially in large networks, as the number of iterations increased slightly with the number of constraints and network size [28]. The latter greatly reduces the number of iterations necessary to obtain the optimal solution. Both methods that were described are implemented in the IPM problem. Nonlinear IPM techniques are applied to the solution of diverse OPF market problems [29]. The OPF-based approach is basically a non-linear constrained optimization problem and consists of a scalar objective function and a set of equality and inequality constraints.

4.2   Deterministic Optimization Method Based on Active Set Algorithm

The active-set method is an algorithm used to identify the active constraints in a set of inequality constraints. The active constraints are then expressed as equality constraints, thereby transforming an inequality-constrained problem into a simpler equality-constrained sub-problem [31].

4.3   Hybrid Optimization Based on Genetic Algorithm and Active Set

Genetic algorithms (GA) belong to the class evolutionary algorithms. Genetic algorithms are efficient stochastic-based search algorithms based on the principles of natural selection and natural genetics. This method is based on a population of potential solutions. The mode of operation is based on the biological principles of natural selection, which coordinate the survival of the samples that are best adapted to their environment [34]. The GA starts with a set of solutions randomly initialized in space. The individuals here are represented by their design variables, named chromosomes. The chromosomes of the initial population are used to produce a new population, going through the different genetic operators, mainly crossover, mutation, and selection. This is motivated by the expectation of creating a new population better than the previous one [35]. In this work, the initial chromosomes are associated with each active power injected (P_i) by the generators in the system. A starting population is generated with the vector of (P_i) and these chromosomes constitute the basis of the research space (starting population). In the reproduction process, the chromosomes representing the possible combinations of P_i solutions are assessed based on the objective function. The best chromosomes will have the highest probability of being the parental candidate for optimization problem solutions. These successful chromosomes (sets of P_i) are then taken forward to the crossover process. Then the new set of chromosomes (the best sets of P_i until this stage) is subjected to the mutation process by enabling new genetic characteristics on the chromosome, preventing the premature stopping of the algorithm in a local solution [32,33].

The optimization approach is explained in Fig. 3.

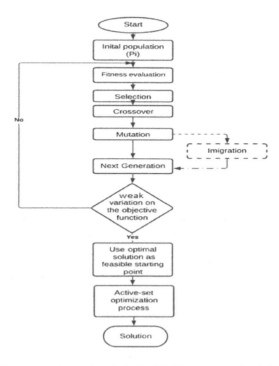

Fig. 3. OPF optimization using hybrid GA/Active-set algorithm flowchart.

5   Results and Discussion

The algorithms' performances were evaluated by their CPU time and capacity to converge to a feasible solution when running the OPF problem for the four scenarios that were previously presented. Since each scenario represents a period of the year, they were computed sequentially from 1 to 4. Thus the curtailed value is updated into the constraint represented by Eq. (13). As the OPF problem was analyzed for each hour of the exemplary days, in each case the algorithms were evaluated 24 times.

In an initial analysis, the algorithms have been exploited by considering only the standard OPF problem constraints and the curtailment linear constraint, formulated in (12). In order to verify the time of convergence, the four case scenarios were evaluated individually, and the total time was recorded, as shown in Table 2.

Table 2. CPU time to converge to the OPF feasible solution.

Case	Active-set (s)	Interior Point (s)	Hybrid GA (s)
1	22.36	31.25	18.96
2	15.88	35.23	17.39
3	23.91	31.50	21.71
4	15.90	31.96	17.86
Total	78.05	129.94	75.92

From the obtained results, the hybrid GA algorithm was faster than the deterministic approaches in general. Regarding the objective function, both deterministic and heuristic approaches were able to converge on the optimal solution.

In a second analysis, characterized by adding the constraint related to non-discriminatory curtailment, as formulated in (13), the hybrid GA was the only algorithm able to achieve the optimal solution in all cases. Both the active-set and interior-point algorithms were unable to converge for an optimal feasible solution in some computations, which prevented the algorithm from determining the optimal set points required by the optimization process. To reach the final decision on power curtailment, all submitted parameters must complete the optimization process for the whole simulation day, which was not accomplished by the optimization process in cases 3 and 4. The results are shown in Table 3.

Table 3. Feasible solution convergence.

Case	Active-set	Interior Point	Hybrid GA
1	Converge	Not converge	Converge
2	Not converge	–	Converge
3	–	–	Converge
4	–	–	Converge

To verify whether the operating conditions required by curtailment regulation were satisfied, the annual RES active power curtailment was calculated by combining the results found in each case scenario. The results are presented in Table 4.

Table 4. Values of OPF inequality constraints.

RES annual maximum energy (MWh)	758452
Annual total load (MWh)	785182
Annual energy losses (MWh)	12157 (1.55%)
DG energy curtailment (MWh)	
G_3	$2.5600 \cdot 10^4$ (4.40%)
G_6	$4.0787 \cdot 10^3$ (4.80%)
G_8	$4.3888 \cdot 10^3$ (4.77%)
Annual total DG curtailment (MWh)	34068 (4.49%)

The results show that the mean curtailment within the renewable source generators was 4,66% of their annual generated power, with a standard deviation of 0.22%; therefore, the constraints added to the problem were satisfied, and the operational requirements were fulfilled. Furthermore, the curtailment values were near their boundaries, which means that the active losses were reduced as much as possible.

6   Conclusion and Future Work

This paper presents an analysis of the application of a GA algorithm to solve the optimal power flow problem in a modified IEEE 14-bus example grid with a high penetration of renewable energy sources. The OPF optimization function seeks to reduce electric grid transmission losses while abiding by the EU energy market regulations' restrictions on the active power curtailment of renewable source generators and its security constraints. To achieve this, non-linear constraints were introduced in the optimal power flow problem, making it necessary to introduce heuristic algorithms to locate the global optimal solution and improve the optimization convergence rate.

Simulation results showed that a hybrid GA algorithm can improve convergence speed and are effective in determining the optimal solution in cases where deterministic algorithms are unable to converge. Therefore, when compared to methods using conventional deterministic algorithms, this approach is effective for solving OPF problems with additional features that increase operational complexity. In future work, the authors intend to extend this research by investigating the effects of other heuristic approaches, such as the Particle Swarm Optimization (PSO) algorithm.

Acknowledgments. The authors are grateful to the Foundation for Science and Technology (FCT, Portugal) for financial support through national funds FCT/MCTES (PIDDAC) to CeDRI (UIDB/05757/2020 and UIDP/05757/2020), SusTEC (LA/P/0007/2021). This work has been supported by NORTE-01-0247-FEDER-072615 EPO - Enline Power Optimization - The supra-grid optimization software.

References

1. Xiong, K., Cao, D., Zhang, G., Chen, Z., Hu, W.: Coordinated volt/VAR control for photovoltaic inverters: a soft actor-critic enhanced droop control approach. Int. J. Electr. Power Energy Syst. **149**, 109019 (2023). https://doi.org/10.1016/j.ijepes.2023.109019
2. Jiao, W., Wu, Q., Huang, S., Chen, J., Li, C., Zhou, B.: DMPC based distributed voltage control for unbalanced distribution networks with single-/three-phase DGs. Int. J. Electr. Power Energy Syst. **150**, 109068 (2023). https://doi.org/10.1016/j.ijepes.2023.109068
3. Grisales-Noreña, L.F., Rosales-Muñoz, A.A., Cortés-Caicedo, B., Montoya, O.D., Andrade, F.: Optimal operation of PV sources in DC grids for improving technical, economical, and environmental conditions by using Vortex Search algorithm and a matrix hourly power flow. Mathematics **11**(1), 93 (2022). https://doi.org/10.3390/math11010093
4. Reddy, S.S., Momoh, J.A.: Minimum emissions optimal power flow in wind-thermal power system using opposition based bacterial dynamics algorithm. In: 2016 IEEE Power and Energy Society General Meeting (PESGM), pp. 1–5, Boston, MA, USA (2016). https://doi.org/10.1109/PESGM.2016.7741635
5. Bhumkittipich, K., Phuangpornpitak, W.: Optimal placement and sizing of distributed generation for power loss reduction using particle swarm optimization. Energy Proc. **34**, 307–317 (2013). https://doi.org/10.1016/j.egypro.2013.06.759
6. Carpentier, J.: Optimal power flows. Int. J. Electr. Power Energy Syst. **1**(1), 3–15 (1979). https://doi.org/10.1016/0142-0615(79)90026-7
7. Tong, X., Zhang, Y., Wu, F.F.: A decoupled semismooth newton method for optimal power flow. In: 2006 IEEE Power Engineering Society General Meeting, pp. 6–pp. Montreal, QC, Canada (2006). https://doi.org/10.1109/PES.2006.1709065
8. Ilyas, M., Alquthami, T., Awais, M., Milyani, A., Rasheed, M.: (DA-DOPF): a day ahead dynamic optimal power flow with renewable energy integration in smart grid. Front. Energy Res. **9**, 696837 (2021). https://doi.org/10.3389/fenrg.2021.696837
9. Frank, S., Steponavice, I., Rebennack, S.: Optimal power flow: a bibliographic survey I. Energy Syst **3**, 221–258 (2012). https://doi.org/10.1007/s12667-012-0056-y
10. Papazoglou, G., Biskas, P.: Review and comparison of genetic algorithm and particle swarm optimization in the optimal power flow problem. Energies **16**(3), 1152 (2023). https://doi.org/10.3390/en16031152
11. Gaing, Z.-L., Chang, R.-F: Security-constrained optimal power flow by mixed-integer genetic algorithm with arithmetic operators. In: 2006 IEEE Power Engineering Society General Meeting, pp. 8–pp. Montreal, QC, Canada (2006) https://doi.org/10.1109/PES.2006.1709334
12. Yan, W., Liu, F., Chung, C.Y., Wong, K.P.: A hybrid genetic algorithm-interior point method for optimal reactive power flow. IEEE Trans. Power Syst. **21**(3), 1163–1169 (2006). https://doi.org/10.1109/TPWRS.2006.879262
13. Mo, N., Zou, Z.Y., Chan, K.W., Pong, T.Y.G.: Transient stability constrained optimal power flow using particle swarm optimisation. IET Gener. Trans. Distrib. **1**(3), 476–483 (2007)
14. Ongsakul, W., Bhasaputra, P.: Optimal power flow with FACTS devices by hybrid TS/SA approach. Int. J. Electr. Power Energy Syst. **24**(10), 851–857 (2002). https://doi.org/10.1016/S0142-0615(02)00006-6

15. Varadarajan, M., Swarup, K.S.: Solving multi-objective optimal power flow using differential evolution. IET Gener. Trans. Distrib.. **2**(5), 720 (2008). https://doi.org/10.1049/iet-gtd:20070457

16. Sinha, P., Paul, K., Deb, S., Sachan, S.: Comprehensive review based on the impact of integrating electric vehicle and renewable energy sources to the grid. Energies **16**(6), 2924 (2023). https://doi.org/10.3390/en16062924

17. Meier, F., Töbermann, C., Braun, M.: Retrospective optimal power flow for low discriminating active power curtailment. In: 2019 IEEE Milan PowerTech, pp. 1–6, Milan, Italy (2019). https://doi.org/10.1109/PTC.2019.8810818

18. Masaud, T.M., Patil, S., Hagan, K., Sen, P.K.: Probabilistic quantification of wind power curtailment based on intra-seasonal wind forecasting approach. In: IEEE Power & Energy Society General Meeting, pp. 1–5, Chicago, IL, USA (2017). https://doi.org/10.1109/PESGM.2017.8274195

19. Wiest, P., Rudion, K., Probst, A.: Optimization of power feed-in curtailment from RES and its consideration within grid planning. In: IEEE Manchester PowerTech, pp. 1–6, Manchester, UK (2017). https://doi.org/10.1109/PTC.2017.7980801

20. Bird, L., et al.: Wind and solar energy curtailment: a review of international experience. Renew. Sustain. Energy Rev. **65**, 577–86 (2016). https://doi.org/10.1016/j.rser.2016.06.082

21. European Commission, "Regulation (EU) 2019/943 of the European Parliament and of the Council of 5 June 2019 on the internal market for electricity(02019R0943 - EN - 23.06.2022)", ed: Official Journal of the European Union, p. 86

22. Illinois Center for a Smarter Electric Grid. http://publish.illinois.edu/smartergrid/. Accessed 30 Mar 2023

23. Angizeh, F., Ghofrani, A., Jafari, A.: Dataset on hourly load profiles for a set of 24 facilities from industrial, commercial, and residential end-use sectors. Mendeley Data **1**, (2020). https://doi.org/10.17632/rfnp2d3kjp.1

24. Open-Meteo. Free Weather API. https://open-meteo.com/. Accessed 28 Oct 2022

25. Yang, H., Lu, L., Zhou, W.: A novel optimization sizing model for hybrid solar-wind power generation system. Sol. Energy **81**(1), 76–84 (2007). https://doi.org/10.1016/j.solener.2006.06.010

26. Bouchekara, H.R.E.H.: Optimal power flow using black-hole-based optimization approach. Appl. Soft Comput. **24**, 879–888 (2014). https://doi.org/10.1016/j.asoc.2014.08.056

27. Torres, G.L., Quintana, V.H.: An interior-point method for nonlinear optimal power flow using voltage rectangular coordinates. IEEE Trans. Power Syst. **13**(4), 1211–1218 (1998)

28. Abido, M.A.: Environmental/economic power dispatch using multi-objective evolutionary algorithms. IEEE Trans. Power Syst. **18**(4), 1529–1537 (2003). https://doi.org/10.1109/TPWRS.2003.818693

29. de Sousa, V.A., Baptista, E.C., da Costa, G.R.M.: Optimal reactive power flow via the modified barrier Lagrangian function approach. Electr. Power Syst. Res. **84**(1), 159–164 (2012). https://doi.org/10.1016/j.epsr.2011.11.001

30. Renewable Energy Production in Portugal on 2023. APREN. (n.d.). https://www.apren.pt/en/renewable-energies/production. Accessed 3 May 2023

31. Na, S., Anitescu, M., Kolar, M.: Inequality constrained stochastic nonlinear optimization via active-set sequential quadratic programming. Math. Prog. (2023). https://doi.org/10.1007/s10107-023-01935-7

32. Hajela, P.: Genetic search - an approach to the nonconvex optimization problem. AIAA J. **28**(7), 1205–1210 (1990). https://doi.org/10.2514/3.25195

33. Alan, H.: Genetic algorithm and programming. In: An Introduction to Computational Physics, pp. 323–346 (2006). https://doi.org/10.1017/cbo9780511800870. 013

34. Amoura, Y., Pereira, A.I., Lima, J.: Optimization methods for energy management in a microgrid system considering wind uncertainty data. In: Kumar, S., Purohit, S.D., Hiranwal, S., Prasad, M. (eds.) Proceedings of International Conference on Communication and Computational Technologies. AIS, pp. 117–141. Springer, Singapore (2021). https://doi.org/10.1007/978-981-16-3246-4_10

35. Amoura, Y., Ferreira, Â.P., Lima, J., Pereira, A.I.: Optimal sizing of a hybrid energy system based on renewable energy using evolutionary optimization algorithms. In: Pereira, A.I., et al. (eds.) OL2A 2021. CCIS, vol. 1488, pp. 153–168. Springer, Cham (2021). https://doi.org/10.1007/978-3-030-91885-9_12

Multi-objective Optimization of the Job Shop Scheduling Problem on Unrelated Parallel Machines with Sequence-Dependent Setup Times

Francisco dos Santos[1,2]([⊠]) [iD], Lino Costa[1,3] [iD], and Leonilde Varela[1,3] [iD]

[1] ALGORITMI Research Centre/LASI, University of Minho, Braga, Portugal
francisco_dos_santos@outlook.pt
[2] Polytechnic Institute, University Kimpa Vita, Uíge, Angola
[3] Department of Production and Systems, University of Minho, Braga, Portugal
{lac,leonilde}@dps.uminho.pt

Abstract. Several optimization criteria are involved in the job shop scheduling problems encountered in the engineering area. Multi-objective optimization algorithms are often applied to solve these problems, which become even more complex with the advent of Industry 4.0, mostly due to the increase of data from industrial systems. In this work, several instances of the multi-objective job shop scheduling problem on unrelated parallel machines with sequence-dependent setup times are solved using evolutionary approaches. In this problem, the goal is to assign a set of N jobs on M unrelated machines considering sequence-dependent setup times. Several objectives such as makespan, average completion time, cost and energy consumption can be optimized. In this work, single and multi-objective optimization problems are solved considering the minimization of makespan and the average completion time. Preliminary results for the comparison of algorithms on different instances of the problems are presented and statistically analysed. Future work will include problems with more objectives, and to extend this approach to the distributed job shop problem.

Keywords: Job shop scheduling problem · multi-objective optimization · evolutionary algorithms

1 Introduction

In industry, the area of job shop scheduling (JSS) has been an area of research with a lot of attraction in manufacturing [17]. This is not only a theoretical field of study, but also an interesting field of application in industry and other different real-world situations. Generally, multi-objective optimization problems

This work has been supported by FCT - Fundação para a Ciência e Tecnologia within the R&D Units Project Scope: UIDB/00319/2020.

ⓒ The Author(s), under exclusive license to Springer Nature Switzerland AG 2023
O. Gervasi et al. (Eds.): ICCSA 2023 Workshops, LNCS 14105, pp. 495–507, 2023.
https://doi.org/10.1007/978-3-031-37108-0_32

are frequent in engineering, and, in particular, in scheduling problems. Thus, it is clear that production problems in practice involve more objectives, and thus it is necessary to extend the solving of single objective JSS problems to multi-objective ones. Makespan, average job completion time, delay, cost savings, latency, energy consumption, and flow time are examples of objectives that comprise a JSS problem in industry [1, 16]. Moreover, the task of scheduling different jobs in an optimal sequence is more challenging with the increasing number of jobs, machines, and criteria [13]. This combinatorial optimization problem consists on ordering jobs for their processing on machines taking into account multiple conflicting criteria.

JSS problems can be solved using different algorithms, such as Genetic Algorithms (GAs) [2, 9], or, when multiple conflicting objectives exist, NSGA-II, NSGA-III, among other algorithms [10]. These algorithms are particularly suited to this kind of problems since they can tackle their combinatorial nature and multiple conflicting criteria.

This paper addresses the unrelated parallel machine scheduling problem considering the scheduling of N jobs that are available at time zero on M unrelated machines. The objective is to find the feasible sequence of jobs in each machine that minimizes the makespan and the average job completion time considering machine-dependent and sequence dependent setup times [7]. A set of small instances of this problem will be used to assess the GA performance on single objective JSS instances. Based on this analysis, NSGA-II [6] is applied to several multi-objective JSS instances.

This paper is organized as follows. Section 2 briefly presents an overview on multi-objective optimization of JSS, the JSS problem description, and a short presentation about multi-objective optimization concepts and genetic algorithms. In Sect. 3, the experimental results are presented and discussed, highlighting the parameters used in the algorithms, as well as performance measures, and the statistical analysis adopted. Finally, Sect. 4 addresses the conclusion and future work.

2   Multi-objective Job Shop Scheduling

2.1   Overview

JSS problems have been studied for over 50 years, either in academic or industrial settings. Most attention is given to JSS as a single objective optimization problem, which results in a schedule for minimizing the time required to complete all jobs, i.e., minimizing the makespan. Several methods have been developed to solve these problems, such as tabu search [12], ant colony [3], as well as genetic algorithms [14]. However, it is clear that the complexity of JSS problems besides being related to the dimension in terms of number of jobs and machines, depends also on the number of objectives and constraints.

JSS problems, in general, involve many objectives. NSGA-II has been applied to solve a set of instances of the flexible JSS problem [15]. In order to improve the efficiency, these authors implemented a grid representation of the solution space and concurrent priority queue to store and dispatch the pending sub-problems to be solved.

There are different representations of the solution space that can be used by GAs for solving JSS problems. These different representation affect application of genetic operators such as recombination and mutation and therefore the performance of the algorithms. In [1], it is provided a computational study to compare the performance of a GA under different representations.

An extension of the NSGA-III algorithm (i-NSGA-III) is proposed in [10] to solve manufacturing JSS problems with multiple objectives. These authors also developed novel problem-specific crossover and mutation operators. The results demonstrated the superiority of the extended version over the original NSGA-III for several instances of multi-objective JSS problems.

2.2   Problem Description

The unrelated parallel machine scheduling problem consists on the scheduling of N jobs on M unrelated machines. The term span is generally used to define the completion time of a given machine, while the term makespan is generally used for the maximum completion time [2]. In spite of makespan being the most common objective to be minimized, there are other relevant conflicting objectives such as the average completion time [16].

The following nomenclature is used for the JSS problem:

- π is the feasible sequence of all jobs assigned to machines, i.e., the vector of all feasible subsequences π_i on each machine i;
- π_i is the feasible subsequence of jobs on machine i;
- $p_{i,j}$ is the processing time of job j on machine i;
- $s_{i,j,0}$ is the setup time to process job j at the initial instant on machine i;
- $s_{i,j,k}$ is the setup time to process job j after job k on machine i;
- $c_i(\pi)$ is the total completion time of jobs on machine i for the feasible sequence π.

The following assumptions are considered in this paper:

- each machine M can only execute one job N at each instant;
- all machines are continuously available;
- all N jobs are independent without any precedence restriction;
- all N jobs are available for being executed at the initial instant;
- no preemption is allowed, i.e., the processing of a job in a machine cannot be interrupted;
- for each machine i, each job j has a processing time $p_{i,j}$;
- for each machine i, to process job j after job k, there is a setup time $s_{i,j,k}$.

In this paper, the goal is to find the feasible sequence of jobs in each machine that minimizes simultaneously the makespan [1] and the average job completion time [8] considering machine-dependent and sequence dependent setup times [7].

Thus, the objectives to minimize are the makespan $(c_{max}(\pi))$ and the average completion time $(\bar{c}(\pi))$.

Mathematically, the makespan and the average completion time can be formulated as:

$$c_{\max}(\pi) = \max_{i=1,\ldots,M}(c_i(\pi)) \qquad (1)$$

and

$$\bar{c}(\pi) = \frac{1}{M}\sum_{i=1}^{M}c_i(\pi) \qquad (2)$$

where $c_i(\pi) = \sum_{j\in\pi_i}p_{i,j} + \sum_{j\in\pi_i}s_{i,j,k}$ with k being the precedent job of job j in the subsequence π_i of the feasible sequence π. Note that if the job j is the first job in the subsequence π_i then k is zero and the setup time $s_{i,j,0}$ at the initial instant is considered.

2.3 Multi-objective Optimization

A multi-objective optimization problem with K objectives and n decision variables can be formulated mathematically as follows:

$$\min \mathbf{F}(\mathbf{x}) = (f_1(x), f_2(x), \ldots, f_K(x))^T \qquad (3)$$

where $\mathbf{x}$ is the decision vector of size n defined in the decision space Ω, and $\mathbf{F}(\mathbf{x})$ is the objective vector defined in the objective space.

When several conflicting objectives are optimized at the same time, the search space becomes partially ordered. In such scenario, solutions are compared on the basis of the Pareto dominance. Without loss of generality, consider a multi-objective optimization problem where K objectives are to be minimized, for two solutions $\mathbf{a}$ and $\mathbf{b}$ from the feasible set Ω, a solution $\mathbf{a}$ is said to dominate a solution $\mathbf{b}$ (denoted by $\mathbf{a} \prec \mathbf{b}$) if:

$$\forall_{i\in\{1,\ldots,K\}} : f_i(\mathbf{a}) \le f_i(\mathbf{b}) \wedge \exists_{j\in\{1,\ldots,K\}} : f_j(\mathbf{a}) < f_j(\mathbf{b}). \qquad (4)$$

Since solutions are compared against different objectives, there is no longer a single optimal solution but a set of optimal solutions, generally known as the Pareto optimal set. This set contains equally important solutions representing different trade-offs between the given objectives and can be defined as:

$$\mathbf{PS} = \{\mathbf{x} \in \Omega \mid \nexists \mathbf{y} \in \Omega : \mathbf{y} \prec \mathbf{x}\}. \qquad (5)$$

The images of the solutions of the Pareto optimal set define a Pareto front in the objective space. This Pareto front allow to identify the trade-offs between solutions and therefore facilitate the decision making.

2.4 Genetic Algorithms

A Genetic Algorithm (GA) is a random search optimization technique that mimics the process of natural selection [5]. It is based on a population that it is generated at random in the beginning of the search. The individuals of the population are, in general, referred as chromosomes and represent potential solutions of the optimization problem. A selection mechanism is used to choose solutions to generate offspring. This mechanism assures that the best chromosomes have higher probabilities of being selected. Genetic operators such as crossover and mutation allow to create new chromosomes that inherit features from the parents. Recombination generates two new child solutions by mating the selected chromosomes, exchanging of specific genes of the parents. Mutation introduces some new elements in the chromosomes in order to increase their ability to reach other points in the search space.

One of the relevant advantages of GAs is that they can work with a population of chromosomes that represent potential solutions of the optimization problem and are adequate to tackle combinatorial problems, since the constraints can be handled by permutation representations. On the other hand, GAs are particularly suited to solve multi-objective optimization problems since they work with population of solutions and therefore can find in a single run an approximation to the Pareto optimal set. Furthermore, diversity-preserving mechanisms can be implemented to spread solutions along the Pareto front to provide a set of good trade-offs to facilitate decision making.

3 Experimental Results

3.1 Test Problems

The test problems were borrowed from previous works [2, 3]. These problems were used to investigate the GA performance and the quality of the NSGA-II results. In this study, from the set of all available problems, only the small problems with balanced processing and setup times for $M \in \{2, 4, 6, 8\}$, and $N \in \{6, 7, 8\}$ were considered. For each combination of the number of machines and jobs, there are 15 different instances of the problems. First, a comparative and statistical analysis of the solutions obtained by GA for the single objective optimization problems considering the makespan and the average completion time, separately, is presented. Then, NSGA-II was applied to solve multi-objective optimization problems considering the makespan and the average completion time, simultaneously.

3.2 Algorithms Implementation and Parameters

In this work, two approaches based on genetic algorithms, GA and NSGA-II, were used to solve the single and multiple-objective JSS optimization problem, respectively. These algorithms were implemented in Python using the PYMOO framework [4].

A permutation representation was adopted to represent the feasible sequences of jobs in each machine (π). A solution is represented by a chromosome that is a permutation of size $N + M - 1$, i.e., a sequence of integer values that can occur only once. In a chromosome, the genes that are superior to N separate the chromosome in M subsequences (π_i) that indicate the set of jobs and the corresponding order assigned to each machine i.

A tournament selection operator was used to select chromosomes for the application of genetic operators. Genetic operators were chosen to guarantee feasibility of the solutions during the search: the order-based crossover and inversion mutation. In the order-based crossover, two chromosomes are combined in order to generate offspring. Two positions are selected at random and the genes between them are swapped. Then, the remaining empty positions are filled with the other parent's genes while preventing repetitions. In the inversion mutation, two positions are generated at random, and the genes in the chromosome are inverted.

In order to find an adequate population size, two different population sizes with 20 and 40 individuals were tested to solve the single objective optimization problems with GA. For the multi-objective optimization problems, NSGA-II was applied with the population size that achieved the best GA performance. The stopping criterion was based on the maximum number of generations and the period of no improvement. In this case, the total number of generations was set to 10,000 and the period to 100 generations. Since the algorithms used are stochastic, for all instances of all test problems, 30 independent runs were performed. In this manner, the results can be statistically analysed. For all statistics tests, a significance level of 5% is considered.

3.3   Single Objective Optimization Results

In this section, the results of the application of GA to single objective JSS optimization problems are presented. Two objectives are considered separately: the makespan and the average completion time. The performance of GA with a population size of 20 and 40 individuals is statistically analysed.

In Table 1, the statistics for the GA performance on single objective problems for the minimization of the makespan for a population size of 20 and 40 individuals is presented. In this table, $AVG(c_{\max}(\pi))_{40}$ $SD(c_{\max}(\pi))_{40}$ and $AVG(c_{\max}(\pi))_{20}$ $SD(c_{\max}(\pi))_{20}$ are the average and standard deviation of the makespan $(c_{\max}(\pi))$ for a population size of 40 and 20 individuals, respectively. These statistics are computed for every combination of M (the number of machines) and N (the number of jobs). For each combination of M and N, the average values of 30 independent runs are calculated and then the statistics (average and standard deviation) for the 15 instances are computed. The p-values for the one-tailed paired t-Student test are also provided [11].

It can be observed that, for all combinations of M and N, the p-values are inferior to 5%, then there are significant differences between the mean values of $c_{\max}(\pi)$ for population sizes of 40 and 20 individuals. Thus, the GA performance with a population size of 40 individuals was significantly superior to the

Table 1. Single objective results for the minimization of the makespan $(c_{max}(\pi))$ for the GA with a population size of 40 and 20 individuals.

M	N	$AVG(c_{max}(\pi))_{40}$	$SD(c_{max}(\pi))_{40}$	$AVG(c_{max}(\pi))_{20}$	$SD(c_{max}(\pi))_{20}$	p-value
2	6	394.773	14.168	395.049	14.173	0.020
	7	491.807	15.805	493.240	15.643	<0.001
	8	521.961	17.087	524.823	17.454	<0.001
4	6	246.220	7.092	247.782	6.850	0.016
	7	255.683	9.676	257.577	8.933	<0.001
	8	270.063	6.301	272.371	5.968	<0.001
6	8	239.093	5.472	241.280	6.157	<0.001

algorithm with a population size of 20 individuals for the minimization of the makespan $(c_{max}(\pi))$.

For illustration purposes, Fig. 1 represents the optimal solution obtained for instance 5 of the minimization of the makespan with 2 machines (m_1 and m_2) and 6 jobs (n_1, n_2, n_3, n_4, n_5 and n_6). In this figure, blue boxes represent the jobs. Additionally, the processing times and setup times are also indicated below the blue boxes and before the jobs, respectively. For instance 5, the processing times $p_{i,j}$ of the job j on machine i are given in the following matrix:

$$p = \begin{pmatrix} 83 \ 77 \ 55 \ 99 \ 86 \ 74 \\ 53 \ 62 \ 90 \ 60 \ 52 \ 83 \end{pmatrix}.$$

The setup times $s_{i,j,k}$ to process job j after job k are given on matrices s_1 and s_2 for machines m_1 and m_2, respectively:

$$s_1 = \begin{pmatrix} 77 \ 91 \ 82 \ 95 \ 50 \ 93 \\ 52 \ 70 \ 94 \ 71 \ 58 \ 85 \\ 67 \ 83 \ 77 \ 69 \ 70 \ 69 \\ 85 \ 68 \ 51 \ 80 \ 58 \ 99 \\ 62 \ 66 \ 53 \ 53 \ 64 \ 98 \\ 74 \ 76 \ 82 \ 58 \ 86 \ 97 \end{pmatrix} \quad s_2 = \begin{pmatrix} 60 \ 72 \ 88 \ 73 \ 60 \ 85 \\ 61 \ 82 \ 53 \ 75 \ 65 \ 53 \\ 68 \ 51 \ 52 \ 58 \ 86 \ 96 \\ 98 \ 69 \ 51 \ 99 \ 71 \ 58 \\ 76 \ 55 \ 73 \ 77 \ 94 \ 85 \\ 98 \ 84 \ 92 \ 79 \ 51 \ 89 \end{pmatrix}.$$

In the diagonal of the matrices, the setup time to process job j at the initial instant on machines ($s_{i,j,0}$) are given. This solution corresponds to the sequence $\pi = \langle \pi_1, \pi_2 \rangle$ where $\pi_1 = [2, 5, 3]$ and $\pi_2 = [1, 4, 6]$. The total completion times are $c_1(\pi) = 399$ and $c_2(\pi) = 387$, and therefore $c_{max}(\pi) = 399$.

In Table 2, the statistics for the GA performance on single objective problems for the minimization of the average completion time for a population size of 20 and 40 individuals is presented. As previously, in this table, the averages and standard deviations of the average completion time ($\bar{c}(\pi)$) for a population size of 20 and 40 individuals are indicated. The statistics and p-values presented in this table were computed similarly as those presented in Table 1.

It can be observed that, for all combinations of M and N, the p-values are inferior to 5%. Thus, the GA performance with a population size of 40

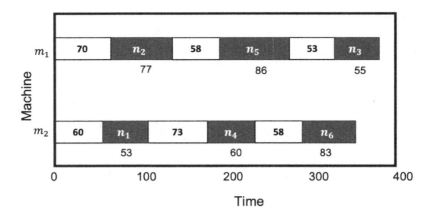

Fig. 1. Representation of the optimal solution ($c_{max} = 399$) obtained for the minimization of the makespan with 2 machines and 6 jobs (instance 5).

Table 2. Single objective results for the minimization of the average completion time
($\bar{c}(\pi)$) for the GA with a population size of 40 and 20 individuals.

M	N	$AVG(\bar{c}(\pi))_{40}$	$SD(\bar{c}(\pi))_{40}$	$AVG(\bar{c}(\pi))_{20}$	$SD(\bar{c}(\pi))_{20}$	p-value
2	6	378.816	12.920	378.979	12.910	0.042
	7	446.227	12.700	447.012	12.627	0.002
	8	504.145	15.717	504.883	15.792	<0.001
4	6	182.536	5.104	183.017	3.873	<0.001
	7	211.641	6.255	212.637	5.928	0.003
	8	240.680	4.525	242.259	4.517	<0.001
6	8	159.232	4.153	160.397	3.951	<0.001

individuals was significantly superior to the algorithm with a population size of
20 individuals for the minimization of the average completion time ($\bar{c}(\pi)$).

Figure 2 represents the optimal solution obtained for instance 5 of the minimization of the average completion time with 2 machines and 6 jobs. This
solution corresponds to the sequence $\pi = <\pi_1, \pi_2>$ where $\pi_1 = [\ ]$ and
$\pi_2 = [3, 4, 6, 5, 2, 1]$. The total completion times are $c_1(\pi) = 0$ and $c_2(\pi) = 735$,
and therefore $\bar{c}(\pi) = 367.5$.

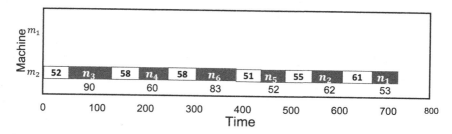

Fig. 2. Representation of the optimal solution ($\bar{c}(\pi) = 367.5$) obtained for the minimization of the average completion time with 2 machines and 6 jobs (instance 5).

For measuring the relative improvement in the GA performance in terms of the objective function values, a δ measure was computed for different statistics. Thus, a δ_{sta} measure was computed according to the following expression:

$$\delta_{sta} = \frac{obj_{40} - obj_{20}}{obj_{40}}$$

where sta and obj are the statistic and the objective considered, respectively. If the δ measure is negative then the best results were obtained by the GA for a population size of 40 individuals. The opposite occurs when the δ measure is positive. If the δ measure is equal to zero then the performance is similar.

In Table 3, the statistics of the δ measure for the comparison of GA with 40 and 20 individuals for the makespan and average completion time objectives is given. The δ measure was computed for the best objective function results (δ_{min}) and the average objective function results (δ_{mean}).

Taking into account the results presented in Table 3, for both $c_{max}(\pi)$ and $\bar{c}(\pi)$, δ_{mean} is always negative and the p-values are all inferior to 5%, meaning that the GA with a population size of 40 individuals significantly achieved a better performance when compared to the GA with a population size of 20. However, for δ_{min}, no significant differences are found for $c_{max}(\pi)$. Finally, for $\bar{c}(\pi)$, no significant differences are found for all combinations of M and N except for $M = 2$ and $N = 7$, and $M = 2$ and $N = 8$. Overall, these results indicate a better performance for a population size of 40 individuals. Moreover, this results in a significant relative improvement of average objective values.

Table 3. Statistics of the δ measure for the comparison of GA with 40 and 20 individuals for the makespan and average completion time objectives.

M	N	$c_{max}(\pi)$				$\bar{c}(\pi)$			
		$AVG(\delta_{min})$	p-value	$AVG(\delta_{mean})$	p-value	$AVG(\delta_{min})$	p-value	$AVG(\delta_{mean})$	p-value
2	6	0.0000	1.000	−0.0007	0.020	0.0000	1.000	−0.0004	0.040
	7	0.0000	1.000	−0.0029	<0.001	0.0004	0.004	−0.0018	0.002
	8	0.0000	1.000	−0.0055	<0.001	0.0005	0.002	−0.0015	<0.001
4	6	0.0000	1.000	−0.0064	0.016	0.0005	1.000	−0.0026	<0.001
	7	0.0000	1.000	−0.0075	<0.001	−0.0003	0.321	−0.0048	0.003
	8	0.0048	0.167	−0.0086	<0.001	0.0000	1.000	−0.0066	<0.001
6	8	−0.0014	0.167	−0.0091	<0.001	−0.0002	0.305	−0.0074	<0.001

3.4 Multi-objective Optimization Results

In this section, the results of the application of NSGA-II to multi-objective JSS optimization problems are presented. Two objectives are considered simultaneously: the makespan and the average completion time.

The hypervolume indicator (H) was used to measure the performance of the NSGA-II [18]. This measure evaluates algorithm performance in terms of convergence to the Pareto front as well as the diversity of the approximation along the Pareto front. The reference point considered was the point $(1000, 1000)^T$ and all hypervolume values were standardized. Thus, all hypervolume values have values belonging to the interval $[0, 1]$. The higher the value of hypervolume, the best performance of the algorithm.

In Fig. 3, the Pareto front obtained for the minimization of the makespan and the average completion time with 2 machines and 6 jobs (instance 5) is depicted. In this figure, it is possible to identify the trade-offs between the objectives for different solutions. The extreme solutions in the Pareto front are the solutions obtained when the single objective JSS problems were solved. Thus, the solutions on the upper-left and lower-right extremes of the Pareto front correspond to solutions presented in Fig. 1 and Fig. 2.

Figure 4 represents a trade-off solution that is a good compromise between the objectives. This solution is in the elbow of the Pareto curve. This solution corresponds to the sequence $\pi = <\pi_1, \pi_2>$ where $\pi_1 = [3, 6]$ and $\pi_2 = [1, 5, 2, 4]$. The total completion times are $c_1(\pi) = 275$ and $c_2(\pi) = 477$, and therefore $c_{max}(\pi) = 477$ and $\bar{c}(\pi) = 376$. that are in the elbow of the curve. This solution is a good compromise between the objectives.

In Table 4, the statistics for the measured hypervolume for Pareto fronts obtained by NSGA-II for 15 instances of the problems for each combination of M and N are presented. In this table, $AVG(H_{max})$, $SD(H_{max})$ are the average and standard deviation of the best hypervolume (maximum hypervolume), and $AVG(H_{mean})$, $SD(H_{mean})$ are the average and standard deviation of the mean hypervolume, respectively. In order to compare this multi-objective results with the single objective ones, the values of $AVG(H_{ref})$ and $SD(H_{ref})$ were also included in this table. These values are the average and standard deviation of the hypervolume computed for the minimum of each objective (the extremes of the Pareto font). It can be seen that the value of $AVG(H_{max})$ is always superior to the value $AVG(H_{ref})$. This highlights the importance of using multi-objective approaches. The values of $AVG(H)$ are for some combinations of M and N inferior to $AVG(H_{ref})$. However, it should be noted that this occurs due to the fact that, for some instances, in a small number of the 30 runs, the approximation obtained is not so close to the optimal Pareto front. Thus, the hypervolume average values are affected by these cases.

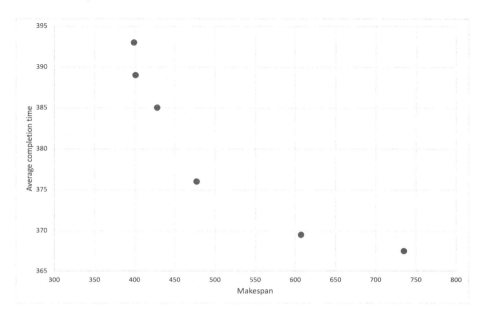

Fig. 3. Pareto front for the minimization of the makespan and the average completion time with 2 machines and 6 jobs (instance 5).

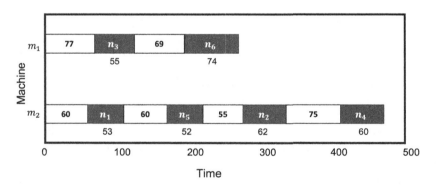

Fig. 4. Representation of a trade-off solution $(c_{\max}(\pi) = 477$ and $\bar{c}(\pi) = 376)$ obtained for the minimization of makespan and the average completion time with 2 machines and 6 jobs (instance 5).

Table 4. Statistics for the measured hypervolume for Pareto fronts on multi-objective JSS problems.

M	N	$AVG(H_{\max})$	$SD(H_{\max})$	$AVG(H)$	$SD(H)$	$AVG(H_{ref})$	$SD(H_{ref})$
2	6	0.375	0.016	0.375	0.016	0.374	0.016
	7	0.281	0.014	0.280	0.014	0.280	0.014
	8	0.239	0.016	0.237	0.017	0.238	0.016
4	6	0.617	0.008	0.615	0.008	0.616	0.008
	7	0.589	0.012	0.586	0.011	0.586	0.012
	8	0.558	0.008	0.553	0.009	0.556	0.008
6	8	0.644	0.008	0.640	0.008	0.643	0.009

4   Conclusions and Future Work

In this paper, several instances of JSS problems on unrelated parallel machines with sequence-dependent setup times were solved as single objective and multi-objective optimization problems. These problems were solved using evolutionary algorithms for different number of machines and jobs. The makespan ($c_{\max}$) and the average completion time ($\bar{c}$) were the objectives considered.

Firstly, a GA algorithm was used to solve instances of the single objective optimization problems consisting on the minimization of the objectives separately. The results of several preliminary tests were analysed to tune the GA parameters, namely, the population size. Then, taking into consideration these results, instances of the multi-objective optimization problem were solved using NSGA-II. In all cases, a permutation was used to represent the sequence of jobs in each machine. All results were statistically analysed. It was concluded that using small population sizes can compromise the performance of the algorithms in this kind of problems. The best results were obtained with a population size of 40 individuals.

The analysis of the hypervolume results for the multi-objective JSS problems confirmed the advantages and importance of using multi-objective approaches since that indicate the existence of conflict between the objectives and multiple trade-offs. The representation of the Pareto front highlights the trade-offs facilitating the decision making process.

Future work will include solving problems with more objectives and the use of other algorithms, and to extend this approach to the distributed job shop problem.

References

1. Abdelmaguid, T.F.: Representations in genetic algorithm for the job shop scheduling problem: a computational study. J. Softw. Eng. Appl. **3**(12), 1155 (2010)
2. Antunes, A.R., Matos, M.A., Rocha, A.M.A., Costa, L.A., Varela, L.R.: A statistical comparison of metaheuristics for unrelated parallel machine scheduling problems with setup times. Mathematics **10**(14), 2431 (2022)

3. Arnaout, J.P., Musa, R., Rabadi, G.: A two-stage ant colony optimization algorithm to minimize the makespan on unrelated parallel machines-part II: enhancements and experimentations. J. Intell. Manuf. **25**, 43–53 (2014)
4. Blank, J., Deb, K.: Pymoo: multi-objective optimization in python. IEEE Access **8**, 89497–89509 (2020)
5. Deb, K.: An introduction to genetic algorithms. Sadhana **24**, 293–315 (1999)
6. Deb, K., Pratap, A., Agarwal, S., Meyarivan, T.: A fast and elitist multiobjective genetic algorithm: NSGA-II. IEEE Trans. Evol. Comput. **6**(2), 182–197 (2002)
7. Feldman, A.: Scheduling algorithms and systems. Columbia University (1999)
8. González-Neira, E.M., et al.: Robust solutions in multi-objective stochastic permutation flow shop problem. Comput. Industr. Eng. **137**, 106026 (2019)
9. Katoch, S., Chauhan, S.S., Kumar, V.: A review on genetic algorithm: past, present, and future. Multimed. Tools Appl. **80**, 8091–8126 (2021)
10. Khan, B., Hanoun, S., Johnstone, M., Lim, C.P., Creighton, D., Nahavandi, S.: Multi-objective job shop scheduling using I-NSGA-III. In: 2018 Annual IEEE International Systems Conference (SysCon), pp. 1–5. IEEE (2018)
11. Montgomery, D.C., Runger, G.C.: Applied Statistics and Probability for Engineers. Wiley, Hoboken (2010)
12. Saidi-Mehrabad, M., Fattahi, P.: Flexible job shop scheduling with tabu search algorithms. Int. J. Adv. Manuf. Technol. **32**, 563–570 (2007)
13. dos Santos, F., Costa, L.A., Varela, L.: A systematic literature review about multiobjective optimization for distributed manufacturing scheduling in the industry 4.0. In: Gervasi, O., Murgante, B., Misra, S., Rocha, A.M.A.C., Garau, C. (eds.) ICCSA 2022, Part II. LNCS, vol. 13378, pp. 157–173. Springer, Cham (2022). https://doi.org/10.1007/978-3-031-10562-3_12
14. Sha, D., Lin, H.H.: A multi-objective PSO for job-shop scheduling problems. Expert Syst. Appl. **37**(2), 1065–1070 (2010)
15. Soto, C., Dorronsoro, B., Fraire, H., Cruz-Reyes, L., Gomez-Santillan, C., Rangel, N.: Solving the multi-objective flexible job shop scheduling problem with a novel parallel branch and bound algorithm. Swarm Evol. Comput. **53**, 100632 (2020)
16. Yenisey, M.M., Yagmahan, B.: Multi-objective permutation flow shop scheduling problem: literature review, classification and current trends. Omega **45**, 119–135 (2014)
17. Zhang, J., Ding, G., Zou, Y., Qin, S., Fu, J.: Review of job shop scheduling research and its new perspectives under industry 4.0. J. Intell. Manuf. **30**, 1809–1830 (2019)
18. Zitzler, E., Thiele, L., Laumanns, M., Fonseca, C.M., da Fonseca, V.G.: Performance assessment of multiobjective optimizers: an analysis and review. IEEE Trans. Evol. Comput. **7**(2), 117–132 (2003)

Radial Basis Function and Bayesian Methods for the Hyperparameter Optimization of Classification Random Forests

Rommel G. Regis[✉][iD]

Saint Joseph's University, Philadelphia, PA 19131, USA
rregis@sju.edu

Abstract. The hyperparameter optimization of a random forest (RF) is a discrete black-box optimization problem that aims to find the settings of the hyperparameters that optimize an overall out-of-bag (OOB) performance measure of the RF. This problem is computationally expensive for high-dimensional data involving many predictors and a large number of data points. This paper explores the use of surrogate-based approaches, particularly radial basis function (RBF) methods and Bayesian optimization techniques, to optimize the hyperparameters of a classification RF. The surrogates approximate the functional relationship between the hyperparameters and the overall OOB performance of the RF, and they are used to guide the search for a global optimum for the hyperparameter optimization problem. While Bayesian optimization methods have been used to tune the hyperparameters of a classification RF, RBF methods have rarely been used for this task, if at all. We compare the performance of the B-CONDOR-RBF algorithm and a Bayesian optimization method with global and local discrete random search methods to tune the discrete hyperparameters of an RF on 10 classification data sets that involve up to 753 predictor variables and up to 19K data points. The global variant of B-CONDOR-RBF obtained better overall OOB prediction error than the discrete random search methods and two Bayesian optimization algorithms given a limited budget of only 100 function evaluations. Furthermore, a local variant of B-CONDOR-RBF outperformed the random search methods and achieved comparable performance with the Bayesian optimization algorithms on the same problems.

Keywords: Random forest · classification problem · hyperparameter optimization · radial basis functions · Bayesian optimization

1 Introduction

Among the most popular predictive modeling techniques is the *random forest (RF)* [3], which is an ensemble of decision trees built from bootstrap samples of the training dataset. It is well-known that the predictive performance of a random forest partly depends on the setting of its hyperparameters, which are the

© The Author(s), under exclusive license to Springer Nature Switzerland AG 2023
O. Gervasi et al. (Eds.): ICCSA 2023 Workshops, LNCS 14105, pp. 508–525, 2023.
https://doi.org/10.1007/978-3-031-37108-0_33

parameters that control the learning process. This paper considers the problem of tuning four hyperparameters of a random forest for classification tasks: number of decision trees in the RF (ntree), number of predictors drawn at random for each split (mtry), minimum number of samples in a node (min.node.size), and the fraction of the training set drawn at random with replacement for constructing each decision tree (sample.frac). We wish to find the settings of these hyperparameters that optimize an overall out-of-bag (OOB) measure of performance of the RF on classification problems. For example, we may wish to determine the RF hyperparameter values that minimize the overall OOB prediction error of the RF or maximize its overall OOB F1 score. A lower OOB prediction error or a higher OOB F1 score is generally expected to lead to better predictive ability of the RF on new or unseen instances.

The hyperparameter optimization of machine learning models for classification can be formulated as a black-box optimization problem where the decision variables are the hyperparameters and the objective function is an estimate of the predictive performance of the model. In this paper, we only consider discrete ordinal settings for the hyperparameters. However, the methods used here can be extended to deal with continuous and non-ordinal hyperparameter settings. More precisely, the hyperparameter optimization problem is to search for an approximate optimal solution to the following discrete optimization problem:

$$\min_{\Theta \in \mathbb{R}^d} \mathcal{E}(\Theta) \qquad (\text{or } \max_{\Theta \in \mathbb{R}^d} \mathcal{P}(\Theta))$$
$$\text{subject to} \qquad \qquad \qquad \qquad \qquad \qquad \qquad \quad (1)$$
$$\theta^{(i)} \in D_i \subset \mathbb{R} \qquad \text{for } i = 1, \ldots, d$$

Here, $\Theta = (\theta^{(1)}, \ldots, \theta^{(d)})$, where $\theta^{(i)}$ is the ith hyperparameter, and D_i is the finite set of all possible ordinal settings of $\theta^{(i)}$. For example, the hyperparameter sample.frac in RFs can take the values in $\{0.5, 0.55, 0.6, \ldots, 0.95, 1\}$. The objective function $\mathcal{E}(\Theta)$ to be minimized is an estimate of the prediction error of the model such as the *overall out-of-bag (OOB) prediction error*, which is the fraction (or percentage) of misclassified instances in the OOB procedure. The alternative objective function $\mathcal{P}(\Theta)$ to be maximized is a measure of predictive ability of the model such as the *overall OOB accuracy, OOB F1 score* or *OOB AUC*. The last two metrics are suitable for unbalanced classification data sets. The *F1 score* is the harmonic mean of the *precision* and *recall* of the model on binary classification tasks. The *precision* of a model is the fraction of true positives among instances that the model labeled as positive while the *recall* is the fraction of true positives among all instances that are actually positive. The *AUC metric* is the area under the *ROC curve* for binary classification problems. This curve is a plot of the true positive rate (recall) vs the false positive rate.

The objective functions $\mathcal{E}(\Theta)$ and $\mathcal{P}(\Theta)$ are black-box since analytical formulas for these functions in terms of the hyperparameters are not available. Moreover, $\mathcal{E}(\Theta)$ and $\mathcal{P}(\Theta)$ are typically random variables, which give rise to stochastic optimization problems. For example, the overall OOB prediction error $\mathcal{E}(\Theta)$ in RFs depends on the bootstrap samples used and the random sample of predictors considered at each of the splits of the decision trees forming the RF. In this case, we minimize an estimate of the expected value of $\mathcal{E}(\Theta)$ over the same search space. For simplicity, we treat problem (1) as deterministic by fixing the random seed when calculating $\mathcal{E}(\Theta)$ or $\mathcal{P}(\Theta)$. The case where the objective function is a random variable will be treated in future work.

Grid search and random search [2] are popular methods for hyperparameter optimization of machine learning models. However, the objective function $\mathcal{E}(\Theta)$ can become computationally expensive when a machine learning model is trained on a large data set with many thousands or millions of instances and hundreds of predictors. In this case, a complete grid search might not be possible while uniform random search might be inefficient in finding optimal hyperparameters. Instead, a natural approach is to utilize an optimization method that uses a surrogate [21] for the objective function. Examples of surrogate-based methods that have been used for hyperparameter optimization include Bayesian optimization techniques [1,7,12,20] and radial basis function (RBF) methods [5,16]. The surrogates approximate the functional relationship between the hyperparameters and the objective function, and so, a surrogate-based method is expected to outperform uniform random search. In fact, Bayesian optimization was shown to be empirically superior to random search [20] on hyperparameter optimization problems on several machine learning models.

This paper explores the use of surrogate-based methods, particularly RBF and Bayesian optimization methods, to optimize the hyperparameters of a classification RF. We focus on hyperparameters that take values on an ordinal finite set. While Bayesian optimization methods have been used for hyperparameter optimization of RFs (e.g., [12]), RBFs have rarely been used for this purpose. In fact, B-CONDOR-RBF [16] is among the few, if not the only RBF method, that has been used to optimize the hyperparameters of an RF. However, this RBF method was only applied to regression tasks in [16]. In this paper, we apply B-CONDOR-RBF and a discrete Bayesian optimization algorithm to optimize the hyperparameters of an RF for classification tasks. Moreover, this study used data sets with much larger numbers of predictors than in [16]. We utilize a global and a local variant of B-CONDOR-RBF both of which use a cubic RBF model augmented by a linear polynomial. We also utilize two variants of the Bayesian optimization method, one of which uses a Gaussian kernel while the other uses the Matérn 5/2 kernel. We compare the performance of these surrogate-based approaches with the widely used uniform random search method and with a local discrete random search approach on 10 classification data sets that involve up to 753 predictor variables and up to about 19K data points. The results show that the global variant of B-CONDOR-RBF obtained better overall OOB prediction error than the two discrete random search methods and the two Bayesian optimization algorithms given a limited budget of only 100 function evaluations on the hyperparameter optimization problems. Furthermore, a local variant of B-CONDOR-RBF outperformed the random search methods and achieved comparable performance with the Bayesian optimization algorithms on the same problems. These results suggest that RBF methods, particularly B-CONDOR-RBF, are promising alternatives to Bayesian optimization for the hyperparameter optimization of classification RFs and possibly other models.

2   Surrogate-Based Methods for Hyperparameter Optimization of Machine Learning Models

For large datasets involving many instances or predictors, the objective function $\mathcal{E}(\Theta)$ or $\mathcal{P}(\Theta)$ is computationally expensive to evaluate, so we consider two methods that use surrogates of the objective function to optimize the hyperparameters of an RF. Both methods are designed to solve the discrete black-box optimization problem in (1) where the hyperparameters take values from an ordinal finite set. In the case of classification RFs in this study, $\mathcal{E}(\Theta)$ represents the overall OOB prediction error of the RF for a given setting of the hyperparameters $\Theta = (\theta^{(1)}, \dots, \theta^{(d)})$, which is a point in the search space. However, the objective function may be replaced by a different metric $\mathcal{P}(\Theta)$ to be maximized such as the overall OOB F1 score or the overall OOB AUC score of the model. Below, we focus on minimizing the objective function $\mathcal{E}(\Theta)$ since maximizing $\mathcal{P}(\Theta)$ is equivalent to minimizing its negative. The two algorithms begin by evaluating $\mathcal{E}(\Theta)$ at initial points randomly selected uniformly from the finite search space. The resulting objective function values at the initial points are then used to fit the initial surrogate for $\mathcal{E}(\Theta)$.

2.1   Bayesian Hyperparameter Optimization

In Bayesian optimization, we build a probabilistic model for the objective function $\mathcal{E}(\Theta)$ that yields a surrogate of the objective and a measure of uncertainty that are used to guide the selection of sample points for function evaluation. In particular, we assume that $\mathcal{E}(\Theta)$ is modeled by a Gaussian Process $\mathcal{GP}(\mu(\Theta), k(\Theta, \Theta'))$ where $\mu(\Theta)$ is the mean function and $k(\Theta, \Theta')$ is the covariance function. In this study, we consider a constant mean function $\mu(\Theta) = \mu$ and two types of covariance functions:

$$k(\Theta, \Theta') = \sigma^2 \exp\left(\frac{-\|\Theta - \Theta'\|^2}{2\ell^2}\right) \quad \text{(Gaussian)}$$

$$k(\Theta, \Theta') = \sigma^2 \left(1 + \frac{\sqrt{5}\|\Theta - \Theta'\|}{\ell} + \frac{5\|\Theta - \Theta'\|^2}{3\ell^2}\right) \exp\left(\frac{-\sqrt{5}\|\Theta - \Theta'\|}{\ell}\right) \quad \text{(Matérn 5/2)}$$

where σ^2 and ℓ are parameters to be determined.

Assume that objective function has been evaluated at n points, yielding $\{(\Theta_1, \xi_1), (\Theta_2, \xi_2), \dots, (\Theta_n, \xi_n)\}$, where $\xi_i = \mathcal{E}(\Theta_i)$ for all $i = 1, \dots, n$. The Gaussian Process is fit using maximum likelihood estimation, and the objective function value at a new point Θ^* will also have a Gaussian distribution with mean and variance given by [14]:

$$\widehat{\xi}(\Theta^*) = \widehat{\mu} + k_*^T K^{-1}(\xi - \widehat{\mu})$$
$$s^2(\Theta^*) = k(\Theta^*, \Theta^*) - k_*^T K^{-1} k_*$$

where $\widehat{\mu}$ is the MLE of μ, $\xi = [\xi_1, \dots, \xi_n]^T$, $k_* = [k(\Theta_1, \Theta^*), \dots, k(\Theta_n, \Theta^*)]^T$, and K is the $n \times n$ covariance matrix whose (i, j) entry is $k(\Theta_i, \Theta_j)$. The predicted value for $\mathcal{E}(\Theta^*)$ is then given by its mean $\widehat{\xi}(\Theta^*)$ while the variance $s^2(\Theta^*)$ provides a measure of uncertainty at the predicted value for $\mathcal{E}(\Theta^*)$.

In this paper, we utilize *Discrete-EI* [16], which is a Bayesian optimization algorithm for bound-constrained black-box optimization problem with discrete decision variables. Discrete-EI uses the Gaussian Process surrogate model described above and the *expected improvement (EI)* criterion [19] as its acquisition function for selecting the next sample point for objective function evaluation. The EI criterion was used in the original Efficient Global Optimization (EGO) method [6]. In each iteration of Discrete-EI, the next sample point is chosen to be a point Θ that maximizes $\text{EI}(\Theta)$ approximately over the search space where

$$\text{EI}(\Theta) = (\xi_{min} - \widehat{\xi}(\Theta))\Phi\left(\frac{\xi_{min} - \widehat{\xi}(\Theta)}{s(\Theta)}\right) + s(\Theta)\phi\left(\frac{\xi_{min} - \widehat{\xi}(\Theta)}{s(\Theta)}\right), \quad (2)$$

if $s(\Theta) > 0$ and $\text{EI}(\Theta) = 0$ if $s(\Theta) = 0$. Here, Φ and ϕ are the cdf and pdf of the standard normal distribution, respectively. Also, ξ_{min} is the current best objective function value.

2.2   The B-CONDOR Algorithm for Hyperparameter Optimization

For the *B-CONDOR* algorithm [16], each iteration generates a large number of random trial points within the search space according to some probability distribution that may adapt as the search progresses. In the *global variant* of B-CONDOR, the trial points are generated uniformly at random throughout the finite search space. In the *local variant*, the trial points are generated in some neighborhood of the current best point. In particular, the trial points in the local variant are obtained by modifying some of the variable settings of the current best point and this process is controlled by two parameters: p_{pert} and $depth_{\text{nbhd}}$. To obtain these trial points, each coordinate of the current best point is modified with probability p_{pert} and the percentage of the number of settings that a variable is allowed to increase or decrease is given by the neighborhood depth parameter $depth_{\text{nbhd}}$. More details can be obtained from [16].

Once the trial points have been generated, the next sample point is selected to be the best trial point according to a weighted ranking of two criteria as in [15]: predicted value of the objective function (*surrogate criterion*), and minimum distance between the trial point and the previous sample points (*distance criterion*). We then evaluate the objective function at the best trial point, which then provides a new data point that is used to update the surrogate model of the objective function for the next iteration. The iterations continue until we reach the maximum number of function evaluations, denoted by n_{max}.

Below is an outline of the B-CONDOR algorithm for problem (1).

The B-CONDOR Algorithm

(1) *(Evaluate Initial Points)* Evaluate $\mathcal{E}(\Theta)$ at space-filling points $\mathcal{I}_0$ from the search space. Set $n \leftarrow |\mathcal{I}_0|$.

(2) *(Iterate)* While $n < n_{\text{max}}$ do:

    (a) *(Build Surrogate)* Build/update the surrogate for the objective, $s_n^{\mathcal{E}}(\Theta)$.

(b) *(Generate Trial Points)* Generate random trial points within the search space according to some probability distribution.

(c) *(Evaluate Surrogate at Trial Points)* Evaluate $s_n^{\mathcal{E}}(\Theta)$ at each trial point and compute the min and max value of $s_n^{\mathcal{E}}(\Theta)$ among the trial points.

(d) *(Compute Minimum Distance of Each Trial Point from Previous Sample Points)* Compute $\Delta_n(\Theta)$ at each trial point and calculate the min and max of $\Delta_n(\Theta)$ among all trial points.

(e) *(Compute Ranks)* For each trial point Θ, compute the *Surrogate Rank* $\mathcal{R}_n^S(\Theta) \in [0,1]$, the *Minimum Distance Rank* $\mathcal{R}_n^{\Delta}(\Theta) \in [0,1]$ and the *Weighted Rank*

$$\mathcal{R}_n(\Theta) = w_S \mathcal{R}_n^S(\Theta) + (1 - w_S)\mathcal{R}_n^{\Delta}(\Theta)$$

(f) *(Select Sample Point)* Choose the next sample point Θ_{n+1} to be the trial point Θ that minimizes $\mathcal{R}_n(\Theta)$.

(g) *(Evaluate Selected Point)* Evaluate $\mathcal{E}(\Theta_{n+1})$, update information, and reset $n \leftarrow n + 1$.

end.

(3) *(Return Best Point Obtained)* Return the best solution obtained Θ_n^* and the value $\mathcal{E}(\Theta_n^*)$.

As in [16], the B-CONDOR method is implemented using an RBF surrogate model, giving rise to *B-CONDOR-RBF*. Given n distinct points and their objective function values, $(\Theta_1, \mathcal{E}(\Theta_1)), (\Theta_2, \mathcal{E}(\Theta_2)), \ldots, (\Theta_n, \mathcal{E}(\Theta_n))$, we use the RBF model of the form [11]:

$$s_n(\Theta) = \sum_{i=1}^{n} \lambda_i \phi(\|\Theta - \Theta_i\|) + c^T\Theta + c_0, \ \Theta \in \mathbb{R}^d,$$

where $\| \cdot \|$ is the 2-norm, $\lambda_i \in \mathbb{R}$ for $i = 1, \ldots, n$, $c \in \mathbb{R}^d$ and $c_0 \in \mathbb{R}$. Note that each point Θ_i is a center and $c^T\Theta + c_0$ is simply a linear polynomial in d variables. Moreover, the basis functions can take various forms such as the cubic $(\phi(r) = r^3)$, thin plate spline $(\phi(r) = r^2 \log r)$, and Gaussian $(\phi(r) = \exp(-\gamma r^2)$ forms. Training this model is fast and is relatively straightforward since it simply involves solving a linear system with good numerical properties [11].

3 Computational Experiments

3.1 Real-World Classification Problems Used for Hyperparameter Optimization of Random Forests

All computational experiments are carried out in R [13] through RStudio [18] on an Intel(R) Core(TM) i7-7700T CPU @ 2.90 GHz, 2904 Mhz, 4 Core(s) Windows-based machine. The RFs are trained and evaluated on the data sets using the *ranger* R package [22], which provides a fast implementation of RFs for high-dimensional data. Specifically, the ranger() function is used to calculate the OOB prediction error of the RF on a dataset.

Table 1. Characteristics of the classification problems for RF hyperparameter optimization. The training set consists of 70% of the data set and is fixed in this study.

Tuning problem	Number of predictors	Number of classes	Number of data points	Size of search space
Job Scheduling	7	4	4331	7700
Gamma Telescope	10	2	19020	11000
Red Wine Quality	11	6	1599	12100
White Wine Quality	11	7	4898	12100
Forest Types	27	4	523	29700
Alzheimer	130	2	333	143000
Urban Land Cover	147	9	675	161700
Hepatic	376	3	281	413600
Madelon	500	2	2000	550000
Parkinson	753	2	756	828300

The B-CONDOR-RBF and Discrete-EI algorithms are applied to optimize the hyperparameters of an RF on 10 classification data sets with no missing values. The characteristics of these hyperparameter optimization problems are given in Table 1. The *High Performance Computing (HPC) Job Scheduling*, *Alzheimer's Disease*, and *Hepatic Injury* data sets are part of the *AppliedPredictiveModeling* R package [8,9]. The *Gamma Telescope, Red Wine Quality, White Wine Quality, Forest Types, Urban Land Cover, Madelon*, and *Parkinson's Disease* data sets come from the UC Irvine Machine Learning Repository [4].

As mentioned earlier, we tune four hyperparameters of a classification RF: (1) number of decision trees, denoted by *ntree*; (2) number of predictors drawn at random for each split, denoted by *mtry*; (3) minimum number of samples in a node, denoted by *min.node.size*; and (4) fraction of the training set drawn at random with replacement for constructing each tree, denoted by *sample.frac*. This results in a 4-dimensional bound-constrained discrete black-box optimization problem. The typical recommended settings of these hyperparameters for classification RFs [12] are: ntree = 500, mtry = $\lceil\sqrt{p}\rceil$ (where p is the number of predictors), min.node.size = 1, and sample.frac = 1 (since we are sampling with replacement). These recommended settings are included in the possible values of the hyperparameters in the optimization problem: ntree $\in \{100, 200, \ldots, 1000\}$, mtry $\in \{1, 2, \ldots, p\}$, min.node.size $\in \{1, 2, \ldots, 10\}$, and sample.frac $\in \{0.50, 0.55, 0.60, \ldots, 0.95, 1.0\}$. Hence, the total number of distinct solutions in the search space for the optimization problem is $10 \times p \times 10 \times 11 = 1100p$.

Before any experiments are performed, we split each data set into a training set (70%) and a test set (30%) only once and the *objective function* is defined as the *overall out-of-bag (OOB) prediction error of the RF on the training set*. We use the same training set and fix the seed in the ranger() function when calculating the OOB prediction error for any setting of the RF hyperparameters. This ensures that each RF tuning problem becomes deterministic. Moreover, all the decision variables of the RF tuning problem are rescaled to range from 0 to 1. After the different optimization methods are used to minimize the objective function for each data set, the best RFs (in terms of OOB prediction error on the training set) obtained by each algorithm are evaluated on the fixed test set.

3.2   Experimental Setup

We run six algorithms for the hyperparameter optimization of the RF on the 10 classification problems: four surrogate-based methods and two random search methods. Among the surrogate-based methods are two variants of B-CONDOR-RBF [16]: B-CONDOR-RBF-Local and B-CONDOR-RBF-Global, which both use a cubic RBF model augmented by a linear polynomial. The cubic type of RBF was chosen due to its simplicity and previous good results when used with RBF methods (e.g., [5,15]). Each iteration of the RBF methods generates $100d$ random trial points from the search space and the RBF surrogate is used to select the most promising trial solution using a weighted combination of the surrogate and distance criteria of 0.95 and 0.05, respectively, as in [15]. In the B-CONDOR-RBF-Local algorithm, the random trial points are generated in the neighborhood of the current best solution. The generation of these random trial points is controlled by two parameters namely, the perturbation probability p_{pert} and the neighborhood depth parameter $depth_{nbhd}$. In particular, the values of p_{pert} and $depth_{nbhd}$ vary through the iterations according to the cycle $\langle(1, 50\%), (0.5, 50\%), (0.5, 25\%), (0.5, 10\%), (0.5, 5\%)\rangle$. This choice of parameter values yields iterations that follow a cycle beginning with a more global search and ending with a more local search. For B-CONDOR-RBF-Global, the random trial points are simply generated uniformly over the entire discrete search space.

As mentioned earlier, the Discrete-EI method that handles ordinal discrete variables uses the expected improvement (EI) criterion from the EGO algorithm [6] to select its sample point. We run Discrete-EI using the Gaussian and Matérn $5/2$ kernels for the covariance function. In Discrete-EI, the next sample point is an approximate maximizer of the EI function over the entire discrete search space obtained by discrete uniform random search for $100d$ iterations. This Discrete-EI implementation uses the km() and EI() functions from the DiceKriging [17] and DiceOptim [10] R packages, respectively.

Random search is the simplest and one of the most widely used method for the hyperparameter optimization of machine learning models. Hence, we include a *Discrete Global Random Search* method to serve as a baseline for comparison with the surrogate-based methods. In this method, the next function evaluation point is simply chosen uniformly at random in the search space of hyperparameters. Moreover, we also implement the *Discrete Local Random Search* method from [16] since it was shown to be consistently better than Discrete Global Random Search on the hyperparameter optimization of RFs for the regression data sets used in that study. In Discrete Local Random Search, the next function evaluation point is generated using the perturbation probability p_{pert} and the neighborhood depth parameter $depth_{nbhd}$ from B-CONDOR-RBF-Local and varying using the same cycle as in the algorithm except there is no RBF involved and only one point is generated in every iteration.

The surrogate-based and random search algorithms are run for 30 trials on the 10 RF hyperparameter optimization problems on classification data sets. For fair comparison, all algorithms used the same $5(d + 1)$ initial points in a given trial run. However, different trial runs used different sets of $5(d + 1)$ initial points where the objective function (overall OOB prediction error) is evaluated. For each set of initial points, we include the typical recommended values of the RF hyperparameters for classification problems given above as the first initial point. Then, we choose $5d+4$ points uniformly at random on the hyperparameter search space for the other initial points. Moreover, we run each algorithm for a limited budget of $20(d + 1)$ function evaluations since the RF hyperparameter optimization problems can be computationally expensive especially on data sets containing many predictor variables and/or a large number of data points. The number of function evaluations is expressed in factors of $d + 1$ since this is the minimum number of points needed to fit the simplest surrogate, which is a linear model. We include the recommended RF hyperparameter settings since they have been known to work well in many cases [12], so this allows us to determine how much further improvement can be made using the surrogate-based hyperparameter optimization methods when there is a very limited budget on the number of function evaluations.

3.3   Results and Discussion

Tables 2 and 3 show the mean and standard error, taken over 30 trials, of the best objective function value (OOB prediction error on the fixed training set) obtained by the surrogate-based and random search algorithms at different computational budgets on the RF hyperparameter optimization problems. In each row of these tables, the best is indicated by a solid blue box while the second best is indicated by a dashed magenta box. Moreover, Figs. 1, 2 and 3 show the plots of the mean of the best overall OOB prediction error obtained by the six algorithms on the RF hyperparameter optimization problems for the classification data sets at different computational budgets beginning with the initial design points of size $5(d+1)$ up to a maximum of $20(d+1)$ function evaluations. These plots also include error bars that represent 95% t confidence intervals for the mean.

The results in Tables 2 and 3 and in Figs. 1, 2 and 3 show that the RBF algorithms and the Bayesian optimization methods are consistently superior to Discrete Global Random Search on the 10 RF hyperparameter optimization problems on classification data sets. This confirms that surrogate-based approaches are promising for hyperparameter optimization of RFs on classification data sets. Among the surrogate-based approaches, B-CONDOR-RBF-Global achieved the best results on most of the problems. In particular, B-CONDOR-RBF-Global obtained generally better results than Discrete-EI with the Gaussian kernel on 9 of the 10 problems (all except on the Forest Types data set). It also obtained better results than Discrete-EI with the Matérn 5/2 kernel on 8 of the 10 problems (all except on the Forest Types and Madelon data sets). Moreover, B-CONDOR-RBF-Global outperformed the local variant B-CONDOR-RBF-Local on 9 of the

Table 2. Mean and standard error of best overall OOB prediction error found by different methods at various computational budgets on the RF tuning problems. The mean is taken over 30 trials. The best and second best results in each row are enclosed by a solid blue box and a dashed magenta box, respectively.

Tuning Problem	Number of evaluations	B-CONDOR-RBF-Local (cubic)	B-CONDOR-RBF-Global (cubic)	Discrete-EI (Matérn 5/2)	Discrete-EI (Gaussian)	Discrete Local Random Search	Discrete Global Random Search
HPC Job Scheduling	10(d+1)	0.1567 (1.54e-04)	0.1570 (1.68e-04)	0.1575 (1.58e-04)	0.1576 (1.57e-04)	0.1572 (1.60e-04)	0.1583 (1.42e-04)
	15(d+1)	0.1566 (1.36e-04)	0.1565 (1.50e-04)	0.1569 (1.51e-04)	0.1570 (1.48e-04)	0.1569 (1.36e-04)	0.1581 (1.51e-04)
	20(d+1)	0.1565 (1.28e-04)	0.1563 (1.37e-04)	0.1567 (1.48e-04)	0.1569 (1.40e-04)	0.1566 (1.34e-04)	0.1581 (1.50e-04)
Gamma Telescope	10(d+1)	0.1207 (5.64e-05)	0.1206 (6.01e-05)	0.1207 (5.47e-05)	0.1208 (6.62e-05)	0.1206 (6.17e-05)	0.1211 (7.50e-05)
	15(d+1)	0.1206 (5.82e-05)	0.1205 (5.58e-05)	0.1206 (4.39e-05)	0.1206 (7.52e-05)	0.1205 (5.59e-05)	0.1208 (6.35e-05)
	20(d+1)	0.1206 (5.48e-05)	0.1204 (5.10e-05)	0.1205 (4.39e-05)	0.1205 (6.13e-05)	0.1204 (5.35e-05)	0.1207 (6.10e-05)
Red Wine	10(d+1)	0.3601 (1.79e-04)	0.3595 (7.71e-05)	0.3598 (1.83e-04)	0.3598 (1.74e-04)	0.3609 (2.07e-04)	0.3630 (2.21e-04)
	15(d+1)	0.3598 (1.35e-04)	0.3593 (3.02e-05)	0.3595 (1.64e-04)	0.3596 (1.65e-04)	0.3602 (1.66e-04)	0.3626 (2.22e-04)
	20(d+1)	0.3596 (1.11e-04)	0.3593 (2.21e-05)	0.3594 (1.60e-04)	0.3595 (1.61e-04)	0.3598 (1.35e-04)	0.3621 (2.43e-04)
White Wine	10(d+1)	0.3745 (5.49e-05)	0.3743 (3.79e-05)	0.3744 (9.29e-05)	0.3746 (1.00e-04)	0.3751 (1.15e-04)	0.3765 (1.26e-04)
	15(d+1)	0.3744 (5.16e-05)	0.3743 (2.11e-05)	0.3743 (9.06e-05)	0.3744 (9.54e-05)	0.3748 (7.16e-05)	0.3764 (1.31e-04)
	20(d+1)	0.3744 (4.99e-05)	0.3742 (8.15e-06)	0.3743 (8.97e-05)	0.3743 (9.05e-05)	0.3746 (7.60e-05)	0.3762 (1.44e-04)
Forest Types	10(d+1)	0.0899 (3.55e-04)	0.0897 (2.95e-04)	0.0895 (3.63e-04)	0.0893 (4.41e-04)	0.0905 (5.36e-04)	0.0907 (4.61e-04)
	15(d+1)	0.0891 (3.10e-04)	0.0891 (2.81e-04)	0.0883 (2.73e-04)	0.0883 (3.25e-04)	0.0892 (4.99e-04)	0.0900 (4.53e-04)
	20(d+1)	0.0890 (3.12e-04)	0.0883 (2.67e-04)	0.0879 (2.30e-04)	0.0881 (2.83e-04)	0.0885 (4.06e-04)	0.0898 (3.87e-04)

Table 3. Mean and standard error of best overall OOB prediction error found by different methods at various computational budgets on the RF tuning problems. The mean is taken over 30 trials. The best and second best results in each row are enclosed by a solid blue box and a dashed magenta box, respectively.

Tuning Problem	Number of evaluations	B-CONDOR-RBF-Local (cubic)	B-CONDOR-RBF-Global (cubic)	Discrete-EI (Matérn 5/2)	Discrete-EI (Gaussian)	Discrete Local Random Search	Discrete Global Random Search
Alzheimer	10(d+1)	0.1565 (8.42e-04)	0.1567 (9.14e-04)	0.1582 (1.04e-03)	0.1592 (8.32e-04)	0.1575 (1.01e-03)	0.1612 (9.13e-04)
	15(d+1)	0.1554 (8.33e-04)	0.1549 (6.93e-04)	0.1565 (8.67e-04)	0.1579 (7.25e-04)	0.1564 (8.15e-04)	0.1587 (8.60e-04)
	20(d+1)	0.1546 (7.83e-04)	0.1541 (7.23e-04)	0.1542 (7.40e-04)	0.1565 (7.05e-04)	0.1551 (8.67e-04)	0.1577 (8.21e-04)
Urban Land	10(d+1)	0.1428 (4.50e-04)	0.1425 (4.65e-04)	0.1433 (4.25e-04)	0.1437 (4.20e-04)	0.1421 (4.65e-04)	0.1441 (4.00e-04)
	15(d+1)	0.1421 (3.93e-04)	0.1415 (4.84e-04)	0.1422 (4.63e-04)	0.1429 (4.73e-04)	0.1415 (4.91e-04)	0.1433 (3.87e-04)
	20(d+1)	0.1416 (3.81e-04)	0.1407 (4.73e-04)	0.1416 (4.55e-04)	0.1423 (4.20e-04)	0.1408 (4.51e-04)	0.1423 (3.95e-04)
Hepatic	10(d+1)	0.4422 (1.53e-03)	0.4417 (1.98e-03)	0.4434 (1.70e-03)	0.4425 (1.83e-03)	0.4423 (1.70e-03)	0.4466 (1.65e-03)
	15(d+1)	0.4403 (1.37e-03)	0.4395 (1.89e-03)	0.4400 (1.52e-03)	0.4395 (1.71e-03)	0.4401 (1.53e-03)	0.4439 (1.62e-03)
	20(d+1)	0.4386 (1.31e-03)	0.4366 (1.69e-03)	0.4378 (1.46e-03)	0.4367 (1.52e-03)	0.4381 (1.48e-03)	0.4401 (1.58e-03)
Madelon	10(d+1)	0.1806 (4.01e-04)	0.1818 (4.92e-04)	0.1813 (4.75e-04)	0.1832 (5.03e-04)	0.1838 (5.75e-04)	0.1868 (7.76e-04)
	15(d+1)	0.1799 (3.27e-04)	0.1805 (3.86e-04)	0.1799 (3.89e-04)	0.1808 (4.67e-04)	0.1826 (5.99e-04)	0.1859 (7.94e-04)
	20(d+1)	0.1790 (4.16e-04)	0.1797 (4.54e-04)	0.1795 (3.10e-04)	0.1804 (4.12e-04)	0.1810 (6.14e-04)	0.1849 (7.42e-04)
Parkinsons	10(d+1)	0.1302 (4.47e-04)	0.1298 (3.18e-04)	0.1302 (4.77e-04)	0.1308 (3.78e-04)	0.1306 (4.28e-04)	0.1317 (3.55e-04)
	15(d+1)	0.1292 (3.90e-04)	0.1290 (3.13e-04)	0.1295 (4.32e-04)	0.1302 (3.78e-04)	0.1301 (4.29e-04)	0.1309 (3.62e-04)
	20(d+1)	0.1285 (4.30e-04)	0.1280 (3.73e-04)	0.1289 (4.74e-04)	0.1295 (4.32e-04)	0.1292 (4.48e-04)	0.1304 (3.14e-04)

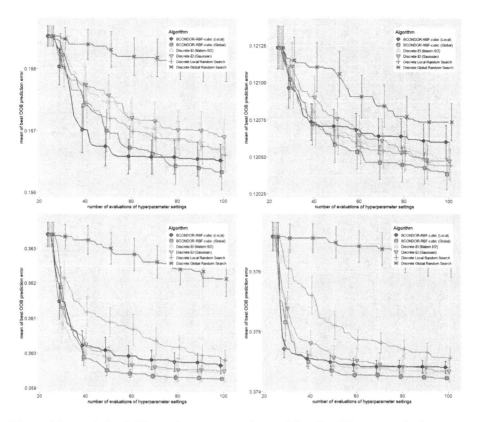

Fig. 1. Mean of the OOB prediction error obtained by the different methods at various computational budgets on four of the hyperparameter optimization problems for classification RFs: Job Scheduling (top left), Gamma Telescope (top right), Red Wine Quality (bottom left) and White Wine Quality (bottom right)

problems, but the latter obtained better results than the former on the Madelon data set involving 500 predictors and 2000 instances. It would be of interest to know for which type of data sets will the local variant yield better results.

Next, as mentioned above, B-CONDOR-RBF-Local consistently outperformed Discrete Global Random Search on all 10 RF hyperparameter optimization problems. It is also better than Discrete Local Random Search on seven of the problems (all except on the Gamma Telescope, Urban Land and Hepatic data sets). Moreover, B-CONDOR-RBF-Local achieved comparable performance with the Bayesian optimization approaches. In particular, B-CONDOR-RBF-Local is better than Discrete-EI with the Gaussian kernel on five of the problems and it is competitive with the latter on another three problems. Also, B-CONDOR-RBF-Local is better than Discrete-EI with the Matérn 5/2 kernel on four of the 10 problems and it is competitive with the latter on another two problems.

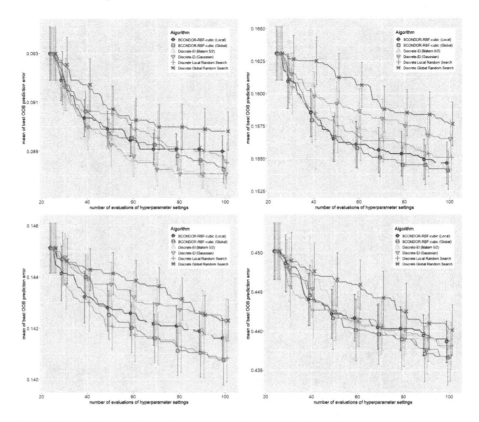

Fig. 2. Mean of the OOB prediction error obtained by the different methods at various computational budgets on four of the hyperparameter optimization problems for classification RFs: Forest Types (top left), Alzheimer's Disease (top right), Urban Land (bottom left) and Hepatic (bottom right).

These results complement those obtained in [16] on the hyperparameter optimization of RFs for regression data sets. In that paper, B-CONDOR-RBF algorithms obtained much better OOB RMSE than Discrete Global Random Search on RF hyperparameter tuning problems on seven regression data sets. They also obtained better or comparable results to Discrete-EI with the Gaussian kernel and the Discrete Local Random Search method. In that paper, Discrete-EI with the Matérn 5/2 kernel was not used.

Next, the Bayesian optimization algorithms (Discrete-EI with the Matérn 5/2 and Gaussian kernels) yielded consistently better results than Discrete Global Random Search on all 10 problems. This is consistent with the findings by Turner et al. [20]. However, compared with Discrete Local Random Search, which does not use any surrogates, the Bayesian approach does not always yield the better result. In particular, Discrete-EI with the Matérn 5/2 kernel obtained better results than Discrete Local Random Search on six of the problems while the

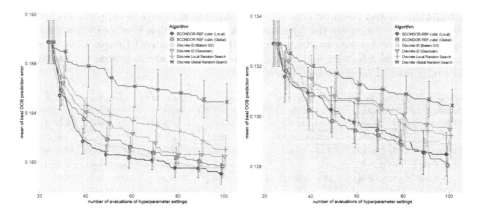

Fig. 3. Mean of the OOB prediction error obtained by the different methods at various computational budgets on two of the hyperparameter optimization problems for classification RFs: Madelon (left), Parkinson's Disease (right).

latter obtained better results than the former on three of the problems. On the Alzheimer's data set, the two methods achieved comparable results. Moreover, Discrete-EI with the Gaussian kernel obtained better results than Discrete Local Random Search on half of the problems, while the latter obtained better results than the former on the remaining half of the problems. For the Bayesian optimization methods, the Matérn 5/2 kernel yielded better results than the Gaussian kernel on seven of the problems while the latter is better than the former only on the Hepatic data set. The two Bayesian methods obtained comparable results on the remaining two problems involving the Gamma Telescope and Forest Types data sets.

As was observed in the hyperparameter optimization of RF for regression problems in [16], Discrete Local Random Search method consistently outperformed Discrete Global Random Search on all 10 RF hyperparameter optimization problems for classification data sets. Moreover, although Discrete Local Random Search does not use a surrogate, it was quite competitive with the Bayesian method Discrete-EI that uses the Gaussian kernel on the same RF tuning problems and it obtained better results than Discrete-EI with the Matern 5/2 kernel on three of the problems. Discrete Local Random Search generates its sample points in the same manner as in B-CONDOR-RBF-Local except no surrogate is involved. This again indicates that this local scheme for choosing sample points is a promising alternative for the widely used global random search for hyperparameter optimization problems, especially when there is a limited budget on function evaluations.

Recall that in each trial run of every algorithm, the first point in the initial design of $5(d+1)$ points consists of the recommended RF hyperparameter settings for classification problems. Table 4 shows the mean and standard error (over 30 trials) of the percentage improvement in the best overall OOB Prediction Error

Table 4. Mean and standard error (over 30 trials) of the percent improvement in OOB prediction error found by the hyperparameter optimization methods after $20(d+1)$ evaluations over the one obtained by using the recommended hyperparameters on RF tuning problems. The best and second best in each row are indicated by a solid blue box and a dashed magenta box, respectively.

Tuning Problem	B-CONDOR-RBF (Local)	B-CONDOR-RBF (Global)	Discrete-EI (Matérn 5/2)	Discrete-EI (Gaussian)	Discrete Local Random Search	Discrete Global Random Search
Job Sched	1.37 (8.1e-02)	1.49 (8.6e-02)	1.25 (9.4e-02)	1.13 (8.8e-02)	1.32 (8.4e-02)	0.37 (9.5e-02)
Telescope	1.07 (4.5e-02)	1.24 (4.2e-02)	1.16 (3.6e-02)	1.17 (5.0e-02)	1.20 (4.4e-02)	0.96 (5.0e-02)
Red Wine	1.19 (3.1e-02)	1.30 (6.1e-03)	1.25 (4.4e-02)	1.23 (4.4e-02)	1.15 (3.7e-02)	0.51 (6.7e-02)
White Wine	0.66 (1.3e-02)	0.71 (2.2e-03)	0.69 (2.4e-02)	0.68 (2.4e-02)	0.62 (2.0e-02)	0.19 (3.8e-02)
Forest Types	9.54 (3.2e-01)	10.28 (2.7e-01)	10.65 (2.3e-01)	10.46 (2.9e-01)	10.00 (4.1e-01)	8.70 (3.9e-01)
Alzheimer	14.21 (4.3e-01)	14.52 (4.0e-01)	14.44 (4.1e-01)	13.17 (3.9e-01)	13.97 (4.8e-01)	12.54 (4.6e-01)
Urban Land	8.45 (2.5e-01)	9.00 (3.1e-01)	8.45 (2.9e-01)	7.99 (2.7e-01)	8.95 (2.9e-01)	7.99 (2.6e-01)
Hepatic	7.56 (2.8e-01)	7.99 (3.6e-01)	7.74 (3.1e-01)	7.96 (3.2e-01)	7.67 (3.1e-01)	7.24 (3.3e-01)
Madelon	45.04 (1.3e-01)	44.84 (1.4e-01)	44.89 (9.5e-02)	44.61 (1.3e-01)	44.43 (1.9e-01)	43.24 (2.3e-01)
Parkinsons	5.60 (3.2e-01)	5.93 (2.7e-01)	5.28 (3.5e-01)	4.86 (3.2e-01)	5.05 (3.3e-01)	4.17 (2.3e-01)

over the recommended hyperparameter settings obtained by the algorithms after $20(d+1)$ function evaluations on the RF hyperparameter optimization problems. As before, the best and second best for each problem are indicated by a solid blue box and a dashed magenta box, respectively. This table also shows that the B-CONDOR-RBF-Global algorithm has the best improvements over the recommended hyperparameters on eight of the problems (all except on the Forest Types and Madelon data sets). The next best improvements were obtained by Discrete-EI with the Matérn 5/2 kernel followed by B-CONDOR-RBF-Local and Discrete-EI with the Gaussian kernel, which have comparable results. These results are somewhat consistent with those obtained in Tables 2 and 3. Moreover, the improvements over the recommended hyperparameters are considerable with the highest mean percentage improvement at 45.04% obtained by B-CONDOR-RBF-Local on the RF tuning problem on the Madelon data set.

Finally, Table 5 shows the mean and standard error (over 30 trials) of the prediction error (percent of misclassified instances) on the test set of the RF whose hyperparameters are obtained by the various methods after $20(d+1)$ evaluations. This table shows that the algorithms that obtained the smallest OOB prediction error do not always get the smallest prediction error on the test set. In particular, B-CONDOR-RBF-Local obtained better test set prediction error than B-CONDOR-RBF-Global on six of the problems. Moreover, it obtained better test set prediction error than Discrete-EI with the Matérn 5/2 kernel on five of the problems while the results are comparable on the Alzheimer data set. These results are not necessarily inconsistent with those in the previous tables since some of the test sets have relatively few instances and the means of the prediction errors are not too far away from one another. In particular, B-CONDOR-RBF-Global, which has the best results in the previous tables, has test set prediction errors that are competitive with the other surrogate methods. In addition, it obtained better or comparable test set prediction errors than Discrete Global Random Search on six of the problems.

Table 5. Mean and standard error (over 30 trials) of the prediction error (expressed as a percentage) on the test set of the RF whose hyperparameters are obtained by the various methods after $20(d+1)$ evaluations. The best and second best in each row are indicated by a solid blue box and a dashed magenta box, respectively.

Tuning Problem	B-CONDOR-RBF (Local)	B-CONDOR-RBF (Global)	Discrete-EI (Matérn 5/2)	Discrete-EI (Gaussian)	Discrete Local Random Search	Discrete Global Random Search
Job Sched	16.49 (3.5e-02)	16.51 (3.6e-02)	16.47 (4.5e-02)	16.58 (4.6e-02)	16.56 (4.2e-02)	16.38 (5.0e-02)
Telescope	11.43 (1.7e-02)	11.46 (1.8e-02)	11.44 (1.5e-02)	11.44 (1.5e-02)	11.45 (1.7e-02)	11.46 (2.0e-02)
Red Wine	29.93 (4.7e-02)	29.78 (6.9e-03)	29.76 (3.7e-02)	29.79 (2.6e-02)	29.74 (8.6e-02)	29.74 (1.2e-01)
White Wine	33.04 (2.4e-02)	33.10 (1.5e-02)	33.12 (2.8e-02)	33.10 (3.2e-02)	33.14 (4.7e-02)	33.74 (5.4e-02)
Forest Types	13.46 (8.5e-02)	13.61 (6.5e-02)	13.69 (6.7e-02)	13.74 (7.3e-02)	13.55 (6.8e-02)	13.55 (7.4e-02)
Alzheimer	10.00 (1.9e-01)	9.80 (1.5e-01)	10.00 (1.9e-01)	10.00 (2.1e-01)	10.00 (1.9e-01)	9.97 (1.8e-01)
Urban Land	11.36 (8.5e-02)	11.36 (7.4e-02)	11.35 (1.0e-01)	11.33 (7.8e-02)	11.44 (8.7e-02)	11.44 (1.1e-01)
Hepatic	40.67 (3.6e-01)	40.86 (4.5e-01)	40.98 (4.0e-01)	40.75 (3.8e-01)	39.96 (4.2e-01)	40.39 (4.8e-01)
Madelon	17.39 (1.2e-01)	17.58 (1.1e-01)	17.59 (9.7e-02)	17.53 (9.4e-02)	17.58 (1.1e-01)	17.83 (1.1e-01)
Parkinsons	9.24 (1.5e-01)	8.96 (1.2e-01)	9.03 (1.2e-01)	9.15 (1.1e-01)	9.57 (1.7e-01)	9.49 (1.2e-01)

4   Summary and Future Work

This paper explored the use of surrogate-based approaches that handle discrete variables, particularly the RBF method B-CONDOR-RBF [16] and a Bayesian optimization method called Discrete-EI, for the hyperparameter optimization of a classification random forest (RF). A global and a local variant of B-CONDOR-RBF and two variants of Discrete-EI are compared with a discrete global random search method and a discrete local random search method on 10 RF hyperparameter optimization problems on classification data sets involving up to 753 predictor variables and up to 19K data points. The B-CONDOR-RBF algorithms used a cubic RBF augmented by a linear polynomial while the Bayesian optimization methods used the Gaussian and Matérn 5/2 kernels. The RF hyperparameter optimization problem involves tuning four RF hyperparameters, so the problem has four decision variables and the objective function to be minimized is the overall out-of-bag (OOB) prediction error of the RF on the training set, which is represented as a fraction of misclassified instances.

The results showed that the B-CONDOR-RBF algorithms (global and local variants) and Discrete-EI algorithms (using the Matérn 5/2 and Gaussian kernels) obtained consistently much better overall OOB prediction error than the Discrete Global Random Search method on all RF hyperparameter optimization problems. Among the four surrogate-based methods, the global variant of B-CONDOR-RBF obtained the best overall OOB prediction error on most of the problems. Moreover, the local variant of B-CONDOR-RBF is an improvement over Discrete Local Random Search and it is better or competitive with the Bayesian optimization algorithm Discrete-EI with the Gaussian kernel on most of the problems. Also, it is competitive with Discrete-EI with the Matérn 5/2 kernel. Among the two Bayesian algorithms, the one that uses the Matérn 5/2 kernel obtained generally better results than the one using the Gaussian kernel. In addition, between the two random search methods, the Discrete Local

Random Search method consistently outperformed the Discrete Global Random Search method. It is also worth noting that the Discrete Local Random Search approach, which does not use a surrogate, was competitive with the Bayesian optimization algorithm that uses the Gaussian kernel on the test problems considered. Compared to random search methods and Bayesian optimization methods, RBF methods are not as popular for the hyperparameter optimization of machine learning models. In fact, this paper is among the few, if not the only one, that used RBF surrogates for the hyperparameter optimization of RFs for classification problems.

Previous work showed that B-CONDOR-RBF works well on regression data sets compared to alternatives such as Bayesian optimization with the Gaussian kernel. This paper showed that it is also promising for the hyperparameter optimization of RF on classification data sets. In future work, we consider other metrics such as the OOB F1 score or OOB AUC score for the objective function of the RF hyperparameter optimization problem on classification data sets. Moreover, we consider other surrogate-based discrete optimization methods that use a different strategy for the selection of sample points. In particular, one can use a nonlinear discrete optimization algorithm to perform a more thorough search on the surrogate surface to determine the next sample point for function evaluation. We can also run B-CONDOR-RBF using other types of RBF such as the thin plate spline or the Gaussian and compare its performance when using the cubic type. When the data set involves thousands of predictor variables and hundreds of thousands or millions of data points, the hyperparameter optimization problem becomes even more computationally expensive. However, the number of decision variables, which is the number of hyperparameters to tune, remains the same. It would be interest to develop more efficient algorithms when dealing with much larger data sets. Finally, it is also of interest to compare the performance of the B-CONDOR-RBF algorithms with the Bayesian methods on hyperparameter tuning problems involving deep neural networks, support vector machines and other machine learning models.

References

1. Archetti, F., Candelieri, A.: Bayesian Optimization and Data Science. Springer, Cham (2019). https://doi.org/10.1007/978-3-030-24494-1
2. Bergstra, J., Bengio, Y.: Random search for hyper-parameter optimization. J. Mach. Learn. Res. **13**, 281–305 (2012)
3. Breiman, L.: Random forests. Mach. Learn. **45**, 5–32 (2001)
4. Dua, D., Graff, C.: UCI Machine Learning Repository. University of California, School of Information and Computer Science, Irvine (2019). http://archive.ics.uci.edu/ml
5. Ilievski, I., Akhtar, T., Feng, J., Shoemaker, C.: Efficient hyperparameter optimization for deep learning algorithms using deterministic RBF surrogates. In: Proceedings of the AAAI Conference on Artificial Intelligence, vol. 31, no. 1 (2017)
6. Jones, D.R., Schonlau, M., Welch, W.J.: Efficient global optimization of expensive black-box functions. J. Glob. Optim. **13**, 455–492 (1998)

7. Joy, T.T., Rana, S., Gupta, S., Venkatesh, S.: Hyperparameter tuning for big data using Bayesian optimisation. In: 2016 23rd International Conference on Pattern Recognition (ICPR), pp. 2574–2579 (2016). https://doi.org/10.1109/ICPR.2016.7900023

8. Kuhn, M., Johnson, K.: Applied Predictive Modeling. Springer, New York (2013). https://doi.org/10.1007/978-1-4614-6849-3

9. Kuhn, M., Johnson, K.: AppliedPredictiveModeling: Functions and Data Sets for 'Applied Predictive Modeling'. R package version 1.1-7 (2018). https://CRAN.R-project.org/package=AppliedPredictiveModeling

10. Picheny, V., Ginsbourger, D., Roustant, O.: DiceOptim: Kriging-Based Optimization for Computer Experiments. R package version 2.1.1 (2021). https://CRAN.R-project.org/package=DiceOptim

11. Powell, M.J.D.: The theory of radial basis function approximation in 1990. In: Light, W. (ed.) Advances in Numerical Analysis, Volume 2: Wavelets, Subdivision Algorithms and Radial Basis Functions, pp. 105–210. Oxford University Press, Oxford (1992)

12. Probst, P., Wright, M.N., Boulesteix, A.-L.: Hyperparameters and tuning strategies for random forest. WIREs Data Min. Knowl. Discov. **9**(3), e1301 (2019)

13. R Core Team: R: A language and environment for statistical computing. R Foundation for Statistical Computing, Vienna, Austria (2021). https://www.R-project.org/

14. Rasmussen, C.E., Williams, C.K.I.: Gaussian Processes for Machine Learning (Adaptive Computation and Machine Learning). The MIT Press (2006)

15. Regis, R.G.: Stochastic radial basis function algorithms for large-scale optimization involving expensive black-box objective and constraint functions. Comput. Oper. Res. **38**(5), 837–853 (2011)

16. Regis, R.G.: Hyperparameter tuning of random forests using radial basis function models. In: Nicosia, G., et al. (eds.) LOD 2022. LNCS, vol. 13810, pp. 309–324. Springer, Cham (2023). https://doi.org/10.1007/978-3-031-25599-1_23

17. Roustant, O., Ginsbourger, D., Deville, Y.: DiceKriging, DiceOptim: two R packages for the analysis of computer experiments by kriging-based metamodeling and optimization. J. Stat. Softw. **51**(1), 1–55 (2012)

18. RStudio Team: RStudio: Integrated Development for R. RStudio, PBC, Boston, MA (2020). http://www.rstudio.com/

19. Schonlau, M.: Computer experiments and global optimization. Ph.D. thesis, University of Waterloo, Canada (1997)

20. Turner, R., et al.: Bayesian optimization is superior to random search for machine learning hyperparameter tuning: analysis of the black-box optimization challenge 2020. In: Proceedings of the NeurIPS 2020 Competition and Demonstration Track, in Proceedings of Machine Learning Research, vol. 133, pp. 3–26 (2021)

21. Vu, K.K., D'Ambrosio, C., Hamadi, Y., Liberti, L.: Surrogate-based methods for black-box optimization. Int. Trans. Oper. Res. **24**, 393–424 (2017)

22. Wright, M.N., Ziegler, A.: Ranger: a fast implementation of random forests for high dimensional data in C++ and R. J. Stat. Softw. **77**(1), 1–17 (2017)

Workshop on Computational Science and HPC (CSHPC 2023)

Optimization of Multiple-Precision LU Decomposition Using Ozaki Scheme

Tomonori Kouya[✉][ID] and Taiga Utsugiri

Shizuoka Institute of Science and Technology, 2022-2 Toyosawa, Fukuroi,
Shizuoka 437-8555, Japan
{kouya.tomonori,2121002.ut}@sist.ac.jp
https://www.sist.ac.jp/

Abstract. LU decomposition, which is typically implemented with matrix multiplication, requires more computational time than any other component of the direct method. To optimize this process, we accelerated the multiple-precision matrix multiplication stage and applied it to solve the ill-conditioned linear system. Although the SIMDized Strassen algorithm yields the best performance among of all existing algorithms, it fails to sufficiently accelerate LU decomposition. Instead, we found that within a limited precision range, the Ozaki scheme is more efficient for accelerating LU decomposition. In this study, we present the results of benchmark tests conducted to compare the Strassen algorithm with the Ozaki scheme in terms of computational time, demonstrating that the latter exhibits superior performance in LU decomposition when solving ill-conditioned linear systems of equations.

Keywords: multiple-precision floating-point arithmetic · Ozaki scheme · matrix multiplication · LU decomposition

1 Introduction

Applications requiring significant amount of floating-point computations, such as AI and scientific simulations, are ubiquitous in numerous areas of modern society. Consequently, multicore CPUs and GPUs are readily available at the consumer level, guaranteeing sufficient computation processing and results for various applications. Although IEEE754-1985 binary64 (53-bit length of mantissa) is a standard that characterizes CPU environments, it is associated with suboptimal conditions that do not satisfy the accuracy required by users, necessitating multiple-precision floating-point operations with longer mantissa lengths. Consequently, a multi-component multiple-precision arithmetic library has been developed to use multiple existing IEEE754-1985 binary32 (24 bit) and binary64 floating-point numbers, extending arithmetic precision using error-free transformation techniques. Furthermore, a fast multi-digit arbitrary precision floating-point arithmetic library has been developed based on GMP [3]'s fast multiple-precision natural number (MPN) kernel. The former is represented by the QD

© The Author(s), under exclusive license to Springer Nature Switzerland AG 2023
O. Gervasi et al. (Eds.): ICCSA 2023 Workshops, LNCS 14105, pp. 529–545, 2023.
https://doi.org/10.1007/978-3-031-37108-0_34

library [1] created by Bailey et al., whereas the latter is represented by MPFR [13]. Both libraries have been in practical use for more than 20 years since their initial development, becoming the de facto standard multiple-long-precision floating-point libraries. Accordingly, MPLAPACK/MPBLAS [11] proposed by Nakata provides the basis for a standard multiple-precision numerical linear computation environment. As of March 2023, its version 2.0.1 stably provides the same functionality as binary32 and binary64 LAPACK.

However, there are currently no optimized basic linear computation libraries with multiple-precision arithmetic such as ATLAS, OpenBLAS, and Intel Math Kernel with binary32 and binary64 arithmetic. Standard optimization methods include using SIMD instructions as in the cases of AVX2, AVX-512, and parallelization with OpenMP, whereas optimization with algorithms such as divide-and-conquer is possible for multiple-precision matrix multiplication. We have constructed a fast multiple-precision basic linear algebra subprogram (BLAS) that incorporates these methods. Consequently, we successfully accelerated the matrix multiplication process using the Strassen algorithm.

Recently, progress has been made on accelerating linear computation using multiple-precision computation; namely, the Ozaki scheme was developed for conducting high-precision operations using fast binary32 and binary64 matrix multiplication (SGEMM and DGEMM). It is necessary to verify whether further algorithmic acceleration incorporating these methods is possible by conducting comparative experiments with the current optimization libraries.

A list of optimization library studies for multiple-precision matrix multiplication is presented in Table 1. A question mark indicates that there are no published studies, and the gray cells indicate that the corresponding precision calculation is not expected to be efficient. The blue "BNCmatmul" denotes our previous work [6,7,9]. The area circled in red denotes our latest work ("Utsugiri"), which is the optimization of DD (Double-Double, 106-bit length mantissa), TD (Triple-Double, 159-bit), QD (Quadruple-Double, 212-bit), and MPFR (arbitrary precision) matrix multiplication using the Ozaki scheme on CPUs, and the implementation of TS (Triple-Single, 72-bit) matrix multiplication using the Ozaki scheme on GPUs [16]. Although we could not confirm the Ozaki scheme's effectiveness on consumer GPUs, its effectiveness on CPUs was confirmed for fixed-precision matrix multiplication with a multi-component scheme, as well as for arbitrary-precision matrix multiplication of up to 768 bits as described later.

The LINPACK test, a benchmark test to determine the 500 fastest supercomputers in the world, involves solving a large set of simultaneous linear equations using a direct method, with LU decomposition being the most computationally time-consuming algorithm in the test. Currently, LU decomposition is usually implemented using fast matrix multiplication (xGEMM). If an optimized multiple-precision BLAS can accelerate this process, it can lead to developing novel fast solvers for more complex adverse nonlinear problems.

Based on the results reported in Table 1, including Lis [4], CUMP [2], and MuPAT [17], we have demonstrated that fast multiple-precision LU decomposition is possible on CPUs within a certain range of precision using fast multiple-

Table 1. List of Optimization Methods and Research for Multiple-Precision Basic Linear Computation

xGEMM	CPU				GPU	
Opt.Method	None	AVX2	OpenMP	Ozaki Scheme	CUDA	Ozaki Scheme
DS	?	?	?	?	Mukunoki	Mukunoki
TS	?	?	?	Utsugiri	Utsugiri	Utsugiri
QS	?	?	?	?	?	?
IEEE754 Binary128	MPBLAS	?	MPBLAS	Mukunoki	Mukunoki	Mukunoki
DD	MPBLAS, BNCmatmul	Lis, MuPAT BNCmatmul	Lis,MuPAT, MPBLAS, BNCmatmul	Utsugiri	Mukunoki	Mukunoki
TD	BNCmatmul	BNCmatmul	BNCmatmul	Utsugiri	Utsugiri	Utsugiri
QD	MuPAT MPBLAS, BNCmatmul	BNCmatmul	MuPAT, MPBLAS, BNCmatmul	Utsugiri	?	?
MPFR	MPBLAS, BNCmatmul	?	MPBLAS, BNCmatmul	Utsugiri	CUMP	?

MPLAPACK/MPBLAS	[11] https://github.com/mahonakata/mplapack
MuPAT	[17] Yagi, H et.al(2020)
Lis	[4] https://www.ssisc.org/lis/
CUMP	[2] https://github.com/skystar0227/CUMP
BNCmatmul	[5] https://na-inet.jp/na/bnc/
Mukunoki	[12] Mukunoki, D et.al.(2021)
Utsugiri	[16] Utsugiri(2021-2023)

precision matrix multiplication implementing the Ozaki scheme. Although we have already reported benchmark results obtained by DD and TD LU decomposition based on the C++ class library [16], we have not obtained benchmark results for QD and MPFR LU decomposition. In this study, we present all the results obtained based on the C-based implementation of matrix multiplication and LU decomposition using DD, TD, QD, and MPFR floating-point arithmetic to avoid the overhead of C++ class libraries.

All benchmark tests conducted on the following Xeon environment show that the Ozaki scheme can also be used to accelerate multiple-precision LU decomposition on CPUs within a certain precision range.

CPU: Intel Xeon W-2295 3.0 GHz 18 cores
OS: Ubuntu 20.04.3 LTS
C/C++ compiler: Intel Compiler version 2021.5.0
MP libraries: MPLAPACK 2.0.1, MPFR 4.2.0

2   Mathematical Notation

Here, we define $\mathbb{F}_{bS}$ and $\mathbb{F}_{bL}$ as sets of the S- and L-bit mantissas of floating-point numbers, respectively. For instance, $\mathbb{F}_{b24}$ and $\mathbb{F}_{b53}$ refer to sets of IEEE754-1985 binary32 and binary64 floating-point numbers, whereas $\mathbb{F}_{b106}$, $\mathbb{F}_{b159}$, and $\mathbb{F}_{b212}$ represent examples of DD, TD, and QD precision floating-point numbers, respectively. Although any mantissa length can be selected in MPFR arithmetic, the set of MPFR numbers is expressed as $\mathbb{F}_{bM}$, which is primarily defined as M-bit using the `mpfr_set_default_prec` function.

Moreover, we use $(\mathbf{x})_i (= x_i)$ as the i-th element of the n-dimensional vector $\mathbf{x} = [x_i]_{i=1,2,..,n} \in \mathbb{R}^n$, and $(A)_{ij} (= a_{ij})$ as the (i, j)-th element of $A = [a_{ij}]_{i=1,2,...,m,j=1,2,...,n} \in \mathbb{R}^{m \times n}$.

3   Why Do We Require a Multiple-Precision Floating-Point Arithmetic Library?

The following is a brief explanation regarding the need for multiple-precision calculations with a mantissa exceeding binary64. First, users may seek to use floating-point arithmetic to obtain a value $F(x)$ from an input value x represented by a floating-point number. Ultimately, $F(x)$ must maintain at least U significant digits. Intuitively, in numerical computations, the initial error due to rounding is assumed to be included in the input value. Suppose the number of mantissa digits for the floating-point arithmetic to be $L(> U)$. Then, the number of significant digits of $F(x)$ is $U–R$, where R denotes the digits lost in the process of computing $F(x)$. Furthermore, it is assumed that the algorithm cannot be modified to ensure accuracy with an L-digit computation.

Unless the calculation algorithm for $F(x)$ is modified, the error propagation minimally changes irrespective of the number of mantissa digits. Therefore, we can increase the number of mantissa digits, slightly exceeding R with some slack of α digits, to $L+R+\alpha$ digits. If the initial error can be significantly minimized, $F(x)$ with U or more significant digits can be subsequently obtained. This process illustrates how multiple-precision calculations are used to ensure accuracy.

In contrast, the multi-fold calculation method proposed by Rump and Ogita [14,15] prevents an increase in the initial error by suppressing the rounding error generated by arithmetic operations to the lower digits using error-free transformation techniques. The computational manner of the error-free transformation process is almost the same as that of multiple-precision calculations. Moreover, in this process, floating-point arithmetic with L or more digits is not used. Accordingly, there is no need to perform renormalization procedures. This offers the advantage of reducing computational complexity compared to that of a multi-component approach that uses error-free transformation techniques.

A conceptual diagram of the two aforementioned approaches is presented in Fig. 1.

Currently, not all algorithms used in numerical computation can be applied using multi-fold arithmetic, especially with nonlinear calculations. Therefore, it is necessary to employ a combination of multi-fold and multiple-precision calculations, where the basic linear calculation part, such as explicit extrapolation process solving initial value problems of ordinary differential equations, uses multi-fold calculations to reduce computational time.

The Ozaki scheme, a matrix multiplication algorithm that we incorporated into our library, is a technique based on the multi-fold calculation approach. By leveraging the speed of existing binary32 and binary64 xGEMM algorithms,

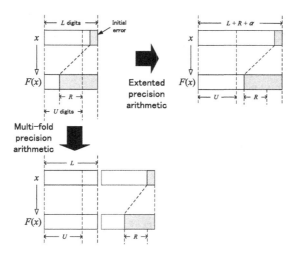

Fig. 1. Extended precision and multi-fold precision arithmetics

it significantly optimizes multiple-precision matrix multiplication under certain conditions, as revealed in our benchmark and previous studies [12,16]. We are confident that the acceleration of multiple-precision linear computation libraries will remain an important theme in guaranteeing the accuracy of broader numerical computation algorithms, following the development trend of multiple-precision numerical algorithms.

4   Algorithms and Performance of Optimized Matrix Multiplication

We focused on the optimization of multiple-precision matrix multiplication, starting with MPI support for arbitrary-precision numerical calculations [5]. Subsequently, owing to current popularity of multi-core CPUs, we accelerated multiple-precision matrix multiplication via parallelization support using OpenMP. As far as multiple-precision calculations are concerned, no other such results have been achieved by incorporating divide-and-conquer methods, such as the Strassen and Winograd algorithms. Although limited to multi-component methods, our proposed method is the only approach that supports AVX2 and has been converted to OpenMP for achieving higher speeds. However, the current code does not improve performance beyond eight threads for OpenMP acceleration, and a drastic reformulation is necessary to further improve parallelization performance. Algorithm 1 is the Strassen matrix multiplication.

The usefulness of the Ozaki scheme is also clear at multiple-precision levels owing to the success of Mukunoki et al. in accelerating the float128 precision matrix multiplication [12]. The float128 arithmetic supported by GCC features TD to QD precision performance for addition and multiplication and is likewise expected to be sufficient for this precision range.

Algorithm 1. Strassen algorithm for matrix multiplication

   Input: $A = [A_{ij}]_{i,j=1,2} \in \mathbb{R}^{m \times l}$, $A_{ij} \in \mathbb{R}^{m/2 \times l/2}$, $B = [A_{ij}]_{i,j=1,2} \in \mathbb{R}^{l \times n}$, $B_{ij} \in \mathbb{R}^{l/2 \times n/2}$

   Output: $C := \text{Strassen}(A, B) = AB \in \mathbb{R}^{m \times n}$

   if $m < m_0$ && $n < n_0$ **then**

      $C := AB$

   end if

   $P_1 := \text{Strassen}(A_{11} + A_{22}, B_{11} + B_{22})$

   $P_2 := \text{Strassen}(A_{21} + A_{22}, B_{11})$

   $P_3 := \text{Strassen}(A_{11}, B_{12} - B_{22})$

   $P_4 := \text{Strassen}(A_{22}, B_{21} - B_{11})$

   $P_5 := \text{Strassen}(A_{11} + A_{12}, B_{22})$

   $P_6 := \text{Strassen}(A_{21} - A_{11}, B_{11} + B_{12})$

   $P_7 := \text{Strassen}(A_{12} - A_{22}, B_{21} + B_{22})$

   $C_{11} := P_1 + P_4 - P_5 + P_7$; $C_{12} := P_3 + P_5$

   $C_{21} := P_2 + P_4$; $C_{22} := P_1 + P_3 - P_2 + P_6$

   $C := [C_{ij}]_{i,j=1,2}$

The Ozaki scheme is an algorithm that aims to simultaneously accelerate performance and improve accuracy by dividing matrices into more matrices with elements represented by shorter digits. Similarly to the "Split" method used in the error-free transformation technique, this approach leverages on the speed of optimized short-precision matrix multiplication (xGEMM) functions. For a given matrix $A \in \mathbb{R}^{m \times l}$ and $B \in \mathbb{R}^{l \times n}$, to obtain a matrix product $C := AB \in \mathbb{R}^{m \times n}$ of long L-bit precision, A and B are divided using the Ozaki scheme, where $D \in \mathbb{N}$ is the maximum number of divisions of short S-bit precision matrices ($S << L$), as depicted in Algorithm 2. The S-bit arithmetic is used for calculations where no particular description is given, and the L-bit arithmetic is used only where high-precision operations are required.

Fig. 2 illustrates an example of the Ozaki scheme when A and $B \in \mathbb{R}^{3 \times 3}$ are divided into three short-digit matrices. The most important feature of the Ozaki scheme is that the matrices A and B are divided into A_1, A_2, A_3, B_1, B_2, and B_3 to fit within a short precision, thereby avoiding rounding errors in fast, low-precision matrix multiplication. An error-free matrix product $C_{ij} := A_i B_j (i, j = 1, 2, 3)$ can be obtained as a result, and a highly accurate matrix product C can be obtained using a multiple-precision matrix addition operation for $C := \sum_{i,j} C_{ij}$. Although the number of divisions of A and B is finite, it is difficult to determine the minimum number of divisions required to guarantee a certain accuracy threshold. As a result, benchmark tests must be performed to determine if the algorithm can be executed faster than other multiplication algorithms.

The following are C-based multi-component multiple-precision floating-point operations: DD (106 bits), TD (159 bits), QD (212 bits), and MPFR-based multi-digit arbitrary precision operations with 256 bits, 512 bits, and 768 bits. We summarize the results of benchmark tests conducted on Xeon to compare

Algorithm 2. Ozaki scheme for multiple-precision matrix multiplication

Input: $A \in \mathbb{F}_{bL}^{m \times l}, B \in \mathbb{F}_{bL}^{l \times n}$
Output: $C \in \mathbb{F}_{bL}^{m \times n}$
$A^{(S)} := A,\ B^{(S)} := B : A^{(S)} \in \mathbb{F}_{bS}^{m \times l},\ B^{(S)} \in \mathbb{F}_{bS}^{l \times n}$
$\mathbf{e} := [1\ 1\ ...\ 1]^T \in \mathbb{F}_{bS}^{l}$
$\alpha := 1$
while $\alpha < D$ **do**
$\quad \boldsymbol{\mu}_A := [\max_{1 \leq p \leq l} |(A^{(S)})_{ip}|]_{i=1,2,...,m} \in \mathbb{F}_{bS}^m$
$\quad \boldsymbol{\mu}_B := [\max_{1 \leq q \leq l} |(B^{(S)})_{qj}|]_{j=1,2,...,n} \in \mathbb{F}_{bS}^n$
$\quad \boldsymbol{\tau}_A := [2^{\lceil \log_2((\boldsymbol{\mu}_A)_i) \rceil + \lceil (S + \log_2(l))/2 \rceil}]_{i=1,2,...,m} \in \mathbb{F}_{bS}^m$
$\quad \boldsymbol{\tau}_B := [2^{\lceil \log_2((\boldsymbol{\mu}_B)_j) \rceil + \lceil (S + \log_2(l))/2 \rceil}]_{j=1,2,...,n} \in \mathbb{F}_{bS}^n$
$\quad S_A := \boldsymbol{\tau}_A \mathbf{e}^T$
$\quad S_B := \mathbf{e} \boldsymbol{\tau}_B^T$
$\quad A_\alpha := (A^{(S)} + S_A) - S_A : A_\alpha \in \mathbb{F}_{bS}^{m \times l}$
$\quad B_\alpha := (B^{(S)} + S_B) - S_B : B_\alpha \in \mathbb{F}_{bS}^{l \times n}$
$\quad A := A - A_\alpha,\ B := B - B_\alpha : L\text{-bit FP arithmetic}$
$\quad A^{(S)} := A,\ B^{(S)} := B$
$\quad \alpha := \alpha + 1$
end while
$A_D := A^{(S)},\ B_D := B^{(S)}$
$C := O$
for $\alpha = 1, 2, ..., D$ **do**
$\quad$ **for** $\beta = 1, 2, ..., D - \alpha + 1$ **do**
$\quad\quad C_{\alpha\beta} := A_\alpha B_\beta$
$\quad$ **end for**
$\quad C := C + \sum_{\beta=1}^{D-\alpha+1} C_{\alpha\beta} : L\text{-bit FP arithmetic}$
end for

---

the computational time (seconds), maximum element-wise relative error of C for MPBLAS (Rgemm), and our Strassen matrix multiplication with 256 bits, 512 bits, and 768 bits as precision operations. Although our previous benchmark test conducted on a Core i7 [16] CPU was based on a C++ implementation, the Intel Math Kernel's DGEMM is common with the C-based codes, so there is approximately a 1% difference in computational time.

The square matrices $A, B \in \mathbb{R}^{n \times n}$ used are set as

$$(A)_{ij} := \sqrt{5}(i + j - 1), (B)_{ij} := \sqrt{3}(n - j + 1). \tag{1}$$

Figure 3 shows three results for DD(upper)-, TD(middle)-, and QD(lower)-precision matrix multiplication on Xeon. The left figures show computational time, whereas the right figures display the maximum of element-wise relative errors in computed matrix C. "OZ" denotes results of the Ozaki scheme. For instance, "OZ 5" denotes the Ozaki scheme with a maximum number of matrix partitions set to 5 ($D = 5$). As mentioned earlier, the Ozaki scheme's performance depends on the distribution of the elements in matrices A and B, number of precision digits of the matrix element calculation required by C, and performance of the xGEMM used. From the righthand side figure in Fig. 3, observe

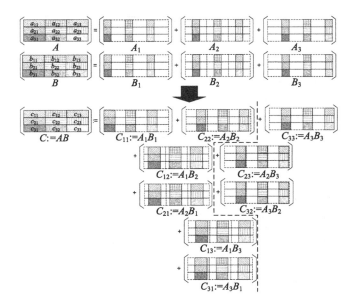

Fig. 2. Matrix multiplication based on Ozaki scheme when the matrices are divided into three components

that the relative error is at least smaller than that of the Strassen matrix multiplication at more than five divisions for DD, more than eight divisions for TD, and more than 12 divisions for QD. In the QD case, however, the accuracy drops by 1–2 decimal places. The Ozaki scheme also yielded faster performance for the three precision calculations. The difference is small for DD but large for TD and QD, which is reasonable as the performance of float128 used by Mukunoki et al. is between TD and QD.

We subsequently increased calculation precision further. Calculation results for MPFR 256 bits, 512 bits, and 768 bits are presented in Fig. 4.

We have already demonstrated that Strassen matrix multiplication is the fastest MPFR matrix multiplication algorithm by a considerable margin [6]; the present results reaffirmed that it is faster than MPBLAS. Furthermore, the Ozaki scheme is faster than the MPBLAS scheme by 256 bits, in addition to yielding the same or lower relative error compared to the Strassen matrix multiplication with more than 14 divisions for 256 bits, more than 25 divisions for 512 bits, and more than 38 divisions for 768 bits. Accordingly, the computational time at 768 bits is equal to or greater than that of the Strassen matrix multiplication. For 38 or more divisions, the Strassen matrix multiplication is expected to be faster in many cases.

To summarize these results, a two-dimensional map of valid matrix multiplication algorithms is presented in Fig. 5.

Strassen matrix multiplication is generally efficient when using long precision and large matrices, as it significantly reduces the amount of arithmetic opera-

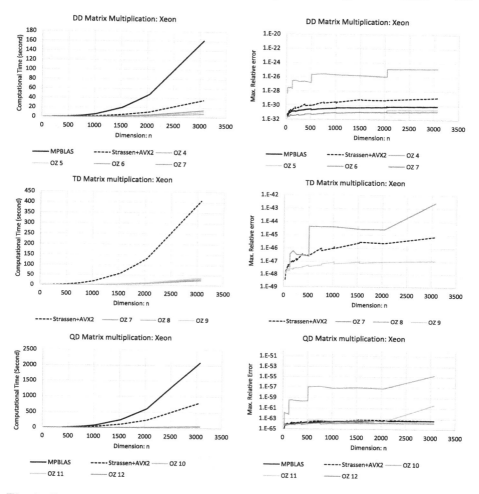

Fig. 3. Computational time (left) and relative error (right) of matrix multiplication using Ozaki scheme: DD prec.(upper), TD prec.(middle), QD prec.(lower)

tions. Blocking is effective when using short precision and mid-sized matrices owing to the presence of cache memory in CPUs. The simple triple-loop method is efficient for small matrices.

The Ozaki scheme is more powerful within a specific range of partitions. When more precision and numerous divisions are necessary to guarantee the output accuracy, the Ozaki scheme tends to be slower than the Strassen algorithm. However, we can confirm that the Ozaki scheme yields high performance within a practical range centered on float128 arithmetic [12].

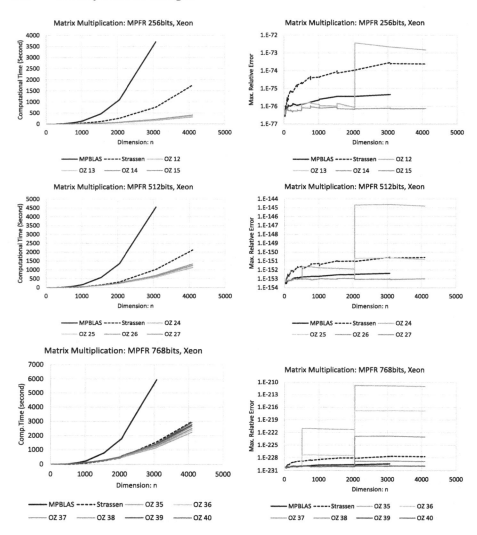

Fig. 4. Computational time (left) and relative error (right) of matrix multiplication using Ozaki scheme: MPFR 256 bits prec.(upper), MPFR 512 bits prec.(middle), and MPFR 768 bits prec.(lower)

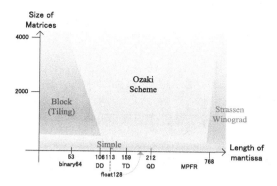

Fig. 5. Map of efficient algorithms for long precision matrix multiplication on Xeon

5 Performance of LU Decomposition Applied with Optimized Matrix Multiplication

As an application of optimized matrix multiplication, we implemented LU decomposition in the direct method for various benchmark tests, including the Top500, and measured its utility on Xeon. The corresponding n-dimensional linear system of equation is:

$$Ax = b, \tag{2}$$

where $A \in \mathbb{R}^{n \times n}$, $\mathbf{x} \in \mathbb{R}^n$, and $\mathbf{b} \in \mathbb{R}^n$ become ill-conditional as follows:

A: The diagonal matrix is $D = \mathrm{diag}[d_1 \cdots d_n]$, where $d_i := 10^{-26(i-1)/n}$. The random matrix is $R \in \mathbb{R}^{n \times n}$; then, A is calculated as $A := RDR^{-1}$ using the mpmath Python library. Therefore, the condition number of A is $\kappa_2(A) = \|A\|_2 \|A^{-1}\|_2 = 10^{26(n-1)/n}$, which requires super-DD precision arithmetic to gain accuracy.

$\mathbf{x}, \mathbf{b}$: After setting $\mathbf{x} = [0\ 1\ \cdots\ n-1]^T$, $\mathbf{b} := A\mathbf{x}$ is calculated using mpmath.

Assuming that LU decomposition in the current LAPACK standard allows using fast matrix multiplications, a constant width $K(= \mathrm{MIN\_DIM})$ is predefined as stated in Fig. 6, and the rectangular component $A - L_{12}U_{21}$ is updated for each K column. Therefore, the complexity of matrix multiplication changes with respect to K; MPLAPACK's LU decomposition (Rgetrf) is also implemented using Rgemm.

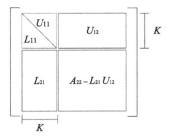

Fig. 6. LU decomposition using matrix multiplication

Various benchmark tests [8,10] have revealed that as long as multiple-precision floating-point operations are used, the typical LU decomposition implementation, wherein calculations are performed column-wise, yields the fastest performance. Furthermore, using the Strassen matrix multiplication does not necessarily improve raw performance. However, we demonstrated that matrix multiplication using the Ozaki scheme was faster than the Strassen matrix multiplication for TD, QD, and MPFR 256 bits, indicating that faster LU decomposition may be achievable.

Results of the multi-component fixed-precision and multi-digit arbitrary-precision calculations are stated below.

5.1   DD, TD, and QD Precision LU Decomposition

LU decompositions were performed for DD, TD, and QD accuracy, with corresponding graphs in Fig. 7 showing the computational time for LU decomposition (left) and maximum element-wise relative error (right) of the numerical solution **x** obtained by performing forward and backward substitutions.

The DD-precision problem is a bad condition problem that can only achieve one order of magnitude accuracy at best. This accuracy drops by 2–3 orders of magnitude further when the Strassen algorithm or Ozaki scheme is used. The computational time required to maximize accuracy also exceeds that required for the usual LU decomposition; for TD- and QD-precision calculations, the difference in accuracy is suboptimal. Moreover, the computational time is sufficiently smaller than that required for the usual LU decomposition.

A table of the minimum computational times and maximum relative errors for each precision calculation, including the MPLAPACK(Rgetrf) results, is provided in Table 2.

Table 2. Computational time (seconds) of DD, TD, and QD LU decomposition, with corresponding maximum relative errors of **x**

Prec	Method	K	Second	Rel.Err
DD 106bits	Rgetrf	N/A	15.8	2.4E − 01
	Normal LU	1	5.1	1.9E − 01
	Strassen+AVX2	32	7.4	1.8E + 01
	OZ 6	128	4.5	9.4E + 01
TD 159bits	Normal LU	1	118.6	3.9E − 17
	Strassen+AVX2	32	95.6	5.9E − 17
	OZ 7	96	19.8	1.7E − 17
QD 212bits	Rgetrf	N/A	207.4	3.8E − 34
	Normal LU	1	155.3	1.4E − 33
	Strassen+AVX2	64	180.8	1.5E − 32
	OZ 12	160	83.2	5.8E − 33

Table 3. Minimum computational time (second) of MPFR LU decomposition and maximum relative errors of **x**

Prec	Method	K	Second	Rel.Err
MPFR 256 bits	Rgetrf	N/A	398.6	2.1E − 50
	Normal LU	1	250.0	1.5E − 49
	Strassen	96	273.7	8.3E − 50
	OZ 13	320	167.6	3.2E − 50
MPFR 512 bits	Rgetrf	N/A	492.3	2.5E − 127
	Normal LU	1	341.1	2.6E − 127
	Strassen	32	390.4	3.1E − 126
	OZ 25	576	333.4	4.1E − 126
MPFR 768 bits	Rgetrf	N/A	627.8	5.1E − 205
	Normal LU	1	481.4	1.9E − 203
	Strassen	32	491.1	3.6E − 203
	OZ 38	736	536.6	3.7E − 203

Generally, observe that our LU decomposition implementation is comparable to Rgetrf in terms of speed. Furthermore, compared to the usual LU decomposition, our LU decomposition is 1.1 times faster with the Ozaki scheme ($D = 6$)

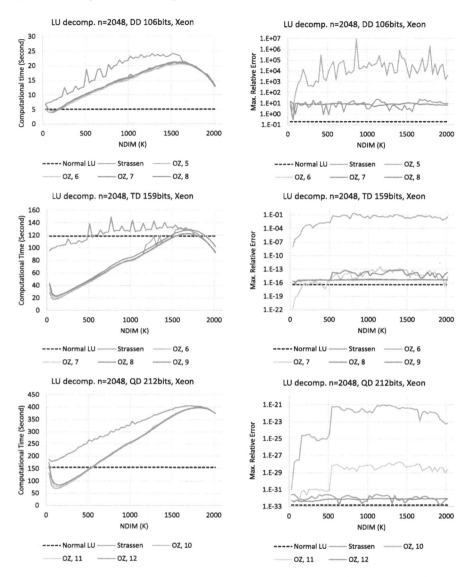

Fig. 7. Computational time (left) and relative error (right) of LU decomposition using the Ozaki scheme: DD prec.(upper), TD prec.(middle), QD prec.(lower)

regarding DD accuracy, 6.0 times faster with the Ozaki scheme ($D = 7$) regarding TD accuracy, and 1.9 times faster with the Ozaki scheme ($D = 12$) regarding QD accuracy. The square matrix multiplication scheme shown above is 6.0 times faster than the Ozaki scheme. These improvements in performance are in line with the results of the square matrix multiplication benchmark test presented earlier.

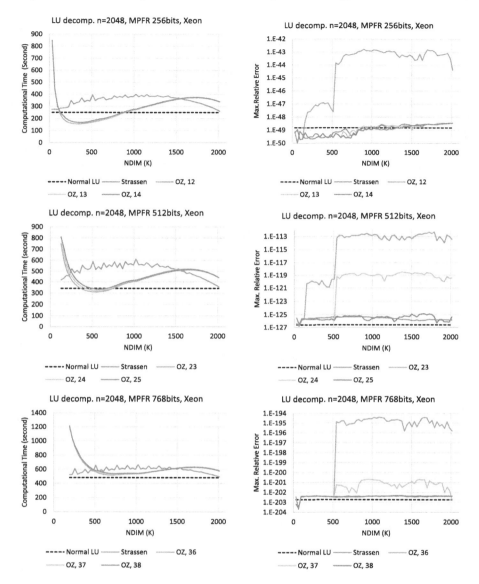

Fig. 8. Computational time (left) and relative error (right) of LU decomposition using Ozaki scheme: MPFR 256 bits(upper), MPFR 512 bits(middle), and MPFR 768 bits(lower)

5.2   MPFR 256-Bit, 512-Bit, and 768-Bit LU Decomposition

We now explain the arbitrary precision calculation in detail. Results for the MPFR 256 bits, 512 bits, and 768 bits calculations are shown in Fig. 8.

Although the Ozaki scheme shows a performance improvement over the Strassen matrix multiplication, there are few areas where the Ozaki scheme can be used effectively beyond 512 bits in the context of this problem.

Table 3 reports the minimal computational times and corresponding maximum relative errors using MPFR calculation.

With fixed precision, observe that our LU decomposition implementation is faster than Rgetrf. Thus, compared to normal LU decomposition, the MPFR 256 bits precision is 1.5 times faster when the Ozaki scheme ($D = 13$) is used, MPFR 512 bits precision is 1.0 times faster when the Ozaki scheme ($D = 25$) is used, and MPFR 768 bits precision is 0.9 times faster when the Ozaki scheme ($D = 38$) is used. Again, observe that the performance is equivalent at 512 bits, and conversely slower at 768 bits.

6   Conclusion and Future Research Directions

As a result of the abovementioned implementation and benchmark tests, we conclude that our implementation of the Ozaki scheme is faster than the Strassen matrix multiplication in the ranges of TD, QD, and MPFR 256 bits and 512 bits accuracy using Intel Math Kernel's DGEMM, specifically for the LU decomposition process.

Future directions of research include the further optimization of our library for multiple-precision linear computation, implementations of the following functions that are not yet supported, and additional performance evaluations via benchmark tests.

1. Optimization of complex linear basic computation and application to the direct method.
2. Implementation of standard-precision basic linear computation using multi-fold precision arithmetic.
3. Development of multiple-precision sparse matrix-vector multiplication (SpMV).

Regarding complex matrix multiplication, it is necessary to evaluate the performance of the Strassen and Ozaki schemes by comparing their accuracies and computational times.

In parallel, it is important to demonstrate the usefulness of the Ozaki scheme for numerical solutions of ordinary and partial differential equations, which are especially important in scientific and engineering simulations, through examples of adverse conditions that require multiple-long-precision linear calculations.

Acknowledgement. This study was financially supported by Kakenhi 20K11843, and also partially supported by the proposed-study fund of Shizuoka Institute of Science and Technology. We appreciate these concerned people and unknown referees who provided helpful comments to improve this paper.

References

1. Bailey, D.: QD. https://www.davidhbailey.com/dhbsoftware/
2. CUMP: Library for arbitrary precision arithmetic on CUDA
3. Granlaud, T., development team, G.: The GNU Multiple Precision arithmetic library. https://gmplib.org/
4. Kotakemori, T., Fujii, S., Hasegawa, H., Nishida, A.: Lis: Library of iterative solvers for linear systems. https://www.ssisc.org/lis/
5. Kouya, T: On BNCpack, multiple-precision numerical computation library with MPFR/GMP. OYO-SURI **21**(3), 197–206 (2011). http://ci.nii.ac.jp/naid/110009426223/
6. Kouya, T.: Accelerated multiple precision matrix multiplication using Strassen's algorithm and Winograd's variant. JSIAM Lett. **6**, 81–84 (2014). https://doi.org/10.14495/jsiaml.6.81
7. Kouya, Tomonori: Performance evaluation of strassen matrix multiplication supporting triple-double precision floating-point arithmetic. In: Gervasi, O. (ed.) ICCSA 2020. LNCS, vol. 12253, pp. 163–176. Springer, Cham (2020). https://doi.org/10.1007/978-3-030-58814-4_12
8. Kouya, T.: Acceleration of LU decomposition supporting double-double, triple-double, and quadruple-double precision floating-point arithmetic with avx2. In: 2021 IEEE 28th Symposium on Computer Arithmetic (ARITH), pp. 54–61 (2021). https://doi.org/10.1109/ARITH51176.2021.00021
9. Kouya, T.: Acceleration of multiple precision matrix multiplication based on multi-component floating-point arithmetic using AVX2. In: Gervasi, O., Murgante, B., Misra, S., Garau, C., Blečić, I., Taniar, D., Apduhan, B.O., Rocha, A.M.A.C., Tarantino, E., Torre, C.M. (eds.) ICCSA 2021. LNCS, vol. 12953, pp. 202–217. Springer, Cham (2021). https://doi.org/10.1007/978-3-030-86976-2_14
10. Kouya, T.: Optimization of mixed-precision iterative refinement using parallelized direct methods. In: 2022 International Conference on Engineering and Emerging Technologies (ICEET), pp. 1–6 (2022). https://doi.org/10.1109/ICEET56468.2022.10007230
11. MPLAPACK/MPBLAS: Multiple precision arithmetic LAPACK and BLAS. https://github.com/nakatamaho/mplapack
12. Mukunoki, D., Ozaki, K., Ogita, T., Imamura, T.: Accurate matrix multiplication on binary128 format accelerated by ozaki scheme. In: 50th International Conference on Parallel Processing. ICPP 2021, Association for Computing Machinery, New York, NY, USA, pp. 1–11 (2021). https://doi.org/10.1145/3472456.3472493
13. Project, M.: The MPFR library. https://www.mpfr.org/
14. Rump, S.M., Ogita, T., Oishi, S.: Accurate floating-point summation part I: faithful rounding. SIAM J. Sci. Comput. **31**(1), 189–224 (2008)
15. Rump, S.M., Ogita, T., Oishi, S.: Accurate floating-point summation part II: sign, k-fold faithful and rounding to nearest. SIAM J. Sci. Comput. **31**(2), 1269–1302 (2008)
16. Utsugiri, T., Kouya, T.: Acceleration of multiple precision matrix multiplication using ozaki scheme (2023). https://doi.org/10.48550/ARXIV.2301.09960, https://arxiv.org/abs/2301.09960
17. Yagi, H., Ishiwata, E., Hasegawa, H.: Acceleration of interactive multiple precision arithmetic toolbox MuPAT using FMA, SIMD, and OpenMP. Adv. Parallel Comput. **36**, 431—440 (2020)

Cities, Technologies and Planning (CTP 2023)

Project Smart SDI: Concept for Improving NSDI for Sustainable Development in Serbia

Ljiljana Živković[(✉)]

Republic Geodetic Authority, Belgrade, Serbia
liliana.zivkovic@gmail.com

Abstract. The recent advancements in the geospatial technologies domain, together with the rapidly growing number of various data collected through the different sources, have launched both global and local initiatives focused on the integration of those data using their locations. In public sector, the aim of these initiatives is to identify efficient approaches for the integration of location information with the public sector non-geospatial data, but also to enhance the usage of public sector geospatial data in general for decision-making and policies management towards the digital and green transformation of today's societies and economies. Thus, an important part of these public sector initiatives deals with the improvement of existing spatial data infrastructures (SDIs), and their integration within the emerging geospatial data spaces and ecosystems intended for the creation of new geospatial knowledge for better understanding of the specific development conditions and informed actions for the SDGs achievement on each location in future. Therefore, in line with the recently adopted European Strategy for data, national SDIs (NSDIs) that are establishing in Europe in accordance with the INSPIRE Directive since 2007 have as well to be improved and integrated into the future common data space for the European Green Deal objectives accomplishment. One of the mandatory or a high value datasets (HVD) that would support directly this new mission of NSDIs is a land use dataset, which is produced and managed following the INSPIRE standards within the spatial and urban planning system of each country. In Serbia, being responsible for the INSPIRE Directive implementation, Republic Geodetic Authority (RGA) has recently adopted the Strategic action plan (SAP) for Serbian NSDI improvement. For starting this SAP implementation, RGA has launched Project "Establishing Smart SDI in Serbia" and developed its concept in partnership with the Swedish counterpart, Lantmäteriet. As main part of this Project, which is supported by the Swedish SIDA, RGA plans generally to implement activities aimed at enhancing usage of the public sector geospatial datasets, particularly those listed as HVDs. Also, Project concept includes digitalization of the land use dataset needed for sustainable spatial and urban planning and development in Serbia, as well as further upgrading of the existing NSDI geoportal, Geosrbija, to a modern platform with the user-centric services and data-driven approach to the decision-making and policies management in line with the Green Agenda for the Western Balkans and SDGs in general.

Keywords: NSDI improvement · public sector geospatial data · land use dataset · sustainable development · Serbia

© The Author(s), under exclusive license to Springer Nature Switzerland AG 2023
O. Gervasi et al. (Eds.): ICCSA 2023 Workshops, LNCS 14105, pp. 549–560, 2023.
https://doi.org/10.1007/978-3-031-37108-0_35

1   Introduction: SDI Evolution

Since their first concept emerged more than 30 years ago, SDI systems' main task has been to provide access to the reliable, standardized and interoperable public sector geospatial datasets and related services, through the geospatial information geoportals to the prevailingly public sector users. In that long period, passing through the different phases of their development on the different administrative levels, so-called jurisdictions [1], these strictly supply-driven systems have been sometimes hard to access and overly rigid for usage by the non-geospatial user communities. Moreover, in recent years, public sector SDIs were even neglecting the new geospatial technologies, new geospatial data sources and large volumes of high-quality geospatial information (from Internet-of-Things, citizen-generated geospatial data, etc.), as well as a growing importance and usage of location for decision-making and daily operations both in public and private sector and for individual purposes [2, 3].

Therefore, relying on the recent advancements in both geospatial and Internet technologies, which today shifts towards Web 3.0 paradigm, it is a time to rethink and restructure public sector SDI systems for embracing the next generation of e-governance processes; user-centric technology platforms and services; application program interfaces (APIs); open data and open analytical software; and new stakeholder collaboration mechanisms. [2, 4] Instead of just providing the standardized public sector geospatial data and services, these future 'beyond SDI' systems as part of the emerging geospatial data spaces and ecosystems should focus on the creation of new insights and a contextual knowledge needed for the evidence-based or data-driven decision-making and policies management aimed at sustainable development on global and local level. For this socio-technical restructuring of existing SDIs to take place in a systematic way, UN-GGIM experts have launched the strategic Project "Integrated Geospatial Information Framework (IGIF)" [5]. As a result, already today the recommendations from this Project lead many countries' institutions and administrations through the digital transformation challenges in the public sector geospatial data and services domain.

Furthermore, the UN New Urban Agenda [6] as well as the Urban Agenda for EU [7] support the use of digital platforms, tools and geospatial information systems for improving a long-term integrated spatial and urban planning, land administration and management. In addition, European Green Deal recognizes the potential of digitalization and digital technologies as the essential enablers for green transformation, while the European Strategy for data emphasizes the digital components as critical ones for both green and digital transformation in Europe. [8] Based on that, it might be even concluded that the green transformation, targeted by the global SDGs and followed by the European Green Deal and Green Agenda for the Western Balkans, would demand the digital transformation, including the improvement of existing public sector SDIs, as a precondition.

Following above described developments, the aim of this article is to present context and Project concept for improvement of the existing national SDI (NSDI) in Serbia. For that reason, after the Introduction, next chapter provides relevant details about the European Strategy for data and its influence on the INSPIRE Directive modernization, which leads public sector geospatial data and related services development in Europe last 16 years. After the European level, the Strategic Action Plan (SAP) for the NSDI improvement in Serbia is presented, followed by the description of used framework or criteria for defining the Project implementation activities for establishment of so-called Smart SDI. Next two chapters in this article, i.e. Project Smart SDI concept and Expected Project results, provide information on the identified Project impact, main outcomes, planned activities and expected outputs in the next 3 years of Project duration, before article finishes with the concluding remarks.

2 European Strategy for Data and INSPIRE Directive

More than a decade after C. Humby claimed that "data is the new oil", European Commission (EC) in a recently adopted 5-year European Strategy for data provides similar view by saying that "data is the lifeblood of economic development". As consequence, in order to take and keep position of "a role model for a society empowered by data to make better decisions – in business and the public sector", EC in this Strategy concludes that Europe Union (EU) should seize the opportunities offered by the ever-increasing production and use of data. In order to achieve this ambitious vision of EU becoming a leader in data-agile economy, this Strategy assumes a number of legal, technological, organizational and financial/investing measures that should be implemented in order for a single European data space -and Single market for data- to be created in accordance with the European values [9].

Also, despite the first electronic government initiatives and digitalization of public sector in general date back to mid 90s, this Strategy confirms that today there is not enough public sector data available for re-use [9], while data is a central to the digital transformation in Europe [8]. Thus, as part of this Strategy implementation, EC has already adopted the Implementing regulation on high-value datasets (HVDs) under the Open Data Directive [10], since HVDs re-use is associated with a significant benefits for the economy and society in general [8]. So, until the middle of 2024, this Implementing regulation is expected to support opening up of these key public sector reference geospatial datasets for free (like administrative units, buildings, cadastral parcels, land uses, etc.) in the machine-readable format, under the standardized open access licenses and through the Application Programming Interfaces (APIs) (besides a bulk download) [3, 8].

As a key part, European Strategy for data plans for the future single European data space to consist of the nine common European data spaces, including the Green Deal data space. (Fig. 1) For this data space to be functional, appropriate data-sharing tools, infrastructure and platform need to be established; data quality, availability and interoperability, particularly for those datasets identified as HVDs, should be secured; while appropriate governance framework and mechanisms should be created for all its stakeholders. Also, in order to stimulate the future use of data and demand for Green Deal-relevant services, EC is currently running "GreenData4All" and "Destination Earth" initiatives, which results would provide input for the INSPIRE Directive modernization and simplification [8, 9].

This forthcoming change of the INSPIRE Directive would lead also to evolvement of the NSDIs from complex and highly specialized geospatial data frameworks into the flexible, open, agile and self-sustainable national data ecosystems. [8] After improvement,

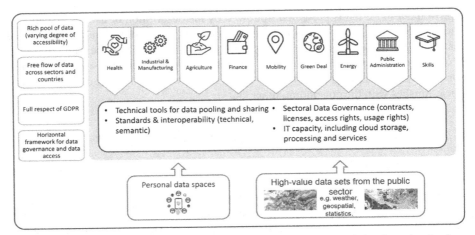

Fig. 1. High-level architecture of the common European data space consisting from the nine large sectoral data spaces[1] (source: Eurogeographics)

these future NSDIs are expected to blend within a larger data space on the European level, where different data users would be able to easily discover, access and use data for different purposes, like research study, policy-making or a business application. In addition, geospatial HVDs that would be part of these future NSDIs should provide a powerful means for integrating and combined use of the existing public sector non-geospatial datasets with the other geospatial datasets for gaining the new geospatial insights and knowledge that would be otherwise difficult to get [2, 4, 9].

Finally, based on the foreseen advantages, INSPIRE Maintenance and Implementation Work Program 2021–2024 [11] defines concrete first actions for transition of the INSPIRE into a sustainable data ecosystem for the environment in Europe. This Work Program includes thus actions on a technical level (like data encoding and sharing), but also actions related to the legal level (like avoiding over-specification and adoption of a simple licensing framework) and organizational (governance) level (like making communities of data users to be an integral part of the governance structure together with data providers).

Once modernized NSDIs become operational part of the geospatial data spaces and ecosystems in Europe, the improved availability and accessibility of various geospatial data would feed the novel application areas, such as Artificial Intelligence [12] and Digital Twins [13], which are important for the future sustainable spatial and urban planning and development in general.

2.1 Land Use Dataset and NSDI Improvement

The leading UN-GGIM's IGIF experts predict that by the time awareness about location as a common feature of virtually all information and, thus, a common basis for integration

---

[1] https://eurogeographics.org/wp-content/uploads/2022/02/7.-INSPIRE-Geoportal-JORDI-ESCRIU.pdf

of information from different sources and contexts would increase. [3] This is particularly important for the spatial and urban planning that relying on a data location and new geospatial technologies can deliver their long-term vision of planning as "a unique place-based systems approach to coordinate multisector efforts to deliver zero-carbon, environmental net gain, a circular economy and a green industrial revolution for a fairer society" [14].

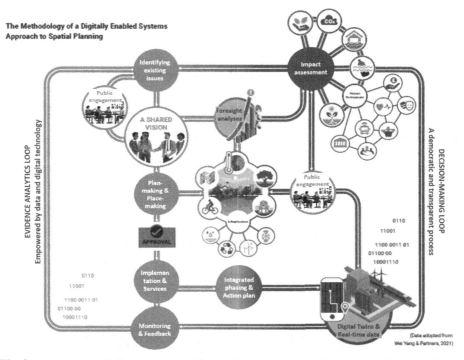

Fig. 2. Integrated digitally enabled spatial planning methodology: The new cyclic methodology for a digitally enabled approach to spatial planning would connect the decision-making loop with the evidence analytics or insight/knowledge creation loop [14]

On one side, this means that land use datasets as a main output of the spatial and urban planning process in each country, and one of the geospatial HVDs, would directly contribute to the capability of future NSDIs to support the meaningful data integration and getting the new geospatial insights and knowledge for the Green Deal achievement in Europe. On the other side, since decisions in the spatial and urban planning aimed at the sustainable development require the new methods and data advancement [14], improved NSDIs would in return additionally strengthen the planning process in every country. This new approach to the spatial and urban planning, which would be supported by Web 2.0 and emerging Web 3.0 paradigms, would trigger also emergence of a new, dynamic and people-centric cyclic planning methodology (Fig. 2), and shifting of the current Planning 1.0 and 2.0 paradigms towards Planning 3.0, where the more responsive planning systems would dominate [4].

Finally, despite that spatial and urban planning and development are strongly tied to the information and communication technologies advancement, elements of previous planning paradigms (Planning 1.0 and 2.0) would likely to persist for many years to come. [4] However, once improved, NSDIs would strongly support sustainable development goals achievement, particularly on the local level, by creating the favorable conditions for centralizing data on one place –on emerging new organizational structure, so-called 'platform'- for the people-centric and data-driven decision-making and policy management [15].

3   Strategic Action Plan for NSDI Improvement in Serbia

In order to systematically improve the current NSDI into a modern SDI system, which would make public sector geospatial data and services open and easier to access by the different users, who would use them to satisfy their own and needs of society and economy in Serbia in general, RGA has adopted the Strategic action plan - SAP [16].

This document is developed using the UN-GGIM's IGIF project recommendations [10] and results of the beforehand prepared studies "Geospatial Alignment to Policy Drivers in the Republic of Serbia" and "Socio-Economic Benefits of Serbian NSDI"[2]. Therefore, aimed at the comprehensive transformation of the current NSDI, the SAP identifies the Key Action Points (KAP) for each of the nine IGIF's strategic pathways (Governance and Institutions; Policy and Legal; Financial; Data; Innovation; Standards; Partnerships; Capacity and Education; Communications and Engagement). Implementation of these KAPs would support accomplishment of the vision (Fig. 3), mission and identified goals for the future modern NSDI in Serbia, namely Smart SDI [16].

VISION

- To establish a value-based "SMART SDI" that strongly facilitates the access, sharing and use of geospatial data and services, responds to the current and future stakeholders needs for geospatial information, enables to apply the most relevant modern (smart) solutions, strengthens the national/regional cooperation and economic development, and enhanced quality of living conditions

Fig. 3. Vision for the Serbian NSDI transformation [16]

Among the overall 35 KAPs there are differences in the timing, cost and risk associated with their implementation. Besides that, variations among the KAPs relate to their mutual relationships or dependencies, important for the efficient and effective delivery of the expected outputs, as well as for successful achievement of the defined outcomes and common vision statement.

---

[2] https://en.rgz.gov.rs/scope-of-works/socio-economic-benefits-study-of-nsdi-impact-on-the-society-in-the-republic-of-serbia.

4 Framework for Project Concept Definition

In order to improve existing NSDI in Serbia, RGA in partnership with its Swedish counterpart, Lantmäteriet, has initiated a Project "Establishing Smart SDI in Serbia", and used the next framework or criteria to define an appropriate Project concept for supporting implementation of a Smart SDI envisaged in the SAP document:

– KAPs activities and outputs that are possible to be implemented in 3-year time, which could be solid basis for further NSDI improvement, i.e. SAP implementation [16];
– Activities identified within the Directive Specific Implementation Plan (DSIP) for INSPIRE Directive for Serbia (part of the Negotiation Chapter 27)[3];
– Specific needs and development priorities of the RGA and Serbia in general, particularly those included in the Sustainable Urban Development Strategy 2030 [17] and Program for the e-Government development in Serbia in period 2023–2025[4];
– Goals and priorities of the Strategy for Sweden's reform cooperation with the Western Balkans and Turkey for 2021–2027 [18]; and
– INSPIRE Maintenance and Implementation Work Program 2021–2024.

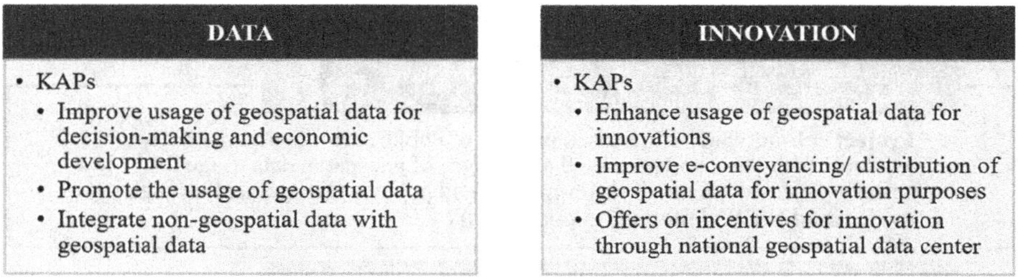

DATA	INNOVATION

• KAPs
  • Improve usage of geospatial data for decision-making and economic development
  • Promote the usage of geospatial data
  • Integrate non-geospatial data with geospatial data
	• KAPs
	  • Enhance usage of geospatial data for innovations
	  • Improve e-conveyancing/ distribution of geospatial data for innovation purposes
	  • Offers on incentives for innovation through national geospatial data center

Fig. 4. Selected KAPs for implementation by the Project "Establishing Smart SDI in Serbia"

Following the criteria listed above, two SAP's strategic pathways (Data and Innovation) and their KAPs listed in the Fig. 4 have been selected as a good starting point for the improvement of NSDI in Serbia in general.

Besides KAPs in the Fig. 4., the activities defined within the other SAP strategic pathways would accompany them as part of the comprehensive socio-technical system approach to the transformation of NSDI into the modern SDI system in Serbia. These activities include: improving cooperation with the local self-governments (Strategic pathway: Partnerships); building capacity of all relevant NSDI stakeholders (Strategic pathway: Capacity and education); promoting the added value of the geospatial data usage (Strategic pathway: Communication and engagements); etc.

---

[3] Access restricted.
[4] In adoption procedure.

5   Project Smart SDI Concept

In order to comply with the previously described geospatial data and technologies trends for the public sector in Europe, and implement the relevant European policies and other development priorities as part of the Serbia EU integration process, RGA together with Lantmäteriet have launched the already mentioned Project "Establishing Smart SDI in Serbia" (Project Smart SDI). This Project, which is today still in the concept form, is going to be implemented in period January 2023 - December 2025, and its activities would be budgeted by the Swedish SIDA with up to 25 million SEK.

The first phase of this Project implementation, so-called Project inception phase, would last until the middle of the first Project year (2023), and would include detail Project planning[5] according to the SIDA project methodology.

Component 1: Project management

• **Project sub-outcome 1** RGA has strategic action plan, established cooperation and capacity to lead establishment of a modern NSDI that supports and facilitates the access, sharing and usage of geospatial data and services, which could respond to the current and future stakeholders' needs for geospatial data for sustainable development on national, provincial and local level

Component 2: Enhancing usage of geospatial data for decision-making and policies management

• **Project sub-outcome 2** Increased number of public sector geospatial data available for re-use, and promoted advantages of geospatial data usage for sustainable development decision-making and policies management through a modernized NSDI platform (3-5 pilot areas)

Component 3: Establishing portfolio management and project planning support for Smart SDI building

• **Project sub-outcome 3** Established portfolio management methodology and project planning support for improvement of NSDI and making RGA more effective as organization

Component 4: Stakeholders capacity building, engagement and communication

• **Project sub-outcome 4** Stakeholders understand and have capacities, tools and cooperation structures and mechanisms for implementing modern NSDI, i.e. establishing Smart SDI

Fig. 5. Project components with their sub-outcomes

Project impact or main outcome to be reached after the 3 years of Project implementation is defined as:

National, provincial and local level public administrations in Serbia are making efficiently and transparently decisions in democratic and socially inclusive manner about

---

[5] Project concept is currently under elaboration by the RGA and Lantmäteriet, so the final list of Project activities was not available at the moment of writing this article.

development activities that improve quality of work and life environment for all citizens through sustainable usage of available land and other natural and manmade resources, processes and services.

The Project main outcome would be achieved by the implementation of different activities grouped under the four Project components that are focused on the accomplishment of four Project sub-outcomes presented above in the Fig. 5.

6 Expected Project Results

While the outcomes of Component 1, 3 and 4 could be generally described as supportive ones for both Project implementation and establishing the right culture and capacity of the social subsystem for modernizing NSDI in Serbia, the outcome of Component 2 would directly contribute to the transformation of current NSDI system. In other words, the assumed outputs from the Component 2 are expected: 1) to create advantages of the future NSDI model and enhance usage of geospatial data and technologies for decision-making and policies management towards the sustainable development; and 2) to stimulate implementation of the other KAPs defined in the SAP document in coming years.

Due to their importance for the technical perspective of planned NSDI modernization, the expected activities and three main results from the Component 2 are outlined below.

Creation of a New Public Sector Geospatial Dataset by Digitalization
Creation of a new public sector geospatial dataset, namely land use dataset, which is categorized as HVD, is planned to be one of the main Project outputs. Since the Project time constraint, this dataset is planned to be created by digitalization of the land uses data for 3–5 pilot spatial and urban plans within the jurisdictions of selected local self-governments, following the relevant INSPIRE standards. Advantages of this pilot land use dataset, and its capacity to support the evidence-based or data-driven sustainable development decision-making, would then be promoted through use case(s) already identified in the SAP, like: transformation and standardization of spatial and urban planning process (targeting SDG 11); process of property legalization (targeting SDG 1.4); support infrastructure projects implementation (highways, railways, infrastructure objects etc.); etc.

Creation of New Public Sector Geospatial Dataset by Integrating Existing Non-geospatial with Geospatial HVD Dataset
This project output would include creation of a new public sector geospatial dataset by integrating one of the already available RGA's HVDs with existing public sector non-geospatial data using their location information, like statistical data, data on energy passports for buildings, SDG indicators data, etc. Also, advantages of the geospatial dataset(s) created in this way as well as their usage for the different purposes, i.e. use cases, would be promoted.

Smart SDI platform

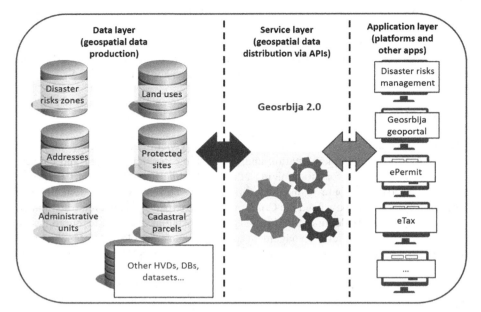

Fig. 6. Future Smart SDI platform

Smart SDI Platform

In line with the increasing demand for re-usable public sector geospatial datasets and services, Project results would include further improvement of the existing NSDI geoportal, Geosrbija, towards the establishment of a modern NSDI platform advantages. This improvement or upgrading of the current Geosrbija geoportal would be focused on establishing the user-friendly platform with the user-centric services, data sharing tools based on APIs and new collaboration services for stakeholders (for co-creation, crowdsourcing, etc.), in line with the SAP solutions as well as foreseen results of the "GreenData4All" initiative, i.e. modernized INSPIRE Directive. (Fig. 6) This upgraded platform, along with the other simplifications and modernization on organizational, legal and financial levels as described in the SAP, should form a solid basis for future green transformation-oriented data space and ecosystem establishment in Serbia towards the Green Agenda for the Western Balkans (and Green Deal) accomplishment.

Finally, besides these three Project outputs on the technical level, other planned Project results would include building appropriate organizational and legal framework for the NSDI modernization, like: establishment of appropriate governance framework for Smart SDI stakeholders; capacity building of RGA and other stakeholders; promotional events for building awareness on the importance of geospatial data; etc.

7   Conclusions

In order to the improve access and enhance usage of the public sector geospatial datasets and related services by the increasingly diversified end-users community, which today demand location-based information to satisfy their various needs, RGA has launched the 3-year Project "Establishing Smart SDI in Serbia". Concept of this Project is based on the recently adopted SAP for the improvement of NSDI in Serbia, which structure and content followed results of the UN-GGIM's IGIF project, as well as provided strategic directions of the European Strategy for data and INSPIRE Directive, related to existing NSDIs modernization and simplification. These improvements of NSDI are needed to support integration of all available public sector data that can contribute to the right decision-making and policies management towards the evolving digital and green transformation in Europe and on global level, which connects today the increasing number of stakeholders from the different sectors, both in developed and developing countries. Once NSDIs and other geospatial initiatives improve and integrate into the future sustainable geospatial data spaces and ecosystems, the new advancements in the geospatial technologies domain are expected to provide a new boost to the sustainable development and SDGs accomplishment on each location, by creating the new geospatial insights and contextual knowledge for the right decision-making. In this aspect, specific focus in future would be on the spatial and urban planning that, due to the support by rapidly developing geospatial and related technologies, would become truly dynamic and more responsive.

References

1. Živković, L.: Towards institutional and organisational framework for the National spatial data infrastructure development in Serbia. Acta. Geogr. Slov. **52**(1), 189–213 (2012). https://doi.org/10.3986/AGS52108
2. Coetzee, S., et al.: EUROGI Towards a sustainable geospatial ecosystem beyond SDI, initiated by the Policies and Portfolio Group of the European Umbrella Organization for Geographic Information (2021). https://doi.org/10.13140/RG.2.2.22555.39203
3. UN-GGIM: Future Geospatial Information Ecosystem: From SDI to SoS and on to the Geoverse Making the Step Change Using the Integrated Geospatial Information Framework, Discussion Paper (2022).https://ggim.un.org/meetings/GGIM-committee/12th-Session/documents/Future_Geospatial_Information_Ecosystem_Discussion_Paper_July2022.pdf
4. Potts, R.: Is a new planning 3.0 paradigm emerging? Exploring the relationship between digital technologies and planning theory and practice. Plann. Theory Pract. **21**(2), 272–289 (2020). . https://doi.org/10.1080/14649357.2020.1748699
5. United Nations Integrated Geospatial Information Framework (UN-IGIF). https://ggim.un.org/IGIF/
6. UN: New Urban Agenda (2017).https://habitat3.org/wp-content/uploads/NUA-English.pdf
7. EC: Urban Agenda for the European Union: Multi-level governance in action (2019). https://ec.europa.eu/regional_policy/sources/docgener/brochure/urban_agenda_eu_en.pdf
8. Kotsev, A., Minghini, M., Cetl, V., Penninga, F., Robbrecht, J., Lutz, M.: INSPIRE – A public sector contribution to the European green deal data space. In: A vision for the technological evolution of Europe's Spatial Data Infrastructures for 2030, EUR 30832 EN, Publications Office of the European Union, Luxembourg (2021). https://doi.org/10.2760/8563.JRC126319

9. EC: Communication from the commission to the european parliament, the council, the European economic and social committee and the committee of the regions a European strategy for data. com (2020) 66 final (2020). https://eur-lex.europa.eu/legal-content/EN/TXT/?uri= CELEX:52020DC0066

10. EC: Commission Implementing Regulation (EU) 2023/138 of 21 December 2022 laying down a list of specific high-value datasets and the arrangements for their publication and re-use (2023). https://eur-lex.europa.eu/legal-content/EN/TXT/?uri=uriserv:OJ.L_.2023. 019.01.0043.01.ENG

11. EC INSPIRE. https://inspire.ec.europa.eu/

12. Andrews, C., et al.: AI in Planning: Opportunities and Challenges and How to Prepare. Conclusions and Recommendations from APA's "AI in Planning" Foresight Community (2022). https://planning-org-uploaded-media.s3.amazonaws.com/publication/ download_pdf/AI-in-Planning-White-Paper-Rev.pdf

13. Logg, A., Naserentin, V.: Modelling and simulating cities with digital twins, GIM International (2022). https://www.gim-international.com/content/article/modelling-and-simulating-cities-with-digital-twins

14. Batty, M., Yang, W.: A Digital Future for Planning - Spatial Planning Reimagined, Digital Task Force for Planning (2022).https://digital4planning.com/wp-content/uploads/2022/02/A-Digital-Future-for-Planning-Full-Report-Web.pdf

15. Geospatial Commission: How GIS and land use modelling can help improve local authority decision-making (2023). https://www.landusedialogues.gov.uk/2023/02/13/how-gis-and-land-use-modelling-can-help-improve-local-authority-decision-making/

16. Republic Geodetic Authority: Strategic action plan for the national spatial data infrastructure of the Republic of Serbia (2021). https://en.rgz.gov.rs/content/pages/english/Structure/ NSDI%20Strategic%20Actions%20Plan-4.pdf

17. MCTI: Sustainable urban development strategy of the Republic of Serbia 2030 (2019). https:// www.mgsi.gov.rs/cir/dokumenti/urbani-razvoj/

18. Strategy for Sweden's reform cooperation with the Western Balkans and Turkey for 2021– 2027, https://si.se/app/uploads/2022/12/strategy-reform-cooperation-western-balkans-and-turkey-2021-27.pdf

"Open Cinema Map" - Open Data and Digital Ethnography as a Means for Grasping the Evolving Spatial Pattern of Cinemas – Athens Case Study

Alkistis Dalkavouki[(⊠)] [ID] and Anastasia Stratigea [ID]

Department of Geography and Regional Planning, School of Rural, Surveying and
Geoinformatics Engineering, National Technical University of Athens, Athens, Greece
dalkavou@mail.ntua.gr, stratige@central.ntua.gr

Abstract. Culture, in its various forms, is currently perceived as a key driver for
urban development and a sector that lies at the heart of SDGs' attainment; while
various studies around the world demonstrate its power in cities' flourishing and
achievement of sustainability objectives. However, rapid technological and other
developments have severely affected certain facets of culture, with cinema being
one of the most impacted ones. This paper explores the evolving spatial pattern of
this specific cultural sector, which is perceived as a vital part of local urban socio-
economic and cultural development and community invigoration. As case study
region, the Athens metropolitan area is considered. The proposed methodological approach is grounded in particular types of open and volunteered geographic
data, as well as spatial tools. More specifically, data are sourced from the Open-
StreetMap platform and supplementary digital sources through digital ethnography; while errors/discrepancies identified in these data are also addressed and
resolved. The time span of the cinemas' spatial pattern exploration in the Athens
area is 2005–2022, with specific interest in 2005, 2012, 2019 and 2022 instances.
Key findings demonstrate a certain decline of enclosed, single-screen enterprises; a
relative stability of open-air, neighborhood and municipal cinemas; and a fragility
of multiplexes.

Keywords: Culture/cinemas · Open data · Open Street Map & Volunteered
Geographic Information · Local urban development · Spatial analysis

1 Introduction

Culture is nowadays perceived as an integral component of the United Nations' Sustainable Development Goals (SDGs) [1], first defined in 2015 in a call to end inequality
and poverty and pave sustainable future pathways for humanity. In this respect, culture, in one of the first times that it is implicitly included in the international agenda
[2], is conceptualized as a factor directly and/or indirectly contributing to the SDGs
in multiple ways. At the same time, culture is considered to be in need of protection

© The Author(s), under exclusive license to Springer Nature Switzerland AG 2023
O. Gervasi et al. (Eds.): ICCSA 2023 Workshops, LNCS 14105, pp. 561–578, 2023.
https://doi.org/10.1007/978-3-031-37108-0_36

and management in both its tangible and intangible aspects. Such ascertainments have definitely informed the United Nations' twenty-year, 17-goal roadmap for sustainable development, gradually adopted by cities around the globe [3].

The UN Agenda 2030 penetrates policy directions of the European Union (EU) as well, with the 17 SDGs demarcating developmental pathways in the European continent. Culture, being pushed towards a "mainstreaming", is considered instrumental to achieving the SDGs in the European context. This is owed to its: intrinsic value, bringing prosperity, social cohesion, and overall well-being; dominance in European identity, image and influence; and potential as a "major economic multiplier". In particular, the Cultural and Creative Industries (CCI) (the two terms will be considered interchangeable for the rest of this paper, despite certain differences in the way they have been historically used) – cinema included – can secure joy, innovation, jobs and profits for the continent [4]. These are transferrable to the local (city) level, with the directions of the New Urban Agenda "localizing" the aforementioned goals, offering practical guidance to interested parties and proposing specific contribution examples [5]. As of this writing, the insistence to propose solutions for cultural development – the "audiovisual sector" included – remains urgent [6].

The role of culture as a significant lever for local urban development is, therefore, definitely recognized. In fact, culture has been conceptualized as an engine of local urban prosperity [7, 8] and a critical component of the "new economy" [9, 10] for over half a century. This view is further galvanized by Florida's proposal [11] on the *creative city*, a concept that has gained worldwide popularity. At around the same time, however, the entire cultural sector suffers from the aftermath of the global 2008 recession [12] and over several years [13]; while local cultural activities are affected even more harshly [14]. The more recent recession, following the outbreak of the Covid-19 pandemic, showcased that culture can be incredibly fragile in times of crises, but also a means for recovery [4]. In the end, culture has long emerged as a significant sector for socio-economic development, worthy of consideration and attentive study; thus, its evolution through time becomes a study priority, in order for more informed policy decisions, supporting and strengthening the role of culture, to be articulated.

Out of all cultural sectors, *cinema* is the focus of this work for several reasons. Firstly, it is a clear engine of multitudinous economic development worldwide, either as an industry or through related activities [15, 16]. Moreover, as one of the CCI [17], cinema has been increasingly regulated since the 1980s and 1990s, both in Europe and Greece [18]. Additionally, cinema's contribution to the social aspect of development is worth mentioning. This is especially witnessed during the first post-war decades, when cinema screens became local reference points, particularly those in smaller neighborhoods. As such, cinemas were spaces of both culture dissemination and socialization, thus strengthening the social cohesion of the population [19]. Since then, various technological, socio-political and demographic changes and crises have reduced the number of cinemas and weakened this relationship. In Greece, for example, such changes relate to the: appearance of television and video; advent of multiplex theaters and the Internet; 1973 and 1979 crises; rise of land prices, affecting the location or even existence of cinemas; shrinkage of production and consumption of local film products and state's apathy; social changes of the '90s; suburbanization of the city of Athens; and piercing economic recession of 2008. However, cinemas in the city of Athens still maintain their cultural role, thanks to both the existence and intertemporal evolution of smaller, private-owned as well as municipal businesses that emphasize cinema's social role [20] and the legal state protection offered to historically significant cinema buildings [21].

That said, it is worth studying the further protection and preservation of cinema as a future-proof form of cultural expression, with important developmental – social, cultural, economic, etc. – repercussions. In such a context, this article attempts to explore the following research questions: how have recent technological, demographic and economic changes impacted the strength of cinemas as a form of culture? How has the spatial pattern of cinemas evolved in the last twenty years in the specific case study region, i.e. the Athens metropolitan area? Which types of cinema enterprises have been mostly affected – either rewarded or degraded – by these changes and why? The response to these questions forms the ground for further research on the developmental potential and protection needs of cinemas, as part of the broader cultural sector. The article is structured as follows: Sect. 2 provides a brief literature overview regarding new, open and digital methods of acquiring geospatial data. In Sect. 3, the methodological approach is presented; while the study context, time span, as well as data acquisition process, are also described. In Sect. 4, the results are presented, discussed and compared to relevant literature. Finally, in Sects. 5 and 6 respectively, results are critically discussed and conclusions are drawn.

2 Literature Review

Before delving into the specifics of the case study, an overview of recent data acquisition literature is presented in this section. Data acquisition currently allows for access to geospatial data of a more niche interest, such as the one explored in this work, thanks to a number of noteworthy trends in digital data creation from the last twenty years. The first is *crowdsourcing*, which is considered to be the exploitation of the expertise of a large number of users to perform tasks at a lower cost [22]. The early-to-mid-2000s advent of Web 2.0 technologies [23] encouraged the cooperation of users, content providers and companies [24] with the aim of creating large amounts of data. This development resulted in revolutionary methods of information production and dissemination, the premiere example of which is Wikipedia [25]. The second trend was what Goodchild [26] named *Volunteer Geographic Information* (VGI) and defined as "geographic information acquired and made available to others through the voluntary activity of individuals or groups, with the intent of providing information about the geographic world" [27]. VGI is the result of several factors, among which are the spread of personal computers, broadband Internet connections and dynamic maps [28]; the democratization of personal GPS devices, which became affordable after being integrated into mobile phones [29]; and the success of open-source software, leading to the creation of open databases for public benefit [26]. These are synthesized into what Sui [30] calls the "wikification" of geographic information; with one of its most popular examples being the OpenStreetMap (OSM) [31].

OSM deserves special mention, as it constitutes one of the main tools for data acquisition in this paper. As a volunteer-made geospatial database, OSM possesses a plethora of inherent advantages that position it as an ideal source of geospatial data, particularly regarding culture. Firstly, it constitutes a democratic, cooperative and remarkably popular work, aiming to provide free geographic data of global coverage [29]. Simultaneously, its information has a local character, as it is often submitted by a place's inhabitants [32]. Its structure further facilitates its popularity, by differing from traditional databases [33]; and making GPS data submission, processing and categorization – in the form of points, lines and polygons [34] – much easier. OSM is also easy to use and is accessible by third-party platforms (QGIS, etc.); while data provided are available in GIS-compatible formats, organized by theme and country [35]. Its legal status offers more advantages: all OSM data are under the "Open Database License 1.0", thus anyone can share and edit them, as well as produce derivatives, as long as the same terms are kept and originals are cited [36]. Finally, the database is constantly maintained [31] and expanded, up to the final research year of this work [35]. As a result, this volunteer effort can provide global, up-to-date and easy-to-use data with few restrictions, in compatible formats and at zero cost, making them an excellent choice for sourcing scientific research.

However, it is also worth examining OSM data's accuracy and reliability, due to the relative laxness of quality control in volunteer cartography [27]. When judged according to more robust spatial data quality standards [37], OSM datasets display errors due to known parameters. These include the: disparate origin of the data, with a variety of sources in different scales and resolutions; lack of clear standards; users' subjective judgment that can lead to undervaluing of individual records; and users' diversification in experience and level of digital literacy [29, 38]. The result is uneven geometric accuracy, quality and completeness of data, with larger errors appearing in poorer, more rural areas and objects thought of as less significant. Moreover, the spatial accuracy of the records is dependent on the users' attention, with the community showing more interest in adding rather than fixing content. Finally, there is no guarantee of logical continuum and linkages between records, because both depend on the users' input and the database's structure [31, 39]. That said, the above does not preclude the use of these data for scientific purposes; quality control is a crucial topic within the OSM community, which is constantly improving and receiving suggestions [25, 29, 31]; OSM's amateur character can be partly useful [40]; and it remains the fastest, most cost-effective alternative to obsolete "official" geographic information [27].

The paper's theoretical background is complemented by *digital ethnography*, with regard to additional data not found through OSM. Ethnography is a discipline that captures the "social meanings and ordinary activities" of subjects in "naturally occurring settings", spaces that are called "fields" [41]; while in recent decades it has expanded further into the Internet. The result is a variety of new methodological tools for the collection and analysis of online data from wider communities [42], gathered quickly and efficiently [43]. The combination of the above allows for the acquisition of data from non-traditional but reliable sources, given the subject matter's niche interest and lack of documentation in official sources. In practice, this paper relies on personal recollections, blog posts and other miscellaneous non-official sources to obtain data on the opening and closing of cinemas. These sources have been legitimized by the discipline of cultural history, a multi-disciplinarian area between history and anthropology that allowed for the discipline's expansion into discussing culture, with attention paid to subjectivity and the values of small groups [44].

3   Data and Methodology

The methodological steps of this work are outlined in Fig. 1. More specifically, the proposed steps aim at creating a geospatial database on cinemas, following the previously discussed literature on open-source geodata and the already explored spatial distribution of cinemas in Greece [19, 21]. The data are then processed and analyzed, in order for inferences as to the trajectory of this specific cultural sector in the Athens metropolitan area to be extracted. This effort has a spatial and temporal focus and is accomplished by the use of up-to-date data. Even with the use of rather large, but deliberately selected, time intervals, this intertemporal view offers a broad but accurate picture of the evolution of the specific cultural dimension, questioning also its resilience to various stresses occurring within the selected time span.

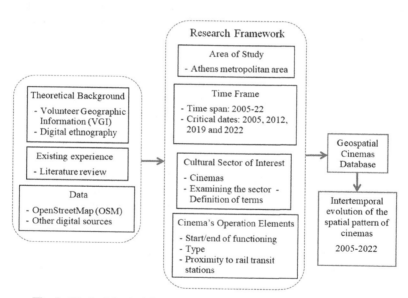

Fig. 1. Methodological flowchart of research, Source: Own elaboration

Before the main data collection process is described, the research is put in its appropriate framing, including the focus region and time span of the study. In particular, the study region concerns the Athens metropolitan area, in an effort to expand upon previous research and focus on an area of specific interest, i.e. the cultural and financial center of Greece [19, 21]. The time span ranges from 2005 to 2022; with data collection being accomplished for the distinct years 2005, 2012, 2019 and 2022. The selected time span encapsulates the two major crises of the last fifteen years in Greece that disturbed consumption patterns in the entertainment market as a whole. The years 2005, 2012, 2019 and 2022 are perceived as 'turning points' in the evolution of consumption patterns of the cinema's cultural activity. In particular, 2005 is considered an indicative year of stability before the Greek financial crisis; 2012 is the year before the recession's peak in the country, which is thought to occur in late 2013 or early 2014, as was reflected in the – at the time – record-breaking unemployment rates [45, 46]; 2019 is thought of as another year of stability before the Covid-19 outbreak [47]; while, finally, 2022 is the year in which the health crisis seems to be over and most institutions resume their "normal" operation. The approach of this work has some disadvantages: e.g., there is a lack of distinction between a cinema's temporary – due to the owner's personal difficulties or possible bureaucracy – and permanent closure. Moreover, no data is available as to the cinemas that were operational in time spans other than those above mentioned (only two such cases were identified in the sample). Nevertheless, the scheme followed provides a satisfactory overview of culture consumption in the study area, apart from a negligible number of exceptions.

Of equal importance is a more strict definition of cinemas' exhibition spaces, as well as their formats and operation schemes. Thus, a "cinema" is considered to be "the space of systematic exhibition of motion pictures (at least 4 times per month, for at least one month, over at least 2 years), delivering its services at a non-symbolic amount of money (a ticket costing over 3 euros)". Moreover, a cinema is considered to be operational at any given "turning point" year, provided that it exhibits motion pictures for up to the first half of that year. This period is considered to be comprised of the months of April and May for enclosed enterprises; and May, June or July for open-air ones. Open-air cinemas that were operational only for August 2005 are excluded. The same holds for some specific categories of movie theaters, e.g. adult theaters and drive-ins. Furthermore, excluded from the data set are cinemas displaying the following attributes: businesses that operated for short periods of time and then ceased to show movies and became theaters or community spaces; spaces whose operation was supported by few data; and charities and art institutions organizing free screenings. Finally, two multiplex cinemas began operations late in the year – they opened in November 2005, to benefit from the Christmas shopping period of their co-located malls – and are excluded from that year's data.

"Multiplex cinema" (called simply "multiplex" for the sake of brevity) is another term in need of clarification. Although this type of cinema possesses a set of identifying traits – its coexistence with a lifestyle and business model of conspicuous consumption, a multitude of screens, and a reliance on car-owning patrons [48] –, its definition depends on both place [49] and time. Older literature [19] and the present paper's sources interpreted it differently over the years. This paper used one uniform, albeit retroactive, definition, namely: a multiplex is "any cinema with at least two screens in operation".

The framing of cinema enterprises for guiding data collection leads to the identification of three general types of businesses and two basic dates, describing their operation. The three general types are: i) open-air, enclosed, or mixed; ii) a single-screen or a multiplex; and ii) municipal or privately-owned. The two fundamental dates relate to a cinema's beginning and end of operation (if it had come). Such decisions follow previous literature on the subject [19, 21].

One final element in need of data collection is each cinema's proximity (distance) to a rail mass transit station. The 5- or 10-min walk criterion is used in this respect as "a threshold for the distance people are typically willing to walk in order to reach a bus stop or other local destination" [50]. This can then be turned into a distance by multiplying it by an average walking speed – about 80 m per minute – and rounding it up to 500 m [51]. These distances can then be turned into circular buffers around mass transit stations in a GIS environment. Despite some drawbacks – the hypothesis of 500 m as an "ideal" distance [52], practical objections [50], etc. –, this assumption is commonly used in transportation studies, including previous studies on the subject [21]. For this paper, circular buffers were created around the stations of the most popular track-based public transport system in Athens, the metro, to gauge the spatial relationship between the metro and cinemas. Lastly, these buffers were dynamic, reflecting the expanding works of the Athens metro network [53].

Data acquisition begins with the OSM database, which provides initial information; and continues with additional sources. Data are retrieved and processed in the QGIS freeware (version 2.18.28) and the QuickOSM (version 2.1.0) add-on. The latter locates and downloads specific data packets, based on user-submitted queries [54]. Another add-on, QOSM (version 0.1.1), is used to place a raster level with the OSM platform's overall map, spot the area of study and subsequently save the features shown in Table 1 in shapefile format.

Table 1. OSM spatial data features through the QuickOSM add-on, Source: Own elaboration

Feature Name	Key	Value
Cinema	amenity	cinema
Mall	shop	mall
Metro Station	route	subway

This was followed by a brief preparatory period, during which all cinemas are turned into point data (centroids are generated from enterprises in polygon form); and distinct levels for the metro stations that were in operation each year are created. The metro's final expansion included all stations that were in operation until July 2022. That said, the most impactful change within the area of study was the addition of two stations – the Keratsini and Elaionas stations – in 2012.

The above procedure offers a first, quick view of the inspected cinemas' phenomenon, while also defusing most of the platform's data errors. Thanks to the relatively privileged position of the study area – Athens is the state capital of a European country –, data collected are rich, reliable and relatively up-to-date. The geometric accuracy of cinema locations is also satisfactory. Some individual errors regarding the shape of buildings that housed cinemas due to the mixed quality of orthophotographs used in OSM's source files are identified; and are easily dealt with, through additional geo-referencing. Furthermore, given that the end product refers to point data for geographic use, they do not prove particularly concerning. Descriptive data prove to be less reliable, and time inaccuracies have to be corrected. Different types of enterprises are incorporated in the above-mentioned cinema categories. Thus retail and outlet stores are grouped with in malls, informal film clubs are thought of as legal cinemas and miscellaneous types of movie theater are included; while several cinemas that had closed the previous years are omitted. The creation of the appropriate tags, the re-organization of categories and the spotting of gaps are manually performed. A sum of *132 cinema enterprises* is located, displaying small but acceptable individual geometry errors that are easily dealt with. Some corrections are carried out to bring the data in line with the above definitions, while omissions are properly filled in.

This first database is complemented, confirmed and expanded thanks to new records from digital sources. The main source of information regarding the cinemas that are open during the aforementioned years is the screening program, provided by the "Athinorama" webpage [55], accessed through the Internet Archive and checked thrice – in January or April, July or August and November or December – for each year. In the case of 2005, additional data is sourced from the online archive of the "Rizospastis" newspaper [56]. Afterwards, details on the history of individual cinemas are identified in specialized blogs, such as "Cinema-Hellas" [57] and "Cinemano" [58]. Specialized books [59] are equally useful for their reproduced material, namely newspaper excerpts, brief interviews with interested parties, photographs, and updated observations. Lastly, the cinemas' official webpages, social media profiles – mostly on Facebook, Twitter and Instagram – and other (mostly local) website news are used to spot operation, pause or reopening announcements, especially for smaller cinema enterprises. All features of existing and new cinemas are tracked and recorded as detailed above. In this way, an extra 70 cinemas are added to the database, most of which had either closed before the creation of the Greek OSM community or had reopened relatively recently. In total, *202 individual cinema enterprises* are identified and organized in QGIS.

Finally, it has to be noted that the errors spotted during data collection are in line with previous studies on the same subject [19] and are similarly corrected. There are few cases where no reliable data could be found as to the founding and operation of cinemas in remote areas, resulting in the removal of 3 such cases from the database. Moreover, individual sources sometimes disagreed with regard to dates, and particularly information as to when a cinema opened. Even then, however, the discrepancies are rather insignificant – a few months on average, with the biggest outlier being 5 years – and are attributed to the imperfections of human memory. In those cases, the dates chosen are those confirmed either from multiple sources or the most authoritative one, i.e. the one closer to the original cinema owners. Finally, name and address changes are combined into one record, with the older data merely being referenced.

4 Empirical Results

Before examining how the cinemas are spatially organized, their overall numbers and related trends are presented, demonstrating the number of cinemas in the years perceived as 'turning points' and related changes in between time intervals (Table 2).

The overall downward trend in the number of cinemas in Athens merits further investigation. Firstly, the peak in the number of cinemas appears in the year 2005, while the cinemas' lowest point and greater losses occurred in 2012, well before the Greek recession peak. Moreover, the number of cinemas in 2019 showed a small rise. Finally, although the 2020 pandemic has affected the number of cinemas in the 2020–2022 time span, this remains larger in 2022 than that of its overall low point in 2012.

Table 2. Operational cinemas by type in 'turning point' years and changes in between time intervals, Source: Own elaboration

Year Cinema Type	2005	2011-2005 number (%)	2012	2019-2012 number (%)	2019	2022-2020 number (%)	2022
Total	174	-36 (-26.1)	138	9 (6.1)	147	-6 (-4.3)	141
Single-Screen	139	-31 (-28.7)	108	7 (6.1)	115	-3 (-2.7)	112
Multiplex	35	-5 (-16.7)	30	2 (6.3)	32	-3 (-10.3)	29
Open-Air	96	-12 (-14.3)	84	9 (9.7)	93	1 (1)	94
Enclosed	63	-23 (-57.5)	40	0 (0)	40	-6 (-17.7)	34
Mixed	15	-1 (-7.1)	14	0 (0)	14	-1 (-7.7)	13
Private-Owned	128	-29 (-29.3)	99	6 (5.7)	105	-7 (-7.1)	98
Municipal	46	-7 (-18)	39	3 (7.1)	42	1 (2.3)	43

Focusing on the specific types of screens is also productive. One can see that the same overall pattern is observed for single-screen and multiplex cinemas, with both exhibiting the same peaks and valleys. However, the former are affected worse than average in 2012 and showed greater resistance in 2022; while the latter behave in the exact opposite way. Open-air cinemas are hit relatively lightly by the pre-2012 changes, while also increasing their numbers in the following years. The exact opposite was observed in the – already relatively lower – number of enclosed cinemas, with greater-than-average losses, especially around 2012 (only stable numbers in 2019); and the much smaller number of mixed cinemas that align with the overall trend, but show greater stability in all instances. Lastly, private-owned cinemas are largely in step with the overall trend, even if they exhibit slightly worse valleys and gains percentage-wise; while municipal cinemas, aside from their smaller-than-average losses in 2012, saw a continuous rise in numbers, even as late as 2022.

A total of 59 cinemas closed during the research period. Mapping of these results for each time interval is shown in Fig. 2a.

From the results obtained, certain inferences can be drawn. The first concerns the date of closure: by far, the greatest number of enterprises (38 cinemas) closes during the research period's first interval (2005–2011), particularly between 2005 and 2008 (31 enterprises). Far fewer cinemas close in the following years, namely 14 in 2012–2019 and 7 in 2020–2022. Those closures also exhibit an interesting spatial variation.

In 2005–2011, closures are observed in the Athens city center, with the western suburbs being most profoundly affected, followed by the southern and eastern ones and the city center itself, to a lesser extent; and several neighborhoods at the north-eastern part of the Athens metropolitan area, such as Artemida, Keratea, Porto Rafti, Rouf, etc. The neighborhoods with the greatest number of closures were those of Piraeus, Kallithea and Plateia Amerikis.

In the 2012–2019 time span, closures are limited to the city center and the previously affected nearby neighborhoods, namely Kallithea, Marousi, Nea Smyrni, Neos Kosmos and Victoria; as well as selected settlements to the north and south, such as Agioi Apostoloi, Agios Stefanos, Lagonisi. The closures beyond 2019 are largely concentrated on the city center – the Kolonaki and Pagkrati neighborhoods – and the already affected or tourism-adjacent neighborhoods, e.g. Glyfada, Neapoli, Palaio Faliro and Amerikis Square. The specific types of cinemas that ceased functioning are also worth highlighting. Thus enclosed cinemas are by far the most stricken at 38 enterprises, 23 of which close between 2005 and 2011; single-screen cinemas suffer 45 closures, with 28 of them occurring between 2005 and 2011; multiplexes also steadily lose their power, decreasing by 10, 2 and 2 enterprises for each interval respectively. Moreover, 50 out of the total closed cinemas are private-owned, while municipal ones keep their strength by exhibiting no losses after 2011.

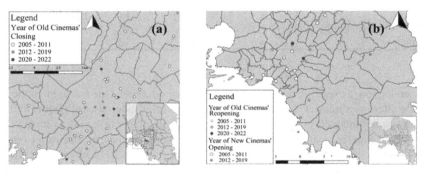

Fig. 2. Map of a) cinema closures, and b) openings and re-openings, by time interval explored, Source: Own elaboration

The opening of new cinemas is far more limited, but still worth mapping (Fig. 2b). Only 14 new cinemas open, mostly during 2005 and 2006 and none after 2016, which is a clear sign of the recession of the Greek economy. Furthermore, only half of those – either mall multiplexes or municipal cinemas – manage to survive till 2022. During the first time interval, the new cinemas are opened in proximity to the city center and the western/southern neighborhoods. Between 2012 and 2019, however, they begin to spread to the southern and western suburbs as well as the eastern neighborhoods of the Athens metropolitan area. Among the cinemas that closed, 1 is located in the Lagonisi neighborhood and the rest are in the city center or its relative proximity; 4 of them are multiplexes within malls, 2 are open-air ventures close to or connected to another commercial activity, and 1 is a similar enclosed case. The opposite is true of the surviving ones, which tend to be located in southern and western suburbs and eastern neighborhoods: 2 are mall multiplexes and 1 is an enclosed multiplex; while all the rest are open-air enterprises, with one being municipal. A more robust trend refers to the 16 reopened cinemas after 2005 – 8 in the first time interval, 6 in the second and 2 in the third one –, all of which remained operational until 2022. These cinemas – mostly open-air (11) and 5 enclosed ones – began appearing in western and southern neighborhoods, but edged closer to the city center after each interval; most are private-owned businesses, though 5 of the earliest reopened enterprises are municipal ones.

It is also worth examining how the aforementioned changes influence the spatial pattern of operational cinemas. Although the overall pattern appears to be strongly concentrated, certain tendencies towards dispersion in later years are noticeable; while as seen in Table 3, more interesting are the results from the patterns of individual categories.

Table 3. The nearest neighbor index (and z-score) of operational cinemas by type and year, Source: Own elaboration.

Year Cinema Type	2005 neighbor index (z-score)	2012 neighbor index (z-score)	2019 neighbor index (z-score)	2022 neighbor index (z-score)
Single-screen	0,51673 (−10,900044)	0,544041 (−9,065023)	0,603457 (−8,135231)	0,627019 (−7,551378)
Multiplex	0,820383 (−2,032885)	0,886375 (−1,1906)	0,905266 (−1,025212)	0,999401 (−0,006176)
Open-air	0,611639 (−7,279517)	0,592359 (−7,147411)	0,64812 (−6,491835)	0,674314 (−6,040789)
Enclosed	0,729975 (−4,100194)	0,830307 (−2,053172)	0,794371 (−2,487972)	0,875122 (−1,393018)
Private	0,438124 (−12,161193)	0,452915 (−10,413650)	0,486532 (−10,065574)	0,537284 (−8,763111)
Municipal	0,869768 (−1,689765)	0,842208 (−1,885165)	0,861426 (−1,718061)	0,865699 (−1,684782)

More specifically, although some categories follow the overall trend, others diverge in interesting ways. Three cinema types – private-owned, open-air, and single-screen ones – remain strongly concentrated for almost the entire research period, but show slight signs of this pattern loosening and easing towards dispersion with time. Another type – municipal cinemas – also displays clustering patterns but weaker, tightening and easing in 2012 and 2022 respectively. Lastly, two categories – enclosed cinemas and multiplexes – switch from a clustered pattern to a random one. The former actually starts as clustered, is weakened with time and ends as random in 2022; while the latter starts from a relatively strong concentrated pattern, which becomes random over the next years and exhibits additional tendencies towards dispersion. As for mixed cinemas, they are too few in number – less than 30 – for their spatial pattern to be meaningful [60]; but they are mentioned here to complement the observations regarding multiplexes, as the two categories overlap significantly. This final category begins in a random pattern and evolves more and more towards a strongly dispersed one.

The above information is easier to comprehend by visualizing the moving average of all points for each year by category (Fig. 3).

Despite the small changes noticed for all operational cinemas – with all points concentrated in the Zografos neighborhood and moving first to the east, then south-west – the individual types exhibit different concentration patterns and routes. The average coordinates of open-air cinemas are clustered between the Papagos and Zografos neighborhoods and follow a trajectory towards the south-west; and municipal ones are concentrated in the city center – the Syntagma and Monastiraki neighborhoods – and follow a western path that deviates slightly south-wise. On the contrary, enclosed cinemas circle the Kolonaki neighborhood and drift towards the east; and private-owned ones follow a similar curve, starting from Zografos and Papagos. Multiplexes and mixed cinemas, the types with the greatest mobility, both move from Neapoli to Kipseli, towards the north, with the latter one category also exhibiting a slight tendency towards the west. Furthermore, single-screen cinemas remain in the Zografos neighborhood and move mainly to the south, with a small inclination towards the east.

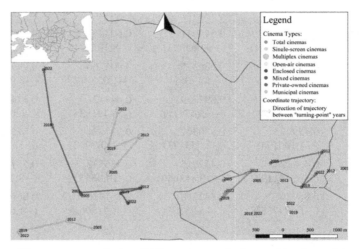

Fig. 3. Map of the average coordinates of Athens cinemas, by type and turning-point year, Source: Own elaboration

Finally, the cinemas' distance from the metro network stations and their subsequent successful operation (i.e. the business remains open up to the year 2022) is examined (Table 4).

By interpreting results presented in Table 4, it appears that the number of cinemas that are located in proximity to the metro decrease, despite the network's expansion and accessibility improvements. Results in the year 2005 actually display the impact of metro infrastructure (deployed in 2004). In fact, the metro's early operation causes slight changes in the functioning of cinemas for the next period. As time goes on, however, improved accessibility gradually loses its influence. The cinema types that benefit the most from this change are private (a total of only 7 municipal cinemas appeared, all of which are enclosed, despite a small reduction in their numbers) and open-air ones to a lesser extent, with their percentages rising in accordance to the aforementioned broader trend. On the contrary, there is a significant number of cinemas (11 specific multiplexes) that are steadily supported by their proximity to metro stations, especially after 2012.

Table 4. Comparison between cinemas within and outside a 10-min distance zone from the nearest metro station, Source: Own elaboration

Year	Cinemas in 10' Zone [number/(%)]	Cinemas out of 10' Zone [number/(%)]	Cinemas in 10' Zone in 'turning point' years in operation in 2022 [number/(%)]	Cinemas in 10' Zone in 'turning point' years in operation in 2022 [number/(%)]
2005	42 (24.14)	132 (75.87)	26 (61.91)	93 (70.46)
2012	41 (29.71)	97 (70.29)	30 (73.18)	87 (89.7)
2019	41 (27.89)	106 (72.11)	36 (87.81)	101 (95.29)
2022	40 (28.37)	101 (71.64)	40 (100)	101 (100)

Simultaneously, there is a large – and after 2012, rising – number of unaffected cinemas outside the 10-min zones, and the percentages of success for each group rise with time.

5 Discussion

Interpreting the findings is complex, since despite the existence of a clear downturn, the results for cinemas are mixed. By far the most affected category is that of enclosed, single-screen cinemas, possibly due to their limited operation window and intense competition from the rising, feature-rich multiplexes. Those cinemas, on the other hand, are trickier to maintain due to the steadily increasing costs [61]. The Covid-19 pandemic caused additional friction, leaving them with either limited or no revenue for several months [4]. The resilience of both types is non-existent, which could be worrying for the sector's overall health in the Attica Region.

The above inference is in line with worldwide trends; however, there are additional complexities to consider. Firstly, the greatest number of losses did not occur during the recession's peak in 2013–2014, but in the time span 2005–2008; while before the Covid-19 outbreak, cinema numbers were making a small recovery. At the same time, the resilience of both open-air and municipal cinemas is noteworthy. In fact, the increase of open-air cinemas is unprecedented and a counter to the overall trend, and could be justified by their lower maintenance costs [19], their connection to tourism [62], and the Greek public's nostalgic affinity for them [21]. In addition, alignment with post-pandemic safety protocols [63] also accounts for the boosting of their attendance and their prominence after 2021. This reveals that the multiple cinema types, which operate in distinct modes and possess different needs, should perhaps be considered separately in terms of study, policy and support.

The multitudinous nature of cinemas as part of the cultural sector is further witnessed in their geographical spread. Firstly, the creation of new cinemas outside the city's center correlates with the suburbanization and population relocation trends of the last few decades in the Attica Region in general and the metropolitan city of Athens in particular, especially the movement towards the northern and eastern suburbs and the creation of multiple peripheral centers [64]. Moreover, and aside from the peripheral neighborhoods, the center of Athens is one of the most affected areas, with multiple closures and few new cinema businesses. This could be a side-effect of the previously-observed rise of land prices [65]; and is owed in part to Greece's entrance into the Eurozone as well as the extensive works in public transit and facilities when the country hosted the 2004 Olympic Games [52, 66]. The competitive, already saturated market could be another factor, as the cinemas which opened in relatively lower-cost areas, where fewer similar businesses are located, seem to be more successful. Simultaneously, the multiple re-openings of smaller cinemas indicate both the emergence of a nostalgic/dormant audience that converge on the neighborhood's remaining screens and the need to utilize valuable and legally-protected real estate [21].

This complexity is reflected in the moving average coordinates: the placement and mobility of cinema groups correspond to particular reclassifications within the space of Attica. Multiplexes and mixed cinemas – two categories that often overlap – moved towards the more expensive northern suburbs [66], but also to the more downgraded western ones, where, due to the many closures of older enterprises, there is little competition. Moreover, municipal cinemas tend to be located in those more traditionally working-class areas, as they tend to be some of the last remaining cinema enterprises in these neighborhoods. This combination of effects covers open-air cinemas as well, which also move towards the southern, more expensive suburbs [66], taking advantage of this nostalgic resonance with audiences of all ages. At the same time, the badly affected enclosed cinemas maintain their traditional concentration around the city center [21], but move eastwards and towards the relatively more upper-middle-class eastern neighborhoods, as this population group can afford leisure spending after the recession more easily. All the above arise from both socio-economic trends and the aforementioned ongoing suburbanization of Athens.

Finally, the metro is a factor that does not, by itself, guarantee a cinema's success, contrary to previous research [20], but only complicates Attica's culture consumption market. It is apparent that the rail network itself cannot reverse the sector's overall trends, but only delay them and preserve – rather than actively support – the enterprises within its reach. The metro has also intensified the co-existence of different modes of cinema-going: rail-supported multiplexes adapt from a car-first service model [48] and accept inflows of people from distant areas – with downtown benefiting either way –, while neighborhood cinemas rely on nearby patrons. Finally, the market somehow rebalanced after the relative novelty of the metro's introduction in 2004, with a significant number of cinemas being completely unaffected.

6 Conclusions

The focus of this paper is on the study of the evolving pattern of cinemas (2005–2022) as a cultural expression and a matter of spatial, social, economic and developmental concern in the Athens metropolitan area. Recent evolutions in geospatial data creation, management and dissemination make the study of the sector significantly easier. Results obtained clearly display a certain decline of the sector that is – in one way or another – felt by most of the multiple types of enterprises in operation. It also unveils the interplay of economy, technology and demographic change as complex issues that are difficult to deal with, while identifying the survival of cinema.

Nevertheless, studying the operation of cinemas and their spatial distribution is not fruitless. Movie-going remains a popular leisure activity, as indicated both by the consistently rising number of open-air and municipally-owned enterprises and the recent boom in attendance, especially after the end of the Covid-19 pandemic. The discovery of more detailed data on the impact these specific businesses have on their local markets, as well as insights into their operation, would greatly enhance those given points.

The presented results should aid in the follow-up to the next parts of this research. Firstly, additional quantitative data – on land values, types of businesses neighboring cinemas and number of tickets per screen – will further illuminate the evolution of the cinemas' phenomenon. Secondly, the addition of qualitative data – interviews and questionnaires with selected cinema owners and exhibitors – will add the perspective of stakeholders involved in the sector; and highlight their particular views and struggles. Both of these steps will highlight important issues that will have to be handled with care and will feed data-enabled policy proposals, addressing the protection of cinema and the enhancement of its role in local urban development.

References

1. What are the Sustainable Development Goals? https://www.undp.org/sustainable-development-goals. Accessed 10 Mar 2023
2. United Cities and Local Governments (UCLG): Culture in the sustainable development goals: A guide for local action (2018). https://www.uclg.org/sites/default/files/culture_in_the_sdgs.pdf. Accessed 11 Jan 2023
3. Hosagrahar, J.: Culture: at the heart of SDGs. UNESCO Cour. (1), 12–14 (2017)
4. Vries, G.D.: Culture in the Sustainable Development Goals: The Role of the European Union (2nd revised edition). Institut für Auslandsbeziehungen, Stuttgart (2020)
5. United Cities and Local Government (UCLG): Culture in the Sustainable Development Goals: A Guide For Local Action. https://www.uclg.org/sites/default/files/culture_in_the_sdgs.pdf. Accessed 10 Mar 2023
6. The Council of the European Union: Council Conclusions on the Work Plan for Culture 2019–2022. Official Journal of the European Union, 2018/C 460/10, 21.12.2018. https://eur-lex.europa.eu/legal-content/EN/TXT/HTML/?uri=CELEX:52018X G1221(01)&from=EN. Accessed 10 Mar 2023
7. Jacobs, J.: The Death and Life of Great American Cities. Vintage Books, New York (2016). ISBN: 0-679-74195-X
8. Hall, P.: Creative cities and economic development. Urban Stud. **37**(4), 639–649 (2000). https://doi.org/10.1080/00420980050003946
9. Brooks, D.: Bobos in Paradise: The New Upper Class and How they Got There. Simon and Schuster, New York (2018). ISBN: 0-684-85378-7
10. Kotkin, J.: The New Geography: How the Digital Revolution is Reshaping the American Landscape. Random House, New York (2000). ISBN: 0375501991
11. Florida, R.L.: The Rise of the Creative Class. Basic Books, New York (2004). ISBN-13: 978-0465024773
12. Mermiri, T.: Private Investment in Culture 2008/09: the Arts in the 'New Normal'. Arts & Business, London (2010). http://cymraeg.aandbcymru.org.uk/uploads/PICS_08-09.pdf. Accessed 24 Mar 2023

13. Bonet, L., Donato, F.: The financial crisis and its impact on the current models of governance and management of the cultural sector in Europe. ENCATC J. Cult. Manag. Policy **1**(1), 4–11 (2011). https://www.encatc.org/media/2703-journal_vol1_issue1_dec201 1512.pdf. Accessed 12 Jan 2023

14. Antoneloul, D., Hatzinikolaou, A.: The Effect of the Recession on the Cultural Activities of the Municipality of Nikaia-Agios Redis. Technological Educational Institute of Peloponnese, Sparta (2017). (in Greek)

15. Scott, A.J.: On Hollywood: The Place, The Industry. Princeton University Press, Princeton (2005). ISBN: 9780691162102

16. Grammatikopoulou, A.: Attracting Foreign Cinema Producers to Greece: Institutions, Production Companies and Communication Strategies. Possibilities and Prospects. Hellenic Open University, Athens (2019). (in Greek)

17. Garnham, N.: From cultural to creative industries: an analysis of the implications of the "creative industries" approach to arts and media policy making in the United Kingdom. Int. J. Cult. Policy **11**(1), 15–29 (2005). http://nknu.pbworks.com/f/FROM+CULTURAL+TO+ CREATIVE+Industries.pdf. Accessed 26 Feb 2023

18. Kontou, M.A.A.: The Character and Evolution of Greek Film Policy. Aristotle University of Thessaloniki, Thessaloniki (2012). (in Greek)

19. Georgikou, A.: The Geographic Distribution of Cinema Screens in the Second Half of the 20th Century in Athens. Harokopio University, Athens (2015). (in Greek)

20. National Center of Social Research: The State of the Exhibition System in Greece. (in Greek). https://www.ekke.gr/projects/estia/gr_pages/gr_cinema/Cinema99/Cinema99. htm. Accessed 10 Mar 2023

21. Paraskevoudakis, M: Cinema and the City: Analyzing the Geographo-temporal Imprint of Athenian Screens during the 1950–2016 Period. National Technical University of Athens, Athens (2017). (in Greek). https://dspace.lib.ntua.gr/xmlui/handle/123456789/45280?locale-attribute=el

22. Tapscott, D., Williams, A.D.: Wikinomics: How Mass Collaboration Changes Everything. Portofolio, New York (2006). ISBN: 978-1-59184-138-8

23. Harrison, T.M., Barthel, B.: Wielding new media in web 2.0: exploring the history of engagement with the collaborative construction of media products. New Media Soc. **11**(1–2), 155–178 (2009). https://doi.org/10.1177/1461444808099580

24. Hudson-Smith, A., Crooks, A., Gibin, M., Milton, R., Batty, M.: NeoGeography and web 2.0: concepts, tools and applications. J. Locat. Based Serv. **3**(2), 118–145 (2009). https://doi.org/ 10.1080/17489720902950366

25. Haklay, M., Singleton, A., Parker, C.: Web mapping 2.0: the neogeography of the GeoWeb. Geogr. Compass **2**(6), 2011–2039 (2008). https://doi.org/10.1111/j.1749-8198.2008.00167.x

26. Goodchild, M.F.: Citizens as voluntary sensors: spatial data infrastructure in the world of web 2.0. Int. J. Spat. Data Infrastruct. Res. **2**, 24–32 (2007)

27. Elwood, S., Goodchild, M.F., Sui, D.Z.: Researching volunteered geographic information: spatial data, geographic research, and new social practice. Ann. Assoc. Am. Geogr. **102**(3), 571–590 (2012). https://doi.org/10.1080/00045608.2011.595657

28. Perkins, C., Dodge, M.: The potential of user-generated cartography: a case study of the OpenStreetMap project and mapchester mapping party. North West Geogr. **8**(1), 18–32 (2008). ISSN 1476-1580

29. Sehra, S.S., Singh, J., Rai, H.S.: Assessment of OpenStreetMap data - a review. Int. J. Comput. Appl. **76**(16), 17–20 (2013). https://doi.org/10.5120/13331-0888

30. Sui, D.Z.: The wikification of GIS and its consequences: or Angelina Jolie's new tattoo and the future of GIS. Comput. Environ. Urban Syst. **32**(1), 1–5 (2008). https://doi.org/10.1016/ j.compenvurbsys.2007.12.001

31. Girres, J.F., Touya, G.: Quality assessment of the French OpenStreetMap dataset. Trans. GIS **14**(4), 435–459 (2010). https://doi.org/10.1111/j.1467-9671.2010.01203.x

32. Goodchild, M.F.: Commentary: whither VGI? GeoJournal **72**, 239–244 (2008). https://doi.org/10.1007/s10708-008-9190-4

33. Goodchild, M.F.: Geographical data modeling. Comput. Geosci. **18**(4), 401–408 (1992). https://doi.org/10.1016/0098-3004(92)90069-4

34. RDF Working Group: W3C Recommendation 10 February 2004. https://www.w3.org/TR/2004/REC-rdf-primer-20040210/. Accessed 6 Mar 2023

35. Zhou, Q., Wang, S., Liu, Y.: Exploring the accuracy and completeness patterns of global land-cover/land-use data in OpenStreetMap. Appl. Geogr. **145**, 102742 (2022). https://doi.org/10.1016/j.apgeog.2022.102742

36. Open Data Commons: Open Data Commons Open Database License (ODbL) v1.0. https://opendatacommons.org/licenses/odbl/1-0/. Accessed 6 Mar 2023

37. Guptill, S., Morrison, J.: Elements of Spatial Data Quality. Pergamon, Oxford (1995). ISBN 978-0-08-042432-3

38. Elwood, S.: Volunteered geographic information: future research directions motivated by critical, participatory, and feminist GIS. GeoJournal **72**, 173–183 (2008). https://doi.org/10.1007/s10708-008-9186-0

39. Haklay, M.: How good is volunteered geographical information? A comparative study of OpenStreetMap and ordnance survey datasets. Environ. Plan.B Urban Anal. City Sci. **37**(4), 682–703 (2010). https://doi.org/10.1068/b35097

40. Coleman, D., Georgiadou, Y., Labonte, J.: Volunteered geographic information: the nature and motivation of produsers. Int. J. Spat. Data Infrastruct. Res. **4**, 332–358 (2009). https://doi.org/10.2902/1725-0463.2009.04.art16

41. Brewer, J.: Ethnography. Open University Press, Buckingham (2001). ISBN: 978-0-335-20268-3

42. Kozinets, R.V., De Valck, K., Wojnicki, A.C., Wilner, S.J.: Networked narratives: understanding word-of-mouth marketing in online communities. J. Mark. **74**(2), 71–89 (2010). https://doi.org/10.1509/jm.74.2.71

43. Beaulieu, A.: Mediating ethnography: objectivity and the making of ethnographies of the internet. Soc. Epistemol. **18**(2–3), 139–163 (2004). https://doi.org/10.1080/0269172042000249264

44. Burke, P.: What is Cultural History? Polity, Cambridge (2008). ISBN-13: 978-0-7456-4409-7

45. Tagkalakis, A.O.: The unemployment effects of fiscal policy: recent evidence from Greece. IZA J. Eur. Labor Stud. **2**(1), 1–32 (2013). https://doi.org/10.1186/2193-9012-2-11

46. Triandafyllidou, A., Mantanika, R.: Migration in Greece: Recent developments in 2014. Report prepared for the OECD Network of International Migration Experts, Paris, 6–8 October, Hellenic Foundation for European and Foreign Policy, Athens, Greece (2014)

47. Akser, M.: Cinema, life and other viruses: the future of filmmaking, film education and film studies in the age of Covid-19 pandemic. CINEJ Cinema J. **8**(2), 1–13 (2020). https://doi.org/10.5195/cinej.2020.351

48. Hanson, S.: Screening the World: Global Development of the Multiplex Cinema. Palgrave Macmillan, London (2019). ISBN 978-3-030-18994-5

49. Park, Y.S., Ham, S.: Spatial analysis of various multiplex cinema types. Front. Archit. Res. **5**(1), 63–73 (2016). https://doi.org/10.1016/j.foar.2015.11.001

50. Moran, M.M.: Walking the Walk: An Assessment of the 5-Minute Rule in Transit Planning. University of Texas, Austin (2013). https://repositories.lib.utexas.edu/bitstream/handle/2152/22683/MORAN-MASTERSREPORT-2013.pdf?sequence=1&isAllowed=y. Accessed 25 Jan 2023

51. O'Sullivan, S., Morrall, J.: Walking distances to and from light-rail transit stations. Transp. Res. Rec. **1538**(1), 19–26 (1996). https://doi.org/10.1177/0361198196153800103

52. Foda, M.A., Osman, A.O.: Using GIS for measuring transit stop accessibility considering actual pedestrian road network. J. Public Transp. **13**(4), 23–40 (2010). https://doi.org/10.5038/2375-0901.13.4.2

53. Efthymiou, D., Antoniou, C.: How do transport infrastructure and policies affect house prices and rents? Evidence from Athens, Greece. Transp. Res. Part A Policy Pract. **52**, 1–22 (2013). https://doi.org/10.1016/j.tra.2013.04.002

54. QuickOSM. https://plugins.qgis.org/plugins/QuickOSM/. Accessed 8 Mar 2023

55. Cinema movies (in Greek). https://www.athinorama.gr/cinema/guide/all/cinemas/. Accessed 8 Mar 2023

56. Cinemas (in Greek). https://www.rizospastis.gr/story.do?id=2926137. Accessed 8 Mar 2023

57. List of Cinemas (in Greek). http://cineanamnisi.blogspot.com/2012/09/blog-post.html. Accessed 8 Mar 2023

58. Cinemas from A to Z (summary list) (in Greek). https://mymovie-diary.blogspot.com/2018/02/blog-post_6.html. Accessed 8 Mar 2023

59. Fyssas, D.: The Cinemas of Athens 1896 – 2013. Histories of the Urban Landscape. Ebooks4greeks, Athens (2019). (in Greek)

60. Waugh, D.: Geography. An Integrated Approach. 3rd ed. Nelson, Surrey (2000). ISBN: 978-0174447061

61. Squire, J.E.: The Movie Business Book. McGraw-Hill Education, New York (2006). ISBN-10: 0335220029

62. Gerasimou, S., Perdicoúlis, A.: Urban renaissance on Athens southern coast: the case of Palaio Faliro. Int. J. Energy Environ. **3**(4), 178–185 (2009)

63. Shah, M.H., Yaqoub, M., Wu, Z.J.: Post-pandemic impacts of COVID-19 on film industry worldwide and in China. Glob. Media J. Pak. Ed. **XIII**(2), 28–44 (2020)

64. Salvati, L., Venanzoni, G.: Work in (slow) progress: latent suburbanization, economic restructuring, and urban–rural convergence in a South Eastern European city. J. Urban Aff. **39**(3), 436–451 (2017). https://doi.org/10.1080/07352166.2016.1251195

65. OECD: OECD Economic Outlook 2012. OECD Publishing, Paris (2012). https://doi.org/10.1787/eco_outlook-v2012-1-en

66. Iliopoulou, P., Stratakis, P.: Spatial analysis of housing prices in the Athens Region, Greece. RELAND Int. J. Real Estate Land Plan. **1**, 304–313 (2018). eISSN 2623-4807

Comparative Study for the Investigation of Safe Movement with the Method of Space Syntax: The Case of Mati, Eastern Attica

Angeliki Papazoglou[✉] and Maria Pigaki

National Technical University of Athens, Heroon Polytechneiou 9, 15780 Athens, Greece
angeliki.papazoglou@hotmail.com, pigaki@survey.ntua.gr

Abstract. Wildfires are destructive incidents of wide range and high impact in urban space, with climate change widely affecting their force and frequency, whereas their impact is extended to environment and society. The purpose of this research was to investigate connectivity and interaction between the "spaces" that were configured in urban space, aiming to contribute in spatial planning in emergency cases, like wildfires. The main concern of this research was how urban planning could take into consideration human movement in urban space and contribute in prevention and disaster management. Methodology was based on analyzing, examining and comparing the spatial configuration between two road network's scenarios, the Syntactic Configuration and the Urban Configuration. Provided that Space Syntax takes into consideration human perceptive in order to simulate human movement in urban space, Space Syntax was combined with Analytic Hierarchy Process (AHP) and criteria closely related to wildfires. Study case and main inspiration was the wildfire of 23/7/2018 at summer location of Mati, Eastern Attica.

Keywords: Space Syntax · Multi-Criteria Decision Methods · Spatial Analysis · GIS · Correlation · Space Planning · Safe Movement · Road Network · Wildfire · Mati

1 Introduction

Last decades, disasters are increasingly concerning the global scientific society due to the incidents' variation and the range of their consequences in society, economy and environment. The effect of climate change in frequency and intensity appear to be strong, making Disaster and Risk Management to be important scientific aspects in the effort of prevention, mitigation and recovery of society, environment and human life. In this recurring effort of research and improvement, technology and all the available means are the most helpful tools.

Mediterranean region is prone to wildfire incidents due to its climatic variety which is characterized by extended summertime with high temperature, long periods of humidity and local strong winds favoring the development of those disasters and complicating the damage control [1]. The continuous extension of urban space near to forest ecosystems

© The Author(s), under exclusive license to Springer Nature Switzerland AG 2023
O. Gervasi et al. (Eds.): ICCSA 2023 Workshops, LNCS 14105, pp. 579–597, 2023.
https://doi.org/10.1007/978-3-031-37108-0_37

and environments makes research about wildfires, fire risk factors and disaster management imperative to be held in order to protect and persevere the Mediterranean ecosystems due to climate change [2, 3]. As regards Greece, the years 2007 and 2018 were two of the most destructive fire seasons in recent history. Nowadays, Greek authorities like Fire Department, General Secretariat for Civil Protection and the relative Ministries are trying to develop strategies to prepare and inform the population for imminent events [1].

To reduce the fire risk, the analytical study of contributing factors is one of the most important measures to be taken into consideration in order to develop an affective prevention plan to protect the environment as much as the urban space. Topography determines fire behavior, whereas factors related to human activities and land use are strongly connected with fire ignition. Furthermore, vegetation and meteorological factors are connected to fire speed [4]. Build environments suffer with extended socio-economic impact in population and aspects of urban environment [1, 4]. Provided that fire spread and ignition factors are closely related to temperature and soil humidity, the continuous transition to warmer and drier conditions has a direct effect in the number of wildfires during fire season.

Based on methodologies related to disasters, this study presents a comparative analysis between two road network's configuration scenarios aiming to investigate the spatial functionality of urban space and contribute in urban design in emergency cases. The main concern leading to this research was to examine how human behavior could be integrated in urban planning in order to improve disaster and risk management. Space Syntax theory is being used to analyze the spatial relationships developed in urban environment taking into consideration human movement. Using the available techniques, spatial configuration was analyzed in various scales starting from pedestrian to vehicular movement. In order to connect Space Syntax theory with wildfires, a Multi-Criteria Decision Analysis method (MCDA) was incorporated in methodology, with Analytic Hierarchy Process (AHP) being the most common method. Fire risk factors were chosen to participate to the creation of fire risk maps for analyzing the functionality of urban space and road network in fire emergency cases. GIS technologies were integral part to the application of methodology. The research is concluded with correlation between the scenarios using Pearson's Correlation analysis and the assessment of the outcome.

The remaining paper is structured in four sections. The first section reports the study area along with the data, analyzes the scenarios and provides the framework of the methodology. Second section reviews the main theory about Space Syntax and AHP, provides a detailed description of the spatial patterns and describes the calculations and the necessary procedures. The third part of this paper refers to the results of the study by the fire risk maps and concludes with discussing the application of the methodology. The final part of this paper includes the study's conclusion followed by the potential improvements for future approaches and developments of the research.

2 Materials and Methods

2.1 Study Area

Four municipalities in Attica, Greece have been chosen as general study area, specifically municipalities of Penteli, Dionisos, Marathonas and Rafina-Pikermi (Fig. 1). Their area has been estimated to 365.928 km^2 and their population is approximately around 128.816 people according to 2011 Population-Housing Census of Hellenic Statistical Authority. The climate of Attica is classified as maritime with dry and very warm summer [5].

Wildfire in summer location Mati, Eastern Attica on 23rd of July 2018, was one of the most devastating fire events in Greece's recent history. Mati is located on Municipality of Marathonas at N 38° 2′ 58.95 and E 23° 59′ 14.86 and due to its seaside location is one of the summer destinations in Eastern Attica, along with Rafina and Nea Makri. As for the topography of the area, follows the tendency from the mountain edges to the sea. However, some longshore elevation differences leading to cliffs, as the Kokkino Limanaki area, differentiate the seaside topography causing problematic access and difficulties in movement at seaside area [6]. Coastal area has mostly dry species of vegetation, like olive trees, kermes and pines [7]. Furthermore, Mati appears to be densely populated with sprawling urban environment and problematic low-quality road network with many dead-ends, parallel roads connected to highways and inadequate signposting and road connectivity. A limited number of highways are the main network of transportation through the area, therefore gathers the majority of the area's traffic [7]. Particularly in summertime, Mati and nearby locations appear to have increase in seasonal population related with touristic activities and movements, according to Hellenic Statistical Authority. Relating to land use, there is a variety of summer and touristic activities in seaside area, with a few agricultural activities to appear in the suburbs [7].

Wildfire on 23rd of July 2018

The wildfire on 23rd of July 2018 and its impacts on the study area were the reason for attempting this research to analyze and compare the spatial configurations in order to suggest an integration of human movement in urban planning in emergency cases. According to Fire Service of Greece, the wildfire at Mati was a result of human negligence. Hellenic National Meteorological Service forecasted strong West/Northwest winds intensifying by noon, whereas Civil Protection Service had published relative fire risk map. At 16:41, Fire Service was informed for fire ignition at Ntaou Penteli, at the east edge of Penteli Mountain [8–10]. The extreme winds that blew that day, combined with topography, led the fire east towards Mati, which burned all through the urban space to coast. Fire speed in association with topography, the specific nature of urban environment and road network minimized residents' available response time leading to traffic problems and resulted in people being trapped, ending with unfathomable consequences for the population killing 103 people and almost destroying the summer location in Eastern Attica [2, 3, 8, 11].

2.2 Data Description

Aiming an all-around approach, data variety was determined from the thorough perusal of the literature [12–14]. Topography, vegetation and land use data were provided from

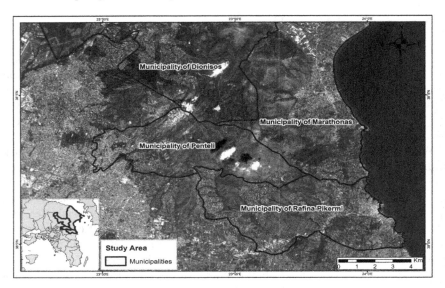

Fig. 1. Study Area

Copernicus program [15]. Digital Surface Model (DSM) with raster resolution of 25 m was used in order to produce the elevation, slope and aspect of the area. As for the vegetation, raster files for Dominant Leaf Type (DLT) and Tree Cover Density (TCD), with 10 m raster resolution, were acquired as well as an Urban Atlas raster file for the analysis of land use. DLT, TCD and Urban Atlas files were referred to 2018, the year of the wildfire in Mati. Hellenic Statistical Authority [16] was used in order to acquire files related to the 2011 Population-Housing Census, in particular excel files about population and buildings and shapefiles about Greek Municipalities, settlements and city blocks of the study area. Considering that wildfire event was part of the study, Fire Service of Greece [10] provided the relative shapefile data for hydrants, water tanks and the boundaries and points of service districts within the study area. Furthermore, daily data about temperature and wind speed and direction, from eight meteorological stations, were provided by the website of National Observatory of Athens (NOA) [17] in excel formats, for the time period 2015 to 2021. Ten-minute data were also acquired from NOA in text formats, from two meteorological stations and were referred to the fire day (23/7/2018). Road network, as one of the most important data, was downloaded from Geofrabrik's website [18]. Considering that a common coordinate system was necessary, the data were reprojected when needed. As for the software programs, ArcGIS 10.5 and QGIS 3.16 were used for executing all the necessary procedures of the methodology so that the final maps to be created.

2.3 Scenarios

In this study, a scenario-based methodology is chosen to analyze and evaluate the contribution of Space Syntax theory into the urban planning in emergency cases, like wildfires in urban environment. Provided that road network configuration is one of the main parameters related to safe movement and evacuation in cases of emergency, two spatial configuration scenarios are chosen. According to Giuliani, Falco and Cutini's research [12], a scenario-based methodology is conducted to analyze and examine the road network's configuration and emergency management after a seismic event in Italian historic centres using Space Syntax techniques. That research consists the main idea for the comparative analysis of syntactic and urban configurational patterns in fire emergency cases that this paper studies. Attempting to combine two different research methods, Space Syntax and AHP, along with fire risk factors, are chosen in order to examine spatial configuration in a case of a fire incident inside the urban space and how this cooperation could provide information to emergency management.

The two road network scenarios are:

- Scenario 1: The Syntactic Pattern of road network is investigated with Space Syntax theory and its techniques, given that Space Syntax takes into consideration the human movement and analyzes the urban configurational patterns in pedestrian and vehicular movement scale.
- Scenario 0: The Urban Pattern of road network is investigated as it is depicted from the road categories, such as major and minor roads and the topography of study area as it is configured from the slope.

2.4 General Framework

The methodology refers to the analysis and examination of spatial configuration patterns of road network and their functionality in fire emergency cases in Eastern Attica area and the settlement of Mati.

The methodology (Fig. 2) is developed on the following stages:

1. First stage includes two analyses. The first is the analysis of the syntactic pattern (Scenario 1) with Space Syntax for investigating the configuration of road network and urban space of the study area. The second one is the analysis of the surveying of urban patterns (Scenario 0) which occur from the categories and the slope of road network.
2. On the second stage, both of the scenarios' functionality is examined with the use of AHP and fire risk factors. This stage is extended in three parts in order to fully analyze the impact of the parameters on road network's configuration pattern.
3. The third stage concerns the comparative analysis of the road network's functionality and usage rates with the use of Pearson's Correlation analysis.

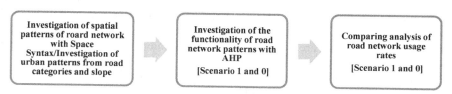

Fig. 2. Study's Conceptual Framework

3 Theory, Methodology and Calculations

3.1 Space Syntax

Urban environment tends to have a diverse morphology starting from neighborhood level to small and metropolitan cities, arising the need to analyze the spatial relationships that develop between urban space and the people living and moving within, making societies spatial phenomena [19]. As a result, human activities affect the shape and pattern of urban space, having consequently urban space affecting people's behavior and their movement and making spatial analysis an important tool in analyzing, designing, maintaining and changing urban functionality [20]. The potential connection of spatial analyses with external spatial factors, like population and land use, could make them more intricate and extend in scale allowing the research of more complex urban systems [20, 21]. Space Syntax theory and methods are based on analyzing how the network is spatially connected and interrelated within the urban space and how its spatial functionality is configured concerning human behavior and movement (pedestrian and vehicular) [22].

There are three potential methods of analyzing the urban space in Space Syntax theory, topological, metric and geometrical (angular) analysis. Every one of the foresaid analyses measures the shortest possible distance through road network's streets between one space to the participating others in the examined urban space [19].

In this paper, Angular Analysis is used in order to analyze the study area's road network. Angular Analysis defines the analysis that every road segment is calculated based on the angle that is connected to every other segment of the system. Thus, Angular Analysis quantifies the possibility of participation of each segment of the network to a possible route and visualizes the human movement and potential route choice within the urban environment [20]. The most commonly used syntactic properties from Space Syntax methodology are Angular Choice, Angular Integration and Connectivity. Angular Choice defines and quantifies the "through movement" in a road network's route, namely the possibility of a road segment to be used in a route. Furthermore, Angular Integration depicts and measures the integration of road segments, the "to movement" in a road network's route, namely the accessibility potential of a road segment through a route [19, 20, 22]. As for Connectivity, it defines the count of direct connections between neighboring street segments. High and low connectivity appears in segments with many and few connections, respectively [20]. Parts of the road network with high connectivity are connected with increased people's mobility and activities [12, 22]. The scale level, distance and radius are important factors in urban analyses. As for distance and radius, they are three alternatives, topological, metric and geometrical distance and radius, similarly defined as Angular Analysis. Metric radius is used in this paper, as it is the mostly used alternative in researches [20]. There are two scales, Local and Global, with Local scales referring to pedestrian movements until 800 m and related to neighborhood patterns and Global Scales referring to vehicular movement, radii farther than 1000 m and related to city and metropolitan patterns [20].

Angular Choice and Integration is used in this Space Syntax analysis and there are seven different radii for Local and Global scales that being examined (200 m, 400 m, 800 m, 1200 m, 1600 m, 3200 m and 6000 m). PST plugin in QGIS is used for the analysis of the chosen radii for Angular Choice and Integration as well as the analysis of hydrants' service areas and accessibility within the study area. The appropriate preparation and topological examination of the network is conducted beforehand in order to assure the accuracy of the research. Figure 3 shows the Space Syntax's framework.

Angular Analysis. Angular Analysis is conducted to study the syntactic pattern through the chosen syntactic properties, Angular Choice and Angular Integration, and provides the relative maps for the examined radii for Local and Global scales. Indicative maps are adduced in Fig. 4 and depict both syntactic properties. In Local scale radii (200 m, 400 m, 800 m), syntactic pattern's spatial configuration gives more emphasis on local street segments. Provided that Local scale refers to pedestrian movement, the neighboring aspect of the road network is appointed for both Choice and Integration, creating local centers within the urban space which appear to have increased mobility and functionality. Apparent distinction among the syntactic patterns for both Choice and Integration is mainly seen between 200 m and 1200 m radii. In Global scale radii (1200 m, 1600 m, 3200 m and 6000 m), there is different configuration in the syntactic patterns considering the fact that these radii are referring to vehicular movement. In Angular Choice, the emphasis is moved to the main road segments of the network which are extended to the whole study area. The configuration of the syntactic pattern shows the movement through the highways of the network connecting distant districts of the study area. In Angular Integration on the other hand, the syntactic pattern appears to have local centres, likewise in local scale radii. However, the centres are configured more extended and refer to the global scale. Road network's connectivity is not developed evenly throughout the whole study area in all syntactic patterns for both syntactic properties. This fact leads to limited mobility and functionality in Angular Choice syntactic patterns, whereas in Angular Integration patterns the centres appear disconnected with one another amplifying their local character and leading to the intermediate study area to have low integration, thus low functionality and usability.

Hydrants Service Areas and Accessibility. The hydrants as firefighting means are used in order to investigate the extension of service areas within the study area. Figure 4 shows indicative maps about the distribution of hydrants within the service areas. The first observation is that there are hydrant gathering centres in similar areas within the network for all the radii. However, as moving from local scale to global scale, the centres seem to appear expanded in size but also in number of connected hydrants serving larger areas in the network. The expansion of the service areas reflects to the connection between the centres and their location relates to dense urban space and road network.

3.2 Analytical Hierarchy Process (AHP)

Multi-Decision Making Methods (MCDM) constitute a wide scope of methods related to the definition of the most effective solution to a problem among a set of alternatives. Analytical Hierarchy Process (AHP), developed by Thomas L. Saaty [23], is used in current paper in order to investigate the two scenarios' spatial patterns (Syntactic Pattern – Scenario 1, Urban Pattern - Scenario 0) functionality combined with fire related factors and analyze their impact to urban configuration in cases of emergency. AHP is one of the most used methods for scientific purposes since it is useful and leads to

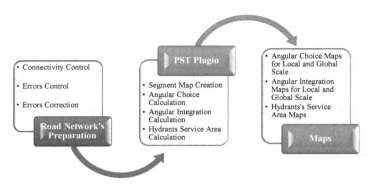

Fig. 3. Space Syntax's Methodology

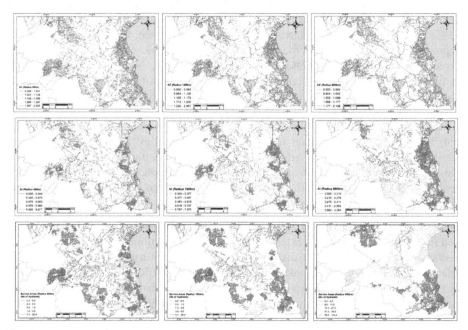

Fig. 4. Angular Choice, Angular Integration and Hydrants' Service Areas Maps (Indicative Radii 800 m, 1600 m and 6000 m)

problem solving results through the evaluation of criteria and studying of alternatives [13]. In a general way, it simplifies the problem in order to examine the relationship between cause and effect [24].

In order to complete AHP, there are four stages need to be followed. On the first stage, the researcher analyzes the problem, constructs the hierarchy leading to the alternative solutions and finalizes the criteria and subcriteria that are going to be used in the process. Furthermore, the criteria are calibrated in a unified scale (from 1 to 5 or 1 to 10) [13]. On second stage, the pairwise comparison is executed in order to rank the criteria and subcriteria's priority using a ranking scale from 1 to 9 to evaluate their importance in the process (Table 1) [13, 25, 26]. The following third stage calculates the weight of every criterion/subcriterion, which provides the contribution rate of each one of them in the final result regarding problem's solution [25, 27].

On the fourth stage, the consistency of the whole process is examined in order to validate the necessary credence and accuracy and allow the conclusion of the process. The calculation of Consistency Ratio (CR) provides the consistency check of pairwise comparisons between the criteria and subcriteria. In order to proceed with the process, the CR should be not greater than 0.10, as it is indicated from the AHP. If not, the comparison should be revised until the CR is 0.10 (10%). However, for the CR to be evaluated, the Consistency Index (CI) calculations precedes. CR and CI equations are given in Eqs. (1) and (2) [13, 25].

$$CR = \frac{CI}{CR} < 0.1 \sim 10\% \tag{1}$$

$$CI = \frac{\lambda Max - n}{n - 1} \tag{2}$$

Therefore, as CI is the Consistency Index, λmax is defined as maximum eigenvalue, n the number of participant criteria/subcriteria and RI is the Random Consistency Index which is based on the number of the participant criteria/subcriteria in the study. This study uses the scale as it is provided from Vargas [25]. This study uses AHP as explorative tool in order to analyze the road network's functionality and safe movement in emergency cases for the two scenarios. Aiming to include factors related to wildfires into road network's examination, the papers of Sivrikaya and Küçük and Sari [13, 14] are studied in order to choose the appropriate criteria and subcriteria to integrate in AHP process. The final maps are created from the AHP and show area's wildfire risk assessment, however the road network's functionality and the pattern's spatial configuration in emergency cases is analyzed through the maps. As for the AHP process, it is concluded in three separate stages with different number of participant subcriteria in each one of them.

Criteria and Subcriteria Analysis. The criteria/subcriteria are closely related to wild-fires in association with road network's configuration. Aiming to an extend analysis of road network's functionality in combination with fire risk factors, AHP is conducted in three stages, where three criteria are used for the First Stage, whereas on Second and Third Stage are used five and four subcriteria respectively. The three main criteria are Topography, Environment and Urban Space. The eleven subcriteria are Elevation, Slope, Aspect, Temperature, Wind Speed, Dominant Leaf Type (DLT), Tree Cover Density (TCD), Population Density, Distance to Settlements, Land Use and Road Network and are calibrated in a scale between 1 to 10 (Table 2). The scores are showing the fire danger with low scores showing low fire danger and high score showing high danger respectively.

Topography is closely related with fire ignition, speed and spread. Slope as a factor plays a crucial part in fire spread due to the fact that fire speed is increased as long as the slope rises contributing to the fire spread [13, 14]. On the other hand, elevation combined with climatic factors as temperature, humidity and wind, effects immensely fire ignition

Table 1. Relative Priorities (Pairwise Comparison) - T. L. Saaty - [13]

Priority Scale	Relations	Explanation
1	Equal Importance	Two activities contribute equally
3	Moderate Importance	One activity is slightly favored over another
5	Strong Importance	One activity is strongly favored over another
7	Very Strong Importance	One activity is very strongly favored over another
9	Extreme Importance	One activity is of the highest possible order of affirmation
2, 4, 6, 8	Intermediate Values	When compromise is needed

danger and spread. Given that aspect of the area and forest play an important role in fire risk and ignition, study area is located in the North hemisphere making south, southern and southwestern aspects more susceptible to fire incidents than northern aspects due to the fact that they receive higher amounts of sunlight [13, 14].

The criterion about Environment refers to the subcriteria of temperature, wind speed, Dominant Leaf Type (DLT) and Tree Cover Density (TCD). More specifically, high temperatures as well as gusty winds result in dry material creating favorable conditions for fire ignition and spread [13, 14]. In this study only temperature and wind speed are participate in the subcriteria. Environmental studies related to fire risk has shown that forest and vegetation type are closely related to fire ignition and evolution in an area. Vegetation is generally a combustible material, however parameters such as its density and moisture have a decisive effect on the speed of spread. Furthermore, leaf type determines vegetation's reaction. Coniferous trees, given their leaf type and the fact that pine needles create a litter layer around trees' trunk which is extremely flammable, are more prone to fire risk than broad-leaved trees whose leafage are moister and have different ignition rate [13, 14].

Urban Space criterion includes the subcriteria of Population Density, Distance to Settlements, Land Use and Road Network. All the above subcriteria are related to urban space, human movement and wildfires. Forests areas near settlements, agricultural lands and areas related to human activities are associated with fire risk. Respectively, population density is strongly connected with fire risk as well [13, 14]. Road network's configuration in Scenarios 1 and 0 is the main variable that examined. Thus, an individual subcriterion is made for every scenario in order to investigate the syntactic and urban patterns that are configured for the two scenarios.

Road Network Subcriteria. For the Scenario 1, according to Yousuf Reja's [28] methodological framework, Angular Choice is chosen for the syntactic pattern's examination for the seven chosen radii. Specifically, only the segments with High Angular Choice values are extracted from every radius and unified in three general scales, Local Scale including 200 m, 400 m and 800 m, Intermediate Scale including 1200 m and 1600 m and Global Scale including 3200 m and 6000 m. Statistical procedures and experiments are conducted for the calculation of the final percentage of the road network's segments that is going to be extracted. We assume that the 86% of road segments is 3 Standard Deviation (3*S.D.) of the mean in a normal distribution, the rest 14% is the percentage with the highest values that is to be extracted for every radius [28].

For Scenario 0, urban pattern's configuration is investigated from two points of view. The first one is how road network's pattern is configured based on Geofabrik's classification [18] for road network's categories, whereas the second one is based on the classification of road network's segments according to the slope that every segment is on. Table 2 contains the participant factors' calibration in order to create the criteria and subcriteria for the execution of AHP process. Tables 3 and 4 indicate the weights and the proceeding CR of every stage of the process. Furthermore, criteria and subcriteria maps are given in Figs. 5 and 6.

Table 2. Fire Risk Factors

	LOW DANGER								*HIGH DANGER*	
	1	2	3	4	5	6	7	8	9	10
DLT	No tree				Broad Leaf					Coniferous
TCD	0-10	11-20	21-30	31-40	41-50	51-60	61-70	71-80	81-90	91-100
Aspect	N	NE, NW	E		Flat	SE, W		S		SW
Slope (%)	0-5			5-15		15-25		25-35		>35
Elevation (m)	0-100		100-200		200-400		400-800			>800
Temperature (°C)	25.5-26.0	26.0-26.5	26.5-27.0	27.0-27.5	27.5-28.0	28.0-28.5	28.5-29.0	29.0-29.5	29.5-30.0	>30.0
Wind Speed (m/s)	<2.5	2.5-3.0	3.0-3.5	3.5-4.0	4.0-4.5	4.5-5.0	5.0-5.5	5.5-6.0	6.0-6.5	>6.5
Urban Atlas	Water/ Wetlands		Urban Areas			Agricultural Areas				Forests
Distance from Settlements (m)	0-250			250-500		500-1000		1000-5000		>5000
Pop. Density (No)	0-1000		1001-5000		5001-10000		10001-15000		>15000	
RN_AC			Global		Intermediate			Local		
RN_Categories		Major Roads		Highway links	Minor Roads		Very small roads		Paths unsuitable for cars	Dead-Ends
RN_Slopes (%)	0-5			5-15		15-25		25-35		>35

Pearson's Correlation. In Statistics, Correlation is defined as the existing and connecting relationship between variables. In this study, Pearson's Correlation is used to analyze and correlate the functionality among the two scenarios' patterns, as it is defined as r and is used for the measurement of the linear correlation between two variables with normal distributions. The value of r ranges between -1 and 1 ($-1 \leq r \leq +1$) and shows the relative correlation between the examined variables [29].

Table 3. AHP's First Stage Criteria/Subcriteria's Weights

Criterion	CR	Weight	Subcriterion	CR	Weight
Topography	0.047725	0.11	Elevation	0.023496	0.10
			Slope		0.65
			Aspect		0.25
Environment		0.63	Temperature	0.049974	0.1443
			Wind Speed		0.4928
			DLT		0.2834
			TCD		0.0795
Urban Space		0.26	Population Density	0.012150015	0.28042
			Distance of Settlements		0.07453
			Road Network		0.36353
			Land Use		0.28152

Table 4. AHP's Second and Third Stage Subcriteria's Weights

AHP's Second Stage			AHP's Third Stage		
Subcriterion	CR	Weight	Subcriterion	CR	Weight
Road Network	0.042247	0.3834	Road Network	0.023127	0.415
Wind Speed		0.2831	Wind Speed		0.299
Slope		0.1770	Slope		0.187
DLT		0.1015	DLT		0.099
Population Density		0.0549			

4   Results and Discussion

4.1   Syntactic Configuration Mapping

Syntactic Pattern's (Scenario 1) functionality and usability is examined through High Angular Choice and mapping fire risk's configuration of the study area. Figure 7 shows the final fire risk maps for the three stages. The depiction follows the Space Syntax Theory's color palette making the comparison and association between fire risk and area's spatial configuration patterns more observable. In all three stages, it is noticeable that areas with low fire risk values are located along the seaside area leaving areas with higher elevation and slope with increased fire risk values.

As for road network's functionality and usability, they are closely related to low fire risk values indicating that in those areas road network's pattern appears to have increasing functionality favoring human movement. The functionality's configuration appears to match the Angular Choice maps (Fig. 4). However, road network appears

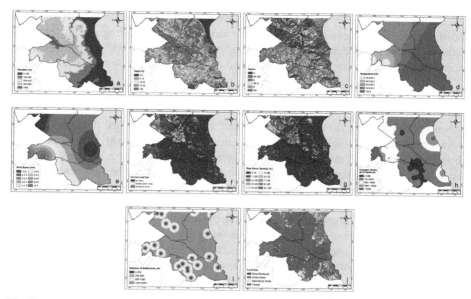

Fig. 5. AHP's Subcriteria Maps: a) Elevation, b) Slope, c) Aspect, d) Temperature, e) Wind Speed, f) Dominant Leaf Type, g) Tree Cover Density, h) Population Density, i) Distance from Settlements and j) Land Use

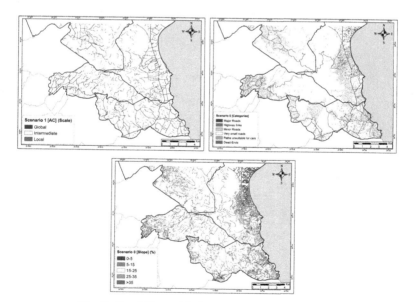

Fig. 6. Road Network's Scenario 1 and 0 Subcriteria

to have limited connectivity within leaving areas disconnected. Local street segments mostly appear disconnected from the main road network forwarding the movement in major roads and inside dense urban space indicating the road network's percentage that is most likely to be used from the population and the areas that is likely to be overcrowded.

4.2 Urban Configuration Mapping

Urban Pattern's (Scenario 0) functionality and usability is examined through road network's categories and road slope, as it was mentioned on the scenarios' analysis. Figure 7 shows the final fire risk maps for the three stages for Scenario 0. As in Scenario's 1 maps, the depiction follows the Space Syntax Theory's color palette. The first observation is that in Scenario 0 maps the road network appears to be connected and available for use in full capacity in contrast with Scenario 1 maps. As in Scenario 1, the general coastal area in Scenario 0 maps appears to have low fire risk values indicating that the functionality and usability appear to be increased favoring the movement in these urban areas, whereas mountainous areas have limited functionality and mobility because of high fire risk values. However, on road categories' maps a lowering functionality in seaside urban area is detected as the study moves through the stages by indicating the dead-end road segments with high fire risk values shifting the human movement in major roads. On road slope maps, slope mainly configures the urban pattern with low slope areas appear to have low fire risk and high functionality, whereas areas with high slope appear to

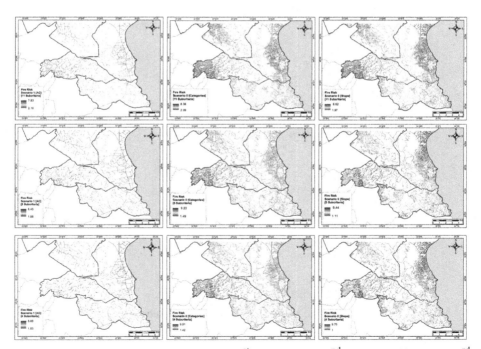

Fig. 7. Final Maps Scenarios 1 and 0 – First (1st line), Second (2nd line) and Third Stage (3rd line)

have low functionality and usability. The progress of the stages indicates through the maps that there are high slope areas in the seaside lowering the area's functionality and limiting the movement in these locations.

Pearson's Correlation Analysis. The comparative analysis is done between the Syntactic Pattern (Scenario 1) and the Urban Pattern (Scenario 0) and is consisted of two parts. The first part analyzes and compares the patterns' functionality between High Angular Choice and the Categories. The second part analyzes and compares the patterns' functionality but as it configures after the AHP's Third Stage.

First Part of Analysis. In order to simplify the calculations, Table 5 shows the classification between the two pattern's functionality. The fire risk calibration scale for the subcriteria is adjusted (0 to 10) and used for the functionality's classification, with 0 meaning low fire risk and high functionality and 10 meaning high fire risk and low functionality respectively. Pearson's Correlation coefficient is calculated to be 0.05, indicating that there is no correlation between the two scenarios' functionality.

Second Part of Analysis. As in first part, the same classification for functionality is used in order to compare and correlate the two scenarios' functionality after the AHP's Third Stage. Table 6 shows functionality's distribution between the two scenarios while Pearson's Correlation coefficient is calculated to be 0.94. Coefficient's value indicates that there is perfect positive linear correlation between the variables, thus as Scenario's 1 functionality increases so does Scenario's 0.

Table 5. Correlation of the Patterns' Functionality (Before AHP Process)

Functionality	AC (No of Segm.)	AC %	Categories (No of Segm.)	Categories %
0–2 [Very High]	0	0%	9909	12.5%
2–4 [High]	13759	45%	260	0%
4–6 [Moderate]	5215	17%	28949	36.5%
6–8 [Low]	11773	38%	29842	38%
8–10 [Very Low]	0	0%	10391	13%
Total	**30747**	**100%**	**79351**	**100%**

In a comparison of Pearson's correlation coefficient before and after AHP process, an increase is observed. Figure 8 shows the combined fire risk map for the two Scenarios after the third stage of AHP.

Table 6. Functionality's Distribution for Scenarios 1 and 0 (After AHP Process - Third Stage)

Functionality	AC (No of Segm.)	AC %	Categories (No of Segm.)	Categories %
0–2 [Very High]	309	1.3%	799	1.2%
2–4 [High]	11030	45.1%	22302	34.8%
4–6 [Moderate]	9727	39.8%	33220	51.9%
6–8 [Low]	3345	13.7%	7490	11.7%
8–10 [Very Low]	34	0.1%	255	0.4%
Total	**24445**	**100.0%**	**64066**	**100.0%**

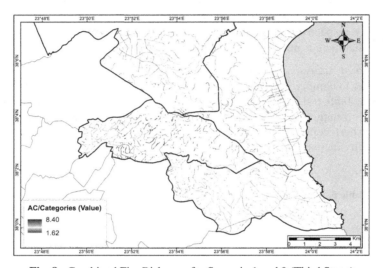

Fig. 8. Combined Fire Risk map for Scenario 1 and 0 (Third Stage)

5   Conclusion

This paper follows a scenario-based methodology in order to investigate the Space Syntax Theory and its potential integration in methodological plans about prevention, mitigation and management in emergency cases, thus its participation in urban planning related to safe movement within urban environment. A comparative analysis between two spatial configuration Scenarios was conducted. Scenario 1 examined the configuration of the syntactic pattern with Angular Choice and Scenario 0 examined the configuration of urban pattern as it occurred from road categories and road slope. Space Syntax's particular characteristics were associated with AHP method in order to examine and compare the functionality and usability of the two scenarios' patterns. Subcriteria and criteria closely related to wildfires were added to the method.

The AHP method was conducted in three stages with a different number of participant subcriteria in each one. Analyzing all the maps that were created from the procedure, this study concludes that Space Syntax theory and techniques can be important tools in urban design. High Angular Choice, provided that it depicted the road segments with the highest angular choice values, pointed out the percentage of the road network that has the higher possibility to be used by people. This percentage was lesser in comparison with the Scenario's 0 pattern which showed that all road network is potentially available for use. Considering the aftermath of the wildfire in Mati, the congestion and high slopes in seaside area leading to people's trapping and casualties, Scenario's 1 final maps seem to match with the references about the conditions that prevailed that day and depicted the spatial configuration of study area's urban space. Therefore, Space Syntax approach depicts a perspective of human movement within urban environment through spatial configuration which can provide important information and potential solutions in urban planning in order to prepare and prevent future consequences from future disaster incidents and design urban movement with the view to safe movement and evacuation if needed.

Positive correlation between the two scenarios' patterns after the AHP method leads to the assumption that the integration of quantitative variables into Scenario's 0 qualitative analysis leads to an increasing correlation between the patterns. Thus, Space Syntax is a technique that can be combined with multiple variables and provide an outcome, however a further research is needed for an extended analysis.

In conclusion, a number of potential improvements could be applied in future relative researches aiming to upgrade the present study. Provided that road network is the main factor, the integration of more features like the road width could allow a more detailed analysis and be a configural factor for the scenarios. An extended analysis of the area's elevation can provide information about the correlation between road network's configuration and people's movement in emergency cases. Given that technology is an important aspect in daily life, the creation of an application for smartphones as a preventative tool which is going to provide safe routes based on user's location through GPS and live feedback for the road networks' situation can be a useful measure in disaster management.

References

1. Adaktilou, N., Stratoulias, D., Landenberger, R.: Wildfire risk assessment based on geospatial open data: application on Chios, Greece. ISPRS Int. J. Geo Inf. **9**, 516 (2020). https://doi.org/10.3390/ijgi9090516
2. Mitsopoulos, I., Mallinis, G., Arianoutsou, M.: Wildfire risk assessment in a typical mediterranean wildland–urban interface of Greece. Environ. Manag. **55**(4), 900–915 (2014). https://doi.org/10.1007/s00267-014-0432-6
3. Rovithakis, A., et al.: Future climate change impact on wildfire danger over the Mediterranean: the case of Greece. Environ. Res. Lett. **17**(4), 045022 (2022). https://doi.org/10.1088/1748-9326/ac5f94
4. Sivrikaya, F., Sağlam, B., Akay, A., Bozali, N.: Evaluation of forest fire risk with GIS. Pol. J. Environ. Stud. **23**, 187–194 (2014)

5. Krina, A., Koutsias, N., Pleniou, M., Xystrakis, F.: Climatic classification of Greece: update – future estimation – relation with forest vegetation. Presented at the 18th Panhellenic Forestry Conference & International Workshop, Edessa, Greece (2017). (in Greek)

6. Technical Chamber of Greece (TCC). Contract for the Preparation of the Regional Application Design Study (Second Stage of the Special Urban Planning) in the Area of "Mati", Attica (2021). http://portal.tee.gr/portal/page/portal/oikonomiko/promitheies/symvaseis1/2021/%D3%D5%CC%C2%C1%D3%C7%20%D1%D5%CC%CF%D4%CF%CC%C9%CA%CF%20%CC%C1%D4%C9%20%C9%C9_%20%CF%D1%C8%C7%20%C5%D0%C1%CD%C1%CB%C7%D8%C7%20-%20%EC%E5%20%F0%E9%ED%E1%EA%E1.pdf

7. Technical Chamber of Greece (TCC) and Ministry of the Environment and Energy. Special Town Planning Plan for the fire-damaged area of the Municipal Units of Nea Makri and Rafina of the Municipalities of Marathon and Rafina-Pikermio, Region of Attica (2020). https://ypen.gov.gr/wp-content/uploads/legacy/Files/ypourgeio/ypourgeio2/mati2_data/EPS_MATI_1_125.pdf

8. Lekkas, E., et al.: The July 2018 Attica (Central Greece) Wildfires (2018). https://doi.org/10.13140/RG.2.2.15202.96966

9. Ligkoni, A.: Forest fires and Climate change in Greece. The case of a fire in Mati Attikis is the result of climate change or human intervention? Master thesis, National and Kapodistrian University of Athens, Department of Geology and Geoenvironment, Greece (2021). https://pergamos.lib.uoa.gr/uoa/dl/object/2943598/file.pdf

10. Fire Service. Fire Service of Greece (2022). https://www.fireservice.gr/el. Accessed 20 Feb 2022

11. Xanthopoulos, G., Mitsopoulos, I.: The catastrophic fire of July 2018 in Greece and the Report of the Independent Committee that was appointed by the government to investigate the reasons for the worsening wildfire trend in the country. Presented at the First General Assembly & 2nd MC meeting, Sofia, Bulgaria (2018)

12. Giuliani, F., De Falco, A., Cutini, V.: The role of urban configuration during disasters. A scenario-based methodology for the post-earthquake emergency management of Italian historic centres. Saf. Sci. **127**, 104700 (2020). https://doi.org/10.1016/j.ssci.2020.104700

13. Sivrikaya, F., Küçük, Ö.: Modeling forest fire risk based on GIS-based analytical hierarchy process and statistical analysis in Mediterranean region. Eco. Inform. **68**, 101537 (2022). https://doi.org/10.1016/j.ecoinf.2021.101537

14. Sari, F.: Forest fire susceptibility mapping via multi-criteria decision analysis techniques for Mugla, Turkey: a comparative analysis of VIKOR and TOPSIS. For. Ecol. Manag. **480**, 118644 (2021). https://doi.org/10.1016/j.foreco.2020.118644

15. European Space Agency. Copernicus Data Hub (2018). https://cophub.copernicus.eu/. Accessed 15 Sept 2022

16. ELSTAT. 'Hellenic Statistical Authority', Hellenic Statistical Authority (2011). https://www.statistics.gr/en/home/

17. NOA. 'National Observatory of Athens'. Meteosearch (2022). https://meteosearch.meteo.gr/. Accessed 24 Mar 2023

18. Geofabrik. Geofabrik Download Server (2022). https://download.geofabrik.de/europe/greece.html. Accessed 10 Apr 2022

19. Hillier, B., Hanson, J.: The Social Logic of Space. Cambridge University Press, Cambridge (1984). https://doi.org/10.1017/CBO9780511597237

20. Van Nes, A., Yamu, C.: Introduction to Space Syntax in Urban Studies. Springer, Cham (2021). https://doi.org/10.1007/978-3-030-59140-3

21. Karimi, K.: Space syntax: consolidation and transformation of an urban research field. J. Urban Des. **23**(1), 1–4 (2018). https://doi.org/10.1080/13574809.2018.1403177

22. Yamu, C., Van Nes, A., Garau, C.: Bill Hillier's legacy: space syntax—a synopsis of basic concepts, measures, and empirical application. Sustainability **13**(6), Article no. 6 (2021). https://doi.org/10.3390/su13063394
23. Saaty, T.L.: The Analytic Hierarchy Process. Agricultural Economics Review, vol. 70. Mcgraw Hill, New York (1980)
24. Saaty, T.L.: Highlights and critical points in the theory and application of the Analytic Hierarchy Process. Eur. J. Oper. Res. **74**(3), 426–447 (1994). https://doi.org/10.1016/0377-221 7(94)90222-4
25. Vargas, R.V., Pmp, I.-B.: Using the Analytic Hierarchy Process (AHP) to Select and Prioritize Projects in a Portfolio. PMI Global Congress (2010)
26. Saaty, R.W.: The analytic hierarchy process—what it is and how it is used. Math. Model. **9**(3), 161–176 (1987). https://doi.org/10.1016/0270-0255(87)90473-8
27. Saaty, T.L.: Decision-making with the AHP: why is the principal eigenvector necessary. Eur. J. Oper. Res. **145**(1), 85–91 (2003). https://doi.org/10.1016/S0377-2217(02)00227-8
28. Yousuf Reja, M.: Investigating the role of open spaces and public buildings for earthquake vulnerability reduction in old Dhaka. Department of Architecture (Arch) (2012). http://lib.buet.ac.bd:8080/xmlui/handle/123456789/3053. Accessed 24 Mar 2023
29. Coolican, H.: Research Methods and Statistics in Psychology, 6th edn, p. xiii, 773. Psychology Press, New York (2014)

Building Collaboration for a Smart and Green Regional Ecosystem: Insights from the Slovak Republic

Ondrej Mitaľ'[(✉)] [iD], Silvia Ručinská[iD], Michaela Lukačínová[iD], and Miroslav Fečko[iD]

Department of Public Policy and Theory of Public Administration, Faculty of Public Administration, Pavol Jozef Šafárik University in Košice, 04011 Košice, Slovak Republic
{ondrej.mital,silvia.rucinska,miroslav.fecko}@upjs.sk,
michaela.lukacinova@student.upjs.sk

Abstract. The study investigates planned collaboration between local and regional stakeholders in the Slovak Republic, which we see as an essential base for smart and green regional ecosystem. The study uses case studies to examine the impact of the implemented solutions on the wider regional ecosystem and how stakeholders collaborate to achieve their goals. The authors argue that systematic and planned collaboration between stakeholders is essential for smart, green, and sustainable development of the region's ecosystem. The study analyzes six cases between 2020 and 2023 and discusses the relationship between stakeholders, the characteristics of stakeholders, and the innovative solutions adopted to solve certain smart and green challenges in the region. The results show that collaboration between local and regional government, higher educational institutions, business, citizens and other stakeholders involved in the Smart city structure has resulted in the implementation of innovative solutions that promote sustainable and environmentally friendly practices, with positive impacts on both entities and the public. The study concludes that smart and green policies operate together and emphasizes the need for planned collaboration between regional stakeholders to address smart and green challenges in the territory.

Keywords: smart city · stakeholder collaboration · regional ecosystem · innovation ecosystem · smart and green public policies · Slovak Republic

1 Introduction

The emergence of Smart cities as a popular approach to address the complex challenges faced by urban areas has captured the attention of academics, policymakers, and practitioners worldwide. As the concept of smart cities gains momentum around the world, it becomes increasingly important to understand the components that make up these innovative urban areas. The growth of urban areas and the associated environmental challenges have spurred the development of Smart city technologies, which aim to mitigate the negative impacts of urbanization. Simultaneously, various practitioners and

© The Author(s), under exclusive license to Springer Nature Switzerland AG 2023
O. Gervasi et al. (Eds.): ICCSA 2023 Workshops, LNCS 14105, pp. 598–612, 2023.
https://doi.org/10.1007/978-3-031-37108-0_38

politicians indicate that Smart city approach can help urban areas in tackling contemporary ongoing environmental climate change. Smart city approach affects not only the city itself but also citizens and various local stakeholders in the wider territory. In this regard, we perceive Smart city as concept that also includes mutual relations not just between local government and citizens, but also complex mutual relationship within the regional ecosystem [9, 45, 53]. For the purpose of this article, we define regional ecosystem as a platform for any mutual relationship between local or regional stakeholders that is associated with positive impact on local challenges and local public policies in the region surrounding a city.

The study has an ambition to realize preliminary research and investigate mutual collaboration between stakeholders of regional innovation ecosystem in the Slovak Republic, which we see as an essential base for smart and green ecosystem. In this sense, the study examines the activities of different stakeholders in the city that aims to answer smart and green challenges, focusing on the relationship between stakeholders and synergic effect of the implemented solutions on regional ecosystem. More precisely, the study examines, with the use of case study method, green and smart solutions adopted by different stakeholders, their impact on mutual relations and synergic effect on regional ecosystem challenges. Focusing on the conditions of the Slovak Republic, altogether 6 cases between 2020 and 2023 were analysed. We perceive regional ecosystem as a term that unifies different approaches to collaboration between stakeholders in the territory, such as innovation ecosystem, regional ecosystem or quadruple helix model [46].

We presume that solutions adopted within the planned collaboration between regional stakeholders have potential to solve both smart and green issues in the territory. Put differently, contemporary smart and green policies operate together, but not as random concurrent activities. They supplement each other, and their interlinking should be seen as welcomed and expected. Smart solutions bring also positive environmental impacts, and green solutions contribute to better and more sophisticated use of smart technologies. In this regard, systematic and planned collaboration of stakeholders in facing smart and green challenges can be seen as approach that contributes to smart, green and sustainable development of regional ecosystem.

2   Sustainable Smart City

As the world population continues to grow and urbanize, cities are facing unprecedented environmental challenges. Currently, more than half of the global population reside in urban areas, and this number is anticipated to rise to 68% by 2050 [55]. It is anticipated that the urban population will increase by more than double its present size by 2050, reaching a point where nearly 70% of the world's population will reside in urban centers [49]. With the rapid growth of urbanization, cities have become focal points for the creation of innovative technological solutions that improve the quality of life for their citizens while simultaneously addressing pressing environmental and socio-economic challenges.

2.1 Perspectives and Components of the Smart City Concept

Smart cities have emerged as a widely popular and fashionable approach to urban development in the present era. Cities worldwide increasingly claim to possess varying degrees of intelligence, with a primary focus on Information and communication technology and infrastructure [4, 15]. In this regard, Smart cities utilize digital technologies to enhance the well-being and quality of life of their residents, thus policymakers tend to initialize the technology-led growth process and allocated municipal budgets towards investments that enable Smart city development [16, 29, 50]. Put differently, Smart cities works through the development of information and communication technologies and the increasing hybridisation of electronic content with the physical world that is often described as augmented reality [40]. Smart city approach should leverage existing urban infrastructure rather than constructing new facilities, thus is expected to result in a safer and more livable urban environment, with improved accessibility to city services and governance [14].

According to the OECD, Smart cities can be defined as initiatives or approaches that increase digitalization to boost well-being and deliver more efficient, sustainable and inclusive services and environments as part of a collaborative, multi-stakeholder process [38]. Accurate assessment and measurement methods are essential for evaluating the effectiveness of a Smart city. The ISO 37120:2014 standard for the sustainable development of communities provides a framework for measuring and reporting the success of Smart city initiatives. Furthermore, the ISO 37120:2014 standard is based on a comprehensive set of 100 performance indicators, divided into 17 categories that encompass various aspects of urban life, such as the environment, economy, energy, education, finance, health, governance, emergency response, safety, recreation, transportation, innovation, solid waste, wastewater, urban planning, water and sanitation, and shelter [20].

Smart cities encompass a range of interdependent elements, including Smart environment, Smart living, Smart mobility, Smart governance, Smart people, and Smart economy, all of which contribute to the creation of a sustainable and livable urban environment [46].

Smart cities refer to the use of mentioned components to improve the quality of life of its citizens, increase the competitiveness of cities, and enhance sustainable development. The interaction between them is the key to the essence of a Smart city as a dynamic system, in which the city and all actors respond and adapt to changes [45]. Additionally, researchers are motivated to develop solutions for Smart cities, taking into account both socio-economic and technical perspectives [48]. The success of the Smart city is based not only on sophisticated digital and smart infrastructure but also on interconnectedness of Smart city components and collaboration of involved stakeholders.

To understand interconnected areas, it is crucial to consider the stakeholders who are part of them and represent them A range of stakeholders, including planners, governments, businesses, citizens, and universities, play a crucial role in the development and functioning of a Smart city. Thus, it is crucial to regularly assess and evaluate the status of these stakeholders in order to achieve the desired outcomes. Additionally, inter-stakeholder interactions are necessary for achieving the objectives of the Smart city. For example, monitoring population growth or economic burdens is critical for ensuring the well-being of citizens, whereas ensuring a high quality of life for urban populations is an essential consideration for planners. The smart city phenomenon has direct implications for enterprises and businesses, necessitating the development of intelligent infrastructure and the implementation of Smart solutions by real estate developers, system integrators, and technology providers. The success of a Smart city largely depends on the government's ability to formulate policies that promote its sustainability. Higher educational institutions, such as universities, have a significant role to play in the planning and operation of Smart cities.

2.2 Evolving Environment and Smart City Concept

The world has a unique opportunity to steer the course of urban development. Despite this, most of the individuals residing in cities lack adequate transportation and housing, and they are plagued by unsanitary conditions, poor waste management, and air quality that fails to meet generally accepted standards. Scholars and policymakers have expressed apprehensions regarding the adverse impacts of higher levels of urbanization on the environmental aspects, such as higher levels of air pollution and CO_2 emissions [13, 47], negative effect on biodiversity [30, 58], public health issues [28, 31, 34]. In this regard, cities contribute to environmental degradation through various factors, including energy and water consumption, mobility, and waste production. Cities have a significant impact on the environment and are therefore key players in the fight against climate change. Based on abovementioned one of the crucial objectives of the Smart city is to prioritize sustainable development, especially in matters related to the environment. The Smart city concept indicate that green aspirations and undertakings are incorporated in almost all of the six Smart city components, its goals (social sustainability, economic sustainability, and environmental sustainability), intelligent initiatives (smart houses, smart energy, smart parking, smart health, etc.) and building blocks in Smart city (smart traffic, smart Sustainability, e-governance, smart technology, smart data, etc.) [48].

As digital transformation consolidates, the Smart City concept helps local government in tackling digital and green challenges. Smart cities present significant opportunities for promoting environmental sustainability, which is critical given the potential negative impact of urbanization on the environment [55]. In response to abovementioned environmental challenges, many economies and cities are turning to the concept of Smart Cities to improve sustainability and livability [23, 45]. Thus, it can be argued that understanding the link between green technological innovation and Smart city development is crucial for promoting sustainable urbanization [56]. Regarding the connection between Smart city and the environment, on average, larger municipalities exhibit a greater degree of ecological awareness, what may be attributed to the emphasis placed on environmental quality by policy makers, urban planners, as well as citizens and communities in Smart cities [4]. Regarding the interconnectedness of smart and green policies, the benefits of co-existing smart city and climate change adaptation explore opportunities as well as reduce the harmful risks of contemporary challenges [8, 19, 42].

The intimate and incontrovertible connection between the Smart City and the environment is reinforced by the European Commission's definition of a smart city, which extends beyond the deployment of digital technologies to achieve enhanced resource utilization and reduced emissions. This encompasses the establishment of more intelligent urban transport networks, upgraded waste disposal facilities and water supply, and more efficient lighting and heating systems for buildings, thus it is explicitly stated that the smart city concept endeavors to attain the European Union's energy and climate objectives [11].

2.3 Stakeholders' Collaboration in Regional Ecosystem

Smart and green challenges have exceeded barriers between the sectors of our society. Both types of challenges affect different types of stakeholders, mainly local governments, business, higher educational institutions and citizens. Put differently, stakeholders of regional ecosystem do not have the capacity to face contemporary ongoing smart and green challenges independently.

Environment with good collaboration of involved stakeholders can lead to various benefits that will emerge in given region or territory, such as the strengthening of cost effectiveness and environmental performance [18, 41, 44], higher identification with cross-sectional and fragmented societal goals [5, 7], as well as general sustainable development of certain environment [17, 24, 27].

However, collaboration between the regional stakeholders cannot be automatically connected to universal success. Collaboration between stakeholders is a complex phenomenon that is determined by several variables, such as the quality of social capital [43, 44], socio-political framework [6], context of city and local government typology [9], as well as involvement of actors in policymaking and relations between stakeholders [22].

Based on abovementioned, collaboration of stakeholders within the region or territory should not be perceived as fortuitous situation that generates new solutions. Collaboration in the case of regional development must be realized under the long-term collaboration. We argue that such collaboration must be also materialized in local government strategies. As it was stated by many scholars, strategic approach in stakeholder collaboration in regional ecosystem can lead to higher intensity of collaboration and mutual benefits for involved stakeholders [10, 21, 37, 53].

In this regard, important precondition of smart and green regional ecosystem is a systematic approach in stakeholder collaboration and involvement of relevant stakeholders in policymaking. Stakeholders' collaboration allow local governments to be more facile in the way they develop infrastructure to meet the needs of its citizens, by removing barriers to innovation [54]. Smart and green challenges represent fragmented and cross-sectional issues of contemporary democratic governance, which can only be solved or mitigated with the mutually beneficial collaboration of stakeholders. We also argue that higher performance of mentioned regional ecosystem leads to higher quality of life, what is also the main aim of local government in contemporary democratic governance.

3   Methods

The study has an ambition to realize preliminary research and investigate mutual collaboration between stakeholders of regional innovation ecosystem in the Slovak Republic, which we see as an essential base for smart and green ecosystem. In this sense, the study examines the activities of different stakeholders in the city that aims to answer smart and green challenges, focusing on the relationship between stakeholders and synergic effect of the implemented solutions on regional ecosystem. More precisely, the study examines, with the use of case study method, green and smart solutions adopted by different stakeholders, their impact on mutual relations and synergic effect on regional ecosystem challenges. Focusing on the conditions of the Slovak Republic, altogether 6 cases between 2020 and 2023 were analysed. Regarding the conditions of the Slovak Republic, each case study focuses on good practice example in the city of regional significance. The selection of cities was determined by the fragmentation of local self-government and the significance of these cities in public service delivery both in the city and in the region surrounding a city.

The case studies represent the appropriate tool, which was used to demonstrate how planned collaboration between stakeholders helps to create smart and green regional ecosystem. Each of six case studies include the description of relationship between stakeholders, character of stakeholders, description of innovative solution adopted to solve certain smart and green challenge in the region, as well as impact on smart and green agenda in the region. Analysed cases of collaboration between stakeholders were selected intentionally.

Theoretical analysis was used to analyse contemporary state of research in the sphere of smart and green agenda. Content analysis was used to analyse the content of strategies adopted by different regional stakeholders, emphasizing selected methodology. Abstraction was used in the context of filtering those aspects of selected cases, which were relevant for our research and smart and green regional ecosystem framework. The method of synthesis was used to systematize new ideas based on our research, as well as to draw conclusions resulting from the analysis.

4   Results

The importance of digital and green challenges is highlighted by the competences assigned to state administration authorities. The Ministry of Environment of the Slovak Republic is the central state authority and the supreme inspection authority in environmental affairs. The central coordination role in digitalization from the central government's perspective is performed by the Ministry of Investments, Regional Development and Informatization of the Slovak Republic. Both state authorities create, with the help of other stakeholders at regional and local levels, basic frameworks that results to policies and strategies.

The Greener Slovakia – Strategy of the Environmental Policy of the Slovak Republic until 2030 is a main national environmental strategy that identifies priorities and basic directions for future environmental and cross-sectional policy goals, mainly sustainable use and effective protection of natural resources, adaptation and mitigation to climate change and air protection, fostering green economy. Envirostrategy 2030 has many ambitious goals, such as reducing individual car traffic and support public transport, including bicycle transport, building green infrastructure in cities, promoting data-based decisions, and fostering inclusion of adaptation measures in strategic documents of cities in general [32]. The 2030 Digital Transformation Strategy for Slovakia is a nationwide strategy of the Slovak Republic that defines policies and priorities of the digital transformation of the society and economy that describes Smart City as the way to a modern and smart territorial development. In addition to digitization, the strategy also underlines the need for green solutions, mainly supporting smart public transport and integrated public transport, preferring emission-free public transport, using of digital technologies to foster communication and participative decision-making at local level, as well as improving collaboration between private, academic and public sector in order to improve quality of life [33].

Framework and priorities defined by the state authorities must be also implemented by the cities. Based on abovementioned, smart and green challenges influence each other. Thus, we presume that local stakeholders naturally develop initiatives that helps cities to improve the quality of live in regional ecosystem. Following case studies demonstrate planned collaboration of regional stakeholders in the Slovak Republic. Simultaneously, case studies concentrate attention on smart and green solutions that we perceive as preconditions for smart and green regional ecosystem.

4.1 Smart Mobility Towards Sustainable Mobility

Collaboration between local government and business has resulted in development of shared transport services and public transport in the city of Košice. This intention of the city of Košice to cooperate with business in the sphere of public transport is declared in recent strategies [25, 26]. This mutual effect was created as an outcome of green and smart solutions. Shared transport services were originally provided by the local business Antik Telecom, mainly bike sharing, e-bike sharing and scooter sharing. Services were available to the public thanks to the mobile app (Antik SmartWay). However, the close collaboration with the city of Košice leads to creation of innovative solutions with positive impacts on both entities, as well as public. Virtual travel tickets for public transport provided by Košice public transport company were added to Antik SmartWay app. In October 2021, both services and information systems were linked, while the application Antik SmartWay can be used to purchase a ticket for public transport and shared transport [26]. Simultaneously, the city of Košice coordinated the construction of the charging stations for electric vehicles with the company. In this regard, the most of them were build next to public transport stops. Summing it up, collaboration was mutually beneficial for each other. This case of smart and green solutions is also contribution to aim Increase the share of sustainable types of mobility and improve traffic service in the city, which is part of priority called Sustainable mobility [25]. Positive impacts of smart and green solutions generate behaviour that motivate citizens to use public transport, shared electric vehicles, as well as creates storage boxes for shared electric vehicles solving one of the biggest problems of shared electronic mobility.

4.2 Smart Solutions Help Reduce Emissions

Higher educational institutions as very specific stakeholders are situated mainly in bigger local self-government units. Universities are also seen as facilitators of sustainable regional development, mainly thanks to their research activities and personal capacities. Collaboration between the city of Košice and Pavol Jozef Šafárik University in Košice play important role in the development of wider territory, as it is also declared in Economic and social development plan 2022–2027 [25]. Planned collaboration between both stakeholders have led to elaboration of document Basic emission balance of the city of Košice, that analyses current state and includes suggestion for more resilient city in the case of climate and energy change. University experts have helped the city to prepare very important document, which is necessary for signatories of Covenant of Mayors, the commitment of local governments to implementing EU climate and energy objectives [12]. Basic emission balance of the city of Košice describes the current level of CO_2 emissions and describe potential smart solutions in various spheres, such as emissions for buildings, emissions for public lighting, emissions in transport, emissions from waste, as well as greenery in the city [39]. This collaboration demonstrates the importance of the higher educational institutions for regional development, also in the spheres of smart and green solutions.

4.3 Green Housing Estates Thanks to Smart Participation Process

Innovative approach to citizens' participation in urban development was applied in the case of Banská Bystrica. This case is based on collaboration between the local government and non-governmental organization that facilitated participation of citizens. Collaboration of mentioned stakeholders is declared to be one of the priorities in the Economic and social development plan 2015–2023 [1]. The aim of the city was to implement citizen friendly environmental solutions in their housing estate. Personal capacities and know-how of non-governmental organization Dialogue Centre were used during participation process. In this regard, data collection process and evaluation of obtained data were carried out exclusively electronically. As a result of this collaboration, the criteria for selecting a processor of project documentation are set with an emphasis on suggestion presented during participation process, explicitly 70% fulfilment of suggestions and 30% economic efficiency [3]. Collaboration between the local government and non-governmental sector have created a space for emphasizing the green demands of citizens. The intention of the city to satisfy the demands of citizens is also expressed in the different strategies, mainly developing the principle of neighbourhood partnerships, which will contribute to the rebuilding of the residential environment housing estate [2] and ensuring the development of green infrastructure and adaptation of the city to the climate changes [1]. Smart and digital solution that helped to obtain data in easier and quicker way have initiated policymaking underlining green and sustainable solutions.

4.4 Innovative Bike Storing as a Support of Cycling Mobility

Another collaboration that combines benefits of green and smart solutions was established in the city of Trnava couple of years ago. Intensive use of bike transport in the city leads to unique solutions, the construct of bike tower. This very specific facility was constructed in the collaboration with BIKETOWER that have already constructed bike towers in 20 cities. Collaboration of the city with the different stakeholders is perceived as very important in the case of public transport and public mobility [51]. Intensive collaboration with the company includes not only the basic annual service works, but also digital services for the citizens. Bike tower is fully automatized. In this regard, citizens can detect the tower's filling status with the use of internet. Besides, Bike tower in Trnava is situated near the train station that encourage citizens to use the combination of public transport and bike rather than the use of own car. This ideal state is in accordance with goals included in the strategies of the Trnava, mainly partial goal Addition of supporting elements for cycle transport [52] and measurement called Development of non-motorized transport, mainly cycling transport [51]. Mentioned combination of green and digital solutions supports green sustainability in the city, as well as helps to mitigate traffic jams and reduce air pollution near the city centre.

4.5 Smart Public Lighting as Part of Mitigating the Impacts of Climate Change

Next case of innovative approach to green and smart solutions in local self-government is based on the collaboration between city and business. Personal capacities of local self-government units are limited, what means that sophisticated analysis and audits must be outsourced. Collaboration with private sector is also reflected as one of the priorities in Program of economic development and social development of the City of Nitra 2015–2023 [35]. The same decision was made by the city of Nitra in the case of public lightning audit. However, this collaboration does not lead to direct impacts on green and smart agenda in the city, audit itself brings innovative green and smart solutions for the city, their citizens and wider region. Energy audit report of the public lighting system elaborated by Arnea Company suggest various smart solutions with positive impacts on environment, such as connection of new smart lightings in the overall integrated smart system of the city, configuration of new smart lightings and control sensors with conditions resulting from climate change, automatization of smart lights in the case of rain, fog and concentrating of citizens [36]. Presented solutions creates smart and green friendly solutions that have potential to minimize negative impacts of public lightning on environment and public finances, but also secure the highest possible safety for citizens. Outcomes of these future solutions comply with the aims of development in the Economic and social development plan 2015–2023, mainly aims increasing the protection of city residents and their property and increasing the energy efficiency of public buildings and city facilities with an emphasis on building and facilities owned by the municipality [35].

4.6 Plant Your Tree Thanks to Your PC or Smartphone

Collaboration between citizens and local self-government units is also very important in the case of smart and green agenda. Involving of citizens in policymaking is defined as one of the priorities in Economic and social development plan 2015–2023 [35]. Web page Green city, created by the city of Nitra and Nitrian Community Foundation gives citizens the opportunity to plant the tree. What's more, citizens can decide where the tree will be planted, and which type of tree will grow in the selected location. Green city initiative is the responsive web application that allows you to participate in the planting of greenery in the city in a simple, modern way [57]. Smart web page solution based on map view can be used to pick the place randomly or intentionally next to the citizen's house. Web page also offers information about every demand of citizens in last years, its evaluation status and an overview of trees planted based on a citizen's request. This case demonstrates how easily cities can encourage their citizens to participate in activities for a greener city, because it is as easy as using PC or smartphone. Presented simple smart solution can help citizens to be more reliable for their environment and be more involved in green, smart and sustainable development of their city.

5 Discussion

As digital transformation and impacts of climate change blurs, cities are being forced to readjust routine activities in policymaking and governance. Smart and green challenges have wider societal impact on local self-government units and their territory. Selected case studies demonstrated that collaboration between other key stakeholders can help cities to mitigate negative impact of digital transformation and climate change. Figure 1 includes comprehensive summarization of the analysed case studies.

	Stakeholders involved	Innovative solutions		Strategy based	
		Smart oriented	Green oriented	Stakeholders cooperation	Compliance with smart and green goals
Case 1	local government, business			yes	yes
Case 2	local government, higher educational institution			yes	yes
Case 3	local government, citizens, non-governmental organization			yes	yes
Case 4	local government, business			yes	yes
Case 5	local government, business			yes	yes
Case 6	local government, citizens			yes	no

Fig. 1. Comprehensive summarization of smart and green case studies. Source: authors

Focusing on the key elements of case studies, important findings should be discussed. As we presumed, solutions adopted within the planned collaboration between local and regional stakeholders have initiated solutions with positive impact on smart and green issues. However, selected cases had different impact on smart and green agenda, because some prioritize green solutions and other were primarily based on smart measures. Smart public lightning initiative from the City of Nitra and Smart mobility case from the city of Košice can be perceived as highly smart oriented, thus these activities need sophisticated digital and smart technologies to be successful. In contrary, collaboration between local government and universities in Košice, as presented in Case 2, has significant impact on green agenda, but also need smart technologies application. Case 2 and Case 3 are mainly green oriented, but outcomes of local governments' activities were amplified thanks to use of smart solutions. Figure 1 also demonstrates the intensity of innovative solutions use. However, case studies with lower intensity also can be perceived as an example of good practice, mainly thanks to collaboration of stakeholders and combination of impacts on digital and green agenda at regional ecosystem.

Selected cases also confirmed, that presented innovative solutions have resulted from intended collaboration between stakeholders, which is also declared by adopted strategies. In this regard, collaboration in demonstrated that smart and green regional ecosystems is not random, and it is far from an ad hoc collaboration. Simultaneously, five out of six cases also confirmed that implemented solutions contribute to aims and priorities included in local government strategies. Put differently, involvement of stakeholders into policymaking also facilitates environment where stakeholders follow initiatives of local and regional governments to increase the performance of local and regional ecosystem. Analysed case studies correspond not only with priorities of local governments' strategies, but also reflect long-term priorities included in national strategies.

Summing it up, we argue that systematic collaboration between the stakeholders contributes to smart, green and sustainable development of a wider region. Smart and green regional ecosystem can be based on abovementioned described as an approach that secures complex sustainable development. However, local and also regional governments can be perceived as the main actor and architect of this ecosystem. Contrary, local government without involved stakeholders is not able to solve contemporary ongoing digital transformation, climate and energy change. Citizens, businesses, nongovernmental organizations and higher educational institutions, as well as relations inside the ecosystem will affect the success of smart and green policies.

6 Conclusion

In conclusion, the concept of smart cities is gaining momentum around the world as a popular approach to address the complex challenges faced by urban areas. The growth of urban areas and the associated environmental challenges have spurred the development of smart city technologies, which aim to mitigate the negative impacts of urbanization and promote sustainable development. The study conducted in the Slovak Republic aimed to investigate the mutual relations between stakeholders in the region to create a smart and green regional ecosystem.

Through the case studies analyzed in this study, it is evident that planned collaboration between regional stakeholders, concentrating mainly on local self-government in the Slovak Republic, can create a smart and green regional ecosystem. The six cases analyzed were intentionally selected to demonstrate how planned collaboration between stakeholders helps to create a smart and green regional ecosystem. Each case study included the description of the relationship between stakeholders, the character of stakeholders, the description of the innovative solution adopted to solve certain smart and green challenges in the region, as well as the impact on the smart and green agenda in the region.

Despite the benefits of the study, there are still limitations to be addressed in further studies. First, our research was based on intentional selection of case studies. Nevertheless, we consider their information value that helped us to demonstrate importance of planned collaboration within local and regional environment. Another limit is based on statement, that smart and green challenges are complex phenomena, thus many other variables affect smart and green agenda. Our research can be further extended from the following aspects, mainly broadening the empirical evidence, further analysis of stakeholders' strategies, as well as interconnectedness to national and European strategies.

In summary, this study has demonstrated the potential for planned collaboration between stakeholders in the Slovak Republic to create a smart and green regional ecosystem. The six cases analyzed show that the solutions adopted within the planned collaboration between regional stakeholders have the potential to solve both smart and green issues in the territory. Smart solutions bring positive environmental impacts, and green solutions also contribute to better and more sophisticated use of smart technologies. Systematic and planned collaboration of stakeholders in answering smart and green challenges can be seen as an approach that contributes to smart, green, and sustainable development of a wider regional ecosystem. Therefore, policymakers and practitioners worldwide should take into consideration the importance of planned collaboration between stakeholders in the development of smart and green solutions in their respective regions. In conclusion, the concept of smart cities is gaining momentum around the world as a popular approach to address the complex challenges faced by urban areas.

Acknowledgments. The article is created as a result of a project supported by the Scientific grant agency of the Ministry of Education, Science, Research and Sport of the Slovak Republic and the Slovak Academy of Sciences, Grant no: 1/0734/22.

References

1. Banská Bystrica. Economic and social development plan 2015–2023 (Plán hospodárskeho a sociálneho rozvoja 2015–2023) (2015). https://cdn.banskabystrica.sk/Dokumenty-mesta/phsr_mesta_banska_bystrica_2015-2023.pdf. Accessed 11 Apr 2023
2. Banská Bystrica: Housing development program the city of Banská Bystrica for the years 2015–2020 (Program rozvoja bývania mesta Banská Bystrica na roky 2015–2020) (2015). https://cdn.banskabystrica.sk/2020/05/Program-rozvoja-bývania-mesta-B.Bystrica_2015-2020_textová-cast.pdf. Accessed 11 Apr 2023
3. Banská Bystrica. Green Housing Estates (Zelené sídliská) (2022). https://www.banskabystrica.sk/zelenesidliska/. Accessed 11 Apr 2023
4. Borsekova, K., Koróny, S., Vaňová, A., Vitálišová, K.: Functionality between the size and indicators of smart cities: a research challenge with policy implications. Cities **78**, 17–26 (2018). https://doi.org/10.1016/j.cities.2018.03.010
5. Bridoux, F., Stoelhorst, J.W.: Stakeholder relationships and social welfare: a behavioral theory of contributions to joint value creation. Acad. Manag. Rev. **41**(2), 229–251 (2016). https://doi.org/10.5465/amr.2013.0475
6. Burns, P.: Tourism, political discourse and post-colonialism. Tour. Hosp. Plann. Dev. **6**(1), 61–73 (2008). https://doi.org/10.1080/14790530801936502
7. Chirico, F., Nucera, G., Szarpak, L., Zaffina, S.: The cooperation between occupational and public health stakeholders and its decisive role in the battle against the COVID-19 pandemic. Disast. Med. Public Health Preparedness **17**(e100), 1–2 (2021). https://doi.org/10.1017/dmp.2021.375
8. Chu, Z., Cheng, M., Yu, N.N.: A smart city is a less polluted city. Technol. Forecast. Soc. Chang. **172**, 121037 (2021). https://doi.org/10.1016/j.techfore.2021.121037

9. Clement, J., Manjon, M., Crutzen, N.: Factors for collaboration amongst smart city stake-holders: a local government perspective. Gov. Inf. Q. **39**(4), 101746 (2022). https://doi.org/10.1016/j.giq.2022.101746

10. Corrêa Gomes, R.: Who are the relevant stakeholders to the local government context? Empirical evidences on environmental influences in the decision-making process of English local authorities. Braz. Adm. Rev. **1**(1), 34–52 (2004). https://doi.org/10.1590/S1807-769220040 0100004

11. European Commission. Smart cities (2023). https://commission.europa.eu/eu-regional-and-urban-development/topics/cities-and-urban-development/city-initiatives/smart-cities_en. Accessed 01 Apr 2023

12. European Commission. Why a Covenant of Mayors? (2023). https://eu-mayors.ec.europa.eu/en/about. Accessed 10 Apr 2023

13. Frick, S.A., Rodríguez-Pose, A.: Average city size and economic growth. Camb. J. Reg. Econ. Soc. **9**(2), 301–318 (2016). https://doi.org/10.1093/cjres/rsw013

14. Giffinger, R.: European smart cities: the need for a place related understanding. Creating smart cities, Napier University, Edinburgh (2011)

15. Gil-Garcia, J.R., Pardo, T.A., Nam, T.: What makes a city smart? Identifying core components and proposing an integrative and comprehensive conceptualization. Inf. Polity **20**(1), 61–87 (2015). https://doi.org/10.3233/IP-150354

16. Glasmeier, A., Christopherson, S.: Thinking about smart cities. Camb. J. Reg. Econ. Soc. **8**(1), 3–12 (2015). https://doi.org/10.1093/cjres/rsu034

17. Harangozó, G., Zilahy, G.: Cooperation between business and non-governmental organizations to promote sustainable development. J. Clean. Prod. **89**, 18–31 (2015). https://doi.org/10.1016/j.jclepro.2014.10.092

18. Hodge, I., McNally, S.: Wetland restoration, collective action and the role of water management institutions. Ecol. Econ. **35**(1), 107–118 (2000). https://doi.org/10.1016/S0921-8009(00)00171-3

19. Huang-Lachmann, J.T.: Systematic review of smart cities and climate change adaptation. Sustain. Account. Manage. Policy J. **10**(4), 745–772 (2019). https://doi.org/10.1108/SAMPJ-03-2018-0052

20. International Organization for Standardization. ISO 37120:2018(en) sustainable cities and communities (2018). www.iso.org/obp/ui#iso:std:iso:37120:ed-2:v1:en. Accessed 01 Apr 2023

21. Jung, T.H., Lee, J., Yap, M.H.T., Ineson, E.M.: The role of stakeholder collaboration in culture-led urban regeneration: a case study of the Gwangju project, Korea. Cities **44**, 29–39 (2015). https://doi.org/10.1016/j.cities.2014.12.003

22. Kijewska, K., Jedliński, M., Stanisław, I.: Ecological utility of FQP projects in the stakehold-ers' opinion in the light of empirical studies based on the example of the city of Szczecin. Sustain. Cities Soc. **74**, 103171 (2021). https://doi.org/10.1016/j.scs.2021.103171

23. Kitchin, R.: Making sense of smart cities: addressing present shortcomings. Camb. J. Reg. Econ. Soc. **8**(1), 131–136 (2014). https://doi.org/10.1093/cjres/rsu027

24. Komninos, N., Kakderi, C., Panori, A., Tsarchopoulos, P.: Smart city planning from an evolutionary perspective. J. Urban Technol. **26**(2), 3–20 (2019). https://doi.org/10.1080/10630732.2018.1485368

25. Košice: Economic and social development plan of the City of Košice and its functional area 2022–2027 (Plán hospodárskeho a sociálneho rozvoja Mesta Košice a jeho funkčnej oblasti 2022–2027) (2021). https://static.kosice.sk/files/manual/phsr/PHRSR_mesta_Kosice_a_jeho_funkcnej_oblasti_2022-2027.pdf. Accessed 10 Apr 2023

26. Košice: Strategy for the development of transport and transport structures of the city of Košice: Document update (Stratégia rozvoja dopravy a dopravných stavieb mesta Košice:

Aktualizácia dokumentu) (2022). https://static.kosice.sk/pages/F3Z5l1YQVXbTrWNA3U9/srd_kosice_aktualizacia.pdf. Accessed 10 Apr 2023

27. Krce Miočić, B., Razović, M., Klarin, T.: Management of sustainable tourism destination through stakeholder cooperation. Manage. J. Contemp. Manage. Issues **21**(2), 99–120 (2016)

28. Kuddus, M.A., Tynan, E., McBryde, E.: Urbanization: a problem for the rich and the poor? Public Health Rev. **41**(1), 1–4 (2020). https://doi.org/10.1186/s40985-019-0116-0

29. Lara, A.P., Da Costa, E.M., Furlani, T.Z., Yigitcanlar, T.: Smartness that matters: towards a comprehensive and human-centred characterisation of smart cities. J. Open Innov.: Technol. Mark. Complexity **2**(2), 1–13 (2016). https://doi.org/10.1186/s40852-016-0034-z

30. Liang, L., Wang, Z., Li, J.: The effect of urbanization on environmental pollution in rapidly developing urban agglomerations. J. Clean. Prod. **234**, 117649 (2019). https://doi.org/10.1016/j.jclepro.2019.117649

31. McMichael, A.J.: The urban environment and health in a world of increasing globalization: issues for developing countries. Bull. World Health Organ. **78**(9), 1117–1126 (2000)

32. Ministry of Environment of the Slovak Republic. Greener Slovakia: Strategy of the Environmental Policy of the Slovak Republic until 2030 (2019). https://www.minzp.sk/files/iep/greener_slovakia-strategy_of_the_environmental_policy_of_the_slovak_republic_until_2030.pdf. Accessed 07 Apr 2023

33. Ministry of Investments, Regional Development and Informatization of the Slovak Republic. Ministry of 2030 Digital Transformation Strategy for Slovakia (2019). https://www.mirri.gov.sk/wp-content/uploads/2019/10/SDT-English-Version-FINAL.pdf

34. Neiderud, C.J.: How urbanization affects the epidemiology of emerging infectious diseases. Infect. Ecol. Epidemiol. **5**(1), 27060 (2015). https://doi.org/10.3402/iee.v5.27060

35. Nitra. Program of economic development and social development of the City of Nitra 2015–2023 (Program hospodárskeho rozvoja a sociálneho rozvoja Mesta Nitry 2015–2023) (2016). Accessed 07 Apr 2023

36. Nitra. Processing of documents for the written report "Energy audit public lighting systems in the city of Nitra" (Spracovanie podkladov pre písomnú správu "Energetický audit sústavy verejného osvetlenia v meste Nitra") (2022). https://nitra.sk/wp-content/uploads/2023/02/Spracovanie-podkladov-pre-pisomnu-spravu-„Energeticky-audit-sustavy-verejneho-osvetlenia-v-meste-Nitra.pdf. Accessed 07 Apr 2023

37. O'Donnell, O.: Strategic collaboration in local government. A review of international examples of strategic collaboration in local government. Local Govern. Res. Ser. **2**, 1–46 (2012)

38. OECD. Enhancing the contribution of digitalization to the Smart Cities of the Future (2019). https://www.oecd.org/cfe/regionaldevelopment/Smart-Cities-FINAL.pdf

39. Pavol Jozef Šafárik University in Košice. Basic emission balance of the city of Košice (2020). https://josephine.proebiz.com/cs/tender/11797/summary/download/89289. Accessed 10 Apr 2023

40. Picon, A.: Smart Cities: A Spatialised Intelligence. Wiley, Chichester (2015)

41. Plaza-Úbeda, J.A., Burgos-Jiménez, J., Vazquez, D.A., Liston-Heyes, C.: The 'win–win' paradigm and stakeholder integration. Bus. Strateg. Environ. **18**, 487–499 (2009). https://doi.org/10.1002/bse.593

42. Polzonetti, A., Sagratella, M.: Smart city and green development. In: Al-Sharhan, S.A., et al. (eds.) I3E 2018. LNCS, vol. 11195, pp. 191–204. Springer, Cham (2018). https://doi.org/10.1007/978-3-030-02131-3_18

43. Pretty, J.: Social capital and the collective management of resources. Science **302**(5652), 1912–1914 (2003). https://doi.org/10.1126/science.109084

44. Robson, M., Kant, S.: The development of government agency and stakeholder cooperation: a comparative study of two Local Citizens Committees' (LCCs) participation in forest management in Ontario. Canada. Economics **9**(8), 1113–1133 (2007). https://doi.org/10.1016/j. forpol.2006.12.002

45. Ručinská, S., Fečko, M.: The use of innovations for smart cities. Transf. inovácií **38**, 81–84 (2018)

46. Ručinská, S.: "Smart city" – conception for local development?, In: CEE e/Dem and e/Gov Days 2015: proceedings of the Central and Eastern European e/Dem and e/Gov Days 2015, pp. 191–205. Austrian Computer Society, Wien (2015)

47. Sadorsky, P.: The effect of urbanization on CO2 emissions in emerging economies. Energy Economics **41**, 147–153 (2014). https://doi.org/10.1016/j.eneco.2013.11.007

48. Shamsuzzoha, A., Nieminen, J., Piya, S., Rutledge, K.: Smart city for sustainable environment: a comparison of participatory strategies from Helsinki, Singapore and London. Cities **114**, 103194 (2021). https://doi.org/10.1016/j.cities.2021.103194

49. The World Bank. Urban Development (2022). https://www.worldbank.org/en/topic/urband evelopment/overview. Accessed 01 Apr 2023

50. Trencher, G., Karvonen, A.: Stretching "smart": advancing health and well-being through the smart city agenda. Local Environ. **24**(7), 610–627 (2017). https://doi.org/10.1080/13549839. 2017.1360264

51. Trnava. Economic development program and social development of the city of Trnava for the years 2014–2023 with an outlook until 2030 (Program hospodárskeho rozvoja a sociálneho rozvoja mesta Trnava na roky 2014–2023 s výhľadom do roku 2030) (2020). https://www.trn ava.sk/userfiles/file/Aktualizacia%20PHSR_na%20web.pdf. Accessed 11 Apr 2023

52. Trnava. Plan of sustainable mobility of the regional city of Trnava and its functional territory (Plán udržateľnej mobility krajského mesta Trnava a jeho funkčného územia) (2021). https:// www.trnava.sk/sk/clanok/pum. Accessed 11 Apr 2023

53. Vitálišová, K., Murray-Svidroňová, M., Jakuš-Muthová, N.: Stakeholder participation in local governance as a key to local strategic development. Cities **118**, 103363 (2021). https://doi. org/10.1016/j.cities.2021.103363

54. Williams, S.: The responsive city: the city of the future re-imagined from the bottom up. In: Haas, T., Olsson, K. (eds.) Emergent Urbanism: Urban Planning & Design in Times of Structural and Systemic Change, pp. 147–158. Ashgate, Farnham (2014)

55. World Health Organization. Urban health (2023). https://www.who.int/health-topics/urban-health#tab=tab_2. Accessed 01 Apr 2023

56. Yan, Z., Sun, Z., Shi, R., Zhao, M.: Smart city and green development: empirical evidence from the perspective of green technological innovation. Technol. Forecast. Soc. Change **191**, 122507 (2023). https://doi.org/10.1016/j.techfore.2023.122507

57. Zelenemestonitra. Green City (Zelené mesto) (2023). https://zelenemestonitra.sk/mapa. Accessed 07 Apr 2023

58. Zhang, L., et al.: Direct and indirect impacts of urbanization on vegetation growth across the world's cities. Sci. Adv. **8**(27), 1–10 (2022). https://doi.org/10.1126/sciadv.abo0095

Typographic Topology/Topographic Typography. Reading the Urban Identity Through the Historical *Typescape*: Hypothesis for an AR Situated Mobile App

Letizia Bollini[(✉)] [iD] and Maria Letizia Mastroianni

Free University of Bozen-Bolzano, 39100 Bolzano, Italy
letizia.bollini@unibz.it

Abstract. Starting from the idea of an alternative way of reading and interpreting the urban space and its evolution through the Farias' concept of *Graphic memory*, the research project proposes the concept of *typescape* as a way of investigating a complex territory from a social, urban, and linguistic point of view. It is an interpretative key that allows to read the *genius loci*, or rather a complex and stratified urban identity, from one side, but also the gentrification processes induced by transformations that have partially modified, overwritten or progressively cancelled the richness of the original identity. The paper presents and discusses the design and prototype of *Bozen-Bolzano AR* situated mobile app that adopts *phygital* storytelling to explore the cultural and intangible heritage of the city according to the methodology already developed and test in different cities such as São Paulo, London, and Venice.

Keywords: Cultural and Intangible Heritage · Typescape · Graphic Memory · generous interfaces design · geo-storytelling

1 Introduction: Cartographies of Emotions

"The only journey possible would now appear to be within signs, images: within the destruction of direct experience." Luigi Ghirri [1].

If it easy to read the urban morphology on a map – showing the planned structures as well as the texture spontaneously shaped by the community or the pattern configured by the buildings and architectures – the living experiences is elusive in this visualization modality and scale, or the more complex the layers of social practices and symbolic values are, the more we need a broad and articulated range of two and three-dimension, multisensorial, multimodal, and synesthetic communication modalities.

Besides, some territories offer a further richness of interpretations thanks to the socio-historical sedimentation they witnessed. If, in some cases, the city has been read as a text, a warp and weft of signs and presences, as in the case of the typographic maps drawn by Paula Scher [2], it is the *peri*-textual references – and their co-location – the *para*-text [3], to reveal the meaning, otherwise not perceivable by adopting a pure editorial

© The Author(s), under exclusive license to Springer Nature Switzerland AG 2023
O. Gervasi et al. (Eds.): ICCSA 2023 Workshops, LNCS 14105, pp. 613–629, 2023.
https://doi.org/10.1007/978-3-031-37108-0_39

metaphor. The tag clouds depicted to recreate the shape of the spatial – urban, national, or worldwide – outline is based on "hand-painted place names, information and cultural commentary" where the personal perspective and the alternative vision of the designer are "expressionistic" as well as "geographical" at the same time. According to Simon Winchester – author of *The Map That Changed the World* [4] – Scher's work reclaims the charm of maps in the age of GPS. These maps charts are more than just a territory: "a mural [...] presents the country's geography and cliwmate, showing networks mountain ranges, rivers, and weather streams in a chaotic, colourful jumble on the map. Scher also created paintings depicting median home prices, driving times and mileage, counties and zip codes." [5]. As she states in an interview: "It's aesthetic, and also emotional [...] I describe it as abstract expressionist information – that you are taking information and manipulating it to create a sensibility. [...] I think the painting is all about being bombarded with media and how you see and hear things" [6] (see Fig. 1a). The letters, used as keywords based on data interpreted by the artistic filter and forming the topology of an actual and abstract place at the same time, derive their own meaningful powers from the expressive side of typography and the significant aesthetic layer rooted in the shape of the character, in their visual emphasis and stylistic morphology and create an impressive and impressionistic narrative of the places. "I began painting maps to invent my own complicated narrative about the way I see and feel about the world. I wanted to list what I know about a place from memory, from impressions, from media, and from general information overload. They are paintings of distortions" Scher finally states about the creation of her imaginative though relatable world [7]. "An irreverent, artful antidote to GPS appification" according to Popova "MAPS is a beautiful antidote to the sterile objectivity of location-aware apps and devices, reminiscent of Ward Shelley's analog data visualization and the poetic subjectivity of *You Are Here: Personal Geographies and Other Maps of the Imagination*" [8]. This approach to maps, then, seems to give back to cartography an emotional dimension able to reconnect with people, more like the community-driven Waze's *live map* app instead of the efficient and commercial representation of Google Maps.

Fig. 1. a) Paula Scher, Tsunami, 2006. *Paula Scher: MAPS*, Princeton University Press, 2011; b) Alighiero Boetti, *Mappa del mondo* 1971–73, embroidered linen canvas. Suzeau & Boetti Collection, Castello di Rivoli, Museo di Arte Contemporanea, Torino (WikiCommons).

A similar elaboration can also be found in the artistic work of Alighiero Boetti. Based on the first experimentation of the *Planisfero politico* (1969) [9] the *Game Plan* cartographies and atlases reproduce the outlines of states and continents on which the corresponding flags are imprinted. However, this weaving of images and colours, seemingly "realistic" in the heraldic symbology of the national flags, is interwoven with the materials and experiences of the author during his travels, e.g., in Afghanistan in 1971 and 1979 (see Fig. 1b). "*Mappa del Mundo* is a colorful, beautifully crafted tapestry showing each country emblazoned with its own flag, examining borders, frontiers, nationalism, and patriotism. The frames are emblazoned with Italian and Persian texts, selected by Boetti and the craftswomen. [...] Geopolitical changes were tracked throughout the world, transforming a simple idea into a political vision by visualizing territory disputes and regime changes." [10].

2 Urban Signs: The Vertical Side of a Horizontal Route

James Clough – a professional calligrapher, scholar, and professor at Politecnico di Milano – in his book about mapping the historical commercial and public sings in Italy mentions how "Intuitive, original and witty, improvised and elegant [...] From the ornate Tuscan style of the 19th century to the eccentric letters of Art Nouveau, from the grandiose architectural inscriptions of the 1930s to the delightful works of the surviving old sign painters, from Fascist ghost lettering to those on manhole covers" the signs and inscriptions are the mirror of the Italian society. "Even before typographic fonts dominated the scene, there was never any real standardisation in letter design in Italy and no manual for sign painters was ever printed. This freedom, detached from pre-established models, the skill of the craftsmen and their creativity make Italian signs so extraordinary." [11]. As Clough underlines, it is possible to follow the evolution of the urban space through shop signs and other signage systems, together with the style/language of graphic design as well as the transformation – political, social, economic – of the urban organism throughout time. Typeface styles – slab-serif and Romans – of the late 19th century, give way to the Deco, linear and then functionalist wave of the 20s and 30s that in some nations hybridise Modernism with political and propaganda connotations, as in the case of the Piacentini's public buildings, or other monumental public buildings that have left a profound identity mark in many Italian cities (see Fig. 2).

Scrolling through the 300 photographic images of the first edition, it is possible to notice how, from north to south, from city to city, the signs change and invent forms of vernacular expression, local aesthetics that represent the specific characteristics of places and in turn contribute to generating their identity: a great local and authorial variety, an intangible, graphic aesthetic, territorial and artistic heritage. Shops, buildings, and places, real or fictional, as narrated visually in extreme illustrative synthesis by Aoi Huber Kono [12], which correspond to places that did exist, every day and familiar places, shops, and workshops, once familiar and now disappearing or dying out.

According to the psychogeography approach, proposed by Gianni Biondillo [13] – architect, writer and professor of *Psychogeography and territory storytelling* at the University of Mendrisio, a "transdisciplinary practice where different areas of knowledge focusing on territory understanding converge: sociology, economy, geography, anthropology, urban planning, but also, literature, art, movie, philosophy and so on" – is by

Fig. 2. Public buildings from the fascist era in Bolzano, details of archigraphy and inscriptions (Photo: Beatrice Citterio)

walking that we experience the city enjoining it at a spatial, time-based and human scale, where the point of view is not the abstract zenithal and aseptic of a map, but rather an eye-vision based on a proprioceptive perspective, a multisensorial, haptic, embodied and situated exploration. Urban Typography, heraldic and commercial signs, wayfinding and signage systems, the visual noise of advertising become structural, meaningful, and connotative elements of the actual, personal, human, and social path through the experienced space. "The physical, emotional and aesthetic experience serves to overcome prejudice towards a space erroneously considered 'banal', predictable, taken for granted, in order to reach a new awareness of the everyday landscape, a palimpsest where the meanings and dreams of the populations that have inhabited it and still inhabit it are deposited. Finally, narrating means sharing the knowledge acquired, in the hope of stimulating in others, through storytelling, the desire to repeat the experience themselves [14]. The approach of walking as a way to access the knowledge of a territory reverberates in the geo-storytelling approaches [15] i.e., the way of narrating a place through geolocated information and contents to be explored *in-situ*, that means mediated by the space as a main driver [16].

3   Inquiring Space Through Typography

The research, then starts from two convergent point of view on typography. The first is deeply connected typographic culture although interpreted according to original perspectives.

Typography, like many other declinations of design culture, has in fact always been a generous and promising field for exploring, experimenting, and innovating design languages. Sometimes even a playful place to express one's personal poetics with relative freedom, as well as a vision – beyond – the times in which designers have found themselves operating. From the intellectual rigour of the Vignellis [17] and their refined formal repertoire concentrated on distilling archetypal forms – masterfully expressed in the New York underground map, indebted to the lesson of the Bauhaus and a certain *Milanese* culture – to the negation, beyond pure textuality, of the use of lettering made by Carson [18] (see Fig. 3a) – which declares the end of typography with the density of its overwriting, precisely to subvert the functional vocation, the readability, of the text and a structural incommunicability – the *dressed word*, as Monguzzi defines it is one of the structural and structuring elements of visual language shaping many experiences in our daily lives. Vice versa, Pierre di Sciullo's synaesthetic and multimodal typography (see Fig. 3b) that shouts or whispers the message [19] recovers the tone of voice, typical of the spoken word, and translates it into the visual dimension, just as Sagmesiter's [20] writing engraved on skin and flesh *physicalises* it by returning to the primordial form of engraving. From the forementioned typographic textures of Paula Scher, which create interwoven worlds of words and emotions, to the dynamic and parametric typography of David Jonathan Ross [21] (see Fig. 3c), which appropriates any possible space, reconfiguring itself to visualise the message it conveys, between graphic transcription of spoken words or unspoken ideas, typefaces are, therefore, a fundamental and indispensable element in the expressive range of visual design and human communication. Fonts are both expression of the vocation of a culture as well of the personal and professional approach of a designer, moreover, they can convey meaning "over-and-above the actual semantic content of whatever happens to be written" as declared by Sara Hyndman – of *Type tasting* research group in London – and the collogues Carlos Velasco, Andy Woods and Charles Spence of the Department of Experimental Psychology of the Oxford University in the liminal study *The taste of typeface* [22]. From this perspective, in fact, typefaces are not just absolving at the most cognitive, functional part of typography, i.e., to convey information and meaning thank the visual transcription or the graphical code, but rather rile on the most expressive side of them. The synesthetic component, pointed out experimentally by Hyndman's work, shows how typefaces activate interactions at a visceral level, that it at a perception one, enabling emotions, feeling connected to implicit values and meaning overcoming the pure visual component in favour of intangible ones deeply rooted on the personal as well as the collective experience.

Fig. 3. Typography a) David Carson b) Di Sciullo; c) Ross

The other approach here explored and adopted as a research format is the one developed by professor at University of São Paulo Prisicilla Lena Farias [23, 24] and further implemented in the Italian context in Venice by professor Bulegato and Bonini Lessing [25] at IUAV. Farias introduces the concept of *graphic memories* as a way to understand visual artifacts as a way to make sense of local identities through signs as contributes of "the design of a local graphic design history […] as a spatially situated and geographically located phenomena" [26] and she establishes the Memoria Grafica Paulistana/Tipografia Paulistana web site started in 2011, to show the results of the research brought out on the graphic memory of the city of São Paulo (2008–13) experience partially replicated in Venezia. While the project aimed to collect data from primary sources – letterpress printing shops heritage, newspaper and so on – and indirect or secondary sources – such as bibliography, literature review and documentary research – then interpreted, visualised and geolocated, to be navigated thank to different approaches, e.g. visual, logical [27] and filters, the experience held in Venice – recently presented by Bulegato & Bonini Lessing at SID conference in 2022 – is more focalised on the signage and way-finding system of the city i.e. the typescape of the city (see Fig. 4) the Venice urban lettering. In this second wave of the research, like the for mentioned exploration brought out by Clough, the focus is on the lettering on façades of commercial establishments able to convey a rich heritage of the evolution of the city, where historical signs are textured with graffiti and tags, transformed, overlapped, or dismissed according to the urban and social evolution of the environment.

Fig. 4. Venezia *typescape*: examples from the *Typographic Landscapes* web site (Photo: https://sites.google.com/usp.br/typescapes/venezia)

As in other cases, visual – such as color [28, 29], architectural styles and systems [30, 31] – sensory – soundscapes [32, 33], smells and/or other synesthetic perceptions– or other values emerge as possible drivers of people experience in connecting, appropriating, building and shaping the urban space and its symbolic and intangible values, typescape seems a promising way to explore and understand the planned environment as well the spontaneous social sedimentations.

4   Research Project: *Poros* u. *Laubengasse*

Poros u. Laubengasse. Typographic topology/Topographic typography is part of the wider research project, namely ALICE developed as a startup fund of the Free university of Bozen-Bolzano coordinated by professor Letizia Bollini, aimed to questioning the elements of the urban identity through intangible or implicit historical, and social values.

Given the cultural, linguistic, political, and architectural complexity of the context under investigation, the project has been divided into three phases, of which the first *Poros u. Laubengasse* explores the historical core of the city center (see Fig. 5).

Although in Italy there are other significant cities with a relevant heritage of covered-walkways, porticoes and colonnades – i.e., Bologna considered and awarded by UNESCO Intangible Heritage 2021 as the town with the world longest extension of arcades (62 km) – nevertheless the "Undergassen" are a significant element in Bolzano's urban morphology in terms of identity and historical evidence. In the western culture the porticoes are a significant structure, from the Stoà Poikìle in Athens to the spontaneous structures of the medieval period (those of bologna date back to the 11th century), from the planned architectures of the urban galleries of the late 19th century – like the Galeries Royales Saint-Hubert in Brussel, or the Galleria Umberto I in Naples – to the interior structures of now-decadent American malls [34], an osmotic poros between the public space of the street and squares and the diaphragm in between and the commercial or private one. The research project, according to the research method developed by Farias, identifies in the depicted heraldic, in the archigraphy, and in the commercial signs, i.e., the *typescape*, the promising key of interpretation of the historic and contemporary meaningful identity of the inner part of the city relating them to the spatial connection and evolution.

Fig. 5. Images of the Laubengasse/Via dei Portici in Bolzano (Photo: Beatrice Citterio)

4.1 Research Questions

The research project, according to the research method developed by Farias [35] and Farias, Bulegato & Bonini Lessing [25], identifies in the depicted heraldic, in the archigraphy, and in the commercial signs, i.e., the typescape, the promising key of interpretation of the historic and contemporary *meaningful* identity of the inner part of the city relating them to the spatial connection and evolution.

The proposed questions are oriented to 3 main research topics [36, 37]: a) the **urban** transformation; b) the **social** transformation; and c) the **cultural** transformation interpreted to indirect mean significant in the transformation of the *genius loci* i.e., the graphic memories and the built typescape. In particular the research questions are organised according to 4 macro areas:

1. Is it possible to adopt the typescape to understand and track back the historical evolution of the city center? And to map time-based thresholds of the urban and social transformation?
2. Is it possible to relay on the typescape to identify recurrent patterns connected to the cultural a linguistic to decodify intertwined aspects of the Bolzano's complex social identity?
3. Is it possible to adopt the typescape as an index of historical preservation or gentrification of the city center?
4. Is it possible to adopt the graphic memory to understand the sense of the local identity and spatial situated or geographically related phenomena?

4.2 Method

The first level of investigation adopted was that of graphic memories, precisely in order to make the study being developed on the typescape of Bolzano replicable and comparable with that already conducted, on the Italian territory, in Venice. A photographic mapping, which started from the street of the porticoes and which in the second and third phase of the research will be extended to the area beyond the Isarco (Oltreisarco) with characters and buildings from the fascist era and to the area of Gries, i.e. the conurbated part of German-speaking, or better to say – Süd Tyroler, culture. The photographic plan includes the mapping of the frontal and perpendicular signs to the internal perimeter of the porticoes with a subsequent correction of the distortion of the images due to the shallow depth of the building body or of the portico itself, thanks to the operational contribution of Beatrice Citterio, a student of the MD course in Eco-social design who collaborated in the mapping phases of the project. The images of individual house, and commercial spaces were then geolocalised and made accessible on Google Map[1] (see Fig. 6). The result should in fact be a potential further contribution to national mapping and the creation of a shared, interoperable database.

However, as the research questions are more extensive and focused on the urban, social and cultural transformations of the city of Bolzano, a second approach, based on time evolution [38] and the visual superposition of changes was adopted to understand and visualise the historical modifications of the urban area. Two strategies were adopted to develop this part of the research.

a) On the one hand, the photographs taken and those available on Street View were compared to understand the changes between the two mappings by referring to the dating of the images uploaded on the Google platform, as well as the collective memory with reference to the last three years (2020 since the beginning of the COVID emergency that has had a significant impact on the commercial activities) thanks to

---

[1] Map available at URL: https://www.google.com/maps/d/u/0/viewer?mid=1OVc6L9nLOndxuy h2cFnyMFk-bG1vz88&ll=46.499331367792706%2C11.35465623927816&z=18.

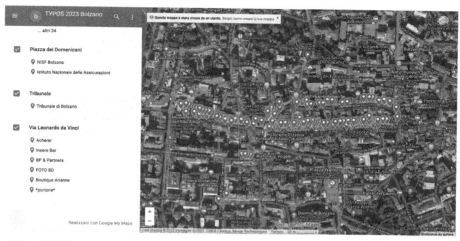

Fig. 6. Urban photography safari geolocated on Google Maps (Credits: Beatrice Citterio)

interviews. How the prospects of the wall curtain from Piazza del Municipio Vecchio to Via del Museo have changed in just 3 years is visible thank to the association between the images and the platform (see Fig. 7).

b) On the other hand, indirect sources have been explored to find the previous destination of the building, nowadays mainly occupied by shops of multinational companies and international brand franchising. Research in the historical archive of the city of Bolzano (Archivio Storico Città di Bolzano[2]) to find historical pictures of the porticoes to compare with the current ones, postcards or any other visual documentation of the previous destination or topology of the area. Secondly an extensive bibliographic and literature review is in progress to find direct or indirect mentions and documental about the destination, private or commercial of the spaces of the covered walk side. In particular, following the suggestions of Dr. W. Kofler Engel [39] director of the Platform Cultural Heritage Cultural Production (https://www.culturalheritage.unibz.it/) of the Free University of Bozen-Bolzano and previously director of the Department for the preservation of Monuments of the Province, the monography *Häsergeschicthe von Altbozen* [40] has been adopted as reference to go back to the intended use of buildings since the eighteenth century. The book in fact tracks back the property of the building of the city center specifying if they were meant for private o company/commercial use. Combining these primary and secondary sources will, then, allow to reconstruct the evolution of the Laubengasse and the rest of the urban territory.

---

[2] http://www.comune.bolzano.it/cultura_context.jsp?ID_LINK=782&area=48.

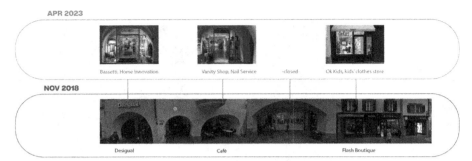

Fig. 7. Comparison between a) Photosafari 2023 (Photo: Beatrice Citterio) and b) Google Street View

4.3   Case Study: Augmenting Experience

However, the original method implies the mapping of the archigraphies and commercial signs on a (*Google*) map, the ALICE research project final scope is to explore the potentialities of *phygital* storytelling [41, 42] in the field of cultural, intangible and landscape heritage. For this reason, a mobile application based on Augmented Reality has been proposed and prototyped in order to offer a different experience when navigating the urban space, together with the geobased-visual and logical information offered on the map [27]. Having the possibility to discover a different story and to visualise a previous configuration of the porticoes make people more conscious and aware of the overall evolution of the street and the surroundings to favor a) a connection between *citisens* – used to the place, but probably blind to the longitudinal as well to the micro transformation constantly reshaping the urban identity – and the historical and contemporary evolution of the city; b) *tourists* attracted by a postcard-picture of the city – crystalised in a stereo-typical image but disconnected from the previous heritage– and not aware of the overall gentrification of the more characteristic area of downtown together with Piazza delle Erbe; c) *off-site students*, a huge community living in the city for a specific period of their lives but somehow reluctant to connect or commit to penetrating deeper into the identity of the city; among the possible persona *spectrums* [43] developed for the project.

The phygital mobile application[3] *Bolzano-Bozen Typescape AR app* (see Fig. 8) becomes the moment in the research development, in which, in a practice-based research perspective, conjectures at a more theoretical level are translated into an interaction model to be subsequently validated. In particular, the application aims to propose to the identified personas, as potential privileged interlocutors of the project, an alternative experience of the city, even in its more historical and everyday parts, but perhaps for this reason the more stereotyped. Inspired by previous case studies developed mainly in the last decade – thank to the raise of geobased social media such as Four Square, primitive metaverses of 3D interactive environments, e.g. Second Life, and, of course, by the

---

[3] Prototype available at URL: https://www.figma.com/proto/fDON9tKYInkT4v3TQC994y/bolzano-ar?node-id=1-2&scaling=scale-down&page-id=0%3A1&starting-point-node-id=1%3A2.

introduction of mobile devices – the application proposes, and hybrid navigation played on a dual level. On the one hand, augmented reality makes it possible –using tags and the idea of proximity – to transform the house and shops under the arcades into touchpoints, i.e. *points of interest* that make it possible to explore the place using the typescape as a key conceptual and visual access key. AR is indeed the way to introduce a different narrative of place based on generous interfaces [44], but above all designed to conduct people to looking at reality from a different perspective. Historical documents, archive images, and direct and indirect testimonies configure an enriched and augmented alternative image, not only in technological standpoint. An immersion in images and stories that restore to the fleeting visit focused on large buildings of historical cultural importance and monuments, to the distracted stroll or daily transit, the depth of the intangible culture that created this heritage and its evolution not only in historical, but above all in human, social and urban terms. Connected to the map and the geolocalised points on it, the application also allows users to take 'historical selfies', i.e. in a process of participation and sharing, to create selfies set on the historical stage or, better still, on the augmented superimposition of images, photos, sketches and archival visual materials.

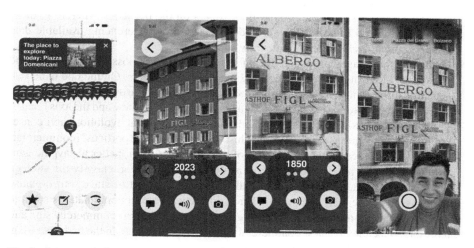

Fig. 8. Images of the *Bolzano-Bozen Typescape AR app* prototype (Credits: Maria Letizia Mastroianni)

The AR mobile application prototype is meant to be tested with people – according to human-centered and qualitative methods – in order to understand main potentialities of the proposed situated interactions:

a) How a phygital approach, namely an hybridization between physical – spaces – and digital – augmented and overlayed information – in exploring a cultural, intangible, distributed heritage environment can improve knowledge sharing and awareness.

b) The role of social perception of the typescape in terms of local culture connected to the specificity of the trilingual history of the city, i.e., Italian, German and Ladin-speaking communities.

c) The impact of mass tourism in the gentrification dynamics of the city center and the progressive falsification of the identity of the place and the sustainability according to the slow movement/tourism approach.
d) The potentialities of using the application in eliciting narrations and testimonies that map the recent evolution of the territory through collective memory.

4.4 Discussion

In this first exploratory phase, some patterns seem to emerge when thinking both to the archighraphy and the commercial signs, that is the typescape.

a) A first pattern seems to emerge from the comparison between the actual occupation of the spaces in the porticoes and the historical records of the ownership transfer of the properties, in the majority of cases [40] the real estate is mainly belonging and presumably for private use and only in recent time have been put to commercial use. The *Häsergeschhichte von Altbozen* monography just mentions if the ownership belongs to a private subject or to a company that allegedly buys it for commercial purposes. However, it is not possible to infer from this data the intended use of the entire building or of the ground-floor rooms on the porticoes. Therefore, these assumptions need to be further verified thanks to cross-referencing available data with additional archival or documentary sources.
b) Gathering the images produced during the photo-safari is possible to classify and cluster the elements depicted according to shared parameters. On the one hand two semantic differentials, to be possibly used interviewing people during the user-testing phase have been proposed: the axis heritage—contemporary/new and the axis local—global. The first couple is aimed to understand the historical evolution, and consequently the renovation, or the erasure of historical traces of the porticos' (commercial) space, while the second is an indicator of the globalisation or, better to say, the gentrification, of this area. After a careful analysis to identify and classify the subject, pictures have been distributed on a scaled timeline – a sort of stave – to organise the materials to be then interpreted. Three different recurrent combinations seem to appear: 1) old commercial signs and a preserved façade; 2) a new commercial sign and a preserved façade; 3) a new commercial sign and a new façade. In the first case – e.g. the Apotheke zur Madonna where the mural inscriptions survived on both sides of the arcades and indeed are intentionally restored (see Fig. 9) – the typescape is preserved and part of the environment heritage, although evolved as a living organism.

Fig. 9. Farmacia Madonna/Apotheke zur Madonna (Photo: Beatrice Citterio)

The second condition is well represented by in Fig. 10. The local apparel company "Maximilian" – a condensed san-serif typeface – is nestled in the ancient frame of the under portico, artistically and richly decorated under portico, a reminder of a bygone time and urban style.

Fig. 10. Maximilian Basic, local apparel company (Photo: Beatrice Citterio)

Finally, the third possible combination, that means when a globalized or multinational company locates a store in the historical context without any connection with it (see Fig. 11). Both the shop signs and the windows are totally indifferent to the porticos structure and identity following standardized guidelines imposing the same architectural style in every country.

The impact of gentrification on urban historical structure and morphology is particularly evident in this last example. Not only the private space has been progressively eroded in favor of the commercial destinations, but the latter are more oriented to satisfy shopping and consumeristic behaviors – also intercepting city-users and tourists – rather than satisfying the daily needs and dynamics of residents and citizens. Furthermore, resident population – according to filtering-down theories – is

Fig. 11. One of the 575 worldwide Terranova's shops/franchising (Photo: Beatrice Citterio)

likely to be pushed away from the city center for the benefit of Airbnb and other short-term rental services and digital platforms.

c) The porticos in Bolzano – compared to those in Bologna, for instance – are rather low and narrow. This characteristic creates several difficulties in the photo mapping. Moreover, perhaps because of this limitation, historical images, such as postcards, do not depict the under portico, but the facades of the houses, making it difficult, if not impossible, to identify historical signs or to infer the private or public use of the spaces (see Fig. 12).

Fig. 12. Historical pictures of the Laubengassen (Source: *AltBozen*)

5   Conclusions

The project described here in its general outline and in its first operational phase, starting in the first quarter of 2023, intends to explore a different key to the level of urban territory, the development and evolution of its identity through parameters linked to the production of graphic signs or graphic memories that constitute its typescape of the city of Bozen-Bolzano. On the one hand, the project proposes an original and alternative approach that explores, through material, spatial, social but at the same time intangible values, the identity of the city and its historical, urban social and political evolution. On the other hand, it uses a methodology that has already been developed and tested in three different urban contexts – as mentioned São Paulo in Brazil, London and Venice – to make the model itself reproducible and interoperable and, in the future, to participate in a possible mapping exercise involving other cities, at least in the Italian territory, rich in experiences, cultures and ideas from the point of view of both local and vernacular cultures and artistic, graphic and typographic.

To do this, two design paths were adopted: a graphic and typographical mapping of heraldic and commercial signs, starting from the central and historically most relevant part of the original urban core, compared with primary and indirect archive and documentary sources mapping and research, which will be expanded in three successive stages to the rest of the urban text with particular attention to the Italian area developed from the 1920s-30s beyond the Isarco river and the German area of Gries.

The second line of research development focused on aspects of experience and interaction for potential target groups identified in the area, translated into a mobile application in which augmented reality becomes the driver of access to and interaction with content and historical-cultural narratives of the area. The forms of reality mediated by technology – augmented, virtual, mixed or blend – allow an exploration that tries to reproduce the three-dimensionality of the world or to enter a direct relationship with it in a situated experience augmented and enriched by the technology itself. Besides, the perspectives opened up by the typescape approach and, in general, by the use of graphic memories as a way to read the urban fabric offers an original point of view both for the people exploring the space thanks to mobile device and the Augmented Reality, as well as for designers widening the 2D possibilities of the visual/touch based interfaces. The combination of these two factors in mobility creates the scenario to transform space-related data into a narrative concept to be explored using one's own situated senses.

Acknowledgements. Although the paper is the joint work of both the authors, Letizia Bollini is author in particular of paragraphs 1, 2, 3, 4 and 5, and Maria Letizia Mastroianni is author of paragraph 4.3 and responsible for the development of the project prototype.

The authors want to acknowledge and thanks Dr. Waltraud Kofler Engel for the precious and generous support in the historical and bibliographical research and the engaging conversations about the city of Bozen-Bolzano and its cultural, social and political evolution.

A special thanks to Beatrice Citterio for the urban photography safari and the visual materials of the city of Bozen-Bolzano pinned on Google Map.

The here presented research is part of the wider project ALICE coordinated by Professor Letizia Bollini, as principal investigator, and funded as a *Start Up project* by the Free University of Bozen-Bolzano.

References

1. Ghirri, L.: Atlante, The place to be MAXXI (1973). https://www.maxxi.art/en/events/luigi-ghirri-atlante/
2. Scher, P.: Maps. Princeton Architectural Press (2011)

3. Gérard Genette, Palimpsestes. La littérature au second degré, SEUIL 1982. (Palinsesti. La letteratura al secondo grado, tr. Raffaella Novità, Torino: Einaudi, 1997)
4. Simon, W.: The Map That Changed the World. http://www.simonwinchester.com/
5. Binlot, A.: A la carte: Paula Scher's American maps chart more than just territory (2022). https://www.wallpaper.com/art/paula-schers-american-maps-chart-more-than-just-territory
6. PRINT. Designer Interviews. Paula Scher's Mind-Bending Maps. Thumbnail for Paula Scher's Mind-Bending Maps. By PrintMagPosted (2020). https://www.printmag.com/designer-interv iews/paula-scher-maps/
7. Scher, P.: All Maps Lie. Design Observer (2011). All maps lie: https://designobserver.com/ feature/all-maps-lie/30828
8. Popova, M.: Paula Scher's Maps.Stunning Subjectivity: Obsessive Typographic Maps by Paula Scher (2011). https://www.themarginalian.org/2011/10/21/paula-scher-maps/
9. Archivio Alighiero Boetti. https://www.archivioalighieroboetti.it/timeline_slider_post/1969/
10. Alighiero Boetti's beautiful Maps of the World, Public Delivery. https://publicdelivery.org/ alighiero-boetti-mappa-del-mundo/
11. Clough, J.: L'italia insegna, Lazy Dog (2015)
12. Kono, A.H.: I negozi, Crazy Dog (2022). https://lazydog.eu/product/i-negozi/
13. Gianni, B.: Sentieri metropolitani. Narrare il territorio con la psicogeografia. Con QR Code, Bollati e Boringhierei (2022)
14. Gianni, B.: Psicogeografia e narrazioni del territorio (2013). http://www.psicogeografia.com/# home
15. Bollini, L., Facchini, C.: I wish you were here. Designing a geostorytelling ecosystem for enhancing the small heritages' experience. In: Gervasi, O., Murgante, B., Misra, S., Ana, M.A., Rocha, C., Garau, C. (eds.) ICCSA 2022, pp. 457–472. Springer, Cham (2022). https:// doi.org/10.1007/978-3-031-10562-3_32
16. Bollini, L.: A human-centered perspective on interactive data visualization. A digital flâneries into the documentation of Historical Italian Mind Science Archive. In: Ceccarelli, N., Jiménez-Martínez, C. (eds.) 2CO Communicating Complexity 2017, pp. 106–114. Universidad de La Laguna, Santa Cruz de Tenerife (2020). https://doi.org/10.25145/b.2COcommunicating.202 0.013
17. Massimo, V., Bob, N.: New York City Transit Authority's Graphic Standards Manual, Unimark (1970)
18. Carson, D.: The End of Print: The Graphic Design of David Carson. Chronicle Books (1995)
19. Po, G. (ed.): Pierre di Sciullo. Pyramyd (2003)
20. Stefan, S.: Things I have learned in my life so far. Abrams (2008)
21. Ross, D.J.: Fit typeface. In: Kerning Conference (2018). https://djr.com/fit
22. Hyndman, S.: Why Fonts Matter: a multisensory analysis of typography and its influence from graphic designer and academic Sarah Hyndman. Random House (2016)
23. Silva Gouveia, A.P., Lena Farias, P., Souza Gatto, P.: Letters and cities: reading the urban environment with the help of perception theories. Vis. Commun. 8(3), 339–348 (2009). https:// doi.org/10.1177/1470357209106474
24. Farias, P.L.: On the concept of graphic memory. Bitácora Urbano Territorial 27(4special), 61 (2017)
25. Emanuela Bonini Lessing Lessing Fiorella Bulegato Priscila Lena Farias 2020 Italian Typographic Heritage: A Contribution to Its Recognition and Interpretation as Part of Design Heritage. ICDHS 12 - 12th Conference of the International Committee for Design History and Design StudiesAt: Zagreb
26. Farias, P.L.: Epígrafes arquitetônicas paulistanas e londrinas: uma comparação sob a perspectiva do design da informação. InfoDesign - Revista Brasileira De Design Da Informação 12(2), 222–238 (2015). https://doi.org/10.51358/id.v12i2.391

27. Bollini, L., Cerletti, V.: Knowledge sharing and management for local community: logical and visual georeferenced information access. In: International Conference on Enterprise Information Systems and Web Technologies (EISWT 2009), pp. 92–99. ISRST (2009)

28. Klinkhammer, B.: The spatial use of color in early modernism. In: FORBES, Geraldine & MALECHA, Marvin. 87th ACSA Annual Meetings, Legacy. 87th ACSA Annual Meeting. ACSA–Association of Collegiate Schools of Architecture (1999)

29. Bollini, L., Limido, C.M.: The role of color in the urban and social image regeneration: from the Zukunftskathedrale to Street art. In: Colour and Colorimetry: Multidisciplinary Contributions-Volume XVB; Proceedings of the 15th Conferenza del Colore, Macerata, Italia, 5–7 Settembre 2019, pp. 63–70. Gruppo del Colore (2019)

30. Davide, L.: The image of the City. MIT Press (1969)

31. Saul, W.R.: Understanding USA, Rswinc (1999)

32. Schafer, R.M.: The soundscape: our sonic environment and the tuning of the world. In: InnerTraditions/Bear & Co., p. 10 (1993)

33. Bollini, L., Fazia, I.D.: Situated emotions. The role of the soundscape in a geo-based multimodal application in the field of cultural heritage. In: Gervasi, O., et al. (eds.) ICCSA 2020. LNCS, vol. 12251, pp. 805–819. Springer, Cham (2020). https://doi.org/10.1007/978-3-030-58808-3_58

34. Bollini, L.: Territorio e rappresentazione. Paesaggi urbani. Paesaggi sociali. Paesaggi digitali. Rimini e l'altro mediterraneo. In: Giovannini, M., Prampolini, F. (eds.) Spazi e culture del Mediterraneo, vol. 3, pp. 28–42. Edizioni Centro Stampa di Ateneo, Reggio Calabria (2011)

35. Michel, L.: Hyper-lieux: Les nouvelles géographies de la mondialisation, SEUIL (2017)

36. Farias, P.L.: Visualizing data on graphic memory research. In: Fadel, L.M., Santa Rosa, J.G., Portugal, C. (eds.) Selected Readings of the 8th Information Design International Conference, pp. 93–114 (2019)

37. Bollini, L.: Territories of digital communities. Representing the social landscape of web relationships. In: Murgante, B., Gervasi, O., Iglesias, A., Taniar, D., Apduhan, B.O. (eds.) ICCSA 2011. LNCS, vol. 6782, pp. 501–511. Springer, Heidelberg (2011). https://doi.org/10.1007/978-3-642-21928-3_36

38. Bollini, L., Begotti, D.: The time machine. cultural heritage and the geo-referenced storytelling of urban historical metamorphose. In: Gervasi, O., et al. (eds.) ICCSA 2017. LNCS, vol. 10406, pp. 239–251. Springer, Cham (2017). https://doi.org/10.1007/978-3-319-62398-6_17

39. Waltraud, K.E. (ed.) La Casa della Pesa a Bolzano. Folio Editore (2022)

40. Heinz, T.B., Seidner, H., Mair, G.: Häusergeschichte von Altbozen. Athesia (2017)

41. Bollini, L.: Virtual & augmented reality representation. Experiencing the cultural heritage of a place. In: Pellegri, G. (ed.) De-sign Environment Landscape City, pp. 572–583. Genova University Press, Genova (2018)

42. Bollini, L.: The third way: hybrid scenarios from multimodal publishing. ArtLab 38, 44–47 (2011)

43. Holmes, K.: Mismatch. How Inclusion Shapes Design. MIT Press (2019)

44. Mitchell, W.: Generous interfaces for digital cultural collections. Digit. Hum. Q. 9(1), 1–16 (2015)

Spatial Tools and ppWebGIS Platforms for Sustainable Urban Development and Climate Change Adaptation

Participatory Planning in Urban Areas with Special Conditions

Eleni Mougiakou[1,2](✉) ⓘ, Yannis Parskevopoulos[1] ⓘ, and Sofia Tsadari[1] ⓘ

[1] Commonspace coop, Akakiou 1 - 3 & Ipirou 60, 10439 Athens, Greece
mougiakou@commonspace.gr
[2] Agricultural University of Athens, Iera Odos 75, 11855 Athens, Greece
https://www.commonspace.gr, https://www.participatorylab.org

Abstract. In the last decades, a shift towards more democratic, participatory processes has occurred, rooted in the need to address environmental problems and climate change threats. Moreover, these participatory processes have been increasingly required in today's spatial plans, strategies, and studies, for example, in Sustainable Urban Mobility Plans, Urban Climate Change Adaptation and Resilience Plans, and Sustainable Development Plans. In this context, academia and industry have built various public participation web-based solutions (ppWebGIS) and other geospatial participation tools to facilitate participatory procedures and support and inform the participants (planners, policymakers, citizens, etc.) towards spatial decision-making.

However, despite the recent advancements in methodological and technological participatory geospatial tools, they are weak in addressing the complex issues found in "outlier" urban areas, i.e., areas with challenging conditions and characteristics. This paper introduces a comprehensive methodological framework for participatory spatial planning that conceptualizes and utilizes geospatial tools and platforms to address the challenges and opportunities in areas with special conditions. As part of an ongoing research program, the paper's main contribution is to provide methodological innovation for participatory spatial planning in areas with special conditions through conceptualizing and implementing participatory geospatial tools to solve complex and multifactorial spatial problems.

Keywords: urban planning · participatory planning · ppWebGIS · ppGIS · geospatial · sustainable development · climate change

1 Introduction

Geographical Information Systems (GIS) can support multicriteria analysis through structured procedures for spatial decision-making [1, 2]. When the involvement of citizens, stakeholders, and experts is decisive in decision-making, then the concept of ppGIS is most appropriate. Public Participation Geographic Information Systems (PPGIS) was

© The Author(s) 2023
O. Gervasi et al. (Eds.): ICCSA 2023 Workshops, LNCS 14105, pp. 630–645, 2023.
https://doi.org/10.1007/978-3-031-37108-0_40

introduced in 1996 during the National Centre for Geographic Information and Analysis (NCGIA) meeting. The term ppGIS appears in the U.S. and is mainly used in developed countries. PGIS is often used to describe participatory design approaches in developing countries' rural areas [3].

In the context of the United Nations' Sustainable Development Goals (SDGs)[1], UN-Habitat[2], the new European Climate Change Adaptation Strategy[3], the new Horizon Missions[4], and the New European Bauhaus initiative[5], the role of advances and multi-level participation is crucial (Table 1). This approach recognizes that effective planning and design requires a collaborative and inclusive process that involves all stakeholders and considers their diverse perspectives and needs.

Table 1. Participation is an essential element in different global approaches

Approach	Participation elements
Sustainable Development Goals (SDGs)	• engaging local communities and marginalized groups to ensure that their needs and aspirations are fully considered • partnerships between governments, civil society, and the private sector in achieving the SDGs
UN-Habitat	• empowering communities and involving them in decision-making processes that affect their lives • recognizes the need to address social exclusion and inequality issues, particularly in urban areas, to promote sustainable development and social justice
Climate Adaptation and Resilience	• engaging stakeholders in developing and implementing strategies to address climate change's impacts • requires a collaborative and inclusive process that involves all stakeholders, including vulnerable populations
Horizon missions	• address some of society's significant challenges, such as climate change, energy, and health • emphasize the importance of involving stakeholders in co-creating and implementing solutions to these challenges
New European Bauhaus	• collaborative, multidisciplinary, multi-stakeholders participation, co-design of transformative projects, initiatives, and measures

---

[1] https://sdgs.un.org/goals.

[2] https://unhabitat.org/.

[3] https://climate.ec.europa.eu/eu-action/adaptation-climate-change/eu-adaptation-strategy_en.

[4] https://research-and-innovation.ec.europa.eu/funding/funding-opportunities/funding-progra mmes-and-open-calls/horizon-europe/eu-missions-horizon-europe_en.

[5] https://new-european-bauhaus.europa.eu/index_en.

This paper intends to present a concept and methodology for participatory spatial planning that employs geospatial tools and participatory platforms to tackle urban areas' unique challenges and possibilities. As an ongoing research program element, the paper's primary contribution lies in its innovative methodology and technology for participatory spatial planning in areas with special conditions through conceptualizing and implementing participatory geospatial tools to solve complex and multifactorial spatial problems.

1.1 Background

This paper is part of the research project "eLEONAS ppWebGIS: PARTICIPATORY PLANNING PLATFORM FOR SUSTAINABLE DEVELOPMENT". The main objective of "eLEONAS ppWebGIS" research project is to design and develop participatory design processes and tools to support spatial decision-making for development, planning, and intervention in urban areas presenting specific challenges and/or potentials. It aims to introduce participatory design in the Integrated Planning for Sustainable Development [4] as a "system" useful for multiple spatial scales and planning applications that directly address public needs.

1.2 Literature Overview and Trends in Public Participation Platforms and Tools

In the last decade, the academy and industry have built numerous digital participation tools and ppWebGIS solutions to support spatial decision-making [5]. The ppWebGIS solutions cover different needs and appear as autonomous tools, plugins, or integrated platforms. An increased interest is noted in strategic, urban, and environmental planning, especially regarding sustainable development, as well as climate change adaptation and resilience.

A semi-systematic approach [6] is employed to explore the progress of public participation tools and platforms in the urban context. Primarily, the database Scopus (https://www.scopus.com/) is used, updated on 20 April 2023. An iteration of three queries to refine the results and highlight the trends in research. All research queries are searched into the papers' titles, abstracts, and keywords. All languages, document types, years, and countries are included. Three subject areas are excluded (Biochemistry, Genetics and Molecular Biology; Medicine; Pharmacology, Toxicology and Pharmaceutics).

The first query[6] explores the presence of public participation web-platforms, integrated with GIS technologies. The result shows **842** documents. As shown in Fig. 1, research interest is increasing, with a maximum in 2019 (75/842 document results). Regarding subject areas, Social science, Environmental science, Computer science, and Earth and Planetary Sciences hold most of the related research.

---

[6] TITLE-ABS-KEY (pp*web*gis OR ppgis OR pgis OR soft*gis) AND (EXCLUDE (SUBJAREA, "BIOC") OR EXCLUDE (SUBJAREA, "MEDI") OR EXCLUDE (SUBJAREA, "PHAR")).

Documents by year

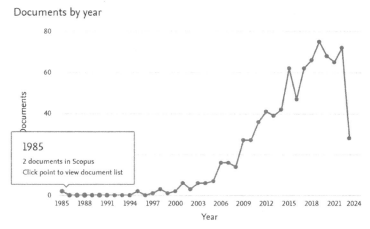

Documents by subject area

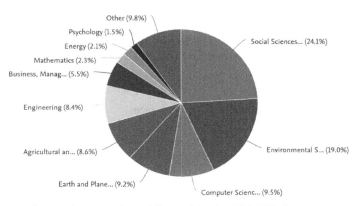

Fig. 1. Progress of research concerning public participation WebGIS platforms, across time and subject areas, through Scopus

The second[7] round of research explores the focus of the first round results in the urban context. The result shows **230** documents. The final[8] refinement search results to only **31** documents from 842, discuss public participation platforms and tools integrated with WebGIS technologies, under the concept of climate change, resilience, or sustainability, in the urban context. As shown in Fig. 2, almost 60% have been published in the last five years; the COVID 19 restrictions impact the field [7, 8]; an ascending number

---

[7] (TITLE-ABS-KEY (pp*web*gis OR ppgis OR pgis OR soft*gis)) AND (TITLE-ABS-KEY (urban OR city OR cities)) AND (EXCLUDE (SUBJAREA, "BIOC") OR EXCLUDE (SUBJAREA, "MEDI") OR EXCLUDE (SUBJAREA, "PHAR")).

[8] (TITLE-ABS-KEY (pp*web*gis OR ppgis OR pgis OR soft*gis)) AND (TITLE-ABS-KEY (urban OR city OR cities)) AND (TITLE-ABS-KEY ("climate change*" OR "resilien*" OR sustainabl*)) AND (EXCLUDE (SUBJAREA, "BIOC") OR EXCLUDE (SUBJAREA, "MEDI") OR EXCLUDE (SUBJAREA, "PHAR")).

of projects explore urban green ecosystem services, whereas 2020 concentrates the maximum number of documents.

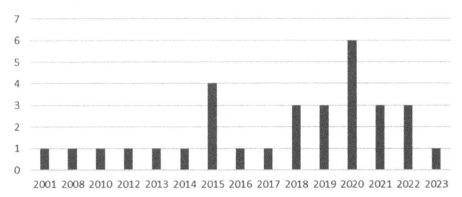

Fig. 2. Documents per year (31 selected by the final query in the Scopus database)

We analyzed the content of the 31 chosen documents related to the different thematic areas relevant to Integrated Planning for Sustainable Development. The eight thematic areas are:

1. Sustainability
2. Adaptation to climate change, risk, or resilience
3. Mobility
4. Ecosystem services
5. Urban Green Spaces
6. Landscape
7. Smart
8. Waste management

Four documents are not included in the following table because they did not meet the criteria of thematic relevance. The remaining 27 documents are presented in Table 2 per thematic area.

Different scales are presented in the selected documents, city [8–10, 16, 22, 28], neighborhood [7, 20, 29, 32], street [11], or other local scales [7, 20, 29]. Most of the documents are related to surveys or spatial questionnaires and ascertain that most cases are limited to low engagement levels (inform or consult) [7–9, 11, 16, 21, 22, 28, 29]. Lastly, an interested critic is deployed [32] to discuss the "elitist and undemocratic" view of ppGIS technologies, exploring contradictory results, empowerment, and dependency.

Table 2. Documents per thematic area

Thematic areas	Documents
Sustainability	[9–15]
Adaptation to climate change, risk or resilience	[12, 16–20]
Mobility	[7, 9, 21–23]
Ecosystem services	[8, 24–27]
Urban Green Spaces	[8, 22, 28, 29]
Landscape	[11, 24, 30]
Smart	[10, 14]
Waste management	[31]

2 Conceptual and Methodological Framework

Planners, consultants, and policymakers use participatory planning combined with WebGIS platforms all over the world to cover the needs of:

- different planning phases [33]
- different levels of engagement [34]
- various methods and technics of public participation [35]

Even though the market offers many solutions regarding basic participatory planning procedures[9], like collaborative whiteboards[10], and teleconference platforms[11], in this paper, we focus on the spatial and online aspects of participatory tools[12,13]. More specifically, we focus on ppWebGIS platforms and tools covering participatory needs of Sustainable Development plans as well as Climate Change Adaptation and Resilience plans and strategies. These emerging and urgent aspects of planning include public and expert participation as fundamental pillars and data-driven spatial decisions (big data).

Drafting Sustainable Development/Climate Change Adaptation and Resilience Plans and Strategies (see Fig. 3) includes different scales (e.g., neighborhood, local, city, regional, national) at different timelines (e.g., months or years until implementation). Those Action Plans and Strategies propose and aim at different goals, depending on the planning phases (assessment, draft, implementation, revision). To achieve those goals, the Action Plan/Strategy describes several projects or actions, in diverse and complementary thematic areas, usually in different spatial units. These plans are inter-disciplinary and trans-disciplinary high complexity problems and need advanced

---

[9] Padlet (https://padlet.com/), Google docs (https://www.google.com/docs/about/).

[10] Miro (https://miro.com/), Mural (https://www.mural.co/).

[11] Zoom (https://zoom.us/).

[12] GISCloud (https://www.giscloud.com/), Maptionnaire (https://maptionnaire.com), ArcGIS online (https://www.arcgis.com/index.html).

[13] ppCITY (https://ppcity.getmap.gr/dev/), participatory LAB (https://platform.participatorylab.org/; https://www.participatorylab.org/).

participation procedures supported by big data (e.g., geodata, climate, Copernicus, census).

To cover those advanced participation needs, planners and consultants use different digital tools, depending on their and the participants' digital skills, according to the project requirements, methods, and technics used. Public participation WebGIS platforms can facilitate multiple users (e.g., experts, stakeholders, the general public, targeted audience), more than the actual numbers to approach through physical meetings. Also, it can easily facilitate procedures, like the Delphi method, that demand several iterations from the participants, usually from experts, to support prediction, prioritization, planning, and generally spatial decision-making.

At the same time, ppWebGIS offers the opportunity to consult and include complex and big geospatial data (e.g., IoT, sensors, city planning datasets, Copernicus data, and many more) during the participatory procedures. Finally, the quick and reliable ways to analyze and summarize results and to export and use the participants' input as another geospatial layer in spatial analysis make the procedure very powerful.

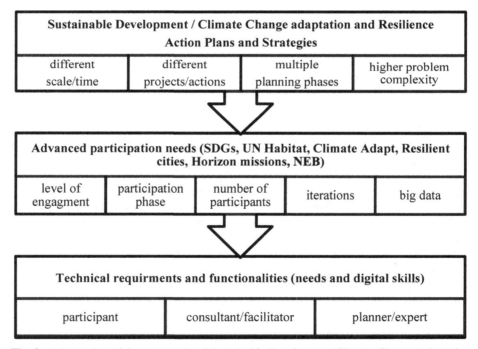

Fig. 3. Advanced participatory needs of Sustainable Development/Climate Change Adaptation and Resilience Action Plans and Strategies

The appropriate functional requirements focus on the three main groups involved in the process **a.** the participants with their diversity, **b.** the consultant/facilitator including the local authority **c.** the interdisciplinary team of planners/experts. The functional requirements are approached step by step by planners and consultants, considering the different participant profiles.

In this context, a significant contribution of this paper is that it introduces a comprehensive methodological framework suitable for urban areas with special conditions but, more importantly, appropriate for different participatory planning applications (i.e., spatial planning, climate change adaptation, and cultural heritage sustainability). The developed methodological framework is structured in the following steps:

- **Investigation, management, and exploratory analysis of available secondary data**; to establish a baseline knowledge of AoI's characteristics and challenges, but more importantly, to identify the information gaps of the secondary data
- **Fieldwork for primary data collection**; to acquire the required detailed knowledge for the Area of Interest, which is key for participatory planning.
- **Analysis of the existing situation of the Area of Interest**; resulting in a comprehensive report describing the characteristics, needs, and challenges of the area of interest, formulating specific questions and objectives as input for the participatory procedures.
- **Participatory procedures**; relevant to different participatory planning applications and multi-level participation of experts, policymakers, stakeholders, and the public.
- **Scenarios and Alternatives**, the different scenarios and alternatives are visualized and included in a WebGIS environment facilitating the participation of various stakeholders.
- **Final consultation, community activation, and engagement**; which refers to innovative tools and methods for community activation and engagement (digital narratives, Location Based Social Network, and Phydigital path.

Table 3 describes the tools developed during the eLeonas project for each methodological step.

The aim is to introduce participatory planning in the **Integrated Planning for Sustainable Development** as a sub-system of it that can deliver on multiple scales while responding directly to public needs. Participatory processes that are emphasized respond to the following design/public needs:

- **Prediction**, where the involvement of experts is critical to the best possible approach and uncertainty reduction.
- **Planning**, where the involvement of multiple stakeholders is vital for the success of development and spatial planning.
- **Prioritization** (risks, measures, and actions), where the involvement of the general public, specialists, and other stakeholders (e.g., policymakers) determines the effectiveness of the proposed interventions.

3 Pilot Area - eLeonas Research Project

Eleonas is an urban area of Athens (see Fig. 4) in a strategic position between the capital city of Athens and the port city of Piraeus. It is intersected by important regional transport infrastructure and thus is a central transport hub for metropolitan Athens. It concentrates a multitude of -often contrasting- uses, functions, and activities such as

Table 3. Description of tools developed for each methodological step

Steps	Tools
Investigation, management, and exploratory analysis of available secondary data	• Geospatial database for storing and managing the data of each participatory planning application (satellite data, vector, tabular data): - Utilization of available open data sources - Utilization of proprietary and commercial datasets - Products from desk research • Project Repository, library (CKAN), for making project data available as open (in the cases that the existing license of the data permits it)
Fieldwork for primary data collection	• Mobile devices (cameras, smartphones, tablets) for fieldwork data collection: - Data collection via 360° spheres - Data collection via thermal camera and wearables - Digital geospatial tools for collecting primary data by filling digital forms (street audits, questionnaires, etc.) • Management and visualization of fieldwork data in a WebGIS environment, with the development of new functionalities for: - managing and visualizing 360° spheres and paths - crowd-sensed data from wearables - georeferenced fieldwork data
Analysis of the existing situation of the Area of Interest	• Development of open-source QGIS plugins as spatial analysis tools regarding: - implementation of various geo-visualization alternatives - custom-made and editable models of spatial analysis • Geo-visualization of the results in WebGIS

(*continued*)

Table 3. (*continued*)

Steps	Tools
Participatory procedures	• Multi-level participation of experts, policymakers, stakeholders, and the public • In a WebGIS environment, the following participatory tools are conceptualized and developed: - Questionnaires: Spatial and non-spatial - Spatial SWOT/PESTLE - Spatial Delphi - Spatial Shang - Pairwise comparison and other relevant methods
Scenarios and Alternatives	• Development as WebGIS functionalities: - Visualization of the analyzed data and relevant Key Performance Indicators (geoKPIs) - Visualization of the different scenarios and alternatives - Comments, "likes," and rating via the online desktop application and smartphone - Visualization of the adaptive capacity to climate change
Final consultation, community activation, and engagement	• Development of Location Based Social Network (LBSN) & Phydigital (Φ-gital) path

residence (formal and informal), industrial uses, logistics, higher education, and urban green. More specifically, logistics is the most prevalent use, followed by industrial uses, and to a lesser extent warehouses. Also, a substantial part of Eleonas is undeveloped land without use, while the residences are limited and concentrated in its northern part. This plethora of layers, identities, and stakeholders constitute Eleonas an ideal case study to conceptualize, develop and pilot a research approach for participatory spatial planning applicable to urban areas with special challenges and opportunities.

Within the eLeonas research project, an online participatory design platform for sustainable development is designed and developed where the user will find tools and methodologies for environmental, developmental, and spatial participatory planning. The platform is created based on innovative technologies and tools, namely:

- Spatial Data Organization, Analysis, and Management (ppWebGIS).
- Participatory planning tools embedded in the geospatial platform (Spatial questionnaire, Spatial SWOT/PESTLE, Spatial Delphi/Shang Method, and other Group Judgment technics) [36, 37].
- Collective awareness, IoT, and social networking tools.

The framework will be tested around three pilot applications (climate change adaptation, sustainable spatial planning, and cultural heritage vulnerability) in Eleonas, Athens (Greece). The tools and supporting toolboxes created can be implemented in other

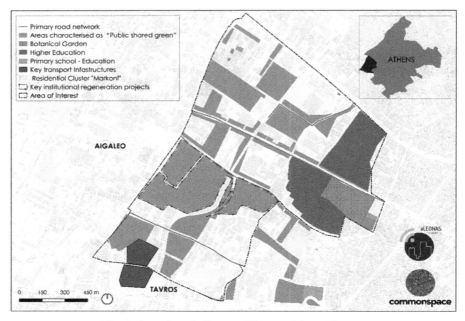

Fig. 4. Location of pilot area Eleonas, Athens (Greece)

regions with similar characteristics. It is essential to test new tools, integrations, and platforms with (almost) real-life pilots (Fig. 5).

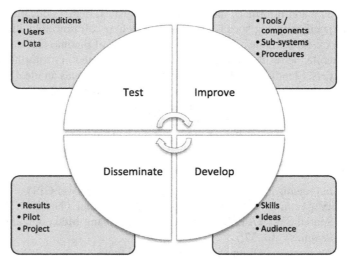

Fig. 5. The importance of real-life pilot cases for ICT research projects

This way, the research can be tested in real conditions, with the actual target group of users and the appropriate volume and complexity of data. Furthermore, the research team, along with the technical partners, can effectively improve tools and components of the digital solution, sub-systems, and procedures, especially participatory ones. This approach leads to the developing skills of the interdisciplinary team, the participants, and the interested parties. Also, to develop new ideas and to expand the audience. Finally, real-life pilots result in better dissemination and exploitation of the results, the project as a whole, and the research outputs.

4 Conclusions

According to the literature [3, 38, 39] and our experience and expertise, the main categories of participatory platforms and tools mainly support procedures of:

- Common vision
- Collective mapping
- Collective planning (or design)
- Expert knowledge (multi-stakeholders)
- Public awareness and final consultation (including scenario)

In addition, there is a need for expert judgment advanced features, at least for the main technics, (spatial) SWOT/PESTLE, (spatial) Delphi/Swang, and Pairwise comparison. Following, in Table 4, are presented the necessary functionalities and integrations.

For the tools to be inclusive, it is necessary to be well-responsive to mobile devices (android and iPhone). Safety of personal data and simplicity are key elements, especially when working with kids.

This paper presents the conceptualization and methodological development of the formal and informal functional requirements of the various ppWebGIS tools developed as part of "eLEONAS ppWebGIS" project. Employs innovative methodological and technological solutions to collect quantitative and qualitative data from the field. Conceptualizes and implements ppWebGIS tools to facilitate advanced participatory procedures (e.g., spatial SWOT/PESTLE, focus groups) tested and assessed for an area with special challenges and characteristics. Further research in this area could focus on implementing and assessing the developed conceptual and methodological framework in other instances to ensure that it fits the needs of spatial planning procedures in diverse spatial and cultural contexts.

Table 4. Functionalities and integrations

Functionalities and integrations	Description & notes
User's registration	Register by themselves or through an e-mail list. Provide statistical analysis—anonymous answers for minors or Expert judgment technics
Profile	"Consultation profile", characteristics for the specific consultation round or the thematic area. Ability to filter or weight the opinion based on the profile
Spatial questionnaire	All question types (i.e., text, multiple, radio button), including Likert, "more than", and image selection
	Answers' format Non-spatial or with geometry (point, line, polygon, Select from predefined features)
Group/expert judgment	(spatial) SWOT/PESTLE, (spatial) Delphi/Swang, Pairwise comparison
	Calculate consensus indicators, during Expert Judgment processes
Supporting material	Supported documents Library, collections, external URL
	Supporting maps, various basemap
Interaction	Voting/Like, Comments, Forum
Analysis	Basic statistical and spatial analysis during and after the participatory process
Visualization	Visualization of results during (preview) and after (final) the participatory process. Publish or hide
Export	Export results as maps, report, csv, json, or other
Integrations	Embed on online forms (i.e., google form, jotform, lime)
	Integrate into whiteboards (i.e., Miro, Mural)
	Integrate into teleconference platforms (i.e., zoom)

Acknowledgments. Research for this paper benefited from the "eLEONAS ppWebGIS: PARTICIPATORY PLANNING PLATFORM FOR SUSTAINABLE DEVELOPMENT" research project, in the framework of the Joint Action of State Aid for Research, Technological Development "Competitiveness, Entrepreneurship and Innovation (EPANEK)", NSRF 2014–2020. The project is implemented by a collaborative group of four partners: the cooperatives Commonspace and Sociality, HERMES NGO and GET Ltd company.

Authors' Contributions. Mougiakou E. devised the main conceptual idea, conceived the methodological framework and steps, and selected methods and tools. In collaboration with Tsadari S. conceived the participatory approach of the eLeonas research project. All authors contributed to the drafting of the document and the figures. Mougiakou E. prepared the final text, tables, and figures included in this publication. All authors provided feedback and reviewed the final manuscript.

References

1. Burrough, P.A., McDonnell, R.A., Lloyd, C.D.: Principles of Geographical Information Systems. Oxford University Press, Oxford (2015)
2. Carver, S., Evans, A., Kingston, R., Turton, I.: Accessing geographical information systems over the World Wide Web: improving public participation in environmental decision-making. Inf. Polity **6** (2000)
3. Brown, G., Kyttä, M.: Key issues and research priorities for public participation GIS (PPGIS): a synthesis based on empirical research. Appl. Geogr. **46**, 122–136 (2014). https://doi.org/10.1016/j.apgeog.2013.11.004
4. PAGE: Integrated Planning and Sustainable Development: Challenges and Opportunities (2016)
5. Somarakis, G., Stratigea, A.: Guiding informed choices on participation tools in spatial planning: an e-decision support system. IJEPR **8**, 38–61 (2019). https://doi.org/10.4018/IJEPR.2019070103
6. Snyder, H.: Literature review as a research methodology: an overview and guidelines. J. Bus. Res. **104**, 333–339 (2019). https://doi.org/10.1016/j.jbusres.2019.07.039
7. Champlin, C., Sirenko, M., Comes, T.: Measuring social resilience in cities: an exploratory spatio-temporal analysis of activity routines in urban spaces during Covid-19. Cities. **135** (2023). https://doi.org/10.1016/j.cities.2023.104220
8. Fagerholm, N., Eilola, S., Arki, V.: Outdoor recreation and nature's contribution to well-being in a pandemic situation - case Turku, Finland. Urban Forestry Urban Greening **64** (2021). https://doi.org/10.1016/j.ufug.2021.127257
9. Kotzebue, J.R.: Integrated urban transport infrastructure development: the role of digital social geo-communication in Hamburg's TEN-T improvement. J. Transp. Geography **99** (2022). https://doi.org/10.1016/j.jtrangeo.2022.103280
10. Szarek-Iwaniuk, P., Senetra, A.: Access to ICT in Poland and the co-creation of Urban space in the process of modern social participation in a smart city-a case study. Sustainability (Switzerland) **12** (2020). https://doi.org/10.3390/su12052136
11. Soares, I., Yamu, C., Weitkamp, G.: The relationship between the spatial configuration and the fourth sustainable dimension creativity in university campuses: the case study of Zernike campus, Groningen, The Netherlands. Sustainability (Switzerland) **12**, 1–21 (2020). https://doi.org/10.3390/su12219263
12. de Carvalho, C.M., Giatti, L.L.: Participatory GIS for urban sustainability and resilience: a perspective of social learning and ecology of knowledge. In: Azeiteiro, U.M., Akerman, M., Leal Filho, W., Setti, A.F.F., Brandli, L.L. (eds.) Lifelong Learning and Education in Healthy and Sustainable Cities. WSS, pp. 21–34. Springer, Cham (2018). https://doi.org/10.1007/978-3-319-69474-0_2
13. Abrantes, P., Queirós, M., Mousselin, G., Ruault, C., Anginot, E., Fontes, I.: Building a prospective participatory approach for long-term agricultural sustainability in the Lezíria do Tejo region (Portugal). Cahiers de Geographie du Quebec **60**, 303–323 (2016). https://doi.org/10.7202/1040537ar
14. Lin, Y., Zhang, X., Geertman, S.: Toward smart governance and social sustainability for Chinese migrant communities. J. Clean. Prod. **107**, 389–399 (2015). https://doi.org/10.1016/j.jclepro.2014.12.074

15. Cusack, C.D., Bills, K.J.: 'Glocalizing' urban sustainability: the case of Nairobi, Kenya. In: Dutt, A.K., Noble, A.G., Costa, F.J., Thakur, R.R., Thakur, S.K. (eds.) Spatial Diversity and Dynamics in Resources and Urban Development, pp. 99–115. Springer, Dordrecht (2016). https://doi.org/10.1007/978-94-017-9786-3_6

16. Zeballos-Velarde, C.: Participatory geographic information systems for integrated risk analysis: a case of Arequipa, Peru. In: Strengthening Disaster Risk Governance to Manage Disaster Risk, pp. 99–106 (2021)

17. Cavan, G., Butlin, T., Gill, S., Kingston, R., Lindley, S.: Web-GIS tools for climate change adaptation planning in cities. In: Filho, W.L. (ed.) Handbook of Climate Change Adaptation, pp. 2161–2191. Springer, Heidelberg (2015). https://doi.org/10.1007/978-3-642-38670-1_106

18. Cavan, G., Kingston, R.: Development of a climate change risk and vulnerability assessment tool for urban areas. Int. J. Disaster Resilience Built Environ. 3, 253–269 (2012). https://doi.org/10.1108/17595901211263648

19. Cavan, G., et al.: Climate change and urban areas: development of a climate change risk and vulnerability assessment tool. Presented at the COBRA 2010 - Construction, Building and Real Estate Research Conference of the Royal Institution of Chartered Surveyors (2010)

20. Saadallah, D.M.: Utilizing participatory mapping and PPGIS to examine the activities of local communities. Alex. Eng. J. 59, 263–274 (2020). https://doi.org/10.1016/j.aej.2019.12.038

21. Vasilev, M., Pritchard, R., Jonsson, T.: Mixed-methods approach to studying multiuser perceptions of an interim Complete Streets project in Norway. Travel Behav. Soc. 29, 12–21 (2022). https://doi.org/10.1016/j.tbs.2022.05.002

22. Heikinheimo, V., Tenkanen, H., Bergroth, C., Järv, O., Hiippala, T., Toivonen, T.: Understanding the use of urban green spaces from user-generated geographic information. Landscape Urban Plan. 201 (2020). https://doi.org/10.1016/j.landurbplan.2020.103845

23. Salonen, M., Broberg, A., Kyttä, M., Toivonen, T.: Do suburban residents prefer the fastest or low-carbon travel modes? Combining public participation GIS and multimodal travel time analysis for daily mobility research. Appl. Geogr. 53, 438–448 (2014). https://doi.org/10.1016/j.apgeog.2014.06.028

24. Fagerholm, N., Torralba, M., Moreno, G., Girardello, M., Herzog, F., Aviron, S., et al.: Cross-site analysis of perceived ecosystem service benefits in multifunctional landscapes. Glob. Environ. Chang. 56, 134–147 (2019). https://doi.org/10.1016/j.gloenvcha.2019.04.002

25. Samuelsson, K.: The Topodiverse City: urban form for subjective well-being. Front. Built Environ. 7 (2021). https://doi.org/10.3389/fbuil.2021.735221

26. Brown, G., Hausner, V.H.: An empirical analysis of cultural ecosystem values in coastal landscapes. Ocean Coast. Manag. 142, 49–60 (2017). https://doi.org/10.1016/j.ocecoaman.2017.03.019

27. Jose, R., Wade, R., Jefferies, C.: Smart SUDS: recognising the multiple-benefit potential of sustainable surface water management systems. Water Sci. Technol. 71, 245–251 (2015). https://doi.org/10.2166/wst.2014.484

28. Schrammeijer, E.A., Malek, Ž., Verburg, P.H.: Mapping demand and supply of functional niches of urban green space. Ecol. Indicators 140 (2022). https://doi.org/10.1016/j.ecolind.2022.109031

29. Ode Sang, Å., Sang, N., Hedblom, M., Sevelin, G., Knez, I., Gunnarsson, B.: Are path choices of people moving through urban green spaces explained by gender and age? Implications for planning and management. Urban Forestry Urban Greening 49 (2020). https://doi.org/10.1016/j.ufug.2020.126628

30. Zhang, K., Liu, M., Huang, L., Tang, X.H.: Tourism community residents' perception of landscape changes and management implications. Presented at the Proceedings of the 7th Academic Conference of Geology Resource Management and Sustainable Development (2020)

31. Arinaitwe, I., Maiga, G., Nakakawa, A.: A theoretical framework for GIS-enabled public electronic participation in municipal solid waste management. In: Paiva, S., Lopes, S.I., Zitouni, R., Gupta, N., Lopes, S.F., Yonezawa, T. (eds.) SmartCity360° 2020. LNICSSITE, vol. 372, pp. 553–567. Springer, Cham (2021). https://doi.org/10.1007/978-3-030-76063-2_37

32. Ghose, R., Huxhold, W.E.: Role of local contextual factors in building public participation GIS: the Milwaukee experience. Cartogr. Geogr. Inf. Sci. **28**, 195–208 (2001). https://doi.org/10.1559/152304001782153017

33. Creighton, J.L.: The Public Participation Handbook: Making Better Decisions Through Citizen Involvement. Jossey-Bass, San Francisco (2005)

34. Organizing Engagement: Spectrum of Public Participation. https://organizingengagement.org/models/spectrum-of-public-participation/

35. COMMONSPACE: Online Guide for Spatial, Urban and Environmental Participatory Planning for Climate Change Adaptation (2021). (in Greek). https://repository.participatorylab.org/dataset/avaqopa-njektpov1kou-odnyou. Accessed Apr 2023

36. Di Zio, S., Pacinelli, A.: Opinion convergence in location: a spatial version of the Delphi method. Technol. Forecast. Soc. Chang. **78**, 1565–1578 (2011). https://doi.org/10.1016/j.techfore.2010.09.010

37. Di Zio, S., Staniscia, B.: A Spatial version of the Shang method. Technol. Forecast. Soc. Chang. **86**, 207–215 (2014). https://doi.org/10.1016/j.techfore.2013.09.011

38. Mougiakou, E., et al.: Participatory urban planning through online webGIS platform: operations and tools. Presented at the ACM International Conference Proceeding Series (2020)

39. De Filippi, F., Coscia, C., Cocina, G.G., Lazzari, G., Manzo, S.: Digital participatory platforms for civic engagement: a new way of participating in society?: Analysis of case studies in four EU countries. Int. J. Urban Plan. Smart Cities **1**(1), 1–21 (2020). https://doi.org/10.4018/IJUPSC.2020010101

Open Access This chapter is licensed under the terms of the Creative Commons Attribution 4.0 International License (http://creativecommons.org/licenses/by/4.0/), which permits use, sharing, adaptation, distribution and reproduction in any medium or format, as long as you give appropriate credit to the original author(s) and the source, provide a link to the Creative Commons license and indicate if changes were made.

The images or other third party material in this chapter are included in the chapter's Creative Commons license, unless indicated otherwise in a credit line to the material. If material is not included in the chapter's Creative Commons license and your intended use is not permitted by statutory regulation or exceeds the permitted use, you will need to obtain permission directly from the copyright holder.

Citizen E-participation: The Experience of LABMET in the Metropolitan City of Cagliari

Nicolò Fenu[1,2](✉) iD

[1] ESOMAS, University of Turin, Turin, Italy
nicolo.fenu@unito.it
[2] SARDARCH Spin Off, Cagliari, Italy

Abstract. The importance of digital transition for Europe's growth and economy cannot be overstated. One of the key components of digital transition is e-participation. In Europe, e-participation has been viewed as a way to increase the legitimacy of public institutions and rebuild trust among citizens. Efforts to integrate information and communication technologies into state processes have been identified as good e-participation practices in European countries. The Metropolitan City of Cagliari has taken a step forward by implementing Decidim within LABMET. LABMET is an experimental metropolitan innovation laboratory promoting citizen engagement in decision-making. LABMET participated in the "OpenGov Project: Methods and Tools for Open Administration", launched by the Department of Public Functions. LABMET can serve as a model for other European cities seeking to embrace digital transition and promote citizen participation.

Keywords: Decidim · città metropolitana di Cagliari · e-participation · Italian Digital Agenda

The European Digital Agenda represents one of the seven pillars of the Europe 2020 strategy [16]. The Digital Agenda aims to leverage the potential of information and communication technologies (ICT) to foster innovation, progress, and economic growth, with the development of the single digital market as its primary objective. Within the European Digital Agenda framework, Italy has developed a national strategy, identifying priorities and intervention methods, as well as the actions to be carried out and measured based on specific indicators, in line with the scoreboards of the European Digital Agenda. The Italian Digital Agenda was developed in partnership with the Conference of Regions and Autonomous Provinces; this agenda aims to revolutionize the country's digital landscape. The Italian Strategy for Ultra-Broadband and the Strategy for Digital Growth 2014–2020 are critical components of this plan, and they are designed to meet the objectives of the Digital Agenda [14].

The Italy Digitale 2026 Plan (Agenda Digitale Italiana) aims to make the country's public administration more digitally accessible. The Italian government has allocated 27% of the resources in its National Recovery and Resilience Plan (PNRR) towards the digital transition of the country.

© The Author(s), under exclusive license to Springer Nature Switzerland AG 2023
O. Gervasi et al. (Eds.): ICCSA 2023 Workshops, LNCS 14105, pp. 646–656, 2023.
https://doi.org/10.1007/978-3-031-37108-0_41

1 PNRR

In the PNRR, ample space is dedicated to digitalization, both of the public administration and of the production system [6].

Mission 1 of the PNRR concerns digitalization, innovation, competitiveness, and culture. Its general objective is "the innovation of the country in a digital key, thanks to which to trigger a real structural change", and it sets out some broad sectors for intervention:

1. Digitalization and modernization of public administration
2. Justice reform
3. Innovation of the production system
4. Implementation of broadband
5. Investment in tourism and cultural heritage.

The intervention lines of the mission are developed around four design components:

1. Digitalization
2. Innovation and security in public administration (PA)
3. Digitalization, innovation, and competitiveness of the production system
4. Tourism and culture 4.0.[1].

The total resources allocated to Mission 1 amount to 40.32 billion euros, in addition to 0.8 billion euros from React-EU and 8.74 billion euros from the Complementary Fund, making a total of 49.86 billion euros.

Digitalization, which is one of the transversal themes of the plan, also recurs in the other missions involving different sectors:

- Educational programmes, the skills of teachers and students, and administrative functions and building infrastructure of schools (Missions 2 and 4).
- Healthcare, hospital infrastructure, medical devices, personnel skills and updating (Missions 5 and 6).
- Technological advances in agriculture, industrial processes, and the tertiary sector (Missions 2 and 3).

The first component of Mission 1, which concerns the digitalization, innovation and security of the PA, is divided into three sectors of intervention: digitalization of the PA, modernization of the PA, and organizational innovation of justice.

The total allocation for the component's interventions amounts to 11.75 billion euros distributed across seven investments and three reforms.

The plan focuses on two main pillars: the digitalization of public administration and the development of high-speed networks. The program includes five ambitious goals: disseminating digital identity and skills; bridging the digital literacy gap; bringing 75% of public administrations onto cloud services; delivery of 80% of essential public services online; and provision of ultra-high-speed broadband to every household and business.

---

[1] https://temi.camera.it/leg18/temi/tl18_informatizzazione_delle_pubbliche_amministrazioni.html

The Italian government has allocated three billion euros to fund the initiative, and the total budget for digital infrastructure and enabling of cloud migration is 1.9 billion euros.

1.1 E-government and E-participation

The future of civic engagement is characterized by both technological innovation as well as new technological user practices that are fuelled by trends towards mobile, personal devices; broadband connectivity; open data; urban interfaces; and cloud computing [5].

E-government or digital administration refers to the use of ICT in administrative processes with the aim of making the action of public administration more efficient, improving the quality of public services provided to citizens, and reducing costs for the community. Local governments have been able to enhance citizen participation and engagement with society through the use of ICT, which has presented an avenue for new initiatives and tools [13].

E-participation is part of the e-government toolbox. E-participation has been recognized as an effective means for governments to engage with citizens and promote transparency and accountability. By leveraging digital technologies, governments can provide citizens with greater access to information and decision-making processes [7].

A growing body of research suggests that e-participation is becoming more widely used to interact with citizens and governments and deepen collaboration between them. E-participation aims to give individuals greater access to data and services, and it encourages their involvement in policy development, ultimately elevating citizens' rights and benefitting society [7]. E-participation is significant for policy-making [8] as well as for urban planning [4].

Over the past few years, there has been significant growth and an emerging e-participation research area [12]. E-participation concerns the extension and transformation of participation in societal democratic and consultative processes mediated by information and ICT [11]. According to the UN,[2] e-participation is about fostering civic engagement and open, participatory governance through ICT.

Several platforms offer the possibility to discuss ideas, participate in online consultations, and interact directly with policy-makers. Among them, Decidim is becoming one of the most employed. Decidim is a participatory democracy platform that allows citizens to participate in the decision-making process in their communities. Decidim is a digital platform for citizen participation. Created in 2015, it is a free/libre, open, and safe technology, and it is based on transparency, collaboration, and citizen empowerment. Various organizations, cities, and countries worldwide have adopted the platform, including NGOs, universities, trades unions, cooperatives, and neighbourhood associations [15].

Decidim is a public commons, free, and open digital infrastructure for participatory democracy [2]. Several research studies have focused on Decidim, especially in the Catalan context [1, 3, 10] (Fig. 1).

---

[2] https://publicadministration.un.org/en/eparticipation.

2   Case Study

2.1   The Metropolitan City of Cagliari (MCC)

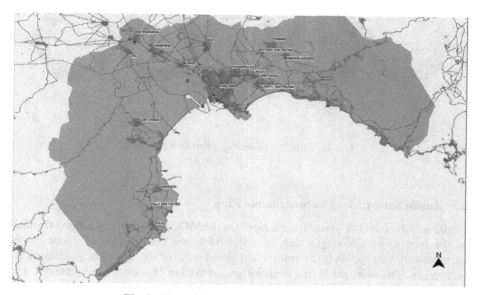

Fig. 1. Map of the Metropolitan city of Cagliari

The MCC is the only metropolitan city in Sardinia. It was established on 4 February 2016 by Article 17 of the regional law, n. 2 "Reorganization of the system of Local Autonomies of Sardinia", replacing the Province of Cagliari from 1 January 2017 (Resolution of the Regional Council, 25 October 2016, n. 57/12) [19].

Its capital is the city of Cagliari and it incorporates 17 municipalities: Assemini, Cagliari, Capoterra, Decimomannu, Elmas, Maracalagonis, Monserrato, Pula, Quartu Sant'Elena, Quartucciu, Sarroch, Selargius, Sestu, Settimo San Pietro, Sinnai, Uta, and Villa San Pietro.

It has a population of 419,022 inhabitants [17] and covers an area of 1,248 km². It is the only Italian metropolitan city established by creating a new aggregation of the capital and its conurbation according to the logic of a metropolitan area, and not by simply changing the name of the old province [9].

2.2   The Metropolitan Strategic Plan

In July 2021, the metropolitan strategic plan was approved. The plan encompasses the development strategies of the metropolitan area for a medium-term period of 10–15 years. The plan consists of a strategic document, which summarizes the objectives, the process, and the forms of participation envisaged for implementation, and 13 projects relating to system actions, five of which are identified as priorities. The five priorities are connected to the project ideas that emerged from the co-planning phase negotiated by the municipalities, which took place during 2021 [20] (Fig. 2).

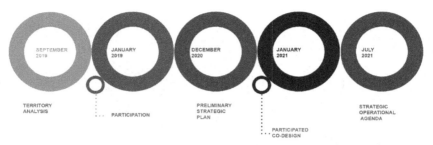

Fig. 2. Time line of Metropolitan strategic plan

2.3 *Anello Sostenibile*: The Sustainable Ring

L'anello sostenibile ("The sustainable ring") of the MCC is the primary action identified by the metropolitan strategic plan. Its objective is the construction of a sustainable infrastructure that connects the natural and urban areas of the 17 municipalities of the vast region. The sustainable ring is an integrated system of social, environmental, and transport infrastructures, interconnected thematically and geographically, and capable of producing sustainable urban regeneration on a metropolitan scale. In particular, the plan aims, through the innovative use of existing buildings and spaces, to create a network of green infrastructures and connections between wetlands, on the one hand, and a network of cultural and sporting services, on the other. In addition, numerous school and sports facilities and civic markets will be the subject of an energy optimization project aimed at saving energy and technological innovation. Many urban and extra-urban green areas have been created to mitigate heatwaves and the presence of pollutants; many places have been valorized and given back to the population, with significant involvement of the third sector (Fig. 3).

2.4 LABMET Platform: Metropolitan Innovation Laboratory – OpenGov

The MCC is one of the local administrations that has joined the OpenGov project,[3] which provides methods and tools for open administration and was launched by the Dipartimento della funzione pubblica (Department of Public Function) to disseminate and support open government methodologies in national and local public policies. The project aims to transfer the methodology and tools for the design of participatory processes, mainly using an open-source technological platform (decidim.org) for online consultation [18] (Fig. 4).

---

[3] https://open.gov.it/. The OpenGov project is funded under the PON Governance and Institutional Capacity 2014–2021, Axis I – Specific objective 1.1 "Increase transparency and interoperability and access to public data" – Action 1.1.1.

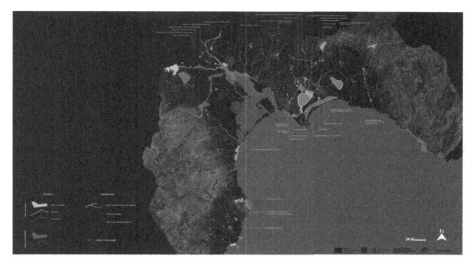

Fig. 3. Masterplan of Anello sostenibile.

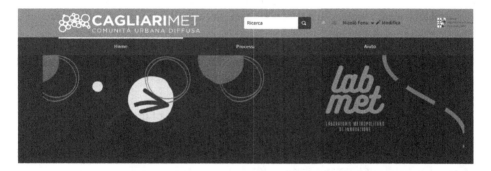

Cosa è la piattaforma LABMET
Laboratorio Metropolitano di Innovazione

Fig. 4. Decidim platform

The MCC decided to employ the Metropolitan Innovation Lab (LABMET) as a pilot project. LABMET is one of the leading activities of the strategic plan of the MCC.

LABMET provides for the population's involvement through opportunities for discussion and workshops activated on the open-source participation platform. In addition, it offers initial responses to the need for multi-institutional and multi-actor partnerships and shared knowledge, and it ensures the construction of durable urban policies and operational projects capable of adapting over time.

LABMET is designed to enable lasting, cross-cutting planning built with territorial actors and, above all, in a way that respects local realities. As such, it pursues the following objectives:

- Strengthen the participatory process with and among civil society actors
- Strengthen the metropolitan city's action in building strategic design and support for municipalities in the metropolitan area
- Involve all actors in innovative experimentation and co-design of common interaction spaces
- Involve all stakeholders in designing and implementing public projects and transformation policies.

The general objectives are to propose participatory methods and tools for public administrations within territorial planning, to implement skills, and to activate a direct line with local stakeholders. The specific goals are, initially, to build an atlas of local resources for the landscape and, subsequently, to develop guiding visions of urban transformation and to integrate the results into the feasibility project on the sustainable ring. The project led the MCC to acquire its own Decidim platform.

To address the primary aims of the project, over 50 participants were invited to contribute, including officials of the MCC and all 17 municipalities. In addition, several stakeholders were involved from various sectors: mobility, sport, sector associations, professional orders, and universities.

The project included teaching and laboratory activities. The training activities were carried out from December 2021 to March 2022 through four online seminars and webinars with around 30 participants. Learning moments were dedicated to:

- Principles of open government
- Involvement of citizens in public decisions as an aspect of transparency
- Open government data as an accountability tool.

After the seminar phase, five workshops with different focuses were conducted online. The topics of the workshops were:

- Sharing of local resources for the landscape and design of the atlas of resources
- Guiding ideas for MCC in 2026 and the role of the sustainable ring; construction of guiding visions
- Visions of the MCC in 2026 and design of the sustainable Cagliari 2026 scenario.

The participatory urban planning laboratory also enabled the transfer of planning methods and languages towards key subjects of public action so that the administrations could autonomously promote participatory paths.

Canale navigabile: navigable canal

The topic for the e-participatory consultation was the Terramaini – La Palma navigable canal project (Fig. 5).

The project offers new connection opportunities through the friendly use and exploration of the areas of the canals, gulf, and lagoons surrounding the city of Cagliari.

The general project of the waterways pursues the objective of offering alternative and sustainable mobility routes to connect the municipalities of Monserrato, Cagliari, Elmas, and Assemini. The theme of connection aims to develop new mobility services, create a

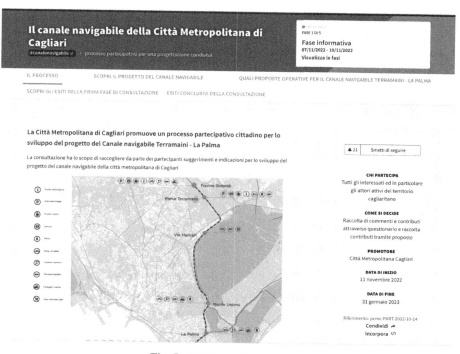

Fig. 5. MCC decidim platform

healthy life and new opportunities for recreation and enjoyment of nature, increase the permeability of the urban fabric, and develop intermodality. The central theme of the general project is to enhance the environmental resources of the territory, such as the salt pans of Molentargius, the park of Molentargius, and the pond of Cagliari, together with the salt pans of Macchiareddu and the lagoon of S. Gilla.

The public consultation, conceived in four phases, aims to gather suggestions and indications from the participants for developing the navigable canal project of the MCC.

11/11/2022 – 10/12/2022

Phase 1 – Collection of feedback on the overall quality of the fairway project.

11/12/2022 – 11/01/2023

Phase 2 – Processing of the intermediate report relating to the feedback on the overall quality of the project.

11/01/2023 – 31/01/2023

Phase 3 – Collection of contributions and proposals for the waterway project.

01/02/2023 – 28/02/2023

Phase 4 – Preparation of the final consultation report on the fairway project.

The objectives of the participatory process are to:

1. Communicate and disseminate the planning strategy and the lines of intervention
2. Promote a citizen debate that allows the channel's vision to be understood in relation to the technical work of planning pre-feasibility

3. Facilitate the comparison and collection of information and proposals to complete the technical design work
4. Facilitate the monitoring of the elaboration process.

The key issues that the consultation addressed were:

1. Placement of stops
2. Stop functions
3. Type of piers
4. Implementation of the paths
5. Management
6. Main function.

The public consultation had a total of 45 contributions from eight different users (Fig. 6).

Fig. 6. Figure 5 MCC decidim platform

3 Conclusion

The experimentation process of the MCC within the OpenGov project is significant. It includes the participatory process using the Decidim platform and a training course regarding digital transition issues. Therefore, the metropolitan city, in addition to adopting digital tools, creates a culture of participation with the active involvement of the administrations.

The *canale navigabile* topic chosen for the experimentation of the participatory consultation is certainly of interest to citizens, but it is not too accessible regarding the direct impact on citizens' lives and is not fully comprehensible. The navigable canals are not typical of ordinary life conditions, although they have high potential for the city's urban development. They constitute a complex subject in which different administrative skills are necessary. Among the critical elements of the first experimentation, there was undoubtedly the tool's novelty and its use: accessing the Decidim platform requires registration. Even though the LABMET project includes the 17 municipalities of the metropolitan city, the planning object of participation is in the Cagliari area and is specifically addressed to its citizens.

There were four phases of the consultation, and they followed the standard consultation times. However, it would be helpful to have more preliminary time to create a communication campaign linked to the Decidim tool to understand its true potential. Furthermore, it would have been appropriate to start the process through a face-to-face meeting on the specific theme of the waterway. The phases have all been managed online; the participatory processes managed with Decidim also include face-to-face meetings, and they build a hybrid path where face-to-face interactions are alternatives to sharing ideas and online proposals. Although a communication campaign was launched using social media tools, such as a dedicated Instagram page, citizens needed more involvement.

Critical issues were found regarding promotion and outside communication, as for all participatory processes. Specifically, there is a risk that only the citizens directly involved in the experimentation and the technicians know the project. On the other hand, the Decidim process has the peculiarity of foreseeing clarity and sharing results from its planning, for which intermediate reports have been developed during the different phases. Furthermore, this participatory approach has the advantage of continuing the project, which will see definitive and executive planning.

The OpenGov project has fully achieved its objectives. By the end of the process, the metropolitan city had its own Decidim platform, and in April 2023, a month after the end of the process, it has already launched a new participatory project for the candidacy of European Green Capital of 2025. However, pilot projects are often not continued once the activities have been completed.

Even from its initial phase, the project had some characteristics that enabled it to achieve results:

(i) The administration adheres to the project philosophy. It activates a series of experts within the organization who have followed the training activities during the pilot project phase and who will follow their implementation.

(ii) A strong territorialization of activities through assistance from the FORMEZ PA[4], in close collaboration with the metropolitan city. Furthermore, the pilot project was part of the activity of the institution's strategic plan, which had seen the involvement of institutional actors and civil society.

The MCC, representing 17 municipalities, has made available a tool for participation and activated a "culture of participation" that allows administrations to start participatory processes. LABMET can be a model for other European cities seeking to embrace digital transition and promote citizen participation.

Funding. This research received no external funding The "Opengov: methods and tools for open administration" is a project financed by PON Governance and Institutional Capacity 2014–2021, Axis I - Specific objective 1.1 "Increasing transparency and interoperability and access to public data" - Action 1.1.1

---

[4] Formez PA - Center for services, assistance, studies and training for the modernization of public administrations. www.formez.it.

References

1. Aragón, P., et al.: Deliberative platform design: the case study of the online discussions in Decidim Barcelona. In: Ciampaglia, G.L., Mashhadi, A., Yasseri, T. (eds.) SocInfo 2017. LNCS, vol. 10540, pp. 277–287. Springer, Cham (2017). https://doi.org/10.1007/978-3-319-67256-4_22

2. Barandiaran, X. et al.: Decidim: political and technopolitical networks for participatory democracy. Decidim's project white pape (2018). http://ajbcn-meta-decidim.s3.amazonaws.com/uploads/decidim/attachment/file/2005/White_Paper.pdf

3. Borge, R. et al.: Democratic Disruption or Continuity? Analysis of the Decidim Platform in Catalan Municipalities. Am. Behav. Sci. 000276422210927 (2022). https://doi.org/10.1177/000276422221092798

4. Bouregh, A.S., et al.: Investigating the prospect of e-participation in urban planning in Saudi Arabia. Cities **134**, 104186 (2023). https://doi.org/10.1016/j.cities.2022.104186

5. Foth, M., Brynskov, M.: Participatory action research for civic engagement. In: Gordon, E., Mihailidis, P. (eds.) Civic Media: Technology, Design, Practice, pp. 563–580. The MIT Press, United States of America (2016)

6. GI: Piano Nazionale di Ripresa e Resilienza (2021). https://www.governo.it/sites/governo.it/files/PNRR.pdf

7. Le Blanc, D.: E-participation: A Quick Overview of Recent Qualitative Trends (2020). https://doi.org/10.18356/0f898163-en

8. Macintosh, A.: Characterizing e-participation in policy-making. In: Proceedings of the 37th Annual Hawaii International Conference on System Sciences, 2004, p. 10 (2004). https://doi.org/10.1109/HICSS.2004.1265300

9. Palumbo, M.E., Mundula, L., Balletto, G., Bazzato, E., Marignani, M.: Environmental dimension into strategic planning. the case of metropolitan city of Cagliari. In: Gervasi, O., et al. (eds.) ICCSA 2020. LNCS, vol. 12255, pp. 456–471. Springer, Cham (2020). https://doi.org/10.1007/978-3-030-58820-5_34

10. Peña-Lopes, I.: Shifting participation into sovereignty: the case of decidim. Huygens Editorial, Barcelona (2019)

11. Sanford, C., Rose, J.: Characterizing eParticipation. Int. J. Inf. Manage. **27**(6), 406–421 (2007). https://doi.org/10.1016/j.ijinfomgt.2007.08.002

12. Steinbach, M., et al.: The diffusion of e-participation in public administrations: a systematic literature review. J. Organ. Comput. Electron. Commer. **29**(2), 61–95 (2019). https://doi.org/10.1080/10919392.2019.1552749

13. Tejedo-Romero, F., et al.: E-government mechanisms to enhance the participation of citizens and society: exploratory analysis through the dimension of municipalities. Technol. Soc. **70**, 101978 (2022). https://doi.org/10.1016/j.techsoc.2022.101978

14. Agenda digitale. https://www.funzionepubblica.gov.it/digitalizzazione/agenda-digitale. Accessed 11 Apr 2023

15. Decidim. https://decidim.org/. Accessed 18 Apr 2023

16. Digital Agenda for Europe | Fact Sheets on the European Union | European Parliament. https://www.europarl.europa.eu/factsheets/en/sheet/64/digital-agenda-for-europe. Accessed 11 Apr 2023

17. Istat.it English. https://www.istat.it/en/. Accessed 11 Apr 2023

18. LABMET. https://partecipa.cittametropolitanacagliari.it/. Accessed 11 Apr 2023

19. Legge Regionale 4 febbraio 2016, n. 2 - Regione Autonoma della Sardegna. https://www.regione.sardegna.it/j/v/80?s=300929&v=2&c=13906&t=1. Accessed 11 Apr 2023

20. Piano Strategico. https://www.cittametropolitanacagliari.it/portale/page/it/piano_strategico_focus?contentId=FCS9131. Accessed 18 Apr 2023

EU Mission on 'Climate-Neutral and Smart Cities' – Assessing Readiness to Join of 12 Greek Cities

Maria Panagiotopoulou(✉), Maria Agalioti, and Anastasia Stratigea[iD]

Department of Geography and Regional Planning, School of Rural, Surveying and Geoinformatics Engineering, National Technical University of Athens, Athens, Greece
mapanagiot@yahoo.gr, stratige@central.ntua.gr

Abstract. Urbanization is currently perceived as a major challenge of the 3rd millennium, with severe repercussions in terms of Climate Change (CC) deterioration and related impacts. In fact, cities are deemed to be the 'source', but also the 'solution' to CC emergency. Such an ascertainment lies at the heart of the European Mission on 'Climate-Neutral and Smart Cities' that falls into the 2050 EU long term strategy towards climate neutrality; and seeks to improve urban sustainability and resilience by leveraging the concept of cities' nature- and technology-enabled climate neutrality. Along these lines, this paper delves into the preparedness or readiness of several Greek cities towards the directions set by the European Mission for Cities. Twelve cities – most thereof capitals of respective regional entities – already active, in one way or another, in the CO_2 reduction endeavor and smart initiatives realm, are explored in this respect. These are evaluated by means of Multicriteria Analysis (MCA), grounded on numerous Mission-oriented criteria, such as CO_2 emissions, participation in the Covenant of Mayors, waste management, deployment of digital infrastructure, smart city applications, governance schemes, etc. Results obtained uncover the diversified state and starting point of Greek cities investigated as to the EU Mission objectives.

Keywords: Urbanization · EU Mission on 'Climate-Neutral and Smart Cities' · Multicriteria analysis · Mission-oriented evaluation criteria · Greek cities

1 Introduction

Urbanization has dramatically escalated over the last few decades, while it is expected to further intensify by 2050 [1]. This ominous urban phenomenon lies among the megatrends of the new millennium [2], featuring resource-intensive pathways and putting at great risk sustainability objectives at the glocal (global/local) level. Urban areas, as engines of growth and prosperity, magnets for habitation, platforms of world's production and innovation, and hubs of government, commerce and transportation, are deemed to be the main source of numerous contemporary problems and overwhelming challenges [3, 4]. Pollution and Climate Change (CC) are the most significant among them, with cities being, at present, imprudent energy consumers (up to 80% of the world's energy is absorbed by cities) and responsible for about 75% CO_2 emissions globally [5], mainly due to transport and building needs.

© The Author(s), under exclusive license to Springer Nature Switzerland AG 2023
O. Gervasi et al. (Eds.): ICCSA 2023 Workshops, LNCS 14105, pp. 657–675, 2023.
https://doi.org/10.1007/978-3-031-37108-0_42

The noticeably accelerating urbanisation trends are anticipated to further affect pollution in a pretty harsh manner [6, 7] due to the increasing volume and intensity of urban functions that stem from the great mass of people, infrastructure, housing and economic activities piled up in cities. The same holds true for the aggravation of CC, owing to the growing levels of Green House Gases (GHG) cities emit, while delivering their services, either directly or indirectly [8, 9]. Both lead to the deterioration of urban living conditions with respect to the poor air quality, energy and water scarcity, land use change / soil sealing, waste overproduction, etc. [6]. At the same time, the rapidly expanding and, in many cases, unplanned urbanization patterns exert massive pressures on the environment, thereby giving prominence to urbanization's role as a key driver of environmental degradation and related impacts on the livelihood of both urban population and natural ecosystems [10–12]. In a bid to simultaneously support economic wellfare, social inclusion and environmental health – the so called "triple bottom line" [13] – urban systems seem to have a critical part as main contributors in the currently evolving *"triple planetary crisis"* – i.e., CC, pollution and biodiversity loss –, a crisis that marks a "code red" for humanity as a whole [14].

Taking into consideration urban systems' pivotal role in coping with the triple planetary crisis and its severe repercussions, cities' future pathways are currently placed at the heart of the global policy and the interdisciplinary planning discourse. This reflects the belief that cities can become avid proponents of sustainable development [15, 16]; and guides the endeavour towards crafting and implementing widely acceptable, innovative, sustainable and resilient future urban pathways and related policy paths that are capable of dealing with the key challenges of contemporary cities; and decreasing their footprint on the planet. Such an effort is largely driven by the conviction that the current urbanization surge appears to be related with two sides of the same coin, since it treats cities as both the source and the means for tackling the aforementioned triple crisis; and offers unprecedented opportunities for establishing sustainable, resilient, livable and climate-neutral future trajectories. These opportunities are currently 'translated' into specific goals by the policy community at the global, European but also national/regional/local level. Therefore, action is undertaken in these spatial contexts and visionary end states are articulated that aim at: motivating reduction of the urban ecological footprint in general and cities' contribution to CC in particular; and shaping the transition towards smart, resilient and climate-neutral cities.

The achievement of *climate neutrality* implies a drastic shift from purely sectoral or 'silo' policy-making approaches to holistic and integrated ones at the urban level [17, 18]. In addition, it calls for a nature-based and technology-enabled orientation, capable of addressing both mitigation and adaptation strategic pathways as two sides of an integral urban response [19, 20]. The former intends to achieve net zero GHG emissions by either reducing or developing trade-off mechanisms to offset remaining unavoidable emissions. The latter targets cities' adaptive capacity strengthening in order to establish resilience to various types of external crises, but also of internal, long-term, persisting trends.

The Mission of the European Commission on "Climate-Neutral and Smart Cities", which constitutes the core of this work, falls under such visionary policy directions. Within such a context, the question as to how prepared to join the climate neutrality strategic vision Greek cities are, is raised. In an endeavor to provide solid answers to the above question, this paper attempts to explore the readiness of 12 Greek cities by use of multicriteria analysis and assessment of their current performance on the basis of several Mission-oriented evaluation criteria. The paper is structured as follows: Sect. 2 provides a succinct description of the idea of climate neutrality, which is perceived as a major strategic policy direction at the global and especially the European level; Sect. 3 delineates the adopted methodological approach; Sect. 4 roughly sketches the explored Greek cities, while it also presents the obtained results on their performance in respect to the EU Mission for cities direction. Finally, in Sect. 5 results are critically discussed and in Sect. 6 certain conclusions are drawn.

2   Framing Climate Neutrality – An Issue of 'Glocal' Policy Concern

CC is currently recognized as a key driving force of global reach [21]. Thus, tackling CC and its ramifications is an issue of immense significance for humanity in general and a critical issue of global governance in particular. As such, overall reduction of GHG emissions and climate neutrality lie at the heart of the United Nations' Agenda 2030 for Sustainable Development. More specifically, this is reflected in SDG 13 (Fig. 1), which is dedicated to "Climate Action" and sheds light on the urgent need to undertake those vital steps that can support transition towards carbon neutrality. Further specialization of SDG 13 into sub-objectives highlights, inter alia, the: boosting of resilience and adaptive capacity of states and regions to climate-related hazards and natural disasters; integration of CC measures into national policies, strategies and planning processes; capacity building and awareness raising of population and institutions, etc. At present, a number of countries are taking mitigation and adaptation actions, targeting the reduction of their national emissions and promoting national and/or regional/local adaptation plans to address CC challenges.

Despite the critical importance of SDG 13 for confronting CC, several SDGs focus also on climate neutrality concerns, such as SDG 7 ('Affordable and Clean Energy'), SDG 9 ('Industry innovation and infrastructure'), SDG 10 ('Reduced inequalities'), SDG 12 ('Responsible production and consumption'), etc. Furthermore, SDG 11 ('Sustainable cities and communities') is of utmost significance, since it stresses the relevance of the local (urban) level and pertinent policies as key factors to the achievement of SDGs overall [22, 23]. SDG's 11 mission is to render cities and human settlements inclusive, safe, resilient and sustainable by addressing topics related to slums and vulnerable population to CC, planning of human settlements, CC mitigation and adaptation, and wealth / resilience of urban economies. Affordable and sustainable transport systems, inclusive and sustainable urbanization, battle against the adverse effects of natural disasters, reduction of cities' environmental impacts, and access to safe and inclusive green and public spaces, are included in the fundamental concerns of SDG 11, which are inextricably linked with climate neutrality dimensions.

Focusing on the European level, the *European Green Deal* (2019) is of substantial importance, as it is considered to be the medium whereby the European Union attempts to harmonize with United Nation's Agenda 2030 and the 17 SDGs; and put forward,

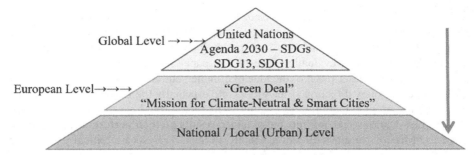

Fig. 1. Climate neutrality as a 'glocal effort' – From global to local (urban) level, Source: Own elaboration

in essence, a new growth strategy. This strategy promotes more sustainable pathways by serving the EU transition towards: a just and prosperous society; a resource-efficient and competitive economy, marked by the decoupling of economic growth from resource use; and a continent seeking to achieve climate neutrality first and foremost, i.e., no net GHG emissions by 2050 [24]. On the way to accomplishing climate neutrality, EU has committed to reduce net GHG emissions by at least 55% until 2030, compared to 1990 levels; and has set up a clear and coherent vision for climate neutrality by 2050. At the same time, Green Deal's strategic objectives are downscaled to the level of the member states by enforcing legislation updates and policy reforms as well as by monitoring their implementation. An ambitious EU strategy, targeting adaptation to CC, is also predicted in the Green Deal; while emphasis is placed on getting access to: data and instruments in support of integrating CC into risk management practices; smart energy infrastructure; and digital transformation, all three being grasped as critical 'vehicles' for reaching the Green Deal objectives [24].

In a bid to deal with the overwhelming challenges of the time, the EU has also put forward five *Missions* that aim at serving its policy priorities, with the Green Deal included. Missions have set quite ambitious goals and are planned to bring concrete results by 2030. For this reason, wide coalitions that are expected to establish the bridges among the research, policy and entrepreneurial communities as well as the European citizens, are provided for. This, in turn, implies that the goals of each Mission are meant to be accomplished by means of a portfolio of actions, incorporating research projects, policy measures or even legislative initiatives, in order to cooperatively attain a measurable goal.

Among the five EU Missions, the present work places its attention on the one seeking to achieve "Climate neutral and smart cities" (henceforth 'Cities' Mission'). This is justified by the fact that Cities' Mission and cities' exceptional role in achieving climate neutrality by 2050, as set by the Green Deal, are tightly intertwined. The significance of the abovementioned role lies in the very nature of cities, considering that these account for more than 70% of global CO_2 emissions [25]. That said, the goal of the EU Mission for Cities is to steer their *climate mitigation efforts* by accelerating green and digital transformation, among others. In doing so, it is supposed to deliver 100 climate-neutral and smart cities by 2030. These will act as pilots and laboratories of innovative and social experimentation, paving thus the way for the rest of the European cities that will follow till 2050. In order to gain one position among the first 100 pilot cities, candidates should satisfy certain criteria (e.g., population size). Furthermore, they should fill out an extended questionnaire that seeks information on: city's vision; current level of emissions; current policies, highlighting climate ambition, actions up to now and existing sectoral or cross-sectoral plans (energy, transport, waste management, etc.) relevant to CC mitigation and GHG reduction; participation in city networks; priorities for abating GHG emissions; partnerships and networking; capital needs and investment strategies; etc. Delving into the necessary requirements for this first selection round of cities by the European Commission has guided the formulation of evaluation criteria for assessing preparedness of 12 Greek cities to join the Cities' Mission, which is actually the primary subject of the following sections.

At the national level, Greece has launched several initiatives for tackling CC, such as the: National and regional strategies for CC [21], actions towards CC awareness raising, National Energy and Climate Plan (NECP) targeting the fulfillment of specific climate and energy objectives by 2030 and 2050, Climate Law, etc. Adhering to the national strategic directions, numerous plans – at the urban level – are conducted, such as Sustainable Urban Development Plans, Sustainable Energy Action Plans (SEAPs), Sustainable Urban Mobility Plans (SUMPs), etc.

3   Methodological Approach

The methodological approach, as presented below, aims at establishing a solid framework for assessing cities' readiness or preparedness to step into the ambitious EU Cities' Mission; and is implemented in the context of 12, unbiasedly selected, Greek urban environments.

3.1   The Steps of the Methodological Approach

The methodological approach consists of two distinct stages, namely (Fig. 2):

- The *development stage*, which aims at picking a number of Greek cities that can potentially fulfill the prerequisites to join the Cities' Mission. In this respect, two specific selection criteria are set: i) population size larger than 50,000 inhabitants; and ii) spatial balance, implying an even coverage across the various Greek regional entities. The output of this stage is a sample of 12 candidate cities, best complying with the aforementioned preselection criteria. These are then subjected to a more in-depth exploration at the evaluation/prioritization stage.
- The *evaluation/prioritization stage*, which represents the core of the Mission-oriented assessment process of the 12 preselected cities. Towards this end, the REGIME multi-criteria evaluation method is used. The adopted procedure starts with the demarcation and definition of the evaluation problem, as previously defined. Then, a range of eval-uation criteria – stemming from the directions given by the EU Mission at the stage of preselecting the 100 pilot cities that are supposed to achieve its goals by 2030 – are set. Afterwards, an exhaustive exploration of the finally selected cities' current state, that incorporates all those dimensions sketched by the evaluation criteria, is

taking place. Based on the cities' thoroughly examined profile and their performance as to the evaluation criteria, the impact matrix – the main input to the evaluation process – is constructed. This is accompanied by the criteria weights that reflect the diversifying importance attached to each single criterion. In the case of this work, equal weights are assigned to all criteria, taking for granted that cities' performance should be measured along all the dimensions introduced by the evaluation criteria, i.e., they all play a crucial role in meeting Mission's objectives. Finally, the impact matrix and criteria weights are used as input to REGIME multicriteria method in order to identify the prioritization of selected cities on the basis of their performance as to the defined criteria.

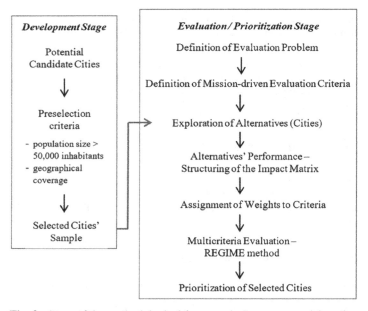

Fig. 2. Steps of the methodological framework, Source: own elaboration

3.2 The REGIME Multicriteria Evaluation Method

REGIME is a discrete multicriteria method, used to evaluate both projects and policies [26, 27]. The advantage of the method lies in its capacity to deal with *mixed data* (quantitative and qualitative) as to the effects and criteria priorities considered in the evaluation problem.

The application of the method is based on two kinds of input data, namely the [28]:

- evaluation (impact) matrix, composed of elements e_{ij} that measure the effect of each alternative i (12 preselected Greek cities in this case), $I = 1, 2, ..., I$ on every evaluation criterion j, $j = 1, 2, ..., J$;

- set of political weights that provide information on the relative importance of criteria to be considered in the evaluation context.

Each value e_{ij} with $i = 1, 2, \ldots I$ (set of alternatives) and $j = 1, 2, \ldots, J$ (set of evaluation criteria), represents the score of alternative i as to the criterion j, but also a short of ranking order of alternative i in respect to the criterion j. Therefore, it can be asserted that if $e_{ij} > e_{i'j}$, then the choice option i is preferable for the evaluation criterion j, compared to I' [29].

REGIME method is founded on a pairwise comparison of all alternatives. It is worth highlighting that the comparison of every set of alternatives is not influenced by the presence and effects of other alternatives, while the potential ranking order of a certain alternative is conditioned by the remaining ones [30].

The development of REGIME method is based on the 'regime' concept. Therefore, the relation $s_{ii'j} = e_{ij} - e_{i'j}$ is defined. In the case of quantitative information, a certain magnitude of $s_{ii'j}$ of the 'regime' is determined. However, when information is of ordinal (qualitative) type, only the sign of the 'regime' matters and not its magnitude. The relation $\sigma_{ii'j} = \text{sign } s_{ii'j} = +$ implies that alternative i is better than i' as regards criterion j, whereas the relation $\sigma_{ii'j} = \text{sign } s_{ii'j} = -$ entails that alternative i is worse than i' as to criterion j. By carrying out comparisons between alternatives i and i' for all $j = 1, 2, \ldots, J$ judgement criteria, a Jx1 regime vector $r_{ii'}$ can be constructed, which is translated into the Eq. 1 [29]:

$$r_{ii'} = (\sigma_{ii'1}, \sigma_{ii'2}, \ldots \sigma_{ii'J})^T, \quad \forall\, i, i', i' \neq I \tag{1}$$

This vector reflects a certain degree of dominance of alternative i over i' for the unweighted effects of all J criteria [29].

For all $I(I-1)$ pairwise comparisons, $I(I-1)$ regime vectors are created, which can be combined into the $J \times I(I-1)$ regime matrix R that has the following form [30]:

$$R = \{r12\, r13 \ldots r1I, \quad \ldots\ldots \quad rI1\, rI2 \ldots rI(I-1)\} \tag{2}$$

Additional information on the relative importance of the set of evaluation criteria is needed. Such information is usually provided by preference weights that are attached to the criteria.

In case of ordinal data, the weights are represented by means of rank orders w_j ($j = 1, 2, \ldots, J$) in a weight vector of the following form [30]:

$$w = (w_1, w_2, \ldots w_j)^T \tag{3}$$

if $w_j > w_{j'}$, criterion j is perceived as more important than j' [29].

These are considered as a rank order representation of the cardinal weights:

$$\underline{w}^* = (\underline{w}_1^*, \underline{w}_2^*, \ldots \underline{w}_j^*)^T \text{ with max } \underline{w}_j^* > 0, \text{ for every } j = 1, 2, \ldots J \tag{4}$$

The ordinal ranking of weights is supposed to be consistent with the quantitative information, incorporated in the unknown cardinal vector w*, that is [30]:

$$\text{if } w_j > W_{j'} \rightarrow w_j^* > w_{j'}^* \tag{5}$$

Then the weighted dominance of alternative i with regard to i' can be represented by the following stochastic expression [30]:

$$v'_{ii} = \sum_{j=1}^{J} \sigma_{ii'j} w_j^*$$ (6)

If $v'_{ii} > 0$, alternative i is dominant with respect to i'. But w_i^* is not known. What is known is only the ordinal value w_j, which is assumed to be consistent with $w_j{}^*$. Therefore, a certain probability can be introduced for the dominance of alternative i with regard to i':

$$P_{ii'} = \text{prob}\,(v_{ii'} > 0)$$ (7)

Then the probability of alternative i to rank higher than the rest of the alternatives can be calculated by the following formula [30]:

$$P_i = [1/(I-1)] \sum_{i \neq i'} P_{ii'}$$ (8)

where P_i is the average probability that alternative i ranks higher than any other alternative [30]. Ranking order of P_i's is then defining the ranking of respective alternative options.

Application of the REGIME method is accomplished by use of the DEFINITE (DEcisions on a FINITE set of alternatives) software.

4   Prioritizing Mission's Readiness of 12 Greek Cities –Implementation and Results

In a bid to explore Greek cities' readiness regarding the objectives of the European Cities' Mission, 12 candidates were finally selected. The aim of such an effort focuses on looking into initiatives and actions already in place that are in alignment with the scope of the Mission's vision.

A profusion of Greek cities was inspected. As already mentioned, these cities should fulfill the requirements of a minimum population of 50,000 inhabitants and their even distribution across the Greek territories. Therefore, the spatial dimension is seriously taken into account in order to attain – to the best possible extent – the equal dispersion of Greek cities of varying population size – large, medium and small. Moreover, it is pretty critical that chosen cities should represent different geomorphological contexts, i.e., located in the coastal or inland part of the country.

Out of the examined potential candidates, 12 cities are finally selected for further exploration (Fig. 3), including the two largest cities of the Greek state, Athens and Thessaloniki. The picked cities share numerous commonalities such as: they have crafted a vision with respect to sustainability and a long-term planning towards its attainment; they have already implemented various environmentally-friendly measures; they have deployed adequate ICT infrastructure and related applications for serving urban functions; they have embraced participatory approaches and governance schemes at the stage of designing policy actions; and they range from frontrunners to less-experienced in the ICT field.

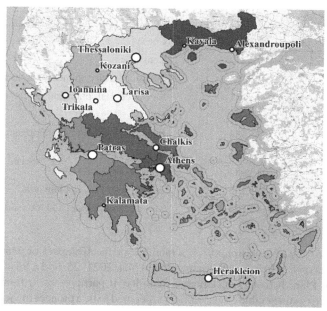

Fig. 3. Spatial distribution of the selected cities across the Greek state, Source: Own elaboration

Figure 3 illustrates the spatial dispersion of the 12 chosen cities, while Table 1 presents the population and type of each one. A brief description of the selected cities is provided the following section.

4.1 The 12 Greek Cities Case Studies

Municipality of Athens is the capital of Greece, a historic city of myths and monuments, characterized by an enduring entrepreneurial spirit that seizes the benefits of digital economy. The city is very active in undertaking action towards CC mitigation, and participates in several pertinent initiatives/networks, such as the Covenant of Mayors and the Compact of Mayors for CO_2 reduction/reporting; Civitas for sustainable mobility; Eurocities for exchange of good practices and cooperation; 100 Resilient Cities for establishing smart and resilient cities; and C40 cities, a global network of mayors that fights against climate crisis. Despite the absence of a Sustainable Energy Action Plan (SEAP), the municipality is determined to decrease CO_2 levels by 40% until 2030; while it also has a Sustainable Urban Mobility Plan (SUMP), a Sustainable Urban Development Plan, etc.; and a number of ICT-enabled applications for serving urban functions (parking, free Wi-Fi, electronic governance, green entrepreneurship, etc.).

Table 1. Population size and type of the selected cities' sample

Municipality	Population Size	Type
1. Athens	664,046	Inland, in plain land
2. Alexandroupoli	72,959	Coastal
3. Herakleion-Crete	173,993	Coastal
4. Thessaloniki	322,240	Coastal
5. Ioannina	112,486	Inland, lake city, in mountainous land
6. Kavala	70,501	Mix of coastal, plain and mountainous parts
7. Kalamata	69,849	Coastal
8. Kozani	71,388	Inland, mix of plain and mountainous parts
9. Larisa	162,591	Inland, in plain land
10. Patras	213,984	Coastal, in plain land
11. Trikala	81,355	Inland, river city, in plain land
12. Chalkis	102,223	Mix of coastal, plain and mountainous parts

Municipality of Alexandroupoli is a member of the Compact of Mayors, while it implements its own SEAP, a waste management plan 2021–25, and a Sustainable Urban Development Plan. It fosters sustainable mobility; it participates in European-funded projects related to sustainable cities; while it is deemed to be a pioneer in the energy sector through the deployment of numerous Renewable Energy applications (photovoltaic, geothermal energy applications, LED lighting, biomass, electric charging stations, etc.).

Municipality of Herakleion-Crete is among the protagonists of the Greek smart cities and possesses a high-quality, advanced, digital infrastructure. The municipality is very active in European-funded projects that target various dimensions of sustainable cities; while it is also a member of various initiatives/networks, such as CIVITAS and Eurocities. In addition, the municipality has drawn up a local waste management plan, a Sustainable Development Strategy, as well as a Resilience Strategy.

Municipality of Thessaloniki – the second largest Greek city, home to the country's second most prominent export and transit port and a gateway to the Balkans – is an active member of initiatives/networks, such as the Covenant of Mayors, Civitas, Eurocities and 100 Resilient Cities. The municipality is engaged in European-funded projects, dedicated to sustainable cities. It has already a SEAP in place, while governance schemes and related platforms are also established, aiming at creating an inclusive and interconnected city through data provision and strengthening of digital innovations for citizens' engagement in decision-making. Furthermore, the municipality has at its disposal a wide spectrum of ICT-enabled applications that fall into the six dimensions of a smart city, as expressed by [31].

Municipality of Ioannina, the capital of the Region of Epirus, at the crossroad of the Via Egnatia ancient road that connects Europe with Asia, is already a member of the Covenant of Mayors and the 100 Intelligent Cities' Challenge European Initiative, which seeks to achieve ICT-enabled, smart, just and sustainable cities. The municipality partakes in European-funded projects, pertinent to various sustainable city dimensions; while it has already developed action plans for sustainable mobility, sustainable urban development, sustainable energy, waste management, etc. Ioannina possesses an adequate ICT infrastructure, which hosts a number of ICT-enabled applications – public participation platforms as well – for serving citizens' needs.

Municipality of Kavala is a member of the Civitas network, 100 Intelligent Cities' Challenge, and Digital Cities Challenge, i.e., European Commission's initiative in support of cities' digital transformation. It is also active in partnerships and coalitions through European-funded projects; while it has crafted strategies and action plans for digital transformation, sustainable urban development and sustainable energy. The latter is accomplished via several city interventions (school energy upgrades, pedestrian networks, etc.). Moreover, various interventions that pursue governance upgrading and strengthening of interaction between the local administration and the citizens are implemented. Along these lines, a participatory GIS platform for coastal zone management is also established.

Municipality of Kalamata is a member of the Covenant of Mayors and has launched many initiatives related to sustainability and CC adaptation, including renewable energy, LED lighting, urban renewal and pedestrian network, bicycle network, waste management, etc. The municipality has already a SEAP, a SUMP, a Sustainable Urban Development Plan and a local waste management plan in place. Furthermore, the development of a resilience plan and the 'Citizens' observatory' – citizens' communication with municipal services and delivery of emergency messages from local government to citizens (G2C) – are in progress.

Municipality of Kozani, the most prominent lignite hub in Greece for more than five decades, is a member of the: Covenant of Mayors; WHO European Healthy Cities Network (raises health issues in the urban agenda); Civitas network; Energy Cities (targets interaction and exchange of good practices for cities' just and sustainable energy transition in the climate neutrality era). The municipality has already applied a SEAP, a SUMP, a strategic plan for shifting into the smart city paradigm, and a Sustainable Urban Development Plan; while a range of smart city applications for serving citizens' needs are deployed.

Municipality of Larisa, located at the most fertile and productive agricultural plain of Greece, is a member of the Covenant of Mayors; Civitas network; UNESCO Global Network of Learning Cities (intends to upgrade long-life learning and digital skills of labour force); Major Cities of Europe – IT Users Group (aims at exchanging ICT-oriented knowledge and good practices in various sectors); River/Cities (promotes interaction among cultural, environmental and political actors for pursuing sustainable development objectives of urban waterfronts); ICLEI-Local Governments for Sustainability (encourages cooperation and cooperative learning of cities committed to sustainable urban development). The municipality of Larisa has also implemented a SEAP, a SUMP and a local waste management plan; while a number of smart applications are at citizens' disposal for satisfying their everyday needs.

Municipality of Patras is one of the largest Greek ports, with intense commercial and passenger activity and connects the Greek mainland with the western European countries and the Ionian Islands. Patras is a member of the Covenant of Mayors; the B-40 Balkan Cities Network (supports cooperation among cities that seek to localize the New Urban Agenda and other international agreements and plans, particularly the SDGs); and the Digital Cities Challenge. The municipality has also developed a SEAP, a strategic plan for sustainable urban development and a local waste management plan. With the assistance of an upgraded ICT infrastructure, a range of digital applications are in place for managing parking, environmental quality, citizens' interaction with municipal services, etc.

Municipality of Trikala, the first Greek smart city, lies at the heart of the country's mainland. It is deeply engaged in cities' networking, and a valuable member of the Covenant of Mayors; Civitas network; and CitiesNet (the first Greek digital community); while it is very active in European-funded projects and serves as a test-bed for numerous digital innovations (e.g., driverless buses). The city has also implemented a SEAP, a SUMP, a sustainable urban development plan, a local waste management plan, installation of two electric vehicle charging stations, etc. The advanced and constantly upgrading ICT infrastructure has allowed Trikala to emerge as one of the most dynamic medium-sized cities in Europe and a pioneer in a wide spectrum of ICT-enabled applications.

Finally, *Municipality of Chalkis*, a distinguished port of the Region of Central Greece, is a member of the Covenant of Mayors and has mapped out a SUMP, a local waste management plan and a strategic plan towards a sustainable and smart city. Its improved ICT infrastructure has offered city the chance to develop plenty of ICT-enabled applications for the benefit of its citizens.

4.2 Multicriteria Analysis and Results

The selection of the evaluation criteria for assessing the 12 selected cities' preparedness or readiness to join the Mission's vision is guided by the directions provided by the Mission at the stage of picking the 100 pilot cities. More specifically, the chosen evaluation criteria – both quantitative and qualitative – their measurement units and directions are presented in Table 2.

The *impact matrix* (Fig. 4), that features the evaluation problem under consideration, is constructed on the basis of the evaluation criteria and the performance (scores) of the selected cities (alternatives) in respect of each single evaluation criterion. Figure 4 provides all the necessary data used as main input to the DEFINITE software, which incorporates the REGIME multicriteria model, among others. Additionally, in this case, equal weights are assigned to all evaluation criteria, implying that each one should be met to the greatest possible degree, since none of them takes precedence.

Taking into consideration the constructed impact matrix, as this is presented in Fig. 4, and treating all 13 evaluation criteria as equal (assignment of equal weights), the results obtained by the application of the REGIME multicriteria evaluation method are displayed in Fig. 5.

Table 2. Evaluation criteria for assessing/prioritizing the selected cities, Source: Own elaboration

Evaluation Criteria	Type	Measurement Unit	Direction*
K1 – Population size	quantitative	Ratio scale (thous. of inh/s)	Benefit
K2 – Total CO_2 emissions	quantitative	Ratio scale (tons)	Cost
K3 – Implementation of Action Plan for Sustainable Energy and Climate	qualitative	Binary scale (yes/no)	Benefit
K4 – Accession to the Covenant of Mayors	qualitative	Binary scale (yes/no)	Benefit
K5 – Current policies for mitigating and adapting to climate change	qualitative	Ordinal Scale**	Benefit
K6 – Implementation of waste management plan	qualitative	Binary scale (yes/no)	Benefit
K7 – Level of digital infrastructure deployment	qualitative	Ordinal Scale	Benefit
K8 – Implementation of Sustainable Mobility Plan	qualitative	Binary scale (yes/no)	Benefit
K9 – Deployment of smart city applications	qualitative	Ordinal Scale	Benefit
K10 – Projects – Cooperative spirit / Participation in national / international city networks	qualitative	Ordinal Scale	Benefit
K11 – Adoption of participatory processes in city management	qualitative	Ordinal Scale	Benefit
K12 – Governance level	qualitative	Ordinal Scale	Benefit
K13 – Implementation of strategic plan for sustainable development	qualitative	Binary scale (yes/no)	Benefit

* Type of criterion – benefit/cost: the higher the value of criterion the better (benefit) or worse (cost) the alternatives' performance with respect to the specific criterion.
** Ordinal scale in REGIME: i) rating performance from 1 (very good) to 5 (very bad) with intermediate values 2 (good), 3 (neutral) and 4 (bad).

	Athens	Alexandroupoli	Herakleion	Thessaloniki	Ioannina	Kalamata	Kavala	Kozani	Larisa	Patras	Trikala	Chalkis
Evaluation Criteria	E1	E2	E3	E4	E5	E6	E7	E8	E9	E10	E11	E12
K1	664046	72959	173993	322240	112486	70501	69849	71388	162591	81355	213984	102223
K2	5069040	435250	880034	2494215	552427	327371	395170	469182	773309	452216	1064886	543006
K3	no	yes	yes	yes	yes	yes	yes	yes	yes	yes	yes	yes
K4	yes	yes	yes	yes	yes	yes	yes	yes	yes	yes	yes	yes
K5	1	2	3	3	3	2	3	1	3	3	2	2
K6	yes	yes	yes	yes	yes	yes	yes	yes	yes	yes	yes	yes
K7	1	4	1	3	3	3	3	3	3	4	1	3
K8	yes	yes	yes	no	yes	yes	yes	yes	yes	yes	yes	yes
K9	2	3	2	2	3	3	4	3	4	3	1	4
K10	1	4	1	1	2	2	3	2	2	4	1	5
K11	3	3	3	3	3	2	2	2	4	4	2	3
K12	4	3	2	1	3	2	2	2	1	3	2	4
K13	yes	yes	yes	no	yes	yes	yes	yes	no	no	yes	no

Fig. 4. Spatial Impact matrix of the evaluation case study, Source: Own elaboration

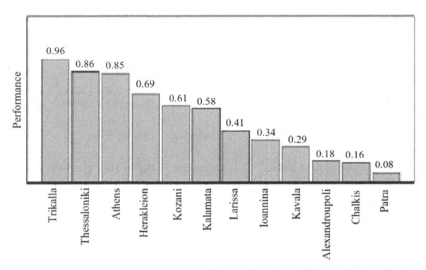

Fig. 5. Prioritization of cities' preparedness with regard to EU Cities' Mission objectives, as emerging from the REGIME multicriteria method, Source: Own elaboration

5 Discussion

The assessment of the 12 inspected Greek cities regarding the alignment of their current state and policy directions with the key objectives of the EU Cities' Mission, carried out in this work, ends up with certain diversifying outcomes. The reason behind this is related to the different city contexts explored in terms of: distinct locational attributes (coastal vs inland, port vs non-port city, plain vs mountainous terrain, etc.); position in the urban network hierarchy and role in the Greek economic system (metropolitan areas of Athens and Thessaloniki vs regional peripheral centers); economic profile (e.g., Kozani as an energy hub of national importance vs Larisa as an agricultural pole); population size; pursued sustainability objectives, starting point and visionary end state; achievements related to the implementation of specific policy pathways; extraversion and interaction by means of being part of various networks/institutions, etc., with specific focus on contemporary city challenges (e.g., Civitas network, Covenant of Mayors, CitiesNet, Energy Cities, etc.).

Considering all the above-mentioned distinct attributes of the explored Greek cities, their prioritization – on the basis of their preparedness to harmonize with the Cities' Mission objectives – leads to the following classification.

The city of *Trikala* ranks first by a wide margin. Trikala – the first Greek smart city since 2008, awarded in 2009, 2010 and 2011 by the Intelligent Community Forum (ICF) [32] – exhibits intense degree of extraversion and networking, and broad partnerships in innovative EU-funded projects; as well as extended ICT infrastructure and relevant smart applications. This is coupled with the city's policy interventions in critical fields, such as energy, transport, waste management, governance and citizens' online engagement. Thus, Trikala appears as a fertile ground for paving the Cities' Mission pathway in the Greek territory, and falls under the group of frontrunner cities, at least for the Greek standards.

The two metropolitan areas of Greece, *Athens and Thessaloniki*, rank second, at a distance from the first (Trikala). Their performance with respect to Cities' Mission objectives appears to be very close, exhibiting, however, certain differences as to the: CC mitigation efforts, state of digital infrastructure, smart city applications for citizens' engagement, and implementation of sustainable development plans. Nevertheless, the large population size of these cities may have a stronger impact in terms of climate neutrality.

Herakleion, Kozani and *Kalamata* are classified in the third group, with Herakleion holding the reins, while the rest two cities exhibit similar performance, with slight difference from Herakleion (Fig. 5). Despite their relatively close hierarchical positions, these three cities are diversified on the basis of several attributes. Herakleion is a coastal city, the economic and administrative center of the Region of Crete, a beacon in smart city development, and a remarkable tourism hub. Kozani is an inland city, with a prominent role as the country's most significant energy hub, but a victim of the national energy decarbonization strategy at the same time. Finally, Kalamata is a regional agricultural urban settlement, a port city of minor importance, and an immature tourism destination that also lags behind in terms of smart city developments. However, all three of them seem to be oriented towards or to have in progress ICT- and non-ICT-enabled policies in critical – for Cities' Mission objectives – fields for achieving sustainability and climate neutrality. Thus, they are perceived as potentially early candidates for Cities' Mission.

Comparable performance is detected among the cities of *Larisa, Ioannina* and *Kavala* that comprise the fourth group. All three constitute important regional poles of Greece, with diversifying roles, namely: Larisa is the agricultural center of the Region of Thessaly and a city that is taking steps towards the implementation of critical for the Mission policy fields; Ioannina is the economic, administrative and research center of the Region of Epirus – one of the poorest regions in the EU – and a city that sets up policy efforts in the direction of sustainable and just future development; Kavala is a regional port city that has acquired noticeable importance in the emerging energy landscape and the energy routes of Greece and Europe as a whole.

Finally, the last group consists of the cities of *Alexandroupoli, Chalkis* and *Patras.* Despite their substantial role in the Greek economy – Alexandroupoli as a rising energy hub in liquified natural gas (LNG) routes and a border of the EU, Chalkis as a satellite city of the metropolitan area of Athens, and Patras as a vital commercial and passenger port – they seem to be really weak in terms of the climate neutrality goal set by EU Cities' Mission.

6 Conclusions

Seeking to attain sustainability and climate neutrality of future cities is currently perceived to be an absolute necessity, considering their ecological footprint on the planet. This view has been transformed into a global concern, articulated through the Agenda 2030, but also the EU Cities' Mission that aims at supporting European cities to reach this visionary end state by tackling the CC challenges and promoting a digital 'metamorphosis'. The EU Mission is formulated as a two-step approach. Initially, 100 cities that will serve as hubs of technological, social and managerial innovation in order to reach the desired climate neutrality end state by 2030, are selected. Afterwards, these 100 frontrunners will establish a pool of good practices, concrete solutions and evidence-based results for feeding the effort of the rest of the European cities towards meeting City Mission's objectives by 2050.

The first step is already complete, and has ended up with a plethora of candidate cities (377 cities) that immediately responded to the European Commission's call. Candidates originate from all EU Member States as well as nine associated or potentially associated countries; and demonstrate remarkable diversity, a critical factor for featuring multiple trajectories that will lead to climate neutrality by 2030, on the basis of different city profiles; and will inform policy efforts and strategies of the rest of the EU cities during their climate neutral journey by 2050. Out of the 362 eligible cities, the first 100 are picked, with six Greek cities falling among them (a number that is considered a great success for Greece), namely: *Athens, Ioannina, Kalamata, Kozani, Thessaloniki* and *Trikala* (in alphabetical order).

The finally selected cities – the result of a multicriteria evaluation process of candidate cities by the Commission (including political and even geographical distribution criteria) – seem to be quite close to the ones obtained in the context of the present work. In fact, selected cities by the Commission incorporate: *Trikala* (the city ranks first in the evaluation of this work), *Athens* and *Thessaloniki* (second best group of cities regarding their performance), *Kozani* and *Kalamata* (third best performing group) and *Ioannina* (fourth best performing group). The slight discrepancy observed between the Commission's final choice and the one of this work as to cities' rating – i.e., selection of Ioannina instead of Herakleion – seems to be well justified considering that the final selection should incorporate – inter alia – cities that exhibit a diversified degree of maturity concerning their climate neutrality performance. That said, Herakleion is left aside, giving thus way to Ioannina, as a city marked by a relatively slow pace towards achieving climate neutrality and digital transformation and as part of one of the poorest regions in the EU.

Ultimately, the multicriteria evaluation exercise conducted in this work seems to be quite fruitful; and may be pretty useful at the national level for: identifying cities' weaknesses in climate neutrality pathways, setting political priorities for treating such weaknesses, and motivating cities to improve their position in the climate neutrality hierarchy.

References

1. UN - United Nations: World Urbanization Prospects: The 2014 Revision, Highlights (ST/ESA/SER.A/352). Department of Economic and Social Affairs, Population Division, United Nations (2015). https://population.un.org/wup/publications/files/wup2014-report.pdf. Accessed 22 Jan 2023

2. Suzuki, H., Dastur, A., Moffatt, S., Yabuki, N., Maruyama, H.: Eco2Cities - ecological cities as economic cities. The World Bank (2010). https://doi.org/10.1596/978-0-8213-8046-8

3. De Filippi, F., Coscia, C., Guido, R.: From smart-cities to smart-communities: how can we evaluate the impacts of innovation and inclusive processes in urban context? Int. J. E-Plann. Res. **8**(2), 24–44 (2019). https://doi.org/10.4018/IJEPR.2019040102

4. Panagiotopoulou, M., Kokla, M., Stratigea, A.: Conceptualizing small and medium-sized smart cities in the mediterranean: an ontological approach. Int. J. e-Plann. Res. **8**(4), 17–41 (2019). https://doi.org/10.4018/IJEPR.2019100102

5. UN Environmental Programme. https://www.unep.org/explore-topics/resource-efficiency/what-we-do/cities/cities-and-climate-change. Accessed 18 Jan 2023

6. OECD: Cities and climate change – Policy Perspectives – National Governments Enabling Local Action (2014). https://www.oecd.org/environment/cc/Cities-and-climate-change-2014-Policy-Perspectives-Final-web.pdf. Accessed 18 Jan 2023

7. IRP - International Resource Panel: The Weight of Cities - Resource Requirements of Future Urbanization. Report by the IRP, United Nations Environment Programme, Nairobi, Kenya (2018). https://www.resourcepanel.org/reports/weight-cities, Accessed 31 Jan 2023

8. Davoudi, S.: Climate change, securitisation of nature, and resilient urbanism. Eviron. Plann. C. Gov. Policy **32**(2), 360–375 (2014). https://doi.org/10.1068/c12269

9. IPCC: Climate Change 2014 - Mitigation of Climate Change. Chapter 12, Human Settlements, Infrastructure and Spatial Planning. Potsdam, IPCC—Working Group III (2014)

10. Liang, L., Wang, Z., Li, J.: The effect of urbanization on environmental pollution in rapidly developing urban agglomerations. J. Clean. Prod. **237**, 117649 (2019). https://doi.org/10.1016/j.jclepro.2019.117649

11. Zipperer, C.W., Northrop, R., Michael Andreu, M.: Urban development and environmental degradation. In: Oxford Research Encyclopedia of Environmental Science (2020). https://doi.org/10.1093/acrefore/9780199389414.013.97

12. Talib, M.N.A., Hashmi, S.H., Aamir, M., Khan, M.A.: Testing non-linear effect of urbanization on environmental degradation: cross-country evidence. Front. Environ. Sci. **10**, 971394 (2022). https://doi.org/10.3389/fenvs.2022.971394

13. UNEP – United Nations Environmental Programme: Making Peace with Nature - A Scientific Blueprint to Tackle the Climate, Biodiversity and Pollution Emergencies. Nairobi (2021). ISBN 978-92-807-3837-7. https://www.unep.org/resources/making-peace-naturelast. Accessed 28 Jan 2023

14. Piñuela, M., Clifton, J.: Action Plan to Tackle the Triple Crisis. Cultivo Land PBC (2021). https://cultivo.land/documents/Cultivo_Action_Plan_Triple-Crisis.pdf. Accessed 17 Jan 2023

15. Girardet, H.: Creating Sustainable Cities. Green Books Ltd., Devon (1999). ISBN 9780857843524

16. Panagiotopoulou, M., Stratigea, A., Leka, A.: Gathering global intelligence for assessing performance of smart, sustainable, resilient, and inclusive cities (S2RIC): an integrated indicator framework. In: Silva, C.N. (ed.) Citizen-Responsive Urban E-Planning: Recent Developments and Critical Perspectives, pp. 305–345. IGI Global (2020). https://doi.org/10.4018/978-1-7998-4018-3. ISBN13 9781799840183

17. Kanter, R.M., Litow, S.S.: Informed and interconnected: a manifesto for smarter cities. Harvard Business School General Management Unit Working Paper 09-141 (2009)

18. Stratigea, A., Leka, A., Panagiotopoulou, M.: In search of indicators for assessing smart and sustainable cities and communities' performance. Int. J. e-Plann. Res. 6(1), 43–73 (2017). https://doi.org/10.4018/IJEPR.2017010103

19. UNECE – United Nations Economic Commission for Europe: Climate Neutral Cities – How to Make Cities Less Energy and Carbon Intensive and More Resilient to Climatic Changes. United Nations, ECE/HBP/168, Geneva, Switzerland (2011)

20. Brunetta, G., Caldarice, O., Tollin, N., Rosas-Casals, M., Morató, J.: Urban Resilience for Risk and Adaptation Governance – Theory and Practice. Springer, Heidelberg (2019). https://doi.org/10.1007/978-3-319-76944-8. ISSN 2524-5988

21. Theodora, Y., Stratigea, A.: Climate change and strategic adaptation planning in mediterranean insular territories: gathering methodological insights from greek experiences. In: Gervasi, O., et al. (eds.) ICCSA 2021. LNCS, vol. 12958, pp. 100–115. Springer, Cham (2021). https://doi.org/10.1007/978-3-030-87016-4_8 ISBN 978-3-030-87015-7

22. Managi, S., Lindner, R., Stevens, C.C.: Technology policy for the sustainable development goals: from the global to the local level. Technol. Forecast. Soc. Chang. **162**, 120410 (2021). https://doi.org/10.1016/j.techfore.2020.120410

23. Ordonez-Ponce, E.: The role of local cultural factors in the achievement of the sustainable development goals. Sustain. Dev. **31**(2), 1122–1134 (2023). https://doi.org/10.1002/sd.2445

24. COM(2019) 640 final: The European Green Deal. Communication from the Commission to the European Parliament, the European Council, the Council, the European Economic and Social Committee and the Committee of the Regions, European Commission, Brussels (2019)

25. Dasgupta, S., Lall, S., Wheeler, D.: Cutting global carbon emissions: where do cities stand? (2022). https://blogs.worldbank.org/sustainablecities/cutting-global-carbon-emissions-where-do-cities-stand. Accessed 29 Jan 2023

26. Nijkamp, P., Rietveld, P., Voogd, H.: Decision Support Model for Regional Sustainable Development. Avebury, Aldershot (1990)

27. Vreeker, R., Nijkamp, P., Ter Welle, C.: A multicriteria decision support methodology for evaluating airport expansion plans. TI 2001-005/3, Tinbergen Institute Discussion Paper (2001)

28. Nijkamp, P., Torrieri, F.: A decision support system for assessing alternative projects for the design of a new road network. Serie Research Memoranda 2000-2 1, Free University Amsterdam (2000)

29. Nijkamp, P.: Culture and region: a multidimensional evaluation of monuments. Research Memorandum 1987-71, Free University of Amsterdam (1987)

30. Hinloopen, E., Nijkamp, P.: Qualitative multiple criteria choice analysis: the dominant REGIME method. Research Memorandum 1986-45, Free University of Amsterdam (1986)

31. Giffinger, R., Fertner, C., Kramar, H., Kalasek, R., Pichler-Milanović, N., Meijers, E.: Smart cities ranking of European medium-sized cities (final report). Centre of Regional Science, Vienna UT (2007). http://www.smart-cities.eu/download/smart_cities_final_report.pdf. Accessed 20 Jan 2023

32. Stratigea, A.: The concept of smart cities – towards community development? NETCOM 26(3–4), 377–390 (2012). https://doi.org/10.4000/netcom.1105

Application and Evaluation of a Cross-Fertilization Methodology in the AEC Industry: New Technologies, Digitalization and Robotization

Daniele Soraggi[1](✉) [iD] and Ilaria Delponte[2] [iD]

[1] Italian Excellence Center for Logistics, Infrastructures and Transport, University of Genoa, 16126 Genoa, Italy
daniele.soraggi@edu.unige.it
[2] Civil Chemical and Environmental Engineering Department, University of Genoa, 16145 Genoa, Italy

Abstract. The construction industry (AEC) has been stuck in a state of lagging innovation for too long, especially when certain processes are deepened. Excluding research into innovative and high-performance materials, it is difficult to stimulate and introduce new updates in other sectors.

In this historical context - NextGenEU, Green Deal, Horizon Europe - the AEC is called upon to assimilate the advances that Industry 4.0, digitization and robotization are introducing. This will have to happen quickly and with different types of innovations: technological, in management processes and in the economic structure of companies.

The aim of this paper is to design a methodology to classify useful innovations for an established sector and to determine which ones are more difficult to adopt and implement successfully. This was done by applying the methodology of the so-called "cross-fertilization" of knowledge spheres. This methodology is based on the principle that multidisciplinary interaction of projects and technologies leads to a network of innovative ideas.

The original contribution of this paper is the definition of the characteristics arising from the cross-fertilization process and the qualitative assessment of their applicability in a stated scenario: the worksite of large-scale infrastructure projects, with a particular focus on the management and monitoring of work progress and the construction of tunnels. The analysis of the results highlights four areas of action for implanting innovations in AEC and how this is only possible through a multi-disciplinary and integrated process.

Keywords: Innovation · Industrial Cross-fertilization · Digitalization

1 Introduction

Over the years, within the AEC industry - Architecture, Engineering and Construction - a status quo in the operative approach and method has been maintained. This has highlighted the difficulty in the introduction of new technologies and innovations on a large

© The Author(s), under exclusive license to Springer Nature Switzerland AG 2023
O. Gervasi et al. (Eds.): ICCSA 2023 Workshops, LNCS 14105, pp. 676–689, 2023.
https://doi.org/10.1007/978-3-031-37108-0_43

scale [1], often one-off and dedicated (e.g. new materials). The latency in the introduction of new technologies in AEC can be traced back to several inhibiting factors: the small number of economies of scale within a highly fragmented sector [2]; the absence of initiatives and training of companies and employees [3]; and the multidisciplinary nature of each project and the presence of multiple teams generate difficulties in recognizing roles, responsibilities and distribution of benefits [4].

With the advent of the fourth industrial revolution, we are witness of an acceleration in the digitalization and automation of work that will have an enormous impact on the work and career experiences of individuals [5]. In the latest recovery plans and new development strategies on an International scale and promoted by the European Union, a key role is played by Digitalization. The European Green Deal identifies digital transition as one of the two pillars on which to formulate its strategies [6] to be implemented through the plans promoted by the NextGenerationEU fund [7]. Within them, a number of themes of interest are highlighted in this contribution: Research and innovation - to boost economies and competitiveness; Employment support and job creation - to support job creation and transition to new sectors and types of work; Connectivity - fast and accessible digital connectivity; Energy efficiency in buildings - investment in energy renovations and compliance with the highest energy efficiency standards [8]. The latter is conceptually extendable to the entire AEC industry.

The Cluster 4 - Digital, Industry and Space - of Horizon Europe itself emphasizes how investment in research in this sector can support Europe's technological and economic competitiveness. Some specific areas of intervention are also highlighted: a human-centered and ethical development of digital and industrial technologies; digital and emerging technologies for competitiveness and fit for the Green Deal [9]. The whole plan outlines a circle of initiatives, strategies, and guidelines at European level on the digitalization of processes and infrastructures. Indeed, the AEC and related industries are stimulating the adoption of advancements in artificial intelligence and Internet of Things (IoT) ecosystems to increase productivity and economics value [1].

This contribution attempts to answer some questions arising from the difficulty of introducing digital and robotic innovations within the AEC; an industrial cross-fertilization methodology will be developed to investigate the main innovative trends: intelligent robotics; cloud VR/AR and AIoT; Digital Twins; 4D printing and Block-chain [10].

Which industries innovate the most?

Do they prefer digital systems or the introduction of robotic systems in a given context? How can these innovations be introduced in AEC?

In order to address these questions, 125 innovations were identified within 9 target sectors. From their analysis, in relation to their possible applicability in the construction of large infrastructures and the management of complex construction sites, four possible alternatives for their classification come out.

The paper is divided into five parts: the second is useful to provide a context around which to focus the research. The concepts of Building Information Model (BIM) and Digital Twin (DT) will be introduced as well as motivating the issues that inhibit innovation within the AEC.

The third part proposes and explains the original methodology used, which cross-fertilizes critical literature analysis. In the first instance, two of the problems present in an AEC are identified: the maintenance of the Tunnel Boring Machine (TBM) head and the tracking of the progress of huge worksites.

In the remaining parts, the results will be analyzed, and conclusions will be drawn regarding the methodology used. For the development of this methodology and its application, reference is made to the activities carried out by UniWeLab, a Joint Lab of the University of Genoa, which involves volunteer students from different disciplines doing research on real problems, identified by the collaboration between the University and Webuild, a leading Italian multinational in the large infrastructure construction sector.

2 Background

Referring to digital innovation in AEC, the thought goes to the modification of operation sequences and processes, caused using digital technologies [11]. The challenge is to have a process that is able to encompass the various components around the realization of an infrastructure, in which engineering and economics aspects are no longer than only few of the branches. From this assumption, new technologies will improve and change operations and processes, requiring changes in overall security, adaptive business, and sustainability. [12–14]. Therefore, at all stages of the infrastructure life cycle, from preliminary design to execution and maintenance, they are required to adopt digital models that facilitate the project management process [15].

Precisely with a view to a circular economy for AEC, several studies focus on the generation, evaluation and valorization of construction and demolition waste (CDW) [16, 17]; this is mainly due to the fact that the current recycling system for these materials has a high environmental impact and a considerable level of resource waste [18, 19]. Bringing CDWs within a circular vision in the AEC industry, as well as digitization, has encountered socio-economic barriers related to resistance to cultural change and the high cost of making a profit only in the long run [16].

In recent years, much attention arose around technologies such as BIM and DT as tools to be implemented and useful for the life cycle management of infrastructure and buildings [20]. BIM is an important tool for a complete digitalization of the building process; however, this innovation process is mainly developed by the tool providers themselves [21] and the innovation itself can be classified as product or service innovation, or related to operational and management practices, methods and processes [22]. Instead, a Digital Twin is a complete simulation of a real system through which to model its behavior as parameters and operational scenarios change in order to predict how it will respond [23]. Although DTs are still in their infancy, BIM systems are already more solid. However, in the literature many researchers refer to DTs interchangeably with BIM [24]. This underlying confusion may be among the problems that prevent a "smooth" implementation of these tools.

In addition to BIM and DT, artificial intelligence (AI) is increasingly being adopted by organizations, but implementation is often done without carefully consideration of the employees who will work with it. If employees do not understand or work with AI, it is unlikely to bring value to the company [25].

Another topic of relevance is the safety of and on construction sites. Focusing on AEC, conceptual designs for safety management based on the use of AI directly on the construction site were first proposed [26]; the influence of site layouts on construction workers' perceptions of robots and how their layouts affect the smooth running of site activities was also studied [27, 28].

Furthermore, among the issues that inhibit investment in digitalization and automation in AEC, it has been noted how they can contribute to wages and careers' inequality in low and medium-skilled jobs [29, 30]. However, it has been shown that in the sectors implementing robotics, inequality in the employment/population ratio is minimal [31], especially when compared to the impact of other capital and technologies [28]. In fact, project management in the construction industry presents unique challenges, which have a clear impact on project success. This is due to the fact that each project has unique characteristics such as: location, number of personnel, specific equipment, integrated logistics, cost variations and business capabilities. These are all factors that influence the design and make up the complex space of maneuvering in management [32].

Thus, referring to the major problems in the construction sector, the following items mainly emerge: labour shortages; site safety; site management and worksite organization; optimal use and processing of materials; personnel training and updating. These are all industrial systems' issues that are responsible for the delay the introduction of new technologies.

3 Methodology

As the previous section has shown, there is neither much past expertise nor novel motivation to introduce new technologies within the AEC and this is mainly due to the specific boundary conditions that differ from project to project.

For this reason, the UniWeLab research group identified the need to introduce a new methodology that could help the development of new solutions. This is the case of a context, such as that of Genoa. The City sees numerous works being carried out, involving excavations in complicated territories and the management of construction sites that are large in terms of the number of activities, companies and workers (e.g. Terzo Valico - Cociv, Sub-port Tunnel, New Outer Dam, New Waterfront).

The methodology proposed and used by the consists of three steps (see Fig. 1): a targeted literature analysis; the identification of the main issues under study; the application of industrial cross-fertilization to identify the industries that innovate the most and their affinity with AEC. This approach investigates if and how technological and cultural cross-fertilization from other industries is possible for AEC (see Fig. 1).

All outputs contribute to the final classification of the four areas of intervention, which will be commented on in the fourth section of the paper.

3.1 Literature Analysis

The literature review is conceived as a preliminary step in the start-up of the methodology, the purpose of which is to provide basic training on the subject of investigation and its issues: in this case, it is about digitalization within the AEC industry.

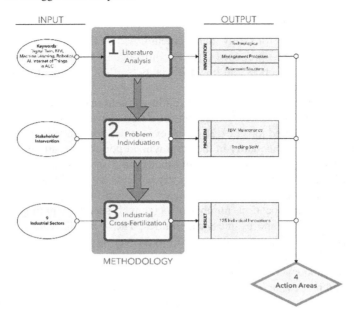

Fig. 1. Example diagram of the proposed methodology.

The first part of the literature analysis consists of identifying articles that make up the starting framework. This was done by asking the students in the research lab to cross-reference some keywords on Google Scholar and Scopus: Digital Twin, BIM or Building Information Model, Machine Learning, Robotics, Artificial Intelligence or AI, Internet of Things or IoT. Each of these had to be accompanied by the terms: AEC or AEC Industry or Construction Sector. Furthermore, some minimum criteria were used to refine the search: published and open access articles, in English. This first part composes the necessary input for the start of phase 1 of the methodology (as in Fig. 1).

The second part of the literature analysis consists of reading and critically reporting on the selected paper. This is done by identifying some of the main components included in each paper: thesis developed by authors, the solution they identified, analysis of the bibliography they used. Finally, the students were asked to summarize the main topic of the paper they analyzed through a guided critical analysis.

The last part is, therefore, the evaluation of results or outputs. Three types of innovation emerge from the literature review: (I) technological innovations; (II) innovations in management processes; (III) innovation in the economic structure of companies.

Technological innovations (I) include robots working autonomously [33] and alongside workers [34]; machine learning applied to real time video capturing infrastructures progress [35, 36] or machines for laser scanning in boundary conditions [37, 38].

In management process innovations (II) there are: software for modelling the entire life-cycle of the worksite [39, 40] such as BIM [15, 22] or digital twin [41]; Decision Support System technologies [42–44]; VR and AR tools to support and simulate design [45] or IoT and OT ecosystems - operational technologies [46]; collaborative BIM Decision Framework [47]; a multi-objective Genetic Algorithm "GA" [48]. When talking about GA in AEC, reference is made to models that aim to provide horizontal and vertical support in the organization of mega-projects. This is done through a digital system programmed to verify operations and capable of reconfiguring itself according to changing boundary conditions in order to minimize project duration and cost, optimize resource and maximize quality [49].

Innovation in economic structure of companies (III) are: digital infrastructure for effective and sustainable circular economies [49, 50]; AI integration model based on socio-technical systems theory (STS) [25], managerial business strategies of investing in innovation trends [51].

Concluding the analysis, it is the advent of Industry 4.0 itself that requires companies to reorganize themselves structurally; furthermore, another innovative aspect that emerges is the conscious use of mobile and social devices, in conjunction with specialized professionals able to facilitate the transition, by incurring minimal costs for the distribution of information and knowledge [52].

3.2 Problem Individuation

In identifying the main issues to be studied, certain notions from the previous phase were considered, but added practical and critical reflections emerged from the dialogue with the company.

The inputs from phase 1 of this methodology, it emerges that there is a little appeal in the introduction of new digital and robotic technologies in the AEC, although there is a demand and a need for them. In addition, among the major challenges faced during the tasks that make up each job order, problems emerged related to the identification of critical elements and full-time site management. In addition to these, an issue of highlighted importance by the Webuild managers of the workshop is the issue of operator safety during the most critical tasks.

From the first stated assumption, the issue of monitoring and controlling site activities emerged: tracking of statement of work (SoW). This operation is still poorly digitalized and too dependent on human judgement; SoW Tracking on the construction site is traditionally a non automated activity requiring visual inspection and dependent on human judgement and, therefore, error [35]. This activity therefore can be a primary test bed for the implementation of new technologies or digital ecosystems.

Among the most complex tasks affecting worker safety and health are those inherent in excavation operations. TBMs are widely used in hard rock tunnel excavation due to their optimal performance; however, during tunnel excavation, the rotary head is element that suffers most from wear and therefore subject to the most frequent maintenance operations [53, 54]. These critical operations occur in critical situations for the operator who, consequently, is put at risk.

Thus, in the next steps of the proposed methodology, the possibilities of introducing digital innovations in these two processes involving AEC through a process of Industrial Cross-Fertilization will be analyzed.

3.3 Cross-Fertilization Application

The last part of the proposed methodology uses an industrial cross-fertilization process to understand in which industries, outside the AEC, the major innovations occur and whether they are importable in the construction sector. Building on cross-fertilization concept, that originates in the natural sciences and accelerates the natural evolutionary process [55], various disciplines-marketing, education sciences, management-have inherited this methodology by readjusting it to their needs [56].

Thus, trying to give a definition of Cross-Fertilization as applied to the field of research and development in industry, it can be said that Cross-Fertilization is done when the combination of interdisciplinary technologies and knowledge generates new broader technological opportunities in terms of Product, Performance and Functionality [57–61]. Therefore, the purpose of interdisciplinary cross-fertilization is to avoid inventing something new that already exists; to fill gaps in a field by synthesizing knowledge dispersed across several disciplines towards a single result [62].

For this phase of the methodology, nine industrial sectors were identified in which to research new digital, robotic technologies introduced in recent times: Aeronautics and Aerospace; Agribusiness; Chemistry and Materials; Electronics and Information; Energetics; Military; Mining-Oilfield; Port; Safety and Health.

The search for innovations in other industries was carried out by the students in the UniWeLab laboratory. For each sector, the search was carried out using different methods: web search, scientific articles, company reports and newsletters, trade journals... The output of this third stage of the methodology is a list of innovations to be evaluated. Each element of this list was classified according to its sector of origin and then validated as specified in Sect. 4; the ultimate goal is to determine in which sectors there are more innovations and which of them can be introduced in the AEC and in which areas.

4 Results' Analysis

Through this method, 125 technological innovations in 9 different industrial sectors were identified. Subsequently, a skimming process was introduced to identify unsuitable innovations, which reduced the list to 111; among the reasons why some were excluded were because they were too generic in relation to the contribution they could make, e.g. digital twin or robotics; or because their applicability was too far removed from the relevant sector, e.g. Synthetic Meat.

Table 1 summarizes the results of the list by breaking down the innovations by industry sector of origin at two different points in time: before and after the validation process (see Table 1). The largest digital and robotic innovations identified come from the broad sectors such as Aeronautics and Aerospace and Port (26 and 22 innovations). These are two areas where the demand for innovation is broad and urgent for the proper handling of complex tasks and activities and where precise execution is required. Also relevant is the interest in digital innovation for the Safety and Health sector, underlining how the topic of safety, which has emerged among the crucial issues for AEC, is among the most proactive.

Looking at those sectors that retained the same number of innovations after the skimming process, Mining-Oilfield and Electronics and Information stand out. This could also be due to the affinity of the two sectors with the two issues that emerged in phase 2: TBM maintenance and SoW tracking: two works that, respectively, refer to the processes of excavation and remote verification of activities and their quantification. In the Agribusiness Sector the introduction of AI and robots that facilitate the harvesting process face some challenges attributable to SoW tracking and processing verification. Computer vision technologies are being investigated to identify fruits and vegetables in plantations and locate their position through image retrieval for algorithm operation [63, 64]; another issue concerns the study of manipulators, which must be robust enough to be able to rip the fruit from its seat, but sensitive enough to avoid compromising its integrity [64, 65].

Finally, the Chemistry and Materials sector is the industry area that has the greatest grip within the AEC, as a large part of today's construction activities include retrofitting: an activity where materials that combine high performance and cost-effectiveness are among the most popular.

Table 1. Innovations by industry sector of origin, before and after the validation process.

Industrial Sector	First List		After Validation	
	n.	%	n.	%
Aeronautics and Aerospace	26	23,4	22	19,8
Agribusiness	10	9,0	9	8,1
Chemistry and Materials	8	7,2	7	6,3
Electronics and Information	9	8,1	9	8,1
Energetics	16	14,4	15	13,5
Military	11	9,9	11	9,9
Mining-Oilfield	5	4,5	5	4,5
Port	22	19,8	18	16,2
Safety and Health	18	16,2	15	13,5
	125		111	

The last step in the analysis of the results was to verify the applicability of the innovations within the AEC. This process investigates how to classify (in a descending scale) each innovation within a reference context of the construction industry. As Table 2 shows, it was possible to identify 4 action areas which can introduce a digital and robotic innovation process: Accessory Innovation, System Innovation, Construction Site Innovation and On Operator Innovation.

4.1 Accessory Innovation

Innovations included in the Accessory Innovations are all those new technologies that do not have a possible direct application with respect to the given tasks. However, they can support of other innovations; they have collaborative value e.g. new materials or Hydrogen combustion cell. Their application is to be considered ancillary to other technologies, in order to achieve a higher level of autonomy, safety, sustainability and innovation.

Table 2. Table identifies the 4 action areas in relation to the number of innovations identified.

Classification	n
Accessory Innovation	28
System Innovation	32
Construction Site Innovation	10
On Operator Innovation	41

4.2 System Innovation

System Innovations fall mainly into process innovations, in which the pivotal goal being increased efficiency, reduced costs and time within a production process. It can be seen that, among the sectors investing the most in these technologies, there are the Port, Aerospace and Information industries e.g. Simulators or IoT ecosystem. System innovations make possible to intervene upstream of the worksite, going preventive and generating a safer and more manageable sensor and monitoring system, or platforms that can independently monitor the progress of construction projects and build a systematic strategy for collecting standardized data [66].

4.3 Construction Site Innovation

Construction Site Innovations possess a characterization such that they can act directly within the shipyard system, with possibly minor or major modifications to it. In this case we see a strong inclusion of robots within the sectors taken as examples: agribusiness, military, port and health e.g. Industrial Robots like [67]. These robots can act in three modes: Local Control; Remote Control; and full Autonomous [68]. Each level through which a robot acts indicates a different type of human-robot interface, this, means that depending on the processing at the site it is necessary to plan which robot technology is best suited. Furthermore, the results suggest that separate human-robot sites increase the perceived safety of workers in robotic tasks [10].

4.4 On Operator Innovation

On Operator Innovation means investing directly in technologies that enhance individual human potential. A worker in the construction industry performs wearisome work both physically and at stress levels, so this area includes technologies that safeguard and monitor the health of the operator e.g. mechanical prostheses. The main goal of this kind of innovation is to minimize the risk for operator - before-during-after work - directly protecting human bodies. Finally, there are innovations that utilize the direct presence of the operator on site to verify operations e.g. smart lens for constant monitoring of accessibility.

5 Discussion and Conclusion

Concluding remarks firstly concern to the analysis of the limitations of this research, mainly arising from the context of application. Referring to existent literature, it is possible to point out that, as far as the subsequent stages of the methodology are concerned, the results obtained are sufficient for the identification of the issues around which the specific case study was developed. However, for a future refinement of this methodology, an updating of the analysis through an established methodology, for instance such as PRISMA (Preferred Reporting Items for Systematic Reviews and Meta-Analyses), can be proposed. This procedure is followed for an objective evaluation of the literature, assuming that a bibliography emerging from key word searches in Scopus can be integrated for a greater accuracy of the result.

The application of this kind of methodology requires a rapid development of digitalization and cannot be done alone. Therefore, once the change due to the Industrial Revolution 4.0 is taken into account by the AEC companies, they will have to adapt to the transformation, caring not to settle for one-off solutions aimed at changing a single process, but evolving into an ecosystem architecture for which a bold, conscious and long-term vision is required [46].

Primarily, it important to highlight that AI changed job structures; for example, the use of robots in pharmacy industry reshaped the employment relations between different occupational groups and created new types of professional figures in new jobs [69]. Is this precisely the definition of new tasks that provides the incipit for the digital development of AEC? Relative to the use of AI are increasing figures such as trainers, explainers, and sustainers [70] who are responsible for the proper functioning of AI. In addition, new figures also call for new government policies to encourage and help the reducing the negative impacts of AI on future jobs [71].

This process cannot be steered by sanctions and penalization, because it is now obsolete and ineffective [22]; it is necessary to establish a collaborative and strategic process of knowledge and technology sharing among different sectors to achieve a higher level of innovation. In order to accelerate this change in a static sector like the EAC, disciplinary interaction under the intuition of individual actors is not enough; policies and initiatives from above are needed. With this in mind, the positions adopted at the European level with the aforementioned NextGenerationUE, Green Deal and Horizon Europe projects are aimed at facilitating digitisation in all sectors. Of course, it is necessary to point out that the import process, which is not present within this paper, will have to take place depending on the characteristics of the target sector, and each technology, where it is possible, will undergo more or less significant modifications. In fact, as is evident from the analysis of the results and the four fields of action identified within the AEC, it is not always the case that a new technology has the characteristics for a right implementation in a new sector, but it is the target sector itself that needs to undertake an evolution and an updating. Perhaps for a better implementation of digital within the AEC's worksites, could it be firstly necessary to rethink their configuration?

In conclusion, it emerges that digitalization is expected to create new opportunities and solve old problems, and this can also happen through an integrative process between separate disciplines, knowledge and sectors. Indeed, the cross-fertilization of knowledge and technologies networking is an advantageous mode of operation for innovation in any sector [59, 63].

References

1. Maureira, C., Allende-Cid, H., García, J.: Optimization in AEC-AI 4.0 industry multi-level adaptive methodology for knowledge mapping. In: Yang, X.S., Sherratt, S., Dey, N., Joshi, A. (eds.) Proceedings of Seventh International Congress on Information and Communication Technology. LNNS, vol. 465, pp. 729–737. Springer, Singapore (2023). https://doi.org/10.1007/978-981-19-2397-5_65
2. Johnson, R.E., Laepple, E.S.: Digital innovation and organizational change in design practice. In: Proceedings of the 23th Annual Conference of the Association for Computer-Aided Design in Architecture (ACADIA), pp. 179–183 (2003). https://doi.org/10.52842/conf.acadia.2003.179
3. Bernstein, P.G., Pittman, J.H.: Barriers to the adoption of building information modeling in the building industry. Autodesk Building Solutions, White Paper **2004**(1), 1–14 (2004)
4. Holzer, D.: Are you talking to me? Why bim alone is not the answer. Association of Architecture Schools in Australasia, March 2007. https://doi.org/10.5130/aab.v
5. Hirschi, A.: The fourth industrial revolution: issues and implications for career research and practice. Career Dev. Q. **66**(3), 192–204 (2018). https://doi.org/10.1002/cdq.12142
6. European Green Deal Homepage. https://digital-strategy.ec.europa.eu/en/policies. Accessed 09 Mar 2023
7. NextGenerationEU Homepage. https://next-generation-eu.europa.eu. Accessed 09 Mar 2023
8. NextGenerationEU – Tematic analyses. https://ec.europa.eu/economy_finance/recovery-and-resilience-scoreboard. Accessed 09 Mar 2023
9. Horizon Europe – Cluster 4 Homepage. https://horizoneurope.apre.it/struttura-e-programmi/global-challenges-european-industrial-competitiveness/cluster-4/. Accessed 09 Mar 2023
10. Pan, Y., Zhang, L.: Roles of artificial intelligence in construction engineering and management: a critical review and future trends. Autom. Constr. **122**. Elsevier B.V (2021). https://doi.org/10.1016/j.autcon.2020.103517
11. Goger, G., Piskernik, M., Urban, H.: Studie: Potenziale der Digitalisierung im Bauwesen Empfehlungen für zukünftige Forschung und Innovationen (Study: Potentials of digitalization in the construction industry Recommendations for future research and innovation). WKO - Wirtschaftskammer Österreich (2018)
12. Kipper, L.M., Iepsen, S., Dal Forno, A.J., et al.: Scientific mapping to identify competencies required by industry 4.0. Technol. Soc. **64** (2021). https://doi.org/10.1007/978-981-19-2397-5_65
13. Gorecky, D., Khamis, M., Mura, K.: Introduction and establishment of virtual training in the factory of the future. Int. J. Comput. Integr. Manuf. **30**(1), 182–190 (2017). https://doi.org/10.1080/0951192X.2015.1067918
14. Li, X., Shen, G.Q., Wu, P., Teng, Y.: Integrating building information modeling and prefabrication housing production. Autom. Constr. **100**, 46–60 (2019). https://doi.org/10.1016/j.autcon.2018.12.024
15. Goger, G., Bisenberger, T.: Digitalization in infrastructure construction – developments in construction operations. Geomechanik Und Tunnelbau **13**(2), 165–177 (2020). https://doi.org/10.1002/geot.201900077
16. Charef, R., Morel, J.C., Rakhshan, K.: Barriers to implementing the circular economy in the construction industry: a critical review. Sustain. **13**(23), 1–18 (2021). https://doi.org/10.3390/su132312989

17. Shooshtarian, S., Maqsood, T., Caldera, S., Ryley, T.: Transformation towards a circular economy in the Australian construction and demolition waste management system. Sustain. Prod. Consum. **30**, 89–106 (2022). https://doi.org/10.1016/j.spc.2021.11.032

18. Rose, C.M., Stegemann, J.A.: From waste management to component management in the construction industry. Sustain. **10**(1), 1–21 (2018). https://doi.org/10.3390/su10010229

19. Gruhler, K., Schiller, G.: Grey energy impact of building material recycling – a new assessment method based on process chains. Resour. Conserv. Recycl. Adv. **18**(February), 200139 (2023). https://doi.org/10.1016/j.rcradv.2023.200139

20. Naderi, H., Shojaei, A.: Digital twinning of civil infrastructures: current state of model architectures, interoperability solutions, and future prospects. Autom. Constr. **149**. Elsevier B.V (2023). https://doi.org/10.1016/j.autcon.2023.104785

21. Aminoff, A., Kaipia, R., Pihlajamaa, M., Tanskanen, K., Vuori, M., Makkonen, M.: Managing supplier innovations: a systematic literature review. Paper presented at 24th Annual IPSERA Conference, Amsterdam, Netherlands (2015)

22. Aminoff, A., Kiviniemi, M.: Driving supplier innovations towards digitalization of infrastructure projects. In: Proceedings of ISPIM Conferences, June 2016

23. Said, M.M., Pilgrim, R., Rideout, G., Butt, S.: Theoretical development of a digital-twin based automation system for oil well drilling rigs. In: Society of Petroleum Engineers - SPE Canadian Energy Technology Conference, CET (2022). https://doi.org/10.2118/208902-MS

24. Sacks, R., Brilakis, I., Pikas, E., Xie, H.S., Girolami, M.: Construction with digital twin information systems. Data-Centric Eng. **1**(6) (2020). https://doi.org/10.1017/dce.2020.16

25. Makarius, E.E., Mukherjee, D., Fox, J.D., Fox, A.K.: Rising with the machines: a sociotechnical framework for bringing artificial intelligence into the organization. J. Bus. Res. **120**(July), 262–273 (2020). https://doi.org/10.1016/j.jbusres.2020.07.045

26. Kontogiannis, T., Kossiavelou, Z.: Stress and team performance: principles and challenges for intelligent decision aids. Saf. Sci. **33**(3), 103–128 (1999). https://doi.org/10.1016/S0925-7535(99)00027-2

27. You, S., Kim, J.H., Lee, S.H., Kamat, V., Robert, L.P.: Enhancing perceived safety in human–robot collaborative construction using immersive virtual environments. Autom. Constr. **96**(March 2017), 161–170 (2018). https://doi.org/10.1016/j.autcon.2018.09.008

28. Berg, A., Buffie, E.F., Zanna, L.F.: Should we fear the robot revolution? (The correct answer is yes). J. Monet. Econ. **97**, 117–148 (2018). https://doi.org/10.1016/j.jmoneco.2018.05.014

29. Guy, M., Natraj, A., Van Reenen, J.: Has ICT polarized skill demand? Evidence from eleven countries over twenty-five years. Rev. Econ. Stat. **96**(1), 60–77 (2014). https://doi.org/10.1162/REST_a_00366

30. Goos, M., Manning, A.: Lousy and lovely jobs: the rising polarization of work in Britain. Rev. Econ. Stat. **89**(1), 118–133 (2007). https://doi.org/10.1162/rest.89.1.118

31. Acemoglu, D., Restrepo, P.: Robots and jobs: evidence from us labour markets. J. Polit. Econ. **128**(6), 2188–2244 (2020). https://doi.org/10.1086/705716

32. Rafiei, M.H., Adeli, H.: Novel machine-learning model for estimating construction costs considering economic variables and indexes. J. Constr. Eng. Manag. **144**(12), 1–9 (2018). https://doi.org/10.1061/(asce)co.1943-7862.0001570

33. Saavedra Sueldo, C., Perez Colo, I., De Paula, M., Villar, S.A., Acosta, G.G.: ROS-based architecture for fast digital twin development of smart manufacturing robotized systems. Ann. Oper. Res. **322**(1), 75–99 (2022). https://doi.org/10.1007/s10479-022-04759-4

34. Cai, J., Du, A., Liang, X., Li, S.: Prediction-based path planning for safe and efficient human-robot collaboration in construction via deep reinforcement learning. J. Comput. Civ. Eng. **37**(1), 1–10 (2023). https://doi.org/10.1061/(asce)cp.1943-5487.0001056

35. Greeshma, A.S., Edayadiyil, J.B.: Automated progress monitoring of construction projects using machine learning and image processing approach. Mater. Today Proc. **65**, 554–563 (2022). https://doi.org/10.1016/j.matpr.2022.03.137

36. Kevin, H.K., Fard, G.: Multi-sample image-based material recognition and formalized sequencing knowledge for operation-level construction progress monitoring. Comput. Civ. Build. Eng. 364–372 (2014). https://doi.org/10.1061/9780784413616.046

37. Mahmoudi, M., Vatankhahan, F., Malekahmadi, O., Goharimehr, R.: Study and performance of three-dimensional laser scanning technology in preparation industrial As-Built plans (2016)

38. Javaid, M., Haleem, A., Pratap Singh, R., Suman, R.: Industrial perspectives of 3D scanning: features, roles and it's analytical applications. Sens. Int. **2**(May), 100114 (2021). https://doi.org/10.1016/j.sintl.2021.100114

39. Hetemi, E., Ordieres-Meré, J., Nuur, C.: An institutional approach to digitalization in sustainability-oriented infrastructure projects: the limits of the building information model. Sustainability (Switzerland) **12**(9), 3893 (2020). https://doi.org/10.3390/su12093893

40. Davies, R., Harty, C.: Implementing site BIM: a case study of ICT innovation on a large hospital project. Autom. Constr. **30**, 15–24 (2013). https://doi.org/10.1016/j.autcon.2012.11.024

41. Rommetveit, R., Bjørkevoll, K.S., Halsey, G.W., et al.: eDrilling: a system for real-time drilling simulation, 3D visualization, and control. In: Society of Petroleum Engineers - Digital Energy Conference and Exhibition 2007, pp. 83–88 (2007). https://doi.org/10.2118/106903-MS

42. Smith, C.J., Wong, A.T.C.: Advancements in artificial intelligence-based decision support systems for improving construction project sustainability: a systematic literature review. Informatics **9**(2), 43 (2022). https://doi.org/10.3390/informatics9020043

43. Rao, H.R., Sridhar, R., Narain, S.: An active intelligent decision support system—architecture and simulation. Decis. Support Syst. **12**, 79–91 (1994). https://doi.org/10.1016/0167-9236(94)90075-2

44. Keen, P.G.W.: Adaptive design for decision support systems. ACM SIGMIS Database **12**(1–2), 15–25 (1980). https://doi.org/10.1145/1017654.1017659

45. Kang, L.S., Moon, H.S., Dawood, N., Kang, M.S.: Development of methodology and virtual system for optimised simulation of road design data. Autom. Constr. **19**(8), 1000–1015 (2010). https://doi.org/10.1016/j.autcon.2010.09.001

46. Woodhead, R., Stephenson, P., Morrey, D.: Digital construction: from point solutions to IoT ecosystem. Autom. Constr. **93**, 35–46 (2018). https://doi.org/10.1016/j.autcon.2018.05.004

47. Gu, N., London, K.: Understanding and facilitating BIM adoption in the AEC industry. Autom. Constr. **19**(8), 988–999 (2010). https://doi.org/10.1016/j.autcon.2010.09.002

48. Aziz, R.F., Hafez, S.M., Abuel-Magd, Y.R.: Smart optimization for mega construction projects using artificial intelligence. Alex. Eng. J. **53**(3), 591–606 (2014). https://doi.org/10.1016/j.aej.2014.05.003

49. Allen, S.D., Sarkis, J.: How can the circular economy-digitalization infrastructure support transformation to strong sustainability? Environ. Res. Infrastruct. Sustain. **1**(3) (2021). https://doi.org/10.1088/2634-4505/ac2784

50. Schröder, P., Bengtsson, M., Cohen, M., et al.: Degrowth within – aligning circular economy and strong sustainability narratives. Resour. Conserv. Recycl. **146**(April), 190–191 (2019). https://doi.org/10.1016/j.resconrec.2019.03.038

51. Gebauer, H., Fleisch, E.: An investigation of the relationship between behavioral processes, motivation, investments in the service business and service revenue. Ind. Mark. Manag. **36**(3), 337–348 (2007). https://doi.org/10.1016/j.indmarman.2005.09.005

52. Bauer, W., Hämmerle, M., Schlund, S., Vocke, C.: Transforming to a hyper-connected society and economy – towards an industry 4.0. Procedia Manuf. **3**(Ahfe), 417–424 (2015). https://doi.org/10.1016/j.promfg.2015.07.200

53. He, J.: Reasonable application, damage causes analysis, and optimization techniques of tunnel boring machine disc cutters in bid 2 project of Lanzhou water source. Tunnel Constr. **42**(S1), 500–507 (2022). https://doi.org/10.3973/j.issn.2096-4498.2022.S1.059

54. Liu, Y., Huang, S., Wang, D., Zhu, G., Zhang, D.: Prediction model of tunnel boring machine disc cutter replacement using kernel support vector machine. Appl. Sci. (Switzerland) **12**(5) (2022). https://doi.org/10.3390/app12052267
55. Hine, R.: A Dictionary of Biology, 8th ed. Oxford University Press, Oxford (2019). https://doi.org/10.1093/acref/9780198821489.001.0001
56. Corazza, L.: Cross-fertilization tra mondo profit e imprese sociali (Cross-fertilisation between the for-profit world and social enterprises). Impresa Sociale **3**(4), 47–60 (2014)
57. Björkdahl, J.: Technology cross-fertilization and the business model: the case of integrating ICTs in mechanical engineering products. Res. Policy **38**(9), 1468–1477 (2009). https://doi.org/10.1016/j.respol.2009.07.006
58. Bogers, M., Horst, W.: Collaborative prototyping: cross-fertilization of knowledge in prototype-driven problem solving. J. Prod. Innov. Manag. **31**(4), 744–764 (2014). https://doi.org/10.1111/jpim.12121
59. González-Piñero, M., Páez-Avilés, C., Juanola-Feliu, E., Samitier, J.: Cross-fertilization of knowledge and technologies in collaborative research projects. J. Knowl. Manag. **25**(11), 34–59 (2021). https://doi.org/10.1108/JKM-04-2020-0270
60. Aparicio, G., Maseda, A., Iturralde, T., Zorrilla, P.: The family business brand: cross-fertilization between fields. Manag. Decis. (2023). https://doi.org/10.1108/md-04-2022-0445
61. Fusco, F., Marsilio, M., Guglielmetti, C.: Co-creation in healthcare: framing the outcomes and their determinants. J. Serv. Manag. **34**(6), 1–26 (2023). https://doi.org/10.1108/josm-06-2021-0212
62. Pan, Y., Froese, F.J.: An interdisciplinary review of AI and HRM: challenges and future directions. Hum. Resour. Manag. Rev (2022).https://doi.org/10.1016/j.hrmr.2022.100924
63. Harvey, J.F.H., Cohendet, P., Simon, L., Borzillo, F.: Knowing communities in the front end of innovation. Res. Technol. Manag. **58**(1), 46–54 (2015). https://doi.org/10.5437/08956308X5801198
64. Boatswain Jacques, A.A., Adamchuk, V.I., Park, J., et al.: Towards a machine vision-based yield monitor for the counting and quality mapping of shallots. Front. Robot. AI **8**(April), 1–12 (2021). https://doi.org/10.3389/frobt.2021.627067
65. Hobbs, J., Khachatryan, V., Barathwaj, S., et al.: Broad dataset and methods for counting and localization of on-ear corn kernels. Front. Robot. AI **8**(May), 1–11 (2021). https://doi.org/10.3389/frobt.2021.627009
66. Alzadjali, A., Alali, M.H., Veeranampalayam Sivakumar, A.N., et al.: Maize tassel detection from UAV imagery using deep learning. Front. Robot. AI **8**(June), 1–15 (2021). https://doi.org/10.3389/frobt.2021.600410
67. Greeshma, A.S., Edayadiyil, J.B.: Automated progress monitoring of construction projects using machine learning and image processing approach. Mater. Today Proc. **65**(2022), 554–563 (2022). https://doi.org/10.1016/j.matpr.2022.03.137
68. Wetzel, E.M., Liu, J., Leathem,T., Sattineni, A.: The Use of Boston Dynamics SPOT in Support of LiDAR Scanning on Active Construction Sites. Paper presented at the Proceedings of the International Symposium on Automation and Robotics in Construction, 2022-July 86–92 (2022). doi: https://doi.org/10.22260/ISARC2022/0014
69. Barrett, M., Oborn, E., Orlikowski, W.J., Yates, J.A.: Reconfiguring boundary relations: robotic innovations in pharmacy work. Organ. Sci. **23**(5), 1448–1466 (2012). https://doi.org/10.1287/orsc.1100.0639
70. Wilson, H.J., Daugherty, P., Bianzino, N.: The jobs that artificial intelligence will create. MIT Sloan Manag. Rev. **58**(4), 14–16 (2017)
71. Waring, P., Bali, A., Vas, C.: The fourth industrial revolution and labour market regulation in Singapore. Econ. Labour Relat. Rev. **31**(3), 347–363 (2020). https://doi.org/10.1177/1035304620941272

Computational Astrochemistry (CompAstro 2023)

Fragmentation Dynamics of Astrochemical Molecules Induced by UV and EUV Photons

Marco Parriani[1]([✉]) [iD], Michele Alagia[2], Robert Richter[3], Stefano Stranges[2,4], Andrea Giustini[5], Simonetta Cavalli[5], Fernando Pirani[5], and Franco Vecchiocattivi[1]

[1] Department of Civil and Environmental Engineering, University of Perugia, Via G. Duranti 93, 06125 Perugia, Italy
marcoparriani@gmail.com, franco@vecchio.it
[2] IOM CNR Laboratorio TASC, 34012 Trieste, Italy
alagia@iom.cnr.it, stefano.stranges@uniroma1.it
[3] Sincrotrone Trieste, Area Science Park, 34149 Basovizza, Trieste, Italy
robert.richter@elettra.trieste.it
[4] Department of Chemistry and Drug Technology, University of Rome Sapienza, 00185 Rome, Italy
[5] Department of Chemistry, Biology and Biotechnologies, University of Perugia, Via Elce di Sotto 8, 06100 Perugia, Italy
andrea.giustini@graduate.univaq.it, simonetta.cavalli@unipg.it

Abstract. The present paper reports on an experimental and computational study aimed at characterizing the microscopic fragmentation dynamics of molecules in space that are subject to double photoionization phenomena by UV and EUV (Extreme Ultraviolet) photons. This kind of processes happening in planetary ionospheres and interstellar medium are simulated at the GASPHASE and CIRCULAR POLARIZATION beamlines of the ELETTRA Synchrotron Facility of Basovizza, Trieste (Italy) using the ARPES (Angle Resolved PhotoEmission Spectroscopy) end station: a molecular beam apparatus coupled with the PEPIPICO (Photoelectron-Photoion-Photoion Coincidence) technique and the TOF (Time-of-Flight) mass spectrometry. The used synchrotron radiation is in the 25.0–45.0 eV photon energy range. Preliminary data are presented for the case of the double photoionization of allene molecules whose photoinduced decomposition highlights 8 different open two-body fragmentation channels and 3 three-body dissociations. For each investigated dissociation channels threshold energies, relative cross sections and the appearing energy for the allene $(C_3H_4)^{2+}$ dication as a function of the photon energy have been measured. Based on a Monte Carlo trajectory simulation, the computational analysis of the PEPIPICO spectra experimentally collected which is still in progress allows the possible extraction of the kinetic energy released (KER) and the angular distributions for the final fragment ions. These observables are very important to rationalize the physical chemistry of the elementary processes induced by the interaction between molecules and ionizing radiations in space.

Keywords: allene · synchrotron radiation · double photoionization · photoelectron-photoion-photoion coincidence · mass spectrometry · astrochemistry

© The Author(s), under exclusive license to Springer Nature Switzerland AG 2023
O. Gervasi et al. (Eds.): ICCSA 2023 Workshops, LNCS 14105, pp. 693–704, 2023.
https://doi.org/10.1007/978-3-031-37108-0_44

1 Introduction

Ionic species can be formed in space in various ways, depending on the specific conditions of the environment [1–5], manly by the interaction of neutral precursors with cosmic rays, UV photons and X-rays. In particular, the absorption of UV and EUV (Extreme Ultraviolet) photons as well as cosmic rays can induce multiple ionization phenomena with formation of doubly charged atomic or molecular species, also named as atomic/molecular dications. They were predicted to exist in the ionospheres of Mars, Venus and Titan and, then, considerable amounts have been detected in such environments highlighting their relevant role, as for example, in the ion escape process from the atmosphere of Mars and Titan [6–10]. Moreover, molecular dications were found in the comet tails, as in the case of the Hyakutake comet. The physico-chemical role of molecular dications in space can be simulated in laboratory using the molecular beam technique coupled with a tunable and intense source of UV and EUV photons as it is the synchrotron radiation. Our research group, since early 2000 is able to produce and characterize molecular dications of atmospheric and astrochemistry interest at the ELETTRA Synchrotron Facility of Basovizza (Trieste, Italy) performing double photoionization experiments. Many molecular species have been studied in the last two decades, as for example N_2O [11, 12], CO_2 [13, 14], C_6H_6 [15, 16], C_2H_2 [17, 18], propylene oxide (CH_2CHCH_2O) [19, 20], ClNO [21, 22], and very recently allene (CH_2CCH_2) molecules.

Allene (C_3H_4) is the first member of the cumulene series C_nH_4. It is well known that allene and the other odd cumulenes belong to the D_{2d} symmetry group, and exhibit stereoisomerism (axial chirality) [23]. The ground state electronic structure is of special interest since the HOMO level is doubly degenerate, having two helical shape MOs of opposite chirality [24]. Although this molecule has no electric dipole moment, and hence could not be directly identified in the interstellar media (ISM), it is thought to be present in space at least as intermediate species [19, 25]. Despite the importance of such a molecule, information on high energy processes involving multiply charged ions of allene is poor. Our research group decided to contribute in order to fill this gap, exploiting our experience in the preparation and generation of effusive molecular beams of simple organic molecules and their employment in a molecular beam apparatus (the ARPES - Angular Resolved PhotoEmission Spectroscopy - end station of the GAS-PHASE). This technique allows photoionization studies to be performed using a tunable and high photon flux of a third-generation synchrotron source. Such experimental studies were mainly based on the use of a PEPIPICO (PhotoElectron–PhotoIon–PhotoIon Coincidence) detector coupled with TOF (Time-of-Flight) mass spectrometer specially designed and built to measure the spatial momentum components of product fragments ions in the double photoionization experiments as we have done in the past [19, 26].

In the case of allene, the investigated process can be schematized by Eq. (1) below:

$$C_3H_4 + h\nu \rightarrow (C_3H_4)^{2+} + 2e^- \rightarrow fragment\ ions \tag{1}$$

where, $(C_3H_4)^{2+}$ is the intermediate molecular dication of allene. This a doubly charged molecular ion can be a stable, unstable or metastable species according to the relative position of the intermolecular potentials describing the fragment ion-ion and neutral-doubly charged ion interactions characterizing the system [26]. Such a variability can be rationalized by the use of the scheme reported in Fig. 1.

Electron excitation and single photoionization processes of allene have been experimentally and theoretically investigated by several research groups. Information on high energy processes involving multiply charged ions of allene is relatively much poorer. Very recently, a detailed experimental and theoretical investigation of double and triple ionization of allene, by single photon absorption, has been carried out [27], providing the energy pattern of dication electronic states, as well as some details on their nuclear dissociation dynamics. The present study is aimed to show preliminary results obtained

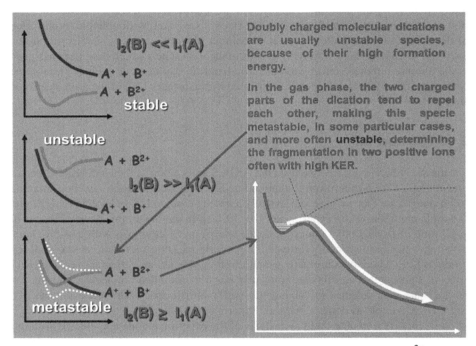

Fig. 1. The scheme of the of the potential energy curves for the simple case of AB^{2+} diatomic molecular dications. *Left upper panel* shows the case of the thermodynamically stable dications; *Center left panel*: the case of unstable species that cannot be detected in gas phase; *Lower left panel*: molecular dications in a metastable state which are the result of an avoided crossing of the potential energy curves involved. In this latter case, the resulting potential energy curve schematized in the *right lower panel*, shows the generation of the two A$^+$ and B$^+$ fragment ions having in general a high relative kinetic energy release. This process is named Coulomb explosion of the metastable dication and produces monocations with a translational energy content that can range between 1–10 eV. In the Figure: i) I$_2$ stands for the second ionization potential of the bounded atom having the lower electronegativity (in this case B); ii) I$_1$ represents the first ionization potential of the other atom (A); iii) the interatomic distance between A and B is shown in the x axis while the energy is shown in the y axis.

in a recent experiment performed at the GASPHASE beamline of the ELETTRA Synchrotron Facility of Basovizza (Trieste, Italy). In this investigation a synchrotron radiation in the 25.0 – 45.0 eV photon energy range has been used in order to conduct a detailed study of the nuclear dissociation dynamics of allene dications $(C_3H_4)^{2+}$ by single photon valence electron double ionization by means of the 3D-ion imaging spectroscopy. This different multi-coincidence technique allows higher mass resolution and much higher sensitivity than before [27], and to shed light into metastable dissociation channels where ions differ by a single unit of mass. Ion-ion coincidence yields, and the associated relative intensities, were measured from below to several tens of eV above the first double ionization threshold. High statistics ion-ion t_1-t_2 [where t_1 and t_2 are the arrival times into the ion-position-sensitive detector (see Fig. 2) of the two fragments ions generated by the Coulomb explosion of the intermediate $(C_3H_4)^{2+}$ molecular dication and detected in coincidence with the electrons ejected by double photoionization of the neutral precursor allene molecule] contour plots are recorded at selected photon energies, just above the lowest lying groups of dication states, which have been assigned to the observed photoelectron-photoelectron bands in the previous study [27], to probe with high sensitivity the topology of potential hypersurfaces [28] of dication electronic states.

2 Experimental

For the study here discussed we used the ARPES end station of the GASPHASE beamline at ELETTRA Synchrotron Radiation Facility, equipped with the same ion-imaging technique device that we have successfully applied before to HX (where X = Cl, Br and I) double photoionization experiments [29, 30, 32]. In particular, this device consists of a 3D-time of flight (TOF) ion coincidence spectrometer equipped with a multi-anode detector. It has been specially designed to properly measure vector momenta of all ion products [29]. The monochromatic synchrotron light beam operating above 22 eV will cross at right angles an effusive molecular beam of the allene molecule, and the ion products are then detected in coincidence with photoelectrons. The allene is used as a commercial sample as done in previous experiments [27].

It is important to note that the analysis of the experimental data, collected with our ion position sensitive detector, is based on the recorded ion imaging coincidence plots, and should allow us to evaluate both the kinetic energy distributions of the final product ions, and their angular distributions with respect to the polarization vector direction (see next section). It is well known [29] that such angular distributions can provide valuable information about the dissociation dynamics of intermediate molecular dications as we have done in previous works [16, 29]. Since allene is a species characterized by a low first ionization energy (9.69 eV, respectively), a conservative estimate of the photon energy range, in which the fixed energy spectra need to be recorded, should approximately be from 22 to 45 eV. Parent $(C_3H_4)^{2+}$ dications and ion-ion coincidence efficiency curves are obtained with a small energy step from the fixed energy spectra in order to measure with good accuracy the appearing potential for the molecular dication, the appearing thresholds for the ion-ion dissociation channels and their branching ratios. At the selected photon energies long acquisition times (6–8 h) were required to achieve sufficiently high statistics in the ion-ion coincidence plots, especially in the case of dication metastable decay processes.

For the present experiments we used 24 shifts (192 h) of beamtime. The employed PEPIPICO experimental device is mounted in the molecular beam ARPES-end apparatus which is schematized in Fig. 2 [29, 30–34], where a typical coincidence plot that can be obtained in this kind of experiments is also shown.

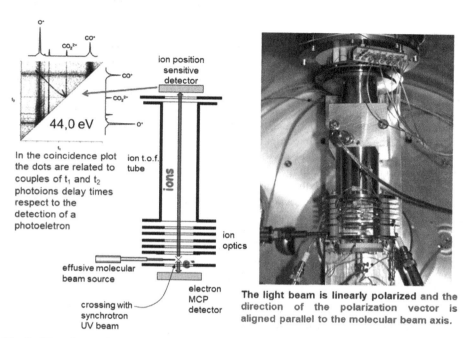

Fig. 2. The scheme of the prototype PEPIPICO (PhotoElectron-PhotoIon-PhotoIon Coincidence) device used in our 3D-ion-imaging TOF (Time-of-Flight) mass spectrometric determinations. On the *right side* is reported a picture of the device mounted inside the molecular beam ARPES (Angle Resolved PhotoEmission Spectroscopy) end station operating at the GASPHASE and CIRCULAR POLARIZATION beamlines of the ELETTRA Synchrotron Facility of Basovizza (Trieste, Italy). In the *center panel* the scheme of our coincidence ion-position-sensitive detector working coupled with a TOF tube mass spectrometer is highlighted. In the *left upper panel*, is shown a typical coincidence plot that can be recorded as a function of the investigated photon energy range using this kind of detector: in the Figure, as an example, are reported the coincidence dots distribution related to couples of t_1 and t_2 delay arrival times of fragments photo-ions respect to the photo-electons ejected in the double photoionization of carbon dioxide investigated at a photon energy of 44 eV.

3 Computational Methods

In Fig. 2 the reader can have an idea of a typical coincidence spectrum that can be recorded in our PEPIPICO experiments: as an example, this kind of observable can be appreciated as it has been collected in the case of the double photoionization of carbon dioxide performed at a synchrotron radiation photon energy of 44.0 eV. On the upper left side panel of the same figure are also visible the mass spectra associated to the ions produced either by single and double photoionization events. Such a coincidence spectrum is characteristic of all double photoionization experiments: i) the two time-of-flight values, indicated as t_1 and t_2 in the figure and text, are shown for a pair of ions (in this case CO^+ and O^+ fragments) and define a point in the diagram since they are produced by the same photoionization event (i.e. the points in the coincidence spectrum represent the coincidence events as a function of the arrival time of the first ion, t_1, and of the second ion, t_2 to the detector - see Refs. [35–37]); ii) the diagonal weak traces correspond to "false" and spurious coincidences that are neglected in the analysis performed by the Monte Carlo computational model adopted (see below).

From the mass spectra, all peaks of the generated ions are well evident as well as the recorded background signal. In the coincidence spectrum of Fig. 2 is also quite evident the "V-shaped" typical trace due to the formation of the metastable CO_2^{2+} dication that evolves by Coulomb explosion towards CO^+ and O^+ with a life time of $\tau = 3.1 \pm 0.9$ μs, experimentally recorded in previous studies [13, 14].

The careful analysis of the coincidence distribution maps (as the one reported in Fig. 2) as a function of the investigated photon energy, permits the determination of the KER (kinetic energy released) of the two ionic product fragments. This can be obtained by analysing the ion intensity maps based on the method proposed by Lundqvist et al. [37] and widely used in double photoionization experiments. In particular, this target can be reached by examining the peak dimensions and shapes recorded for each ion pair product in the coincidence diagrams.

As mentioned above, a crucial experimental observable is the coincidence dots density distribution in the diagram's area of the clearly visible "tail" and the "V-shaped" traces in the coincidence plots of Fig. 2.

By using a powerful computational method introduced by Field and Eland [35], an accurate analysis of this kind of distributions as a function of the arrival time differences (t_2-t_1) of the fragment ions to our MCP (multi-channel plate) ion-position-sensitive detector (see Fig. 2), can be performed to extract the lifetime of the intermediate molecular dication which is formed in a metastable electronic state (as is the case of CO_2^{2+} [13, 14]). As a confirmation test, a second data analysis is generally carried out determining the lifetime of the metastable dications, with an alternative procedure using a Monte Carlo trajectory simulation performed in our laboratory (see for instance Ref. [13, 14]). For such a purpose, we developed a proper computer routine able to determine the t_1 and t_2 distribution delay times once the kinetic energy released (KER) by the two ionic fragments and the dissociation lifetime, τ, of the metastable dication have been fixed. The experimental distribution of the coincidence dots density $I(t_2-t_1)$ is simulated adjusting KER and τ. Then, we evaluate the standard deviation as a reliability level of the simulation with 10^6 trajectories. The $I(t_2-t_1)$ behavior is analized in order to obtain the lifetime of the metastable dication during the dication dissociation. This can achieve by plotting the number of coincidence points along the track of the tail as a function of the $(t_2 - t_1)$ difference. After that we perform a data fitting by a Monte Carlo simulation of the trajectories of fragment ions inside the TOF mass spectrometer [38, 39].

The reader interested in a detailed description of such a computational routine can find details in Refs. [40–43].

By this procedure, we are able to determine also:

i) the KER distributions of the fragment ions as previously done in recent papers [20–22];
ii) the angular distribution of final ions with respect to the polarization vector direction of the used synchrotron radiation [11,12]: as specified in Fig. 2, in our experiments performed at the CIRCULAR POLARIZATION beamline of ELETTRA, the synchrotron light beam is linearly polarized, and the direction of the polarization vector is aligned parallel to the molecular beam axis.

It has been well demonstrated [44, 45] that the angular distributions of fragment ions so recorded, give crucial information about the dissociation microscopic dynamics of the Coulomb explosion of intermediate molecular dications. Such distributions are in general represented by $I(\theta) \sin\theta$, according to Eq. (2) below:

$$I(\theta)sin\theta = \frac{\sigma_{tot}}{4\pi}\left[1 + \frac{\beta}{2}\left(3cos^2\vartheta - 1\right)\right] \tag{2}$$

where $I(\theta)$ and σ_{tot} are the differential and total cross sections of the dissociation process, respectively; θ represents the angle between the velocity vector of the fragment ion and the polarization vector of the synchrotron light; β is the so called "anisotropy parameter" and, in general, ranges from $\beta = -1$, in the case that product ions are emitted along a direction perpendicular to the polarization vector, up to the value of $\beta = 2$ for a parallel direction. Angular distributions of fragment ions characterized by an isotropic behavior are associated to a value of $\beta = 0$ or almost zero.

4 Results

New information provided by the present study is the energetics and dissociation dynamics of allene dications by direct double photoionization of the precursor molecule, thus avoiding the core hole formation involved in previous measurements [27]. The direct approach is the most effective type of investigation of $(C_3H_4)^{2+}$ dication energetics and topology of their potential energy surfaces (PESs) [28]. The observables aimed to be recorded are: i) the threshold energies for the formation of different ionic products; ii) the related branching ratios; iii) the angular and kinetic energy distribution of fragment ions at different photon energies. These important experimental data are mandatory information for further investigations of the topology of PESs of the relevant electronic states characterizing the dissociation dynamics of $(C_3H_4)^{2+}$ dications.

The study described here is a first attempt to investigate the role of excited electronic states on the reactivity of allene dication which is a relevant species in astrochemistry.

In Fig. 3 is shown the coincidence plot (analogous to the one of the left upper panel of Fig. 2 and discussed in detail in Sects. 2 and 3) recorded in the double photoionization of allene molecule at a synchrotron photon energy of 40.8 eV. In this type of plot, which is typical of double photoionization experiments, the two time of flight values of a couple of ions, t_1 and t_2 (both reported in the x and y axis in ns), produced in the same photoionization event define a point. In the Figure are also shown the mass spectra related to the recorded double coincidences (red color).

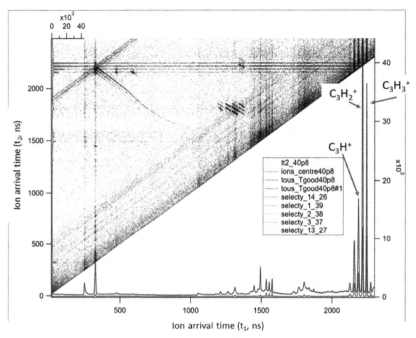

Fig. 3. The coincidence plot recorded in the double photoionization of allene molecule at a photon energy of 40.8 eV. In the figure, the mass spectra related to the double coincidences are shown in red color, while in blue color (on the x axis) the mass spectrum of the single ionization can be appreciated.

Preliminary results are here presented for the double photoionization experiment on allene (C_3H_4) molecules performed at the ELETTRA Synchrotron Radiation Facility (GASPHASE Beamline), recording data from 25.0 up to 45.0 eV photon energy. During the assigned beam time it was possible to explore the energetics of formation and the fragmentation microscopic dynamics of the intermediate $(C_3H_4)^{2+}$ dication.

First of all, it was possible to extract the energy thresholds for several fragmentation channels produced by double photoionization of C_3H_4 recording the relative cross sections for the formation of the different open dissociation channels. They are listed below with the relative threshold energy in eV:

$$C_3H_4 + h\nu \rightarrow H^+ + C_3H^+ + H_2 + 2e- \quad h\nu \geq 30.0\,eV \tag{3}$$

$$\rightarrow H_2^+ + C_3H^+ + H + 2e- \quad h\nu \geq 30.0\,eV \tag{4}$$

$$\rightarrow H_3^+ + C_3H^+ + 2e- \quad h\nu \geq 30.0\,eV \tag{5}$$

$$\rightarrow H^+ + C_3H_2^+ + H + 2e- \quad h\nu \geq 35.0\,eV \tag{6}$$

$$\rightarrow H_2^+ + C_3H_2^+ + 2e- \quad h\nu \geq 34.0\,eV \tag{7}$$

$$\rightarrow H^+ + C_3H_3^+ + 2e- \quad h\nu \geq 28.0\,eV \tag{8}$$

$$\rightarrow CH^+ + C_2H_2^+ + 2e- \quad h\nu \geq 37.5\,eV \tag{9}$$

$$\rightarrow CH^+ + C_2H_3^+ + 2e- \quad h\nu \geq 33.0\,eV \tag{10}$$

$$\rightarrow CH_2^+ + C_2H^+ + 2e- \quad h\nu \geq 38.0\,eV \tag{11}$$

$$\rightarrow CH_2^+ + C_2H_2^+ + 2e- \quad h\nu \geq 32.5\,eV \tag{12}$$

$$\rightarrow CH_3^+ + C_2H^+ + 2e- \quad h\nu \geq 33.5\,eV \tag{13}$$

The measured threshold energies reported above were obtained by accumulating 6–8 h at each investigated photon energy with a 200 meV photon energy step.

Furthermore, by recording the coincidence plots along 4–8 h accumulation period (see, for example, the Fig. 3 where is reported the coincidence plot recorded at 40.8 eV) as well as the mass spectra by using the PEPIPICO device mounted in the ARPES end station and described in Sect. 2, we could be able to extract:

i) the threshold energy for the formation of the allene dication $(C_3H_4)^{2+}$, whose preliminary value of 27.8 ± 0.1 eV is determined on the basis of the analysis of the recorded mass spectra as a function of the photon energy which is shown in Fig. 4;

ii) for each fragment ion produced, the respective kinetic energy released (KER);

iii) the angular distributions of the final product ions at various investigated photon energies in the range of 25.0–45.0 eV.

Such data are still in analysis in order to get the beta anisotropy parameter for the collected angular distributions (accordingly to Eq. (2)) in order to fully characterize the microscopic dynamics of recorded fragmentation reaction channel (3)–(13) listed above. In this respect, further theoretical efforts will be done with the aim of calculating the potential energy surfaces of interest, investigating the location of the lowest stationary points at the B3LYP level of theory, in conjunction with the 6–311 + G(d) basis set as we have done in various previously studied systems [26, 46–49].

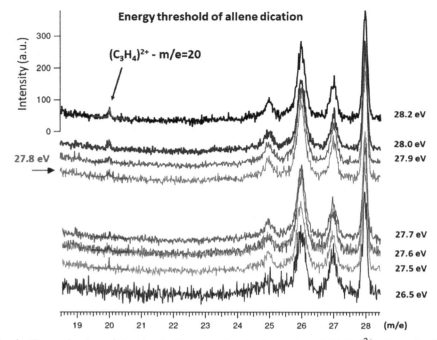

Fig. 4. The evaluation of the threshold energy for the formation of $(C_3H_4)^{2+}$ allene dication collecting mass spectra of ions produced by the double photoionization of allene in the 25.0–45.0 eV photon energy range. On the left side of the figure, the appearance energy value of 27.8 ± 0.1 eV for the allene dication is highlighted in red color next to the mass spectrum to which it refers.

Acknowledgments. This work was supported and financed with the "Fondo Ricerca di Base, 2018, dell'Università degli Studi di Perugia" (Project Titled: Indagini teoriche e sperimentali sulla reattività di sistemi di interesse astrochimico). Support from Italian MIUR and University of Perugia (Italy) is acknowledged within the program "Dipartimenti di Eccellenza 2018–2022". The scientific staff of the GASPHASE beamline of ELETTRA Synchrotron Facility of Basovizza (Trieste, Italy) is warmly acknowledged.

References

1. Alagia, M., et al.: Production of ions at high energy and its role in extraterrestrial environments. Rendiconti Lincei Scienze Fisiche e Naturali **24**, 53–65 (2013)
2. Pei, L., Carrascosa, E., Yang, N., Falcinelli, S., Farrar, J.M.: Velocity map imaging study of charge-transfer and proton-transfer reactions of CH3 radicals with H3+. J. Phys. Chem. Lett. **6**(9), 1684–1689 (2015)
3. Candori, P., Falcinelli, S., Pirani, F., Tarantelli, F., Vecchiocattivi, F.: Interaction components in the hydrogen halide dications. Chem. Phys. Lett. **436**(4–6), 322–326 (2007)
4. Stäuber, P., Doty, S.D., Van Dishoeck, E.F., Benz, A.O.: X-ray chemistry in the envelopes around young stellar objects. Astron. Astrophys. **440**(3), 949–966 (2005)

5. Thissen, R., Witasse, O., Dutuit, O., Wedlund, C.S., Gronoff, G., Lilensten, J.: Doubly-charged ions in the planetary ionospheres: a review. Phys. Chem. Chem. Phys. **13**(41), 18264–18287 (2011)

6. Gronoff, G., et al.: Modelling dications in the diurnal ionosphere of Venus. Astron. Astrophys. **465**(2), 641–645 (2007)

7. Falcinelli, S., et al.: Kinetic energy release in molecular dications fragmentation after VUV and EUV ionization and escape from planetary atmospheres. Plan. Space Sci. **99**, 149–157 (2014)

8. Falcinelli, S., et al.: The escape of O+ ions from the atmosphere: an explanation of the observed ion density profiles on Mars. Chem. Phys. Lett. **666**, 1–6 (2016)

9. Falcinelli, S., Pirani, F., Vecchiocattivi, F.: The possible role of penning ionization processes in planetary atmospheres. Atmosphere **6**(3), 299–317 (2015)

10. Falcinelli, S.: Mass spectrometric detection of alkaline earth monohalide dications. Mol. Phys. **88**(3), 663–672 (1996)

11. Alagia, M., et al.: Double photoionization of N2O molecules in the 28–40 eV energy range. Chem. Phys. Lett. **432**(4–6), 398–402 (2006)

12. Alagia, M., et al.: Anisotropy of the angular distribution of fragment ions in dissociative double photoionization of N 2 O molecules in the 30–50 eV energy range. J. Chem. Phys. **126**(20), 201101 (2007)

13. Alagia, M., et al.: Double photoionization of CO2 molecules in the 34–50 eV energy range. J. Phys. Chem. A **113**(52), 14755–14759 (2009)

14. Alagia, M., et al.: Dissociative double photoionization of CO 2 molecules in the 36–49 eV energy range: angular and energy distribution of ion products. Phys. Chem. Chem. Phys. **12**(20), 5389–5395 (2010)

15. Alagia, M., et al.: Dissociative double photoionization of benzene molecules in the 26–33 eV energy range. Phys. Chem. Chem. Phys. **13**(18), 8245–8250 (2011)

16. Alagia, M., et al.: Dissociative double photoionization of singly deuterated benzene molecules in the 26–33 eV energy range. J. Chem. Phys. **135**(14), 144304 (2011)

17. Alagia, M., et al.: Angular and energy distribution of fragment ions in dissociative double photoionization of acetylene molecules at 39 eV. J. Chem. Phys. **136**(20), 204302 (2012)

18. Falcinelli, S., et al.: Angular and energy distributions of fragment ions in dissociative double photoionization of acetylene molecules in the 31.9-50.0 eV photon energy range. J. Chem. Phys. **145**(11), 114308 (2016)

19. Falcinelli, S., et al.: Double photoionization of propylene oxide: a coincidence study of the ejection of a pair of valence-shell electrons. J. Chem. Phys. **148**(11), 114302 (2018)

20. Falcinelli, S., et al.: Angular distribution of ion products in the double photoionization of propylene oxide. Front. Chem. **7**, 621 (2019)

21. Falcinelli, S., et al.: The fragmentation dynamics of simple organic molecules of astrochemical interest interacting with VUV photons. ACS Earth Space Chem. **3**(9), 1862–1872 (2019)

22. Salén, P., et al.: Electronic state influence on selective bond breaking of core-excited nitrosyl chloride (ClNO). J. Chem. Phys. **157**(12), 124306 (2022)

23. Hendon, C.H., Tiana, D., Murray, A.T., Carbery, D.R., Walsh, A.: Helical frontier orbitals of conjugated linear molecules. Chem. Sci. **4**(11), 4278–4284 (2013)

24. Garner, M.H., Hoffmann, R., Rettrup, S., Solomon, G.C.: Coarctate and mobius: the helical orbitals of allene and other cumulenes. ACS Central Sci. **4**(6), 688–700 (2018)

25. Kaiser, R.I., Stranges, D., Lee, Y.T., Suits, A.G.: Neutral-neutral reactions in the interstellar medium. I. Formation of carbon hydride radicals via reaction of carbon atoms with unsaturated hydrocarbons. Astrophys. J. **477**(2), 982 (1997)

26. Falcinelli, S., Rosi, M.: Production and characterization of molecular dications: experimental and theoretical efforts. Molecules **25**(18), 4157 (2020)

27. Ideböhna, V., Sterlingb, A.J., Wallnera, M., et al.: Phys. Chem. Chem. Phys. **24**, 786–796 (2022)
28. Falcinelli, S., Vecchiocattivi, F., Pirani, F.: The topology of the reaction stereo-dynamics in chemi-ionizations. Commun. Chem. **6**(1), 30 (2023)
29. Lavollée, M.: A new detector for measuring three-dimensional momenta of charged particles in coincidence. Rev. Sci. Instrum. **70**(7), 2968–2974 (1999)
30. Alagia, M., et al.: The double photoionization of HCl: an ion–electron coincidence study. J. Chem. Phys. **121**(21), 10508–10512 (2004)
31. Alagia, M., Brunetti, B.G., Candori, P., Falcinelli, S., et al.: J. Chem. Phys. **120**(15), 6980–16984 (2004)
32. Biondini, F., et al.: Penning ionization of N 2 O molecules by He*(2 S 3, 1) and Ne*(P 2, 0 3) metastable atoms: Theoretical considerations about the intermolecular interactions. J. Chem. Phys. **122**(16), 164308 (2005)
33. Alagia, M., et al.: Mass spectrometric study of double photoionization of HBr molecules. J. Chem. Phys. **117**(3), 1098–1102 (2002)
34. Teixidor, M.M., Pirani, F., Candori, P., Falcinelli, S., Vecchiocattivi, F.: Predicted structure and energetics of HCl2+. Chem. Phys. Lett. **379**(1–2), 139–146 (2003)
35. Taylor, S., Eland, J.H.D., Hochlaf, M.: Fluorescence and metastability of N 2 O 2+: Theory and experiment. J. Chem. Phys. **124**(20), 204319 (2006)
36. Alagia, M., et al.: The double photoionization of hydrogen iodide molecules. J. Chem. Phys. **124**(20), 204318 (2006)
37. Lundqvist, M., Baltzer, P., Edvardsson, D., Karlsson, L., Wannberg, B.: Novel time of flight instrument for doppler free kinetic energy release spectroscopy. Phys. Rev. Let. **75**(6), 1058 (1995)
38. Field, T.A., Eland, J.H.: Lifetimes of metastable molecular doubly charged ions. Chem. Phys. Lett. **211**(4–5), 436–442 (1993)
39. Alagia, M., et al.: The soft X-ray absorption spectrum of the allyl free radical. Phys. Chem. Chem. Phys. **15**(4), 1310–1318 (2013)
40. Schio, L., et al.: NEXAFS and XPS studies of nitrosyl chloride. Phys. Chem. Chem. Phys. **17**(14), 9040–9048 (2015)
41. Falcinelli, S., et al.: The escape probability of some ions from mars and titan ionospheres. In: Murgante, B., et al. (eds.) ICCSA 2014. LNCS, vol. 8579, pp. 554–570. Springer, Cham (2014). https://doi.org/10.1007/978-3-319-09144-0_38
42. Brunetti, B., et al.: Dissociative ionization of methyl chloride and methyl bromide by collision with metastable neon atoms. J. Phys. Chem. A **101**(41), 7505–7512 (1997)
43. Brunetti, B.G., Candori, P., Falcinelli, S., Pirani, F., Vecchiocattivi, F.: The stereodynamics of the Penning ionization of water by metastable neon atoms. J. Chem. Phys. **139**(16), 164305 (2013)
44. Bartocci, A., et al.: Catching the role of anisotropic electronic distribution and charge transfer in halogen bonded complexes of noble gases. J. Chem. Phys. **142**(18), 184304 (2015)
45. Zare, R.N.: Photoejection dynamics. Mol. Photochem **4**(1), 1–37 (1972)
46. Dehmer, J.L., Dill, D.: Photoion angular distributions in dissociative photoionization of H 2 at 304 Å. Phys. Rev. A **18**(1), 164 (1978)
47. Arfa, M.B., et al.: Ionization of ammonia molecules by collision with metastable neon atoms. Chem. Phys. Lett. **308**(1–2), 71–77 (1999)
48. Lago, N.F., Albertí, M., Laganà, A., Lombardi, A.: Water (H2O) m or Benzene (C6H6) n Aggregates to Solvate the K + ? In: Beniamino, M., et al. (eds.) Computational Science and Its Applications – ICCSA 2013, ICCSA 2013, vol. 7971, pp. 69–83. Springer, Berlin (2013). https://doi.org/10.1007/978-3-642-39637-3
49. Balucani, N., et al.: Collisional autoionization dynamics of Ne∗(3P2, 0)–H2O. Chem. Phys. Lett. **546**, 34–39 (2012)

Computational Investigation of the N(^{2}D)+ C$_2$H$_4$ and N(^{2}D)+ CH$_2$CHCN Reactions: Benchmark Analysis and Implications for Titan's Atmosphere

Luca Mancini[1($\boxtimes$)] (iD), Emília Valença Ferreira de Aragão[1,2] (iD), and Marzio Rosi[3] (iD)

[1] Dipartimento di Chimica, Biologia e Biotecnologie, Università degli Studi di Perugia, 06123 Perugia, Italy
luca.mancini2@studenti.unipg.it
[2] Master-tec srl, Via Sicilia 41, 06128 Perugia, Italy
[3] Dipartimento di Ingegneria Civile ed Ambientale, Università degli Studi di Perugia, 06125 Perugia, Italy
marzio.rosi@unipg.it

Abstract. In the present contribution we report a theoretical investigation of the reactions of atomic nitrogen, in its first electronically excited ^{2}D state, with two different molecules: ethylene (C$_2$H$_4$) and acrylonitrile (CH$_2$CHCN), which appear to be important processes for the chemistry of Titan's atmosphere. The main reaction channels have been investigated through *ab initio* electronic structure calculations. Accurate quantum chemical calculations allowed the identification of the available pathways as a sequence of minimum and transition state structures, leading to the formation of different products, mainly related to H-displacement processes. Single point energy calculations have been performed at different levels of theory in order to establish a reasonable computational strategy for the analysis of astrochemically relevant gas phase neutral-neutral reactions.

Keywords: Computational chemistry · *Ab initio* calculations · Astrochemistry · Titan's atmosphere

1 Introduction

The appearence of life on Earth led to massive transformations of its geomorphology. As a result, studying planets and moons that are similar to the early Earth can be very helpful in providing a good picture of the early stages of our prebiotic chemistry. The best candidate for this purpose appears to be Titan, the largest moon of Saturn, that represents one of the only few moons of the Solar System which possess a thick atmosphere. Different space missions, including the

© The Author(s), under exclusive license to Springer Nature Switzerland AG 2023
O. Gervasi et al. (Eds.): ICCSA 2023 Workshops, LNCS 14105, pp. 705–717, 2023.
https://doi.org/10.1007/978-3-031-37108-0_45

last and famous Cassini-Huygens mission [1], provided new information about the composition and atmosphere of Saturn's moon. Titan's inner structure isn't completely known. Data coming from the latest missions can help to build a general model, according to which Titan's structure is characterized by five primary layers. The inner one is composed by a core of water-bearing silicate rock. The first core is surrounded by an ice-VI layer. This second layer is surrounded by a third layer of salty liquid water, covered by an outer crust of water ice. Finally, the surface is cover by a layer of organic molecules which grant to the moon the typical orange color. Despite several similarities of Titan's surface with the surface of our planet, the different temperature leads to different characteristic of Saturn's moon. In details the temperature reaches values down to 94 K on the surface of Titan (also resulting from 'greenhouse effects') and around 175 K in the stratosphere, while the overall surface pressure is 1.5 bar. As a consequence the surface is covered by water ice, which plays the role of Earth's rocks. The conditions of temperature and pressure appears to be closer to the ones typical of the triple point of methane, therefore, Titan's surface is crossed by rivers of flowing methane, which fills lakes and seas. The surface, in which few visible impact craters can be found, is covered by 'sand' composed of hydrocarbons, forming also dark dunes extending across Titan's equatorial region's landscape. Moreover, similarly to Earth, Titan shows several types of clouds formed by a plethora of different volatile species [2]. The main component of Titan's atmosphere has been revealed to be N_2 [3], followed by methane, and different other hydrocarbons (e.g. C_2H_6, C_2H_4, C_2H_2) [4]. In the recent years, different photochemical models have been developed [5–7], with the aim to include results from physical and chemical investigations to derive a representative simulations of Titan's atmosphere. Therefore, the analysis of chemical reactions involving molecular species containing nitrogen appears to be pivotal for the understanding of the chemistry of the atmosphere of Titan. From a chemical point of view, the N_2 molecule appears to have a high chemical stability. As a consequence, the main actor to drive the chemistry of Titan's atmosphere is "active nitrogen", namely atomic nitrogen in its ground and excited states $N(^4S)$ and $N(^2D)$, respectively. The main formation mechanisms for the two aforementioned species are related to the interaction of N_2 with EUV photons, as well as the impact of N_2 with energetic particles, including high energy free electrons. Unfortunately, the $N(^4S)$ ground state appears to be unreactive with closed-shell molecules, while $N(^2D)$ appears to be more reactive. This last species is metastable with a relatively long radiative lifetime [8] and an high energy content (it is 230 kJ mol^{-1} higher than the ground state) [9,10]. The reactivity of $N(^2D)$ with various partners has been the subject of several theoretical and experimental studies, with potential uses in the modeling of Titan atmosphere (i.e. $N(^2D)+ C_2H_2$; C_2H_6; HC_3N) [11–13]. Together with the common and abundant C_2H_4 molecule, [14] another particularly relevant N-bearing molecule detected on Titan's atmosphere is acrylonitrile (CH_2CHCN). Interestingly, this last species is considered to be a promising candidate, considering also the possibility to form more complex and prebiotic species. After the initial data, obtained from the Cassini orbiter, regarding the detection of the CH$_2$CHCNH$^+$ cation [15–18], the acrylonitrile molecule has been definitely detected using the ALMA interferometer [19,20]. One of the accepted formation routes of CH$_2$CHCN is the CN + C$_2$H$_4$ reaction [21–28], in which the dominant mechanism appears to be the elimination of atomic hydrogen, followed by the formation of CH$_2$CHCN. On the contrary, a lack of information is present regarding the possible destruction mechanisms of acrylonitrile. Following the directions of the aforementioned photochemical models, possible destruction routes of acrylonitrile are represented by the reactions with N(^{2}D) and CN radical. The two reactions analysed in the present contribution, N(^{2}D)+C$_2$H$_4$ and N(^{2}D)+CH$_2$CHCN, have already been investigated [29,30] combining an experimental investigation, performed through the crossed molecular beam (CMB) technique with mass spectrometric (MS) detection and time-of-flight (TOF) analysis, with accurate ab initio calculations in order to unveil the global reaction mechanism. In this work we present a theoretical investigation, performed at different levels of theory, of the main reaction pathways for the N(^{2}D)+C$_2$H$_4$ and N(^{2}D)+CH$_2$CHCN, which allows to derive a feasible computational strategy to be used for the study of different reaction between atomic nitrogen and hydrocarbons and/or nitrile molecules.

2 Theoretical Methods

The global doublet Potential Energy Surface (PES) for the two reactions, N(^{2}D) + C$_2$H$_4$ and N(^{2}D) + CH$_2$CHCN, has been analysed adopting a well-established computational strategy, already used for the investigation of several reactions [31–33]. In details, a first analysis has been performed through density functional calculations, with the B3LYP [34,35] functional, in conjunction with the correlation consistent valence polarized basis set aug-cc-pVTZ [36–38]. The same level of theory has been employed to calculate harmonic vibrational frequencies, in order to determine the nature of each stationary point, i.e. minimum if all the frequencies are real and saddle point if there is one, and only one, imaginary frequency. Subsequently, the energy of each stationary point has been computed with the more accurate coupled cluster theory including both single and double excitations and using a perturbative estimate of the effect of the triple excitations (the CCSD(T) level) [39–41], with the same basis set aug-cc-pVTZ. The zero-point correction (computed using the scaled harmonic vibrational frequencies obtained at the B3LYP/aug-cc-pVTZ level) has been added in order to correct the energies at 0 K. Additionally, more accurate calculations for the stationary points involved in the main reaction channels have been performed at the CCSD(T) level corrected with a Density Fitted (DF) MP2 extrapolation to the complete basis set (CBS) and with corrections for core electrons excitations. In particular, the energies have been computed as:

$$E = E(CCSD(T)/aug-cc-pVTZ) + [E(CCSD(T, core)/cc-pVTZ)$$
$$- E(CCSD(T)/cc-pVTZ)] + [E(DF-MP2/CBS) - E(DF-MP2/aug-cc-pVTZ)]$$

where E(DF-MP2/CBS) is defined as:

$$E(DF - MP2/CBS) = E[(DF - MP2)/aug - cc - pVQZ)]$$
$$+ 0.5772 * [E(DF - MP2/aug - cc - pVQZ) - E(DF - MP2/aug - cc - pVTZ)]$$

The E(DF-MP2/CBS) extrapolation has been performed using Martin's two parameter scheme [42], by performing a series of ab initio calculations using the MP2 method and different basis set (including aug-cc-pVTZ and aug-cc-pVQZ).

The experimental separation [43] $N(^4S)$-$N(^2D)$ of 230.0 kJ mol^{-1} has been added to the energy of $N(^4S)$ at all the levels of calculations in order to have a more accurate estimation of the energy of $N(^2D)$. All calculations have been carried out using GAUSSIAN 09 [44] and Molpro [45] while the analysis of the vibrational frequencies has been done using MOLDEN [46,47].

3   Results

3.1   The $N(^2D)$+C_2H_4 Reaction

The potential energy surface obtained for the $N(^2D)$+C_2H_4 reaction is reported in Fig. 1. As already explained, the energy of the stationary points has been evaluated at different levels of theory (B3LYP/aug-cc-pVTZ, CCSD(T)/aug-cc-pVTZ, CCSD(T)/CBS). The results obtained from the different investigations are reported in Table 1. For the sake of simplicity, in the following description only the more accurate results (i.e. the CCSD(T)/CBS energy values) are described. As is evident, the interaction of atomic nitrogen with the ethylene system, which results in the attack of $N(^2D)$ on the C-C double bond of C_2H_4, and the subsequent formation of the MIN1 intermediate (located 447 kJ mol^{-1} below the reactant energy asymptote), represents the first step of the reaction. When MIN1 is created, it can immediately go through an H-displacement process, which creates the cyclic $CH_2(N)CH$ radical. The process has a total exothermicity of 264 kJ mol^{-1}, while the product channel has a barrier of 195 kJ mol^{-1}. With a bond distance of 2.075 Å, the associated transition state, TS2, exhibits the dissolution of a C-H bond. For the aforementioned MIN1, an alternative outcome is represented by the isomerization to MIN2, through the breaking of the C-C σ-bond. The process is characterized by a barrier (represented by TS1) of 114 kJ mol^{-1}. Once formed, MIN2, located 517 kJ mol^{-1} below the energy of the reactants, can result in the atomic hydrogen and the CH_2NCH linear radical being formed. This reaction channel is located 226 kJ mol^{-1} under the energy of the $N(^2D)$+C_2H_4 reagents. A transition state, TS3, located 226 kJ mol^{-1} below the energy of the reactants, was identified for the H-displacement process. This last process is characeirzed by a barrier almost equal to the endothermicity of

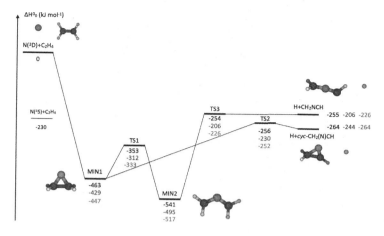

Fig. 1. Schematic representation of the potential energy surface for the N(^{2}D) +C$_2$H$_4$ reaction with energies evaluated at the B3LYP/aug-cc-pVTZ (in black), CCSD(T)/aug-cc-pVTZ (in blue) and CCSD(T)/CBS (in red) level of theory. (Color figure online)

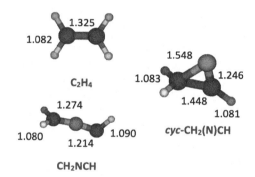

Fig. 2. Bond distances (in Å) for the reactant (C$_2$H$_4$) and products of the N(^{2}D) +C$_2$H$_4$ reaction.

the reaction at all the levels of theory. Therefore, the barrier is not very relevant and can be neglected in the global PES. Figures 2 and 3 show the geometry (bond distances in Å) of all the stationary points, including the C$_2$H$_4$ reactant and the two products, evaluated through the previous described DFT calculations.

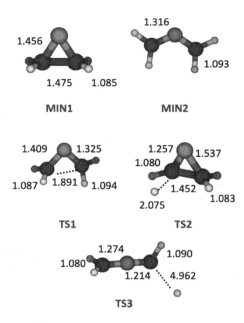

Fig. 3. Bond distances (in Å) for the minima and transition states of the $N(^2D) + C_2H_4$ reaction.

Table 1. Enthalpy changes (ΔH_0^0) and barrier height, in kJ mol^{-1}, for the main channels of the $N(^2D) + C_2H_4$ reaction evualated at the B3LYP/aug-cc-pVTZ, CCSD(T)/aug-cc-pVTZ and CCSD(T)/CBS level, respectively.

Reaction Channel	B3LYP/aug-cc-pVTZ		CCSD(T)/aug-cc-pVTZ		CCSD(T)/CBS	
	ΔH_0^0	Barrier	ΔH_0^0	Barrier	ΔH_0^0	Barrier
$N(^2D) + C_2H_4 \rightarrow MIN1$	−463	−	−429	−	−447	−
$MIN1 \rightarrow H + cyc - CH_2(N)CH$	199	207	185	199	183	195
$MIN1 \rightarrow MIN2$	−78	110	−66	117	−70	114
$MIN2 \rightarrow H + CH_2NCH$	286	287	289	289	291	291

3.2   The N(^{2}D)+ CH$_2$CHCN Reaction

The potential energy surface obtained for the $N(^2D)+CH_2CHCN$ reaction, reported in Fig. 4, shows some similarities with the one obtained for the previous reported reaction. The main difference is due to the presence of a CN group in the place of an hydrogen atom, which removes the symmetry of the molecule. As a consequence, the PES appears to be more complex and characterized by an increased number of possible reaction pathways.

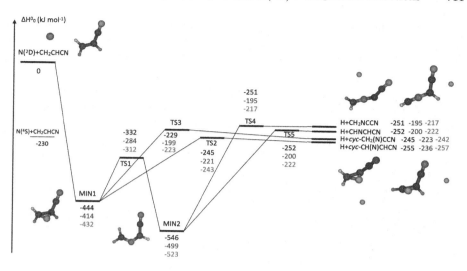

Fig. 4. Schematic representation of the potential energy surface for the N(^{2}D) +CH$_2$CHCN reaction with energies evaluated at the B3LYP/aug-cc-pVTZ (in black), CCSD(T)/aug-cc-pVTZ (in blue) and CCSD(T)/CBS (in red) level of theory. (Color figure online)

Also in this case, among all the calculated values of energy, only the more accurate results (i.e. the CCSD(T)/CBS energy values) are described. The values of enthalpy changes and barrier heights evaluated at the different level of theory are reported in Table 2. Similarly to case of the N(^{2}D)+C$_2$H$_4$ reaction, the first step is represented by the attack of N(^{2}D) to the C-C double bond of CH$_2$CHCN, with the formation of the MIN1 intermediate, located 432 kJ mol^{-1} below the reactant energy asymptote and characterized by a cyclic C(N)C structure. Once formed, MIN1 can undergo two different H-displacement process, depending on which H atom is eliminated, leading to the formation of two cyclic isomers CH$_2$(N)CCN and CH(N)CHCN. The global exothermicity of the two products is 242 kJ mol^{-1} and 257 kJ mol^{-1}, respectively. Two different transition states have been identified for the related H-displacement process, TS2 and TS3, representing a barrier of 189 kJ mol^{-1} and 209 kJ mol^{-1} respectively. The breaking of the C-C bond in MIN1, represented by the TS1 transition state (which shows an energy of 312 kJ mol^{-1} below the reactant energy asymptote), leads to the formation of the linear intermediate MIN2, whose global exothermicity is 523 kJ mol^{-1}. Once formed, MIN2 can lead to the formation of atomic hydrogen, together with the two CH$_2$NCCN and CHNCHCN linear radicals, located 217 kJ mol^{-1} and 222 kJ mol^{-1} under the energy of the N(^{2}D)+CH$_2$CHCN reactants. Two possible transition states, TS4 and TS5, have been identified in the PES. Similarly to the case of the previous described reaction, the energy of the two saddle points is almost equal to the endothermicity of the reaction channel at all the levels of theory. Therefore, the barriers are not very relevant and can be neglected in the global PES. Figures 5 and 6 show the geometry (bond distances in A) of all the stationary points, including the CH_2CHCN reactant and the four products, evaluated through the previous described DFT calculations.

Table 2. Enthalpy changes (ΔH_0^0) and barrier height, in kJ mol^{-1}, for the main channels of the $N(^2D) + CH_2CHCN$ reaction evuialated at the B3LYP/aug-cc-pVTZ, CCSD(T)/aug-cc-pVTZ and CCSD(T)/CBS level, respectively.

Reaction Channel	B3LYP/aug-cc-pVTZ		CCSD(T)/aug-cc-pVTZ		CCSD(T)/CBS	
	ΔH_0^0	Barrier	ΔH_0^0	Barrier	ΔH_0^0	Barrier
$N(^2D) + CH_2CHCN \rightarrow MIN1$	−444	−	−414	−	−432	−
$MIN1 \rightarrow H + cyc - CH_2(N)CCN$	199	215	191	215	190	209
$MIN1 \rightarrow H + cyc - CH(N)CHCN$	189	199	178	193	175	189
$MIN1 \rightarrow MIN2$	−55	112	−85	130	−91	120
$MIN2 \rightarrow H + CH_2NCCN$	248	248	304	304	306	306
$MIN2 \rightarrow H + CHNCHCN$	247	247	299	299	301	301

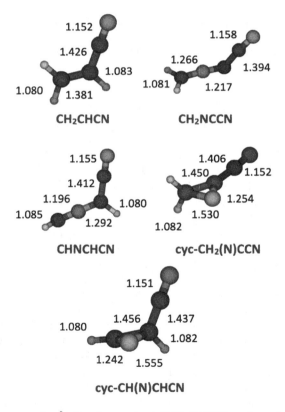

Fig. 5. Bond distances (in Å) for the reactant (CH_2CHCN) and products of the $N(^2D)$ + CH_2CHCN reaction.

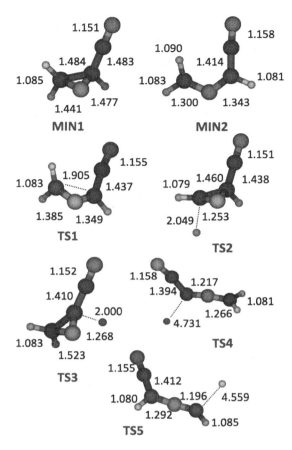

Fig. 6. Bond distances (in Å) for the minima and transition states of the N(^{2}D) + CH$_2$CHCN reaction.

4 Discussion

The two reactions N(^{2}D)+C$_2$H$_4$ and N(^{2}D) +CH$_2$CHCN show some similarities, especially considering the initial bimolecular approach. The main differences can be ascribed to the presence of the CN group. Indeed, the acrilonitrile molecule (CH$_2$CHCN) can be considered as ethylene (C$_2$H$_4$) with a CN group in place of an H atom. The presence of this cyano moiety removes the symmetry of the molecule, leading to a more complex reaction scheme, characterized by a double number of possible reaction paths and product channels. The high electrophilicity of the nitrogen, drawn to the double bond's electron density in both processes, is what propels N(^{2}D)'s attack on the companion molecule. Due to the presence of two C-N bonds involving the two ethylenic carbon atoms in a cyclic structure, the two reactions result in the development of a cyclic intermediate. In the case of the N(^{2}D)+C$_2$H$_4$ reaction, the formation of a cyclic species is possible, thanks to a H-displacement process directly after the initial attack. In the case of the reaction with acrylonitrile, instead, two main cyclic products can be formed. Alternatively, the C(N)C ring opening process has been identified as the cause of the generation of linear intermediates, which can immediately undergo an H-displacement process, depending on the hydrogen atom which is eliminated from the different carbon atoms. In the present work, after a first identification of the main reaction paths in the PES, the energy of the various stationary points have been calculated at different levels of theory. As can be seen from the data reported in Table 1 and Table 2, some differences can be noticed in the values of energy. In particular, DFT calculations tend to overestimate the energy, while the more accurate CCSD(T)/CBS level provides more reliable data. Considering the difference between the obtained data, the use of coupled-cluster theory, in conjunction with the aug-cc-pVTZ basis set leads to accurate data in a less time consuming approach.

5   Conclusions

In the present contribution we report a theoretical investigation of the potential energy surface for the two $N(^2D)+C_2H_4$ and $N(^2D) +CH_2CHCN$ reactions, that are important for the chemistry of planetary atmospheres, in particular in the atmosphere of Titan. Both the processes have been found to be barrierless. This is a key component for astrochemical reactions, along with the existence of stationary points below the reactant energy asymptote. In actuality, Titan's low temperatures indicate a hostile chemical environment where only exothermic and barrierless reactions may occur. Following this formalization, it appears that the two $N(2D)+C_2H_4$ and $N(2D) +CH_2CHCN$ reactions are viable and significant paths to add knowledge about the chemistry of nitrogen-bearing molecules on Titan's atmosphere. A complete analysis of the overall PES, together with a kinetic investigation of the rate constants and branching ratios, will allow to understand the importance of the title processes and to improve the chemical models of the atmosphere of Titan. Additionally, a combined approach using DFT methods for geometry optimizations, followed by a CCSD(T) analysis of the energy, appears to be the best compromise between chemical accuracy and computational cost for the analysis of reactions involving $N(^2D)$ and hydrocarbons in Titan's atmosphere.

Aknowledgements. This project has received funding from the Italian MUR (PRIN 2020, "Astrochemistry beyond the second period elements", Prot. 2020AFB3FX) and from the European Union's Horizon 2020 research and innovation programme under the Marie Skłodowska-Curie grant agreement No 811312 for the project 'Astro-Chemical Origins' (ACO). The authors thank the Herla Project - Università degli Studi di Perugia (http://www.hpc.unipg.it/hosting/vherla/vherla.html) for allocated computing time. The authors thank the Dipartimento di Ingegneria Civile ed Ambientale of the University of Perugia for allocated computing time within the project "Dipartimenti di Eccellenza 2018-2022".

References

1. Brown, R.H., Lebreton, J.P., Waite, J.H.: Titan from cassini-huygens (2009)
2. Hörst, S.M.: Titan's atmosphere and climate. J. Geophys. Res. Planets **122**(3), 432–482 (2017)
3. Lindal, G.F., Wood, G., Hotz, H., Sweetnam, D., Eshleman, V., Tyler, G.: The atmosphere of titan: an analysis of the voyager 1 radio occultation measurements. Icarus **53**(2), 348–363 (1983)
4. Hanel, R., et al.: Infrared observations of the saturnian system from voyager 1. Science **212**(4491), 192–200 (1981)
5. Yung, Y.L., Allen, M., Pinto, J.P.: Photochemistry of the atmosphere of titan: comparison between model and observations. Astrophys. J. Suppl. Ser. **55**(3), 465–506 (1984)
6. Lavvas, P., Coustenis, A., Vardavas, I.: Coupling photochemistry with haze formation in titan's atmosphere, part ii: results and validation with Cassini/Huygens data. Planet. Space Sci. **56**(1), 67–99 (2008)
7. Vuitton, V., Yelle, R., Klippenstein, S., Hörst, S., Lavvas, P.: Simulating the density of organic species in the atmosphere of titan with a coupled ion-neutral photochemical model. Icarus **324**, 120–197 (2019)
8. Dutuit, O., et al.: Critical review of n, n$^+$, n$_2^+$, n^{++}, and n$_2^{++}$ main production processes and reactions of relevance to titan's atmosphere. Astrophys. J. Suppl. Ser. **204**(2), 20 (2013)
9. Herron, J.T.: Evaluated chemical kinetics data for reactions of n(^{2}d), n$_2$)), and n$_2$(* 3* u+) in the gas phase (1999)
10. Schofield, K.: Critically evaluated rate constants for gaseous reactions of several electronically excited species. J. Phys. Chem. Ref. Data **8**(3), 723–798 (1979)
11. Balucani, N., et al.: Cyanomethylene formation from the reaction of excited nitrogen atoms with acetylene: a crossed beam and ab initio study. J. Am. Chem. Soc. **122**(18), 4443–4450 (2000)
12. Balucani, N., et al.: Formation of nitriles and imines in the atmosphere of titan: combined crossed-beam and theoretical studies on the reaction dynamics of excited nitrogen atoms n(^{2}d) with ethane. Faraday Discuss. **147**, 189–216 (2010)
13. Liang, P., et al.: Combined crossed molecular beams and computational study on the n(^{2}d)+ HCCCN (x^1 σ+) reaction and implications for extra-terrestrial environments. Mol. Phys. **120**(1–2), e1948126 (2022)
14. Vinatier, S., et al.: Analysis of Cassini/CIRS limb spectra of titan acquired during the nominal mission: I. hydrocarbons, nitriles and co$_2$ vertical mixing ratio profiles. Icarus **205**(2), 559–570 (2010)
15. Cui, J., et al.: Analysis of titan's neutral upper atmosphere from Cassini ion neutral mass spectrometer measurements. Icarus **200**(2), 581–615 (2009)
16. Vuitton, V., Yelle, R., McEwan, M.: Ion chemistry and n-containing molecules in titan's upper atmosphere. Icarus **191**(2), 722–742 (2007)
17. Magee, B.A., Waite, J.H., Mandt, K.E., Westlake, J., Bell, J., Gell, D.A.: INMS-derived composition of titan's upper atmosphere: analysis methods and model comparison. Planet. Space Sci. **57**(14–15), 1895–1916 (2009)
18. Müller-Wodarg, I., Griffith, C.A., Lellouch, E., Cravens, T.E.: Titan: Interior, Surface, Atmosphere, and Space Environment, vol. 14. Cambridge University Press, Cambridge (2014)
19. Palmer, M.Y., et al.: ALMA detection and astrobiological potential of vinyl cyanide on titan. Sci. Adv. **3**(7), e1700022 (2017)

20. Lai, J.Y., et al.: Mapping vinyl cyanide and other nitriles in titan's atmosphere using alma. Astron. J. **154**(5), 206 (2017)
21. Sims, I.R., et al.: Rate constants for the reactions of CN with hydrocarbons at low and ultra-low temperatures. Chem. Phys. Lett. **211**(4–5), 461–468 (1993)
22. Balucani, N., et al.: Crossed beam reaction of cyano radicals with hydrocarbon molecules. iii. chemical dynamics of vinylcyanide (c_2h_3 CN; x^1a') formation from reaction of CN ($x^2\sigma$ $^+$) with ethylene, c_2h_4 (x^1a_g). J. Chem. Phys. **113**(19), 8643–8655 (2000)
23. Balucani, N., et al.: Formation of nitriles in the interstellar medium via reactions of cyano radicals, CN (x $2\sigma+$), with unsaturated hydrocarbons. Astrophys. J. **545**(2), 892 (2000)
24. Balucani, N., Asvany, O., Osamura, Y., Huang, L., Lee, Y., Kaiser, R.: Laboratory investigation on the formation of unsaturated nitriles in titan's atmosphere. Planet. Space Sci. **48**(5), 447–462 (2000)
25. Leonori, F., Petrucci, R., Wang, X., Casavecchia, P., Balucani, N.: A crossed beam study of the reaction CN+C_2H_4 at a high collision energy: the opening of a new reaction channel. Chem. Phys. Lett. **553**, 1–5 (2012)
26. Balucani, N., et al.: A combined crossed molecular beams and theoretical study of the reaction CN+C_2H_4. Chem. Phys. **449**, 34–42 (2015)
27. Vereecken, L., De Groof, P., Peeters, J.: Temperature and pressure dependent product distribution of the addition of CN radicals to C_2H_4. Phys. Chem. Chem. Phys. **5**(22), 5070–5076 (2003)
28. Gannon, K.L., Glowacki, D.R., Blitz, M.A., Hughes, K.J., Pilling, M.J., Seakins, P.W.: H atom yields from the reactions of CN radicals with c_2h_2, c_2h_4, c_3h_6, trans-2-c_4h_8, and iso-c_4h_8. J. Phys. Chem. A **111**(29), 6679–6692 (2007)
29. Balucani, N., et al.: Combined crossed beam and theoretical studies of the n(^{2}d)+ c_2h_4 reaction and implications for atmospheric models of titan. J. Phys. Chem. A **116**(43), 10467–10479 (2012)
30. Vanuzzo, G., et al.: The n(^{2}d)+ ch_2chcn (vinyl cyanide) reaction: a combined crossed molecular beam and theoretical study and implications for the atmosphere of titan. J. Phys. Chem. A **126**(36), 6110–6123 (2022)
31. Marchione, D., et al.: Unsaturated dinitriles formation routes in extraterrestrial environments: a combined experimental and theoretical investigation of the reaction between cyano radicals and cyanoethene (c_2h_3cn). J. Phys. Chem. A **126**(22), 3569–3582 (2022)
32. Rosi, M., et al.: Possible scenarios for sis formation in the interstellar medium: electronic structure calculations of the potential energy surfaces for the reactions of the SiH radical with atomic sulphur and S_2. Chem. Phys. Lett. **695**, 87–93 (2018)
33. Mancini, L., Trinari, M., de Aragão, E.V.F., Rosi, M., Balucani, N.: The $s^+(^4s)+$ sih_2 ($^1a_1$) reaction: toward the synthesis of interstellar SiS. In: Gervasi, O., Murgante, B., Misra, S., Rocha, A.M.A.C., Garau, C. (eds.) Computational Science and Its Applications – ICCSA 2022 Workshops. ICCSA 2022. LNCS, vol. 13378, pp. 233–245. Springer, Cham (2022). https://doi.org/10.1007/978-3-031-10562-3_17
34. Becke, A.D.: A new mixing of Hartree-Fock and local density-functional theories. J. Chem. Phys. **98**(2), 1372–1377 (1993)
35. Stephens, P.J., Devlin, F.J., Chabalowski, C.F., Frisch, M.J.: Ab initio calculation of vibrational absorption and circular dichroism spectra using density functional force fields. J. Phys. Chem. **98**(45), 11623–11627 (1994)

36. Dunning Jr, T.H.: Gaussian basis sets for use in correlated molecular calculations. I. The atoms boron through neon and hydrogen. J. Chem. Phys. **90**(2), 1007–1023 (1989)

37. Woon, D.E., Dunning Jr, T.H.: Gaussian basis sets for use in correlated molecular calculations. III. The atoms aluminum through argon. J. Chem. Phys. **98**(2), 1358–1371 (1993)

38. Kendall, R.A., Dunning Jr, T.H., Harrison, R.J.: Electron affinities of the first-row atoms revisited. Systematic basis sets and wave functions. J. Chem. Phys. **96**(9), 6796–6806 (1992)

39. Bartlett, R.J.: Many-body perturbation theory and coupled cluster theory for electron correlation in molecules. Annu. Rev. Phys. Chem. **32**(1), 359–401 (1981)

40. Raghavachari, K., Trucks, G.W., Pople, J.A., Head-Gordon, M.: A fifth-order perturbation comparison of electron correlation theories. Chem. Phys. Lett. **157**(6), 479–483 (1989)

41. Olsen, J., Jo/rgensen, P., Koch, H., Balkova, A., Bartlett, R.J.: Full configuration-interaction and state of the art correlation calculations on water in a valence double-zeta basis with polarization functions. J. Chem. Phys. **104**(20), 8007–8015 (1996)

42. Martin, J.M.: Ab initio total atomization energies of small molecules-towards the basis set limit. Chem. Phys. Lett. **259**(5–6), 669–678 (1996)

43. Moore, C.E.: Atomic Energy Levels. US Department of Commerce, National Bureau of Standards (1949)

44. Frisch, M., et al.: Gaussian 09, rev. A. 02, Gaussian. Inc., Wallingford, CT (2009)

45. Werner, H.J., et al.: The molpro quantum chemistry package. J. Chem. Phys. **152**(14), 144107 (2020)

46. Schaftenaar, G., Noordik, J.H.: Molden: a pre-and post-processing program for molecular and electronic structures. J. Comput. Aided Mol. Des. **14**(2), 123–134 (2000)

47. Schaftenaar, G., Vlieg, E., Vriend, G.: Molden 2.0: quantum chemistry meets proteins. J. Comput. Aided Mol. Des. **31**(9), 789–800 (2017). https://doi.org/10.1007/s10822-017-0042-5

A Computational Study of the Reaction Between N(^{2}D) and Simple Aromatic Hydrocarbons

Marzio Rosi[1,2(✉)] (ID), Nadia Balucani[3] (ID), Piergiorgio Casavecchia[3] (ID),
Noelia Faginas-Lago[3] (ID), Luca Mancini[3] (ID), Dimitrios Skouteris[4] (ID),
and Gianmarco Vanuzzo[3] (ID)

[1] DICA, Università di Perugia, 06125 Perugia, Italy
marzio.rosi@unipg.it
[2] CNR-SCITEC, 06123 Perugia, Italy
[3] DCBB, Università di Perugia, 06123 Perugia, Italy
{nadia.balucani,piergiorgio.casavecchia,
gianmarco.vanuzzo}@unipg.it, luca.mancini@studenti.unipg.it
[4] Master-Tec srl, 06128 Perugia, Italy

Abstract. In this contribution, we will present a computational study of the reactions involving N(^{2}D) and simple aromatic hydrocarbons, like benzene or toluene. The aim is to determine the chemical reactivity of N(^{2}D) with aromatic species after previous investigations with aliphatic molecules, in order to establish which level of calculation is necessary to get reliable results.

Keywords: Computational chemistry · Potential energy surfaces · Ab initio calculations · Density Functional Theory · Coupled Cluster calculations

1 Introduction

The reactivity of atomic nitrogen in its ground state (^{4}S) with closed shell molecules, like hydrocarbons, is very low, while atomic nitrogen in the ^{2}D state is much more reactive with hydrocarbons. N(^{2}D) was detected in the water-poor comet C/2016 R2 (Pan-STARRS) [1] and in a plethora of strongly photon-irradiated environments including the Orion Nebula (M42), low-ionization H II regions (M43), planetary nebulae (*i.e.* the Ring Nebula), supernova remnants (*i.e.* the Crab Nebula), and Herbig-Haro objects [2–5]. Polycyclic aromatic hydrocarbons (PAHs) and related species are presumed to be omnipresent in the interstellar medium (ISM) and aromatic chemistry is widespread in the earliest stages of star formation. Nitrogen, in its molecular form, and hydrocarbons, both aliphatic and aromatic, are also the main components of the atmosphere of Titan [6, 7]. This atmosphere is similar, in some aspects, to the primordial atmosphere of Earth [8, 9] and for this reason has been extensively studied by several missions [10, 11]. Among the hydrocarbons identified on Titan there is benzene [12, 13], while toluene is easily produced by the reaction of C_6H_5, obtained by photodissociation of benzene, and CH_3 [14]. Dinitrogen in the atmosphere of Titan can dissociate into atomic nitrogen both in its ground state or ^{2}D excited state in similar amounts [15, 16] and N (^{2}D) can easily

© The Author(s), under exclusive license to Springer Nature Switzerland AG 2023

O. Gervasi et al. (Eds.): ICCSA 2023 Workshops, LNCS 14105, pp. 718–734, 2023.
https://doi.org/10.1007/978-3-031-37108-0_46

react with other constituents of the upper atmosphere of Titan or with species present in the ISM medium [17–24].

The reaction of N(^{2}D) with several aliphatic hydrocarbons of increasing complexity, starting from methane, have been already investigated both theoretically, using accurate ab initio methods and kinetic calculations, and experimentally through crossed molecular beams techniques [25–32]. A similar approach is employed for the reactions between N(^{2}D) and aromatic hydrocarbons, starting from benzene [33–35] and toluene [36, 37] with the intention to extend the study to more complex aromatic systems, like polycyclic aromatic hydrocarbons (PAHs). In this study we will present the results of calculations performed on the reactions of N(^{2}D) with benzene and toluene paying particular attention to the computational aspects, in order to determine the best approach to the ab initio study of these systems computationally very demanding.

2   Computational Details

The theoretical investigation of the reaction of N(^{2}D) with benzene and toluene was performed adopting a well-established computational strategy previously used for the study of many other bimolecular reactions [38–42]. The optimization of all the stationary points (minima and transition states) was performed at the B3LYP [43, 44] level of theory in conjunction with the 6-311+G(d,p) basis set [45, 46] and, in particular cases, using the ωB97X-D [47, 48] functional with the same 6-311+G(d,p) basis set [45, 46]. The geometry of the optimized stationary points was then refined by the use of the B3LYP functional with a larger basis set, *i.e.* the Dunning aug-cc-pVTZ [49]. The geometry optimizations were always followed by the computation of the vibrational frequencies. IRC calculations [50, 51] were performed to assign the transition states to the relative minima. The energy of all the stationary points was computed then at the CCSD(T) level [52–54] using the aug-cc-pVTZ basis set [49]. All the energies were corrected to 0 K by adding the zero point energy (ZPE) correction computed using the scaled harmonic vibrational frequencies evaluated at the same level of the corresponding geometry optimization. The energy of N(^{2}D) was estimated using the N(^{4}S) – N(^{2}D) experimental energy difference of 55 kcal mol^{-1} [55]. For selected stationary points, very accurate calculations were performed at the CCSD(T) level corrected with a Density Fitted (DF) MP2 extrapolation to the complete basis set (CBS) and with corrections for core electrons excitations. In particular, we compute the energies as:

ECBS   =
E(CCSD(T)/aug-cc-pVTZ) + [E(CCSD(T,core)/cc-pVTZ)-E(CCSD(T)/cc-pVTZ)] +
[E(DF-MP2/CBS)-E(DF-MP2/aug-cc-pVTZ)]

where E(DF-MP2/CBS) is defined as:

E(DF-MP2/CBS) = E[(DF-MP2)/aug-cc-pVQZ)] + 0.5772*[E(DF-MP2/aug-cc-pVQZ)-E(DF-MP2/aug-cc-pVTZ)]

The E(DF-MP2/CBS) extrapolation was performed using Martin's two parameter scheme [56]. These energies will be denoted as CBS although they include also the core-valence correlation correction. The accuracy of these calculations should be within ± 1 kcal mol^{-1}.

The DFT and CCSD(T) calculations were done using Gaussian 09 [57] while the CBS calculations were done with MOLPRO [58, 59]. Molekel was used for the analysis of the optimized structures and the vibrational frequencies [60, 61].

3   Results and Discussion

3.1   Attack of N(^{2}D) to the Aromatic Ring

Table 1 reports the energy difference between the energy of atomic nitrogen in its ^{4}S ground state and in its first excited ^{2}D state. As expected, the description of a lowest spin excited state is a difficult task and the results obtained with a single-reference method are unsatisfactory. In particular, we have an error of 9 kcal mol^{-1} at B3LYP level using a split valence basis set, which is reduced to 8 kcal mol^{-1} using a more extended basis set like the aug-cc-pVTZ. Using a method which includes more extensively correlation effects like the CCSD(T) does not improve significantly the description, being the error still 7 kcal mol^{-1}. Even a very accurate method wich includes at CCSD(T) level an extrapolation to the complete basis set and the core-valence correlation effects, *i.e.* the CBS scheme, provides an unsatisfactory description, being the error still 6 kcal mol^{-1}. For this reason, we decided to evaluate the energy of N (^{2}D) adding the experimental energy difference to N(^{4}S) which is well described at any level of approximation. The energy of nitrogen in its excited ^{2}D state will be estimated in this way in all the calculations.

Table 1. Total energy (hartree) and energy differences Δ (kcal mol^{-1}) between nitrogen in its ground ^{4}S state and in the ^{2}D state computed at various level of calculation compared to the experimental value [56].

Method	N(^{4}S)	N(^{2}D)	Δ
B3LYP/6-311+G(d,p)	−54.600723	−54.499263	64
B3LYP/aug-cc-pVTZ	−54.602891	−54.502416	63
CCSD(T)/aug-cc-pVTZ	−54.516924	−54.417503	62
CBS	−54.585385	−54.488412	61
Experiment			55

The approach of N(^{2}D) to benzene leads first of all to the formation of an adduct where the distance between the nitrogen atom and the benzene ring is very long, more than 3 Å. In Fig. 1 we have reported the optimized geometry computed at B3LYP/aug-cc-pVTZ level for the initial adduct derived from the interaction of N(^{2}D) with benzene and toluene; for benzene we have performed the geometry optimization also at ωB97XD/6-311+G(d,p) (parameters reported in red in parentheses) and from Fig. 1 we can notice that no significative differences in the optimized parameters are present.

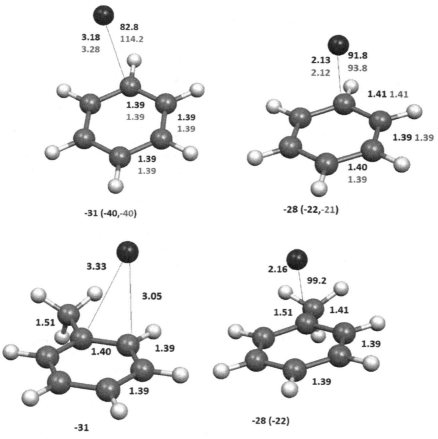

Fig. 1. Optimized structures of the initial adduct obtained for the attack of N(^{2}D) to benzene (top) or toluene (bottom) and the transition state for the isomerization of the adduct to the first stable species. Geometry optimization has been performed at B3LYP/aug-cc-pVTZ (in black) and ωB97X-D/6-311+G(d,p) (in red) level. Bond lengths in Å, angles in degrees. Relative energies (kcal mol^{-1}) with respect to N(^{2}D) + aromatic ring have been evaluated at B3LYP/aug-cc-pVTZ and, in parentheses, at CCSD(T)/aug-cc-pVTZ//B3LYP/aug-cc-pVTZ and CCSD(T)/aug-cc-pVTZ//ωB97X-D/6-311+G(d,p) (in red) level of theory. Carbon atoms in green, nitrogen in blue, hydrogen in white. (Color figure online)

The nitrogen atom approaches the ring almost in a perpendicular way, being the NCH angle 82.8° at B3LYP/aug-cc-pVTZ level and 114.2° at ωB97XD/6-311+G(d,p) level. Due to the very long distance between the nitrogen atom and the aromatic ring, the geometry of benzene is almost unchanged with respect to that of isolated benzene. This electrostatic adduct evolves to the first intermediate, **w1**, through the transition state shown in Fig. 1. The geometry of this saddle point is very close to that of the adduct, the only significant difference being the N—C distance which changes from 3.18 to 2.13 Å. Although the optimized geometries seem to be reasonable, the relative energies of these species with respect to the reactants are not. The adduct is more stable with respect to the reactants by 31 kcal mol^{-1} at B3LYP/aug-cc-pVTZ level and by 40 kcal mol^{-1} at CCSD(T)/aug-cc-pVTZ level using both the B3LYP/aug-cc-pVTZ or the ωB97XD/6-311+G(d,p) optimized geometries. This energy does not seem to be correct, since an electrostatic adduct where the interaction between the two species is very weak cannot be stabilized so strongly. The energy of this adduct is so low with respect to the reactants because in this species there is a very bad description of N(^{2}D), which is almost not interacting with benzene, which lowers unrealistically the energy of the adduct. This adduct is formed by a nitrogen atom and a benzene ring almost not interacting; its energy should be almost equal to the sum of the energies of N(^{2}D) and C_6H_6. Also the energy of the transition state is too low with respect to the reactants being 28 kcal mol^{-1} under the reactants and 22 or 21 kcal mol^{-1} at CCSD(T)/aug-cc-pVTZ level, depending on the use of the optimized geometry at B3LYP/aug-cc-pVTZ or ωB97XD/6-311+G(d,p) level. In order to solve this problem, we computed the energy of both species, minimum and saddle point, at CBS level. The energy of the adduct was computed to be 4 kcal mol^{-1} over the reactants starting from the B3LYP/aug-cc-pVTZ optimized geometry and 5 kcal mol^{-1} over the reactants using the ωB97XD/6-311+G(d,p) geometry. This point suggests that the description of the initial attack of N(^{2}D) to benzene cannot be described properly at this level of calculation. Multirefence methods, as CASPT2 for instance, should be employed, but their use could be too computer resources demanding for systems as big as the ones here considered. A more affordable alternative could be the use of semiempirical methods, as the Improved Lennard-Jones (ILJ) which provides realistic description of long range interactions [62–65]. Since we are interested in the exit channels and relative branching factors of the investigated reactions we decided to considered the reaction starting from the first intermediate, *i.e.* species **w1**, as previously done by Chin et al. [66].

The interaction of N(^{2}D) with toluene shows a behaviour similar to that of benzene. In Fig. 1 we can see the formation of an initial adduct where the nitrogen atom is very far from the toluene ring (more than 3 Å) and the toluene ring is almost unperturbed. This species is more stable than the reactants by 31 kcal mol^{-1} at B3LYP/aug-cc-pVTZ level (the CCSD(T) calculation did not converge). Also the transition state lies under the reactants by 28 kcal mol^{-1} at B3LYP/aug-cc-pVTZ level and 22 kcal mol^{-1} at CCSD(T)/aug-cc-pVTZ level. These energies clearly overestimate the strength of the interaction between the nitrogen atom and the toluene molecule. Also in this case this description cannot be considered correct and, therefore, we will start our analysis for this reaction starting from the first intermediate, *i.e.* **w1**.

3.2 Interaction of N(^{2}D) with Benzene

We will focus our attention only to the main reactive channel, *i.e.* the one leading to the formation of hydrogen cyanide and the cyclopentadienyl radical, since we are interested in computational requirements. The other reactive channels have been reported elsewhere [34–36]. The potential energy surface (PES) relative to this reaction channel is reported in Fig. 2, while the optimized geometries of the intermediates and transition states considered in Fig. 2 are reported in Fig. 3 and 4, respectively. We can notice from Fig. 2 that the first intermediate is species **w1** where the nitrogen is bonded to a carbon atom of the ring, together with an hydrogen atom. This carbon center therefore changes its hybridization from sp^2 to sp^3 and the ring is distorted. This attack to a carbon of the ring is in agreement with the structure of the initial adduct reported in Fig. 1. Species **w1** can evolve towards the products following two different pathways: the first (in red) implies the evolution of **w1** through **w2, w4, w6, w9**, while the second (in blue) implies a pathway which goes through **w3, w5, w7, w8, w9**. The second pathway shows the presence of an initial saddle point higher in energy. However, in order to establish which one is the preferred pathway kinetic calculations are necessary and they have been presented elsewhere [36].

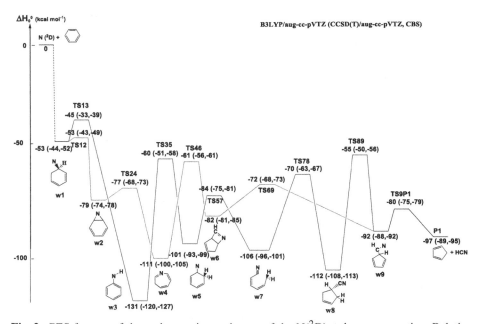

Fig. 2. PES for two of the main reaction pathways of the N(^{2}D) + benzene reaction. Relative energies (kcal mol^{-1}) respect to N(^{2}D) + benzene, computed at B3LYP, CCSD(T) (in parentheses, first entry) and CBS (in parentheses, second entry) level with inclusion of ZPE.

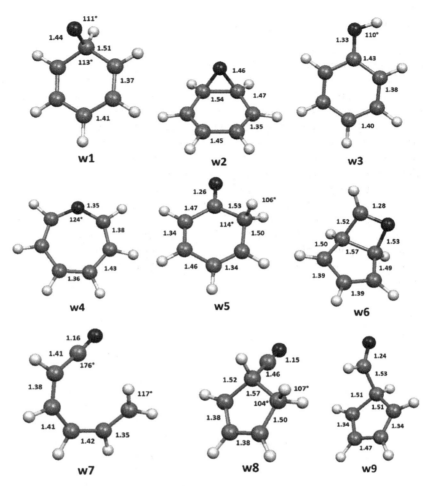

Fig. 3. Optimized geometries of the minima reported in Fig. 2. Geometry optimization has been performed at B3LYP level. Distances in Å, angles in °. Carbon atoms in green, nitrogen in blue, hydrogen in white. (Color fgure online)

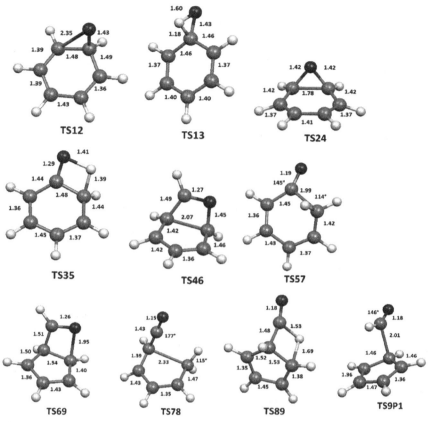

Fig. 4. Optimized geometries of the transition states reported in Fig. 2. Geometry optimization has been performed at B3LYP level. Distances in Å, angles in °. Carbon atoms in green, nitrogen in blue, hydrogen in white. (Color fgure online)

For each stationary point we have reported the energy computed at B3LYP/aug-cc-pVTZ, CCSD(T)/aug-cc-pVTZ and CBS level. We can notice that there are significant differences among the three approaches. In particular we can notice that there is an overestimation of the binding energies at B3LYP level as expected, and an underestimation of the binding energies at CCSD(T) level due to the basis set incompleteness. These two errors somehow cancel each other, with the result that the B3LYP energies are closer to the CBS ones, than the CCSD(T) energies. However, if we change the reference energy, considering that of the first intermediate **w1**, the difference among the energies of the three methods considered are lower, as we can see from Fig. 5, suggesting that also the B3LYP method can provide reasonable semi-quantitative results, also for energies besides those for geometries. This is encouraging in view of the possible investigation of more complex systems. The comparison between the energies computed at CCSD(T)/aug-cc-pVTZ and CBS level allows us to estimate the absolute basis set

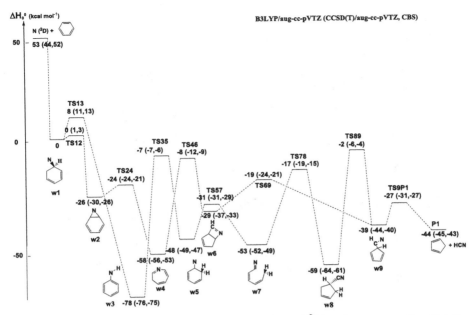

Fig. 5. PES for two of the main reaction pathways of the $N(^2D)$ + benzene reaction. Relative energies (kcal mol^{-1}) respect to **w1** intermediate, computed at B3LYP, CCSD(T) (in parentheses, first entry) and CBS (in parentheses, second entry) level with inclusion of ZPE.

superposition error (BSSE) which is around 3–4 kcal/mol. However, this error is not so relevant as far as we are interested in relative energies.

3.3 Interaction of N(^{2}D) with Toluene

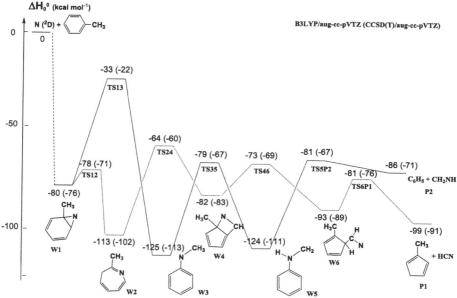

Fig. 6. PES for two of the main reaction pathways of the N(^{2}D) + toluene reaction. Relative energies (kcal mol^{-1}), respect to N(^{2}D) + toluene, are computed at B3LYP and CCSD(T) (in parentheses) level with inclusion of ZPE.

Figure 6 shows the PES of the reaction between N(^{2}D) and toluene, while the optimized structures of the minima and transition states are reported in Figs. 7 and 8, respectively. Also in this case we have considered only the channel leading to the formation of hydrogen cyanide, since the other reaction channels will be presented elsewhere. For analogy with the reaction of benzene we have considered also the evolution of intermediate **w3**, which in this case however leads to different products. The first intermediate, **w1**, shows the nitrogen center bonded η^2 to two carbon atoms; this is in agreement with the optimized structure of the initial adduct reported in Fig. 1, where it is clear that the nitrogen atom approaches two carbon atoms. From Fig. 6 we can see that species **w1** can evolve to the formation of hydrogen cyanide and methylcyclopentadyenil radical through the intermediates **w2**, **w4** and **w6** (red pathway). **w1** can isomerize also to **w3**, which is the species corresponding to the intermediate **w3** in the PES of N(^{2}D) + benzene. However, this species shows a different reactivity since the migration of an hydrogen of the CH$_3$ group to the nitrogen is preferred with respect to the migration of the whole CH$_3$ group to the adjacent carbon atom of the benzene ring. **w3** can dissociate into a phenyl radical and methanimine. Fron Fig. 6, where we have reported the energies relative to the reactants computed at B3LYP/aug-cc-pVTZ and CCSD(T)/aug-cc-pVTZ (in parentheses) levels, we can notice significant differences between the values obtained with the two methods. In Fig. 9 we have reported the PES changing the reference energy. Also in this case we can notice that there is a smaller difference between the two methods. However, it seems clear that for a quantitative treatment at least CCSD(T) calculations are necessary. B3LYP can provide reasonable semi-quantitative results which anyway can be important when other methods are unfeasible.

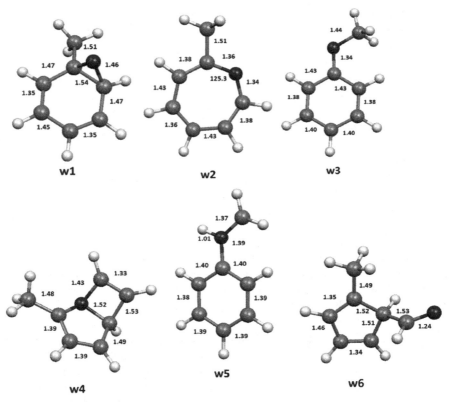

Fig. 7. Optimized geometries of the minima reported in Fig. 6. Geometry optimization has been performed at B3LYP/aug-cc-pVTZ level. Distances in Å, angles in °. Carbon atoms in green, nitrogen in blue, hydrogen in white. (Color fgure online)

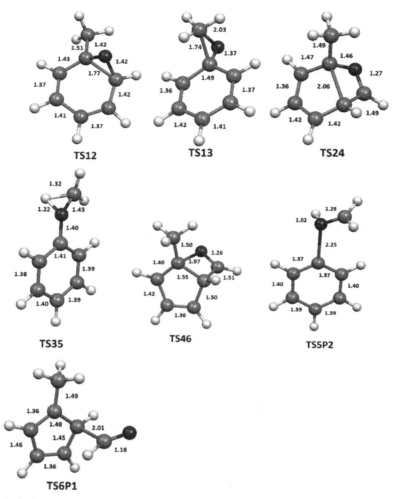

Fig. 8. Optimized geometries of the transition states reported in Fig. 6. Geometry optimization has been performed at B3LYP/aug-cc-pVTZ level. Distances in Å, angles in °. Carbon atoms in green, nitrogen in blue, hydrogen in white. (Color fgure online)

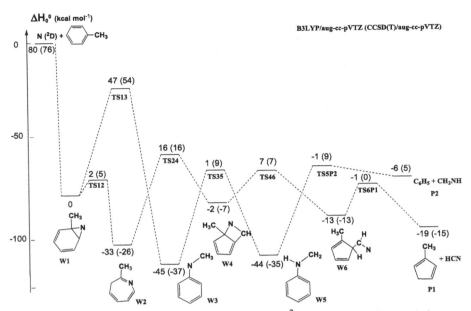

Fig. 9. PES for two of the main reaction pathways of the N(^{2}D) + toluene reaction. Relative energies (kcal mol^{-1}), respect to **w1** species, are computed at B3LYP and CCSD(T) (in parentheses) level with inclusion of ZPE.

4 Conclusions

The theoretical investigation of the interaction of N(^{2}D) with benzene and toluene, focusing the attention on computational requirements, suggests that a quantitative treatment of these reactions requires extensive inclusion of correlation effects as well as extrapolation to the basis set completeness limit. Particularly challenging is the initial approach of N(^{2}D) to the aromatic system, which cannot be described properly by single reference methods. Multireference methods, which could be unfeasible for most of the aromatic systems, should be employed, although an alternative worth of consideration could be represented by semiempirical methods which describe properly long range interactions. The comparison between DFT and CCSD(T) calculations suggests that useful semi-quantitative results can be obtained also at DFT level of approximation. This is an important result in order to extend our study to complex PAHs.

Acknowledgments. The authors acknowledge the MUR (Italian Ministry of University and Research) for "PRIN 2017" funds, project "MAGIC DUST" (Prot. 2017PJ5XXX_002).

References

1. Raghuram, S., Hutsemékers, D., Opitom, C., Jehin, E., Bhardwaj, A., Manfroid, J.: Forbidden atomic carbon, nitrogen, and oxygen emission lines in the water-poor comet C/2016 R2 (Pan-STARRS). Astron. Astrophys. **635**, A108 (2020)

2. Ferland, G.J., Henney, W.J., O'Dell, C.R., Porter, R.L., van Hoof, P.A.M., Williams, R.J.R.: Pumping up the [N i] nebular lines. Astrophys. J. **757**, 79 (2012)
3. Dopita, M.A., Mason, D.J., Robb, W.D.: Atomic nitrogen as a probe of physical conditions in the interstellar medium. Astrophys. J. **207**, 102–109 (1976)
4. Ferland, G.J., Rees, M.J.: radiative equilibrium of high-density clouds, with application to active galactic nucleus continua. Astrophys. J. **332**, 141 (1988)
5. Bautista, M.A.: Continuum fluorescence excitation of [N I] and [O I] lines in gaseous nebulae. Astrophys. J. **527**, 474 (1999)
6. Hörst, S.M.: Titan's atmosphere and climate. J. Geophys. Res.: Planets **122**, 432–482 (2017)
7. Vuitton, V., Yelle, R.V., Anicich, V.G.: The nitrogen chemistry of Titan's upper atmosphere revealed. Astrophys J. **647**, L175–L178 (2006)
8. Vuitton, V., Dutuit, O., Smith, M.A., Balucani, N.: Chemistry of Titan's atmosphere. In: Mueller-Wodarg, I., Griffith, C., Lellouch, E., Cravens, T. (eds.) Titan: Surface. Atmosphere and Magnetosphere. Cambridge University Press, Cambridge (2013)
9. Balucani, N.: Elementary reactions of N atoms with hydrocarbons: first steps towards the formation of prebiotic N-containing molecules in planetary atmospheres. Chem. Soc. Rev. **41**, 5473–5483 (2012)
10. Brown, R., Lebreton, J.P., Waite, J. (eds.): Titan from Cassini-Huygens. Springer, Netherlands (2010)
11. Lai, J.C.-Y., et al.: Mapping vinyl cyanide and other nitriles in Titan's atmosphere using ALMA. Astron. J. **154**(206), 1–10 (2017)
12. Vuitton, V., Yelle, R.V., Cui, J.: Formation and distribution of benzene on Titan. J. Geophys. Res. **113**, E05007 (2008)
13. Clark, R.N., et al.: Detection and mapping of hydrocarbon deposits on Titan. J. Geophys. Res. **115**, E10005 (2010)
14. Loison, J.C., Dobrijevic, M., Hickson, K.M.: The photochemical production of aromatics in the atmosphere of Titan. Icarus **329**, 55–71 (2019)
15. Lavvas, P., et al.: Energy deposition and primary chemical products in Titan's upper atmosphere. Icarus **213**, 233–251 (2011)
16. Dutuit, O., et al.: Critical review of N, N$^+$, N$_2$$^+$, N^{++} and N$_2$$^{++}$ main production processes and reactions of relevance to Titan's atmosphere. Astrophys. J. Suppl. Ser. **204**, 20 (2013)
17. Balucani, N.: Nitrogen fixation by photochemistry in the atmosphere of Titan and implications for prebiotic chemistry. In: Trigo-Rodriguez, J.M., Raulin, F., Muller, C., Nixon, C. (eds.) The Early Evolution of the Atmospheres of Terrestrial Planets. Springer Series in Astrophysics and Space Science Proceedings, vol. 35, pp. 155–164. Springer, New York (2013). https://doi.org/10.1007/978-1-4614-5191-4_12
18. Balucani, N.: Elementary reactions and their role in gas-phase prebiotic chemistry. Int. J. Mol. Sci. **10**, 2304–2335 (2009)
19. Imanaka, H., Smith, M.A.: Formation of nitrogenated organic aerosols in the Titan upper atmosphere. PNAS **107**, 12423–12428 (2010)
20. Balucani, N., et al.: Dynamics of the N(^{2}D) + D$_2$ reaction from crossed-beam and quasiclassical trajectory studies. J. Phys. Chem. A **105**, 2414–2422 (2001)
21. Balucani, N., et al.: Experimental and theoretical differential cross sections for the N(^{2}D) + H$_2$ reaction. J. Phys. Chem. A **110**, 817–829 (2006)
22. Homayoon, Z., Bowman, J.M., Balucani, N., Casavecchia, P.: Quasiclassical trajectory calculations of the N(^{2}D) + H$_2$O reaction elucidating the formation mechanism of HNO and HON seen in molecular beam experiments. J. Phys. Chem. Lett. **5**, 3508–3513 (2014)
23. Balucani, N., Cartechini, L., Casavecchia, P., Homayoon, Z., Bowman, J.M.: A combined crossed molecular beam and quasiclassical trajectory study of the Titan-relevant N(^{2}D) + D$_2$O reaction. Mol. Phys. **113**, 2296–2301 (2015)

24. Israel, G., et al.: Complex organic matter in Titan's atmospheric aerosols from in situ pyrolysis and analysis. Nature **438**, 796 (2005)

25. Balucani, N., et al.: Combined crossed molecular beam and theoretical studies of the $N(^2D)$ + CH_4 reaction and implications for atmospheric models of Titan. J. Phys. Chem. A **113**, 11138–11152 (2009)

26. Balucani, N., et al.: Cyanomethylene formation from the reaction of excited nitrogen atoms with acetylene: a crossed beam and ab initio study. J. Am. Chem. Soc. **122**, 4443–4450 (2000)

27. Balucani, N., Cartechini, L., Alagia, M., Casavecchia, P., Volpi, G.G.: Observation of nitrogen-bearing organic molecules from reactions of nitrogen atoms with hydrocarbons: a crossed beam study of $N(^2D)$ + ethylene. J. Phys. Chem. A **104**, 5655–5659 (2000)

28. Balucani, N., et al.: Formation of nitriles and imines in the atmosphere of Titan: combined crossed-beam and theoretical studies on the reaction dynamics of excited nitrogen atoms $N(^2D)$ with ethane. Faraday Discuss. **147**, 189–216 (2010)

29. Balucani, N., et al.: Combined crossed beam and theoretical studies of the $N(^2D)$ + C_2H_4 reaction and implications for atmospheric models of Titan. J. Phys. Chem. A **116**, 10467–10479 (2012)

30. Vanuzzo, G., et al.: Reaction $N(^2D)$ + CH_2CCH_2 (Allene): an experimental and theoretical investigation and implications for the photochemical models of Titan. ACS Earth Space Chem. **6**, 2305–2321 (2022)

31. Mancini, L., et al.: The reaction $N(^2D)$ + CH_3CCH (Methylacetylene): a combined crossed molecular beams and theoretical investigation and implications for the atmosphere of titan. J. Phys. Chem A **125**, 8846–8859 (2021)

32. Mancini, L., de Aragão, E.V.F., Rosi, M., Skouteris, D., Balucani, N.: A theoretical investigation of the reactions of $N(^2D)$ with small alkynes and implications for the prebiotic chemistry of titan. In: Gervasi, O., et al. (eds.) ICCSA 2020. LNCS, vol. 12251, pp. 717–729. Springer, Cham (2020). https://doi.org/10.1007/978-3-030-58808-3_52

33. Balucani, N., Pacifici, L., Skouteris, D., Caracciolo, A., Casavecchia, P., Rosi, M.: A theoretical investigation of the reaction $N(2D)$ + C6H6 and implications for the upper atmosphere of Titan. In: Gervasi, O., et al. (eds.) ICCSA 2018. LNCS, vol. 10961, pp. 763–772. Springer, Cham (2018). https://doi.org/10.1007/978-3-319-95165-2_53

34. Balucani, N., et al.: A Computational Study of the Reaction $N(^2D)$ + C_6H_6 Leading to Pyridine and Phenylnitrene. In: Misra, S., et al. (eds.) ICCSA 2019. LNCS, vol. 11621, pp. 316–324. Springer, Cham (2019). https://doi.org/10.1007/978-3-030-24302-9_23

35. Balucani, N., et al.: An experimental and theoretical investigation of the $N(^2D)$ + C_6H_6 (benzene) reaction with implications for the photochemical models of Titan. Faraday Discuss. (2023). https://doi.org/10.1039/D3FD00057E

36. Rosi, M., et al.: A computational study on the attack of nitrogen and oxygen atoms to toluene. In: Gervasi, O., et al. (eds.) ICCSA 2021. LNCS, vol. 12953, pp. 620–631. Springer, Cham (2021). https://doi.org/10.1007/978-3-030-86976-2_42

37. Rosi, M., et al.: A computational study on the insertion of $N(^2D)$ into a C—H or C—C bond: the reactions of $N(^2D)$ with benzene and toluene and their implications on the chemistry of titan. In: Gervasi, O., et al. (eds.) ICCSA 2020. LNCS, vol. 12251, pp. 744–755. Springer, Cham (2020). https://doi.org/10.1007/978-3-030-58808-3_54

38. Balucani, N., Skouteris, D., Ceccarelli, C., Codella, C., Falcinelli, S., Rosi, M.: A theoretical investigation of the reaction between the amidogen, NH, and the ethyl, C_2H_5, radicals: a possible gas-phase formation route of interstellar and planetary ethanimine. Molec. Astrophys. **13**, 30–37 (2018)

39. Sleiman, C., El Dib, G., Rosi, M., Skouteris, D., Balucani, N., Canosa, A.: Low temperature kinetics and theoretical study of the reaction CN + CH_3NH_2: a potential source of cyanamide and methyl cyanamide in the interstellar medium. PCCP **20**, 5478–5489 (2018)

40. Berteloite, C., et al.: Low temperature kinetics, crossed beam dynamics and theoretical studies of the reaction S(^{1}D) + CH$_4$ and low temperature kinetics of S(^{1}D) + C$_2$H$_2$. Phys. Chem. Chem. Phys. **13**, 8485–8501 (2011)
41. Rosi, M., et al.: Possible scenarios for SiS formation in the interstellar medium: electronic structure calculations of the potential energy surdaces for the reactions of the SiH radical with atomic sulphur and S$_2$. Chem. Phys. Lett. **695**, 87–93 (2018)
42. Troiani, A., Rosi, M., Garzoli, S., Salvitti, C., de Petris, G.: Vanadium hydroxide cluster ions in the gas phase: bond-forming reactions of doubly-charged negative ions by SO$_2$-promoted V-O activation. Chem. Eur. J. **23**, 11752–11756 (2017)
43. Becke, A.D.: Density functional thermochemistry. III. The role of exact exchange. J. Chem. Phys. **98**, 5648–5652 (1993)
44. Stephens, P.J., Devlin, F.J., Chablowski, C.F., Frisch, M.J.: Ab initio calculation of vibrational absorption and circular dichroism spectra using density functional force fields. J. Phys. Chem. **98**, 11623–11627 (1994)
45. Krishnan, R., Binkley, J.S., Seeger, R., Pople, J.A.: Self-consistent molecular orbital methods. XX. A basis set for correlated wave functions. J. Chem. Phys. **72**, 650–654 (1980)
46. Frisch, M.J., Pople, J.A., Binkley, J.S.: Self-consistent molecular orbital methods 25. Supplementary functions for Gaussian basis sets. J. Chem. Phys. **80**, 3265–3269 (1984)
47. Chai, J.-D., Head-Gordon, M.: Long-range corrected hybrid density functionals with damped atom-atom dispersion corrections. Phys. Chem. Chem. Phys. **10**, 6615–6620 (2008)
48. Chai, J.-D., Head-Gordon, M.: Systematic optimization of long-range corrected hybrid density functionals. J. Chem. Phys. **128**, 084106 (2008)
49. Dunning, T.H., Jr.: Gaussian basis sets for use in correlated molecular calculations. I. The atoms boron through neon and hydrogen. J. Chem. Phys. **90**, 1007–1023 (1989)
50. Gonzalez, C., Schlegel, H.B.: An improved algorithm for reaction path following. J. Chem. Phys. **90**, 2154–2161 (1989)
51. Gonzalez, C., Schlegel, H.B.: Reaction path following in mass-weighted internal coordinates. J. Phys. Chem. **94**, 5523–5527 (1990)
52. Bartlett, R.J.: Many-body perturbation theory and coupled cluster theory for electron correlation in molecules. Annu. Rev. Phys. Chem. **32**, 359–401 (1981)
53. Raghavachari, K., Trucks, G.W., Pople, J.A., Head-Gordon, M.: Quadratic configuration interaction. A general technique for determining electron correlation energies. Chem. Phys. Lett. **157**, 479–483 (1989)
54. Olsen, J., Jorgensen, P., Koch, H., Balkova, A., Bartlett, R.J.: Full configuration–interaction and state of the art correlation calculations on water in a valence double-zeta basis with polarization functions. J. Chem. Phys. **104**, 8007–8015 (1996)
55. Moore, C.E.: Atomic energy levels. Natl. Bur. Stand. (U.S.) Circ. N. 467. U.S., GPO, Washington, DC (1949)
56. Martin, J.M.: Ab initio total atomization energies of small molecules—towards the basis set limit. Chem. Phys. Lett. **259**, 669–678 (1996)
57. Frisch, M.J., et al.: Gaussian, Inc., Wallingford CT (2009)
58. Werner, H.-J., Knowles, P.J., Knizia, G., Manby, F.R., Schütz, M.: Molpro: a general-purpose quantum chemistry program package. WIREs Comput. Mol. Sci. **2**, 242–253 (2012)
59. Werner, H.-J., et al.: The Molpro quantum chemistry package. J. Chem. Phys. **152**, 144107 (2020)
60. Flükiger, P., Lüthi, H.P., Portmann, S., Weber, J.: MOLEKEL 4.3, Swiss Center for Sci-entific Computing, Manno (Switzerland) (2000–2002)
61. Portmann, S., Lüthi, H.P.: MOLEKEL: an interactive molecular graphics tool chimia, vol. 54, pp. 766–769 (2000)
62. Richardson, V., et al.: Fragmentation of interstellar methanol by collisions with He.$^+$: an experimental and computational study. PCCP **24**, 22437–22452 (2022)

63. de Aragao, E.V.F., Mancini, L., Faginas-Lago, N., Rosi, M., Skouteris, D., Pirani, F.: Semiempirical potential in kinetics calculations on the $HC_3N + CN$ reaction. Molecules **27**, 2297 (2022)

64. de Aragão, E.V.F., et al.: Coding cross sections of an electron charge transfer process. In: Gervasi, O., Murgante, B., Misra, S., Rocha, A.M.A.C., Garau, C. (eds.) ICCSA 2022. LNCS, vol. 13382, pp. 319–333. Springer, Cham (2022). https://doi.org/10.1007/978-3-031-10592-0_24

65. de Aragao, E.V.F., Mancini, L., Faginas-Lago, N., Rosi, M., Balucani, N., Pirani, F.: Long-range complex in the $HC_3N + CN$ potential energy surface: ab initio calculations and intermolecular potential. In: Gervasi, O., et al. (eds.) ICCSA 2021. LNCS, vol. 12958, pp. 413–425. Springer, Cham (2021). https://doi.org/10.1007/978-3-030-87016-4_31

66. Chin, C.-H., Zhu, T., Zhang, J.Z.H.: Cyclopentadienyl radical formation from the reaction of excited nitrogen atoms with benzene: a theoretical study. PCCP **23**, 12408–12420 (2021)

Author Index

© The Editor(s) (if applicable) and The Author(s), under exclusive license
to Springer Nature Switzerland AG 2023
O. Gervasi et al. (Eds.): ICCSA 2023 Workshops, LNCS 14105, pp. 735–736, 2023.
https://doi.org/10.1007/978-3-031-37108-0

Printed in the United States
by Baker & Taylor Publisher Services